Black Women in America

BLACKS IN THE DIASPORA

Darlene Clark Hine, John McCluskey, Jr., and David Barry Gaspar
General Editors

Black Women in America
An Historical Encyclopedia

Editors
DARLENE CLARK HINE
ELSA BARKLEY BROWN
ROSALYN TERBORG-PENN

VOLUME II
M–Z

INDIANA UNIVERSITY PRESS
BLOOMINGTON & INDIANAPOLIS

First published in 1993 by Carlson Publishing, Inc.
First Indiana University Press Edition 1994

The paper used in this publication meets the minimum requirements of American
National Standard for Information Sciences–Permanence of Paper for Printed
Library Materials, ANSI Z39.48-1984.

Manufactured in the United States of America

Library of Congress Cataloging-in-Publication Data

Black women in America : an historical encyclopedia / edited by Darlene
Clark Hine, Elsa Barkley Brown, and Rosalyn Terborg-Penn.
    p. cm. – (Blacks in the diaspora)
    Originally published: Brooklyn, N.Y. : Carlson Pub., 1993.
    Includes bibliographical references and indexes.
    ISBN 0-253-32774-1 (set, pbk.)
    1. Afro-American women–Encyclopedias. I. Hine, Darlene Clark.
II. Brown, Elsa Barkley. III. Terborg-Penn, Rosalyn.
E185.86.B542 1994
920.72'089'96073–dc20
[B]   93-14369
ISBN 0-253-32775-X (v. 1, pbk.)
ISBN 0-253-32776-8 (v. 2, pbk.)

1 2 3 4 5 99 98 97 96 95 94

Cover photo: Anna Julia Cooper (1858-1964), scholar and educator;
principal of M Street High School in Washington, D.C.; president of
Frelinghuysen University; author of *A Voice from the South by a
Black Woman of the South* (1892). (Scurlock Studio, Washington, D.C.)

Cover design: Harakawa Sisco Inc.

Contents

Volume I

Volume II

Black Women in America

THE ENTRIES

M-Z

M

MABLEY, JACKIE "MOMS"
(1897-1975)

Jackie "Moms" Mabley had a grandmother who lived to be 104 years old. "Moms" herself was a salty, wise, hilarious granny onstage for so long that, though she actually died at 78, it seemed that she had outdone that ancient slave grandmother.

Born Loretta Mary Aiken in Brevard, North Carolina, in 1897, Mabley was one of seven children. Her grandmother advised her to leave home if she wanted to make something of herself, and when she was thirteen years old, she did. She joined a minstrel show, claiming to be sixteen, and started performing on the Theater Owners Booking Association circuit. Shortly after leaving home, she met and became engaged to a young Canadian man named Mabley. They were never married, but as she explained later, he took a lot from her, so she could at least take his name. She adopted "Jackie" as a first name simply because she liked it.

In Houston, Texas, a husband and wife dance team called "Butterbeans and Susie" saw her perform and persuaded her to join their act. As part of their routine, she performed her first significant role in *The Rich Aunt from Utah*.

When Mabley began her career, there was an extensive network of Black-owned and -managed halls. They had arisen during the early years of the Jim Crow era, and, though they owed their existence to discrimination and racism, they provided a home for Black entertainers and audiences. Here the entertainers could perfect their craft, and the audiences could hear their own music, see their own dances, and relax in congenial laughter. In a sense, these clubs were sanctuaries shutting out an oppressive larger society. Whites might be admitted, but they clearly were there on the sufferance of the Black majority. Dorothy Gilliam describes the Howard Theatre as the "one place in Washington where Blacks and whites, school teachers and domestics, doctors and laborers mingled as equals" (Gilliam 1986).

This was Mabley's venue. She worked with Dusty (Open-the-Door-Richard) Fletcher in Washington, D.C. She walked onstage with a stepladder and the American flag and "hipped her children" at the Earle Theater in Philadelphia. She was a standby at the Apollo in New York. In a 1941 letter to Arna Bontemps, Langston Hughes mentions his fondness for Mabley's performances at the Apollo, to the extent of "splitting his money" with her. Mabley appeared at the Apollo more often than any other performer in its history.

In the 1920s, during the Harlem Renaissance, Mabley began performing at nightclubs such as the Cotton Club, Connie's Inn, and the Savoy Ballroom. She shared billing with Duke Ellington, Louis Armstrong, Benny Goodman, Count Basie, and Cab Calloway. Later she created comedy routines from her encounters and supposed love affairs with these immortals of entertainment. During the 1910s and 1920s, she also worked in the Black theater, in revues such as *Bowman's Cotton Blossoms, Look Who's Here,* and *Miss Bandanna.* In these revues, Mabley sometimes appeared in blackface.

During the Depression, Black clubs and theaters had great difficulty staying open. Mabley found work at church socials, rent parties, movie houses, and show theaters. She recalled doing fifteen "jailhouse bits" in one day at the Monogram in Chicago, where she worked with Fletcher and Spider Bruce John Mason. She also appeared in the revues *The Joy Boat, Sidewalks of Harlem,* and *Red Pastures.*

Connoisseurs of the remarkable and the odd must cherish the thought of the Broadway play *Fast and Furious: A Colored Revue in 37 Scenes* in 1931. In this production Mabley collaborated with Harlem Re-

The salty, wise, wisecracking Jackie Mabley was called "Moms" for so many years that it was easy to believe that she was ancient when she started out in show business. Hers was a remarkably durable career that stretched from minstrel shows to the Harlem Renaissance to movies to record albums to television. [Schomburg Center]

naissance literary light Zora Neale Hurston, writing scenes and performing. In one skit, they appeared together as cheerleaders.

In 1933, Mabley appeared in her first film, playing a small role as a bawdy house matron in O'Neill's *The Emperor Jones,* which starred Paul Robeson. In 1939, she played Quince in a jazz adaptation of *A Midsummer Night's Dream.* Inspired by the rude mechanicals' version of "Pyramus and Thisbe," she added that kind of satire of the classics to her comedy routine. Mabley returned to film in 1947 in *Killer Diller.* In 1948, she had the lead role in *Boarding House Blues,* in which she played the character of Moms, who ran a boarding house for out-of-work entertainers.

Mabley acquired the name "Moms" from the fellow entertainers whom she helped and cared for, but she soon discovered the persona was one that she could use to good effect on stage. It brought both protection and freedom. Female entertainers were often seen as either immoral or threatening, but Moms was safe. Mabley was, of course, not the first to draw on the power and associations of the maternal. There were Ma Rainey (Gertrude Pridgett), Big Mama Blues (Lillie Mae Glover), Sweet Mama Stringbean (Ethel Waters), and the Last of the Red Hot Mamas (Sophie Tucker), to name a few. Mabley, however, took the role to its limits, creating a character with the authority of a community elder in expounding folk wisdom, advising presidents, leveling bigots, and instructing the people about what and how to teach their young.

That persona proved durable, taking Mabley into television in the 1960s. She appeared on *The Smothers Brothers Comedy Hour* and on variety and talk shows hosted by Merv Griffin, Mike Douglas, Ed Sullivan, Garry Moore, and Flip Wilson. She appeared at Carnegie Hall with Nancy Wilson and Cannonball Adderley and at the Playboy clubs, the Copacabana, and the Kennedy Center. She was invited to the White House by John F. Kennedy. She was also a highly successful recording artist, making more than twenty-five comedy records. Her first, *Moms Mabley: The Funniest Woman in the World,* sold more than a million copies.

Mabley gave birth to three daughters and adopted a son. She made her home in Washington, D.C.; Cleveland, Ohio; and White Plains, New York.

In 1974, Mabley appeared in the motion picture *Amazing Grace.* Shortly after it was completed, she died on May 23, 1975.

BIBLIOGRAPHY

Bennetts, Leslie. "The Pain behind the Laughter of Moms Mabley," *New York Times* (August 8, 1987); Bogle,

Donald. *Brown Sugar: Eighty Years of America's Black Female Superstars* (1980); Brown, Geoffrey F. "Moms Mabley Didn't Die; She Just Chuckled Away," *Jet* (June 12, 1975); Calloway, Earl. "Moms Mabley Makes Mirth in New Movie," *Pittsburgh Courier* (June 8, 1974); Debenham, Warren. *Laughter on Record: A Comedy Discography* (1978); Fox, Ted. *Showtime at the Apollo* (1983); "Friends Gave Her 'Moms' Nickname," *Jet* (June 12, 1975); Gilliam, Dorothy. "Filming the Howard Theatre Tale," *Washington Post* (July 7, 1986); Hall, Nathaniel. "The Negroes of Transylvania County, 1861-1961." In *Transylvania Times: A History*, ed. Mary Jane McCrary (1961); Hamilton, Willie L. "Harlemites Applaud 'Moms' for the Last Time," *New York Amsterdam News* (June 4, 1975); Harris, Tex. "A Solemn Crowd in Harlem Recalls Churchgoing 'Moms,' " *New York Amsterdam News* (June 4, 1975); *The Howard Theatre: A Class Act*. VHS videotape, District of Columbia Humanities Council (June 26, 1985); Jacobson, Mark. "Amazing Moms," *New York* (October 14, 1974); Kellner, Bruce. *The Harlem Renaissance: A Historical Dictionary for the Era* (1984); Levine, Lawrence W. *Black Culture and Black Consciousness: Afro-American Folk Thought from Slavery to Freedom* (1977); Mantle, Burns, ed. *Best Plays of 1931-32* (1932); "Moms Mabley, 75, Comedienne of TV, Stage and Radio, Dead," *New York Times* (May 24, 1975); Moritz, Charles H., ed. "Moms Mabley," *Current Biography Yearbook* (1979); Nichols, Charles H., ed. *Arna Bontemps and Langston Hughes Letters* (1980); Sampson, Henry T. *Blacks in Black and White: A Source Book on Black Films* (1977), and *The Ghost Walks: A Chronological History of Blacks in Show Business, 1865-1910* (1988); Sandford, John E. and Norma Miller. *The Redd Foxx Encyclopedia of Black Humor* (1977); Schiffman, Jack. *Harlem Heyday* (1984); Southern, Eileen. *Music of Black Americans* (1971); Terrell, Bob. "Jim Aiken's Place," *Asheville Citizen-Times* (February 6, 1972); Toll, Robert. *On with the Show* (1976); Trescott, Jacqueline. "Moms: 'Keeping God in Front,' " *Washington Star-News* (October 4, 1974); Williams, Elsie A. "Moms Mabley." In *Women's Comic Visions*, ed. June Sochen (1991).

DISCOGRAPHY

For a discography, see Smith, Ronald L. *Comedy on Record: The Complete Critical Discography* (1988).

ELSIE ARRINGTON WILLIAMS

MADAME SELIKA *see*
SELIKA, MARIE SMITH

MADGETT, NAOMI LONG (1923-)

With seven volumes of her own poetry published by 1988, two edited collections of poems by other African-American poets published by 1991, and two textbooks—one college level creative writing (1980) and one secondary level language and literature (1967)—Naomi Long Madgett belongs to the long tradition of African-American women writers who work as hard on their own literary career as on teaching and encouraging others to be artists. Her poems have been included in more than 100 anthologies, as early as 1949 in *The Poetry of the Negro, 1746-1949* edited by Langston Hughes and Arna Bontemps and as recently as 1992 in *Adam of Ife: Black Women in Praise of Black Men* which she edited and published herself through her own Lotus Press. Madgett's poetry has appeared in journals and magazines such as *Callaloo, Essence, Michigan Quarterly Review, Sage*, and *Obsidian*.

Born in Norfolk, Virginia, on July 5, 1923 Naomi Cornelia Long spent her early childhood in East Orange, New Jersey, where her father, Clarence Marcellus Long, served as a Baptist minister. Madgett's mother, Maude (Hilton) Long, was a schoolteacher. Both of her parents taught her to value education and encouraged her to read at an early age. She often sat on the floor of her father's study reading Aesop's fables or Robert T. Kerlin's anthology *Negro Poets and Their Poems* (1923). In the autobiographical foreword to her *Phantom Nightingale: Juvenilia* (1981), Madgett lists many American and English poets whose work she read as a child, and whom she then unwittingly imitated as she progressed through her own poetry-writing phases: Edgar A. Guest, Longfellow, Langston Hughes, Georgia Douglas Johnson, Tennyson, and Robert Browning.

Naomi's parents moved the family from East Orange to St. Louis, Missouri, in December 1937. The poet looks back on this move as an important transition in her life because in St. Louis she attended the all-Black Sumner High School where her knowledge of African-American achievement was expanded. At Sumner High School academic standards were high and Naomi Long's efforts to write poetry were encouraged. Following her high school graduation at age seventeen in June 1941, she published her first volume of poetry, *Songs to a Phantom Nightingale*, as Naomi Cornelia Long. She entered college, her mother's alma mater Virginia State University, that same year. During her years at Virginia State, Long visited the African-American poet Countee Cullen, who encouraged her to continue writing.

When reflecting in a 1992 interview on her long career as a poet, Naomi Long Madgett assessed the first twenty-two years, between 1934 and 1956, as a lonely time: "I didn't know other Black poets. I didn't follow trends. I just tried to write honestly but my own timing was against me." At this early stage in her career Madgett had followed her own interests in writing lyrical and romantic poetry on a range of topics, while publishers at the time sought poems emphasizing the African-American experience. Her numerous poems written during these years and published in her first two volumes, *Songs to a Phantom Nightingale* (1941) and *One and the Many* (1956), and in one comprehensive collection, *Phantom Nightingale: Juvenilia (Poems 1934-1943)* (1981), repeat the theme of loneliness to characterize her early childhood, adolescence, and young adult years through the mid-1950s. Her repeated references to the small, melodious, Old World migratory bird, the nightingale in her poems reflect her preoccupation with lyrical poetry as well as her belief that the bird "was a phantom . . . as elusive as my dream of happiness, as otherworldly as my youthful fantasies" (*Phantom Nightingale: Juvenilia*).

Long earned her B.A. from Virginia State in 1945. She then began graduate school at New York University, withdrawing after one semester to marry Juan F. Witherspoon on March 31, 1946. She moved with him to Detroit that same year where she worked as a reporter and copyreader for the *Michigan Chronicle*, an African-American weekly, until the birth of her child, Jill, in 1947. During this time some of her poems began to appear in anthologies under the name Naomi Long Witherspoon. In 1948, she started divorce proceedings at the same time that she began working in an all-Black branch office of the Michigan Bell Telephone Company in Detroit as a service representative. She was granted a divorce in 1949 and continued working for the telephone company until 1954. She married William H. Madgett on July 29, 1954. This second marriage ended in divorce in 1960, but the poet continues to publish under the name Madgett. She began teaching in the Detroit public junior high and high schools in 1955. While working as a teacher in Detroit, Madgett completed a Master's degree in English education at Wayne State University in 1956. In 1961 and 1962, she took postgraduate courses at the University of Detroit. She introduced a course in creative writing and the first structured African-American literature course in Detroit public schools in 1965.

During the academic year 1965-66, Madgett was awarded a $10,000 Mott Fellowship to work as a resource associate at Oakland University in Rochester, Michigan. During this year she published the third collection of her own poems (*Star by Star*), and wrote an African-American literature textbook (with

Ethel Tincher and Henry B. Maloney), *Success in Language and Literature/B* for use in high schools. It was published in 1967, the same year that she was honored by the Metropolitan Detroit English Club as the Distinguished English Teacher of the Year. One of Madgett's high school students, Pearl Cleage, is a recognized author of short stories and poetry and has acknowledged Madgett as having first recognized her talent and encouraged her to consider a writing career. Madgett resigned from the Detroit public schools in 1968 to accept a position as associate professor of English at Eastern Michigan University in Ypsilanti. There she taught courses in creative writing and African-American literature in the Department of English Language and Literature until 1984, when she retired as a full professor.

In 1972, three of Madgett's friends interested in publishing her fourth book of poetry, *Pink Ladies in the Afternoon*, founded Lotus Press. Two years later, Naomi Madgett arranged to take over the existing stock of books and name. In 1978, Lotus Press published Madgett's fifth book of poetry, *Exits and Entrances*. In 1980, Madgett, along with her third husband Leonard Andrews and her daughter Jill W. Boyer, incorporated the press as a nonprofit, tax-exempt corporation. Retirement in 1984 allowed Madgett to devote full attention to the growth and development of Lotus Press. The press had gained a reputation as one of the few companies in the country dedicated to keeping Black poetry alive, and has published seventy-five titles, sixty-six of which are still in print. Madgett runs the press by herself, reading and responding to each manuscript personally. Many African-American writers (Houston Baker, Tom Dent, James Emmanuel, Ronald Fair, Lance Jeffers, Gayl Jones, Pinkie Gordon Lane, and Paulette Childress White) were first published by Madgett's Lotus Press. In commemoration of the twentieth anniversary of Lotus Press in 1992, Madgett edited an anthology of poems by Black women to pay tribute to the Black American man: *Adam of Ife: Black Women in Praise of Black Men*.

In 1980, Naomi Long Madgett earned a Ph.D. in literature and creative writing from the International Institute for Advanced Studies. Between 1982 and 1988, she was honored by the Detroit City Council, the Michigan state legislature, the Black Caucus of the National Council of Teachers of English, the Stylus Society of Howard University, Your Heritage House with the Robert Hayden Runagate Award, the College Language Association with its Creative Achievement Award, and Wayne State University with the Arts Achievement Award. In late 1986, she received a Creative Artist Award from the Michigan Council for the Arts to underwrite her seventh book of poetry, *Octavia and Other Poems*.

Published by Third World Press in Chicago in 1988, *Octavia and Other Poems* is divided into three sections, the first of which contains a sequence of thirty-three poems that explore Madgett's family history. The title poem, "Octavia," is based on Madgett's great-aunt, Octavia Cornelia Long, who died of tuberculosis at the age of thirty-four in Charlottesville, Virginia, three years before Madgett was born. The emphasis in the entire collection is on the lives of Madgett's grandparents, uncle, aunts, and father during the first two decades of the twentieth century. The appendix consists of family pictures, biographies, and a family tree that provides a context for the poems about her family. In some ways, *Octavia and Other Poems* is a narrative of the experiences of many African-American families at that time.

In the course of her more than fifty years as a poet, publisher, and teacher, Naomi Long Madgett has either been influenced by or participated in the Harlem Renaissance, the civil rights movement, the Black arts movement, and the women's movement in the United States. When she began writing poetry in early 1940 there were few if any other African-American women publishing poetry. By the mid-1960s, Madgett was part of a circle of Black poets in Detroit and other cities who encouraged one another's development. Since the mid-1970s, she has been contributing to the tradition of African-American poetry both as poet and as an independent publisher. She currently lives with her husband, Leonard Andrews, in Detroit, Michigan.

BIBLIOGRAPHY

Bailey, Leaonead Pack. *Broadside Authors and Artists: An Illustrated Biographical Directory* (1974); *BAW*; *DLB*; *IWW*; Madgett, Naomi Long. Personal Interview (June 7, 1992), and "A Short History of Lotus Press: 1972-1992," typescript (1992); *The Writer's Market* (1986). Madgett's papers are in the Special Collections of Fisk University Library, Nashville, Tennessee.

ALICE A. DECK

MAHONEY, CAROLYN R. (1946-)

Carolyn Mahoney's creative talents have been employed since 1989 as the first mathematician on the faculty of a new college, California State University at San Marcos. Known as an effective teacher, she was invited by the Committee on Student Chapters of the Mathematical Association of America (MAA) to speak about "Contemporary Problems in Graph Theory" at the national MAA meeting in Baltimore in January 1992. She has given talks on both mathematical research (combinatorics, graph theory, and matroids) and pedagogy throughout the United States and the People's Republic of China.

Carolyn Mahoney was born in Memphis, Tennessee, on December 22, 1946, to Stephen and Myrtle Boone. In 1970, she received her B.S. in mathematics from Siena College in Memphis. Her M.S. and Ph.D. in mathematics were awarded by Ohio State University in 1972 and 1983, respectively. She has taught at Denison University in Granville, Ohio (1984-89), and Ohio State University (1987-89). She and her husband Charles have three daughters.

She is coordinator of the Young Scholars Program, a year-round, comprehensive, precollege program for low-income Appalachian, Hispanic, and Black students in Ohio. She directed a program to improve the achievement of Black students in mathematics at four Ohio liberal arts schools. From 1986 to 1989, she was a member of the test development committee of the College Board. She has served on many boards and prestigious committees, contributed to numerous policy-setting documents, won several grants, and given dozens of invited talks. On March 20, 1989, Carolyn Mahoney was inducted into the Ohio Women's Hall of Fame.

BIBLIOGRAPHY

Mahoney, Carolyn R. "On the Independent Set Numbers of a Class of Matroids," *Journal of Combinatorial Theory* (1985); Mahoney, Carolyn R. and Franklin Demana. "Filling the Math and Science Pipeline with Young Scholars," *Notices of the American Mathematical Society* (February 1991).

PATRICIA CLARK KENSCHAFT

MAHONEY, MARY ELIZA (1845-1926)

The first trained Black nurse in the United States, Mary Eliza Mahoney was born in Dorchester, Massachusetts, on May 7, 1845, to Charles and Mary Jane Stewart Mahoney. On August 1, 1879, she completed a sixteen-month diploma program in nursing at the New England Hospital for Women and Children in Boston, at a time when the institution's charter stipulated that each class include only one Black student and one Jewish student.

Mahoney registered with the Nurses Directory at the Massachusetts Medical Library in Boston upon receipt of her diploma. Like the vast majority of new nurses, she first entered private-duty nursing. Not until after World War II would the majority of nurses secure staff employment in hospitals, and Black nurses would wait even longer for hospital staff appointments.

Mahoney was able to secure membership in the Nurses Associated Alumnae of the United States and Canada, organized in 1896 and later renamed the American Nurses' Association (ANA). By the turn of the century, few Black nurses were allowed to become members of the ANA because nurses were required to become members of state nursing associations before they were granted membership in the national organization and southern associations refused to admit Black women.

After Black nurses organized their own organization, the National Association of Colored Graduate Nurses (NACGN), in 1908, Mahoney delivered the welcoming address at its first convention in Boston in August 1909. The members honored Mahoney in 1911 by awarding her life membership in the NACGN and electing her national chaplain, a position that bore the responsibility for the induction of new officers.

In 1911, Mahoney became supervisor of the Howard Orphan Asylum for Black children in Kings Park, Long Island. She retired in 1922, but continued to participate in and observe the activities of the NACGN until her death on January 4, 1926.

As a lasting tribute, the NACGN established in 1936 an award in her name to honor distinguished Black nurses. When the NACGN merged with the ANA in 1951, the practice of giving the Mary Mahoney Award was preserved. In 1976, she was named to nursing's Hall of Fame.

BIBLIOGRAPHY

Davis, Althea T. "Architects for Integration and Equality: Early Black American Leaders in Nursing," Ed.D. diss. (1987); Miller, Helen S. *Mary Eliza Mahoney, 1845-1926: America's First Black Professional Nurse* (1986); National Association of Colored Graduate Nurses, Minutes, 1908-17, 1917-37, Schomburg Center for Research in Black Culture, New York Public Library.

DARLENE CLARK HINE

MAMMY

The Mammy figure remains a staple of plantation legend and continues as a powerful icon well into the present. Her status as a historical figure remains disputed, but most scholars agree that her role in popular culture reflects a deliberate manipulation of stereotype for racial exploitation and commercial gain.

The myth of the Mammy revolves around two basic principles. First, that a slave woman within the white household devoted her maternal instincts and skills to the white family who owned her and that she took pleasure and pride in this service. Second, that she gained status from this role and was revered within the Black community.

The roots of this myth are planted deep in Old South nostalgia. It is true that many Black women were forced to devote their time and energies to the white family in the "Big House," but most were not slave women of advanced age who lorded over the white household. Rather most slave women who tended children were young, interchangeable nurses. The maternal affection Black women were alleged to have lavished on their white charges was more likely the mask demanded by racist slaveowners. White southerners wished to believe that slaves preferred white children to their own, not merely as a strategy for currying favor but as a recognition of white superiority. White employers have demanded this deception from Black household help well into the modern era.

The letters and diaries of antebellum white slaveowners reflect the ambivalence many felt concerning slave women within the household. In fact, many were young mulattoes, rather than the mature, "unmixed" Black women portrayed in legend. The presence of these women in planter homes could be disruptive to family harmony if planters sexually exploited the situation. Even if these tensions were absent, many white mistresses expressed fears for their children entrusted to Black surrogates, with exaggerated claims of Black incompetence. The image of the Mammy has obscured the large body of evidence that suggests she was more a product of fiction than of antebellum life. Furthermore, Black women possibly emerged in these Mammy roles only after slavery—the Mammy was not merely a member of white southerners' postwar households but the Lost Cause's most powerful ideological weapon.

The status of the Mammy within the Black community has almost always been derived from white authority, seriously limiting any accurate measure of

In Gone with the Wind *(1939), Hattie McDaniel played Mammy to the headstrong
Scarlett O'Hara (Vivien Leigh). For her performance, McDaniel won the first Academy
Award ever presented to a Black actor, male or female. She had not been allowed to attend the
Atlanta premiere of the film, however.*

regard within the Black community. African-American men and women have recognized white celebrations of the Mammy as a means of emasculating Black men within American society. Although men and women unite in this indictment, gender has created some intense debates within the Black community on these explosive issues, addressed in Michele Wallace's *Black Macho and the Myth of Superwoman* (1980).

Despite conflicting intents, white authors of the North and South contributed to this mythmaking. Harriet Beecher Stowe's Aunt Chloe in *Uncle Tom's Cabin* (1852) is a literary godmother of the many popular variations on this theme in modern literature, from William Faulkner's Dilsey in *The Sound and the Fury* (1929) to Margaret Mitchell's Mammy in

Gone with the Wind (1939) to Carson McCullers's Berenice in *The Member of the Wedding* (1946). The mammies represented in this genre, as Trudier Harris has illuminated, are warm, nurturing figures who live to serve. They appear not only in fiction but in films and television, advertising, and other media.

Black actresses like Hattie McDaniel and Louise Beavers were confined to these stereotypical roles because the image of the Black woman as happily sacrificing her needs to those of whites served national as well as regional myths. Trapped within the racist film community, McDaniel struggled against repressive forces during the 1930s. Irony was her strong suit on and off the screen. When asked how she felt about playing only maids in the movies, she replied that she was a lot happier earning her Hollywood salary playing a domestic instead of having to be one, pointing out the economic realities that women of color faced. Further, her Oscar for her role in *Gone with the Wind* (1939) reflected not only her talent to convincingly play the role of Mammy but her superb skill at being able to turn the stereotype inside out. At the same time, it was perhaps no accident that until 1991 no Black female screen performance *except* the Mammy was singled out for American film's highest accolade.

This image should have outlived its usefulness as a literary device; a pointedly different image of the Black domestic appeared in the television series *I'll Fly Away* (1991-), and the role was explored sensitively in the 1990-91 season of the popular Black situation comedy *A Different World*. Protests and consciousness-raising campaigns have made inroads.

Regardless of this progress, Mammy continues her reign. The reappearance of Mitchell's Mammy—in one of the most traditional and stereotyped modes, on her deathbed being nursed by her former white owner—in the runaway best-seller *Scarlett* (1991) demonstrated her tenacious hold on the white American imagination. From minstrel shows of the nineteenth century to Al Jolson in blackface singing "I'd walk a million miles for one of her smiles" in the first talking picture, *The Jazz Singer* (1927), to Mandy Patinkin (not in blackface) belting out the same song in his 1989 Broadway one-man show, *Dress Casual*, American musical theater celebrates Mammy, often masquerading in the guise of nostalgia. The exploitation of this icon in country collectibles and other popular commercial fare in shopping malls and airports throughout the country diminishes the image of Black women in America. Most treacherous of all, for over 100 years she has haunted kitchen shelves; even with the handkerchief removed from her head after a 1980s update, we still recognize this pernicious incarnation grinning down at us—Aunt Jemima.

[*See also* DOMESTIC WORKERS IN THE SOUTH; MEMORABILIA.]

The servant Dilsey is a central character in William Faulkner's great novel The Sound and the Fury. *She is played superbly in the film version by Ethel Waters. [Donald Bogle]*

BIBLIOGRAPHY

Bogle, Donald. *Toms, Coons, Mulattoes, Mammies, and Bucks* (1989); Harris, Trudier. *From Mammies to Militants: Domestics in Black American Literature* (1982); McDowell, Deborah, and Arnold Rampersad, eds. *Slavery and the Imagination* (1989); Morris, Sarah. "From Griddle Cake to Hip-Hop: Reading the Aunt Jemima Stereotype in Literature and Popular Culture," undergraduate thesis (1991); White, Deborah. *Ar'n't I a Woman?: Female Slaves in the Antebellum South* (1985).

CATHERINE CLINTON

MAPP, ZYLPHA *see* BAHA'I FAITH

MARSHALL, HARRIET GIBBS (1868-1941)

Educator, concert pianist, and author Harriet Gibbs was born in Vancouver, British Columbia, Canada, on February 18, 1868. The daughter of Marie A. Alexander and Judge Miflin Wistar Gibbs, she grew up in Oberlin, Ohio, where she attended Oberlin Conservatory of Music, the first African-American woman to complete the course in piano (1889). She concertized early in her career, and, after serving as the first director of music at Eckstein-Norton College (Cane Springs, Kentucky), she supervised music activities for colored students in Washington, D.C.'s public schools (1900-1903). Her official title, however, was Assistant Director of Music for the District of Columbia Public Schools. In 1903, she founded the Washington Conservatory of Music and School of Expression. On June 3, 1906, she married Napoleon B. Marshall.

The Washington Conservatory was important to the city not only because it offered opportunity for college level instruction in music but also because it provided cultural programs for the city from 1910 to its closing in 1960. Harriet Marshall had conceived of the school as part of a National Center of Negro Music, which she opened in 1936. From 1922 to 1928 she lived in Haiti where her husband had been appointed a member of the American legation. While there, Harriet Marshall became interested in the country and its culture, cofounding the industrial school l'Oeuvre des Femmes Haitienne pour l'Organization de Labour and researching the achievements of Haitian women. She later wrote *A Story of Haiti* (1930).

Another literary effort was an unpublished drama titled *Last Concerto* based on the life, love, and music of Samuel Coleridge-Taylor. Harriet Gibbs Marshall died in Washington, D.C., on February 25, 1941.

[*See also* BAHA'I FAITH.]

BIBLIOGRAPHY

BDAAM; *DANB*; McGinty, Doris E. "The Washington Conservatory of Music and School of Expression," *Black Perspective in Music* (Spring 1979); Washington Conservatory of Music and James Hunt Collections in Moorland-Spingarn Research Center. Howard University, Washington, D.C.

DORIS EVANS McGINTY

MARSHALL, PAULE (1929-)

"We (as people of African descent) must accept the task of 'reinventing' our own images and the role which Africa will play in the process will be essential" (Williams 1986). This statement summarizes the content as well as the ideological thrust of Paule Marshall's fiction, for although she focuses primarily on the experiences of English- and French-speaking African peoples from the Caribbean, she also writes about the Black experience in North and South America. Her writing as a whole explores and reconstructs the African presence throughout the diaspora.

She was born Valenza Pauline Burke on April 9, 1929, in Brooklyn, New York, the daughter of Ada (Clement) and Samuel Burke, emigrants from Barbados, and she grew up in a tightly structured West Indian-American community. At nine years of age she visited the homeland of her parents and wrote a series of poems reflecting her impressions. However, it was not until her young adult life, when she began to write serious fiction, that she drew upon the power of Barbadian speech to describe a distinct racial and ethnic heritage.

Marshall graduated cum laude and Phi Beta Kappa from Brooklyn College in 1954. From her first marriage to Kenneth Marshall (1950) she has one son, Evan Keith, who is a naval architect living in London. She divorced Kenneth Marshall in 1963. In 1970, she wed for the second time, marrying Nourry Menard, a Haitian businessman.

Marshall's fiction writing began when she started composing short vignettes at the end of her work day as a researcher and staff writer for *Our World* magazine in New York City. These exercises later developed into her first short story, "The Valley Between" (1954).

Paule Marshall draws upon her experience as the daughter of emigrants from Barbados to examine in her fiction what she calls "the task of 'reinventing' " the images of people of African descent. [Schomburg Center]

National Endowment for the Arts and Humanities Award (1967-68 and 1978-79), the American Book Award (1984), the Langston Hughes Medallion Award (1986), the New York State Governor's Award for Literature (1987), the John Dos Passos Award for Literature (1989), and John D. and Catherine T. MacArthur Fellowship (1992).

With her multicultural background, Marshall is uniquely suited to examine points of convergence and divergence between various cultures, and her emphasis on Black female characters addresses contemporary feminist issues from an Afrocentric perspective. The ultimate objective of Marshall's fiction is to dismantle all forms of personal, social, and political oppression and to celebrate the triumph of the human spirit.

BIBLIOGRAPHY

Benston, Kimberly. "Architectural Imagery and Unity in Paule Marshall's *Brown Girl, Brownstones*," *Negro American Literature Forum* (Fall 1975); Brathwaite, Edward K. "West Indian History and Society in the Art of Paule Marshall's Novels," *Journal of Black Studies* (1970); Bröck, Sabine. "Transcending the 'Loophole of Retreat': Paule Marshall's Placing of Female Generations," *Callaloo* (Winter 1987); Brown, Lloyd W. "The Rhythms of Power in Paule Marshall's Fiction," *Novel: A Forum on Fiction* (Winter 1974); Busia, Abena P. A. "What Is Your Nation? Reconnecting Africa and Her Diaspora through Paule Marshall's *Praisesong for a Widow*." In *Changing Our Own Words: Essays on Criticism, Theory, and Writing by Black Women*, ed. Cheryl A. Wall (1989); Christian, Barbara. *Black Women Novelists: The Development of a Tradition, 1892-1976* (1980), and "Paule Marshall." In *African-American Writers*, ed. Valerie Smith (1991), and *Black Feminist Criticism: Perspectives on Black Women Writers* (1985); Cook, John. "Whose Child? The Fiction of Paule Marshall," *College Language Association Journal* (September 1980); DeVeaux, Alexis. "Paule Marshall: In Celebration of Our Triumph," *Essence* (May 1979); Denniston, Dorothy L. "Paule Marshall." In *American Woman Writers*, ed. Lina Mainiero and Langdon Faust (1981); *DLB*; Gabbin, Joanne A. "A Laying On of Hands: Black Women Writers Exploring the Roots of Their Folk and Cultural Tradition." In *Wild Women in the Whirlwind: Afra-American Culture and the Contemporary Literary Renaissance*, ed. Joanne M. Braxton and Andrée Nicola McLaughlin (1990); Kapai, L. "Dominant Themes and Techniques in Paule Marshall's Fiction," *College Language Association Journal* (September 1972); Keiz, Marcia. "Themes and Style in the Works of Paule Marshall," *Negro American Literature Forum* (Fall 1975); Kubitscheck, Missy Dehn. "Paule Marshall's Women on Quest," *Black American Literature Forum* (Spring-Summer 1987); Pannill, Linda. "From the 'Workshop': The Fiction of Paule Marshall," *MELUS: Journal of the Society for Multiethnic Literatures of the United States* (Summer 1985); Pollard, Velma. "Cultural Connections in Paule Marshall's *Praisesong*

Her subsequent fiction includes *Brown Girl, Brownstones* (1959), *Soul Clap Hands and Sing* (1961), "Reena" (1962), "Some Get Wasted" (1964), "To Da-Duh: In Memoriam" (1967), *The Chosen Place, the Timeless People* (1969), *Praisesong for the Widow* (1983), and *Daughters* (1991).

Marshall combines a writing career with teaching and currently holds an appointment as professor of English and creative writing at Virginia Commonwealth University in Richmond. She has received several prestigious awards, including a Guggenheim fellowship (1960), the Rosenthal Award (1962), a Ford Foundation grant for fiction writers (1964-65), the *for the Widow," World Literature Written in English* (Autumn 1985); Sandiford, Keith. "Paule Marshall's Praisesong for the Widow: The Reluctant Heiress, or Whose Life Is It Anyway?" *Black American Literature Forum* (Winter 1986); Spillers, Hortense J. *"Chosen Place, Timeless People*: Some Figurations for the New World." In *Conjuring: Black Women, Fiction, and Literary Tradition*, ed. Marjorie Pryse and Hortense J. Spillers (1985); Talbert, L. Lee. "The Poetics of Prophecy in Paule Marshall's *Soul Clap Hands and Sing*," *MELUS: Journal of the Society for Multi-ethnic Literatures of the United States* (1977); Troester, Rosalie Riegle. "Turbulence and Tenderness: Mothers, Daughters, and 'Other Mothers' in Paule Marshall's *Brown Girl, Brownstones*," *Sage* (Fall 1984); Turner, Darwin T. "Introduction." In *Soul Clap Hands and Sing* (1988); Washington, Mary Helen. "Afterword." In *Brown Girl, Brownstones* (1981); Welch, Sharon D. "Memory and Accountability." In *A Feminist Ethic of Risk* (1990); Williams, John. "Return of a Native Daughter: An Interview with Paule Marshall and Maryse Conde," *Sage* (Fall 1986); Willis, Susan. "Describing Arcs of Recovery: Paule Marshall's Relationship to Afro-American Culture." In her *Specifying: Black Women Writing the American Experience* (1987). For a special issue on Paule Marshall's fiction, see *Callaloo* (Spring-Summer 1983); see also several essays in *Black Women Writers (1950-1980): A Critical Evaluation*, ed. Mari Evans (1983).

DOROTHY L. DENNISTON

MARTIN, MARY B. *see* BAHA'I FAITH

MARTIN, ROBERTA EVELYN (1907-1969)

American composers of art music in the Western European tradition who studied with Nadia Boulanger take pride in having studied with the most important teacher of composition in the twentieth century. Gospel singers who sang with Roberta Martin are accorded a special position, for while Mahalia Jackson is considered the "Greatest Gospel singer of all times" and Thomas Andrew Dorsey is called the "Father of Gospel Music," Martin "created and left a dynasty of gospel singers and a portfolio of unduplicated gospel music." Equally significant is the fact that Martin was able to accomplish what few other composers have: the effective combination of emotion, style, and form.

Gospel singer, pianist, composer, and publisher Roberta Evelyn Martin was one of six children born to William and Anna Winston in Helena, Arkansas. She began taking piano lessons from her oldest brother's wife at the age of six, at which time she played the piano for the local Sunday school. When she was eight, the family moved to Cairo, Illinois, and then to Chicago when she was ten. Roberta graduated from Wendell Phillips High School in Chicago, where she studied piano with the choral director, Mildred Bryant Jones. While preparing for a career as a concert pianist, she accepted her first church position as pianist for the Young People's Choir at Ebenezer Baptist Church.

Martin initially was not attracted to the new gospel music being sung in Sanctified churches. In 1932, when Thomas Dorsey and Theodore R. Frye organized one of the first gospel choirs at Chicago's Pilgrim Baptist Church, Martin was recruited as pianist. However, in 1933, after she heard the Bertha Wise Singers of Georgia, she adopted the Wise gospel piano style and, with the help of Frye, organized a group of male singers, first called the Martin-Frye Singers. The members were Willie Webb, Robert Anderson, Eugene Smith, and Narsalus McKissick. In 1935 she severed her relationship with Frye and renamed the group the Roberta Martin Singers. In the 1940s, she added female singers Delois Barrett Campbell and Bessie Folk and refined the "Roberta Martin gospel style." Her style is marked more by the potential of gospel than by its tradition, since she cultivated the well-modulated voice, as opposed to the encumbered, raspy tone so often associated with gospel; she eschewed the low bass voice, instead creating a vocal harmony of soprano, alto, tenor, and high baritone; she favored the aggressive rather than passive lead, supported by background voices that more often hum a response than repeat the lyrics of the lead, thereby placing more emphasis on the lyrics and the leader; and she created a gospel piano style marked more by nuance and refinement than virtuosity and flamboyance. Her piano style was wholly adopted by her piano student and stepdaughter Lucy Smith Collier, the granddaughter of the legendary Chicago preacher Reverend Lucy Smith.

In 1939, Martin opened her publishing firm, the Roberta Martin Studio of Music, and one of her first successes came in 1941 with the publication of "He Knows How Much We Can Bear" by Phyllis Hall. She composed her first gospel song, "Try Jesus, He Satisfies," in 1943. Before her death she had composed over 100 songs under her own name and that of Fay Brown. Among her best-known compositions, in addition to "Try Jesus," are "God Is Still on the Throne" (1959), "No Other Help I Know" (1961),

"Let It Be" (1959), and "Teach Me Lord" (1963). Less concerned with publishing her own compositions than those of other composers, her firm published compositions by James Cleveland, Alex Bradford, Lucy Matthews, Sammy Lewis, Kenneth Woods, and Dorothy Norwood. Her most famous publication was her theme song, "Only a Look" by Anna Shepherd.

Martin began recording in the late 1930s, and during her career earned six gold records for selling a million copies of a song or an album. She received gold records for the songs "Only a Look" and "Old Ship of Zion" on the Apollo label and "Grace," "God Specializes," "God Is Still on the Throne," and "I'm So Grateful" on the Savoy label. Adamant that her name never appear on a marquee, she refused engagements at New York's Apollo Theatre and Las Vegas night clubs, but the Roberta Martin Singers appeared in almost every other gospel venue. From the huge tents of New York's Reverend A. A. Childs, to the small churches of Cocoa, Florida, to the elegant auditoriums of Los Angeles, to the domed cathedrals of Italy, where they were invited to perform at the Spoleto Festival by its creator, Gian Carlo Menotti, in 1963, the Roberta Martin Singers carried their gospel message throughout the world for over thirty-five years. Other singers associated with the group include Archie Dennis, Sadie Durrah, Gloria Griffin, Myrtle Jackson, Romance Watson, Louise McCord, Myrtle Scott, Delores Taliaferro (Della Reese), and James Lawrence. Roberta Martin was honored by a colloquium and concert at the Smithsonian Institution in 1982.

[*See also* GOSPEL MUSIC.]

BIBLIOGRAPHY

Boyer, Horace Clarence. "Black Gospel Music." In *The New Grove Dictionary of American Music*, ed. H. Wiley Hitchcock and Stanley Sadie (1986); Heilbut, Anthony. *The Gospel Sound—Good News and Bad Times* (1985); Jackson, Irene V. "Afro-American Gospel Music and Its Social Setting with Special Attention to Roberta Martin," Ph.D. diss. (1974); Williams-Jones, Pearl. "Roberta Martin: Spirit of an Era." In *Roberta Martin and the Roberta Singers: The Legacy and the Music*, ed. Bernice Johnson Reagon and Linn Shapiro (1982).

HORACE CLARENCE BOYER

MARTIN, SALLIE (1895–1988)

Gospel singer and composer Sallie Martin is acknowledged as "the mother of gospel music" because of her ground-breaking work as a promoter and pub-

lisher. Born in Pittfield, Georgia, she eventually moved to Baltimore, Maryland, where she met and married Wallace Martin. The Martins, including one son, finally settled in Chicago. There, in 1932, Sallie Martin began her involvement in gospel music, winning a spot singing with a group headed by Thomas A. Dorsey, "the father of gospel music." With Dorsey, and later with singer/composer Roberta Martin (no relation), Sallie Martin helped popularize gospel music during its "golden age," 1945 to 1960. They established numerous choirs and created "the gospel highway circuit," a loosely formed network of churches and other performance venues that welcomed gospel music at a time when it was not always embraced by elite Black congregations.

Martin, who had only a seventh-grade education, served as Dorsey's song demonstrator, promoter, and bookkeeper, and she is credited with encouraging

Sallie Martin, known as "the mother of gospel music," helped to popularize that style as a promoter and publisher. She formed the first all-female gospel group and influenced many artists, including Dinah Washington. [Mary Wilkes]

him to copyright and publish his music. The pair cofounded the National Convention of Gospel Choirs and Choruses in 1933, the first such convention for gospel performers. Later, she joined with composer Kenneth Morris to found the Martin and Morris Publishing Company that issued such classics as "Just a Closer Walk with Thee" and "Dig a Little Deeper." She is also credited with forming the first all-female gospel group, the Sallie Martin Singers. Among the many artists she influenced was blues great Dinah Washington, who performed with Martin as a teenager. Once, in assessing her life, Sallie Martin said, "I've never been the greatest . . . never claimed to be the greatest, yet and still I've been everywhere the greatest have been" (Heilbut 1985).

BIBLIOGRAPHY

Heilbut, Anthony. *The Gospel Sound: Good News and Bad Times* ([1971] 1985); "A Homecoming Victory Celebration to the Loving Memory of the Late Sallie Martin, 'Mother of Gospel Music,' " funeral program, Chicago (1988).

DISCOGRAPHY

Say Amen, Somebody, DRG SB 2 12584 (1983); *God Is Here*, the Sallie Martin Singers, Vee Jay 5041 (n.d.); *The Legends*, Savoy SL 14742 (n.d.).

DEBORAH SMITH BARNEY

Cora Martin-Moore is among the second generation of gospel pioneers who serve as role models for today's young musicians. As such, she continues a tradition established by her adoptive mother, Sallie Martin. [J. C. DjeDje]

MARTIN-MOORE, CORA (1927-)

Cora Juanita Brewer Martin-Moore (gospel singer, choir director, composer, and publisher) was born November 4, 1927, in Chicago, Illinois. She is the oldest child of Lucious Bruer and Anne Claude James Bruer. When Martin-Moore was just a youngster, she was adopted by pioneer gospel singer Sallie Martin. Martin-Moore is married to Henry A. Moore.

Martin-Moore began her musical career in Chicago at an early age as a member of Mount Pleasant Baptist Church. Later, as a featured contralto soloist, she traveled extensively throughout the United States and made several recordings with her mother's group, the Sallie Martin Singers. Since moving to Los Angeles in 1947, she has been associated with Saint Paul Baptist Church, one of the first churches on the West Coast to promote and make recordings of gospel music (Capitol Records, 1947). She has served as a member of Saint Paul's legendary Echoes of Eden Choir (1947-58), director of the John L. Branham Crusaders Youth Choir (1952-58), and minister of music and director of the Echoes of Eden Choir

(1958-present). In 1959, the latter group performed with Nat "King" Cole in the Hollywood Bowl.

Martin-Moore's formal educational training was obtained from several schools in the Los Angeles area: University of California, Los Angeles Extension; Los Angeles Southwest College (A.A. degree); and California State University, Dominguez Hills (B.A. degree). She has owned and managed a religious music studio and record shop (Los Angeles Gospel Music Mart) and served as an instructor at Crenshaw-Dorsey Community Adult School for over thirteen years.

Not only was Martin-Moore featured as a religious disc jockey for two years on her own gospel radio program, but also she has composed, arranged, and published a number of gospel songs, spirituals, and anthems. Among her more famous are "Heaven Sweet Heaven" (1953), "Do You Know the Lord Jesus for Yourself?" (1955), "What a Wonderful Savior I've Found" (1957), and "He Is a Friend of Mine" (1965). Her song "He'll Wash You Whiter Than Snow" (1954) was featured in a Universal motion picture produced by Quincy Jones (*The Lost Man*, 1969), starring Sidney Poitier. During the 1970s she began to tour and perform as a solo artist which led to two recordings with Savoy Records: *James Cleveland Presents Cora Martin* and *I Found God*. In 1974, she was awarded best soloist album by James Cleveland's Gospel Music Workshop of America (GMWA), and since 1987, she has been a member of the board of directors of GMWA. Also, she has received many tributes and proclamations from the city of Los Angeles.

Since arriving on the West Coast in the 1940s, Martin-Moore has become a nationally recognized gospel performer in her own right. Along with others (e.g., James Cleveland, Albertina Walker, Delois Barrett Campbell) who had their early gospel music training in Chicago (a city now regarded as the birthplace and center for gospel music), she is among the second generation of gospel music pioneers who serve as role models for today's young musicians, continuing a tradition established by her mother, Sallie Martin.

BIBLIOGRAPHY

DjeDje, Jacqueline Cogdell. "Gospel Music in the Los Angeles Black Community: A Historical Overview," *Black Music Research Journal* (Spring 1989); Martin-Moore, Cora. Interviews (July 8 and 23, 1987, and November 21 and 25, 1991).

JACQUELINE COGDELL DJEDJE

MARYLAND FREEDOM UNION

On February 9, 1966, some twenty Black women, working as nurses' aides, housekeepers, and kitchen staff, walked off their jobs at Lincoln Nursing Home in Baltimore, Maryland. They called field secretaries from the Congress of Racial Equality (CORE) with whom they had met the previous week, and told them that Lincoln was "on strike," that the workers had named their union "Maryland Freedom Local No. 1," and that the CORE organizers had better come down to Lincoln Nursing Home immediately to show the workers how to "run a proper picket line." The workers, who made as little as 25¢ an hour and worked up to seventy-two hours a week, became the nucleus of what they called a "new kind of union," the Maryland Freedom Union (MFU).

The concept of a "freedom union" of poverty-wage workers had been advanced by CORE staff frustrated with failed efforts to assist Black workers in

The Maryland Freedom Union (MFU) was born out of frustration by CORE staff in their failed attempts to assist Black workers in attaining union rights and benefits. With encouragement from CORE field secretaries, some twenty employees of the Lincoln Nursing Home in Baltimore went out on strike in February 1966 and became the nucleus for the new union. The MFU transcended the traditional limits of trade unions by organizing low-wage workplaces as an integral part of a movement to transform American society. [Raya Dunayevskaya Collection, Wayne State University]

struggles for union rights and benefits. Convinced that the American Federation of Labor and Congress of Industrial Organizations (AFL-CIO) unions were not interested in organizing such workers, and exhilarated by the success of the Student Nonviolent Coordinating Committee's (SNCC) 1965 Mississippi Freedom Labor Union project, CORE selected Baltimore as the site of its own freedom union experiment.

The Lincoln Nursing Home strikers were soon joined by Black women workers at two other nursing homes. Meeting jointly, they elected Vivian Jones, a nurses' aide at Bolton Hill Nursing Home, as MFU president, and Ola Mae Johnson, an aide at Lincoln, as secretary. The union members, with no prior public speaking experience, spoke to church groups, student meetings, and outdoor rallies to explain the strike and appeal for funds.

Together with CORE members and supporters from local churches and schools, they picketed the suburban homes of nursing home owners and marched on city hall. By March 1966, they created a union study group on Black and labor history, reading a history of Black struggles, *American Civilization on Trial* (1963), and inviting its author, political philosopher Raya Dunayevskaya, to lecture at the MFU's Freedom House. Dunayevskaya's suggestion that the workers view themselves as "self-developing thinkers" made an impact (Raya Dunayevskaya Collection 1969).

After completing a covert study of retail stores along the mall shopping streets of the West and East Baltimore ghettos, the MFU opened an organizing drive among retail workers there. For the campaign, MFU President Vivian Jones designed a large button showing two Black hands breaking a chain and the union slogan, "Breaking Free at Last." Thousands of the buttons, distributed in the Black community, helped garner support for an MFU plan that any store they picketed was to be boycotted by Black shoppers. The boycotts proved effective, and MFU strikers succeeded in winning union contracts at three of the largest retail chain stores in the ghettos by August 1966.

The campaigns aroused opposition from both merchants' associations and AFL-CIO unions. The unions accused the MFU of organizing in direct competition with them. Walter Reuther, then head of the AFL-CIO's Industrial Union Department, complained to Floyd McKissick, national director of CORE, about CORE becoming a union. McKissick, citing CORE's deep financial crisis, soon severed formal ties with the MFU.

Later MFU campaigns included food stores, hospitals, and a print shop, but its momentum slowed under the impact of tight finances and the ideological crises afflicting civil rights organizations in the late 1960s. The inner-city stores and nursing homes organized by the MFU closed in the early 1970s, victims of economic decline or neighborhood gentrification.

While it flourished, the MFU's membership, nearly all Black and 90 percent women, and many of them recently arrived from the rural South, created a union quite different from the typical AFL-CIO affiliate. What drew so many of these workers to the MFU was not only that it was a union willing to accept them as members. It was that this organization called itself a *freedom* union and sought to organize low-wage workplaces as an integral part of a movement to transform the whole of American society. As a forerunner of both the Black caucuses within established unions and Black feminist critiques of civil rights organizations, the Maryland Freedom Union was a unique learning experience.

BIBLIOGRAPHY

Allen, J. Linn. "Got 35¢ to 61¢ an Hour," *Afro-American* (February 12, 1966); Flug, Michael. "Organized Labor and the Civil Rights Movement of the 1960s: The Case of the Maryland Freedom Union," *Labor History* (Summer 1990); Johnson, Ola. "Low-Paid Workers Win Fight for Union," *News and Letters* (August-September 1966); Meier, August and Elliott Rudwick. *CORE: A Study in the Civil Rights Movement, 1942-1967* (1973); Congress of Racial Equality papers, 1941-67. State Historical Society of Wisconsin, Madison; Raya Dunayevskaya Collection. Archives of Labor and Urban Affairs, Wayne State University, Detroit, Michigan (1969).

MICHAEL FLUG

MASON, (BRIDGET) BIDDY (1818-1891)

(Bridget) Biddy Mason, an illiterate slave and plantation-trained midwife, walked across the United States from Mississippi to California to become a powerful force in the economic, educational, spiritual, and health-care developments of the nascent Black community of Los Angeles.

Born a slave in Hancock County, Mississippi, on August 15, 1818, Biddy's parents remain unknown. However, records indicate that she was of mixed blood, Black and three kinds of Indian—Choctaw, Seminole, and Geegi. Biddy was owned in turn by three families who operated plantations: the Smithsons of South Carolina, the Bankses of Georgia, and the Crosby family of Mississippi. Biddy Mason's childhood was spent in Mississippi where she was trained to assist the house servants and midwives in the Smithson household. When his cousin Rebecca married Robert Marion Smith in 1836, John Smithson made her a present of Mason, along with three other slaves—two house servants, Hannah and Ella, and Buck, a blacksmith and horse trainer. Mason managed the plantation's business affairs and cared for the sickly Rebecca. Robert Smith became the father of Mason's three daughters, Ellen, Ann, and Harriet. He also was father to nine children by Hannah and six children with his wife.

Around 1844, Robert Smith was converted to Mormonism by Elder John Brown. By March 1848, the Smith clan had joined the Crosbys, Bankses, and Smithsons in the third Mormon migration into Indian territory. Biddy Mason, Hannah, and forty other slaves accompanied the Mormons on this migration.

They were promised their freedom at the completion of this journey if they chose to accompany the family.

During this trip to Utah, Mason herded the cattle, cared for her newborn daughter, Harriet, and made camp at the end of the day. She also made the first meal of the day and broke up camp. Because hers was the last wagon, she literally ate the dust of the entire wagon train.

They lived in Utah for three years. In 1851, Brigham Young requested volunteers to establish a settlement in southern California. After camping at Cajon Pass for three months, they moved into San Bernardino. During this time, Mason came into contact with the Black community of Los Angeles.

In December 1855, Charles Owens notified his father, Robert Owens, that Smith was planning to remove Biddy and her three daughters to Texas. Lizzy Flake Rowan, a friend to Mason, joined Robert Owens in a petition to Judge Benjamin Hayes that resulted in freedom papers for Biddy Mason and thirteen other of Smith's slaves. Hayes asked Sheriff Burnside to place Mason and her three daughters in his protective custody. This lawsuit set a precedent regarding the legal rights of Black settlers in the American West.

Freedom was officially achieved on January 21, 1856, ending Biddy Mason's long and arduous quest for freedom for herself and for her children. She became a nurse and midwife to Dr. John S. Griffin, serving members of the Los Angeles, San Bernardino, San Diego, and Santa Barbara communities. She saved her wages of $2.50 per day to purchase her homestead at Spring Street. Mason was a founding member of the First African Methodist Episcopal Church in 1872, and she established a nursery and day-care center for the children of Black working parents. Mason also visited and nursed the sick and insane in the hospitals and in jail. She was always available to assist persons in need regardless of color and creed.

Biddy Mason died on January 15, 1891, and was mourned by the community that she had served faithfully for over forty years. She was a compassionate woman who endeared herself to those with whom she came in contact.

BIBLIOGRAPHY

Atwood and Ernst. *Los Angeles City and County Directory, 1884* (1885); Bancroft, Hubert Howe. *Register of Pioneer Inhabitants of California, 1542-1848* (1892); Beasley, Delilah Leontium. *The Negro Trail-Blazers of California* (1919); Bell, Horace. "Reminiscences of a Ranger, 1860-1890." Manuscript, Huntington Library Collection, San Marino, California; Brown, John Zimmerman. *An Autobiography of Pioneer John Brown (1820-1896)* (1941); Hayes, Judge Benjamin. "A Suit for Freedom," *Los Angeles Star* (February 2, 1856); Jansen, Joan and Gloria Lothrop. *California Women: A History* (1987).

BOBI JACKSON

MASON, LENA DOOLIN (b. 1864)

Lena Doolin Mason is one of only a handful of nineteenth-century preaching women for whom we have visual images. She was born in the Soldiers' Barracks on Hampshire Street in Quincy, Illinois, on May 8, 1864. Her mother, Relda Doolin, had taken refuge in the barracks after escaping from slavery, and her father, Vaughn Poole Doolin, was fighting in the Civil War. Lena was the fifth of ten children and one of eight girls. She attended Douglass High School in Hannibal, Missouri, as well as Knott's School in Chicago.

At the age of seven, Lena experienced her first call to preach, and in January 1872 she joined the African Methodist Episcopal Church of Hannibal, Missouri, under the pastorate of Reverend John Turner. At the age of twelve, she was again called to preach. On March 9, 1883, Lena married George Mason. The couple had four sons and two daughters, but only Bertha May is known to have survived to adulthood.

Lena Doolin Mason actively began her ministry at the age of twenty-three and for the first three years she preached exclusively to white congregations. She traveled and preached in almost every state and was especially acclaimed during her five months in Minneapolis, Minnesota. Mason is credited with having influenced some 1,617 persons to convert to Christianity.

BIBLIOGRAPHY

AME Church. *Centennial Historical Souvenir of "Mother" Bethel AME Church* (c. 1916); Culp, Daniel W., ed. *Twentieth-Century Negro Literature* (1969).

JUALYNNE E. DODSON

MASON, VIVIAN CARTER (1900-1982)

"I've never been afraid to speak my mind . . . and I don't back away from things, just because some people might consider them controversial" (Lake

The third president of the National Council of Negro Women, Vivian Carter Mason, helped the organization devise strategies to work toward implementation of the Brown v. Board of Education *Supreme Court decision. She is shown here standing between Eleanor Roosevelt and Ed Sullivan (Mary McLeod Bethune is second to her right). [Bethune Museum and Archives]*

1982). In her many roles as a clubwoman, social worker, and social activist, Vivian Carter Mason lived up to her words. The daughter of a Methodist minister, George Cook Carter, and Florence Williams Carter, a music teacher, she credited her parents with instilling values that inspired her social concerns. Born in Wilkes-Barre, Pennsylvania, on February 10, 1900, Vivian Carter received her early education in the public schools of Auburn, New York, and graduated from the University of Chicago, where she studied political economy and social welfare. She later pursued graduate course work at Fordham University and at New York University.

While a student at the University of Chicago, Vivian Carter met her future husband, William T. Mason, a native of Trinidad, West Indies. They married in Brooklyn, New York, where Vivian Carter Mason worked as a Young Women's Christian Association (YWCA) program director. Their only child, William T. Mason, Jr., was born in 1926 in Norfolk, Virginia, where his father established a lucrative real estate and insurance business. William Mason, Sr., was an astute businessman who weathered the Great Depression and amassed a considerable fortune before his death in 1976.

Unwilling to place her son in poorly equipped schools in segregated Norfolk, Mason moved with her son to New York City in 1931. In New York, she worked her way through the ranks to establish herself professionally as the first Black woman administrator in the city's Department of Welfare and also gained prominence in a number of local and national organizations. A member of the National Association for the Advancement of Colored People, Mason sat on the national board of the YWCA and on the executive board of the National Council of Negro Women (NCNW). She also founded the Committee of 100 Women, an organization that sent poor New York City children to summer camp.

In the mid-1940s, she returned to Norfolk where she continued to devote herself to social and political reform. Mason represented the NCNW at the inaugural meeting of the International Women's Democratic Federation (IWDF) in Paris in 1945. She served on the executive board of the IWDF and as vice president of its American affiliate, the Congress of American Women. From 1949 to 1953, Mason served as president of the Norfolk chapter of the NCNW and founded the Norfolk Women's Council for Interracial Cooperation. In 1953, she was elected to the first of two terms as president of the NCNW. During her term of office, she steered the council through the tumultuous years following the Supreme Court's historic ruling in *Brown* v. *Board of Education*. As the organization's leader she emphasized interracial coalition building and support for grassroots efforts to bring about racial justice.

Following her tenure as NCNW president, Mason turned her attention back to local politics. She urged women to become involved. "We have to educate women to realize that they have a right to share in the legislative process," she said (Gagliardi 1971). She challenged women not only to vote but also to run for office themselves. As she put it, "any governing body is better for having women on it" (Gagliardi 1971). She led the way. In 1968, she was the only Black woman on Virginia's Democratic central committee.

Long an outspoken critic of local school administration, Mason was nonetheless appointed to the Norfolk City School Board in 1971—the first Black woman to serve on the board. In 1971, Virginia Press Women named Mason "Newsmaker of 1971," citing "her work with Black and white women to achieve equality" and "her demonstrated belief in the American political system" (*Journal and Guide* 1971). Yet Mason saw perhaps more clearly than those who honored her that although Black and white women might find common cause, the agenda of Black women sometimes differed from that of white women: "Black women realize that to get ahead they have to work with the Black man because he has been so beaten down it would be a form of self-destruction to do otherwise." Still, she believed, "Black women have unique capabilities, tempered by decades of oppression and indignities. . . . they have the qualities of endurance, determination, and foresight" (*Virginia Pilot* 1974).

Her own involvement in conventional party politics toward the end of her life did not prevent Mason from supporting the more radical choices other Black women made. In 1972, for example, Mason risked her reputation and political standing to defend the rights of Communist party member Angela Davis. It also did not alter her course—one that always sought new avenues for social change and social justice. In 1978, Mason resigned from the Norfolk school board to focus attention on founding a local chapter of the National Urban League, feeling that the need for direct support to Black economic enterprise was pressing. Vivian Carter Mason died in Norfolk, Virginia, on May 10, 1982.

[*See also* NATIONAL COUNCIL OF NEGRO WOMEN.]

BIBLIOGRAPHY
Collier-Thomas, Bettye. *NCNW, 1935-1981* (1981); Gagliardi, Martha. "Vivian Mason Never Gives Up," *Virginia Pilot* (September 24, 1971); *Journal and Guide.* "Newsmaker of Year Award to Mrs. Mason" (October 4, 1971); Lake, Marvin Leon. "Mrs. Mason, Rights Crusader, Dies at 82," *Virginia Pilot* (May 12, 1982); Mason, Vivian C. Files of the National Council of Negro Women and Women's Interracial Council. Norfolk Public Library, Norfolk, Virginia; National Council of Negro Women. Records in the Bethune Museum archives, Washington, D.C.; U.S. House of Representatives, Committee on Un-American Activities. *Report on the Congress of American Women* (1949); *Virginia Pilot.* "Black Women Work with Men" (August 28, 1974).

V. A. SHADRON

MATHEMATICS

Although the first woman in the United States to receive a Ph.D. in mathematics did so in 1886, and the first Black man did so in 1925, it was not until 1949 that the first Black woman received a Ph.D. in mathematics. That year there were two, but the third was not until 1962. Until 1969, meetings of mathematical organizations in the South, where most Black mathematicians were employed, were held in white-only facilities.

However, outside the academic world, there were Black women, even in the nineteenth century, who found outlets for their mathematical talents and interests. Susie Johnson McAfee, for example, was denied a teaching certificate in Texas because her father refused to bribe a public official. However, of her nine children, five earned college degrees in mathematics, and two earned degrees in chemistry. Among these seven, three were daughters. Of the two remaining sons, one studied mathematics for two years before becoming a plumber, and the other, having received his degree in physical education, went back to school in later years and received a certificate in mathematics.

As Black women began to gain access to higher education, they still faced double-barreled discrimination. Many have stated that before college graduation, racism is a more serious problem than sexism because the nation's schools are steeped in racism. However, after graduation, sexism is the greater obstacle because of the attitudes of white men who dominate the field and who believe that any woman's place is in the home.

Teaching in elementary and high schools was long the fallback for Black women interested in mathematics. Ironically, the 1954 Supreme Court decision in *Brown* v. *Board of Education* hurt many of them. When white children joined Black children in southern classrooms, many Black mathematics teachers who had been teaching in all-Black schools were fired or forced to retire.

World War II, on the other hand, proved a boon. Black women were able to find jobs doing computational work that would now be done by computers. As technology took over, some of them were able to become computer specialists. Today there are hundreds of Black women with college degrees who have mathematical careers involving computers. They include programmers, systems analysts, technical salespeople, statisticians, and managers. Even more are teachers of mathematics.

A National Science Foundation report in 1988 stated that in 1986, there were 2,300 Black women "mathematical scientists," of whom 300 were employed by the federal government and 700 each by "business and industry" and "education institutions." The last number seems suspiciously small if it includes secondary teachers.

By 1980, twenty-five Black women had received Ph.D.s in mathematics, and, since then, thirteen more have been added. They include Elayne Arrington-Idowu (University of Cincinnati, 1974); Danielle Carr (Duke University, 1992); Shannon Cobb (University of Southwestern Louisiana, 1990); Suzanne Craig (University of California, Los Angeles, 1980); Debra Curtis (Stevens Institute, 1991); Geraldine Darden (Syracuse University, 1967); Mary Lovenia DeConge-Watson (St. Louis University, 1968); Teresa Edwards (Georgia Institute of Technology, 1990); Etta Falconer (Emory University, 1969); Emma Rose Fenceroy (University of Alabama, 1979); Annie Marie Garraway (University of California at Berkeley, 1967); Fannie Gee (University of Pittsburgh, 1979); Rada Higgins (Ohio State University, 1974); Fern Hunt (New York University, 1978); Corlis Powell Johnson (Emory University, 1981); Eleanor Green Dawley Jones (Syracuse University, 1966); Iris M. Mack (Harvard University, 1986); Vivienne Lucile Malone Mayes (University of Texas, 1966); Shirley Mathis McBay (University of Georgia, 1966); Janis Oldham (University of California at Berkeley, 1990); Wanda Patterson (Georgia Tech, 1988); Evelyn Patterson Scott (Wayne State University, 1970); Daphne Smith (Massachusetts Institute of Technology, 1985); Geor-

gia Caldwell Smith (University of Pittsburgh, 1961); Vernise Steadman-Toler (Howard University, 1988); Frances Sullivan (City University of New York, 1980); Thyrsa Franzier Svager (Ohio State University, 1965); Evelyn Thornton (University of Houston, 1973); Bessie Tucker (University of Mississippi, 1983); Argelia Velez-Rodriguez (University of Havana, 1960); Janice Brown Walker (University of Michigan, 1982); and Roselyn E. Williams (Florida State University, 1988).

Of the 401 U.S. citizens who received a Ph.D. in mathematics in 1989-90, only four were Black, and eighty-nine were women; of these, one was a Black woman.

BIBLIOGRAPHY

Bozeman, Sylvia T. "Black Women Mathematicians: In Short Supply" *Sage* (Fall 1989); Donaldson, James. "Black Americans in Mathematics." In *A Century of Mathematics in America* (1988); Gerdes, P. "On Culture, Geometrical Thinking, and Mathematics Education," *Educational Studies in Mathematics* (1988); Kenschaft, Patricia Clark. "Black Women in Mathematics in the United States," *American Mathematical Monthly* (October 1981), and "Blacks and Women in Mathematics." Educational Policy Seminar Papers (1986), and "Black Men and Women in Mathematics," *Journal of Black Studies* (December 1987), and "Black Women in Mathematics," *Association for Women in Mathematics Newsletter* (September/October 1988), and "Successful Black Mathematicians of New Jersey," *UME Trends* (December 1989), and "What Are They Doing Now? Careers of 75 Black Mathematicians," *UME Trends* (May 1990), and *Winning Women in Mathematics* (1991); Mayes, Vivienne Malone. "Black and Female," *Association for Women in Mathematics Newsletter* (1975); National Science Foundation. *Women and Minorities in Science and Engineering* (1988); Newell, Virginia K., Joella H. Gipson, L. Waldo Rich, and Beauregard Stubblefield. *Black Mathematicians and Their Works* (1980); Zaslavsky, Claudia. *Math Comes Alive: Activities from Many Cultures* (1987), and *Africa Counts* (1973).

PATRICIA CLARK KENSCHAFT

MATTHEWS, MIRIAM (1905-)

Miriam Matthews is a foremost authority on California Black bibliography. She is also a dedicated librarian, a civil rights activist, a lecturer on race relations, a photographer, a collector of African-American art and literature, and a writer.

Miriam Matthews was born in Pensacola, Florida, on August 6, 1905, one of three children born to Reuben and Fannie (Elijah) Matthews. The family moved in July 1907 to Los Angeles, where Miriam received her early education.

Miriam Matthews received an A.B. from the University of California in 1926, a certificate in librarianship from the University of California in 1927, and an M.A. from the University of Chicago in 1945. The title of her Master's thesis was "Library Activities in the Field of Race Relations."

In 1927, Matthews was appointed to the Los Angeles Public Library system—the first Black professional librarian hired by the library. From 1929 to 1949, she served as a branch librarian, and in 1949 she became a regional librarian for the Los Angeles Public Library, supervising twelve branch libraries. In this capacity, she served on top administrative committees, representing all the branch librarians in Los Angeles. She also served on numerous committees and boards representing more than fifty organizations, not only concerned with libraries and archives but also with civil rights, health, youth problems,

The first Black professional librarian of the Los Angeles Public Library system, Miriam Matthews has been documenting the history and contributions of African-Americans in California for decades. [Miriam Matthews]

education, race relations, history, and art. During her membership in the American and California library associations, Matthews, as a national councillor, played a prominent role in promoting the cause of intellectual freedom in California and throughout the United States. Significantly, she served as chair of the Committee for Intellectual Freedom of the California Library Association from 1946 to 1948. She served on numerous other committees.

Governor Edmund G. Brown in 1977 appointed Matthews to the California Heritage Preservation Commission and to the California State Historical Records Advisory Board, where she was active in the preservation and use of archives throughout California. In addition, she helped transmit evaluations of archival grant proposals from California institutions to the National Historical Publications and Records Commission for funding. In 1979, she was instrumental in securing a permanent archival program for Los Angeles. During this time, she served on the supervisory committee for the California Historical Records Educational Consultant Service.

While a member of the Los Angeles Bicentennial Committee, Matthews proposed and fought to have a monument erected honoring all the multiethnic founders of the city of Los Angeles. In 1981, a large monument was erected on the spot where the city was founded. A small plaque below the monument credits Matthews as the originator of the project.

Among the many committees Matthews has served on are the advisory board of the National Youth Administration, Los Angeles (1938-39); Youth Committee, Los Angeles (1938-40); and the executive board of the National Intercollegiate Christian Council, Asilomar area (1937-38). She is also a member of the American Association of University Women, the National Association for the Advancement of Colored People (life member), the University of California and University of Chicago alumni associations, and the Southern California, San Diego and Western Historical Society.

Throughout her career, Matthews has accepted numerous city, county, state, and national awards. Most important is the Miriam Matthews Award, established in February 1988 by California State University, Dominguez Hills. It is presented annually to individuals who have made outstanding contributions in the field of African-American history and culture. Matthews was named Woman of the Decade in Literature in 1960 (*Los Angeles Sentinel*), Newsmaker of 1975 (National Association of Media Women), and Gran Dama of the City and County of Los Angeles in 1984 (City Council and County Board of

Supervisors). In 1982, she received the Award of Merit (California Historical Society), and in 1988 she was appointed one of the first five Fellows of the Historical Society of Southern California. In 1984, she received the U.S. House of Representatives Award.

An interest in the history and contributions of African-Americans to California led Matthews to research this subject back to 1781. As a result, she acquired a large collection of books, documents, historical photographs, and art over the years. She has shared her collection with researchers and writers of TV documentaries. She has loaned her paintings and sculptures to museums for exhibitions, and she has made donations to many permanent collections in museums. She was the first person in Los Angeles to initiate an interest in the celebration of Negro History Week.

Matthews has given lectures at educational institutions and meetings of organizations and appeared on radio and television. In March 1959, she presented a paper entitled "Weeding and Replacement" at the University of Southern California workshop, "Improving the Book Collection."

BIBLIOGRAPHY

Abajian, James de T. *Blacks and Their Contributions to the American West* (1974); Arvey, Verna. "Librarian Stimulates Community Thought," *Opportunity* (April-June 1947); Williams, Ora. *American Black Women in the Arts and Social Sciences: A Bibliographical Survey* (1978); *WWBA*; *WWCA*; personal correspondence.

SELECTED WORKS BY MIRIAM MATTHEWS

"Alice Taylor Gafford," *Family Savings Community News Letter* (October 1967); "Library Activities in the Field of Race Relations," Master's thesis (1945); "The Negro in California from 1781 to 1916: An Annotated Bibliography," unpublished manuscript (n.d.); "Race Relations on the Pacific Coast: A Select Bibliography," *Journal of Educational Sociology* (November 1945); "Report Submitted to the Graduate School of Library Science, University of Southern California, in Partial Fulfillment of the Requirements for the Research Course in Library Science 290 ab" (February 1944); "William Grant Still—Composer," *Phylon* (Second Quarter 1951).

DOROTHY PORTER WESLEY

MATTHEWS, VICTORIA EARLE (1861-1907)

Victoria Earle Matthews was "a Salvation Army field officer, a College Settlement worker, a missionary, a teacher, a preacher, and a Sister of Mercy, all in

Although she was born into slavery and had little formal education, Victoria Earle Matthews became a journalist, lecturer, social reformer, and pioneer in travelers' aid work at the turn of the century. [Schomburg Center]

one" (*New York Age* 1907). Matthews, as described by a New York City reporter who was her contemporary, dedicated her life to helping others. She volunteered for settlement activities, social welfare work, and club organizations with relentless zeal. Matthews was resourceful, assertive, and had great foresight.

Matthews was born on May 27, 1861, in Fort Valley, Georgia, one of nine children born to Caroline Smith. Her mother, a native of Virginia, escaped from slavery to New York during the Civil War, but returned to Georgia for her children after Emancipation. Victoria, her mother, and the family arrived in New York City around 1873, after spending three years in Richmond and Norfolk.

Matthews received very little formal education. She attended Grammar School 48 in New York City until poverty and the illness of a family member forced her to leave. She began working as a domestic, but continued to read and attend special lectures. In 1879, at the age of eighteen, she married William Matthews, a coachman and native of Petersburg, Virginia. During the early years of her marriage, Matthews wrote short stories and essays for *Waverly* magazine and other publications.

In 1893, under the pen name "Victoria Earle," she published *Aunt Lindy,* her most ambitious work. Matthews did free-lance writing for the *New York Times,* the *New York Herald,* and the *Brooklyn Eagle.* She wrote articles for the leading Black newspapers, the Boston *Advocate, Washington Bee, Richmond Planet,* and *Cleveland Gazette.* She edited *Black Speeches, Addresses, and Talks of Booker T. Washington* (1898).

A journalist with the *New York Age,* Matthews was sympathetic to the antilynching crusader and writer Ida B. Wells. Matthews helped organize a testimonial for Wells on October 5, 1892, at Lyric Hall in New York City that brought together Black women from Boston, Philadelphia, and New York. This event inspired the founding of the Woman's Loyal Union of New York City and Brooklyn two months later. Matthews was a founder and the first president of the women's club.

Matthews attended the first national conference of Black women in July 1895. She presented a stunning address on "The Value of Race Literature," praising the creative ability of Black men and women and their contributions to race literature and race building. The national conference sparked the founding of the National Federation of Afro-American Women (NFAAW). Matthews was appointed to the executive board and to the editorial staff of the *Woman's Era,* the official journal of the NFAAW.

In July 1896, the National Colored Women's League of Washington and the Federation of Afro-American Women held their conventions in Washington, D.C. Seven women from the two national organizations, including Matthews, formed a joint committee to consider uniting. Their recommendations led the two women's organizations to join together as the National Association of Colored Women (NACW). Mary Church Terrell was elected president of the NACW. Matthews became the first national organizer of the NACW and the New York State organizer for the Northeastern Federation of Women's Clubs.

In December 1895, Matthews attended the Congress of Colored Women of the United States in Atlanta. Black clubwomen from twenty-five states attended the women's congress. Immediately after the congress, she toured the South. She visited the red-light districts and employment agencies in New Orleans and other southern cities. Following her investigations, Matthews returned to New York determined to continue her "uplift" and improvement work there.

Victoria Matthews' concern for social welfare work in the Black community increased after the death of her son and only child, Larmartine, at the age of sixteen. At this time, she began to focus on issues related to the well-being of children and young women. She began to visit local families and held mothers' meetings in the various homes.

The White Rose Mission, established by Matthews, opened on February 11, 1897. It was founded with the purpose of "establishing and maintaining a Christian, non-sectarian Home for Colored Girls and Women, where they may be trained in the principles of practical self-help and right living" (Richings 1897). It offered a social center for community women and children as well as shelter and protection to young women coming from the South in search of employment. Matthews organized a group of women from different religious denominations to assist in operating her program.

With the desire to do practical, useful work, Matthews began to lecture. With a talent for dramatic and forceful speeches, she often spoke before Black audiences on the political and social responsibilities of self-improvement. She encouraged respect for Black women, their work, and accomplishments. Matthews was invited to represent Black American women at the annual convention of the Society of Christian Endeavor in San Francisco. On July 11, 1897, in her address "The Awakening of the Afro-American Woman," she stated that it was the responsibility of the Christian womanhood of the country to join in "elevating the head, the heart, and the soul of Afro-American womanhood."

Matthews voiced concern about Black women who came to the North seeking employment. Employment agents went into the rural districts of the South with convincing stories of the "North" and of "New York." Agents pressured women into signing contracts. These unfortunate young women were then at the mercy of agencies that had financed the trip to the North.

A pioneer in travelers' aid work, Matthews and her assistants met the boats at the Old Dominion pier and helped the inexperienced young women from the South. Matthews, as superintendent of the White

Rose Mission, established a series of social services from Norfolk to New York. In 1905, she organized the White Rose Travelers' Aid Society. White Rose agents watched the docks to prevent Black women from the South from becoming victimized. The appointed agents were Dorothy Boyd in New York and Hattie Proctor in Norfolk.

Matthews established a special library of books by and about Black people at the White Rose Home for Working Girls. Many of the books were used in her teachings on "Race History." As her health gradually failed, her duties as superintendent of the White Rose Home were assumed by her assistants, including Frances Reynolds Keyser.

Matthews maintained her Brooklyn residence at 33 Poplar Street and her membership at St. Philips Episcopal Church. A plaque outside the brownstone distinguishes it as "The White Rose Home" and a large photograph of Victoria Earle Matthews which dominates the entry hall are memorials to her inspiring and dedicated service. She died on March 10, 1907, of tuberculosis at the age of forty-five and was buried in the Maple Grove Cemetery, New York City.

[*See also* WHITE ROSE MISSION, NEW YORK CITY; WOMAN'S LOYAL UNION OF NEW YORK AND BROOKLYN.]

BIBLIOGRAPHY

Brown, Hallie Q. *Homespun Heroine and Other Women of Distinction* ([1926] 1988); *DANB*; Davis, Elizabeth. *Lifting As They Climb: An Historical Record of the National Association of Colored Women* (1933); Meier, August. *Negro Thought in America, 1880-1915, Racial Ideologies in the Age of Booker T. Washington* (1963); *NAW* (1971); *New York Age* (March 14, 1907); Richings, G. F. *Evidence of Progress among Colored People* (1897); Scruggs, Lawson A. *Women of Distinction: Remarkable in Works and Invincible in Character* (1893).

FLORIS BARNETT CASH

MAYNOR, DOROTHY (1910-)

Dorothy Maynor not only had a long and successful career as a concert singer, she also established a school to ensure that other aspiring African-Americans would have the opportunity to become artists as well. Dorothy Maynor was born Dorothy Leigh Mainor in Norfolk, Virginia, on September 3, 1910. She began vocal study at Hampton Institute in her native state where, starting at the age of fourteen, she completed her formal education (B.S., 1933). Origi-

Concert artist Dorothy Maynor never appeared on the opera stage in her long career, but in 1965, she was able to fulfill a lifelong dream by founding the Harlem School of the Arts. [Schomburg Center]

nally majoring in home economics, she attracted the attention of R. Nathaniel Dett, who enrolled her in the institute's choral ensemble and to whose music she remained dedicated.

Following additional vocal study at the Westminster Choir College, she was encouraged in her career by Serge Koussevitsky in 1939, who heard her at the Berkshire Music Festival, and she presented her recital debut that November at Town Hall. Her singing was characterized by a lyric legato with which she particularly endowed her French repertoire.

Her career included concerts and recitals throughout the Western hemisphere, Europe, and Australia, as well as broadcasts and telecasts. The repertoire included Lieder, spirituals, sacred works of Bach and Handel, and opera arias (particularly "Depuis le jour" from Charpentier's *Louise*), but she never appeared on the opera stage. Retired from concert life in 1965, she realized a long-standing dream by founding the Harlem School of the Arts, serving as its director until 1980.

In 1975, she was appointed to the board of directors of the Metropolitan Opera. Honorary doctorates were bestowed on her by Bennett College, Howard University, Oberlin College, Carnegie-Mellon University, and Duquesne University.

BIBLIOGRAPHY

Ewen, David. "Dorothy Maynor, 1910- ." *Musicians since 1900: Performers in Concert and Opera*, ed. David Ewen (1978); Schauensee, Max de. "Maynor, Dorothy." *The New Grove Dictionary of Music and Musicians*, ed. Stanley Sadie (1980); Slonimsky, Nicolas. "Maynor, Dorothy." *Baker's Biographical Dictionary of Musicians*, ed. Nicolas Slonimsky (1978).

DISCOGRAPHY

The Art of Dorothy Maynor. RCA LCT-1115 (1953). *Legendary Recordings*. LR-139 ([1944] 1980).

DOMINIQUE-RENÉ de LERMA

McCABE, JEWELL JACKSON (1945-)

Businesswoman Jewell Jackson McCabe is president of her own management consulting firm, a distinguished spokesperson for professional Black women, and founder and chair of the National Coalition of 100 Black Women, an organization designed to meet the needs of professional Black women and facilitate their access to mainstream America. Notable not only for her successful career in the world of business, McCabe's dedication to the advancement of women and minorities has been described as "impressive and much to be admired" (Noel 1984).

Jewell Jackson McCabe, daughter of broadcast pioneer Harold ("Hal") B. Jackson and Julia O. (Hawkins) Jackson, was born on August 2, 1945, in Washington, D.C. She graduated from Bard College in 1966. She married her first husband, Frederick Ward, at age nineteen and later married Eugene McCabe. Twice divorced, she has no children.

McCabe served as director of public affairs for the New York Urban Coalition from 1970 to 1973 and as public relations officer for the Special Service for Children, New York City, from 1973 to 1975. She then held a position as associate director of public information for the women's division of the Office of the Governor, New York, for two years. In 1977, McCabe became director of the government and community affairs department of WNET-TV, a public broadcasting station in New York City. As director, she helped maintain and improve the station's relationship with federal, state, and city governments for the purpose of securing tens of millions of dollars in financial assistance. More recently, McCabe has served as president of Jewell Jackson McCabe Associates, a consulting firm specializing in government relations, minority marketing, and establishing links between government and the private sector.

The National Coalition of 100 Black Women, an extension of the New York Coalition of 100 Black Women, was founded by McCabe in 1981. The coalition has a membership of 7,000 women in twenty-two states and is organized along lines similar to its counterpart, 100 Black Men. Described as "a coalition of high achievers combined with highly energetic women," the group provides a leadership forum for professional women, places important emphasis on the concept of alliance, and sets special priorities in the areas of voter registration and mobilization (Noel 1984). The coalition also serves as a resource network for young people. Every year the coalition honors ten Black women for achievement in the arts, science, technology, and business through the presentation of the Candace Award. The title of the award (pronounced Can-day-say) is the Ethiopian word for "queen."

McCabe has served on numerous corporate boards, including Reliance Group Holdings. Her gubernatorial appointments range from chair of the New York State Jobs Training Partnership to member of the New York State Council on Fiscal and Economic Priorities and the New York State Council on Families, where her assigned committee was teen pregnancy prevention. McCabe's affiliations have spanned a broad spectrum of business and community groups, such as the National Alliance of Business, United Way of America, the Association for a Better New York, and the United Hospital Fund.

Honored by several national organizations, McCabe has received tributes from the Women's Equity Action League, a leading advocacy group for women, and the national Young Women's Christian Association (YWCA) for her endeavors on behalf of women in business. In 1980, she served as deputy grand marshal in the annual Martin Luther King, Jr., parade in New York City; that same year she was awarded the Outstanding Community Leadership Award by Malcolm/King College. McCabe has received two honorary doctorates. Her published works, or works composed under her direction, include *Commemorative Book: Motown Returns to the Apollo* (fiftieth anniversary) (1984); *Women in New York* (1975-77), a newsletter published by New York State; and *Give a Damn* (1970-73), published by the New York Urban Coalition.

With a wide range of experience in both the public and private sectors, Jewell Jackson McCabe has been both an influential and a dedicated force in the business world.

[*See also* NATIONAL COALITION OF 100 BLACK WOMEN.]

BIBLIOGRAPHY

Fortune. "On the Rise: Jewell McCabe" (August 17, 1987); Lanker, Brian. *I Dream a World* (1989); *New York Times.* "Volunteerism: New Paths" (June 3, 1979); Noel, Pamela. "New Battler for Black Women," *Ebony* (February 1984).

FENELLA MACFARLANE

In addition to running her own management consulting firm, Jewell Jackson McCabe is founder and chair of the National Coalition of 100 Black Women, an organization dedicated to the needs of professional Black women. [UPI/Bettmann]

McCARROLL, ERNEST MAE (1898-1990)

Ernest Mae McCarroll was the first Black physician permitted to practice at Newark City (Martland) Hospital in 1946, in an era when, as she said, "Negro doctors had no other choice than to leave their patients at the front door" (Kukula 1990).

Born in Birmingham, Alabama, on November 29, 1898, McCarroll earned a B.A. from Talladega College in 1917 and entered medical school at the Woman's Medical College of Pennsylvania in 1919. She graduated in 1925, interned at Kansas City General Hospital No. 2 and entered general practice in Philadelphia.

In 1929, she moved to Newark, New Jersey, where she established a private practice and pioneered in the fight against sexually transmitted diseases. In that year she also married Leroy Baxter, a dentist. Ten years later they were divorced. McCarroll had two subsequent marriages (1958, 1983).

During the 1930s, McCarroll worked as a clinic physician with the Newark Department of Health, lecturing about hygiene and venereal diseases to women throughout the city.

She received her M.S. in public health from Columbia University in 1939, and she did postgraduate work at the Harvard University School of Public Health. McCarroll was a member of the board of trustees of the National Medical Association (NMA) 1949-55 and 1963-73. She was named First Lady of the NMA for her work and the New Jersey Medical Society named her the first General Practitioner of the Year in 1955.

She retired in 1973 and died in a Florida nursing home on February 20, 1990.

BIBLIOGRAPHY

Cobb, W. Montague. "E. Mae McCarroll," *Journal of the National Medical Association* (November 1973); Kukula, Barbara. "Mourners Recall Life of a Pioneering Physician," *Star-Ledger* (March 12, 1990); Lloyd, Esther Vincent. "Ernest Mae McCarroll." In *Past and Promise: Lives of New Jersey Women*, ed. Joan N. Burstyn (1990).

SUSAN SHIFRIN

McCLAIN, LEANITA (1952-1984)

Leanita McClain, the first Black member of the *Chicago Tribune* editorial board, was born in 1952. Named by her parents, Lloyd, a factory worker, and Elizabeth McClain for her two older sisters, Leatrice and Anita, she grew up in a public housing project named for the pioneer Black woman journalist Ida B. Wells-Barnett. McClain was a high achiever in the public schools, and while a student at Chicago State University she decided to pursue a career in journalism. She received a full scholarship to the Medill School of Journalism at Northwestern University, completed her Master's degree in 1973, and went to work as a general assignment reporter at the *Chicago Tribune*, where she met and married Clarence Page. The marriage ended in divorce.

McClain's superior journalistic abilities earned her frequent promotion. She moved from general assignment reporter to working on the copy desk, to the picture desk, to the Perspective department. Soon she was editor of the Perspective section and then a weekly columnist, the second Black person to become a staff columnist in the 137-year history of the newspaper. And in fewer than ten years after joining the *Tribune*, she became a member of the editorial board. McClain was barely thirty years old.

Her writings and professional accomplishments have been honored outside the *Chicago Tribune*. She received the Chicago chapter of Sigma Delta Chi's Peter Lisagor Award, the 1983 Kizzy Award for an outstanding Black female role model, and the Chicago Association of Black Journalists' top award for commentary, as well as being listed by *Glamour* magazine as one of the country's ten most outstanding career women.

After accomplishing so much so quickly, she painfully asked of herself and her friends: "I have made it, but where?" In an article that was an important catalyst to her career, she answered quite clearly by saying: "I have overcome the problems of food, clothing, and shelter, but I have not overcome my old nemesis, prejudice. *Life is easier, being black is not*" (McClain 1980). As an accomplished Black professional woman from the housing projects of Chicago's South Side, McClain was caught with one foot in each world. "Whites won't believe I remain culturally different. . . . Blacks won't believe I remain culturally the same" (McClain 1980). Leanita McClain committed suicide in May 1984 at the age of thirty-two, and though she left a stack of suicide notes, including one labeled "generic suicide note," it is possible that her publications reveal some of the conditions of her life that led her to choose that end.

McClain began her professional career just after the pressures of the civil rights movement opened some doors for talented young African-Americans, and she was extremely conscious of the privileges that the movement enabled her to enjoy. Her first major article, published in *Newsweek* in 1980, on the responsibilities and burdens of the Black middle class, addressed the frustration that Black professionals felt over being accused of having forgotten where they came from when she in fact had not. McClain was committed to her race as well as to her professional position. She was optimistic about her ability to bridge these two worlds, but she was not a romantic. She noted in that article:

I am burdened daily with showing whites that blacks are people. I am, in the old vernacular, a credit to my race. I am my brothers' keeper, and my sisters', though many of them have abandoned me because they think that I have abandoned them. I run a gauntlet between two worlds, and I am cursed and blessed by both. I travel, observe and take part in both; I can also be used by both. I am a rope in a tug of war. If I am a token in my downtown office, so am I at my cousin's church tea. I assuage white guilt. I disprove black inadequacy and prove to my parents' generation that their patience was indeed a virtue. I have a foot in each world, but I cannot fool myself about either.

McClain also achieved prominence just before Chicago politics turned its ugliest—when Harold Washington won the Democratic primary in the mayoral contest. She was appalled and apparently shocked by the incessant virulent racist attacks, and the equally persistent efforts after Washington's election to prevent his governing effectively. Ultimately, her anger led her to write an article that was published in the *Washington Post* under the title "How Chicago Taught Me to Hate Whites" (so titled by *Post* headline writers). McClain's point was that until the 1983 campaign she had always believed that race relations were improving and that ultimately racism and bigotry would be eradicated, but the campaign and its aftermath were so vile that she had to acknowledge that "an evilness still possesses this town, and it continues to weight down my heart"; the constant meanspiritedness confounded her and led her to "begin that morning [after the election] to build my defenses brick by brick" (McClain 1983). She realized she could never trust even her own judgment as easily as she had before. Worse still, the campaign and its aftermath made her realize that she had the capacity to hate. McClain worked to reclaim her old working relationships and to shed her hate, but many Chicagoans never forgave her for exposing them in the national press.

In her essays for *Newsweek* and *The Washington Post*, as well as in her weekly and then twice weekly columns for the *Tribune*, it is clear that Leanita McClain was a crusader, and she was a responsible one. She fought for better government, better schools, better housing. She worked to convince people that politics and race were inseparable, that privilege came with responsibility, that public schools could work, that public housing did not have to be a scourge, and that racism, sexism, and bigotry could and would destroy us all.

BIBLIOGRAPHY

Klose, Kevin. "A Tormented Black Rising Star Dead by Her Own Hand," *Washington Post* (August 5, 1984); McClain, Leanita. "How Chicago Taught Me to Hate Whites," *Washington Post* (July 24, 1983), and "The Middle-Class Black's Burden," *Newsweek* (October 13, 1980); Page, Clarence, ed. *A Foot in Each World: Essays and Articles by Leanita McClain* (1986).

STEPHANIE J. SHAW

McCLENDON, ROSE (1884-1936)

While watching Rose McClendon descend the winding staircase in the opera *Deep River*, the producer, Arthur Hopkins, whispered to Ethel Barrymore, "She can teach some of your most hoity-toity actresses distinction." Barrymore later remarked, "She can teach them *all* distinction" (Johnson 1930).

Rose McClendon was born Rosalie Virginia Scott in Greenville, South Carolina, in 1884, the daughter of Sandy and Lena Jenkins Scott. Around 1890 the family moved to New York, where Rosalie attended public schools. In 1904, she married Henry Pruden McClendon, a chiropractor, who supplemented his income as a Pullman porter. During the early years of marriage, McClendon directed and acted in church plays and cantatas at Saint Mark's AME Church, but it was not until she received a scholarship to the American Academy of Dramatic Arts in 1916 that she devoted her life to theater.

Hailed by the *Afro-American* as the "Negro first lady of the dramatic stage" (July 18, 1936), her acting credits included *Justice* (1919); *Roseanne* (1926) with Charles Gilpin (and later with Paul Robeson); *Deep River* (1926) with Jules Bledsoe; *In Abraham's Bosom* (1926), Paul Green's Pulitzer Prize-winning drama for which she received the *Morning Telegraph* Acting Award the following year, along with Ethel Barrymore and Lynn Fontanne; *Porgy* (1927); *House of Connelly* (1931); *Black Soul* and *Never No More* (1932); *Brainsweat* and *Roll Sweet Chariot* (1934); *Panic*; and her last appearance, as Cora in *Mulatto* (1935), a role Langston Hughes created for her.

In the late 1920s, McClendon was a director for the Negro (Harlem) Experimental Theatre, and in the 1930s she worked in a supervisory capacity with the Federal Theatre Project. It was she who suggested that separate Negro units be established "to insure the production of plays dramatizing Black themes and exhibiting black talents" (Ross 1986).

McClendon always envisioned the establishment of a permanent "Negro Theatre" that produced plays dealing "with Negro problems, with phases of Negro life, faithfully presented and accurately delineated"—a theater that would not merely develop "an isolated Paul Robeson, or an occasional Bledsoe or Gilpin, but a long line of first-rate actors" (McClendon 1935). Toward this end, she and Dick Campbell founded the Negro People's Theatre in Harlem in 1935. Unfortunately, on July 12, 1936, Rose McClendon died of pneumonia. To keep her dreams alive, Dick Campbell and his wife, Muriel Rahn, organized the Rose McClendon Players. Later, in 1946, philanthropist Carl Van Vechten established the Rose McClendon

Called the "Negro first lady of the dramatic stage," Rose McClendon worked with artists such as Paul Robeson, Ethel Barrymore, and Langston Hughes. [Moorland-Spingarn]

Memorial Collection of Photographs of Distinguished Negroes at Yale and Harvard universities.

BIBLIOGRAPHY

Anderson, Jervis. *This Was Harlem, 1900-1950* (1981); Bordman, Gerald. *The Concise Oxford Companion to the American Theatre* (1987); *DANB*; *DBT*; Houseman, John. *Run Through, 1902-1941* (1972); Johnson, James Weldon. *Black Manhattan* ([1930] 1988); Kellner, Bruce. *The Harlem Renaissance: A Historical Dictionary of the Era* (1987); McClendon, Rose. Letter to the Editor, *New York Times* (June 30, 1935); Mitchell, Lofton. *Black Drama* (1967); Rampersad, Arnold. *The Life of Langston Hughes: 1902-1941* (1986); Ross, Ronald. "The Role of Blacks in the Federal Theatre, 1935-1939." In *The Theatre of Black Americans*, ed. Errol Hill (1979-1980); Woll, Allen. *Black Musical Theatre: From Coontown to Dreamgirls* (1989).

ANNETTA JEFFERSON

McCOY, MARY ELEANORA (1846-1923)

Mary Eleanora Delaney Brownlow McCoy rose from humble beginnings to become a person of great influence in social improvement and philanthropic clubs and organizations in Michigan.

Born on January 7, 1846, in an Underground Railroad station in Lawrenceburg, Indiana, she was the daughter of Jacob C. Delaney and Eliza Ann (Montgomery) Delaney. Her formal education was limited to attending classes first at mission schools taught in private homes in Indiana and later at the Freedman's School in St. Louis, Missouri, in 1869. Moving to Michigan in the early 1870s, Mary met and later married Elijah McCoy on February 25, 1873, the second marriage for both. Elijah, born in 1843 in Colchester, Ontario, Canada, to former slaves who had also escaped on the Underground Railroad, studied mechanical engineering in Edinburgh, Scotland, for five years before looking for a job in the United States. Elijah's career as an inventor began when he was working as a railroad fireman on the Michigan Central Railroad. It was necessary to stop railroad trains after a certain amount of use to oil the moving parts. Elijah invented several types of self-lubricating devices that made it unnecessary to stop trains merely to lubricate them. His inventions led to the popular saying, "Is it the real McCoy?," warning people to beware of imitations. Prolific as an inventor, Elijah received six patents for lubricating devices and one for an ironing table between 1872 and 1876 and another forty-four patents (thirty-six of which were for lubricators) between 1882 and 1926. Elijah organized the Elijah McCoy Manufacturing Company in Detroit in 1920 and died in October 1929.

The McCoys had moved to Detroit by 1882. In the 1890s, Mary McCoy became a leader in founding and in serving as an official of Black women's clubs, earning her the title "Mother of Clubs." In 1895, Mary was one of the founders of the "In as Much Circle of King's Daughters and Sons Club," said to be the first Black women's club founded in Michigan. She was also the only Black woman to be a charter member of the prestigious Twentieth Century Club, started in 1894. In 1898, Mary was one of the co-founders of the Michigan State Association of Colored Women and eventually became its vice president. The Michigan association became a member of the National Association of Colored Women, widening its scope of activity. Mary called the first meeting, which led in 1898 to the establishment of the Phillis Wheatley Home for Aged Colored Women in Detroit, and later she served as its vice president. She was also the major financial supporter of the McCoy Home for Colored Children, vice president of the Lydian Association of Detroit, and president of the Sojourner Truth Memorial Association, whose purpose was to erect a monument to Truth, a former slave and powerful speaker for abolition and women's rights who lived in Battle Creek, Michigan, from the 1850s until her death in 1884, and to establish University of Michigan scholarships in Truth's name.

McCoy was a charter member of the Detroit chapter of the National Association for the Advancement of Colored People in the 1910s, a member of the Order of the Eastern Star, Prince Hall Affiliate, and at the Bethel African Methodist Episcopal Church she was a member of the Willing Workers and the King's Daughters clubs. One of the early Black supporters of the Democratic party, McCoy also campaigned for women's right to vote in all elections. Consequently, she was chosen as flag bearer from Michigan in a women's suffrage parade held as part of the inaugural ceremonies for President Woodrow Wilson in 1913. Governor Ferris of Michigan appointed McCoy to the socially prestigious Michigan Commission for the Half-Century Exposition of Freedmen's Progress to be held in Chicago in 1915. As a member of the commission, Mary was a "Field Agent, Eastern Michigan," charged with finding materials to be put on display at the Chicago exposition and information to be listed, with photographs, in the companion book, the *Michigan Manual of Freedmen's Progress.* Both Mary and Elijah McCoy are prominently referred to in the book, and Elijah's work was on display in Chicago. In early 1920, Mary and Elijah were in a traffic accident, and Mary was seriously injured. Her health declined, and she died in early 1923.

BIBLIOGRAPHY

Dannett, Sylvia G. L. *Profiles of Negro Womanhood* (1964); Marshall, Albert P. *The "Real McCoy" of Ypsilanti* (1989); Mather, Frank Lincoln, ed. *Who's Who of the Colored Race* ([1915] 1976); Michigan Freedmen's Progress Commission, *Michigan Manual of Freedmen's Progress,* comp. Francis H. Warren ([1915] 1985); *NBAW;* Peebles, Robin S. "Detroit's Black Women's Clubs," *Michigan History* (January/February 1986); Wesley, Charles Harris. *The History of the National Association of Colored Women's Clubs* (1984).

DE WITT S. DYKES, JR.

McCROREY, MARY JACKSON (1869-1944)

Mary Jackson McCrorey became one of the first African-American women to run for public office in the South when she sought a seat on the Charlotte, North Carolina, school board in 1937. McCrorey's pursuit of elective office, which came toward the end of her long career as a political activist, reflected her commitment to Black education and accomplishments.

Mary Jackson was born in 1869, the first child in her large family to be born as a free person. Her parents, Alfred and Louise Jackson, had been the slaves of a professor at the University of Georgia at Athens who taught them how to read and write. The Jacksons emphasized the value of education to their eighth child, Mary, who graduated from Atlanta University. Mary Jackson later pursued graduate courses at Harvard University and the University of Chicago.

From the late 1880s through the mid-1890s, Mary Jackson taught in Georgia and Florida. In 1895 she joined the illustrious Lucy Laney, another Atlanta University graduate, at the Haines Institute, Laney's school in Augusta, Georgia. Jackson was the assistant principal at Haines until 1916, when she became the second wife of Henry Lawrence McCrorey, president of Biddle University in Charlotte, North Carolina. (During their marriage, Biddle became Johnson C. Smith University.) McCrorey taught at Biddle part-time and, after the admission of women to the university, served as an advisor to women students and supervised their campus conduct.

After moving to Charlotte, McCrorey became involved in civic affairs. In 1916, she founded a Young

Women's Christian Association (YWCA) for African-Americans, one of the first in the South. She served as chairperson of the Phyllis Wheatley YWCA branch from 1916 to 1929, reporting to a committee of local YWCA white women. She became president of the African-American auxiliary of the Charlotte Associated Charities, serving from 1916 until 1944. When Methodists founded the Bethlehem Center, a settlement house for African-Americans, they named McCrorey to the board. A Presbyterian, McCrorey served on regional and national denominational boards. She also joined the Priscilla Art and Literary Club, a leading women's organization in Charlotte, and worked with the North Carolina Federation of Colored Women's Clubs.

McCrorey's abilities quickly became apparent to state and national leaders. A member of the regional and the North Carolina Commission on Interracial Cooperation from 1920 to 1944, she also held a seat on the advisory board of the State Commission of Welfare and Public Charity from 1924 to 1944. She served on the executive board of the National Council of Negro Women, an organization founded by her friend Mary McLeod Bethune to give African-American women a greater voice in politics. From 1922 to 1944, McCrorey was corresponding secretary of the International Council of Women of the Darker Races.

Although McCrorey did not succeed in her 1937 bid for a Charlotte school board seat, her competent campaign was well received and created a precedent for the participation of African-American women in local government. In 1941, Benedict College in Columbia, South Carolina, recognized her contributions to African-American education with the honorary degree of Doctor of Pedagogy. Mary Jackson McCrorey died in 1944 in a fire at her home, the president's residence at Johnson C. Smith University.

BIBLIOGRAPHY

Gilmore, Glenda Elizabeth. "Black Women and Ballots in a 'Progressive' Southern State: North Carolina, 1898-1937," Southern Historical Association Meeting (1989); Hall, Jacquelyn Dowd. *Revolt against Chivalry: Jesse Daniel Ames and the Women's Campaign against Lynching* (1974); Lucas, Doris, Tom Parramore, and Earlie Thorpe, eds. *Paths toward Freedom* (1976); Neverdon-Morton, Cynthia. *Afro-American Women of the South and the Advancement of the Race, 1895-1925* (1989); Parker, Inez Moore. *The Biddle-Johnson C. Smith University Story* (1975); *Quarterly Review of Higher Education among Negroes* (January 1944); Rouse, Jacqueline Anne. *Lugenia Burns Hope: Black Southern Reformer* (1989); *WWCA*.

GLENDA ELIZABETH GILMORE

McDANIEL, HATTIE (1895-1952)

Character actress Hattie McDaniel presents a troubling figure on the landscape of American race relations. On the one hand, she had a fruitful career in the competitive industry of Hollywood cinema in the 1930s and 1940s, an era when the star system that enshrined white stars created few opportunities for Black talent. On the other hand, she became famous for portraying mammy-like figures and thus perpetuated one of the most hated stereotypes of Black women. Her admirers could point to her commitment to her race in providing an example of success for Black youth and, when she could, by making small improvements for Black actors in the industry. It is almost impossible to reconcile these two opinions, because McDaniel was so firmly defined by a paradoxical nature.

Fittingly, her early life was rooted in contradiction. Hattie McDaniel, the youngest of thirteen children, was born on June 10, 1895, to Henry and Susan (Holbert) McDaniel. In spite of her later fame as a deep-southerner, McDaniel was not raised in the South (she later had to teach herself southern dialect for film roles). Her birthplace was Wichita, Kansas, and her family soon moved to Colorado, where she grew up. The McDaniels first lived in Fort Collins and in 1901, when Hattie was six, moved to Denver where they remained throughout her life.

Although certainly not free from racism, Denver at the turn of the century was a relatively liberal town. Schools were not segregated, and, in fact, McDaniel attended predominantly white public schools. McDaniel eventually dropped out of Denver's East High School in 1910 to perform in minstrel shows, a form of vaudeville performed by Black entertainers playing stereotypical roles. One of the groups with which McDaniel performed was the Henry McDaniel Minstrel Show, which costarred two of her brothers, Sam and Otis. The troupe was headed by her father, who had frequently supported himself and his family through minstrel shows since his emancipation from slavery at age twenty-five.

After her father went into semiretirement in 1916, Hattie McDaniel went solo. At first she toured the Southwest and Pacific Northwest with fellow Black entertainer Professor George Morrison and his orchestra, the Melody Hounds. Then, in late 1924, while continuing to tour, she began singing on Denver radio station KOA with the Melody Hounds. These successes led to extensive travel on the Black entertainment circuit in the late 1920s.

She was booked as a blues singer primarily through the Theater Owners Booking Association (TOBA), an organization that launched the careers of many blues greats. Bessie Smith, Ethel Waters, Ma Rainey, Ida Cox, Mamie Smith, and Alberta Hunter all got their start on the TOBA circuit, which was infamous for cheating entertainers out of their hard-earned money and for giving them grueling schedules. As a result, TOBA came to be nicknamed Tough on Black Asses. Nevertheless, the organization did provide the performers with food and shelter and a certain amount of job security. McDaniel even got the chance to sing some of her own compositions, such as "I Wish I Had Somebody," "Just One Sorrowing Heart," "Any Man Would Be Better Than You," and "BooHoo Blues."

McDaniel's personal life during this early period in her career was as heartbreaking as her music. In 1922, she married George Langford, but soon after the wedding he died, reportedly of a gunshot wound. McDaniel remained a widow for sixteen years. In addition, her father, Henry, also died that year at the age of eighty-two.

After the stock market crash of 1929, the TOBA circuit went bust, and McDaniel found herself without a job. She worked for a while in the washroom of the Club Madrid in Milwaukee, Wisconsin, until she got her big break singing there on a night when the club was short on entertainment. She proved popular and soon became one of the club's regular performers.

In 1931, McDaniel was persuaded by her brothers, Sam and Otis, to join them in Los Angeles, where they had relocated. She found a few jobs singing in choruses and appearing in uncredited bit parts in Hollywood movies, including *The Golden West* (1932), set in the South. Every Friday she performed on Los Angeles Black radio station KNX's *Optimistic Do-Nut Hour* as Hi-Hat Hattie, a bossy maid. Ironically, because McDaniel was paid only $5 a week at KNX, and $5 per movie appearance, she had to support herself as a maid.

In late 1932, McDaniel was finally cast in a role big enough to be credited. Her early films included Josef von Sternberg's *Blonde Venus* (1932), in which McDaniel appeared briefly as a protectress of bombshell fugitive Marlene Dietrich. McDaniel also appeared in *I'm No Angel* (1933), which infamously paired Mae West and Cary Grant. As with *The Golden West*, these roles were primarily servile-but-sassy types with exaggerated southern accents. There were simply no other roles available for large Black women in Hollywood. As a result, McDaniel began to find herself in competition with a small group of women who collectively portrayed all of Hollywood's mammies

and maids. The group included Ethel Waters and Louise Beavers (who forced herself to overeat so that she would appear more mammy-like).

Hattie McDaniel's reputation grew throughout the mid-1930s, and she was contracted to play bigger parts. In *Judge Priest* (1934), she portrayed Aunt Dilsey, Judge Priest's (Will Rogers) spiritual-singing servant. She also played Mom Beck in the 1935 Shirley Temple vehicle, *The Little Colonel*, which glorified antebellum plantation life. Other roles included Malena Burns in *Alice Adams* (1935), with Katharine Hepburn in the title role; Queenie in *Show Boat* (1936); Lizzie in *Can This Be Dixie?* (1936); and Hilda in *The Mad Miss Manton* (1938), starring Barbara Stanwyck. She also appeared in many *Our Gang* shorts. Thus, by the end of the decade, McDaniel had established herself as one of the most successful mammy/maids of all time. By 1939, she had over fifty credits in feature films and shorts. In 1936 alone, she appeared in fourteen movies.

It is clear that McDaniel relished her fame. She was able to move into an upscale Los Angeles neighborhood, and she gave generous donations to several

The controversy surrounding Hattie McDaniel's career playing Hollywood "mammies" is exemplified by her being barred from attending the Atlanta premiere of Gone with the Wind, *and then winning a Best Supporting Actress Oscar for her role in the film. [Schomburg Center]*

charities. She began to count many of her glamorous white costars as her friends and enjoyed giving advice to fledgling Black actors, choosing not to dwell on the unavailability of nonracist, nonstereotypical roles for them in Hollywood. Indeed, she outwardly dismissed any criticism of her success as a mammy figure, saying, "I'd rather play a maid than be one" (Jackson 1990). The only setback in McDaniel's life during this period was a mysterious, virtually unrecorded marriage to Howard Hickman, which ended in 1938.

On December 6, 1938, McDaniel tested for a choice role: Mammy in *Gone with the Wind*, the well-publicized movie adaptation of Margaret Mitchell's best-selling novel. After much deliberation, producer David O. Selznick offered McDaniel a contract on January 27, 1939, disappointing dozens of other actresses who also had auditioned.

McDaniel found herself being paid $500 a week to participate in a film shoot that took months and achieved mythical status even as it was unfolding. The sets and costumes were elaborate, even by Hollywood standards. The film's stars, Vivien Leigh and Clark Gable, were enshrined in movie magazines. While the minutiae of the filming were eagerly followed by millions of Americans, however, few thought to question why McDaniel was called "Mammy" both on screen and on the set. So great was the appeal of *Gone with the Wind* to a white public that the voices of those who worried about the film's possible racist message were lost in the uproar. When at last the film was complete, Selznick made a decision that clearly delineated the low status of Black actors in Hollywood. He forbade McDaniel and all of *Gone with the Wind*'s other Black actors to attend the Atlanta premiere in December 1939. He was afraid their presence would anger southerners. McDaniel, as usual, accepted this injustice without complaint.

Except for a few critics who were outraged by the portrayal of Black characters in the film, white Americans loved *Gone with the Wind*. Especially appealing was McDaniel's beturbaned Mammy scolding Scarlett O'Hara (Vivien Leigh) in voice-coached Georgia sass. When McDaniel won a best supporting actress Oscar for the role, Mammy's status as an indelible figure in America's cultural psyche was assured. As for McDaniel, she saw the award, the first ever given to a Black actor, as a victory not only for herself but also for the Black community. "[The Oscar] makes me feel very humble, and I shall hold it as a beacon for anything that I may be able to do in the future," McDaniel said as she accepted the award. "I sincerely hope that I shall always be a credit to my race and to the motion picture industry" (Jackson 1990).

McDaniel's words proved prophetic. *Gone with the Wind* was the beacon—or perhaps the burden—for her future. Soon after the Oscar awards ceremony, McDaniel toured the country on a series of David O. Selznick-conceived, ill-attended tours targeted at Black communities to promote *Gone with the Wind*. She promoted herself as Mammy incarnate, publishing recipes for "Mammy's fried chicken à la Maryland" and posing for photographs in which she happily gazed at her prized collection of mammy figurines. In addition, McDaniel's career for most of the 1940s consisted mainly of Mammy-esque roles in *Gone with the Wind* imitations, such as *Maryland* (1940) and *The Great Lie* (1941). She also played cheerful mammy Aunt Tempey in *Song of the South* (1946), the undeniably racist Disney version of antebellum days. The Old South roles were otherwise alternated with modern versions of Mammy: sassy maid roles in watered-down retreads of screwball comedies such as *Affectionately Yours* (1941), *George Washington Slept Here* (1942), *Three Is a Family* (1944), and *Family Honeymoon* (1948).

One important exception to the string of mammy and maid parts was Minerva Clay, McDaniel's role in the 1941 movie *In This Our Life*, starring Bette Davis and Olivia de Havilland. The movie was the first to represent Black characters who were not one-dimensional smiling servants/slaves but complex characters unjustly forced to cope with racism. McDaniel's character, Minerva Clay, whose son is falsely accused of killing someone, sums up the movie's sentiment when she sighs, "Well, you know those policemen. They won't listen to what a colored boy says."

For McDaniel, the 1940s were otherwise defined by her troublesome relationship with the National Association for the Advancement of Colored People. Led by executive secretary Walter White, the NAACP attacked the core group of Black actors who perpetuated servile stereotypes. Waters and Beavers were chastised for their portrayal of mammies, while Stepin Fetchit and Clarence Muse were blasted for Uncle Tom roles. Because of her Oscar, McDaniel was the most visible Black actor and received the harshest criticism. In response to the NAACP's condemnation, McDaniel and her fellow actors formed their own group, the Fair Play Committee (FPC), which emphasized slow change in the movie industry. The FPC pointed out the actors' own small attempts at change, such as asking that the word "nigger" be removed from their scripts or refusing to speak in dialect. For White, these small efforts were not enough.

After winning the Academy Award for her portrayal of Mammy in Gone with the Wind, *Hattie McDaniel found herself playing similar roles in* Gone with the Wind *imitations, such as* Maryland *(1940), with Ben Carter. [Donald Bogle]*

In addition to her woes with the NAACP, McDaniel's 1941-45 union with Lloyd Crawford, though by far the longest of her four marriages, proved troublesome. Crawford found himself in financial difficulty and resented McDaniel's star status. In 1944, McDaniel announced (at the age of forty-nine) that she was pregnant, and she even received baby gifts from her Hollywood friends. When McDaniel was later diagnosed as having a so-called false pregnancy, she was crushed and slipped into depression. Not long after, she and Crawford divorced.

When White's campaign died out, McDaniel moved on to playing the role of Beulah, the maid on an extremely popular radio show of the same name starting in 1947. McDaniel's health had begun to decline, however, a development her biographer, Carlton Jackson, partially attributes to the harassment by the NAACP. Her four-month marriage (1949-50) to Larry Williams probably contributed as well. She suffered from weight loss and had a series of slight strokes and heart attacks. After each physical setback, she would recuperate and then go back to work. For example, in the summer of 1951 McDaniel prepared to replace archrival Ethel Waters on the ABC-TV version of *Beulah*, which had been airing since 1950. She shot six episodes before becoming ill; the six shows were never aired. During the first few months of 1952, McDaniel improved and even recorded a season's worth of *Beulah* on the radio, but in May it was revealed that she had breast cancer, and from then on she was too ill to perform. Hattie McDaniel died on October 26, 1952, at the Motion Picture Country Home and Hospital in Woodland Hills, California. She was fifty-seven years old.

[*See also* MAMMY; FILM.]

BIBLIOGRAPHY

Bogle, Donald. *Toms, Coons, Mulattoes, Mammies, and Bucks: An Interpretive History of Blacks in American Films* (1989); Jackson, Carlton. *Hattie: The Life of Hattie McDaniel* (1990).

SARAH P. MORRIS

McKINNEY, NINA MAE (1913-1967)

The first African-American actress to make her name in the American cinema, Nina Mae McKinney also presents an archetype of the exploitation and oppression of African-American women in Holly-wood. Born Nannie Mayme McKinney in Lancaster, South Carolina, McKinney was reared by her grandmother on the estate of Colonel LeRoy Sanders, where her family had worked for many generations. Her parents lived in New York City. When she was twelve, they sent for her, and she went to live in the city where, just four years later, she began her entertainment career.

She was dancing in the chorus line of Lew Leslie's *Blackbirds* when she was spotted and cast in the role of Chick in the film *Hallelujah* (1929), directed by King Vidor. Some say that, in this role, McKinney originated the stereotype of the "Black temptress" that has haunted African-American actresses from that day to the present. Critics described her characterization of Chick as "half woman, half child"—McKinney was only seventeen years old when she played the role. She was a beautiful young woman and, on the strength of her performance, she was given a five-year contract at Metro-Goldwyn-Mayer (MGM).

That five years was a time of frustration for the young actress. She was a leading lady in an industry that had no leading lady roles for an African-American woman. MGM did not know what to do with her. As a result, she was cast in only two films, *Safe in Hell*

An actress and singer who was once called the "Black Garbo," Nina Mae McKinney, right, was a victim of Hollywood exploitation and oppression. Her film debut, some claim, originated the stereotype of the "Black temptress." Her last film was Pinky *(1949), which starred Jeanne Crain (left). [Schomburg Center]*

(1931) and *Reckless* (1935). Her parts in both films were small. In the latter, she also dubbed Jean Harlow's songs. When her contract ended, so did her career in Hollywood.

In 1929, McKinney went to Europe. She toured with a pianist, Garland Wilson, and sang in major nightclubs in Paris and London. Billed as the "Black Garbo," she was greeted with enthusiasm by European audiences. She twice starred with Paul Robeson: in the play *Congo Road* and the English film *Sanders of the River* (1935). The former took her back to New York City for its Broadway premiere. Yet her native country was still unprepared to offer McKinney a career. She appeared in several independent films, including *Pie Pie Blackbird* with Eubie Blake, and then returned to Europe in 1932.

Eight years later she returned to the United States. She married jazz musician Jimmy Monroe and toured the United States with her own band. She also appeared in a number of Black-cast films. Her last film was *Pinky*, released in 1949.

McKinney died in New York City on May 3, 1967, at the age of fifty-four. In 1978, she was inducted into the Black Filmmakers Hall of Fame.

BIBLIOGRAPHY

CBWA; *EBA*; *NBAW*.

KATHLEEN THOMPSON

McLIN, LENA JOHNSON (1928-)

Composer, conductor, and educator Lena Johnson McLin was born in Atlanta, Georgia, on September 5, 1928. As a young woman she moved to Chicago, where, for approximately nine years, she lived with her uncle, Thomas A. Dorsey, the father of gospel music.

She graduated from Booker T. Washington High School in Atlanta. Later she received a B.A. from Spelman College in Atlanta and a Master's degree from the American Conservatory of Music in Chicago, and she completed additional graduate study at Chicago State University and Roosevelt University, both in Chicago. She also received an honorary doctor of humanities from Virginia Union University in Richmond.

McLin taught for thirty-six consecutive years in the public high schools of Chicago, where she earned superior ratings annually at local music festivals. At Kenwood Academy, she created a conservatory-like environment with a curriculum for music majors, an

unusual achievement for a high school that is not focused on the performing arts.

McLin has served as a consultant for twenty years at forty-eight major universities, including Westminster Choir College in New Jersey, where she served for ten consecutive years. When she retired in 1991, many prominent former students attended the celebration, including opera stars Nicole Heaston and Mark Rucker and jazz singer Kim English. Her son, Nathaniel McLin, is a composer and critic of art and music, and her daughter, Beverly Leathers, is a composer and surgical assistant. In addition to composing music, McLin serves as a consultant and is a pastor at the Holy Vessel Baptist Church in Chicago.

Almost 100 of her more than 2,000 works have been published by Neil Kjos in San Diego, California. These works include art songs, cantatas, anthems, piano pieces, orchestral works, and arranged spirituals as well as *Free at Last*, a cantata written in tribute to Martin Luther King, Jr., and *Pulse: A History of Music.*

[*See also* COMPOSERS.]

BIBLIOGRAPHY

McLin, Lena J. *Pulse: A History of Music* (1977); Southern, Eileen. *The Music of Black Americans: A History* (1983); Spencer, Jon Michael. *As the Black School Sings* (1987); White, Evelyn Davidson. *Choral Music by Afro-American Composers: A Selected Annotated Bibliography* (1981); Williams, Ora. *American Black Women in the Arts and Social Sciences: A Bibliographic Survey* (1978).

SANDRA CANNON SCOTT

McMILLAN, ENOLIA PETTIGEN (1904-)

The first woman president of the National Association for the Advancement of Colored People, Enolia Pettigen McMillan has had a long and distinguished career as an educator and administrator and is renowned for more than five decades of service to the cause of civil rights. Firmly believing in the need for increased educational and employment opportunities for Black Americans, McMillan has worked through many different organizations to help bring an end to discrimination.

Enolia Pettigen was born on October 20, 1904, in Willow Grove, Pennsylvania, the daughter of Elizabeth (Fortune) Pettigen and John Pettigen, who had been born into slavery in Virginia. When Enolia was eight, her family moved to Baltimore, where they became active members of the Calvary Baptist Church. In 1922, after graduating from high school, and with much encouragement from her family and her high school principal, McMillan enrolled in Howard University in Washington, D.C., and graduated in 1926. Six years later she received her M.A. from Columbia University in New York City. In 1935, she married Betha D. McMillan, with whom she had one son, Betha D., Jr.

From 1926 to 1928, McMillan taught at Pomonkey High School. She was named principal of the school in 1928, a position she held until 1935. McMillan then taught junior high school students in Baltimore until 1956, when she was made vice principal of Clifton Park and Cherry Hill junior high schools, positions she held until 1969. In 1963, she also was made vice principal of Paul Laurence Dunbar Senior High School. Throughout her tenure as a teacher and administrator, McMillan worked hard to improve the status of Black American schools. She was appointed as a lifelong principal by the Baltimore City School System in 1985.

McMillan's long service with the NAACP began in 1935 in the Baltimore chapter, and she became chapter president in 1969. McMillan's seventeen-year presidency was a busy and successful one as she strove to increase membership, especially of young people, and improve its fund-raising potential. In 1985, McMillan became the first woman to be elected president of the national association. She was reelected to this unsalaried position each year until her retirement in December 1989. During her tenure as NAACP president, McMillan initiated moving the group's national headquarters to Baltimore, and she worked hard to raise funds for the building of its new headquarters, which opened in 1986.

In addition to her long-standing involvement with the NAACP, McMillan's community service includes being the only woman to be elected president of the Maryland State Colored Teachers Association, the first woman to chair the Morgan State College Trustee Board, and the first Black person to serve as trustee to the executive committee of the Public School Teachers Association. She also has been a member of the Governor's Commission on the Structure and Governance of Education in Maryland and chairperson of the Joint Committee to Equalize Teachers Salaries in Maryland.

McMillan is the recipient of many awards and honors, including the NAACP Merit Medal in 1938 and the Distinguished Citizen Award from the Democratic Ladies Guild in 1984. She was named one of the Top 100 Black Business and Professional Women

of 1986. In 1984, McMillan received an honorary doctorate of humane letters from Sojourner-Douglass College and was inducted into the Douglass High School Hall of Fame in 1972. In honor of her dedication to education for Black students, the Baltimore chapter of the NAACP created a scholarship fund in her name for students from low-income families.

Although her earliest ambition to become a doctor was never realized, Enolia Pettigen McMillan has dedicated much of her life to ensuring that the future ambitions of every young child, regardless of race or class, may be pursued to the fullest.

BIBLIOGRAPHY
Baltimore *Afro-American* (June 1984); Baltimore *News American* (May 8, 1984); Baltimore *Sun* (January 16, 1984); *USA Today* (January 12, 1984); *WWBA* (1990).

FENELLA MACFARLANE

McMILLAN, TERRY (1951-)

Funny, outspoken, and able to communicate with and move her readers, Terry McMillan is a serious and successful novelist.

Terry McMillan was born October 18, 1951, in Port Huron, Michigan, to Madeline Washington Tilman and Edward McMillan. Her father, a sanitation worker, died when McMillan was sixteen. Her mother held a variety of jobs, from auto worker to domestic to pickle factory employee. According to McMillan, her mother was responsible for "teaching me and my five siblings how to be strong and resilient. She taught us about taking risks" (Max 1992).

McMillan attended public schools in Port Huron and, when she was sixteen years old, worked in the public library. There she discovered Black writers when she was shelving a book by James Baldwin. "I remember feeling embarrassed," she admits now, "and did not read his book because I was too afraid. I couldn't imagine that he'd have anything better or different to say than Thomas Mann, Henry Thoreau, Ralph Waldo Emerson." Eventually she did read Baldwin, as well as other classic Black writers; she was amazed and moved.

From 1973 to 1979, McMillan attended the University of California at Berkeley, graduating with a Bachelor's degree in journalism. While there, she wrote and published her first short story, "The End." After Berkeley, she moved to New York to study film at Columbia University, where she earned a Master's degree. She made her living as a word processor and enrolled in a writing workshop at the Harlem Writers Guild. During this time her son, Solomon Welch, was born. In 1983, McMillan was accepted at the MacDowell Colony, where she wrote the first draft of her first novel, *Mama*. The book was published in 1987.

McMillan took the marketing of *Mama* into her own hands. She sent out thousands of letters, primarily to Black organizations, asking them to promote her book and offering to read from it to their members. Conventional wisdom among white publishers had been that Black people do not buy books. McMillan proved that when someone reaches out to them, Black readers are indeed there. Her second novel, *Disappearing Acts* (1989), did even better than her first. And *Waiting to Exhale* (1992) was on *The New York Times* best-seller list for months; the paperback rights were sold for $2.64 million. McMillan has been hailed as a "crossover" success, but the book buyers, according to her, are mostly Black. "I've had 1,500 people show up for a reading of *Waiting to Exhale*. Twelve hundred in Chicago, a thousand people waiting in line in Washington. I think I've signed more than 10,000 books, and the people who come are 90 percent black. In some cities 98 percent" (Max 1992).

After the publication of *Disappearing Acts*, McMillan was involved in a landmark legal battle. Her former living partner sued her for defamation of character. He charged that the central male character in the novel was recognizably himself and that the depiction was injurious. Fiction writers around the country breathed a sigh of relief when his claim was dismissed in court.

In 1988, McMillan became associate professor at the University of Arizona and retains her tenure there even though she has moved to Danville, California. She tours extensively, reading from her work and teaching workshops. In 1990, she was a judge for the National Book Award for fiction. The same year, she edited the anthology *Breaking Ice*, to introduce other Black authors to her readers.

When reviewing *Disappearing Acts*, Robert G. O'Meally made an astute estimate of McMillan as a writer: "with eloquence and style, McMillan gives her work a voice that is her own, one tough enough to speak across color and class lines, daring enough to make a statement about our country and our times" (O'Meally 1986).

BIBLIOGRAPHY

Max, Daniel. "McMillan's Millions," *The New York Times Magazine* (August 9, 1992); O'Meally, Robert G.

Terry McMillan proved that Black people do buy books when she successfully undertook the marketing of her first novel, Mama, *by reaching out to Black readers through direct mail advertising. [Marion Ettlinger]*

"The Caged Bird Sings," *Newsday* (August 13, 1986); Sayers, Valerie. "Someone to Walk over Me," *The New York Times* (August 6, 1989); Trescott, Jacqueline. "The Urban Author, Straight to the Point," *Washington Post* (November 17, 1990); *WWBA* (1992).

KATHLEEN THOMPSON

McNEIL, CLAUDIA (1917-)

Claudia McNeil was born in Baltimore, Maryland, on August 13, 1917, to Marvin Spencer McNeil and Annie Mae Anderson McNeil. Shortly after her birth, the family moved to New York City, where Claudia lived for most of her life. Annie McNeil was six feet four inches tall and an Apache Indian. She owned a grocery store and ran the household single-handedly after telling her husband to leave. Claudia credits her mother as her inspiration for her acting successes; but as a young girl, her relationship with her mother was not always harmonious. At the age of twelve Claudia went to work for the Heckscher Foundation as a mother's helper. Through this position, she met the Toppers, a Jewish couple of Romanian descent, who later adopted her. She became fluent in Yiddish, a skill she would use years later to score a comedic coup as a stereotypical (well, almost) Jewish mother named Sarah Goldfine in Carl Reiner's farce *Something Different* (1967).

At the age of twenty, with $500 from the Toppers, McNeil set out to become a professional singer. Her first job, at the Black Cat in Greenwich Village, paid $13.50 a week. Soon she moved on to bigger and better engagements, such as vocalist for the Katherine Dunham Dance Troupe on its tour of South America. She sang in vaudeville and nightclubs for years before she began acting on the advice of Ethel Waters, and so, in her thirties, she landed her first Broadway role as a replacement in *The Crucible* in 1953.

Langston Hughes asked her to audition for his play *Simply Heavenly* (1957), based on his "Simple Takes a Wife" and other "Simple" stories. She won critical acclaim as Mami in *Simply Heavenly*, and two years later solidified her critical and popular appeal with her success in Lorraine Hansberry's *A Raisin in the Sun* (1959). As Lena Younger, McNeil played a widow who mediates among the feuding factions in her family and leads them to take the first step toward integrating a lily-white Chicago suburb. She repeated the role in the 1961 film version as well.

Claudia McNeil became a star with her portrayal on stage and screen of the powerful, God-fearing matriarch. She so strongly identified with this role that she said, "There was a time when I acted the role. . . . Now I live it" (Morrison 1960). She went on to play the part of Mama in Peter S. Feibleman's *Tiger, Tiger, Burning Bright* (1962), based on his novel *A Place without Twilight*. Again, she received widespread praise, as well as a Tony nomination, for her acting.

Claudia McNeil (second from the right) became a star in 1959 with her portrayal of Lena Younger in Lorraine Hansberry's groundbreaking play A Raisin in the Sun. *The cast also included Sidney Poitier, Ruby Dee, and Diana Sands, who reprised their roles in the film version (1961). [Donald Bogle]*

In 1965, McNeil toured abroad as Sister Margaret in James Baldwin's *The Amen Corner*, performing in Paris, Israel, Edinburgh, and London, where she received the London Critics Poll award for best actress. After *Something Different* (1967), she played Ftatateeta in *Her First Roman* (1968), an expensive musical flop based on George Bernard Shaw's *Caesar and Cleopatra*, and starring Leslie Uggams (McNeil's roommate for a time) and Richard Kiley. She then played Mrs. Devereaux, a tenant in a Brooklyn tenement, in John Golden's *Wrong Way Light Bulb* (1969), and starred in two of the three one-act plays in Ted Shine's *Contributions* (1970).

Claudia McNeil acted in several films, beginning with *The Last Angry Man* (1959), starring Paul Muni. She began acting on television in the 1950s, and in the 1970s she acted in television more than in any other medium. She performed in television productions such as *The Member of the Wedding* (DuPont Show of the Month, 1958), *Do Not Go Gentle into That Good Night* (CBS Playhouse, 1967), and *To Be Young, Gifted and Black* (NET Playhouse, 1972). She was nominated for an Emmy Award for an episode of *The Nurses* in 1963. She retired in 1983 and in 1985 moved into the Actors' Fund Nursing Home in Englewood, New Jersey.

BIBLIOGRAPHY

BAFT; Bogle, Donald. *Toms, Coons, Mulattoes, Mammies, and Bucks* ([1973] 1989); *DBT*; Freeman, Lucy, ed. *Celebrities on the Couch: Personal Adventures* (1970); Klotman, Phyllis Rauch. *Frame by Frame—A Black Filmography* (1979); Mapp, Edward. *Directory of Blacks in the Performing Arts* (1978); McNeil, Claudia. Personal interview (December 10, 1991); Morrison, Allan. "Mother Role Brings Broadway Fame," *Ebony* (May 1960); Talese, Gay. *The Overreachers* (1965); *Who's Who in the Theatre* (1977).

JOEL BERKOWITZ

McQUEEN, BUTTERFLY (1911-)

Butterfly McQueen achieved fame primarily as a film actress in the 1940s. Noted for portraying seemingly dimwitted domestics prone to outbursts of hysteria, she elevated that convention to something

The slave Prissy in the film Gone with the Wind *speaks the controversially immortal line, "Lawdy, Miz Scarlett, I don't know nuthin' 'bout birthin' babies!" Decades later, the actress who played her, Butterfly McQueen, said about that type of role, "I didn't mind being funny, but I didn't like being stupid." Her integrity by and large cost her a career in Hollywood.*
[Donald Bogle]

In 1975, at the age of sixty-four, Butterfly McQueen earned a college degree. She immersed herself in various social welfare projects, and when this photo was taken in the early 1980s, she was working with Black and Hispanic students in Harlem, primarily at Public School 153. "They're my children and I love them all." [Schomburg Center]

approaching an art form with her first motion picture role as the slave, Prissy, in *Gone with the Wind* (1939). In later years she devoted herself to volunteer work with youth in Harlem.

She was born Thelma McQueen on January 8, 1911, in Tampa, Florida, the only child of a stevedore and a cleaning woman. She attended grammar school in Augusta, Georgia, and graduated from a Long Island, New York, high school where she was able to cultivate her interests in music and dance. She studied ballet with Mabel Hunt and modern dance with Venezuela Jones in the latter's Negro Youth Project. In a production of *A Midsummer Night's Dream* at City College of New York, she danced in the "Butterfly Ballet" and thus acquired her stage name. After a

brief stint with the Federal Theater Project, she made her Broadway debut in George Abbott's *Brown Sugar* in 1937; although the revue closed after only three days, McQueen received good critical notices. She went on to play in several other productions, including *Swingin' the Dream*, a Benny Goodman-Louis Armstrong collaboration. The musical brought her to the attention of David O. Selznick, producer of *Gone with the Wind*.

McQueen won excellent reviews for her labors in the classic Civil War epic, although, in retrospect, many African-Americans regretted some of the excesses of the performance. Malcolm X, for example, recalled feeling both anger and shame the first time he saw Prissy on screen (Haley 1966). In fairness to McQueen, however, it is important to note that she herself regarded Prissy as backward and that, on the set, she resisted offensive characterizations and situations. For instance, she refused to eat watermelon in one scene, and only after registering her displeasure did she submit to the scene in which Scarlett O'Hara (played by Vivien Leigh) slaps her in the face upon hearing her tearful confession, "Lawdy, Miz Scarlett, I don't know nuthin' 'bout birthin' babies!" Then, too, *Time* magazine cited the "sly humor" McQueen brought to the role: Although obliged to scream, "De Yankees is comin'!" as Sherman approaches Atlanta, Prissy also quietly sings to herself, "Jes' a few mo' days ter tote de wee-ry load" (Cripps 1977). (According to historian Thomas Cripps, her casual reading material between takes included the critics George Jean Nathan and Alexander Woollcott.)

McQueen's subsequent screen appearances constituted, for the most part, variations on the Prissy theme; she reprised squeaky-voiced foolish maids, for example, in *Affectionately Yours* (1941), *Mildred Pierce* (1945), and *Duel in the Sun* (1947). As Peter Nobel observed in *The Negro in Films* (1970), McQueen was fated "to act stereotypes or starve." In a sense, she decided to starve. To protest the lines she was asked to speak as a colored servant on Jack Benny's radio program, she walked out of the studio, and when she declined similar motion picture assignments, casting agents boycotted her for more than a year. The actress retired from films in 1947. "I didn't mind playing a maid the first time, because I thought that was how you got into the business," she told an interviewer decades later. "But after I did the same thing over and over I resented it. I didn't mind being funny, but I didn't like being stupid" (Stark 1986). For a brief period in the early 1950s she played Oriole, the dizzy neighbor on the television series *Beulah*, but then left

Hollywood altogether. From the standpoint of her acting career, the next twenty-five years were not encouraging. She held menial jobs more often than not.

During this time McQueen returned to Augusta, took a course in nursing at the Georgia Medical School, and managed Les Belles, a community service club for Black children. Relocating in a one-room apartment in New York, she enrolled as an undergraduate at City College of New York (CCNY) and, in 1975, at the age of sixty-four, earned a Bachelor of Arts with a major in Spanish. She then immersed herself in various social welfare projects, such as the Mount Morris Marcus Garvey Recreational Center. Since the early 1980s she has worked with Black and Hispanic students in Harlem, primarily at Public School 153. "They're my children," McQueen, who never married, stated, "and I love them all" (Stark 1986).

Although she was lauded, in 1989, at the fiftieth anniversary celebration of the release of *Gone with the Wind*, movie offers have remained infrequent; she played small roles in *Amazing Grace* in 1974 and *The Mosquito Coast*, starring Harrison Ford, in 1986. Occasionally she performs in churches, singing, dancing, signing autographs, and talking about the making of *Gone with the Wind*. (She has an abiding fondness for Clark Gable.) In 1978, she wrote, produced, and starred in a bilingual one-act play, *Tribute to Mary Bethune*, in Washington, D.C.

For every bit of acting she ever did, Butterfly McQueen received uniformly fine reviews; had she come along a generation or so later, she might have enjoyed great artistic and commercial success, but fate and the historical calendar mitigated against her. For her stand against racist stereotyping she was, in effect, punished by the Hollywood establishment and never recovered. This unfortunate turn in a promising career was the result of McQueen's decision to live by her principles. The children of Public School 153 no doubt love her all the more because of it.

BIBLIOGRAPHY

Belmer, Rudy, ed. *Memo from David O. Selznick* (1972); Bogle, Donald. *Brown Sugar: Eighty Years of Black Female Superstars* (1980), and *Toms, Coons, Mulattoes, Mammies, and Bucks* (1989); Cripps, Thomas R. *Slow Fade to Black: The Negro in American Film, 1900-1942* (1977); Haley, Alex, ed. *The Autobiography of Malcolm X* (1966); Mapp, Edward. *Blacks in American Films: Today and Yesterday* (1972); Nobel, Peter. *The Negro in Films* (1970); Sampson, Henry T. *Blacks in Black and White: A Source Book on Black Films* (1977); Stark, John. "Lawd, Miss Scarlett, Look at What Butterfly McQueen Is up to Now," *People Weekly* (December 1, 1986).

FILMOGRAPHY
Gone with the Wind (1939); *Affectionately Yours* (1941); *Cabin in the Sky* (1943); *I Dood It* (1943); *Since You Went Away* (1944); *Flame of the Barbary Coast* (1945); *Mildred Pierce* (1945); *Duel in the Sun* (1947); *The Phynx* (cameo, 1970); *Amazing Grace* (1974); *The Seven Wishes of Joanna Peabody* (ABC television production, 1978); *The Mosquito Coast* (1986).

THOMAS J. KNOCK

McRAE, CARMEN (1922-)

Carmen McRae is that rarest of jazz singers, as comfortable with modern pop songs and Tin Pan Alley tunes as she is with the tongue-twisting music of composer Thelonious Monk. Born and raised in New York, the crucible of modern jazz creativity, McRae studied piano extensively as a child, a talent she still nurtures, often nudging aside her regular pianist during a set or concert.

Early on McRae came under the spell of the great Billie Holiday. To say that Billie Holiday was her greatest influence is to understate the case; McRae's albums, as well as a portion of nearly every nightclub set or concert she gives, are devoted to the memory of Lady Day. McRae herself has often summed it up by exclaiming, " 'Lady' has always been my mentor."

Although Holiday's influence remains strong, make no mistake about it; Carmen McRae is one of the singular vocal talents in the history of jazz song. Her straightforward, no-frills approach to a vocal line and her tender touch with ballads are unmistakable McRae characteristics, and her often brusque, sassy manner, as well as her salty retorts to misbehaving audiences, are some of her most enduring qualities.

McRae's professional career began in 1944 with a stint as what was then called a girl singer with the Benny Carter Orchestra. Thereafter she worked with the big bands of Count Basie and later Mercer Ellington, the Duke's son. She became thoroughly immersed in the burgeoning bebop craze as an intermission singer and pianist at New York clubs, particularly those in Harlem. One of those clubs, Minton's Playhouse, is credited with having provided a nightly laboratory for such mid-to-late-1940s jazz explorers and alchemists as Charlie Parker, Dizzy Gillespie, Thelonious Monk, drummer Kenny Clarke (to whom McRae was later married for a short time), and others. These clubs were not merely places to work; it was here that McRae absorbed the coming sounds of bebop and where she came under the influence of the great Sarah Vaughan.

"Sassy [as Vaughan was known] was a phenomenon," McRae has said. "She took the art of improvisation and did it better than anybody. Plus, Sarah was blessed with the best voice *ever*. I, like many others, have always considered the human voice to be another instrument, and no one proved that better than Sarah. What great happiness she gave."

Accolades and recognition began to come McRae's way as early as 1954, when she was named "best new female singer" by *Down Beat* magazine following the release of her first recording as a lead singer. Since that time she has recorded dozens of albums, ranging from ballad interpretations to lending her personalized touch and breathing new life into seemingly mundane pop material to her much-acclaimed 1990 recording of Thelonious Monk material.

Carmen McRae has always enjoyed a particularly strong following in the Pacific Rim, most notably in northern California. She scored many of her triumphs at the famed Monterey Jazz Festival. At the 1962 festival she worked opposite Louis Armstrong, performing an adaptation of Dave Brubeck's musical, *The Real Ambassadors*. A particular favorite in Japan, McRae has traveled to the Far East on many occasions.

One of the hallmarks of McRae's art is her impeccable enunciation of a lyric. Ralph J. Gleason, San Francisco-based critic and longtime McRae admirer, stated it very eloquently when he said, "Carmen McRae sings the lyrics of a song like Sir Laurence Olivier delivering a Shakespearean speech. She gives lessons in elocution. There are songs which take on multiple additional meanings by the manner in which Carmen McRae delivers the lines. You can hear a song for years and then hear Carmen sing it and all of a sudden the lyrics become a story, they literally come to life." A singer's singer in every sense of that overused cliché, Carmen McRae is a true original.

BIBLIOGRAPHY

Feather, Leonard. *The Encyclopedia of Jazz in the Sixties* (1967); Gleason, Ralph J. *Celebrating the Duke* (1975); Kernfeld, Barry, ed. *New Grove Dictionary of Jazz* (1988).

WILLARD JENKINS

A singer whose name is mentioned in the same breath with Billie Holiday and Sarah Vaughan, Carmen McRae is comfortable with a wide range of musical styles, though she is best known for her jazz vocals. She is seen here with talk show host Dick Cavett. [Schomburg Center]

McWORTER, LUCY *see* ENTREPRENEURS IN ANTEBELLUM AMERICA

MEMORABILIA

Black collectibles are commercial items depicting the image of a Black person. Thousands of such items, produced in the United States and abroad from the 1880s to the late 1950s, were originally intended for everyday use as advertising cards, postcards, housewares, toys, and household decorations. Almost universally derogatory, with racially and sexually ex-aggerated features, they consistently showed Black people in servile roles and thus consolidated prevailing ideas of Black inferiority. Although it was widely believed that these objects died out in the late 1950s, manufacturers have been making reproductions of these same images since the mid-1970s. These reproductions can be found at flea markets, "country collectibles" boutiques, and can also be ordered through national mail houses. Within this genre of reproductions, the most prolific are mammy and pickaninny dolls.

These objects were drawn according to stereotypes, portraying African-Americans as very dark, generally bug-eyed, nappy-headed, childlike, stupid, lazy, and deferential. African-American children of both sexes were depicted as pickaninnies; adult males generally were portrayed as sambos, bums, or faithful older servants, whereas adult females were represented as mammies or harlots.

Although scholars clearly have demonstrated that the faithful "mammy" was a myth, the image has persisted as a popular icon in the American consciousness. Indeed, members of the United Daughters of the Confederacy were so taken with the mythology that they raised money and petitioned Congress in 1923 to erect a monument to the mammy in our nation's capital. The bill was killed in Congress (only after an acrimonious debate), but the myth has persisted, for example, in the "mammy" character in Margaret Mitchell's 1936 novel, *Gone with the Wind*, and in Hattie McDaniel's Oscar-winning portrayal of her in the 1939 screen version. Mitchell's characterization of the faithful, deferential, but happy servant was later translated into a mammy cookie jar manufactured by the McCoy pottery company of Roseville, Ohio, one of the largest manufacturers of memorabilia.

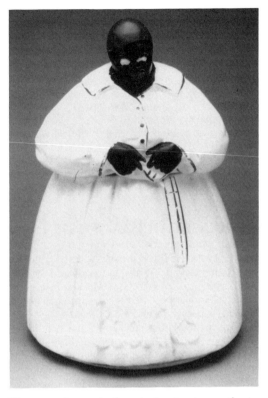

The mammy is a popular figure in American iconography. This cookie jar is just one example. [Professor Kenneth Goings]

Aunt Jemima, a variant of the mammy, was given life by Nancy Greene, who portrayed Aunt Jemima at the 1893 Chicago World's Fair and who toured the country for years thereafter promoting *her* cooking products. More recent depictions of Aunt Jemima have shed many of the typical slave trappings—she is now shown without a bandanna and wearing a house dress.

The harlot, a different but equally derogatory image, can be seen throughout the history of Black memorabilia: an African-American woman with large breasts, usually dressed very scantily and often depicted in provocative poses, enticing men to use her sexually. The harlot always appears happy to be used in such a manner, and her provocative clothing and attitude worked to justify the degradation and abuse of African-American women of all ages.

Such collectibles, by denigrating the appearance and status of African-Americans, helped create and perpetuate racial and gender stereotypes. The recent resurgence in the reproduction of these objects clearly signals a return to earlier racist ideas.

BIBLIOGRAPHY

Congdon-Martin, Douglas. *Images in Black: One Hundred Fifty Years of Black Collectibles* (1990); Goings, Kenneth W. "Memorabilia That Have Perpetuated Stereotypes About African-Americans," *Chronicle of Higher Education* (February 14, 1990); Reno, Dawn. *Collecting Black Americana* (1986).

KENNETH W. GOINGS

MENKEN, ADAH ISAACS (1835-1868)

What would make a dirty Colorado gold miner of the 1860s drop his pick, slick down his hair, and go to the theater to watch an adaptation of Lord Byron's poem "Mazeppa"? Adah Isaacs Menken in a body stocking charging onto the stage strapped to a horse. This actress knew how to draw a crowd.

Menken loved to wrap herself and her life in mystery, but she was probably Creole, born in 1835 in Chartrain, Louisiana, to Auguste Theodore, a storekeeper referred to as a "free man of color," and Marie Theodore, a native of Bordeaux. Her father died shortly after her birth, and her mother remarried, to a man named Josephs. In 1856, twenty-one-year-old Adah married Alexander Isaac Menken, a Jewish musician from Cincinnati. After he suffered serious financial setbacks, she went on the stage to support them. She made her theater debut under the name Adah Isaacs Menken in 1857 as Pauline in *The Lady of Lyons*. She was well received in spite of her inexperience and average acting talent, probably because she had a good voice, a pretty face, a remarkable figure, and stage presence. Managed by her husband, she traveled around the South and the Midwest.

Menken and her husband separated in July 1859, shortly after her New York debut. Thinking that she was divorced, she quietly married a boxer named John Carmel Heenan in September. When her secret marriage was revealed, Alexander Menken said that there had been no divorce. Heenan left for England, and Adah Menken was left pregnant and alone. Her child died shortly after birth.

Scandal had surrounded Menken, and she decided to exploit it. She discovered the role of the Tartar youth in *Mazeppa*. During the Victorian era, boys' roles, in which actresses wore tights, were the theater's cheesecake. *Mazeppa* offered the additional lure of a boffo ending when the naked youth—Menken wore neck-to-toe tights—was strapped to a horse that walked up a narrow runway through the crowd to the stage. From its opening on June 3, 1861, until her death, Menken had a guaranteed crowd pleaser. She took the show west. Her third husband, journalist Robert Henry Newell, went with her to San Fancisco, where her first run in that city brought in $9,000. Her western tour thrilled miners and literary lights equally, her considerable skills as a poet making it respectable for people such as Bret Harte and Joaquin Miller to admire her.

After divorcing Newell, Menken took *Mazeppa* to England, where she caused a terrific scandal and received $500 a performance, making her the highest-paid actress on record at the time. She was adopted by the British literati and had a romantic relationship with the poet Algernon Swinburne. She was married once more, in 1866, to James Paul Barkley; the marriage lasted three days, and a son was born three months later. Then Menken hit Paris. When she wasn't delighting audiences, she was scandalizing the city by posing for photographs embracing Dumas *père*.

After Paris, Menken's career began to slide. Six weeks after her last performance, at Sadler's Wells on May 30, 1868, her health failed. She died, probably of tuberculosis complicated by peritonitis, in August. A volume of her poetry published after her death received some attention, and she is listed in many literary reference works as a poet and keeper of salons. Yet Adah Menken's place in history is more truly marked by the image of the "naked lady" riding her horse across the American frontier in defiance of Queen Victoria and all her kind.

BIBLIOGRAPHY

Burke, William J. and Will D. Howe. *American Authors and Books 1604-1940* (1943); *NAW*; *NBAW*.

KATHLEEN THOMPSON

MERCER, MABEL (1900-1984)

"Mabel Mercer is a person of true maturity, of profound perception, of a lovingness seldom encountered and the guardian of the tenuous dreams created by the writers of songs" (Wilder 1965). Thus composer Alec Wilder, many of whose songs were introduced by Mabel Mercer, described the singer, whose regal bearing, crisp diction, and attention to lyric interpretation made her the toast of café society and a major influence on such singers as Frank Sinatra, Nat "King" Cole, Peggy Lee, Johnny Mathis, Barbara Cook, Bobby Short, and Leontyne Price. Legend has it that Billie Holiday was nearly fired from a job because she spent so much time at the club across the street, where Mercer was performing.

Born in Burton-on-Trent, Staffordshire, England, in 1900, Mabel Mercer was the daughter of an American jazz musician and a British variety actress. She attended a convent school in Manchester until age fourteen. She left school to go on tour with members of her family and then, after World War I, began working on the Continent, as both a dancer and singer.

In 1924, she met Bricktop, who was herself an entertainer at that time. After Bricktop opened her famous Paris nightclub on the rue Pigalle in 1930, Mercer joined Bricktop and Louis Cole as an entertainer there, performing in ensemble and solo numbers. Her appearances at Bricktop's throughout most of the 1930s made Mercer a star and enabled her to develop her distinctive style and approach to a song. She characteristically performed seated, as if on a throne, wearing a dark dress, with her hands folded in her lap.

Mercer first appeared in the United States in 1938 at the New York City club Ruban Bleu in a successful engagement that lasted several weeks. She then traveled to the Bahamas for an appearance there; with the outbreak of World War II, she was unable to attain an entry permit to return to the United States until 1941.

Back in the States, Mercer returned to the Ruban Bleu for six months. She then became a regular at Tony's, a club on West 52nd Street, from 1942 until 1949, when the building Tony's was in was torn down. Other engagements followed, notably at the Byline Room from 1949 to 1957, and later at Downstairs at the Upstairs, the St. Regis Room of the St. Regis Hotel, and the Café Carlyle.

In addition to her club appearances, Mercer appeared in 1972 in a PBS television special, *An Evening with Mabel Mercer & Bobby Short & Friends*. In 1977, she appeared at Carnegie Hall and then in London, where she also starred in a five-part BBC television series, *Miss Mercer in Mayfair*. In 1982, after a three-year absence from performing, she appeared at the Kool Jazz Festival in a program of songs by Alec Wilder. Her final public appearance was in November 1983, at a benefit for the SLE Foundation, which combats lupus.

Among the songs she introduced or saved from unjustified obscurity were "The End of a Love Af-

fair" (by Edward Carolan "Bud" Redding), "While We're Young" (cowritten by Wilder), "Fly Me to the Moon" (by Bart Howard), "Remind Me" (by Jerome Kern and Dorothy Fields), "By Myself" (by Arthur Dietz and Howard Schwartz), and "Little Boy Blue" (by Richard Rodgers and Lorenz Hart); the last-named song was recorded by Frank Sinatra, Lena Horne, and Margaret Whiting after they heard Mercer's rendition of it.

She died April 20, 1984, in Pittsfield, Massachusetts, of respiratory arrest. A brief marriage to Kelsey Pharr, a jazz musician, had ended in divorce; she left no survivors.

BIBLIOGRAPHY

Clarke, Donald, ed. *The Penguin Encyclopedia of Popular Music* (1989); Kramer, Gary. Liner notes to *The Art of Mabel Mercer*. Atlantic SD2-602 (1965); *Variety*. Obituary (April 25, 1984); Whitaker, Rogers. Liner notes to *Once in a Blue Moon*. Atlantic 1301; Wilder, Alec. Liner notes to *The Art of Mabel Mercer*. Atlantic SD-602 (1965).

SELECTED DISCOGRAPHY

Once in a Blue Moon, Atlantic 1301; *Merely Marvelous*, Atlantic 1322; *The Art of Mabel Mercer*, Atlantic SD2-602; *At Town Hall* (with Bobby Short), Atlantic SD2-604.

BARBARA BERGERON

MERIWETHER, LOUISE (1923-)

"I have been deeply concerned for many years by the way African Americans fell through the cracks of history," writes Louise Meriwether, "and I reacted by attempting to set the record straight" (In Letter to Rita Dandridge 1981). Her attempt was to involve herself with race issues and to write about the remarkable exploits of African-Americans, which, she insists, are not Black history but American history.

Louise Meriwether was born May 8, 1923, in Haverstraw, New York, to Marion Lloyd Jenkins and Julie Jenkins, South Carolinians who had migrated to New York via Philadelphia in search of a better life. The only daughter and the third of five children, she had moved with her family to Brooklyn and later to Harlem, where, trapped by the Great Depression, her father became a numbers runner. She grew up on welfare and attended P.S. 81. Meriwether was graduated from Central Commercial High School in downtown Manhattan, received a B.A. in English from New York University, and an M.A. in journalism from the University of California in Los Angeles, where she moved with Angelo Meriwether, her first husband. That marriage ended in divorce, and so did her second marriage, to Earl Howe. Meriwether currently lives in New York City with her mother.

Primarily as a writer, Meriwether has raised the consciousness of Black Americans about their history. While a newspaper woman for the *Los Angeles Sentinel* from 1961 to 1964, she published articles on significant but little-known African-Americans (Grace Bumbry, a singer; Audrey Boswell, an attorney; and Vaino Spencer, a Los Angeles judge) who overcame great odds to achieve success. She also published an article on Matthew Henson, the African-American who was the first man to stand atop the North Pole. She revised and published one of her graduate theses as "The Negro: Half a Man in a White World" in the October 1965 issue of *Negro Digest*. In 1970, she published her first novel, *Daddy Was a Number Runner*, which documents the corrosive effects of the economic depression on the Coffins, a Black Harlem family on welfare. The novel received favorable reviews and was reissued by the Feminist Press in its Black women writers series. It garnered two grants for Meriwether in 1973: one from the National Endowment for the Arts in Washington, D.C., and the other from the Creative Arts Service Program, an auxiliary of the New York State Council on the Arts. In addition to a number of history-related short stories and essays, Meriwether has published three children's books on historical figures: *The Freedom Ship of Robert Smalls* (1971), *The Heart Man: Dr. Daniel Hale Williams* (1972), and *Don't Ride the Bus on Monday: The Rosa Parks Story* (1973). Her forthcoming work, *Fragments of the Ark*, is a Civil War novel told from the point of view of several slaves and deals with, perhaps for the first time, the 150,000 Black soldiers and the thousands of field hands who deserted their masters' plantations—crippling the Confederacy—to work as laborers for the Union army.

Meriwether has frequently interrupted her writing to participate in civil rights activities. In 1965, she trekked to Bogalusa, Louisiana, to work with the Congress of Racial Equality (CORE) and tote guns for the Deacons, a Black coalition that maintained a twenty-four-hour patrol to secure the area's Black citizens from the forays of the Ku Klux Klan. Two years later, she opposed Hollywood director Norman Jewison and Twentieth Century-Fox producer David L. Wolper, who wanted to make a movie about Nat Turner based on William Styron's *The Confessions of Nat Turner* (1967). Because Styron's book emasculated the insurrectionist and distorted historical truths, Meriwether and Vantile Whitfield, founder of Performing Arts Society of Los Angeles (PASLA), formed the Black Anti-Defamation Association to protest the making of the film. Tremendous support came from the Black community, including that of John Henrik Clarke, noted historian, who edited a volume of essays entitled *William Styron's Nat Turner: Ten Black Writers Respond* (1968). As a result of these efforts, the motion picture was not made.

In the early 1970s, Meriwether and others formed Black Concern, a committee to protest South Africa's offering large sums of money to American Black entertainers to break the boycott of the Organization of African Unity (OAU) and perform in that country. Meriwether and John Henrik Clarke wrote and distributed *Black Americans Stay Out of South Africa*, a pamphlet detailing the flagrant injustices against Black South Africans. She carried her message to radio audiences and to the United Nations, receiving support from their Committee Against Apartheid, the United Council of Churches, and other national organizations. Black Concern was instrumental in persuading Muhammad Ali, then heavyweight boxing champion, to cancel a match in Johannesburg, and in convincing other Black entertainers to uphold the OAU's boycott.

The crisis over, Meriwether returned to her writing, publishing short stories and articles. From 1979 to 1985, she was a faculty member at Sarah Lawrence College in Bronxville, New York (and one semester, while on leave, an instructor at the University of Houston), teaching creative writing. During that time, she received a grant from the Mellon Foundation through Sarah Lawrence College to assist her in researching the Civil War novel, which required several trips to the Sea Islands, Charleston, and North Carolina.

Meriwether's "weakness" has been in taking time away from her writing to organize the community in political activities that she felt were of prime importance. While trying to write, she has actively protested the Gulf War, the Vietnam War, the invasions of Panama and Grenada, and the covert actions of the United States in Chile and Cuba.

BIBLIOGRAPHY

Dandridge, Rita B. "From Economic Insecurity to Disintegration: A Study of Character in Louise Meriwether's *Daddy Was a Number Runner*," *Negro American Literature Forum* (Fall 1975); *DLB*; Meriwether, Louise. Letters to Rita B. Dandridge (September 8, 23; October 19; November 20, 1991); Schraufnagel, Noel. *From Apology to Protest: The Black American Novel* (1973).

RITA DANDRIDGE

MERRITT, EMMA FRANCES GRAYSON (1860-1933)

Emma Merritt's contributions as teacher and administrator in the Washington, D.C., public schools changed the face of education for Black Americans around the country. That she was able to carve out a career in education in Washington, D.C., in the 1870s was a remarkable feat in itself for a young Black woman. At the same time, her accomplishments were impressive for any educator of any race, gender, or period in history.

Emma Frances Grayson Merritt was born on January 11, 1860, in Dumfries (Cherry Hill), Prince William County, Virginia. She was one of seven children of John Merritt, a Black man, and Sophia Cook Merritt, a Cherokee woman. When Emma was three years old, the Merritt family moved to Washington, D.C., where she attended the Black public schools that had been funded by Congress in 1864.

The first school Merritt attended was a part of the Ebenezer African Methodist Episcopal Church, which was publicly subsidized as a school. She graduated from high school and became a teacher herself at the age of fifteen. After eight years of teaching in grammar school, in 1883, Merritt entered Howard University. There she studied under both James M. Gregory and Wiley Lane. In 1887, she became principal of the Banneker Elementary School. She also continued her own education. From 1887 to 1890, she studied at Columbian University (now George Washington University) and then went back to Howard in 1889 to focus on mathematics. In 1890, she took over as principal of Garnet School and established the first kindergarten for African-American students, an astounding move at a time when kindergartens were almost unheard of in the general population.

In 1898, Merritt became director of primary instruction and in 1927 supervising principal of all Black schools in Washington, D.C. She remained in the latter position until her retirement in 1930. Throughout her career, she was an innovator. She developed a primary department for Black students and modernized instruction in that department, organized "demonstration and observation" schools to improve teaching methods, classified students in homogeneous learning groups, established excursions and field trips, and introduced silent reading into the schools—all in the first quarter of the twentieth century.

Her innovations carried far beyond the District of Columbia, in part because she corresponded with former students who were teaching in the rural South and kept them apprised of new ideas in education. She also lectured on her methods at a variety of institutions, including the State College in Delaware, Howard University, Cheyney Institute in Pennsylvania, Manassas Industrial School and Hampton Institute in Virginia, the Normal School in Baltimore (now Coppin State College), West Virginia State College, and Dallas Institute in Texas. While she made such major contributions to education, she was herself continuing to be educated. She spent some time between 1898 and 1901 at the Cook County Normal School in Chicago studying mathematics and child psychology. She also completed a course of study at the Phoebe Hearst (Kindergarten) Training School in Washington, D.C., and at the Berlitz School of Languages.

Merritt's educational genius was widely recognized in her own time. The District of Columbia superintendent of schools, F. W. Ballou, praised her highly and asked his board of education to establish two laboratory schools in which her methods could be used and observed. In 1925, Howard University awarded her an honorary Master of Arts degree.

Merritt was also active in community affairs. She organized and presided over the Teachers' Benefit and Annuity Association of Washington, D.C., and the Prudence Crandall Association for needy children. From 1930 to 1933, she was president of the District of Columbia branch of the National Association for the Advancement of Colored People. She was also a founding member of the National Association of Colored Women.

Emma Merritt died on June 8, 1933. Eleven years later, an elementary school was named in her honor in the District of Columbia.

BIBLIOGRAPHY

CBWA; DANB; Dannett, Sylvia. Profiles of Negro Womanhood (1964-66); Du Bois, W. E. B. "Along the Color Line," Crisis (September 1903); EBA; Franklin, John Hope. From Slavery to Freedom (1969); Journal of Negro History. "Educators of the First Half Century of Public Schools in the District of Columbia" (April 1932); NA; Quarles, Benjamin. The Negro in the Making of America (1969); Robinson, Omelia. "Contributions of Black American Academic Women to American Higher Education," Ph.D. diss. (1978); Taylor, Estelle. "Emma Frances Grayson Merritt: Pioneer in Negro Education," Negro History Bulletin (August-September 1975); Thomas, Emma Merritt Wormley. Personal interview; Woodson, Carter G. "Emma Frances Grayson Merritt," Opportunity (August 1930); WWCA (1932).

GERRI BATES

METOYER, MARIE THÉRÈSE *see* COINCOIN

THE MIDDLE CLASS

While social differences, especially those centered around free or enslaved status, were not unknown to the antebellum Black community, class formation and social stratification became increasingly characteristic of postbellum Black urban life. Increased educational opportunities and urbanization greatly enlarged the social distinctions among Black people in the United States. Until recently, however, the fluidity of the class structure in the Black community as well as the tendency in race-dominated white America to view Black citizens as a monolithic group have combined to limit scholarly attention to issues of class in the Black community. The dearth of women property holders and their limited occupational range have made women invisible in most of the scholarship dealing with issues of class in the Black community.

Yet a major force in the expansion of the Black middle class during the late nineteenth and early twentieth centuries was the rise in the number and importance of educated, professional (and, sometimes, financially successful) Black women. Moreover, male class identity was frequently affirmed and, on occasion, determined by the social position and even physical appearance of the women they married. Gender and class issues were and remain inextricably intertwined in the lives and social structure of most groups; Blacks were and are no different. This essay

This formal dance of the Baltimore upper middle class took place around 1915. [Scurlock Studio]

focuses on the formation of the Black female middle-class community, the community roles of Black middle-class women, and the tensions within and across women's class lines during the decades from 1880 to 1930.

At the turn of the twentieth century, women who belonged to the small but expanding middle class tended to be either college or normal school graduates; if employed, they were to be found in either professional or white-collar positions or as businesswomen; and they were active in the organizational and institutional life of the Black community, locally and, sometimes, nationally. Educated middle-class Black women excluded from professional positions on the basis of either their race or gender, or both, also occupied domestic service and semi-skilled positions, which placed them at the lower end of the middle class.

A racially restricted job market often meant that middle-class status in the Black community was not always tied to either income or job description. Other determinations of social status such as decorum, respectability, and moral refinement could be as important as occupation and income. As representatives of the race's advancement, especially its moral progress, since emancipation, generations of middle-class Black women were expected to conduct themselves with the utmost decorum and to be of the highest moral character. For the most part, no amount of money or family background could substitute for morals and manners.

Although Black women who belonged to the middle class shared certain characteristics, it was not a monolithic, unambiguous group. There was considerable difference in family background, income, and occupation as well as in the attitudes and in the nature and level of community roles of the Black female middle class. With the expansion of the Black middle class in the early twentieth century, social distinctions within the middle class became even more noticeable. With some overlapping, Black middle-class women can be categorized loosely as belonging to three basic groups—the upper-middle-class social elite, the new professional middle class, and the lower middle class.

Personal income and property ownership had less to do with determining social status for Black women than for Black men. Few women achieved financial success on their own; Maggie Lena Walker and Madam C. J. Walker were among the exceptions. The economic success that most middle-class women enjoyed traditionally was tied to their husbands or to their jobs during a period when there was no real job security. Domestic workers often had more job security than female teachers, who often had to resign from their teaching jobs when they married and who lacked anything close to a permanent position.

Women like Mary Church Terrell and Josephine Bruce belonged to the Black upper middle class. The combination of a prominent familial background, income, and very light skin with "barely a trace of African blood" differentiated them from most of the middle class as well as the Black masses. Descended from racially mixed parentage, the women of this class were often light in skin color. As such, they were frequently sought after as mates by upper-middle-class men or men with such aspirations. The social status attached to their family backgrounds often centered around their free Black ancestry; the educational, financial, and professional standing of their parents and even grandparents; and, occasionally, their descent from prominent white ancestry.

As part of the Black middle-class elite, these women were frequently touted as the most representative of Black womanhood, partly to combat widespread racist theories about Black female immorality and lack of respectability. As a consequence, middle-class Black women in the upper rungs of the Black social structure occupied many of the major leadership positions in the Black women's secular club movement, locally as well as nationally. Oberlin graduate and daughter of millionaire Robert Church, Mary Church Terrell was elected the first president of the National Association of Colored Women because she was considered the "best" representative of Black women's progress.

Yet, even as they embarked upon moral and social uplift campaigns among the "lowly" as members of Black women's clubs, upper-middle-class African-American women regularly attempted to distinguish, if not distance, themselves from the less fortunate. Moreover, few domestics and even middle-class women of lesser social standing could be found at the "full-dress" New Year's Day receptions or other social soirees of the Black middle-class elite.

Not a birthright, middle-class status came to a larger group of Black women as an outgrowth of their educational and professional success. As educational opportunities in privately and federally supported normal schools and colleges and job opportunities became more accessible to women of color at the turn of the twentieth century, the ranks of the Black female middle class grew. Teachers (without prominent familial background) in Black urban and rural school systems for colored youth, and white-collar office workers in small Black business concerns and increasingly in the federal government, formed the core of the new Black female middle-class life.

Middle-class Black women in this category ranged from Anna J. Cooper, the recipient of a Ph.D. from the Sorbonne and the second female principal of the highly acclaimed M Street High School (for colored youth) in Washington, D.C., and bank president Maggie Lena Walker to entrepreneur Madam C. J. Walker and school president Nannie Helen Burroughs.

For the most part, the major difference between these individuals and those in the upper-middle-class social elite was family background. Often raised in poverty and with the cultural values of ordinary Black folk, this group of middle-class women often differed in self-perceptions and attitudes toward the Black masses as well as in the nature and level of their community roles from those upper-middle-class women whose families were part of the old aristocracy. Moreover, unlike the upper-middle-class elite, they represented the complete gamut of physical features and skin colors in the Black community, from very light to very dark.

Coming from humble backgrounds and often growing up in the Baptist church tradition, most of these middle-class women shared less of the elitist feelings characteristic of their upper echelon middle-class sisters. Early on, they were personally aware of the abilities and strengths of hardworking, church-going ordinary Black folk. Thus, a person's education, occupation, or family background did not automatically indicate her moral character. Few would link "respectable" domestic servants with the "lowly" or the "vicious" members of the race. One of the primary goals of Burroughs's National Training School for Women and Girls—professionalizing domestic service work—was deemed a worthy cause by most members of this group and by legions of ordinary Black women and men (some of whom eventually constituted the lower middle class) who donated nickels and dimes to keep the school afloat.

Like Burroughs, Maggie Lena Walker, the daughter of a washerwoman, who went on to graduate from the Colored Normal School in Richmond, Virginia, and to teach in the local school system prior to becoming the first female president of a bank in the United States, represented this new middle class of Black women. Her affiliation with a mutual benefit society, the Independent Order of Saint Luke, was not unusual for those in the new Black middle class. The Independent Order in which Walker served as Right Worthy Grand Secretary for over three decades never restricted its membership to any particular stratum of Black society. Middle-class women active in mass-based organizations, like the Order of Saint Luke, seldom distanced themselves from their less formally trained sisters.

In her analysis of the womanist consciousness of Walker, historian Elsa Barkley Brown asserts that Walker succeeded as the leader and spokeswoman of the Order of Saint Luke "not merely because of her own strengths and skills, considerable though they were, but also because she operated from the strength of the Saint Luke collective as a whole and from the special strengths and talents of the inner core of the Saint Luke women in particular" (Brown 1989).

Racial solidarity to middle-class women who were true race women, like Burroughs and Walker, meant joining in with and accepting all classes within the Black community. They did not feel that women at the lower ends of the social structure could either represent themselves or act on their own behalf.

It would be hard to imagine Walker or Burroughs describing the role of educated women in Tuskegee, Alabama, as "bringing up the light of knowledge and the gospel of cleanliness to their poor benighted sisters," or referring to the Black female masses as the "Negro's . . . most illiterate and vicious representatives," and, at the same time, referring to educated women as "the more intelligent and worthy classes," as Mary Church Terrell did in response to the query "What Role Is the Educated Negro Woman to Play in the Uplifting of Her Race?"

Rosa D. Bowser, founder of the Woman's League and president of the Richmond Mothers' Club, responded differently; she emphasized the need for educated, middle-class women to "be WITH the element to be uplifted." She argued that "It is impossible to help a fallen or weak sister to rise if the helper, like the Levite, pass by on the other side, and merely call out, Arise and stand in the beauty of pure womanhood—rather than like the Samaritan, she goes to her and lifts her to her feet." When Terrell spoke of coming "into the closest possible touch with the masses of our women," it is doubtful that she meant as close as Bowser, Burroughs, and Walker did.

Even when operating at a social and physical distance, however, the Black middle-class elite were imbued with the same spirit of sacrifice that compelled practically all members of the Black middle class to assist in the advancement of the race. Education and means (however limited) obligated members of the Black middle class to assume important community roles and to work to better their race. Thus, free time that could have been devoted to purely leisure-time activities often went to conducting mothers' meetings, operating kindergartens, teaching

Sunday school, and aiding working women. Belonging to the middle class was as much, if not more, a call to duty for most educated middle-class Black women than it was a status symbol. Incomes were often too low, job security too elusive, and racial discrimination too widespread for most middle-class Black women to boast of being anything other than servants of their people. Despite differences in motivation, personal circumstances, and attitudes, educated middle-class Black women served important roles as community builders, role models, and public symbols of the race's progress at a critical juncture in the development of Black community life and race relations in the United States.

BIBLIOGRAPHY

Barnett, Evelyn Brooks. "Nannie Burroughs and the Education of Black Women." In *The Afro-American Woman: Struggles and Images* (1978); Bowser, Rosa D. "What Role Is the Educated Negro Woman to Play in the Uplifting of Her Race?" In *Twentieth Century Negro Literature; Or, A Cyclopedia of Thought on the Vital Topics Relating to the American Negro*, ed. Daniel W. Culp (1902); Brown, Elsa Barkley. "Womanist Consciousness: Maggie Lena Walker and the Independent Order of Saint Luke." In *Black Women in America*, ed. Micheline R. Malson et al. (1989); Bruce, Josephine. "What Has Education Done for Colored Women?" *Voice of the Negro* (July 1904); Fields, Emma L. "The Women's Club Movement in the United States, 1877-1900," M.A. thesis (1948); Harley, Sharon. "Mary Church Terrell: Genteel Militant." In *Nineteenth Century Black Leaders*, ed. Leon Litwack and August Meier (1988); Silone-Yates, Josephine. "The National Association of Colored Women," *The Voice of the Negro* (July 1904); Terrell, Mary Church. "The Progress of Colored Women," Mary Church Terrell Papers, Manuscript Division, Library of Congress, Washington, D.C., and "What Role Is the Educated Negro Woman to Play in the Uplifting of the Race?" In *Twentieth Century Negro Literature; Or, A Cyclopedia of Thought on the Vital Topics Relating to the American Negro*, ed. Daniel W. Culp (1902).

SHARON HARLEY

MIDWIVES

Black women have been prominent in the provision of health care since the colonial period, but their service as midwives has been especially remarkable. In the antebellum South, many older slave women became the acknowledged healers in the slave quarters, proffering botanical remedies, tending to injuries, and assisting women in childbirth. Black slave midwives attended virtually all normal, or nonproblematic, births to slave women; in rural areas, slave and free midwives attended both Black and white women. So commonplace were the Black birth attendants in the antebellum South that one Virginia physician estimated they attended the births of half the white women in the state. Slave midwife Mildred Graves, for example, served her slave community and many of the neighboring white women. Her obstetrical services—the fees redounding to her master—kept her very busy and increased her value to her master.

In freedom as in slavery, the African-American midwife continued to serve her community, and some freedwomen were able to earn their living as midwives. Black midwives usually were older women, with children of their own, who believed they had been divinely called to their vocation. Similarly, a Black midwife usually recruited her successor in response to a dream or other supernatural instruction. Many midwives also were the daughters and granddaughters of midwives, the call to this special work extending through generations. Black midwives usually were called grannies or granny midwives, a respectful acknowledgment of age and status, and often they were addressed with a fictive familial name, such as Aunt or Auntie. From at least the antebellum period through most of the twentieth century, the Black midwife was a revered member of her community, the "local wise woman" and "charismatic leader."

African-American lay midwifery has been a syncretic mix of traditional folk remedies and practices, reliance upon divine guidance and care, select aspects of medical practice such as aseptic technique, a conviction in the normalcy of parturition, and a willingness to watch and wait upon nature. Also, in caring for women in childbirth, the Black midwife offered emotional support, encouragement, and (often) prayer along with her specific expertise. The training of these lay midwives was traditionally empirical in an apprentice relationship to an experienced midwife. In this way, Black midwives preserved and transmitted both knowledge and culture from the past to the present.

Despite the revolution in childbirth practices that has occurred in the United States in the past 150 years—the birth place moved from the home to the hospital and the birth attendant changed from the female midwife to the male physician—Black midwives continued to be the obstetrical caregivers for substantial numbers of Black women in the rural South well into the twentieth century. For example, in the early 1900s, Black midwives may have delivered most of the babies born in South Carolina; in 1914, Black midwives probably attended half of all births in

Virginia; in 1936, sixty-seven percent of all North Carolinian Black women giving birth were attended by Black midwives; and as late as 1950, the majority of childbearing Black women in Alabama relied on the care of granny midwives. In fact, when late-twentieth-century regional statistics for midwife-attended births are analyzed, midwifery emerges as a primarily rural, southern, and non-white institution.

Historically, Black midwives have been much more prevalent in the southern United States than in other regions because of the region's large African-American population, but segregation, racism, rural isolation, poverty, and the lack of alternative institutions have all been factors that kept the Black midwife in business despite the growing trend toward hospital births. The quality of the Black midwife's services also maintained her popularity among select populations. In addition to the assistance rendered during childbirth, the midwife usually stayed with the new mother for the early postpartum period, caring for new mother and new baby and, if necessary, attending to various domestic tasks. Moreover, hospital births, or even physician-attended home births, were economically out-of-reach for many rural Black families through the first half of the twentieth century. In 1924, a Black Texas woman reported that she could get a midwife for seventy-five cents while a doctor would charge fifteen dollars. Some midwives cultivated relationships with rural general practitioners to better serve their rural community: the midwife attended normal deliveries and called on the doctor when complications arose.

The Black midwife came under vicious attack in the early decades of the twentieth century as part of a nationwide, physician-led campaign against all midwives who, ostensibly, were to blame for alarming rates of maternal and infant mortality. This movement coincided with efforts by obstetricians to raise the status of their fledgling medical specialty. Although several contemporary studies vindicated lay midwives—the immigrant midwife in the North and the Black granny midwife in the South—physicians succeeded in persuading state legislatures that lay midwives should either be prohibited by statute or carefully regulated. At that time, in the South, physicians were unprepared to take over the midwives' large caseload. Thus, most southern states accepted the granny midwife as an interim necessary evil and proposed that her alleged abuses be curbed through education, licensure, and supervision.

Some states began identifying and licensing midwives in the early 1990s, but most states did not begin midwife training programs until federal funds through the Sheppard-Towner Act became available. The Black granny midwives who sought licensure and who participated in the training programs often achieved a new sense of authority about their vocation and a collective identity as women with a special—divinely sanctioned—knowledge and skill.

Although most training classes for Black lay midwives were organized by state agencies and taught by white medical professionals, in several southern states Black nurses and Black physicians were recruited to assist in the midwives' education. There also were at least two Black initiatives for midwife education: in cooperation with the Maternity Center Association of New York, Dillard University (through the Flint-Goodrich Hospital in New Orleans) and Tuskegee Institute both offered midwifery training courses for graduate nurses for a brief time during the early 1940s.

The withdrawal of federal aid for midwifery training in the late 1920s, additional legal restrictions regarding lay midwifery, the growth of urban centers in the American South, the postwar boom in hospital construction, the establishment of medical schools with teaching hospitals in need of clinical material, and, finally, the availability of health care insurance and subsidized care all contributed to the dwindling number of Black midwives in the late twentieth century. Some Black granny midwives continue in their vocation, however. In Harris County, Texas, in 1970, for example, one study identified four Black midwives. All were older women with children, empirically trained, who had been practicing for many years.

BIBLIOGRAPHY

Baughman, Greer. "A Preliminary Report upon the Midwife Situation in Virginia," *Virginia Medical Monthly* (October 1928); Bureau of Child Hygiene, Texas State Board of Health. "Report on the Midwife Survey in Texas" (1924); Chapin, Charles V. "The Control of Midwifery," *The Medical Progress* (April 1923); Darlington, Thomas. "The Present Status of the Midwife," *American Journal of Obstetrics and Gynecology* (1911); Devitt, Neal. "The Statistical Case for Elimination of the Midwife, Part 1," *Women and Health* (Spring 1979), and "Part 2," *Women and Health* (Summer 1979); Dougherty, Molly C. "Southern Lay Midwives as Ritual Specialists." In *Women in Ritual and Symbolic Roles*, ed. Judith Hoch-Smith and Anita Spring (1978), and "Southern Midwifery and Organized Health Care Systems in Conflict," *Medical Anthropology* (Spring 1982); Freedman, Alex S. "The Passing of the Arkansas Granny Midwife," *Kentucky Folklore Record* (1974); Gardner, Sarah. "Medical Men Versus Granny Women: The Professionalized Obstetricians' Campaign to Eliminate

Midwifery in the Rural South, 1920-1950." Paper presented at the second annual meeting of the Southern Association of Women's History, Chapel Hill, North Carolina (June 1991); Hanson, Henry and Lucile Spire Blachly. "Present Status of Midwifery in Florida," *Southern Medical Journal* (December 1931); Hardin, E. R. "The Midwife Problem," *Southern Medical Journal* (May 1925); Hine, Darlene Clark. *Black Women in White: Racial Conflict and Cooperation in the Nursing Profession, 1890-1950* (1989); Holmes, Linda Janet. "African American Midwives in the South." In *The American Way of Birth*, ed. Pamela S. Eakins (1986), and "Louvenia Taylor Benjamin, Southern Lay Midwife: An Interview," *Sage: A Scholarly Journal on Black Women* (Fall 1985), and "Medical History: Alabama Granny Midwife," *Journal of the Medical Society of New Jersey* (May 1984); Johnson, Charles S. *The Negro in American Civilization: A Study of Negro Life and Race Relations in Light of Social Research* (1930); Kobrin, Frances E. "The American Midwife Controversy: A Crisis in Professionalization." In *Women and Health in America*, ed. Judith Walzer Leavitt (1984); Leavitt, Judith Walzer. *Brought to Bed: Childbearing in America, 1750-1950* (1986); Lee, Florence Ellen. "Role of Lay Midwifery in Maternity Care in a Large Metropolitan Area," *Public Health Reports* (November/December 1984); Levy, Walter Edmond. "Our Midwife Problem," *Southern Medical Journal* (September 1931); Litoff, Judy Barrett. *American Midwives, 1860 to the Present* (1978), and *The American Midwife Debate: A Sourcebook on Its Modern Origins* (1986); Lobenstine, Ralph Waldo. "The Influence of the Midwife Upon Infant and Maternal Morbidity and Mortality," *American Journal of Obstetrics and Diseases of Women and Children* (1911); Logan, Onnie Lee, as told to Katherine Clark. *Motherwit: An Alabama Midwife's Story* (1989); McCoy, Samuel. "Ketchin' Babies: A Hundred Thousand Births that Need Safeguarding," *The Survey* (August 1925); Mongeau, Beatrice, Harvey L. Smith, and Ann C. Maney. "The 'Granny' Midwife: Changing Roles and Functions of a Folk Practitioner," *American Journal of Sociology* (March 1961); Parsons, Alice. "South Carolina Pays Tribute to Lay Midwives," *Journal of Nurse-Midwifery* (Winter 1975); Plecker, W. A. "The Midwife in Virginia," *The Virginia Medical Semi-Monthly* (January 1914), and "The Midwife Problem in Virginia," *The Virginia Medical Semi-Monthly* (December 1914), and "Virginia Makes Efforts to Solve Midwife Problem," *Nation's Health* (December 1925); Savitt, Todd. *Medicine and Slavery: The Diseases and Health Care of Blacks in Antebellum Virginia* (1978); Starr, Paul. *The Social Transformation of American Medicine* (1982); Susie, Debra Ann. *In the Way of Our Grandmothers: A Cultural View of Twentieth-Century Midwifery in Florida* (1988); Underwood, Felix J. "The Development of Midwifery in Mississippi," *Southern Medical Journal* (September 1926).

MEGAN SEAHOLM

THE MILITARY

While serving one's country is widely held to be an honor and an act of patriotism, historically most governments have been reluctant to enlist women into their armed services. Combat, in particular, has been considered unnatural for women. Yet, some women have defied traditional norms and become soldiers in various parts of the world.

Achieving the status of soldier in the United States has been a long and arduous process for women. Black women in particular have gone through a number of phases in the quest to serve their country. The first phase consisted of individual acts of heroism and displays of patriotism. Next came the spirited efforts of individuals and groups to provide organized support. From these efforts sprang a number of support organizations in which serving the soldier and his family were primary objectives. A major turning point for Black women and the military occurred during World War II, when Black and white women finally donned the military uniform. At the next major transitional juncture Black women successfully tackled double integration: that of integration into white female units and then integration into all-male forces. While serving in an increased number of combat-support roles and technical specialties, a large number of women were placed on the battlefield. Some even lived in coed facilities, which was a first for the military. Many women experienced these increases and changes during the Persian Gulf War. Today, Black women contribute to most aspects of the United States military.

Although there were a number of conflicts during the colonial period, the American Revolution was the first war waged by the nation. The war, which began in 1775, was made official with the 1776 signing of the Declaration of Independence. Like their white counterparts, Black Americans were torn between supporting Great Britain or supporting the United States. Black men and women, however, were indecisive because of their status. Most were slaves, and free Black Americans were treated little better than slaves in most instances. Moreover, it was unclear whether the British—who promised freedom to all Black soldiers supporting the crown—or the Americans offered the greatest opportunity for change. As a result, thousands of Black men fought on both sides during the American Revolutionary War.

Though Black men were able to enlist in the militia, Black women were relegated to support roles. Little is known of their activities. One nameless free Black maid contributed a large portion of her meager

This company of the Black Women's Army Auxiliary Corps is shown at their camp near Monrovia, Liberia, during World War II (1942/1943). They are being reviewed by the Hon. Lester A. Walton, U.S. Minister to Liberia. [National Archives]

monthly wage to the war effort. Another unnamed free Black woman gave soup and bread to hungry, incarcerated patriots. Phillis Wheatley composed an inspirational poem for General George Washington while he was stranded that dreadful winter at Valley Forge. Some Black women probably were among the camp followers providing services such as cooking, washing, and caring for the sick, but existing records show no evidence of this.

The records recall the names of only a few women who actually took up arms and fought during the Revolution. These include Nancy Hart, the six-foot Georgian; Margaret Corbin, known as Captain Molly, who was wounded in the 1776 attack on Ft. Washington; and Deborah Sampson Gannett. Some historians have identified Gannett as a Black heroine.

After the Revolutionary War ended, records indicate that escaped Black slaves had taken shelter in Florida at a fort abandoned by the British during the war. General Andrew Jackson considered the fort a threat to United States security and ordered its destruction. At "Fort Negro," as it was known, Black women and men died in the confrontation. The fort was completely destroyed.

Black women played more varied military support roles in the Civil War (1861-65), the bloodiest war in U.S. history. Slave women in the South kept plantations going by planting and harvesting cotton, which the Confederate government relied on to help finance the war. The Union army relied on Mary Elizabeth Bowser, a slave girl, to spy on the Confederate president, Jefferson Davis. The most noted Black woman spy of the period is Harriet Tubman. She served in South Carolina, gathering information from informants based behind Confederate lines. Tubman was also a nurse and a scout who led Union soldiers during several expeditions to the South. In effect, she became the first Black woman in U.S. history to lead men to war. Though this legendary leader of the Underground Railroad was a civilian employed by the U.S. military, she was buried with full military honors.

The fiery abolitionist speaker Sojourner Truth participated in the Civil War. Truth organized fundraisers for Black troops and nursed wounded soldiers confined to Freedman's Hospital in Washington, D.C. She worked with Clara Barton, the white nurse who organized the American Red Cross.

Susie King Taylor, a native of Georgia, worked for the Union Army as a nurse and teacher to Black soldiers. Charlotte Forten was another who taught Black soldiers during the Civil War. Two others, Mary Chase and Mary Peake, opened schools for the freedmen, who were considered contrabands of war, in Alexander and Hampton, Virginia, respectively. Elizabeth Keckley supported the war effort in a slightly different way. Keckley, seamstress for the president's wife, Mary Todd Lincoln, organized the Contraband Relief Association of Washington, D.C., during the summer of 1862 to help Black Americans displaced by the war. Starting with forty members, the highly successful organization quickly expanded as it attracted the attention of Black churches across the North. Keckley's Contraband Relief Association was the forerunner to twentieth-century Black women's organizations designed to serve the military. Some of these organizations were the Negro War Relief, Women's Committee of the Council of National Defense, and the women's auxiliaries to various military units.

Evidence of Black women's participation in military events in the West is sketchier still, but there are at least two accounts of Black women being present in confrontations with Native Americans. In the colonial period, Lucy Terry wrote a poem describing one of the battles between white settlers and Native Americans. The poem, entitled "A Slave Report in Rhyme on the Indian Attack on Old Deerfield, August 25, 1746," helped to establish Terry as the first published Black woman in the United States. Over 125 years later, a Black woman known as "Aunt Sally" Campbell traveled with General George Custer before his defeat by the Sioux Indians at the Battle of Little Big Horn (1876). She probably served as his cook and washerwoman. When Custer left the Dakota Territory to search for the Sioux in Montana, Campbell remained in South Dakota, where she became the first non-Indian woman to reside in the territory.

Much of the Spanish-American War (1898) took place in Cuba and in the Philippines. As Teddy Roosevelt made his famous charge up San Juan Hill, the Twenty-fourth Infantry, an all-Black unit, provided cover. Additionally, the Ninth and Tenth Cavalry and the Twenty-fifth Infantry were all-Black units that participated in combat during the ten-week war. Though the United States won the war, thousands of Black and white soldiers contracted a number of tropical diseases. In July 1898, the Surgeon General asked that a corps of Black women be organized to nurse infirm Black soldiers. Thirty-two Black women were sent to nurse Black troops located at Camp Thomas, Georgia. These trailblazers were so well received that Congress created a permanent Army Nurse Corps in 1901. The Navy Nurse Corps was established in 1908. Thus, women had finally become an official part of the military, but ironically, Black women did not serve in either of these corps for another four decades.

However, Black nurses were accepted into the Red Cross. The opportunities created for Black nurses to serve the military directly and through the Red Cross were important during the era of Jim Crow, when there were very few Black hospitals and health care facilities and when Black nurses were barred from working in white hospitals.

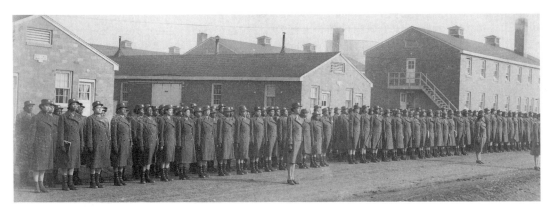

Company 8 of the Women's Army Auxiliary Corps is shown here in formation at Fort Des Moines, Iowa. One of its officers was Charity Adams Earley, the first Black woman commissioned in the army. [Charity Adams Earley]

During World War I, 650,000 Black men served in the U.S. military, with approximately a third of these serving in France. Hundreds of Black nurses registered with the American Red Cross. In June 1918, the secretary of war issued a call for Black nurses who were affiliated with the Red Cross to volunteer for overseas duty as well as for service at home. Among those who responded was Adah B. Thoms, the president of the National Association of Colored Graduate Nurses. Many others served the more than 38,000 Black troops confined to base hospitals in Kansas, Illinois, Iowa, Kentucky, Ohio, and New Jersey. Elizabeth Miller was assigned to a government military plant in Alabama. Black women were mobilized into serving in practically every state in the country through local organizations under various names. These included Hostess Houses in states with military bases. Mary McLeod Bethune worked with the Emergency Circle, Negro War Relief in Florida. Black women in Colorado formed the Negro Women's Auxiliary War Council, a Negro Women's League for Service, and a Red Cross auxiliary. Alice Dugged Carey headed the war relief work in Georgia under the umbrella of the Georgia State Federation of Colored Women's Clubs. The Phyllis Wheatley Club served as a clearing house for war relief activities in South Carolina. The Circle of Negro War Relief and the Crispus Attucks Circle were organized in Philadelphia, and Detroit had a Josephine Gray Colored Lady Knitters Club. Black women in New York formed a woman's auxiliary to the Fifteenth Regiment, an all-Black unit that became the first New York State Guard. These and numerous other clubs knitted for soldiers, provided comfort kits, organized letter writing campaigns, cooked food, provided entertainment, and even raised money. One of the most successful fund-raisers by Black women during World War I was staged in Savannah, Georgia, where $.25 million was raised. Black women nationally raised a total of about $5 million for the war effort.

Another important aspect of Black women's support during World War I was employment in the Department of Defense War Industries. These included factories and plants located in Detroit, St. Louis, Louisville, Baltimore, Philadelphia, and Washington, D.C.

Then, in December 1941, the United States entered World War II. During World War II and throughout the 1940s, a number of developments improved opportunities for Black women who wanted to participate in the military. Pressure from civil rights activists such as A. Philip Randolph, from the National Association for the Advancement of Colored People and the Black press, and the efforts of Mary McLeod Bethune and other members of Franklin D. Roosevelt's "Black Cabinet," combined with the military's changing needs to open new doors.

Perhaps the most important development for Black women during World War II was the creation of the Women's Army Auxiliary Corps (WAAC) in May 1942. The WAAC was incorporated into the U.S. Army in 1943 when it became the Women's Army Corps (WAC). Black and white women were accepted into both of these organizations, but segregation and discrimination often occurred. By the end of World War II more than 4,000 Black women had enlisted into the WAC.

The first Black woman in U.S. history to be commissioned as an officer was a WAC, Charity Early Adams. She was also the highest ranking Black woman during World War II. Adams described her military experience in the book *One Woman's Army: A Black Officer Remembers the WAC* (1989). The 6888th Central Postal Battalion, comprised of 800 women, was the first all-Black female unit to deploy overseas. They served in England. The WAC trained in Des Moines, Iowa. The first graduating class consisted of thirty-nine Black women representing every region of the country. Included were: Charity Early Adams, Frances Alexander, Myrtle Anderson, Violet Askens, Veraneal Austin, Mary Bordeaux, Geraldine Bright, Annie Brown, Harriet Buhile, Abbie Campbell, Mildred Carter, Irma Cayton, Natalie Donaldson, Sarah Emmert, Geneva Ferguson, Ruth Freeman, Evelyn Green, Elizabeth Hampton, Vera Harrison, Dovey Johnson, Alice Jones, Mary Kearney, Mary Lewis, Ruth Lucas, Charline Mary, Ina McFadden, Mary Miller, Glendora Moore, Sarah Murphy, Doris Norrel, Mildred Osby, Gertrude Peebles, Corris Sherard, Jessie Ward, and Harriet West. The WACs also had a renowned Black band known as the 404th Army Service Band. The band sang and performed at Black and white military, civilian, and church functions across the country.

The navy opened its doors to Black women during World War II with a plan to raise Black recruitment to 10 percent of the navy's total personnel and to form the Women's Reserve of the United States Navy, most commonly known as the WAVES (an acronym for Women Accepted for Volunteer Emergency Service). In 1944, Bessie Garret became the first Black woman accepted. The first WAVES officer graduates from Smith College included two Black women, Frances Wills and Harriet Pickens. The Coast Guard admitted five Black women during World War II. Among them were Olivia J. Hooker, currently a practicing clinical psychologist. The first Black WAVES to enter the Hospital Corps were Ruth C. Isaacs, Katherine Horton, and Inez Patterson.

While the navy announced big plans, it fell short of its goals. The 10 percent Black quota was never achieved during World War II, and as of 1945 there were only fifty-six Black WAVES. However, the navy became the first armed service to incorporate women in its regular forces when, in 1948, the WAVES were incorporated into the regular navy. The WACs, in contrast, did not become part of the regular army until 1978. With the elimination of these separate auxiliaries, the navy and the army decreased some problems with sexism and made more soldiers (regardless of sex) part of the core organization.

The army and the navy, despite these changes, continued to maintain separate nurse corps. While both branches formed their nurse corps at the beginning of the twentieth century, Black nurses were not admitted until the introduction of World War II. Susan Elizabeth Freeman became one of the first Black women to join the Army Nurse Corps (1941), while Phyllis Mae Daley was the first Black inducted into the Navy Nurse Corps (March 8, 1945). There were considerably more Black females, however, in the army's nurse corps than in the navy's. Black nurses served in all-Black military hospitals as well as in four general hospitals, the regional hospitals, and at least nine station hospitals. Additionally, Black women nurses served in Africa and in Europe during World War II.

The U.S. military assisted the United Nations and its mission in Korea during the early 1950s, and the women who went to Korea were nurses with the Red Cross, the Army Nurse Corps, or the Navy Nurse Corps. A few others served during the Korean War in Tokyo, Japan, and other places in the Far East Command that were not in the battle zone. When the Korean War began, there were about 29,000 total women in all branches of the military services. The numbers increased to nearly 100,000 by 1956. It is not known how many of these were Black, but it is clear that most were white. (One Black soldier, I. C. Rochell, was on duty in Korea for more than 17 months and reported seeing only one Black woman, a nurse with the Red Cross.)

One of the lasting achievements for women during the Korean War was the formation of the Defense Advisory Committee on Women in the Armed Services (DACOWITS), a group that still functions today in the interest of women in the military. One of the Black women who later served on this powerful com-

First Lieutenant Nancy C. Leftenant, a graduate of Lincoln Hospital School for Nurses in New York, joined the Reserve Corps of the Army Nurse Corps in February 1945. In March 1948 she became the first Black member of the Regular Army Nurse Corps. [Moorland-Spingarn]

mittee was Clara Adams-Ender, a general in the Army Nurse Corps.

President Truman's executive orders in the late 1940s and the 1954 Brown v. Board of Education Supreme Court ruling began the long desegregation process. By 1973, toward the end of the Vietnam War, almost 10 percent of the American troops who served in Vietnam were Black, including thousands of Black women. From this point on, a series of new firsts signaled the gains made by Black women. The Reverend Alice Henderson became the first woman chaplain in the country in 1974. During that same year, Jill Brown became the first Black woman to qualify as a pilot in U.S. military history. In 1975, the Naval Medical Corps appointed its first Black female physician, Donna P. Davis. Black women were being admitted to all of the military academies by 1976 where the entrance requirements were the same for both sexes, except for weight and height. In March 1980, Hazel W. Johnson (later Hazel Johnson-Brown) became the first Black woman in U.S. history to hold the rank of general. Johnson, who also had a Ph.D., was the Chief of the U.S. Army Nurse Corps. Two other Black women generals were promoted during the 1980s as well, General Sherian Cadoria, in the army, and General Clara Adams-Ender in the Army Nurse Corps. The fourth Black female general, Marcelite J. Harris, in the air force, received her rank in 1990.

Today, Black women are allowed to join all areas of the U.S. armed services, except combat arms units (infantry, armor, artillery, and combat engineers). Women are attached to the combat arms units in support capacities. During operations Desert Shield and Desert Storm, Captain Cynthia Mosley com-

manded Alpha Company of the Twenty-fourth Forward Support Battalion, Twenty-fourth Infantry Division. Mosley's company was responsible for refueling vehicles and resupplying troops located in the war zone. Moreover, the first Scud missile was shot down in the Gulf War by a Black woman, Lieutenant Phoebe Jeter. As many as 40 percent of the 35,00 female soldiers involved in the Gulf War were Black, and three Black women lost their lives.

The responsibilities of Black (and white) women during Operation Desert Storm suggest a still expanding role for women in the armed services as the controversy over whether women should or should not be allowed in combat proceeds. The post-Cold War era, shrinking military budgets, and changes in the world economy all pose new challenges to Black women's careers in the military. There is every reason

Commander Thomas A. Gaylord of the U.S. Navy administers the oath of office on March 8, 1945, to five new navy nurses commissioned in New York. A graduate of Lincoln School for Nurses, Phyllis Mae Daley (second from right) became the first of four Black nurses sworn into the Navy Nurse Corps as an ensign. [National Archives]

to believe they will be as successful in the future as they have been in the past.

[*See also* GANNETT, DEBORAH SAMPSON; NURSING, WORLD WAR I.]

BIBLIOGRAPHY

"Black Women's World War II Military Experiences: A Roundtable," Association for the Study of Afro-American Life and History (October 30-November 3, 1991); "Blacks in the Military: The Ultimate Sacrifice, With No Guarantees," Association for the Study of Afro American Life and History (October 30-November 3, 1991); Claybrook, Clint. "Clerk Is Top NCO at Home of the Infantry," *Benning Patriot* (January 10, 1992); Drotning, Phillip T. *Black Heroes in Our Nation's History* (1970); Earley, Charity Adams. *One Woman's Army: A Black Officer Remembers the WAC* (1989); *Ebony.* "The Untold Story of Black Women in the Gulf War" (September 1991); *Essence.* "Women in the Military" (April 1990); Foner, Jack D. *Blacks and the Military in American History* (1974); Franklin, John Hope. *From Slavery to Freedom* (1989); Gasperette, Elio. *Patriots and Loyalists in Petticoats: Women in the American Revolution* (1976); Greene, Robert Ewell. *Black Defenders of America, 1775-1973* (1974); Holm, Jeanne. *Women in the Military: An Unfinished Revolution* (1982); Katz, William Loren. *Eyewitness: The Negro in American History* (1967); MacGregor, Morris J. and Bernard C. Nalty, eds. *Blacks in the United States Armed Forces: Basic Documents* (1977); McPherson, James M. *The Negro's Civil War* (1965); *NA*; Scott, Emmett J. *The American Negro in the World War*; Smith, Graham. *When Jim Crow Met John Bull: Black American Soldiers in World War II* (1987); Stevenson, Lisbeth Gant. *Afro-American History: Heroes in Hardship* (1992).

LINDA ROCHELLE LANE

An outstanding woman playwright of the Harlem Renaissance, May Miller focused in her works on social and political issues. Unlike most of her contemporaries, who wrote for all-Black casts, Miller often included white characters as a way to deal with racial issues of the day. [Moorland-Spingarn]

MILLER, MAY (SULLIVAN) (1899-)

May Miller is recognized as one of the most outstanding Black female playwrights of the Harlem Renaissance. Miller was also the most widely published Black woman playwright of her era. Of her fifteen plays, nine were published; many of them were staged at numerous colleges and little theater groups throughout the country.

May Miller was born January 26, 1899, in Washington, D.C. One of five children born to Kelly and Annie May Miller, she grew up on Howard University's campus, where her father was a prominent professor and dean. Kelly Miller's position as a nationally recognized sociologist and educator put him in close social and political contact with many eminent Black Americans. He was also a published poet, and his creative and oratorical skills influenced the young May. She attended the noted M Street School (later Dunbar High School), where she studied under playwrights Mary P. Burrill and Angelina Grimké. Under Burrill's tutelage, May Miller was encouraged to write her first play, *Pandora's Box*, published in 1914. Miller graduated from Dunbar High School in 1916 and entered Howard University that same year. She continued to develop her dramatic writing skills through the Howard Drama Club. Academically at the head of her class, she earned a B.A. in 1920. In recognition of her abilities, Howard University awarded Miller a playwright's award for best play for her play *Within the Shadows*, making her the first Howard student to win such an award.

The 1920s and 1930s were Miller's most prolific and productive years. After graduating from Howard University, she taught drama, speech, and dance at the Frederick Douglass High School in Baltimore. While in Baltimore, she wrote most of her plays. Miller was among those enriched by poet/playwright

Georgia Douglas Johnson's "S Street Salon," which was a gathering place at Johnson's Washington, D.C., home for writers to share their works. Miller commuted on weekends to S Street, where she cultivated an array of friendships among such writers as Langston Hughes, Carter G. Woodson, Willis Richardson, and Zora Neale Hurston. During the summer months, Miller studied playwriting at Columbia University under the prominent theater scholar Frederick Koch.

In 1925, her play *The Bog Guide* placed third in the Urban League's *Opportunity* contest. *Opportunity* also awarded her an honorable mention the next year for *The Cuss'd Thing*. During the 1930s, Miller wrote history plays to educate her students at Douglass High School. In 1935, Miller collaborated with playwright Willis Richardson on *Negro History in Thirteen Plays*, an anthology dramatizing the lives of Black heroes and heroines. Miller contributed four plays to the anthology and earned national recognition.

Like many of the Black women writers of the 1920s and 1930s, Miller's plays focused on social and political issues. Her work stands out from that of other Black women because she dared to venture from the home, and in several plays she incorporated white characters in major roles. While most of her contemporaries utilized an all-Black cast, Miller included white characters in many of her works as an effective method of dealing with the racial issues of the time.

Miller wrote her last play, *Freedom's Children on the March*, in 1943. The same year, she retired from the Baltimore school system and began to focus on writing poetry. She retired to Washington, D.C., with her husband, John Sullivan, a high school principal whom she had married in 1940.

Miller's career as a poet is just as outstanding and expansive as her life as a playwright. Upon returning to Washington, D.C., in 1943, she joined a poetry workshop conducted by Inez Boulton. Miller's poetry speaks of humanist issues. Like her plays, her poetry poses the moral questions that confront a society without humanist values. Her poems have been published in many periodicals, anthologies, and journals; she has conducted readings throughout the Washington, D.C., area.

In 1986, May Miller won the Mister Brown Award (William Brown was manager of the African Company in New York from 1816 to 1823) for Excellence in Drama and Poetry, an award sponsored by the National Conference of African-American Theatre. Though Miller has given up playwriting, the 1990s have seen a resurgence in the production and publication of her plays. Miller resides in Washington, D.C.

BIBLIOGRAPHY
Brown-Guillory, Elizabeth, ed. *Wines in the Wilderness* (1990); Hatch, James V. and Ted Shine, eds. *Black Theatre U.S.A.: Forty-five Plays by Black Americans, 1847-1974* (1974); Hatch, James V. and Leo Hamalian, eds. *The Roots of African-American Theatre* (1991); Miller, May and Willis Richardson, eds. *Negro History in Thirteen Plays* (1935); Perkins, Kathy Anne, ed. *Black Female Playwrights: An Anthology of Plays before 1950* (1989); Randolph, Ruth Elizabeth and Lorraine Elena Roses, eds. *Harlem Renaissance and Beyond: Literary Biographies of 100 Black Women Writers, 1900-1945* (1989); Richardson, Willis, ed. *Plays and Pageants from the Life of the Negro* (1930).

SELECTED WORKS BY MAY MILLER
Plays: *The Bog Guide* (1925); *Christophe's Daughters* (1935); *The Cuss'd Thing* (1926); *Freedom's Children on the March* (1943); *Moving Caravans* (193?); *Nails and Thorns* (1933); *Pandora's Box* (1914); *Riding the Goat* (1925); *Samory* (1935); *Scratches* (1929); *Sojourner Truth* (1935); *Stragglers in the Dust* (1930); *Within the Shadow* (1920). Poetry: *Collected Poems* (1989); *The Clearing and Beyond* (1974); *Dust of Uncertain Joy* (1975); *Halfway to the Sun* (1981); *Into the Clearing* (1959); *The Ransomed Wait* (1983).

KATHY A. PERKINS

MILLS, FLORENCE (1896-1927)

Born in total poverty in Washington, D.C., on January 25, 1896, Florence Mills rose through dedication and talent as a singer and dancer to become the outstanding Black woman in American musical comedy during the Jazz Age and the most popular personality in Harlem during the Harlem Renaissance. Her parents, John and Nellie Simons Winfrey, were illiterate migrants from Lynchburg, Virginia. "Baby Florence" was on stage full time beginning in childhood, first as a "pickaninny" in white vaudeville, then in a sister act on the Black popular entertainment circuit.

After working in a wild South Side Chicago cabaret, her big break came when Mills was given the opportunity to play the ingenue in Noble Sissle and Eubie Blake's phenomenal *Shuffle Along*, the 1921 show that introduced syncopated song and dance to white America. She went on to star in *Plantation Revue* in New York and *Dover Street to Dixie* in London, where British intellectuals began to perceive African-American music as serious art. Florenz Ziegfeld offered Mills a major role in the *Follies*, but the deeply race-conscious performer turned him down in order to create an all-Black revue.

So popular was the musical comedy star Florence Mills during the Jazz Age that 150,000 people jammed the streets of Harlem for her funeral in 1927. [Richard Newman]

After her *From Dixie to Broadway* played in the heart of the theater district, and after she earned another first as a Palace Theatre vaudeville headliner, she opened *Blackbirds of 1926* in London. It was an extraordinary hit. Soon afterward, however, poor health forced her to return to New York, where she died on November 1, 1927. With 150,000 people in the streets, the people gave their beloved "Blackbird" the largest funeral in Harlem's history.

BIBLIOGRAPHY
NBAW.

RICHARD NEWMAN

MISSISSIPPI FREEDOM DEMOCRATIC PARTY

Created in the spring of 1964, the Mississippi Freedom Democratic party (MFDP) was a predominantly Black independent political party set up alongside the state Mississippi Democratic party at the height of the civil rights movement. At the time of the party's creation, Black voters constituted 6.7 per- cent of the state's registered voters (the lowest figure for any state in the union), due largely to a variety of legal and extralegal voting restrictions ranging from literacy and poll tax requirements to economic intimidation and widespread indiscriminate violence. Thus, as the brainchild of many Student Nonviolent Coordinating Committee (SNCC) members and local activists throughout the state, the MFDP was formed in response to the state's history of keeping Black residents from registering as voters and participating in regular party activities such as precinct, district, and county meetings as well as primary and general elections. Contributing much to the MFDP's notable historical achievements were the activities of many well-known women civil rights leaders.

Arguably, the year of the MFDP's founding proved to be its most historically significant. With financial support from the Council of Federated Organizations, a coalition of various civil rights organizations set up to administer voter-registration drives throughout the Deep South, the grass-roots party ran a slate of candidates on a platform of statewide political inclusion and social justice. Black women candidates Victoria Gray and Fannie Lou Hamer were two of the four MFDP candidates running for office that spring of 1964, and Black women constituted a sizable portion of the party's voter-registration workers during the campaign. Among the Freedom party's local achievements that spring and early summer were the registration of more than 80,000 disenfranchised Black voters in its Freedom Ballot campaign, a political demonstration that involved mock or protest elections, and voter registration sign-ups with the MFDP.

In the late summer of 1964, the Freedom party challenged the seating of the all-white Mississippi state delegation to the Democratic National Convention in Atlantic City, New Jersey. Among the MFDP's sixty-eight-member delegation and large, nationally based staff were such civil rights notables as Ella Baker, Fannie Lou Hamer, Annie Devine, and Victoria Gray. In its challenge, the MFDP argued that it best represented Mississippi's Democratic party because it was open to all Mississippians of voting age, unlike the lily-white party which engaged in violence, intimidation, and other measures to keep Black citizens from exercising their fundamental right. Thus, MFDP contenders argued that, even though the Freedom party was not recognized legally by its home state, only its delegates deserved seating and recognition because only they had faithfully adhered to the rules of the national party.

The highlight of the MFDP's summer challenge was the moving presentation of Hamer, who recounted one of the many instances of anti-civil rights violence, the horrible beating that she and five others received in a Winona, Mississippi, jail cell in 1963. By recounting the Winona incident in such vivid detail, Hamer tried to expose Mississippi's long and infamous history of political repression against Black people and, by most accounts, was quite successful. Following her powerful presentation, hundreds of telegrams in support of the MFDP's challenge poured into the Freedom party's temporary convention headquarters. In this regard, the MFDP attracted national attention and support for the civil rights movement.

Although the Democratic party's credentials committee offered two at-large seats in response to the challenge, the Freedom Democrats rejected such an offer on the basis of its being a back-of-the-bus compromise that they could not accept and expect to return to their communities with their heads held high. Although the Freedom Democrats failed in their primary political crusade, they did influence the rules committee of the Democratic party to make some

In 1964, the Mississippi Freedom Democratic party challenged the seating of the all-white Mississippi state delegation at the Democratic National Convention in Atlantic City, New Jersey. The highlight of the summer challenge was Fannie Lou Hamer's moving account of a beating she and five other civil rights activists received in a Mississippi jail cell in 1963. Although the party wasn't seated, the Democrats did make some changes to ensure fairer representation of African-Americans at future conventions. [Schomburg Center]

changes by the 1968 and 1972 conventions. Beginning with the 1968 convention, the Democratic party refused to seat any delegation that had been constituted through racially discriminatory means. Beginning with the 1972 convention, the party added to such a restriction a provision barring any delegation that failed to meet a sex quota for delegation membership.

After the 1964 challenge, the MFDP returned home and continued running candidates in local, county, and state elections. Before returning to full-time local organizing, however, the MFDP decided to issue yet another challenge in the national arena. In January 1965, Annie Devine, Victoria Gray, and Fannie Lou Hamer challenged the seating of the newly elected congressmen from their respective districts. Again, the charge was made that the three white men had won the election because Black Mississippians had been effectively excluded from participating in the primary and general elections. Hamer, Devine, and Gray spent six months living in Washington, D.C., lobbying members of the U.S. House of Representatives to give fair consideration to their cause. Although this challenge also attracted a great deal of attention, it too ended in defeat, but not before the three women were given symbolic representation by being allowed to sit on the floor of Congress during the debate, which made them the first Black women in history to be given official recognition by the U.S. Congress. As with the previous challenge, however, Devine, Gray, and Hamer saw this as tokenism and dismissed its importance as they returned home to continue the struggle in their home districts.

During 1965-66, like many SNCC activists, many members of the MFDP returned to civil rights activities in the state with a more radical mindset, particularly as it pertained to economic justice and international struggles against colonialism. In 1965, the Mississippi Freedom Labor Union (MFLU), a union of cotton and domestic workers, formed and received a great deal of organizational and moral support from the Freedom party. This was particularly the case during the 1965 MFLU maid strike in Bolivar County, Mississippi, in which scores of women struck against several local hotels. By 1967, the MFDP added to its platform planks calling for a fair distribution of the nation's wealth and an end to U.S. involvement in the Vietnam War. The MFDP also continued running candidates, many of whom were women, including local activist Emma Sanders, who participated in the landmark 1967 statewide elections where, among other historic achievements, twenty-two Black Americans were elected to office in Mississippi, the most since Reconstruction.

By 1967-68, the MFDP was facing challenges from moderate Black leaders and local white liberals within its own ranks. This eventually resulted in a faction of the party breaking off and forming the Loyal Democratic party, a more moderate wing of the MFDP that had always desired a closer working relationship with the mainstream, national Democratic party. Although momentarily left in disarray, the original MFDP rose again in true grass-roots form not more than a year later when it resumed sponsoring candidates for election and participating in voter registration drives, labor activities and poor peoples' cooperatives, all of which it continued to do through the mid-1970s.

BIBLIOGRAPHY

Lawson, Steven. *Black Ballots: Voting Rights in the South, 1944-1969* (1976); McLemore, Leslie. "The Mississippi Freedom Democratic Party," Ph.D. diss. (1971); Parker, Frank R. *Black Votes Count: Political Empowerment in Mississippi after 1965* (1990); Romaine, Anne. "The Mississippi Freedom Democratic Party through 1964," Master's thesis (1969).

CHANA KAI LEE

MISSISSIPPI STATE FEDERATION OF COLORED WOMEN'S CLUBS

The 1,000-member Mississippi State Federation of Colored Women's Clubs, established in 1903, is the oldest statewide Black women's group in Mississippi. The Mississippi clubwomen's movement was inspired by the National Association of Colored Women. One of its officers, native Mississippian Margaret Murray Washington (Mrs. Booker T. Washington), encouraged the women of Mississippi to elevate themselves through club work during the 1901 annual session of the Southeastern Federation of Colored Women's Clubs in Vicksburg, Mississippi.

Many Black women had been engaged in isolated club work in the state. Among these were Ursala J. Wade Foster, a dietitian and matron at Alcorn and Jackson State colleges and first president of the Mississippi Federation (1903-7); Mattie Foote Rowan, wife of President L. J. Rowan of Alcorn A & M College and third president of the federation (1909-13); and Lizzie W. Coleman, a Greenville elementary school principal and loyal member of the federation.

When these three women issued the call to organize as an affiliate of the national federation in 1903, the Phyllis Wheatley Club of Jackson served as host under the leadership of its president, Mrs. D. H. Butler, and the chair of local arrangements, Frankie D. Robinson. At the organizational meeting Mrs. Butler was named recording secretary, and Frankie Robinson was named vice president. Margaret Murray Washington, Mary Church Terrell, Mary Talbert, and Hallie Q. Brown are among the national federation presidents who visited the developing Mississippi federation.

Women of all ages answered the 1903 call to organize, and they declared in the preamble to their constitution that "We, Colored Women of the State of Mississippi, feeling the need of united and systematic effort, and hoping to furnish evidence of moral, mental, and material progress made by our people, do hereby unite in a state organization." These college-educated women became the cultural and civic role models for generations of upwardly mobile Black women who were neither submissive and passive nor protestors. They actively communicated their goals and projects in the *Woman's Herald*, at annual meetings, and through altruistic service. They established homes for working girls, established libraries and reading rooms for the Black community, awarded scholarships, provided institutional care for physically and mentally disabled people, and purchased and ran clubhouses for adults and camps and recreational centers for youth. The Old Folks Home in Vicksburg, Mississippi, one such project, was maintained by the federation between 1910 and 1920.

While many affiliated clubs chose projects in small-town settings, some chose to work with rural women. For example, a mothers' club for rural women was initiated by the fifth federation club president, Grace Jones (1920-24), wife of the founder of Piney Woods School. She organized mothers who had to walk miles to her home for club meetings. Mothers also came to the school to participate in projects that taught them how to care for their families by preparing proper meals and making clothes that their children modeled during club meetings.

Although a few of these clubwomen voted, their political tactics more often included subtle persuasion of the legislature through white women's groups, petitions, personal contact, civic organizations, letters, and the press. They used these tactics to get more space for Black patients at the Tuberculosis Hospital in Magee, Mississippi, and to get state support for the blind at Piney Woods School. An outstanding club project started with a petition to the Mississippi legislature in 1923 that culminated in the creation of a new youth center. On May 11, 1940, Governor Paul B. Johnson signed the Mississippi state legislature's bill to establish the Oakley training school for troubled Black boys and girls.

The practices of the state federation were circumscribed by Jim Crow-era approaches that affected the types of civic projects it sponsored and the locations for annual meetings—in Black churches and community institutions such as Natchez College, Jackson College, and Piney Woods School. Since the death of Jim Crow laws and the integration of white hotels and restaurants in the 1970s, the federation now often holds its annual meetings in formerly segregated conference facilities.

Although other Mississippi Black women's groups have emerged, the federation's economic projects are among the most substantial ones serving the housing needs of Black Mississippians. The federation's headquarters are in Clinton, located on part of a 147-acre property purchased in 1927, and they include a modern home for low-income senior citizens and disabled persons called Federation Tower Apartments, the state club office, recreational facilities, and valuable timber. These and other properties in Hattiesburg, Clarksdale, and Grenada, Mississippi, are valued at approximately $20 million. The federation's properties are symbolic of its vision, economic vitality, and willingness to address the needs of Mississippi's Black women.

BIBLIOGRAPHY

Davis, Elizabeth Lindsay. *Lifting as They Climb* (1933); Federation of Colored Women's Clubs. Subject file. Mississippi Department of Archives and History, Jackson, Mississippi; Harrison, Alferdteen. *Piney Woods School: An Oral History* (1982); McMillen, Neil R. *Dark Journey: Black Mississippians in the Age of Jim Crow* (1989); Thompson, Cleopatra D. *History of the Mississippi State Federation of Colored Women's Clubs, 1903-1950* (forthcoming); Wesley, Charles Harris. *The History of the National Association of Colored Women's Clubs: A Legacy of Service* (1984); White, Geneva Brown Blalock and Eva Hunter Bishop, eds. *Mississippi's Black Women: A Pictorial Story of Their Contributions to the State and Nation* (1976).

ALFERDTEEN B. HARRISON

MITCHELL, ABBIE (1884-1960)

In 1929, while performing in Chicago with Helen Hayes in *Coquette*, Abbie Mitchell said, "All my work as an actress has been done with my singing in my mind" (*DANB*). Despite the numerous roles she played on and off Broadway, Mitchell was first and foremost a singer.

Born on New York's Lower East Side in 1884 to a musically inclined African-American mother and a German-Jewish father, Abbie Mitchell was early discovered to be a prodigy. After completing her public school training in Baltimore, she returned to New York in 1897 to study voice with Harry L. Burleigh and to audition for *Clorindy, the Origin of the Cakewalk*. Recognizing her unusual talent, lyricist Paul Laurence Dunbar and composer Will Marion Cook cast her in their musical. A year later, Mitchell married Cook and, in 1899, was given the principal role in the next Dunbar-Cook collaboration, *Jes Lak White Folks*.

In 1903, she was cast in *In Dahomey*, a Bert Williams-George Walker production written by Jesse Shipp. After playing in New York, the company moved to London's Shaftesbury Theatre. While in London, Edward VII invited the company to perform at a birthday celebration for the Prince of Wales. When the king noted that Abbie Mitchell was not there, he sent his private coach for her so that he could hear her sing "Brownskin Baby Mine," the song she had made famous (*DANB*).

Back in New York, Mitchell became immersed in the theatrical life centered at the Marshall Hotel on West Fifty-third Street. She joined the Memphis Students, a playing, singing, and dancing group that opened at Proctor's Twenty-third Street Theatre, played at Hammerstein's Victoria Theatre and the Roof Garden in New York, the Olympia in Paris, the Palace Theatre in London, and the Schumann Circus in Berlin.

Between 1904 and 1912, in addition to giving recitals, Mitchell appeared in *The Southerner* (1904) and *Bandanna Land* (another Williams and Walker show, 1908), and sang the lead in *The Red Moon*, which later was performed for Czar Nicholas II of Russia. Beginning in 1912, a throat ailment prevented Mitchell from singing for a few years, during which time she became involved with the Lafayette Players, a Harlem theater company, as a lead actress until she left for Paris to study voice with Jean de Reszke and de Reszke's famous teacher, Szbrilla. She performed in concert throughout Europe, singing French classics, German lieder, and Negro folk songs.

When Mitchell returned to America, she appeared in *In Abraham's Bosom* at the Provincetown Theatre (1926), *The House of Shadows* (1927), and *Coquette* in Chicago (1929). Two years later, she accepted the position of head of the voice department at Tuskegee

King Edward VII of England once sent his private carriage for Abbie Mitchell so he could hear her sing "Brownskin Baby Mine," the song this theatrical performer made famous. [Schomburg Center]

Institute. However, her work at Tuskegee did not prevent her from singing in concert. She appeared at Town Hall in New York City on November 22, 1931, and at the Mecca Temple and Aeolian Opera Company in *Cavalleria Rusticana* in 1934. That same year she also appeared as Binnie in *Stevedore* and, in 1939, as Addie in Lillian Hellman's *The Little Foxes*.

On March 16, 1960, Abbie Mitchell died in Harlem Hospital. She was survived by her son, Mercer Cook, and three grandchildren. Her husband had died in 1944, her daughter in 1950.

BIBLIOGRAPHY

DANB; *DBT*; Isaacs, Edith. *The Negro in American Theatre* (1947); Johnson, James Weldon. *Black Manhattan* ([1930] 1988); Kellner, Bruce. *The Harlem Renaissance: An Historical Dictionary for the Era* (1987); Woll, Allan. *Black Musical Theatre: From Coontown to Dreamgirls* (1989).

ANNETTA JEFFERSON

MITCHELL, JUANITA JACKSON (1913-1992)

Juanita E. Jackson Mitchell was the first national youth director of the National Association for the Advancement of Colored People (NAACP) and, later, the first African-American woman to be admitted to practice law in Maryland. Although these distinctions significantly marked her transition from one career to another, Mitchell's prominence is primarily a consequence of her civil rights advocacy for more than half a century.

Juanita E. Jackson was born in Hot Springs, Arkansas, on January 2, 1913, to Lillie M. Carroll Jackson, a school teacher, and Keiffer Albert Jackson, a traveling promoter and exhibitor of religious films. With the exception of occasions when the family traveled with Keiffer Jackson on business, Jackson was raised in Baltimore with her two sisters and her brother, Virginia, Marion, and Bowen Keiffer. Jackson graduated from the Frederick Douglass High School with honors in 1927. For two years she attended Morgan State College in Baltimore but then transferred to the University of Pennsylvania in Philadelphia; she graduated in 1931 with a B.S. in education. Racial consciousness nurtured by her parents and her sorority, Alpha Kappa Alpha, and her leadership in the interracial national Methodist youth movement motivated her to return home during the Great Depression to try to improve conditions for African-Americans in Baltimore.

Jackson saw the crises of the economic depression—massive unemployment, racial segregation, other forms of racist discrimination, and continued lynching—as challenges. Implementing her idea to hold a forum to address such challenges, Jackson, along with Lincoln University (Pennsylvania) graduate and friend Clarence M. Mitchell, Jr., and approximately one dozen other African-American youth of high school and college ages, founded the City-Wide Young People's Forum of Baltimore. As its first president, Jackson collaboratively developed programs and projects with other officers, older advisers, and many of Baltimore's African-American citizens. The forum held well-attended weekly public meetings featuring Black leaders and prominent educators. The forum also sponsored antilynching petition drives and various demonstrations and employment campaigns for African-Americans in Baltimore. Jackson led the forum through 1934, even after she found employment in 1932 as a secondary school teacher in the Baltimore public schools. As Jackson had hoped, the forum proved to be a boon to the Baltimore African-American community from 1931 through 1940.

In 1935, having observed the success of Baltimore's forum in mobilizing youth as well as adults, and having been impressed by Jackson's skills, talent, and education (she had earned an M.A. in sociology), Walter White, the executive secretary of the NAACP, invited Jackson to assume the leadership of the NAACP's first nationwide youth program. From 1935 to 1938, headquartered in New York City but traveling throughout the nation, Jackson served as national youth director and special assistant to Walter White. She wrote a constitution, organized youth councils, revived junior NAACP branches, established a national network, and worked with youth primarily on four problems—education, jobs, civil rights, and lynching—doing for youth what Ella Baker had done for the NAACP's branches. Support from other women for this youth work came as a result of Jackson's participation with Mary McLeod Bethune in the founding conference of the National Council of Negro Women (NCNW) and its subsequent activities.

Juanita Jackson's August 1938 marriage to Clarence M. Mitchell, Jr. (then the National Youth Administration's Maryland director of the Division of Negro Affairs, but later the NAACP's chief lobbyist until 1978) interrupted her employment with the NAACP but did not end either her association with the NAACP or her political activism. As a new wife and mother in the early 1940s, Mitchell coordinated a civil rights march of 2,000 citizens on the state capital, participated in a White House conference on children, and directed the first NAACP citywide voter registration campaign in Baltimore. After giving birth to four sons, Clarence III, Keiffer, Michael, and George, and desiring to be better armed for the civil rights struggle, she decided to change vocations. She studied law at the University of Maryland, served on the *Law Review*'s staff, and earned her law degree by 1950.

When Mitchell became the first African-American woman admitted to practice before the courts of Maryland, she had one objective in mind: to litigate on behalf of African-Americans seeking an end to racial discrimination. Her legal achievements were notable throughout the 1950s and 1960s. She was counsel in Maryland litigation initiated in 1950 to eliminate the racial segregation of state and municipal beaches and swimming pools, which she won in November 1955. A Baltimore secondary school desegregation case filed in 1953 and handled successfully by Mitchell resulted in Baltimore becoming the first southern city to desegregate public schools after *Brown v. Board of Education*. During the 1960s she served as counsel for students who had engaged in sit-ins to desegregate Maryland restaurants, in *Robert Mack Bell v. Maryland*. On appeal in 1964, the students represented by Mitchell and the NAACP Legal Defense Fund prevailed in the U.S. Supreme Court. Viewing the Baltimore commissioner of police's authorization of mass searches of private homes without warrants, known as the Veney raid, as a particular affront to African-American residents and a gross violation of civil liberties affecting all citizens, Mitchell represented several homeowners in proceedings to enjoin further such mass searches. As counsel for the homeowners she won the Veney raid cases on appeal from the U.S. District Court for Maryland to the U.S. Court of Appeals, Fourth Circuit, in September 1966.

Although Mitchell devoted considerable time and energy to the firm of Mitchell, Mitchell and Mitchell (both her husband and her son Michael eventually earned law degrees) during the late 1950s through the 1980s, public advocacy of civil rights continued to be a priority. Recognition of Mitchell's particular talents and expertise resulted in her holding several important positions with the NAACP and other organizations. She directed, both in 1957-58 and in 1960, two major voter registration campaigns that placed more than 50,000 new voters on the books. She presided over the Baltimore NAACP branch, later served as the legal redress chairperson of the Maryland state conference, and, in the 1970s, succeeded her mother as president of the state conference of NAACP branches. A life member of NCNW, Jackson also chaired for a time that organization's legal committee.

Juanita Jackson Mitchell slowed her pace after her husband's death in 1984 and her subsequent illness, but she continued to maintain a lively interest in protecting the rights of African-Americans, including opposition to official repression of activists and African-American elected officials during the 1980s. Her distinguished careers and activism of more than fifty years have resulted in her being the recipient of such honors as the NCNW's award for Special Distinction in Law, the Outstanding Service Award of the Youth/College Division of the NAACP and the Bicentennial Award of the University of Maryland's Black American Law Students Association. As was her mother, in recognition of achievements as a state citizen and woman, Juanita Jackson Mitchell was inducted into Maryland Women's Hall of Fame in 1985.

On July 7, 1992, at the age of seventy-nine, Juanita Jackson Mitchell, who had been in poor health for some time, succumbed to a heart attack and stroke. Benjamin Hooks, the executive director of the NAACP, praised her as "one of the greatest freedom fighters in the history of Maryland and the nation," and Maryland Governor William Donald Shaefer paid tribute to Mitchell as "an inspiration, a fighter . . . [who] never deviated from her principles." A memorial service attended by many admirers and friends was held at the Sharpe Street Memorial Methodist Episcopal Church where she had so often met to further civil rights causes and to worship a God in whom she had great faith. Her principal legacy was a life of courageous and consistent struggle for civil rights.

BIBLIOGRAPHY

McNeil, Genna Rae. *Groundwork: Charles Hamilton Houston and the Struggle for Civil Rights* (1983); Mitchell, Juanita Jackson. Personal papers, Baltimore, Maryland; National Association for the Advancement of Colored People. Papers at Library of Congress, Washington, D.C.; Wagandt, Charles. Interviews with Juanita Jackson Mitchell, *Washington Post* (July 8, 1992); Watson, Denton. *Lion in the Lobby: Clarence Mitchell Jr.'s Struggle for the Passage of Civil Rights Laws* (1990).

GENNA RAE McNEIL

MITCHELL, NELLIE B. (1845-1924)

My motto is excelsior. I am resolved to give myself up wholly to the study of music, and endeavor, in spite of obstacles, to become an accomplished artist (Nellie B. Mitchell c. 1865).

The worth of an artist can often be measured by the impact she or he has on the local level. It is at this level that the most enduring impressions are made, for the true artist in full bloom has often been well planted and tilled in home soil. Nellie B. Mitchell was a concert singer, educator, and arts function organizer whose presence was known and felt in and around New England. Her vocal talents, charm, and grace won her admiration and praise from seasoned critics and local audiences alike.

Born in Dover, New Hampshire, in 1845, Nellie B. Mitchell was devoted to music from an early age until her death, in Boston in 1924, at the age of seventy-nine. As a child she studied voice in Dover and began her career as a church soloist in local churches in Dover, New Hampshire, Haverhill, Massachusetts, and Boston between 1865 and 1886. She trained at both the Boston and the New England conservatories of music as well as the School of Vocal Arts in Boston, from which she received a performance diploma in 1879. In 1874, she made her New York singing debut in Steinway Hall; she made an appearance in Philadelphia in 1882.

Many performances followed. In 1885, Mitchell did a concert tour of the South, and in 1886 she formed her own touring company to travel around New England. Critics mentioned her attractive voice as well as her charm as an artist. "Miss Nellie Brown showed a particularly well-modulated voice, trained study, and appreciative method, which served her well in the pleasant rendering given by her so graciously and unaffectedly," said the Boston *Traveller* in 1874. "This lady is fortunate in her exceedingly sweet and well-trained voice, which, in conjunction with her fine personal appearance and stage manners, rendered her reception unusually enthusiastic," said the Boston *Globe* in 1874.

During the later years of her career, between 1890 until her death in 1924, she devoted her time to teaching and organizing and attending concerts and arts events. Mitchell organized the "Centennial Musical Festival" to benefit Boston's young people, and for the festival she organized and conducted fifty young girls in the performance of the operetta *Laila, the Fairy Queen*. This concert was given May 16-17, 1876, and then repeated in Haverhill, December 13, 1876. She was the primary organizer and financier of a Boston concert performed on March 21, 1918, with other prominent Boston artists. Among the concert patrons and sponsors were William Dupree, James Monroe Trotter, and Mme. Mamie Flowers. Sponsored by the Shamut Congregational Church in Boston, the concert was a benefit for the great Black prima donna of the time, Madame Selika.

Nellie B. Mitchell spent her later summers teaching at the Hedding Chautauqua summer school in East Epping, New Hampshire. In addition to starting her own singing company, she was also a founding member of the Chaminade Club. This club was organized by Black women in order to study light classical music, notated spirituals, and the accomplishments of women artists. Also during this time, Mitchell was an active member of the music teachers' national association.

Although Nellie B. Mitchell certainly became an artist of national reputation (to the extent that a Black artist during her lifetime could be so recognized), her most enduring impact has been in her native New England.

BIBLIOGRAPHY

BDAAM; Lewbrew, Arthur. Personal collection (letters, papers, programs on Afro-American artists from c. 1790-present), Detroit, Michigan; Trotter, James Monroe. *Music and Some Highly Musical People* (1881).

WILLIAM C. BANFIELD

MOLTON, FLORA (1908-1988)

Flora Molton was born in Louisa County, Virginia, in 1908. She was partially blind at birth and was plagued by impaired vision for all of her life. She grew up in a religious and musical family. Her father was a Baptist preacher in a local congregation, where her mother played the organ; he played the accordion, which was the first instrument that Flora mastered as a child. While in her teens, Flora Molton learned to play the guitar; she also joined the Holiness Church, and there commenced her own career as a preacher. In the late 1930s, she moved to Washington, D.C., where she continued to preach occasionally. During World War II, she began to perform her own unique brand of "holy blues" on the streets of the nation's capital, in order to supplement her meager income. Her guitar style combined finger-picking techniques from her native Piedmont region with the Mississippi Delta slide technique. By the postwar era, she was also writing her own songs.

In the early 1960s, Molton teamed up with Ed Morris, a local guitarist. He was instrumental in getting her bookings in folk music venues and organizing her initial backup bands. During this period, she wrote her best known songs, especially "The Train Song" and the tribute "Louis Armstrong." Throughout the next two decades, she continued to compose songs, play solo in the streets, and appear at folk festivals with her bands. She also recorded an album and was the subject of a short documentary film. Flora Molton died at her home in Washington, D.C., in 1988.

BIBLIOGRAPHY

BWW.

WILLIAM BARLOW

MONTGOMERY BUS BOYCOTT

Black women played a crucial role in the thirteen-month Montgomery, Alabama, bus boycott (December 1955-December 1956) that succeeded, through a combination of nonviolent direct action and judicial efforts, in ending bus segregation in the city. The boycott not only culminated years of community organizing by Montgomery Black activists, particularly women, but also launched the Black freedom movement. As leaders, as a large cadre of activists, and as a corps of several thousand committed followers, African-American women were central actors: first, in heightening community consciousness and setting the stage for the boycott; second, in initiating the mass protest; third, in the day-to-day planning, organizing, and sacrificing that sustained it through many trials.

Montgomery had had racially segregated buses since the city bus line began operation in the mid-1930s, enforced by a city ordinance first enacted in 1900 to segregate street cars. Montgomery's bus customs were harsher than those in many other Southern cities. Not only were Black passengers often required to pay their fare at the front and then reboard through the back door, but also they frequently had to stand over vacant seats reserved for whites. If the forward white section was full, drivers ordered Black riders to relinquish their seats in the unreserved middle section for arriving white passengers—and they often did so rudely, with racial slurs. Black females bore the brunt of the abusive treatment. Because women comprised fifty-six percent of the city's Black population, and because the majority of employed women worked as domestics in white homes across town and depended on public transportation, they rode the buses in much greater numbers than did Black men.

SETTING THE STAGE

For more than a decade before the boycott, individual women defied the injustice of segregated seating. Indeed there is a long tradition of resistance by Black women, including Elizabeth Jennings and Ida B. Wells in the nineteenth century, to unequal treatment in public transportation, North and South. In 1944, for instance, Viola White was arrested on a bus in Montgomery for violating the segregation code, and then was beaten and jailed. She was released from jail, but when she died ten years later, the appeal of her conviction had still not been heard.

In 1946, Dr. Mary Fair Burks, head of the Alabama State College English Department in Montgomery, founded the Women's Political Council (WPC) as a means to promote voter registration and civic activism by Black women, especially by professional women, and to address community problems such as inadequate parks and playgrounds and mistreatment on buses. In the fall of 1949 a newly hired English professor at Alabama State College, Jo Ann Gibson Robinson, joined the WPC. After a painful experience of abuse by a bus driver, she dedicated herself to remedying the bus situation. When she succeeded Burks as council president in the early 1950s she made this issue its prime concern. Robinson and other WPC activists met regularly with city officials to discuss the segregation policy, without success. In May 1954, four days after the *Brown* v. *Board of Education* school desegregation decision, Robinson wrote a letter to Mayor W. A. Gayle warning him of a boycott if conditions did not improve. "Please consider this plea," she concluded, "for even now plans are being made to ride less, or not at all, on our buses" (Robinson 1987).

A major turning point in the bus campaign came in March 1955 with the arrest and trial of fifteen-year-old Claudette Colvin, a junior at Booker T. Washington High School, for refusing to give up her seat in the unreserved midsection of a bus. The Colvin incident galvanized the Black community and made bus seating an issue, for the first time, in the municipal election that month. Robinson acted as the main spokesperson at two meetings the WPC and other Black groups held with city commissioners and bus company officials. One member of the Black delegation was Rosa Parks, a longtime civil rights activist and mentor of the National Association for the Advancement of Colored People Youth Council of which Colvin was a member. The meetings yielded only empty promises from city and bus company officials. When Colvin was convicted, even though the bus company manager admitted that the driver had violated company policy, boycott sentiment grew. A sizable number refused to ride for several days. Robinson pushed for an organized boycott, but civil rights leader E. D. Nixon decided that Colvin, who was pregnant at the time, would not be a fitting symbol around which to mobilize protest; nor did hers seem a promising test case to challenge bus segregation in federal court. The men "were afraid," Robinson later asserted. "Women are more daring when it comes to what we face" (Robinson 1984).

In July 1955, the Black community was heartened when the U.S. Court of Appeals for the Fourth Circuit in Richmond, Virginia, declared in *Flemming* v. *South Carolina Electric and Gas Company* that intrastate bus segregation was unconstitutional. Sarah Mae Flemming, arrested on a Columbia, South Carolina, bus the year before, had sued the bus company for violating her Fourteenth Amendment rights to equal protection. (The ruling was upheld by the U.S. Supreme Court in April 1956 but was not enforceable in Montgomery and the city ignored it.) When, in October 1955, eighteen-year-old Mary Louise Smith was arrested on a Montgomery bus, community leaders again decided not to press the case for federal appeal.

INITIATING THE BOYCOTT

In the early evening of Thursday, December 1, 1955, after a long day of tailoring at Montgomery Fair department store, Rosa Parks was arrested on a city bus when she refused to give up her seat in the unreserved section to a white man. Although Parks had not planned her calm protest, she recalled that she had "a life history of being rebellious against being mistreated because of my color." The time had come "when I had been pushed as far as I could stand to be pushed. . . . I had decided that I would have to know once and for all what rights I had as a human being and a citizen" (Raines 1983; Parks 1956). Reflecting later on her motives, Parks stated that she refused to obey the driver's command "because I was so involved with the attempt to bring about freedom from this kind of thing. . . . I felt just resigned to give what I could to protest against the way I was being treated, and felt that all of our meetings, trying to negotiate, bring about petitions before the authorities . . . really hadn't done any good at all" (Hill 1991).

Parks was bailed out of city jail by E. D. Nixon, with whom she had worked for twelve years in the Montgomery NAACP. He was accompanied by Clifford Durr, a prominent local attorney who had served on the Federal Communications Commission under President Franklin D. Roosevelt, and his wife, Virginia Durr; these southern whites were outspoken opponents of segregation. All four returned to Parks's home, where Nixon persuaded her, against her husband's wishes, to make hers the major test case challenging segregation laws. Parks's virtuous character and high stature in the Black community made her the ideal representative of Black grievances and aspirations.

Meanwhile, when Jo Ann Robinson learned of Parks's arrest, she decided to commence the boycott. After phoning Nixon and getting his support, she hastily drafted a flyer that called on all Black residents to stay off the buses on Monday, the day of Parks's trial. "Another Negro woman has been arrested and thrown into jail," Robinson wrote, "because she refused to get up out of her seat on the bus for a white

person to sit down. . . . Negroes have rights, too, for if Negroes did not ride the buses, they could not operate. . . . The next time it may be you, or your daughter, or mother" (Robinson 1987). Around midnight she drove to the Alabama State College campus where, risking her job, she and a Business Department colleague stayed up all night mimeographing 50,000 copies. The next day—utilizing distribution routes that the WPC had mapped out several months prior—Robinson and two male students drove all over town, delivering bundles to schools, businesses, stores, factories, taverns, beauty parlors, and barbershops. Having launched the boycott, Robinson, Burks, and other WPC leaders took part in a large planning meeting at Dexter Avenue Baptist Church, whose pastor was Dr. Martin Luther King, Jr. At Sunday services the Baptist, African Methodist Episcopal, and other Black ministers urged their congregations to join the protest.

The boycott on Monday, December 5, proved a spectacular success; very few Blacks rode the buses. In the afternoon the leaders formed a new organization, the Montgomery Improvement Association (MIA), to direct the protest, and they elected King president. Several women were chosen to serve on the MIA executive committee, including Robinson, Rosa Parks, Irene West, Euretta Adair, and Erna Dungee. That night a few thousand boycotters, more women than men, gathered at Holt Street Baptist Church and resolved to continue the mass protest until they won decent treatment. Robinson and the WPC not only initiated the boycott but acted as catalysts to mobilize leadership by other women and by the ministers.

SUSTAINING THE PROTEST

Once the boycott started, King and other men took charge and assumed the major leadership positions. In a short time the young preacher was universally recognized as the paramount leader in fact as well as name. Yet if King, Nixon, Ralph Abernathy, and other male leaders dominated the policy-making, women leaders took responsibility for much of the hands-on organizing, including the efficient car pool system, that sustained the boycott for over a year. "We really were the ones who carried out the actions," MIA financial secretary Erna Dungee Allen recalled. For a number of reasons—including sexism, the need to protect their jobs, and deference to a long tradition of community leadership by Black ministers—female leaders remained less visible and rarely if ever served as speakers at mass meetings or press conferences. The women "passed the ideas to men to a great extent," Allen remembered. Burks and

Robinson "were very vocal and articulate, especially in committee meetings." Yet in the mass meetings, women "let the men have the ideas and carry the ball. They were the power behind the throne" (Millner 1989).

Numerous women exercised informal leadership but Robinson's multifaceted role was probably second only to King's in its impact. She chose to keep a low public profile, however, in order not to endanger either her teaching position at Alabama State College, a Black institution dependent on the white legislature, or the supportive college president, H. Councill Trenholm. King reported that "more than any other person," the indefatigable Robinson "was active on every level of the protest" (King 1958). Besides her influential role on major committees, she served as a key MIA negotiator since she had had the most experience dealing with white officials. She also edited and produced the monthly MIA newsletter that was sent all over the country. Moreover, despite a full teaching load she drove in the car pool most mornings and afternoons.

While Robinson, Irene West, Euretta Adair, Hazel Gregory, Johnnie Carr, and other middle-class women served on committees, managed the MIA office, and played vital leadership roles, dozens of less-educated women supported the boycott. Georgia Gilmore, a self-employed cook, organized a club that sold pies and cakes, and she donated the proceeds at the mass meetings. Inez Ricks formed a rival club, and the meetings were enlivened by a weekly contest over which club raised more money.

The female leadership network was indispensable to the boycott's success, but the backbone of the long protest was several thousand working-class women who, in the face of intimidation and threats, rode in the car pools or walked as far as twelve miles a day, even in the rain. "I'm not walking for myself," said an elderly woman refusing a ride. "I'm walking for my children and my grandchildren" (King 1958). Another woman, Mother Pollard, promised King that she would walk until it was over. "But aren't your feet tired?" he inquired. "My feets is tired," she answered, "but my soul is rested" (Raines 1983). Many domestic workers secured the tacit support or acquiescence of their white female employers, who in some cases actually drove them to and from work. As role models whose commitment, sacrifice, and ingenuity inspired leaders and followers alike, the women who stayed off the buses were the protest's prime movers and underlying leaders.

Finally, even in the judicial arena, women were makers of history in Montgomery. While Rosa Parks's appeal was delayed in state court, MIA and NAACP lawyers filed a federal lawsuit in the name of Claudette Colvin, Mary Louise Smith, and two older women whose rights also had been violated on buses. The *Browder* v. *Gayle* lawsuit resulted in the November 1956 U.S. Supreme Court decision striking down Alabama's city and state bus segregation laws. Montgomery's Black citizens called off the boycott when the ruling took effect in December and buses were no longer segregated. With the bus victory bolstering their morale and confidence, many of the women activists turned their attention to other pressing community issues such as school desegregation and voter registration.

[*See also* PARKS, ROSA.]

BIBLIOGRAPHY
Black Women Oral History Project, ed. Ruth Edmunds Hill (1991); Burks, Mary Fair. "Trailblazers: Women in the Montgomery Bus Boycott." In *Women in the Civil Rights Movement: Trailblazers and Torchbearers, 1941-65*, ed. Vicki L. Crawford, Jacqueline Anne Rouse, and Barbara Woods (1990); Garrow, David J. "The Origins of the Montgomery Bus Boycott," *Southern Changes* (October-December 1985); King, Martin Luther, Jr. *Stride Toward Freedom* (1958); Millner, Steven M. "The Montgomery Bus Boycott: A Case Study in the Emergence and Career of a Social Movement." In *The Walking City: The Montgomery Bus Boycott, 1955-1956*, ed. David J. Garrow (1989); Parks, Rosa. Interviewed by Sidney Rogers (1956); Raines, Howell. *My Soul is Rested* (1983); Robinson, Jo Ann Gibson. *The Montgomery Bus Boycott and the Women Who Started It* (1987); Robinson, Jo Ann Gibson. Interviewed by David J. Garrow (April 5, 1984); Thornton, J. Mills, III. "Challenge and Response in the Montgomery Bus Boycott of 1955-1956," *Alabama Review* (July 1980).

STEWART BURNS

MOODY, ANNE E. (1940-)

Born on September 15, 1940, Anne Moody was the oldest child born to Fred and Elmire Moody in Wilkinson County, Mississippi. From the hardships of rural poverty, Moody would emerge as a vital civil rights activist and critically acclaimed writer.

As a child, Moody attended segregated schools and in 1964 received her Bachelor of Science degree from Tougaloo College. Upon graduating, Anne Moody was already a veteran of the struggle for civil rights; between 1961 and 1963 she served in the Congress of Racial Equality (CORE) and afterward carried her activities north to Cornell University, where she served as civil rights project coordinator (1964-65). Moody's youth and her participation in the civil rights struggle are revealed in her autobiography *Coming of Age in Mississippi* (1968), an articulate and moving account of the often frustrating struggle of growing up Black in the Deep South. She vividly recalls the succession of shacks in which her family lived, hunger, white prejudice, Black apathy, and the birth of her racial consciousness.

Coming of Age, moreover, represents a confluence of the personal and historical and the reciprocal interaction between them. As part of a historical maelstrom, Moody's racial consciousness was raised by the lynching of Emmett Till. In her desire to combat race hatred she became a vital force within the civil rights struggle. Unfortunately, Moody would later break with the movement; frustration with northern whites and doubts about the direction of Black liberation culminated in her departure.

BIBLIOGRAPHY

Moody, Anne. *Coming of Age in Mississippi* (1968); *SBAA*.

GINA BEAVERS

MOON, MOLLIE (1908-1990)

Two months to the day before her death on June 24, 1990, the *New York Times* described Mollie Moon as "an organization unto herself." The occasion was a presidential award ceremony marking National Volunteer Week and honoring Mollie Moon's career of civic volunteerism. The description was apt; Moon had devoted nearly half a century to the presidency of the National Urban League Guild. Since 1942, the organization she helped found had grown to eighty-three affiliates nationwide. Moon remains best known,

On May 23, 1963, Anne Moody (right) participated with John R. Salter and Joan Trunpauer in a sit-in at a Jackson, Mississippi, lunch counter. A crowd of white teenagers sprayed the demonstrators with mustard, catsup, and sugar, and one white man beat Salter on the back and head several times. [UPI/Bettmann]

however, as the guiding force behind the guild's famous Beaux Arts Ball, which, since 1942, has contributed millions of dollars to the National Urban League.

Working in an admittedly elite milieu, Moon was nonetheless a pioneer of the civil rights movement. Her vision was modest, yet it proved far reaching: to foster cooperation and understanding among Black and white individuals while they worked together to advance the cause of racial equality and social justice in America. She accomplished this goal by bringing Black and white middle-class people together for social, cultural, and educational activities. Unlike other interracial organizations, the guild's focus was always social—doing good while having a good time. In the 1940s and 1950s, racial segregation by law and by custom discouraged Black and white people from interacting socially. In cities across America, however, National Urban League Guild activities brought Black and white people into each other's homes and offices, fostering personal friendships and underscoring common interests. Consequently, the guild cemented important bonds between Black and white urban, middle-class Americans, helping to build a solid foundation for the burgeoning civil rights movement.

Mollie Moon's proudest single achievement, however, was breaking the color line at Rockefeller Center's Rainbow Room. Naming Winthrop Rockefeller her cohost for a 1948 guild event, Moon quashed any attempt to bar Black patrons from the posh nightclub. "Nobody was going to buck the landlord," she declared.

Moon served for many years as secretary to the National Urban League's board of trustees. In addition, she was a board member of the Dance Theatre of Harlem, one of the Coalition of 100 Black Women, and a leader in several Catholic women's organizations. After her husband's death in 1985, she raised money to establish the Henry Lee Moon Civil Rights Library and Archives at the headquarters of the National Association for the Advancement of Colored People (NAACP) in Baltimore. A pharmacist by training, she served as an adviser to the U.S. Food and Drug Administration. In addition to her volunteer work, Moon owned and operated a public relations firm on New York's Fifth Avenue.

Born July 31, 1908, in Hattiesburg, Mississippi, Mollie Lewis Moon was educated at Meharry Medical College, Columbia University Teachers College, the University of Berlin, and the New School for Social Research. She spent her adult life at the center

Mollie Moon sought to foster cooperation and understanding among individuals by bringing Black and white middle-class people together for social, cultural, and educational activities. She devoted nearly half a century to furthering this goal through the National Urban League Guild and its famous Beaux Arts Ball. [National Urban League Guild]

of Black America's civic, social, and cultural life. In 1932, she traveled with poet Langston Hughes, future husband Henry Lee Moon, and others to the Soviet Union to make a film about race relations in America. This youthful adventure, however, turned into a political and artistic debacle; the film was never made. In 1938 she married Moon, a respected journalist, scholar, *Crisis* editor, and NAACP official. Their daughter, Mollie Lee Moon Elliot, a mother of five who is also committed to the guild and the Henry Lee Moon Library, lives in Manhattan with her husband, film producer Stephen Elliot.

Mollie Moon's imprint on the National Urban League Guild and on America's urban middle class remains an important yet overlooked part of the history of American race relations in the twentieth century.

[See also NATIONAL URBAN LEAGUE GUILD.]

BIBLIOGRAPHY

Nieman, Linda. "National Urban League Guild." In *Women's Issues Interest Groups*, ed. Sarah Slavin (forthcoming); personal interviews with Helen Harden, Sylvia Hughes, Anita Marina, Mollie Moon, Mollie Lee Moon Elliot and Guichard Parris; printed and photographic documents in the collection of the National Urban League Guild's archives in New York City.

LINDA NIEMAN

MOORE, AUDLEY (QUEEN MOTHER) (1898-)

In recalling the events of her life, "Queen Mother" Moore stated its theme: "there wasn't nothing to do but get into the struggle" (Lanker 1989). A powerful street speaker and adept political organizer, Moore has been involved for almost a century in a host of crucial campaigns in support of Garveyism, the Harlem boycott and renters' rights movements, the Republican and Communist parties, the Scottsboro defense, Pan-Africanism, and the reparations movement.

Born in New Iberia, Louisiana, on July 27, 1898, Moore's experiences growing up in the South profoundly influenced her political vision. Her parents' lives had been shaped by white violence and her own memories included lynchings, manhunts, and overt discrimination. Moore's father, St. Cyr Moore, born as a result of his mother's rape by a white man, ran a livery stable. Moore's mother, Ella Henry, was raised in a middle-class French Creole household after her father was lynched by whites and her mother driven from their property. Both parents died by the time Moore was in the fourth grade, ending her formal schooling. Moore trained in the Poro hairdressing system and at age fifteen became the primary supporter of herself and her two younger sisters, Eloise and Lorita.

Moore worked as a volunteer nurse during the 1918 influenza epidemic. She and Eloise lived in Alabama during World War I. They organized support services for Black soldiers that were denied by the Red Cross. Moore joined the Universal Negro Improvement Association in New Orleans and embraced its tenets. She was attracted by Marcus Garvey's oratory and the beauty and self-fulfillment she found in his talk of the grandeur of ancient African civilization and pride in African culture and heritage. Moore often described an incident in New Orleans when she and other audience members defied white authorities by mounting benches and waving weapons while chanting for Garvey to speak. She remembered this as a victorious experience that contributed to the militancy of the grass-roots methods she used in later struggles.

Moore moved to Harlem in the 1920s. She organized domestic workers in the Bronx labor market and helped Black tenants to defy evictions by white landlords. Arrested repeatedly for her activities, she used her jail sentences to organize fellow inmates. In the 1930s, she joined the International Labor Defense and the Communist party, becoming one of the leading Black Communist woman organizers in New York. An extraordinary and persuasive speaker, she agitated on such issues as the Scottsboro defense, the Italo-Ethiopian war, economic boycotts, Black political representation, racial prejudice in film, and a myriad of other causes. She was a Communist party candidate for the New York State Assembly in 1938 and for alderman in 1940, and she was campaign manager for Benjamin Davis's successful bid for the New York City Council in 1943.

Moore left the Communist party in 1950. She and Eloise joined Mother Langley and Dara Collins in founding the Universal Association of Ethiopian Women, which worked on welfare rights, prisoners' rights, antilynching, and interracial rape issues. In the 1960s she formed the Reparations Committee of Descendants of U.S. Slaves, Incorporated, demanding federal reparations to Blacks as partial compensation for the gross exploitations of slavery and its aftermath.

In 1972, Moore traveled to Africa to attend Kwame Nkrumah's funeral. During the trip she was honored with the title of "Queen Mother" and spoke at the All African Women's Conference in Dar es Salaam. Her tours of African farms and industries inspired her to found the Queen Mother Moore Research Institute and the Eloise Moore College of African Studies and Vocational and Industrial School in the Catskills (destroyed by fire in 1978).

Moore was a member of the National Association of Colored Women and a founding member of the National Council of Negro Women. Her view of the women's movement in the 1970s was negative, however, and she has described feminism as an "alien ideology emanating from the white woman," whereas the Black woman's fight is "alongside of her man" (*Black Scholar* 1973).

Moore's long career of political activism merged Black nationalism, Pan-Africanism, and the Left. Her simultaneous support of Black women's organizations and alienation from the white feminist agenda speaks to the racial bifurcation of the women's movement.

BIBLIOGRAPHY

Ahmad, Muhammed. "Queen Mother Moore." In *EAL*; "The *Black Scholar* Interviews: Queen Mother Moore." *Black Scholar* (March-April 1973); Lanker, Brian. "Queen Mother Audley Moore." In his *I Dream a World: Portraits of Black Women Who Changed America* (1989); Moore, Audley. Oral history interview by Cheryl Townsend Gilkes. Black Women Oral History Project, Schlesinger Library, Radcliffe College, Cambridge, Mass., and oral history interviews by Mark Naison and Ruth Prag. Oral History of the American Left Project, Tamiment Library, New York University, New York; Naison, Mark. *Communists in Harlem during the Depression* (1983); "Queen Mother Moore," *New Afrikan* (December 18, 1983); "Queen Mother Moore Receives Garvey Award," *Burning Spear* (January-March 1987).

BARBARA BAIR

A founding member of the Society of Black Composers, Dorothy Rudd Moore says that the main influences on her music have been J. S. Bach and Duke Ellington. [Schomburg Center]

MOORE, DOROTHY RUDD (1940-)

She is a poet, composer, singer, lecturer, and teacher, but ask her what she enjoys most, and Dorothy Rudd Moore will say that she thinks of herself primarily as a composer. However, although she is partial to her opera, *Frederick Douglass*, she insists that all of her compositions are her favorites because she thinks of them as her children.

Born on June 4, 1940, Dorothy Rudd spent her childhood in New Castle, Delaware, where the strong influence of her mother, a singer, seemed naturally to guide her toward a musical career. In 1963, she earned a B.M. in theory and composition from Howard University, having studied composition under Mark Fax. She received a Lucy Moten Scholarship and was accepted in the summer studies program at Fontainebleau where she studied under Nadia Boulanger. She later settled in New York City and studied composition with Chou Wen-chung and voice with Lola Hayes.

Moore has taught at the Harlem School of the Arts, New York University, and Bronx Community College, and she was a founding member of the Society of Black Composers. In 1975, she made her Carnegie Recital Hall debut. She is married to Kermit Moore, a cellist and conductor.

As a composer, Moore leaves nothing to chance, working to achieve structure and logic. Although she bases her choice of style on the intent of a particular piece, the primary influences on her music have been J. S. Bach and Duke Ellington—Bach because of his structure and Ellington for both structure and inventiveness. Her works include a song cycle, other vocal music, a symphony, chamber music, and "Dream and Variations" for piano.

[*See also* COMPOSERS.]

BIBLIOGRAPHY

Jackson, Barbara G. Program notes, North Arkansas Symphony Orchestra (April 6, 1986); Moore, Dorothy Rudd. Personal interview (January 3, 1992); Southall, Geneva. "In Celebration of Black Women Composers." Program notes, fourth annual Music of the Black American Composer program (May 1988); Tischler, Alice. *Fifteen Black American Composers: A Bibliography of Their Works* (1981).

MELLASENAH MORRIS

MOORE, MELBA (1945-)

In her eighteen months in the rock musical *Hair*, Melba Moore did more than move up from the chorus to female lead. She also grew from an ex-schoolteacher who supported herself doing background vocals and singing commercial jingles to a coming Broadway star. Since then, she has become a respected singer and actress in theater, film, and television.

Born in New York City on October 27, 1945, Moore is the daughter of singer Melba (Bonnie) Smith and jazz saxophonist Teddy Hill. She was brought up in Harlem and later in Newark, New Jersey. The pain and danger she saw around her in Harlem drove Moore into herself, making her shy, withdrawn, and able to communicate her emotions only through music. She attended the Arts High School in Newark and then Montclair State Teachers College. After graduation, she taught music at Pershing Avenue Elementary School before quitting to work in show business. She was a stand-up singer on the Catskills resort circuit for a time and was doing a background session in a recording studio when she was heard by the composers of *Hair*. They asked her to audition for a new production of the musical, and she was cast as part of the "tribe." After eighteen months, having moved to a leading role, she left to play Lutiebelle in *Purlie*, the musical version of Ossie Davis's *Purlie Victorious*. Her performance drew raves and won her a Tony Award, a New York Drama Critics Circle Award, and a Drama Desk Award.

Since then, Moore has appeared in two other Broadway musicals and five films, including *Lost in the Stars*, a musical adaptation of Alan Paton's *Cry, the Beloved Country*. She has also appeared frequently on television, including appearances on the nighttime soap *Falcon Crest*. She shared star billing in the miniseries *Ellis Island* and was the first Black actress to have a situation comedy named after her. *Melba*, however, did not air for long. She also has had a successful recording career, winning two Grammy Award nominations.

Melba Moore is married to Charles Huggins, and they have one daughter, Charli.

BIBLIOGRAPHY

BAFT; CBWA; NA; NBAW; WWBA (1992).

KATHLEEN THOMPSON

MOORE, UNDINE SMITH (1905-)

Undine Smith Moore, born on August 25, 1905, in Jarratt, Virginia, is a composer and educator. She earned Bachelor of Arts and Bachelor of Music degrees from Nashville's Fisk University, where she studied piano and organ with Alice M. Grass. Moore later studied at Juilliard School of Music in New York City and the Eastman School of Music in Rochester, New York. She also received a Master of Arts degree and a professional diploma from Columbia University Teachers College.

Moore began her teaching career in the public schools in Goldsboro, North Carolina, but taught at Virginia State College in Petersburg, Virginia, from 1927 until her retirement in 1972. She cofounded and codirected the Black Music Center at Virginia State College from 1969 to 1972.

Moore served as a visiting professor at Virginia Union University in Richmond, Virginia; Carleton College in Northfield, Minnesota; and Howard, Fisk, and Indiana universities. With Altona Trent-Johns, Moore founded the Black Man in American Music program at Virginia State College. She also has lectured extensively.

[*See also* COMPOSERS.]

BIBLIOGRAPHY

Baker, David N., et al., eds. *The Black Composer Speaks* (1978); Cohen, Aaron I. *International Encyclopedia of Women Composers* (1981); Green, Mildred. *Black Women Composers: A Genesis* (1983); Hitchcock, H. Wiley and Stanley Sadie, eds. *The New Grove Dictionary of American Music* (1986); Jones, R. D. "The Choral Works of Undine Smith Moore: A Study of Her Life and Work," Ph.D. diss. (1980); Kenyon, Nicholas. "Scenes from the Life of a Martyr: Carnegie Hall, New York Concert Reviews," *New Yorker* (February 1, 1982); Mapp, Edward. *Directory of Blacks in the Performing Arts* (1978); Roach, Hildred. *Black American Music: Past and Present* (1984); Sadie, Stanley, ed. *The New Grove Dictionary of Music and Musicians* (1980); Southern, Eileen. *The Music of Black Americans: A History* (1983); Spencer, Jon Michael. *As the Black School Sings* (1987); Stern, Susan. *Women Composers: A Handbook* (1978); White, Evelyn Davidson. *Choral Music by Afro-American Composers: A Selected Annotated Bibliography* (1981); Williams, Ora. *American Black Women in the Arts and Social Sciences: A Bibliographic Survey* (1978). The Special Collections of the Johnston Memorial Library of Virginia State University includes a vertical clippings file of newspaper articles on Moore, as well as audiotapes of concerts and lectures sponsored by the Black Man in American Music program. The J. Harold Montague

Collection includes a photo of Moore as accompanist with the 1931-32 Choral Society directed by Alston Burleigh. A rare interview with her is included in Fisk University's Black Oral History Collection.

SANDRA CANNON SCOTT

MORRISON, TONI (1931-)

Pulitzer Prize winner Toni Morrison is a giant in the literary world. Her creative rigor, her intellectual and critical depth, and her prophetic vision of the role of literature in interpreting the African-American experience in the United States are unsurpassed. Morrison has written six novels, one short story, one play, and numerous critical essays and has come to be regarded as one of the preeminent writers of our time. In all of her writings, Morrison is concerned about crafting a special, clarifying angle for remembering the past and making it a useful mechanism for survival in the contemporary world. "I think long and hard about what my novels should do," says Morrison. "They should clarify the roles that have become obscured, they ought to identify those things in the past that are useful and those things that are not and they ought to give nourishment" (LeClair 1981).

Morrison began writing during the 1970s when there was a ready audience in the United States for works by women, particularly Black women. Although she has been concerned in her works with a female quest for selfhood, the major thrust of the Morrison canon has been the "elaborately socialized world" of Black people as a whole. Her women protagonists have been representatives of the challenges that face all those within the Black community. For Morrison, the major challenge in the late twentieth century in the aftermath of the civil rights movement and integration is forgetfulness. Morrison wants to record and restore in her works the sustaining values that she believes were part of the cohesive Black communities of the past. Through penetrating and enhancing analyses of historical experience and creative use of the myths, music, language, and worldview of African-Americans, Morrison has created a body of work that is as well regarded for its pure aesthetic beauty as for the magnitude of its interpretive power.

Born Chloe Anthony Wofford on February 18, 1931, Morrison grew up in the small midwestern town of Lorain, Ohio. She was the second of George and Ramah Wofford's four children. Her parents had migrated from the South with their families in the early 1900s. Her maternal grandparents had been sharecroppers in Greenville, Alabama. They had lost their land in the late 1890s and were never able to get out of debt. Her father's family were Georgia sharecroppers, and the racial strife they endured left him with painful memories of the South and a bitter attitude toward white people. With both parents from migrant families, Morrison was brought up—as many in such families were—with a strong distrust of whites and an understanding that the only tangible or emotional aid on which she could depend would come from her own community. Group loyalty was among the earliest values she was taught as a child. It was, her parents believed, one of the most important lessons that she could learn in order to survive in the harsh racial environment of the 1930s and 1940s.

In the Wofford household, the distinctiveness of Black cultural life was richly lived and affirmed by Morrison's parents on a daily basis. Her growing years were filled with the jokes, lore, music, language, and myths of African-American culture. Her mother sang to the children, her father told them folktales, and they both told "thrillingly terrifying" ghost stories. It was at their knee that she heard tales of Br'er Rabbit and of Africans who could fly; heard the names, the imagery, the rhythms of the language; and observed the naming ritual that would become a significant part of her later work as a novelist.

Education was also expected and encouraged during her growing years. Morrison was taught to read at home by her parents before she entered first grade. During her adolescent years, she read Dostoyevsky, Jane Austen, and Tolstoy. They wrote so specifically about their culture, Morrison remembers, that even a little Black girl in Lorain, Ohio, could enjoy their stories. Later, as a beginning writer, Morrison wanted to bring that kind of specificity to the experiences of her culture as well.

In 1949, Morrison graduated with honors from Lorain High School and entered Howard University the following fall. At Howard, Morrison was an English major and a classics minor. She also joined the Howard Repertory Theater, and here she had the opportunity to make her first trips to the South. During these trips she was able to see, firsthand, the harsh realities of southern life for Blacks that her father had recounted, but more importantly, in the Black communities that she visited she saw the similarities between core Black cultural life in the North and South. The knowledge of that shared worldview of Black people in both the North and the South would help her later to achieve the group cultural resonance in her works for which she has become famous.

In 1953, Morrison graduated from Howard and entered graduate school in English at Cornell University. She wrote a dissertation on Woolf and Faulkner and graduated from Cornell in 1955. Morrison taught briefly in the English department at Texas Southern University in Houston, then returned to Howard in 1957. While at Howard she joined a writers' group, where she first began to work seriously on her writing. She also met and married Jamaican architect Harold Morrison. The couple lived in Washington and had two sons, Slade Kevin and Harold Ford. The marriage, challenged by the differing cultural expectations of the roles of each partner, ended in divorce in 1964.

With two children to support alone, Morrison accepted a job in 1966 as a textbook editor with a subsidiary of Random House in Syracuse, New York. During the 1960s, many publishing companies, as a result of demands by civil rights groups, were trying to revise their textbook selections, and Morrison thought that she could make a contribution. It was in Syracuse during the nights after the children were asleep that she began to work on a story she had started in her writers' group at Howard about a little Black girl who wanted blue eyes. Morrison sent the story to Holt; it was published in 1970 as *The Bluest Eye*. Still considered a favorite by many of her readers, *The Bluest Eye* tells the story of a young girl, Pecola Breedlove, and her family who fall victim to the debilitating effects of racism, poverty, urban life, and, most significantly for this novel, the Anglo-Saxon standards of physical beauty, accepted not only by the larger society but by the Black community as well. The family destruction and the consequent madness of Pecola were a stinging indictment by Morrison of what happens to individuals whose personhood and beauty are negated summarily by the society in which they live.

In 1968, Morrison moved from Syracuse to New York City to become a trade book editor in the New York office of Random House. Over the next sixteen years, Morrison would rise to become senior editor at Random House, one of few Blacks and the only Black woman to hold such an esteemed position. Morrison was a highly regarded editor and oversaw the publication of Black writers such as Gayl Jones, Toni Cade Bambara, John McCluskey, Muhammad Ali, and Andrew Young.

Working as an editor by day and a writer by night, Morrison completed her second novel, *Sula*, in 1973. In this novel, the protagonist is not a passive victim of the imposed values of the larger society that take her away from the true values of her culture, as was Pecola. Sula, in a search for an existential self, defies the values of the community willingly. Unlike her childhood friend, Nel, who gives up the rebellion and quest for self of adolescence and settles into womanhood in the same way as the others in her community, Sula never conforms. She comes to church suppers without underwear, she sleeps with Nel's husband, she puts her grandmother in a nursing home, and, worst of all for the people in her community, Sula sleeps with white men. Her words to Nel on her deathbed are a commentary on the restricted lives she sees Black women living: "I know what every Black woman in the country is doing. . . . Dying. Just like me. But the difference is they dying like a stump. Me I'm going down like one of those redwoods." While Morrison understands the desire for self-definition outside the community, she believes it is a futile effort. Racism and sexism in the society allowed no such definition for the Sulas of the 1950s, and so ultimately they had to depend on their communities even if they did so in defiance. The community ostracizes Sula and keeps its distance from her, but despite her defiance of their values, she is never put out of the community. In her characterization of Sula, Morrison demonstrates the larger values of the Black community regarding evil: "They let it run its course, fulfill itself and never invented ways either to alter it, annihilate it or prevent its happening again." She also affirmed, as she would do in all of her novels, the value of community allegiance over the desire for an existential self.

During the early 1970s, Morrison also was involved in the publication of a unique pictorial history of African-American life in the United States called *The Black Book*. Although her name appears nowhere on the work and her official capacity on the project was that of in-house editor, *The Black Book* was Morrison's idea, and she participated as much in collecting materials as did the official editors of the project: Middleton Harris, Morris Levitt, Robert Furman, and Ernest Smith. The book chronicles Black life from slavery to roughly the 1940s. It contains newspaper clippings, bills of sale, sheet music, announcements, dream books, definitions, letters patent, crafts, photographs, sport files, and other memorabilia taken largely from the collection of its editors, but it also includes an array of contributions from attics, scrapbooks, and trunks gathered by Morrison and other supporters of the project. In explaining her desire to do this kind of book, Morrison says she had gotten tired of histories of Black life that focused only on leaders, leaving the everyday heroes to the "lump of statistics." She wanted to bring those lives to the forefront—to create a genuine Black history book "that simply recollected life as lived." *The Black Book* was not a major commercial success, but Morrison's work on the project, which exposed her to the first-hand documents of the everyday lives of Black people—their joys, triumphs, and creations—would be invaluable to her work as a novelist. Here she saw head braces used on slaves, read the newspaper account of a slave woman who killed her children rather than have them returned to slavery, saw the patents of unsung accomplishments, and saw the photographs of Harlem life and the loves that grew and died there. The kernel of many of the conflicts that would appear in her later novels had been suggested through the view of Black life she gained from compiling the materials for this project.

Perhaps nowhere was the evidence of her work on *The Black Book* more prevalent than in her next novel, *Song of Solomon*. Filled with the lore, the songs, and the myths of African-Americans, *Song of Solomon*, published in 1977, was a treasury of history and culture. It is the story of Milkman Dead, a young man who, in his attempts to find a family fortune in the caves of Virginia, finds instead the songs, myths, lore, and love of his ancestors. It is a redemptive tale of a young boy who has been cut off from his family and knowledge of his ancestry by his father, who believes that the way to achieve manhood in this country is to own things. The only link Milkman has to his ancestry in the town where he grows up is his Aunt Pilate, a wise old woman who sings the stories of her history. She lives with very little, supporting herself and her daughters with only the bootleg wine she sells from her house, and her special joy is loving and caring for the living and the dead of her family. In an ironic twist that has Milkman finding the treasury of his ancestry rather than a bag of gold, *Song of Solomon*, with the most drama of any previous Morrison novel, affirms the value of connecting with the past. Morrison also explores material wealth and violence as solutions to problems in contemporary society, but she affirms, once again, the validity, the richness, and the empowerment of a knowledge of ancestral heritage. *Song of Solomon* was received with much fanfare and high critical acclaim. It sold over 3 million copies and was on the *New York Times* best-seller list for sixteen weeks. It won the American Academy and Institute of Arts and Letters Award and the National Book Critics' Circle Award in 1978. It was chosen as a Book-of-the-Month Club selection, the only novel by

a Black writer since *Native Son* (1940) to have achieved such recognition.

Tar Baby, Morrison's fourth novel, was published in 1981. It was an instant commercial success, appearing on the *New York Times* best-seller list less than one month after it was published. With a *Newsweek* cover story and a stunning lineup of promotional tours, *Tar Baby* had made Morrison, said one reviewer, "the toast of the literary world." In the novel, Morrison focused on the effects that access to material success and its trappings can have on the viability of the village values that had been a sustaining part of the African-American past. Set in the Caribbean on the fictional Isle de Chevalier, it combines mythical landscape, traditional peasant and patrician class culture, a Black male longing to return to the past, and a Black woman enjoying the material benefits of money and fame. The relationship between Son and Jadine turns into a romantic Armageddon between old ways

The critical and commercial success of two of her novels, Song of Solomon *and* Tar Baby, *catapulted Toni Morrison to the upper echelon of modern American writers. [Schomburg Center]*

and the new. The novel dramatizes the way in which the larger sociopolitical choices of Blacks during the late 1970s manifested themselves on a personal level. The outcome of this debate, however, is not hopeful. Unable to resolve their differences, Son and Jadine end the romance as individuals understanding more about the value of each other's outlook on life but unable to reconcile these ways into a unifying relationship. Morrison not only sets up a thematic argument against Jadine, pointing out that she is one who has "forgotten her ancient properties," but she also unravels the story against a natural landscape so mythically rendered that the setting, too, suggests the superiority of that which is timeless, rooted, and unshaken by contemporary realities.

With the financial and critical success of *Song of Solomon* and *Tar Baby*, Morrison was able to leave her position at Random House. In 1984, she was named to the Albert Schweitzer Chair in the Humanities at the State University of New York (SUNY) at Albany. While at Albany she taught courses in literature and was commissioned by the New York State Writers Institute to write a play in honor of the first national observance of the birthday of Dr. Martin Luther King, Jr. The play, *Dreaming Emmett*, was based on the life of the young boy Emmett Till, who was killed by a lynch mob in Mississippi in 1954. The play was performed by the Capital Repertory Theater of Albany, New York, on January 4, 1986.

While at Albany, Morrison also completed writing her fifth novel, *Beloved*, published in 1987. The writing of *Beloved* suggested a settling period for Morrison. A minority writer, she had said, must go through four stages: a period of anger, a period of self-discovery, a period of celebratory use of the culture, and finally an arrival at a "conceptual notion of the ethnic experience." With the writing of *Beloved*, Morrison had come through all of these stages. She was not just writing the story of the effects of slavery on the rights and responsibilities of the mother-love of one woman, but trying, through the characterization of Sethe, to understand the full human meanings and implications of the slave experience. Motherhood and infanticide provided a powerful medium through which to reveal the effects of the horror of slavery on the humanity of individuals. The story is based on the life of Margaret Garner, a Kentucky slave who, with her four children, escaped to Cincinnati, Ohio. When caught, she tried to kill all of the children but succeeded in killing only one, by cutting her throat. When Morrison read this story while working on *The Black Book*, she was deeply moved by the humanistic and symbolic nature of this story. Here was a woman who did a courageous thing, says Morrison: "She took the lives of her children into her own hands" (Rothstein 1982). This incident proved not only how slavery robbed individuals of their most basic human rights, but it also demonstrated the way in which slaves, sometimes in violent and paradoxical ways, insisted on their humanity in spite of slavery's horror. Even as she reveals the most brutal and humiliating aspects of slavery, Morrison does not explain away Sethe's deed. In fact, the story is largely about how Sethe accepts her guilt and seeks forgiveness. In the novel, Sethe is revisited by what she believes is the ghost of her daughter, and the story pivots around Sethe, her family, and her community coming to terms with this awful deed and finding the strength and courage to live clearer, fuller lives as a result of it.

Beloved has been called Morrison's most successful novel, technically and thematically. The complexity that it assigns to slavery, an event too often "summarized away" in American history, gives the novel its greatest moral and historical merit. Full of intertwining plots and layered time sequences, the novel keeps readers challenged and attentive. The order of revelation, always out of chronological sequence in Morrison's novels, is doubly complicated in this novel by characters "remembering what they were remembering in a time past." The infanticide that is the cause of the action in the story gives way to the labor of working out symbolic meanings of the ghost's presence and understanding the quests for psychological and moral wholeness that it inspires in all the characters. *Beloved* touched a major chord in the American reading public. It has been a widely read and studied text, taught in history courses and literature courses as well as courses in women's studies and creative writing. Never before had Morrison been so successful in achieving her own standard for good literature: *Beloved* was a novel "unquestionably political and irrevocably beautiful at the same time" (Evans 1984). It won the Pulitzer Prize for fiction.

In 1989, Morrison was named the Robert F. Goheen Professor in the Council of the Humanities at Princeton University. At Princeton she teaches courses in American literature and is writer-in-residence in the humanities. With her professorships at both SUNY and Princeton, Morrison began to write critical essays as highly regarded as her fictional works. Her essays in critical anthologies, and for such journals as the *Michigan Quarterly* and *Thought*, have been widely read and have provided useful insights for interpretations of her works and of American literature in general. In 1990, Morrison delivered the prestigious Massey Lectures in American Civilization at Harvard University and the Clark Lectures at Trinity College, Cambridge. The Massey Lectures, which explore the presence of Blackness or "Africanism" in literature by white writers and the reflexive implications of that presence on the writers themselves and the culture out of which they wrote, were published by Harvard University Press in 1992 (*Playing in the Dark: Whiteness and the Literary Imagination*).

While at Princeton, Morrison's artistic works also continued to flourish. She was commissioned by Carnegie Hall to write the lyrics for the operatic piece *Honey and Rue* performed there in January 1992 featuring soprano Kathleen Battle with music by André Previn. In the spring of 1992, she completed her sixth novel, *Jazz*, her intricate and improvisational telling of the story of Black city life in the 1920s and 1930s. *Jazz* is the second in a trilogy, which began with *Beloved*, mythologizing Black life throughout various periods in history.

Morrison has served as a trustee of the New York Public Library and of the National Humanities Center, as co-chair of the Schomburg Commission for the Preservation of Black Culture, and for six years as a member of the National Council of the Arts. She is a member of the American Academy and Institute of Arts and Letters and the American Academy of Arts and Sciences. She has received honorary degrees from Harvard, the University of Pennsylvania, Sarah Lawrence College, Oberlin College, Spelman College, Dartmouth College, and Yale, Georgetown, Columbia, and Brown universities. In 1978, she received the Distinguished Writer Award from the American Academy of Arts and Letters. She was the first recipient of the Washington College Literary Award in 1987 and was a New York State governor's awardee in 1986. She has also been a subject of the highly regarded PBS interview series *A World of Ideas with Bill Moyers*. In 1989, she was the recipient of the Modern Language Association of America Common Wealth Award in Literature and the Sara Lee Corporation Front Runner Award in the Arts.

Because the challenge in Morrison's writing is one undertaken in service to her people and not to herself, and because she sincerely believes that the story, the novel, is the mode through which African-Americans can be led out of the cultural confusion and complexity of contemporary society, Morrison has become a kind of literary Moses. In her works, she strips away the idols of whiteness and of Blackness that have prevented Blacks in the United States from knowing themselves and gives them their own true, mythical, remembered words to live by. She takes on the whole culture and seeks to restore the mythos and the ethos that will clarify the meaning of the journey of African-Americans in the United States. She is healer and prophet; she is nurturer and guide; and because she achieves these tasks with such grace, such love, and such confidence, courage, and skill, Morrison holds an indelible position of prominence in African-American history and in the history of great writers throughout the world.

BIBLIOGRAPHY

Bandler, Michael J. "Novelist Toni Morrison: We Bear Witness." *African Woman* (September-October 1979); Denard, Carolyn. "Toni Morrison." In *Modern American Women Writers*, ed. Elaine Showalter (1991); *DLB*; Dowling, Colette. "The Song of Toni Morrison." *New York Times Magazine* (May 20, 1979); Evans, Mari, ed. *Black Women Writers (1950-1980)* (1984); Giddings, Paula. "The Triumphant Song of Toni Morrison." *Encore* (December 12, 1977); LeClair, Thomas. " 'The Language Must Not Sweat.' A Conversation with Toni Morrison." *New Republic* (March 21, 1981); Randolph, Laura. "The Magic of Toni Morrison." *Ebony* (July 1988); Rothstein, Mervyn. "Toni Morrison's *Beloved* Inspired by a Slave Who Chose to Kill Her Child, *New York Times* (August 26, 1982); Strouse, Jean. "Toni Morrison's Black Magic." *Newsweek* (March 30, 1981).

SELECTED WORKS BY TONI MORRISON

Essays: "Behind the Making of *The Black Book*," *Black World* (February 1974); "City Limits, Village Values: Concepts of Neighborhood in Black Fiction." In *Literature and the Urban Experience: Essays on the City and Literature*, ed. Michael C. Jaye and Ann Chalmers Watts (1981); "A Knowing So Deep," *Essence* (May 1985); "Memory Creation and Writing," *Thought* (December 1984); *Playing in the Dark: Whiteness and the Literary Imagination* (1992); "Recitatif." In *Confirmation: An Anthology of African American Women Writers*, ed. Amiri Baraka and Amina Baraka (1983); "Rootedness: The Ancestor as Foundation." In *Black Women Writers (1950-1980): A Critical Evaluation*, ed. Mari Evans (1984); "The Site of Memory." In *Inventing the Truth: The Art and Craft of Memoir*, ed. William Zinsser (1987); "Unspeakable Things Unspoken," *Michigan Quarterly Review* (Winter 1989); "What the Black Woman Thinks about Women's Lib," *New York Times Magazine* (August 22, 1971). Novels: *Beloved* (1987); *The Bluest Eye* (1970); *Jazz* (1992); *Song of Solomon* (1977); *Sula* (1973); *Tar Baby* (1981). Plays: *Dreaming Emmett* (1986).

CAROLYN DENARD

MORTON-JONES, VERINA *see* JONES, VERINA MORTON HARRIS

MOSEKA, AMINATA *see* LINCOLN, ABBEY

MOSSELL, GERTRUDE E. H. BUSTILL (1855-1948)

Through her books, articles, and newspaper columns, Gertrude Mossell wrote about her political and social ideology, reflecting the views of a feminist and social reformer in the late nineteenth and early twentieth centuries. She encouraged women to go into professions such as medicine and journalism, and she dismissed the notion that a woman had to choose either to have a family or a career. Mossell and other Black women leaders of her era combined roles as activists and professionals with those of wife and mother. Taken together, her views would not be seriously considered by most African-Americans for at least another generation.

Gertrude E. H. Bustill Mossell, educator, journalist, and feminist, was born in Philadelphia, Pennsylvania, on July 3, 1855. She died at the age of ninety-two at Frederick Douglass Memorial Hospital in Philadelphia, the city where she spent most of her life, on January 21, 1948. She had been ill for about three months.

Her parents, Charles H. and Emily (Robinson) Bustill, were among the free-Black elite of nineteenth-century Philadelphia. The prominent Bustill family included generations of achievers, including Gertrude's great-grandfather, the former slave Cyril Bustill (1732-1806), who earned his freedom and served on George Washington's staff as a baker during the American Revolution. One of Cyril's daughters, Grace Bustill Douglass (1782-1842), was an abolitionist and a member and officer of the Philadelphia Female Anti-Slavery Society, as was her daughter, Sarah Mapps Douglass (1806-82), who also married a Douglass. Sarah was not only an abolitionist but a feminist and noted educator. Perhaps the most illustrious member of the Bustill family was Gertrude's cousin, the actor and political activist Paul Bustill Robeson (1898-1976), who became a Rhodes scholar after graduating from Rutgers University.

Gertrude Bustill and her elder sister (who later became Mrs. William D. Robertson) were raised as Quakers, as were many of the Bustills. Both women later followed the lead of several family members and joined the Presbyterian church. They were educated in Philadelphia "colored" schools.

After completing Roberts Vaux Grammar School, Gertrude Bustill taught school for seven years at various places, including Camden, New Jersey, and Frankford, Delaware. As was the custom, her marriage to physician Nathan F. Mossell of Lockport, Pennsylvania, probably in the early 1880s, ended her formal teaching career. She returned to live in Philadelphia, where she raised two daughters, Mazie and Florence. A few years after her marriage, however, Gertrude Mossell resumed her writing and developed a career as a journalist, educating the public about women's rights and social reform movements.

Mossell's career goal emerged from her exceptional ability as a writer who came from a family of political activists and feminists. Reverend Benjamin Tucker Tanner discovered her writing potential, probably in the late 1860s, as a guest at the closing exercises of the Roberts Vaux Grammar School, where he heard Bustill read her essay "Influence." He invited her to submit it for publication to the periodical he edited, the *Christian Recorder*. As a result of this first literary success, Gertrude Mossell began an outstanding literary career, writing essays and columns for numerous newspapers and periodicals and eventually writing two books, *The Work of the Afro-American Woman* (1894) and *Little Dansie's One Day at Sabbath School* (1902).

Mossell developed a national reputation as a journalist writing for African-American newspapers. Her articles and columns appeared in the *AME Church Review*, the (New York) *Freeman*, and the (Indianapolis) *World*. In Philadelphia, she wrote for leading papers with syndicated columns in the *Echo*, the Philadelphia *Times*, the *Independent*, and the *Press Republican*. In addition, Mossell assisted in editing the *Lincoln Alumni Magazine*, the journal of her husband's alma mater.

African-American women journalists were few and far between during the 1880s when Mossell wrote the column "Our Woman's Department," which appeared in the first issue of T. Thomas Fortune's New York *Freeman*, in December 1885. Mossell introduced her column by titling the first one "Woman Suffrage." She wrote that her column would "be devoted to the interest of women" and that she would "promote true womanhood, especially that of the African race." Mossell encouraged readers ignorant about the issues of woman suffrage to read books and periodicals to educate themselves. She hoped that those who thought unfavorably about votes for women would be convinced to change their opinions with new awareness. Married women, Mossell argued, supported woman suffrage. Her words indicated a significant political awareness and sophistication shared by only a few outspoken Black woman suffragists in the 1880s.

Mossell's column appeared every other week throughout 1886, and in it she promoted career development in business and the professions. She called for the training of women in skills that would prepare them for businesses such as the restaurant industry. As for literary and journalistic careers, Mossell introduced her readers to role models such as Frances Ellen Watkins Harper, Josephine Turpin, and Charlotte Ray, to essayists such as Mary Ann Shadd Cary, and to journalists such as Ida B. Wells-Barnett, Clarissa Thompson, and Mattie Horton, using her column to promote women and encourage them to seek their rights.

Gertrude Mossell believed that all types of African-American women needed to ally themselves in order to help one another in a process that she and others of her era called "racial uplift." Although she was known as a product of Philadelphia's Black elite, Mossell looked beyond the lines of status when she called for women of color to come together to work on behalf of their race.

BIBLIOGRAPHY

DANB; Majors, Monroe, ed. *Noted Negro Women: Their Triumphs and Activities* (1893); Mossell, Gertrude. *The Work of the Afro-American Woman* ([1894] 1908); Penn, I. Garland, ed. *The Afro-American Press and Its Editors* (1891).

ROSALYN TERBORG-PENN

MOTEN, LUCY ELLA (1851-1933)

Born in Farquier County, Virginia, near White Sulphur Springs, Lucy Moten was the daughter of free African-Americans, Benjamin and Julia (Witchers) Moten. Young Lucy's parents were so impressed with her early intellectual development that they relocated to Washington, D.C., so that she could attend a school for free African-Americans conducted by John F. Cook, Sr. When public schools for African-Americans opened in the District of Columbia in 1862, the Motens saw to it that their daughter was enrolled. It was probably this early thrust into the world of academia that resulted in Moten's lifetime commitment to education.

After graduating from Howard University in 1870, Moten began her teaching career in the primary division of the O Street School in Washington, D.C. As a teacher she continued to pursue her academic and professional training, graduating from the Normal School at Salem, Massachusetts, in 1876. In addition, she graduated with honors from the Spencerian Business College in 1883 and took classes in public speaking with Alfred Townsend, a respected Washington, D.C., teacher of the period.

Armed with an excellent academic record and a recommendation from Frederick Douglass, Moten was appointed and served as principal of Miner Normal School in Washington, D.C., from 1883 to 1920. For twenty-five years Miner Normal School was recognized as one of the top teacher training institutions in America. Under Moten's leadership, the school's faculty and admission standards were raised, and the curriculum was extended to a two-year program. Also during her tenure, a new Miner facility was built in 1914. Moten helped plan the design, securing well-lighted and well-ventilated stairs and corridors inside the structure. According to official documents and correspondence dating to her tenure at Miner Normal School, Moten had strong opinions about teacher qualifications. "The teacher must be first class in every particular, a professionally trained person whose personality will impress itself on . . . pupils always for their best good. The aesthetic must be looked after as well as the moral and the physical." Moten trained meticulous, punctual, accurate, and thorough teachers who were recruited by state superintendents throughout the country.

After Moten received a medical degree from Howard Medical School in 1897, she was able to treat the medical needs of her students and establish a course in physical hygiene. By linking her professional advancement with that of the school, Moten became an inspiration to her students, instilling cultural pride, dedication, and discipline as well as developing their intelligence. Her emphasis on personal morals also influenced her students, provoking them to reach for higher goals. For four decades Miner trained the majority of teachers employed in Washington's African-American schools. Her teaching was not limited to Miner, however. Moten spent many summers training teachers in the South, which led to further graduate work at New York University in the field of education. Her commitment to education also led her to Europe, where she broadened her educational perspective and came upon the architectural style that she decided would be used in building the new Miner Normal School, a replica of Christ's College in Cambridge, England.

Lucy Ella Moten was struck and killed by a taxi in New York's Times Square on August 24, 1933. A pioneer in education even in death, she bequeathed more than $51,000 to Howard University. Ironically, given her cause of death, the money was to be used to fund student travel regardless of the recipient's sex, color, or creed. In 1954, a Washington, D.C., elementary school was named in her honor.

BIBLIOGRAPHY

Carruthers, Thomasine. "Lucy Ella Moten," *Journal of Negro History* (January 1934); Dabney, Lillian G. *The History of Schools for Negroes in the D.C., 1807-1947* (1949); *NAW*; Wormle, G. Smith. "Educators of the First Half Century of Public Schools of the D.C.," *Journal of Negro History* (April 1932).

TOMIKA DePRIEST

MOTLEY, CONSTANCE BAKER
(1921-)

In the 1950s and 1960s, the courts of our country were battlegrounds in the war for civil rights. One of the leaders in the effort was Constance Baker Motley, long-time counsel for the National Association for the Advancement of Colored People (NAACP) and later a federal court judge.

Constance Baker was born September 14, 1921, in New Haven, Connecticut, to Willoughby Alva and Rachel Huggins Baker, both West Indian emigrants. Her father was chef for a Yale fraternity. She attended the New Haven public schools and learned Black history through lectures given in her Sunday school. She became active in community activities while she was still in high school, becoming president of the New Haven Youth Council and secretary of the New Haven Adult Community Council.

After graduation from high school, she went to work for the National Youth Administration because college was financially impossible. Then Clarence Blakeslee, a local businessman, heard Baker speak at a New Haven community center. Blakeslee had built the building and wanted to know why it was not used by Black citizens. Baker's answer so impressed him that he wondered why she was not in college. When Baker said she wanted to go to law school but could

Before being appointed the first Black woman judge in the federal district court system, attorney Constance Baker Motley tried some of the most important civil rights cases of the twentieth century. In 1956, Motley and Arthur Shores of the NAACP brought a contempt of court suit against the University of Alabama after the university refused to admit a Black applicant, Polly Ann Hudson, on moral grounds. The contempt charge was dismissed. [UPI/ Bettmann]

not afford the tuition, Blakeslee offered to pay for her schooling.

Baker attended Fisk University and then transferred to New York University, graduating from its Washington Square College in 1943 with an A.B. in economics. She went on to Columbia Law School, graduating in 1946. That same year, she married Joel Wilson Motley, an insurance broker. Then she went out to find a job.

"My first job interview," she remembers, "was an accurate sign of the times. . . . When I appeared for my interview, a balding middle-aged white male appeared at a door leading to the reception room where I was standing. The receptionist had not even asked me to have a seat. Even after the door to the reception room quickly closed, she still did not invite me to sit down. She knew as well as I that the interview was over" (Motley 1991).

Fortunately, Motley heard that there was a vacancy for a law clerk at the NAACP Legal Defense and Education Fund and went to make an application. Thurgood Marshall interviewed Motley for the job and hired her at once. At the interview he told her the first of many stories about successful Black women. "Over the years," says Motley, "he told me about every successful African-American woman he encountered" (Motley 1991).

As a clerk, Motley was responsible for a great deal of research. Marshall suggested that in order to have access to its library, she should join the New York City Bar Association. Having done so, she went to use the library. "When I got there," she says, "I saw the 'gate keeper' standing at his desk immediately inside the door. He was an elderly white man with snow-white hair who appeared to be one year older than God." After some time, Motley got his attention, only to be told that the library was for members only. She told him she was a member and, recovering from his shock, he asked what her name was. " 'Mrs. Motley,' I said, guarding against what all African-American women guarded against in those days. When he found my name on the membership list, he exclaimed, 'Oh, right this way, *Constance*' " (Motley 1991). Respect did not come quickly or easily.

In 1965, Constance Baker Motley was elected to the office of Manhattan Borough President, the highest and best-paid job ever held by a Black woman in the United States to that time. She was sworn in on February 24, 1965, by New York City Mayor Robert F. Wagner (left), while her son and husband looked on proudly. [UPI/Bettmann]

In 1950, Motley became assistant counsel for the Legal Defense and Education Fund and became involved in trying cases. She helped write the briefs filed in the U.S. Supreme Court in the school desegregation case, *Brown* v. *Board of Education*. Her reputation as a fine lawyer and a dedicated civil rights proponent grew. "Among the better known cases I personally tried," she says, "were those against the Universities of Mississippi, Georgia, and Alabama, and Clemson College in South Carolina. As a result, James Meredith, the plaintiff in the University of Mississippi case, became a national hero in 1962. Charlayne Hunter-Gault and Hamilton Holmes, the plaintiffs in the University of Georgia case, brought Georgia kicking and screaming into the twentieth century in 1961. George Wallace and Alabama finally gave up massive resistance to desegregation in 1963. And now South Carolina brags about Harvey Gantt, the plaintiff in the Clemson College case in 1962, who became mayor of Charlotte" (Motley 1991).

In 1963, leaders of the Democratic party in New York asked her to fill the unexpired term of New York State Senator James Watson. She agreed and was then elected to the New York State Senate in 1964, becoming the first Black woman in that legislative body. She resigned to run in a special election to fill a one-year vacancy as president of the Borough of Manhattan. She was then reelected to a full four-year term.

Over the years, Motley argued ten civil rights cases in the Supreme Court, winning nine. During one of those cases, Ramsey Clark, who was then Attorney General of the United States, was in court and heard her. Afterward, he went back to the White House and suggested to President Lyndon Johnson that he appoint Motley to the federal bench. Initially, Johnson submitted her name for a seat on the Court of Appeals for the Second Circuit, but, according to Motley, "the opposition to my appointment was so great, apparently because I was a woman, that Johnson had to withdraw my name. I remember how stunned both Johnson and Marshall were at the strength and intensity of the opposition" (Motley 1991).

In January 1966, Johnson submitted Motley's name to the U.S. Senate for confirmation of her nomination as a U.S. District Judge. At that time, only two other women were federal district judges. Over fierce opposition from a group headed by James Eastland of Mississippi, Motley was finally confirmed in August.

"When I was introduced as a new judge at a Second Circuit Judicial Conference," relates Motley, "the master of ceremonies said, 'And now I want to introduce Connie Motley who is doing such a good job on the District Court.' In contrast, everyone else was introduced with a full-blown curriculum vitae" (Motley 1991).

In 1982, Motley became Chief Judge of the Southern District of New York. She is now a Senior U.S. District Judge.

BIBLIOGRAPHY

CBWA; *EBA*; Motley, Constance Baker. "My Personal Debt to Thurgood Marshall," *Yale Law Journal* (November 1991); *NA*; *NBAW*; *WWBA* (1992).

KATHLEEN THOMPSON

MOUTOUSSAMY-ASHE, JEANNE (1951-)

"Research on black women is a difficult task, but . . . historical research on the black woman photographer seemed impossible," stated Jeanne Moutoussamy-Ashe in the introduction to her book *Viewfinders* (1986). Nonetheless, she devoted herself to that task in the mid-1980s, producing a work that documents the lives and work of Black female photographers as far back as 1860. Even prior to the publication of *Viewfinders*, she had visually recorded the cultural heritage of the South Carolina coastal region in the book *Daufauskie Island* (1982) and had developed a series of lectures and a traveling exhibit around that photo essay.

Jeanne Moutoussamy was born in Chicago, Illinois, in 1951. Both of her parents were active professionals in the visual arts and nurtured their daughter's interest and talent. She moved to New York City to attend Cooper Union, where she earned a B.F.A. in photography in 1975. She then worked in television photojournalism for both WNBC and WNEW in New York and for *PM Magazine*. In addition to her books, she has had several individual and group exhibits in New York City, Boston, Chicago, Houston, Washington, D.C., Detroit, Los Angeles, London, Florence, and Paris and has contributed photographs to numerous magazines and newspapers, including *Life*, *Smithsonian*, *Sports Illustrated*, *People Weekly*, *Ebony*, *Black Enterprise*, *World Tennis*, *Self*, and *Essence*. She has also done official photo-portraits of several U.S. Cabinet members, including Patricia Roberts Harris. Her work has received awards and is in the permanent collections of several museums.

Moutoussamy-Ashe currently lives in New York City with her husband, Arthur Ashe, and their daughter, Camera. Much of her current work focuses on the Black family. She is a founding member of the Black Family Cultural Exchange, a group of African-American women from New York City and nearby Connecticut who have organized a series of successful book fairs for and about Black children. Profits are contributed to scholarship funds and to book funds for local community centers.

BIBLIOGRAPHY

Ashe, Arthur. *Getting Started in Tennis* (1977) (photographs by Jeanne Moutoussamy); Moutassamy-Ashe, Jeanne. Champions and Challengers Series: *Tracy Austin, Björn Borg, Franco Harris, Reggie Jackson* (1977-78), and *Daufauskie Island: A Photographic Essay* (1982), and *Viewfinders: Black Women Photographers* (1986); *New York Times.* "Style Makers" (March 3, 1991); *Songs of My People* (1991) (photographs by Jeanne Moutoussamy-Ashe).

ADELE LOGAN ALEXANDER

MUM BETT *see* FREEMAN, ELIZABETH

MURRAY, PAULI (1910-1985)

Pauli Murray, lawyer, teacher, poet, and minister, was also a strong advocate of women's rights. She once remarked, "I entered law school preoccupied with the racial struggle and single-mindedly bent upon becoming a civil rights lawyer but I graduated an unabashed feminist as well" (Murray 1956). She was nominated by the National Council of Negro Women as one of the twelve outstanding women in American life for the year 1945 and was named Woman of the Year by *Mademoiselle* magazine in 1947. Murray became a founding member of the National Organization for Women, formed in 1966.

Anna Pauline (Pauli was a nickname) Murray was born on November 20, 1910, in Baltimore, Maryland. Her parents, William Henry and Agnes Georgianna Fitzgerald Murray, were middle class and of mixed ancestry. In late March 1914, when she was three years old, Anna Murray's mother died. Since her father was unable to care for all six of his children, Anna Murray's mother's oldest sister, Pauline Fitzgerald Dame, adopted her and took her to live in North Carolina. Three years after her mother's death

A "freedom rider" in the 1940s and a student leader of sit-ins in Washington, D.C., restaurants, courageous attorney Pauli Murray was also a founding member of the National Organization for Women. [Schomburg Center]

her father was committed to a mental institution, where he remained until his death in 1923.

Murray attended the public schools in Durham, North Carolina. After graduation from Hillside High School in Durham in 1926, she attended Richmond Hill High School in New York City for one year in order to meet college entrance requirements. In September 1928, she entered Hunter College in New York City. Her years at Hunter were interrupted by the Depression and a brief marriage. She eventually earned an A.B. degree from Hunter College, graduating in January 1933.

In 1938, Murray unsuccessfully attempted to break the color line by applying for admission to graduate school at the University of North Carolina—Chapel Hill. She later was accepted at the Howard University Law School where she graduated in June 1944 with an LL.B. degree. She was first in her class and the only woman. Also in 1944, Murray applied to Harvard University Law School to study for an advanced law degree but was denied because the law school was not open to women. Instead she did a year of graduate study at the Boalt Hall of Law at the University of California at Berkeley, where she earned an LL.M. degree in 1945.

In 1965, Murray was the first Black person to be awarded a Doctor of Juridical Science degree from the Yale University Law School, with a dissertation entitled "Roots of the Racial Crisis: Prologue to Policy." She also received many honorary degrees.

Pauli Murray was a crusading human rights attorney, a teacher, a civil rights and women's rights activist, a poet and writer, and a priest. She was admitted to practice law in California, New York, and the U.S. Supreme Court. For nine months in 1946 she practiced law with the Commission on Law and Social Action, an agency of the American Jewish Congress. She later opened a private law practice in New York City, where she worked until 1960. From 1960 to 1961, she was a senior lecturer (the equivalent of a full professor) and taught the first course in constitutional and administrative law at the Ghana Law School in Accra. While in Accra she coauthored (with Leslie Rubin, a senior lecturer in law at the University College of Ghana) the first textbook in a series of books on law in Africa, *The Constitution and Government of Ghana* (1961). An earlier book, *States' Law on Race and Color* (1951), became an invaluable reference for civil rights lawyers. She served as vice president of Benedict College in South Carolina and a professor of law at Brandeis University in Waltham, Massachusetts.

Murray became active in the early civil rights movement during the New Deal. She was a freedom rider in the early 1940s and was arrested for protesting segregated seating on interstate buses. While at Howard University Law School she was one of the student leaders of the sit-ins in Washington, D.C., restaurants.

In 1972, at the age of sixty-two, Murray had a call to the Episcopal ministry and applied for admission to holy orders. She completed an M.Div. degree from General Theological Seminary in 1976 and was consecrated and ordained the first Black female priest of the Episcopal Church in 1977 at the National Cathedral in Washington, D.C.

In addition to her other achievements, Pauli Murray was a poet and writer. She authored an autobiography, *Song in a Weary Throat: An American Pilgrimage* (1987), *Proud Shoes: The Story of an American Family* (1956), *Dark Testament and Other Poems* (1970), and numerous monographs and articles.

Pauli Murray died on July 8, 1985 in Pittsburgh, Pennsylvania.

BIBLIOGRAPHY

EBA; Smith, Jessie Carey, ed. *Notable Black American Women* (1992); *WWBA*.

SYLVIA M. JACOBS

MUSLIM WOMEN

Any discussion of Black women who are Muslim must encompass their Islamic identity and situate their activities within the understandings of Muslim women in general. The primary belief of Muslims is based in the revelation of the Qur'an (the Glorious Recitation), which asserts that Islam is the *way* that God has given for the welfare of humanity. Muslims believe the Qur'an to be the last revelation, spoken to the Prophet Muhammad by God for the guidance of humanity. The Qur'an sits at the center of Islamic intellectual activity, from philosophy and jurisprudence to art and music. The first Muslim community is the paradigm for all Muslim communities.

Some of the principles of Islam are: (1) the belief that there is only one God; (2) the belief that God has provided every human community with guidance through prophets and scriptures (the Qur'an lists at least twenty-five prophets, including Jesus, in a line from Adam to Muhammad); (3) the belief that there will be a final accounting for earthly life; and (4) the belief that all Muslims are in a constant struggle (Jihad) within themselves to be Muslim. Believing in one God, praying five times daily, fasting, sharing wealth, and a possible once-a-lifetime pilgrimage become central in the continual remembrance of God.

The worldview of Muslim women anywhere in the world has at its center Islamic legal injunctions regarding women, which are focused primarily on marriage, divorce, inheritance, and ownership of property. Dress, although not a legal situation, is a cultural consideration whose social affirmation is rooted in theological tradition. In addition to these concerns, all Muslim women spend a great amount of time in spiritual practice. Common concerns for Muslim women include the practice of Islam, marriage, divorce, dress, the home, health, and travel.

Estimates of the number of Muslims (immigrant and indigenous) in the United States range from 3 to 9 million, depending on which source is consulted. In this article, the range of possibilities is used. Given this range, Muslims of African descent are said to account for between 30 percent and 50 percent of all Muslims in America. From this estimate, we can approximate the number of Black women who are Muslim to be between 200,000 and 900,000 on the lower end and 300,000 to 1.5 million on the higher end. There are at least 17 distinct Islamic communities in the United States to which these women belong. Because communities of Muslims of African descent have existed since the turn of the century, by 1970 there were, in some communities, families with three generations present. Contrary to popular understanding, many of these Black women who are Muslim did not belong to the Nation of Islam, and the communities to which they did belong have grown in large numbers in subsequent decades. Truly, Black women who are Muslim represent the diversity of Islam. They belong to Sunni, Shi'i, and Sufi communities, more specifically, Ansar, Ahmadi, Moorish Science, Sufi, Twelver Shi'i, Nation of Islam, American Muslim Mission, Fuqra, and university communities to name a few.

Women's Islamic practice differs little from that of men. Islam is very clear and specific about behaviors that are prohibited and practices that are obligatory. Women pray five times daily beginning before sunrise; they are exempted only during their menstrual cycles and immediately after childbirth for a period of up to forty days. Fasting during the month of Rahmadan (the month during which the Qur'an was revealed to Prophet Muhammad) is an obligation on all Muslims. Fasting during pregnancy is not encouraged and, in some communities, is actively discouraged. Women generally organize the providing of charity and set up the network for acknowledging need. They direct, along with men, the educational networks. The Hajj, the pilgrimage to Mecca, is an act of worship in which women participate if they are financially able and can secure a male escort, usually a husband or other male family member. Women go to the Friday congregational prayers at a Masjid (Mosque), usually near their homes. Although separated from men, most women do not find this to be a subjugating experience because they are not there to socialize but to pray.

Women's lives are lived inside a network of women, studying Islam, performing their religious obligations, working at careers, pursuing education, tending husbands and children. Islam places the greatest stress on the individual's accountability to God. Older women or those with infirmities are generally cared for by the community as a whole, as are widows. At the time of death, the body of a deceased woman is attended (washed, perfumed and prayed over) by women. Muslims are not embalmed (this is Islamic law); they are wrapped in a shroud and placed in a wooden casket and buried within three days of death. In some cities Muslims have burial grounds; in others, their families contract with cemeteries for plainly or unmarked graves.

It is this core of concerns that forms the framework around which the lives of Black women who are Muslim are structured and their experiences explained. Muslim girls are introduced early on to the traditional gender separation in Islam. Whether in the Masjid (Mosque), Muslim schools or at social events, gender separation is the norm. Girls learn quickly that their primary social contacts, their models for behavior and their teachers, will be women. At seven years of age, Muslim girls generally are encouraged to dress modestly, as this is the age when their training in making formal prayers and fasting begins. Black mothers who are Muslim generally keep their daughters close to them and accompany them in play or on outings. Most Muslim girls attend weekend Islamic studies classes taught by women where they learn how to perform prayers, read the Qur'an, and speak and read Arabic. The weekend schools (rarely composed of only one nationality) also provide an opportunity for women's community.

Puberty is a significant time in the lives of Black girls who are Muslim. They have learned their prayers, fasted for several years, and are now considered young women, accountable for their actions. Mothers are even more vigilant about their daughters' associations and, in some instances, begin to look around the community for a potential future husband. Casual social mixing of boys and girls is prohibited in order to safeguard the integrity of both. At puberty, girls are taught to exercise propriety in conversations, appearance, and behavior.

Morality emerges as a key issue and marriage as its testimony. The Qur'an asserts that marriage is foundational, and tradition asserts that marriage is half of faith. Marital age patterns among Black women who are Muslim follow those in the general Black community—young women and men marry soon after high school. There is, however, a stronger inclination for marriage in the Black Muslim community primarily because of prohibitions against dating and premarital sex. Black women who are Muslim generally marry using two traditions—Islamic and secular. Islamically, marriage is a contract that requires some negotiations prior to agreement. Women usually draw up their contracts in consultation with mothers and/or women from the community. Contracts include the request and stipulations of a dowry (a gift given to the bride, ranging from money to houses), the couple's living arrangements, educational and career considerations, and so on. After a contract is agreed upon and a date set, the accompanying ceremony can be held either in a home or at a Masjid (Mosque) with witnesses. Generally couples go to the local city hall to get a marriage license, either prior to or immediately following the religious ceremony.

Black women who are Muslim marry from all over the Muslim world in significant numbers. Among Black women who are Muslim, arranged marriages are rarely if ever enacted. Education and careers are actively sought by most Black women who are Muslim but not to the exclusion of marriage. There are no limits on the type of career a woman can pursue, except those generally thought to intrude upon the Islamic understanding of modesty. The problems that Black women who are Muslim have encountered in seeking an education or a career have, for the most part, been generated by the larger American community. Black women who are Muslim generally have been discriminated against both in educational institutions and the workplace due to their dress and their refusal to participate in social events.

Dress for Muslim women has several fundamental criteria; first and foremost it must be modest—loose-fitting garments that do not expose legs, chest area, and arms. The hair, by tradition, is covered in a variety of ways, usually depending on taste, from scarves to the more traditional veil that covers the breast as well as the hair. Black women who are Muslim feel that their modest dress protects them from unwanted advances from males and also, and perhaps more significantly, that it marks off their personal space. Most Muslim women in America create their dress by arranging Western styles, but they also purchase modest clothing from numerous Muslim stores owned by Muslims from other countries. Although there is definitely an American Muslim woman's dress, Black women who are Muslim are just as likely to wear clothes from Pakistan, Saudi Arabia, or Senegal.

The homes of Black women who are Muslim also reveal the centrality of Islam in their lives. Generally there is a great deal of framed Arabic calligraphy on the walls instead of pictures; bookcases are filled with Qur'ans and Hadith, texts on the sayings and actions of the Prophet Muhammad; and floors are covered in oriental rugs. Space is important in the Muslim home because the family is constantly making prayers. In some homes a room is set aside for this purpose, while in others there is a minimal amount of furniture so that prayers can be made anywhere. Shoe stands and baskets are kept near the door because outside shoes are not worn in the house. Cleaning is done continuously, also primarily because of formal prayers. Grocery shopping is a serious matter for Muslim women because they cannot buy food that contains pork or any of its by-products. Usually a group of women in the community continuously makes and updates lists of which products contain pork and then distributes the lists at the Masjid (Mosque).

Black women who are Muslim travel extensively throughout the Muslim world, as they have an expanded sense of community. With male guardians, they have made the pilgrimage to Mecca in increasing numbers since the 1970s. Some have taken their educational skills to Muslim countries in Africa to teach in schools, practice medicine, and to study Islamic sciences. All Muslim countries welcome them and their families, often providing financial support. Women engaged in import/export businesses travel to buy materials and artifacts. In an effort to get their children out of the drug culture of America, several Black women who are Muslim have opened schools specifically for Black American Muslim children in countries such as Senegal and the Sudan. Marriage to foreign Muslims also has significantly increased travel for Black women who are Muslim. Women work in all areas of U.S. industry, from television broadcasting, to medicine, education, business, and engineering.

Health care elicits a variety of concerns among Black women who are Muslim. They prefer Muslim female physicians first and then female physicians who are at least willing to understand the cultural difference. Generally, Black women who are Muslim prefer homeopathic medicines and home remedies, and they are users of midwives and birthing centers. Hospital stays are accompanied by the normal anxieties plus the additional apprehension of being different.

BIBLIOGRAPHY

Abdul-Rauf, Muhammad. *The Islamic View of Women and the Family* (1977); Haddad, Yvonne Y., ed. *Muslim Communities in America* (1991); Haneef, Suzanne. *What Everyone Should Know about Islam and Muslims* (1979).

BEVERLY McCLOUD

MUTUAL BENEFIT SOCIETIES

Theory and practice neatly converge in explaining the critical presence of women among the ubiquitous mutual benefit societies in African-American history. In theory, the millions of Black women who organized and participated in these societies were giving institutional life to traditional gender roles associated with religion, sickness, death, education, household economies, social welfare, and above all, family and kinship—what Herbert Gutman (1976) identified as a web of social obligations reaching back to family and gender responsibilities in Africa. In practice, these obligations became a social fortress against the crushing weight of American racism and slavery, producing a symbolic, but nonetheless protective, African-American kinship system that embraced non-related, fictive kin who turned to one another as brothers and sisters in need of mutual assistance. Family became community and vice versa—the perfect precondition for the vast array of voluntary associations that freedwomen and freedmen would usher in after emancipation.

Before emancipation, organized mutual aid, like organized religion, took place in two worlds: the visible and the invisible, the world the free Blacks made, and the world the slaves made. Given the importance of women in African mutual aid, it is inconceivable that first-generation African-American slave women did not transfer these social assignments to the New World, where the need was all the more urgent and extensive. The African connection may have been lost from consciousness over time, but the "female slave network," emphasized by Deborah Gray White (1985) as a cultural mainstay on American plantations, evolved pragmatically as a less formal but widespread system of community cooperation, especially in regard to collective care for children, the sick, and the elderly.

The Independent Order of St. Luke was founded in 1867 by an ex-slave, Mary Prout. By 1899, the order had fallen on hard times, and might have ceased to exist had it not been for Maggie Lena Walker. Under her leadership, by 1920 the Order of St. Luke had more than 100,000 members in twenty-eight states and had created the St. Luke Penny Savings Bank, a weekly newspaper, and a department store, and generally had become a collective force to reckon with in Richmond, Virginia, where the organization was headquartered. Pictured here is their office force. [National Park Service]

In the meantime, free Black men and women could afford to organize a more visible infrastructure of mutual aid. As a rule, mutual benefit societies, like most other Black institutions, came out of the church. Sometimes it was the other way around, with the mutual benefit society, an institution nearly as basic as the family, taking the lead. The African Methodist Episcopal Church, for example, evolved out of the Free African Society, a mutual assistance organization founded in 1787 by the free Black citizens of Philadelphia to provide their community the rudiments of social welfare. In 1793, the welfare functions of the Free African Society were absorbed by the Female Benevolent Society of St. Thomas, one of hundreds of such societies organized by free Black women in antebellum cities. By 1838 there were 119 mutual aid societies in Philadelphia alone, more than half of which were female associations, and women made up nearly two-thirds of the membership of all benefit societies. A sample of the earliest established female societies in Philadelphia would include the Benevolent Daughters (1796), the Daughters of Africa (1812), the American Female Bond Benevolent Society of Bethel (1817), the Female Benezet (1818), and the Daughters of Aaron (1819).

In general, benefit societies collected dues, which they distributed among their members to relieve the sick and to bury the dead. Just as often, especially in church-related societies, their activities embraced a larger commitment to community uplift and moral reform. Surely this was the case with the Female Wesleyan Association of Baltimore, or New York City's Abyssinian Benevolent Daughters of Esther, as well as another New York society, the African Dorcas Association, founded in 1827 for the expressed purpose of providing clothing for Black school children. The Colored Female Charitable Society of Boston (1832) pledged itself to "mitigate [the] sufferings" of widows and orphans. The African Female Benevolent Society of Newport, Rhode Island, sponsored that city's school for Black children from 1809 until 1842 when Newport finally opened a public school. In neighboring Massachusetts, the Colored Female Religious and Moral Society of Salem (for dues of 52¢ per year) offered weekly prayer, religious conversation, profitable reading, and friendly advice along with sickness and death benefits to members who would "resolve to be charitably watchful over each other" and not "commit any scandalous sin, or walk unruly" (Sterling 1984). The 1846 charter of the New Orleans Colored Female Benevolent Society of Louisiana, in addition to providing insurance benefits, called for the "suppression of vice and inculcation of virtue among the colored class" (Curry 1981). The Female Lundy Society in Albany and its sister institution in Cincinnati, both founded in the 1840s, combined antislavery with social welfare. Indeed, with the rapid expansion in the number and variety of Black organizations, especially after 1830, the lines of demarcation among moral reform movements, political protest groups, mutual benefit societies, secret lodges, insurance associations, credit unions, orphanages, schools, library companies, and literary societies became difficult to discern. There existed at once a division of labor and a melding of functions—the sacred, the secular, and the sororal—in order to serve the all-encompassing purpose of racial deliverance.

This distinctive mission widened into a war for survival after emancipation. The invisible became visible; self-help and racial solidarity coincided with the advancing career of Jim Crow; hence, as four million ex-slaves sought institutional support and expression, voluntary associations among Black women multiplied by the thousands. At the turn of the twentieth century, W.E.B. Du Bois's pioneering studies in sociology uncovered so many mutual aid societies that he found it "impractical to catalog them" (Du Bois 1899). Among women in the black belt of Alabama, Du Bois concluded that "The woman who is not a member of one of these [benevolent societies] is pitied and considered rather out of date" (Du Bois 1898). In Petersburg, Virginia, Du Bois gave up after listing twenty-two mutual benefit societies, at least half of which were women's associations like the Sisters of Friendship, the Ladies Union, the Ladies Working Club, the Daughters of Zion, the Daughters of Bethlehem, the Loving Sisters, and the Sisters of Rebeccah. It was in nearby Richmond, however, that the mutual benefit society among Black women assumed its highest stage of development in a century-long evolution from folk networks among female slaves to national organizations among professional women.

By the close of Reconstruction, Black women in Richmond had organized twenty-five "female benevolent orders" (Rabinowitz 1978). Doubtless, the most important among these was the Independent Order of St. Luke, which had expanded to Richmond from Baltimore, where it had been founded in 1867 by an ex-slave, Mary Prout. By 1899, the order had fallen on hard times, and might have expired had it not come under the leadership of Maggie Lena Walker. Born in Richmond (1867), Walker had been active in the Order of St. Luke since the age of fourteen, while also teaching in Richmond's public schools and helping to found an insurance company, the Woman's Union. It was the Order of St. Luke, however, that became the instrument of her vision for community development. By 1920, with more than 100,000 members in twenty-eight states, the order had created the St. Luke Penny Savings Bank; a weekly newspaper, the *St. Luke Herald*; a department store, the St. Luke Emporium; and generally had emerged as a collective force to reckon with in Richmond. Walker and St. Luke women, for example, funded scholarships, helped to found a school for delinquent girls, fought for women's suffrage, protested racial disfranchisement, denounced lynching, and took the lead in the 1904 boycott against Richmond's segregated streetcars. The Order of St. Luke (which included men) represented a holistic movement guided by Walker's "womanist" consciousness, wherein "dichotomous thinking" about domestic vs. public, male vs. female, and Black vs. female had little meaning in a historic struggle that subsumed antithetical notions of race and gender (Brown 1989).

The Order of St. Luke symbolized a major transition in the evolution of African-American institutions. By the turn of the twentieth century, the functions of the benefit society increasingly passed into the more modern and secular hands of Black insurance companies, savings banks, settlement houses, hospitals, civil rights organizations, and government agencies. However, many of these functions passed into the caring hands of Black clubwomen who, as descendants of the mutual aid tradition, continued to offer substance and hope in the vast spaces where modern institutions seldom reached. The connection between the Daughters of Africa and the National Association of Colored Women may not have been direct, nor perfectly aligned across the social strata, but it was nonetheless linear and ran through the Independent Order of St. Luke and thousands of earlier such societies who also lifted as they climbed.

BIBLIOGRAPHY

Berkeley, Kathleen C. " 'Colored Ladies also Contributed': Black Women's Activities from Benevolence to Social Welfare, 1866-1896." In *The Web of Southern Social Relations: Women, Family, and Education*, ed. Walter J. Fraser, et al. (1985); Brown, Elsa Barkley. "Womanist Consciousness: Maggie Lena Walker and the Independent Order of St. Luke," *Signs: Journal of Women in Culture and Society* (Spring 1989); Curry, Leonard P. *The Free Black in Urban America, 1800-1850* (1981); Du Bois, W.E.B. *The Philadelphia Negro: A Social Study* (1899), and *Some Efforts of American Negroes for Their Own Social Betterment* (1898); Giddings, Paula. *When and Where I Enter: The Impact of Black Women on Race and Sex in America* (1984); Gutman, Herbert G. *The Black Family in Slavery and Freedom, 1750 1925* (1976); Henderson, Alexa Benson. *Atlanta Life Insurance Company: Guardian of Black Economic Dignity* (1990); Hine, Darlene Clark. *When the Truth Is Told: A History of Black Women's Culture and Community in Indiana, 1875-1950* (1981); Jones, Jacqueline. *Labor of Love, Labor of Sorrow: Black Women, Work, and the Family from Slavery to the Present* (1985); Meier, August. *Negro Thought in America, 1880-1915* (1963); Neverdon-Morton, Cynthia. *Afro-American Women of the South and the Advancement of the Race, 1895-1925* (1989); Rabinowitz, Howard N. *Race Relations in the Urban South, 1865-1890* (1978); Salem, Dorothy. *To Better Our World: Black Women in Organized Reform, 1890-1920* (1990); Scott, Anne Firor. "Most Invisible of All: Black Women's Voluntary Associations," *Journal of Southern History* (February 1990); Shaw, Stephanie J. "Black Club Women and the Creation of the National Association of Colored Women," *Journal of Women's History* (Fall 1991); Smith, Susan. " 'Sick and Tired of Being Sick and Tired': Black Women and the National Negro Health Movement, 1915-1950," Ph.D. diss. (1991); Sterling, Dorothy, ed. *We Are Your Sisters: Black Women in the Nineteenth Century* (1984); Terborg-Penn, Rosalyn and Sharon Harley, eds. *The Afro-American Woman: Struggle and Images* (1978); Weare, Walter B. *Black Business in the New South: A Social History of the North Carolina Mutual Life Insurance Company* (1973); White, Deborah Gray. *Ar'n't I a Woman? Female Slaves in the Plantation South* (1985).

WALTER WEARE

N

NAPIER, NETTIE LANGSTON (1861-1938)

Nettie Langston Napier worked hard as the president of the Day Homes Club and as a member of the National Association of Colored Women (NACW) to help meet the needs of families who faced discrimination and economic hardship. Although her own life was free of economic deprivation, Napier was a generous philanthropist dedicated to improving life for all Black people.

Born on June 17, 1861, in Oberlin, Ohio, Nettie DeElla Langston was the daughter of Caroline M. (Wall) Langston and John Mercer Langston. John Langston was the son of white plantation owner Ralph Quarles and his mistress, a woman of Indian and African-American descent. He went on to become a prominent lawyer and founder and head of Howard University's law school. He is considered by many to have been one of the first great Black orators, second only to Frederick Douglass. Both of Nettie Langston's parents were educated at Oberlin College.

When Nettie was nine years old, the family moved from Oberlin to Washington, D.C., where she attended public schools and then Howard University. After one year at Howard, she transferred to her hometown in order to complete her education in music, attending the Oberlin conservatory from 1876 to 1878. In 1878, she married James Carroll Napier.

The couple probably lived in Nashville, Tennessee, where James Napier had grown up, before moving to Washington, D.C., in 1910. The Napiers had one adopted daughter, Carrie Langston Napier.

In Washington, the Napiers lived in the historic Hillside Cottage located at Fourth and Bryant streets near Howard University. The couple moved within an elite social circle. Booker T. Washington was a close friend, and he would make their home his headquarters whenever he was in the city. James Napier rose within his profession, the law, and, as a Republican, became prominent within political circles at the local and national levels. Nettie Langston Napier was considered a dedicated wife and mother and an elegant, stately hostess. In 1913, however, following James Napier's resignation from his two-year office in the Register of the Treasury in protest against President Woodrow Wilson's policy on segregation, the couple returned to Nashville.

In Nashville, James Napier dedicated himself to the One Cent Savings Bank (later Citizen's Savings Bank) in which he was an investor, while Nettie Napier focused on community concerns. As in many other cities, numerous children in Nashville were left unattended at home while their parents were at work. Napier believed these children needed food, health care, and training, and in order to accomplish these tasks she proposed the establishment of the Day Homes Club, a Black women's organization designed to help meet the needs of poor communities in a manner similar to that of the Phyllis Wheatley Club, which was associated with the City Federation of Colored Women's Clubs.

The club was formed in 1907, with Napier as its president. It was housed at 618 Fourth Avenue South, later known as Porter Homestead. On January 14, 1907, a meeting of interested women supporters framed a constitution; elected officers; appointed Josie E. Wells, a specialist in diseases of women and children, as physician-in-charge; and decided to seek a woman superintendent for the home as well as vice presidents for the city's wards. The following month, Napier convened a large meeting of Black women to debate the day home concept in Nashville and to generate interest in her organization. After a general discussion of contemporary issues involving women, such as temperance and education, Napier delivered the key item on the agenda, her presentation on neglected children.

Initially daytime hours were set for the home, but it soon became apparent that because of irregular work hours, arrangements would have to be made to keep some children overnight; thus, some ten to twelve children became boarders. Although there was a pressing need for the home, and even though the local newspapers were more than sympathetic, within eighteen months the home was in financial trouble. Food and clothing were badly needed. The club needed more members in order to receive adequate funding. Napier said in an article published in *The Globe* on October 30, 1908, that although the club was trying desperately to raise enough money to keep the day home running, it would be forced to close if further contributions did not arrive. It should have been possible to secure funding for the home, but enough contributions were not forthcoming. The exact date—and the exact cause—of the day home's closure have yet to be established.

Napier's community efforts did not stop with the failure of this venture, however. Having been instrumental in bringing the NACW to Nashville in 1897, she attended their meeting in Buffalo in 1901 and was thereafter an active member of the organization. She held various positions in the NACW national body, including auditor and national treasurer. She served on many of the organization's most important committees and was president of the Douglass Memorial Fund. Napier also was chairperson of the executive committees of the New Idea Club and the City Federation. Her work as head of the Committee of Colored Women assisted the Red Cross campaign during World War I.

Nettie Langston Napier died on September 27, 1938, at her home in Nashville. She is buried in Nashville's Greenwood Cemetery.

BIBLIOGRAPHY
Davis, Elizabeth Lindsay. *Lifting as They Climb* (1933); *The Globe* (Nashville). "Meeting of the Day Home Club" (October 30, 1908), and "Women's Meeting Held in the Interest of 'Day Home' Project" (February 22, 1907), and "Emancipation Anniversary" (January 11, 1907; January 18, 1907); Langston, John Mercer. *From the Virginia Plantation to the National Capitol* (1898); *NBAW*; Neverdon-Morton, Cynthia. *Afro-American Women of the South and the Advancement of Race, 1895-1925* (1989); Washington, Margaret Murray. "The Beginnings of the National Club Movement: Club Work Among Negro Women." In *Black Women in White America*, ed. Gerda Lerner (1972); Wesley, Charles Harris. *The History of the National Association of Colored Women's Clubs: A Legacy of Service* (1984).

FENELLA MACFARLANE

NASH, DIANE (1938-)

Civil rights activist Diane Nash was born on May 15, 1938, in Chicago and grew up on the city's South Side with her mother and stepfather, Dorothy and John Baker. Nash was raised Roman Catholic, attended parochial elementary school, and then Hyde Park High School. She attended Howard University for a year and then transferred to Fisk University in Nashville, Tennessee.

Moving to Nashville was a pivotal experience for Nash, who had never before experienced the horrors of southern segregation. Feeling stifled, she began looking for a group that was fighting segregation and found James Lawson's workshops on nonviolence. At first, she was unconvinced by nonviolence as an approach to political and social change, but as the Nashville movement began to use it, Nash saw its power. Her own commitments had their roots and basis in Christianity, and Nash became an activist who saw nonviolence not only as a tactic but also as a lifestyle. She was elected chairperson of the Student Central Committee in Nashville, and they began organizing sit-ins at Woolworth, Walgreen, Kress, and two department stores. As a leader in the Nashville movement, Nash attended the first meeting of the Student Nonviolent Coordinating Committee (SNCC) in Raleigh, North Carolina, April 16-18, 1960, and was elected to the committee. Nash was not elected chair of the (temporary) committee only because she came late to the meeting, and Marion

Barry, another Nashville student, had already been elected.

In February 1961, Nash was one of eleven students to be jailed in Rock Hill, South Carolina, the first group to go to jail and refuse to pay bail. The students spent one month in jail, a time of personal growth for the group. Nash, along with the Nashville group, also mobilized to keep the Freedom Rides going after the Congress of Racial Equality (CORE) pulled out. Nash was elected coordinator for the SNCC rides, which meant she had to stay out of jail and coordinate student efforts and act as liaison with the press and the U.S. Justice Department. In August

1961, SNCC, after a heated discussion, decided to develop two agendas: Diane Nash was to head direct action, and Charles Jones was to coordinate voter registration.

Also in 1961, Diane Nash married James Bevel, another civil rights activist, and they moved to Jackson, Mississippi, where they continued to organize. Expecting her first baby and facing a two-and-a-half-year jail sentence, Nash decided to turn herself in at the end of April 1962 and have her baby in jail in order to keep with the movement's idea of "jail-no-bail" and to dramatize the situation of Black Americans in the South. The judge chose not to sentence her on

One of the original members of the Student Nonviolent Coordinating Committee, Diane Nash was in the first group of students to go to jail and refuse bail. Later, Nash joined the staff of the Southern Christian Leadership Conference. Her civil rights work eventually led her to the peace movement and later to the women's movement. [State Historical Society of Wisconsin]

that longer charge but instead convicted her for refusing to move to the back of the courtroom. Sherrilynn was born on August 5, 1962, in Albany, Georgia, where Bevel was working for the Southern Christian Leadership Conference (SCLC). Nash joined the staff of SCLC in 1962-63 and became a field staff organizer. She and Bevel made an effective organizing team; their ideas were instrumental in initiating the 1963 march on Washington and the 1964-65 Selma campaign. For their work, Nash and Bevel together received SCLC's highest award in 1965, the Rosa Parks Award. Their second child, Douglass, was born on May 15, 1964.

Diane Nash's civil rights work led her to the peace movement, and at the end of 1966 she traveled with a group of women from the United States to North Vietnam. Her trip to Vietnam coincided with the rising feminist movement, and the combination profoundly affected Nash's growing feminism. She continued her political work through the 1970s, 1980s, and into the 1990s in Chicago, doing tenant organizing, welfare support, and housing advocacy. She has one granddaughter and one grandson.

[See also STUDENT NONVIOLENT COORDINATING COMMITTEE.]

BIBLIOGRAPHY

Nash, Diane. "Inside the Sit-ins and Freedom Rides: Testimony of a Southern Student." In *The New Negro*, ed. Matthew Ahmann (1961); Powledge, Fred. *Free at Last? The Civil Rights Movement and the People Who Made It* (1991).

JEANNE THEOHARIS

NASH, HELEN E. (1921-)

"Sell a house and send her to medical school," said Helen Nash's grandfather on his death bed in 1941. A successful Atlanta property owner, he knew that one of his assets would be enough to support her for the first year. Though her father was a physician, he was skeptical of his daughter's commitment to medicine. Supporting Helen Nash's medical education proved a wise investment with a rich return. In 1989, Dr. Helen Nash celebrated her fortieth anniversary in practice. During those years, she became a distinguished pediatrician and child advocate. Now Clinical Professor of Pediatrics at the Washington University School of Medicine, in 1949 she was the only woman among the first four Black doctors to integrate the medical staff there.

Helen Nash was born on August 8, 1921. She grew up in a prosperous family where education and culture were highly valued. Her father was Homer Erwin Nash, M.D., and her mother was Marie Graves Nash, a music teacher. A graduate of Spelman College in her native Atlanta, and of Meharry Medical College in Nashville, Helen Nash performed well academically. Despite harsh discrimination against Black Americans and women in medicine, she was determined to become a physician, and her upbringing and education had given her the self-confidence necessary to succeed.

In 1945, she arrived in St. Louis to take a rotating internship at Homer G. Phillips Hospital, one of the few institutions in the country then offering postgraduate training to minority physicians. Opened in 1937 as a segregated hospital to serve the Black community, "Homer G." (as it was known) was famous for giving young doctors superb clinical experience. Dr. Nash worked on twelve services during her internship year and took three additional years of residency training in pediatrics. There she met Dr. Park J. White, the senior supervising pediatrician from the Washington University School of Medicine. Unlike many colleagues at this time, he felt a deep commitment to improving medical care for Black children. Concerned about the rate of Black infant mortality since 1924, when he surveyed the problem in St. Louis, White saw a great need for well-trained Black physicians and immediately saw Helen Nash's promise. He encouraged her to become board-certified, and she passed the examination without difficulty.

Despite differences in age, race, and gender, an extraordinary collaboration developed between these two pediatricians. By 1947, they had helped mobilize some of the pressure necessary to integrate St. Louis Children's Hospital, the city's major pediatric teaching institution. They pressed successfully for improved standards of care and hygiene at Homer Phillips Hospital—where newborns were still sleeping in partitioned group spaces, rather than in individual bassinets. Supported by funds from the U.S. Children's Bureau, Dr. White and Dr. Nash raised standards and lowered mortality. The mean details of segregation infuriated Dr. Nash. Sick Black children received no ice cream, and bananas only on rare occasions, while they were routinely given to other pediatric patients at City Hospital No. 1. She took pride in confronting bureaucrats to change this policy. By 1949, as a result of her work with Dr. White, the premature babies' death rate had dropped from 80 percent to 16 percent.

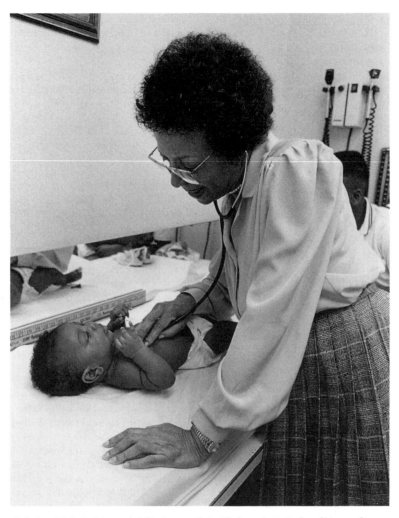

A distinguished physician and child advocate, Helen Nash revolutionized conditions at St. Louis Children's Hospital. [Tom Heine]

Infant mortality remains a major concern for Helen Nash today. She is indignant that infants in the United States die more often than children in twenty-two other nations, with Black babies dying at twice the rate of others—a ratio that has not changed since her mentor, Dr. White, surveyed the problem in 1924. Over her long career Dr. Nash has built both a thriving practice and an outstanding reputation as a child advocate. When many local physicians moved to the suburbs, she continued to maintain a busy office in downtown St. Louis where she now treats her third generation of patients. Some families who have moved to outlying areas bring their youngsters back to her for care. Dr. Nash's bonds with children are all-inclusive; her concerns reach well beyond the confines of private practice. As a 1976 honor citation from the St. Louis Medical Society states: "She has given of her time and herself unstintingly throughout her career in improving the health of all children regardless of socioeconomic or ethnic status." In 1974, she spent six weeks developing rural health clinics in the Philippines because, as she said in an interview: "I had always been envious of Peace Corps volunteers and wanted to see if I could do something like that myself."

Dr. Nash has a long record of commitment to family planning services for the Black community and sees no conflict between this and her role as a pediatrician. Indeed, she feels a special responsibility to make sure that children are born to parents ready to nurture them. Her pediatric practice extends beyond adolescence, when necessary, and includes the provision of contraceptive counseling because, as she says, "By the time an adolescent is pregnant, it's already too late."

She calls herself a "rabid feminist," and believes that women must learn to speak up for themselves. She has been a powerful role model for many; indeed an unusual number of former women patients have become physicians. Others have achieved success in various fields, among them Harry Hampton (the well-known producer of *Eyes on the Prize*, a documentary film history of the civil rights movement). At her fortieth anniversary celebration, he said: "Helen's life is a broad, rich quilt. She is a pioneer for both her race and her gender. . . . Our chief want in life is to find someone who can help us to do what we can—Helen is that for many. . . . She is a long-distance runner, who connects the now to then and to what will be."

In addition to her responsibilities at the Washington University School of Medicine, Helen Nash holds an Honor Membership in the St. Louis Medical Society, is a member of the American Medical Association, the Missouri State Medical Association, and the St. Louis Pediatric Society. She is a trustee of the St. Louis Symphony and a trustee of the Missouri Botanical Gardens. In 1992, she also received two honorary degrees: a Doctor of Humane Letters from Webster University and a Doctor of Humane Letters from the University of Missouri in St. Louis.

BIBLIOGRAPHY

Nash, Helen. Personal interviews.

MARION HUNT

NATIONAL ASSOCIATION FOR THE ADVANCEMENT OF COLORED PEOPLE

Women played a large part in the early development of the National Association for the Advancement of Colored People (NAACP), founded in 1909. Among the more well-known Black women activists were Ida B. Wells-Barnett of Chicago, Illinois, Mary Church Terrell and Nannie Helen Burroughs of Washington, D.C., and Mary McLeod Bethune of Daytona Beach, Florida. These women used existing social and community organizations established by Black women to generate and sustain the NAACP's membership.

Until recently, few scholars have focused on the importance of women's roles in the association. Usually historical accounts of the NAACP focus on its male membership—most noticeably on the prominent scholar W.E.B. Du Bois. However, there is a growing body of work documenting the crucial early contributions of women to this organization.

In 1905, a select group of concerned, prominent Black and white American citizens were prompted by W.E.B. Du Bois to begin a civil rights organization known as the Niagara Movement. Although the Niagara Movement had a predominantly Black male membership, it also hosted a women's auxiliary whose members included Maria Baldwin, Carrie Clifford, and Mary White Ovington. Ovington was possibly the only participating white woman. Members of the Niagara Movement pushed for social equality and voting rights for Black Americans. Within about four years of its founding, the organization faced bankruptcy and was forced to dissolve. Its members, however, remained dedicated to the cause of civil rights for Black Americans, and they became some of the earliest members of the NAACP.

The NAACP began in response to a horrible race riot in Springfield, Illinois, in 1908. Socialist southern journalist William English Walling wrote an article about the riot in the *Independent* newspaper and challenged his readers to come forth and join forces to combat the rampant racism. Oswald Garrison Villard, the liberal activist grandson of famed abolitionist William Lloyd Garrison, was among the white supporters who responded to Walling's article. Villard was editor of the *New York Evening Post*. He issued what is referred to as "the call," inviting those who believed in justice for all in a true democracy to attend a national meeting. Sixty men and women signed the call. One-third were women, but only two were Black women (Mary Church Terrell and Ida B. Wells-Barnett). Among those who responded to the call were several Black activists and educators such as W.E.B. Du Bois and Francis Grimké. Many white philanthropists and social activists, including Mary White Ovington, Jane Addams, William Walling, and William Dean Howells, signed the document as well. Although the majority of executive office holders were white, this generally did not diminish the Black members' commitment to the association.

One of the chief concerns of the newly founded organization was the issue of lynching. The early years of the twentieth century were plagued with reported and unreported lynchings of Blacks. These heinous crimes not only were inflicted on usually innocent Black men but also on Black women and children. Between 1909 and 1917, antilynching crusader Ida B. Wells-Barnett became increasingly disgusted with the NAACP's approach to this problem. Wells-Barnett thought the association was far too lenient concerning lynching. Moreover, Wells-Barnett disliked the dominance of white leadership in the NAACP, in part because she thought they were insensitive to the impact of lynching on Black Americans.

Women played important roles in the NAACP, at all levels. Modjeska Simkins (right) was elected secretary of the South Carolina state organization in 1939, when James M. Hinton (left) was elected president. Under their leadership, the state organization launched several court cases to establish equality for Black Americans, including Briggs v. Elliot, *which ultimately was combined with* Brown v. Board of Education. *Thurgood Marshall (center) was the NAACP's attorney for this case. [Barbara Woods]*

Kathryn Johnson, a Black woman, served as the first field secretary for the NAACP from 1910 to 1916. Johnson's work was strictly voluntary until 1914. After a few disagreements with the national office, Kathryn Johnson resigned her position. It was not until 1920 that a Black man, James Weldon Johnson, held a key position in the NAACP as national field secretary.

Several Black women successfully pooled their talents to work with established women's club networks and the NAACP. For example, Mary Talbert, a key clubwoman from Buffalo, New York, served as president of the Empire State Federation of Colored Women and worked for a branch organization of the NAACP at the same time. Talbert was well trained in fund-raising techniques and membership recruitment. Her skills contributed to the record growth in the number of branch organizations between 1909 and 1920.

During the early years of the NAACP, many Black women served in various capacities to boost its membership, raise funds, increase its social and community service, and implement the association's commitment to woman's suffrage. Educators Mary McLeod Bethune and Nannie Helen Burroughs remained on the board of advisors for at least three decades. In 1920, Catherine Lealtad became the assistant director of branch organizations. Lealtad had previous experience working with the Young Women's Christian Association (YWCA). Once again, a Black woman used her previous administrative and organizational talents to nurture the development of the NAACP.

The early women workers in the NAACP established a tradition of excellence that was maintained by women such as Daisy Lampkin of Pittsburgh, Pennsylvania, Ella Baker of New York, and, much later, Daisy Bates of Little Rock, Arkansas. The Black women who worked with the NAACP were dedicated to the cause of securing civil rights for all—men and women. The NAACP was largely a grass-roots organization that used its existing community, church, and professional networks to sell subscriptions to the association's official news publication, the *Crisis*. The *Crisis*, which began publication in 1910, was available at the subscription price of 10¢ a copy or $1 a year—affordable even for those with low or modest incomes.

In 1914, the NAACP instituted the renowned Spingarn Award, the brainchild of Joel E. Spingarn, who was then chairman of the NAACP board of directors. The award was established to honor African-Americans who have excelled in their vocation. A modest number of women have been recipients of this medal; many of them were members or officers of the NAACP. Past female recipients include Mary B. Talbert (1922), Mary McLeod Bethune (1935), Daisy Bates and the Little Rock Nine (1958), and Rosa L. Parks (1979).

Black women remain a strong presence in the NAACP. Within the past decade and into the 1990s, women occupy a significant number of local and executive positions within the association.

BIBLIOGRAPHY

Duster, Alfreda M. *Crusade for Justice: The Autobiography of Ida B. Wells* (1970); Finch, Minnie. *The NAACP: Its Fight for Justice* (1981); Fishel, Leslie H., Jr., and Benjamin Quarles, eds. *The Black American: A Brief Documentary History* (1970); Giddings, Paula. *When and Where I Enter: The Impact of Black Women on Race and Sex in America* (1984); Kellogg, Charles Flint. *NAACP: A History of the National Association for the Advancement of Colored People* (1967); Neverdon-Morton, Cynthia. *Afro-American Women of the South and the Advancement of the Race, 1895-1925* (1989); Lerner, Gerda, ed. *Black Women in White America: A Documentary History* (1973); Osofsky, Gilbert, ed. *The Burden of Race: A Documentary History of Negro-White Relations in America* (1968); Rouse, Jacqueline Anne. *Lugenia Burns Hope: Black Southern Reformer* (1989); Salem, Dorothy. *To Better Our World: Black Women in Organized Reform, 1890-1920* (1990); Terrell, Mary Church. *A Colored Woman in a White World* (1940); Zangrando, Robert. *The NAACP Crusade against Lynching, 1909-1950* (1980). The National Association for the Advancement of Colored People (NAACP) papers are in the Manuscript Division, Library of Congress, Washington, D.C. These materials contain board meeting minutes, annual reports, branch meeting notes, and miscellaneous correspondence. See also the eightieth anniversary edition of *Crisis* (January 1989), particularly the reprinted essay by Mary White Ovington, "How the NAACP Began," Felicia Kessel's "The NAACP: The History of a Promise," and "NAACP Highlights, 1909-1988."

LISA BETH HILL

NATIONAL ASSOCIATION OF COLORED GRADUATE NURSES

At the end of the nineteenth century the status of Black nurses was appalling. Throughout the United States they were denied adequate training. They were kept out of most hospital and private duty nursing. When they found employment, they were paid significantly lower wages than white nurses. They were not allowed to serve as nurses in the armed forces. Their inferior status in the profession was reinforced by separate state board examinations and exclusion from nursing organizations. Worst of all, they had to stand by helplessly as their own people were denied health care which they themselves could have provided.

On August 25, 1908, a group of fifty-two Black graduate nurses met at St. Mark's Methodist Church in New York City to try to change these conditions. The force behind the gathering was Martha Franklin, from New Haven, Connecticut. She had recently surveyed hundreds of Black nurses about their professional situations and the results had made her decide that they must take matters into their own hands. Franklin was elected president of the organization at that first meeting, and the major issues were aired. When the women left, they had three goals: to advance the standards and best interests of trained nurses, to break down discrimination in the nursing profession, and to develop leadership within the ranks of Black nurses. They were also fiercely determined to improve health care for Black patients.

In the years that followed, the National Association of Colored Graduate Nurses (NACGN) battled on all fronts. In 1909, the organization set out to destroy the practice of separate state boards of nursing. One member, Ludie A. Andrews, instituted legal proceedings against the state of Georgia and fought for the next ten years for the right to sit for the same professional licensing examination as her white peers. In 1917, the organization created a national registry of Black graduate nurses to help its members find employment, especially private duty employment. In 1920, it began a campaign to improve Black-operated nursing schools.

In 1934, the NACGN established a national headquarters and hired a nurse executive secretary, Mabel Keaton Staupers. Two years later, three Black schools of nursing were accredited by the New York State Board of Nurse Examiners. In the same year, a public health nursing program for graduate Black nurses was established at St. Phillip Hospital in Richmond, Virginia.

In the years that followed, the NACGN worked for legislation that would improve the lot of its members and the Black community as a whole. In 1943, it supported an amendment to the Bolton Bill for the creation of the Cadet Nurse Corps, ensuring that Black nursing students would be able to join the corps. More than 2,000 Black students had participated by the war's end. The organization also worked with the army, pressuring it to drop its restrictions against Black nurses. As a result, more than 500 Black nurses served in the army in World War II. The

In 1908, fifty-two Black graduate nurses met in New York City and formed the National Association of Colored Graduate Nurses to address the inferior status of Black women in the nursing profession. In 1934, the NACGN established a national headquarters and hired Mabel Keaton Staupers as nurse executive secretary. It was Staupers, who later became president of the organization, who spearheaded the fight to eliminate quotas for Black nurses in the U.S. army and navy nurse corps. [Schomburg Center]

group was less successful with the navy, in which only four Black nurses served.

The final obstacle to full participation in professional nursing was the American Nurses' Association (ANA). By 1949, through the efforts of the NACGN, only nine states and the District of Columbia still barred Black nurses from their local ANA chapters, and provisions had been made for individuals to bypass those chapters and join the ANA directly.

On January 25, 1951, the board of directors of the National Association of Colored Graduate Nurses, having decided that its job was done, voted itself out of existence.

[*See also* NURSING.]

BIBLIOGRAPHY

Carnegie, Mary Elizabeth. *The Path We Tread: Blacks in Nursing, 1854-1984* (1986); Durham, Claudia Marie. "Opinions of Selected Negro Nurses Concerning Inter-Group Race Relations in Hospitals," Master's thesis (1955); Hine, Darlene Clark. *Black Women in White: Racial Conflict and Cooperation in the Nursing Profession, 1890-1950* (1989); Ravitz, Mel J. "Integration of Nurses: A Latent Function of Hospital Discrimination," *Phylon* (Fall 1955); Robinson, Alice M. "Black Nurses Tell You: Why So Few Blacks in Nursing," *RN* (July 1972); Staupers, Mabel Keaton. *No Time for Prejudice: A Story of the Integration of Negroes in Nursing in the United States* (1961); Thoms, Adah B. *Pathfinders: A History of the Progress of Colored Graduate Nurses* (1929).

MARIE MOSLEY

NATIONAL ASSOCIATION OF COLORED WOMEN

The national club movement developed as a response to increasingly complicated social welfare demands on community resources, a reaction to the growing racism of the late nineteenth century, a need to build a national reform network, and a mission to demonstrate the abilities of Black women. Reflecting the spirit of progressive reform, Black women subordinated denominational, regional, and ideological identities to forge a national club movement dedicated to racial betterment. The northeastern urban areas dominated the early years of national organization, influencing the direction and leadership during the formative years. As a result of these efforts the National Association of Colored Women (NACW), through its regional, state, and city federations, developed institutions to serve the race for generations.

The groundwork for successful club work emerged from their experiences in beneficial, church, and literary societies in northern urban areas, where Black women used their relative freedom to develop social organizations for serving the race. Philadelphia, the city with the largest nineteenth-century Black population in the North, was a leading city for mutual aid societies by 1890. Church-related missionary societies, often called Dorcas societies after the biblical Dorcas who dedicated her life to good deeds, maintained several organizations to provide aid to ill and dependent women and children. The African Dorcas Association in New York City provided clothing, hats, and shoes for children attending the African Free School. Other women held fairs in New York City to support the Colored Orphan Asylum.

Literary societies, primarily social improvement associations meeting in a member's home, provided a structure through which women became informed about issues and skilled in effecting change. The literary societies provided poetry readings and musical performances, experience with parliamentary procedures, opportunities to develop leadership skills unhampered by either male or white dominance, and increased educational awareness of racial issues which included segregation in transportation, lynching, debt peonage, and voting rights. Such literary societies often adopted projects to benefit the race. Their fund-raising skills supported local homes for the aged, colored schools, or orphanages.

Responding to specific community needs, these early club efforts were narrow in scope, limited to a particular denomination or social clique, and short-lived due to lack of administrative knowledge or finances. By the late nineteenth century, the potential for organized action increased as the Black population gained education, settled in urban areas, developed organizations to respond to local needs, and faced intensified racial discrimination and violence. During the last decade of the nineteenth century, all these preconditions came together and resulted in the national club movement to improve life for Black Americans.

The national club movement emerged from three centers of club life in the North and East: Washington, D.C., New York, and Boston. Washington, D.C., a center of the Black elite, attracted a national audience through conventions, conferences, and a forum, the Bethel Literary and Historical Association (founded in 1881). This public platform engaged the intellectual elite, including Mary Ann Shadd Cary, the first Black female editor of *Provincial Freeman*; Hallie Q. Brown, lecturer for the British and American temperance movements; Mary Church Terrell, daughter of the first Black millionaire; Fannie Barrier Williams, Chicago community leader and Anna Cooper, leader in Black secondary education. Most of the Washington women were teachers, aware of children's problems. Many were volunteers at the Home for Friendless Girls, founded in 1886 by Caroline Taylor. Leaders in education, benevolence, and literary societies, these women joined together during the summer of 1892 to form the Colored Woman's League of Washington, D.C.

Black women in New York City were also involved in a variety of activities. On October 5, 1892, the Black female leadership from the New York-Brooklyn community held a testimonial dinner to honor the antilynching crusader, Ida B. Wells. Organized by Victoria Earle Matthews, a contributor to several New York dailies; Maritcha Lyons, a public school teacher; Sarah Smith Garnet, principal of a Manhattan grammar school; Susan Smith McKinney, a Brooklyn physician; and others, the testimonial dinner recognized Wells for her courage in researching, writing, and lecturing about lynching, one of the major injustices experienced by Black men. This dinner stimulated the formation of two important women's clubs: the Woman's Loyal Union, organized by Mathews and Lyons later that month, and the Woman's Era Club of Boston, founded by Josephine St. Pierre Ruffin in January 1893.

The Boston women reflected the town's educational and community activism. Ruffin had served on the Sanitary Commission and in Kansas Relief Association, Women's Industrial and Educational Union, and Moral Education Society. With her daughter, Florida Ridley, and Maria Baldwin, principal of Agassiz School, one of the most prestigious white schools in Cambridge, she met to collect data, publish and disseminate tracts and leaflets, and develop any other service to improve the image of Black women through example.

While these three centers were developing services for their communities, several events soon drew these women together in a national collective effort. In preparation for the Columbian Exposition in Chicago, a Board of Lady Managers encouraged women from other countries to participate in this international demonstration of progress commemorating the discovery of America. When Black women's groups from Washington, D.C., and Chicago petitioned for inclusion in the planning process, they were rejected since they had no national organization to represent them. The Colored Woman's League of Washington, D.C., attempted to organize a convention to become a national group, but lack of cooperation from other centers resulted in failure to gain exposition participation. Soon after, the Washington League invited women in all parts of the country to affiliate for racial advancement. Women's clubs from Kansas City, Denver, Norfolk, Philadelphia, and South Carolina responded. The Black women in Chicago also responded to the rejection from the Columbian Exposition. In September 1893, the Chicago Women's Club was formed to take leadership in civic and community reform.

The move to develop a national representative body quickened. In January 1894, the Colored Woman's League incorporated with affiliated leagues. Two months later, the Boston Woman's Era Club launched the first monthly magazine published by Black women, the *Woman's Era*, which informed subscribers about fashion, health, family life, and legislation. Women from Chicago, Kansas City, Washington, Denver, New Orleans, and New York contributed to the magazine and served as heads of the magazine's departments. In October 1894, the National Council of Women invited the Colored Woman's League to become a member and send delegates to the spring 1895 convention. Eligibility required the Colored Woman's League to call itself a national organization. Through the columns of the *Woman's Era*, the league requested delegates from other clubs, but only a few accepted. Even though the announcement appeared in the *Woman's Era*, the Woman's Era Club sent no delegates since the Boston leadership was seeking a similar national role. Although the league behaved as a national organization at the spring 1895 National Council of Women's convention, no national convention of Black women had yet taken place.

The catalyst for calling a national convention was a slanderous letter sent by a southern journalist to a British reformer. The British reformer sent the letter to Josephine Ruffin, editor of the *Woman's Era*, who included a copy in a communication to subscribers. The Black elite reacted with moral outrage, leading to Ruffin's call for a national conference in Boston. The newly elected leaders of the First National Conference of Colored Women of America represented an alliance of competing groups: Ruffin (Boston) as president, Helen Cook (Washington, D.C.) and Margaret Murray Washington of the newly formed Tuskegee Woman's Club as vice presidents, and Elizabeth Carter (New Bedford, Massachusetts) as secretary. Before leaving the conference, the delegates voted to form a permanent organization, the National Federation of Afro-American Women (NFAAW) to correct the image of Black women. The conference's 104 delegates and fifty-four clubs represented fourteen states and the District of Columbia and reflected the middle-class interest in home life and racial uplift. The women sought to lead the masses to the social righteousness that these leaders embodied.

As a result of this meeting, NFAAW was invited to participate in the Women's Congress at the 1895 Cotton States and International Exposition in Atlanta, Georgia. Prominent Black women from twenty-five states attended to demonstrate the race's skills, culture, and talents. The separate Black exhibition provoked conflict among the women. Josephine St. Pierre Ruffin expressed the northern integrationist opinion when she declined the invitation due to the racial segregation of contributions. She did not speak for all northern women. Victoria Matthews attended and gathered information for the New York women. The participating group declared itself the Colored Women's Congress of the United States. The group met once more in Nashville during the Tennessee centennial (1897), during which time they disbanded to strengthen the national aspirations of Black women, aspirations threatened by the proliferation of so-called national organizations.

To strengthen these aspirations the National League of Colored Women and the National Federa-

Ida B. Wells-Barnett brought her four-month-old son, Charles Aked Barnett, to the 1896 meeting at which the National Association of Colored Women was formed. They were such a ubiquitous presence that he was voted "baby of the association." This photo was taken a few months later. [The Joseph Regenstein Library, The University of Chicago]

tion of Afro-American Women had to clarify their interrelationships as national organizations. The women realized that competition for members, financial resources, and the attention of the white press could endanger the emerging club movement. Both groups held their national conventions in Washington, D.C., during July 1896, a duplication of effort that made their organizational quest seem ridiculous. The leadership of both groups sought unity. Therefore, a representative body of seven women from each organization deliberated together to overcome the factionalism and conflicts that historically had constrained the effectiveness of these Black women's clubs. The joint committee elected Mary Church Terrell as chair and recommended the two organizations merge to form the National Association of Colored Women (NACW). For self-protection, self-advancement, and social interaction, the NACW gradually lessened the city and/or class divisions that had historically prevented national unity.

Mary Church Terrell became the first president of the NACW, aided by vice presidents from Boston, Philadelphia, Kansas City, and New Orleans. The strength of the NACW remained in the Northeast with Washington, D.C., and the Boston area predominating. These women valued self-help, protection of women, honesty, and justice. They honored past and present Black leadership with organizations named the Sojourner Truth Club, Phyllis Wheatley Club, Lucy Thurman WCTU Club, Ada Sweet Club, and Ida B. Wells Club. The religious roots appeared in clubs such as the Calvary Circle and Christian League. Joining heroines of the past with younger, ambitious women filled with hopes for the future, merging old traditions with new scientific methods of social organization, the NACW became a major vehicle through which Black women attempted reform during the next four decades.

After founding the NACW, the women responded to the general reform context. As educated, elite women, they actively supported the major women's reform movements seeking moral purity, temperance, self-improvement, and suffrage. Their racial identity, however, complicated participation in national organizations that included the National Congress of Mothers, the Women's Christian Temperance Union, the National Council of Women, the General Federation of Women's Clubs, the National American Woman Suffrage Association, and the Young Women's Christian Association. Black women had different perspectives on the women's issues; they possessed a triple consciousness because they were American, Black, and women.

They reassembled in Nashville (1897) to formalize the organizational structure of the NACW and to demonstrate Black female worth and capabilities. Held during the Nashville centennial, the first annual conference (the first biennial was in Chicago in 1899) became a platform for racial self-defense. Unlike the Chicago Exposition, the Nashville centennial's woman's department recognized the NACW, a national organization representing about five thousand members.

The leadership wanted to develop and protect women. They wanted less criticism and more emphasis on the progress of the race. Self-help and racial solidarity appeared in every speech.

The defensive nature of the NACW was evident in the organization's mission to furnish evidence of the moral, mental, and material progress made by people of color. The present status of the race required Black women's leadership in self-help beginning in the home and through mothers' congresses, kindergartens, and schools to develop the intellect and to prepare for jobs. The elite leaders were duty bound to protect and sympathize with their fallen sisters, not only preaching but also practicing race unity and race pride. By the end of the Nashville meeting, the NACW had gained both a formal structure and a communications network in the publication of the *National Notes*, a means through which local, reform-minded Black women could disseminate information, discuss issues, and stimulate further organization.

The strength of the North in leadership, conference locations, and issues appeared in the biennials of the NACW during the pre-World War I period, a time when 90 percent of the Black population resided in the South. During these early years, regional, personal, and ideological conflict threatened to halt the precarious unity of the national club movement. At the first biennial in Chicago (1899), all three types of conflict were present. Mary Church Terrell had to rely on the local Chicago women for assistance in planning and executing this meeting. The Chicago clubwomen warned Terrell that the participation of Ida B. Wells-Barnett would result in their lack of cooperation.

Since Terrell had to rely upon the local women for the planning and program, she decided to omit Wells-Barnett during these stages. Wells-Barnett, offended by the exclusion, charged that Terrell feared losing her position to Wells-Barnett. Terrell, however, was more a practical politician than a jealous competitor. Terrell did not include Wells-Barnett in the planning stages for many reasons. First, since the convention took place in Chicago, Terrell could not offend the leading clubwomen who specifically disliked working with Wells-Barnett. Second, Wells-Barnett, as the secretary to the Afro-American Council, which was holding its annual meeting in Chicago during the same week, would be involved in other activities. Third, Wells-Barnett's reputation for creating controversy was not a desirable commodity in an organization attempting to unite factions of Black women and to provide a public image of reserved, ladylike leadership. Terrell personally admired Wells-Barnett's courage and direct approach to many issues, but that very style of interaction could threaten the loosely organized, infant federation. Terrell was an excellent judge of the politically expedient. She understood the need to build a structure with which Black women could then effectively attack racial injustices.

A second conflict emphasized regional jealousies. When the organization began to function with the recognition of credentials, selection of officers, and parliamentary procedures, disagreements developed. Some of the delegates arrived with no credentials. To avoid setting a negative precedent for the NACW, Mary Church Terrell ruled that those delegates lacking proper credentials could not take part in the proceedings. When Josephine St. Pierre Ruffin attempted to speak on a subject, Terrell ruled her out of order. The past rivalry of the Boston-Washington clubs was reinforced by the credential/parliamentary procedure difficulties.

The regional rivalries erupted again during the election process. The NACW constitution prevented a president from serving more than two consecutive terms. Since Terrell had served as the head of the joint committee and as president of the NACW when formally organized at Nashville in 1897, many delegates thought Terrell ineligible. The constitutional issue was resolved and Terrell won reelection. The position of first vice-president had Ruffin, Libby Anthony, and Josephine Bruce in competition. Ruffin and Anthony withdrew, giving that office to Bruce. The position of recording secretary, too, produced conflicts. Chicago's Connie A. Curl, New Bedford's Elizabeth C. Carter, and Pittsburgh's Mary Sutton vied for the position. Even though the South had won only three of the eleven offices, Carter withdrew, charging the NACW with playing power politics in using the Northeast for money and influence to help the expansion of the NACW. Due to the election conflicts, Carter announced the withdrawal of the Northeast federation, the only regional federation. The Woman's Era Club of Boston and Northeast

federation took their complaints to the press. The NACW responded with public refutations of the charges and persuaded the northern women to remain for the sake of unity.

The next seven biennials deliberately attempted to balance the centers of club activity in biennial location and leadership to lessen the regional conflicts. Hence, the northern interests received four biennials: 1901 Buffalo, 1906 Detroit, 1908 Brooklyn, and 1914 Wilberforce. Centers of club activity received recognition in the election of their leaders to the presidency: Josephine Silone Yates (1901-6) of the Kansas City league, Lucy Thurman (1906-8) of the Michigan State federation, Elizabeth Carter (1908-12) of the Northeast federation, and Margaret Murray Washington (1912-16) of the Tuskegee Women's Club and the National Federation of Afro-American Women. The clubs of the North were satisfied, but conflict did not cease. The election of the darkest-skinned candidate, Lucy Thurman, demonstrated the color consciousness of the Black female network, which was seeking to prove that leadership skills had no relationship to the percentage of white blood. The publication of *National Notes* at Tuskegee provoked charges of "Tuskegee machine" censorship from Ida B. Wells-Barnett at the Louisville meeting. More a personal than ideological conflict, the charges failed to gain adherents and Tuskegee continued publishing the newsletter through 1922.

The clubwomen shared more in common as the decades progressed. During the pre-World War I years, the NACW expanded in numbers, regions, and interests. Only one regional and six state federations existed in 1901, yet by 1909, the southern federation and twenty state federations had developed. By 1916, 300 new clubs had joined the NACW since the last biennial. The departments within the NACW grew and changed from social science, domestic science, juvenile court, humane and rescue work, religion, temperance, music, literature, and publication, to include mothers' clubs, kindergartens, and business/professional women. The expansion and increased specificity of interests responded to the participation of educated women in business, social work, and the professions while still showing interest in women's issues and the family. The clubwomen stressed the responsibility of the privileged to help their social inferiors, since white Americans increasingly judged the race by its lowest elements. By training the lower classes to adopt attitudes, manners, and other behavior acceptable to the middle class, these "missionaries" hoped to improve the white perceptions of the race. The self-help method fit the careers of the overwhelming majority of the NACW leaders and was the most acceptable path to advancement supported by white reformers and philanthropists alike.

These self-help efforts to uplift and serve the community are best seen in the local club activities in the North. Typically, care for the race's aged was the first type of organized reform initiated by clubwomen. Lack of programs to care for aging ex-slaves mobilized groups of women to organize, charge membership fees, hold socials, and solicit county funds, to raise money to cover services, purchase facilities, and hire qualified personnel to manage these homes for the aged. The Alpha Home in Indianapolis, the Cleveland Home for Aged Colored People, and similar services in Chicago, Brooklyn, New Bedford, Newark, and Philadelphia emerged from the efforts of individual women joined by clubs that adopted the project. For example, Gabrella Smith of Chicago founded the Home for Aged and Infirm Colored People by taking homeless elderly into her house. She interested other women in her project and soon, Anna Hudlin organized a club for the placement of aged in the home. The club raised funds, obtained other properties, provided furnishings and managed an endowment for the home's operation. Many of the daily responsibilities were assumed by clubwomen through a network of volunteers. The Woman's Loyal Union established a Home for Aged Colored People. The same group provided the support for a venture started by clubwoman Elizabeth Carter. Her New Bedford Home for the Aged soon received recognition from the NACW as the greatest such enterprise established by the race. Soon, clubs accepted responsibility for the aged in their communities. New Haven's Twentieth Century Club assumed the financial obligations for the Hannah Gray Home. Detroit's club with the same name developed the Phyllis Wheatley Home for Aged Colored Women under the leadership of Mary E. McCoy, wife of the inventor Elijah McCoy and founder of the Detroit club.

Closely related to care for the aged were the local programs to aid the infirm and dependent populations. Women's clubs aided the colored departments or wards in hospitals, created medical facilities for Black communities, and developed specialized medical services. The New York clubwomen contributed food, clothing, and services in the form of lectures and performances to the Lincoln Hospital and Home. New Jersey women formed the Charity Club to assist Christ Hospital in Jersey City. Berean Church clubwomen helped Dr. Caroline Still Anderson establish a dispensary in Philadelphia, while the Yates Women's Club supported a small Black hospital in Cairo, Illinois. The need for health care for tubercu-

Margaret Murray Washington (seated) of the Tuskegee Women's Club was one of the officers of the National Federation of Afro-American Women, which evolved into the National Association of Colored Women. Washington served as president of the NACW from 1912 to 1916. [Library of Congress]

losis patients led the Indianapolis Woman's Improvement Club to establish the Oak Hill Tuberculosis Camp, the first of its kind in the nation. Gradually, these health care efforts emerged from their charity roots to reflect the general trends in Progressive reform calling for investigation, planning, and alteration of the environment rather than the patient.

Such mixtures of charity and social welfare approaches were also evident in the clubwomen's efforts for youth. As with the homes for the aged, many of the orphanages started out with one woman's concern for dependent children. Amanda Smith, international evangelist and temperance lecturer, used her own money to start a children's home in Harvey, Illinois. Joined by the Illinois clubwomen and aided by the State of Illinois, the home expanded to care for over sixty children by 1908. Smith was over sixty at the time she began the effort, but her dream prospered and continued after her death through the organized efforts of the clubwomen. Chicago clubwomen aided the Louise Children's Home and Home for Dependent Children. The New Bedford Women's Club supported a children's home founded in 1904. As with the homes for the aged, the segregated facilities did not provoke conflict due to their charitable nature and to the belief that the race could better care for its own.

Black clubwomen thought that the most efficient way to reform society was to care for and instruct the young. As a result of that belief, clubwomen developed day nurseries and kindergartens that required little expenditure for facilities or staff. Provided in a church basement, a clubwoman's home, or a rented house, day nurseries needed only to rely on the women as volunteers. Kindergartens (a concept imported from German liberals) were usually established by the educated leadership in clubs. In many kindergartens, the clubwomen provided instruction for mothers in child care, health, and hygiene. The Chicago clubwomen helped Wells-Barnett establish a kindergarten at Bethel Church in 1897. The Women's Christian, Social and Literary Club of Peoria, plus several others in the Illinois Federation, supported similar kindergarten/day nursery projects. Due to the integration of social services in Boston, the clubwomen there supported a kindergarten for Black children in Atlanta through their Georgia Educational League. Before the Great Migration of Black Americans came from the South to these northern cities, women had developed self-help services for the aged, infirm, and/or dependent populations from New York to Chicago to Detroit.

The seeds for the development of urban multiservice centers grew out of the homes or missions for the protection of women coming to the northern population centers. The travelers' aid services could not or did not meet the expanding needs of Black women migrating in search of better wages, working conditions, or opportunities. Victoria Earle Matthews, president of the Brooklyn Women's Club and Woman's Loyal Union, had been concerned about young women since her trip to attend the Atlanta Exposition. Upon her return, she gathered clubwomen together to develop a social service for young working girls: the White Rose Home. These clubwomen had served as founders, administrators, and teachers and/or volunteers in kindergartens and industrial training programs in cooking, laundry, sewing, chair caning, and wood burnishing. The White Rose Home in New York City became a model settlement house for other institutions in the North.

The National League for the Protection of Colored Women, one of the three organizations that merged to form the National Urban League, was directly influenced by the White Rose Home. Soon, such homes for working women as the Phyllis Wheatley Home in Evanston and Chicago, Lincoln Settlement in Brooklyn, and the Phyllis Wheatley Association in Cleveland expanded as community needs grew with the Great Migration.

As jobs opened during World War I, Black Americans left the South for northern opportunities. Between the 1910 census and the 1920 census, Detroit's Black population expanded by 623 percent, Cleveland's by 308 percent, and Gary, Indiana's, by 1,284 percent. New York gained the highest urban Black population, while Chicago went from eighth place to fourth place in similar population growth. By 1920, 85 percent of Black Americans outside the South were urban residents. These numbers exacerbated the conditions that Black women had been trying to improve through their self-help efforts. These centers filled the needs for lodging, job placement, night classes, industrial training, day nurseries, kindergartens, libraries, boys and girls clubs, savings clubs, choir and music programs, and social gatherings. They became the training ground for Black visiting nurses and social workers graduating from the newly formed educational programs. These multiservice community centers cooperated with the National Urban League through affiliation and laid the foundation for major social services in Black communities for generations. As these services changed, so too did the women.

The biennials of the NACW demonstrated the growth of competence and confidence among club workers. The 1916 Baltimore biennial highlighted trends toward racial pride and interorganizational

In the spirit of progressive reform, Black women subordinated denominational, regional, and ideological identities to forge a national club movement dedicated to racial betterment. The National Association of Colored Women, through its regional, state, and city federations, developed institutions to serve the race for generations. Among the distinguished women who served as president were (left to right) Mary McLeod Bethune (1924-28), Mary Church Terrell (1896-1901), Mary Waring (1933-37), and Elizabeth C. Brooks (1908-12). [Bethune Museum and Archives]

cooperation. By the time the women reconvened, the NACW had passed formal resolutions to support the woman suffrage amendment, to cooperate with the Young Women's Christian Association, National Urban League, and the National Association for the Advancement of Colored People, and to support federal antilynching legislation. The newly elected president, Buffalo clubwoman Mary B. Talbert, directed the NACW to assume financial obligations for the redemption and restoration of the Frederick Douglass home. Talbert's creative fund-raising and participation techniques appealed to racial identity, to female pride, and to individual needs for recognition. All ages, regions, and institutions assisted. The campaign was so successful that the 1918 Denver biennial held a ceremonial burning of the mortgage on the Frederick Douglass home, which came to symbolize the success of one Black man and the triumph of organized Black clubwomen.

While rescuing the Douglass home, international conflict influenced the American homefront. The First World War provided the occasion for clubwomen to prove their patriotism, their abilities, and their solidarity. The war meant an end to laissez-faire social policy as the government guided national health campaigns, mobilized housing and urban development, and encouraged reforms such as industrial education, social insurance, and community activism. This surge in organizational activity created a growth in confidence and self-image because women felt needed. They proved their abilities, performed nontraditional jobs, and increased their expectations for postwar progress. The clubwomen raised money through Liberty Loans, War Savings Stamps, and United War Work campaigns. Many club leaders served in the six Black base hospitals and hostess houses. The Circle for Negro War Relief called on the national club movement for help. The clubwomen used the war years to garner services for their communities and to demonstrate racial pride.

As the war ended, demobilization produced thousands of returning soldiers, unemployment caused by reversion to peacetime economy, and readjustment to civilian life. Economic and social tensions exploded in the Red Summer of 1919. By year's end, seventy-seven lynchings included eleven soldiers, and twenty-six cities suffered race riots killing hundreds. The postwar period provided the context in which rising expectations collided with reality. Black clubwomen armed with better training, interorganizational connections, and confidence sought less charity and more justice. They embodied both the New Negro and the New Woman as they attacked the chronic injustice of lynching.

Mary Talbert built on wartime networks to mobilize women against lynching. She utilized women's imagination, money, and volunteer time to spread the information and raise the funds to cooperate with the NAACP in the national campaign against lynching. Talbert formed an ad hoc group for fund-raising and publicity that became known in 1922 as the Anti-Lynching Crusaders. Broader based than the NAACP, the crusaders directed religious fervor into their attempt to unite one million women to suppress lynching and to pass the Dyer Anti-Lynching Bill. Although federal legislation was never achieved, the public and political awareness of lynching injustices changed and lynchings declined. Talbert completed her term of office with the NACW and became a board member of the NAACP. The clubwomen approached the 1920s as activists in the NACW, NAACP, and National Urban League. These multilayered commitments modified the clubwomen and the NACW.

The change in the NACW was gradual at first. The biennials of 1920 and 1922 were held in the South (Tuskegee and Richmond) under the leadership of a northern clubwoman, Hallie Q. Brown, of Wilberforce, Ohio. With the NAACP fighting the legal and political battles and the National Urban League negotiating and investigating social and economic problems in the communities, the NACW had

to carve out a special niche for itself. Brown's leadership started to shape that role in education through what came to be known as the Hallie Quinn Brown Scholarship Loan Fund.

Ohio clubwomen honored Brown by leading the states in contributions to the fund. The letters NACW came to mean: National pride, Achievement, Cooperation, and Willingness to serve. The publication of *National Notes* was turned over to Myrtle Foster Cook of Kansas City, Missouri, who developed the newsletter into a magazine with reports, comments, and items of interest to clubwomen. The departments of the NACW had changed to include Frederick Douglass Memorial and Historical Association, Education, Child Welfare, Health and Hygiene, Social Service, Legislation and Law Enforcement, Big Sisters Movement, Fine Arts, Business, and Interracial Cooperation.

The biennial attempts to balance location of meeting and national presidency continued under the leadership of the Southeast federation's leader, Mary McLeod Bethune, president of the NACW 1924-28. The biennials during her leadership took place in Chicago and in Oakland, a recognition of the regional and numerical expansion of the NACW, which in 1924 included over 100,000 members. The NACW, now in the consolidation phase of its growth, gave Bethune authority to establish a national headquarters in the nation's capital and to compile the first official directory.

A generational transition was also in progress. The founding leaders of the NACW were dead or aging; thus, the organization initiated plans to attract younger women into membership through a junior division. The younger generation had its own interests that reflected the social life of the 1920s. The NACW adapted to these changes.

When the clubwomen came to the fifteenth biennial in Washington, D.C. (1928), the NACW dedicated the national headquarters at Twelfth and O Streets and the caretaker's cottage at the Frederick Douglass home, both physical examples of achievement. The new president, Sallie W. Stewart of the Indiana federation, reported that the junior division work was growing rapidly. The women memorialized past leaders and looked to the future, not knowing that this would be their last, great celebration of club work.

The Great Depression modified the optimism. The women met for the next biennial in Hot Springs, Arkansas (1930). Two days of executive sessions focused on the financial problems confronting the organization. As if to escape the unpleasant realities surrounding them, the clubwomen toured a model house, viewed exhibits of beautiful homes and fine art, and expressed optimism about the scholarship fund, expansion, and the nation's future. The departments merged to form the Board of Control (a financial monitor), a National Association of Colored Girls, and Women in Industry, Mother, Home, and Child.

The NACW did not meet again in biennial until 1933, when clubwomen came to celebrate the Chicago Exposition. Dr. Mary Waring, one of the original clubwomen in Chicago, became president. The discussions, although permeated with references to the causes of and solutions to the Depression, focused on traditional women's issues: standardize the home; create a good environment for the child; train girls to be industrious, artistic and gracious; improve working conditions for women and girls; and increase community service. At the 1935 Cleveland biennial, Waring informed members about threatened court action against the NACW for the printing costs of the official history compiled by Elizabeth L. Davis. Past president Mary McLeod Bethune, director of the National Youth Administration's Division of Negro Affairs, reported on the financial condition of the NACW headquarters.

Bethune's position in the Roosevelt administration had demonstrated to her a need for a united coalition of all Black women's organizations able to pressure the political system into action to help the race. Criticized by many of the older leaders of the NACW for attempting to weaken or destroy the national club movement, Bethune nevertheless organized the National Council of Negro Women (NCNW) in 1935. With this united coalition, Bethune continued to influence the national direction of Black women through national political structures. Her efforts in the National Youth Administration provided work experience for over 400,000 Blacks and utilized over 700 to administer these programs. Self-help could make no such claims. Just as some years earlier, local clubwomen united to form a national club movement, now Bethune saw a need to influence national politics through a united coalition of all Black women's groups.

With the creation of the NCNW in 1935, the NACW declined in its original importance. With the NACW's cooperation and support, other organizations had taken over responsibilities to the Black community by specializing in goals and tactics. City, state, and private organizations provided institutional support for many of the services started by the clubwomen. The Depression brought economic devastation to Black communities and a changing political context through which reform was directed. The younger generation joined the NACW more as a social outlet than as a means to serve the community. They sought means to effect their personal mobility, not to uplift their sisters.

As the political and ideological contexts changed, the NACW persisted with fewer members and a different direction after 1935. It was during the period of the club movement's greatest growth, 1890-1920s, that the NACW achieved its legacy—shaping the leadership, the institutions, and the identity of a people through its women.

BIBLIOGRAPHY

Brawley, Benjamin. *Women of Achievement* (1919); Brown, Hallie. *Homespun Heroines* (1926); Cash, Floris. "Womanhood and Protest: The Club Movement among Black Women, 1892-1922," Ph.D. diss. (1986); Culp, D. W., ed. *Twentieth Century Negro Literature: Or, a Cyclopedia of Thought on the Vital Topics Relating to the American Negro* (1902); Dannett, Sylvia. *Profiles of Negro Womanhood* (1964); Davis, Elizabeth. *Lifting as They Climb* (1933); Du Bois, W.E.B., ed. *Social and Physical Conditions of Negroes in Cities* (1897); Duster, Alfreda, ed. *Crusade for Justice* (1970); Field, Emma. "The Women's Club Movement in the United States," M.A. thesis (1948); Hamilton, Tullia. "The National Association of Colored Women, 1896-1920," Ph.D. diss. (1978); Harley, Sharon and Rosalyn Terborg-Penn, eds. *The Afro-American Woman: Struggles and Images* (1978); Loewenberg, Bert and Ruth Bogin, eds. *Women in Nineteenth-Century American Life* (1976); MacBrady, J. E., ed. *A New Negro for a New Century* (1900); Majors, Monroe. *Noted Negro Women* (1893); Mossell, Gertrude. *The Work of the Afro-American Women* (1908); Salem, Dorothy. *To Better Our World: Black Women in Organized Reform, 1890-1920* (1990); Terrell, Mary. *Colored Woman in a White World* (1940); Wesley, Charles H. *The History of the National Association of Colored Women's Clubs: A Legacy of Service* (1984). Manuscript Collections with a special focus on the North include: Ida B. Wells papers, J. Regenstein Library, University of Chicago; Information Dames and Prudence Crandall Club folders, St. Louis Association of Colored Women's Clubs Collection, Western Historical Joint Collection, University of Missouri—St. Louis; Minerva Club folder, Myrtle Bell papers, Western Reserve Historical Society, Cleveland, Ohio; Margaret Washington papers and Monroe Works clipping files, Frissell Library, Tuskegee, Alabama; Mary Church Terrell papers, Library of Congress, and Moorland-Spingarn Center, Howard University, Washington, D.C.; the *Woman's Era*, Rare Book and Manuscript Department, Boston Public Library, Boston; Schomburg Center for Research in Black Culture, New York Public Library, New York.

DOROTHY SALEM

NATIONAL ASSOCIATION OF TEACHERS IN COLORED SCHOOLS *see* AMERICAN TEACHERS ASSOCIATION

NATIONAL BLACK SISTERS' CONFERENCE

The civil rights movement gave the U.S. Roman Catholic church a singular opportunity to witness concretely the meaning of unity in faith and diversity in race, culture, and ethnicity. While individual Catholic lay men and women, sisters, and priests participated in marches and sit-ins, and while individual bishops denounced the sin of racism, the Catholic church as a whole made no substantial contribution to this organized effort. While liberal faintheartedness and indifference dismayed Black Catholics, it did not prevent them from resourceful and programmatic activity. In fact, the resurgence of their one-hundred-year-old struggle for justice and equality within the Roman Catholic church coincides with their engagement in the civil rights movement. The National Black Sisters' Conference, an organization of Black Roman Catholic nuns, is a product of this effort.

The National Black Sisters' Conference (NBSC) was founded in August 1968 by an international gathering of 155 Black Roman Catholic nuns from 79 different religious congregations, 45 U.S. cities, the Caribbean, and the continent of Africa. The conference's position paper pledged to work unceasingly for the liberation of Black people. Since then, the NBSC has been the chief means through which Black nuns have cooperated across congregational lines to confront individual and institutional racism in the Roman Catholic church and in U.S. society; to maintain a network for personal and communal support, self-criticism, study, and prayer; and to develop initiatives to promote systemic change in religious life. The founding president and executive director of the Conference was (former) Religious Sister of Mercy, Mary Martin de Porres Grey (now Dr. Patricia Grey Tyree).

Since the organization's founding, NBSC leadership, staff, and members have sponsored annual meetings; conducted spiritual retreats and workshops for Black laity, vowed members of Catholic religious orders, and clergy; provided consultative services to parochial and community schools, Catholic and Protestant parishes, and dioceses; published a quarterly newsletter, *Signs of Soul*, as well as four monographs; and developed and implemented workshops on the training and preparation of Black sisters. From 1973 to 1975, the conference provided technical and personnel assistance to the Roman Catholic Bishop of Benin City, Nigeria, in the founding of an indigenous order of Roman Catholic sisters. In the early 1980s, the conference founded Sojourner House in Detroit, Michigan. Sojourner House is a national facility grounded in African-American values, spirituality, and culture. It is a place for prayer, counseling, spiritual discernment, training, and support for Black lay women and lay sisters in ministry.

During the decade of the 1970s, the NBSC sponsored or contributed to several projects aimed directly at the cultural, social, and economic conditions of African-Americans. Two important collaborative projects included a tutorial and recreational program for the children of Louisiana sugar-cane workers and formal participation in the National Black Political Assembly, a grass-roots organization that sought to create a national political agenda responsive to the conditions of Black poor. To address the crisis of education in the Black community, the NBSC developed and maintained for five years Project DESIGN (Development of Educational Strategies in the Growing Nation). This consulting agency prepared diagnostic evaluations of schools, provided curriculum and pedagogical assistance to instructors, lent organizational support to community school boards, trained parents in curriculum assessment and teacher evaluation, and cosponsored a graduate degree program in education with Antioch-Putnam Graduate School of Education, Washington, D.C., and Carlow College, Pittsburgh, Pennsylvania.

The national office of the NBSC currently is located in Washington, D.C.

BIBLIOGRAPHY

National Black Sisters' Conference. *Black Survival: Past, Present, Future: A Report of the Second National Black Sisters' Conference* (1970), and *Black Celibate Commitment: Report of the Third Annual National Black Sisters' Conference* (1971), and *Making a Way Out of No Way: Conference Proceedings 1982* (1982), and *Tell It Like It Is: A Black Catholic Perspective on Christian Education* (1983).

M. SHAWN COPELAND

NATIONAL COALITION OF 100 BLACK WOMEN

In 1970, a small group of women met in New York City to address the problems and opportunities facing Black women in the wake of the civil rights and women's movements. Calling themselves the Coalition of 100 Black Women, they initiated programs that dealt with the following issues: the crisis of the Black family; career advancement, especially in the corporate sector; and political and economic empowerment. Through these programs the women also were able to identify and develop their leadership potential and encourage the use of their leadership skills.

The group's efforts were so successful that the number of members in the coalition soon surpassed the "100" in its name. In 1981, under the leadership of its president, Jewell Jackson McCabe of New York, the coalition expanded into a national organization, the National Coalition of 100 Black Women (NCBW). By 1991, under McCabe's leadership as president and then chair of the NCBW board of directors, fifty-nine chapters in twenty-two states and the District of Columbia had become NCBW affiliates—with a membership of 7,000 women.

Chapters, the basic organizational units of NCBW, are governed by the national board of directors, which consists of national officers, directors appointed by the national president, and members elected by chapter delegates at biannual meetings.

A volunteer, nonprofit organization, NCBW seeks to empower African-American women through programs that meet their diverse needs. These programs enable NCBW (1) to provide effective networks among Black female leaders and establish links between NCBW and the corporate and political sectors; (2) to make Black women a visible force in the socioeconomic and political arenas and, through role modeling and mentoring, expose the next generation to new career opportunities, especially in the corporate arena; (3) to develop and position the leadership talent within the community of Black women; and (4) to recognize the historic and current achievements of Black women.

Since its inception, NCBW has secured $550,000 for its Women in Partnership program, a role-modeling project for pregnant teenagers that is being carried out by approximately half the NCBW chapters; generated $750,000 for a career exploration program for high school students, which included a summer internship with major businesses and corporations and a career education course at Hunter College in New York City; established a model mentoring program,

in conjunction with Spelman College in Atlanta and City College in New York, that has been replicated by the Alabama, New Jersey, Texas, California, and Indiana chapters; presented the annual Candace Awards, a program established in 1982 to recognize Black women of achievement nationally, one of the most significant forums of its kind; held an NCBW Colloquy in 1986, supported by a Louis Harris study of leadership values among high-ranking Black women and by eminent Black female scholars who presented research papers at the colloquy establishing a twenty-year blueprint for NCBW action in the areas of education, economic development, and society governance; launched, in 1989, a nationwide reproductive health rights education program; and became, in 1991, a partner with Time-Warner in sponsoring Time-Warner's Time to Read program at NCBW chapters in Atlanta, Los Angeles, Houston, Richmond, and Washington, D.C.

BIBLIOGRAPHY

Haynes, Eleanor. "Doing My Thing: The Coalition of 100 Black Women," *New York Voice* (February 4, 1972); Powell, Bernice F. "Assembly: The National Coalition of 100 Black Women," *Elan* (February 1982).

SHIRLEY POOLE

NATIONAL COUNCIL OF NEGRO WOMEN

The National Council of Negro Women (NCNW), the first Black organization of organizations, and the first national coalition of Black women's organizations, was founded on December 5, 1935, by Mary McLeod Bethune. During the fifty-seven years of its existence, it has had four presidents, Mary McLeod Bethune (1935-49); Dorothy Bolden Ferebee (1949-53); Vivian Carter Mason (1953-57); and Dorothy Irene Height (1957-). Modeled after the National Council of Women (NCW), a white association that included few Black women's organizations, the NCNW was proposed by Bethune as an effective structure to "harness the great power of nearly a million women into a force for constructive action."

Prior to 1935, the National Association of Colored Women (NACW) was the foremost national organization of African-American women. Founded in 1896 as a national coalition of Black women's clubs, many of which were of local and regional significance, it had established an enviable record of achievement and attracted a significant number of Black women leaders. As a young woman seeking national support and visibility for her fledgling school, the Daytona Normal and Industrial Institute, Bethune affiliated with the NACW (1912). Moving through the ranks, Bethune served as president of the Florida Federation of Colored Women's Clubs (1917-1924), founder and president of the Southeastern Association of Colored Women (1920-25), and as the eighth president of the NACW (1924-28). It was the latter experience that convinced Bethune of the need for a National Council of Negro Women.

Between 1896 and 1935, over thirty national organizations of African-American women were founded. In addition to the NACW, there were college-based professional sororities and a number of religious, political, and professional organizations. The effectiveness of these organizations was frequently undermined by program duplication and competitiveness. Although a number of their members joined the NACW, few national organizations affiliated. It was Bethune's perception that the NACW's membership structure in some ways prevented it from affirming the level of power that the NCW wielded. When asserting their right to speak for Black women, NACW presidents frequently quoted membership numbers. With the exception of Bethune, presidents serving between 1900 and 1934 cited a membership of 50,000. In 1927, Bethune laid claim to an organizational base of 250,000 members. The NCW, an umbrella organization for national women's organizations, claimed to represent millions of women, members of its diverse affiliates.

Beyond the issue of structure, as president of the NACW, Bethune had experienced significant opposition to the promotion and implementation of her organizational agenda. Her primary goal was to have Black women fully represented in national public affairs. Achievement of this purpose required establishing a headquarters in the nation's capital and employing an executive secretary. She was also concerned about the lack of a clear feminist focus and commitment in NACW to women's issues and especially to working-class and poor Black women. While Bethune was an ardent supporter, and frequently a part of the Black leadership that defined key race issues and strategies, by 1928 she was extremely concerned about the lack of financial support NACW members and African-American women gave to causes and issues specifically related to the NACW and to Black women. Bethune noted that Black women spent an inordinate amount of time and effort raising money for male-dominated organizations and male-defined causes. Bethune's focus on securing and maintaining a national headquarters brought her and her program into direct conflict with the old guard NACW leadership, which for years had made retrieval, restoration, and maintenance of the Frederick Douglass home a major fund-raising and organizational priority.

Bethune's decision to found the NCNW was based on an astute analysis of the issues of the time, the weaknesses of the NACW, and her personal need for continued recognition as the leader of a major organization of Black women. In 1928, at the end of her tenure as NACW president, Bethune began to recruit supporters for the development of a new organization. In December 1929, she invited the heads of all national Black women's organizations to meet in Daytona Beach, Florida, to discuss the development of a "National Council of Colored Women." Bethune argued that women's organizations were "more numerous and diversified and more keenly alive to the needs of the group" and "in a better position to make use of the Negro's purchasing power as an effective instrument to keep open the doors that have remained closed" (Bethune, n.d.). She stated that the proposed meeting would forge new relationships among Black women and that the new organization would provide an unprecedented base of power for Black women.

Between 1929 and 1935, Bethune held a number of planning meetings that were attended by key Black women leaders. A national promotion committee, chaired by Bethune, was authorized to contact and inform every national organization of the purpose of the national council plan. Organizations were asked to consider the idea at their annual conventions, or in executive committee meetings, and to send representatives to the council planning meetings.

After six years of recruitment, discussion, and planning, Bethune had garnered the support of the fourteen Black women's organizations represented at the 1935 founding meeting, held in New York City at the 137th Street Branch of the Young Women's Christian Association. Although the National Association of Colored Women did not affiliate with the National Council of Negro Women, a number of its prominent members, including Mary Church Terrell and Charlotte Hawkins Brown, attended the founding meeting. Both Terrell and Brown argued against the founding of the NCNW. Brown, the president of the North Carolina Federation of Colored Women's Clubs, a supporter of Bethune and the national council concept, anticipated that NACW president Mary F. Waring would accuse Bethune of splitting the NACW; thus, for political expediency she contested a permanent organization. Terrell, the venerable first president of the NACW, had mixed feelings about the new organization. She told the gathering that "Theoretically I believe everything that has been said. But I can't see how this organization can help. I do not see how the mistakes made by other groups will not be made by this one" (Collier-Thomas 1980).

Charlotte Hawkins Brown accurately gauged the NACW response, immediately delivered by Waring. Waring criticized and impugned the motives of Bethune and the founding members of the NCNW. Responding to Waring's criticism, Brown stated that the NACW had "so devoted itself to politics that it could do nothing constructive. The main idea has been to elect a president." Brown argued that the NACW had become "a political machine, a ballyhoo for section[alism]" (Collier-Thomas 1980). She pointed out that there was no discussion of issues related to the place and problem of women in American life and that no committees were appointed to investigate issues concerning African-American women.

THE BETHUNE YEARS, 1935-49

The founding of the NCNW was controversial, and effectively split the Black women's club movement, leading to the eventual decline of the NACW. Unanimously elected as president, Mary McLeod Bethune set about the difficult task of unifying the divergent national groups into a national council that could at once tap the expertise of member organizations and harness their memberships and spheres of influence. The founding organizations were widely differentiated in purpose, membership, and organizational strength. Several organizations required that members be college educated; others required that members possess professional training in specified occupations; one group focused primarily on problems of organized labor; another had no requirements other than the payment of dues. Some organizations had extensive programs and received wide recognition. Thousands of Black women throughout the United States belonged to one or more of these associations.

The National Council of Negro Women was clearly an ambitious undertaking. Beginning as a national organization that proposed to carry out activities on a national level, the council, by virtue of its constitution, theoretically co-opted the membership of the affiliate organizations. The initial success of the organization depended upon unconditional support from member organizations, a well-trained volunteer staff, a cadre of highly articulate and visible volunteers, and carefully chosen projects and interpretations that could justify the council's existence to the general public and the constituent membership. The election of Charlotte Hawkins Brown, Mary Church Terrell, Lucy D. Slowe, and several other key women to serve as NCNW officers helped to quell some of the criti-

This formal portrait was taken at the NCNW's 1940 annual convention. [Bethune Museum and Archives]

cism and projected an image of unity to thousands of Black women who closely scrutinized the public actions of their leaders.

The NCNW constitution defined the national council concept and the role of the organization in rather broad terms. The specific purpose of the council was to unite national organizations in a powerful bloc that could function as an instrument for distributing information from the leadership to the constituent memberships, and as a vehicle through which Black womanhood could cooperate with national or international movements affecting questions of peculiar interest to women.

During the first year of operation, the NCNW consisted of national women's organizations (affiliates) and life members. Within a short period of time, it became apparent that this structure was inadequate for implementing a national program. In 1937 local councils, known as metropolitan councils, were established in communities where five or more affiliated branches were located. Affiliates were asked to urge their local chapters to work with the metropolitan councils. Registered councils were set up in rural areas, and junior councils were authorized for youth. During the 1940s, regional directors were elected to aid in the coordination of programming with affiliates and local councils. Regional directors were seen as the lifeline between the national and the regional and local communities because the national office could not directly address the need for field services. In the early 1950s, the regional director's broad powers were expanded by both constitutional redefinition and common practice. Under Dorothy Height local councils became known as sections and the regional system was supplanted by the state mechanism.

During the early years, the council was administered by a board of directors consisting of twelve officers, four members-at-large, and the chairpersons of thirteen standing committees. The board was comprised of the president and affiliate representatives. During the 1970s and 1980s, as affiliate representation became more pro forma and their attendance and involvement more sporadic, the board was expanded to include nonaffiliated women and additional sectional leaders. The national office was operated by a series of volunteer executive secretaries. The council had no paid staff until 1942, when Jeanetta Welch Brown became the first paid executive secretary. She was assisted by a stenographer, a clerk, and a team of volunteers. The addition of paid staff and the purchase of a national headquarters in 1943 provided the base necessary to propel the organization toward becoming a clearinghouse for information related to

Black women's organizations and for projecting the NCNW's national agenda.

During Bethune's administration, the NCNW's national program, administered through thirteen committees, was carefully designed to achieve credibility for the council through affiliation and collaboration with organizations and associations in every area of American life. In addition to national women's organizations, the NCNW extended its contacts to every major social, educational, governmental, and community organization. Focusing upon public affairs, employment, citizenship, family life, religion, postwar planning, consumer education, rural life, membership, personnel, and the publication of the *Aframerican Woman's Journal*, the committees successfully utilized the media and collaborated with key national organizations, governmental agencies, educational institutions, and individuals to educate and to effect change.

Working with the Young Men's Christian Association (YMCA), labor unions, and other organizations, the NCNW collected, analyzed, and distributed data regarding the employment of Black Americans on federal jobs, particularly in the Civilian Conservation Corps and the National Youth Administration. The NCNW exposed the discriminatory practices of local communities that excluded Black workers from government training programs. During World War II, the council systematically documented Black employment in plants engaged in war work and, as a result of pressures brought to bear from many sources, the Fair Employment Practice Committee was established.

While the NCNW exposed discriminatory practices, it also impressed upon Black workers their responsibility to maintain a professional attitude and appearance and to develop job-related skills. Utilizing public meetings nationwide, contacts with employees and employers, newspaper articles, and the dissemination of materials, the NCNW conducted a "Hold Your Job" campaign.

The NCNW campaigned for integration of Black Americans into the military and fought for the admission of women into the women's divisions of the army, navy, and air force. As a result of a series of conferences between Bethune and army leaders, Black women were accepted into the Women's Army Corps (WACS). Bethune personally recruited many of the first thirty-nine WACS. She inspected training camps and, when necessary, lodged complaints against discriminatory practices. The metropolitan councils sponsored programs for the WACS and took a special interest in their activities.

The National Council of Negro Women actively cooperated with the YWCA, the NAACP, the League of Women Voters, and other groups to eliminate racism and sexism. The council was an active participant in and planner of several conferences called by President Franklin D. Roosevelt and Eleanor Roosevelt. Here, Mary McLeod Bethune, Mary Church Terrell (center), and other NCNW members stand at the White House gate in 1946. [Bethune Museum and Archives]

While the NCNW closely monitored the government, it also gave strong support to government programs. By sponsoring "We Serve America" programs, encouraging local councils to "Buy Bonds and Be Free," and launching the Harriet Tubman Liberty Ship, the NCNW membership stressed its patriotism.

The council did not limit its associations to Black women's organizations. It actively worked with the national board of the YWCA, the National Association for the Advancement of Colored People (NAACP), the National Council of Women, the National Urban League, the League of Women Voters, the National Council of Church Women, the National Council of Jewish Women, and the National Council of Catholic Women to educate and to effect programs targeting the elimination of racism and sexism. In 1944, the council sponsored a conference to address the status of minorities in the United States. The council was an active participant and planner in numerous conferences called by President Roosevelt and Eleanor Roosevelt. Conferences on employment, on child care, and on women's participation in the war were attended by Black women representing diverse organizations. Black women were appointed to serve on boards and conference committees for the War Manpower Commission, the Women's and Children's Bureau, the Department of Labor, and other government bureaus.

Bethune possessed a worldview. She felt that people must be aware of and become actively involved in the struggles for peace throughout the world. Her concern led her to join the Moral Rearmament Movement and to support the idea of a United Nations.

Accompanied by Dorothy Boulding Ferebee and Edith Sampson, Mary McLeod Bethune traveled to San Francisco to witness the founding of the United Nations. As one of two consultants to the NAACP, she was able to attend this historic meeting and to project the image and program of the NCNW. The NCNW was the only national Black woman's organization represented at that meeting. The NCNW sent representatives and observers to meetings throughout the world and since that time has maintained an official observer at the United Nations.

At the end of Bethune's tenure, the National Council of Negro Women was recognized as the major advocate for Black women. Its advocacy was well articulated in the pages of the *Aframerican Woman's Journal.* Edited by Sue Bailey Thurman, the journal informed Black women of the major issues concerning women, targeted legislation that affected women and Black Americans, highlighted the accomplishments of individual women, and projected the work of the NCNW. In 1949, the name of the journal was changed to *Women United.* The council also published *Telefact,* a newsletter that informed members of the council and its affiliates of news and important issues and events relevant to legislation, international affairs, and economic developments.

DOROTHY BOULDING FEREBEE, 1949-53

In November 1949, at the fourteenth annual convention, Dorothy Boulding Ferebee was elected the second national president of the National Council of Negro Women. Ferebee was one of several young women whom Bethune had groomed and identified as a possible successor. Ferebee was a physician who came from a distinguished family of organizers and club leaders. She was the grandniece of Josephine St. Pierre Ruffin, the founder of the Boston New Era Club and a founder of the first national secular organization of Black women, the National Association of Colored Women. Prior to her election as president of NCNW, Dr. Ferebee had served as the tenth national president of Alpha Kappa Alpha sorority and the national treasurer of the NCNW. Earlier in her ca-

reer she had founded the Southeast Settlement House in Washington, D.C. Her credentials and achievements were impressive.

Dr. Ferebee served as NCNW president from November 1949 to November 1953. By supporting the United Nation's policies of human rights and peace, and through more focused programmatic thrusts aimed at eliminating the segregation of and discrimination against Blacks and women in health care, education, housing, and the armed forces, Dr. Ferebee's administration succeeded in maintaining the established NCNW program of advocacy and in expanding the understanding of the national council concept. Ferebee began by immediately announcing a "Nine Point Program" that affirmed NCNW goals and set forth a few new specific programmatic approaches. She proposed to address most problems through brochures and pamphlets informing the membership of the issues, and to collaborate and cooperate with federal agencies and nonprofit organizations in sponsoring conferences and distributing data. In particular, she proposed that the council implement its commitment to basic civil rights through education and legislation by conducting voter-registration campaigns for local and national elections; by recommending the appointment of qualified Black citizens to high level government positions; and by promoting the passage of legislation which would address lynching, the poll tax, genocide, federal aid to education, women's status, national health, and the establishment of a Fair Employment Practices Commission.

Dorothy Ferebee's job was not easy. It was difficult to fill Mary McLeod Bethune's shoes, and although Bethune had relinquished the presidency, she was constantly sought as the official representative of the NCNW. She graciously helped to smooth the path for Ferebee, but as the founder and president emeritus, she outshone all of the existing and aspiring Black female leadership. It took at least a year or more before Ferebee received the recognition associated with her position. Hampered by a limited budget and staff, and having to maintain a full-time job while being a full-time president, was no easy task. However, Ferebee, highly motivated, success-oriented, and committed, was able to guide the council smoothly through the transitional period.

Still, the need for a clearly defined program was a major issue until the late 1960s. Dorothy Ferebee and her successor, Vivian Carter Mason, understood the problem, but with a limited financial base, they were unable to solve it. The delivery of tangible program services was not realized until the administration of Dorothy Irene Height, the fourth president of NCNW. Yet, though the NCNW lacked the traditional programming associated with voluntary organizations, it continued to diversify its activities and to address issues of major significance.

VIVIAN CARTER MASON, 1953-57

At the first biennial convention, held in 1953, the National Council of Negro Women elected its third president, Vivian Carter Mason. Having served as vice president under Ferebee, and having worked closely with Bethune, she was well known to the membership. During Ferebee's extended trips to represent the council at conferences and meetings, both within the United States and abroad, it was Vivian Carter Mason who had chaired the meetings and addressed crucial organizational issues.

Vivian Carter Mason served as NCNW president from November 1953 to November 1957. By 1953, basic program activities were broadly defined under eleven national departments whose titles differed little from the original committees established in the late 1930s. The departments included Archives and Museum, Citizenship Education, Education, Human Relations, International Relations, Labor and Industry, Public Relations, Religious Education, Social Welfare, Youth Conservation, and Fine Arts. The NCNW's special projects and programs tended to reflect the apparent needs of its national affiliates and local councils, and during Mason's administration there was a special emphasis on interracial cooperation.

The NCNW had grown in stature, membership, and influence. Its structure incorporated a rather comprehensive program emphasis; its internal composition included local councils and national affiliates; and its cooperative endeavors, extending to every major program affecting Black people, required a national office with the professional expertise and physical resources necessary for administering what had become a large organization. It was the scope of the NCNW's work, not the size of the membership, that defined the necessary level of administration.

Vivian Carter Mason introduced a tighter and more sophisticated administration and further interpreted the organization's program. The national headquarters became the center in which the council greeted national leaders, hosted social functions, and built coalitions with other national organizations.

At the NCNW's annual meeting in 1947 at Shiloh Baptist Church, Washington, D.C., president Mary McLeod Bethune (far right) posed with Daisy Lampkin (second from left), Dorothy Ferebee (far left), and an unidentified woman. [Bethune Museum and Archives]

The building was painted, refurbished, and physically realigned to provide additional office space, privacy, and improved working conditions.

Mason understood constitutional law and the importance of developing an instrument that could govern the organization effectively. Under Mason's administration, the constitution was amended to include additional membership categories such as the Life Members Guild and to incorporate specific items aimed at curtailing the free-wheeling activities of some local councils and individuals who were acquiring property, soliciting funds, and engaging in partisan political activities not sanctioned by the national office. The NCNW began to require that local councils hold annual elections. Local councils were permitted to structure their own constitutions, with the stipulations that the constitutions conform to the legal scope of the national organization, and that a copy of the document be forwarded to the national office. In 1955 and 1957, revised local council manuals and handbooks for regional directors were distributed to the membership. Mason felt that these materials both explained and enhanced the administrative process.

Vivian Carter Mason was thrust into leadership during one of the most critical and historic periods in American history: on May 17, 1954, the U.S. Supreme Court struck at the heart of the "separate but equal" dictum by ruling that segregation in public schools was unconstitutional. Mason's administration was dominated by the civil rights struggle that emerged in the 1950s. The NCNW joined with the National Association for the Advancement of Colored People and other national organizations to devise strategies to implement the 1954 Supreme Court decision. Following the court decision, the NCNW met with affiliate presidents and experts in education and group relations to discuss program development throughout the nation. In October 1954, the heads of eighteen national organizations of women met to share information concerning both implementation of the Supreme Court decision and educational programs. Two years later, the twenty-first annual convention was an interracial conference of women. This conference explored how women of all colors and all persuasions could work to surmount barriers to human and civil rights. Other activities included public programs supportive of Rosa Parks, Autherine Lucy, and the Birmingham bus boycott. Mason visited Alabama to acquire first hand information on the situation there.

During her four years as NCNW president, Vivian Carter Mason succeeded in moving the council to another level. Assessing her administration, she said that many of the goals had not been reached. In her recommendations for the future, she cited a number of areas that needed the immediate attention of the next president. She suggested that the NCNW develop more local councils and strengthen existing ones by continuing to hold the leadership conferences begun in 1952 and by extensively promoting programs; that the NCNW sponsor at least two meetings per year with national affiliates to insure greater participation and cooperation; and that the council build a strong public relations program. After twenty-two years of operation under three administrations, the NCNW had built a solid base of credibility, had developed an extensive network of contacts and supporters, and had created a sound constitution and operational structure that could easily be amended and expanded. The organization still needed money and clearly defined program service areas.

DOROTHY IRENE HEIGHT, 1957-

In 1957, Dorothy Irene Height became the fourth president of the National Council of Negro Women. Introduced to Bethune and the council in 1937, she had served for twenty years in a number of appointive positions that provided her a unique opportunity to understand every aspect of the NCNW. Prior to her election as NCNW president, she served for thirteen years as a member of the YWCA National Board staff and for eight years as the president of Delta Sigma Theta sorority. By 1957, she understood the many dimensions of a national organization and was ready to assume the leadership of the major national Black women's organization. She had several mentors, but none had more impact than Mary McLeod Bethune.

Coming to power on the eve of the civil rights revolution of the 1960s, Dorothy Height was determined to make the National Council of Negro Women the organization Bethune intended it to be. The groundwork necessary to achieve this goal was laid between 1958 and 1965; between 1966 and 1980, the growth of the organization was little less than phenomenal. The election of Ronald Reagan as president of the United States in 1980 effectively checked the NCNW's growth and to some extent the growth of other major Black organizations that had become dependent on the federal government's largess. The NCNW had in the 1980s received a number of government and foundation grants that allowed it to enlarge the national staff and relocate its headquarters. Struggling to maintain the large staff and NCNW offices catapulted the organization into debt and forced it to scale back its national staff. While it continues to maintain a high profile and a commitment to international programs, it has not been able to mount major domestic programs.

During the late 1960s and 1970s, Height developed the NCNW into an international corporation with a highly trained professional staff and with capabilities for program delivery and advocacy seldom realized by voluntary organizations. In spite of many contradictions and problems, Dorothy Height has been able to maintain the illusion of power that Bethune affected during the early years. During the late 1930s, Bethune frequently stated that the NCNW represented 500,000 women, which was the collective membership of the fourteen NCNW affiliates. In the 1940s, the figure was adjusted to one million. Until the late 1980s, Height maximized this image of power and gained political capital by stating that she represented four million women. Bethune and Height were accurate in their projections of the number of Black women represented through the membership of affiliate organizations; however, the public, particularly white Americans, perceived the NCNW, Bethune, and Height as more powerful than they actually were. The idea of NCNW's representative power has been particularly attractive to predominantly white, politically oriented governmental agencies or organizations seeking to identify one representative of a diverse constituency for a variety of purposes, including sponsorship of government-funded community service projects.

Dorothy Height during her tenure has moved the NCNW to a new level. Following her election, the NCNW began to move in new directions to solve a number of old problems, to introduce program initiatives more tailored to the times, and to find new ways to institutionalize the legacy of Mary McLeod Bethune and the national council concept. Questions regarding finances, membership development, public relations, interpretation of the national council concept, and the functioning of local councils and regions were candidly addressed by Dorothy Height and the board of directors.

In particular, Dorothy Height saw the acquisition of tax-exempt status as the key to solving many financial problems, for it would make the NCNW more attractive to philanthropists, foundations, and other potential donors who were reluctant to give large sums of money for which they would be taxed. Because of the council's emphasis on legislative and political activities, this status had been consistently denied to the council under Bethune. Under Height's direction the Articles of Incorporation were revised and the base of the NCNW's educational and charitable programs were broadened. In 1966, the Internal Revenue Service ruled that NCNW was tax-exempt.

Acquiring tax-exempt status was viewed by many as the biggest news in NCNW's history, because it paved the way for grants and contributions that made growth and expansion possible. The simultaneous announcement of two major grants for programs to recruit and train African-American women for volunteer community service was cause for great celebration. Grants of $300,000 from the Ford Foundation and $154,193 from the Department of Health, Education and Welfare meant that for the first time in its thirty-one-year history, the NCNW would be able to expand its quarters and staff and develop more effective community service programs. Height announced that the grants provided the NCNW with resources to mobilize a nationwide network to work within a variety of communities, middle-class and poor, Negro and white, to carry out needed community service and social action programs.

After 1965, major program priorities focused on issues related to youth, employment, housing, health, consumerism, hunger and malnutrition, civil rights, volunteerism, women's issues, international problems and family life. From 1965 to 1980, they sponsored at least forty national projects; about one-fourth were related to youth; another fourth targeted women's issues. Operation Sisters United, Youth Career Development, Health Careers, National Collaboration for Children and Youth, New Roles for Volunteers, the National Immunization Program, the Fannie Lou Hamer Day Care Center, Volunteers Unlimited, and Ujamma are some of the programs designed to respond to problems concerning youth unemployment, delinquency, teenage pregnancy and parenthood, and health care and to stress the need for education in areas where Black professionals are underrepresented. Operation Cope, Women's Rights and Housing, Women's Opportunity, Project Woman Power, the NCNW Leadership Development Project, and the Women's Learning Center explored problems related to lower-income women, single heads of households, sexism, employment, the acquisition of management skills, education, household workers, and affirmative action.

Under Height's direction, the NCNW's historic concern for working with women in the African-American diaspora and for maintaining advocacy on international issues has been a key focus. Following forty years of international program emphasis, in 1975 the NCNW, with a grant from the Agency for International Development, established an international

*In 1974, a seventeen-foot statue of Mary McLeod Bethune (with two children) was placed a
short distance from the Capitol. Shown here admiring the model are the three women who
succeeded Bethune as president of the National Council of Negro Women (left to right): Vivian
Carter Mason, Dorothy Height, and Dorothy Ferebee. [Bethune Museum and Archives]*

division. The division formalized ongoing NCNW
work in this area and provided a unique opportunity
for Black American women to work with women in
Africa, the Caribbean, and other parts of the world. In
1979, this division concluded an agreement with the
director for educational and cultural affairs of the
International Communication Agency for a "Twin-
ning" program involving the NCNW and the national
women's organizations of Senegal and Togo.

Employment issues have been central to the
NCNW's efforts to advance the economic status of
Black women and their families. With the "Hold
Your Job" campaigns of the 1940s, the NCNW had
sponsored seminars and conferences and developed
extensive program materials on this topic. The 1970
opening of the Women's Center for Education and
Career Advancement for Minority Women extended
the NCNW's commitment to minority women employed at all levels of business. The center, located in
New York City, now offers a variety of programs and
services. Education and career consultation and an
educational program geared toward gaining and keeping employment are features of the center. In
cooperation with Pace University, the center sponsors an associate degree program that emphasizes the

skills and knowledge necessary for advancement in
business. In 1976, the center published a detailed
curriculum guide that offered all NCNW sections
and affiliates, government agencies, and business training programs an instructional package useful for the
development of educational programs for women
employed in entry-level positions in large corporations and financial institutions.

In the last five years, the NCNW's domestic
program has focused largely on Black Family Reunion celebrations. To address the many negative
images of the Black family, in 1986 the NCNW
launched a culturally based event emphasizing the
historic strengths and traditional values of the Black
family. The celebrations are reminiscent of the large
state fairs and festivals of the past. The events consist
of workshops, issue forums, exhibits, and demonstrations anchored by extensive entertainment. They have
helped to renew the NCNW's public role, and sig-
nify its reentry into national public policy discussions.

CONCLUSION

The development of the national council concept
was a stroke of genius. Mary McLeod Bethune conceived the idea and founded the organization; Dorothy

Ferebee and Vivian Carter Mason sustained the idea; and Dorothy I. Height implemented important elements of the concept. Handicapped by a lack of resources, Ferebee and Mason were unable to develop and maintain clearly identifiable programs that could be replicated and sustained at the local level. Bethune brought to the council talented women representative of diverse affiliates and other national organizations, utilizing their skills and personal resources to expand the understanding of the national council concept and to provide a level of advocacy unknown to Black women of that time. They spoke for women and they spoke for Black America in such a forceful manner that within a short period of time, NCNW was able to mobilize thousands of Black women through its affiliate and organizational network.

By 1960, the most profound changes in the status of Black Americans since Emancipation were well under way. As the Southern Christian Leadership Conference (SCLC), the Student Nonviolent Coordinating Committee, and other civil rights groups began to utilize the techniques of nonviolence to force social and political change, violence erupted in Alabama, Mississippi, and other southern cities. The NCNW, through its volunteer network, which included a number of militant young Black women, moved into rural communities and urban areas and immediately began to set up workshops to define problems and develop strategies for addressing the needs of Black Americans. The NCNW identified local, state, and national resources that were available for program development in these areas. The NCNW was one of the first national organizations of Black women to be recognized by the federal government as possessing the capabilities for coordinating and implementing major government-sponsored programs.

Beginning with President John F. Kennedy and continuing with President Lyndon B. Johnson, there seemed to be a solid commitment to providing opportunities for Black Americans and women. As the Great Society and War on Poverty programs were launched, the federal government sought organizations and institutions capable of implementing programs at the local level. They turned to the NAACP, the Urban League, the NCNW, the SCLC and several other organizations for guidance and direction in defining the needs and programs that would serve the poor and dispossessed. The NCNW, utilizing the skills of both educated and uneducated Black women, developed self-help programs such as Wednesdays in Mississippi, the Okolona Day Care Center, Project Homes, and Operation Daily Bread.

Mary McLeod Bethune understood the nature and function of power and believed that if Black women could be united in purpose they could be a potent force for effecting economic, political, and social change. She knew that they could not be as effective as individuals and separate organizations as through an organization of organizations. In effect, Bethune was asking Black women's organizations to give up a little power to acquire great power. Some heads of Black women's organizations interpreted unification as a threat to their personal power bases, frequently defined by their leadership in a national organization.

Prior to the 1940s, there had been many Black female leaders but Mary McLeod Bethune became the first to function as an equal with Black male leaders. The NCNW records demonstrate that W.E.B. Du Bois, Walter White, Carter G. Woodson, and others had immense respect for her. Indeed, she frequently opened new doors by taking the views of the Black leadership into areas unknown and inaccessible to even the most prominent race leaders. Yet even though Bethune had immense personal power and was able to build respect and credibility for her new organization, she was not able to build the kind of financial and administrative capability necessary to sustain the national council concept.

The accomplishments of Dorothy Height's administration have enhanced NCNW's prominence and recognition. Achievements notwithstanding, the NCNW has yet to realize the goal of unifying national Black women's organizations. The goal is as elusive today as it was fifty-seven years ago. The growth in numbers and power of the major sororities, Alpha Kappa Alpha and Delta Sigma Theta, and the advent of new organizations, such as the National Coalition of 100 Black Women, present powerful challenges to the NCNW's goal of unification. Many national Black women's organizations have become disillusioned with the NCNW's leadership and its fiscal instability. Some maintain a pro forma relationship with the NCNW—they pay the annual affiliate membership fee to keep a place on the board. Many are concerned about the lack of new leadership and are looking forward to the identification of Height's successor. Members of many affiliate groups feel that their organizations are more viable than the NCNW. Nonetheless, in less than half a century the National Council of Negro Women achieved many of the goals articulated by Mary McLeod Bethune. Collaboration and coalition building have proven key to harnessing the power of 4 million women.

BIBLIOGRAPHY

Bethune, Mary McLeod. "NCNW Must Provide Vision and Organized Power," *Women United: Souvenir Year Book* (1951), and "The National Council of Negro Women 1935-1949." Unpublished typescript, Bethune Museum and Archives, Washington, D.C. (n.d.); Collier-Thomas, Bettye. *Black Women in America: Contributors to Our Heritage* (1984), and *NCNW, 1935-1980* (1980), and "Toward Black Feminism: The Creation of the Bethune Museum and Archives." Unpublished typescript (n.d.); Holt, Rackham. *Mary McLeod Bethune: A Biography* (1964); Leffall, Delores C., and Janet L. Sims. "Mary McLeod Bethune—The Educator," *Journal of Negro Education* (Summer 1976); *NAW*; Noble, Jeanne. *Beautiful, Also Are the Souls of My Black Sisters: A History of the Black Woman in America* (1978). The papers of the National Council of Negro Women are housed at the Bethune Museum and Archives National Historic Site in Washington, D.C.

BETTYE COLLIER-THOMAS

NATIONAL DOMESTIC WORKERS UNION

In early 1968, formal efforts to organize domestic workers began in Atlanta when eight women met at Perry Homes, a low-income housing project, to discuss the idea of an organization. This effort to organize was spearheaded by Dorothy Lee Bolden, who had worked as a maid for thirty-eight years. The women continued to hold meetings at the Butler Street Young Men's Christian Association, and as the group grew they moved to the Wheat Street Baptist Church. Reverend William Holmes Borders, the church's pastor, was prominent in the African-American community and an encouraging force behind Bolden's organizing efforts. The group also received support and aid in the form of office space and telephone and secretarial help from John McGowan, executive director of the Georgia Human Relations Council. Although Bolden had in earlier years sought advice from organized labor representatives in Atlanta, the group decided not to affiliate with any existing labor organization but to create their own group, the National Domestic Workers Union (NDWU).

By August 1968, the group had coalesced into a "mutual-benefit association," defined by social scientists and organizational theorists Peter M. Blau and W. Richard Scott (1962) as one "in which the membership is expected to be the prime beneficiary." Thus, it was not a "union" in the true sense of the term. According to Bolden, she used the word "union" to "give the organization strength of its own. . . . The word union gave it clout, and working class members understood the word." Members were taught how to negotiate with and communicate their desires to their employers. The instruction proved successful, and most members got the wage increases and better working conditions they sought. Wages increased from $3.50 to $5.00 per day to $13.50 to $15.00 plus carfare.

The NDWU from its inception was characterized by volunteerism and an evangelical fervor. Members felt that by banding together, they could improve their lot. On September 19, 1968, Bolden was elected president, due to her charisma, self-confidence, competence, commitment to the mission of the group, and ability to articulate its ideological goals. She has served as president to the present.

The group agreed that its objective would be to "promote . . . organized and unionized Domestics, including all people." The group's charter, granted by the state of Georgia in 1968, states:

> This corporation is organized and chartered for the purpose of enhancing, protecting, and promoting the economic, social, and educational welfare of its members in Atlanta, Georgia, its environs and in the American Nation as a whole. The primary purpose of this organization shall be to benefit the community as measured by the increased wages, better working conditions, and more benefits to its members as reflected in improved living standards rather than monetary profits to its members.

To increase its membership, NDWU members agreed to promote the organization by contacting individuals, organizing meetings in various communities, distributing leaflets advertising the group at bus stops and other places frequented by domestic workers, and advertising on the radio. The group held spirited meetings, where community leaders were invited to speak. These tactics were extremely successful, and membership grew.

By the 1970s, the organization was considered a powerful political force in the community. Members participated in voter registration drives, protested against the Atlanta Mass Transit Authority (to get routes and fares that better accommodated domestic workers), and worked on local, state, and national political campaigns.

In an effort to pursue the goal of professionalizing the field of domestic work, the NDWU implemented several projects between 1971 and 1978 funded by government grants. Its homemakers' skills program was designed to train welfare recipients in consumer affairs, problem solving, resource use, and job hunting.

Another grant allowed the NDWU to develop a profile of Atlanta's domestic workers, which indicated that the group needed improved child care and training. As a result, the Office of Equal Opportunity and Economic Opportunity in Atlanta funded a career-training center, which operated for three years. Participants were paid a weekly stipend and received six months of training in reading, writing, mathematics, early childhood education, monetary budgeting, food preparation, first-aid, and general household duties.

In an attempt to create financial stability for the organization and honor women in domestic service, Bolden established a fund-raiser called Maids Honor Day in 1970. Employers nominated domestic workers for the Maid of the Year Award, and the winner and runners-up received cash and gifts. Former President Jimmy Carter's maid Minnie Fitzpatrick received the award in 1978. The fund-raiser was discontinued after 1978.

A major focus of the NDWU has been providing a nonprofit employment placement and counseling service for its members. Between 1972 and 1980, over 13,000 members were served.

In 1979, Bolden was accused of misusing government funds. After a federal investigation, she was found innocent of the charge. However, her image was tarnished, and her credibility has continued to be questioned by some.

Between 1979 and 1984, the NDWU continued to provide counseling and placement services despite financial difficulties. During this period it was funded totally by donations from individuals and Bolden's personal funds. From 1984 to 1988, the NDWU received an annual grant of $12,000 from the Fulton County Board of Commissioners, to be used for job placement, training, and counseling. Since 1988, the NDWU has been dependent upon contributions and Bolden's personal funds.

By 1990, membership in the NDWU had declined considerably. In 1991, the NDWU placed and counseled approximately 300 members. During that time, members received domestic jobs paying from $50 to $80 per day. In spite of the organization's financial problems, Bolden continues to be committed to its goals.

BIBLIOGRAPHY

Blau, Peter M. and W. Richard Scott. *Formal Organizations* (1962); Bolden, Dorothy Lee. Personal interviews (September 15, 1982; February 1, 1983; June 25, 1985; and November 11, 1991). Records of the NDWU can be found in the Southern Labor Archives, Georgia State University, and the organization's office, Atlanta.

DOROTHY COWSER YANCY

NATIONAL LEAGUE FOR THE PROTECTION OF NEGRO WOMEN

see

ASSOCIATIONS FOR THE PROTECTION OF NEGRO WOMEN

NATIONAL NEGRO HEALTH WEEK

The dismal state of Black health care in the United States spawned a grass-roots Black health movement that began largely as a local effort by Black women's groups. Midwives, mothers, nurses, teachers, and sororities organized and participated in activities that provided health services and information to the community. "From 1890 to 1920 the health activities of organized women's clubs laid the foundation for the Black health movement" (Smith 1991).

Slavery was a flagrant violation of fundamental human rights, one of which was the right to health and an inadequate health care system. African-Americans, however, in direct response to racism and segregation, built hospitals and medical schools to address Black health care needs. Howard University and Meharry Medical College were among the first fourteen Black medical schools founded in the United States.

The health care deficits established during slavery continued well into the twentieth century. "For example, in 1900 the Black death rate was 25 per 1,000 compared to 17 per 1,000 in whites. Although the Black rate dropped in 1930 to 14 per 1,000, it was still considerably higher than the white rate of 10" (Morais 1967).

In 1915, Booker Taliaferro Washington founded National Negro Health Week (NNHW) in an effort to increase the awareness and improve the health status of African-Americans. This observance brought national attention to the Black health care crisis, and it was the catalyst for the National Negro Health Movement, officially launched in 1932.

The Negro Organization Society of Virginia also played a major role in providing the foundation for the National Negro Health Movement. Under the direction of Robert Russa Moton in 1912, this organization started day-long campaigns to clean up the farms and neighborhoods in Virginia. With the support of the Virginia Board of Health the campaign expanded to a week.

In 1914, Monroe Nathan Work, a sociologist at Tuskegee Institute, provided an alarming statistical analysis of Black Americans' health in the South. His calculations indicated that nearly half of all Black deaths were premature and could have been prevented. These data, combined with the activity of local health activists, inspired Booker T. Washington to envision a national health movement. In 1915, he initiated a Health Improvement Week at Tuskegee Institute. This became National Negro Health Week (NNHW), to promote health and disease prevention among African-Americans. Sixteen states participated during the first year. Lectures at schools and churches, distribution of health pamphlets, and special clean-up services took place across the country. After Washington died on November 14, 1915, plans for a National Negro Health Week in 1916 did not materialize. In 1917, however, under the leadership of Tuskegee faculty Moton and Work, Washington's efforts were renewed and the institutionalization of NNHW began.

They decided to honor Booker T. Washington as founder of the movement by celebrating National Negro Health Week during the first week in April, to commemorate his birth on April 5. They also wanted to expand the week into a year-round program. Health leaders concluded that the best way to do this was to get the U.S. Public Health Service (USPHS) to take over NNHW.

In 1932, NNHW came under the purview of the USPHS, and this branch of the government became the center for all activity concerning Black health issues. The name National Negro Health Movement was coined and the USPHS opened the Office of Negro Health Work under the direction of Dr. Roscoe C. Brown. Activities sparked by NNHW survived well into the 1940s and were supported by minority and nonminority associations and public health departments. Various health education and special clinical services were sponsored nationwide. During this time, Dr. Brown kept records of participation throughout the country. He reported that the number of people reached with NNHW increased from 500,000 in 1933 to 5,000,000 in 1942. These figures suggest it was indeed a mass movement.

From 1932 to 1950, a quarterly newsletter chronicling the movement, the *National Negro Health News*, was published. In 1950, the USPHS declared the end of the Black health program and closed the NNHW office. Although the health status of African-Americans had improved significantly, a two-tiered health care system remained, one for white Americans and one for Black Americans.

BIBLIOGRAPHY

Brown, Roscoe C. Annual reports. U.S. Public Health Service, Washington, D.C. (1930-32, 1933, 1942); Morais, Herbert. *The History of the Negro in Medicine* (1967); Smith, Susan. " 'Sick and Tired of Being Sick and Tired': Black Women and the National Negro Health Movement, 1915-1950," Ph.D. diss. (1991); Work, Monroe. "The South and the Conservation of Negro Health," *Negro Year Book* (1914-1915).

LESA WALDEN

NATIONAL ORGANIZATION OF BLACK ELECTED LEGISLATIVE WOMEN

The National Organization of Black Elected Legislative Women (NOBEL) was founded in 1985 in Philadelphia, Pennsylvania, by California State Senator Diane Watson. NOBEL is an organization of Black women state legislators seeking to improve the lives of Black women by furthering their education about public policy issues, promoting participation in the development of public policy, and introducing and supporting legislation that improves the lives of Black women.

NOBEL's purpose is to train and educate Black women and thus increase the number of Black women in local, state, and national elected and appointed offices. NOBEL's primary goal is to assess the needs of all women and provide a national voice in policy debates addressing these needs. Another objective is to work with governments to create programs to further legal, social, economic, and educational opportunities for women.

NOBEL has addressed various issues in national forums and has coordinated numerous activities. In 1989 the main issue for the organization was at-risk youth; the organization lobbied successfully for legislation that would help Black youth. NOBEL also pressed for the rights of political refugees in South Africa. In 1990 NOBEL's second annual legislative conference in New York featured a symposium,

"Women's Health Update," that drew attention to diseases affecting women and the Black community.

NOBEL's agenda for the 1990s is geared to policy implementation and programs adopted to meet the basic needs of women, particularly Black women. Among concerns are the health crisis in the Black community, particularly the impact of tobacco, and the increased occurrence of breast cancer among women of color.

An ongoing activity is the Mother's March for Peace that occurs twice annually, once at the National Black Caucus of State Legislators' Conference. NOBEL members also work with other communities of color.

All Black women legislators are considered members of NOBEL; total membership in 1992 comprised 102 Black women legislators serving thirty-two state legislatures.

BIBLIOGRAPHY

Center for the American Women and Politics, Eagleton Institute of Politics, Rutgers University, New Brunswick, New Jersey.

CAROLE ECHOLS
GRETCHEN E. MACLACHLAN

NATIONAL POLITICAL CONGRESS OF BLACK WOMEN

The National Political Congress of Black Women (NPCBW) was founded in 1984 in Washington, D.C., by Shirley Chisholm, the first Black woman to run for president of the United States, to provide a political forum for Black women. The NPCBW primarily targets Black women of voting age but also encourages women under eighteen years of age to enter and participate in the political process.

The purpose of the NPCBW is to rally Black women to participate in elective politics, to encourage them in public policy formulation, and to educate them about all levels of the political process. The special focus of the NPCBW is to bring masses of Black women into political leadership roles at all levels of government. The NPCBW builds on the experience of Black women, who historically have been beacons of progressive political change, to empower them for the future. The NPCBW acts as a catalyst for this empowerment.

The mission of the NPCBW is to "develop and advocate public positions, at every level of govern-ment, and engage in dialogue with the political parties, to encourage the development of policy, platform and strategy beneficial to the needs and aspirations of the Black community."

The organization has addressed many issues since its founding. It has pressed for affirmative action, access to nontraditional jobs, economic development, education, health, leadership development, the legislative process, and housing and urban development. It has documented patterns of housing market discrimination against Black men and women by holding hearings in Atlanta, St. Louis, San Francisco, and New York. These hearings stimulated legislative action and informed Black women of their rights under the law. The NPCBW also focuses on the social and economic status of the Black family and encourages family reunions to reaffirm the importance of family to the Black community. The first reunion, held in 1986 in Washington, D.C., drew 200,000 people. Besides serving as a social outlet, it offered information on job skills, health issues, and the transmission of historical tradition.

The NPCBW's future agenda concentrates on critical issues of job discrimination, health care, drug abuse, single parenting, lack of education and of daycare facilities, and job training. The organization has already initiated programs in some of these areas, including a Black Parents Drug Prevention Program, Parent Education Teleworkshops, the Fannie Lou Hamer Day Care Center in Ruleville, Mississippi, and Education 2000.

The NPCBW is an independent, nonpartisan organization. Its membership, made up primarily of Black women, is nationwide. The organization's main office in Rancocas, New Jersey, is staffed by one full-time staff member and five volunteers. Some distinguished members and officers of the NPCBW are Shirley Chisholm, former congresswoman (chairperson); C. DeLores Tucker, former secretary of state of Pennsylvania (vice chairperson); and Mable Thomas, member of the Georgia Legislature (board of directors).

BIBLIOGRAPHY

Hernandez, Aileen C. *National Women of Color Organizations: A Report of the Ford Foundation* (1991); National Political Congress of Black Women, Inc., Rancocas, New Jersey.

GRETCHEN E. MACLACHLAN
CAROLE ECHOLS

NATIONAL TRAINING SCHOOL FOR WOMEN AND GIRLS

The National Training School for Women and Girls, a boarding school that opened in 1909 and trained students in domestic science, business, and sewing in the first half of the twentieth century, prepared young Black women to both "uplift" the race and earn a living. School founder Nannie Helen Burroughs (1879-1961) first presented the idea of a training school for young Black women in her role as corresponding secretary for the women's auxiliary of the National Baptist Convention at the turn of the century. She found a receptive audience among Baptist women who declared in a 1908 meeting: "We are not here to discuss the necessity of the institution. The preparation of our women for domestic and professional service, in the home and communities, ranks next in importance to preparation of their souls for the world to come" (Burroughs Papers). In 1907, Burroughs worked with a committee of the National Baptist Convention to purchase a site for a school in Lincoln Heights in Washington, D.C., and two years later the school enrolled its first thirty-one students.

The school was chartered independently of the National Baptist Convention, and Burroughs deliberately excluded the word "Baptist" from the school's name to emphasize its openness to students of all denominations. This original charter incited a debate in the 1920s and 1930s within the Black Baptist community about who had control over the school's operations and finances. Burroughs, however, maintained control over the school and ensured that nearly all of the members of the board of trustees were Black women. Funding was drawn primarily from individual contributions within the Black community, in contrast to many other private Black schools that were dependent on support from white foundations. Fund-raising projects carried out by the students and staff of the National Training School included recitations, plays, and concerts. These performances raised money, advertised the school, and gave students practice in public speaking and performance. Other revenue was raised through operating a laundry, which also served as a training center, selling student-made goods, and running a summer school for adult women offering courses in social service and community organizing.

The school's motto was the three B's—Bible, bath, and broom. The bath and broom symbolized training in cleanliness and housekeeping skills as part of racial advancement. Burroughs placed particular stress on the need for young Black women to be trained in domestic science, a skill they could use in the workplace and the home. The central tenet of the school was the Bible, which emphasized spirituality and moral conduct. The students of the National Training School lived in the campus dormitories, and they came from different regions of the United States

LAUNDRY

Dainty Linens Handled with Care

Prompt and Courteous Service.

We CAN and WILL Please our Patrons

If our work does not please you TELL US

If it pleases you TELL YOUR FRIENDS

We are anxious to secure their patronage.   Price List sent on request.

LAUNDRY DEPARTMENT

The National Training School for Women and Girls, Inc.

Lincoln Heights, D.C.   Phone Lincoln 1777

The motto of the National Training School was the three B's—Bible, bath, and broom. The founder, Nannie Helen Burroughs, placed particular stress on training in domestic science. This card advertises services for which the students are being trained.

as well as Africa and the Caribbean. They took courses in missionary work, domestic science, social work, clerical work, printing, sewing, music, beauty culture, and agriculture. This training was aimed at providing the skills needed for Black women to become simultaneously wage workers, housewives, and community activists.

The National Training School also emphasized "race pride" through its required courses in "Negro history." Burroughs was a friend of Carter G. Woodson and a strong advocate of the teaching of Black history. Every student was required to complete the course and pass a written and oral examination. In their 1929 yearbook the students wrote of their appreciation for the opportunity to study the history of their race: "this school teaches History and Negro History and the students are tremendously inspired by learning the truth about their own race. We know now that our race has been a valuable part of all that has been going on in the building of world civilizations. Dr. Carter G. Woodson's books are used as the text here and we have a room, a real library—if you please—set apart for the study of Negro life and history."

After 1953 the school, then called the National Trade and Professional School for Women and Girls, narrowed its training solely to the field of missionary service, and Burroughs continued as the school's president until her death in 1961. For the first half of the twentieth century the National Training School prepared young Black women for their dual roles as wage workers and "uplifters" of the race, and served as a model institution for the Black community.

[*See also* BURROUGHS, NANNIE HELEN.]

BIBLIOGRAPHY

Barnett, Evelyn Brooks. "Nannie Burroughs and the Education of Black Women." In *The Afro-American Woman: Struggles and Images*, ed. Sharon Harley and Rosalyn Terborg-Penn (1978); Burroughs, Nannie Helen. Papers. Library of Congress, Washington, D.C.; Clark-Lewis, Elizabeth. "This Work Had an End: African-American Domestic Workers in Washington, D.C., 1910-1940." In *To Toil the Livelong Day: America's Women at Work, 1780-1980*, ed. Carol Groneman and Mary Beth Norton (1987); Collier-Thomas, Bettye. "The Impact of Black Women in Education: An Historical Overview," *Journal of Negro Education* (1982); Dill, Bonnie Thornton. " 'Making the Job Good Yourself': Domestic Service and the Construction of Personal Dignity." In *Women and the Politics of Empowerment*, ed. Ann Bookman and Sandra Morgan (1988); Fisher, Berenice M. *Industrial Education: American Ideas and Institutions* (1967); Giddings, Paula. *When and Where I Enter: The Impact of Black Women on Race and Sex in America* (1984); Green, Constance M. *The Secret City: A History of Race Relations in the Nation's Capital* (1967); Harley, Sharon. "Black Women in a Southern City: Washington D.C., 1890-1920." In *Sex, Race, and the Role of Women in the South*, ed. Joanne V. Hawks and Sheila L. Skemp (1983), and "Beyond the Classroom: The Organizational Lives of Black Female Educators in the District of Columbia, 1890-1930," *Journal of Negro Education* (Summer 1982); Higginbotham, Evelyn Brooks. "Religion, Politics, and Gender: The Leadership of Nannie Helen Burroughs," *Journal of Religious Thought* (Winter/Spring 1988); Jones, Jacqueline. *Labor of Love, Labor of Sorrow: Black Women, Work, and the Family from Slavery to the Present* (1985); Lerner, Gerda. *Black Women in White America: A Documentary History* (1972); Palmer, Phyllis. *Domesticity and Dirt: Housewives and Domestic Servants in the United States, 1920-1945* (1989); Terborg-Penn, Rosalyn. "Survival Strategies among African-American Women Workers: A Continuing Process." In *Women, Work and Protest*, ed. Ruth Milkman (1985).

VICTORIA WOLCOTT

NATIONAL URBAN LEAGUE

The first decades of the twentieth century were years of significant demographic change within the African-American population in the United States, as a predominantly southern and rural people became increasingly northern and urban. Believing that greater economic, educational, and political opportunities would result, a number of people and organizations encouraged this migration. Many others, however, worried about the impact these population shifts would have on the migrants themselves, on the Black communities into which they moved, and on the cities as a whole. Among the organizations founded to address these issues were the various local associations for the protection of women that united in 1906 into the National League for the Protection of Colored Women (NLPCW), the Committee for Improving Industrial Conditions in New York (CIICNY), and the Committee on Urban Conditions among Negroes (CUCAN). In 1911 the NLPCW, CIICNY, and CUCAN merged to form the National League on Urban Conditions among Negroes (the National Urban League after 1920), an interracial organization. The National Urban League's principal focus was economic: opening up opportunities to migrants; providing job training, housing assistance, and wholesome recreational activities; and educating migrants on life in the city. To support its programs, the National Urban League (NUL) recognized the need for trained social workers and thus it also developed a program to train young African-American men and women in social work. As with other organizations of the time operating in the Black community, "the existing social services and reform networks developed by black women" were key to the development of the National Urban League and the carrying out of its programs (Salem 1990).

Unlike the National Association for the Advancement of Colored People (NAACP), where early work focused at the national level, the NUL's initial work was concentrated in local affiliates, many of which grew out of existing clubs, settlement houses, and organizations. Beginning in the nineteenth century, Black clubwomen had served as their community's social workers, and the women who organized local affiliates provided the Urban League with important ties to existing community organizations. In Chicago, for example, the Urban League, endorsed by the local Federation of Colored Women's Clubs, received its major financial support initially from the Baptist Women's Congress, and Mrs. William Carey, president of that organization, served as the Chicago Urban League's first director. The board of directors included major figures in the local Black women's club movement and thirty women, called Urban League Volunteers, helped to carry out the programs. Half of the Urban League of Greater Boston's executive board was female; they brought to the league their work with the Abraham Lincoln Settlement, Baby Hygiene Association, Boston Society for the Care of Girls, Children's Aid Society, Church Home Society, Episcopal Mission Work among Colored People, Girls' Trade School, Harriet Tubman Home, Home for Aged Women, and the Young Women's Christian Association (YWCA).

One of the most influential locals was Atlanta's Neighborhood Union, founded in 1908. The Neighborhood Union (NU) had developed a systematic plan of work on issues such as housing, child care, educational and recreational activities, and health care in Atlanta by the time the Urban League sought affiliation. The NU's method included dividing the city into zones and districts each with its own captain, conducting community investigations aided by Morehouse College sociology students. The NU's "zone-neighborhood-district organization" became the model for Urban League work in cities such as Jacksonville, Louisville, Philadelphia, Newark, Norfolk, and Tallahassee (Salem 1990). The NU emphasized a professional social work approach to community problems. Its founding president, Lugenia Burns Hope, organized a Social Service Institute at Morehouse College in 1919 that was the predecessor to the Atlanta School of Social Work (incorporated 1925; becoming in 1938 the Atlanta University School of Social Work).

The Urban League affiliates were many migrants' first contacts with life in their new city. In Chicago in 1917 the Urban League appointed a representative to work with the Travelers' Aid Society at the Illinois Central Railroad station to assist migrants on their arrival. The league also kept a "certified lodging list" and provided employment assistance. Historian James Grossman contends that the "Urban League was by far the largest employment agency for black Chicagoans" (Grossman 1989). At the same time as the Urban League provided valuable employment and other assistance, it also attempted to socialize migrants into behavior patterns league workers thought suitable to urban life, which often meant to behavior that employers or others in the larger white community would find acceptable. This emphasis on "respectable" behavior took many forms. The Neighborhood Union, the Atlanta affiliate, used its district organizing as a way to pressure out of the community those they considered undesirable. In Chicago, the Urban League conducted "Strangers Meetings," passed out leaflets at train stations and other places where migrants might be found in large numbers, and oversaw hundreds of clubwomen who went door-to-door advising newcomers on appropriate behavior, dress, food, and housekeeping. One leaflet developed by the Chicago Urban League demanded that migrants pledge "I will refrain from wearing dust caps, bungalow aprons, house clothing and bedroom shoes out of doors. I will arrange my toilet within doors and not on the front porch. I will insist upon the use of rear entrances for coal-dealers, hucksters, etc. I will refrain from loud talking and objectionable deportment on street cars and in public places. I will do my best to prevent defacement of property either by children or adults" (Grossman 1989). The Urban League affiliates attempted to assist migrants in obtaining the better living conditions—housing, jobs, education—that were the goals of their migration and at the same time to impose a uniform standard of behavior as the price paid for these opportunities. Yet despite the patronizing attitudes that often accompanied them, the services offered by the Urban League were often invaluable to those new to the urban life in both the North and the South.

Not all the Urban League's services were specifically for migrants, the unemployed, or the working class. Some health care and recreational opportunities benefitted African-Americans of all classes who were denied access to the predominantly white social services in the urban areas. Among these services were birth control clinics. Through its established networks and its professional orientation, the Urban League was able in the 1920s and the 1930s to bring together teachers, physicians, nurses, social workers, labor leaders, and clubwomen to establish birth control clinics in several urban areas, such as Baltimore and Harlem, often receiving the support of (or at least no opposition from) local ministers. Here, as in other avenues of work, the networks and commitment of Black women were central to the efforts of the Urban League.

In turn, the Urban League, with its focus on professional social work, provided early educational and employment opportunities for a select group of women. Urban League Fellowships supported social work education; by 1920 seventeen African-Americans, eight of them women, had received these fellowships. More were trained in the coming decades. A significant portion of these found employment within the Urban League: in 1923 its forty local organizations employed approximately 150 social workers, about half of whom were women. "Three [were] executive secretaries, about ten special industrial workers, and others case workers, home economic workers, health nurses, girls' club workers, juvenile court workers, etc." (Bowles 1923). The fellowships also benefited women who then sought employment in the YWCAs and other organizations providing services to the Black community.

By the 1940s a number of professionally trained women came to head many of the local affiliates. E. Fannie Granton, for example, who became executive director of the Englewood, New Jersey, Urban League in 1944, was a graduate of Shaw University (Raleigh, North Carolina) with a graduate degree from the Atlanta University School of Social Work.

Through its journal, Opportunity, the National Urban League was also instrumental in the careers of another group of Black women: literary and visual artists. Along with the NAACP's Crisis, throughout the 1920s and 1930s Opportunity encouraged and rewarded literary production by African-American men and women, sponsoring literary contests and providing an avenue for publication. In 1925, the first year of the Opportunity contest, it received 732 entries. Women were particularly prominent among the entrants and winners in the drama category. Four of Opportunity's seven 1925 playwright awards went to work authored by women: two to works by Zora Neale Hurston, Colorstruck and Spears, and one each to works by May Miller and Eloise Bibb Thompson.

Hurston also won a fiction prize for her short story "Spunk." In 1926 and 1927 two other women received playwright awards, Georgia Douglas Johnson and Eulalie Spence. The awards dinners sponsored by Opportunity were an unprecedented opportunity for the winners, many of whom were new young writers, to be introduced to established writers and intellectuals, Black and white. In addition to its contests, Opportunity also regularly published African-American writers; for example, Marita Bonner's play The Pot Maker appeared in 1927 and her short story "Tin Can" in 1933. Opportunity also encouraged artists: Gwendolyn Bennett's work provided the covers of the January 1926, July 1926, and December 1930 issues.

Thus the National Urban League in its first three decades of existence provided support for working-class women adjusting to life in the city and for the more well-to-do professional women and artists seeking opportunities and support for their careers. In turn, the support and expertise of Black women in the local Urban League affiliates was crucial to the development of the Urban League, laying the foundation of the organization that would emerge in the next decades as a major force in the continuing struggle for civil and economic rights for African-Americans.

BIBLIOGRAPHY

Bowles, Eva D. "Opportunities for the Educated Colored Woman," Opportunity (March 1923); Grossman, James. Land of Hope: Chicago, Black Southerners, and the Great Migration (1989); Moore, Jesse Thomas, Jr. A Search for Equality: The National Urban League 1910-1961 (1981); Opportunity (1920-45); Perkins, Kathy, ed. Black Female Playwrights: An Anthology of Plays before 1950 (1989); Rodrique, Jesse. "Birth Control Movement" (in this volume); Rouse, Jacqueline Anne. Lugenia Burns Hope: Black Southern Reformer (1989); Salem, Dorothy. To Better Our World: Black Women in Organized Reform, 1890-1920 (1990); Weiss, Nancy. The National Urban League (1974).

ELSA BARKLEY BROWN

NATIONAL URBAN LEAGUE GUILD

Best known for its annual sponsorship of New York's legendary Beaux Arts Ball, the National Urban League Guild is a nonpartisan, nonprofit, interracial service organization. As an independent fund-raising auxiliary to the National Urban League, the guild shares the league's dedication to improving the quality of life for urban minorities. Changing over time to reflect contemporary exigencies, the issues and goals both groups embrace demonstrate a deep concern for social justice and equal opportunity: racism, employment, housing, health care, economic development, criminal justice, social welfare, and education are major areas of commitment.

The National Urban League was organized in 1910 to provide assistance and guidance to the large numbers of African-Americans migrating to northern industrial cities form the rural south. Guided by the standards, objectives, and methods of professional social work, the organization has been an effective national force for improving the lives of urban racial minorities and fostering cooperation and understanding among racial and ethnic groups. Today, the Urban League's activities include researching how Blacks and other minorities live and work in urban communities across the nation, analyzing policies affecting urban life, consulting with government agencies and community groups, providing direct services to disadvantaged city dwellers, disseminating educational information about all aspects of the changing conditions of urban life, and advocating policies and programs to improve and enrich the quality of urban life.

To support the league's research, policy, and program initiatives, the guild conducts its own fundraising, publicity, and educational projects. Over the years, its art exhibitions, literary evenings with famous authors, membership drives, public relations campaigns, and educational forums have supported the league's work in a variety of ways. In addition, by attracting the participation and support of Black and white middle-class people, guild activities have helped foster interracial cooperation and understanding.

Fund-raising, however, remains the organization's primary focus. Since 1942, the Beaux Arts Ball has been its major annual project. At this star-studded gala—held until 1958 at Harlem's famed Savoy Ballroom and subsequently at the Waldorf-Astoria Hotel—celebrities and guests come together for an all-night extravaganza of dancing, dining, and entertainment. Elaborately costumed according to each year's theme, guests celebrate the Urban League's achievements while contributing thousands of dollars toward its ongoing work.

A small group of young New York City professionals—Blacks, whites, women, and men—began meeting in members' homes in June 1942. Their desire to promote racial harmony through organized action led them to initiate a program of educational, cultural, and social activities aimed at improving race relations. In an era when racial segregation was widely practiced by both custom and law, these visionaries developed a successful and highly visible model for interracial cooperation as they undertook programs aimed at enriching community life while calling attention to the concerns and work of the Urban League. This fledgling group grew quickly into a national organization. Today, guild officers and committees conduct the organization's business from a volunteer-staffed office in the National Urban League's headquarters in New York City.

The guild's membership has always included men and women of both races. In the early years, most members were social workers and teachers, while others were artists, journalists, librarians, and medical professionals. Some of the women were homemakers whose husbands were professionals and businessmen. At a time when fewer women worked outside the home and when racial prejudice discouraged the participation of African-American women in many civic groups, the Urban League Guild proved an important outlet for middle-class women's talents and energies.

Indeed, the dynamic force behind the founding of the group was a committed nucleus of Harlem women. Well connected in the arts, professions, and civic organizations, they brought together an impressive array of professional expertise, leadership skills, and influence. Mollie Moon presided over the organization for nearly half a century, from its founding in 1942 until her death in 1990. Co-founder Helen E. Harden, a teacher in the New York public schools, served until 1991 as the organization's first vice president. In 1991, Sylvia Hughes became the group's second elected president.

Soon after the guild's founding in 1942, its leaders began receiving requests to help organize affiliate groups in other cities. In its first fifty years, the guild chartered eighty-three chapters throughout the United States. Today, local guild chapters in cities across America promote the National Urban League's goals within their own communities, adapting them to local circumstances and concerns. Affiliates serve as auxiliaries to their own local Urban Leagues, patterning many of their activities after those originated by the national guild. Ten years after its founding, the National Urban League Guild group joined with its affiliates in forming the National Council of Guilds, a confederation of autonomous organizations. In 1952, Mollie Moon was elected the first of many council presidents; today Anita Marina of Carrolton, Texas, presides over the confederation.

As successful as the guild's efforts have been throughout its history, two significant contributions

The National Urban League Guild is an interracial fund-raising auxiliary to the National Urban League. The goals it embraces demonstrate a deep concern for social justice and equal opportunity. This group photograph includes guild founder Alta Taylor (seated, center), president Mollie Moon (left foreground), and vice president Helen Harden (seated on floor, right, wearing white blouse). [National Urban League Guild]

to African-American life merit recognition. Among national organizations whose membership includes women and men of all races and creeds, the guild is unique in affording urban middle-class Black women a half-century of leadership and control of a national organization. While leadership posts are filled without regard to race or sex, Black women as a group have consistently enjoyed unlimited leadership opportunities. By establishing a separate organizational entity, the guild's founders ensured that its members would control their own leadership. Moreover, because its financial contributions to the league have been considerable, the guild has become a significant voice within the National Urban League's historically male-dominated leadership hierarchy. At least one guild official traditionally sits on the league's board of trustees. President Mollie Moon, for ex-

ample, served for many years as an Urban League officer. The league's formal recognition of the guild also includes providing office space in its national headquarters in New York City and appointing staff liaisons to work with the National Urban League Guild and the National Council of Guilds.

A second guild achievement—rooted in the days of segregation—has remained unrecognized despite its significance. As it expanded to cities across America, the National Urban League Guild's organizational network became an invaluable social and professional resource for members of the Black middle class. In a racially segregated America, middle-class Blacks had to rely heavily on personal and organizational contacts for social entree wherever they moved or traveled. Like affiliation with a historically Black college or university or membership in a national Black fraternity or sorority, league and guild connections proved an important social credential, recommending members to prominent social circles wherever they traveled. There was a practical side to this as well, for Blacks of every class risked humiliation and rebuff when seeking dining or lodging accommodations in unfamiliar areas. Consequently, the hospitality and guidance of prominent locals helped middle-class Black travelers to insulate themselves from potentially unpleasant—and possibly dangerous—situations. Because the guild was interracial, this important network extended into parts of the white community as well. Thus guild affiliation formed an important thread in the tapestry of Black middle-class social identity, enabling its members to manipulate Jim Crow America within the comfort and security of their class.

Like the National Urban League, the guild has been criticized for being elitist and conservative. A broad historical evaluation, however, must take into account each group's accomplishments, both in terms of its own goals and in terms of what was possible at the time. By these criteria, both organizations made important and lasting contributions to America's urban masses and to its middle class.

BIBLIOGRAPHY

Moore, Jesse T., Jr. *A Search for Equality: The National Urban League, 1910-1961* ([1981] 1987); Nieman, Linda. Essay on the Guild. In *Women's Issues Interest Groups*, ed. Sarah Slavin (forthcoming); Personal interviews with Helen Harden, Sylvia Hughes, Anita Marina, Mollie Moon, and Guichard Parris; Printed and photographic documents in the collection of the National Urban League Guild's New York offices; Weiss, Nancy J. *The National Urban League, 1910-1940* (1974).

LINDA NIEMAN

NATIONAL WELFARE RIGHTS MOVEMENT

Throughout the 1960s and the early seventies, a militant grass-roots movement of welfare recipients challenged the local, state, and national welfare bureaucracies. The National Welfare Rights Organization (NWRO) effectively coordinated the actions of numerous local welfare rights groups across the country between 1967 and 1975. This movement of poor, mostly African-American women and their supporters represented an important example of the active presence of the poor in the political process. It also brought attention to the ways in which race, sex, and class relations informed welfare policy decisions.

In 1966, a veteran civil rights activist and former associate director of the Congress of Racial Equality (CORE), George Wiley, created the Poverty Rights Action Center (PRAC) to establish a national communications network for the numerous welfare rights organizations that began emerging in the early 1960s. PRAC eventually became the headquarters for NWRO, established a year later in an effort to provide a tightly organized structure for the national efforts of local groups to challenge oppressive welfare policies. Several years before the national organization emerged, however, local organizations, like the one started by welfare recipient Johnnie Tillmon in Watts, began appearing around the country. Some of these organizations empowered welfare clients to plan their own job training programs—programs that stressed adequate opportunities for career advancement, education, and effective day-care facilities. Other organizations, like the Brooklyn Welfare Action Council (B-WAC) gained the attention of local politicians who requested endorsements from welfare organizations and viewed welfare rights activists as viable political actors.

The NWRO emerged during the turbulent era of the 1960s when the nation's attention was directed at the stark contradiction of poverty existing in a country as affluent as the United States. President Lyndon Johnson spoke of the nation's ability to eliminate poverty and his newly developed national antipoverty programs were based upon the notion of "maximum feasible participation of the poor" (Piven and Cloward 1978). Within this climate, the NWRO was able to utilize funds from middle-class liberal churches and government poverty programs for the operation of a national network.

In entering the highly contested welfare debate, welfare recipients added their voices to policy discussions that had historically excluded them. At its height in the late 1960s, NWRO-educated recipients and others eligible for benefits under existing laws pressured welfare agencies to provide such benefits in a dignified manner and articulated a unique and complex vision of welfare that guaranteed an adequate income for all families regardless of their composition. Welfare rights activists led sit-ins in welfare departments and utilized other direct action tactics to obtain immediate benefits for their members. Prior to the welfare activism of this era, many who were eligible for benefits were reluctant to apply for public assistance and many who did were denied relief. The assertive posture of the NWRO fueled an explosion in the welfare rolls as many more poor women applied for funds and became informed of their rights as recipients. As a result, many local welfare agencies were forced to change restrictive and demoralizing policies.

African-American welfare recipients/activists like Johnnie Tillmon, Beula Sanders, and Etta Horn gained national prominence as spokespersons and lobbyists for the national organization. The NWRO lobbied the Congress for a guaranteed national income and fought against social security amendments that violated the constitutional rights of welfare recipients. As lobbyists, welfare women demanded that they be provided with the resources to manage their own lives. They criticized nonexistent or inadequate day-care facilities, ill-planned job training programs, degrading, low-wage employment, and welfare practices that scrutinized their personal lives before providing benefits they desperately needed. Furthermore, they exposed the problematic nature of white society's definitions of concepts like "illegitimacy" and matriarchy, and they affirmed the integrity and legitimacy of female-headed households. They criticized policies that purported to stabilize families by forcing mothers to accept low-wage work without guaranteeing adequate day-care facilities and transportation costs. Most important, these women asserted that their roles as mothers constituted valuable work for which they should be compensated. Their vision challenged existing assumptions about the proper composition of the family as well as notions about the meaning of work and welfare. The political participation of welfare women was met with fierce resistance from a powerful antiwelfare backlash in the early seventies. The organization was forced to file for bankruptcy in 1975 when financial support declined dramatically.

The NWRO represents a unique moment in the struggle for Black liberation, because it brought together welfare rights and civil rights within a unified struggle. Welfare activists conceptualized the two as connected and stressed the impact of gender and race in the formulation of welfare policies. Women in the movement conceptualized welfare as a women's issue and undoubtedly influenced feminists who incorporated welfare into their agenda after the demise of the NWRO.

This empowering moment for women on welfare did not occur without many of the gender, race, and class hierarchies against which the movement defined itself. Black female organizers resisted the initiatives of professional organizers who were often sent by the national coordinating committee to direct the organization of local and state activities. Struggles of Black women for autonomy within the NWRO were rooted in the organization's two-tiered leadership structure, which employed full-time organizers who were mostly male, white, and middle-class while the elected leaders were all welfare recipients and mainly African-American women. Nonetheless, the strong challenge to the state represented in this movement exemplified the radical potential of organizations led by and for the poor.

BIBLIOGRAPHY

Piven, Frances Fox and Richard Cloward. *Poor Peoples' Movements: Why They Succeed, How They Fail* (1978); Pope, Jacqueline. *Biting the Hand That Feeds Them: Organizing Women on Welfare at the Grass Roots Level* (1981); West, Guida. *The National Welfare Rights Movement: The Social Protest of Poor Women* (1981).

AMY JORDAN

NATIONALISM *see* BLACK NATIONALISM

NAYLOR, GLORIA (1950-)

Gloria Naylor has become widely associated with a line from her novel, *The Women of Brewster Place* (1982), "All the good men are either dead or waiting to be born." While Naylor explores the violence inflicted upon Black women by their men, she also writes about the possibilities of transformation of men. Primarily, however, Naylor has made a commitment to illuminate the condition of Black women in America.

A short-story writer and novelist, Gloria Naylor was born on January 25, 1950, to Roosevelt, a transit worker, and Alberta McAlpin Naylor, a telephone operator, in Brooklyn, New York. Born and reared in the South, her parents left her a rich legacy from which to draw fictional characters. Naylor earned a Bachelor's degree in English from Brooklyn College of the City University of New York in 1981 and a Master's degree in Afro-American Studies from Yale University in the early 1980s.

Before choosing writing as a primary career, Naylor worked as a missionary for Jehovah's Witnesses in New York, North Carolina, and Florida from 1968 to 1975. Between 1975 and 1981, she worked for several hotels, including the Sheraton City Square in New York City, as a telephone operator. Since the 1980s, Naylor has taught at George Washington

Gloria Naylor, talented author of The Women of Brewster Place, *has made a commitment to illuminate the condition of Black women in America. [Schomburg Center]*

University, New York University, Boston University, and Cornell University.

Naylor achieved national acclaim with the publication of her first novel, *The Women of Brewster Place*, which won the American Book Award for first fiction in 1983. Her novel centers on the lives of seven Black women, of different backgrounds and ages, who find themselves on a dead-end ghetto street that seems to have a life of its own. The novel weaves together broad topics like sex, birth, death, love, and grief to convey the common burden that Black women experience because of their race and gender. With their backs literally up against a brick wall, these women act as mothers to each other as they share their trials and triumphs.

Naylor's second novel, *Linden Hills* (1985), explores the lives of affluent but spiritually dead African-Americans who are trapped by the American dream. While these upwardly mobile African-Americans pride themselves on having arrived, their achievements are undermined by their disdain for the more humanistic values like mutual support of family and kindness to others and their preoccupation with material possessions.

With the support of a grant from the National Endowment for the Arts, Naylor wrote her third novel, *Mama Day* (1989). Steeped in mysticism, the novel resembles Toni Morrison's *Beloved* (1987), Sherley Anne Williams's *Dessa Rose* (1987), and Alice Walker's *The Temple of My Familiar* (1990). In a timeless world where traditionalists practice herbal medicine and worship their ancestors, Mama Day, a stalwart matriarch, has magical powers that she must conjure up in order to save her great niece from the island's evil forces. A compelling generational saga, *Mama Day* tells a story of pride, pain, and woman-healing.

Winner of a Guggenheim fellowship in 1988, Gloria Naylor joined the ranks of the select few Black women who have won the coveted creative writing award. Naylor's three novels have established her as one of the most talented contemporary fiction writers in America.

Naylor is currently working on a film version of *Mama Day*.

BIBLIOGRAPHY

CA; *Contemporary Literary Criticism*, vol. 28; Kubitschek, Missy Dehn. *Claiming the Heritage: African American Women Novelists and History* (1991); *NA*; Walker, Melissa. *Down from the Mountaintop: Black Women's Novels in the Wake of the Civil Rights Movement, 1966-1989* (1991).

ELIZABETH BROWN-GUILLORY

NEGRO WOMEN'S CLUB HOME, DENVER

Black women, like their white counterparts, were well aware of the significant role of club work in bringing about improvements to their communities. Yet, because Black women had fewer resources to bring to their clubs during the early twentieth century, it was often necessary for clubs to join forces. One outstanding example of combined efforts among Black clubwomen was the establishment of the Negro Women's Club Home in Denver, Colorado.

By the early 1900s, Denver's Black community had a distinct and growing need to provide accommodations for single working girls, as well as a day nursery for working mothers. While this was too great a task for any individual club, Georgia Contee of the Self-Improvement Club suggested that it might be possible to get other clubs to contribute to this effort. The Self-Improvement Club invited presidents of the various Black women's clubs in the city to a meeting to determine the level of interest. Seven clubs responded to the challenge—Taka Art and Literary Club, Pond Lily Art and Literary Club, Self-Improvement Club, Carnation Art, Literary and Charity Club, Progressive Art, Sojourner Truth, and Twentieth Century—and these became known as the Negro Women's Club Home Association.

After two years of planning and raising funds for the home, the seven clubs were able to move into a modern, two-story brick structure at 2357 Clarkson Street in Denver on December 16, 1916. The home, which consisted of eight rooms, was incorporated for $5,000, with each club buying equal shares of stock ($10 per share). The new home was a dormitory for "deserving" girls and a day nursery for children. The upper floor of the building was used for the dormitory while the lower floor housed the nursery.

The maintenance of the home required a tremendous amount of effort on the part of the clubs. Fund raising efforts were constant and on-going, but the club members also contributed whatever the home needed—dishes and other utensils, milk, bread, clothing for the children in the nursery, sheeting for the exterior of the building, screens for the windows, and rakes for the yard. Yet perhaps more important than any of these contributions was the amount of time spent in the home. Club members regularly changed diapers, cleaned the building, and cooked meals. The board of directors ran a very tight ship; every aspect of the home's functioning was taken seriously—from establishing the rules for the dormitory and nursery and having the cupboards repaired, to hiring and firing a yard man.

By far the most important individual in the home was the matron. She was responsible for seemingly endless tasks, especially surrounding the running of the dormitory. Young working girls could rent a room in the dormitory for $1.25 per week including kitchen privileges (the price was increased to $1.50 in 1920, and $2.00 in 1924).

The "inmates," as the residents were called, were governed by strict rules regarding washing and ironing, making beds, use of kitchen facilities, use of club dishes and other utensils, and when lights were to be out. The rules clearly indicate the clubwomen's desire to instill proper training and morality in the girls. Specific requirements concerning the washing of dishes ("must use pan instead of sink; must use soap when washing dishes"), personal grooming ("arrangements of toilet, including the straightening of hair must be done in one's room"), and entertainment of "company" ("must use the parlor and matron must be present") were rigidly upheld by the matron ("Minutes," June 1, 1919).

The matron's duties did not end with dormitory maintenance. She also opened the building at 7:00 A.M. and closed it at 6:00 P.M.; she was responsible for all cases of emergency and for itemizing weekly reports of transactions in the home (accounts for dormitory and nursery were to be kept separately). She also collected fees for entertainments held in the home, and was responsible for the behavior of the children, including teaching them proper table manners, as well as preparing the menus. As if these duties were not enough, she was also admonished to "make the home comfortable and at all times, take the place of mother for the girls entering the home" ("Minutes," September 2, 1919). For all of these responsibilities, the matron's salary was $40 per month in 1920.

Both the nursery and dormitory continued to prove successful, and in 1921 the association's report to the State Board of Charities and Corrections indicated that the home had four paid officers. The nursery had cared for thirty children, and the dormitory housed nine girls.

In addition to the dormitory and nursery, the home allowed various community organizations to rent its facilities for entertainments, stipulating, of course, that these could not be card parties, dancing parties, or political meetings. In this way the association contributed to the home's income and became a community center.

In spite of what was clearly an enormous undertaking to maintain the home, the association also sponsored yearly fund-raisers, established mothers' meetings, and in 1921 established a health clinic in the home.

As community needs changed, so did the home. For example, the Young Women's Christian Association had completed a new building by 1924, causing less demand for the dormitory, but at the same time there was a growing need to expand the nursery. Thus, the dormitory was eliminated and the association devoted its energies toward maintaining the nursery.

Three of the seven clubs in the association eventually disbanded, but the remaining clubs—Pond Lily, Self-Improvement, Carnation, and Taka Art—still today comprise the Negro Women's Club Home Association. The name of the nursery was changed to George Washington Carver Day Nursery in 1946, and it is now housed in a modern building in Denver.

[See also DENVER, COLORADO, CLUB MOVEMENT.]

BIBLIOGRAPHY

"Annual Report to the State Board of Charities and Corrections," year ending June 20, 1921. Dorothy Reaves, Denver, Colorado; *Brochure*. The Negro Women's Club Home (1924); Dickson, Lynda F. "African-American Women's Clubs in Denver: 1890-1925." *Essays and Monographs in Colorado History* (1991); "Minutes of the Negro Women's Club Home," "Rules Governing Dormitory" (June 1, 1919), "Rules for Matron" (July 1 and September 2, 1919; February 2 and June 1, 1920).

LYNDA F. DICKSON

NEIGHBORHOOD UNION, ATLANTA

On Thursday, July 8, 1908, community activist Lugenia Burns Hope assembled her neighbors to discuss the need for settlement work on Atlanta's West Side. Out of this meeting evolved the Neighborhood Union, a community service organization designed to improve the moral, social, intellectual, and religious life of Black Atlantans. Adopting the motto "Thy Neighbor as Thyself," the union sought to build playgrounds, clubs, and neighborhood centers; to develop a spirit of helpfulness among neighbors; to promote child welfare; to impart a sense of cultural heritage; to abolish slums and houses of prostitution; and to improve the overall moral quality of the community. Toward this end, Atlanta was divided into zones, districts, and neighborhoods led by neighborhood presidents and district directors and supervised by a board of directors and a board of managers. By 1915, branches of the union were stretched across the city.

The union's legacy is one of varied civic service. It hosted medical fairs, bazaars, clinics, and carnivals in order to provide much needed medical attention to the Black citizens of Atlanta; it set up kindergartens and day care centers; its settlement house provided temporary shelter for homeless families; it offered classes in motherhood training, child care, and care for the elderly, vocational training in the arts for boys, and sewing and millinery for girls. Its most outstanding and ongoing project, however, was the union's drive for quality education for Atlanta's African-American children. For decades the group petitioned Atlanta's board of education, the mayor, and the city council, asking for additional schools, the restoration of dilapidated facilities, and the elimination of double (sometimes triple) sessions in order to increase the pay of African-American teachers. It protested the lack of a high school for Black students and the lack of special education classes, vocational arts classes, and literary classes beyond the sixth grade. Joining with other groups and leaders, the union was able to work for or against the passage of school bonds in special and municipal elections. However, because funds appropriated for Black schools were not always forthcoming, even after elections, the union often found itself rallying and protesting in order to ensure that Black schools actually received the funds that had been budgeted to them. The Neighborhood Union also helped realize a long-held dream—the opening of Booker T. Washington High School in 1924, the first high school in Atlanta for African-American students.

The female members of the union viewed their organization as an experiment in community cooperation designed to enhance ethnic pride, promote citizenship, and strengthen families. For more than seven decades the union served Atlanta's most neglected population. Financially reliant on fund-raisers and membership fees, the Neighborhood Union received very little county and municipal support until 1920, when the city made the union responsible for the health care of African-American preschoolers. For the next fifty years the agency that was created did indeed serve "Thy Neighbor as Thyself." From the early years of the century until the Neighborhood Union disbanded in the 1970s, it was a continuous voice of protest against social and racial injustice.

BIBLIOGRAPHY

Frazier, E. Franklin. "The Neighborhood Union in Atlanta," *Southern Workman* (September 1923); Rouse, Jacqueline Anne. *Lugenia Burns Hope* (1989); Shivery, Louie D. "The Neighborhood Union," *Phylon* (1942).

JACQUELINE A. ROUSE

NEW ERA CLUB

The New Era Club was founded in 1893 in Boston, Massachusetts, by Josephine St. Pierre Ruffin, a prominent African-American community worker; her daughter, Florida Ruffin Ridley; and Maria Louise Baldwin, the first African-American female principal in a Massachusetts public school. As one of the first African-American women's civic organizations in the country, the New Era Club enabled African-American women to organize and devote themselves to their own needs as well as those of the larger African-American community.

The membership of the New Era Club was typical of emerging African-American women's organizations. As middle-class educated women, these clubwomen had distanced themselves from the larger African-American urban community. They did not see their involvement in the African-American clubwomen's movement as a reaction against American middle-class values; indeed, these values were upheld as the goal for all African-Americans, and they emphasized education and social advancement as the means of solving the problems of the urban environment.

The club movement borrowed from women's involvement in church-related work. Participation in church activities had introduced women to community service work and raised their consciousness and understanding of larger social issues. In the club network, such activities provided women with a strong sense of sisterhood. African-American clubwomen organized their own movement in support of voluntary efforts to ameliorate urban problems during the Progressive era. They enlarged the scope of their movement, and their interest in the urban environment was informed by a combined perspective of race and gender.

The emergence of the New Era Club signaled the efforts of African-American women to break away from the white women's club movement and form their own clubs in order to place middle-class African-American women in positions of power and leadership. Ruffin, the first and only president of the New Era Club, considered the club's importance to be its ability to guarantee that African-American women would have an autonomous role in the efforts of Progressive reformers. A primary goal of the African-American club movement was to demonstrate to white clubwomen, and to society at large, the capabilities of African-American women and to demonstrate to African-American women the opportunities that were available to them.

The two most significant achievements of the New Era Club were its involvement in forming the first national African-American women's organization and its creation of the *Woman's Era*, the club's journal. Together, these accomplishments demonstrated the ability of African-American women to organize successfully—without the assistance of white women.

In July 1895, Ruffin convened a conference in Boston, assembling representatives from thirty-six African-American women's organizations from twelve states. The meeting was held to increase the visibility of African-American women and the efforts of their club movement. A second motive for the conference was to protest charges of immorality that had been lodged against African-American women by the male editor of a Missouri newspaper in a letter to a British suffragist. At the three-day conference held from July 29 to 31, conference members organized the National Federation of Afro-American Women. The formation of this national organization, spurred by the efforts of the New Era Club, gives a strong indication of the cooperation that existed among the various African-American women's clubs.

The New Era Club became a charter member of the National Association of Colored Women (NACW) the following year, when the National Federation of Afro-American Women joined with the National League of Colored Women at a meeting held in Washington, D.C. By helping to effect the union of these two national organizations, the New Era Club secured greater awareness for the African-American clubwomen's movement.

First issued on March 24, 1894, the *Woman's Era* reported the organization's activities, but its greatest service was as a source of news about the activities of a growing network of African-American women's clubs throughout the country. The publication further expanded its influence when it became the official organ of the NACW in 1896. Devoted to social and political issues of interest to the African-American community, the *Woman's Era* acted as a powerful instrument for the New Era Club. In addition, the New Era Club maintained a prominent position in the newly formed national organization because the *Woman's Era* continued to report the local concerns of the Boston club but reserved space for the more national concerns of the NACW. As a result, the local activities of the New Era Club were nationally known to African-American clubwomen. In November 1897, the *Woman's Era* shifted focus from reporting local and national club activities to calling attention to the need for prison reform in the South. The journal ceased publication in 1898.

The New Era Club continued to struggle against discrimination of African-American women's clubs by white clubwomen. Initially accepted into the Massachusetts Federation of Women's Clubs, the New Era Club attempted to increase its influence in the white clubwomen's movement by gaining membership in the General Federation of Women's Clubs, and, in 1900, the federation's executive committee granted provisional membership to the club. The same year, however, Ruffin, as the official representative of the New Era Club, attempted to secure membership into the Milwaukee Convention of the

General Federation of Women's Clubs, but conference organizers, all white women, denied admission to Ruffin as the representative of an African-American women's club and refused to ratify the membership of the New Era Club in the General Federation of Women's Clubs. Despite her failure to gain entrance into the national convention, the New Era Club brought into full view the discriminatory practices of the white clubwomen's movement, which limited the effectiveness of the movement as a whole.

The New Era Club disbanded in 1903, but it left a legacy of achievement of African-American women in the Progressive era.

BIBLIOGRAPHY

Giddings, Paula. *When and Where I Enter: The Impact of Black Women on Race and Sex in America* (1984); selected papers of the New Era Club and issues of the *Woman's Era*, Boston Public Library, Boston, Massachusetts.

SHELAGH REBECCA KENNEDY

Camille Lucie Nickerson, a notable music educator and authority on Creole music, established the Junior Department of the Howard University School of Music. [Moorland-Spingarn]

NICKERSON, CAMILLE LUCIE (1887-1982)

Camille Lucie Nickerson was born in New Orleans, Louisiana, in 1887. She attended Xavier Preparatory School in New Orleans and did her undergraduate and graduate work at Oberlin Conservatory of Music in Oberlin, Ohio, where she received both a Bachelor's and a Master's degree in music and was elected to Pi Kappa Lambda National Music Honor Society. She wrote her Master's thesis on Creole music. Later known as Miss NAACP, Nickerson became a nationally recognized authority on Creole music.

Camille Nickerson founded the Nickerson School of Music, and many of her students became teachers of music. One of them, Beryl Thornhill Richardson, remembers her "as an excellent teacher, demonstrating correct piano playing positions, technique of wrist control and all fundamentals. She played and sang for the class and clapped the rhythm. She was kind, thorough, impeccably dressed, and loved her students." In 1917, Nickerson founded the B Sharp Music Club, consisting of her piano pupils, in New Orleans. Two of the original members remain—Lucille Levy Hutton, who was the first Black music consultant in the New Orleans public schools, and Charles B. Rousseve, pianist, organist, author, and public school principal.

Nickerson also served as president of the National Association of Negro Musicians (1935-37). The B Sharp Music Club became affiliated with the national association in 1921 and continues to be an important cultural organization in New Orleans, having celebrated its seventy-fifth anniversary in 1992. Nickerson appeared in many concerts with the B Sharp Music Club, and she represented Louisiana as a composer on stage at the Kennedy Center in Washington, D.C.

In 1926, Nickerson joined the faculty of Howard University in Washington, D.C., where she was professor of piano and an authority on Creole music. She established the Junior Department of the Howard University School of Music.

Her music lives on in the hearts of her music club and the extended community. The Robert Perry Singers of the B Sharp Music Club continue to sing her Creole songs. Five of her arrangements have been published by the Boston Music Company: "Chere, Mo Lemmé, Toi" (Dear, I Love You So) (1942); "Lizette, To Quitté la Plaine" (Lizette, My Dearest One); "Danse, Conni, Conné" (Dance, Baby, Dance) (1942); "Fais Do Do" (Go to Sleep) (1948); and "Michieu Banjo" (Mister Banjo) (1942). Her arrangement of "Oh, Susanna" was published in the Silver Burdett music textbooks.

Camille Lucie Nickerson died on April 27, 1982, in Washington, D.C. The B Sharp Music Club paid tribute to her on June 27 of that year.

BIBLIOGRAPHY

Nickerson, Camille. Personal interviews.

LILLIAN DUNN PERRY

NORMAN, JESSYE (1945-)

Overnight sensations are rare in opera, considering the time required for the voice to be trained and mature, the obligations for serious study of historical traditions and legacies, the commitment to comprehensive understandings of musical structures, the necessary mastery (not only of diction) of French, German, and Italian, and required stage experience as both recitalist and actor.

Jessye Norman, born September 15, 1945, in Augusta, Georgia, is one of those exceptions. Her vocal talents were discovered while she was still in high school, and she was at age sixteen a contestant in the Marian Anderson competitions. Although she did not win, she stopped on the trip to audition for Carolyn Grant at Howard University, who unconditionally accepted her for study, not immediately realizing the young soprano did not yet have her high school diploma, a matter promptly addressed. Her undergraduate studies culminated with the B.Mus. degree in 1967, after which she moved to Baltimore's Peabody Conservatory to study with former Howard University faculty member Alice Duschak. Thereafter she entered the graduate program at the University of Michigan, where her teachers were Elizabeth Mannion and Pierre Bernac. While those degree plans were in progress, she secured a travel grant which allowed her to enter the 1968 International Music Competition in Munich. With performances of "Dido's Lament" (Purcell) and "Voi lo sapete" from Mascagni's *Cavalleria rusticana*, she won first place and was immediately engaged for her operatic debut as Elisabeth in *Tannhäuser* by the Deutsche Oper (1969), later performing in *Aida, Don Carlo, L'africaine,* and *Le nozze di Figaro*. She first appeared at Milan's Teatro alla Scala in 1972 as Aida and, at London's Covent Garden, as Cassandre in *Les troyens* (Berlioz), with New York and London recital debuts the next year. She was first seen on the American stage November 22, 1982, as both Jocasta in *Oedipus rex*

An overnight sensation whose outstanding vocal talents were recognized while she was still in high school, Jessye Norman has achieved international success in opera, on the concert stage, and as a recording artist. In 1988, she received an honorary degree from Harvard University; among her fellow honorees was Costa Rican president Oscar Arias. [AP/Wide World Photos]

(Stravinsky) and Dido in *Dido and Aeneas* (Purcell) with the Opera Company of Philadelphia. Her Metropolitan Opera debut took place on September 26, 1983, returning to the role of Cassandre in Berlioz's *Les troyens*, subsequently offering New Yorkers her interpretation of Didon in the same opera, as well as the Prima Donna and Ariadne in *Ariadne auf Naxos* (Richard Strauss). She was simultaneously active as recitalist, guest orchestral soloist, director of master classes, and recording artist, rapidly securing international respect as a musician of the highest rank.

Hers is a voice which can range from a dark and lusty mezzo-soprano (Carmen, as an example) to a dramatic soprano that more than satisfies the highest expectation of the Wagnerite. A person of commanding bearing, among her many strengths are an uncommon ability for emotional communication, a concern for repertoire beyond the traditionally expected, and an ability to bring new significance even into more popular repertoires.

BIBLIOGRAPHY

Bernheimer, Martin. "Norman, Jessye." *The New Grove Dictionary of Music and Musicians*, ed. Stanley Sadie (1980); Ewen, David, ed. *Musicians since 1900: Performers in Concert and Opera* (1978); "Norman, Jessye." *Current Biography*, ed. Charles Moritz (1976); Rich, Maria. "Norman, Jessye." *Who's Who in Opera* (1976); Smith, Patrick J. "Norman, Jessye." *The New Grove Dictionary of American Music*, ed. H. Wiley Hitchcock and Stanley Sadie (1986).

SELECTED DISCOGRAPHY

Carmen. Philips 422 366-2 (1989); *A German Requiem*. Angel DSB DSB-3983 (1985); *Tristan und Isolde*. Philips 9500 031 (1975); see also Turner, Patricia. *Afro-American Singers: An Index and Preliminary Discography of Opera, Choral Music and Song* (1977).

DOMINIQUE-RENÉ de LERMA

NORTH CAROLINA FEDERATION OF COLORED WOMEN'S CLUBS

Formed in Charlotte, North Carolina, in 1909, the North Carolina Federation of Colored Women's Clubs (NCFCWC) united numerous African-American women's groups that had been active in the state throughout the 1890s, including temperance chapters, literary societies, and mutual aid associations. The names of member organizations suggest the breadth of interests and traditions among African-American women: the Eastern Star, the Pansy Literary Society, the Sisters of the Household of Ruth, and the King's Daughters. On college campuses, women students participated in Young Women's Christian Associations (YWCA), and by 1890 African-American temperance workers had formed a statewide Woman's Christian Temperance Union (WCTU). Thus the statewide federation established a formal network for preexisting clubs while it encouraged the formation of new ones.

The new federation elected Marie Clay Clinton as its first president in 1909. Clinton, a native of Huntsville, Alabama, had married George C. Clinton, bishop of the African Methodist Episcopal (AME) Zion Church, and moved to Charlotte in 1901. An accomplished musician, Clinton founded the Buds of Promise, the national children's organization of the AME Zion Church, and prior to the formation of the NCFCWC she became a national officer of the denomination's Woman's Home and Foreign Missionary Society. She also joined one of the state's oldest clubs, the Priscilla Art and Literary Club, which exists today.

Clinton served as president of the NCFCWC until the election of Charlotte Hawkins Brown in 1911. Brown, a native of Henderson, North Carolina, moved to Cambridge, Massachusetts, as a child and attended Massachusetts State Normal School at Salem. In 1902, prior to graduation, Brown returned to North Carolina as a teacher for the American Missionary Association (AMA) at Sedalia. Soon she founded her own school there, Palmer Memorial Institute, independent of AMA support.

The federation's activities during its first two decades of existence illustrated the concerns and priorities of its members. Upon Brown's election as president, Clinton began to travel throughout the state to organize clubs and encourage existing clubs to join the federation. National organizer Elizabeth Lindsay Davis and past national president Lucy Thurman visited North Carolina to boost the effort during those early years. By 1913, at least one prototype of a city federation existed in North Carolina at Salisbury. There, under the auspices of the Salisbury Colored Women's Civic League, African-American women from literary societies, neighborhood clubs, and temperance associations federated into a citywide association. The Civic League promoted unity with the statewide federation and launched numerous ser-

vice projects such as anti-tuberculosis work, mothers' clubs, healthy baby programs, and recycling days.

Also in those early years, before any formal structure for interracial cooperation existed, NCFCWC leaders worked diligently to establish communication with white women's clubs, sponsoring joint cleanup days, delegate exchanges at conventions, and bond campaigns during World War I. When the North Carolina Commission on Interracial Cooperation formed in the 1920s, NCFCWC officers served as board members.

After the Nineteenth Amendment giving women the vote passed in 1920, the federation led an effort to conduct citizenship schools for Black women and to encourage them to register and vote. The state federation encouraged city federations to sponsor moonlight schools to teach male and female adults to read in order to pass the state literacy test that was required for voting. In the 1920s, in cooperation with the state federation of white women's clubs, NCFCWC founded and gained state support for Efland Home, a training school for delinquent and dependent African-American girls.

Brown, who earned several honorary degrees, stepped down as federation president in 1935, and Minnie Pearson succeeded her, serving from 1935 until 1941. Pearson continued the federation's voting rights program by encouraging African-American women in the state to register and vote during the later years of the Great Depression. Lulu Spaulding Kelsey, founding president of the Salisbury Colored Women's Civic League, became federation president in 1941. Kelsey, educated at Scotia Seminary, operated a chain of funeral homes and had been active in club work since 1913. Ill health ended her term in 1946, when she was succeeded by Ruth G. Rush, who served as federation president until 1953. Rose Douglass Aggrey, another veteran of the Salisbury Colored Women's Civic League, followed Rush. In the 1940s, Aggrey had established and edited the *Federation Journal*, a statewide newspaper. Aggrey's term ended in 1957, but the district structure she built has served the organization into the present, resulting in broad geographical representation among officers. Presidents have served three- or four-year terms since the 1950s, and each district sponsors a local service project. The state federation continues to support work among young people in correctional institutions.

For more than eight decades the North Carolina Federation of Colored Women's Clubs has served as a catalyst for, and been a reflection of, African-American women's activism. Since its inception the federation has brought together women from a myriad of backgrounds and interests, uniting them in their quest for a stronger political voice, racial justice, and better communities.

BIBLIOGRAPHY

Brown, Charlotte Hawkins. Manuscript collection, Arthur and Elizabeth Schlesinger Library, Radcliffe College, Cambridge, Massachusetts; Davis, Elizabeth Lindsay. *Lifting as They Climb: The National Association of Colored Women* (1933); Gilmore, Glenda Elizabeth. "Gender and Jim Crow: Women and the Politics of White Supremacy in North Carolina, 1895-1920," Ph.D. diss. (1992); Kelsey, A. R. Personal interview (May 14, 1991); Lancaster, Abna Aggrey. Personal interview (June 25, 1991); Lerner, Gerda. "Early Community Work of Black Club Women," *Journal of Negro Education* (1974), and *Black Women in White America: A Documentary History* (1972); Wesley, Charles Harris. *The History of the National Association of Colored Women's Clubs: A Legacy of Service* (1984).

GLENDA ELIZABETH GILMORE

NORTHWEST TERRITORY

The lives and historical experiences of Black women in the midwestern states of Illinois, Michigan, Wisconsin, Ohio, and Indiana that were carved out of the Northwest Territory are known only through widely scattered and fragmented sources. Although the much-heralded Northwest Ordinance of 1787 expressly prohibited slavery and mandated that this region be free, slavery in various guises—ranging from outright lifetime indenture to long-term apprenticeship—existed into the 1850s. As late as the 1840s there were still approximately 350 slaves in the region, most located in the river counties of southern Illinois. One of the connecting threads in the history of Black women in the Northwest is the relentless quest for freedom and for the equal enjoyment of educational, social, and economic opportunities.

From the outset Black women established a pattern of fighting for the freedom of their children and struggling to survive in the Northwest region. Beginning in the 1830s, for example, a number of petitions were filed in Illinois courts on behalf of Black women challenging the indenture and apprentice claims of their white masters on their children. In the case of *Boon* v. *Juliet* (1836), Bennington Boon claimed that although his indenture agreement with Juliet had expired, he retained the rights to the service of her three children under provisions of an 1807 statute. Juliet, with the aid of white antislavery supporters, won this suit and the state court ruled that the chil-

dren of African-Americans registered under the territorial laws of Indiana and Illinois were unquestionably free. However, not until 1845 did the Illinois Supreme Court declare the holding of all Black apprentices illegal.

A small number of Black women in the nineteenth century were born and raised in the Northwest Territory, and others were transported into the region as members of manumitted slave families from North Carolina, Virginia, Kentucky, and Tennessee. Still other Black women came to reside in the Northwest after escaping slavery via the Underground Railroad. Margaret Garner, the slave woman made famous through the fictionalized tale of her escape and subsequent killing of her daughter by novelist Toni Morrison in *Beloved* (1987), crossed the frozen Ohio River in the winter of 1856 and arrived in Cincinnati, where she was ultimately captured by local police and returned to slavery in Louisville. Finally, a few free Black women living in southern or border states voluntarily migrated into the Northwest. Often, as was true of Louisa Picquet of Cincinnati, Ohio, these women expended considerable energy, time, and resources trying to secure the freedom of their relatives. Louisa spent twelve years searching for her mother, saving money earned from washing and begging for funds from white Cincinnatians. As long as her mother remained enslaved, she could not feel truly free, and she eventually located her mother and purchased her freedom.

Most of the white settlers in Illinois, Indiana, and Ohio were relentlessly hostile to African-Americans because they feared that their proximity to slave states exposed them to being overrun by escaping slaves. One of the Illinois Black Laws, adopted in 1819, decreed that anyone employing an uncertified African-American could be fined $1.50 for each day of work performed. In 1829 the Illinois legislature raised the amount of bond to be paid by African-Americans migrating into the state from $500 to $1,000. Many such laws were largely unenforced, reflecting sentiment more than practice. The passage of the Fugitive Slave Law as part of the Compromise of 1850, however, underscored the vulnerability of African-Americans in the steady exodus to Canada during the decade before the outbreak of the Civil War.

Proscriptions notwithstanding, Black women pursued a variety of jobs wherever they lived in the Northwest. The largest numbers worked as domestics, cooks, washerwomen, and agricultural laborers. Like white females, they could not vote or hold political office. Other rights were even more circumscribed. Ohio denied African-Americans the benefits of welfare relief and mandated racially segregated schools. Indiana and Illinois denied public education to Black children altogether. In spite of these limitations, some Black women were able to make strides toward greater freedom and autonomy. They had many advantages over sisters in slavery. Life in the small midwestern towns increased opportunities to become involved in religious and community activities. A few Black women and their families found islands of racial toleration in frontier settlements in Wisconsin. Like Lucy, the wife of Free Frank of Illinois, these women cultivated gardens, raised poultry, sold dairy produce, and engaged in a number of money-generating tasks. Without their labor many families would have perished.

Black schoolteachers were often the only professional women in the Northwest region prior to the Civil War. Those Black women interested in acquiring higher education found Oberlin, Ohio, a particularly promising haven. The first coeducational and interracial institution of higher learning, Oberlin College, held great attraction for Black women. Sarah Jane Woodson, born on November 15, 1825, in Chillicothe, Ohio, was one of the first Black women to attend Oberlin College. She was the youngest of the eleven children of Thomas and Jemimma Woodson, two emigrants from Greenbriar County, Virginia. After moving into Ohio in 1820, the Woodsons had joined with several other Black families to found an all-Black farming community at Berlin Crossroads, Jackson County, Ohio. In 1852, Sarah enrolled in Oberlin College. During vacations, she earned money by teaching in the segregated schools in Circleville and Portsmouth, Ohio. After her graduation in 1856, Woodson served on the faculty of Wilberforce University in Ohio, becoming one of the earliest Black women to teach at the college level.

Black women played a crucial role in the development of religious and social welfare institutions within small Black Northwest communities. Virtually all of the Black churches, regardless of denomination, depended upon the fund-raising activities and support of Black women. Sarah Woodson, an astute observer of Black women's participation in community efforts, recorded that while Black women seldom occupied visible positions of leadership, they often bore a heavy burden: "They would make great provisions to feed the multitudes that would gather" at camp-meetings, and "in raising funds with which to build churches no difficulties deterred them from their efforts and no dangers affrighted them from their purpose. Through heat and cold and storms and fatigue and hardships they gathered a little here and there, while they made

what they could with their own hands, which many times was only the widow's mite; but when these small sums were put together they were sufficient to raise a monument in the name of God to dedicate to his worship."

Black women also played a major role in the antislavery struggle. They joined antislavery societies, raised funds, and attended lectures. By far one of the most outstanding and outspoken Black women of this era was Isabella Baumfree, who took the name Sojourner Truth in the mid-1840s. She lectured across the country on behalf of Black freedom and women's rights. Truth moved to Battle Creek, Michigan, in 1856 where she died in 1883.

As the number of Black women increased in Northwest communities, so too did the number of clubs devoted to self-improvement and social or racial uplift. In 1843, a group of Black women in Detroit formed what eventually became known as the Detroit Colored Ladies Benevolent Society. Similar organizations were established in Chicago, Cleveland, and other midwestern communities. These clubs worked to ameliorate the suffering of the poor, aged, orphaned, and sick. But the clubs had a distinct personal purpose. Everywhere Black women went, they were hounded by the negative stereotype of low morality. These clubs often provided a nurturing sanctuary where they could engage in self-improvement activities freely and talk among themselves.

Within the Black townships, enclaves, settlements, or communities, gender roles were fluid yet bounded. The boundaries, of necessity, were often permeable. Black women did perform both male and female sex-stereotyped work. Along with the men, they worked in the fields and helped to create and sustain the major community institutions. They also bore a great deal of the responsibility for maintaining kin networks, socializing the young, providing elementary education and rudimentary health care, and laboring in the home. The survival of African-Americans in the Northwest depended upon the contributions of women, men, and children. These struggling people could ill afford to worship a cult of true womanhood or to erect symbolic pedestals upon which to perch idle and ornamental women.

BIBLIOGRAPHY

Hine, Darlene Clark. *Black Women in the Middle West: The Michigan Experience* (1990), and *When the Truth Is Told: Black Women's Culture and Community in Indiana, 1875-1950* (1981); Lawson, Ellen Nickenzie. *The Three Sarahs: Documents of Antebellum Black College Women* (1984).

DARLENE CLARK HINE

NORTON, ELEANOR HOLMES
(1937-)

Eleanor Holmes Norton was the first female chair of the Equal Employment Opportunity Commission (EEOC). Born on June 13, 1937, in Washington D.C., she is a fourth-generation Washingtonian. After she received her B.A. from Antioch College in 1960, she attended Yale University, where she earned a Master's degree in American history in 1963 and a J.D. in 1965.

From 1965 until 1970, she worked for the American Civil Liberties Union (ACLU) in New York City. In 1968, she received national attention for her representation of former Alabama Governor George Wallace, who wanted to hold an outdoor political rally at Shea Stadium in New York City. This case set

a precedent for her staunch stand on legal and constitutional principles. After the Wallace case, she became assistant director of the ACLU in New York City.

In 1970, she became head of the New York City Commission on Human Rights, appointed by Mayor John V. Lindsay. Her appointment was renewed by Mayor Abraham D. Beame in 1974.

In 1977, President Jimmy Carter appointed her chair of the EEOC, a position she held until 1981. When she took the post, she inherited a backlog of 130,000 cases, and the commission had the reputation of being a swamp of bureaucratic mismanagement. After only two years in office, she had transformed the EEOC into a highly productive and efficient agency. For example, she cut the backlog of cases in half and increased the productivity of EEOC

Shown here protesting the racial policies of the government of South Africa, Eleanor Holmes Norton had a life-long commitment to civil rights causes that began with her membership in the Student Nonviolent Coordinating Committee in the 1960s. She was chair of the Equal Employment Opportunity Commission from 1977 to 1981. [AP/Wide World Photos]

area offices by 65 percent. She later became a professor of law at Georgetown University and, in 1990, made a successful bid to become the congressional representative for the District of Columbia.

Her lifelong commitment to civil rights began with her membership in the Student Nonviolent Coordinating Committee (SNCC) and her participation in the Mississippi Freedom Democratic Party (MFDP). In 1963, she was a member of the national staff of the March on Washington.

In addition to her career as an activist and politician, Eleanor Holmes Norton is a recognized legal scholar and coauthor of *Sex Discrimination and the Law: Causes and Remedies* (1975). She and husband Edward Norton and their two children, Katharine and John, reside in the District of Columbia.

BIBLIOGRAPHY

"A Conversation with Commissioner Eleanor Holmes Norton," the American Enterprise Institute Studies in Government Regulation (June 29, 1979); Lanker, Brian. *I Dream a World: Portraits of Black Women Who Changed America* (1989).

MECCA NELSON

NURSING

The history of the development of the nursing profession is the story of the struggle of a group of women to overcome social and economic adversities. Within this history, however, is another, almost parallel chronicle of the effort of Black women to acquire nursing education, to end economic discrimination, and to win professional acceptance from their white counterparts.

During the formative phases of the nursing profession in America, a plethora of concerns riveted the attention of most white nurse leaders: exploitation of student nurses in hospital training schools, limited employment opportunities for graduate nurses exacerbated by competition from untrained women, absence of certification or licensing boards, and the need to develop collegiate nursing programs while raising the low social status and esteem accorded to nurses.

The first three American nurse training schools were established in 1873. These early schools operated within hospitals, but in keeping with traditions initiated in Florence Nightingale's movement in 1850s Britain to establish an organized system for training nurses, they were characterized by a degree of faculty

autonomy, a separate funding apparatus, and the use of women as nurse supervisors. However, insufficient capital and endowment and the demand for more scientific-based instruction determined that this type of relatively autonomous nurse training school was soon eclipsed by hospitals, which came to dominate nursing education.

There were fifteen hospital nurse training schools in 1880 and 431 schools twenty years later. The number of graduates increased from 157 to 3,456 within this time. The proliferation of nurse training schools continued as hospitals garnered increased respectability from the public, which began to accept them as places of good care, not dens of death. By 1926 there were 2,150 schools with 17,000 graduates, virtually all of which excluded Black women.

As hospital nurse training schools mushroomed on the educational landscape, nurse leaders questioned the instructional quality and low admission standards. The inadequate, random instruction provided at the hospitals, the exploitation of student nurses, and the general low status accorded to even trained nurses motivated nurse leaders to organize what would be renamed, in 1911, the American Nurses' Association (ANA). Its official organ, the *American Journal of Nursing*, had commenced publication in 1901. The National League of Nursing Education, the ANA, and the many other emergent national societies struggled to upgrade the status of and to professionalize nursing.

The professionalization of nursing had a negative impact on Black nurses. Black women had long worked as nurses on slave plantations and, after Emancipation, in the homes of white southerners. However, as the number of nurse training schools grew and nursing became another way out of domestic service for thousands of European immigrant and poor white women, Black women were increasingly denied the opportunity to acquire this training. Mary Eliza Mahoney, a Black 1879 graduate of the New England Hospital for Women and Children in Boston, was an exception to the rule of exclusion practiced by the majority of hospital schools in the North and all such institutions in the South. Left with little alternative, African-Americans founded their own network of nursing schools and hospitals.

In 1886, John D. Rockefeller contributed the funds for the establishment of a school of nursing at the Atlanta Baptist Seminary (now Spelman College), a school for Black women. This was the first school of nursing established within an academic institution in the country. The earliest Black hospital nursing schools came into existence in the 1890s, established mostly by Black physicians and Black women's clubs. In 1891, Daniel Hale Williams, the famed open-heart surgeon, founded Provident Hospital and Nurse Training School in Chicago. In 1894, he was also instrumental in creating the Freedmen's Hospital and Nurse Training School in Washington, D.C. Under the aegis of Booker T. Washington, the Tuskegee Institute School of Nurse Training in Alabama came into existence in 1892. In the same year, the Hampton Nurse Training School at Dixie Hospital in Hampton, Virginia, began accepting students. In October 1896, the Black women of the Phyllis Wheatley Club founded the only Black hospital and nurse training school in New Orleans. The Phillis Wheatley Sanitarium and Training School for Nurses began rather inauspiciously in a private residence consisting of seven beds and five patients. This institution was later renamed the Flint Goodridge Hospital and Nurse Training School. Finally, on October 4, 1897, Alonzo Clifton McClennan, an 1880 graduate of the Howard University Medical School, founded the Hospital and Nursing Training School in Charleston, South Carolina. Anna De Costa Banks, one of the first graduates of the Dixie Hospital School of Nursing, became the first head nurse of the South Carolina institution. By 1920 there were thirty-six Black nurse training schools.

The impetus leading to the founding of Black schools of nursing was an effort to respond to an array of perceived and real needs of Black Americans. Providing adequate training and educational opportunities for Black women was only one of many motivational factors. McClennan, for example, was angered by the stubborn refusal of the white municipal hospital administrators in Charleston to allow Black physicians to attend their patients, even in segregated wards. He and his Black colleagues initially created their hospital in order to advance their practices and to care for their patients. They added the nursing school in order to acquire help in the delivery of medical care to the hordes of poor, superstitious African-Americans of Charleston and surrounding counties who sought their services. The Black women of the Phyllis Wheatley Club were inspired to establish a nursing school after observing the poor quality of health and the high mortality rates of African-Americans in New Orleans. Between 1890 and 1900, the overall death rate in New Orleans dropped from 25.4 to 23.8 per thousand, while that of the city's Black population increased from 36.6 to 42.4 per thousand. These conditions were similar in cities both above and below the Mason-Dixon line. The lack of adequate hospital facilities and Black health care professionals lessened the already slim chances of survival for African-Americans.

The establishment of the Phillis Wheatley Sanitarium and Nurse Training School marked the first attempt by African-Americans to improve Black health care in the city.

Other founders and heads of Black nursing schools articulated different reasons for their actions. Alice Bacon, the white founder of the Hampton Nurse Training School at Dixie Hospital, justified the establishment of the school as a means to retain "in the hands of trained colored women a profession for which, even without training, the Negro women have always shown themselves especially adapted." She declared that Black women had "to take up the work laid down by the home trained women of the old days, and to hold for their race throughout the South a profession that has always been theirs." Likewise, Booker T. Washington declared, "Colored women have always made good nurses. They have, I believe, a natural aptitude for that sort of work."

These early Black nursing schools were, for the most part, as deficient in quality and standards as were many of their white counterparts. In keeping with prevailing practices, student nurses were exploited as an unpaid labor force. In every institution they performed all of the domestic and maintenance drudgery, attended the patients, and dispensed medicine. Many student nurses at Tuskegee Institute required extended leaves of absence to recover from damage done to their health while working in the hospital. It was not inconsequential that one of the early Tuskegee catalogs noted that the major admission requirement into the nursing program consisted of a strong physique and stamina to endure hardship.

The most oppressive aspect of Black nursing training at some of these early schools, notably at Tuskegee and Charleston's Nursing Training School, involved the hiring out of student nurses to supplement a hospital's income. In the Charleston school, the student nurses were required to turn over to the hospital the dollar a day they earned on private cases. These nurses also managed the hospital's poultry operation, tended the vegetable gardens, and organized public fund-raising activities. In spite of the attendant hardship and the mediocre instruction, hundreds of Black women graduated from these segregated hospital nursing programs and went on to render invaluable service to Black patients.

Although, with financial assistance from wealthy philanthropists, African-Americans had, by 1928, fashioned an extensive nursing training school network, the process of becoming a respected member of the nursing profession involved more than the acquisition of basic training and a diploma. Access to specialized training or graduate education was of equal importance. Black women desiring to secure graduate education or specialized training, however, were consistently denied admission into many of the country's leading graduate nursing programs.

At every juncture in their quest for professional acceptance and advancement, Black nurses encountered entrenched racist attitudes. Challenging career opportunities such as employment in hospitals, visiting nurse associations, and municipal departments of health proved to be as elusive as sympathetic work environments that held out possibilities for promotion to supervisory or administrative positions. In fact, the vast majority of Black graduate nurses, like their untrained predecessors, worked in private-duty jobs, where they frequently were expected to perform domestic chores in addition to providing nursing care. When asked about the absence of Black women in supervisory positions at her hospital, the white superintendent of nurses at the Lincoln Hospital in New York asserted that "colored" head nurses did not have the capacity to fill positions that entailed heavy responsibility and that discipline could not be maintained unless there was firm, competent white direction. As bleak as the situation was in the North, the advancement opportunities for Black graduate nurses were even more limited in the South. Almost all Black graduate nurses in the South worked for lower wages than their white colleagues.

Besides the injustice of unequal pay, Black women graduate nurses considered the denial of membership in the American Nurses' Association the most visible and demeaning manifestation of professional ostracism. Barred from membership in local and state ANA affiliates, the majority of Black women nurses could not participate in the largest professional association of nurses. The only significant number of Black women in the ANA had become members when the Alumnae Association of the Freedmen's Hospital in Washington, D.C., had merged with the ANA in 1911.

The ANA's exclusionary practices motivated Martha Franklin, a Black graduate of the Women's Hospital in Philadelphia, to launch a separate Black nursing organization. Beginning in 1906-7, Franklin mailed over 2,000 inquiries to Black graduate nurses, superintendents of nursing schools, and nursing organizations to determine whether interest existed for a separate Black society. Her letters struck a responsive chord among the members and leadership of the Lincoln Hospital nursing school. Adah Belle Thoms, president of the Lincoln School of Nursing Alumnae Association, arranged a meeting. In August 1908,

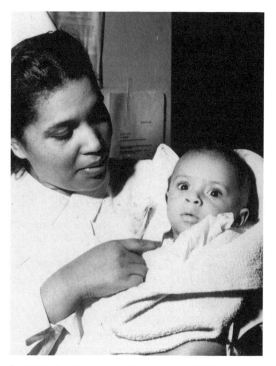

By 1942, when this photograph of nurse Irene Hill was taken in Chicago, the status of Black nurses had greatly improved since the late nineteenth century, thanks in part to the efforts of the National Association of Colored Graduate Nurses. [National Archives]

fifty-two nurses convened at St. Mark's Episcopal Church in New York City to found the National Association of Colored Graduate Nurses (NACGN). In 1912, the NACGN members numbered 125, and by 1920 it boasted a membership of 500.

Under the leadership of two of its more forceful presidents, Adah B. Thoms (1915-20) and Carrie E. Bullock (1927-30), the NACGN accomplished much. It secured a temporary headquarters in 1918, which consisted of a room in New York City's Young Women's Christian Association's 137th Street Branch. In 1920 Thoms filed the NACGN incorporation papers and established a national registry of Black graduate nurses to assist them in finding employment. Bullock, a 1909 graduate of the Provident Hospital School of Nursing, was supervisor of Black nurses at the Chicago Visiting Nurses Association during her presidency. She focused on two key issues during her tenure. In 1928, to facilitate communication and to foster a greater sense of professional involvement among Black nurses, Bullock founded and edited the organization's official organ, the *National News Bulletin*. Second, to encourage Black women nurses to pursue postgraduate education, Bullock secured the support of managers of the Julius Rosenwald Fund for the establishment of a Rosenwald fellowship program for Black graduate nurses.

In spite of these accomplishments, problems remained. Salary inequities in hospitals and public health agencies persisted; the multiplication of unaccredited Black hospital nurse training schools that grossly exploited their students and produced poorly trained nurses continued; and white nurses remained unresponsive to the entreaties of Black women for recognition and acceptance within the nursing profession. Under the auspices of the Hospital Library and Service Bureau, Donelda Hamlin, in 1925, conducted a survey of state board of health officials and visiting nurse association heads to determine their evaluation and perceptions of Black women public health nurses. In her subsequent report, Hamlin emphasized, as representative of the overall response, the comments of the superintendent of the Public Health Nursing Association in Louisville, Kentucky. The respondent declared that "the type of training the average colored nurse received in this part of the country is far inferior to that given to white nurses. Even the best training for colored nurses hardly approximates the poorest training given to white nurses. From another standpoint, their educational background is not so good. Therefore I think the type of service rendered would necessarily be of lower grade than under other circumstances."

In late 1925, the Rockefeller Foundation employed Ethel Johns to examine the status of Black women in the nursing profession. Johns visited twenty-three hospitals and nurse training schools for Black women during a four-month period. In Chicago, Johns interviewed the chief nurse of the city's health department, which employed 10 Black graduate nurses and 154 white nurses. She asserted that Black nurses' "technique is inferior to that of the white nurses, they are not punctual, and are incapable of analyzing a social situation." She maintained that there was a marked tendency among them "to organize against authority" and "to engage in political intrigue." Not surprisingly, Johns ended her report on a discouraging if understated note. She wrote, "Negro nurses in every part of the country feel very keenly that they are debarred from qualifying themselves for leadership and it is true that most doors are closed to them."

Black graduate nurses and the NACGN made the opening of doors to their profession a top priority. It would take twenty years, the emergence of a cadre of resourceful Black nurse leaders, and a world war crisis for them to break through the negative attitudinal barriers, gain entry into the ANA, and win acceptance as full members in the profession of nursing. In the mid-1930s the NACGN's situation improved when grants from the General Education Board of the Rockefeller Foundation and from the Julius Rosenwald Fund made it possible for the NACGN to employ Mabel K. Staupers as executive secretary and to move into permanent headquarters at Rockefeller Center in New York City, where all the major national nursing organizations had offices. Following a long and relentless struggle, Staupers and NACGN president Estelle Massey Osborne succeeded in winning recognition and acceptance for Black nurses.

Staupers's fight to eliminate quotas established by the U.S. Army Nurse Corps constitutes one of the finest periods in NACGN history. Although many Black nurses volunteered their services during World War II, they were refused admittance into the navy, and the army allowed only a limited number to serve. In 1943, although the navy had notified Staupers that it had decided to place the induction of Black nurses under consideration and the army had raised its quota of Black nurses to 160, the situation had not greatly improved. In an effort to draw attention to the unfairness of quotas, Staupers requested a meeting with Eleanor Roosevelt. In November 1944 the First Lady and Staupers met, and Staupers described in detail Black nurses' troubled relationship with the armed forces. In January 1945, when Norman T. Kirk announced the possibility of a draft to remedy a nursing shortage within the armed forces, Staupers made a well-publicized response, "If nurses are needed so desperately why isn't the Army using colored nurses?" Afterward she encouraged nursing groups of all races to write letters and send telegrams protesting the discrimination against Black nurses in the army and navy Nurse Corps. The groundswell of public support for the removal of quotas on the number of Black nurses in the Nurse Corps proved effective.

Buried beneath an avalanche of telegrams from an inflamed public, Kirk, Rear Admiral W.J.C. Agnew, and the War Department declared an end to quotas and exclusion. On January 20, 1945, Kirk stated that nurses would be accepted into the army Nurse Corps without regard to race, and five days later Agnew announced that the navy Nurse Corps was open to Black women. Within a few weeks, Phyllis Daley became the first Black woman to break the color barrier and receive induction into the corps.

The end of discriminatory practices by a key American institution helped to erode entrenched beliefs about the alleged inferiority of Black health care professionals and paved the way for the integration of the American Nurses' Association. In 1948, the ANA opened the gates to Black membership, appointed a Black nurse as assistant executive secretary in its national headquarters, and elected Estelle Osborne to the board of directors. The decision to grant individual memberships to Black nurses barred from state associations in Georgia, Louisiana, South Carolina, Texas, Virginia, Arkansas, Alabama, and the District of Columbia was followed by the adoption of a resolution to establish biracial committees in district and state associations to implement educational programs and promote development of harmonious intergroup relations.

With the removal of the overtly discriminatory barriers to membership in the ANA, members of the NACGN recognized that their needs would now be served by the ANA, which agreed to take over the functions of the NACGN and to continue to award the Mary Mahoney Medal honoring individuals for their contributions to interracial understanding. Thus, during the NACGN's 1949 convention, the members voted the organization out of existence, and the following year, Staupers, then president, presided over its formal dissolution.

[See also THE MILITARY; NATIONAL ASSOCIATION OF COLORED GRADUATE NURSES.]

BIBLIOGRAPHY

For an extensive bibliography, see Hine, Darlene Clark. *Black Women in White: Racial Conflict and Cooperation in the Nursing Profession, 1890-1950* (1989).

DARLENE CLARK HINE

NURSING, WORLD WAR I

A little-noted aspect of America's involvement in World War I was the struggle of Black women nurses to serve in the U.S. Army Nurse Corps. Although this particular quest for unfettered access to professional opportunities proved futile, it is nevertheless a revealing case study in both the military history of America and in the history of Black women. An examination of the nature and extent of the U.S. government's staunch resistance to the inclusion of Black women nurses in "the fight to make the world safe for democracy" illuminates some of the implications of armed forces interracial relations and policies.

More than 367,000 Black men were called into service during World War I, and, following an effective Black protest campaign and lobbying effort, the U.S. Congress authorized the establishment of a separate reserve officers' training camp for Black soldiers. At this time African-Americans were barred altogether from the marines and the pilot section of the aviation corps, but they were permitted to serve in almost every branch of the army and in menial jobs in the navy. Yet Black women who fervently desired to use their professional talents and expertise to aid their country during this period were consistently denied the right to serve in the Nurse Corps.

Black Americans had been understandably cautious when in 1914 Woodrow Wilson, a southerner, became president of the United States. However, in spite of their already low expectations of his administration insofar as Black rights were concerned, even the most cynical African-Americans were shocked by the depth of Wilson's apparent commitment to racial segregation and discrimination. Wilson had not been in office long, for instance, before he issued an executive order establishing separate eating and restroom facilities in government buildings; other laws segregated and eliminated large numbers of African-Americans from civil service jobs. With Wilson's re-election to the presidency came America's plunge into World War I. Black Americans immediately offered their services in the armed forces. Even radicals such as W.E.B. Du Bois and several leaders of the National Association for the Advancement of Colored People urged Black men to volunteer for the army. Ironically, confronted with the warm response of African-Americans to the draft, the U.S. Congress continued to debate legislation for the drafting and training of African-Americans in separate military units.

Of all Black professionals, women nurses needed no special persuasion to volunteer their services to aid and care for their wounded countrymen. The advent of World War I helped to raise their expectations and excite their professional dreams. Black women nurses had long despaired over their status as professional outcasts. They could not attend the better equipped and managed nurse training schools, were denied individual membership in the American Nurses' Association (ANA), and were denied supervisory or administrative positions in hospitals, nurse training schools, and public health agencies and bureaus. At every level of employment, they earned lower salaries than white nurses. Furthermore, the general low regard and esteem they possessed in the public mind exacerbated their unfair treatment.

In the pre-war years, Black women nurses had engaged in a number of largely unsuccessful activities designed to improve their position within the ranks of organized nursing. In 1908 they had founded their own professional body, the National Association of Colored Graduate Nurses, to better structure and intensify their struggle to win membership and integration into the ANA. Yet professional equality eluded them. Thus Black women nurses desired to seize the opportunity created by the war emergency to accomplish these objectives.

Although the first wave of Black women nurses who attempted to enlist in the U.S. Army Nurse Corps expected to encounter racism, they were not prepared for the total rejection of their services during one of America's greatest crises. Disillusioned and hurt, Black women nurses focused their anger initially on the American Red Cross, reorganized and incorporated by an act of Congress on January 5, 1905. The Red Cross, an auxiliary of the U.S. Army Nurse Corps, recruited and enrolled nurses, then classified them as First Reserve nurses or Second Reserve nurses. The First Reserve was composed of nurses with the educational, moral, and professional qualifications required by the military Nurse Corps. The Second Reserve consisted of nurses available for critical civilian nursing who, because of some technicality, such as being over forty years old, were not eligible for the First Reserve. In effect, the American Red Cross enjoyed quasi-governmental status, particularly within the army nursing group. Indeed, the second superintendent of the Nurse Corps, Jane Delano, served simultaneously as head of the Red Cross Nursing Service.

Black nurses demanded to know why so few of them were called or enrolled into either the First or Second Reserve. Delano's response to their inquiries was both evasive and defensive: "We are enrolling colored nurses at the present time," she explained, "and shall continue to do so in order that they may be available if at any time there is an opportunity to assign them to duty in military hospitals." That time and opportunity never seemed to come, and most Black nurses waited in vain for the call. Later, criticized for their failure to enroll Black nurses, Red Cross leaders shifted blame to the office of the surgeon general, who, they insisted, had simply not called for Black nurses. Red Cross officials further asserted that many Black nurses had not met the Red Cross prerequisite of graduation from a fifty-bed hospital

nurse training school. The Red Cross also steadfastly insisted that it had given Black nurses who lacked the necessary credentials a provisional enrollment until they registered or acquired additional training.

In spite of these unconvincing rationalizations and evasions, Black nurses in particular and Black Americans in general felt the injustice deeply. Black criticism of the Red Cross increased as the war continued. The army was markedly reluctant to tap the nursing services of Black women, and the navy refused even to consider the matter. As Black pressure and anger mounted, the Red Cross belatedly prepared a list of Black nurses to serve in a proposed segregated hospital to be established in Des Moines, Iowa. The signing of the armistice on November 11, 1918, and the end of the war, however, aborted the proposed installation. A month before the war's end, though, two dozen Black nurses were called for service at Camp Sherman, Ohio; Camp Grant, Illinois; and Camp Sevier, South Carolina. This number represented only a fraction of the 21,000 white women who had been given the opportunity to serve their country as nurses. Commensurately, as the status of the white nursing profession skyrocketed in the aftermath of the war emergency, that of Black nurses plummeted. Because Black nurses had not served their country, they apparently bore no claim to a share of nursing's newly earned public esteem.

Black educators and leaders such as Robert R. Moton, successor to Booker T. Washington as president of Tuskegee Institute, and Emmett J. Scott, special assistant for Negro Affairs in the War Department, had joined the chorus of protests against the exclusion of Black women nurses from service in the Nurse Corps. Moton and Scott informed the secretary of war and the surgeon general of the widespread dissatisfaction of African-Americans with the war effort, emphasizing that they were particularly disillusioned with the American Red Cross. Moton wrote, "The Red Cross's exclusion of colored nurses . . . results in a certain sort of indifference on the part of colored people which ought not to be when the country needs every ounce of effort along every available line." In the face of the war emergency, some African-Americans had accommodated themselves to the exclusion and segregation practiced by the U.S. War Department, convinced that it was temporarily important to do so given the worldwide threat to democracy. The discrimination practiced by the Red Cross was a different matter, however, because that institution symbolized humanitarianism in its most pure form. Black nurses especially believed that the

Red Cross had not vigorously pushed for their entry into the Nurse Corps and had failed to uphold its democratic principles.

The intransigence of the Nurse Corps and the inertia of the Red Cross had motivated some Black nurse leaders and liberal white allies to take matters into their own hands. In a fashion reminiscent of Booker T. Washington's emphasis on racial solidarity and self-help, an interracial group of some of New York City's most prominent, wealthy, and influential citizens met on November 2, 1917, to launch the Black or, more precisely, interracial counterpart of the American Red Cross. The new organization, incorporated as the Circle for Negro War Relief, was structured similarly to the Red Cross. Officers of the Circle were Emilie Bigelow Hapgood, president; George Foster Peabody, treasurer; and Grace Neil (Mrs. James Weldon) Johnson, secretary. The vice presidents were ex-governor Charles S. Whitman, W.E.B. Du Bois, Robert R. Moton, Charles Young, and Ray Stannard Baker. Other members of the board of directors included Gertrude Pinchot, Arthur B. Spingarn, Edward Sheldon, R. J. Coady, and Russell Janney.

The primary objectives of the Circle included the promotion of the interests and improvement in the conditions of Black soldiers and sailors at home and abroad. Beyond this, Circle members pledged to aid those people related to or dependent upon Black servicemen. Within two years, the Circle had fifty-three local chapters in seventeen states and boasted a membership of more than three thousand. Circle committees on the local levels initiated many activities designed to serve Black servicemen and their families. Committee members sewed, knitted, baked, and collected supplies to send to servicemen via channels established by the American Red Cross. This sharing of Red Cross information and a transfer network was the extent of the cooperation between the Circle and the Red Cross throughout the war years. The Circle also raised money for Black soldiers who returned from the war penniless and for those discharged from hospitals without money. In such cases, government funds were, more often than not, both late and inadequate.

The successful execution of all Circle work depended largely on Blue Circle nurses. Through arrangements similar to those of Red Cross nurses, Blue Circle nurses provided relief to needy Black families. Furthermore, they instructed many poor rural African-Americans on the importance of sanitation, proper diet, and adequate clothing. The nurses also maintained necessary contact with city, county, and state health officials, often alerting them to serious community health problems.

After the war ended, the board of directors voted to continue a revised program of the Circle's work. On May 19, 1919, the board changed the name of the organization to the Circle for Negro Relief, dropping "War" from its title. Circle leaders then turned their attention to seeking funds and developing a new peacetime program. In an effort to raise money, Circle leaders submitted grant proposals to the heads of the major white philanthropic foundations, but with discouraging results. Edwin Embree of the Rockefeller Foundation assured the Circle of the foundation's sympathy and commitment to improving the health of Black people but denied its request for funds. In a private memorandum, Embree observed that as far as he could determine, most of the Circle's meager resources were used to cover overhead expenses. More importantly, however, he maintained that it was against the Rockefeller Foundation's policy to contribute to private voluntary health agencies.

Circle leaders thus drafted a new program, this time with more success. They attempted to construct a national plan that included raising scholarship funds to train and pay part of the salaries of Black visiting Circle nurses in southern communities. Their new peacetime program also called for the creation of day nurseries and kindergartens and for providing financial assistance to small community hospitals. Under the new Circle program, each local Circle committee was instructed to organize a County Health Club and to appeal to its respective county Board of Health for financial support to pay half of the salary of a Blue Circle public health nurse. Will W. Alexander of the Commission on Interracial Cooperation in Atlanta attested to the feasibility of the county health plan in a wire to Circle headquarters on January 15, 1921. He enthusiastically claimed that the Board of Health of South Carolina was "greatly interested" in public health nursing for African-Americans and would look upon the Circle's plan with favor. Circle leaders justified their plan by noting that the white nursing services such as the Red Cross devoted little attention and meager resources to addressing the health needs of African-Americans, especially in the South. They argued that the new Circle plan would improve general Black health care, help the families of poor Black servicemen, and provide more employment for Black women nurses. The Circle for Negro Relief continued throughout the 1920s until the Great Depression.

Black women nurses had looked to the war crisis and the peacetime need for trained nurses to allow them a chance to serve their country, demonstrate their usefulness and value, and enhance their image in the American mind. But they soon discovered that not even a war crisis could lend them that stature. Although they were able to provide some service in the Circle, American racism emerged from World War I unscathed and more entrenched than ever. Integration of Black women into the army and navy Nurse Corps would have to await another crisis: the coming of World War II.

[This article was originally published in *Indiana Military History Journal* (January 1983).]

BIBLIOGRAPHY

American Red Cross Papers, National Archives, Washington, D.C.; Bullough, Bonnie and Vern L. Bullough. *The Emergence of Modern Nursing* (1964); Du Bois, W.E.B. *The Autobiography of W.E.B. Du Bois* (1968); Elmore, Joyce Ann. "Black Nurses: Their Service and Their Struggle," *American Journal of Nursing* (March 1936); Flikke, Julia O. *Nurses in Action: The Story of the Army Nurse Corps* (1943); Franklin, John Hope. *From Slavery to Freedom* (1974); Rockefeller Foundation Papers, Rockefeller Archive and Research Center, Pocantico Hills, New York; Spingarn, Arthur B., Papers, Manuscript Division, Library of Congress, Washington, D.C.; Staupers, Mabel Keaton. *No Time for Prejudice: A Story of the Integration of Negroes in Nursing in the United States* (1961), and "Story of the National Association of Colored Graduate Nurses," *American Journal of Nursing* (April 1961); Thoms, Adah B. *Pathfinders: A History of the Progress of Colored Graduate Nurses* (1929); Wilkins, Roy. "Nurses Go to War," *Crisis* (February 1943).

DARLENE CLARK HINE

O

OAKLAND, CALIFORNIA, BLACK WOMEN'S CLUBS

The twelve women who founded the Fannie Jackson Coppin Club in 1899 could not have known that their organization would persist through the twentieth century and come to be known as the mother of Black women's clubs in California. That it did is both a tribute to the women who were its leaders and members and a consequence of their historical place and time. Societies, circles, church groups, and women's auxiliaries to male fraternal orders had already been part of Oakland's Black (and white) society for at least three decades, but most were short-lived and did not survive the death or departure of key members. The longevity and effectiveness of the Coppin club and others that soon followed it into existence were possible for two reasons: by the turn of the century, Black society in Oakland and the East Bay had reached a critical mass able to support permanent institutions, and a successor generation of women appeared in the 1920s for whom the clubs were an important route to new opportunities.

Oakland was a young city in 1899, still three years shy of celebrating the fiftieth anniversary of its incorporation by land speculators in 1852. The first Black settlers had arrived by 1854. In 1860, the census recorded forty-one Black residents, including ten children. By 1899, the Black population numbered about 1,000, attracted by employment opportunities created when the Western Pacific Railroad located the western terminus of its transcontinental line there in 1869. Pullman porters, redcaps, and maids working on passenger trains—required to live near the depot—formed the nucleus of a significant Black community that expanded steadily as word spread that Oakland offered opportunities for employment, education, and home ownership. By the 1890s, the Black population was large enough to support Black professionals and require social services not available from public agencies and denied by white-controlled institutions.

Black Oaklanders had a tradition of service and struggle for civil rights. Even when they numbered only a few dozen, they had fought against slavery and school segregation, campaigned for equal access to the courts and for Black suffrage, and supported Black newspapers based in San Francisco; they had organized churches, fraternal lodges, and mutual aid societies; and they had played important roles in statewide networks of Black political activists. In 1897, an ad hoc group of Black women opened the Home for Aged and Infirm Colored People after five years of fund-raising among individuals and churches. No single institution with a broader resource base was responsible for the facility, and women's clubs would play a critical role in providing financial and organizational support until the Home closed in 1938.

Like those in other parts of the country, Black women's clubs in Oakland expanded the resources for community service and promoted personal and community improvement while providing an organizational framework for identifying a leadership group—a function with particular significance in the context of rapid growth (Black Oaklanders would number 3,000 by 1910 as San Franciscans relocated to the East Bay after the 1906 earthquake). Hence it was not surprising that new clubs proliferated. The Art and Industrial Club was founded in 1906 to encourage members to develop talents in art and needlework, and the Mothers' Charity Club was organized in 1907 to provide direct assistance to needy children and families. In 1912 came the Imperial Art and Literary Club and the Elmhurst Progressive Club. All of the clubs shared elements that characterized Black women's clubs throughout the country: programs that combined social service, cultural activities (such as literary study, theatrical performance, musical training, and sponsorship of public cultural events), and social activities ranging from luncheons served at club meetings to elaborate balls and soirees, often billed as fund-raisers for social service projects.

In a regionally distinct role, Oakland clubs also served as a vehicle for boosterism, which the Black community used both to claim a place in the growing city and to insert club leaders into national Black organizations. The original purpose of the Fannie Jackson Coppin Club, for example, was to encourage distinguished Black visitors to Oakland. The club would provide accommodations, so that such visitors could be spared the embarrassment of being refused service in a public facility.

By 1913, there were clubs in San Francisco, Sacramento, San Jose, and Stockton as well as Oakland. In a move calculated to expand their scope and effectiveness and to affirm Oakland's leadership, Elizabeth Brown organized them into the Northern [California] Federation of Colored Women's Clubs, which immediately affiliated with the National Association of Colored Women. A Southern [California] Federation had been formed in 1906, and the two groups joined to form the California Association of Colored Women. In choosing the motto with which it summarized its purposes to the public, the northern federation deliberately supplemented the "Lifting as We Climb" slogan of the National Association. "Deeds Not Words" would appear on all its printed materials, frequently set in context in a single line:

"Lifting as We Climb Service Deeds Not Words."

The usefulness of the northern federation as an instrument for both service and political activism in different arenas was apparent almost immediately. No sooner was the northern federation established than it announced plans to establish an orphanage and home for adolescent girls. Its plans were modeled after the Phyllis Wheatley homes that Black women were opening in eastern cities where young women were coming without families to supervise them. Fund-raising began immediately, and the Northern Federation Home opened its doors in 1918, accepting full-time residents ages five to fourteen and providing day care for children ages three to fourteen. It was later renamed the Fannie Wall Home, after its first president.

Meanwhile, the federated clubs demonstrated their ability to boost Oakland and thereby promote Black achievement. In 1915, the California Association of Colored Women met in Oakland and, in a hotly contested election, chose Elizabeth Brown over the Southern California incumbent as president. She was followed in 1917 by Hettie Tilghman, also of Oakland. Oakland clubwomen were key organizers of an Alameda County Black presence at the 1915 Panama Pacific International Exposition in San Francisco, the world's fair that celebrated the city's reconstruction from the wreckage of the 1906 earthquake. Led by a women's club known as the Civic Center, and with about two weeks' notice, the Colored Women's Clubs assembled a float that carried about fifty women and children in the Alameda County parade. They made a special point of publicizing the race of fourteen-year-old Virginia Stephens, who had won a newspaper contest to invent a nickname for the exposition. "As very few of our white friends knew that Miss Stephens was colored," reported the Oakland *Sunshine* on June 12, 1915, "the clubs took this means to inform the public by a large banner of her presence in the float and her nationality."

The high point of the clubs' booster role came in 1926, when the northern federation hosted the fifteenth biennial meeting of the National Association of Colored Women. Oakland was a surprising choice for an organization with its membership overwhelmingly from the East and South, and the Oakland clubwomen used the occasion to display not only the natural attractions of the city but its relatively benign racial climate. Journalist Delilah Beasley, an active clubwoman, boasted, for example, that Black women attending interracial meetings were served meals with their white peers rather than being asked to leave when the tables were set. California Lieutenant Governor Clement C. Young and Oakland Mayor John

Davis welcomed the 500 delegates. Beasley claimed in 1928 that the (white) *Oakland Tribune*'s coverage of the event had "in a great measure influenced the recognition of Negro clubwomen of Oakland by the national organization," which chose one Oakland woman as national auditor and another to be editor of the organization's official publication in that year.

In the 1920s, the northern federation proved a staging ground for women who were preparing for larger opportunities in an integrated society. Like their counterparts elsewhere, Black Oakland clubwomen organized and supported a Black Young Women's Christian Association (Linden branch), provided a women's auxiliary for the Black Young Men's Christian Association, took part in interracial exchanges based in both clubs and churches, and participated in such politically oriented organizations as the National Association for the Advancement of Colored People and the Alameda County League of Colored Women Voters. In these contexts they defined a broadening mission for which they educated themselves by developing study curricula and regularly inviting social service and civil service professionals to speak at their meetings. Their proximity to the University of California enabled them to go further. Having accepted students of all races from its inception, the university was training a steady trickle of Black students by the 1920s. On campus, they were generally ignored by white fellow students; off campus, they had difficulty in finding housing and part-time jobs. Black clubwomen took a leading role in creating a network of support for students and challenging local youth to seek higher education and professional careers. In addition to offering practical help, they put the students on display as experts and leaders, inviting them to deliver papers and speeches at club meetings and public assemblies, highlighting their achievements as artists, and helping to sponsor their collegiate social activities. Not surprisingly, young women graduates became club activists and at the same time launched careers as the first Black teachers, lawyers, social workers, nurses, and civil servants in white-dominated environments.

Along with churches, Black women's organizations would take the lead in organizing voluntary relief work during the Great Depression. As the scale of the disaster expanded, they used interracial ties and organizational competence forged during the 1920s to facilitate their participation in Community Chest campaigns. Eventually, New Deal programs would dwarf the efforts of voluntary associations, but some of the Black women professionals nurtured in the clubs were able to find positions in the new agencies.

Other clubwomen worked politically to create openings for Black workers in jobs as diverse as public school teaching and public works construction, but the clubs themselves were no longer the moving force. By the time World War II transformed the Bay Area with its mammoth influx of new workers for the war industries, the women's clubs had become auxiliaries, continuing to provide a community base from which leadership emerged and continuing to act creatively to fill gaps in public programs but no longer institutionally capable of shaping events. The process is symbolized by the evolution of the Fannie Wall Home, which joined the Community Chest in 1923, and reorganized as an independent corporation with a board of directors and a professional executive director in 1941. Its building was razed for redevelopment in 1962; after several abortive attempts to reopen, in 1978 it leased its new building to the city of Oakland for a children's day nursery. The women's clubs must, however, share the credit for the emergence in Oakland and the East Bay of a body of Black political and professional leaders who moved to center stage in the mid-1970s.

BIBLIOGRAPHY

Beasley, Delilah L. "Activities among Negroes," *Oakland Tribune* (1923-34); Crouchett, Lawrence P., Lonnie G. Bunch, III, and Martha Kendall Winnacker. *Visions toward Tomorrow: The History of the East Bay Afro-American Community, 1852-1977* (1989); Hausler, Donald. "Blacks in Oakland: 1852-Present," Manuscript (1988); *Miscellaneous Negro Newspapers of California*, Reel 1, microfilm newspaper collection, University of California Library, Los Angeles; Women's clubs papers. Northern California Center for Afro-American History and Life, Oakland.

MARTHA KENDALL WINNACKER

OBERLIN COLLEGE

Trustees at American colleges and universities are not known for radical pronouncements. Yet in 1835, the trustees of the Oberlin Collegiate Institute, sparked by an evangelical commitment to abolitionism, declared: "the education of people of color is a matter of great interest and should be encouraged and sustained at this institution."

As the first coeducational college in America, the school had been on the cutting edge of educational reform ever since its founding two years earlier. At a time when other college doors were closed to Black students, or, in a few instances, open to only a single Black male student, Oberlin's commitments had a profound impact on the educational aspirations and achievements of free Black women. Aside from short-lived New York Central College in McGrawville, N.Y. (1848-58), Oberlin was the only college in America open to Black women until after the Civil War. Over 140 Black women had enrolled at Oberlin by 1865.

In 1835, the trustees of Oberlin College initiated a strong commitment to the education of people of color. However, when Mary Church Terrell (class of 1884) arrived at the school in 1913 to enroll her two daughters, she discovered that the segregationist practices of the society at large had eroded some of that commitment. She lashed out at the administration in a letter, suggesting that "if colored students are to be segregated at Oberlin . . . it seems to me it would be wiser and kinder to exclude them altogether." [Moorland-Spingarn]

The school included a Preparatory Department (PD) that became especially important to Black students and women who had received inadequate or discriminatory public secondary education. Oberlin was best known, however, for its two college-level courses: a Young Ladies' Course (LC), comparable to the curriculum at women's seminaries; and a more rigorous College Course (sometimes called the "gentlemen's course") leading to a baccalaureate degree. Highest enrollments were in the school's preparatory department, but sixty-one Black women enrolled in either the Ladies' or College Course by 1865. Twelve completed the Ladies' Course and three earned the A.B. degree.

This group of Oberlin-educated Black women became leading educators and social activists in emerging Black institutions across the country. Among them were Mary Jane Patterson (AB 1862) and Fanny Jackson Coppin (AB 1865), who became principals at historic Black high schools. Sarah Woodson Early (LC 1856) probably became the first Black woman on a college faculty when, in 1866, she began teaching at Wilberforce University. Black Oberlin women served with the American Missionary Association (AMA) as teachers in southern Black schools after the Civil War; they included Louisa Alexander (LC 1856), Emma Brown (LC), Clara Duncan (PD), Blanche Harris (LC 1860), and Sarah Stanley (LC). Mahala McGuire (LC) became an AMA missionary teacher in Africa as did African-born Margru, known in America as Sarah Kinson (LC). Others, like Lucy Stanton Day (LC 1850), taught in the South without organizational support. A few women achieved prominence outside the field of education: Edmonia Lewis, a student in the Ladies' Course in the 1860s, became a well-known sculptor; and Frances Norris (AB 1865) became a businesswoman in Atlanta after the war, specializing in real estate and catering.

Many of these women remembered Oberlin as an interracial utopia, recalling that they had been members and officers of the literary society, and had roomed and eaten along with their white classmates in college dormitories and dining halls. Although Fanny Jackson realized that Oberlin was not the "pool of Bethesda for the sin of prejudice," she always maintained that it "came nearer to it than any other place in the United States." Bigotry, she explained, was not found in the Oberlin administration or faculty; indeed, "prejudice at Oberlin is preached against, prayed against, sung against, and lived against" (Perkins 1978).

After the Civil War, Oberlin's Black graduates played an important role in establishing the first Black colleges and serving on their faculties. As these colleges grew and other white colleges began admitting Black students, Oberlin began to lose some of its distinctiveness. However, in the 1880s, Mary Church Terrell, Anna Julia Cooper, and Ida Wells Gibbs Hunt (all AB 1884) still found Oberlin a comfortable and inspiring place to be. Terrell valued both her Black and white friends as well as the opportunity for social integration in dormitories and campus organizations. Less is known about the Oberlin experiences of two women who became early Black physicians, Matilda Evans (PD) and Caroline Still Anderson (LC 1880).

Unfortunately, as segregationist practices grew in American society so they did at Oberlin, especially after 1900. In 1913, when Mary Church Terrell came to Oberlin to enroll her two daughters, she learned that only two college dormitories were open to Black women and that literary societies were no longer admitting Black students. She lashed out at the administration, writing, "If colored students are to be segregated at Oberlin with such a wonderful record as it once made for itself even in the dark days of slavery, it seems to me it would be wiser and kinder to exclude them altogether" (Terrell 1914).

To counteract growing social segregation, Black students began to establish organizations of their own, and newly integrated liberal associations, such as the Young Women's Christian Association and the National Association for the Advancement of Colored People, provided forums for race-related issues to be discussed and addressed. After World War II, special programs were offered to expose students to Black culture, including exchange programs with historic Black colleges.

During the civil rights and Black Power movements, renewed pride in Oberlin's early commitment to racial justice resurfaced. Compelled by this tradition, new and successful efforts were made to increase Black enrollment and retention. Unlike Mary Church Terrell and earlier generations of Black students, many Black students did not wish to be assimilated into white society. Their outspoken presence required the college to reassess what it offered in the way of academic and social support, with the result that, among many changes, Oberlin stepped up Black recruitment through a special nondiscriminatory program for disadvantaged youths, added a Black Studies Program (now a department), established an African Heritage House, and formed a Black Alumni group within the Alumni Association.

Oberlin's twentieth-century Black women continue to be very much a part of the Oberlin experience and to play important roles in American society. Most would agree with Johnnetta Betsch Cole (AB 1957), president of Spelman College, that their Oberlin experience has greatly influenced their lives by its "staunch commitment to a liberal arts curriculum [and] emphasis on taking responsibility for oneself and the world" ("Oberlin College" 1991).

BIBLIOGRAPHY

Bigglestone, William. "Oberlin College and the Negro Student, 1865-1940," *Journal of Negro History* (July 1971); Fletcher, Robert Samuel. *A History of Oberlin College* (1943); Henle, Ellen and Marlene Merrill. "Antebellum Black Coeds at Oberlin College," *Oberlin Alumni Magazine* (January-February 1980); Horton, James Oliver. "Black Education at Oberlin College: A Controversial Commitment," *Journal of Negro Education* (Fall 1985); Jones, Adrienne Lash. "Black Students Helped Oberlin from the Beginning," *[Oberlin] Observer* (November 13, 1986); Lawson, Ellen Nickenzie with Marlene Merrill, eds. *The Three Sarahs: Documents of Antebellum Black College Women* (1984); Nickenzie, Ellen and Marlene Merrill. "The Antebellum 'Talented Thousandth': Black College Students at Oberlin before the Civil War," *Journal of Negro History* (Spring 1983); "Oberlin College: A Unique African-American Heritage." Oberlin College Archives (1991); Perkins, Linda. *Fanny Jackson Coppin and the Institute for Colored Youth* (1987); Terrell, Mary Church. Letter to President King. King Papers, Oberlin College Archives (January 26, 1914).

MARLENE DEAHL MERRILL

OBLATE SISTERS OF PROVIDENCE

Twenty-two vessels from the island of Saint Domingue anchored off Fell's Point near Baltimore, Maryland, on July 9, 1793, with more than 500 Black and white people on board. All were fleeing the Haitian Revolution. The well-to-do French-speaking Black Haitians would join the 15,800 Black Roman Catholics already in Maryland and bring new life to Black Catholicism in America. That new life began with a Sulpician priest, Father Jacques Hector Nicholas Joubert, and Elizabeth Lange, a Haitian refugee.

Joubert, who had been assigned pastoral charge of the refugees, soon discovered that the children had difficulty learning their catechism because they were unable to read French or English. The priest approached Lange, who had already begun operating her own day school, about establishing a teaching community consecrated to God in which the children could be taught to understand their catechism. Lange and another teacher, Marie Madeleine Balas, had already considered such an idea, however, and on July 2, 1829, it was realized with the establishment of the Oblate Sisters of Providence.

The beginnings of most religious communities are difficult, but this was particularly true for the four original Oblates, Lange, the founder, and Balas, plus Rosine Boegue and Almeide Duchemin Maxis. The white residents of Baltimore were sympathetic to southern attitudes and did not peacefully accept the formation of these Black women into a religious society, especially while some 400,000 of their brethren were enslaved in Maryland. One record reports that when the Oblate Sisters first appeared on the street they were stoned by angry white residents. With encouragement from Joubert, however, they were nonetheless able to combine the activities of teaching and devotional living into a religious community. In their habits of black dress, with a white collar and a large white bonnet for convent wear, they taught Black children arithmetic, English, penmanship, religion, and housekeeping. In a black bonnet and cape for outside wear they also tended to sick people outside the convent. The sisters had a great influence on their students, some of whom became Oblates, while others went on to establish their own schools.

When Joubert died on November 5, 1843, the order faced four desperate years. When it appeared that the church had deserted them, the sisters took in washing, sewing, and embroidery to support themselves. Believing that the order would be disbanded, some of the sisters withdrew in 1845. In 1847, however, when a Redemptorist priest named Thaddeus Anwander came to their assistance, the community began a resurgence and the order began to grow and flourish. During the Civil War years, a Jesuit priest named Father Peter Miller carried them through. Still later, the Josephite fathers helped to solidify the struggling but determined order.

The Oblates proved that virtue and intelligence know no race, sanctity heeds no color, and determination has no end. They demonstrated courage and tenacity in perilous times and gave hope to their persecuted race. Most of all, they contributed to the history of Black Catholics in America.

BIBLIOGRAPHY

Fitzpatrick, Sandra and Maria R. Goodwin. *The Guide to Black Washington* (1990); Gilliard, John T. *The Catholic Church and the American Negro* (1929), and *Colored Catholics in the United States* (1941); Marrow, Gloria R. "A Narrative of the Founding and Work of the Oblate Sisters of Providence," Master's thesis (1976); *The New Catholic Encyclopedia* (1967); *News American* (May 14, 1973); Oblate Archival Materials. *Annals of the Oblate Sisters of Providence* (1842-77), Baltimore, Maryland; Sherwood, Grace. *The Oblates Hundred and One Years* (1931).

GLORIA MARROW

OCCOMY, MARITA BONNER *see* BONNER, MARITA

ODETTA (1930-)

Odetta sings folk songs and plays a guitar she calls "her baby" in a career that has spanned four decades. She has performed internationally, appeared in numerous films and plays, and lectured throughout the United States. Odetta has been said to be "authentic"; she is an artist who captured the soul of the folk revival movement and who has been embraced by the feminist community.

Odetta Holmes Felious Gordon was born on December 31, 1930, in Birmingham, Alabama. Odetta grew up in a southern Baptist music tradition that focused on the spiritual. Odetta and her family moved to Los Angeles, California, when she was six. She began singing lessons at the age of thirteen. Odetta's father exposed her to big band and country music, and she also enjoyed listening to the Metropolitan Opera broadcasts on the radio.

Odetta was introduced to folk music while she was in the chorus of a production of *Finian's Rainbow* in Los Angeles. She traveled to San Francisco with a friend and emerged on the folk music scene in San Francisco in 1953. Music critics have compared her to Bessie Smith. Odetta has said that her artistic progenitors are Paul Robeson for his political conviction and Marian Anderson for her character. Dignity, love of self, and political commitment permeate Odetta's songs and words.

Odetta has toured in Europe with two other great vocal artists, Nina Simone and Miriam Makeba. She says that she is an "ancestor worshiper." She gives praise to and honors the ancestors who have taught her the importance of positive energy in vanquishing the negative forces that keep the struggle from advancing.

BIBLIOGRAPHY

Armstrong, Don. "Odetta a Citizen of the World," *Crisis* (June/July 1983); Budds, Michael. "Odetta," *New Grove Dictionary of American Music*, ed. H. Wiley Hitchcock

Since the 1950s, America's folk music world has been enhanced by the proud presence of the magnificent Odetta. [Schomburg Center]

and Stanley Sadie (1986); *BWW*; Feather, Leonard. *Encyclopedia of Jazz* (1960); Garland, Phyl. "Roll On Odetta," *Stereo Review* (March 1988); Greenberg, Mark. "Power and Beauty: The Legend of Odetta," *Sing Out* (August-October 1991); Leder, Jan. *Women in Jazz* (1985); Tudor, Dean and Nancy Tudor. *Black Music* (1979); Vann, Kimberly R. *The Bibliography* (1990).

SELECTED DISCOGRAPHY

And the Blues. Riverside RLP 9417; *Sometimes I Feel Like Cryin'*. RCA LSP 2773 (1962).

NOMALONGA DALILI

OGLESBY, MARY (1915-)

"I've been fooling people for years," teacher, aviator, and community activist Mary Oglesby once said, "letting them think I've been working, but I've been having fun." Mary Oglesby was born January 6, 1915, to Melinda (Dunham) and Charles Owings in Portsmouth, Ohio. Her mother's family came from Madagascar, and her father was pureblood Cherokee Indian from Oklahoma. They met and married in Chicago when Melinda was fifteen and Charles was fifty-one. Mary's mother died on January 8, 1915, leaving behind an eleven-month-old daughter and two-day-old Mary. Charles Owings raised Mary and her sister during their early years with the help of a German woman who came in to cook, clean, and do the laundry.

Charles Owings had already contributed to history before his daughters were born as a soldier in the Civil War. In 1865, he presented the flag to President Abraham Lincoln at the Appomattox Courthouse in Virginia during General Lee's surrender to General Ulysses S. Grant, signalling the end of the Civil War. By 1918, Owings had moved the girls to Glenellen, Indiana, where Mary began elementary school at age four because her sister was already in school and her father was at work—there was no one home to take care of her. When the school sent Mary home because she was too young to attend, her father took her to the school and insisted that they would have to accept her because he would not leave her home unattended.

The family moved between Chicago and various sections of Ohio. The girls completed East High School in Xenia, Ohio, about three miles from Wilberforce. When their father died they moved back to Chicago and lived with the family of their first cousin, Katherine Dunham, a renowned choreographer, dancer, and anthropologist. Both Mary and her sister received scholarships for academic achievement and attended Joliet Junior College in Illinois. From there they completed their Bachelor's degrees at Howard University, where Mary majored in physical education and her sister majored in home economics. Mary had the counsel of surrogate mother Mary Rose Reeves Allen at Howard, whom she addressed as "Lady Allen." Lady Allen was head of physical education at Howard and guided primarily Mary, but also her sister, toward their professional careers. While at Howard Mary studied African history with Leo Hansberry (Lorraine Hansberry's uncle), dance with Violet Warfield, and anatomy, kinesiology, physical therapy, and physiology with Allen. Oglesby graduated from Howard in 1937 and accepted a teaching offer in Indianapolis, where she has remained ever since. She has continued her graduate work at Butler, Purdue, and the University of Michigan.

As a child Mary Owings always "dreamed of jumping off a house and floating away." She used to take umbrellas down to the barn and jump out of the hayloft window. She always wanted to fly. Mary married in 1944, after which she and her husband began to travel the country by car. One day she suggested that they start flying. They located a training school at the Plainfield Airport in Plainfield, Indiana, that provided basic training, classroom work on the mechanics and the parts of an airplane, and hands-on experience in flying aircraft. Mary Oglesby received her student pilot's license on August 8, 1946, and her private pilot's license on October 27, 1946. She and her husband took lessons together. Mary's husband was jealous because on September 21, 1946, Mary soloed across country in an airplane before he did.

Oglesby was in one crash on December 4, 1948. The plane was piloted by a third party and she and her husband were passengers. They were flying in inclement weather when the pilot descended too rapidly and hit a tree limb; Mary's head hit the gyro-compass, resulting in a compound fracture of the skull. Mary had a cranial operation during which a permanent plate was placed in her head. She immediately resumed flying in 1949.

Oglesby is a major in the Indiana Wing Civil Air Patrol, which participates in search and rescue missions for downed aircraft. She is a commandant for women cadets during drill competitions. For more than forty years she has flown a Cessna 150 on search and rescue missions.

Mary Oglesby has devoted her life to others. For approximately forty-eight years she has taught health classes, physical education, driver education, and safety at Crispus Attucks High School. She was a swimming coach for fifteen years and a basketball, track, and volleyball coach for three years. She taught swimming for fifteen years for the Fall Creek Young Women's Christian Association and continues to substitute teach swimming at the Washington High School in Indianapolis. Although retired and widowed, Oglesby continues to serve others. She drives daily up and down the roads of Indiana picking up food from farmers and merchants to donate for the homeless. She organizes volunteers who come to a church on Sundays to cook and serve a decent dinner to the homeless community. She is still physically fit, active in the Civil Air Patrol, and teaches swimming. Her daughter Mona is an international flight attendant and interpreter for deaf travelers.

BIBLIOGRAPHY
Oglesby, Mary. Personal interviews (1989, 1990).

ELIZABETH HADLEY FREYDBERG

OGLESBY, SADIE *see* BAHA'I FAITH

ORMES, ZELDA JACKSON "JACKIE" (1917-1986)

Jackie Ormes is a name familiar to many Black newspaper readers of the 1930s, 1940s, 1950s, and 1960s, for she was the creator of the nationally syndicated cartoon strips "Torchy Brown," "Patty Jo 'n' Ginger," and "Candy."

Zelda Jackson was born in Pittsburgh, Pennsylvania. Her father was an artist and Jackson studied art in schools in her hometown before joining the *Pittsburgh Courier* staff around 1936. She began as a feature writer and contributed pieces of art work, soon developing the strip "Torchy Brown in Dixie to Harlem," which first appeared May 1, 1937. Jackson had married Earl Ormes and her pen name, "Jackie Ormes," was taken from her family name and her married name. In the initial strip, Torchy, a young woman "who doesn't know a thing about life—but suspects an awful lot," lives on a "little dixie farm" with her aunt and uncle, but the visit of Dazzling Dinah soon leads her to migrate to New York City where she tries to make it in the entertainment business in Harlem. In later incarnations Torchy Brown becomes a newspaper reporter.

When Ormes began drawing "Torchy," most women in comic strips did "things like dangle from window ledges and scream for help, or look up at their heroes with round, admiring eyes. 'Torchy' Brown [was] a jump into the unexpected. . . . She was the first woman to star in a black strip. . . . Torchy was smart, self-reliant and constantly butting up against bigotry and sexism" (Heise 1986).

Zelda Jackson Ormes moved to Chicago in the early 1940s; her husband worked for Supreme Life Insurance Company of America and she worked as a general assignment reporter for the *Chicago Defender*, at the same time attending classes at the Art Institute of Chicago. Her second cartoon, "Patty Jo 'n' Ginger," was a little-sister-big-sister strip that addressed sex roles, segregation, educational inequalities, and other political issues. A strip in 1947, for example, showed Patty-Jo and Ginger, unable to buy fireworks for their Fourth of July celebration, with the caption, "Shucks—Let's go price Atom Bombs—They haven't outlawed them yet!!!" (*Pittsburgh Courier*, July 5, 1947). Other strips commented on the quality, content, and availability of education. Patty-Jo, having failed history, announces, "But I'm proud to flunk my history course. I can't help it if the school hasn't got the right text book on Negro Americans. . . . I jus' *feel good* contradictin' the teacher when she's wrong!" (*Pittsburgh Courier*, December 1, 1951). When Ginger volunteers to collect donations for the Negro college

fund, Patty-Jo responds, "Gosh—Thanks if you're beggin' for me—But, how's about gettin' our rich Uncle Sam to put good public schools all over, so we can be trained fit for any college?" (*Pittsburgh Courier*, June 26, 1948). Following the murder of fourteen-year-old Chicagoan Emmett Till by Mississippi white men who alleged Till had whistled at one of their wives, Ormes blasted the absurdity of U.S. racial ethics with a strip in which an indignant Patty-Jo announces, "I don't want to seem touchy on the subject . . . but, that new little white tea-kettle just whistled at me!" (*Pittsburgh Courier*, October 8, 1955). These overtly political strips were interspersed with numerous strips featuring a scantily clad Ginger, but even the latter carried a political, if more subtle, message, by suggesting the absurdity of women who exist for others merely as helpless sex objects. For example, Patty-Jo handing Ginger an umbrella: "For your birthday, sis—it's guaranteed not to open without the help of a MAN!" (*Pittsburgh Courier*, July 9, 1949). The "Patty Jo 'n' Ginger" strip was so popular that Ormes developed "Patty Jo" character dolls.

Jackie Ormes's strips were syndicated in Black newspapers across the country, making her the only nationally syndicated Black woman cartoonist until Barbara Brandon's 1990s "Where I'm Coming From" strip. Ormes retired from cartooning in the late 1960s after drawing became too difficult due to rheumatoid arthritis. She remained active in the Chicago community, and was on the board of directors of the DuSable Museum of African-American History and Art. Ormes died in Chicago on January 2, 1986; she was sixty-eight years old. Her contributions to cartooning are briefly acknowledged in the New Day Films video *Funny Ladies*.

BIBLIOGRAPHY

Heise, Kenan. "Jackie Ormes, 68; Drew Comic Strip 'Torchy,' " *Chicago Tribune* (January 3, 1986); *Jet*. "Jackie Ormes, 68, Artist, Journalist Dies in Chicago" (January 20, 1986); Jones, Lisa. "Girls on the Strip," *Village Voice* (March 10, 1992); *Pittsburgh Courier*. "Patty Jo 'n' Ginger" (1945-56), and "Torchy Brown in Dixie to Harlem" (1937-38), and " 'Torchy Brown' Will Be Big Hit in *Courier*" (August 12, 1950).

ELSA BARKLEY BROWN

OSBORNE, ESTELLE MASSEY (1901-1981)

Estelle Massey Osborne devoted her life to nursing—as a practitioner and as an advocate for improved training and better job opportunities for Black nurses.

Estelle Massey was born on May 3, 1901, in Palestine, Texas, eighth of the eleven children of Hall and Bettye Estelle Massey, a remarkable couple with strong opinions about childrearing. The Massey children raised and sold vegetables for spending money. The Massey daughters were not allowed to work for white employers because their mother did not want

A courageous advocate for Black nurses, Estelle Massey Osborne fought to lift the color ban in the army and navy nurse corps. [Moorland-Spingarn]

them exposed to racism. The Masseys brought up their children to be strong, confident, and proud.

Estelle Massey continued her parents' dreams for her by attending Prairie View State College. After graduation, she taught, became a nurse, and then taught nursing. At that point, she decided that she needed more education.

While attending Teachers College at Columbia University in New York, Massey taught at Lincoln Hospital School for Nurses in the Bronx. Later she was hired by Harlem Hospital School of Nursing, becoming the first Black nursing instructor there. After receiving her Bachelor's degree at Columbia in 1931, she became the first educational director of nursing at Freedmen's Hospital School of Nursing (now Howard University College of Nursing). Her goal while at Freedmen's was to provide Black student nurses with the same quality education that white students were receiving at the best nursing schools, but Osborne had another goal as well. She wanted to change the quality of education for Black nurses across the country.

Working through the National Association of Colored Graduate Nurses (NACGN), as well as on her own, Osborne organized conferences, gave seminars, and conducted workshops all over the country. For five years she was president of the NACGN.

In 1936, Osborne became the first Black director of nursing at City Hospital No. 2 (now the Homer G. Phillips Hospital Training School). In 1943, she served as a consultant to the National Nursing Council for War Service. As the first Black consultant on the staff of any national nursing organization, she helped increase the number of white nurses' training schools admitting Black students from fourteen to thirty-eight in just two years. She also fought to lift the color ban on Black nurses attempting to enlist in the army and navy nurse corps and, with the army, was successful.

In 1946, she received her Master's degree and became the first Black member of the nursing faculty at New York University in New York City. This position brought Osborne a great deal of visibility and prestige and allowed her to make even greater strides in her fight for the advancement of Black nurses. In 1948, she won a position on the board of directors of the American Nurses Association.

In the years that followed, Osborne served in an executive position with most of the important nursing organizations in the country. When she retired in 1967, she was associate general director of the National League for Nursing. Estelle Massey Osborne died in 1981.

BIBLIOGRAPHY

Dannett, Sylvia G. L. *Profiles of Negro Womanhood* (1966); *New York Times.* Obituary (December 17, 1981); Osborne, Estelle Massey. Papers, 1943-67, and clipping file. Schomburg Center for Research in Black Culture, The New York Public Library, New York City; Safier, Gwendolyn. *Contemporary Leaders in Nursing: An Oral History* (1977).

MARIE MOSLEY

P

PARKS, ROSA (1913-)

Rosa Louise McCauley Parks, held in high esteem because of her defiance of southern law and tradition, frequently has been called the mother of the modern civil rights movement. Parks's act on December 1, 1955, of sitting down to stand up for equal chances at riding the bus in Montgomery, Alabama, took on enormous meaning. It became legendary, resulting in 42,000 Black people's boycotting city buses. The Montgomery bus boycott lasted 381 days, and when it ended on December 21, 1956, the U.S. Supreme Court had ruled segregation on city buses unconstitutional, Martin Luther King, Jr., had become a national leader, and a mass movement of nonviolent resistance had begun that would continue into the 1960s.

When Leona McCauley gave birth to Rosa in Tuskegee, Alabama, on February 4, 1913, *Plessy* v. *Ferguson* and Jim Crow were in their second decade. McCauley reared her daughter in Montgomery, where Rosa attended the all-Black Alabama State College. Rosa married Raymond Parks, a barber, in 1932, and they both became active in the local chapter of the National Association for the Advancement of Colored People (NAACP). Raymond Parks volunteered his time to help free the defendants in the Scottsboro cases of the 1930s. Rosa Parks served as youth advisor for the Montgomery NAACP, becoming its secretary in the 1950s. She first worked as a clerk and

an insurance saleswoman, and then she became a tailor's assistant at the Fair Department Store, making 75¢ an hour in 1955.

Sometime that year, E. D. Nixon, Pullman porter and president of the Montgomery NAACP, recommended Rosa Parks to white activist Virginia Durr, who sought a part-time seamstress. The Durrs on numerous occasions listened to Parks's complaints about segregation in the South, especially the situation involving Montgomery's public transit system. Parks deplored the custom of having to enter the front of the bus to pay the fare and then having to exit to reenter in the back of the bus. Frequently, white bus drivers pulled away before Black riders could reboard at the back. Moreover, Parks kept the Durrs abreast of the efforts for a test case to end Montgomery segregated busing or at least improve the situation. Then, in March 1955, authorities arrested Claudette Colvin, a fifteen-year-old high school student, for refusing to give up her seat to a white passenger. At Parks's invitation, Virginia Durr attended an NAACP meeting concerning Colvin's case. An informal bus boycott had begun, but NAACP leaders decided not to initiate an organized resistance around this particular case. Upon learning that a scholarship was available for a 1955 summer workshop at the Highlander Folk School in Monteagle, Tennessee, the Durrs urged Rosa Parks to accept it. A reluctant Parks consented to go when friends of the Durrs offered to pay her travel expenses to and from Tennessee.

The Highlander Folk School was a training ground for labor organizers, and having been active in the NAACP in Montgomery, Parks knew of the struggle for justice and equality that that organization had maintained since 1910. Her mother, a schoolteacher, had benefited from the NAACP's efforts to secure equal salaries for Black and white teachers in the 1940s. Parks believed that the historic *Brown* v. *Board of Education* Supreme Court ruling in 1954 made most Black Americans optimistic about their future in a newly desegregated America.

The Supreme Court decision marked a turning point in the long struggle against segregation, but the decision embraced only one aspect of racial equality, public education. Black Americans now had to overcome inequities in economic and political arenas. On the heels of *Brown*, Black citizens made it evident in Montgomery that they would no longer tolerate racial injustice. This stand was sparked by Rosa Parks's refusal to give up her seat so that a white man could sit in the first row of a section of a transit bus reserved for nonwhites. According to de facto custom, when the section reserved for white passengers was filled, Black passengers were expected to give up their seats to those whites left standing. Parks was arrested for not complying and fined $14. Within four days of Parks's arrest and bond release, the Black community of Montgomery rallied around the quiet, reserved, and hard-working woman as its symbol of courage.

Parks has said that she simply was too tired to move that day. The Durrs accompanied E. D. Nixon to get Parks from jail. Indeed, the Durrs, Fred D. Gray (her Black defense attorney), and E. D. Nixon (a principal organizer of the boycott) all played critical roles in organizing and sustaining the boycott. Though the gains from the Montgomery boycott were won by the many unsung participants who made it a success, Rosa Parks must be credited with providing the spark that made it all begin to happen.

For her actions in 1955, Parks lost her job, but history continues to reward her. When she moved with her husband and mother to Detroit in 1957, she again worked as a seamstress, but Congressman John Conyers later hired her as a staff assistant. Detroit renamed its Twelfth Street in her honor in 1969. She continues to receive numerous awards and honorary degrees. *Ebony* readers chose her in 1980 as the living Black woman who had done the most to advance the cause of Black America, and the Martin Luther King, Jr., Center for Nonviolent Social Change awarded her the Martin Luther King, Jr., Nonviolent Peace Prize that same year. She fulfilled a personal dream in 1987 by founding the Rosa and Raymond Parks Institute of Self Development in Detroit. The institute addresses her lifelong commitment to career training for Black youth, and affirms the Parkses' devotion and dedication to human rights struggles.

[*See also* MONTGOMERY BUS BOYCOTT.]

One day in December 1955 in Montgomery, Alabama, Rosa Parks refused to give up her seat on a bus to a white man. A year later, the Supreme Court had ruled segregation on city buses was unconstitutional, Martin Luther King, Jr., had become a national leader, and a mass movement of nonviolent resistance had been launched. [Schomburg Center]

BIBLIOGRAPHY

Barnard, Hollinger F., ed. *Outside the Magic Circle: The Autobiography of Virginia Foster Durr* (1985); Bennett, Lerone, Jr. "Great Moments in Black History No. 12: The Day the Black Revolution Began," *Ebony* (September 1977); Brown, Roxann. " 'Mother of the Movement': Nation Honors Rosa Parks with Birthday Observance," *Ebony* (February 1988); Garrow, David J., ed. *The Montgomery Bus Boycott and the Women Who Started It: The Memoir of Jo Ann Gibson Robinson* (1987); King, Martin Luther, Jr. *Stride toward Freedom: The Montgomery Story* (1958); Marshall, Marilyn. "Forty Who Made a Difference: Movers and Shakers," *Ebony* (November 1985); Nash, Tom. "Essence Woman," *Essence* (May 1985); "100 That Shook America," *Esquire* (December 1964); Reed, Linda. *Simple Decency and*

Honored in 1980 by Ebony *as the living Black woman who had done the most to advance the cause of civil rights, Rosa Parks was invited to the podium at the Democratic National Convention in 1988 by the Reverend Jesse Jackson and his wife, Jacqueline, before Jackson's prime-time address. [UPI/Bettmann]*

Common Sense: The Southern Conference Movement, 1938-1963 (1991); "Thirty-fifth Anniversary Service Awards: *Ebony* Readers Pick Rosa Parks and Jesse Jackson as Most Outstanding Blacks," *Ebony* (November 1980).

LINDA REED

PARSONS, LUCY (1853-1942)

A veteran of the anarchist, socialist, and communist movements in Chicago during the late nineteenth and early twentieth centuries, Lucy Parsons was the first Black woman to play a prominent role in the American Left. A committed revolutionary, Parsons devoted sixty years of her life to improving the situation of the poor, the jobless, the homeless, women, children, and people of color.

Born in 1853 in Waco, Texas, of African, Indian, and Mexican ancestry, Lucy met and subsequently married Albert Parsons, a former Confederate army scout turned radical. Because of their mixed marriage, the couple was forced to flee Texas in 1873. They ultimately ended up in Chicago, where they both joined the socialist-oriented Workingmen's party in 1876. Within three years, Lucy Parsons began contributing articles to the *Socialist* and became a primary speaker on behalf of the Working Women's Union. The Parsonses were eventually drawn to anarchism, which emphasized cooperative organization of production, the abolition of the state, and the free exchange of products without profit or market intervention. Along with her husband and several other white Chicago radicals, Lucy Parsons helped form the International Working People's Association (IWPA) in 1883. She continued to develop as a talented propagandist and radical intellectual, publishing a popular article in *Alarm* (a revolutionary socialist newspaper) in 1884 that called on the jobless to "learn to use explosives!"

The first Black woman to play a prominent role in the American Left, legendary anarchist Lucy Parsons wrote powerfully on lynching and racial violence. [Archives of Labor and Urban Affairs, Wayne State University]

Less known, however, are her early writings on lynchings and racist violence in the South, which were published several years before Ida B. Wells's famous pronouncements on the subject. She viewed racial oppression as primarily a class question and suggested that African-American working people adopt violent strategies of self-defense. Commenting on a multiple lynching that had occurred in Carrollton, Mississippi, in 1886, Parsons insisted that race had nothing to do with the brutal murders. "It is because [the Black man] is *poor*. It is because he is dependent. Because he is poorer as a class than his white wage-slave brother of the North" (Ashbaugh 1976). Her tendency to focus on economic causes and de-emphasize the role of racism might be linked to her own denial of her Black heritage. Her complexion and features not only enabled her to pass as Spanish, but her social world consisted almost entirely of white Leftists. Because racism was not something she had to endure all of her life, it was difficult for her to see

how it could have shaped the lives of African-Americans.

Like so many other anarchists and radical labor leaders, Lucy Parsons helped organize the famous attempted general strike on May 1, 1886, demanding a general eight-hour work day. Three days into the strike, Albert Parsons and eight other IWPA members were arrested for allegedly throwing a bomb at police during a demonstration at Chicago's Haymarket Square. Lucy Parsons led a campaign to free her husband and the other seven political prisoners, but her efforts were to no avail: Albert Parsons and three other defendants were executed in 1887. (Just two years later she lost her youngest of two children, eight-year-old Lulu, to lymphadenoma.)

Despite these tragedies, Lucy Parsons continued her work on behalf of anarchist and socialist causes, addressing radical gatherings throughout the United States as well as England. In 1891, she published and edited a short-lived newspaper called *Freedom: A Revolutionary Anarchist-Communist Monthly*, in which she began dealing with the woman question much more rigorously, publishing essays on rape, divorce, marriage, and the role of women's oppression as a function of capitalism. Like her views on racism, Parsons believed that sexism would automatically disappear with the construction of a socialist society.

By the turn of the century, Parsons had become somewhat of a legend of the Left. She was one of two women in attendance at the founding convention of the Industrial Workers of the World (IWW) in 1905, she gained some notoriety for leading mass demonstrations of homeless and unemployed people in San Francisco (1914) and Chicago (1915), and she was a vocal opponent of World War I. In 1927, Parsons joined the International Labor Defense, a Communist-led organization devoted to defending "class war prisoners," notably incarcerated labor organizers like Tom Mooney and African-Americans unjustly accused of crimes (e.g., the Scottsboro Nine and Angelo Herndon). After working closely with the Communists for more than a decade, the eighty-six-year-old Parsons joined the party in 1939. Three years later her life came to an end when a fire engulfed her home.

BIBLIOGRAPHY

Ashbaugh, Carolyn. *Lucy Parsons, American Revolutionary* (1976); Davis, Angela. *Women, Race, and Class* (1981); Parsons, Lucy E. *The Life of Albert R. Parsons* (1889).

ROBIN D. G. KELLEY

PATTERSON, LOUISE THOMPSON (1901-)

An educator, cultural critic, early civil rights activist, and pioneering advocate of Black women's rights in Harlem, Louise Thompson brought to the Communist party an unusually sophisticated understanding of the complexities of race and gender oppression—a unique perspective for an organization that emphasized class exploitation above all else.

Born in Chicago, Illinois, on September 9, 1901, she was raised in several predominantly white, often racist communities in the West. Her family eventually settled in Oakland, California, in 1919. She earned a degree in economics from the University of California at Berkeley in 1923, but racism limited her career opportunities. She chose to go back to the Midwest and work toward a graduate degree at the University of Chicago, but she abandoned the idea soon thereafter. Giving up school, as well as a lucrative position at a Black-owned Chicago firm, Thompson headed south to accept a teaching job in Pine Bluff, Arkansas, in 1925, and a year later accepted a faculty position at Hampton Institute in Virginia. Because of her open support of a student strike in 1927, the Hampton administration pressured Thompson to resign, after which she headed to New York City to accept an Urban League Fellowship to study at the New School for Social Work.

Unimpressed with social work paternalism as a means to improve the lives of the Black poor, she discontinued her education in 1930 and turned to New York's Congregational Educational Society (CES), a liberal organization interested in the problems of race relations and labor. Simultaneously, she became a prominent figure in Black cultural circles, serving as editorial secretary for Langston Hughes and Zora Neale Hurston, and offering her spacious apartment as a meeting place for Black artists and intellectuals. Her involvement in social problems and cultural politics, compounded by the Great Depression, the Scottsboro case, and the growing strength of the Communist party in Harlem, radicalized Thompson. She and artist Augusta Savage formed a left-wing social club called the Vanguard, out of which developed a branch of the Friends of the Soviet Union (FOSU). Soon thereafter, Thompson attended classes at the Workers' School, moving deeper into the party's inner circle.

As secretary of the Harlem chapter of FOSU, she became principal organizer of a group of Black artists invited to the Soviet Union in 1932 to make a film about African-American life. Although the project was abandoned, she returned to New York with a deeper appreciation of socialism and a greater affinity for Communist politics. In 1933, she left CES and served as assistant national secretary of the National Committee for the Defense of Political Prisoners (NCDPP), through which she was officially asked to join the Communist party. A year later she accepted a full-time position in the International Workers' Order (IWO) and continued to organize cultural and political events on behalf of the Communist party in Harlem and elsewhere (including Alabama, where in 1934 she spent a night in a Birmingham jail). As Black artists joined the Works Progress Administration (WPA) in the late 1930s, Thompson became an increasingly critical liaison linking Black popular culture and Harlem's literati with Communist popular front politics. In 1938, for example, she and Langston Hughes organized the IWO-sponsored Harlem Suitcase Theatre that performed a number of works by Black playwrights.

In 1940, Louise Thompson married long-time friend and veteran party leader William L. Patterson—who over a decade earlier had suggested she read Marx and look seriously at events in the Soviet Union. Soon afterward she joined "Patt" in Chicago and continued her work nationally and locally. Among other things, she served as national recording secretary of the IWO and helped establish a Black community center on Chicago's South Side. Following World War II, she was among the founders and leading activists of the Civil Rights Congress (CRC), and in the 1950s she joined such luminaries as Charlotta Bass, Shirley Graham, and Alice Childress in forming the Sojourners for Truth and Justice, a Black woman's auxiliary of the CRC.

BIBLIOGRAPHY

Horne, Gerald. *Communist Front?: The Civil Rights Congress, 1946-1956* (1988); Naison, Mark. *Communists in Harlem during the Depression* (1983); Patterson, Louise. Interview by Ruth Prago, Oral History of the American Left, Tamiment Institute, New York University (November 1981); Patterson, William L. *The Man Who Cried Genocide: An Autobiography* (1971); Rampersad, Arnold. *The Life of Langston Hughes: I, Too, Sing America, Volume I: 1902-1941* (1986).

ROBIN D. G. KELLEY

PATTERSON, MARY JANE (1840-1894)

The 1860 census lists Mary Jane Patterson as one of fourteen residents in her parents' household in

Oberlin, Ohio. Two years later she graduated from Oberlin College, becoming the first Black woman to receive a B.A. degree from an established American college. Patterson devoted the rest of her life to the education of Black children.

Born in Raleigh, North Carolina, in 1840, Patterson was the oldest of Henry and Emeline Patterson's seven children. In 1856, she and her family moved to Oberlin, Ohio, where they joined a growing community of free Black families who worked to send their children to the college. Henry Patterson worked as a master mason, and for many years the family boarded large numbers of Black students in their home. Eventually, four Patterson children graduated from Oberlin College. All became teachers.

Mary Jane Patterson's first known teaching appointment was in 1865, when she became an assistant to Fanny Jackson in the Female Department of the Institute for Colored Youth in Philadelphia. In 1869, when Jackson was promoted to principal, Patterson accepted a teaching position in Washington, D.C., at the newly organized Preparatory High School for Colored Youth—later known as Dunbar High School. She served as the school's first Black principal, from 1871-72, and was reappointed from 1873-84. During her administration, the name "Preparatory High School" was dropped, high school commencements were initiated, and a teacher-training department was added to the school. Patterson's commitment to thoroughness as well as her "forceful" and "vivacious" personality helped her establish the school's strong intellectual standards (Terrell 1917).

Patterson also devoted time and money to other Black institutions in Washington, D.C., especially to industrial schools for young Black women, as well as to the Home for Aged and Infirm Colored People. She never married, nor did her two Oberlin-educated sisters (Chanie and Emeline), who later joined her and taught in District schools.

Mary Jane Patterson died in Washington, D.C., September 24, 1894, at the age of fifty-four. Her pioneering educational attainments and her achievements as a leading Black educator influenced generations of Black students.

BIBLIOGRAPHY

Bigglestone, William. *They Stopped in Oberlin: Black Residents and Visitors of the Nineteenth Century* (1981); Oberlin College Archives. Alumni Records. "Mary Jane Patterson" file (1981), and Lawson-Merrill papers, "Mary Jane Patterson" file, and "Patterson Family" file; Perkins, Linda. "Fanny Jackson Coppin and the Institute for Colored Youth," Ph.D. diss. (1978); Terrell, Mary Church. "History of the High School for Negroes in Washington," *Journal of Negro History* (July 1917).

MARLENE DEAHL MERRILL

PAYNE, ETHEL L. (1911-1991)

Known as the "first lady of the Black press," Ethel L. Payne built a reputation as a hard-hitting and insightful reporter for the *Chicago Defender*, covering and participating in the major events of the modern civil rights movement and becoming the first Black woman journalist to specialize in international news.

Ethel Lois Payne was born in Chicago on August 14, 1911. Her father worked as a Pullman porter; her mother taught high school Latin. After briefly attending two colleges and working as a clerk at the Chicago Public Library, Payne, in 1948, became a hostess for an Army Special Services club in Japan.

Payne, who never married, was led into journalism by a diary she kept while in Japan. She showed her diary to a *Chicago Defender* reporter who had traveled to Japan on his way to cover the Korean war. The reporter took the diary back to Chicago, and the *Defender* ran excerpts on its front page. After the editor telephoned Payne and offered her a job, she returned to Chicago and began reporting full time in 1951. After two years in Chicago, Payne became the *Defender*'s one-person bureau in Washington, D.C.

Payne arrived in the nation's capital as the modern civil rights movement was beginning. She doggedly covered legislative and judicial battles on Capitol Hill and then presented the results—or lack of results—in her blunt, straightforward style. By 1954, Payne had established herself as a tough reporter and powerful writer. That same year Black reporters named her their "newsman's newsman," the Washington reporter who best exemplified high journalistic standards.

Payne received national attention in 1954 when, during a White House press conference, she asked President Dwight D. Eisenhower when he planned to ban segregation in interstate travel. Eisenhower barked back that he refused to support any special interest. Front-page stories in the *Washington Post* and *Washington Evening Star* characterized Eisenhower as being "annoyed" by the question and described him as responding in "clipped words." After the incident, Eisenhower refused to recognize Payne during press conferences, but members of the White House press corps said her question helped move civil rights onto the national agenda.

"The first lady of the Black press," Ethel Payne was the Chicago Defender's one-person Washington bureau during the 1950s. During the 1952 Democratic National Convention, she interviewed presidential candidate Adlai E. Stevenson. [Rodger Streitmatter]

Payne never claimed to be an objective reporter. Instead, she called herself an advocacy journalist. During an interview for an oral history project, Payne said:

If you have lived through the black experience in this country, you feel that every day you're assaulted by the system. You are either acquiescent, which I think is wrong, or else you just rebel, and you kick against it. I wanted to constantly, constantly, constantly hammer away, raise the questions that needed to be raised (Currie 1987).

Although Payne was assigned to Washington, she volunteered to traverse the Deep South in order to chronicle the historic events erupting there. In 1956, she reported on the Montgomery bus boycott and desegregation efforts at the University of Ala-

bama. In 1957, she traveled to Arkansas to cover efforts to desegregate Central High School in Little Rock. She carried a sign during the 1963 demonstrations in Birmingham, and when 250,000 activists marched on Washington that same year, Payne was among them. Two years later, she joined 15,000 marchers who walked from Selma to Montgomery to demand voting rights, and when President Lyndon B. Johnson signed the Civil Rights Act of 1964 and the Voting Rights Act of 1965, he asked Payne to join him in the Oval Office for the historic occasions.

Because Payne both reported on and participated in history as it was being made, she suffered much verbal and physical abuse from segregationists. During her oral history interview, Payne recalled the angry mob that faced her in Selma:

You could just feel the hatred. It was just like an enveloping cloak around you. I'll never forget the faces, the contorted faces of housewives, standing out and screaming like they were just lunatics from the asylum: "Nigger! Nigger! Nigger!" (Currie 1987).

In the mid-1960s, Payne shifted her attention to international affairs and reported from thirty countries on six continents. In 1966, Payne traveled to Vietnam to report on Black troops fighting in the war. In 1969, she covered the Nigerian Civil War. A year later, she joined Secretary of State William P. Rogers for a ten-nation tour of Africa and two years after that traveled to Zaire to attend the First Ordinary Congress of the Popular Revolution Movement. Later in the 1970s, Payne visited the People's Republic of China, reported on the International Women's Year Conference in Mexico City, and accompanied Secretary of State Henry Kissinger on a six-nation tour of Africa.

Payne broke new ground for journalists of her race and gender by becoming the first Black female commentator employed by a national broadcast network. Three times a week from 1972 to 1982, Payne shared her views with listeners and viewers of the *Spectrum* public affairs program on CBS, first on radio and later on television.

In 1973, at the same time that she worked part time as a network commentator, she was promoted to associate editor of the *Defender*, in charge of its Chicago news operation. Payne left the *Defender* in 1978 and wrote a syndicated column for Black newspapers from Florida to California. She died in her Washington home on May 28, 1991.

Throughout her forty years of covering the modern civil rights movement and international affairs, Payne was respected as a professional journalist of the highest caliber. Her pithy writing style and fearless reporting combined to raise the standard of Black female journalists. After her death, the *Washington Post* on June 2, 1991, carried a tribute to Payne, stating:

> Her voice was low, but her questions were piercing, and her reports on the world were cherished by millions of readers. The proof of professionalism—fairness, straightforward accounts of all sides and independence of views—were in her writings.

BIBLIOGRAPHY

Currie, Kathleen. Interview with Ethel L. Payne. Women in Journalism Oral History Project of the Washington Press Club Foundation, Oral History Collection, Columbia University, New York, New York (August 25-November 17, 1987); Mitchell, Grayson. "Ethel Payne: First Lady of the Black Press," *Essence* (March 1974); *NBAW*; Payne, Ethel L. "Loneliness in the Capital: The Black National Correspondent." In *Perspectives of the Black Press: 1974*, ed. Henry G. LaBrie III (1974); Streitmatter, Rodger. "No Taste for Fluff: Ethel L. Payne, African-American Journalist," *Journalism Quarterly* (Autumn 1991).

RODGER STREITMATTER

PEAKE, MARY SMITH KELSEY (1823-1862)

Mary Smith Kelsey was born in Norfolk, Virginia, the daughter of a light-skinned free Black woman and a white European, whom Virginia law forbad marriage. She was educated in Alexandria, Virginia, living with an aunt until she returned to Norfolk at the age of sixteen. In 1847, her mother married Thomas Walker, and Mary moved with the couple to Hampton, Virginia, where she worked as a seamstress. She was already deeply committed to Christianity and active in charity, founding an organization called Daughters of Benevolence sometime between 1847 and 1851. She also began illegally teaching both slaves and free Black Americans to read. In 1851, she married Thomas Peake, and the couple were part of Hampton's antebellum Black elite. Her daughter, Daisy, was born about 1856.

At the start of the Civil War, her teaching was given official sanction by Union officers at Fort Monroe, and she became one of the first teachers in the South to be supported by the American Missionary Association. By early 1862, she was teaching over fifty children in her day school as well as twenty adults in the evenings. Deeply religious herself, she taught the Bible and singing, reading, writing, and simple mathematics, and she founded a Sunday school for children. She died of tuberculosis in February 1862.

[*See also* FREEDMEN'S EDUCATION.]

BIBLIOGRAPHY

Engs, Robert Francis. *Freedom's First Generation: Black Hampton, Virginia, 1861-1890* (1979); Hucles, Michael. "The Nineteenth Century." In *"Don't Grieve for Me": The Black Experience in Virginia, 1619-1986*, ed. Philip Morgan (1986); Lebsock, Suzanne. *Virginia Women, 1600-1945: A Share of Honor* (1987).

MARILYN DELL BRADY

PECK, FANNIE B. *see* HOUSEWIVES' LEAGUE OF DETROIT

PERRY, CARRIE SAXON (1931-)

Carrie Saxon Perry went from Hartford's housing projects to its mayor's office. She was born on August 10, 1931, in Hartford, Connecticut, to Mabel Lee Saxon. Reared in the poverty of the Depression, she attended the Hartford public schools and then went on to Howard University in Washington, D.C., encouraged and supported by her mother, grandmother, and aunt. At Howard, she studied political science and spent two years in the School of Law.

Returning to Hartford, Saxon married James Perry, whom she later divorced, and bore a son, James Perry, Jr. She also began a career in social work, quickly becoming administrator for the Community Renewal Team of Greater Hartford and then executive director of Amistad House. Her experiences with Hartford's poor moved her to work for broader solutions by going into politics. Her first bid for the Connecticut State General Assembly, in 1976, was so narrowly defeated that only the absentee ballots turned the trick for her opponent. Her second bid, in 1980, was successful. In neither race had she received an endorsement from any newspaper, fellow politician, or political organization.

In her first year in the state house, Perry was appointed assistant majority leader. She was active on a variety of committees and subcommittees, always fighting for human rights. Before going on to other political arenas, Perry served four terms in the state legislature. She also attended two Democratic national conventions. In 1987, Perry, having established wide visibility and credibility, ran for mayor of Hartford. She won the election, becoming the first Black woman to serve as mayor of a major American city.

BIBLIOGRAPHY
NBAW; *WWBA* (1992).

KATHLEEN THOMPSON

PERRY, FREDERICKA DOUGLASS SPRAGUE *see* SPRAGUE, FREDERICKA DOUGLASS (PERRY) AND ROSABELLE DOUGLASS (JONES)

PERRY, JULIA AMANDA (1924-1979)

A prolific composer and conductor extraordinaire, Julia A. Perry was born in Lexington, Kentucky, on March 25, 1924. She studied composition, conducting, piano, and voice at the Westminster Choir School in New Jersey, earning a Master of Music degree in 1948. Further study was done at Juilliard School of Music in New York City and the Berkshire Music Center in Lenox, Massachusetts.

Perry's studies also took her to the Accademia Chigiana in Siena, Italy, where she studied with Emanuel Balaban, Aleco Galliera (conducting), Nadia Boulanger, Henry Switten, and Luigi Dallapiccola (composition). Her compositions include symphonic works, operas, and chamber music. *The Cask of Amontillado*, an opera, was finished at Columbia University on November 20, 1954.

In 1957, under the auspices of the United States Information Service, Perry conducted a series of European concerts, primarily performing her own works. She once referred to conducting as her "most rewarding performing medium." She also lectured extensively throughout Europe and America.

Perry's honors include two Guggenheim fellowships, an award from the National Institute of Arts and Letters, and a Boulanger Grand Prix. Her neoclassical style featured dissonant harmonies, contrapuntal textures, and intense lyricism. She also used Black folk idioms in her *Soul Symphony*, which she composed in 1972.

Julia Perry died on April 29, 1979, in Akron, Ohio.

[*See also* COMPOSERS.]

BIBLIOGRAPHY
Green, Mildred. *Black Women Composers: A Genesis* (1983); Handy, D. Antoinette. *Black Women in American Bands and Orchestras* (1981); Hitchcock, H. Wiley and Stanley Sadie, eds. *The New Grove Dictionary of American Music* (1986); *NA*; Sadie, Stanley, ed. *The New Grove Dictionary of Music and Musicians* (1980); Slonimsky, Nicolas, ed. *Baker's Biographical Dictionary of Musicians* (1978); Southern, Eileen. *The Music of Black Americans: A History* (1983); Spencer, Jon Michael. *As the Black School Sings* (1987); White, Evelyn Davidson. *Choral Music by Afro-American Composers: A Selected Annotated Bibliography* (1981); Williams, Ora. *American Black Women in the Arts and Social Sciences: A Bibliographic Survey* (1978). Many of Perry's works are in the Raymond I. Johnson Collection, Department of Music, Jackson State University, Jackson, Mississippi.

SANDRA CANNON SCOTT

PETIONI, MURIEL MARJORIE
(1914-)

Soon after Muriel Petioni, M.D., opened her medical practice in Harlem in 1950, she learned the necessity of integrating medical treatment with the social and economic realities that impacted upon her patients. Many could not afford the $2 or $3 she charged for an office visit or house call, and so they sometimes paid her with food. Popular because of her holistic approach to treatment, Dr. Petioni worked as New York City Department of Health School Physician between 1950 and 1980. In her practice at 114 W. 131 Street she pioneered in the successful treatment of drug addiction, for which she was honored by the city of New York in 1983. She remains an activist for health care delivery and is affiliated with many health-related and community institutions.

Petioni has been concerned throughout her career with women's issues and women's advancement in the male-dominated medical profession. In 1974, she started one of the first organizations of Black women doctors, the New York-area Susan Smith McKinney Steward Medical Society, named for the prominent nineteenth-century Brooklyn physician. She continued as its first president until 1984. In 1977, Dr. Petioni organized Black women physicians nationally in Medical Women of the National Medical Association. It was the first female physicians' group admitted officially as a component of the Black National Medical Association formed in 1895.

Muriel Marjorie Petioni was born in Port of Spain, Trinidad, on January 1, 1914, the daughter of Rose Alling, a department store clerk, and Charles Augustin Petioni, a newspaper reporter. The family immigrated to New York City when Muriel was five. Her father became a prominent Harlem physician, activist, and champion of Caribbean independence. She attended public schools 68, 136, and Wadleigh High School. After two years at New York University she entered an accelerated program at Howard University, one of two Black medical schools in Washington, D.C., and graduated with a B.S. in 1934 and an M.D. in 1937.

In 1939, she completed her internship at Harlem Hospital, one of the few hospitals admitting Black interns to its training program, and then did her residency at the Black-operated Homer Phillips Hospital in St. Louis, Missouri. In 1942, she married Mallalieu S. Woolfolk, a lawyer. They have one son, Charles M. Woolfolk, a New York businessman.

Before returning to New York City in 1950, Dr. Petioni practiced as a college physician at several Black institutions. In 1951, after her father's death, she established a family practice in her father's office

A pioneer in the successful treatment of drug addiction, Muriel Petioni started one of the first organizations of Black women doctors, the New York-area Susan Smith McKinney Steward Medical Society, named for the well-known nineteenth-century physician.

in Harlem, where she continued to practice until her retirement in 1990.

In some ways Dr. Petioni's career is characteristic of Black women physicians of her generation, whose approach to medical practice brought them into direct contact with community and family concerns. Typically excluded from surgical specialties, these medical women were the organizers within local and national medical societies and were more often leaders in the larger community than their male colleagues. Dr. Petioni's initiation of formal organization among Black women physicians in the 1970s reflected growing feminist concerns among Black professional women who were encouraged by their expanding numbers and the need to organize the support they could only receive from other women.

BIBLIOGRAPHY

Petioni, Muriel. Interview (November 21, 1991); *WWBA* (1988).

IRMA WATKINS-OWENS

PETRY, ANN LANE (1908-)

If working in the family drugstore had not been, literally, a 365-days-a-year job, Ann Petry once speculated to a class of young pharmacy students, she might have applied for a license from the state of New York rather than seek a job in journalism when she moved there in the late 1930s. Had that happened, the world would have missed an acclaimed novelist. As it is, Ann Petry's writing captures the full scope of her life and heritage, including her brief career in pharmacy.

Ann Lane was born in Old Saybrook, Connecticut, on October 12, 1908. Her father, Peter C. Lane, was one of the first Black pharmacists registered in Connecticut and the only Black pharmacist in the nearly all-white Old Saybrook of the early 1900s. He built a successful practice despite early threats from some members of the community, harassment that extended to young Ann and her sister as well. Her mother, Bertha James Lane, owned several businesses at various times, and two of her aunts received college educations. One of them, Anna L. James, the first Black woman pharmacist in Connecticut, practiced with her brother in the family drugstore. "I don't think it ever occurred to them there were things they could not do because they were women," Petry remembers (Finholm 1986).

It was to her father's drugstore that Ann Lane went upon her graduation from Connecticut College of Pharmacy in 1931. Petry's childhood, drugstore life, and New England life—and their particular tensions for Black professional families—are fictionalized in *Country Place* (1947), "Miss Muriel" (1971), and "The New Mirror" (1965).

Ann Lane married George Petry and moved to New York City. Her early fiction found regular publication in the *Crisis*, a Black journal that particularly nurtured promising writers. Her experiences as a reporter in Harlem taught her stark lessons that have been captured in such works as "Like a Winding Sheet" (1946), "In Darkness and Confusion" (1947), and Petry's first novel, *The Street* (1946), which sold 1.5 million copies and won a Houghton Mifflin Literary Fellowship Award in 1946. Petry also has written historical novels for young readers that reflect her desire to nurture knowledge of and pride in the achievements and humanity of Black women throughout history.

Petry's contribution to literature has been acknowledged by membership in the Authors' Guild and American P.E.N. (Association of Poets, Playwrights, Editors, Essayists, and Novelists), and by honorary doctorates from several colleges and universities. Literary critics have praised her writing for various qualities, some seeing her as a chronicler of New England, referring primarily to *The Narrows* (1953), which tells of a doomed interracial love affair in a closed New England community. Others classify her as the most successful follower of the "Richard Wright school" of urban realism. Still others praise her hard-hitting short stories about the tragedies and ironies of Black life. More recent critics, who look at her work within the tradition of Black women writers, compare her strong urban women characters with Zora Neale Hurston's characterizations of strong rural women.

Ann and George Petry have one child, a daughter, Elizabeth. They live today in Old Saybrook, a short distance from the James Pharmacy, which still bears her aunt's name.

BIBLIOGRAPHY

Bone, Robert A. *The Negro Novel in America* (1965); Christian, Barbara. *Black Feminist Criticism: Perspectives on Black Women Writers* (1985); Davis, Arthur P. *From the*

The Street, *Ann Petry's novel about the Harlem she knew as a newspaper reporter, sold 1.5 million copies in 1946. [Moorland-Spingarn]*

Dark Tower: Afro-American Writers 1900-1960 (1974); Finholm, Valerie. "Women Carve Paths for Others to Follow," *Hartford Courant* (March 2, 1986); Spillers, Hortense. *Conjuring: Black Women, Fiction, and Literary Tradition* (1985); Wade-Gayles, Gloria. *No Crystal Stair: Visions of Race and Sex in Black Women's Fiction* (1984).

SELECTED WORKS BY ANN PETRY

The Street (1946); *Country Place* (1947); *The Drugstore Cat* (1949); *The Narrows* (1953); *Harriet Tubman: Conductor on the Underground Railroad* (1955); *Tituba of Salem Village* (1964); *Legends of the Saints* (1970); *Miss Muriel and Other Stories* (1971).

SUZANNE POIRIER

PETTEY, SARAH E. C. DUDLEY (1869-1906)

Sarah Dudley Pettey originated the Woman's Column in the *Star of Zion*, the weekly newspaper of the African Methodist Episcopal (AME) Zion Church. She began writing the column in 1896, during a period in which she toured the United States, speaking on behalf of woman suffrage and African-American political rights. Pettey championed equal opportunity for women in the AME Zion Church hierarchy, and her husband, Bishop Charles Calvin Pettey, ordained the first woman elder in that denomination in 1897. In her column, Pettey argued for full political participation for Black Americans in the South and for the right of African-American men and women to pursue a classical education and to participate in the industrialization of the New South. Her article "What Role Is the Educated Negro Woman to Play in the Uplifting of Her Race?" appeared in D. W. Culp's *Twentieth-Century Negro Literature* (1902).

Sarah Dudley was born in New Bern, North Carolina, in 1869, the daughter of a state representative. She graduated with honors from Scotia Seminary in Concord, North Carolina, in 1883. After graduation she taught at New Bern's grade school and at the state normal school located there. Six years later she married Charles Calvin Pettey, a North Carolina native who had graduated from Biddle Memorial Institute in Charlotte. In addition to Pettey's two daughters, the couple had five children. Bishop Pettey supported his wife's journalistic career and her suffrage activism. Sarah Dudley Pettey served as a national officer in the AME Zion Woman's Home and Foreign Missionary Society from 1892-1900, during which time she and her husband traveled widely in the United States and Europe. Widowed at the age of

thirty-one, Pettey died in 1906 after a short illness. She was thirty-seven.

BIBLIOGRAPHY

Culp, D. W. "Mrs. Sarah Dudley Pettey." In *Twentieth-Century Negro Literature: or A Cyclopedia of Thought on the Vital Topics Relating to the American Negro*, ed. D. W. Culp (1902); Gilmore, Glenda Elizabeth. "Gender and Jim Crow: Sarah Dudley Pettey's Vision of the New South," *North Carolina Historical Review* (July 1991); Hood, Bishop J. W. "Mrs. Sarah E. C. Dudley Pettey." In *One Hundred Years of the African Methodist Episcopal Zion Church* (1895); Pettey, Sarah E. C. Dudley. "What Role Is the Educated Negro Woman to Play in the Uplifting of Her Race?" In *Twentieth-Century Negro Literature*, ed. D. W. Culp (1902).

GLENDA ELIZABETH GILMORE

PHILADELPHIA FEMALE ANTI-SLAVERY SOCIETY

For thirty-six years, from 1833 until 1870, the members of the Philadelphia Female Anti-Slavery Society labored in the crusade against slavery and discrimination. Besides being champions of Black emancipation, the members of the Society pursued their work as a pioneering interracial group steadfastly dedicated to racial and sexual equality. Black women played significant roles in charting the Society's progressive philosophical agenda over those years.

The Society had a modest beginning, when on December 9, 1833, an interracial group of twenty-one women met at Catherine McDurmot's school room in Philadelphia. The constitution they adopted set forth their firm belief that slavery and prejudice against color were contrary to both the laws of God and the ideals stated in the Declaration of Independence. Opposed to the use of physical force or political affiliations, the Society employed a moral suasion strategy to meet its goals.

Of the forty-two women who became the Society's charter members, nine were Black. Lucretia Mott, Esther Moore, Rebecca Buffum, and other white abolitionists were joined by their Black colleagues, namely Charlotte Forten and her three daughters, Harriet D. Purvis, Sarah Louisa Forten, and Margaretta Forten. Grace Douglass, Mary Woods, Lydia White, Margaret Bowser, and Sarah McCrummel also signed the charter, while Sarah Mapps Douglass, Grace Douglass's daughter, joined the organization shortly thereafter. In subsequent years, other Black women,

918

including Anna Woods, Debrah Coates, Hannah Coates, Amerlia M. Bogle, and Amy Matalida Cassey, became members.

The Black members' activism characterized the organization. The Society's powerful board of managers, which set policy and allocated finances, typically had one or two Black members. During 1836, Sarah Forten and Sarah McCrummel served on the twelve-member board. In 1837, Sarah Forten and Grace Douglass joined their white colleagues, Lucretia Mott and three others, to form a six-member board of managers. Black members helped coordinate the Society's annual fairs to raise funds for the emancipation cause. From 1866 to 1868, Harriet Purvis and her daughter, Hattie Purvis, Jr., worked on the fairs. The Society also actively supported Black education in Philadelphia by visiting schools and distributing books to students. For nine consecutive years, from 1840 to 1849, the Society's education committee, which included several Black members, allocated $120 annually to finance a school taught by Sarah Mapps Douglass. Additional funds were spent in January 1847 to purchase a stove for the school.

Other activities involving the Society's Black members included raising money to build an antislavery hall, distributing antislavery literature and periodicals, and spearheading petition campaigns to abolish slavery in the District of Columbia. In 1857, Sarah Parker Remond, a Black abolitionist from Boston, reported to the Society on her antislavery work in Ohio. Harriet Purvis introduced Remond to the Society. The women also worked with Robert Purvis and other Black Americans of the Philadelphia Vigilant Committee by donating money to clothe, feed, and transport slaves fleeing the South.

Thus, with the close of the Civil War and the ratification of the post-Civil War constitutional amendments, members of the Society determined that their work was finished. Resolutions offered at the final meeting of the Society, on March 21, 1870, celebrated the occasion. "Whereas," began the resolution offered by Margaretta Forten, "the object for which this Association was organized is thus accomplished, therefore resolved, that the Philadelphia Female Anti-Slavery Society, grateful for the part allotted to it in this great work, rejoicing in the victory which has concluded the long conflict between slavery and Freedom in America, does hereby disband." The women of the Society had much to celebrate. As a model of racial equality and cooperative sisterhood for almost four decades, the Society's members could rejoice that their efforts to achieve Black emancipation had been successful.

BIBLIOGRAPHY

"Constitution of the Philadelphia Female Anti-Slavery Society" (December 14, 1833) and "Minutes of the Philadelphia Female Anti-Slavery Society" (1833-70), The Historical Society of Pennsylvania, Philadelphia; Quarles, Benjamin. *Black Abolitionists* (1969); Sumler-Lewis, Janice L. "The Forten-Purvis Women of Philadelphia and the American Anti-Slavery Crusade," *Journal of Negro History* (Winter 1981-82).

JANICE SUMLER-EDMOND

PHILLIPS, ESTHER *see* RHYTHM AND BLUES

PHILLIPS, VELVALEA ROGERS (1924-)

Velvalea Rogers was born in Milwaukee, Wisconsin, on February 18, 1924. She earned her B.S. in 1946 from Howard University and her LL.B. in 1951 from Wisconsin Law School. In 1971, she graduated from the University of Nevada Summer College for Juvenile Court Judges.

Vel Rogers Phillips has been a juvenile court judge; county court judge; Milwaukee Alderman; Wisconsin Secretary of State (1978); Milwaukee children's court judge (1972-74); and a visiting lecturer in the University of Wisconsin Department of African-American Studies. She also has been active in several organizations, including the American Association of University Women, Women's International League for Peace and Freedom, Delta Sigma Theta, the National Association for the Advancement of Colored People (NAACP), and the Day Care and Child Development Council, John F. Kennedy School.

Among her many accomplishments, Phillips was the recipient of the Milwaukee Star Award for Service (1967) and the Woman of the Year Award (1968) of Milwaukee University Chapter of Theta Sigma Phi Sorority. She was the first Black American elected to the Milwaukee Common Council (1956) and the first Black American to serve on the Democratic National Convention Committee on Rules and Order of Business. She served on the committee for six years and in 1960 she cochaired it.

She and her husband, W. Dale Phillips, share a law practice and have two children, Dale and Michael.

BIBLIOGRAPHY

NA; *WWBA* (1992).

JUDY WARWICK

PHINAZEE, ALETHIA ANNETTE LEWIS HOAGE (1920-1983)

A good library, to Alethia Phinazee, is as essential to the nourishment of the mind as food is to the nourishment of the body. Her single-minded dedication to this premise has had a lasting impact on the practice of librarianship in America.

Born on July 25, 1920, in Orangeburg, South Carolina, Alethia received a Bachelor of Arts degree from Fisk University in 1939 and a Bachelor of Library Science degree in 1941 from the University of Illinois. After teaching library science at Caswell County Training School in North Carolina, she returned to the University of Illinois, where she earned a Master's degree in 1948. In 1961, she became the first woman to receive a doctorate in library science from Columbia University.

After she received her doctorate, she taught at the Atlanta University School of Library Science from 1963 to 1969, when she resigned to found the Cooperative College Library Center in Atlanta. She served as director of the center through 1970. She also held various nonteaching posts as librarian at Talladega College, Lincoln University (Missouri), Southern Illinois University, and Atlanta University.

In 1970, she became dean of the School of Library Science at North Carolina Central University. Working tirelessly to win accreditation for the school from the American Library Association (ALA), she eventually succeeded and established the school's program in early childhood librarianship. Having distinguished herself as a national leader in the profession, she distinguished herself in North Carolina when she was elected the first African-American president of the state ALA. In 1978, Governor Jim Hunt granted her the first two four-year terms on the Public Librarian Certification Commission. In the same year, she also served as chair of the Council of Deans and Directors of the Association of American Library Schools.

An ALA activist, she was cochair of an ALA-sponsored Institute on Use of Library of Congress Classification, served four years on the ALA Council, and was first chair of its Standing Committee on Library Education. In 1980, friends and colleagues throughout the country nominated her to run for the presidency of the ALA. She described herself at the time as a "possible-ist" seeking effective ALA continuing-education programs, equitable dues, and shorter conferences.

A prolific author and respected speaker, Phinazee was chair and editor of proceedings for two major library conferences: "Materials by and about American Negroes" in 1965 and "The Georgia Child's Access to Materials Pertaining to Negro Americans" in 1967.

She died on September 17, 1983.

BIBLIOGRAPHY

Phinazee, Alethia Annette Lewis Hoage. Manuscript Collection, Clark Atlanta University, Atlanta, Georgia; and Manuscript Collection, Shepherd Library, North Carolina Central University, Durham, North Carolina.

ARTHUR C. GUNN

PHYLLIS (PHILLIS) WHEATLEY CLUBS AND HOMES

Throughout their history, Black American women have always celebrated the accomplishments of "one of their own," especially the "firsts" of their race and sex. Each accomplishment served to validate the worth of all Black women. Therefore it is no surprise that during the latter part of the nineteenth century and early in the twentieth century, when Black women organized in large and small communities, the name most frequently given to their clubs and institutions was that of the slave poet, Phillis Wheatley. The story of Wheatley's rise from illiteracy and slavery to become the first published Black woman in America served as inspiration to all, especially women who were suffering the trauma of separation from family and familiar surroundings. Thus her name (originally spelled *Phillis*, but most often updated to *Phyllis*) became almost synonymous with residences for Black women, young and old.

Although there is no record to establish the earliest Phillis Wheatley Club, it appears as a popular nomenclature at the organization of the national Black women's club movement. At the first meeting of the newly formed National Association of Colored Women (NACW) in 1896, Phyllis Wheatley clubs from New Orleans, Chicago, and Jacksonville, Florida, were represented. Also, delegates from the Phyllis Wheatley Club of Nashville, Tennessee, were noted in attendance at the 1895 Atlanta Congress of Colored Women. In later years, Phyllis Wheatley Club affiliates of the NACW were commonplace.

The first known Phyllis Wheatley Home was established in 1897 by Black clubwomen as a home for aged women in Detroit. Originally, a small group of women pooled their own funds to rent a small building to house seven "inmates." By 1901, the group, which had expanded to twenty-four members, purchased a property that could accommodate twelve persons. A similar project of the Nashville Phyllis Wheatley Club evolved when, after years of charitable work with the needy, the group established a Phyllis Wheatley Room at Mercy Hospital and finally purchased a home for aged women in 1925.

More popularly, use of the name Phyllis Wheatley was associated with homes for young women. Of these, the first was a home in Chicago sponsored by the Chicago Phyllis Wheatley Club. The home was the third project of the group and seems to have evolved in tandem with the needs of Black women in the city. During their first five years, for example, the group operated a sewing school for children of all nationalities. The school closed when the women shifted their focus to the needs of working women and opened a day nursery in a much-congested dis-

trict. Finally, in 1906, the club purchased a home for Black women migrants, which provided living accommodations, social facilities, and an employment bureau for single Black women. It also offered classes and club activities for nonresident girls.

Exclusion of Black women from all-white Young Women's Christian Association (YWCA) facilities prompted the establishment of Phillis Wheatley Homes in cities across the country. Most were created out of concern for the moral and social well being of young Black women during the period of the Great Migration. Typical of the young women's residences was the Phyllis Wheatley YWCA in Washington, D.C., which was organized as the Colored Women's Christian Association (CWCA) in 1905. The group struggled for years as a charitable organization that tried to minister to needy men and women while also trying to negotiate to affiliate with the national board of the YWCA. Finally, during World War I, through the YWCA War Work Council, the CWCA became the Phyllis Wheatley Branch of the YWCA. This pattern was repeated in at least thirty-three communities.

Through its "Colored Work" department, the YWCA's national board provided the best-known

Jane Edna Hunter was head of the Phillis Wheatley Home Department of the NACW. She was the founder of the independent Phillis Wheatley Home in Cleveland, Ohio, and firmly believed in educating women for domestic work. This is a cooking class at her Sarah T. Hills Training School in Cleveland in 1937. [Phillis Wheatley Association, Cleveland, Ohio]

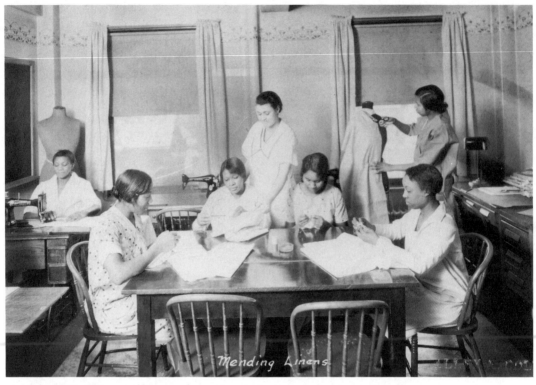

The Cleveland Phillis Wheatley Home was the largest independent facility in the country, with an eleven-story building and several satellite centers. This is a sewing class in the 1930s. [Phillis Wheatley Association, Cleveland, Ohio]

organizational model for Phillis Wheatley residences for single women. These "colored branches" offered skills training, club activities, employment services, and industrial girls' organizations that mostly duplicated selected services of white associations on a smaller scale. In all cases, Black members of a committee of management made decisions related to programs, classes, and activities, while fiscal and personnel decisions were subject to the authority of white boards of directors of the central association. Altogether, at least seventeen segregated branches of the YWCA were named after Phillis Wheatley, including those in Indianapolis, Louisville, Little Rock, St. Louis, Charlotte, Harrisburg, Richmond, Chattanooga, and Atlanta.

Phyllis Wheatley branches of the YWCA were the best-known residences for young Black women, but the YWCA did not have facilities in all of the cities where there was a need. Moreover, the paternalistic governance structure of the YWCA was

considered by some as an inappropriate model for Black self-determination. In response to these and other concerns, the NACW formed the Phillis Wheatley Home Department in 1931 to coordinate and promote work among young women in cities where the YWCA did not have branches.

The head of the department for the NACW was Jane Edna Hunter, founder of the independent Phillis Wheatley Home in Cleveland, Ohio. The Cleveland home was the largest independent facility for Black women in the country, with an eleven-story building and several satellite centers. Hunter consistently resisted efforts to have her institution become affiliated with the YWCA and instead established the Phillis Wheatley Department of the NACW. In her 1940 autobiography, *A Nickel and a Prayer*, she boasted that since the Cleveland association was founded, "the National Association of Colored Women has established like-named institutions in nine cities of the United States." In this model, Hunter provided materials with suggestions for programs and services. However, each of these homes was locally funded, and governance was left to independent boards of directors.

There were also Phillis Wheatley clubs and club houses affiliated with the NACW. For example, the Phyllis Wheatley House in Oberlin, Ohio, sponsored by the local Women's Progressive Club, served as a meeting center for Black youth in the city. Phyllis Wheatley clubs in cities such as Billings, Montana; Jackson, Mississippi; Middlesboro, Kentucky; and New Orleans carried out a variety of activities including temperance and suffrage work.

BIBLIOGRAPHY

Davis, Elizabeth Lindsay. *Lifting as They Climb* (1933); Jones, Adrienne Lash. *Jane Edna Hunter: A Case Study of Black Leadership, 1905-1950* (1990); Lerner, Gerda, ed. *Black Women in White America* (1972); Neverdon-Morton, Cynthia. *Afro-American Women of the South and the Advancement of the Race, 1895-1925* (1989); Salem, Dorothy. *To Better Our World: Black Women in Organized Reform, 1890-1920* (1990); Spear, Alan H. *Black Chicago: The Making of a Negro Ghetto, 1890-1920* (1967); Terborg-Penn, Rosalyn and Sharon Harley. *The Afro-American Woman: Struggles and Images* (1978); YWCA National Board. "Branches Organized before 1950," typescript (1971).

ADRIENNE LASH JONES

PHYSICIANS, NINETEENTH CENTURY

The African-American woman physician of the late nineteenth century remains an enigma due to the scarcity of records on the subject. We do know that in the quarter century after the demise of slavery and during the height of racial segregation and discrimination, there were 115 Black women physicians in the United States. These women's personal and professional lives were quite different from those of other physicians—men or white women—in several ways. Most obviously, Black women physicians were an integral part of the communities in which they practiced, working at Black colleges, in community clinics and hospitals, and as clubwomen and successfully combining their careers with their roles as wives and mothers. Moreover, they also established hospitals and clinics, trained nurses, taught basic health guidelines, and founded homes and service agencies for poor women and unwed pregnant women of both races.

In 1864, fifteen years after Elizabeth Blackwell became the first American woman medical graduate, the first Black woman graduate, Rebecca Lee, received a doctor of medicine degree from the New England Female Medical College in Boston. Three years later, the second Black American woman physician, Rebecca J. Cole, graduated from the Woman's Medical College of Pennsylvania. In 1870, Susan Smith McKinney Steward completed her studies at New York Medical College for Women. Lee, Cole, and Steward signaled the emergence of Black women in the medical profession.

Black women physicians such as Rebecca J. Cole skillfully combined private medical practice with community service among white and Black women. Cole worked for a time with Elizabeth and Emily Blackwell at the New York Infirmary for Women and Children as a "sanitary visitor." The infirmary's Tenement House Service, begun in 1866, was the earliest practical program of medical social service in the country. As a sanitary visitor or tenement physician, Cole made house calls in slum neighborhoods, teaching indigent mothers the basics of hygiene and "the preservation of health of their families." Elizabeth Blackwell described Cole as "an intelligent young coloured physician" who conducted her work "with tact and care" and thus demonstrated that the establishment of a social service department "would be a valuable addition to every hospital."

The late nineteenth century witnessed a dramatic increase of women doctors in America. Their numbers rose from nearly 200 in 1860 to 2,423 in 1880 and to more than 7,000 by 1900. During this period nineteen medical schools for women were founded, although by 1895 eleven had disbanded. By the 1920s, the U.S. Census listed only sixty-five Black women as practicing physicians. Not surprisingly, Black male physicians far outnumbered their female counterparts. In 1890, there were 909 Black male physicians, and by 1920 the number had jumped to 3,885. The increase was due largely to the existence of several medical schools founded for African-Americans in the post-Reconstruction South. According to one contemporary Black male physician, M. Vandehurst Lynk, Howard University School of Medicine in Washington, D.C., Meharry Medical College in Nashville, Leonard Medical School of Shaw University in Raleigh, North Carolina, and Flint Medical College (originally the Department of Medicine of New Orleans University) in New Orleans labored to keep up with quickly evolving medical standards. By 1914, however, of the approved Black medical schools, only Howard and Meharry remained open. These two institutions played the most significant role in the education of Black women physicians during that period.

The Howard University Medical School was chartered in 1868 and was supported by the U.S. government as an institution to train African-Americans. By 1900, it had graduated 552 physicians, 25 of whom were Black women.

Meharry Medical College graduated the largest number of Black women physicians (thirty-nine by 1920). Originally the Department of Medicine at Central Tennessee College in 1876, Meharry was the first medical school in the South to provide for the education of Black physicians. Meharry's location in the South made it the logical place for the majority of Black women to pursue a medical education. In 1893, seventeen years after its opening, Meharry graduated its first Black women physicians, Annie D. Gregg and Georgiana Esther Lee Patton. The first woman to teach at Meharry and attain a position of leadership as superintendent of Hubbard Hospital was Josie E. Wells, a member of the class of 1904.

By the turn of the century, the Woman's Medical College of Pennsylvania, established in 1850 as the first regular medical school for women, had graduated approximately a dozen Black women physicians. This institution blazed a new trail by providing medical training to women of every race, creed, and national origin. Indeed, all of the women's medical colleges, which in most instances were founded as temporary expediencies, enabled women to escape social ostracism, subtle discrimination, and overt hostility throughout their training in a male-dominated profession. However, the trend toward coeducation in the 1870s did not result in an increase in the percentage of Black women physicians. Only one or two Black women attended the integrated coeducational institutions.

Among the early Black women graduates of the Woman's Medical College were Rebecca J. Cole (1867), Caroline Still Wiley Anderson (1878), Verina Morton Jones (1888), Halle Tanner Dillon Johnson (1891), Lucy Hughes Brown (1894), Alice Woodby McKane (1894), Matilda Arabella Evans (1897), and Eliza Anna Grier (1897). Three of these graduates—Johnson, Jones, and Brown—became the first Black women to practice medicine in Alabama, Mississippi, and South Carolina, respectively. The successes achieved by the Woman's Medical College's Black graduates possibly attest to a high quality of education and underscore the advantage of a more nurturing and supportive sex-segregated environment in which students learned from female faculty role models. Other factors, including family background,

prior education, and social status, may also have influenced their securing a medical education in the first place and subsequently their success.

The majority of early Black women physicians were the daughters of socially privileged Black families or others who, perhaps to protect them from menial labor or domestic servitude, encouraged their daughters to educate themselves. That family background and prior education were important determinants of success in acquiring a medical education is reflected in the lives of a few of the early Black women physicians. Caroline Anderson was the daughter of William Still, a founder of the Underground Railroad, chairman of the General Vigilance Committee in antebellum Philadelphia, and author of *The Underground Railroad* (1872), which chronicled the escape of runaway slaves. Halle Johnson was the daughter of Bishop B. T. Tanner of the African Methodist Episcopal Church in Philadelphia. Susan Steward was the daughter of a prosperous Brooklyn, New York, merchant. Sarah Logan Fraser's father was Bishop Logan of the Zion Methodist Episcopal Church in Syracuse, New York. Like William Still, Bishop Logan had aided and harbored escaping slaves in his home. Unlike Anderson, Johnson, and Steward, Fraser received her medical degree from the Medical School of Syracuse University. Sarah G. Boyd Jones's father, George W. Boyd, was reputed to be the wealthiest Black man in Richmond. Sarah Jones attended the Richmond Normal School before completing medical training in 1893 at Howard University Medical School. After graduation she returned to Richmond, where she became the first woman to pass the Virginia medical board examinations. She later founded the Richmond Hospital and Training School of Nurses, which in 1902 was renamed the Sarah G. Jones Memorial Hospital.

To be sure, not all of the first generation of Black women physicians belonged to illustrious families. Some, such as Eliza Grier, were former slaves who worked their way through college and medical school, occasionally receiving limited financial assistance from parents or siblings. In 1890, Grier wrote to the Woman's Medical College concerning her financial straits, "I have not money and no source from which to get it only as I work for every dollar. . . . What I want to know from you is this. How much does it take to put one through a year in your school? Is there any possible chance to do any work that would not interfere with one's studies?" Grier apparently completed the medical program by working every other year, since she graduated seven years later, in 1897.

Black women who were fortunate enough to receive medical education encountered additional obstacles after graduation. Racial customs and negative attitudes toward women dictated that Black women physicians practice almost exclusively among African-Americans, and primarily among Black women, many of whom avoided treatment since the payment of medical fees was a great hardship. Poverty was often accompanied by superstition and fear. Consequently, new Black women doctors frequently had to expend considerable effort persuading, cajoling, and winning confidence before being allowed to treat physical illness.

It is significant that many Black women who were able to establish private practices also founded hospitals, nurse training schools, and social service agencies. Since Black professionals and patients were prohibited from or segregated within local health care facilities, these Black institutions became adjuncts to their medical practices and simultaneously addressed the needs of the Black community.

Several Black graduates of the Woman's Medical College, most notably Lucy Brown and Matilda Evans, established such institutions. After her 1894 graduation, Brown took up practice in Charleston, South Carolina. In 1896, she joined a small group of eight Black male physicians led by Alonzo C. McClellan and established the Hospital and Nursing Training School in Charleston. Evans moved to Columbia, South Carolina, in 1897, where she practiced medicine for twenty years. Since there were no hospital facilities open to African-Americans in the city, Evans initially cared for patients in her own home. Eventually, as her number of clients grew, she was able to rent a separate building with facilities for thirty patients, and she established a full-scale hospital and nurse training school. She also founded the Negro Health Association of South Carolina.

Other Black women physicians accepted appointments as resident physicians in segregated Black colleges and universities established in the South during Reconstruction. Such appointments provided small but steady stipends and much-needed experience at working in an institutional setting. Moreover, they assured a degree of professional autonomy, status, and visibility and enabled the development of greater self-confidence.

During the 1890s and early 1900s, Halle Johnson, Ionia R. Whipper, Verina Jones, and Susan Steward became resident physicians at Black colleges. Not only did they minister to the health care needs of the college students and faculty, but they often taught courses and lectured on health subjects. Johnson served

as the first Black woman resident physician at Tuskegee Institute from 1891 to 1894. She was responsible for the medical care of 450 students as well as for 30 officers and teachers and their families, she was expected to make her own medicines, and she taught one or two classes each term. For her efforts she was paid $600 per year plus room and board and was allowed one month of vacation.

In 1903, Ionia R. Whipper, a member of the 1903 graduating class of Howard Medical School, succeeded Johnson as resident physician at Tuskegee Institute. Reflecting social change, however, Whipper was restricted to the care of female students at the institute. After leaving Tuskegee, Whipper returned to Washington, D.C., where she and a group of seven friends established a home for unwed, pregnant, school-age Black girls, initially in her own home. In 1931, she purchased property and opened the Ionia R. Whipper Home for Unwed Mothers, which had a policy of nondiscrimination as to race, religion, or residence.

After completing her education at the Woman's Medical College, Verina Jones accepted an appointment as resident physician of Rust College in Holly Springs, Mississippi. Like Johnson and Whipper, she doubled as a teacher, conducting classes at the industrial school connected with the university.

Later generations of Black women physicians were further encumbered in their pursuit of medical careers as the requirements for certification were raised. Medical graduates increasingly were expected to secure internships and residencies for specialization and to pass state medical board examinations for certification. Only a small number of the highly rated hospitals in the country accepted African-Americans or women for internships and residencies. Consequently, Black women faced fierce competition for available slots. Most of the all-Black hospitals preferred to grant internships and residencies to men, while the few women's hospitals usually selected white women. The confluence of sexual and racial segregation strengthened the barriers blocking the aspirations and careers of Black women physicians.

Like their white women counterparts, Black women physicians remained sensitive to the prevailing social attitude that higher education and professional training threatened a woman's femininity. However, since economic necessity and racism so circumscribed the opportunities of Black men that Black women, regardless of marital status, had to contribute to the well-being of the family, Black Americans were more tolerant of women working outside the home. Indeed, the Black woman physician was frequently a much sought-after marriage partner. Many Black women physicians married Black ministers, physicians, or educators. Susan Steward, commenting on the marriageability of Black women physicians, observed, "Fortunate are the men who marry these women from an economic standpoint at least. They are blessed in a three-fold measure, in that they take unto themselves a wife, a trained nurse, and a doctor." Furthermore, since nineteenth-century medical practices were frequently located in the home, marriage and career could be conducted in the same place.

Self-reliant, committed, and talented, these women successfully combined a multiplicity of roles as physicians, wives, mothers, daughters, and community leaders. The convergence of racism, sexism, and professionalization undoubtedly contributed to the significant reduction in the number of Black women physicians in the 1920s. For the contributions, sacrifices, and services of those women who did persevere, all Black Americans owe a great debt of gratitude, one that is only beginning to be acknowledged.

BIBLIOGRAPHY

Aptheker, Bettina. "Quest for Dignity: Black Women in the Professions, 1885-1900." In her *Woman's Legacy: Essays on Race, Sex, and Class in American History* (1982); Brown, Sara W. "Colored Women Physicians," *Southern Workman* (1923); Hine, Darlene Clark. "Co-Laborers in the Work of the Lord: Nineteenth Century Black Women Physicians." In *Send Us a Lady Physician: Women Doctors in America, 1835-1920*, ed. Ruth J. Abram (1985).

DARLENE CLARK HINE

PHYSICIANS, TWENTIETH CENTURY

During the twentieth century, medicine assumed a position as one of the most prestigious professions in the United States. In order to succeed in it, Black women have had to overcome obstacles based on both their race and gender. They have had to battle not only sexism, including that of Black men, but also racism, including that of white women. Dr. Dorothy Ferebee, a 1924 honors graduate of Tufts University Medical School, accurately described the challenges faced by twentieth-century Black women physicians when, discussing her years at Tufts, she noted: "It was not easy. The medical school had five women out of 137 students. We women were always the last to get assignments in amphitheaters and clinics. And I? I was the last of the last because not only was I a woman, but a Negro, too" (Smith 1991). Yet, the history of these women also reveals that despite these barriers, they have advanced in and made important contributions to their profession.

Only a small number of Black women have become physicians. In 1920, sixty-five Black women practiced medicine. Fifty years later, the number had increased to 1,051. By 1989, the number had grown to 3,250, but this represented less than 1 percent of the practicing physicians in the United States. Until the advent of affirmative action programs in the 1970s, most Black women graduated from the two predominantly Black medical schools, Howard University and Meharry Medical College.

After 1920, hospitals became increasingly important to physicians' careers. In contrast to their nineteenth-century counterparts, twentieth-century Black women physicians had to secure access to hospitals. Hospitals had become essential for medical education, medical practice, and medical specialization. Several states had even passed laws requiring the completion of an internship as a prerequisite for medical licensure.

These changes in medical practice threatened the future of Black physicians and placed an additional burden on Black women's advancement in the profession. African-American physicians seeking internships and residencies were expected to pursue them at Black hospitals, which usually had inferior programs. Moreover, Black hospitals preferred to admit Black men, and the few women's hospitals did not always welcome Black women.

The opportunities, therefore, for Black women to obtain hospital appointments and specialty training were severely limited. Isabella Vandervall, a 1915 graduate of the New York Medical College for Women, was rejected for an internship by four hospitals, including the one affiliated with her medical school, not because she was unqualified—she had graduated first in her class—but because of her race. Fortunately, she was able to practice, having obtained licenses in New York and New Jersey before the laws on compulsory internship had gone into effect. In 1923, Lillian Atkins Moore, a senior medical student at Woman's Medical College of Pennsylvania, applied for an internship at the college's hospital. She too was rejected because she was Black. The hospital's medical director admitted that race had been the deciding factor in the hospital's action and offered to get her an appointment—at one of the "colored" hospitals. Moore finally secured a position at Douglass Hospital, a Black hospital in Philadelphia.

A few Black women were able to gain admission to programs at government hospitals. Dorothy Ferebee, after several rejections from white hospitals, secured an internship at Freedmen's Hospital in Washington, D.C. In 1926, May Chinn became the first Black woman intern at Harlem Hospital. This was not the first time that Chinn had been a pioneer. She was also the first Black woman to graduate from Bellevue Hospital Medical College. Chinn also found that racial discrimination prohibited Black physicians from appointments to private hospitals. Therefore Chinn was forced during the 1930s to perform major surgery in patients' homes. Margaret Lawrence also completed her internship at Harlem Hospital. She had not been allowed to work at New York's Babies' Hospital, ostensibly because housing could not be provided for a Black woman in the nurses' dormitory, where female interns were housed. This was not the first time that Lawrence encountered racial barriers. When she arrived at Cornell University in 1932 she was the only Black undergraduate on campus and was not allowed to live in the dorms. She supported herself by working as a domestic for white families. Nonetheless, she did well academically and expected to be admitted to Cornell Medical School. She was not admitted, however, and was told that it was because a Black man who had been admitted twenty-five years earlier had contracted tuberculosis. Lawrence eventually gained admission to Columbia Medical School and, once again, was the only Black student. In 1946, she became the first Black trainee at the Columbia Psychoanalytic Clinic.

Racism was not the only obstacle in the professional paths of twentieth-century Black women physicians. When Chinn first went into practice in Harlem, she encountered resistance from her Black male colleagues. She later noted that they appeared to be divided into three distinct groups. "The first group," she stated, "didn't believe that a woman should be a doctor, so they pretended that I didn't exist. The second group actively discouraged patients from coming to me: 'What can she do for you that a man cannot do better?' The third group said they were helping me by sending me on their night calls after midnight" (Davis 1979). Margaret Lawrence also had to battle sexism. At Meharry Medical College she was the only woman on the faculty during the early 1940s and encountered blatant sexism. She was excluded from intellectual camaraderie, overburdened with responsibilities, and poorly paid in comparison with her male colleagues.

An examination of the work of twentieth-century Black women physicians demonstrates the significant contributions that they have made to medicine and their communities. These women founded hospitals, established civic organizations, practiced medicine among the underserved, and challenged barriers in a profession that has been and continues to be white and male dominated. Matilda Evans, the first Black woman to practice in South Carolina, established three hospitals between 1898 and 1916. In 1930, she established a free-of-charge child and maternal clinic in the basement of a Black church. Virginia Alexander, a 1925 graduate of Woman's Medical College of Pennsylvania, established the Aspiranto Health Home in 1931 to provide health care for poor women and children in North Philadelphia. She also worked as a civil rights activist. Dorothy Ferebee directed the Alpha Kappa Alpha Mississippi Health Project, which had been designed by the sorority to bring much-needed health care to the poor of the Mississippi Delta every summer from 1935 to 1942.

Throughout most of the twentieth century, most Black women physicians had general practices because of their limited opportunities to obtain specialty training. Since World War II, more have entered the more prestigious and financially rewarding medical specialties. In 1946, Helen O. Dickens, the daughter of a former slave, received her certification from the American Board of Obstetrics and Gynecology. Four years later, she became the first Black woman admitted to the American College of Surgeons. The American Board of Surgery certified its first Black woman, Hughenna L. Gauntlett, in 1968, and the American Board of Neurological Surgery certified its first, Alexa Canady, in 1984.

Black women have also begun to assume leadership roles within the profession. In 1958, Edith Irby Jones broke the racial barriers of southern medical schools when she became the first Black person, male or female, admitted to the University of Arkansas School of Medicine. In 1985, Jones became the first woman president of the National Medical Association, a predominantly Black medical society. By 1991, two other Black women, Vivian Pinn-Wiggins and Alma R. George, had headed the organization. In 1991, Pinn-Wiggins was appointed the first permanent director of the National Institutes of Health Office of Women's Health Research. Roselyn Payne Epps, in 1990, became the first Black physician to be president of the American Medical Women's Association. Despite these achievements, only a few Black women have assumed prominent roles in the medical

927

hierarchy. Few have been named department chairs and none has been named a medical school dean.

In their pursuit of medical careers, twentieth-century Black women physicians have had to challenge stereotypical notions about Black women and their work. Chinn once recalled that a Black woman patient wept when she approached because "she felt she had been denied the privilege of having a white doctor wait on her." While Margaret Lawrence was in medical school, white women often stopped her on the street to offer her daywork as a maid. The tenacity of these stereotypes about Black women and their work continues. Even in the late twentieth century, Black women medical students are at times assumed to be members of the cleaning staff. These examples illustrate that there is a dissonance between these women's ambitions to succeed in a socially prestigious and scientifically rigorous profession and their presumed place in society.

BIBLIOGRAPHY

Blount, Melissa. "Surpassing Obstacles: Black Women in Medicine," *Journal of the American Medical Women's Association* (1984); Brown, Sara W. "Colored Women Physicians," *Southern Workman* (1923); Davis, George. "A Healing Hand in Harlem," *New York Times Magazine* (April 22, 1979); Du Bois, W.E.B. "The Woman's Medical College," *Crisis* (1923); Epps, Roselyn Payne. "The Black Woman Physician—Perspectives and Priorities," *Journal of the National Medical Association* (1986); Gamble, Vanessa Northington. "On Becoming a Physician: A Dream Not Deferred." In *The Black Women's Health Book: Speaking for Ourselves*, ed. Evelyn C. White (1990); Hunter-Gault, Charlayne. "Black Women M.D.s: Spirit and Endurance," *New York Times* (November 16, 1977); Lightfoot, Sara Lawrence. *Balm in Gilead: Journey of a Healer* (1988); Smith, Susan Lynn. " 'Sick and Tired of Being Sick and Tired': Black Women and the National Negro Health Movement, 1915-1950," Ph.D. diss. (1991); Vandervall, Isabella. "Some Problems of the Colored Woman Physician," *Women's Medical Journal* (July 1917).

VANNESSA GAMBLE

PIERCE, BILLIE GOODSON (1907-1974)

Billie Goodson Pierce (a.k.a. Willie Madison Goodson) was born in Marianna, Florida, in 1907 and raised in Pensacola. She came from a musical family; her six sisters were all pianists. At ten, Billie temporarily worked as Bessie Smith's accompanist. Later in her career, she also accompanied blues great Ida Cox.

Drawn to the music of bands that traveled in and around the South, Billie decided to leave home at fifteen to play blues and ragtime jazz. For nearly ten years, she worked throughout the South in various bands. She started with the Mighty Wiggle Carnival Show, with her sister Edna, as a pianist. She also played with Mack's Merrymakers, the Nighthawks Orchestra, the Joe Jesse Orchestra, the Douglas Orchestra, and Slim Hunter's Orchestra.

Her first job in New Orleans was as a substitute for her sister Sadie Goodson with Buddy Petit's Band on a steamliner—*The Madison*. She worked with Alphonse Picou in 1930 and then performed with Punch Miller and Billy, and Mary Mack's Merry Makers.

She had her own band in the mid-1930s with George Lewis (clarinet) and De De Pierce (trumpet). She married Pierce in 1935, and they gained international recognition, and as the result of several recordings and tours, they became established successes in New Orleans and enjoyed fame throughout the 1960s.

Billie Pierce died on September 29, 1974, in New Orleans, shortly after her husband's death.

BIBLIOGRAPHY

Carr, I., D. Fairweather and B. Priestley. *Jazz: The Essential Companion* (1988); Dahl, Linda. *Stormy Weather: The Music and Lives of a Century of Jazzwomen* (1984); Handy, D. Antoinette. *Black Women in American Bands and Orchestras* (1981); Placksin, Sally. *American Women in Jazz, 1900 to the Present: Their Words, Lives, and Music* (1982); Sampson, Henry T. *Blacks in Blackface: A Source Book on Early Black Musical Shows* (1980).

SELECTED RECORDINGS

Billie and De De Pierce: New Orleans Music, Arhoolie-2016 (1959); *Billie and De De Pierce: Vocal Blues and Cornet in the Classic Tradition*, Riverside RLP-370 (1961); *Jazz at Preservation Hall*, Atlanta ATC-1409 (1962).

PAULETTE WALKER

PINDELL, HOWARDENA (1943-)

Howardena Pindell has made significant contributions to the visual arts as well as to scholarship on racism in the art world. She was born on April 14, 1943, in Philadelphia. Her art training began at eight years old when she was enrolled in free Saturday morning classes at the Fleischer School. In 1965 she received a B.F.A. from Boston University's School of Fine and Applied Arts and in 1967 an M.F.A. from Yale University's School of Art and Architecture.

After graduating from Yale she moved to New York City where she began working at the Museum of Modern Art as an exhibition assistant. She held three other curatorial titles there before leaving the museum in 1979 to teach at the State University of New York at Stony Brook.

Pindell was trained as a figurative painter at Yale, where she produced urban landscapes and studied skeletal forms. While she was in New York City, the necessity of maintaining full-time employment impeded her art-making because she could not devote as much time to it. By the time she finished work in the evenings there was very little natural light, so she would experiment with color, light, and texture using dots and grids, and because of space constraints her work remained small and abstract.

Pindell's distinctive abstract style was inspired by many sources throughout the 1970s. She initiated this style by making stencils or templates of punched-out holes and then spraying paint through them. The product of so many hole punches was bags and bags of tiny dots, which she began to add to the surfaces of her works. In addition, she numbered many of these dots and then arranged them randomly over an underlying grid of graph paper. In these numbered works she was toying with notions of distance, size, mass, quantity, and identification. The use of numbers was partly influenced by her father's odometer books in which he would keep track of mileage on family road trips, and by Pindell's experiments in surface light and shadow, randomness, and interpretation. She chose numbers for their visual quality instead of their associative value.

The unnumbered dot works became studies in accumulation of color, space, and surface texture, tension, and contrast. The effects were three-dimensional and sculptural. The surfaces were built upon a regimented grid which accentuated the juxtaposition of the random and the rigid. Pindell used the grid as a metaphor for technological society with its square computers, televisions, and vertical and horizontal format. Her abstract works of the 1970s can be categorized as having a very tactile quality, and clearly deal with issues of confinement, control, order, and the elusive quality of boundaries. As Pindell began to move away from the strict confines of the stretched canvas, and still utilizing the basic structure of the grid, she began to experiment with sewing her canvases. The sewing added an internal geometry and tension as well as a physical quality.

Pindell's abstract works of the 1970s were indicative of many of her personal struggles during this time. They were reflective of issues that affected her experience as a Black woman artist. The racism, sexism, discrimination, exclusion, isolation, and rejection that she experienced in her life translated into an obsessive quality in her works that was her means of escape and avoidance. The tedious process of her work was meditative and the aesthetic quality of her product was a means to deal with her anger by making everything beautiful.

Ironically, this abstraction in itself created problems for her because it placed her work in a limited category. Since she was not using explicit political imagery in these works, they were considered by Black art institutions to be invalid. She found temporary acceptance in the women's movement and helped to found a collective alternative exhibition space for women artists called Artists-in-Residence Gallery. Still, she was frustrated with a primarily white women's movement that did not address issues relevant to her situation as a Black woman.

These factors, along with her feelings of powerlessness to help other Black artists and women artists despite her position at the museum, led to disillusionment and to the realization that her work was masking her pain and anger. Almost simultaneous to these recognitions, her move toward open political activism was reinforced by a Black art community protest of a show at Artists Space in New York City in 1979 entitled "Nigger Drawings." Pindell was active in this protest and her own outrage led to a decisive change in her visual imagery. Her video work *Free, White and 21* (1980) seems to mark this change and the beginning of more explicitly political content in many of her works. In this important twelve minute work, Pindell focuses on the image of herself as she recounts experiences in her life that clearly demonstrate racial prejudice and reactions to skin color.

Along with the changes that took place in 1979, Pindell was also in a serious car accident from which she experienced memory loss. This experience led her to use artistic production as an exercise in memory. She began to use the postcards and photographs she had collected in her extensive travels to recreate her impressions of places she had visited. From this point in time, memory and personal experience became integral parts of her artistic vision.

In 1982, Pindell traveled to Japan on a United States-Japan Friendship Commission Creative Artist grant for about eight months. The works inspired by her experience in Japan are more circular and organic in shape than her earlier works and they tend to focus on nature and landscape while reflecting the rigidity she found in that culture. The work *Hiroshima Disguised: Japan* (1982) is asymmetrical, oddly shaped, and maze-like. The surface is built up so that its texture resembles a Japanese ornamental dry garden and is reminiscent of her dot works. It consists of ten separate canvases arrayed like the islands and its pale lavender tone resembles ash. The surface is embedded with shattered metal and cut glass and contains small photographic images that make reference to the devastating effects of nuclear war. This work is characteristic of her near-far style which, when viewed from afar, gives the impression of abstraction while upon close scrutiny revealing its political content.

Pindell traveled to India in 1984 on a National Endowment for the Arts painting fellowship. Her works from this period became more sinuous and S-shaped, like coiled snakes or flowing rivers. They have a meditative quality and reflect a spirituality with an undercurrent of poverty and suffering. The works from India and Japan resemble travelogues of her personal physical and emotional journeys.

Pindell's Autobiography series is her most recent body of work and presents a coming together of her past focuses and a distinct emphasis on personal identity and self-definition. This series focuses on key issues, such as notions of self, racial heritage, women of color, hierarchical imagery, omission, appropriation, and stereotyping. These works utilize near-far contrast in both canvas and photographic mediums. They deal with public as well as private spheres and both comment and reflect upon issues of history, culture, politics, personal experience, and identity.

The Autobiography series, for which she received a College Art Association award in 1990, and her extensive published research on art world racism attest to her prominence as a key Black woman artist. Her work addresses multifaceted aspects of her experience and her multiple consciousness as a Black woman. Through her work she expresses her rejection of superimposed categories and definitions and emphasizes that Black women define themselves in diverse manners in response to their own personal experience. Her visual and written works battle against the silencing of people of color by omission and promote inclusive and egalitarian practices in art history and in the art world at large.

BIBLIOGRAPHY

Failing, Patricia. "Black Artists Today: A Case of Exclusion," *Art News* (March 1989); Feinberg, Mark. "Painter Pindell Discovers That More Than the Gallery Walls Are White," *In These Times* (September 20, 1989); Jacobs, Joseph. *Since the Harlem Renaissance: Fifty Years of Afro-American Art* (1985); Patton, Sharon. "The Search for Identity." In *African-American Artists, 1880-1987*, ed. McElroy, Guy C. et al. (1989); Pindell, Howardena. "Art World Racism: A Documentation," *The New Art Examiner* (March 1989), and *Autobiography: In Her Own Image* (1988); Robins, Corinne. *The Pluralist Era* (1984); Rouse, Terrie S. *Howardena Pindell: Odyssey* (1986); Sheffield, Margaret. *Howardena Pindell: Autobiography* (1989); Stein, Judith E. and Ann Sargent Wooster. "Making Their Mark." In *Making Their Mark: Women Artists Move into the Mainstream, 1970-85*, comp. Randy Rosen and Catherine C. Brawer (1989); Wilson, Judith. "Howardena Pindell Makes Art That Winks at You," *Ms.* (May 1980); *WWBA* (1978).

NADINE WASSERMAN

PITTMAN, PORTIA MARSHALL WASHINGTON (1883-1978)

Portia Marshall Washington was born on June 6, 1883, to Booker T. Washington and Fanny Norton Smith Washington. Much of her early life was shaped by the fact that her father was the famous Booker T. Washington, and that heritage opened important doors of opportunity for her. She began her formal schooling at Tuskegee Institute, which her father founded, and went from there, in 1895, to Framingham State Normal School in Massachusetts, her first stepmother's alma mater. In 1899, she returned to Tuskegee for her senior year of high school and then spent one year at Wellesley College, whose first president, Alice Freeman Palmer, was a member of Tuskegee's Board of Trustees. After spending an intervening year back at Tuskegee, she returned to Massachusetts to attend Bradford Academy (now Bradford Junior College) and in 1905 became its first Black graduate. Portia Washington's educational odyssey was atypical for girls at the time, white or Black, yet the very same privilege that afforded her a fine education also encouraged a variety of restrictions. Moreover, it did not prevent the racism, sexism, a bad and possibly violent marriage, and ultimately the poverty that she would experience.

At the New England schools, she either lived in the only single dorm rooms on campus or she was not allowed to live on the campus at all because she was Black. Her movements in New England also were severely circumscribed because of the number of reporters who sought information that would embarrass her father. Even while she studied in Europe, she admitted that she continued to make decisions about her life and lifestyle in such a manner as to protect his as well as her own reputation. In 1907, she abandoned her music studies when William Sidney Pittman, a promising young architect, proposed and threatened to marry someone else if she did not marry him soon. Unable to break out of the traditional social conventions of the time, she decided that "every girl had to marry a good man when she can get him" (Stewart 1977). Portia Washington left Europe and married Pittman in October 1907.

Sidney Pittman had been a student at Tuskegee Institute before the turn of the century, and Washington had advanced him money to attend Drexel Institute and study architecture. He returned to Tuskegee after the completion of the course to work off his debt, but after he and Portia married they moved to Washington, D.C., where he established his own architectural firm and worked successfully for several years. Their children—Sidney, Jr., Booker, and Fannie—were born in the District in 1908, 1909, and 1912, respectively. Although Portia Pittman confined her work primarily to their household, she sometimes gave private music lessons and public benefit concerts, and she accompanied her father during his many visits to the city. After Sidney Pittman's business began to falter (which was probably why she began to give private music lessons), he moved the family to Dallas, Texas, in 1913.

As was the case in Washington, D.C., Pittman's business started out well in Texas but soon began to falter. Portia Pittman was flourishing, however, directing several church and school choirs, giving private music lessons, presiding over the Texas Association of Negro Musicians' Education Department, and eventually teaching in the public school system. As her fame as a musician increased and her husband's architectural business declined, he became moody, despondent, and even violent. After an episode in 1928 during which he struck their daughter, Fannie, the only child still living at home, Portia left him and returned to Tuskegee Institute to teach. The rising professional standards in the field of education and the necessary interest of Tuskegee administrators in their school rating and accreditation led the school to retire her in 1939. She returned to giving private music lessons until 1944, when she began to devote herself to work designed to memorialize her father. (One project concerned a scholarship fund in his name for needy Black students.)

While she was younger, Portia Washington Pittman's music training had enabled her to enhance the family economy by teaching piano, but in her old age she had to depend more, but not exclusively, on her children. Her teaching career spanned the period during which the feminized professions went through a standardization of credentials, which left her with reduced teaching opportunities. Moreover, the gender and racial stratification of wage work, coupled with class conventions of the time, further restricted her to working in her home or in private Black institutions. Consequently, despite having worked for wages much of her life, she could not benefit from New Deal public pension programs such as Social Security. In the 1950s, she lived in Washington, D.C., with her older son, Sidney, Jr., and later she and Fannie shared a home. All three children died within five years of each other, however, beginning with Sidney in 1967. In her old age, the Washington, D.C., branch of the Tuskegee Institute Alumni Association helped support Portia Washington Pittman by providing her with an apartment, which she kept until her death on February 26, 1978.

BIBLIOGRAPHY

Harlan, Louis and Raymond Smocks, eds. *The Booker T. Washington Papers* (1977-81); Stewart, Ruth Ann. *Portia: The Life of Portia Washington Pittman, the Daughter of Booker T. Washington* (1977); see also the Booker T. Washington papers in the Library of Congress, Manuscript Division, Washington, D.C.

STEPHANIE J. SHAW

PLAYER, WILLA B. (1909-)

Willa B. Player is counted as a rare figure within education, not only for her historic place as first Black woman president of a four-year women's college, but also for her commitment to the civil rights movement and equal opportunity for women. Her achievements reflect her enlightened beliefs and her dedication to the betterment of opportunity for young Americans.

The youngest child of Clarence E. and Beatrice D. Player, Willa Player was born on August 9, 1909, in Jackson, Mississippi. When she was seven, the family moved to Akron, Ohio, where she completed her elementary and high school education. Brought up in a devout Methodist family, Player decided to attend a Methodist college, Ohio Wesleyan University, in Delaware, Ohio. She graduated with a B.A. in 1929 and in 1930 received an M.A. from Oberlin College, Ohio. Player continued to study French at the University of Grenoble, France, and was awarded the Certificat d'Etudes in 1935. She earned a Ph.D in 1948 from Columbia University in New York City.

In 1930, Player became an instructor of French and Latin at Bennett College, a historically Black college in Greensboro, North Carolina. For the next fifteen years she worked her way up the academic career ladder, eventually becoming vice president. In 1955, Bennett College made history when Player was appointed university president, a position she held for the next ten years. Not only was Player the first Black woman to preside over Bennett College; she was also the first Black woman nationwide to be named to such a position at a four-year women's college. As college president during the years of the civil rights movement, Player considered student participation in sit-ins and other nonviolent protests as entirely reasonable forms of dissent. Indeed, she said she was proud of the Bennett students who attempted to de-segregate Greensboro during the 1960s.

After she retired from Bennett College in 1966, Player became director of the Division of Institutional Development in the Bureau of Postsecondary Education in Washington, D.C. During her tenure there, Player distinguished herself by establishing Title III as a major source of categorical support for historically Black and other minority institutions of higher education. In an era marked by the neglect of categorical programs that had been won through the civil rights movement, Player succeeded in not only maintaining but further developing funding for Title III programs, often in the face of reactionary opinion. She retired from the bureau in April 1977.

Willa Player has served on many boards, committees, and organizations. Some, such as the United Negro College Fund, reflect her dedication to improving educational opportunities for Black students, whereas others, such as the United Methodist Women (whom she assisted in establishing a charter for racial policy), testify to her lifelong involvement in the church. In addition to several honorary doctorates, Player has been the recipient of the Stepping Stone to Freedom Award for her contribution to the civil rights movement. In 1972, she was awarded both the Superior Service Award and the Distinguished Service Award from the U.S. Department of Health, Education and Welfare. In 1984, she was inducted into the Ohio Women's Hall of Fame in Columbus.

BIBLIOGRAPHY

Atlanta Daily World, "Educator Honored" (May 1, 1984); *CBWA*; *EBA*; Guy-Sheftall, Beverly. "A Conversation with Willa B. Player," *Sage* (Spring 1984); Lumpkins, Barbara. "Black Women: Special Challenges, Rewards," *Akron Beacon Journal* (February 4, 1985); *NBAW*; *WWBA* (1992). Information on Willa B. Player can be found in the Bennett College Archives, Greensboro, North Carolina. Interviews with Player are contained in the Black Oral History Collection, Fisk University Library, Nashville, Tennessee, and the Civil Rights Movement Project, Greensboro Public Library, Greensboro, North Carolina.

FENELLA MACFARLANE

PLEASANT, MARY ELLEN (1814-1904)

Mary Ellen Pleasant arrived in San Francisco during the Gold Rush heyday, probably sometime in 1849. In the next fifty years she worked as cook, accountant, abolitionist, and entrepreneur in the bustling town on the bay. Histories of the West describe her as madam, voodoo queen, and prostitute. Pleasant herself requested that the words "she was a friend of John Brown's" be printed on her gravestone, indicating her own desire to be remembered as an abolitionist. She was the target of what one historian calls an "avid conspiracy" that sought to silence her, and it was said that she harbored the skeletons of San Francisco's elite in her closet (Bennett 1979).

Sources report conflicting stories of her background (some say she was from Georgia, others Virginia), but Pleasant herself claimed she was born on August 19, 1814, in Philadelphia. She described her mother as a free colored woman and her father as a wealthy planter. Pleasant was educated on Nantucket by the Hussey family. She appeared to have spent time in Boston where she met William Lloyd Garrison and other abolitionists, including Alexander Smith, whom she married. Smith was a wealthy Cuban planter and, upon his death, willed Pleasant a considerable sum that most sources estimate at $45,000. Smith intended her to use the money for abolitionist causes. Her second husband, John James Pleasant, joined Mary Ellen in San Francisco sometime between 1848 and 1852, but he does not figure prominently in the records of her California career. Pleasant had one child, Elizabeth Smith, but little is known of her beyond the Black newspaper, the *Elevator*, report in 1866 that Pleasant sponsored a lavish wedding for her daughter at the African Methodist Episcopal Zion Church in San Francisco.

Pleasant spent time in Canada West in the late 1850s, working in the community of Black abolitionists and fugitive slaves stationed near Chatham. She and John Pleasant, along with Mary Ann Shadd Cary, Martin Delaney, and others, were members of the Chatham Vigilance Committee, organized to aid escaped slaves after the passage of the 1850 Fugitive Slave Act. Pleasant also bought real estate in Chatham in 1858. She reported that she met John Brown in Chatham, where the raid on Harpers Ferry was planned, and that she gave him financial support for his activities.

By the 1860s, she had returned to San Francisco and become a restaurateur and investor. San Francisco's thriving elite provided an eager market for her elegant restaurants and boardinghouses where she entertained some of the West's most famous financiers. Her best-known establishment, at 920 Washington Street (in the heart of today's Chinatown) was the meeting spot for some of the city's most prominent politicians, including Newton Booth, elected as governor of California in 1871. In the private domain of Pleasant's kitchens and dining rooms, she was privy to information about San Francisco's most powerful businessmen and politicians.

Pleasant also ran laundries in which she employed Black men and women. She operated an extensive employment network for the Black population of the city, supplying the chief employers of African-Americans—mining moguls turned hotel owners—with most of their labor force. In this way she functioned as a city boss, running an informal employment agency in Black San Francisco. Her efforts to improve conditions for African-Americans in the West extended beyond the workplace; she harbored fugitive slaves and fought for passage of an 1863 law guaranteeing Black Americans the right to testify in court. Pleasant also challenged Jim Crow laws in her landmark case against the North Beach Railroad Company in 1868. She was awarded $500 in damages after drivers refused to allow her to board the streetcar, but the case was appealed.

In 1884, Pleasant again appeared in court. This time it was as a witness in the highly publicized trial *Sharon* v. *Sharon*. Stories of the trial and Pleasant's testimony were common fare in national as well as local papers, indicating that Pleasant's entrepreneurial reputation was well known. Further, her role in the trial was pivotal as she testified to the authenticity of a marriage contract between mining mogul and Nevada Senator William Sharon and Sarah Althea Hill. Pleasant reportedly funded Hill's case, which was eventually thrown out of court, and press coverage of Pleasant likened her to a scheming voodoo queen.

Pleasant was well aware of the distortions her character suffered in the press: "You tell those newspaper people that they may be smart, but I'm smarter. They deal with words. Some folks say that words were made to reveal thought. That ain't so. Words were made to conceal thought" (Fraser 1901). Pleas-

ant died in San Francisco in 1904. All that remains of the mansion she had built, on the corner of Octavia and Bush streets in San Francisco, are the eucalyptus trees she planted. Her legend—although tangled—reveals the financial genius of a nineteenth-century African-American woman whose power, at the very least, inspired mythology and imagination.

BIBLIOGRAPHY

Beasley, Delilah L. *The Negro Trail-Blazers of California* (1919); Bennett, Lerone. "A Historical Detective Story: The Mystery of Mary Ellen Pleasant. Parts I and II," *Ebony* (April and May 1979); Fraser, Isabel. "Mammy Pleasant: The Woman," *San Francisco Call* (December 1901); Holdredge, Helen. *Mammy Pleasant* (1953), and *Mammy Pleasant's Partner* (1954); " 'Mammy' Pleasant Memoirs and Autobiography," *The Pandex of the Press* (January 1902); Thurman, Sue Bailey. *Pioneers of Negro Origin in California* (1952).

LYNN HUDSON

A legend in San Francisco, where she was restaurateur, entrepreneur, labor boss, and possibly madam, Mary Ellen Pleasant also supported abolitionists around the country. She was the target of what one historian calls an "avid controversy" that sought to silence her, and it was said that she harbored the skeletons of San Francisco's elite in her closet. [Schomburg Center]

POE, L. MARIAN FLEMING (1890-1974)

Lavinia Marian Fleming Poe became perhaps the first Black female lawyer in any southern state. Born August 13, 1890, the second of three children of Archer R. Fleming and Florence M. (Carter) Fleming, she grew up in Newport News, Virginia, with her parents and her brothers, Daniel and Archer, Jr. She excelled at school.

In the early 1910s, Marian Fleming worked in Newport News as a stenographer for a Black banker, notary, and real estate agent, E. C. Brown, president of the Crown Savings Bank. On September 20, 1911, she married a waiter named Abram James Poe, and they had two children, Florence Alice (November 30, 1912), and Abram James, Jr. (January 28, 1918). For a time around 1920, Marian Poe worked in the office of J. Thomas Newsome, a Black attorney, and her experience with Newsome convinced her that she wished to become a lawyer.

Success was a long shot. The law schools in Virginia—Washington and Lee University, the University of Virginia, the University of Richmond—excluded all Black applicants. Moreover, until 1920, Virginia law did not permit women to be licensed to practice the profession. Poe had two young children; but she went off to Washington, D.C., earned a law degree from Howard University in 1925, and later that year passed the Virginia bar examination.

For nearly a half-century, Marian Poe practiced her profession as a general practitioner in Newport News, one of a handful of Black attorneys who served the Black community there. Across those years, Poe did what she could, too, to help young Black lawyers get started, much as Thomas Newsome had done for her.

She participated in the profession in ways that stretched far from Newport News. A charter member of the (predominantly Black) Old Dominion Bar Association, she served throughout the 1940s as its secretary, and she served for a time as an assistant secretary of the (predominantly Black) National Bar Association. In addition, Poe served once at mid-century and twice in the 1960s as the Virginia delegate to the national convention of the National Association of Women Lawyers, a predominantly white but clearly biracial group. Thus she participated in the support systems that promoted the work of Black lawyers, particularly in Virginia, and of female lawyers across the nation.

Still, she emphasized her own community. The focal point of her life remained the building where she lived and had her office in the center of the Black business district in Newport News. She owned that building, at 628-630 Twenty-fifth Street, and for a time it also housed Alice's Beauty Shop, which her daughter ran, and her son-in-law's enterprise, Webb's Grill and Guesthouse. She was active in civic organizations and, at the First Baptist Church of Newport News, she taught Sunday school, sang in the choir, and became the first woman on the board of trustees. Following her own advice, she kept busy to the end.

Marian Poe died in a local hospital on March 20, 1974, at the age of eighty-three. After services at the First Baptist Church, she was buried at Pleasant Shade Cemetery in Newport News. By the time she died, the number of Black female lawyers in Virginia had risen into double digits, and Black men and Black women alike could be admitted to any law school in the state.

BIBLIOGRAPHY

Ashby, William M. *Tales without Hate* (1980); "Atty. L. Marian Poe Says 'Keep Busy' to Succeed," *Norfolk Journal and Guide* (September 17, 1955); Dark, Okianer Christian, and Allen R. Moye. "L. Marian Poe: A Model of Public Service," *Virginia Lawyer* (March 1990); *Ebony*. "Lady Lawyers" (August 1947); *Richmond News Leader* (March 23, 1974); Wallenstein, Peter. " 'These New and Strange Beings': Women in the Legal Profession in Virginia, 1890-1990," *Virginia Magazine of History and Biography* (1993); *WWCA* (1927); Zimmerman, Mary H., comp. *Seventy-five Year History of National Association of Women Lawyers, 1899-1974* (1975).

PETER WALLENSTEIN

POLITE, CARLENE (1932-)

Carlene Polite is among the most talented and versatile Black artists to emerge from the "second renaissance" of Black culture in the 1960s and 1970s. An innovative novelist, an accomplished dancer, and a political activist, Polite has been firmly committed to the cultural and political liberation of Black Americans.

Born in Detroit on August 28, 1932, to John and Lillian (Cook) Hatcher, Carlene Polite attended Sarah Lawrence College and the Martha Graham School of Contemporary Dance before embarking on her multifaceted career. From 1955 to 1963, Polite concentrated her energies on dance; in addition to performing with the Concert Dance Theatre of New York City (1955-59), the Detroit Equity Theatre (1960-62), and the Vanguard Playhouse (1960-62), she taught modern dance at the Detroit Young Men's

Christian Association (1962-63) as well as at Wayne State University.

In the early 1960s, Polite was one of numerous Black artists and intellectuals who turned to political activism. During this period, which she later described as her freedom fighter days, Polite held a number of political positions, including organizer of the Northern Negro Leadership Conference in 1963, elected member of the Michigan State Central Committee of the Democratic party from 1962 to 1963, and coordinator of the Detroit Council for Human Rights in 1963. She participated in the historic June 23, 1963,

Walk for Freedom and the Freedom Now rally in November 1963 to protest the Birmingham bombings.

After the Detroit Council for Human Rights closed in 1964, Polite worked briefly in a nightclub and then moved to Paris, where she lived for the next seven years. During these years, Polite focused on her writing. Her first novel, *The Flagellants*, was published in French in 1966, and in English the following year. While residing in Paris, Polite sustained her preoccupation with the political condition of Black Americans: in an article entitled "Speak, Brother!"

The remarkably talented and versatile Carlene Polite emerged from the "second renaissance" of Black culture in the 1960s and 1970s as an innovative novelist, an accomplished dancer, and a committed political activist. [Schomburg Center]

935

that appeared in *Mademoiselle* in January 1968, Polite presented four different approaches to the issue of Black Power in four distinct Black speech styles. Her second novel, *Sister X and the Victims of Foul Play*, was published in 1975, four years after her return to the United States. Polite is currently a full professor in the English department at the State University of New York at Buffalo, which she joined as an associate professor in 1971. Divorced from Allen Polite, she has two daughters, Glynda Bennett and Lila Polite.

In keeping with the Black Nationalist aesthetic of the 1960s and 1970s, Polite's work urgently conveys the need for political liberation: from the disabling stereotypes of matriarchs and emasculated Black men portrayed in *The Flagellants*, and from the oppressive cultural and political system of capitalism portrayed in *Sister X*. Polite's novels have not achieved the recognition they deserve; their dense prose and uneven style are offset by the dazzling originality and exuberance of her writing. In her attempt to introduce the rhythms of Black oral expression into her novels, and her playful experimentation with form, Carlene Polite helped to shape the development of Black fiction, opening the way for later innovators such as Gayl Jones and Ishmael Reed.

BIBLIOGRAPHY

BABB; BW; DLB; Gross, Robert A. "The Black Novelists: 'Our Turn.' " *Newsweek* (June 16, 1969); Houston, Helen Ruth. *The Afro-American Novel 1965-1975: A Descriptive Bibliography of Primary and Secondary Material* (1977); Lottmann, Herbert R. "Authors and Editors," *Publishers Weekly* (June 12, 1967); Polite, Carlene. *The Flagellants* (1967), and *Sister X and the Victims of Foul Play* (1975), and "Speak, Brother!" *Mademoiselle* (January 1968); *WWBA* (1990).

MADHU DUBEY

POWERS, GEORGIA MONTGOMERY DAVIS (1923-)

The soft-gray hair and the sparkling eyes belie the strength and determination that mark the life of Georgia Montgomery Davis Powers. The first Black and first woman to be elected to the Kentucky State Senate (1967-1989), her life has been characterized by the "breaking of barriers" (Powers 1989). Born in Springfield, Kentucky, on October 19, 1923, Powers was the only female among nine children. A graduate of Louisville Municipal College (1942) and the mother of four children, she says she did not know what she wanted to do until she was forty-four. She had held

thirty jobs, including owning a business, when she decided that politics was her calling. She ran for and won the senate seat from District 33 in Louisville in 1967. However, this was not the beginning of Powers's activism but rather a milestone along the way of a dedicated civil libertarian.

Powers was at the center of the Kentucky civil rights movement in the early 1960s and continued the struggle within the chambers of the state senate. In 1964, she organized a march in Frankfort, Kentucky's capital. The march's success was instrumental in the passage in 1966 of Kentucky's Public Accommodations and Fair Employment Law, and it was a key experience in her decision to run for public office.

Her activities in Kentucky brought her into the inner circle of Dr. Martin Luther King, Jr., and she was one of the organizers of the Kentucky affiliate of the Southern Christian Leadership Conference. She participated in the Selma, Alabama, march in 1965, pushed for open housing in 1967 in Kentucky, and on April 4, 1968, she was in Memphis, Tennessee, at the request of Dr. King, to participate in the sanitation workers' march. From her room in the Lorraine Motel, she heard the shots that killed Dr. King.

During her more than twenty years in the Kentucky State Senate, Powers was a successful advocate for women's issues, as well as civil rights. She sponsored Kentucky's Equal Rights Amendment, Kentucky's Affirmative Action Plan, legislation to eliminate race descriptors from Kentucky drivers' licenses, and legislation on sex and age discrimination. In 1980, she introduced legislation to require that at least one Black member be appointed to the Board of Regents at each of Kentucky's public universities. Within the senate, she served as chairperson of the Labor and Industry Committee, the Elections and Constitutional Amendments Committee, and the Cities Committee.

Powers's political skills were developed from adversarial situations, yet adversary relations have a personal price. Powers has had to work through what she calls "diminishing rage" (Powers 1989). Each act of racial or sexual discrimination diminishes the spirit of a person, and it must be regained. Nevertheless, her struggles for justice, she believes, have earned her the right, borrowing a phrase from her favorite poem by Jenny Joseph, to say—"When I am an old lady I shall wear purple, with a red hat, which doesn't go and doesn't suit me" (Powers 1989).

BIBLIOGRAPHY

"Black Women in American Politics: A Public Symposium." Program Brochure. University of Kentucky,

Lexington (October 12-13, 1989); Lanker, Brian. *I Dream a World: Portraits of Black Women Who Changed America* (1989); Powers, Georgia Montgomery Davis. "The Breaking of Barriers." Speech given at "Black Women in American Politics: A Public Symposium," University of Kentucky, October 12, 1989; *Who's Who in American Politics* (1989).

PAULA D. McCLAIN

POWERS, HARRIET (1837-1911)

There is only one way to understand the significance of Harriet Powers, and that is to look at her quilts (one of which is pictured here). Their originality and joyful spirit cannot be described. On seeing them, one experiences an undeniable feeling that this woman was an artist.

Harriet Powers was born a slave on October 29, 1837, in Georgia. Her maiden name is unknown, as are the circumstances of her birth and childhood. She was married to Armstead Powers and had three children, two of whom were born in slavery; the third was born in 1866, just after the end of the Civil War. Most of this information comes from the 1870 census, which also states that Powers's occupation was keeping house and that her husband was a farmhand.

The family was fairly prosperous. They owned animals and tools and, sometime in the 1880s, bought two two-acre plots of land. In 1873, they were living in the Buck Branch, Winterville district of Clarke County, Georgia. At other times between 1870 and 1894, when Armstead seems to have left the farm, they lived in the Sandy Creek district. Harriet Powers remained in that district, living an independent and reasonably comfortable life until her death in 1911.

Born into slavery, Harriet Powers went on to live an independent and reasonably comfortable life, and to create quilts characterized by originality and a joyful spirit. The quilt illustrated here is The Creation of the Animals, *dated 1895-98 and made in Athens, Georgia, of pieced and appliquéd cotton with plain and metallic yarns. [Bequest of Maxim Karolik; Courtesy, Museum of Fine Arts, Boston]*

Powers's existence and her quilts are known to us because of Jennie Smith, a white artist from Athens, Georgia, who was head of the art department of the Lucy Cobb School. Smith first saw a Powers quilt at the Athens Cotton Fair of 1886. She was enormously impressed and resolved at once to find its maker. She visited Powers at her farm and offered to buy the quilt, but Powers refused to sell. Then, in 1890, the Powers family went through a very difficult time financially. A year later they would have to sell off one of their pieces of land. Smith received word that she could now buy the quilt. Unfortunately, she was unable to do so. The next year, Smith sent word to Powers that she was ready to buy the quilt if it was still for sale. At the end of this back-and-forth, Powers brought the quilt, carefully wrapped, to Smith's home and handed it over in return for $5. Before she left, she related to Smith the story of each of the quilt's fifteen squares. The quilt depicts events of her lifetime that Powers considered significant, such as a dark day apparently caused by forest fires in New York and Canada. Smith wrote down and preserved what she had been told. Powers returned a number of times to Smith's house to visit her quilt.

It was Smith's purpose to exhibit the quilt in Atlanta at the Cotton States Exposition of 1895. The Black community had raised $10,000 for a special building at the exposition, and there were exhibits from eleven southern states. Powers's name is not on the list of exhibitors, but there is evidence that her quilt was there; in 1898, a group of faculty wives from Atlanta University commissioned Powers to create a second quilt as a gift for Reverend Charles Cuthbert Hall, president of Union Theological Seminary.

The quilt owned by Smith passed, at her death, into the hands of a friend, Hal Heckman. He kept the quilt for some time and then gave it to the Smithsonian Institution. It is now on exhibit there. The quilt owned by Hall was inherited by his son, Reverend Basil Douglas Hall, who sold it to collector Maxim Karolik. Karolik gave it to the Museum of Fine Arts in Boston in 1964. Entitled *The Creation of the Animals*, it is reproduced here. Powers dictated her explanations of this quilt to Jennie Smith as well.

Looking at these two quilts today causes profoundly mixed feelings. It is wonderful to see the work of an artist preserved, but it is impossible not to feel great sadness that she was denied the opportunity to fulfill her potential.

BIBLIOGRAPHY

Adams, Marie Jeanne. "The Harriet Powers Pictorial Quilts," *Black Art* (1979); Fry, Gladys-Marie. "Harriet Powers: Portrait of a Black Quilter," *Sage* (Spring 1987); McDaniel, M. Akua. "Black Women: Making Quilts of Their Own," *Art Papers* (September/October 1987).

KATHLEEN THOMPSON

PREER, EVELYN (1896-1932)

"Evelyn Preer ranks first as a Movie Star," wrote Floyd J. Calvin, a reporter for the *Pittsburgh Courier*, in 1927. Preer had worked hard to earn that accolade. The daughter and the oldest of Frank and Blanch Jarvis's three children, Evelyn Preer was born on July 26, 1896, in Vicksburg, Mississippi. While she was still quite young, Preer was taken to Chicago by her widowed mother. It was in Chicago that she received her formal education, and Chicago also was where her theatrical career had its dramatic beginnings. While street preaching for her mother, a devout member of the Apostolic Church, Preer attracted the attention of the Black movie producer/director Oscar Micheaux. In 1917, she appeared in Micheaux's first Black silent film, *The Homesteader*. The first of many profitable collaborations of the director and his young star, it was followed by seven other successful films: *The Brute* (1920); *Within Our Gates* (1920); *Deceit* (1921); *The Gunsaulus Mystery* (1921); *Birthright* (1924); *The Conjure Woman* (1926); and *The Spider's Web* (1926). Preer considered the latter film her best movie work.

In October 1920, Preer joined the Lafayette Players, who were then performing at the Lincoln Theatre in Chicago. Remaining with the Players for twelve years, until her death in 1932, she became one of their most popular leading ladies and a favorite with audiences all over the country. By 1924, Preer was the star of the traveling group of Players who toured extensively through the southern states, and she married her leading man, Edward Thompson. Their union produced one child, a daughter, Ed Eve, born shortly before Preer's death in November 1932. Lauded by the leading Black critics of the time, Preer was once referred to as "a shining jewel in Ethiope's ear." Because she was a star of the Lafayette Players, Preer performed in the leading plays of the time: *Porgy*; *Over the Hill to the Poor House*; *Salome*, in which she was advertised as "The Most Beautiful Colored Woman in the World!"; *Dr. Jekyll and Mr. Hyde*; *Madam X*; *The Chip Woman's Fortune*, written by the Black dramatist Willis Richardson; *Bought and Paid For*; *Branded*; *The Warning*; *Anna Christie*; *Desire under the Elms*; *The Hunchback of Notre Dame*; and *Rain*, to name just a few of her successes.

Star of eight successful Black silent films, Evelyn Preer was a leading actress with the Lafayette Players until her untimely death at the age of thirty-six. [Sister Francesca Thompson]

Evelyn Preer made several popular phonograph records and, in 1924, appeared in the Broadway production of *Lulu Belle*, directed by the famous producer and playwright, David Belasco. She appeared in *Shuffle Along*, by Eubie Blake and Noble Sissle, in 1921 and in *Rang Tang*, by Miller and Lyles, in 1927. Multitalented, Preer was widely acknowledged to be a pioneer for the other Black actresses who were to follow her.

After her untimely death at thirty-six, Oscar Micheaux wrote of her meteoric career: "She was beautiful, intelligent ... and a born artist ... more versatile than any actress I have ever known ... her early passing will leave her missed greatly by the profession." In Clarence Muse's eloquent eulogy at Preer's funeral in Los Angeles, he concluded by saying, "And so, Evelyn Preer, go on! The Lafayette Players have profited by your visit here. The world has been uplifted." It was a fitting tribute to a dedicated artist who had given her last bow and made her final exit.

BIBLIOGRAPHY
Blake, Eubie. Personal interview (1978); Bush, Anita. Personal interview (1969); *California Eagle* (November 25, 1932); Muse, Clarence. Personal interview (1969); *New York Age* (October 24, 1925; November 26, 1932); *Pittsburgh Courier* (April 16, 1927); Private collection, Sister Francesca Thompson, New York City; Thompson, Sister Francesca. "The Lafayette Players, 1915-1932," Ph.D. diss. (1972).

SISTER FRANCESCA THOMPSON

PRENDERGAST, SHIRLEY (1932-)

In 1973, Shirley Prendergast became the first Black woman lighting designer on Broadway with the production of *The River Niger*, as well as one of the first Black women to be admitted into the lighting division of United Scenic Artists Association (USAA), the major stage designers' union.

Born Merris Shirley Prendergast on June 15, 1932, in Boston, Massachusetts, she is the daughter of Dorita and Wilford A. Prendergast. Before working in theater, she earned a degree in microbiology at Brooklyn College. As a dancer during college, she became interested in lighting design.

During the 1960s, Prendergast attended the famous Lester Polakov's Studio and Forum of Stage Design in New York City, where she studied with some of Broadway's most prominent designers. Through the Negro Ensemble Company (NEC), Prendergast was provided the opportunity to design numerous productions and develop professionally as a designer. Her first production with NEC was *Summer of the Seventeenth Doll*. In 1969, she passed the lighting examination and was admitted into USAA, local no. 829.

The NEC's production of *The River Niger*, which opened at the St. Mark's Theatre, moved to Broadway—allowing Prendergast to have her first Broadway show. Since the *The River Niger*, Prendergast has designed other Broadway productions, including *The Amen Corner* (1983), *Don't Get God Started* (1989), *The Waltz of the Stork* (1981), and *Robeson* (1990). She also has designed for the Alvin Ailey American Dance Theatre, New York Shakespeare Festival, Crossroads Theatre, the New Federal Theatre, and numerous regional companies, while maintaining close ties with NEC.

BIBLIOGRAPHY
Negro Ensemble Company Playbills. Billy Rose Theatre Collection, Library of the Performing Arts, New

York, New York; Prendergast, Shirley. Personal interviews (1982, 1991).

KATHY A. PERKINS

PRESTAGE, JEWEL LIMAR (1931-)

Jewel Limar Prestage is a pioneer with a long list of firsts, the most prominent being that she was the first American Black woman to secure a Ph.D. in political science. A major highlight of her academic career was the founding of the School of Public Policy and Urban Affairs at Southern University, where she served as its first Dean—a position from which she retired in 1989 after a thirty-three-year association with that university.

Jewel Limar, born in 1931 into a large family in Hutton, rural Louisiana, grew up in nearby Alexandria. During the height of segregation, she earned a B.A. summa cum laude in 1951 and then a Ph.D. from the University of Iowa in 1953. Limar married James J. Prestage, a biologist and former university chancellor; they are the parents of five children.

Since 1954, Prestage has held directorships, memberships, and offices in major scholarly organizations, including vice president of the American Political Science Association and president of both the Southern Political Science Association and the Southwestern Social Science Association. Her initiative led to the founding of the National Conference of Black Political Scientists in 1969, and she later served as its president. She has served on editorial boards of six scholarly journals, contributed articles to the *Journal of Politics*, *Social Science Quarterly*, and other journals, and coauthored a textbook on women in politics.

Appointed to the National Advisory Council on Women's Educational Programs by President Jimmy Carter, she became the first minority person to chair that body. Prestage served as chair of the Louisiana State Advisory Committee to the U.S. Commission on Civil Rights and served on the Judicial Council of the Democratic party. As a result of her scholarship, her advocacy of women and minorities, and her leadership in higher education, Prestage was the recipient of Distinguished Alumni Achievement awards from both Southern University and the University of Iowa, as well as the Fannie Lou Hamer Award. She also was inducted into the Women's Pavilion at the 1984 World's Fair in New Orleans. In 1991, the Policy Studies Organization established the Jewel L. Prestage Award for the Study of Minorities and Public Policy. The American Political Science Association presented awards to her in 1984 and 1989 for contributions to the development of the profession.

Now dean of the Benjamin Banneker Honors College at Prairie View A & M University, the nation's first full honors college at a historically Black institution, Prestage plans to continue her academic affiliations, work with the development of honors education in the nation, and do research on women in politics.

BIBLIOGRAPHY

SELECTED WORKS BY JEWEL LIMAR PRESTAGE

Prestage, Jewel Limar. "Black Politics and the Kerner Report: Concerns and Directions," *Social Science Quarterly* (December 1968), and "Quelling the Mythical Revolution in Higher Education: Retreat from the Affirmative Action Concept," *Journal of Politics* (August 1979), and "In Quest of the African-American Political Woman," *Annals of the American Academy of Political and Social Science* (May 1991), and with James Prestage. "The Consent Decree as an Instrument for Desegregation in Higher Education," *Urban League Review* (Winter 1986-87), and with Marianne Githens. *A Portrait of Marginality: The Political Behavior of the American Woman* (1977).

IFE WILLIAMS-ANDOH

PRICE, FLORENCE SMITH (1888-1953)

Florence Smith Price was among the first Black women composers to earn widespread recognition. Her award-winning compositions have been performed by major orchestras and renowned solo artists. The North Arkansas Symphony Orchestra, the Detroit Symphony, and pianists Althea Waites and Selma Epstein have given performances of her music.

Born on April 9, 1888, in Little Rock, Arkansas, she studied piano with her mother, Florence Smith, a concert pianist and accomplished soprano. She was a published composer while still in high school. In 1906, she graduated from the New England Conservatory of Music, where she studied piano, organ, and composition. Her teachers included George Chadwick and Frederick Converse. She also studied at the Chicago Musical College, the American Conservatory of Music, and the Chicago Teachers College. She taught at Shorter College in Little Rock and at Clark College in Atlanta.

In 1912, she married Thomas Price, a lawyer in Little Rock, and devoted her time to composition and teaching in her private studio. She had two daughters, Florence and Edith, and a son who died during infancy. Price moved to Chicago in 1927 and remained there until her death in 1953.

Price won Holstein awards in 1925 and 1927. Her Symphony in E minor won the Wanamaker Prize in 1932 and was premiered by the Chicago Symphony Orchestra at the 1933 Chicago World's Fair. Influenced by the more traditional melodic and rhythmic characteristics of Black music, her works are considered neoromantic and nationalistic. She wrote symphonies, concerti, sonatas, chamber music, choral music, and various pieces for organ, piano, and voice.

BIBLIOGRAPHY

Cohen, Aaron I., ed. *International Encyclopedia of Women Composers* (1987); Green, Mildred Denby. *Black Women Composers: A Genesis* (1983), and "A Study of the Lives and Works of Five Black Women Composers in America," Ph.D. diss. (1975); Jackson, Barbara G. Program notes, North Arkansas Symphony Orchestra (April 6, 1986); Southall, Geneva. "In Celebration of Black Women Composers." Program notes, fourth annual Music of the Black American Composer program (May 1988); Southern, Eileen. *The Music of Black Americans: A History* (1983).

MELLASENAH MORRIS

Among the first Black women composers to earn widespread recognition, Florence Smith Price heard her Symphony in E minor performed by the Chicago Symphony Orchestra at the 1933 Chicago World's Fair. [Moorland-Spingarn]

PRICE, LEONTYNE (1927-)

"La diva di tutte le dive" (opera's foremost goddess) and "La prima donna assoluta" (the absolute first lady)—these are among the evaluations critics have made of soprano Mary Violet Leontyne Price, a native of Laurel, Mississippi, where she was born on February 10, 1927.

Her family life centered around the church, where both parents were active. She began piano lessons when only four and joined her mother in the church choir not many years later. In 1936, she attended a recital in Jackson, Mississippi, by Marian Anderson, and she firmly decided she would be a musician. At that time, the only role for a Black woman in music other than performing was teaching, and with that major she attended Central State College in Ohio. Before her graduation in 1949, she was encouraged to apply for admission to New York's Juilliard School of Music as a voice major. She was admitted, though she had learned no foreign languages and her only contact with opera had been the Saturday afternoon broadcasts from the Metropolitan Opera. Her student colleagues remember how cordially, but resolutely, she passed them in the hall, scores in her arms, on the way to the practice rooms to prepare for her lessons with Florence Kimball and to study for her classes.

She was cast in the role of Mistress Ford in a school production of Verdi's *Falstaff*, and attracted the attention of the composer Virgil Thomson, who was seeking new singers for the 1952 revival of his *Four Saints in Three Acts*, an opera calling for an all-Black cast. He engaged Price for the role of Cecilia, which she performed in New York and at the Paris International Arts Festival. In turn, this won her the role of Bess in Gershwin's *Porgy and Bess*, in which she toured in Berlin, Paris, and Vienna into 1954. That November, she made her New York debut at Town Hall. The next February found her on national television, in the title role of Puccini's *Tosca*, and later in

Mozart's *Die Zauberflöte* and *Don Giovanni*, and in Poulenc's *Dialogues des Carmélites*.

The San Francisco Opera engaged her as Madame Lidoine when they staged the Poulenc opera in 1957, and continued to call on her talents for *Il trovatore* and *Madama Butterfly*. A European career was critical to the profession, and she appeared that year at the Arena di Verona, Covent Garden, and the Vienna Staatsoper. Her Chicago debut with the Lyric Opera was as Liù in Puccini's *Turandot* (1959).

Beginning in 1955, the Metropolitan Opera had added Black singers: Marian Anderson and Robert

Her extraordinary voice and her deep commitment to excellence have helped Leontyne Price achieve one of the most brilliant operatic careers of our time. In 1955, she sang Tosca *on network television. [Schomburg Center]*

McFerrin (1955), Mattiwilda Dobbs (1956), Gloria Davy (1958), and Martina Arroyo (1959). In April of 1953, Price had, in fact, performed "Summertime" from *Porgy and Bess* in a broadcast gala to raise funds for the company, but her formal debut came with Verdi's *Il trovatore* (January 27, 1961) when, in the role of Leonora, she won forty-two minutes of cheers from the audience. There was no doubt that she would open the Metropolitan Opera's next season (as Puccini's Minnie in *La fanciulla del west*) and the next year she opened again by repeating her 1957 Vienna role as Aida. During the final seasons that the Metropolitan remained in its old quarters, she was celebrated for her artistry in the Italian repertoires of Puccini's *Turandot* (Liù) and *Madama Butterfly* (Cio-Cio-San), and as Elvira in Verdi's *Ernani*, in her repertoire since the 1962 Salzburg Festival, when she had been selected by Herbert von Karajan.

When the Metropolitan Opera moved to Lincoln Center in 1966, she inaugurated the new hall in Samuel Barber's *Antony and Cleopatra*, which the composer had written specifically for her. Her operatic career continued internationally to set new vocal standards until January 3, 1985, when, as Aida at the Metropolitan Opera, she concluded an almost unprecedented one-third of a century on the stage.

She had demonstrated her interpretive leadership in the Italian repertoires of Verdi and Puccini, and expanded the previously practiced limits to excel in German, Spanish, French, and Slavic works, as well as spirituals and other American music. Her principal opera roles, in addition to those mentioned, were the Prima Donna and Ariadne (*Ariadne auf Naxos*), Amelia (*Un ballo in maschera*), Fiordiligi (*Così fan tutte*), Donna Anna (*Don Giovanni*), Tatiana (*Eugene Onegin*), Leonora (*La forza del destino*) and Manon (*Manon Lescaut*). These and other works are richly documented in her many recordings.

As her voice matured, it transformed from an almost coloratura soubrette to a *lirico spinto*, the luxuriously and richly textured sound Verdi had desired, critics commented; but she unhesitatingly attributed her success to a voice that she described as "dark" and "smoky," and to the "luxury of her Blackness." Her continued work at the piano facilitated her deep knowledge of the structure of music. Her understanding of her own voice endowed her with the mechanics needed to accommodate its uniqueness. Moreover, her interpretations betrayed the profound intellectual probings to which she subjected every work from the recital, opera, and concert repertoires, in which she was first among the stars.

BIBLIOGRAPHY
Blyth, Alan. "Price, Mary Violet Leontyne." *The New Grove Dictionary of Music and Musicians* (1980); Ewen, David. "Price, Leontyne, 1927- ." *Musicians Since 1900: Performers in Concert and Opera* (1978); Lyon, Hugh Lee. *Leontyne Price: Highlights of a Prima Donna* (1973); Rich, Maria. "Price, Leontyne." *Who's Who in Opera* (1976); Sargeant, Winthrop. *Divas* (1973); Slonimsky, Nicolas. "Price, Leontyne." *Baker's Biographical Dictionary of Musicians* (1978).

DOMINIQUE-RENÉ de LERMA

PRIMUS, PEARL (1919-)

Pearl Primus was born in Trinidad in 1919 and moved to New York at an early age. She attended Hunter College and graduated in 1940 majoring in biology and pre-medicine. Primus received a dance scholarship to the New School for Social Research and began to study what were called at the time "primitive dances." Her first choreographed work, *African Ceremonial*, premiered at the Ninety-second Street Young Women's Hebrew Association on February 14, 1943. This was considered her professional debut, and the work received positive reviews. After a ten-month engagement at a club called Café Society Downtown, she left to prepare her first solo concert. This performance took place at the Belasco Theater on Broadway in the fall of 1944. This was an extraordinary achievement for a young Black woman in the 1940s. Primus went on to study with some of the great modern dance teachers of that time including Martha Graham, Doris Humphrey, Charles Weidman, Hanya Holm, and Sophie Maslow.

Primus traveled the South observing the lifestyles of the common people, living with sharecroppers, and visiting Black churches. It was that experience that inspired much of her subsequent choreography. Dances like *Strange Fruit* became classics, because of her bold statement of social protest. Some of the other works choreographed by Pearl Primus are *Shango* (1947), *Impinyuza* (1951), *Naffi Tombo* (1960), the legendary *The Negro Speaks of Rivers* (1943), choreographed to a poem by Langston Hughes, and *Michael Row Your Boat Ashore* (1979), which was about the horror of the Birmingham, Alabama, church bombings. Primus's choreography chronicled the Black experience in the United States and the traditional dances of Africa and the Caribbean. Primus also worked on Broadway dancing in and choreographing such shows as *Show Boat* (1945), *Caribbean Carnival*

Whether traveling the American South living with sharecroppers, or working with the National Dance Company of Liberia, Pearl Primus has always used her exceptional talents as a choreographer and dancer to explore the lives of her people. [Moorland-Spingarn]

(1947), *The Emperor Jones* (1947), and *Mister Johnson* (1956).

Like her predecessor, Katherine Dunham, Primus received the last and largest Rosenwald Fellowship to finance her travel to Africa for eighteen months. In 1949, she was able to visit what was then known as the Gold Coast (Ghana), Angola, the Cameroons, Liberia, Senegal and the Belgian Congo (Zaire). Later, on another trip to Africa with her husband, Percival Borde, she was named "Omowale" which means "the child returns home" by the Nigerians in Yoruba. In 1959, on her second major trip to Africa, Primus was named director of Liberia's Performing Arts Center. Her work with the National Dance Company of Liberia and her stylization of the Liberian dance "Fanga" earned her that country's highest award, the

Order of the Star of Africa, which was bestowed on Primus by the late President William V. S. Tubman.

Primus was married to Percival Borde, a dancer and choreographer. After their two-year stay in Liberia, they returned to the States and formed the Earth Dance Company in the 1970s. In 1976, two of Primus's dances, *Fanga*, a dance of welcome, and the *Wedding Dance*, were performed by the Alvin Ailey American Dance Theater. The American Dance Festival in Durham, North Carolina, reconstructed Primus's *The Negro Speaks of Rivers* and presented the dance in its Black dance classic series.

Primus has taught dance and anthropology at Hunter College, the State University of New York at Buffalo, New York University (where she received her Ph.D. in dance education), and at Smith College where she was a Five College Professor of Humanities. She was honored by President George Bush for her contributions to dance and received the National Medal of Arts at the White House on July 9, 1991.

[*See also* DANCE COMPANIES, ARTISTIC DIRECTORS.]

BIBLIOGRAPHY

Clarke, Mary and David Vaughan, eds. *The Encyclopedia of Dance and Ballet* (1977); Cohen-Stratyner, Barbara Naomi. *Biographical Dictionary of Dance* (1982); *EBA*; Emery, Lynne Fauley. *Black Dance: From 1619 to Today* (1988); Long, Richard. *The Black Tradition in American Concert Dance* (1990); *NA*; *NWAT*; Patterson, Lindsay, ed. *Anthology of the Afro-American in the Theater: A Critical Approach* (1978); Rollins, Charlemae. *Negro Entertainers of Stage, Screen, and T.V.* (1967); Thorpe, Edward. *Black Dance* (1990); Toppin, Edgar A. *A Biographical History of Blacks in America Since 1528* (1971); *WA*; Willis, John, ed. *Dance World* ([1967] 1976); *WWBA* (1990).

KARIAMU WELSH ASANTE

PRINCE, LUCY TERRY (c. 1730-1821)

Lucy Terry Prince led a remarkable life as advocate, devoted mother, wife, and poet. Since documentation of her early life is sketchy, biographers speculate that Lucy Terry was born in Africa, enslaved there, and brought to Bristol, Rhode Island, where at about age five she was bought by Ebenezer Wells. Records show that Wells had her baptized in his home in Deerfield, Massachusetts, on June 15, 1735, and that he apparently taught her to read and write. Lucy Terry remained in slavery until 1756 when she married Abijah Prince, who bought her freedom from Wells.

Lucy Terry Prince is perhaps best known for her rhymed poem "Bars Fight," which has been called the most accurate account of an Indian raid that occurred on August 25, 1746, in that part of Deerfield known as "The Bars." Although Prince's poem was not published until 1855 (in Josiah Gilbert Holland's *History of Western Massachusetts*), it was written over a century earlier in the year of the raid and almost certainly makes Prince the first Black poet in America.

"Bars Fight" is Prince's single poem, but it is not the only accomplishment in her long, full life. She was twenty-six when she married Abijah, who was twenty-five years her senior and by all accounts an extraordinary man. Abijah had served four years in the militia during the French and Indian War (1744-48), and perhaps because of this military service (no

one knows for certain) was granted his freedom and three parcels of land in Northfield, Massachusetts. The Princes paid taxes in Northfield but remained in Deerfield until they moved in the 1760s to Guilford, Massachusetts, on a hundred-acre lot that had been left to Abijah by an employer, Deacon Samuel Field. Later, Abijah became one of the fifty-five original grantees and founders of the town of Sunderland, Vermont, where he owned another one-hundred-acre farm.

It was while they lived in Guilford that Lucy Prince first demonstrated a willingness to defend her rights in a public debate. In 1785, white neighbors, the Noyeses, threatened the Princes' lives and property (tearing down fences and burning haystacks). Lucy appealed in person to Governor Thomas Chittenden and his Council for protection from these assaults, and on June 7, 1785, the Council ordered the selectmen of the town to defend the Princes.

Between 1757 and 1769, Lucy and Abijah had six children: Caesar (January 14, 1757), Durexa (June 1, 1758), Drucella (August 7, 1760), Festus (December 12, 1763), Tatnai (September 2, 1765), and Abijah, Jr. (June 12, 1769). The two oldest sons, Caesar and Festus, enlisted in the militia during the American Revolution. Although Festus was only fifteen at the time of enlistment, he falsified his age and served for three years as an artilleryman. After the war he married a white woman and settled on a farm in Sunderland. Not much is known of the other children except that Durexa acquired a reputation as a poet, and Tatnai became a shopkeeper in Salem, New York.

We do know that the education of her youngest child, Abijah, Jr., was the impetus for another of Prince's appeals to public authority, when she tried, unsuccessfully, to gain her son's admission to Williams College. On that occasion Prince spoke for three hours before the college trustees, recounting her family's military contributions, quoting the law and the Bible, and reminding her audience of what she considered her friendship with the late Col. Ephraim Williams, whose property bequeathal had established the Free School that became Williams College in October 1793. Despite her efforts, however, Prince's son was not admitted.

A short time later Prince once again engaged in public debate to establish her rights by pleading a property dispute case before the U.S. Supreme Court. Her neighbor, Col. Eli Bronson, had claimed part of the Sunderland lot that Abijah had been granted by King George III. The town could not settle the matter and the lawsuit eventually reached the Supreme Court. Prince was represented by Isaac Tichnor, who later became governor of Vermont, but it was she who presented the argument before the court with Justice Samuel Chase of Baltimore presiding. Bronson's attorneys, prominent jurist Stephen R. Bradley and Royall Tyler, the poet and later chief justice of Vermont, faced a formidable adversary in Lucy Prince. Although there is no surviving record of this case, George Sheldon, a nineteenth-century historian, writes that the court ruled in her favor and Justice Chase declared her argument exceptional, "better than he had heard from any lawyer at the Vermont bar" (Sheldon 1972).

In 1803, at age seventy-three, Prince moved to Sunderland. Abijah had died nine years earlier and was buried at Bennington, some eighteen miles from Sunderland. As evidence of her fortitude and strength, Prince made an annual visit by horseback to her husband's grave up until 1821, the year of her death. The August 21, 1821, obituary that appeared in the *Franklin Herald* of Greenfield, Massachusetts, is a fitting summary of Lucy Prince's life: "In this remarkable woman there was an assemblage of qualities rarely to be found among her sex. Her volubility was exceeded by none, and in general the fluency of her speech captivated all around her, and was not destitute of instruction and edification. She was much respected among her acquaintance, who treated her with a degree of deference."

BARS FIGHT

August 'twas the twenty-fifth,
Seventeen hundred forty-six
  The Indians did in ambush lay,
  Some very valient men to slay,
The names of whom I'll not leave out.
  Samuel Allen like a hero fout,
And though he was so brave and bold,
  His face no more shall we behold.
Eleazer Hawks was killed outright,
Before he had time to fight,—
Before he did the Indians see,
Was shot and killed immediately.
Oliver Amsden he was slain,
Which caused his friends much grief and pain.
Simeon Amsden they found dead,
Not many rods distant from his head.
Adonijah Gillett we do hear
Did lose his life which was so dear.
  John Sadley fled across the water,
And thus escaped the dreadful slaughter.
Eunice Allen see the Indians coming,
And hopes to save herself by running,
  And had not her petticoats stopped her,

The awful creatures had not catched her,
Nor tommy hawked her on her head,
And left her on the ground for dead.
Young Samuel Allen, Oh lack-a-day!
Was taken and carried to Canada.

BIBLIOGRAPHY

DANB; Dannett, Sylvia G. L. "America's First Negro Poet," *Profiles of Negro Womanhood* (1964); Holland, Josiah Gilbert. *History of Western Massachusetts* (1895); Kaplan, Sidney and Emma Nogrady Kaplan. "Lucy Terry Prince." In *The Black Presence in the Era of the American Revolution, 1770-1800*, ed. Sidney Kaplan (1989); Katz, William Loren. "Lucy and Abijah Prince," *The Black West* (1973); Proper, David R. "Lucy Terry Prince," unpublished manuscript (n.d.); Robinson, William H., Jr. "Lucy Terry." In *Early Black American Poets*, ed. William Henry Robinson (1969); Sheldon, George. *A History of Deerfield, Massachusetts* ([1895-96] 1972), and "Negro Slavery in Old Deerfield," *New England Magazine* (March 1893).

JAN FURMAN

PRINCE, NANCY GARDNER
(1799-c. 1856)

The preface to the second edition of Nancy Prince's autobiography, *A Narrative of the Life and Travels of Mrs. Nancy Prince* (1853), is brief, but it reflects the essential nature of her character: she was a courageous, resilient, fervently religious reformer who chose different paths from the ones that most women were expected to follow during the era of slavery, as mounting tensions led to the Civil War. Prince had traveled to Europe; she had lived and worked in Russia (1824-33) and Jamaica (1840-41; 1842), bridging cultural and geographical gaps in her fight against slavery, her evangelical work, and her advocacy for women's rights.

Nancy Gardner was born in 1799 in Newburyport, Massachusetts, to free parents. Her maternal grandfather, Tobias Wornton, a slave, fought at Bunker Hill; her maternal grandmother was a Native American captured by the English. Prince's father, Thomas Gardner—a Black seaman who survived at sea better than on land—died when she was three months old. Gardner's stepfather, Money Vose, entertained her with stories of his escape from slavery. After his death, Gardner's mother suffered a mental collapse and Gardner essentially took over the parenting role for six children. The family experienced dire poverty and homelessness, forcing Gardner, on one occasion, to rescue her sister from a brothel.

After marrying Nero Prince, a seaman, a founding member of the Prince Hall Freemasons, and a servant in Russia's imperial court in 1824, Prince traveled through Europe en route to Russia. Her narrative relates romantic and harrowing adventures in Russia, where Prince boarded children, operated a sewing business, and became involved in religious affairs.

Prince went to Jamaica in 1840 and 1842, believing she could help convert and educate Jamaica's emancipated slaves. Identifying with their struggles, she felt vindicated against apologists of slavery when she saw that newly freed Jamaicans could prosper. However, because of widespread violence between former slaves and masters, corruption within the ranks of evangelists, and their alleged abuse of her (she stated that they attempted to rob her), Prince made a perilous journey home.

Little is known of Prince after the 1856 edition of her narrative, but the aspects of her life that are omitted from the narrative—perhaps for her own protection—are just as revealing, such as her 1841 letter to William Lloyd Garrison protesting racist treatment aboard a steamboat, her leadership in attacking a slaveholder tracking a runaway (1847), and her participation in the 1854 National Woman's Rights Convention.

BIBLIOGRAPHY

Andrews, William L., ed. *Sisters of the Spirit: Three Black Women's Autobiographies of the Nineteenth Century* (1986); Barthelemy, Anthony G., ed. *Collected Black Women's Narratives* (1988); Blakely, Allison. *Russia and the Negro: Blacks in Russian History and Thought* (1986); Bolster, Jeffrey W. " 'To Feel Like a Man': Black Seamen in the Northern States, 1800-1860," *Journal of American History* (forthcoming); Curtin, Philip D. *Two Jamaicas: The Role of Ideas in a Tropical Colony, 1830-1865* (1955); Grimshaw, William H. *Official History of Freemasonry among the Colored People in North America* (1969); Loggins, Vernon. *The Negro Author* (1931); Loewenberg, Bert James and Ruth Bogin, eds. *Black Women in Nineteenth-Century American Life: Their Words, Their Thoughts, Their Feelings* (1976); Prince, Nancy. Letter to William Lloyd Garrison. *Liberator* (September 17, 1841); Prince, Nancy. "Announcement of Lecture on Russia." *Liberator* (March 8, 1839); Shockley, Ann Allen, ed. *Afro-American Women Writers, 1746-1933: An Anthology and Critical Guide* (1988); Spradling, Mary M., ed. *In Black and White* (1980); Sterling, Dorothy, ed. *We Are Your Sisters: Black Women in the Nineteenth Century* (1984); Walters, Ronald G. *A Black Woman's Odyssey through Russia and Jamaica: The Narrative of Nancy Prince* (1990).

AUSTRALIA TARVER HENDERSON

PROPHET, NANCY ELIZABETH (1890-1960)

Nancy Elizabeth Prophet was a master sculptor who studied in Europe and taught at Atlanta University and Spelman College. Prophet was born March 19, 1890, apparently the only child of William H. Prophet and Rose Walker Prophet, in Providence, Rhode Island. Her father was employed by the city. Her mother was a housewife. Prophet attended public school in Providence and as she advanced through the system, she exhibited an exceptional aptitude for art. Encouraged by her teachers and friends, she entered the renowned Rhode Island School of Design, often working as a domestic to pay her tuition.

After graduation Prophet lived for a brief period of time in New York City. This was the age of the Harlem Renaissance, and she wanted to go to France where she could study with master teachers and exhibit her work in the salons of Paris. With financial assistance from Gertrude Vanderbilt Whitney, Prophet went to Paris in 1922. She studied at l'Ecole Nationale des Beaux Arts from 1922-25. While in Europe, Prophet came to the attention of Henry Tanner, who was so impressed with her talent that he recommended her for the Harmon Foundation prize. She won this prestigious award, which included money she could use to support herself while she continued her studies.

Prophet returned to the United States in 1932 and was received in Newport, Rhode Island, society as a master sculptor. One year later, on the advice of her friend W.E.B. Du Bois she accepted a teaching position at Spelman College. By 1939, however, she had left Spelman and was working in the art department at Atlanta University. Prophet ostensibly realized that there was virtually no opportunity for her, as a Black woman, to become a part of the art community in Atlanta. And so, in 1945, she returned to Providence, where she expected to make a comeback. Unfortunately, she had lost contact with many of her supporters over the years. She could not obtain the financial backing needed to allow her to live as a sculptor. Having no other means of support, Prophet went to work as a domestic, just as she had done as a student twenty years earlier.

Prophet's most productive years were between 1920 and 1930, and she received several awards; for example, her *Head of a Negro* earned the Harmon Foundation prize for best sculpture in 1930. In 1932, at the annual meeting of the Newport Association, she won first prize (the Richard Greenbough Prize) for her sculpture *Discontent*, but because she was not a member of the association, she was initially ineligible to receive the award. The association hurriedly elected her to membership minutes before the show opened. This was a special honor for Prophet, because the exhibition included over 200 works by forty-one artists. Prophet's three other head carvings at this exhibit received excellent reviews from the judges.

Her work was exhibited in the Paris August Salons from 1924-27 and at the Salon d'Automne in 1931 and 1932. In the United States, Prophet's work was included in group exhibitions throughout the 1930s at the Harmon Foundation and the Whitney Sculpture Biennial. In 1978, her pieces were part of the "Four from Providence" exhibit at the Bannister Gallery of Rhode Island College. Other group exhibitions include the Bellevue Art Museum and the Art Association of America tour in 1985. Prophet's only known one-person exhibit was in 1945 at the Providence Public Library.

Prophet sculpted in both marble and stone. Her surviving sculptures are heads carved in wood in a style described as "stark, aggressive," "naturalistic and non-sentimental." Her subjects were always Black. Prophet's best-known sculpture is *Congolaise*, which she completed in 1930. It is not known who posed for this piece or for any of her other works, or even if she used a model. *Congolaise* is described as very similar to

a Masai tribesman, and this strong African influence is characteristic of the heads she sculpted. Prophet's other works include *Silence* and *Head in Ebony*. She eventually destroyed some of her pieces and others rotted out-of-doors because she could not afford to pay for storage. Consequently, very few of her works survive. Some of those that do are housed in the Black Heritage Society of Rhode Island in Providence, the Rhode Island School of Design, and the Whitney Museum of American Art in New York City.

Elizabeth Prophet died in 1960 in Providence in poverty and obscurity. In her lifetime she overcame the barriers of sex and race to become a respected sculptor, whose surviving works are a testimony to her special talent and race consciousness.

BIBLIOGRAPHY
CBWA; NBAW.

GLORIA V. WARREN

PROUT, MARY ANN (c. 1800-1884)

"During the early days of Bethel [African Methodist Episcopal Church] when it was poor and in debt, she was constantly devising ways and means of

Although her work was exhibited at Paris salons and at the Whitney Sculpture Biennial, Nancy Elizabeth Prophet ended her life working as a domestic, and few of her works survive. [National Archives]

relieving it. She lived to a great old age and was never married." These words, from Sylvia G. Dannett's *Profiles of Negro Womanhood, 1619-1900* (1964), sum up the life of Mary Ann Prout, reformer, educator, and church worker.

Prout was born in Baltimore, Maryland, in 1800 or 1801. According to Dannett she was born a slave, but the papers of Daniel Murray indicate that she and her two older brothers, William A. and Jacob W., were born free and were of mixed African parents. Since William and Jacob immigrated to Liberia—a colony in West Africa for free Negroes—in 1824 and 1834, respectively, it is probable that the Prout siblings were free persons.

While there is no evidence of where or how the Prouts were educated, all records that mention them refer to their intelligence and superior education. All three were noted teachers and lecturers and made their mark historically. William was for a time governor of Liberia, and Jacob's son Samuel was postmaster general of that country for many years.

Mary Ann Prout remained in Baltimore. In 1820 or 1830, depending on the source, she founded the Day School and taught there until 1867. It was presumably this school that kept her in the United States when her brothers immigrated to Africa.

The year that the school closed, Prout founded a secret order from which evolved the Independent Order of St. Luke. Early in her life Prout had recognized the need for a Black organization that would administer financial aid to the sick and ensure proper burial for the dead. Later, there was a split in the order. The part that split off was headquartered in Richmond, Virginia, and was developed by Maggie Lena Walker into one of the most significant financial institutions in Black American history. Walker always credited Prout as founder of the order.

That same year, 1867, the Gregory Aged Women's Home officially opened in Baltimore. Prout was the president of the association in charge of the home and was one of its two Black trustees.

Prout was, throughout her life, a dedicated member of the Bethel AME Church, where she belonged to a group called the Daughters of Conference and appears to have been an active member of the choir. She died in 1884 in Baltimore.

BIBLIOGRAPHY

Baltimore Afro-American Ledger (October 31, 1903); Bragg, George F., Jr., ed. *Men of Maryland* (1925); Daniel, Sadie Iola. *Women Builders* (1970); Graham, Leroy. *Baltimore: The Nineteenth Black Capital* (1982); Major, Monroe. *Noted Negro Women: Their Triumphs and Activities* ([1893] 1986); *NAW*; Wolff, Jane and Eleanor McKay. *The Papers of Daniel Murray* (1977).

MARGARET REID

Q

QUAKERS

After the American Revolution, members of the Society of Friends (Quakers) often encouraged slaves and freedmen to adopt their religious practices. However, many Quakers did not want people of color to join their group officially, favoring instead separate meetings for Black Friends conducted under their guidance. Rather than bowing to discrimination and accepting the racial homogeneity of meetings, a few African-American women attended the predominantly white meetings and sought official membership in the Society of Friends. Their actions, which usually met with formidable opposition, demonstrate the determination of African-American Friends to adhere to their religious beliefs and fight intolerance.

In 1781, Abigail Franks applied to join the meeting in Delaware County, Pennsylvania. Because she was "half-white, one-eighth Negro, and three-eighths Indian," a committee was formed to look into her membership application (Cadbury 1936). Although the committee reported being pleased with her sincerity and her skin color, her application was not immediately accepted; rather, it was referred to the yearly meeting. Finally approved in 1784, her membership made Franks the first person of color to belong to the American Society of Friends.

Franks's eventual success did not wipe out Quaker sentiments of racial exclusivity, however. When Cynthia Miers sought membership, her application generated so much debate that her case was first forwarded to the quarterly meeting and then to the yearly meeting. (Quaker polity works on the basis of consensus.) Outraged at her treatment, Quaker John Wiggins decried the Friends who deemed it "unsafe to receive her on account of her color" (Cadbury 1936). In 1796, the yearly meeting finally approved her application, ruling that "membership in the Society of Friends was not limited with respect to nation or colour."

This ruling may have played a role in the 1799 decision to make David and Grace Mapps members of the Little Egg Harbor Meeting. However, questions about whether some Friends would feel uncomfortable sitting next to them continued to arise. At a dinner party, for example, their host circumvented a challenging situation by saying to his guests, "David Mapps and his wife will come with me; and as I like to have all accommodated, those who object to dining with them can wait til they have done."

Their daughter, Grace A. Mapps, also was a practicing Quaker. After graduating from college at McGrawville, New York, in 1852 (making her one of the first African-American women to receive a college degree), Mapps became principal of the girl's department of the Institute for Colored Youth, a Friends high school in Philadelphia, in 1853, a position she held until 1864. In addition to teaching Greek, Mapps wrote poetry; one of her poems appeared in the *Anglo-African* magazine in 1859.

Sarah Mapps Douglass, an in-law of Grace A. Mapps, was a Quaker and one of the first members of the Philadelphia Female Anti-Slavery Society. She also belonged to the Anti-Slavery Women of the United States and attended their 1837 New York convention. Her solid academic background, attained by expensive private tutoring, enabled her to lecture on physiology and hygiene. In 1853, with extensive teaching experience, Douglass went to work at the Preparatory Department of the Institute for Colored Youth, where she remained until 1877. Besides teaching, she was involved in numerous activities, including serving as the vice chair of the Women's Pennsylvania branch of the American Freedman's Aid Commission after the Civil War.

In spite of her accomplishments, Douglass was deterred from formally joining the Society of Friends because non-European applicants were discouraged from applying for membership. Intolerance did not prevent her from adhering to her religious faith and attending Quaker meetings, however. Following in the footsteps of her mother, Grace Bustill Douglass, and her grandfather, Douglass became a practicing, albeit unofficial, member. She attended meetings even though she was forced to sit in the "Negro pew" and even though many members refused to associate with her. On the few occasions when white Friends would sit next to her, other Quakers voiced their disapproval. Sarah Grimké commented in a letter to Elizabeth Pease (April 18, 1840), "I do not think the present generation have or would receive a colored member. I have heard it assigned as a reason that of course no white member would marry them and then if they infringed the Discipline they must be disowned." Sarah Grimké and her sister, Angelina, as well as Lucretia Mott, three white Quaker women, became friends of Douglass and denounced her mistreatment. Eventually Sarah Mapps Douglass, recognizing the futility of her struggle to be accepted as an equal in the Society of Friends, left this church and joined her father's First African Presbyterian Church. But her mother, Grace Bustill Douglass, continued to attend Quaker meetings and press for acceptance of Black Friends on an equal basis.

Although only a small circle of nineteenth-century African-American women were affiliated with Quakerism, meeting records demonstrate the extent of their participation at services. For example, nineteenth-century African-American poet Hetty Saunders, described as "a Friend in everything except official membership," was buried in the Friends Cemetery in 1862 (Cadbury 1936). Sarah Antone's appearance in the records of the 1875 New Bedford,

Massachusetts, meetings indicates that she was a practicing Quaker, and Emily Rodman Williams officially joined the Friends in 1891.

African-American sociologist Vera Green, herself a Quaker since 1961, found Black people reluctant to join the Society of Friends, which, at the time of her survey, had a membership of less than one percent African-American. According to her survey, many Black respondents felt that Friends meetings seldom focused on issues pertaining to African-Americans, Puerto Ricans, or the Third World; also peace testimony was sometimes seen as reminiscent of "the former passivity forced on blacks" (Ives 1986). For many reasons, political as well as religious, African-Americans remain underrepresented at Quaker meetings.

BIBLIOGRAPHY

Cadbury, Henry. "Negro Membership in the Society of Friends," *Journal of Negro History* (1936); Ives, Kenneth. *Black Quakers: Brief Biographies* (1986); Soderlund, Jean. *Quakers and Slavery: A Divided Spirit* (1985).

NICOLETTA KARAM

QUARLES, NORMA R. (1936-)

As the first woman in New York City to coanchor a six P.M. news program, television journalist Norma R. Quarles is a pioneer in the field of broadcasting, paving the way for women in a traditionally male-dominated domain. She has won many awards for her incisive reporting, including an Emmy, and she was inducted into the National Association of Black Journalists Hall of Fame in 1990.

Norma Quarles was born in New York City on November 11, 1936. She is an alumna of Hunter College and City College of New York. She began her career first as a retail buyer and then as a real estate broker from 1957 to 1965, when she moved into the field of broadcasting as a reporter, disc jockey, and public service director for WSDM Radio in Chicago. The following year, Quarles transferred to television and attended a one-year news training program sponsored by NBC in New York. In 1967, she moved to Cleveland, Ohio, where she was news reporter and anchor for WKYC-TV for three years. She then went back to WNBC-TV in New York, this time as a reporter. While filling in as host of a women's show for three weeks, Quarles performed so well that the network offered her the position of anchor of the six P.M. newscast—the first time a woman had been given such a significant broadcasting position in New York.

In her work for WNBC over the next twenty-one years, Quarles was the recipient of many awards. In 1973, her news reporting about the documentary *The Stripper* won Quarles the Front Page Award. That same year she also was awarded a Sigma Delta Chi Deadline Club Award. While working for WMAQ-TV, the NBC affiliate in Chicago, Quarles received an Emmy Award for outstanding reporting on her

Urban Journal series. In 1984, she was chosen as a panelist for the League of Women Voters-sponsored vice presidential debate. Quarles is a member of the National Academy of Television Arts and Sciences and Sigma Delta Chi, and she is a member of the board of governor's of the National Academy of Television Arts and Sciences.

Norma Quarles left NBC in 1988 to join Cable News Network (CNN), where she has served as coanchor of the *Daybreak* and *Daywatch* programs.

Emmy Award-winning reporter Norma Quarles was the first woman to anchor a six P.M. newscast in New York City. She is currently a correspondent and reporter for Cable News Network, based in CNN's New York office. [CNN]

She also is a correspondent and reporter based in CNN's New York office. Divorced, she is the mother of two children, Lawrence and Susan. A notable success in her own right, Norma Quarles has also helped open doors for a new generation of women and Black reporters.

BIBLIOGRAPHY

Cable News Network (CNN). "Norma Quarles Biography" (1990); *CBWA*; *Ebony*, "Upsurge in TV News Girls" (June 1971); *EBA*; Gelfman, Judith S. *Women in Television News* (1976); *NA*; *NBAW*; Scheuer, Steven H., ed. *Who's Who in Television and Cable* (1983); *WWBA* (1992).

FENELLA MACFARLANE

R

RADIO

There are more than 12,000 radio and television stations, commercial and noncommercial, operating in the United States. Black women comprise approximately 4.5 percent of the total number of employees. They hold positions in virtually every aspect of the industry as owners and managers, sales employees, technicians, and professionals. Radio has been the beneficiary of the rich contributions made by Black American women since the 1920s when broadcasting developed. Through music, drama, and comedy, as on-air personalities, station managers, and owners, Black women have been integral to shaping the contours of American broadcasting.

MUSIC

Among the Black women who made early contributions to radio was singer Bessie Smith, whose live blues performance was transmitted across the South from Beale Street over a Memphis radio station in 1924. Throughout the 1920s, 1930s, and 1940s, Black women across the nation stepped before microphones and poured out their souls in song and music to radio audiences. Gospel singer Lucille Barbee continued the live tradition well into the 1960s on Nashville's WVOL.

Women were also members of groups such as the Hampton Singers, who performed on radio in New York City in 1924. Women's voices were vital to the renowned spiritual singing group Wings over Jordan, which performed many years over NBC radio on Sunday mornings during the 1930s. The autobiographies of Tom Fletcher (1954) and Perry Bradford (1965), and the biography of Eubie Blake (Rose 1979), are sprinkled with citations on contributions made to radio by gifted Black women such as Artie Bell McGinty, Adelaide Hall, and Eva "The Dixie Nightingale" Taylor.

DRAMA AND COMEDY

When network radio programmers turned away from music shows and embraced drama and vaudeville-style comedy in the 1930s, the rate of Black performances dropped noticeably. Network drama producers ignored Black actors almost completely. Exceptions were the fine performances of Rose McClendon and Dorothy Caul who performed on *John Henry, Black River Giant*. In the early 1950s, the National Negro Network produced and aired a soap opera, *The Ruby Valentine Story*, featuring the highly acclaimed actress Juanita Hall, who had starred in the Broadway musical *South Pacific*. However, by that time, network radio drama was a dying art form and negative Black images predominated.

Blackface minstrelsy, promulgated in radio by the enormous success of the *Amos 'n' Andy Show*, forced Black women to accept demeaning, stereotypical roles to survive. Amanda Randolph applied considerable talents to the role of Sapphire's nagging mother, Mama, on the *Amos 'n' Andy Show*, and Ernestine Wade, in the role of Sapphire, was directed to act in broken English as white producers perceived "negroes" to speak. Hattie McDaniel, who won an Academy Award for her role in *Gone with the Wind*, initially showcased her "mammy" character on KNX radio in Los Angeles and joined the network series *Showboat* in the early 1930s. Later, McDaniel magnificently played the lead role of maid in the radio network series *Beulah*. Georgia Burke was cast stereotypically as a humorous maid in the radio soap opera *Betty and Bob*.

RADIO PERSONALITIES

Some talented Black actors and entertainers got an opportunity to help improve and reshape the image of Black Americans in broadcasting when network radio declined after World War II and disc jockeys became popular by playing recorded music. In 1947,

there were seventeen known Black American radio disc jockeys in the United States. By 1951, at least nine women attracted national recognition for excellence in their respective markets: Cecilia Violenes at WWRL in New York; Carrie Terrell and Helen Lawrence at WERD in Atlanta; Ruth Ellington James at WLIB in New York City; Roberta Polk at WEDR in Birmingham; Jessie Morris at WFPG in Atlantic City; Willa Monroe at WDIA in Memphis; France White at WOOK in Washington, D.C.; and Mary Dee at WHOD in Homestead, Pennsylvania. On the national scene, Una Mae Carlisle was broadcasting coast to coast daily on the American Broadcasting Company.

Women air personalities were essential to the dissemination of new Black music, bebop and rhythm and blues. They also pioneered radio station outreach service programs in communities and helped lead a radio movement that informed the disenfranchised about politics, health care, culture, economics, and

Hattie McDaniel, seen here with a group of students at a Black college, won an Academy Award for her performance in the film Gone with the Wind. She initially showcased her mammy character on KNX radio in Los Angeles, and later joined the radio casts of Showboat and Beulah. [National Archives]

spiritual life. They helped restore humanness to the public Black image.

Their contributions laid the groundwork for the next generation of legends, Black women broadcasters such as Vivian Carter, Dorothy Brunson, Bernadine Washington, Martha Jean "The Queen" Steinberg, and Yvonne Daniels (who earned the title "First Lady of Chicago Radio"). Daniels was perennially number one among listeners of Chicago's WSDM-FM, which featured an all-female lineup in the 1970s. Earlier in her career she was a noted jazz authority at WCFL-AM, a 50,000-watt radio station in Chicago. She died in 1991.

MANAGEMENT AND OWNERSHIP

Many of these Black women were businesswomen. Vivian Carter, in addition to her air personality work, cofounded and managed Chicago's famous Vee Jay Record Company, which became a major program supplier for radio stations nationally and internationally. Also in Chicago, Bernadine Washington, having established a reputation in community affairs and service, became one of the nation's first Black female station managers in 1975 at WVON-AM and WSDM-FM. Vernele Blackburn later managed WVON, and in Detroit, Verna Green used her MBA from Michigan State University to take WJLB from the bottom of the pack to become the perennial leader.

Dorothy Brunson, the first African-American female to own a radio station, commenced her distinguished radio career in accounting and moved into broadcast management with Sonderling Broadcast. She purchased her first properties in 1979. She is president of her own corporation—one that wholly owns broadcast and cable operations.

Martha Jean "The Queen" Steinberg earned national recognition for outstanding air personality and community work in Memphis and Detroit, where she combined station management and co-ownership with her other talents. She is among more than a dozen Black women who own and manage radio stations. Prime examples are Mary Bell, Detroit; Mutter Evans in Raleigh; Kathy Hughes in Washington, D.C.; and Nancy Waters in Hart, Michigan.

Collectively, African-American women have competed successfully in the white male business environment of radio, employed and trained thousands of men and women, and excelled in all aspects of the business.

BIBLIOGRAPHY

Blackburn, Verlene. Telephone interview (September 6, 1991); Bradford, Perry. *Born with the Blues* (1965);

Stage, screen, and recording star Ethel Waters was among the Black entertainers who also performed on radio. [Donald Bogle]

Brunson, Dorothy. Telephone interview (August 28, 1991); Chenault, Julie. "Verna Green," *Essence* (July 1984); *Ebony*, "New Radio Station in Michigan" (April 1957); *Ebony*, "Speaking of People, Cecilia Violenes" (July 1952); *Ebony*, "Una Mae Carlisle, Only Negro Musician with Coast to Coast Radio Show" (January 1951); Fletcher, Tom. *100 Years of the Negro in Show Business* (1954); *Jet*, "Bernadine

Washington: First Black Woman Radio GM, VP" (March 16, 1975); *Jet*, "Yvonne Daniels, First Lady of Chicago Radio, Succumbs" (July 1991); Kahlenberg, Richard S. "Negro Radio," *Negro History Bulletin* (March 1966); McCoy, Sid. Telephone interview (September 9, 1991); McDonald, J. Fred. *Don't Touch That Dial: Radio Programming in American Life, 1920-1960* (1979); Morrow, Herman. Telephone interview (September 10, 1991); *Our World*, "The Captain's Mate" (September 1951); *Our World*, "Crashing New Employment Field, Negro Women Are Winning Recognition as Radio Disc Jockeys" (August 1951); *Our World*, "Lady Is a Huckster" (February 1952); *Our World*, "Ruby Valentine" (April 1954); Redd, Lawrence N. *Rock Is Rhythm and Blues* (1974); Rose, Al. *Eubie* (1979); Ross, Mark. "The Rapid Ascent of Mutter Evans," *Black Enterprise* (December 1980); *United States Federal Communications Commission Reports*, "Waters Broadcasting Company" (December 1981); Washington, Bernadine. Telephone interview (August 29, 1991).

LAWRENCE N. REDD

RAINEY, MA (1886-1939)

In a Black theater in 1925, curtains open to reveal a huge hand-cranked Victrola. A slim chorus girl approaches the giant stage prop and puts an oversized record on the turntable, and from inside the machine a full, gravelly voice sings the popular hit "Moonshine Blues." Then the phonograph doors open and out steps a short, dark woman with broad features and luminous eyes, wearing a necklace of gold coins and a satin dress glittering with spangles and sequins. Her name is Ma Rainey, the earliest well-known woman blues singer. Her style, the Classic Blues, was a female-dominated mixture of folk blues and Black professional entertainment that flourished in the 1920s. She was a great vocalist, comedienne, and songwriter; a star in minstrelsy, vaudeville, and recording; a dancer, producer, and theater manager. She sang blues as early as 1902, earning the title Mother of the Blues, and leads a great tradition of women blues singers from Bessie Smith and Memphis Minnie to Big Mama Thornton, Koko Taylor, and many others.

She was born Gertrude Pridgett on April 26, 1886, in Columbus, Georgia, the second of Thomas and Ella Allen Pridgett's five children. Her family came from Alabama, and a grandmother may have been in show business after Emancipation. At the age of fourteen she debuted in "A Bunch of Blackberries," a revue at the Springer Opera House in Columbus, and she trained professionally in southern minstrel shows, where she first heard the blues in Missouri

around 1902 and added them to her act. On February 2, 1904, she married William "Pa" Rainey, a singing comedian, and performed with him as Rainey and Rainey, Assassinators of the Blues.

In her mid-teens she was already an established minstrel star and soon became leader of the famed Rabbit Foot Minstrels. These Black variety shows included jugglers, acrobats, chorus lines, and comedians, but "Madame" Rainey was the star, singing blues and ragtime tunes, flirting outrageously with the young men in her band, and dancing nimbly despite her weight. The shows traveled by train, following cotton and tobacco harvests in the South and Midwest, and performing under a large circus tent with a portable wooden stage and Coleman lanterns for footlights.

Sometime during her minstrel days Rainey worked with Bessie Smith, whose fame would one day eclipse her own. Despite popular legend, she never kidnapped Smith or taught her to sing, but the two were close friends, and as a young chorus girl Smith clearly was impressed with the older star. They also may have been lovers: both were bisexual, and Rainey later recorded a frankly lesbian song, "Prove It on Me."

Madame Rainey ran a disciplined show and paid employees on time, unlike many managers who stranded their companies on the road. Fellow performers have recalled her warmth and the way she encouraged younger musicians. She even adopted a son, Danny, billed as "the world's Youngest Juvenile Stepper," who sang, danced, and did female impersonations in her show (*Chicago Defender*). Because of her age (she was at least ten years older than most performers), her nurturing personality, and her act with Pa Rainey, she gained the nickname "Ma."

By the 1920s she had separated from Pa Rainey, and in 1923, at the age of thirty-seven, she emerged from the rural tent-show circuit to national stardom through a recording contract with Chicago-based Paramount Records. Although popular Harlem entertainer Mamie Smith made the first Black blues recording in 1920, sparking a nationwide blues craze, Ma Rainey brought an authentic Deep-South sound to the blues. Dubbing her "the Mother of the Blues," Paramount aggressively promoted her in the Black press, especially the *Chicago Defender*. Her records were sold to southerners by mail order and to northerners through stores in Black neighborhoods.

From 1923 to 1928 she recorded at least ninety-two songs for Paramount, with accompanists ranging from jazz greats to downhome slide guitarists and jug bands. Superbly backed by Louis Armstrong, she made the first recording of the blues standard "See, See Rider," and her rich contralto, slurs and moans, and lisping diction deeply moved her audience, whether struggling down South or homesick up North.

Her brisk record sales resulted in tours on the Theater Owners' Booking Association (T.O.B.A. or Toby-time) circuit, a network of Black vaudeville theaters in southern and midwestern cities. Working conditions could be feudal, and lesser acts grumbled that T.O.B.A. meant "tough on Black asses," but

these tours brought Ma Rainey standing-room-only audiences and national exposure (Albertson 1972). Her arranger and band director on the road was future gospel composer Thomas A. Dorsey.

A white singer with her talent would have earned more money, but Ma Rainey lived well. She dressed in diamonds and bought a house in Georgia and a $13,000 touring bus with a power generator to light her tent shows. Like most Black musicians, though, she was paid a flat fee for recording sessions, and she

One of the last great minstrel artists—shown here in performance in a touring show—and one of the first professional woman blues singers, Ma Rainey was dubbed "Mother of the Blues" when her classic recordings were first issued in the 1920s. [AP/Wide World Photos]

never received royalties. Unlike most blues women of her day, she composed more than a third of the songs she recorded.

By the late 1920s her style was threatened by competition from radio, talking pictures, and the emergence of swing music. Record companies began recording male country blues singers for much lower fees, and in 1928 her Paramount contract was canceled. Ma Rainey continued to tour the ailing Toby-time and tent-show circuits, but Paramount went bankrupt in the early 1930s, and the Great Depression killed Black vaudeville.

Her recording and vaudeville days were over, and when her sister, Malissa, died in 1935, Ma Rainey retired from active performance, returning to Columbus to live with her family; that same year her mother died. During this time she purchased and managed the Lyric and Airdrome theaters in Rome, Georgia, and in later life she joined the Friendship Baptist Church where her brother, Thomas Pridgett, Jr., was a deacon. On December 22, 1939, at the age of fifty-three, she died of heart disease and was buried in the family plot in Porterdale Cemetery in Columbus. The Black press ignored her passing, and her death certificate lists her occupation as housekeeping.

Ma Rainey was one of the last great minstrel artists and one of the first professional woman blues singers. She was Paramount's most recorded female star and one of its best-selling artists. Because of her lisp and heavy Georgia accent, because Paramount lacked the superior recording facilities of larger companies, and because her recordings were played so often, surviving seventy-eights are frequently scratchy or unclear, and her LP reissues suffer in comparison to Bessie Smith's. Nonetheless, her records should be heard and reheard for their timeless songs of wandering lives, broken family ties, and disappointed love affairs, as well as for their humor, strength, and resilience in new environments.

Ma Rainey has continued to influence other Black artists. Country blues singer Memphis Minnie recorded a tribute in 1940; poets Sterling Brown and Al Young wrote about her in the 1920s and 1960s, respectively; and August Wilson's critically acclaimed 1984 Broadway play, *Ma Rainey's Black Bottom*, testifies to her continuing vitality for Black culture.

BIBLIOGRAPHY

Albertson, Chris. *Bessie* (1972), and Liner notes. In *Oh My Babe Blues: Ma Rainey, Volume 2* (1989); Barlow, William. *Looking Up at Down: The Emergence of Blues Culture* (1989); Brown, Sterling A. "Ma Rainey." In his *The Collected Poems of Sterling A. Brown* (1980); *BWW*; Dixon, Robert M. W.

and John Godrich. *Blues and Gospel Records, 1902-1943* (1982); Evans, David. *Big Road Blues* (1982); Fulbright, Thomas. "Ma Rainey and I," *Jazz Journal* (March 1956); Harrison, Daphne Duval. *Black Pearls: Blues Queens of the 1920s* (1988); Lieb, Sandra. *Mother of the Blues: A Study of Ma Rainey* (1981); *NAW*; Oliver, Paul. *Blues Fell This Morning: The Meaning of the Blues* (1961), and *The Story of the Blues* (1969); Pridgett, Thomas. "The Life of Ma Rainey," *Jazz Information* (September 6, 1940); Stewart-Baxter, Derrick. *Ma Rainey and the Classic Blues Singers* (1970); Titon, Jeff Todd. *Early Downhome Blues: A Musical and Cultural Analysis* (1977); Young, Al. "A Dance for Ma Rainey." In *Dancing; poems* (1969).

DISCOGRAPHY

(Unless noted otherwise, all are monophonic 33-1/3 LPs.) *Blues the World Forgot, 1924-28*. Biograph 12001; *Complete Recordings in Chronological Order* (British). VJM VLP 81 (LP, cassette, and CD); *The Immortal Ma Rainey*. Milestone M-2001; *Ma Rainey*. Milestone M-47021 (2-album set); *Ma Rainey's Black Bottom*. Yazoo 1071; *Oh My Babe Blues, Vol. 2, 1924-28*. Biograph 12011; *Queen of the Blues, Vol. 3, 1923-24*. Biograph 12032.

FILM/VIDEOTAPE

Wild Women Don't Have the Blues. Video, California Newsreel (1989).

SANDRA LIEB

RANDOLPH, AMANDA (1902-1967)

Amanda Randolph was a gifted actress and singer whose talents far outweighed the opportunities she received in the course of her long stage, radio, television, and film career.

Amanda Randolph was born in 1902 in Louisville, Kentucky. Gifted with musical talent and a powerful singing voice, she began performing at age fourteen in Cleveland's musical comedies and night clubs. She toured Europe in 1930 with the Scott and Whaley show. In 1932, Randolph and Catherine Handy, daughter of composer W. C. Handy, sang together as the "Dixie Nightingales," appearing in several shows, including the Glenn and Jenkins Revue. During the 1930s, she performed in several hit musical revues such as *Chilli Peppers, Dusty Lane*, and *Radiowaves*.

Randolph's film career probably began in 1936, the year she appeared in the musical short, *The Black Network*. This film and others, such as *Lying Lips* (1939) and *The Notorious Elinor Lee* (1940), written and produced by Oscar Micheaux and in which Randolph appeared, belonged to the genre called race movies, so named for their focus on Black American characters and plot lines designed to appeal to a Black audience. Although often of poor technical quality, these films offered a fairer representation of Black life than did most Hollywood productions. During the 1940s, Randolph and her sister, Lillian, were featured on the long-running and extremely popular radio show *Amos 'n' Andy*. Randolph also worked on other radio productions during this time, such as *Kitty Foyle* and *Big Sister*.

During the 1950s, Randolph appeared in several Hollywood movies, including *She's Working Her Way Through College* (1952) featuring Ronald Reagan. In this film and many others, Randolph was consigned to comic roles as maids and housekeepers. Repeatedly assigned such stereotypical roles, Randolph was unable to perform to the full extent of her talent. Although many postwar films attempted to portray Black American men in a more favorable light, the situation of limited roles for Black women changed little during Randolph's career.

Also during the 1950s, Randolph made the transition to television. She was one of only two members of the radio cast to be accepted for the television version of *Amos 'n' Andy*, which, despite the controversy that led to its cancellation in 1955, was the first television series to feature an all-Black cast. In 1953, Randolph was assigned the role of the family housekeeper, Louise, on *The Danny Thomas Show* (also known as *Make Room for Daddy*), a popular show that ran for more than a decade. Amanda Randolph died, following a stroke, in 1967.

Despite the limited parts to which she was consigned, Amanda Randolph brought dignity to the tough-talking character she so often played. The long, cold stare directed at a foolish or pretentious character was something she had honed to perfection, as was the flagrant scorn she conveyed by a special roll of her eyes. Beyond this characterization, however, was a wealth of talent rarely drawn upon. Films such as *The Black Network* (1936), one of the few in which Randolph was given an opportunity to demonstrate her deep singing voice, suggest that, had richer roles come her way, Amanda Randolph would be much better known today.

BIBLIOGRAPHY

BAFT; Brooks, Tim and Earl Marsh. *The Complete Directory to Prime Time Network TV Shows, 1946-Present* (1985); Cripps, Thomas. *Slow Fade to Black: The Negro in American Film, 1900-1940* (1977); *Ebony*, "Negroes Get Better Roles in TV Than in Any Other Entertainment" (June 1950); Klotman, Phyllis Rauch. *Frame by Frame: A Black Filmography* (1979); *NBAW*; *New York Times*, "Amanda Randolph, Actress in 'Amos 'n' Andy,' Was 65" (August 25, 1967); Sampson, Henry T. *Blacks in Black and White: A Source Book on Black Films* (1977); Terrace, Vincent. *Radio's Golden Years: The Encyclopedia of Radio Programs, 1930-1960* (1981).

FENELLA MACFARLANE

RANDOLPH, LUCILLE CAMPBELL GREEN (1883-1963)

Lucille Randolph was the wife of activist A. Philip Randolph and provided critical financial assistance for his publication, the *Messenger*. The youngest of seven children of William and Josephine Campbell, former slaves, Lucille Campbell was born April 15, 1883, in Christiansburg, a small town in western Virginia.

To enhance her skills as a teacher, she attended Howard University, where she met a law student named William Joseph Green. After he graduated in 1911, they married and moved to New York City, where he worked in the U.S. Customs Service, but he soon died.

Her life took a new turn. By 1914, she had gone into business with Amy E. Weddington, operating a Madam Walker beauty parlor on West 135th Street, and she had met and married another newcomer from the South, A. Philip Randolph. In 1915, after she met Chandler Owen at a party at Madam Walker's, she introduced her new friend to her new husband, and Owen became his partner and a central figure in his development.

When A. Philip Randolph and Chandler Owen began publishing the *Messenger* in 1917, Lucille Randolph's earnings at the beauty salon produced crucial financing for the enterprise. Speaking for himself and for Owen about those early years, A. Philip Randolph later said, "She carried us." More specifically, he declared that without his wife's money, "We couldn't have started the *Messenger*" (Anderson 1973). It was the *Messenger* that brought him to the attention of the people who, in 1925, asked him to take the lead in organizing what became the Brotherhood of Sleeping Car Porters, the foundation for all his subsequent work.

By the mid-1920s, her beauty business had faded, and in subsequent years she appears to have spent much of her time in community work, particularly with the men and women in porters' families. While he spent much of his time traveling about the country, and she stayed in Manhattan, they kept in touch by mail, "Buddy" writing "Buddy," as their limited surviving correspondence from the 1940s and 1950s shows. They had no children. By the early 1950s, she was an invalid. She died in New York on April 12, 1963, just months before her husband led the great March on Washington.

BIBLIOGRAPHY

Anderson, Jervis. *A. Philip Randolph: A Biographical Portrait* (1973); Dufty, William. "A Post Portrait: A. Philip Randolph," *New York Post* (December 29, 1959); Pfeffer, Paula F. *A. Philip Randolph, Pioneer of the Civil Rights Movement* (1990).

PETER WALLENSTEIN

RANDOLPH, VIRGINIA ESTELLE
(1874-1958)

Virginia Estelle Randolph was born June 8, 1874, to former slaves Sarah Elizabeth Carter and Edward Nelson Randolph, in Richmond, Virginia. The former owner of Randolph's mother, a professor at Old Richmond College, witnessed the parents' marriage and was responsible for naming each of the four children. Virginia's mother, widowed when her youngest child was only one month old, worked day and night to afford the rent on their one-room dwelling. According to Randolph, other necessities were provided by white friends and those who employed her mother as a domestic. The second oldest of the four children, Randolph attributed her discipline, self-reliance, creativity, and belief in God to her mother. She was reared in Virginia during the turbulent Reconstruction period and began her teaching career just six years prior to *Plessy v. Ferguson* (1896), which endorsed "separate but equal" facilities and privileges for Black and white Americans. Thus, times were socially, economically, and politically difficult.

In 1880, at age six, Randolph enrolled in the Baker School in Richmond. She was an excellent student and received a medal for highest honors at the end of her first term. At sixteen, in 1890, she passed her teaching examination but she was too young to qualify for a school. Because an uncle assumed full responsibility for her, she was given a job teaching in Goochland County. Two years later, she passed another exam for a more challenging position at the one-room Mountain Road School in Henrico County.

Randolph enrolled fourteen boys and girls on the first day at the Mountain Road School. She immedi-

ately improved the condition of the school building and the grounds. To support structural repairs and educational services, Randolph organized a Willing Workers Club and a Patrons Improvement League. With the support of the league, Randolph purchased twelve sycamore trees for the school grounds. Each tree was named for a disciple. As a result of the tree-planting campaign, Randolph was the first individual in the state of Virginia to celebrate Arbor Day.

Jackson T. Davis, the first appointed superintendent of Negro instruction in Henrico County, Virginia, was impressed with Virginia Estelle Randolph and the Mountain Road School when he inspected the Black schools in the county in 1902. Davis's educational beliefs were reinforced by industrial education for Black Americans, which he observed while visiting Hampton Institute. Convinced that Randolph's teaching methods should be communicated to other Black teachers in one-room rural schools throughout and the state, Davis sought funds from the Anna Thomas Jeanes Fund, which had been established in the name of a Philadelphia Quaker for the purpose of providing financial assistance to Black rural schools. Davis's request was approved on October 26, 1908, and Randolph became the first Jeanes Supervising Industrial Teacher.

As a Jeanes Teacher, Randolph administered, supported, and/or coordinated activities that ensured professional growth for rural teachers and, at the same time, provided resources and information to meet community needs. Teacher training and supervision were acute problems; adults needed literacy training and self-help projects to improve nutrition, health care, and hygiene. Randolph provided the link needed between the schools and the communities.

Randolph's ideas were practical, simple, and reflective of the needs of an agrarian rural community. She believed in the all-around development of the child. She taught girls to cook and sew and boys to make useful handicrafts from honeysuckle vines and hickory. In addition, Randolph believed in the industrial training philosophy that taught manual skills as well as religious and moral precepts. She argued that a mind is of little value if one has not learned to use one's hands. She was undoubtedly influenced by Booker T. Washington, a graduate of Hampton Institute. In addition to reading, writing, and arithmetic, Hampton's industrial education program taught gardening, woodworking, serving, and cooking. Most of all, students were trained to be resourceful, self-reliant, obedient, and docile.

The emphasis on manual labor and docility caused grave concerns, and at times Randolph met resistance. All parents were not interested in having their children taught industrial skills; rather, they wanted their children to learn the "classical or liberal arts." Some teachers were unaccepting of Randolph's industrial training, too. However, possessed of an indomitable spirit, Randolph eventually secured the support of her opponents.

Randolph received the William E. Harmon Award for Distinguished Achievement in 1926; she was the first Black American to receive this award. That year she was also honored by the Richmond Community Fund and the Black teachers of Henrico County. As a further testament to her work, a Virginia Estelle Randolph Fund was established to assist boys and girls in southern rural schools.

Although she never married, Randolph usually had at least a dozen children living in her home. She owned a private bus that transported them to and from school and over her lifetime she gave shelter to approximately fifty-nine children. Randolph was not selective in her support; she assisted the juvenile youth, the handicapped, and the rural poor.

Randolph retired in 1949, after a long and productive career as an educator, social worker, and humanitarian. As the first Jeanes Supervisor, she provided the first formal in-service teacher training for rural Black teachers, which led eventually to improved educational preparation and certification. She introduced supervision for Black teachers and organized community development through adult education activities. Randolph's work improved dramatically the educational practices of the rural one-room southern schools. The school term lengthened, attendance improved, school buildings were maintained, and county training schools for teacher training were introduced. The county training schools later developed into secondary schools. Moreover, she accomplished these changes during an era that supported a "separate and unequal" public school system.

Virginia Estelle Randolph died March 16, 1958. In 1970, the old Mountain Road School was dedicated as a museum in her honor. It is one of the few in the South to honor a Black female educator. In 1976, the Virginia Historic Landmarks Commission dedicated the Virginia E. Randolph Museum and the ten remaining original sycamore trees as a National and State Historic Landmark.

BIBLIOGRAPHY

Brawley, Benjamin. *Doctor Dillard of the Jeanes Fund* (1971); Bristow, Eliza Stickley. "Her Level Best: The Story of a Brave Woman," typescript (n.d.); Bowie, Walter Russell. *Women of Light* (1963); Crawford, R. A., ed. *National Association of Jeanes Supervisors Bulletin* (1958); Dannett, Sylvia G. L. *Profiles of Negro Womanhood* (1966); Davis, Jackson. *The Jeanes Visiting Teacher* (1936); Fosdick, Raymond B. *Adventure in Giving: The Story of the General Education Board* (1962); Furley, O. W. and T. Watson. *A History of Education in East Africa* (1978); Haynes, George Edmund. "The Harmon Awards," *Southern Workman* (March 1926); Jones, Lance G. E. *The Jeanes Teacher in the United States, 1908-1933* (1937); Jones, Thomas Jesse. *Education in East Africa* (1929); Jones, Warner M., Sr. Interview (April 8, 1988), Virginia Estelle Randolph Museum, Glen Allen, Virginia; King, James Kenneth. *Pan-Africanism and Education* (1971); NASC Interim History Writing Committee. *The Jeanes Story: A Chapter in the History of American Education 1908-1968* (1979); Richardson, Archie G. *Development of Negro Education in Virginia, 1831-1970* (1976); Spivey, Donald. *Schooling for the New Slavery: Black Industrial Education, 1868-1915* (1978); Wright, Arthur D. *The Jeanes Fund and The Jeanes Teachers* (1936).

BERNADINE S. CHAPMAN

RANSOM, EMMA S. COMER
(d. 1941)

Emma Ransom was one of many women married to prominent African Methodist Episcopal ministers, who expanded the role of pastor's wife through careers in social and civic work. Born and educated in Selma, Ohio, Emma Comer married Reverdy C. Ransom in 1887. He would later become an influential bishop of the AME Church. Emma Ransom was the cofounder of the Ohio Conference Branch Missionary Society and edited and published *Women's Light and Love*, the society's periodical. From 1896 to 1904 the couple founded and operated the Institutional Church and Social Settlement in Chicago, which forged an important link between the concerns of the church and issues facing African-Americans in urban settings. This would remain a focus of the work of both Emma and Reverdy Ransom throughout their lives.

The Ransoms moved to New York City in 1907 and, from that time until 1924, Emma was an important figure in activist circles in the city. She served as president of the Committee of Management of the Harlem Branch of the New York City Young Women's Christian Association from 1909 to 1924. Ransom was one of the central figures in helping the Harlem branch to establish itself as an important community institution, one that dealt with the range of issues facing young women in the city. The Harlem YWCA paid tribute to her great role in this when it named the branch residence the Emma Ransom House in 1926.

After Reverdy Ransom was named bishop, the family moved to Wilberforce, Ohio, where Emma continued to be an important figure in women's missionary work in the church, as well as an advisor to the YWCA, until her death in 1941.

BIBLIOGRAPHY

Ransom, Reverdy C. *The Pilgrimage of Harriet Ransom's Son* (n.d.); Weisenfeld, Judith. "The More Abundant Life: The Harlem Branch of the New York City Young Women's Christian Association, 1905-1945," Ph.D. diss. (1992); Wright, Bishop Richard R., Jr. *The Bishops of the AME Church* (1963).

JUDITH WEISENFELD

RAP MUSICIANS

The explosion of rap music during the 1980s was dominated by male rappers—the political rap of Public Enemy and others, the African nationalist rap of Brand Nubian and the Jungle Brothers, the message rap of KRS-One and Boogie Down Productions, the dub inspired rap of Shaba Ranks, the crossover rap of M.C. Hammer, and the white rappers led by Vanilla Ice. For all of its complexity, however, it is the evolution of female rap that promises to expand the dimension of rap music and place it into the ongoing sexual politics of post-modern America.

The origins of female rap date back to 1979 and the early 1980s when rap music was still confined to its Bronx and Queens club roots. One of the pioneers of female rap was The Sequence, who recorded a neglected single, "Funk You Up," for Sylvia and Joe Hill's Sugar Hill Records, one of the first labels to explore the various dimensions of this new inner-city sound. This was followed by Lisa Lee's collaboration with Afrika Bambataa and the establishment of Us Girls in 1984. Salt-N-Peppa burst out of the role that the male rap establishment had created for women when their 1986 album, *Hot, Cool, and Vicious*, went platinum. Receiving a Grammy Award in 1989, Salt-N-Peppa have mainstreamed female rap.

The early rhymes of Lisa Lee were mild compared to what followed. Lisa Lee's efforts paved the way for one of the first major battles in rap music, the "Roxanne, Roxanne" dispute, which in turn led to a new trend in rap music. In 1984, UTFO, a four-man group from Brooklyn, recorded "Roxanne, Roxanne," the story of a ghetto girl who rejects the overtures of several male suitors:

Yo, EMD
Yeah, what's up man?
There goes that girl they call Roxanne.
She's all stuck up
Why do you say that?
'Cause she wouldn't give a guy like me no rap.

"Roxanne, Roxanne" prompted an immediate response from a fifteen-year-old rapper from Queens, Roxanne Shanté. A big fan of Millie Jackson (whose lengthy raps on sex, eroticism, and love have bordered on pornography and who is herself one of the major influences on women rappers), Shanté initiated a response called "Roxanne's Revenge," which was responsible for the development of response rap, rappers responding to other rappers' rhymes. It also represents an element of the verbal style called "dissin'" (short for disrespect) that has deep roots in the combative verbal styles of inner-city Afro-America. Shanté's rap was characterized by a bold and raunchy style that set the tone for female rappers.

Roxanne Shanté's success made room for an entire wave of women rappers whose rhymes represent a determined challenge to the patriarchal macho of male rappers. M. C. Lyte from Brooklyn followed in Roxanne's steps by developing a style she has described as a sort of female hard-rock, characterized by a deep voice "smackin' people" with her rhymes. Queen Latifah, of Newark, emerged on the rap scene in 1990 with her smash debut recording, "Ladies First," which really catapulted women rappers into the formerly all-male mainstream. Combining the African nationalist message with a distinct feminist orientation, Latifah's presence suggests that the days of Black macho in rap are long over:

The ladies will kick it,
the rhyme it is wicked
Those who know how to be pros get evicted
A woman can bear you, break you, take you
Now it's time to rhyme. Can you relate to
A sister dope enough to make you holler and
    scream?

("Ladies First")

Harmony, from the Boogie Down Productions stable, has as the theme of her raps positive images of sisters and sisterhood. At the first major conference on rap music, held at Howard University in early 1991, she introduced her rap "What You Need" from her debut album, *Let There Be Harmony*, by pronouncing: "Rap about what / A break beat or a cut / I ain't no slut who sells records with her butt!" Harmony's rap style is a definite response to the newest trend in women's rap music, the "skeezer" (gold-diggin', money-grabbin' women) genre characterized by BWP (Bytches with Problems) and HWA (Hoes with Attitude). This genre emerged from Los Angeles and is a counterpoint to the macho gangster rap of Ice-T, N.W.A, and Ice Cube. BWP's smash hits "Two-Minute Brother" and "Money" seem to point to another wave of response raps, pitting message-oriented feminists against the gold-diggin' skeezers.

In between lies the music of Yo-Yo, a protégé of Ice Cube who, in 1991, released her first album, *Make Way for the Motherlode*, and signaled a bold assertiveness without succumbing to the gold-diggin' image. Yo-Yo has formed an organization, the Intelligent Black Women's Coalition, specifically designed to deal with the problems of young Black women: teen pregnancy, economic opportunity, crack, and Black male attitudes.

In mid-1992, Sister Souljah, a protégé of Public Enemy, became the center of national political debate. Known for her blistering public speeches on drug abuse, Black-on-Black crime, male rappers, and U.S. politicians, Sister Souljah suffered a wicked political attack by Democratic party presidential nominee Bill Clinton, who attacked her debut rap album *360 Degrees of Power* for contributing to the climate of violence in the aftermath of the 1992 Los Angeles riots. Souljah's paramilitary raps are reminiscent of the guerrilla rhetoric of the 1960s, and along with Public Enemy's "By the Time I Get to Arizona," signal a marked shift in the already militant Black nationalist rap from rhetoric to armed struggle.

The continuing growth of female rappers can only deepen and strengthen one of the most powerful cultural forces in contemporary American society but it also can be a vehicle—through the use of easily understood popular idiom—to challenge, and indeed transform, the attitudes of African-American boys and men. At a time of cultural and social malaise within Afro-America, this is no small task.

WILLIAM ERIC PERKINS

RAY, CHARLOTTE E. (1850-1911)

Charlotte Ray was the first Black woman regularly admitted to the practice of law in any jurisdiction in the United States. She was born in New York City on January 13, 1850, one of the seven children of the Reverend Charles Bennett Ray, of African, Indian, and white ancestry, and his second wife, Charlotte

Augusta Burroughs, a native of Savannah, Georgia. Charles Ray, editor, later owner, of the *Colored American* and pastor of the Bethesda Congregational Church in New York, was one of the distinguished Black leaders of his day, known for his fearless work for the Underground Railroad. His daughter, Charlotte, described in the *Woman's Journal* (May 25, 1872) as "a dusky mulatto," had the benefit of educated parents. In 1869, she was a teacher in the Normal and Preparatory Department of Howard University.

Shortly thereafter Charlotte began the study of law at the university. A classmate years later remembered her as "an apt scholar"; a contemporary visitor to the law school was impressed by "a colored woman who read us a thesis on corporations, not copied from the books but from her brain, a clear incisive analysis of one of the most delicate legal questions" (*President's Report*, Howard University, 1870). She graduated from the Howard University Law School in February 1872, reading an essay on "Chancery" that was well received.

Rules for bar admission were set by the Supreme Court of the District of Columbia, a court of general jurisdiction established during the Civil War to replace the circuit court. Charlotte Ray's application caused no debate. As a graduate of Howard University Law School she was not required to take a bar examination. She was admitted to practice in the lower courts of the District of Columbia on March 2, 1872, and to practice in the Supreme Court of the District of Columbia on April 23, 1872. After bar admission Charlotte Ray opened a law office in Washington where she hoped to practice a specialty within real estate law that did not entail trial appearances. It was the very beginning of women's entry into the legal profession, years before a woman could make a living from the law. Reminiscing in 1897, the Wisconsin lawyer Kate Kane Rossi recalled that "Miss Ray ... although a lawyer of decided ability, on account of prejudice was not able to obtain sufficient legal business and had to give up ... active practice" (*Chicago Legal News* 1897). The Panic of 1873 and the ensuing economic depression had further dampened her chances for success.

Charlotte Ray attended the annual convention of the National Woman Suffrage Association in New York City in 1876. By 1879, she had returned to New York to live. For a time, like her two younger sisters, she taught in the Brooklyn public schools. Sometime before 1886, she was married to a man with the surname of Fraim, of whom nothing is known. By 1897, she was living in Woodside, Long Island. Charlotte Ray Fraim died of acute bronchitis at her

Woodside home on January 11, 1911, at the age of sixty. She was buried in the Ray family plot in Cypress Hills Cemetery, Brooklyn.

In becoming a lawyer Charlotte Ray justified the dreams of many abolitionists, woman suffragists, and free Black Americans. Enabled by the Civil War and Reconstruction to gain a law degree and bar admission, Charlotte Ray, with marked intellectual capacity and family support, took advantage of the opportunity. She remains an unsung pioneer.

BIBLIOGRAPHY

Alexander, Sadie T. M. "Women as Practitioners of Law in the U.S.," *National Bar Journal* (July 1951); *Chicago Legal News* (October 23, 1897); Death record. New York City Department of Health, Queens Borough (1911); *New National Era* (February 29, 1872); Ray, F. T. *Sketch of the Life of Rev. Charles B. Ray* (1887); Stanton, Elizabeth C., et al. *History of Woman Suffrage* (1886); Thomas, Dorothy. "Charlotte E. Ray," *NAW; Woman's Journal* (May 25, 1872).

DOROTHY THOMAS

RAY, HENRIETTA GREEN REGULUS (1808-1836)

Henrietta Green Regulus Ray was an activist among free African-Americans in New York City during the 1820s and 1830s. She was one of many urban women whose access to education and property propelled them into benevolent, self-help, and community uplift work in the antebellum years.

Little is known of Henrietta Green's early life, except that she was a native New Yorker, lived in the home of African-American newspaper editor Samuel E. Cornish for three years, acquired a basic education, and pursued a "useful trade." Sometime before 1828, she married Laurent (Lawrence) D. Regulus, the shoemaker son of Dominique Regulus, a French merchant residing in both St. Thomas (Virgin Islands) and New York, and an Afro-Caribbean woman named Delaydo. Regulus died in 1828, leaving Henrietta a house in which she lived with her second husband, Charles B. Ray, after their 1834 marriage. Charles Ray was a young Massachusetts native who, driven from theological seminary by racial prejudice, had moved to New York City in 1832 where he opened a boot and shoe store. Later he became a well-known New York minister, newspaper editor, political activist, and community leader. The Rays had one child, Matilda, born in January 1836, who at the age of six months died of tuberculosis, the same ailment that killed her mother.

From 1828 until her death on October 27, 1836, Henrietta Regulus Ray played an active part in forming and running free Black women's educational and self-help organizations. After participating in establishing the African Dorcas Association, a group devoted to providing clothing to children attending the African Free School, she became the Association's assistant secretary in 1828. Six years later, she became the first president of the New York Female Literary Society (sometimes referred to as the Colored Ladies' Literary Society), "formed for the purpose of acquiring literary and scientific knowledge" (*Emancipator*, November 24, 1836) and dedicated both to women's self-help and self-improvement and to racial uplift. Like African-American women's literary societies in other northern cities, the Female Literary Society combined educational activities with abolitionist concerns, raising funds to assist runaway slaves and donating money to support a petition campaign aimed at ending slavery in Washington, D.C.

In her brief life, Henrietta Regulus Ray exemplified the experiences of members of northern free Black women's organizations: creating multifaceted groups, combining benevolence with reform, and associating individual improvement with the advancement of the race. Her husband and his second wife, Charlotte Burroughs, honored her by naming one of their seven children for her, Henrietta Cordelia Ray, whose career as a student at New York University and as a poet perhaps fulfilled some of the aspirations of the woman for whom she was named.

BIBLIOGRAPHY

Barber, Gertrude. "Index of Letter of Administration of New York County, 1743-1875" (typescript, New York Public Library); *DANB; Emancipator.* Obituary (November 24, 1836); *Freedom's Journal* (February 15, 1828); Perkins, Linda. "Black Women and Racial 'Uplift' Prior to Emancipation." In *The Black Woman Cross-Culturally*, ed. Filomena Chioma Steady (1981); Porter, Dorothy B. "The Organized Educational Activities of Negro Literary Societies, 1828-1846," *Journal of Negro Education* (October 1936); Ray, Florence T. *Sketch of the Life of Rev. Charles B. Ray* (1887); Sawyer, Ray C. "Abstracts of Wills for New York County, 1801-1855" (typescript, New York Public Library).

ANNE BOYLAN

RED CROSS NURSING SERVICE *see* NURSING, WORLD WAR I

REESE, DELLA (1931-)

Pop and soul singer and actress Della Reese was born Deloreese Patricia Early on July 6, 1931, in Detroit, Michigan. She began singing professionally with Mahalia Jackson's gospel troupe from 1945 to 1949, and then performed with Erskine Hawkins in the 1950s.

In 1957, she began a solo career, and achieved three Top Forty hits in the late 1950s: "And That Reminds Me" (1957), which reached number twelve; "Don't You Know" (1959), which reached number two; and "Not One Minute More (1959), which reached number sixteen. Her RCA album *Della* (1960) reached the Top Forty and earned her a Grammy Award nomination for Female Vocal, Album. Her other albums include *Special Delivery* (1961) and *Classic Della* (1962).

As an actress, Reese made many television appearances, including starring in the syndicated *The Della Reese Show* (1969-70) and performing as a series regular in *Chico and the Man* (NBC, 1976-78), *It Takes Two* (ABC, 1982-83), *Charlie & Co.* (CBS, 1986), and *The Royal Family* (1991-92). She made many guest appearances on television variety, talk, and panel shows including *The Ed Sullivan Show, Perry Como's Kraft Music Hall, To Tell the Truth,* and *The Tonight Show Starring Johnny Carson;* in television movies and miniseries including ABC's *Nightmare in Badham County* (1976) and *Roots: The Next Generation* (1979); and as a guest star in drama and comedy series such as *The Bold Ones, Police Woman, McCloud, The Love Boat,* and notably *The A-Team,* in which she played the mother of series regular Mr. T.

Her film appearances include *Let's Rock* (1958) and *Harlem Nights* (1989).

BIBLIOGRAPHY

Clarke, Donald, ed. *The Penguin Encyclopedia of Popular Music* (1989); Inman, David. *The TV Encyclopedia* (1991); Whitburn, Joel. *The Billboard Book of Top 40 Hits* (1992).

BARBARA BERGERON

RELIGION

The importance of religion in the African-American experience cannot be overstated. Religion can be seen as both worldview and human organization, and from both perspectives, women have been at the center. The African-American religious experience, especially as it has been actualized by women, combines African sensibilities, New World experiences, Western Christianity, and an activist orientation toward injustice and racial oppression. As a worldview it encompasses mythic, experiential, doctrinal, ethical, ritual, and social dimensions and transcends specific organizational or denominational forms. Women, historically, have taken great responsibility for all of these dimensions, framing and shaping the contexts of religious life and practice. They are the primary teachers of religious doctrine and tradition within the churches. Religious life and practice, in turn, have been central to the psychic and spiritual strengths women have used to cope with the oppressive realities of life in the United States. In their everyday language of struggle with economic, political, and cultural oppression, women within and outside of churches draw on the traditions of spirituals and biblical images. Within Christian churches, women are the most significant force, although their leadership roles vary widely.

AGENTS OF HISTORY AND ORGANIZATION

The vital religious role of women begins in slavery. The African background contained models of women priestesses, cult leaders, and healers. These were not forgotten in the confrontation with the masculinism of Western Christianity. Although Black women were initially excluded from church memberships, "whenever colonists introduced Christianity to Africans, black women quickly played a prominent role" (Webb 1983). Isabella, an African woman who arrived the year before the *Mayflower*'s landing in 1620, may already have been baptized. Some early bondwomen may have become Christian to help their families.

Women were prominent leaders in the slave quarters community. They were prayer leaders and exhorters. As exhorters and professors, they often admonished the community to maintain their hope for freedom. Toni Morrison, in her novel *Beloved* (1987), provides a portrait of one such woman, Baby Suggs, whose informal preaching of self-love to enslaved women, men, boys, and girls reflected the activities of nineteenth-century preaching women such as Jarena Lee, Amanda Berry Smith, Julia Foote, and Zilpha Elaw. The importance of African sensibilities can be seen in the role of women in translating African traditions of cult leadership, prophecy, healing, and divining into the slave community's emphasis on conversion and encounters with the Holy Spirit. The role of Tituba in precipitating the witch hunts of Salem, Massachusetts, is an important although confusing example. Women prophets often wielded considerable power and influence in slave communities, occasionally, as with a woman named Sinda, bringing plantation routine to a halt.

Christian missions to slaves led to the prominence of the Methodist and Baptist traditions among African-Americans. John Wesley's first two Black baptisms were enslaved women. The presence of Africans and their descendants at Baptist and Methodist revivals also helped to fuel the growth of these traditions. During slavery, Black women and men in Philadelphia and New York organized the African Methodist Episcopal (AME) Church and the African Methodist Episcopal Zion (AMEZ) Church. In the South, Africans and African-Americans became overwhelmingly Baptist, so much so that an Afro-Baptist faith has been seen as dominant, regardless of denomination. Within these churches women exercised ritual and social leadership. In Baptist churches during slavery, church discipline was enforced by boards of deacons and deaconesses who oversaw the lives of men and women respectively.

The most prominent aspect of women's organizational church history took place in the women's departments and missionary societies of their congregations and denominations. After slavery, the masculinism of Western Christianity asserted itself in an assault on women preachers and worship leaders. In spite of this assault, the freed women and men seemed to bind into a religious leadership class of educators. The AME Church was quite explicit in charging its elders in the South to organize and to teach for the purposes of citizenship and economic development. Black and white women missionaries were most prominent among the educators in the rural and urban South. Baptist educational activities usually supported women teachers who also functioned as community organizers and leaders. Most women who rose to prominence as national leaders were at once church women and teachers such as Ida B. Wells, Anna Julia Cooper, and Fannie Jackson Coppin. These women all left writings that advocated racial justice for African-Americans and challenged Black men to be more egalitarian in their approaches to women leaders.

Women shared the pulpit with men during the 1880s, in the early days of what came to be the National Baptist Convention. The AME Church saw the emergence of two women's missionary societies in 1874 and 1904, the older Women's Parent Mite Missionary Society and the predominantly southern Women's Home and Foreign Missionary Society. In 1900, the Women's Auxiliary of the National Baptist Convention was formed. One of its most prominent

leaders was Nannie Helen Burroughs, who in 1907 introduced a resolution establishing Women's Day. Although criticized as tokenism, Women's Day has continued to be celebrated as a day where women provide the sermons and lead the worship. It has become one of the most important public expressions of Black Christian women and a cherished tradition, spreading to every Black denomination and to predominantly Black congregations in white denominations. In her day, Burroughs complained that this had become the chief day for raising money rather than raising women. It was women's ability to raise funds, however, that also defines their historical role in African-American church history.

The Holiness movement of the late nineteenth century and the Pentecostal movement of the early twentieth century had a profound impact on church life and women's roles within it. Emphasizing the person and work of the Holy Spirit, a tradition carried forward from its African antecedents largely by women, these movements created new denominations in which women played diverse but highly prominent roles. In Holiness denominations, women were fully ordained and pastoring churches. It was to Holiness women pastors such as Neely Terry that William Seymour, the apostle of American Pentecostalism, came when seeking a pulpit to air his views about speaking in tongues. The earliest Pentecostal denomination in the United States was the Church of God in Christ (COGIC). Its founder, Bishop Charles Harrison Mason, organized a women's department that became characteristic of the denominations of the Sanctified Church. It was first headed by Mother Lizzie Woods Roberson, who was succeeded by Mother Lillian Brooks Coffey, who, like Nannie Helen Burroughs, was active in national women's organizations. The roles that emerged in the Sanctified Church (COGIC and many other Holiness and Pentecostal denominations) were highly diverse.

In denominations such as COGIC that did not officially ordain women, women's departments encouraged the development of strong traditions of service and evangelism. In other denominations women were ordained, and in some cases, they formed denominations such as the Mount Sinai Holy Church, founded by Bishop Ida Robinson, in which women could serve as bishops and preside. The diversity of women's roles in the Sanctified Church has made possible the existence of strong role models for women in other denominations; in some cases, the growth of women's preaching and pastoral ministries among Baptists and African Methodists has been fueled by the movement of Pentecostal and Holiness women into these denominations.

In addition to their organizational roles within church history, church women have established an important political history. It was church women who became the prominent organizers of the club movement that culminated in the formation of the National Association of Colored Women. Possibly because they could not lead from the pulpit, these women moved into the community, forming clubs and organizations that addressed the diverse social and cultural needs of the Black community of the late nineteenth and early twentieth centuries. Eschewing separatism, these women invited men to join them in a movement led by women for the benefit of women and men. In their move to uplift women, the basic

Christian orientation of these women was evident in their biblical language and the dual roles they played as both community and church leaders. Their organizing was so successful that in 1935 Mary McLeod Bethune was able to form the National Council of Negro Women from the many national Black women's organizations that had been formed.

The explicitly Christian ideologies and practices of many of these groups continued to demonstrate the activist orientation of church women and the infusion of their religious worldview into their cultural and community activities. Women such as Nannie Helen Burroughs and Mary McLeod Bethune, both of whom organized schools, left dramatic legacies within their denominations. The ethical orientation of these Christian women is epitomized in

The ethical orientation of activist church women is epitomized in the famous "Last Will and Testament" of Mary McLeod Bethune, in which she encourages a legacy of faith, hope, and love alongside such practical strategies as education, dignity, harmonious living, and devotion to youth. Her "Last Will" is quoted on the base of the statue of Bethune in Washington, D.C., the model for which is reproduced here. [Schomburg Center]

the famous "Last Will and Testament" of Mary McLeod Bethune, in which she encourages a legacy of faith, hope, and love alongside such practical strategies as education, dignity, harmonious living, and devotion to youth. Blocked from her desire to preach Christianity in Africa after graduating from Moody Bible Institute, her work to develop and sustain Bethune-Cookman College in Florida remains a testimony to finding her "Africa" in Florida.

AGENTS OF RELIGIOUS TRADITION

In addition to their organizational and historical roles, African-American women have been the principal agents of a distinctive Afro-Christian tradition. There are four basic pillars of this tradition—preaching, prayer, music, and testimony. Women have traditionally led devotional worship and been responsible for emphases on prayer, music, and testimony. Regardless of the obstacles they faced in attaining roles as ordained ministers, pastors, bishops, or elders, women have managed to make their voices heard in preaching of the gospel. In many traditions, "teaching" and "speaking" have been discriminatory euphemisms for women's preaching.

The basic language of the Afro-Christian worship is rooted in the English Bible. Women play a significant role in appropriating and maintaining the Bible as a foundation, integrating it imaginatively into their prayers, their testimonies, and the songs they compose. Hymnists such as Lucie E. Campbell are known for vibrant biblical images. Although a focus of some controversy because of its male-centeredness, the Bible has been central to the mythic dimension of the African-American Christian worldview. Black women have especially emphasized the role of Jesus as fellow sufferer and model of service. For many women in the churches, their devotional life enables them to focus on Jesus as friend in the depths of all kinds of physical and emotional suffering. Women have appropriated the Bible's stories and images to create sacred and secular literature. Nannie Helen Burroughs, a prominent Baptist leader and educator, wrote a "Roll Call of Biblical Women" that reworked and extended biblical stories about women in order to give them the prominence in church life she felt they deserved.

The most prominent religious role of women both in churches and in popular culture has been in the area of music. Historical accounts point to women in slave communities as song leaders. In addition to composing hymns, women gained prominence as musical directors in denominations, exercising power by shaping hymnbooks. Lucie Campbell and Willa

Townsend played such roles in the National Baptist Convention and Mattie Moss Clark has overseen such work in the Church of God in Christ.

Gospel music is one of the most significant contemporary expressions of the music tradition. The most internationally famous singer has been Mahalia Jackson. However, Sallie Martin (in partnership with Thomas Dorsey) and Mother Willie Mae Ford Smith played significant roles in carrying the gospel music tradition into mainstream, particularly Baptist, churches. Mother Smith, who trained generations of soloists through the National Convention of Gospel Choirs and Choruses, traveled widely throughout Black churches conducting revivals. Leading evangelists and church mothers in Pentecostal and Holiness churches (the Sanctified Church) were also known for their singing. In a manner similar to the growth of the blues tradition, men were often prominent as itinerant singers and members of quartets traveling through the South, while women such as Sallie Martin, Roberta Martin, Clara Ward and the Ward Singers, the Caravans, the Davis sisters, and evangelist Shirley Caesar were responsible for the urban prominence of gospel music.

Prayer is another area of prominence for women. It was often women who provided the prayer prior to the sermon. Not only did women gain prominence as prayer warriors and prayer band leaders within denominations and congregations, some women also maintained independent prayer ministries in their homes and communities. The spiritualist tradition incorporated this tradition of prayer ministry for both individuals and groups, and the (mostly women) pastors in this tradition had both congregations and clients. Although the subject of some controversy, these independent women were occasionally the principal contacts for unchurched Black people. During slavery, the initial socialization of boys and girls took place through their observations of mothers and aunts at prayer in the cabins and hush harbor congregations. After slavery, women retained their prominence in the prayer tradition. Narratives and missionaries' accounts describe the vivid prayers of women such as Aunt Jane, whose powerful prayer on behalf of "poor Ethiopian women" provides stunning images of divine invocation in a context of suffering and struggle.

The testimony tradition is easily observable since most congregations today hold weekly prayer meetings, monthly love feasts, and periodic revivals with extended devotional periods where women lead. The testimony periods provide a central fulfillment for the church's role as a therapeutic community. It is here that church members are able to talk about the troubles, struggles, and victories they have experienced. Women are highly represented in Baptist and Methodist congregations, while 90 percent of the members of Sanctified Church congregations are women. Aware of their predominance, women often make extended efforts to provide opportunities for male prominence and leadership, efforts sometimes criticized in the face of the discrimination they experience in spite of their numbers. Women show no such restraint when it comes to the expressive dimensions of religious life. Their testimony sometimes functions as a form of protest at their sufferings.

Preaching is central to the ritual experience and it is one of the most contested areas with regard to women's roles. As far as we know, the first African-American woman to seek ordination was Jarena Lee in the AME Church. Anticipating the continuing debate over the legitimacy of women's preaching, she reminded her listeners that Mary first preached the resurrection, the event upon which depends all of Christian faith and doctrine. Amanda Berry Smith, also of the AME Church, was the most famous of the preaching women in the nineteenth century. Her ministry was international, carrying her to Africa and to India. A staunch advocate of African women's education, her work reflected the combination of religious fervor and social activism that characterized Black Christian women of the nineteenth and twentieth centuries.

A DIVERSE EXPERIENCE

There is great diversity among the religious experiences of late-twentieth-century women, but that diversity arises largely out of a shared historical experience of oppression and creative response. As an organizational experience, the religious experience is historically, primarily, and predominantly Christian with a distinctive emphasis on the person and the work of the Holy Spirit and on the person of Jesus as fellow sufferer and member of the disinherited and

The role of women in churches has been most prominent in the area of music. Pictured here is the Excelsior Temple Band, Brooklyn, New York, 1929. [Moorland-Spingarn]

the dispossessed. In spite of the dominance of Christianity, African-American women exhibit a wide range of spiritual and organizational expressions and interact across diverse religious settings, including Baha'i, Islam, Buddhism, and traditional African and African-Caribbean religions, especially Yoruba religion, in the form of Lucumi or Santeria.

[See also AFRICAN METHODIST EPISCOPAL PREACHING WOMEN; BAHA'I FAITH; BAPTIST CHURCH; CATHOLIC CHURCH; CHURCH OF GOD IN CHRIST; MUSLIMS.]

BIBLIOGRAPHY

Andrews, William. *Sisters of the Spirit: Three Black Women's Autobiographies of the Nineteenth Century* (1986); Barnett, Evelyn Brooks. "Nannie Helen Burroughs and the Education of Black Women." In *The Afro-American Woman: Struggles and Images*, ed. Sharon Harley and Rosalyn Terborg-Penn (1978); Brooks, Evelyn. "The Feminist Theology of the Black Baptist Church, 1880-1900." In *Class, Race, and Sex: The Dynamics of Control*, ed. Amy Swerdlow and Hannah Lessinger (1983); Higginbotham, Evelyn Brooks. "African American Women's History and the Metalanguage of Race," *Signs* (Autumn 1992); Carter, Harold. *The Prayer Tradition of Black People* (1976); Church of God in Christ. *Official Manual with the Doctrines and Discipline of the Church of God in Christ* (1973); Cornelius, Lucille. *The Pioneer History of the Church of God in Christ* (1975); Dodson, Jualyne E. and Cheryl Townsend Gilkes. "Something Within: Social Change and Collective Endurance in the Sacred World of Black Christian Women." In *Women and Religion in America: Volume Three—The Twentieth Century*, ed. Rosemary Radford Ruether and Rosemary Skinner Keller (1986); Fauset, Arthur Huff. *Black Gods of the Metropolis* (1944); Gilkes, Cheryl Townsend. "Together and in Harness: Women's Traditions in the Sanctified Church," *Signs* (Summer 1985), and "The Roles of Church and Community Mothers: Ambivalent American Sexism or Fragmented African Familyhood?" *Journal of Feminist Studies in Religion* (Fall 1986), and "The Role of Women in the Sanctified Church," *Journal of Religious Thought* (1986), and " 'Some Mother's Son and Some Father's Daughter': Gender and Biblical Language in the Afro-Christian Worship Tradition." In *Shaping New Vision*, ed. Clarissa W. Atkins, Constance H. Buchanan, and Margaret R. Miles (1987); Hurston, Zora Neale. *The Sanctified Church* (1982); Keller, Rosemary Skinner. "Lay Women in the Protestant Tradition." In *Women and Religion in America—Volume One: The Nineteenth Century*, ed. Rosemary Radford Ruether and Rosemary Skinner Keller (1981); Johnson, James Weldon. *God's Trombones* (1927); Smart, Ninian. *Worldviews: Crosscultural Explorations of Human Beliefs* (1983); Sobel, Mechal. *Travelin' On: The Slaves' Journey to an Afro-Baptist Faith* (1979); Trulear, Harold Dean. "Reshaping Black Pastoral Theology: The Vision of Bishop Ida B. Robinson," *Journal of Religious Thought* (1989); Webb, Lillian Ashcraft. "Black Women and Religion in the Colonial Period." In *Women and Religion in America—Volume Two: The Colonial and Revolutionary Periods*, ed. Rosemary Radford Ruether and Rosemary Skinner Keller (1983); White, Deborah Gray. *Ar'n't I a Woman: Female Slaves in the Plantation South* (1985); Zikmund, Barbara Brown. "The Struggle for the Right to Preach." In *Women and Religion in America—Volume One: The Nineteenth Century*, ed. Rosemary Radford Ruether and Rosemary Skinner Keller (1981).

CHERYL TOWNSEND GILKES

REMOND, SARAH PARKER (1826-1894)

"I appeal on behalf of four millions of men, women, and children who are chattels in the Southern States of America. Not because they are identical with my race and color, though I am proud of that identity, but because they are men and women. The sum of sixteen hundred millions of dollars is invested in their bones, sinews, and flesh—is this not sufficient reason why all the friends of humanity should not endeavor with all their might and power, to overturn the vile systems of slavery." Sarah Parker Remond, a lady of no ordinary character, made this statement during a lecture on slavery that she was giving in Warrington, England, in 1859. A free person of color, she was touring throughout England hoping to impress the English people on the evils of slavery in the United States and to implore them to endorse propositions protesting this evil as a blot on the civilized world.

Sarah Parker Remond was born in Salem, Massachusetts, on June 6, 1826, one of eight children of John and Nancy Lenox Remond. She received a limited education in the primary schools and was primarily self-educated by reading newspapers, books, and pamphlets she borrowed from friends or purchased from the Anti-Slavery Society depositories, which sold many titles at a cheap price.

Raised in a family that included many abolitionists, Remond from childhood learned of the horrors of slavery and witnessed many incidents involving the Underground Railroad. Her home was a haven for Black and white abolitionists. She regularly attended antislavery lectures in Salem and Boston. Charles Lenox Remond, her older brother, was a well-known antislavery lecturer in the United States and Great Britain. Along with household duties, cooking and sewing, Nancy Remond taught her daughters to seek

Sarah Parker Remond's commitment to the cause of abolition took her to England in 1859. She gave more than forty-five speeches from 1859 to 1861 to British audiences, enlisting their aid in the antislavery movement. [Courtesy, Essex Institute, Salem, Massachusetts]

liberty in a lawful manner and that to be Black was no crime, but an accident of birth.

Sarah Remond determined early in life to fight the prejudice she constantly faced because of her color. In May 1853, she was denied a seat, for which she had a ticket, to attend a performance of the opera *Don Pasquale* at the Howard Athenaeum in Boston. Remond was forcibly ejected from the theater and pushed down the stairs, from which she suffered an

injury. She sued the managers of the theater and won her suit. The small award of $500 she received did not compensate for her injury and embarrassment. Her object, however, was not to make money on the case but to vindicate a right.

In 1856, Remond accompanied her brother Charles on his antislavery lecture tour in New York State. She spoke briefly at some of the meetings, gaining confidence in her ability to lecture. She addressed several antislavery meetings in New York, Massachusetts, Ohio, Michigan, and Pennsylvania between 1856 and 1858. Sarah and her brother faced prejudice on many occasions. Some boarding houses and hotels refused to accept them, and special accommodations for them had to be found in private homes.

On December 28, 1858, Sarah Parker Remond left Boston in the steamer *Arabia* for Liverpool to enlist the aid of the English people in the American antislavery movement. Accompanied by Samuel May, Jr., she arrived in Liverpool on January 12, 1859, after a frightening trip. The ship had been covered with ice and snow. It rolled and tossed so much that many passengers were sick, including Remond, who regained her strength after a few days of recuperation in the home of William Robson in Warrington.

At Tuckerman Institute on January 21, 1859, Remond gave her first antislavery lecture on the free soil of Britain. Without notes she eloquently spoke of the inhuman treatment of slaves in the United States. Her shocking stories of atrocities brought tears to the eyes of many listeners.

Between 1859 and 1861, Remond gave over forty-five lectures in eighteen cities and towns in England, three cities in Scotland, and four cities in Ireland. Everywhere the press reported her speeches and the reactions of her audiences. In spite of a heavy lecture schedule, Remond, desirous of furthering her education, attended classes at Bedford College for Ladies, later a part of the University of London, from October 1859 to mid-1861. She studied history, elocution, music, English literature, French, and Latin.

At the end of the Civil War, Remond lectured on behalf of the freedmen. She was an active member of the London Emancipation Society and the Freedmen's Aid Association in London. These organizations solicited funds and clothing for the ex-slaves.

In 1865, she published a letter in the *Daily News* protesting attacks on Black people in the London press after an insurrection in Jamaica. One lecture that she delivered in London, "The Freeman or the Emancipated Negro of the Southern States of the United States," was published in *The Freedman* (London) in 1867.

Remond visited Rome and Florence on several occasions while living in England. In 1866, she left London and entered the Santa Maria Nuova Hospital in Florence, Italy, as a medical student. She received a diploma certifying her for professional medical practice in 1871. She practiced medicine in Florence, Italy, for more than twenty years.

In Florence, on April 25, 1877, Sarah Parker Remond married Lazzaro Pintor, a native of Sardinia.

This remarkable woman from a unique African-American family died on December 13, 1894. She was buried in the Protestant Cemetery in Rome.

[*See also* ABOLITION MOVEMENT.]

BIBLIOGRAPHY

DANB; May, Samuel J. Diary (January 1-10, 1859), Anti-Slavery Collection, Cornell University Library, Ithaca, New York; *NAW*; Porter, Dorothy B. "The Remonds of Salem, Massachusetts: A Nineteenth-Century Family Revisited," *Proceedings of the American Antiquarian Society, Worcester, Massachusetts, October 16, 1985* (1986), and "Sarah Parker Remond, Abolitionist and Physician," *Journal of Negro History* (July 1935); Protestant Cemetery Archives, Rome, Italy; Warrington *Times* (January 29, 1859).

DOROTHY PORTER WESLEY

RHYTHM AND BLUES

As in all forms of Black expression, women played a significant role in the evolution of rhythm and blues, a style of music that became prominent during the 1940s in the aftermath of World War II. More rhythmically assertive and upbeat than the popular blues of the 1920s and 1930s, this music, which came to be called R & B, reflected the increasingly confident mood of Blacks. Although they had been relegated to segregated units, many Black Americans had gotten their first taste of freedom from racism while serving abroad in the military. At home, a huge migration northward by Black Americans seeking prosperity in industrial jobs had endowed them with a confident urban edge. City life also brought Black women new opportunities to work as entertainers, offering the talented an alternative to servitude.

While jazz was regarded as the music of urban sophisticates, rhythm and blues fused instrumental elements of that established form with the gritty directness and storytelling qualities of the blues. The result was an exciting and readily accessible kind of music that dominated Black popular taste from the 1940s to the 1960s. Rhythm and blues also supplied the foundation for the development of rock and roll when young whites began to listen to this music, recording their own versions of Black hits and borrowing heavily from their stylistic elements. The latter development is typified by the example of "Big Mama" Willie Mae Thornton, an exuberant, foot-stomping singer and harmonica player whose recording of "Hound Dog" became a number one R & B hit in 1953; the song sold far more and ensured the future success of a young Elvis Presley when he recorded it in 1957.

Women played a critical role in providing the linkages from blues to jazz to R & B, with a frequent blurring of the lines that separated them. The "classic Blues" period of the 1920s had been built on the work of powerful female vocalists like Gertrude "Ma" Rainey and Bessie Smith, whose 160 recordings formed the backbone of a lucrative market in "race" records, those that would be sold to a Black audience. Smith was a major influence on singers who followed her, regardless of genre. Although Billie Holiday was indisputably a jazz singer identified with the swing era, she listened to Bessie Smith records as a child and retained a blues feeling in all of her work.

Most women who played leading roles in the evolution of rhythm and blues generally credit Holiday with influencing them, especially in terms of her phrasing and ability to lend subtle nuances to lyrics. Foremost among these was Dinah Washington, who started in 1943 as a jazz vocalist with the Lionel Hampton big band, but whose earthy style and choice of blues-inflected material quickly made her a rhythm and blues star. She became known as "Queen of the Blues" during the 1950s when she had several top R & B hits. Later in that decade and in the early 1960s, she crossed over into the mainstream with such popular hits as "What a Diff'rence a Day Makes" and "This Bitter Earth," but she interpreted them in a style that retained the integrity of her R & B roots.

Rhythm and blues supplied the foundation for the development of rock and roll when white artists "covered"—made their own recordings of—songs by Black artists. "Big Mama" Willie Mae Thornton had a number one hit with "Hound Dog" on the rhythm and blues charts in 1953, but it was Elvis Presley's subsequent cover four years later that really established both the singer and the song. [Amy Van Single]

Esther Phillips began her career when she was thirteen, and went on to become a recording star under the name Little Esther. Some critics called her the greatest teenaged singer ever, who sometimes sounded like a junior edition of the great Dinah Washington. [Schomburg Center]

She also continued to perform and record material in a more straight-ahead jazz vein throughout her career. A tempestuous woman who was married seven times, Dinah Washington died in 1963 at the age of thirty-nine, after mixing pills with alcohol. Like Billie Holiday, who also died tragically after a tumultuous life, Washington left her mark on young singers. Four years after Washington's death, when singer Aretha Franklin was being hailed as the First Lady of "soul music," an R & B derivative drawing heavily on Black gospel music, she demurred at being granted such a title, saying, "The queen of the blues was and still is Dinah Washington."

A singer whose style bore a strong resemblance to that of Washington was Esther Phillips. She began her career in 1949, when she was thirteen, after winning a talent show in her native Los Angeles, and went on to become a recording star under the name Little Esther. Some critics have called her the greatest teen singer ever, for even as an adolescent, she sang with a rare authority, etching her vocals with a distinctive vinegarish tone. Phillips sounded at times like a junior edition of Dinah Washington, who had encouraged her and who remained her idol. During the 1950s, Phillips had several top R & B hits, among

them "Cupid's Boogie" and "Deceivin' Blues." Her adult years were marred by bouts with drug addiction, but she was greatly admired by the Beatles and recorded a broad range of material during the 1960s, including the country tune "Release Me." Phillips enjoyed a new surge of popularity during the early 1970s with impressive performances on recordings like "Baby I'm for Real" and "Home Is Where the Hatred," a searing musical commentary on the wages of addiction. Her albums *From a Whisper to a Scream* and *Alone Again (Naturally)* on the Kudu label were critically acclaimed best-sellers. She was nominated for a Grammy as best R & B vocalist in 1973, but when she lost to Aretha Franklin, Franklin gave the trophy to Phillips, saying it was she who should have won. Phillips died at the age of forty-eight in 1984, due to kidney and liver failure.

Tragedy seemed to stalk many of these gifted rhythm and blues women, but certainly not all of them. Ruth Brown launched the first phase of her career back in the 1950s when she was considered the only real competitor to Dinah Washington as R & B queen. An admirer of Billie Holiday, she had intended to become a jazz singer and got a job as vocalist with the Lucky Millinder orchestra in 1948. Shortly afterwards the two fell out and Brown continued on her own, becoming one of the first artists signed by Atlantic Records, which was to become perhaps the greatest business force in R & B recording history. Though Brown said she did not like the blues, she was asked to sing them, and thus ended up recording fresh popular material that had a blues flavor, resulting in songs that applied to both Black and white audiences. Her first record, "So Long," released in 1949, became a top R & B hit, as did subsequent releases such as "Teardrops from My Eyes," "5-10-15 Hours" and "(Mama) He Treats Your Daughter Mean." Brown was billed as "Miss Rhythm" and sold so many records that some referred to Atlantic as "the House that Ruth Built." She inadvertently contributed to the enrichment of the popular mainstream when white singers like Patti Page and Georgia Gibbs recorded versions of songs she had released previously. After the early 1960s, Brown seldom recorded and fell into obscurity, taking a job as a domestic to raise her son. She had a second coming, however. During the 1980s, she sued Atlantic for past royalties, arrived at an amicable settlement, and took the initiative in establishing the Rhythm and Blues Foundation, an ongoing organization that provides aid to needy R & B artists and annually honors stars of yesteryear with major financial awards. Brown also was featured in the film

Hairspray, won a Tony Award for her starring role on Broadway in the musical *Black and Blue*, and won a Grammy Award for her recording of *Blues on Broadway*. This time around she was acknowledged as a star in the mainstream.

While few stories have such a happy ending, other leading women of R & B were also rediscovered during the 1980s. LaVern Baker, who was a major R & B singer during the 1950s with hits on Atlantic like "Tweedle Dee" and "Jim Dandy," performed abroad as well as in the United States. When Ruth Brown left the cast of *Black and Blue* in 1991, Baker assumed the role on Broadway. Etta James, whose sassy ribaldry on hits like "Roll With Me, Henry" had made her a star during the 1950s, was rediscovered by a younger generation. Several of her older recordings were reissued, and new releases indicated that her power was undiminished.

If there is a single artist who linked earlier R & B singers to the later soul era, it was Aretha Franklin, who had started out as a child prodigy performing gospel music in her father's Detroit church. She emerged in the 1960s as a dominant force, combining gospel fervor and personal passion with sheer musical brilliance as a singer, pianist, and composer. Spanning the music spectrum, from the gospel majesty of Mahalia Jackson, who was a major influence, to the tart stylings of Dinah Washington, and infusing her art with the hard realities of the modern inner-city world that spawned her, Franklin was the defining artist of soul music, an aesthetic developing with strong political ramifications. Her 1967 recording of Otis Redding's "Respect" became the anthem of the Black revolution, and fans eagerly awaited each of her releases. By the early 1980s, Aretha Franklin had released more million-selling singles than any other woman in the history of recording. Her popularity had waned somewhat by the 1990s, when she veered toward less substantial pop-oriented material, but her overall contribution could not be questioned.

BIBLIOGRAPHY

Albertson, Chris. *Bessie* (1972); Clarke, Donald, ed. *The Penguin Encyclopedia of Popular Music* (1989); Garland, Phyl. "Aretha Franklin: Sister Soul," *Ebony* (September 1967), and "Coast-to-Coast Comeback: Esther Phillips," *Ebony* (October 1972), and "Crossover: A Bridge over Pop Waters," *Billboard* (June 9, 1979), and "No More Blues," *Essence* (May 1985); George, Nelson. *The Death of Rhythm and Blues* (1988); Heckman, Don. *Five Decades of Rhythm and Blues: BMI 1943-1975* (1976); Lieb, Sandra. *Mother of the Blues: A Study of Ma Rainey* (1981); Shaw, Arnold. *Honkers and Shouters: The Golden Years of Rhythm and Blues* (1978).

DISCOGRAPHY
For discographies, see Allen, Daniel. *Bibliography of Discographies, Vol. 2: Jazz* (1981); Gray, Michael. *Bibliography of Discographies, Vol. 3: Popular Music* (1983); Osborne, Jerry. *Blues, Rhythm and Blues, Soul* (1980).

PHYL GARLAND

RICHARDS, BEAH (c. 1933-)

Sidney Poitier, Bill Cosby, and Robert Hooks have played her sons and grandsons. She played a grandmother in her first professional role, in 1956 off-Broadway, and her career, now in its fourth decade, is still going strong. "I've been everybody's mother," says the actress, poet, and playwright with the marvelous voice.

She was born Beulah Richardson around 1933 in Vicksburg, Mississippi. Being a realist in a racist society left her no illusions, but surrounded by a close, compassionate community, Richards never entertained the idea of failure. She cites her mother, Beulah Molton Richardson, who was a seamstress and president of the Parent-Teacher Association (PTA), as her model for perseverance and community spirit; the poetry came from her father, Wesley R. Richardson. In a 1977 taped interview, Richards described him as "a minister with a gift for shaping words into images so sharp and clear that they became living and moved people to action." His daughter inherited both the gift and the will to move people.

The youngest in the family, Richards followed her sisters, Muncie and Ann, to the local school, where she remembers being inspired by a teacher named Mrs. M. A. Bell, whose great love for poetry, drama, and music gave all her students a strong sense of art. In high school, Richards shone in debating guild, drama, and Latin clubs, winning prizes and praise. There was no theater in the town, and the moviehouse was not open to Black people, but everyone told her she was going to become a star. After high school graduation, Richards studied drama with Randolph Edmonds at Dillard University in New Orleans and centered her dreams around Paul Robeson and Marian Anderson. Although she greatly admired her English professor, Rudolf Moses, Richards left the university after one horrifying year, angered by the racism she found there.

Richards moved to San Diego, where she studied dance and apprenticed at the Globe Theatre, appearing in *The Little Foxes* and *Another Part of the Forest*. She also acted and choreographed for the San Diego

Community Theatre, winning three Atlas Awards for her performances. After three years, Richards moved to New York. She wrote poetry and taught at the Ophelia DeVore Charm School. In 1955, she performed at the Greenwich Mews Theatre in *Trouble in Mind*; in 1956 she appeared in Brecht's *Arturo Ui*. In an off-Broadway revival of *Take a Giant Step*, Richards was cast as a cantankerous eighty-three-year-old who is not afraid to fight back; she earned her union card and the praise of the critics, only one of whom thought she looked a little young for the part. She repeated her role in the film version, which was released in 1961. Richards was the understudy for Claudia McNeil in *A Raisin in the Sun* in 1959 and made her Broadway debut in October of that year in *The Miracle Worker*. She subsequently toured nationally with the play and appeared in the 1962 film version. In 1961, Richards was back on Broadway as Idella Landy in Ossie Davis's *Purlie Victorious*, and she repeated her role in the 1963 film version, entitled *Gone Are the Days*.

Richards returned to California to work with the Theatre of Being and Frank Silvera, who was her acting teacher, her director, and her co-star in James Baldwin's *The Amen Corner*. The play opened in Los Angeles in March 1964, bringing Beah Richards more acclaim than ever. She said that prior to this time she had merely acted at acting without really knowing what it was about—that she did not really become an actress until *The Amen Corner*. The role was Sister Margaret Alexander, who has to choose between loyalty to her storefront Harlem church and her alcoholic and wayward husband, who is dying. After a successful run in Los Angeles, the play moved to Broadway, where Richards won a Theatre World Award, a Tony nomination, and topped *Variety*'s drama critics poll for her performance.

In 1965, Richards began a new chapter in her career when she guest starred on the television series *The Big Valley*, with Barbara Stanwyck. Appearances on *Dr. Kildare* and *I Spy* followed, in 1966 and 1967, respectively, and television began to represent an increasing portion of her work. To date she has appeared in over thirty TV series and a dozen TV movies, including *Roots II: The Next Generation*; *The Bill Cosby Show* (a series regular as his mother, Rose Kincaid, 1970-71); *Ironside*; *Room 222*; *Sanford and Son*; *Frank's Place* (Emmy Award); *Murder, She Wrote*; *Benson*; *Equal Justice*; *Designing Women*; and *Beauty and the Beast*.

Richards did not give up her work on the big screen or on the stage, however, and 1967 saw the release of three feature films: *In the Heat of the Night*, *Hurry Sundown*, and *Guess Who's Coming to Dinner?*,

which earned her an Academy Award nomination. She enjoyed working with Spencer Tracy and Katharine Hepburn as well as with Sidney Poitier, who played her son. Other films include *The Great White Hope* (1970), *The Biscuit Eater* (1972), *Mahogany* (1975), *Big Shots* (1987), and *Drugstore Cowboy* (1989). On stage she performed in *The Crucible* at the Mark Taper Forum and *The Little Foxes* at Lincoln Center and on a national tour. Richards performed in *A Raisin in the Sun* at the Inner City Repertory Company in 1968 and 1974, and in the twenty-fifth anniversary production at the Yale Repertory Theatre in 1983.

Richards has been associated with Inner City Rep and the Inner City Cultural Center of Los Angeles since 1967. This continuing relationship has provided Richards with an oasis in which to nourish herself as an artist, as both actress and writer. Her play *One Is a Crowd* was produced by Inner City in 1971 and again in 1973, with Richards starring as Elizabeth Dundee. Much earlier, in 1957, Richards had published a poem in *Freedomways* entitled "A Black Woman Speaks." The work is both a reproach and a plea to white women to bring an end to racism. In 1974, Inner City published *A Black Woman Speaks and Other Poems*. The following year Richards adapted her poems to the stage in a one-woman show of the same name. She has performed this piece at theaters and colleges all over the country, including Dillard University in New Orleans and the New Federal Theatre in New York. *A Black Woman Speaks*, taped by KCET-TV in Los Angeles and broadcast in 1975, won an Emmy Award. Richards's commitment to Inner City includes sharing her skills and vision as a teacher of both professionals and beginners. She teaches scene exploration and the ideal of achieving a "skinless view of life." In spite of her involvement with youth, Richards made a conscious decision not to have children of her own. (She was married in 1963 to Virginia-born artist Hugh Harrel; the couple divorced after three years.) She is committed to creating a society that welcomes all children.

The Hills/Hollywood chapter of the National Association for the Advancement of Colored People (NAACP) presented Richards with its Second Annual Award for Lifetime Achievement in Theatre in 1989, and her television work has earned five nominations for the NAACP Image Award. In addition to the Theatre World Award (*The Amen Corner*, 1965), the Academy Award nomination (*Guess Who's Coming to Dinner?*, 1967) and the Emmy Award listed above, Richards has received the All-American Press Association Award, 1968; the Black Filmmakers Hall of

Fame Award, 1974; the NAACP Hall of Fame Image Award, 1986; and the ACE award, for best actress on a cable TV movie or miniseries, 1986.

BIBLIOGRAPHY

American Film (September 1978); *Amsterdam News* (July 31, 1976); Beckley, Paul V. Review of *Take a Giant Step,* New York *Herald Tribune* (September 20, 1956); Billops, Camille. Personal interview with Beah Richards, Los Angeles (March 25, 1975); Bronner, Edwin, ed. *The Encyclopedia of the American Theatre 1900-1975* (1980); Brooks, Tim, and Earle Marsh. *The Complete Directory to Prime Time Network TV Shows 1946 to the Present* (1985); *CBWA; DBT; Ebony,* "The Long Distance Runner Beah Richards: Talented Actress Pursued Her Dream from Mississippi to Broadway to Hollywood" (October 1987); Hammond, Sally. "Baldwin Heroine," *New York Post* (April 23, 1965); Mapp, Edward. *Directory of Blacks in the Performing Arts* (1990); Parish, James Robert. *Actors' Television Credits: 1950-1972* (1973); Parish, James Robert, with Mark Trost. *Actors' Television Credits Supplement I, 1978* (1978); Parish, James Robert, with Vincent Terrace. *Actors' Television Credits Supplement II, 1977-81* (1982); Patterson, Lindsay, ed. *International Library of Negro Life and History: Anthology of the American Negro in the Theatre* (1967); Richardson, Beulah. *A Black Woman Speaks* (1957); Sullivan, Kaye. *Films for, by and about Women Series II* (1985); *Take a Giant Step,* theater program. Billy Rose Theatre Collection, Library of the Performing Arts, New York City; Watts, Richard, Jr. Review of *Take a Giant Step, New York Post* (September 26, 1956); Wilding, Stephen. Interview with Beah Richards, *Black Stars* (March 1980); Woll, Allen. *Dictionary of Black Theatre* (1983); *WWBA* (1988).

SHAUNA VEY

RICHARDS, FANNIE M. (1841-1922)

Educator and clubwoman Fannie M. Richards was the first Black person to teach in Detroit's public schools.

Richards was born on October 1, 1841, in Fredericksburg, Virginia. She was one of fourteen children of Maria Louise Moore, a free person of color born in Toronto, and Adolphe Richards, a British-educated Hispanic with some African ancestry. All of the children received the best private education available, even as Virginia tightened restrictions on Black education. The Richardses risked expulsion from the state for educating their children.

When her husband died in 1851, Maria Richards moved the family to Detroit to escape the increasingly hostile atmosphere. Detroit had gained a reputation as a center of antislavery activity and had many Black settlers. The Richards family soon took its place among the Cultured 40, the educated, white-collar segment of the Black community. Fannie's brother John was a barber who was active politically and became known as Detroit's most eloquent orator.

Richards was educated in the then-segregated public schools of Detroit and decided to go into teaching. However, no normal school or university in the area would accept Black students at that time, so Richards moved to Toronto to study. After graduation from Toronto Normal School in 1863, she returned to Detroit and founded a private school for Black children. There was, at the time, only one public school for Detroit's Black students.

When Richards learned that a second public school for Black children was to open, she applied for a teaching position. She was hired over several other applicants and became the first Black teacher in Detroit's public schools. Four years later, she joined with a group of liberal citizens to sue the Detroit Board of Education over the board's refusal to comply with a Michigan Supreme Court order to integrate the state's schools. She provided funds for the suit and probably served as an advisor to the man who led it, future Michigan governor John Bagley.

Two years later, because of the court ruling in this action, Richards became the first Black teacher of white students in Detroit. For the next forty-four years she taught a wide variety of students at Everett School and developed a reputation as an outstanding teacher. She introduced the kindergarten concept to Detroit schools at a time when only Boston and New York had experimented with the idea.

Richards was also a clubwoman, active in charitable pursuits. She helped to found Detroit's Phyllis Wheatley Home for Aged Colored Ladies in 1897 and served as its first president.

Fannie M. Richards died in Detroit on February 13, 1922.

BIBLIOGRAPHY

DANB; Hartgrove, W. B. "The Story of Marie Louise Moore and Fannie M. Richards," *Journal of Negro History* (1916); Katzman, David M. *Before the Ghetto: Black Detroit in the Nineteenth Century* (1973); Moehlman, Arthur B. *Public Education in Detroit* (1925); *NBAW;* Peebles, Robin S. "Fannie Richards and the Integration of the Detroit Public Schools," *Michigan History* (1981).

JOHN REID

RICHARDSON, GLORIA ST. CLAIR HAYES (1922-)

Violent conflict raged in the streets and in the hearts of Black and white citizens when Gloria Richardson tried to lead the people of Cambridge, Maryland, to peace and freedom. "We live in a town where a man might be killed tomorrow," Richardson said in 1963, "where civil war might break out next week. It cannot get better while the white people fail to understand the mood of the Negro community and to realize that unless they grant the means of progress, their houses and ours may fly apart" (Brock 1990).

Gloria St. Clair Hayes Richardson came from a family of leaders. She was born on May 6, 1922, in Baltimore, the only child of John Edwards Hayes and Mabel Pauline St. Clair Hayes. When she was six years old, the Hayeses moved to Cambridge to be near other members of the prominent St. Clair family. Her grandfather, H. Maynadier St. Clair, was the second Black American to be elected to the city council of Cambridge, serving from 1912 to 1946. He was not, however, considered to be a strong voice for his people, and when his son, Herbert, made a bid to replace him, Herbert was defeated.

In the meantime, Gloria St. Clair Hayes attended Frederick Douglass High School and Howard University. She married and had a daughter, Donna. She grew increasingly angry about the conditions of life in Cambridge. In 1962, she took up the leadership of the town's Black community, but not by running for the city council. New methods were emerging in the struggle for justice, so Richardson assumed her leadership role as cochair of the Cambridge Nonviolent Action Committee (CNAC). She and others in Cambridge had been inspired to organize by a group of young freedom riders from New York and Baltimore. "There was something direct," she said, "something real about the way the kids waged nonviolent war. This was the first time I saw a vehicle I could work with" (Brock 1990). Richardson and other members of the St. Clair family became the nucleus of the new group, which was given support by the Student Nonviolent Coordinating Committee (SNCC).

On March 25, 1963, Richardson and her cochair, Inez Grubb, went before the city council with their demand—complete integration immediately. The alternative was public protest. Demonstrations began a few days later. There were sit-ins and picketing, demonstrations at the theater, the skating rink, city hall, the county courthouse, and the jail. Eighty protesters were arrested in seven weeks, including Richardson.

They were brought before the courts in May at the notoriously paternalistic "Penny Trials." Each defendant was given a suspended sentence and fined a penny. Judge W. Laird Henry lectured Richardson about disgracing her family name, and he trivialized the protesters' concerns.

Richardson went back out onto the streets. On May 14, 1963, three generations of women in her family were arrested. Donna Richardson was in a group of fourteen who were arrested for a sit-in in the lobby of the Dorset Theater. Gloria Richardson and her mother, Mabel St. Clair Booth, were arrested at the Dizzyland Restaurant. When protesters marched around the jail where they were being held, more were charged. That day, sixty-two Black people fighting for their rights were put behind bars.

Four days later, Judge Henry, realizing that his judicial rap on the knuckles had not been effective, announced that he and other members of the white community were ready to take the demonstrators seriously. He would free those arrested and organize a committee to negotiate a settlement with the Black community. The Committee on Interracial Understanding was set up, and the prisoners were released. The committee agreed that the basic demands of the demonstrators would be met. These included: complete desegregation of public places; complete desegregation of public schools; equal employment opportunities in industries and stores, with an initial quota of 10 percent; a public housing project and study of sewer and sidewalk needs; and an end to police brutality and appointment of a Black deputy sheriff. There was, for a few days, peace.

Then arrests began again as peaceful demonstrations and an economic boycott continued. On May 31, Richardson asked Attorney General Robert F. Kennedy to investigate the violations of constitutional rights that were occurring in Cambridge. One fifteen-year-old girl, Dinez White, was being held without bond after having been arrested for praying outside a segregated bowling alley. Kennedy did not respond to Richardson's appeal. Dinez White was released on a writ of habeas corpus, but on June 10 she was sentenced to an indeterminate term in a correctional school, along with another juvenile protester. When violence broke out, Richardson again asked Kennedy for help.

Three days later, state troopers surrounded the Black district. The governor of Maryland declared a state of martial law and sent in the National Guard. The Guard remained in Cambridge until July 8. When it left, students again tried to enter the Dizzyland Restaurant, and again violence broke out. Just three days after they had left, the National Guard was back but could not stop the violence. On July 16, a commission of both Black and white citizens was appointed to find a solution. A moratorium was called on demonstrations.

During this time, Gloria Richardson continued to search for peaceful solutions. She met with other civil rights leaders, Black and white, to try to find a way to bring calm without compromise. On July 15, upon her return from a conference on racial problems in Annapolis that was chaired by Maryland's governor, she was arrested on the streets of Cambridge. On July 17, Robert Kennedy gave a speech in which he suggested that she was responsible for the violence there. She sent him a letter protesting the charge. Again, at a rally at a local church, she warned that the situation could no longer be controlled by guns and promises. Only justice would avert further violence.

On July 22, 1963, a conference was held in Washington, D.C. Gloria Richardson and other civil rights leaders met with Robert Kennedy, General George Gelston, who was in charge of the National Guard in Cambridge, and Maryland State Attorney General Thomas B. Finon, among others. A treaty was signed.

That might have been the end of the open conflict. It might have been the beginning of progress toward justice. It covered five points: (1) complete and immediate desegregation of the public schools and hospitals in the county; (2) construction of 200 units of low-rent public housing; (3) employment of a Black advocate in the Cambridge office of the Maryland Department of Employment Security and in the Cambridge post office; (4) appointment of a human relations commission; and (5) adoption of the Charter Amendment providing for desegregation of public accommodations.

The fifth point contained a loophole. The Charter Amendment, by law, could be subjected to public referendum, so that treaty point was not firm. All present at the conference expressed the hope that no referendum would be called, but the hope proved baseless. Petitions were circulated, and more than enough signatures were obtained. When the referendum was placed on the ballot, Richardson took a highly controversial stand. She insisted that Black Americans already had, by virtue of the U.S. Constitution, the rights outlined in the referendum and refused to ask Black voters to support the referen-

Civil rights activist Gloria Richardson was deeply involved in sit-ins, demonstrations, and protests held by the Black community in Cambridge, Maryland, in the early 1960s. She is pictured at a 1963 meeting with Attorney General Robert Kennedy and Cambridge mayor Calvin Mowbray to discuss implementation of community demands for change. [UPI/ Bettmann]

dum. When it failed, many people blamed Richardson.

In the years that followed the days of conflict and violence in Cambridge, Black children began to enter white schools. The U.S. Civil Rights Commission issued a report vindicating the CNAC and criticizing Richardson's opponents. An on-the-job-training program was instituted in Cambridge. In the same month that the National Guard finally withdrew from Cambridge, President Lyndon Johnson signed into law the 1964 Civil Rights Act. However, when Richardson participated in a demonstration on the night that George Wallace spoke in Cambridge, she was arrested.

Gloria Richardson left Cambridge in August 1964. She moved to New York and married her second husband, Frank Dandridge. Her commitment to the rights of others has led her to work with the Department of Aging in New York City.

BIBLIOGRAPHY
Brock, Annette K. "Gloria Richardson and the Cambridge Movement." In *Women in the Civil Rights Movement: Trailblazers and Torchbearers, 1941-1965,* ed. Vicki L. Crawford, Jacqueline Anne Rouse, and Barbara Woods (1990); *CBWA*; Giddings, Paula. *When and Where I Enter: The Impact of Black Women on Race and Sex in America* (1984); *NBAW*.

KATHLEEN THOMPSON

RIDLEY, FLORIDA RUFFIN (1861-1943)

Florida Ruffin Ridley had for her role model a mother who had achieved distinction in her own right. Born in 1861 in Boston, Massachusetts, Florida Ruffin was the daughter of George Lewis Ruffin and Josephine St. Pierre Ruffin, one of the Black community's leading clubwomen. She was educated at Boston Teachers College and Boston University and then taught in the Boston public schools. She married Ulysses A. Ridley and had two children. Like her mother, Ridley had a multifaceted career as clubwoman and community activist.

Ridley was, throughout her life, active in her community. However, it is her work with her mother for which she is primarily remembered. In 1893, along with Maria Baldwin, Ruffin and Ridley founded the Woman's Era Club, which was open to women of all races, and Ridley's report to the first meeting is a matter of record. In the report, she talked about an antilynching leaflet published by the club, which indicates that the aims of the organization were not primarily social. Ridley spent three years, at one point, working with a kindergarten in Atlanta, Georgia, that was partially supported by the Woman's Era Club.

In 1895, Ridley was one of the organizers of the first national conference of Black women. Out of this Boston conference, which was attended by delegates from sixteen states and the District of Columbia, came the National Federation of Afro-American Women, of which Ridley was recording secretary. She was editor of its official magazine, the *Woman's Era,* until 1900. She was also active in the suffrage movement and was a member of the Brookline Equal Suffrage Association from 1894 to 1898.

During World War I, Ridley became deeply involved in activities supporting American soldiers. From 1917 to 1919, she was executive secretary of the Soldiers Comfort Unit, which evolved into the League of Women for Community Service. She was executive secretary of the League until 1925. At the same time, she was a member of the board of directors of the Robert Gould Shaw Settlement House. When the Cooperative Committee of Social Agencies was formed to coordinate the services of that house, the Harriet Tubman House, and the Boston Urban League, Ridley returned to her role as editor and took responsibility for its journal, the *Social Service News.*

Florida Ruffin Ridley died in March 1943 in Toledo, Ohio, where she had gone to live with her daughter. She was eighty-two years old.

BIBLIOGRAPHY
Brown, Hallie Q. *Homespun Heroines and Other Women of Distinction* ([1926] 1988); *CBWA*; *NBAW*.

KATHLEEN THOMPSON

RINGGOLD, FAITH (1934-)

Faith Ringgold, painter, sculptor, and performance artist, is perhaps one of the most famous contemporary Black women artists in America. Her work draws upon many artistic styles and media and has been exhibited throughout the world. She has received several awards in honor of her artistic achievement: a grant from the National Endowment for the Arts for sculpture, a Creative Artistic Public Service Grant, and a Guggenheim fellowship. Her work has always been intensely political, and in an art world characterized by conformity, racism, and sexism, Ringgold continues to be an independent, resistant voice for African-American women.

Faith Ringgold was born in 1934 in New York City. She grew up in Harlem where her father was a truck driver for the sanitation department and where her mother, after separating from Ringgold's father, was a dress designer. In high school, Ringgold realized she wanted to be an artist. She attended City College, but because women at that time were not accepted in the School of Liberal Arts, she had to attend the School of Education. She received a B.A. in art in 1955 with a minor in education and then went on to earn an M.A. in art in 1959. After graduation, she worked as an art teacher in the New York public school system.

The artistic training Ringgold received at City College focused on traditional, Western conceptions of high art. She was told that good art had its origins in classical Greece and could be traced through the work of European artists. When Ringgold tried to paint Black people, her teachers did not know how to mix the skin tones, and when she created purple and green flesh colors they criticized her for being exotic. Discouraged, she decided to follow the more acceptable route and went to Europe, where she adopted the French Impressionist style of painting. When she returned to America in 1960, however, bringing her Impressionist flowers and still lifes to the Ruth White Gallery in New York, she was told that a person like herself—a Black woman—could not create good European art. This was a reaction that Black artists repeatedly faced; they were told they could not paint in the high art style but were refused any other kind of formal training.

In 1963, Ringgold left New York City and the white art scene and decided to train herself. She began by reading James Baldwin and Amiri Baraka (LeRoi Jones) and studying African art. Like many other Black artists of the time, she adopted Alain Locke's philosophy that Black Americans had to learn from their African past and incorporate it into their own artistic styles. She was heavily influenced also by the changes taking place in Black political movements. The emphasis was shifting away from civil rights toward Black revolution, and when she heard Adam Clayton Powell and Stokely Carmichael urging Black people to stand up for Black Power, she knew she wanted her art to speak for those who were standing up and resisting with pride and dignity.

Out of this period emerged a series of paintings, including *The Flag Is Bleeding, U.S. Postage Stamp Commemorating the Advent of Black Power,* and *Die.*

These images contained the flat, matte style and interlocking geometric shapes that characterize much African art. In 1971-72, Ringgold painted a mural at the Women's House of Detention at Rikers Island, New York City, depicting the many different jobs women can do, in order to show that inmates could be rehabilitated. More and more, Ringgold's work began to focus on Black women speaking out. In the early 1970s, she started making portrait masks of women from Harlem. These African-like masks were made of bead fringe, embroidery, and fabric; many had their mouths open to show the need for women to find their own voices. By 1972, Ringgold was using these techniques to celebrate types of women's artistic expression that for so long had been devalued. She wanted to show that not only do women need to speak out, they can do so by claiming the ways in which women have been expressing themselves for generations.

Increasingly, Ringgold's work met with resistance, both from the white art world and Black male artists. White people found her art too politicized and overly concerned with Black issues. Black male artists found her art too influenced by African styles and soft media. They called her pieces weavings, wall hangings, crafts—anything but art. Ringgold believed they reacted this way because of the strong need to identify with the white art world's standards of excellence, standards that have no place for African influences or traditional female art forms.

Also in the 1970s, Ringgold was involved in numerous protests against racism and sexism in the art world. In 1970, the Whitney Museum of American Art organized an exhibit of artists from the 1930s in which not one Black artist was included. Although Ringgold helped organize the demonstration, neither she nor any of the other women involved were acknowledged. That same year, the leading male artists in the Venice Biennale took their work out of the show in a strike against racism, sexism, and the Vietnam War. They set up an alternative show, but, as Ringgold pointed out, no women or Black artists were represented. As a result of her protest, the exhibit was opened to women and minority artists. She joined the Ad Hoc Committee on Women Artists and Students for Black Liberation, which pressured museums to exhibit the work of women artists. In 1971, Ringgold, with Kay Brown and Dinga McGannon, put together a show of Black women artists called "Where We At."

In 1976, Ringgold began a new phase of artistic and political expression; she started to do performance art. Using her masks and soft sculptures, she created characters and stories that spoke about the Black experience in America. One of her most famous performance pieces, *The Wake and Resurrection of the Bicentennial Negro*, is about a young man who dies of an overdose and his wife who dies of grief. Both are resurrected by the love of the man's mother. More recently, Ringgold has turned to the medium of quilting. In her quilts entitled *Who's Afraid of Aunt Jemima*, *The Purple Quilt*, and *Slave Rape Story Quilt*, she uses fabric squares and narrative text to talk about the lives of different Black women. She tells her own story in *Change: Faith Ringgold's over 100 Pounds Weight Loss Story Quilt*, because she believes the traditional women's art of quilting is a powerful way to tell the story of women's lives.

BIBLIOGRAPHY
Lippard, Lucy. "Flying Her Own Flag," *Ms.* (July 1976); Miller, Lynn and Sally Swenson. *Lives and Works* (1981).

EMILY COUSINS

RIPERTON, MINNIE (1948-1979)
Known for her angelic five-octave range, Minnie Riperton became one of the most memorable songstresses of the 1970s.

Born in Chicago on November 8, 1948, Minnie Riperton began her career by training in opera, but as a teenager she joined a girl-group known as the Gems.

Riperton later landed a job as a receptionist at Chess Records. There, she did session background vocals for Etta James and Fontella Bass. After several session jobs, she joined the soul/psychedelic group Rotary Connection.

Riperton's solo career began under the pseudonym Andrea Davis, but the first solo album under her real name was the critically acclaimed *Come to My Garden*. Riperton augmented her career by touring with such luminaries as Quincy Jones and Roberta Flack and by doing session work with Stevie Wonder.

In 1974, she moved to Epic Records and recorded the aptly titled *Perfect Angel*. Produced by Stevie Wonder, *Perfect Angel* became Riperton's biggest seller, containing the haunting hit single "Lovin' You" (cowritten with her husband, Dicky Rudolph). Her next two Epic releases, *Adventures in Paradise* and *Stay in Love*, also sold well.

In 1976, Riperton was diagnosed with breast cancer, and she later became a spokesperson for the American Cancer Society. Still focused on her sing-

ing career, however, Riperton moved to Capitol Records, where she recorded the eponymous *Minnie* in 1979. *Minnie* contained such classics as "Memory Lane" and "Lovers and Friends."

On July 12, 1979, shortly after the release of *Minnie*, Riperton succumbed to cancer. In 1980, Capitol Records released the posthumous *Love Lives Forever*, a collection of 1978 tracks with new, studio-dubbed backing.

Although considered more of a cult songstress than a superstar, Riperton's crystal-clear, angelic voice has influenced the likes of Teena Marie and Mariah Carey.

BIBLIOGRAPHY
Jet. "Family Plans to Build Memorial Building for Minnie Riperton" (May 1, 1980), and "Many Toasts Lifted to Minnie Riperton as She Rests in Peace" (August 2, 1979); *New York Times*. Obituary (July 13, 1979); Norment, Lynn. "Minnie Riperton: 'Perfect Angel' Leaves Legacy of Love," *Ebony* (October 1979).

DISCOGRAPHY
For a discography, see Cordell, John. "Minnie Riperton Discography," *Goldmine* (October 1979).

JOHN MURPH

RIVERS, EUNICE *see*
LAURIE, EUNICE RIVERS

ROBERTS, LILLIAN DAVIS (1928-)
"Lillian Roberts Day" was proclaimed by New York Governor Hugh Carey on January 9, 1981, in tribute to the labor leader's importance to the political and economic struggles of working people. As associate director of New York City's District Council 37, American Federation of State, County and Municipal Employees (AFSCME), Lillian Roberts had been at the forefront of labor battles for decades. Two months later Carey named her New York's State Industrial Commissioner; she was the first Black woman appointed to this position. Such honors from the state were in stark contrast to her stand against Governor Nelson Rockefeller in 1968 and her subsequent jailing, despite mass protests, for organizing a state hospital workers' strike in violation of a public employees no-strike law.

Lillian Davis was born on January 2, 1928, on Chicago's south side to Lillian and Henry Davis, the second of five children. As part of the great migration of Black people out of the South, her parents came to Chicago from Mississippi two years before her birth. Her mother's prayers and religiosity gave strength and emotional protection to the family while her leadership in community struggles for better education, humane welfare services, and housing provided young Lillian Davis with a model of committed womanhood. With her family's encouragement, she finished high school and was awarded a scholarship to the University of Illinois in 1945, but the scholarship did not cover her living expenses. After a year and a half, when the brother who was helping her was drafted and the welfare then supporting her family would not provide room and board, she was forced to quit her only formal higher education and to return to Chicago to find work.

Lillian Davis was hired in 1946 as the first Black nurses' aide in the nursery at Chicago's Lying-In Hospital when war-related positions were still pulling white women into better-paying jobs and Black women's work in hospitals was primarily limited to the kitchens. The work fascinated her and she took every opportunity to ask questions, to learn more, to become more skilled. As a so-called non-professional, she was never included in the shift report meetings of nurses, but she was often informally left in charge of the nursery and given teaching responsibilities with the new medical students. Davis married silkscreen operator William Roberts in 1948 and settled into a life of paid labor and homemaking.

After ten years, an overwork grievance pushed Roberts into work with the hospital workers' union, AFSCME. Her aggressiveness and sense of fair play quickly made her a shop steward and brought her into conflict with hospital management. The AFSCME organizer, Victor Gotbaum, recognized her skills and offered her a job with the union. It was the beginning of a life-long labor alliance. Lillian Roberts quickly demonstrated her organizing skill, bringing both white and Black workers together and into the union. Deeply committed to working-class empowerment, she fought against racism in all forms and for the union she saw as vital to democracy. Amid these struggles, tragedy struck her family. A brother was killed by the Chicago police and her sister was murdered by her husband, leaving three young sons that Roberts and her husband began to raise.

By 1965, Victor Gotbaum had become executive director of District Council 37 of AFSCME in New York City and he called Roberts to assist on a social service workers' strike. She subsequently directed a hard-fought campaign against the Teamsters Union that led to AFSCME's victory as the union for New York City's nonprofessional workers in nineteen municipal hospitals. Her organizing, three years later, of the state hospital workers led to violations of the state's no-strike law and her two-week jailing. At home, her mother assisted in the raising of her sister's sons while Roberts's marriage to William ended in divorce after twenty years.

Rising to director of the hospital division, then associate director of District Council 37 with its 600-person staff and 110,000 members, Roberts continued to fight for improved working conditions, better wages, and her own union project: a training program that made it possible for working union members to certify as licensed practical nurses. With Gotbaum, she built the union into a strong voice for labor in the maelstrom of New York City labor and municipal politics, and into the leader in worker education, with the creation of a District Council 37 campus at the College of New Rochelle. In recognition of her skills and renown, in 1981 Governor Carey named Roberts the state's Industrial Commissioner, a title she fittingly had changed to Labor Commissioner. She was reappointed to this position by Governor Mario Cuomo in 1982, as she was leading a fight against sweat shop conditions in the garment industry, promoting employment opportunities, organizing training programs, and working to see that surplus food was dispensed to the needy. She was awarded numerous honors, including an honorary doctorate from the College of New Rochelle, the National Association for the Advancement of Colored People's Roy Wilkins Award, and the Adam Clayton Powell Government Award.

Roberts was forced to resign in 1987 from the Labor Commissioner post after internal struggles with the governor. She became senior vice-president of Total Health Systems, a health maintenance organization in New York, and directed their marketing to union, government, and commercial sectors. She is remembered for her dignity, her militancy, and her commitment to democracy and to the education of working-class people of all races.

BIBLIOGRAPHY

Dionne, E. J., Jr. "District 37 Aide Named by Carey to Fill Labor Job," *New York Times* (March 31, 1981); Ferretti, Fred. "Tribute to a Trade Unionist Draws the City's Leaders," *New York Times* (January 12, 1981); Johnson, Rudy. "Lillian Roberts: A First Lady of Labor." Unpublished manuscript (1992); Reverby, Susan. "From Aide to Organizer: The Oral History of Lillian Roberts." In *Women of America: A History*, ed. Carol Berkin and Mary Beth Norton (1979); Reverby, Susan. "The Oral History of

Lillian Roberts." In *The Twentieth-Century Trade Union Woman: Vehicle for Social Change*, ed. Joyce Kornbluh (1979).

SUSAN M. REVERBY

ROBERTS, RUTH LOGAN (1891-1968)

"The basic cause of most problems in Harlem is segregation. Segregation makes ghettoes, which breed riots, unemployment, disease" (Woltman n.d.). With these words Ruth Logan Roberts made known her views about the community in which she lived for over fifty years. One of Harlem's more renowned cultural salons, her home at 130 West 130 Street was known throughout New York City's "elite" Black community as a place where aspiring young people could come to enjoy a warm welcome, excellent food, and stimulating conversation. Often called a Harlem society leader, Ruth Logan Roberts disliked such pretensions, and although she enjoyed international travel, elegant clothes, and the company of intellectuals, she often immersed herself in a wide variety of volunteer activities.

Ruth Logan Roberts, daughter of suffragist Adella Hunt Logan, was born in Tuskegee, Alabama, in 1891. She served on the national board of the Young Women's Christian Association (YWCA) as well as the board of directors of the Harlem YWCA, and Governor Thomas E. Dewey appointed her to the New York State Board of Social Welfare. Roberts's most significant contributions came, however, through her involvement with health-related organizations. She was the wife of one physician, Eugene Percy Roberts, and the sister of two others; a graduate of Sargeant School of Physical Education, where she was trained in physical therapy; and a director of physical education for girls at Tuskegee Institute. Roberts was a member of the boards of the New York Tuberculosis and Health Association, the Katy Ferguson Home for Unmarried Mothers, and, most significantly, the National Association of Colored Graduate Nurses. Her association with the latter organization centered on her unwavering efforts to desegregate training facilities and to equalize treatment of Black nurses. She protested discrimination against Black nurses in the military by writing directly to President Franklin Delano Roosevelt and other government officials during World War II. At Tuskegee, as early as 1913 she lobbied for woman's suffrage, and for many years she was active in Republican party politics.

She had no children of her own but raised her far-younger siblings, and she worked with organizations dedicated to the youth of New York City, where she lived until her death in 1968.

[*See also* LOGAN, ADELLA HUNT; LOGAN, MYRA ADELE.]

BIBLIOGRAPHY

Hine, Darlene Clark. *Black Women in White* (1989); "Ruth Logan Roberts." Obituary, *New York Times* (October 3, 1968); Roberts, Ruth Logan. Personal interviews; Booker T. Washington Collection, Library of Congress, Washington, D.C.; Woltman, Frederick. "The Little Known Harlem," *New York Post* (n.d.).

ADELE LOGAN ALEXANDER

ROBESON, ESLANDA GOODE (1896-1965)

Intellectual, writer, and activist Eslanda Goode Robeson was born on December 12, 1896, in Washington, D.C., where she grew up in a middle-class African-American family. Her maternal grandfather was Francis Lewis Cardozo, a noted Black politician in South Carolina during Reconstruction. In the early 1900s, Eslanda's family moved to New York City where she finished high school and studied chemistry at Columbia University, receiving a B.S. in 1923. She later attended the London School of Economics and then earned a doctorate in anthropology from Hartford Seminary.

In 1921, she married Paul Robeson, then one of the few African-American students attending Columbia University's Law School. In 1927, they had a child, Paul, Jr. Her husband eventually earned an international reputation as a singer, actor, and outspoken left-wing political activist.

Eslanda Robeson's main political activity, from the 1930s through the mid-1960s, was on behalf of the colonized people of the world, primarily Africans. Along with her husband, she traveled all over the world and lived for extended periods of time in London and Moscow. In 1936, she visited Africa for the first time, accompanied by her young son, and later published a book, *African Journey*, which was the diary of her trip. In 1938, she traveled to Spain to support anti-Fascist troops fighting in the Spanish Civil War against Franco. These experiences fueled an international perspective and a commitment to decolonization and independence for all nations.

Often overshadowed by her brilliant husband, Eslanda Goode Robeson had a distinguished career as an opponent of racism, colonialism, and all forms of oppression. In 1951 she was one of three protesters who disrupted the United Nations' postwar conference on genocide to argue, unsuccessfully, that ending vigilante violence against African-Americans should be a part of the group's agenda. [Schomburg Center]

She was a pioneer advocate for African self-determination. In 1941, Robeson cofounded the Council on African Affairs, a group of African-Americans who lobbied aggressively against colonialism in Africa. The group hoped that in the wake of World War II the reordering of the world political map would include decolonization. Robeson represented the council as a delegate observer to the founding convention of the United Nations in 1945. In 1951, she was one of three protesters who disrupted the United Nations

postwar conference on genocide to argue, unsuccessfully, that ending vigilante violence against African-Americans should be a part of the agenda. In 1958, she attended the All-African Peoples Conference in the newly independent African nation of Ghana as a representative of the Council on African Affairs and one of the few women delegates.

In addition to her staunch opposition to colonialism, Eslanda Robeson was also a strong supporter of Socialist countries like the Soviet Union and China after its 1949 revolution, and although neither she nor her husband was ever an open member of the Communist party, many of their friends were, and the couple made no apologies for these associations or their left-wing sympathies. Her dissident political views led to her being called before the House Un-American Activities Committee (HUAC) in 1953 to defend her past political affiliations. Robeson refused to cooperate with what she deemed the anti-Communist hysteria that was the impetus for the committee's investigations. She was reprimanded by HUAC chairman, Senator Joseph McCarthy, for her actions. In the late 1940s and early 1950s, Paul Robeson was denied work because of his political views, and both he and Eslanda were labeled Communist subversives. In 1958, the couple moved to the Soviet Union to escape the political persecution and racial discrimination they faced in the United States. They lived there for five years. When they returned to the United States in 1963, the Vietnam War was under way. Eslanda did not hesitate to immediately speak out against the war and in support of the growing peace movement. It was one of her last acts of political defiance. Two years later, in 1965, she died of cancer.

BIBLIOGRAPHY

Duberman, Martin Bauml. *Paul Robeson: A Biography* (1988); *DANB*; *NAW*; Ransby, Barbara. "Eslanda Goode Robeson, Pan-Africanist," *Sage* (Fall 1986). The Eslanda Goode Robeson papers are in the Moorland-Spingarn Research Center, Howard University, Washington, D.C.

BARBARA RANSBY

ROBINSON, BERNICE (1914-)

Bernice Robinson was an educator and activist during the civil rights movement in the American South. She served as the first teacher in the citizenship school program developed in the South Carolina Sea Islands in the late 1950s. This program eventually spread across the South and was responsible for encouraging thousands of Black Americans to register to vote in the early 1960s, changing the political face of the South.

Robinson was born in Charleston, South Carolina, on February 7, 1914. Her father, James Christopher Robinson, a bricklayer, was a union organizer, although his daughter did not know this until she became an activist herself many years later. Her mother, Martha Elizabeth Anderson Robinson, was a seamstress and homemaker. Both parents taught their children to be self-reliant and, in particular, to avoid relying on the white community. This would be an important factor for Robinson when she became politically active.

Finishing high school in the segregated system in Charleston, Robinson hoped to pursue studies in music. She decided to live with her sister in New York City and work in order to earn tuition for a music conservatory in Boston. Over the next ten years she held a variety of jobs in New York City in the garment industry, as a beautician, and in civil service. In 1947, when her parents became ill, she postponed her hope of entering the conservatory and returned to Charleston. By this time she had married and divorced and was raising a daughter, Jacquelyn, on her own.

Her time in New York heightened her awareness of racial discrimination and injustice, and when she returned to South Carolina she became active in the NAACP and the YWCA working on the issues of job discrimination and political disenfranchisement. In 1954, an aunt, Septima Clark, invited Robinson to attend a workshop at the Highlander Folk School in Tennessee.

The workshop experience was a pivotal one. There she worked with another South Carolina low country leader, Esau Jenkins, who spoke of the need for an adult education class to help rural Black residents learn basic literacy skills in order to pass the voter registration test. The Highlander Folk School and Jenkins joined forces to begin the citizenship education program in the Sea Islands. Septima Clark became director of the program and Robinson was asked to be the first teacher.

Reluctant at first, she eventually agreed, acknowledging that as an independent person (a beautician who did not rely on white customers) and as someone not wedded to formal ideas about teaching, she could play an important role in this unusual school. She told the students, "I'm really not going to be your teacher. We're going to work together and teach each other" (Carawan 1989). Robinson and Clark built the curriculum for the adult classes around the specific needs and interests of the students. The schools were so popular they spread quickly throughout the Sea Islands. As word of them spread, requests came in from across the South for literacy classes aimed at political empowerment and for the training of teachers like themselves. The citizenship school program became the prototype for the southern voter education program that was eventually taken over by the Southern Christian Leadership Conference (SCLC).

Robinson spent the 1960s and 1970s as a civil rights activist and teacher. She worked first at Highlander, and later for SCLC. She traveled the South providing workshops on political empowerment. When she returned to live in Charleston, she was urged to run for the state legislature in 1972. Though unsuccessful, she remained active in local politics and community affairs. She served on Highlander's board of directors for many years.

Bernice Robinson continues to live in Charleston. She has been honored with a distinguished service award from the NAACP and from the Black caucus of the South Carolina State Legislature. She maintains a lively interest in political and social developments and urges people not to become complacent.

[See also HIGHLANDER FOLK SCHOOL.]

BIBLIOGRAPHY

Brown, Cynthia Stokes. *Ready from Within. Septima Clark and the Civil Rights Movement* (1986); Carawan, Guy and Candie Carawan. *Ain't You Got a Right to the Tree of Life? The People of Johns Island, South Carolina* (1989); Horton, Aimee Isgrig. *The Highlander Folk School, A History of Its Major Programs, 1932-1961* (1989); Horton, Myles (with Judith Kohl and Herbert Kohl). *The Long Haul* (1990); Oldendorf, Sandra Brenneman. *Highlander Folk School and the South Carolina Sea Island Citizenship Schools: Implications for the Social Studies.* Ph.D. diss. (1987); Phenix, Lucy Massie. *You Got to Move.* Video production, First Run Features (1986); Tjerandsen, Carl. *Education for Citizenship: A Foundation's Experience* (1980); Wigginton, Eliot, ed. *Refuse to Stand Silently By: An Oral History of Grass-roots Social Activism in America, 1921-1964* (1992); Williams, Juan. *Eyes on the Prize, America's Civil Rights Years, 1954-1965* (1987).

CANDIE CARAWAN

ROBINSON, JO ANN GIBSON (1912-)

As president in the early 1950s of the Women's Political Council (WPC) of Montgomery, Alabama, Jo Ann Gibson Robinson was one of several crucial initiators of the Montgomery Bus Boycott of 1955-56. Robinson was an influential and leading figure both during the two years of Black civic activism leading up to the boycott and as a major player in the significant events that transformed the arrest of Rosa Parks into a communitywide protest movement.

Jo Ann Gibson was born near Culloden, Georgia, on April 17, 1912, the youngest of twelve children. Educated in the segregated public schools of Macon and then at Fort Valley State College, she became a public school teacher in Macon, where she was briefly married to Wilbur Robinson. After their one child died in infancy, Robinson left Macon after five years of teaching and went to Atlanta, where she earned an M.A. in English at Atlanta University. In the fall of 1949, after teaching one year at Mary Allen College in Crockett, Texas, Robinson accepted a position at Alabama State College. She was a professor of English at Alabama State throughout the boycott.

In Montgomery she joined both the Dexter Avenue Baptist Church and the WPC, which had been founded three years earlier by another Alabama State English professor, Mary Fair Burks. At Christmastime in 1949, Robinson endured a deeply humiliating experience at the hands of an abusive and racist Montgomery City Lines bus driver, and she resolved then and there that the WPC would target racial seating practices on Montgomery buses. Many other Black citizens had had similar experiences, and for the next several years the WPC repeatedly asked city authorities to improve racial seating practices and address the conduct of abusive bus drivers. In May 1954, more than eighteen months before the arrest of Rosa Parks but just several days after news of the U.S. Supreme Court's *Brown* v. *Board of Education* decision began to sweep the country, Robinson wrote to Montgomery's mayor as WPC president, gently threatening a Black boycott of city buses if abuses were not curtailed.

Following Rosa Parks's arrest in December 1955, Robinson played a central role in beginning the protest by immediately producing the leaflets that spread word of the hoped-for boycott among the Black citizens of Montgomery. She became one of the most active board members of the Montgomery Improvement Association, the new Black community group created to lead the boycott, but she remained out of the limelight in order to protect her teaching position at Alabama State as well as those of her colleagues. In 1960, Robinson left Alabama State (and Montgomery), as did other activist faculty members.

After teaching one year at Grambling College in Grambling, Louisiana, Robinson moved to Los An-geles, where she taught English in the public schools until her retirement in 1976 and where she was active in a number of women's community groups. Robinson's health suffered a serious decline just as her memoir, *The Montgomery Bus Boycott and the Women Who Started It*, was published in 1987. She was honored by a 1989 publication prize given by the Southern Association for Women Historians, but was unable to accept the award in person.

[*See also* MONTGOMERY BUS BOYCOTT; WOMEN'S POLITICAL COUNCIL, MONTGOMERY, ALABAMA.]

BIBLIOGRAPHY

Burks, Mary Fair. "Trailblazers: Women in the Montgomery Bus Boycott." In *Women in the Civil Rights Movement*, ed. Vicki L. Crawford et al. (1990); Garrow, David J., ed. *The Montgomery Bus Boycott and the Women Who Started It: The Memoir of Jo Ann Gibson Robinson* (1987), and *The Walking City* (1989).

DAVID J. GARROW

As a professor of English at Alabama State College and as president of the Women's Political Council of Montgomery, civil rights activist Jo Ann Robinson was an influential and leading figure in the Montgomery Bus Boycott of 1955-56.

ROBINSON, RUBY DORIS *see* SMITH-ROBINSON, RUBY DORIS

THE ROLLIN SISTERS

During the Reconstruction period, the five Rollin sisters were well known socially and politically among the people of Columbia, the South Carolina capital. The sisters were Frances Anne (1845-1901), Charlotte, known as Lottie (b. 1849), Kate (1851-76), Louisa (b. 1858), and Florence (b. 1861). They have been celebrated for their cultural and political influence within the Black and white Radical Reconstruction government in South Carolina.

The Rollin family was among the elite South Carolina families of color, descendants of emigres who fled the Haitian Revolution in the late eighteenth century. The parents, William and Margaretta Rollin, were married in 1844. They lived in an elegant mansion on American Street in Charleston. William was a fair-skinned mulatto who operated a successful lumber yard and transported lumber by ship between the port of Charleston and South Carolina coastal plantations. He and Margaretta sent all their daughters to private, Catholic parish schools for free "colored" people in Charleston and then to the North for secondary education in Boston and Philadelphia. Both of these urban centers had large free-Black networks. Frances, Lottie, Louisa, and Kate attended school in Philadelphia. Lottie and Kate also enrolled at Dr. Dio Lewis's Family School for Young Ladies in Boston.

After the Civil War, the family moved to Columbia. Of the five sisters, Frances, Lottie, and Louisa were the most active in Reconstruction politics. Kate's illness and death, at the age of twenty-five, in 1876 prevented her from participating as fully as did her other sisters. Kate was said to have been engaged to marry a white South Carolina senator from Colleton County. Little else is known about her.

Of the three political activists, the youngest was Louisa. She addressed the South Carolina House of Representatives in 1869 to urge support for universal suffrage. Like her sisters, Louisa was a feminist and woman suffragist.

Lottie Rollin was well known in South Carolina and in the American Woman Suffrage Association (AWSA). In 1870, she was elected secretary of the South Carolina Woman's Rights Association, an affiliate of the AWSA. In 1871, Lottie led a meeting at the state capital to promote woman suffrage. By 1872, she was elected by her state organization to represent South Carolina as an ex-officio member of the executive committee for AWSA, which met in New York City.

Frances Rollin, who became the wife of William J. Whipper, appears to have been the only sister who married. Through her descendants, more information about her life has survived than about her siblings. Like Lottie and Louisa, Frances was a feminist. She was also an educator and a civil rights activist. She kept company with the leading Black abolitionist women in Philadelphia during the antebellum period, including Sarah M. Douglass and Charlotte Forten.

Like Charlotte Forten, Frances kept a diary, written during her 1868 sojourn in Boston, the same year she published the biography of the abolitionist and emigrationist Martin R. Delany. She published the book, *The Life and Times of Martin Robison Delany*, under the name Frank A. Rollin. Delany wanted a competent and sympathetic author to write about his life but felt the public would not accept the book seriously if the author was known to be female.

Frances Rollin had met Delany when he was a Freedmen's Bureau agent in Charleston and she was teaching with the bureau in the Sea Islands. It was with the help of the bureau that Frances sued the captain of a Sea Islands steamer for refusing to honor her first-class ticket because she was Black. Frances won the suit, and the captain was fined.

After completing her book on Delany in 1868, Frances began working for William James Whipper as a law clerk in his Columbia law office. He was born free in Philadelphia, the nephew of Black abolitionist William Whipper. In an attempt to escape the racial prejudice in the United States, Whipper's parents took him to Chatham, Canada, to live in a Black settlement. During the Civil War, he returned to the states, joined the Union Army, and settled in South Carolina. Whipper served in the state constitutional convention and became a state senator and later a judge. He was a supporter of women's rights, and he married the talented Frances Rollin shortly after he hired her in 1868.

After marriage, Frances taught at Avery Institute, a well-respected Black postsecondary education institution in the 1870s and 1880s. She also began a family. Frances and William Whipper conceived five children. The three who survived grew to be successful adults. Their only son, Leigh Whipper, became a stage and screen actor, well known in the 1940s and 1950s.

The eldest surviving Whipper was Winifred. She taught in the "colored" schools at the turn of the century in the District of Columbia. The youngest surviving daughter, Ionia Rollin Whipper, attended Howard University Medical College in the 1890s. She did so with the help of her mother, who by then had separated from William Whipper. Frances wrote Whitefield McKinlay, Washington realtor and political ally of Booker T. Washington, asking for a loan to help pay Ionia's tuition. Frances's investment in her daughter was worthwhile: Ionia Whipper became a gynecologist and the founder of the Whipper Home for Unwed Mothers, the only facility of the kind that accepted Black girls in the racially segregated nation's capital.

Frances Anne Rollin Whipper died in 1901, shortly after her daughter completed medical school but not before Frances saw Ionia provide services to the Black middle-class Washington, D.C., community that they had adopted. There appear to be no extant records of what happened to Lottie and Louisa Rollin after the Reconstruction era. They both were living in Columbia during the 1880s after their parents separated, and Margaretta moved in with Frances when William Rollin died. The sisters lost most of their wealth and property at the end of the century, as did many Black Americans during the depressions of the 1890s and the political setbacks resulting from the conservative Democratic backlash that drove out the Radical Republicans following Reconstruction. Nonetheless, the Rollin sisters remain part of the legacy and social history remembered from the era when Black Americans significantly influenced the politics of South Carolina.

BIBLIOGRAPHY

Bennett, Lerone. *Black Power USA: The Human Side of Reconstruction, 1867-1877* (1969); *DANB*; Ione, Carole. *Pride of Family: Four Generations of American Women of Color* (1991); Terborg-Penn, Rosalyn. "Nineteenth-Century Black Women and Woman Suffrage," *Potomac Review* (Spring-Summer 1977).

ROSALYN TERBORG-PENN

ROLLINS, CHARLEMAE HILL
(1897-1979)

When children ask baffling questions about life, parents and teachers must find answers that are honest and satisfying. Artists offer answers through their pictures, musicians through their music, and authors through honest portrayal of people in books. This was the view of Charlemae Hill Rollins, librarian, author, and children's literature specialist, who led a lifelong crusade to change the image of Black people in children's literature and promote the publication of books about the Black experience in American life and culture. During the thirty-six years of her professional career, Rollins taught children's literature, lectured widely, and wrote articles about the importance of storytelling and the role of books in helping young people understand themselves and the peoples of other cultures.

Charlemae Hill was born in Yazoo City, Mississippi, on June 20, 1897, to Allen G. and Birdie (Tucker) Hill. The family moved to Oklahoma before it became a state. She was educated in her hometown of Beggs but later attended secondary schools in St. Louis, Missouri, and Holly Springs, Mississippi. Hill attended Howard University and taught school for a short period of time. She received her library training at the University of Chicago and Columbia University. In 1918, she married Joseph Walker Rollins. Shortly after the birth of their son, Joseph, Jr., the family moved to Chicago, where Charlemae lived until her death on February 3, 1979.

Rollins joined the staff of the Chicago Public Library as a junior assistant in 1926. When the George C. Hall Branch of the Chicago Public Library opened in 1932, Rollins was placed in charge of the children's room. At this branch, in the heart of the Black community, Rollins became popular and widely known for her storytelling, which she believed helped children escape from hate, rejection, and injustice. For middle- and working-class families and their children, she emphasized planning programs and developing the book collection so that they could find information about their heritage.

Rollins decried the absence of books about prominent Black Americans and their contributions to American history, and she disparaged the distorted images of Black characters in books for children and young adults. With characteristic creativity and energy she solicited help from publishers and worked with her colleagues at the Chicago Public Library to select those materials that presented realistic portrayals of Black life. Later in life she published an anthology of Black folklore about Christmas and wrote accurate and respectful biographies about Black poets and entertainers as well as eminent Black men and women.

Rollins gained national attention for initiating, coordinating, and revising *We Build Together*, a bibliography of acceptable children's books about Black people. Published by the National Council of Teachers of English in 1941, the list was revised in 1948 and 1967, during the postwar years and the civil rights movement when there was growing concern about racial prejudice. The theme of the list, that Black people are human beings and should not be depicted as stereotypes, gave tangible expression to Rollins's lifelong crusade. Acknowledged as an expert on intercultural relations and children's literature, she lectured widely on these topics, taught children's literature at Roosevelt and other universities, conducted workshops on storytelling, and contributed articles to professional journals.

A recipient of numerous awards for her humanitarianism, community service, and contributions to education, Rollins received the American Brotherhood Award from the National Conference of Christians and Jews (1952), the Woman of the Year Award, Zeta Phi Beta (1956), the Good American Award of the Chicago Committee of One Hundred (1962), and the Women's National Book Association Constance Lindsay Skinner Award (1970). She was awarded the Doctor of Humane Letters from Columbia College, Chicago in 1974. Her book *Black Troubador: Langston Hughes* won the Coretta Scott King Award in 1971.

During the 1950s, Rollins was an active member of the American Library Association (ALA). She was a member of the ALA Council for four years, held the office of treasurer for the Children's Library Association, and served as president of the Children's Services Division (1957-58). ALA honored her contributions to children's work and literature by awarding her the American Library Association Letter (1953), the Grolier Society Award (1955), and the Children's Reading Round Table Award (1963). ALA also extended its highest award, Honorary Membership, to Rollins in 1972.

BIBLIOGRAPHY

American Libraries, "Charlemae Rollins—Librarian and Storyteller" (September 1974); *BAW*; Commire, Ann. *Something about the Author* (1972); *Dictionary of American Library Biography*, supplement (1990); Hopkins, Lee Bennett. *More Books by More People* (1974); Saunders, Doris. "Charlemae Rollins," *ALA Bulletin* (February 1955); *SBAA*; Shaw, Spencer G. "Charlemae Hill Rollins, 1897-1979: In Tribute," *Public Libraries* (Fall 1982); Thompson, Era Bell. "Crusade in Children's Books," *Negro Digest* (August 1950).

SELECTED WORKS BY CHARLEMAE HILL ROLLINS

Black Troubador: Langston Hughes (1970); *Call of Adventure* (1962); *Christmas Gift* (1963); *Famous American Negro Entertainers of Stage and Screen* (1967); *Famous American Negro Poets for Children* (1965); *Magic World of Books* (1952); *They Showed the Way: Forty American Negro Leaders* (1964); *We Build Together: A Reader's Guide to Negro Life and Literature for Elementary and High School Use* ([1941] 1948, 1967).

BETTY L. JENKINS

ROSS, DIANA *see* THE SUPREMES, DIANA ROSS AND

RUDOLPH, WILMA GLODEAN (1940-)

At the 1960 Rome Olympics, Wilma Glodean Rudolph made her mark in track by becoming the first American woman ever to win three gold medals. That achievement established her as one of the outstanding female athletes in the world.

The twentieth of twenty-two children, Wilma was born near Clarksville, Tennessee, on June 23, 1940, to Ed and Blanche Rudolph. Polio had left Wilma at four years old with little chance of ever walking, but with her family's help Wilma was able to discard her brace and corrective shoes by the age of twelve. By age sixteen, six-foot-tall "Skeeter," as she was nicknamed, had already been named an All-State player in basketball and won a bronze medal at the 1956 Olympics in the 4 x 100 meter relay. Just two years later, Rudolph believed her dreams of a college education and Olympic gold medal were over when she discovered she was pregnant.

With the support of coach Ed Temple, Rudolph attended Tennessee State University on a full track scholarship. In 1960, she returned to the Olympics and won gold medals in the 100 meter dash, 200 meter dash, and 4 x 100 meter relay. She held world records in all three events at the time she retired from amateur competition in 1962. After graduating from Tennessee State University in 1963, Wilma married high school sweetheart Robert Eldridge, with whom she had four children: Yolanda (1958), Djuanna (1964), Robert, Jr. (1965), and Xurry (1971). Since then she has worked as a teacher, coach, and director of youth foundations, finally settling in Indianapolis, Indiana.

Wilma Rudolph is one of the most celebrated female athletes of all time. During her competitive years she was voted the United Press Athlete of the Year (1960), the Associated Press Woman Athlete of

A victim of polio at age four, Wilma Rudolph overcame many obstacles to become the first American woman ever to win three gold medals in the Olympics. Shown here at far left with her 400-meter relay teammates Lucinda Jones, Barbara Jones, and Martha Hudson in 1960, she has since received numerous honors and awards, including being named one of America's Greatest Women Athletes. [National Archives]

the Year (1960, 1961), the James E. Sullivan Award (1961), and the Babe Didrickson Zaharias Award (1962). Rudolph's more recent honors include being inducted into the Black Sports Hall of Fame (1973), the Women's Sports Hall of Fame (1980), and the U.S. Olympic Hall of Fame (1983). In 1984, she was one of five sports stars selected by the Women's Sports Foundation as America's Greatest Women Athletes.

During a period of reemergence of the female athlete, Wilma Rudolph had a significant impact. She was one of the first major role models for both Black and female athletes, and her success and popularity during the 1960 Olympics gave a tremendous boost to women's track in the United States. In addition, her celebrity caused gender barriers to be broken in previously all-male track and field events such as the Millrose Games and the Penn Relays.

Although remembered primarily for her Olympic achievements, Rudolph also has made significant contributions through her work with youth. In 1977, her autobiography, *Wilma*, was published and adapted for a television movie. Now divorced, she currently heads the Wilma Rudolph Foundation, a nonprofit organization she started in 1981 to train young athletes.

BIBLIOGRAPHY

Adams, Lucinda Williams. "My Olympic Experience," *JOHPERD* (March 1988); Bernstein, Margaret. "That Championship Season," *Essence* (July 1984); Biracree, Tom. *Wilma Rudolph* (1988); DeFrantz, Anita. "Woman and Leadership in Sport," *JOHPERD* (March 1988); *Ebony* "Whatever Happened to Wilma Rudolph?" (February 1984); Gerber, Ellen, et al. *The American Woman in Sport* (1974); Guttman, Allen. *The Games Must Go On* (1984); Hart, M. Marie. "On Being Female in Sport." In *Out of the Bleachers*, ed. Stephanie Twin (1979); Jacobs, Linda. *Wilma Rudolph: Run for Glory* (1975); Lanker, Brian. *I Dream a World: Portraits of Black Women Who Changed America* (1989); Markel, Robert, Nancy Brooks, and Susan Markel. *For the Record: Woman in Sports* (1985); Rudolph, Wilma. *Wilma* (1977); Uglow, Jennifer S., ed. *The Continuum Dictionary of Women's Biography: New Expanded Edition* (1989); Wallechinsky, David. *The Complete Book of the Olympics* (1984); *Wilma*. RCA/Columbia Pictures (1977).

BRENDA MEESE

RUFFIN, JOSEPHINE ST. PIERRE (1842-1924)

Josephine St. Pierre Ruffin was a women's club activist, journalist, and suffragist. She was born in Boston in 1842 to John St. Pierre, a man of African, French, and Indian ancestry, and Eliza Matilda (Menhenick) St. Pierre, a native of Cornwall, England. Her education began in Salem and finished in Boston after its schools were integrated. At sixteen she married George Lewis Ruffin (1834-86), and the couple promptly moved to England to spare themselves and their future family the trials of American racism.

At the outbreak of the Civil War, however, they returned to the United States to help with efforts to abolish slavery. Josephine Ruffin recruited for the colored Fifty-fourth and Fifty-fifth Massachusetts regiments and worked for the U.S. Sanitation Commission. She also became extensively active in women's clubs and in professional and charitable organizations such as the Associated Charities of Boston, the Massachusetts State Federation of Women's Clubs, and the Boston Kansas Relief Association for Black migrants. Through her work for the Black weekly paper the *Courant* she became a member of the New England Women's Press Association.

In February 1893, Ruffin founded the New Era Club with her daughter, Florida, who joined her mother in much of her work, and Maria Baldwin, a Boston school principal. Its purpose was to organize a number of kindergartens in Boston and one in Georgia and to keep the women's clubs in touch with each other with regular reports. Ruffin served as editor of the club's monthly journal, the *Woman's Era*, which was the first newspaper published by Black women. As president of the club, Ruffin became a member of the Massachusetts State Federation of Women's Clubs.

Ruffin participated in two nineteenth-century traditions: Black women's alliance with white abolitionists and suffragists, and their separation into their own service-oriented clubs. African-American women began organizing antislavery and literary societies in the 1830s and joined white women in the suffrage movement that began in the 1840s. Antislavery work, in particular, introduced white women and free northern Black Americans to activism and trained them for future agitation in other areas.

Ruffin helped found both colored organizations and integrated ones, such as the Massachusetts School Suffrage Association, and she became friends with such prominent activists as Julia Ward Howe and Lucy Stone. As the reaction against integration stiffened in the late nineteenth century, however, Ruffin and other Black women stopped trying to join white organizations and formed their own.

Ruffin was at the center of a well-publicized incident. In 1900, the General Federation of Women's Clubs held its biennial meeting in Milwaukee. Ruffin was eligible to attend through her membership in the Massachusetts Federation of Women's Clubs, and because she was the New Era Club's president, she was automatically a vice president of the general federation. She was also an alternate delegate for the meeting through her membership in another predominantly white organization, the New England Women's Press Association. Ruffin insisted, however, on going as the president of the New Era Club. When the executive board discovered that all of the club's members were Black women, they would not accept Ruffin's credentials or seat her as a vice president. Someone even tried to snatch her badge on the convention floor, but Ruffin resisted. She also refused

When racists moved to oust her from the biennial meeting of the General Federation of Women's Clubs, Josephine St. Pierre Ruffin refused to compromise. "It was an opportunity which I did not seek," she said in a historic explanation of her courageous actions, "but which I did not shirk." [Schomburg Center]

the attempt to refund her registration fee. The policy that she was acceptable only as a delegate from a white club was typical of a number of national organizations, such as the Women's Christian Temperance Union and the Young Women's Christian Association.

The Massachusetts delegation sent a letter of protest to the executive board. Delegates from Iowa, Utah, and a majority of the delegates from northern states sided with them, but the southern delegates, led by president Rebecca Lowe, skillfully used parliamentary procedures to keep the issue from discussion in an open meeting. Ironically, Lowe herself had done a great deal of work to establish kindergartens for Black children.

Ruffin regarded the matter calmly, reporting that "I did not feel angry. It was an issue clearly set before the women of the country. It was an opportunity which I did not seek, but which I did not shirk" (Giddings 1984). The president of the Massachusetts general federation opined that Ruffin had "demonstrated the splendid possibilities of her race."

During the controversy, a letter of support for Ruffin was written to the *Woman's Journal*, a feminist newspaper. The writer decried "American women's desire to inflict shame and humiliation upon other women," then warned that "it is a most dangerous policy to alienate from the common national interest so large a body as is constituted by the colored population of the United States. . . . The Negro has hitherto been intensely American in his feelings and ambitions," and white people should not recklessly seek to "denationalize him." The many undesirable results, according to the writer, might include "weakening our strength in case of war."

One of Ruffin's greatest accomplishments came in response to an inflammatory letter concerning Black women's character. In 1895, the president of the Missouri Press Association, James W. Jacks, wrote to Florence Belgarnie, an Englishwoman who served as secretary of the Antislavery Society of England. Belgarnie had become sympathetic to the struggles of Black Americans through the work of Ida B. Wells. Jacks's letter accused Black women of having "no sense of virtue and of being altogether without character," as well as being "prostitutes, thieves, and liars" (Giddings 1984). This was no isolated charge. The defense of their moral character was a recurring, important issue for Black women. The ability of white men to coerce Black women into sexual relations, both during slavery and afterward, paradoxically led to a stereotype of Black women as being of easy virtue.

Copies of Jacks's letter were circulated among clubs across the country. Ruffin responded with a manifesto titled "A Call: Let Us Confer Together." Extending her invitation "to all colored women of America, members of any society or not," Ruffin proposed the first national convention of Black women, to carry out what she called "our right and our bounden duty . . . to teach an ignorant and suspicious world that our aims and interests are identical with those of all good aspiring women." This and other goals must be achieved, she wrote, "for the sake of thousands of self-sacrificing young women, teaching and preaching in lonely southern backwoods, for the noble army of mothers . . . whose intelligence is only limited by their opportunity to get at books, for the sake of the fine cultured women who have carried off the honors in school here and often abroad" (Giddings 1984).

She proposed to spread the message "not by noisy protestations of what we are not, but by a dignified showing of what we are and hope to become." She emphasized that "We are not drawing the color line. . . . We are not alienating or withdrawing, we are only coming to the front, willing to join any others in the same work" (Giddings 1984).

Ruffin maintained that the conference could provide mutual encouragement and inspiration as well as the chance to discuss Black people's special interests. She also was interested in general questions of the day—temperance, morality, higher education, hygiene, and the home. Most important, she believed, was the chance to offer help to Black women who lacked "opportunity, not only to do more, but to be more." Ruffin was irked that too many Americans "glibly" described Black women as, "for the most part, ignorant and immoral, some exceptions of course, but these don't count." Ruffin argued that "because all refutation has only been tried by individual work, the charge has never been crushed" (Lerner 1973).

The conference's resolutions included working to end discrimination against Black labor and championing homemaking and purchasing homes. The participants called for the abolition of segregated transportation and the convict lease system, and they proposed measures to be taken against the destruction of Black people's rights that had resulted from the withdrawal of federal troops from the South. They also commended the Republican party for condemning lynching in its platform and voiced regret that the Democrats did not.

One hundred women from twenty clubs in ten states attended the conference and formed the National Federation of Afro-American Women. It ultimately united thirty-six clubs in twelve states. The federation merged in 1896 with the Colored Women's League to form the National Association of Colored Women, of which Ruffin became the first vice president.

In some ways, Black and white women's clubs were similar: they were primarily middle class with mostly Protestant members, and they emphasized education, material progress, and the importance of the home and women's influence in it. The clubs differed, however, in that for Black Americans the gap between the upper class and others was not as great as within white society. Black clubwomen were more likely to see their heritage and future as tied to those of the less fortunate. The motto of the National Association of Colored Women made this clear: "Lifting as We Climb."

The charitable aims of Black clubs also tended to be direct and specific: providing an individual with money for an education, granting money to a school district, and generally addressing the needs of the aged, the poor, the sick, and the young. Clubwoman Fannie Barrier Williams observed that "among white women the club is the onward movement of the already uplifted. Among colored women the club is the effort of the few competent in behalf of the many incompetent" (Giddings 1984). Because Black women were largely excluded from major national organizations except in certain areas, usually New England, and from labor unions, including the Black National Labor Union, local clubs took on a greater significance.

Ruffin was able to pursue her philanthropic callings because of the financial position that she and her family enjoyed. Her husband was born to a prominent Black family that had moved from Richmond to Boston. Upon the young couple's return from England in 1858, George Ruffin worked as a barber—a common occupation among the African-American upper class—until he graduated from the Harvard Law School in 1869. Later he became a state legislator, a Boston city councilman, and, in 1883, Boston's first Black municipal judge. Of their three sons, one became a lawyer, another an inventor and manufacturer, and the third an organist; their daughter taught in Boston's public schools. Josephine Ruffin provided convincing evidence against those who argued that Black women who were college graduates might not be fit to manage households and rear children.

In 1889, Ruffin gave a speech, "An Open Letter to the Educational League of Georgia," that demonstrated both the diplomacy that Black leaders often had to employ when dealing with white people and

the boldness of this particular woman. She complimented the group of southern white women on undertaking "the moral training of the colored children of Georgia" but chastised them nonetheless:

One of the saddest things about the sad condition of affairs in the South has been the utter indifference which Southern women, who were guarded with unheard of fidelity during the [Civil] war, have manifested to the mental and moral welfare of the children of their faithful slaves, who, in the language of Henry Grady, placed a black mass of loyalty between them and dishonor. This was a rare opportunity for you to have shown your gratitude to your slaves and your interest in their future welfare.

These words possess an intriguing subtext; they mine the Confederacy's lost-cause romance of the faithful slaves in order to invoke the notion of paternalism that the Old South used to defend slavery as not merely a benign institution but a benevolent one. Ruffin took her audience to task, especially for persecuting northern teachers "simply because they were doing your work," which she said southern women were too bitter or too poor to do. Speaking of the antilynching campaign, she called on southern women "to join in this great altruistic movement of the age and endeavor to lift up the degraded and ignorant, rather than to exterminate them. . . . If you had done your duty to them at the close of the war," she argued, "you would not now be confronted with a condition which you feel it necessary to check, in obedience to that great first law of nature—self-protection" (Ruffin 1889). She argued that these women should dismiss any critics, since "the South has suffered too much already from that kind of false pride to let it longer keep her recreant to the spirit of the age" (Ruffin 1889). Clearly, Black leaders of the late nineteenth century had to maintain a delicate balance as they tried to help create a New South.

After the New Era Club disbanded in 1903, Ruffin helped found the Association for the Promotion of Child Training in the South, the Boston branch of the National Association for the Advancement of Colored People, and the League of Women for Community Service, adding to the long list of organizations with which she had been affiliated. She also served in the New England Women's Club and organized funding for the Mount Coffee School in Liberia.

Two weeks before Ruffin's death, she attended the annual meeting of the League of Women for Community Service, where she cast her vote and waited until 1:00 A.M. for the outcome. She died of nephritis at the age of eighty-one and was buried in Cambridge at the Mount Auburn Cemetery.

BIBLIOGRAPHY

Brown, Hallie Q. *Homespun Heroines and Other Women of Distinction* ([1926] 1988); Dunbar, Alice Moore, ed. *Masterpieces of Negro Eloquence: The Best Speeches Delivered by the Negro From the Days of Slavery to the Present Time* (1970); Fields, Emma L. "The Women's Club Movement in the U.S., 1877-1900," Master's thesis (1948); Flexner, Eleanor. *Century of Struggle: The Woman's Rights Movement in the United States* (1975); Giddings, Paula. *When and Where I Enter: The Impact of Black Women on Race and Sex in America* (1984); Lerner, Gerda, ed. *Black Women in White America: A Documentary History* (1973); Wesley, Charles Harris. *The History of the National Association of Colored Women's Clubs, Inc.: A Legacy of Service* (1984); *Woman's Journal* (June 16, 23, 30, 1900).

ELIZABETH FORTSON ARROYO

RUSH, GERTRUDE E. DURDEN (1880-1918)

Gertrude E. Durden, composer and playwright, was born August 5, 1880, in Navasota, Texas, to Reverend Frank and Sarah E. (Reinhardt) Durden. Gertrude attended high schools in Parsons, Kansas, and Quincy, Illinois. She studied at the Westerman Music Conservatory in Des Moines, Iowa, and received her A.B. in 1914 from Des Moines College.

Gertrude E. Durden married James B. Rush, of Des Moines, on December 23, 1907. She taught in the government district schools in Oklahoma for four years and in the Oswego, Kansas, public schools for three years. She became a lecturer in 1911 and started her career as a playwright when she staged *Paradise Lost* under the title *Satan's Revenge*. Her other writings include *Sermon on the Mount* (1907), *Uncrowned Heroines* (1912), and *Black Girls Burden* (1913). Rush was also a composer whose songs include: "If You But Knew," "Jesus Loves the Little Children," and "Christmas Day."

Rush was a member of the Associated Charities in the Interests of Poor Black People, the Colored Woman's Suffrage Club, and the Order of the Eastern Star. She organized the Woman's Law and Political Study Club, was a delegate to the Half-Century Exposition of Negro Emancipation in Philadelphia, and was a member of the committee that secured an appropriation for the Iowa Federation Home for Women and Girls.

Rush died on September 8, 1918, in Des Moines, Iowa.

BIBLIOGRAPHY

Mather, Frank Lincoln, ed. *Who's Who of the Colored Race: A General Geographical Dictionary of Men and Women of African Descent* ([1915] 1976).

JUDY WARWICK

RUSHEN, PATRICE (1954-)

Patrice Rushen was giving classical piano recitals by the age of six. In her teens, she branched into jazz and soon evolved into a consummate, multifaceted artist, combining singing, composing, producing, arranging, and performing into a blend of rhythm and blues, jazz, and pop.

Born to Ruth and Allen Rushen on September 30, 1954, in Los Angeles, Patrice was enrolled in a special college eurhythmics course at age three. She began piano lessons at five and at a very early age developed the discipline that has allowed her to continue her growth and study of music as well as the development of her own unique style of music.

She has recorded nine albums, received two Grammy nominations for "Number One" (best rhythm and blues instrumental performance) and "Forget Me Nots" (best rhythm and blues vocal performance) in 1982, and developed a passion for film composing. "Film composing allows me to explore more aspects of music and meet a lot more people," she explained in an interview (November 2, 1991). "As I get older, my priorities are shifting off myself and onto other people."

Patrice Rushen's musical diversity handed her a new challenge when she composed the score for Robert Townsend's film *Hollywood Shuffle* (1987). Her television composing credits include the series *Brewster Place* and the comedy special *Robert Townsend and His Partners in Crime*. She is distinguished as the first woman to be musical director of a network television show, *The Midnight Hour* for CBS. She has also been musical director for Emmy Awards and the NAACP Image Awards ceremonies.

Rushen's early career included session work for such artists as Diane Reeves, Peabo Bryson, Jean-Luc Ponty, Teena Marie, Hubert Laws, Eddie Murphy, Terri Lyne Carrington, Lee Tineour, Con Funk Shun, Wayne Shorter, Flora Purim, Ronnie Laws, the Temptations, Sonny Rollins, and Herbie

Composer and instrumental recording artist Patrice Rushen was the first woman to be musical director of a network television show, The Midnight Hour *for CBS. She is the only woman to emerge from jazz and rhythm and blues as a self-contained recording artist—responsible for composing, producing, and arranging her own work. [Schomburg Center]*

Hancock. A highly regarded arranger, Rushen has arranged strings and horns for Ramsey Lewis, Sheree Brown, the Dazz Band, and Prince, to name a few. She is the only woman to emerge from jazz and rhythm and blues as a self-contained recording artist—responsible for composing, producing, and arranging her own work.

Patrice Rushen combines a career and marriage. She married Marc St. Louis, actor, concert tour manager, and technician, in 1986.

BIBLIOGRAPHY

Rushen, Patrice. Personal interviews.

REGINA JONES

S

SAAR, BETYE (1926-)

Betye Saar is a visual artist with thirty years of experience. Her artistic style is distinguished by her use of assemblage in forms ranging from three-dimensional frames to installations.

She was born in Pasadena, California, in 1926. She earned a Bachelor of Arts degree in design from the University of California at Los Angeles in 1949, and did graduate work in printmaking at California State University at Long Beach (1958-62) and the University of Southern California (1962). At the time, Black students were not encouraged to enter art programs except in design.

Saar's work of the early 1960s was inspired by her training in graphics and by her experience as mother and wife. Her visual representations frequently depicted her children, women, women and children, and nature. From an early age Saar had been a collector, so her progression from printmaking to mixed media was natural. After finding an old leaded window she experimented with filling each panel with a print or drawing. When she saw an exhibition of works by Joseph Cornell, she realized the potential of assemblage.

Although Saar's work has gone through many stylistic changes, it always conveys history, memory, ritual, cultural diversity, and spirituality. Her *Black Girl's Window* (1969) marks her move toward collage and assemblage, as it combines a window frame with prints as well as photographs and three-dimensional objects. The theme revolves around Saar's own life and encompasses elements of the past, present, and future. A central panel contains skeletal images that refer to the death of her father when she was six years old, but the panel relates to death as part of the cycle of life. The bottom panel depicts Saar herself as a silhouette of a young Black girl peering out into the world. Her palms contain astrological symbols that represent destiny or fate. The overall work explores Saar's quest for enlightenment through her identity as a Black woman and in a collective human identity that is revealed through diverse cultural practices. The imagery seems inspired by Saar's lifelong fascination with mysticism and ritual.

Saar's combination of elements has its source in the African ritual notion of vital force or collective energy. She generally combines thrift store objects that have a history of their own, to create a powerful charm. Saar uses the idea of accumulation as an extension of an African cultural heritage, and her work reflects a tie to cultures that relate to the earth, nature, and mysticism.

As an artist Saar acts as a shaman, who combines special ingredients and found objects into charms or mojos. She alters, manipulates, recycles, and transforms her materials into boxes, altars, and installations. The products come together like allegorical stories for which she is the author or griot. Each work is a

Prominent artist Betye Saar creates distinctive assemblages that convey issues of history, memory, ritual, cultural diversity, and spirituality. [Tracey Saar]

vehicle for conveying human spirit and emotion. She sounds a collective chord in the public by focusing on issues of memory and personal experience. Saar's work touches her audience both at the heart and in the mind by projecting a familiar space through intimate emotions. She reaches into the depths of human memory and retrieves sentimental images and fragments of the past, making her viewers feel as if they are returning to the comforts of childhood, taking a sentimental sojourn triggered by the recognition of objects that were once familiar but had been forgotten.

By communicating her own emotions and experiences as a Black woman, Saar reveals commonalities in cultures and histories and exposes the mystical in time and space. Her work attempts to break through the barriers of time, space, energy, history, culture, memory, and human emotion.

During the 1960s and 1970s, when African-Americans were concerned with cultural awareness, civil rights, and a search for identity, Saar began to focus on her anger and hurt due to the negative imagery projected in popular culture. Saar's work contributed a strong political statement of protest, such as *The Liberation of Aunt Jemima* (1972), which focused on the historical use of derogatory images of Black people. By using commercial images, Saar calls to question

the mechanisms of racism and exposes how deeply they are embedded in our culture. This particular work raises the consciousness of her viewer as well as asserts her control of her own image as a Black woman. Her use of derogatory images was a vehicle not only for transformation but also for empowerment through self-proclaiming and exposing.

Saar takes the familiar image of Aunt Jemima and transforms her into a woman in active pursuit of her own liberation. She is taking initiative and is capable and self-reliant. The traditional symbol of Aunt Jemima is reclassified to demonstrate how Black women can and do control their own identities despite the images imposed upon them by traditional Western notions of Black womanhood.

In this series of works, Saar infiltrates stereotypical images with messages of reality. *The Liberation of Aunt Jemima* is a box assemblage that contains the powerful image of Aunt Jemima in a vibrant and assertive red dress. Saar manipulates Jemima's role as servant and raises her to a postion of power. By exposing the objectification of Black people and by confronting white American exploitation, this representation rattles the very foundations of racism. Jemima is proud, confident, and self-assured. Saar actively reclaims the history of her foremothers and her cultural heritage.

In the 1970s, Saar's work became more introspective, as she began to focus more on her own personal history. Her Aunt Hattie, who had been like a grandmother to her, died in 1974. With her death Saar felt a resurfacing of feelings of pain and sadness similar to those she had felt at the loss of her father. This inspired a new body of work based in private, intimate memories. From Aunt Hattie she inherited drawers and closets full of clothing and objects. Instead of found objects from thrift stores with unknown histories, Aunt Hattie's memorabilia inspired a nostalgic vision of a real woman from recent time past. Saar captured the power and magic elicited from everyday, ordinary lives in these works. They were testaments to Aunt Hattie as well as a celebration of Black history and heritage, and they evoke memories of a collective past in which there is a shared emotional spirit.

After this series of works Saar made a stylistic switch from boxes to altars. The viewer was often invited to participate physically by the ritual leaving or exchanging of offerings. In the 1980s Saar again expanded her vision by creating installations, often incorporating her altars into these sites. These walk-in versions of her smaller works break free of boundaries by magnifying the intimacy of her boxes.

They evolve as ritual by combining old, familiar objects with nature and personal energy. She continues to focus on shared emotion and experience, and in her most recent body of works she returns to the power of nostalgia and memory. These works are frames in which she combines found objects and photographs in order to reconstruct the identities of the people in the photographs, whom she does not know. She continues to pursue the notion of a collective identity in which there is a shared emotional space.

Saar's philosophical content is consistent throughout her body of work. With each progression, her ideas become more intricate and informed. Her work is continuously evolving along with the events in her life. She is a prominent artist whose significant contributions are underscored by her many achievements, exhibitions, awards, and commissions.

BIBLIOGRAPHY
"Betye Saar." In *Shrovetide in Old New Orleans*, ed Ishmael Reed (1978); Campbell, Mary Schmidt. *Rituals: The Art of Betye Saar* (1980), and *Tradition and Conflict: Images of a Turbulent Decade* (1985); Clothier, Peter. *Betye Saar* (1984); Lewis, Samella. *Art: African-American* (1978); Munro, Eleanor. *Originals: American Women Artists* (1979); Nemser, Cindy. "Conversations with Betye Saar," *Feminist Art Journal* (Winter 1975-76); Saar, Betye. "Installation as Sculpture," *International Review of African-American Art* (1984); Shepard, Elizabeth, ed. *Secrets, Dialogues and Revelations: The Art of Betye and Alison Saar* (1990); Stein, Judith E. and Ann Sargent Wooster. "Making Their Mark." In *Making Their Mark: Women Artists Move into the Mainstream, 1970-85*, ed. Randy Rosen and Catherine C. Brawer (1989); Wright, Beryl. *The Appropriate Object* (1989).

NADINE WASSERMAN

SADDLER, JUANITA (c. 1892-1970)

Speaking and writing against the evils of discrimination in the 1920s and 1930s was not a popular activity, but that is what Juanita Saddler did in her position as an employee of the national Young Women's Christian Association (YWCA). She was born and grew up in Guthrie, Oklahoma, but seems to have regarded Tulsa, Oklahoma, as her hometown. She received her Bachelor's degree from Fisk University in Nashville, Tennessee, in 1915 and her Master's degree from the Teachers College at Columbia University.

Saddler was branch secretary for interracial education with the national YWCA from 1920 to 1935. In that capacity she distinguished herself—and her employer—by developing a policy statement on the responsibility of the student YWCA in the struggle for integration. This statement formed the basis of the national YWCA's interracial charter, adopted in 1946. Saddler also established a program to integrate welfare programs for youth in Washington, D.C., as well as programs to help Black girls in Boston. In addition, she helped organize church women to support ecumenical and interracial activity in New York City. She has been described as gracious, possessing a keen intellect and a good sense of humor, and as an articulate public speaker.

Juanita Saddler was a woman of many firsts. She was the first Black female dean at Fisk University and the first Black woman to hold a position as deacon at Christ Chapel at the Riverside Church in New York City. Juanita Saddler died in 1970 in New York City. She was seventy-eight years old.

BIBLIOGRAPHY
New York Times. "Juanita Saddler of the Y.W.C.A. Dies: Leader of Integration in Many Fields was 78" (n.d.); Pratt, Mildred. Personal interview with Elizabeth Norris, YWCA historian, National Board, New York, New York (August 29, 1991), and personal interview with Mary Woods, Pittsburgh, Pennsylvania (September 10, 1991); Snyder, Ida Sloan. "Juanita Saddler's Obituary" (January 12, 1970); YWCA U.S.A., National Board Archives, New York, New York.

MILDRED PRATT

SAINT FRANCES OF ROME ACADEMY, BALTIMORE

The year 1829 saw the simultaneous establishment of two historic Black Roman Catholic institutions in Baltimore, the Oblate Sisters of Providence and the Saint Frances of Rome Academy. These two institutions were, and still are, inextricably woven together. The Oblates, the first order of Black nuns, became the teachers at the new academy, which was the genius of Father Nicholas Joubert, a Sulpician priest who, because he understood the needs of Haitian refugees and the social climate of the time, believed that the school was necessary.

The academy was established to educate Black girls in subjects that would be applicable to their social and economic environment. Under the guidance of the Oblates, students were taught religion, English, penmanship, geography, arithmetic, history, orthography, and art as well as washing, ironing, cleaning, care of children, and sewing.

The first school was located on Richmond Street. The facility was small, and this limited educational operations, but because the work of the Oblates pleased the Catholic leadership, they were able to initiate a move to larger quarters. In 1867, they purchased a lot on a hill between Greenmount Avenue and Jones Falls, facing Chase Street. In 1870, the cornerstone was laid for the new school, and by 1871 the new structure was completed. After forty-two years in cramped spaces, the Oblates, including their founder, Sister Elizabeth Lange, then ninety years old, moved into their new building. The site served as both the convent and the school. The school was well patronized, and wealthy white people often sponsored deserving students. Most of the girls who enrolled in the private institution came from the South, but some came from Washington, D.C., and Philadelphia, and still others came from the Caribbean. Although it was a Catholic school, non-Catholic girls were enrolled also, and the school was held in high regard by Catholics and non-Catholics alike.

Students were identified according to their class or tuition status as either boarders, the upper-class students, or pensionnaires, the day students. When the new school opened, there were twenty-three students—eleven boarders and twelve pensionnaires. Boarding students paid a fee of $4 a month, plus $1 for fuel during the winter months, whereas pensionnaires paid $2 a quarter, plus $.50 for fuel in the winter.

In its time, the school was an improvement over those institutions formerly open to Black students. Indeed, the establishment of Saint Frances of Rome Academy marked the birth of a kind of social and educational elite within the Black community. It forged scholastic achievement among Black women who shared what they learned with others of their race. If length of continuance is any indicator of success, Saint Frances Academy has proven to be one of America's most successful and enduring institutions.

BIBLIOGRAPHY

Fitzpatrick, Sandra and Maria R. Goodwin. *The Guide to Black Washington* (1990); Gilliard, John T. *The Catholic Church and the American Negro* (1929), and *Colored Catholics in the United States* (1941); Marrow, Gloria R. "A Narrative of the Founding and Work of the Oblate Sisters of Providence," Master's thesis (1976); *The New Catholic Encyclopedia* (1967); *News American* (May 14, 1973); Oblate

Archival Materials. *Annals of the Oblate Sisters of Providence* (1842-77); Sherwood, Grace. *The Oblates Hundred and One Years* (1931).

GLORIA MARROW

SAMPSON, DEBORAH *see* GANNETT, DEBORAH SAMPSON

SAMPSON, EDITH (1901-1979)

Edith Sampson was the first Black woman appointed as a judge in Illinois, the first woman to graduate from the Loyola University Law School in Chicago, the first Black delegate to the United Nations, and the first Black person to hold an appointment with the North Atlantic Treaty Organization (NATO).

Edith Spurlock was born on October 13, 1901, in Pittsburgh, Pennsylvania, one of eight children in the family of Louis and Elizabeth (McGruder) Spurlock. Her father earned $75 a month working in a cleaning and pressing establishment, and Elizabeth worked at home, making hat frames and switches for false hair. Louis and Elizabeth Spurlock owned their home and they lived comfortably.

Spurlock was educated in the Pittsburgh public schools. However, periodically she was forced to leave school to earn her tuition; at one time she worked in a fish market. After graduation she entered the School of Social Work at Columbia University in New York. Three years later she married Rufus Sampson, a field agent for Tuskegee Institute, and moved with him to Chicago. This marriage ended in divorce and she later remarried, to Chicago jurist Joseph Clayton.

During her first few years in Chicago, she was a homemaker, raised her sister's two small children after the sister's death, worked full time as a social worker, and earned an LL.B. in 1925 from the John Marshall Law School in Chicago by attending night classes. Sampson failed the bar examination that year. Then, in 1927, she enrolled in the Loyola University Law School and went on to become the first woman to receive an LL.M. from that school. She passed the Illinois bar in 1927 and was admitted to practice before the Supreme Court in 1934.

Sampson's public service career began in earnest shortly after she completed law school. Between 1934 and 1942, she worked simultaneously as a probation officer, a lawyer with a private law practice, and a referee in the Cook County Family Court. In 1949, she was selected by the National Council of Negro Women as their representative to participate in America's Town Meeting of the Air Program, with twenty-five other national, civic, cultural, welfare, and labor leaders. The group traveled to twelve countries, debating political issues of world concern. At the group's banquet in a Washington, D.C., hotel, Sampson was refused service and the activity was moved to another location. Many guests were upset, but when Sampson was asked how she could eat under the circumstances, she smiled, saying, "I've been colored a long time and if I stopped eating every time something like this happened, I'd be thin as a rail."

In 1950, Sampson was appointed by President Harry Truman as an alternate delegate to the United Nations General Assembly, where she was a strong advocate for the world's underprivileged children. Sampson's appointment was made at a time when the United States was being criticized for its treatment of Black Americans, and Communist governments' officials charged that her appointment was merely window dressing to divert attention from the oppressive racial policies of the United States. Her response was that the president did not ask her to represent 6 million Negroes, but to represent 150 million Americans. She urged Black Americans not to fall prey to Communist propaganda and separate themselves from white American society. She argued that under a democracy, Black Americans at least have the freedom and opportunity to improve their situations. While a member of the United Nations General Assembly, Sampson also served as a member-at-large of NATO. Sampson was reappointed to the General Assembly in 1952. Also in 1952, Sampson served as a member-at-large of the United Nations Educational, Scientific, and Cultural Organization (UNESCO). Twelve years later, she was appointed to the U.S. Commission on NATO as a member of its U.S. Citizens Commission.

Sampson was an energetic speaker, urging full citizenship for Black Americans. She was in great demand as a lecturer, traveling extensively throughout the Middle East, Scandinavia, Europe, and South America. She was as active in public service in Chicago as she was in national activities, holding the offices of assistant corporation counsel, associate judge of the Municipal Court, and judge of the Cook County Circuit Court.

Sampson died on October 8, 1979, in Chicago. In her long and distinguished career in public service,

Edith Sampson worked tirelessly for equality for Black citizens in this country. Her efforts are summed up best in her own words, "When we Negroes achieve first class citizenship in America, we will not drape our mantles over our shoulders and return anywhere; we are already there."

BIBLIOGRAPHY
CBWA; NBAW.

GLORIA V. WARREN

SANCHEZ, SONIA (1934-)

Uh Huh, But How Do It Free Us, the title of Sonia Sanchez's 1970 drama, best sums up her commitment to improving the life of Black Americans. Sanchez was a leading activist during the civil rights movement of the 1960s. Like her contemporaries, including Amiri Baraka, Addison Gayle, Don L. Lee, Nikki Giovanni, Tom Dent, and Lorenzo Thomas, Sanchez called for a change in American politics. She became a spokesperson for the millions who demanded a revamping of a society in which the masses of African-Americans were impoverished and undereducated. When meager gains were made by select Black politicians, many of whom she believed had been bought, Sanchez was quick to ask, "Uh huh, but how do it free us?"

Sonia Sanchez was born on September 9, 1934, in Birmingham, Alabama, to Wilson L. and Lena Jones Driver. She earned a Bachelor's degree from Hunter College in 1955 and holds an honorary doctorate from Wilberforce University. The mother of three children, Anita, Morani, and Mungu, Sanchez has held several faculty positions since 1965 in California, New York, New Jersey, and Massachusetts before moving to Philadelphia in the late 1970s to teach English and write at Temple University. She has been the recipient of several major awards, including the P.E.N. Writing Award in 1969, the National Institute of Arts and Letters Grant in 1970, a National Endowment for the Arts fellowship, and an American Book Award for poetry in 1978-79.

Evocative, moving, and militant are words that best describe the poetry and plays of Sonia Sanchez, who manipulates Black street speech to illuminate the deplorable conditions that the Black masses endure. Sanchez also writes about imperialism, capitalism, racism, sexism, child abuse, ineffectual and womanizing men, initiation rites for women, drug abuse, the

Sonia Sanchez's uncompromising view of Black life is skillfully presented in her evocative, moving, and militant poetry and plays. [Schomburg Center]

destruction of great Black leaders, Black on Black crime, and generational conflicts.

A leading poet since the 1960s, Sanchez has published several major collections: *Homecoming* (1969), *We a BaddDDD People* (1970), *It's a New Day: Poems for Young Brothers and Sisters* (1971), *Love Poems* (1973), *A Blues Book for Blue Magic Women* (1974), *I've Been a Woman* (1978), *Home Girls and Handgrenades* (1984), and *Generations: Selected Poetry; 1969-1985* (1986). In many of these collections, Sanchez calls for new Black heroes and heroines to lead a revolution that will save Black children from destruction.

Sanchez's uncompromising vision of the meaning of Black life is as pervasive in her plays as it is in her poetry. She warns African-Americans against moving toward a vacuous America that places value on material possessions and devalues human life. Sanchez also warns white Americans that African-Americans will no longer tolerate disenfranchisement and degradation and that blood will be spilled as a corrective measure. Blending poetry with drama, Sanchez has published several poemplays, including *The Bronx Is Next* (1970), *Uh Huh, But How Do It Free Us?* (1970), *Sister Son/ji* (1972), *Dirty Hearts* (1972), *Malcolm/Man*

Don't Live Here No Mo (1972), and *I'm Black When I'm Singing, I'm Blue When I Ain't* (1982).

Sonia Sanchez was one of the leading proponents of the Black Arts movement. Increasingly since the 1960s, Sanchez has concerned herself with racism globally, recognizing that the unjust treatment of one Black person anywhere threatens Black people everywhere. Her poetic voice of the 1960s expressed the violence and turmoil of the period. Her voice continues to appeal to audiences nationally and internationally, as Sanchez warns that tumultuous times may come again if people of color and women continue to be victimized by capitalist America.

BIBLIOGRAPHY

Brown-Guillory, Elizabeth, ed. *Wines in the Wilderness: Plays by African-American Women from the Harlem Renaissance to the Present* (1990); *CA*.

ELIZABETH BROWN-GUILLORY

SANCTIFIED CHURCH

Sanctified Church is an indigenous term African-Americans use to refer to Holiness, Pentecostal, Independent, Community, Spiritual, and Deliverance denominations and congregations collectively. Although there is a history of conflict with larger and older Baptist and Methodist denominations, Sanctified Church represents an alternative to more pejorative and hostile terms and recognizes similarities in prayer, preaching, testimony, and music. Many denominations emerged during the late nineteenth and twentieth centuries emphasizing some aspect of sanctification and sharing ritual practices emphasizing the Holy Ghost (Spirit) and such activities as "shouting," the "holy dance," speaking in tongues, and other spiritual gifts. Pentecostals highlight speaking in tongues in statements of doctrine and discipline.

Novelist and anthropologist Zora Neale Hurston pointed to the Sanctified Church as a song-making and cultural protest movement that preserved aspects of African-American worship considered primitive and unseemly by an emerging middle class. Usually classified as sects, cults, and storefronts because of their marginal status in northern urban ghettos, these churches often have their roots and hold their annual convocations in the South. The Sanctified Church congregations tend to be around 90 percent female. Some denominations ordain women and were founded by women such as Bishop Ida Robinson. The Church of God in Christ, the largest denomination, does not ordain women to be pastors, elders, or bishops, but women are central to the history and growth of the denomination as church founders, missionaries, evangelists, supervisors, and church mothers. Organization of a prominent, somewhat autonomous, powerful women's convention or department is a characteristic feature of these churches.

BIBLIOGRAPHY

Dodson, Jualyne E. and Cheryl Townsend Gilkes. "Something Within: Social Change and Collective Endurance in the Sacred World of Black Christian Women." In *Women and Religion in America: Volume Three: 1900-1968*, ed. Rosemary Radford Ruether and Rosemary Skinner Keller (1986); Fauset, Arthur Huff. *Black Gods of the Metropolis* (1944); Gilkes, Cheryl Townsend. "The Role of Women in the Sanctified Church," *Journal of Religious Thought* (1986), and "The Roles of Church and Community Mothers: Ambivalent American Sexism or Fragmented African Familyhood?" *Journal of Feminist Studies in Religion* (Fall 1986), and "Together and in Harness: Women's Traditions in the Sanctified Church," *Signs: Journal of Women in Culture and Society* (Summer 1985); Hurston, Zora Neale. *The Sanctified Church* (1982); Trulear, Harold Dean. "Reshaping Black Pastoral Theology: The Vision of Bishop Ida B. Robinson," *Journal of Religious Thought* (1989).

CHERYL TOWNSEND GILKES

SANDERS, MAUDE (1903-)

Teacher, physician, and crusader for medical justice, Maude Sanders was born in New Orleans, Louisiana, in 1903 to John E. and Sophronia Sanders. She was the youngest of ten children. Her father was born in Natchez, Mississippi, in 1860. It is speculated that he was the son of a white slave master. Sanders remembers her father as a carpenter who built his own house and worked for a shipbuilding company in New Orleans. In an interview, Sanders said her father was a brilliant man who knew how many nails were required to build a warmer house and who could calculate the amount of wall paper required to paper a house as efficiently as a college graduate, although he had only a grade school education. While working with her father, Sanders learned to hammer a nail "as efficiently as any man." Her mother, Sophronia, was born in Natchez, Mississippi, in 1871. She did not finish school but had enough education to teach grade school. She also took in laundry to help meet the family's economic needs. Sanders's mother taught her to sew, and both parents taught their children the value of education.

Maude Sanders's formal education began at age seven, when she entered Miro School, the first school for Black students to be built in her district. Prior to the construction of Miro, Black children had to walk nine miles to school. She entered the school in 1910 and graduated in 1918. By the time of her graduation from elementary school, New Orleans had built one high school for all Black school children in the city. Sanders enrolled in the McDonough High School and graduated in 1922. Like most of her peers, Sanders decided to take a job teaching. She found a job in Convent, Louisiana, a small rural area where she taught for two years. She boarded with a mulatto family whose young daughter told Sanders that she was too Black to take a bath in the same tin wash tub used by the family. Unhappy that children only went to school two months of the year and worked on farms the other ten, Sanders left Convent in 1924 and returned to New Orleans. She enrolled at Xavier, a Black Roman Catholic college, and entered the two-year teaching program because teaching seemed to be the only career available to Black women other than working in someone's kitchen. There were few teaching jobs, however, because there were only a few schools for Black children, and few Black children were able to attend school anyway because they had to work. When she graduated, Sanders was unable to find a teaching job because the public schools would not hire teachers trained in Catholic schools. So, she resigned herself to substitute teaching and making suits in a tailor shop owned by a German Jew, who had hired her over a white applicant because she was more diligent and wanted to learn how to make perfect buttonholes on men's suits. The sewing skills her mother had taught her turned out to be very useful in that job.

In 1928, after working in the tailor shop for a year, Sanders, now twenty-five, married a man with an eighth-grade education. Most Black men at the time did not have the opportunity to get an education, because they had to work. Unfortunately, her husband thought of himself as inferior to her and so they were divorced after a few years.

Maude Sanders's chance to pursue a career in medicine came shortly after her divorce, when her two sisters, Naomi, a teacher, and Lillian, a beautician, after consulting with one of Maude's former teachers, suggested that she study medicine. Since childhood, Sanders had been interested in anything that was sick—human or not. In early childhood she put a splint on a dog's broken leg and nursed a chicken back to health after it had swallowed a fishing hook. At age thirty-two, however, Sanders thought that such a career move, especially for a Black woman, would be impossible, but her sisters insisted that with their financial help and her job with the National Youth Administration she would be able to finance a medical education. Because she had no Bachelor's degree, Sanders spent two years at Xavier and New Orleans University taking the science courses necessary to be accepted at the Meharry Medical School in Nashville. However, neither would accept her courses at the other and award her a Bachelor's degree. Fortunately, the Meharry Medical School admitted her without the Bachelor's degree because she had all of the required science courses.

Maude Sanders and three other women were the first women admitted to Meharry in 1934; one of them (Doris Sanders) graduated with Maude Sanders in 1939. During her years of medical school, Maude Sanders was the oldest student at Meharry and it embarrassed her. Meharry required all women to study five years, and men four, in order to graduate

After graduating from medical school, Sanders faced another hurdle—internship. Most programs discriminated against women and Black students, and Sanders was both. She and Doris Sanders were the first women accepted at City Hospital (Homer Philips) in St. Louis, Missouri. Denied an opportunity to specialize in surgery, however, Sanders accepted a place in urology. The female interns shared men's quarters and were paid $75 a month, while the men were paid $125 per month. Sanders and the other woman were so happy to have a place to intern that they did not complain.

When Sanders completed her internship, she learned through a friend that the one Black male physician in Peoria was leaving. So, in 1942, she relocated. In Peoria she rented quarters that had been vacated by the physician for $25 a month. As the only Black physician in Peoria, Sanders's office was always overflowing with patients. Most of her patients were Black residents who were too poor to pay, but Sanders served them anyway. Not surprisingly, therefore, Sanders worked from early morning to late at night, and even after she returned home, patients would call and come to her for help. As a general practitioner, she also took on the roles of sister, mother, lawyer, and marriage counselor to her patients.

When Sanders retired in 1990, Mayor James Maloof declared October 17 of that year Maude Sanders Day. Sanders received several other awards for her service to the citizens of Peoria, among them the Martin Luther King, Jr. Award, the United Way Award, the Illinois State Medical Society Award, the Outstanding Business/Woman Award, the Distinguished Service Award, the Career Center Award, and the Outstanding Physician Award.

As a Black female, Sanders had to overcome a great deal of race and sex discrimination, but she never allowed adversity to overcome her principles. For instance, although she was accepted as a member of the Peoria American Medical Society, because the society met at the segregated Jefferson Hotel she was not allowed to attend meetings. Because of this rebuff, Sanders never attended meetings, even after the policy was changed. Also, a physician once asked Sanders to marry him, but she had to refuse his offer because he did not want her to continue to practice medicine. Relating the incident in an interview, Sanders said, "He didn't want a woman whom he felt might be equal or above his professional ability." In addition, although she was permitted to practice medicine in three local hospitals, the hospitals themselves were segregated when she came in 1942, and she had problems getting her patients admitted because only a designated number of rooms was allocated for Black patients. "We resented it," Sanders said. "We fought it for years. They were reluctant to put whites next to Blacks. I had patients die before they could get in" (Olsen 1990).

Maude Sanders lives in a wooded area near Peoria.

BIBLIOGRAPHY

Flowers, Debra. Personal interview (February 26, 1990); Hall, Millie. "One of Peoria's Great Pioneers," *Traveller Weekly* (November-December 1990); Olsen, Dean. "Doctor's Work the Best Medicine: Peoria's First Black Woman Doctor Fought Prejudice to Win Respect," *Peoria Journal Star* (October 14, 1990); Pratt, Mildred. Personal interview (May 17, 1991).

MILDRED PRATT

SANDS, DIANA (1934-1973)

"Look at me. Never mind my color. Please just look at me!" (Stang 1964). Diana Sands eventually got her wish—she starred in Broadway's *The Owl and the Pussycat*, a role written specifically for a white actress. Not one line in the 1964 play was altered to accommodate or explain her race. Her sensational performance shattered the misconceptions of integration, an important subject in Sands's life. "The Negro female has been categorized as the neuter, a mammy, an exotic. Why isn't she a mother, wife . . . a woman desired . . . someone who embodies all the characteristics of American womanhood?" (Gussow 1967).

Diana Sands was born on August 22, 1934, in the Bronx, New York, and was raised a Catholic. Her father, Rudolph Thomas Sands, Sr., was a carpenter. Her mother, Shirley Sands, was a milliner. The youngest of three, she had an older brother and sister, Sleegie Rudolph Thomas, Jr., and Joan Crawford Sands Harris, "named for you know who" (Wahls 1965). Her parents approved of her acting career and helped her during bad financial times.

Diana Sands went to elementary school in Elmsford, New York, a town with a small Black minority. Racial discrimination forced the family back to Manhattan, where Sands attended the High School of the Performing Arts and made her stage debut in George Bernard Shaw's *Major Barbara*. After graduation in 1953, Sands toured as a carnival singer and then returned to New York. Sands pursued her craft with devotion and persistence in $15-a-week roles at the Greenwich Mews, and in show tours, and lived with night jobs, daytime classes, furnished flats, and hunger.

A 1957 role in *Land Beyond the River* spared Sands from becoming a permanent key-punch operator for Con Edison. In 1958, she sang in *Egg and I* and *Another Evening with Harry Stoones*. In 1959, Lorraine Hansberry's *A Raisin in the Sun* brought her a new opportunity, but "they had to come and get me. I wouldn't even audition . . . I'd given up" (Bunce 1970). Her Broadway performance as Beneatha Younger led to two awards in 1959: the Outer Critics Circle Award as best supporting actress and the *Variety* Critics' Award for the most promising young actress. Sands's performance in the film version won the 1961 International Artists' Award.

In 1964, a banner year for Sands, she won an Obie for *Living Premise* and a Tony nomination for her role in James Baldwin's *Blues for Mr. Charlie*. She also married Lucien Happersberg, a Swiss artist and Baldwin's manager (the marriage ended in divorce a few years later). Then, with controversy and opposition, Sands was cast opposite Alan Alda in *The Owl and the Pussycat*. Her performance brought her whirlwind fame and another Tony nomination. An acclaimed 1965 London production followed.

Two television Emmy nominations came for *Beyond the Blues* and for "Who Do You Kill?," an *East Side/West Side* episode. Other television roles included *I Spy*, *Dr. Kildare*, *The Fugitive*, and *Julia*. Film credits include *An Affair of the Skin*, *Ensign Pulver*, *Four Boys and a Gun*, *Executive Suite*, *Garment Jungle*, and *The Landlord*. Tour appearances include the lead roles in

Caesar and Cleopatra, *Antony and Cleopatra*, and *Phaedra*. In 1968, she performed at the Lincoln Center Theater as Cassandra in *Tiger at the Gates*, and the lead in George Bernard Shaw's *St. Joan*, which many consider to be her finest work.

In the early 1970s the good roles became fewer and Sands's stardom faded, though she continued to fight for effective change behind the scenes. In an interview with Maurice Peterson for *Essence* magazine (1972), Sands talked about stardom: "I did get mar-

The first Black American to create on Broadway a role that had been written for a white actress, Diana Sands was propelled by her success in The Owl and the Pussycat *into a brilliant career. Her 1968 performance in the title role of Shaw's* Saint Joan *was considered by some critics to be her best. [Schomburg Center]*

velous notices and won awards, but of course, it was not possible for me to become a star." Together with Ossie Davis and others, Sands founded Third World Cinema which produced two of her last films: *Georgia, Georgia* and *Honey Baby, Honey Baby*.

In autumn of 1973, Sands was due to marry director Kurt Baker and star opposite James Earl Jones in the Third World production of *Claudine*. A sudden illness interrupted both plans. Diahann Carroll took the role. Sands was hospitalized at Memorial Sloan-Kettering Hospital in New York City, where she died of an inoperable tumor, the result of lung cancer, on Friday, September 21, 1973.

Diana Sands's versatile talent, persistence, courage, and vision enabled her to transcend the color barrier on stage. Her pioneering accomplishments during the tumultuous civil rights era of the 1960s are a theater legacy. Sands broke many barriers, but discrimination ultimately denied her the continual stardom she so richly deserved.

BIBLIOGRAPHY

Bradley, B. "Making of a Broadway Star," *Sepia* (July 1960); Bunce, A. "Black Bonanza," *The Christian Science Monitor* (August 19, 1970); Caston, S. "Diana Sands: Notes on a Broadway Pussycat," *Look* (February 9, 1965); Coombs, Orde. "Lunching with Diana Sands," *Essence* (August 1970); Dee, Ruby. ". . . Swinging Gently," *New York Amsterdam News* (September 3 1977); "Diana Sands: Collecting Acting Prizes Is Her Hobby," *Sepia* (May 1966); "Diana Sands, First Tan Cleopatra," *Sepia* (August 1967); "Diana Sands in Death Struggle with Cancer," *Jet* (October 4, 1973); Fields, S. "Sands Stops Drifting," *New York Daily News* (November 27 1964); "Final Rites Held for Diana Sands," *Jet* (October 11, 1973); Gussow, Mel. "And Now, Diana at the Stake," *New York Times* (December 31, 1967); Lapole, Nick. "Diana Sands Reached for a Star," *New York Journal American* (February 21, 1965); "Mime: To Speed up Her Progress on the Stage, Diana Sands Turned to Pantomime." *Our World* (July 1955); Peterson, Maurice. "Diana, Diana," *Essence* (June 1972); Sands, Diana. Clippings File. Billy Rose Theatre Collection, Lincoln Center Library of the Performing Arts, New York City; Schaap, Dick. "A Girl Playing a Girl," *New York Herald Tribune* (November 15, 1964); Stang, Joanne. "The Carpenter's Daughter. Diana Sands, Praised for Her Performance in Baldwin Drama Discusses Her Past and the Future," *New York Times* (May 10, 1964); Wolf, A. "The Passion of Diana Sands," *Look* (January 9, 1968); Wahls, R. "Diana the Pussycat," *New York Daily News* (July 4, 1965); Wilson, Earl. "Says Diana of Diahann," *Newark Evening News* (August 4, 1970).

DELIA REYES

SAPPHIRE

One of the most pervasive stereotypes of Black women, historically and contemporarily, is that of the dominating, emasculating female. This stereotype grew through radio, television, and scholarly studies to have a significant impact on popular conceptions of Black women. In 1926, a radio serial premiered in which two white actors, Freeman Gosden and Charles Correll, portrayed two southern Black men who had migrated North to Chicago. The roots of this new radio show, *Sam 'n' Henry*, were nineteenth-century minstrel shows and blackface vaudeville acts. After becoming a regional hit, *Sam 'n' Henry* moved to another Chicago radio station, and in 1928 Gosden and Correll renamed their main characters Amos and Andy. In 1929, *Amos 'n' Andy*, which eventually became the most popular radio show in the United States, joined NBC and within a short period of time became something of a national obsession. A third character, the Kingfish, head of the Mystic Knights of the Sea (a fraternal order), became a prominent feature of the show, along with his wife, Sapphire, the precise origins of whose role are unknown.

In June 1951, the television show *Amos 'n' Andy* premiered, and the broadcast was shown at the annual convention of the National Association for the Advancement of Colored People in Atlanta, Georgia. After the broadcast, the convention passed a unanimous resolution condemning *Amos 'n' Andy* for its derogatory stereotypes of Black people. Despite the controversy that continued to swirl around this enormously popular television show, both within and without the Black community, it won an Emmy nomination in 1952. CBS cancelled the show after its second season, but it was syndicated to hundreds of local stations, and *Amos 'n' Andy* remained a staple of American commercial television until the mid-1960s.

As the series evolved, more characters, especially female ones, emerged. In 1929, Ernestine Wade, a Black actress and musician, auditioned for the part of the Kingfish's wife, whose character went unnamed in the early years of the show. As a result of Wade's handling of the role, Sapphire eventually became the most popular, and the most stereotypical, female character on the series. As the Kingfish's domineering wife, Sapphire embodied many of the most prevalent stereotypes about African-American women as overbearing, bossy, sharp-tongued, controlling, and emasculating. The most memorable scenes of their marriage consisted of Sapphire scolding the Kingfish, especially about his dishonesty, laziness, and unreliability. Their relationship conformed to the stereotype of the matriarchal Black family, which Black sociologist E. Franklin Frazier immortalized in his classic *The Negro Family in the United States* (1939).

Amos 'n' Andy reinforced notions about problematic relationships between Black men and women and sketched an indelible portrait of the stereotypical domineering Black woman in the psyches of Black and white Americans. Sapphire would become, long after the name's association with the program had faded, an acceptable and unquestioned term for so-called emasculating Black women. Sapphire also became a pervasive image in the folk culture of African-Americans and one of the most damaging and pervasive stereotypes of Black women, which still has currency in contemporary conceptions of Black womanhood.

BIBLIOGRAPHY

Kelley, Melvin Patrick. *The Adventures of Amos 'n' Andy: A Social History of an American Phenomenon* (1991).

BEVERLY GUY-SHEFTALL

SAUNDERS, CECELIA CABANISS (1883-1966)

The Harlem branch of the New York City Young Women's Christian Association, founded in 1905, assumed a position of prominence in the Harlem community and among Black New Yorkers in general largely through the efforts of Cecelia Cabaniss Saunders. Born Cecelia Holloway in Charleston, South Carolina, she grew up as a member of the nation's Black aristocracy. The Holloways, a free family of color, had produced many educators, business people, and politicians in the eighteenth and nineteenth centuries. Cecelia's father, James H. Holloway, served as principal of the Timmonsville School in Charleston during Reconstruction and she would follow in his footsteps through her lifelong commitment to education. Cecelia Holloway graduated from Fisk University in 1909 and worked for the national board of the Young Women's Christian Association before becoming executive secretary of the Harlem branch in 1914. She married Dr. James E. Cabaniss in 1912, was widowed, and was remarried in 1915 to John D. Saunders, a real estate agent in New York City.

Cecelia Cabaniss Saunders was tireless in her work with the Harlem YWCA, guiding it from a small organization in a make-shift rented building to

an established community institution with an imposing physical plant. By the late 1930s, Saunders's Harlem YWCA consisted of a main building with offices and meeting rooms, a thriving trade school, the Emma Ransom Home residence, and summer camp facilities. Saunders dedicated herself, through the YWCA, to assisting young African-American women in entering into fields of work from which they were previously barred because of racism. Her philosophy was that industry would not reject women who were well trained. Over the years, the branch was successful in opening up new fields of work for Black women in New York City. Saunders was also involved in many other organizations, but her love and life's work went to the Harlem YWCA.

BIBLIOGRAPHY

Morris, Robert C. *Reading, 'Riting, and Reconstruction: The Education of Freedmen in the South, 1861-1870* (1981); Weisenfeld, Judith. "The More Abundant Life: The Harlem Branch of the New York City Young Women's Christian Association, 1905-1945," Ph.D. diss. (1992).

JUDITH WEISENFELD

SAVAGE, AUGUSTA (1892-1962)

Augusta Savage is one of the most enigmatic figures in American art. Although she was one of the most influential individuals in Harlem during the later part of the Harlem Renaissance, her life and career remain a somewhat sketchy mystery. She championed social and political causes and effected cultural and economic opportunities, particularly for African-American artists and the Harlem community in the 1930s, but choose to leave that community later in life.

Her efforts in establishing the Harlem Community Art Center, where Black people had the unprecedented and rare opportunity to study fine arts, was heralded throughout the nation. The center was one of the most exciting programs of its kind in America. It became a model for other urban centers and a symbol of race pride, as did her best known work, *The Harp*, which she produced for the 1939 World's Fair.

Cast in plaster and painted, this sixteen-foot-high sculpture stood in the court of the Contemporary Arts Building on the Fair grounds. The sculpture depicted a choir supported by the arm and hand of the Creator. The kneeling figure held a bar of musical notes and the text of James Weldon Johnson's poem

"Lift Every Voice and Sing." The work received wide publicity and became well known nationally throughout Black communities.

Augusta Savage was one of four women artists, and the only Black artist, to receive a commission from the Fair Corporation. She was awarded twelve hundred dollars to design and produce the sculpture. *The Harp*, which became popularly known as *Lift Every Voice and Sing*, executed at the pinnacle of her career, represented Augusta Savage's most monumental achievement. Regrettably, there were no funds to cast the work and it was destroyed at the close of the Fair.

Augusta Savage made a tremendous personal sacrifice to be an artist and a teacher. She had to fight for virtually everything that she believed in and wanted to be. From the outset, she fought her father's disapproval of making art, and as a young single woman in New York, she fought against racism, sexism, and discrimination. Yet, in spite of the early deaths of two husbands, another short-lived marriage that ended in divorce, and the constant emotional demands placed on her by her family, she managed to live a life of artistic intensity and exert great influence on younger artists.

Born Augusta Christine Fells in 1892, in Green Cove Springs, Florida, she was the seventh of fourteen children. Her father was a carpenter, fisherman, farmer, and minister and disapproved of her making "graven" objects. Savage indicates in her autobiographies that she came from a hard-working family. Her early years were spent working in the house with her mother, going to school, and making small clay objects. As she says:

> at a very early age, [I] demonstrated the artistic talent which shaped my career. . . . From the time I can first recall the rain falling on the red clay in Florida, I wanted to make things. When my brothers and sisters were making mud pies, I would be making ducks and chickens with the mud.

Her father was not impressed with her fascination and love for making clay objects. She later stated that her parents "practically whipped the art out of me."

At the young age of fifteen, Augusta married John T. Moore, her first husband, and a year later had her only child, Irene Connie Moore. Her husband died a few years after the birth of their daughter.

In 1915, Augusta's father moved the family to West Palm Beach, Florida. At this time she gave up clay making. However, she resumed modeling in clay when a school principal who recognized her talents persuaded her to teach a clay modeling class in the Black high school for a term. This experience inspired her to be a teacher and she enrolled at Tallahassee State Normal School (now Florida A&M University) for one year. She returned to West Palm Beach and entered the county fair there. Her work was greatly admired. Fairgoers, including many northern tourists, purchased her work. Impressed by her entries, George Graham Currie, superintendent of the fair, suggested that she go to New York to study. But Augusta moved to Jacksonville, Florida, where she attempted to earn a living sculpting portrait busts of prominent Black Americans. She soon discovered that this plan was not feasible. The expected patron-

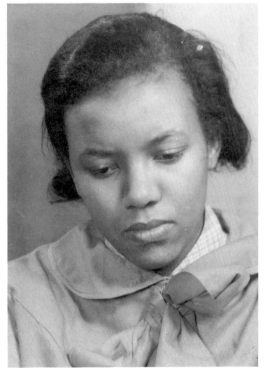

A groundbreaker in the creation of a vital Black artistic community, Augusta Savage was the first director of the Harlem Community Art Center, the only Black artist to receive a commission for the 1939 World's Fair, and the only director of the Salon of Contemporary Negro Art in Harlem. [National Archives]

age did not materialize and after a few months, she moved to New York City.

In 1921, at the outset of the Harlem Renaissance, Augusta arrived in New York. She was twenty-nine and had not yet formally studied sculpture or art. Currie provided Augusta with a letter of introduction to his friend, sculptor Solon Borglum, founder of the School of American Sculpture. Since Augusta could not afford the tuition of the school, Borglum directed her to Kate L. Reynolds, principal of Cooper Union, where tuition was not required.

Savage was accepted into the program and began a formal course of study with portrait sculptor George Brewster. To support herself, Savage took a job as an apartment caretaker.

By her second year at Cooper Union, she was taking fourth-year courses but had financial difficulties. After losing her job, she informed Reynolds that she would be unable to complete her studies. Reynolds found temporary employment for her and special funds to pay for her living expenses.

In 1923, Savage was engulfed in a controversy over a scholarship for foreign study. She sent an application to an American summer program for architects, painters, and sculptors at the Palace of Fontainebleau near Paris. She was accepted in the program, but the scholarship was withdrawn when two Alabama girls who also won scholarships complained to the committee that they could not be expected to travel or room with a "colored girl." Herman MacNeil, president of the National Sculpture Society and a member of the committee, attempted to reverse the decision of the committee, but their minds could not be changed. Ashamed of their decision, he invited Savage to study privately that summer with him at his studio in College Point, New York.

The incident was extensively published in the press. It brought Augusta Savage sympathetic public attention and notoriety. On the political front she had the support of W.E.B. Du Bois and other prominent and distinguished people. It was during this time that she met and married Robert Poston, a Garveyite and brother of journalist Ted Poston. Robert Poston died five months after their marriage.

Du Bois arranged for Savage to receive a working scholarship to Italy. Sponsored by Countess Irene Di Robilant, manager of the Italian-American Society in New York, the scholarship covered tuition and materials at the Royal Academy of Fine Arts in Rome. Unable to raise the money for travel and living expenses, she had to postpone the trip. What she earned working at a laundry was sent to West Palm Beach to care for her father, who was now paralyzed. She even-

tually brought her parents to New York to live with her and postponed her trip indefinitely.

Although she worked and cared for her parents, she was able to continue her art work. She succeeded in producing several important works, such as *Green Apples* and a bust of musician Theodore Upshure. She exhibited periodically with the Harmon Foundation and at the 135th Street Branch of the New York Public Library. She also participated in major group exhibitions that included the works of artistic giants, painter Henry O. Tanner and sculptor Meta Warrick Fuller.

Another family tragedy struck. A brother drowned in a flood in the aftermath of a Florida hurricane. She then had to shoulder the cost of bringing the remainder of her family to New York to live with her.

As a recipient of the Julius Rosenwald Fellowship, Savage was finally able to study abroad. She departed for Paris in 1929. Because she had won a consecutive award, she was able to stay for two years. The initial award was for her sculpture titled *Gamin*. Using her nephew Ellis Ford as a model, she captured the quintessential character of youth. The work expresses the tenderness and streetwise sharpness of the boy. *Gamin*, in the collection of the Schomburg Center for Research in Black Culture, is a work that straddles the boundary between portraits and types. It is an important marker in the shift of African-American art toward the representation of Black people by Black artists. The work reflected the new realism that was beginning to emerge.

While in Paris, she studied with Felix Beauneteaux at the Grande Chaumière and Charles Despiau. She exhibited at the Salon d'Automne, at the Grand Palais, Salon Printemps, and at the Société des Artistes Français Beaux Arts. During this period, she also received a Carnegie Foundation grant that allowed her to travel to Belgium and Germany.

Shortly after returning to New York at the age of forty, she opened her own school—The Savage Studio of Arts and Crafts, located at 163 West 143rd Street in Harlem. She attracted young artists Ernest Crichlow, Norman Lewis, William Artis, and others. By the mid-1930s, her school, through an association with the State University of New York, had become the largest art school of its type in New York and had attracted the attention of both the Carnegie Foundation and the Federal Art Project of the Works Progress Administration (WPA).

By 1936, Savage became an assistant supervisor for the WPA Federal Art Project and became an advocate for other Black artists. She was responsible for bringing many of them onto the rolls as art instructors and studio artists. Her vigor and advocacy role led to her appointment as the first director of the Harlem Community Art Center in 1937.

Savage took a leave of absence in 1938 from the Harlem Community Art Center in order to execute the commission for the World's Fair. During her absence, her position was taken over by artist and writer Gwendolyn Bennett.

Following her triumphant success at the World's Fair, she was awarded a silver medal by the Women's Service League of Brooklyn in recognition of her pioneering efforts. She was the first Black member of the National Association of Women Painters and Sculptors, the first director of one of the most important art centers in the nation, the only Black artist to receive a commission for the World's Fair, and the first and only director of the first Black-owned corporation to open a gallery devoted to the work of Black artists.

The gallery, named the Salon of Contemporary Negro Art in Harlem, opened in 1939. It was the culminating project in Savage's long career of promoting Black artists and art, and of her efforts to build economic support and opportunities for them. Over thirty artists participated in the show. Among the more popularly known women artists were Meta Warrick Fuller (exhibiting for the first time in twenty years), Gwendolyn Knight, Sara Murrel, Georgette Seabrooke, Lois Mailou Jones, Grace Mott Johnson, Selma Burke, and Elba Lightfoot. Due to a lack of funding, the gallery closed after a few months.

Savage's attention shifted away from the intense involvement that characterized her work, and in 1945, she moved to Saugerties, New York. There she supported herself with odd jobs, taught art to children in local summer camps, wrote short stories, and reestablished ties with her daughter Irene. During this time, her artistic production was virtually nonexistent, although she completed a few works.

Her influence as a teacher was demonstrated often when her students were praised and awarded for their excellent work and achievements. Norman Lewis, Gwendolyn Knight, Ernest Crichlow, Morgan Smith, and Marvin Smith are among the many talented artists that she nurtured artistically and intellectually. They were the direct beneficiaries of her personal sacrifice, dedication, and love.

Savage contributed substantially and uniquely to the shaping of African-American art. She was among the earliest African-American artists to consistently and sympathetically use Black physiognomy in her work. She is most appreciated for her ability to give dignity to her subjects in spite of the obstacles of racism, sexism, and discrimination. She gave her sitters quiet will and perseverance like her own.

BIBLIOGRAPHY

Abrams, Alyse. *WPA Writers Project Papers*, Archives, Manuscripts and Rare Books Division, Schomburg Center for Research in Black Culture, New York City (November 27, 1939); *Against the Odds: African-American Artists and the Harmon Foundation*, exhibition catalogue, Newark Museum (1989); *Augusta Savage and the Art Schools of Harlem*, exhibition catalogue, Schomburg Center for Research in Black Culture (1988); Fax, Elton C. "Augusta Savage—An Appraisal," *American Society of African Culture Newsletter*, Schomburg Center Clipping File (n.d.); Harmon Foundation. *Negro Artists: An Illustrated Review of Their Achievement* (1935); Michelson, S. "The Federal Art Project in Harlem," *WPA Writers Project Papers*, Archives, Manuscripts and Rare Books Division, Schomburg Center (June 24, 1942); Rubinstein, Charlotte. *American Women Sculptors* (1990).

DEIRDRE BIBBY

SCHUYLER, PHILIPPA DUKE (1931-1967)

Philippa Duke Schuyler's career was as remarkable as her background was unusual. Her father was George S. Schuyler, a well-known Black American writer. Her mother, Josephine Cogdell, came from a wealthy white Texas ranching and banking family. Philippa was brought up in an atmosphere of intense interest in intellectual matters and the arts. Though her mother attributed the child's genius to a diet of raw foods, it is more likely to have resulted from constant intellectual challenge.

Schuyler was born on August 2, 1931. Newspaper and journal articles chronicled the prodigy's development as she crawled at four weeks, walked at eight months, read at two years, and played the piano at age three. At four she could spell forty-letter words and was performing her own piano compositions over the radio. When she was seven, her IQ was measured as 180, and she was playing the piano on tour. She graduated from elementary school at ten, had written more than 100 compositions by thirteen, and, for that birthday, completed her first orchestral work. Scored for 100 instruments, *Manhattan Nocturne* was performed by the New York Philharmonic under the direction of Rudolph Ganz during the last performance of the 1944-45 Young People's Concerts season.

Schuyler graduated from high school at fifteen. A few years later, she wrote *The Rhapsody of Youth* in honor of the inauguration of Haitian president Paul Magloire and received the Haitian Decoration of Honor and Merit. A young woman now, she continued to tour and was well received, visiting more than eighty countries. She was knighted in Haiti and gave command performances for Ethiopia's Haile Selassie and Queen Elizabeth of Belgium.

A devoted Catholic, Schuyler wrote five books during her career, including one with her mother. She was fluent in several languages, and in demand as a lecturer across the globe. The budding writer had begun working as a news correspondent just before her death. She died on May 9, 1967, in a helicopter crash in Da Nang during the Vietnam war. She was trying to help remove Catholic schoolchildren from

In addition to being a composer, Philippa Duke Schuyler was also noted as a concert pianist and, later, as a news correspondent. She died at the age of thirty-five in a helicopter crash, while trying to help remove Catholic school children from the site of fighting during the Vietnam war. [Library of Congress]

A child prodigy, Philippa Duke Schuyler began composing for the piano at age four. For her thirteenth birthday, Schuyler completed her first orchestral work. Scored for one hundred instruments, Manhattan Nocturne *was performed by the New York Philharmonic under the direction of Rudolf Ganz. [Schomburg Center]*

the site of fighting in Hue to the relative safety of a school in Da Nang.

Schuyler's best-known musical works include *Fairy Tale Symphony*, *Sleepy Hollow Sketches*, and *The Nile Fantasy*, also known as *Le Nile* and *White Nile Suite*.

[*See also* COMPOSERS.]

BIBLIOGRAPHY

BDAAM; Cherry, Gwendolyn, Ruby Thomas, and Pauline Williams. *Portraits in Color: The Lives of Colorful Negro Women* (1962); "Far Lands," *Courier Magazine* (July 28, 1951); McIntosh, India. "Harlem Prodigy," *Negro Digest* (September 1944); Mitchell, Joseph. "Evening with a Gifted Child," *Negro Digest* (October 1943); "On the Cover: Young Artist Abroad," *Musical Courier* (January 1956); "Original Girl," *Time* (March 25, 1946); "Philippa Schuyler in Stadium Debut," *New York Times* (July 15, 1946); "Philippa Schuyler, Pianist, Town Hall, May 12 (Debut)," *Musical America* (June 1953); Reno, Doris. "Young Pianist Gives

Skillful Concert Here," *Miami Herald* (February 25, 1950); "Super-Girl," *Ebony* (March 1946); Talalay, Kathryn. "Philippa Duke Schuyler, Pianist, Composer, Writer," *Black Perspective in Music* (Spring 1982).

SELECTED WORKS BY PHILIPPA SCHUYLER
Adventures in Black and White (1960); *Good Men Die* (1969); *Jungle Saints: Africa's Heroic Catholic Missionaries* (1963); *Who Killed the Congo?* (1962); *Kingdom of Dreams* with Josephine Schuyler (1966).

DEBORRA A. RICHARDSON

SCIENCE

In 1876, Edward A. Bouchet became the first Black man to earn a doctorate in the United States, graduating from Yale University with a degree in physics. One hundred years later, in 1976, Shirley A. Jackson became the first Black woman in the United States to earn a doctorate in physics, from the Massachusetts Institute of Technology (MIT). This century-long gap between Bouchet and Jackson reflects the very different experiences of Black men and Black women in the sciences in this country. In few other professions has the gap between Black male and female participation been so great. From 1876 to 1940, only ninety Black people earned doctorates in the sciences—95 percent of the recipients were male, and 5 percent were female. These pioneering Black women scientists included Ruth E. Moore, bacteriology, Ohio State University, 1933; Jessie Jarue Mark, botany, Iowa State University, 1935; Flemmie P. Kittrell, nutrition, Cornell University, 1936; Roger Arliner Young, zoology, University of Pennsylvania, 1940; and Ruth Lloyd, anatomy, Western Reserve University, 1941.

In contrast, by 1940 more than 25,000 white men and 2,000 white women held doctorates in the sciences. It was not until the early 1980s that Black women gained parity with Black men in the sciences, earning 50 percent of all doctorates awarded to Black Americans. Overall, however, by 1987 Black women earned only 6 percent of all science degrees awarded in engineering, mathematics, and the physical sciences, the smallest percentage of any racial/ethnic group.

To understand the disparity in the participation of Black women in the sciences it is necessary to look at the periods before and after 1940. From the late nineteenth century until 1940, Black women who wanted to become scientists were hindered by factors related both to race and gender. First, in this period

few women in the United States were allowed to enter educational institutions in which they could be trained as scientists. The small number of Black women who earned doctorates in the sciences during this period were largely educated at the undergraduate level in the historically Black colleges in the South. These colleges had few of the resources needed for the training of scientists, such as laboratory equipment, advanced courses, or extensive library holdings. Furthermore, many educators at these colleges did not view science as a viable occupation for Black students because few scientific institutions employed Black graduates. These same educators also felt that Black women should train to be teachers, for which there was a critical need in Black communities. However, the biggest barrier faced by all Black people who wanted to study science in this period was the belief held by many white scientists that "the exact and intensive habit of mind, the rigorous mathematical logic demanded of those who would be scientists is not natural to the Negro race" (Du Bois 1939).

Against this background, the few Black women who managed to earn doctorates in the sciences were unique and committed women. Those who succeeded had to overcome stereotypes about appropriate women's roles both inside and outside their communities as well as the prejudice of white scientists. Typically they pursued their scientific careers in institutions that required them to teach a great deal, thus allowing them little time for research. It is not surprising that all of these first Black women scientists earned degrees in the biological sciences, the fields most open to women in general in this period.

After 1940—and especially after World War II—scientific institutions in the United States experienced a tremendous amount of growth. The successful use of sophisticated technology such as radar during the war fueled the growth of many new industries in the postwar era. Surely the most visible sign of the new spirit of scientific development emerged in the 1960s with the drive to put a man on the moon. Expanded employment opportunities for scientists, coupled with the breakdown of laws supporting racial segregation, made it possible for many more Black women to pursue careers in the sciences. Black women began to earn degrees in many fields, among them mathematics (Marjorie Lee Browne, University of Michigan, 1949, and Evelyn Boyd Granville, Yale, 1949); geology (Margurite Thomas, Catholic University, 1942); chemical engineering (Jenny Patrick, MIT, 1979); and mechanical engineering (Christine Darden, George Washington University, 1983). These women have had successful careers as educators and researchers. In addition, they have served as positive role models encouraging young Black women to prepare themselves for careers in science.

In spite of these efforts, however, the number of Black women in science has remained small. Science is still largely viewed as a male activity in U.S. society, and such views continue to make young women uncomfortable about their interest in science. The National Science Foundation and the National Institutes of Health are two federal institutions that have attempted in recent years to counter such views and provide additional encouragement to outstanding Black female undergraduates by offering them scholarships and summer research opportunities at the most prestigious laboratories in the country. As a result, Black women scientists are conducting research in the most innovative scientific disciplines, including neuroscience, computer science and artificial intelligence, ecology, and oceanography.

By and large, Black women scientists in the United States have succeeded in spite of numerous barriers and in the face of tremendous odds. Most Black women scientists have never had other Black women as study companions, colleagues, or mentors. Indeed, many have had the experience of being the lone Black female in their respective fields. Those who succeed do so by overcoming their isolation and the difficult working environments they often encounter. Success in science requires hard work, long hours, and a commitment to the pursuit of knowledge for knowledge's sake. The training is long and arduous. For much of this century, successful male scientists have been afforded the opportunity to pursue their scientific interests with few interruptions. Only in the last decade of the twentieth century have Black women been provided equal access to such opportunities. Having demonstrated their commitment to the highest ideals of science, Black women scientists will no doubt make greater tangible achievements in the future.

BIBLIOGRAPHY

Du Bois, W.E.B. "The Negro Scientist," *American Scholar* (Summer 1939); Jay, James M. *Negroes in Science: Natural Science Doctorates 1876 to 1969* (1971); Malcolm, Shirley. "Increasing the Participation of Black Women in Science and Technology," *Sage: A Scholarly Journal on Black Women* (Fall 1989); Rossiter, Margaret. *Women Scientists in America: Struggles and Strategies to 1940* (1982).

EVELYNN M. HAMMONDS

SCOTIA SEMINARY

For more than sixty years after its founding in 1867, the rigidly straight-laced Presbyterian girls' school located about fifteen miles north of Charlotte in the old cotton-mill town of Concord, North Carolina, existed as Scotia Seminary. On November 22, 1870, the state of North Carolina had chartered it as such. By 1932, as the junior college movement swept the United States and southern public authorities assumed greater responsibility for Black secondary education, this elementary-secondary-normal institution, through a merger with Barber College for Women in Anniston, Alabama, became the nineteenth recognized Black junior college in the country. The transformed school, Barber-Scotia College, typified the Black junior college in its private sponsorship, state accreditation, small enrollment, low tuition—$50 for nine months—and its combination of secondary and collegiate programs. The college was atypical, however, in that more than 50 percent of its faculty—seven out of twelve—held the Master's degree rather than just the Bachelor's. Moreover, most of its students—fifty-nine out of ninety-five—were enrolled in the collegiate curriculum, and, as previously, all of the students were women. In the evolving pattern of other postsecondary Black schools, the institution awarded its first four-year state approved college degrees in 1945; as earlier, it continued to enroll relatively small numbers. In 1947, it counted 157 students; in 1954, 191. That changed in 1955 when, shattering an eighty-seven-year tradition, it registered a white male. This resulted from a 1954 amended charter that permitted acceptance of students regardless of gender and race. In 1958, again in keeping with contemporary currents in Black higher education, Barber-Scotia College became a member of the regional accrediting agency, the Southern Association of Colleges and Schools. This occurred under the administration of Leland Stanford Cozart, who had been president since 1932. The institution continues under Presbyterian auspices to be a vital educational force in the Carolinas.

Just as the evolution of the Concord institution into a reputable senior college commands attention and respect, so should its extended phase as Scotia Seminary. Scotia enjoyed the distinction of becoming the first major boarding school for Black girls in the vanquished Confederacy and thus being a prototype for other schools in the region. Existing in an era of virulent racial segregation, discrimination, and repression, it and kindred subcollegiate institutions before World War I offered the highest leadership training available in the South to a majority of upwardly mobile Black women who lacked access to the college education available not only to white men and women but also to Black men.

On behalf of the freedman's committee of the Northern Presbyterian Church, Scotia's founder, Reverend Luke Dorland of Toledo, Ohio, cast it in the mold of antebellum girls' seminaries. Specifically, Scotia modeled itself after Mount Holyoke Female Seminary in South Hadley, Massachusetts, which opened in 1837 and was noted for its independence, permanency, and intellectual rigor. Scotia was always an under-financed missionary enterprise—it had a paltry endowment of only $1,000 by 1894. It could not match its mentor, but, nevertheless, it aimed high. Its purpose was "to educate colored girls in religion, and in the Arts and Science usually taught in seminaries of a high order; and in those domestic duties which belong to the highest type of wife, mother, and teacher" (*Annual Report* 1872). Clearly students were trained to occupy a woman's place in segregated society. Scotia's leadership believed that no higher place existed for its graduates in this society than the home because it accepted the late-nineteenth-century notion of women as civilizers; women were to instill higher virtues in family members.

Although this was the most prominent raison d'être for Scotia, a close second was to educate teachers. "Especially does it [the Seminary] aim to raise up effective teachers," Scotia announced in the mid-1870s, "now so much needed and sought by freed people" (Cozart 1976). It was the teachers, not the homemakers—though often they were one and the same—about whom Scotia characteristically boasted. In 1894, roughly seven-eighths of its alumnae were teachers.

Under the leadership of President David Satterfield in 1891, it erected a new dormitory, Faith Hall, the second major building on campus. The new dormitory facilities meant that annual enrollments could expand, but had to be capped at a little below 300 students. In addition, the school found accommodations for twice the number of teachers, increasing from eleven to twenty-two. The growth never threatened the seminary's commitment to certain continuities. All of the presidents were well-credentialed white males. Most teachers were white women. Probably stemming most from a perceived need to shield students from deleterious influences, the institution isolated itself both physically and psychologically from Concord's Black and white communities. Students submitted to school authority

in all aspects of their lives, including what they wrote in personal letters.

Moreover, the seminary subscribed completely to the era's popular head-hand-heart approach to educating Black youth. It fostered logical thinking and encouraged the acquisition of useful information, particularly through drill for mental development. It offered two curricula: a four-year grammar program of English, arithmetic, algebra, geography, science, history, and literature; and a three-year normal and scientific course that included geometry, astronomy, physics, chemistry, history, Latin, and rhetoric. The industrial department taught courses in sewing and cooking, and the students participated in a housekeeping program to minimize operating expenses. Consequently, the girls washed, ironed, set tables, scrubbed floors, and dusted furniture. The seminary's curriculum also embraced training in refinement, teaching qualities such as a gently modulated voice, quiet dignity, and conservative dress. Most of all, it centered on promoting Christianity as "an intelligent faith" (Satterfield 1892). Students participated in worship services and studied the Bible daily. Most, for the first time, saw Christianity reflected in egalitarian relationships between white and Black faculty members. When, through merger, the seminary became a junior college, a liberalizing wind blew away some traditions, but others remained to anchor the school in a new era.

BIBLIOGRAPHY

Cozart, Leland Stanford. *A Venture of Faith: Barber-Scotia College, 1867-1967* (1976); Guzeman, Jessie Parkhurst, ed. *Negro Year Book* (1947); Hartshorn, William Newton. *An Era of Progress and Promise 1863-1910* (1910); Hobson, Elizabeth C., and Charlotte Everett Hopkins. *A Report Concerning the Colored Women of the South* (1896); Jenkins, Martin D. "Enrollment in Institutions of Higher Education of Negroes," *Journal of Negro Education* (Spring 1954); Jones, Thomas Jesse, ed. *Negro Education: The Study of the Private and Higher Schools for Colored People in the United States* (1917); Lane, David A., Jr. "The Junior College Movement Among Negroes," *Journal of Negro Education* (July 1933); Logan, Frenise A. *The Negro in North Carolina, 1876-1894* (1964); Lyons, James E. "In the Beginning of Faith: An Oral History of Barber-Scotia College" (1976), Barber-Scotia College Library, Concord, North Carolina; Parker, Inez Moore. *The Rise and Decline of the Program for Black Presbyterians of the United Presbyterian Church, U.S.A. 1865-1970* (1977); Presbyterian Board of Missions for Freedmen. *Annual Report*, 1871-1905, Presbyterian Historical Society, Philadelphia; Richings, G. F. *Evidence of Progress among Colored People* (1896); Satterfield, David J. "The Education of Afro-American Girls," *American Missionary Magazine* (July 1892); "Scotia," *Home Mission*

Monthly, 1887-1905, Presbyterian Historical Society, Philadelphia; Scruggs, L. A. *Women of Distinction* (1893); U.S. Department of Interior. *Survey of Negro Colleges and Universities* (1929); Williams, W.T.B. "Typical Negro Schools and Colleges in North Carolina," *Southern Workman* (April 1904); Work, Monroe N., ed. *Negro Year Book, 1918-1919* (1919).

ELAINE M. SMITH

SCOTT, GLORIA DEAN RANDLE (1938-)

Recognized in the exhibit, I Dream a World, Seventy-five Black Women Who Changed America, Gloria Dean Randle Scott has played, and continues to play, an outstanding role in American higher education. As college president and member of numerous professional and voluntary organizations, Scott is also a strong proponent of women's rights. She describes herself as a "race woman," saying, "Giving something back, influencing what happens to Black people has always been important. . . . I suppose I'm one of the vestiges of what you call 'race women,' people who really believe in African-Americans" (Mercer 1990).

Daughter of Randle Scott and Juanita (Bell) Randle, Gloria Dean Randle Scott was born on April 14, 1938, in Houston, Texas. She graduated from Jack Yates High School in 1955 as salutatorian. Her B.A. (1959), M.A. (1960), and Ph.D. in higher education, zoology, and botany (1965) were earned at Indiana University. In 1959, she married Will Braxton Scott, currently a professor of sociology and social work at Bennett College in Greensboro, North Carolina. Scott's career reflects her special interest in educational research and planning as well as her ongoing dedication to the needs of women and Black youth.

In 1967, after holding teaching positions at Marian College in Indianapolis, Indiana, and Knoxville College in Tennessee, Scott went to North Carolina Agricultural and Technical State University in Greensboro, where she developed long-range institutional planning and set up the Office of Institutional Research and Planning. Between 1968 and 1973, Scott served as director of that office and also worked as a teaching faculty member. In 1977, Scott served as assistant to the president for educational planning and evaluation at Texas Southern University in Houston. She then moved to Atlanta, where she served as vice president of Clark College

for nine years. From 1978 to 1987, Scott returned to teaching, holding positions at several colleges, including Bryn Mawr in Pennsylvania, Atlanta University, and Grambling State University in Louisiana. In 1987, Scott was elected president of Bennett College, a historically Black liberal arts college that enrolls more than 600 women students. Scott is the second woman president in the history of the college.

Scott has said she views the Black college not only as the provider of education for economic, social, and intellectual betterment but also potentially as a "corporate citizen" representing the interests of Black students. Scott has worked hard, both within her institution and in the larger community, to develop leadership qualities in young Black women and improve access to higher education for Black students. Having served on the President's Board of Advisors on Historically Black Colleges since 1990, Scott and the board of advisors successfully petitioned President George Bush in 1991 to overturn a Department of Education ruling that stated it was unlawful to provide minority-only scholarships for college students.

Scott has maintained a long association with the Girl Scouts (USA) and has been a member of its board of directors since 1969. In 1975, she became the organization's first Black president. Scott views scouting as both an opportunity for personal growth as well as a means to enhance the lives of poor and minority children. The nature trips that Scott experienced as a teenager were instrumental in generating her lifelong interest in the outdoors. As Girl Scouts president, Scott worked vigorously to update the concerns and issues addressed by the organization, including women's issues, attitudes toward the natural environment, and justice for juveniles. She oversaw programs designed to increase participation by Black and Puerto Rican youths and adults in the organization, particularly in its leadership, as well as programs aimed at mentally handicapped youth. Classes on venereal disease also were developed during Scott's tenure as president.

Scott's activities in national and regional organizations have been both varied and numerous. Between 1973 and 1976, she was active in dismantling dual systems in higher education and conducted program review and evaluation for the U.S. Office of Education in states where the dual system still operated. Currently she holds a position on the external review board for minority participation at Stanford University. From 1966 to 1982, Scott was a founding member and secretary of Persons Responsive to Educational Problems, and she served as vice chair of the National

Advisory Committee on Black Higher Education and Black Colleges and Universities from 1976 to 1983.

Both President Gerald Ford and President Jimmy Carter appointed Scott to the National Commission on International Women's Year between 1976 and 1978. President Carter also appointed her to the National Commission on International Year of the Child, a position she held from 1978 to 1980. In 1985, Scott convened Clark College's Conference on American Black Women, entitled "Have We Come a Long Way, Baby?," and she led a delegation to the International Women's Decade meeting in Nairobi, Kenya. She has been a member and chairperson of SERO (Service Employment Redevelopment Operation)/ National Scholarship for Negro Students, 1982-85; a member of InRoads Atlanta, 1986-88; and member of the board of directors and cochairperson of the minority task force, National Association of Independent Colleges and Universities, 1989-92.

She also has been the recipient of numerous awards, including receiving the Indiana Governor's Award and being named Outstanding Negro Student in Indiana in 1964; being selected as a Legendary Woman, Birmingham Southern College, in 1977; receiving a citation from the Texas House of Representatives for outstanding leadership and contribution through services in 1978; and being inducted into the Academy of Women Achievers, the Young Women's Christian Association (YWCA) of Atlanta in 1986. In 1977, Scott was awarded an LL.D. from Indiana University, and in 1978 Fairleigh Dickinson University honored her with an honorary doctor of humane letters degree.

Gloria Scott is remarkable not merely for her spectacular achievements as a dynamic and determined leader within the field of education but also for her dedicated service to the needs and aspirations of women, Black communities, and young people across America.

BIBLIOGRAPHY

CBWA; Demaret, Kent. "The Old Girl Scout Cookie Crumbling? No Way, It's Got a New Activist—And Its First Black—Prez: Gloria Scott," *People Weekly* (July 25, 1977); *Ebony*, "Speaking of People" (August 1977); *Essence*, "Essence Women" (January 1978); *Jet*, "Bush's Black College Board Lauds Call for Review of Minority Scholarship Plan" (January 21, 1991); Jones, M. Colleen. "An Interview with Gloria Scott," *Journal of the National Association of Women Deans, Administrators, and Counselors* (Spring 1979); *Ladies' Home Journal*, "Women of the Year 1977" (June 1977); Lanker, Brian. *I Dream a World: Portraits of Black Women Who Changed America* (1989); Mercer, Joye. "Difficult Winds Ahead: Five Women Chart the Course for HBCUs in the 1990s," *Black Issues in Higher Education* (September 27, 1990); *NBAW*; Scott, Gloria Dean Randle. "The Economic Future: Institutional and Student Financial Aid for Blacks in Higher Education." In *Black Students in Higher Education: Conditions and Experiences*, ed. Gail E. Thomas (1980), and "Educational Needs of Black Women." In *Occupational and Educational Needs of Black Women* (1977), and special collections, Atlanta Public Library, Atlanta, and archives of Bennett College, Greensboro, North Carolina; *Who's Who of American Women* (1978); *WWBA* (1992).

FENELLA MACFARLANE

SCOTT, HAZEL (1920-1981)

After making her musical debut at age three, Hazel Dorothy Scott went on to become a star of Broadway, radio, television and film. Described as gifted, sophisticated, elegant, glamorous, outspoken, and uncompromising, Scott was renowned not only for her outstanding achievements as musician, singer, and actress but also for her commitment to speaking out against racial injustice.

Hazel Scott was born in Port of Spain, Trinidad, on June 11, 1920. Under the guidance of her mother, Alma Long Scott, she began playing the piano at age two, and at age three she made her musical debut in Trinidad. In 1924, her family moved to the United States where Scott, again thanks to her mother, began formal music training. Two years later, five-year-old Scott was making her American debut at New York's renowned Town Hall. Within three years, she had won a six-year scholarship to the Juilliard School of Music in New York City, but at the time the entrance age was sixteen. Around age fourteen, Scott joined her mother in Alma Long Scott's All-Woman Orchestra, where she played both piano and trumpet. By 1936, at age sixteen, Scott was not only a radio star on the Mutual Broadcasting System; she also was playing at the Roseland Dance Hall with the great Count Basie Orchestra.

In the late 1930s, Scott's career expanded when she appeared in the Broadway musical *Singing Out the News* and then, a few years later, *Priorities of 1942*. In 1939, she recorded her first record, with the sextet Rhythm Club of London. The early 1940s were busy years for Scott, with successful appearances in several films, including *Something to Shout About, I Dood It, Tropicana,* and *The Heat's On* in 1943, *Broadway Rhythm* in 1944, and *Rhapsody in Blue* in 1945. National recognition also came as a result of Scott's association with

Musician, singer, actress, and activist, the gifted and glamorous Hazel Scott made her musical debut at three, and by sixteen was a radio star. In the late 1930s and 1940s, she appeared in Broadway shows and films, and in the late 1940s and early 1950s, she became the first Black woman to have her own television show. [Scurlock Studio]

Barney Josephson's Café Society Downtown and Uptown in New York between 1939 and 1945.

In one of the year's most glittering social events, Hazel Scott married the charismatic preacher and powerful politician Adam Clayton Powell, Jr., in 1945. After the birth of their son, Adam Clayton Powell III, and following several years of separation, the couple divorced in 1956. During the late 1940s and early 1950s, Scott became the first Black woman to have her own television show, but in 1950 she was accused of being a Communist sympathizer, and her show was canceled. Scott defended her participation in fund-raising performances for groups fighting for equal rights and was widely recognized for her efforts in the struggle for racial freedom and justice. Speaking of her contract, which during the 1940s contained a clause allowing her to refuse to perform before racially segregated audiences, Scott once said in an interview, "What justification can anyone have who comes to hear me and then objects to sitting next to another Negro?" (*Washington Post* 1970).

In 1967, following five years of living abroad, primarily in Paris, Scott returned to the United States.

She appeared in television shows such as *Julia* and *The Bold Ones* and held nightclub residences at Emerson Ltd. in Washington, D.C., and Ali Baba East and Downbeat in New York City. In 1978, she was inducted into the Black Filmmakers Hall of Fame. Scott continued to perform until her death in the fall of 1981.

Famous for her ability to blend classics with high jazz as well as for her wit, personality, and talent, Hazel Dorothy Scott will be remembered for her dignity and determination in the struggle for racial equality and justice.

BIBLIOGRAPHY

CBWA; BDAAM; Handy, D. Antoinette. *Black Women in American Bands and Orchestras* (1981); Lewis, Claude. *Adam Clayton Powell* (1963); NBAW; Placksin, Sally. *American Women in Jazz* (1982); Powell, Adam Clayton, Jr. *Adam by Adam* (1971); Shaw, Arnold. *Black Popular Music* (1986); Taylor, Arthur. *Notes and Tones* (1977); *Washington Post*, "Hazel Scott Reflects" (July 4, 1970).

FENELLA MACFARLANE

SCOTT, MINNIE TAYLOR
(1872-1914)

Clubwoman Minnie Taylor Scott of Indiana represents many women of her era—second generation out of slavery, member of an extended family of achievers, and a hard worker dedicated to racial uplift. She also represents African-American women who have kept the family legacy and passed it down to others. The major source of information about her life comes from her family Bible, which was maintained and passed from her grandmother, Marie Woods, to other generations of women in the family.

Scott's mother, Emma Woods Taylor, maintained a list of all of the women in her family, beginning with her mother, Marie Woods, a mulatto slave from North Carolina. Both Emma and her husband, William Taylor, were born into slavery. Like many North Carolina freed people, they migrated to the Midwest after emancipation, where they settled in Indianapolis, Indiana. Their daughter, Minnie, was born October 25, 1872, and named for one of her mother's sisters. Their son, Marshall Woods Taylor, was born in 1878. By the time he was twenty-one, he had become nationally acclaimed as a cyclist, nicknamed Major. In 1899, he won the U.S. and World sprint championships. Racial prejudice, however, drove Major Taylor to become an expatriate who took his celebrated skill to Europe and Australia. In 1982, the city of his birth honored him by naming its first cycling arena the Major Taylor Velodrome.

Minnie Taylor decided to take a different path by staying in her home state to work with other women of her race who assisted their own people. She married William Aaron Scott, whose parents had been freed by their North Carolina master before Emancipation and sent by ox cart to the Midwest. The Scotts also settled in Indianapolis, where several of their descendants achieved success in education, business, and the arts. One son, Rufus, became a vaudeville actor and performed with Bert Williams. Another son, Edward, went to college and became a teacher. His son, William Edouard Scott, became a celebrated artist whose works can be found in the Indiana Museum of Art, the Tuskegee University Museum, and the DuSable Museum in Chicago.

Minnie Scott lived in one of the houses on the Scott family compound with an extended family of achievers. Her two children, Aaron and Emma, were encouraged to become professionals at a time when Black families paid dearly for higher education. Nonetheless, Aaron became a pharmacist and the owner of a drug store in Indianapolis. Emma became a teacher.

Their grandmother, Emma Taylor, cared for them during most of their lives as Minnie Scott traveled throughout the state and the country organizing other Black women to uplift their communities.

She began in Indianapolis during the 1890s while her children were small. Minnie Scott was one of the early presidents of the Alpha Home in Indianapolis. The home was founded in 1886 by the former slave Elizabeth Goff as a refuge for impoverished and homeless former slave women. By 1887, the home opened to former slave men. Although Marion County, Indiana, allocated funds to assist the home, the meager amount was never enough. As a result, Black Indianapolis clubwomen like Minnie Scott regularly raised funds for the support of the home. Throughout the 1890s and 1900s, the Alpha Home picnic in July and the Emancipation picnic in August raised funds for the Alpha Home.

As a pioneer in the Indiana women's club movement, Minnie T. Scott functioned on the state and national levels. She was the second president of the Indiana State Federation of Colored Women's Clubs, serving from 1907 until her sudden death in 1914. As president, she represented the women of her state on the national level in the National Association of Colored Women (NACW) conventions. The year of Scott's death, Minnie M. Scott of Toledo, Ohio, became prominent in the NACW leadership. As a result, the activities of the two women are sometimes confused, and Minnie T. is listed in NACW as the person from Toledo.

Minnie T. Scott's untimely death at the age of forty-two left a void for her family and the women she served. Her daughter, Emma, was still in high school, and her son, Aaron, was in college. Minnie Scott's legacy and extended family continued as her mother, her husband, and his relatives kept the family together. Consequently, the children were able to complete college. Family members say that Minnie Scott died of overwork and the pressures of being a leader in the women's club movement. Similar reasons have been given for the early demise of many other Black women leaders who labored to uplift their race.

BIBLIOGRAPHY

Hine, Darlene Clark. *When the Truth Is Told: A History of Black Women's Culture and Community in Indiana, 1875-1950* (1981); Wesley, Charles Harris. *The History of the National Association of Colored Women's Clubs* (1984).

ROSALYN TERBORG-PENN

SELIKA, MARIE SMITH
(c. 1849-1937)

Marie Smith Selika, concert and operatic soprano, was one of the small group of internationally recognized Black women singers during the second half of the nineteenth century. Selika, like her contemporaries, studied with European voice teachers and entrusted her career to a series of concert managers.

Marie Smith Williams adopted the stage name "Selika," the name of the leading female character in Meyerbeer's opera *L'Africaine*. The Black press reported that Selika performed this role in a stage production at the Academy of Music in Philadelphia. She was often referred to as "Queen of Staccato" for

Musical history was made on October 12, 1896, when Marie Selika joined Sissieretta Jones and Flora Batson on the stage of New York's Carnegie Hall. The three leading Black singers of their time thrilled a rapt audience. [Schomburg Center]

her sensational singing of E. W. Mulder's "Polka Staccato."

Little information is available on Selika prior to 1875 except that she was born c. 1849 in Natchez, Mississippi, and that soon thereafter the family moved to Cincinnati, Ohio. She studied voice as a child under the patronage of a wealthy white family who arranged for her lessons with a professional teacher. Between 1873 and 1876, she moved to San Francisco where she continued her voice studies with Signora G. Bianchi and made her West Coast debut in 1876. She met her husband, Sampson Williams, in Chicago, where both studied with Antonio Farini, who taught the so-called Italian method.

Selika first appeared in Philadelphia on November 21, 1878, accompanied by Thomas A. Beckett at the Academy of Music. The following year she appeared at Steinway Hall in New York. From 1882 to 1885, Selika and her husband toured Europe, performing in Paris, Russia, Germany, and England, and giving a command performance for Queen Victoria at St. James's Hall in October 1883. She performed at the Musée du Nord in Brussels and sang Weber's *Der Freischütz* in Germany. The press reported that the European trips provided excellent musical experiences for Selika and Sampson Williams, who was now performing with her.

From 1885 to 1891, the Williamses toured the United States giving benefit recitals and making church appearances, sometimes with other artists. After a second European tour in 1891, Selika and her husband, now called "Signor Velosko," sang in the West Indies. Selika performed at the Chicago World's Fair in 1893 and soon thereafter the couple settled in Cleveland, Ohio. On October 12, 1896, Selika, Sissieretta Jones, and Flora Batson—the three leading Black singers of the period—sang together at New York City's Carnegie Hall.

After her husband's death in 1911 and with her career in decline, Selika accepted a teaching position at the Martin-Smith Music School in New York City. A testimonial concert in her honor was given in 1919 at which she performed. She was active as a private teacher until her death on May 19, 1937, in New York City.

Selika reigned for almost three decades as a queen of song in the United States and Europe. She was the first concert coloratura in African-American music culture. As a tribute to her vocal excellence, Frederick G. Carnes wrote *Selika, A Grand Vocal Waltz of Magic*, which included staccato passages, trills, and vocal cadenzas.

BIBLIOGRAPHY

BDAAM; Jordan, Carolyne Lamar. "Black Female Concert Singers of the Nineteenth Century." In *Feel the Spirit: Studies in Nineteenth-Century Afro-American Music,* ed. George Keck and Sherrill Martin (1988); Southern, Eileen. *The Music of Black Americans: A History* (1983), and "In Retrospect: Black Prima Donnas of the Nineteenth Century," *Black Perspective in Music* (Spring 1979), and "Selika, Marie." In *The New Grove Dictionary of American Music,* ed. H. Wiley Hitchcock and Stanley Sadie (1986).

ELLISTINE P. LEWIS

SEXUAL HARASSMENT

As a crime, it did not exist. As an act, it had no name. Yet, from the time that women first entered the labor market, they suffered it, fought it, and sometimes succumbed to it.

Sexual harassment arises from deep-seated cultural disorders that reflect disrespect for women and that stem from the structures of male domination in such institutions as marriage and prostitution. However, to provide a context for sexual harassment and its relevance in the lives of Black women, it is necessary to go back to their sexual exploitation by men who considered themselves their legal owners.

The sexual exploitation of domestic servants—whether slave or free, Black or white—has been endemic throughout Western history. Historically, women servants seldom had many options. Compliance with their employers' sexual demands preserved them not only from unemployment but also from starvation or prostitution. The situation was so common that the seduced housemaid was a comic figure in fiction and on the stage. In real life, of course, her case was far from comic. If, after being abused by her employer, she became pregnant, she lost her occupation and often her life. If she refused to submit, the power of her employer to deprive her of other jobs was such that dismissal often meant the same thing.

In the earliest days of the American colonies, employers frequently sexually exploited servants, especially indentured servants. African women, in the years between 1619—when they first came to this country—and 1640, shared this oppression. Then, after 1640, when virtually all African servants were reduced by law to the condition of slavery, their condition became far worse.

The laws of the time gave mixed signals with regard to the sexual exploitation of slaves. On the one hand, sexual intercourse between Black and white

The calm and eloquent testimony of Anita Hill before the Senate Judiciary Committee considering the Supreme Court nomination of Clarence Thomas brought the issue of sexual harassment before the American people more forcefully than it ever had been before. [Reuters/Bettmann]

people was considered an even more serious sin—and therefore crime—than that within one "race." A white man who was convicted of having sexual relations with a Black woman faced a more severe punishment than one who slept with his white neighbor. That punishment extended to sexual relations between a man and his slave. However, if he forced a woman slave to have intercourse and she bore a child, that child was, by law, his slave as well, giving his action a significant financial advantage. As Paula Giddings points out, "Being able to reproduce one's own labor force would be well worth the fine, even in the unlikely event that it would be imposed" (Giddings 1984).

From the earliest years of America, then, white men were encouraged by law and custom to force sexual acts upon women who tilled their fields and cleaned their houses. However, Black women did not accept this exploitation without resistance. Even though their families were hostage to the slaveowner, they refused, fought, poisoned, and aborted in their determination not to lose their sexual self-respect or to participate in the breeding of new slaves. The struggle was, however, grossly unequal.

As the conditions of slavery changed, so did the forms of sexual exploitation. In the nineteenth century, women who were slaves were often rewarded for compliance and for pregnancies—relieved of onerous duties and given certain privileges. At this point, resistance was clearly a question of refusing to accept the status of property, especially as that status applied to one's most personal being. There were, of course, still punishments for refusal, and refusal was frequently futile.

A strange ambivalence on the part of male slaveowners emerged and can be seen in power relations within other relationships. Hazel Carby explains the significance of this ambivalence when she comments on the analysis of historian John Blassingame. "A slave woman, he argued, could be 'neither pure nor virtuous'; existing in circumstances of sexual subordination, 'women were literally forced to offer themselves willingly' to their masters. The interpretive ambivalence evident in the juxtaposition of 'forced' and 'willingly' indicated the spectrum of representation of the female slave from victim to active collaborator and a historical reluctance to condemn as an act of rape what is conceived in patriarchal terms to be sexual compliance" (Carby 1987).

One begins to yearn, not for the first time, for another word to replace "sexual" in this context. An act that is the result of dominance—whether it be physical, economic, or legal—should not bear the same name as an act entered into out of shared desire. It confuses discussion and it confuses people. When a historian can say that women were *forced* to offer themselves *willingly* and suggest that the act reflected on their virtue, the confusion is clearly profound. Yet it serves to point up one specific male attitude that is at the root of sexual harassment.

Some men are apparently able to believe that forced sex is the same act as consensual sex, in every way except its origin. For this reason, these men can exercise "conjugal rights" on women who shudder at their touch. They can pay for intercourse with women who despise them; and white men could, for two centuries in this country, force female slaves to accept them "willingly" as sexual partners.

Some men are also able to derive satisfaction by using their power in the workplace to force unwanted attentions on coworkers and employees. There are other men, of course, who have no illusions about or interest in the desires of the women they exploit. For these men, sexual harassment, like rape, is rewarding *because* it is forced sex. It is the act of domination that satisfies. They often harass women who threaten their power. Harassment is a tool for keeping women in their place, by causing them embarrassment, undermining their confidence, and defining them as sexual beings in the eyes of coworkers. The behavior of all of these men is not aberrant. It has been sanctioned by society, in other forms, throughout America's history and beyond. It is, to a large degree, part of male psychology in this country. This is one of the reasons that sexual harassment cases are difficult to prosecute.

The progress of the industrial revolution did nothing to mitigate the problem. While domestic servants tried to fend off attack in private homes, women in factories faced the forced attentions of foremen and supervisors. One account tells of women in a broom factory who carried knives to protect themselves.

Today, the problem is formidable. In a 1980 study by the U.S. Merit Systems Protection Board of federal employees, 42 percent of women reported being sexually harassed at some time in the two years covered by the study. Other studies have yielded equally discouraging figures.

Black women's position in this society, which has long condoned sexual harassment, is once more complicated by the way white society tried long ago to justify the behavior of slaveowners. A myth was propagated of the inordinately sexual Black woman. Her "animal lustfulness" made her irresistible to any normal man, and therefore no white man could be blamed for failing to resist her. In addition, she was essentially corrupt, so the white man could not be held responsible for her corruption. This myth, born out of the economic considerations of the slave culture and out of the rampant sexism of men who would exploit any woman who fell under their control, has haunted Black women ever since.

However, their history may also explain why Black women have played such an important role in the development of legal redress for sexual harassment. This legal process is of fairly recent date. Until sexual discrimination was made illegal in this country, there was no satisfactory machinery for attacking the problem. Before the law, it did not exist. A woman who was raped by a coworker could charge him with rape and try to take him to court. A woman who was subjected to forced touching and fondling by her boss could make an attempt to charge him with sexual assault, though that would almost certainly be a fruit-less act. A woman who, day in and day out, was constrained to listen to sexual innuendo and humili-ating remarks could do nothing at all.

Then, in 1976, things began to change. Within a very short time, a number of women brought suit charging that sexual harassment was sex discrimina-tion. Among these were several Black women; Paulette Barnes and Margaret Miller brought two of the earli-est cases. These cases were unsuccessful in the lower courts, the judges ruling in Miller's case that the acts in question were not sufficiently tied to the workplace and in Barnes's case that sexual harassment is not treatment "based on sex" within its legal meaning. Paulette Barnes appealed her case and was upheld when a three-judge panel ruled that when an em-ployer abolishes a woman's job because she refuses his advances it is sex discrimination. The ruling was another landmark in the legal definition of sexual harassment.

Another Black woman brought the case that was the turning point in sexual harassment prosecution. Diane Williams, a public information specialist in the Justice Department, refused the sexual advances of her supervisor; she was fired. After several hearings, the judge of the appeals court stated that "the con-duct of the plaintiff's supervisor created an artificial barrier to employment which was placed before one gender and not the other, despite the fact that both genders were similarly situated." Defense attorneys argued that since either gender could be harassed, harassment was not discrimination on the basis of gender. The judge returned that, regardless of who *could* be harassed, if one gender, primarily, *was* ha-rassed, discrimination was being practiced.

Maxine Munford, another Black woman, was hired as an assistant collections manager at James T. Barnes and Company. Her supervisor, Glen D. Harris, be-gan making sexual advances and threats the next day. When she persistently refused and threatened to re-port him, he fired her. She protested and the company upheld the dismissal. In court, the judge held Barnes and Company responsible because they did not inves-tigate the situation when she protested.

One of the greatest contributions a Black woman has made to this struggle was not a court case at all. In 1991, college professor Anita Hill agreed to appear before a congressional committee that was hearing testimony on the confirmation of Judge Clarence Thomas to the U.S. Supreme Court. It was not her choice to make her charges against Thomas public. She had answered questions in a confidential investi-gation, and her answers had been leaked to the press.

At that point she was asked to testify publicly and she did. During her testimony before an all-male com-mittee, all of the cultural biases already discussed here—and more—were apparent in her questioners.

Whether they believed Hill's statements about Thomas or not, many observers were appalled by the questions that were asked her and the attitudes they revealed. There was the implication that no woman's career could be important enough to provide a plau-sible reason for silence about harassment. There was the insinuation that women who receive sexual atten-tions must in some way provoke them. Arguments were presented based on Hill's attractiveness, as judged by the male members of the committee and the press. The lack of awareness on the part of men in both the government and the media was stunning. The suspi-cion began to arise in many minds that the widespread sexual harassment of women in a country where 98 percent of the Senate is male might not be accidental.

All of this was exacerbated, if not caused out-right, by Hill's status as a Black woman. It is possible that a white woman with Hill's professional reputa-tion and credentials might have been subjected to the same interrogation but, to many social critics, it does not seem likely: not by white men who hoped to be re-elected and not on national television.

Whatever the reasons, from the time that sexual harassment began to be defined and treated as a crime, Black women have been in the forefront of the struggle against it. Catharine MacKinnon has outlined several probable reasons for this.

First, the white apologist's myth of Black women's sexuality may make them more vulnerable to harass-ment. This may stretch credulity in the last decade of the twentieth century, but that myth still has adher-ents. Second, the scarcity of job opportunities for most Black women might make men believe that they would be less likely to complain about harassment, again increasing the probability of its occurring. Third, that same abysmal job situation may actually make Black women as a whole *more* likely to protest, be-cause they must use any means to protect the little they have against a threat of loss, including a threat brought by a sexual harasser. As MacKinnon says, "Compared with having one's children starving on welfare, for example, any battle for a wage of one's own with a chance of winning greater than zero looks attractive. In this respect, black women have been able to grasp the essence of the situation, and with it the necessity of opposition, earlier and more firmly than other more advantaged women" (MacKinnon 1979). All of these probably contribute to Black women's leadership in the fight against sexual harassment.

However, if sexual harassment is seen primarily in terms of power, the most important reasons for the place of Black women at the forefront of this struggle probably relate to their position in the hierarchy of power. A man who resists giving up power to a woman, or who takes out his anger and frustration on a woman because she is less powerful, may be more likely to try to victimize a Black woman than a white one. Black women, because of their historical position in American society, are likely to have fewer resources outside of the courts for resisting this victimization. For better or worse, many Black Americans have come to see the law as their most dependable ally in the struggle for justice and equality, and many Black women see on the horizon no more effective defender of their honor.

BIBLIOGRAPHY

Carby, Hazel V. *Reconstructing Womanhood* (1987); Giddings, Paula. *When and Where I Enter: The Impact of Black Women on Race and Sex in America* (1984); Hill, Anita. "The Nature of the Beast." In *Sexual Harassment: Know Your Rights*, ed. Martin Eskenazi and David Gallen (1992); MacKinnon, Catharine A. *Sexual Harassment of Working Women* (1979); Medea, Andra and Kathleen Thompson. *Against Rape* (1974); Paludi, Michele A. and Richard B. Barickman. *Academic and Workplace Sexual Harassment* (1991).

KATHLEEN THOMPSON

SHABAZZ, HAJJ BAHIYAH BETTY (1936-)

Betty Shabazz, the widow of Malcolm X (El Hajj Malik El Shabazz, the Black Muslim civil rights leader assassinated in 1965), has definite goals for carrying on the work for which her husband lived and died. Shabazz (Mrs. Malcolm X Little) devotes her time to Black community affairs in the areas of health, child care, and education.

Born May 28, 1936, in Detroit, Michigan, she attended Tuskegee Institute, Brooklyn State Hospital School of Nursing (R.N.), and Jersey City State College (Certified School Nurse and B.A. Public Health Education). She has certification in early childhood education and completed a thesis on sickle-cell anemia for her Master's degree in public health administration, and then completed a Ph.D. in education

administration at the University of Massachusetts at Amherst. She is the mother of six children.

Shabazz shows a strong interest in education and children and devotes her time to improving conditions for the disadvantaged. She is a volunteer in early childhood education and on the Sickle-Cell Telethon Advisory Board, and performs local PTA work in a high school for pregnant students. Shabazz has served as director of the African-American Foundation, the Women's Service League, and the Day Care Council of Westchester County, and she is a trustee of the National Housewives League. She is a member of the board of education of the Union Free School (District 13) and is cochair of the advisory board of the *Amsterdam News* in New York City.

She has worked as a university instructor, community activist, and registered nurse. She has served as director of institutional advancement, in Alumni Affairs at Medgar Evers College in New York City, and as chairman of the forty-first National Council of Negro Women Convention in New York City. At Mount Holyoke College in South Hadley, Massachusetts, a cultural center has been named in her honor. She remains active in Delta Sigma Theta Sorority.

BIBLIOGRAPHY

Cain, Joy D. "Dr. Betty Shabazz," *Essence* (February 15, 1985); *Ebony Success Library* (1973); *NA*; Richardson, Marilyn. *Black Women and Religion: A Bibliography* (1980); Shabazz, Betty. "Malcolm X as Husband and Father." In *Malcolm X: The Man and His Times*, ed. John Henrick Clarke (1969); Spradling, Mary Mace. *Black and White* (1985).

LAVONNE ROBERTS-JACKSON

SHADD, MARY ANN *see* CARY, MARY ANN SHADD

SHANGE, NTOZAKE (1948-)

"Somebody almost walked off wid alla my stuff" best characterizes the sentiments expressed by playwright, poet, short-story writer, novelist, and essayist Ntozake Shange (En-to-ze-ke Shong-ge). The above line from Shange's *For Colored Girls Who Have Considered Suicide/When the Rainbow Is Enuf*, which appeared on Broadway in 1976, struck a chord that appealed to women of every race, class, and age. Shange's heroines recall experiences of women who have been rejected, verbally and physically abused, and discredited. Her characters draw strong emotional responses because of their determination to survive destructive forces and to build a future that will allow women to soar. While Shange has been heralded as a leading feminist author, she is as much concerned with the plight of Black men as with that of women globally. Some common themes in Shange's works include hypocrisy, racism, women's self-effacement, stereotyped roles for Black people, and infidelity. Her works link race, class, and gender issues, thereby illuminating the condition of the masses of African-Americans.

The oldest of four children, Ntozake Shange was born Paulette Williams on October 18, 1948, in Trenton, New Jersey. Shange's parents, surgeon Paul T. Williams and psychiatric social worker and educator Eloise Williams, provided her with intellectual stimulation and love. When Shange was eight, her parents moved to St. Louis, where they remained for five years. During her years in St. Louis, Shange was exposed to opera, music, dance, literature, and art but was also introduced to blatant racism when she was bused to a German-American school.

Shange's method of coping with the tumultuous racial tensions of the late 1950s and early 1960s was to immerse herself in the works of her favorite authors: Mark Twain, Herman Melville, Simone de Beauvoir, and Jean Genet. Shange also associated with nationally and internationally renowned musicians and singers such as Dizzy Gillespie, Charlie Parker, Josephine Baker, Chuck Berry, and Miles Davis, all of whom were friends of her parents and who influenced Shange's writing. Political leader W.E.B. Du Bois was also a close family friend who influenced Shange. When she was thirteen, Shange's family returned to New Jersey, where she completed high school.

Always sensitive to the plight of women in a sexist society, Shange attempted suicide at age eighteen after the dissolution of an early marriage. Plagued with a deep sense of alienation and rage, Shange tried to end her life several times, including sticking her head in a gas oven, slashing her wrist, overdosing on Valium, and drinking toxic chemicals.

Though Shange's personal life was unstable, she excelled academically. She earned a Bachelor's degree, with honors, in American studies from Barnard College in 1970 and a Master's degree in 1973 from the University of Southern California, Los Angeles. After the civil rights movement of the 1960s raised her consciousness, Shange assumed an African name in 1971 that empowered her to rechannel her ener-

Ntozake Shange's powerful play For Colored Girls Who Have Considered Suicide/When the Rainbow Is Enuf *earned a 1977 Obie for best original play and was later nominated for Tony, Grammy, and Emmy awards. [Library of Congress]*

gies. "Ntozake" means "she who comes with her own things" and "Shange" means "who walks like a lion." It was while she was in graduate school between 1971 and 1973 that Shange discovered a Black literary heritage, reading voluminously the works of Ralph Ellison, Jean Toomer, Claude McKay, Amiri Baraka, Margaret Walker, and others.

From 1972 to 1975, Shange held several English teaching positions at Sonoma State College and the University of California Extension while choreographing poems with the Third World Collective, Raymond Sawyer's Afro-American Dance Company, West Coast Dance Works, and her own company, For Colored Girls Who Have Considered Suicide.

Shange's move to New York City in 1975 marked the beginning of her professional career. Her choreopoem *For Colored Girls* was produced professionally at Studio Rivbea in July 1975, at the New Federal Theatre in 1976, at the Public Theatre in

June 1976, and at Broadway's Booth Theatre in September 1976. Not since Lorraine Hansberry's long-running *A Raisin in the Sun* in 1959 had a play by a Black woman appeared on Broadway. *For Colored Girls* earned a host of awards—a 1977 Obie for best original play, the Outer Critics Circle Award, the AUDELCO Award, and the Mademoiselle Award—and was nominated for Tony, Grammy, and Emmy awards.

For Colored Girls comprises twenty choreographed poems and vignettes that portray women in a state of pain, rage, anguish, or disillusionment. These women tell of their exploitation and resolve to stand together against pernicious men who lie, seduce, beat, and abandon them. The choreopoem ends with a laying on of hands, a self-empowering ritual that helps the women become self-confident, self-sufficient, and self-loving.

Shange's rise to fame brought with it increased speaking engagements. Between 1976 and 1981, Shange lectured and performed scenes from her Broadway hit as well as from *Sassafrass*, a 1977 novella, and *Nappy Edges*, a 1978 collection of poems, at a host of institutions, including Yale, Brown, Rice, Howard, Southern, and New York universities.

Shange's writing career was secured in 1981 with the publication of *Three Pieces*, a collection of three plays: *Spell #7*, *A Photograph: Lovers-in-Motion*, and *Boogie Woogie Landscapes*. A prolific writer, Shange produced several major works in the 1980s, including the novels *Sassafrass, Cypress, and Indigo* (1982) and *Betsey Brown* (1985); two poetry collections, *A Daughter's Geography* (1983) and *From Okra to Greens* (1984); and a collection of essays, *See No Evil: Prefaces, Essays and Accounts, 1976-1983* (1984).

The major theme in Shange's works is the abuse of women and children. Her female characters survive in the face of loneliness, rejection, and rape. One scene in *For Colored Girls*, "Latent Rapists," focuses on women who have been raped by friends, men in prestigious positions, but who are afraid to press charges. These women fear double victimization because they live in a society that treats a woman who has been raped as the villain instead of the victim. Another scene in *For Colored Girls*, "Sorry," centers on the multitude of excuses that men give when they hurt women. Perhaps the most powerful scene in the choreopoem is "A Nite with Beau Willie Brown," which tells the story of an emotionally disturbed Vietnam veteran who flings his two children out of the window when his abused wife refuses to reconcile. This choreopoem had mass appeal and drew women together to discuss their abuse and be healed.

Beginning in 1981, Shange was the recipient of several honors and awards, including a Guggenheim fellowship in 1981; artist-in-residence at the Equinox Theatre in Houston; a Medal of Excellence from Columbia University; an Obie Award for the Public Theatre production of *Mother Courage and Her Children*, an adaptation of Bertolt Brecht's play; and an appointment to the New York State Council on the Arts Program.

While writing and performing during the 1980s, Shange also taught English at Rice University and the University of Houston before moving to Philadelphia, where she currently resides with her eleven-year-old daughter, Savannah. Ever undertaking new projects, Shange's *The Love Space Demands*, a collection of poems, was published in 1991.

Though her theater pieces are extremely experimental, Ntozake Shange carved a place for her poetry on the American stage, historically dominated by males. Her most significant achievement is that she, in grand style, successfully moved her poetry from the spoken word to dramaturgy, thus popularizing the choreopoem. She blends music, dance, and poetry to characterize the Black experience in America, particularly the Black female experience. Her works empower women to take responsibility for their lives by learning to love themselves and to challenge their oppressors. Shange's life and works give clarification and direction to the current feminist movement.

Prior to Shange, no other playwright had drawn such an emotional response from Black men and from women of every race. Her plays initiated a dialogue between men and women, a discussion that continues as sexual harassment policies are being revamped. On one level, Shange's heroines accuse men of abuse, but on another, perhaps higher, level her characters grapple with the constraints that have been placed on Black men and women in America.

"Somebody almost walked off wid alla my stuff" refers to women who have been violated by men, but the statement has also become a metaphor for the lives of poor, uneducated, dispossessed Black people in America and around the world who refuse to be trampled upon and who fight mightily for a chance to seize the rainbow.

BIBLIOGRAPHY

Brown-Guillory, Elizabeth. *Their Place on the Stage: Black Women Playwrights in America* (1988); CB (1978); Latour, Martine. "Ntozake Shange: Driven Poet/Playwright," *Mademoiselle* (September 1976); "Ntozake Shange: Interviews," *New Yorker* (August 2, 1976); Tate, Claudia. "Ntozake Shange." In her *Black Women Writers at*

Work (1983); Richards, Sandra L. "Conflicting Impulses in the Plays of Ntozake Shange," *Black American Literature Forum* (Summer 1983).

ELIZABETH BROWN-GUILLORY

SHARECROPPERS UNION (SCU) *see* THE LEFT

SHIPP, OLIVIA (PORTER) (1880-1979)

Olivia Shipp performed in jazz bands and chamber music ensembles, in theater orchestras and ragtime bands, from the turn of the century until the post-World War II era.

She was born Olivia Sophie L'Ange on May 17, 1880, in New Orleans. As a child, she taught herself to play keyboard on an old pump organ given to her family. She also took some voice lessons from Abbey Lyons, a member of the Fisk Jubilee Singers.

When the Black Patti Troubadour Company came through the city, Olivia L'Ange's sister, May, joined them as an actress, touring and then settling in New York to form the Bob and Kemp vaudeville team. (She adopted the name Kemp to protect her family from the stigma of association with show business.) When she left New Orleans, she promised to send for her sister as soon as she could; when Olivia was about twenty, May did so.

Olivia D'Ange worked in vaudeville while studying the piano. After hearing a cello in a vaudeville performance, she decided that that was the instrument she wanted most to play. She began teaching piano to another musician in exchange for cello lessons. Later, she used the money she earned from vaudeville and her music teaching to pay for lessons from an eminent Hungarian cellist, Professor Turkisher. She also studied with Black cellists Wesley Johnson and Leonard Jeter. Through Jeter, she gained a position with the Martin-Smith Music School, serving as Jeter's assistant and as a member of the school's orchestra. She also performed with Black violinist Charles Elgar and his chamber ensemble on radio and in a trio with two women on violin and piano. Olivia, too, adopted a stage name, Porter, and used that name until her marriage to a man named Shipp. Thereafter, she performed as Olivia Shipp.

Though not a member of the original group, Shipp played with the Lafayette Theatre Ladies' Orchestra in the late 1910s and early 1920s. In order to play with Marie Lucas's popular group, Shipp learned to play the bass violin, studying with a bassist for the New York Philharmonic.

Shipp worked with a variety of bands, orchestras, and small groups. She also formed her own orchestra, Olivia Shipp's Jazz-Mines. Shipp's most important contribution was founding the Negro Women's Orchestral and Civic Association. With the backing of Local 802 of the American Federation of Musicians, it became an important performing group during the Harlem Renaissance.

Olivia Shipp died in February 1979, with a remarkable record of achievement.

BIBLIOGRAPHY

Handy, D. Antoinette. *Black Women in American Bands & Orchestras* (1981); *NBAW.*

KATHLEEN THOMPSON

SHOCKLEY, ANN ALLEN (1927-)

Ann Allen Shockley, librarian, novelist, newspaper columnist, teacher, and feminist political activist, has made contributions in a wide range of fields, yet she remains one of countless Black women whose achievements remain invisible to most of mainstream America. The subjects of her major writings illuminate some of the reasons for this lack of recognition, as do the social and political environments in which she has written.

Shockley was born June 21, 1927, in Louisville, Kentucky, the daughter of Bessie Lucas and Henry Allen, both social workers. She was encouraged by her parents to pursue her love for reading and writing at an early age. She was the editor of her junior high school newspaper and went on to become a fiction editor and columnist for the *Fisk University Herald* during her undergraduate years. She received her B.A. from Fisk University (1944-48) and a Master's degree in library science from Case Western Reserve University (1959-60). In August 1949, she married William Shockley, a teacher. They had two children, William Leslie, Jr. and Tamara Ann.

In 1945, while still an undergraduate at Fisk, Shockley became a staff writer for the *Louisville Defender.* She was eighteen. Some of her earliest published writings appeared in the newspaper, among them teen columns and short stories. In 1949, she began writing a weekly column called "Ebony Topics" for Maryland's white-owned *Federalsburg Times*. For about three years beginning in 1950, she wrote a similar weekly column for the *Bridgeville News* in Delaware, where she lived with her husband. Shockley also published articles in the *Afro-American* (Baltimore) and *Pittsburgh Courier* newspapers.

In 1959, Shockley wrote the first of several works in the area of librarianship with special emphasis on Black collections, *A History of Public Library Services to Negroes in the South, 1900-1955* (unpublished). In 1969, she began working at Fisk University Special Negro Collection. Since then, she has co-authored *Living Black American Authors: A Biographical Directory* (1973) and published her well-received *Handbook of Black Librarianship* (1977). Both of these works are significant to the fields of Black librarianship and African-American history. In addition to these major books, Shockley has published numerous essays and articles in the professional journals of her field.

In addition to her writings on librarianship and history, Shockley is also a prolific short-story writer and novelist. Before the appearance of her first published novel, *Loving Her*, in 1974, she had published more than thirty short stories in newspapers and periodicals. In most of her stories, Shockley grapples with such socially and politically charged issues as racism, sexism, homophobia, interracial relationships, and the everyday trials and tribulations of being Black in America. These themes reflect some of her personal experiences as a Black feminist as well as the larger collective experiences of the political and social struggles of the 1960s and 1970s. The influences of civil rights, Black Power, the second wave of women's liberation in North America, and the lesbian and gay liberation movements echo through the pages of her stories, where they are interpreted and challenged.

Of particular historical, political, and social significance have been Ann Allen Shockley's published novels and collections of short stories. *Loving Her* was the first novel written by a Black woman with a Black lesbian as its central character that explored a lesbian relationship in depth. The novel details the experiences of Renay, the protagonist, who flees a physically and emotionally abusive husband to pursue a relationship with Terry, a wealthy white woman. Her second novel, *Say Jesus and Come to Me* (1982), confronts the issue of homophobia in the Black church in a satirical and biting manner. The main character, Reverend Myrtle Black, is a Black lesbian minister who, like her male heterosexual counterpart, uses her power from the pulpit to seduce young women in the congregation. Shockley wrote that the intent of this piece was to "bring out the homophobic hypocrisy of the black church, which is filled to the pulpit with closet gays and lesbians from all walks of life. . . . I wanted to expose the conservatism and snobbishness of the black middle class and academicians, which I see all the time; black male oppression of women; [and] the superior attitudes and opportunism of some white women towards black women in the women's liberation movement" (Dandridge 1987).

In her collection of ten short stories, *The Black and White of It* (1980), Shockley offers glimpses into relationships between lesbians living within the constraints of a racist and heterosexist society. Although her plots and themes incorporate many different living situations and relationship issues, Shockley has been criticized for her overall negative outlook regarding the possibility of lesbians finding fulfilling and enduring loving relationships. Her two novels have been extensively reviewed in lesbian, Third World, and women's publications. She has received mixed responses to both novels, including favorable yet critical assessments from Alice Walker, Barbara Smith, and Rita Dandridge, as well as a scathingly homophobic response to *Loving Her* from Frank Lamont Phillips. All three of these major works nonetheless represent important steps toward exposing and confronting important issues both within and outside of Black communities.

BIBLIOGRAPHY

Dandridge, Rita B. *Ann Allen Shockley: An Annotated Primary and Secondary Bibliography* (1987); *DLB*; Roberts, J. R. *Black Lesbians: An Annotated Bibliography* (1981).

TRACYE A. MATTHEWS

SIGMA GAMMA RHO SORORITY

"Greater Service, Greater Progress" was to become the slogan and call of the organization that made November 12, 1922, a significant date in the history of the Black Greek system, for this date would mark the establishment of the first sorority of Black women—Sigma Gamma Rho—on a predominantly white campus, Butler University in Indianapolis, Indiana. Three other sororities of Black women, all established at Howard University, and four fraternities of Black men, two at Howard, one at Cornell, and one at Indiana University, had already been established in the early 1900s. Because Black students could not join the all-white Greek sororities at Butler, a tough and determined Black female, Mary Allison Little, envisioned the need to pull Black women together into the bonds of sisterhood. Six other Butler students who had chosen teaching as their profession joined Mary Little in laying the foundation for a new sorority and further advancing the Black fraternal movement.

Originally the new sorority was to be composed of teachers, and it was to provide support and opportunities for networking to young people, with a focus on professional development. Soon, however, the members recognized that teaching went far beyond the walls of the classroom and that community service and interaction were needed in order to educate the whole child. Education was to be the mainstay of the sorority, but the organization also wanted to develop broad horizons with diverse dimensions in order to reach into communities and serve all people. Thus, Sigma Gamma Rho membership had to be expanded; it could not be restricted to teachers.

National conventions were not called in the early years because too many other issues needed to be addressed. Under the leadership of Mary Little, who was to become the first grand basileus (national president), members became immersed in developing unity and broad-based goals. After the first national meeting (Boule) in 1925, it was evident that an education-focused legacy was evolving, but it was during the fifth Boule, in 1929, that the sorority mandated an aggressive scholarship program that required alumnae chapters to maintain a scholarship fund. This led to the establishment of the Sigma Gamma Rho National Education Fund, which focuses on education, research, health, and the awarding of scholarships and grants to students regardless of race, gender, or nationality.

The torch of leadership passed through several hands during the 1920s, and the goal of involving women from various regions of the country was reflected in the selection of leaders from coast to coast. The Roaring Twenties ended with the sorority poising itself and moving aggressively to charter more chapters on Black college campuses, particularly the land grant colleges that were experiencing considerable growth in enrollment. The first West Coast chapter was established in Los Angeles and a charter member of that chapter, Hattie McDaniel, became the first Black Academy Award winner in 1939 when she received an Oscar for her performance in *Gone with the Wind*.

In response to the dire economic conditions of the times, the sorority established Sigma Gamma Rho's Employment Aid Bureau. In further pursuing its agenda, programs to assist in community education and uplift also were established; for example, circulating libraries on wheels, national literary contests, book exhibits, and book showers for Black colleges were adopted as national programs. The African Book Shower Project, designed to send books to Wilberforce Institute in South Africa, was the sorority's first international involvement, and it later expanded into the Linens for Africa Drive and other international projects.

During World War II, the sorority suspended its national conventions so that members could support the war effort at home and on foreign soil. Sigma Gamma Rhos were visible in the military, the Red Cross, the USO, and similar organizations.

Against the backdrop of the war, and with an upswing of juvenile delinquency, the sorority was stirred to develop programs to address this problem. Sigma "Teen Towns," centered around art, music, literature, games, and other forms of wholesome recreation, became a thrust of the organization, and they carried over into the 1950s. Sigma Gamma Rho was fully involved in the Mid-Century Conference on Children, and its leaders were summoned to White House conferences that dealt with many pertinent issues.

The 1960s and 1970s were a time of great social, political, and moral change. In response to these changes, Sigma Gamma Rho intensified its support for the United Negro College Fund, the National Association for the Advancement of Colored People (NAACP), the Urban League and other national organizations that offered service to the community and furthered in every possible way the dignity and worth of all people. Academic excellence, moral responsibility, political involvement, social awareness, and community outreach were built into the on-going thrust of the sorority as it concerned itself with civil rights, human dignity, moral decency, and the strengthening of a new breed of poised and informed women.

As the number of Black students increased on predominantly white campuses in subsequent decades, there was a noticeable expansion of the Black Greek system. During these years Sigma Gamma Rho modified its agenda to better address this expansion and the resulting societal changes. A national program called Project Reassurance was designed to deal with teenage pregnancy. Also, after the publication of Alex Haley's book *Roots*, and with heightened concern for Africa, the sorority established Project Africa, Project Mwanamugimu, and related programs to give assistance to the people of Africa and to help young

African-Americans understand and appreciate their ancestral history.

From that cold November day in 1922 when Alpha chapter sank its roots into the campus of Butler University, Sigma Gamma Rho has progressively evolved into a thriving sisterhood that comprises more than 70,000 college-trained women across the United States, and in Bermuda, Africa, the Virgin Islands, and the Bahamas.

BIBLIOGRAPHY

Brown, Roxanne. "Sigma Gamma Rho," *Ebony* (February 1991); Cook, Nannie, ed. "Project Reassurance Director Presents Health Forum," *The Aurora* (September 1978), and "$12,000 Raised for the New Provident Hospital," *The Aurora* (September 1978); Tillman, Vivian, ed. "Project Africa," *The Aurora* (Fall 1990), and "The Mwanamugimu Project," *The Aurora* (Fall 1990), and "Public Program at the 1990 Chicago Boule," *The Aurora* (Fall 1990), and "Yearly Involvement—Mwanamugimu Project," *The Aurora* (Summer 1991), and "Black Fraternity, Sorority Take Root," *The Aurora* (Summer 1991); White, Pearl Schwartz. *Behind These Doors A Legacy: The History of Sigma Gamma Rho Sorority* (1974); Wilkes, Lillie, ed. "Curbing Juvenile Delinquency," *The Aurora* (May 1967), and "Teen-age Pregnancy," *The Aurora* (May 1976), and "Undergrads Attend War on Poverty Programs," *The Aurora* (September 1968).

KATIE KINNARD WHITE

SIMKINS, MARY MODJESKA MONTEITH (1899-1992)

"I cannot be bought and I will not be sold!" These words of Mary Modjeska Monteith Simkins characterize the bold, outspoken and defiant stance that the human rights activist of Columbia, South Carolina claimed for herself. Born in that city on December 5, 1899, Modjeska Simkins, as she was popularly known, lived for ninety-two years, during which she became legendary in her hometown, native state, and beyond for the role she played in furthering the cause of justice and equality among all peoples.

Henry Clarence Monteith and Rachel Evelyn Hull Monteith were a prosperous married couple who decided to make a secure home for the large family they planned; much to their joy, their first child was a daughter, whom they named both for Rachel's younger sister, Mary Ellen, and for a favorite Polish actress, Helena Modjeska. To provide the best family life possible, the couple purchased a farm on the outskirts of Columbia so that Modjeska and their other seven children could grow and develop into women and men with few distractions from outside influences.

Modjeska's mother, a public school teacher, exposed her daughter to culture and erudition to the greatest possible extent. The young girl was taken to church and given a leadership role; she was taught the rudiments of reading, writing and mathematics before she entered grade school; and she was exposed to music, to cultural affairs and education, to drama and the social graces, to all that a nineteenth-century mother thought would refine a little girl into a southern lady, replete with the charms and eloquence that would make her the choice of a fine southern gentleman when it came time for her to marry.

The Monteith home was filled with various reading materials, both on classical subjects and on worldly affairs. This inspired the children to read and explore the world outside their home, to open their minds to problems that lay outside of Columbia, South Carolina, and even America. Her younger siblings looked to Modjeska for guidance and for an example in academic pursuits. She was placed into the second grade upon enrollment at Benedict College for she had been so well trained that she was head and shoulders above the other young children her age who were entering the school. (Benedict College, like many private Black institutions of higher education in this period, offered quality primary and secondary curriculums in addition to college courses in order to provide the education denied Black Americans in segregated public schools.) Modjeska excelled in mathematics and decided to become a mathematics teacher after she graduated from the college course.

A few months after she received an A.B. degree in 1921, Monteith started teaching in the teacher-training department of Benedict; the next year she found employment in the elementary division of Booker T. Washington School in Columbia. Two years later she was assigned to teach mathematics at the school. She maintained this position until December 1929, when she married Andrew Whitfield Simkins, and had to resign because married women were not allowed to teach in the city's schools. By 1931, she had found employment at the South Carolina Tuberculosis Association as the agency's first Director of Negro Work. This position lasted until 1942, when she was released because of her involvement in civil rights activities. Before she retired she worked at Victory Savings Bank in Columbia, where she held various positions, including heading a bank branch and serving on the board of directors.

The historical and familial circumstances into which Modjeska was born and reared—including an emphasis on education, racial uplift, and activism—prepared her for a public career. Columbia was the state's capital and the seat of two private Black colleges, Benedict College and Allen University. Within forty miles, there were three other Black colleges, Morris College in Sumter, and Clafin College and South Carolina State College in Orangeburg. Living in the center of Black higher education in the state prompted her to complete graduate studies. She attended Columbia University in New York, the University of Michigan at Ann Arbor, and Michigan State Normal School (now Eastern Michigan University). This commitment to education was in harmony with the Monteiths' family heritage of participation in racial uplift projects, and she continued the tradition. Moreover, older relatives, particularly her mother and two maternal aunts, Rebecca Walton and Mayme Dunmore, were active in the Columbia branch of the National Association for the Advancement of Colored People (NAACP), and they brought Modjeska into the organization.

In the 1930s, Modjeska Simkins was active with the Civil Welfare League, a local organization that sought improved municipal conditions for Black residents in Columbia, including securing better housing, ending police brutality, and regaining the franchise. Also, she worked diligently with the Columbia branch of the NAACP as publicity director and she took part in the founding meeting of the South Carolina Conference of Branches of NAACP in 1939.

Perhaps her greatest public work during the 1940s and 1950s was with the South Carolina NAACP. From the outset, she worked as corresponding secretary; in 1941, she was elected as head of the publicity committee and a member of the speakers' bureau. In 1942, she was elected state secretary, a position she held until 1957. During the period in which she held elective office, the South Carolina NAACP launched several court cases to establish equality for Black Americans, and Simkins was at the heart of these proceedings. They won their first lawsuits, for equalization of teachers' salaries, in Charleston in 1944 and in Columbia in 1945. The NAACP set up a Teachers Defense Fund, and Simkins was secretary of this project. Then, with *Elmore* v. *Rice* in 1947 and *Brown* v. *Baskins* in 1948, the South Carolina NAACP dismantled the all-white primary. The most significant lawsuit in which Simkins played a major role was the NAACP lawsuit to end segregation in South Carolina's public schools and, ultimately, the nation's public schools. *Briggs* v. *Elliott* was filed in federal district court in May 1950, the initial hearing before a three-judge court was in May 1951, and it later be-

came the first of five cases to be decided by the U.S. Supreme Court as *Brown* v. *Board of Education* in May 1954.

Simkins was active in many organizations that fought racism and injustice on local, regional, and national levels in voter registration, education, and health care. In the mid-1940s, she worked with the Columbia Women's Council and with the Richland County Citizens Committee; both were political action groups. She participated in regional organizations such as the Commission on Interracial Cooperation, the Southern Regional Council, the Southern Conference for Human Welfare, the Southern Organizing Committee for Economic and Social Justice, and the Southern Negro Youth Congress. At the national

Named for Polish actress Helena Modjeska, Modjeska Simkins was prepared by her upbringing, with its emphasis on education, racial uplift, and activism, for a public career. An activist for more than six decades, she worked with over fifty progressive reform organizations to advance the struggle for human and civil rights in the United States. [Barbara Woods]

level, she was a member of the Civil Rights Congress, the National Negro Congress, and the United Negro and Allied Veterans of America.

Her work with political parties spanned more than half a century. Her activities in the early years were tied to the national Republican party; in 1948 she was named to the National Convention Committee on Permanent Organization from South Carolina. She became disenchanted with the Republicans during this period because many politicians who had disapproved of President Harry Truman and Democrats' support of civil rights moved into the Republican party, and later, she changed party affiliation. Simkins never was a strict one-party person even so. In 1948, she supported Henry Wallace's candidacy for the U.S. presidency. In South Carolina, she also supported two predominantly Black third-party platforms, the Progressive Democratic party in the 1940s and the United Citizens party in the 1970s. Her involvement in politics led her to run for public office four times, but she was never elected.

Because of her work with more than fifty progressive reform organizations over a period of six decades, Modjeska Simkins is a major figure in South Carolina history and a major figure in women's history. She was a steadfast, persistent, and courageous activist in the struggle for human rights in the United States.

She received many honors in her lifetime, including being awarded the highest commendation given by her home state, the Order of the Palmetto. The Columbia branch of the NAACP named a scholarship for her—the Modjeska Simkins Scholarship Award. In 1980, the Modjeska Simkins Endowment Fund was established "to make small grants to nonprofit organizations whose grass roots activities in South Carolina exemplify Mrs. Simkins's spirit and work on behalf of human rights, social dignity, and economic justice." The American Civil Liberties Union of South Carolina Foundation is a trustee of this fund. At Benedict College, the research archives have been named in her honor to keep her memory alive.

BIBLIOGRAPHY

Aba-Mecha, Barbara Woods. "Black Woman Activist in Twentieth-Century South Carolina: Modjeska Monteith Simkins," Ph.D. diss. (1978); *Ante Bellum: A New South Carolina Journal for Women.* "Modjeska" (Summer/Fall 1977); Beardsley, Edward. *A History of Neglect: Health Care for Blacks and Mill Workers in the Twentieth-Century South* (1987); Bodie, Idella. *South Carolina Women* (1991); Horne, Gerald. *Black and Red: W.E.B. Du Bois and the Afro-American Response to the Cold War, 1944-1963* (1986); *NBAW;* Reed, Linda. *Simple Decency and Common Sense: The Southern Conference Movement, 1938-1963* (1991); Woods, Barbara

"I cannot be bought and I will not be sold!" These words of Modjeska Simkins characterize the bold, defiant, and outspoken nature of this longtime activist, a major figure in South Carolina history. [Barbara Woods]

A. "Modjeska Simkins and the South Carolina Conference of the NAACP, 1939-1957." In *Women in the Civil Rights Movement: Trailblazers and Torchbearers, 1941-1965,* ed. Vicki Crawford, Jacqueline Rouse, and Barbara Woods (1990), and "Portrait of an Activist: Modjeska Monteith Simkins." In *African American Women: A Biographical Dictionary* (1992); The personal papers of Modjeska Monteith Simkins are located at the University of South Carolina, Columbia, South Carolina, and Winthrop College, Rock Hill, South Carolina.

BARBARA WOODS

SIMMONS, ALTHEA T. L.
(1924-1990)

Civil rights activist Althea Simmons was born in Shreveport, Louisiana, on April 17, 1924, to Lillian Littleton Simmons and M. M. Simmons. She attended Southern University in New Orleans, from which she received a B.S. with honors. From there she went to the University of Illinois at Urbana, earning a Master's degree in marketing, and then to Howard University, where she received a law degree.

After graduation from law school, Simmons went to work for the W. J. Durman law office in Dallas, Texas. She soon became active in the National Association for the Advancement of Colored People (NAACP), first serving as a volunteer and later as a paid staff person. She was executive secretary of the Texas State Conference of NAACP branches and chairperson of the executive committee of the Dallas branch. She then moved to Los Angeles as a field secretary. From 1964 to 1974, she was secretary for training for the entire country, developing handbooks and setting up training sessions, coordinating the entire massive educational program of the NAACP at that time.

When the 1964 Civil Rights Act passed, Simmons was director of the NAACP's National Voter Registration Drive. She also went to Mississippi to help teach Black citizens how to use the new law.

In 1979, Simmons became chief lobbyist for the NAACP in Washington, D.C. Her position was an enormously important one, as she worked to persuade legislators to pass laws that would give Black Americans justice and opportunity. Her predecessor in the job, Clarence Mitchell, was legendary. "I recall quite vividly when Mr. [Benjamin] Hooks took me to the White House to introduce me to President Carter," she said in an interview for *I Dream a World.* "The president said, 'Miss Simmons, you've got some very big shoes to fill.' And I said respectfully, 'Mr. President, nobody can fill Clarence Mitchell's shoes. I'll have to walk in my own footsteps' " (Lanker 1989).

Simmons's own footsteps turned out to be legendary as well. She became one of the most effective lobbyists in Washington, playing a crucial part in the 1982 extension of the Voting Rights Act, sanctions against South Africa, and the naming of a national holiday to honor Dr. Martin Luther King, Jr.

Althea T. L. Simmons died in September 1990 in Washington, D.C.

BIBLIOGRAPHY

Lanker, Brian. *I Dream a World* (1989); *NBAW; WWBA* (1992).

KATHLEEN THOMPSON

SIMMONS, DOROTHY VERNELL
(1910-)

Dorothy Vernell Simmons, gospel singer, choir director, and publisher, was born September 10, 1910, in Powhatan, Louisiana. The only child of Martha Jones and George Smith, Simmons lived most of her early life in Louisiana. After a brief stay in New Orleans, her family moved to Chicago when she was seven years old. She married Allen Simmons in 1940, and they have one son, Cornelius Webb, who is a salesman.

As a young person living in Chicago, Simmons learned much about singing from attending Tabernacle Baptist Church. In the early 1940s, she worked with Sallie Martin and Kenneth Morris at the Martin and Morris Music Studio in Chicago (a music store and publishing company), and she later joined a group organized by Kenneth Morris called the Martin and Morris Singers. She became a member of the Sallie Martin Singers when it was formed and traveled extensively with the group for several years. Her first trip to Los Angeles occurred in 1944 when the Sallie Martin Singers toured the city, and Simmons decided to move there in 1947. Around the same time, she and Doris Akers formed the Simmons-Akers Singers, a female gospel trio, which stayed together until the late 1950s. Through concert tours and recordings, the Simmons-Akers Singers became a highly respected, nationally known group. In addition, they served as choir directors at the Opportunity Baptist Church and Sky Pilot Church in Los Angeles and at the Upper Room Community Church in Richmond, Cali-

A member of the Simmons-Akers Singers, one of the most sought-after gospel groups in the United States in the 1950s, Dorothy Simmons later became one of the first Black performers to take gospel music to a western music audience. [J. C. DjeDje]

fornia. They also organized their own publishing company and music store, the Simmons-Akers Music House, in Los Angeles.

During the 1960s, Simmons established herself as a solo artist and moved to Colorado, where she became one of the first Black performers to take gospel music to a western music audience. Her Pilgrim Rest Baptist Church Choir in Denver had a weekly radio broadcast, and each month she appeared on two television stations. Because of this exposure and a guest appearance on a hootenanny television show in Denver, she regularly received generous offers to sing in nightclubs. However, she declined because of her belief that gospel singing should always be associated with and performed in a religious context. When Simmons returned to Los Angeles in the 1970s, she continued to perform in churches in the city and received formal training to become a licensed practitioner of the Religious Science Church.

Simmons's musical career began to decline in the late 1970s. But her high lyric soprano voice, which seemed to be an inspiration from a higher source, is one of the reasons that the Simmons-Akers Singers were one of the most sought-after groups in the United States during the 1950s.

BIBLIOGRAPHY

DjeDje, Jacqueline Cogdell. "Gospel Music in the Los Angeles Black Community: A Historical Overview," *Black Music Research Journal* (Spring 1989); Simmons, Dorothy. Interviews (June 21, 1988, and November 25, 1991).

JACQUELINE COGDELL DJEDJE

SIMONE, NINA (1933-)

Born in Tryon, North Carolina, in 1933, Nina Simone exhibited musical talent at an early age. By the age of seven, she was a self-taught organist and pianist and a member of the church choir. Her early musical talents led to formal training at both Asheville (North Carolina) High School and the Juilliard School of Music in New York City. Simone's career began to blossom after her family moved to Philadelphia; thereafter she sang in nightclubs up and down the East Coast, primarily as a vocalist/pianist. Immersed in jazz, in the 1960s she became an eclectic vocalist, singing and recording compositions ranging from blues and jazz to soul. Specific examples include "I Loves You Porgy" (1959) and "I Put a Spell on You," originally recorded by Screaming Jay Hawkins around 1965. In 1967, after her switch from Phillips to RCA, she entered a very successful commercial period. Both commercial singles "Ain't Got No—I Got Life," from *Hair*, and "To Love Somebody," originally recorded by the Bee Gees, were successful for Simone. In addition, the successful albums *Nina Simone Plays the Blues*, *Silk and Soul*, and *Here Comes the Sun* all were issued between 1967 and 1972.

Simone's vocal style is characterized by a soul-searching, mostly alto, vocal range that appears to disdain ornamentation, preferring to squeeze meaning from individual words. Her vocal style emits a believable purity, giving the impression that she truly feels, or has lived, the text of her songs. The believable aspect of Simone's singing style is reflected in her social consciousness. In the 1960s, she made significant contributions to the civil rights movement via protest songs such as "Old Jim Crow," "Mississippi Goddam," and "Young, Gifted, and Black,"

Eclectic vocalist Nina Simone translated great commercial success into powerful political protest. [Schomburg Center]

and since the 1970s she has devoted more time to political causes. In part because of her political beliefs, since the late 1970s Simone has recorded only two albums, *Baltimore* (1978) and *Let It Be Me* (1987), in the United States; all of her other albums have been released in Europe.

Simone currently resides in both Los Angeles and Switzerland and continues to concertize, primarily in Europe.

BIBLIOGRAPHY

Cleary, Steven and Nina Simone. *I Put a Spell on You: Autobiography of Nine Simone* (1991); Meadows, Eddie S. Personal interview with Carrol W. Waymon, brother of Nina Simone (November 26, 1991); Zwerin, Michael. "The Real Nina Simone," *Downbeat* (January 1968).

DISCOGRAPHY

Baltimore, CTI 7084 (1978); *Best of Nina Simone*, Phillips 600298 (Reissue 1985); *Best of Nina Simone*, RCA AFLI-4374 (1970); *Black Is the Color*, 2 Trip 8021-2 (1959); *The Blues*, Novus 3101-2 (Reissue 1991); *Finest* ("I Loves You Porgy"), Bethlehem 6003 (1959); *Here Comes the Sun*, RCA AFL 1-4536 (1967); *Let It Be Me*, Verve 831437-1 (1987); *Live in Europe*, 2 Trip 8020-2 (1975); *Portrait*, Trip 9521 (1973).

EDDIE S. MEADOWS

SIMPSON, CAROLE (1940-)

Broadcast journalist Carole Simpson was born on December 17, 1940, in Chicago, Illinois, to Doretha Viola Wilbon Simpson and Lytle Ray Simpson. She attended the University of Illinois from 1958 to 1960 and then transferred to the University of Michigan, where she graduated in 1962 with a B.A. She later did graduate study in journalism at the University of Iowa. From 1968 to 1970, Simpson worked as a news reporter at WCFL Radio in Chicago. She went from there to WBBM Radio, where she was special correspondent and weekend anchor.

Her move into television came while she was working at WBBM. She appeared as commentator on a minority affairs program on Chicago's public television station, WTTW, which led to a position as a news correspondent at WMAQ-TV. The next year, she also began teaching at Northwestern University's prestigious Medill School of Journalism.

As Chicago's first Black woman television newsperson, Simpson quickly established her credibility and competence. Her on-the-air persona was likable but serious. In 1974, she moved to a Washington, D.C., public affairs show and then to the network. First she was substitute anchor for the *NBC Nightly News* and weekend anchor for *Newsbreak*; then, from 1978 to 1981, she was a Capitol Hill correspondent. Following her appearance as a perimeter reporter at the 1980 political conventions, she was lured away from NBC to become a general assignment correspondent for ABC, covering Vice President George Bush and his 1988 campaign for president.

In 1988, Simpson became anchor of ABC's *World News Saturday*. Along with her anchor duties, she has done three news specials and reports for other ABC news shows, covering a wide variety of issues, such as teen pregnancy, acquired immune deficiency syn-

One of this country's most respected broadcast journalists, Carole Simpson did graduate work in journalism before becoming Chicago's first Black woman television newsperson. She was a Capitol Hill correspondent for NBC before moving to ABC, where she anchors World News Saturday *and hosts news specials and reports. [Brent Petersen]*

drome (AIDS), and battered women. While in South Africa to cover the release of Nelson Mandela from prison, Simpson was assaulted by a South African police officer and declared that she would not return to that country until apartheid had ceased.

Carole Simpson continues to be one of this country's most respected broadcast journalists.

BIBLIOGRAPHY

CBWA; NBAW; WWBA (1992).

KATHLEEN THOMPSON

SIMPSON, GEORGIANA (1866-1944)

In 1921, at the age of fifty-five, Georgiana Simpson became the first Black American woman to earn a Ph.D. Georgiana Simpson was born and raised in the District of Columbia. She attended Washington, D.C., public schools and graduated from the Normal School under the leadership of Dr. Lucy Moten. In 1885, at the age of nineteen, Simpson became an elementary school teacher.

Simpson studied German language and literature in Germany and then returned to Washington, D.C.,

When, in 1921, Georgiana Simpson became the second Black American woman to earn a Ph.D., she was fifty-five years old. At sixty-five, she became a professor at Howard University. [Moorland-Spingarn]

to teach German at Dunbar High School (formerly the M Street School). Throughout her teaching career, Simpson attended summer sessions at the University of Chicago and Harvard University. During this period she received her B.A. degree in German from the University of Chicago.

Simpson was awarded a Ph.D. in German from the University of Chicago in 1921. (Two other Black women received Ph.D.s in 1921: Sadie Tanner Mossell [Alexander] and Eva Dykes, but in order of actual receipt, Simpson's was awarded first.) After completing her Ph.D., Simpson undertook postdoctoral study in French language and literature. A dedicated and hard-working scholar, Simpson edited Grangon La Coste's *Toussaint L'Ouverture* in 1924. This text is frequently used by college French instructors.

Simpson left Dunbar High School in 1931, accepting a professorship at Howard University. A beloved and respected teacher and scholar, Simpson retired from Howard University in 1939. She died in 1944. In 1976, she received a posthumous achievement award from the National Association of Black Professional Women.

BIBLIOGRAPHY

CBWA; Robinson, Omelia. "Contributions of Black American Academic Women to American Higher Education," Ph.D. diss. (1976).

CATHERINE JOHNSON

SIMPSON, VALERIE (1948-)

"It was a dream come true. We were just writers, and Motown was it. When they called us we didn't hesitate. With a whole slew of artists there our songs would get the chance to be recorded. It was the best thing that happened to us" (Davis 1988). This is how vocalist-songwriter Valerie Simpson has described her entry into the Motown studio stable with her eventual husband and songwriting partner, Nickolas Ashford.

Best known in the 1970s and 1980s for her in-studio and onstage partnership with Ashford, which produced a string of hits and opened many ears to her vivacious vocal charms, Valerie Simpson is a crafter of unforgettable lyrics and haunting melodies. She was barely out of high school when she teamed up with Ashford to churn out hits, which they began selling at $75 each. Ashford and Simpson's first hit was "Let's Go Get Stoned," which was written for Ray Charles. Together they produced such memorable pop classics as "Ain't No Mountain High Enough" and "You're All I Need to Get By" for Marvin Gaye and Tammi Terrell, and Diana Ross's anthem, "Reach Out (And Touch Somebody's Hand)," as well as her "Remember Me."

Both Simpson and Ashford wanted to strike out on solo and duo careers, but their contract with Motown kept them from doing so. Simpson managed to record two solo albums for Motown's Tamla label, *Exposed* in 1971 and 1972's *Valerie Simpson*, both of which have become collector's items. Shortly after the release of Simpson's eponymous LP, the duo's desire to perform led them to leave Motown and move to a long-term deal with Warner Brothers. They later moved to Capitol Records, where Ashford and Simpson became hitmakers in their own right, scoring particularly big during the late 1970s and 1980s with such hits as "Send It," "Don't Cost You Nothing," "Is It Still Good to Ya," and a host of others, while at the same time making their mark, due in no small part to Valerie Simpson's soaring voice.

BIBLIOGRAPHY

Davis, Sharon. *Motown: The History* (1988); Stambler, Irwin. *The Encyclopedia of Pop, Rock & Soul* (1976).

WILLARD JENKINS

SIPUEL, ADA LOIS *see* FISHER, ADA LOIS SIPUEL

SIPUEL v. BOARD OF REGENTS

Under Oklahoma law, it was a misdemeanor for school officials to admit "colored" students to white schools or to instruct classes of mixed races. *Ada Lois Sipuel* v. *Board of Regents* (1948) struck a death blow against this law on the graduate level of education in Oklahoma and prepared the way for the momentous *Brown* v. *Board of Education* decision in 1954. During the Oklahoma state convention of the National Association for the Advancement of Colored People (NAACP) in 1945, the delegates decided to make a bold move against segregated education by attempting to enroll Black students on the graduate and professional level at the University of Oklahoma and Oklahoma State University. One of the students was Ada Lois Sipuel.

In 1946, she applied for admission to the University of Oklahoma School of Law, which, at the time, was the only law school in the state. Following its segregationist policies, the university rejected her application solely on the basis of her race. Two Oklahoma courts upheld the university's decision. Thurgood Marshall, then a litigator with the NAACP Legal Defense and Education Fund, argued her case before the U.S. Supreme Court, which in 1948 issued a *per curium* decision that summarily reversed the Oklahoma courts. Relying on precedent set in *Missouri ex rel. Gaines* v. *Canada*, a 1938 case involving the University of Missouri School of Law in which the higher court reversed the Missouri courts, the Supreme Court ordered the University of Oklahoma School of Law to admit Sipuel.

The Sipuel case was a part of the national strategy of the NAACP, which was designed to attack the legality of racial segregation in education and ultimately to overthrow the dictum of "separate but equal." As a result of the Sipuel case, southern states could not require Black Americans to wait until they established the requisite graduate or professional schools.

BIBLIOGRAPHY

Aldrich, Gene. *Black Heritage of Oklahoma* (1973); Swain, Ruth E. *Ada Lois: The Sipuel Story* (1978); Teal, Kay M. *Black History in Oklahoma: A Resource Book* (1971); Thompson, John H. "The Little Caesar of Civil Rights: Roscoe Dunjee in Oklahoma City, 1915 to 1955," Ph.D. diss. (1990).

JOHN H. THOMPSON

SISTERS OF THE HOLY FAMILY

The Sisters of the Holy Family is the second oldest Catholic congregation for women of color organized in the United States. Despite racial prejudice and discrimination, the order, founded in 1842, has a long history of providing services for Black people. These services have included religious education for slaves and, after the Civil War, academic training for African-Americans in Louisiana, Texas, California, Oklahoma, and in Belize, Central America. In addition, the sisters have provided a home for the aged, orphanages, and a day-care center for the working poor.

Henriette Delille (1813-1862), the founder of the congregation, was an educated free woman of African descent, born in New Orleans. A feminist, social worker, and educator, she rebelled against the convention of the quadroon women of her family who became concubines of wealthy white men during the era of slavery. She and the women who joined with her to organize their religious order challenged the prevailing belief that women of color were not capable of practicing celibacy or being nuns. Among the Catholics of New Orleans during the early nineteenth century, it was believed that only white women were called to religious congregations. As a result, it took three attempts in the seventeen years from 1825, the year their charitable work began, to 1842 for the congregation to be recognized and officially founded.

The African-American women were inspired by two French women who worked with Black Catholics in New Orleans, Sr. St. Marthe Fontier of the Ursuline Sisters, and Marie Jeanne Aliquot. As a result, Delille and a friend, Cuban-born Juliette Gaudin (1808-1888), began to teach religion to the slaves. The young women soon became interested in dedicating their lives to this work and sought to become the Black branch of the Ursuline Sisters. Unfortunately, their plans were not well received by the all-white order.

Throughout the 1830s, Delille and Gaudin worked in the slave communities of New Orleans. In 1835, when Delille was declared of legal age, she sold all of her property with hopes of founding a community of Black nuns, separate from the Ursulines, to teach in a school for free girls of color. A campaign waged by civil authorities against those who sought to educate Black people thwarted the effort. In the meantime, Delille and Gaudin began a campaign to encourage free quadroon women to select men of their own class, and to marry in the church. In addition, they encouraged slave couples to have their unions blessed by the church.

Finally, in November 1842, Delille and Gaudin received permission from the diocese to begin their new order in St. Augustine's Church, property earlier donated to the diocese by the Ursulines. A year later, the novices were joined by Josephine Charles, another quadroon.

Despite the barriers, their philosophy made a mark on other men and women of the quadroon class. When in 1847 the state legislature passed an incorporation act that required the sisters to form an association, several prominent quadroons came to their rescue. The Association of the Holy Family was organized with Delille as president. Financial and moral support made it possible for the association to build a home in 1849 for the sick, aged, and poor Black residents of the city. The home was called the Hospice of the Holy Family.

The first three novices led the order throughout much of the nineteenth century—Delille, 1842-62; Gaudin, 1862-67; and Charles, 1867-82. The three are considered the founders of the congregation. The primary work of the sisters in the nineteenth century was in the area of education. Between 1852 and 1898, they opened six schools in New Orleans. These various schools met the needs of middle-class families as well as the poor. St. Mary's school, for example, was founded as a night school in 1867 for freed slaves who could not attend classes in the day. Outside of New Orleans the sisters opened six additional schools in Louisiana, Texas, and Belize. The Sacred Heart school was founded in Belize in 1898.

In addition to schools, the sisters administered other institutions during the nineteenth and twentieth centuries. In 1876, the Louisiana Asylum for Negro Girls was placed under their supervision by the state. In 1896, the sisters organized Lafon, the first Black home for orphan boys in the city of New

Orleans. Continuing their mission to meet the needs of Black Americans into the twentieth century, in 1920 the sisters reorganized the former boys' home into the Lafon Home for the Aged. Fifty years later they were using one of their former convents as a day-care center, which they operated across the street from the historically Black Dillard University. Nonetheless, primary and secondary religious and academic training continue to be a major goal of the Sisters of the Holy Family.

BIBLIOGRAPHY
Detiege, Sister Audrey Marie. *Henriette Delille, Free Woman of Color* (1976); Hart, Sister Mary Francis Borgia. *Violets in the King's Garden: A History of the Sisters of the Holy Family of New Orleans* (1976).

ROSALYN TERBORG-PENN

SIZEMORE, BARBARA (1927-)

The accomplishments of Black women in education have been formidable, but these women have seldom achieved appropriate positions of responsibility and authority. Barbara Ann Laffoon Sizemore is one educator who has achieved eminence as the first Black woman to head the public school system of a major city.

Barbara Laffoon was born in Chicago, Illinois, on December 17, 1927, the only child of Sylvester Walter Laffoon and Delila Alexander Laffoon. She grew up in Terre Haute, Indiana, where she attended Booker T. Washington Elementary School. Her father died when she was eight years old, and her mother later married Aldwin E. Stewart. After graduating from Wiley High School, she went to Northwestern University in Evanston, Illinois, earning a B.A. in classical languages in 1947 and an M.A. in elementary education in 1954.

From 1947 until 1963, Sizemore was a teacher in the Chicago public schools. Her special subjects were Latin, English, and English for Spanish speakers. In 1963, she became one of the first Black women to be appointed principal of a Chicago school when she went to Anton Dvorak Elementary School. She remained there for two years before becoming principal of Forrestville High School. After two years at Forrestville, Sizemore became involved in an important attempt to improve the education of Black children in the city. She was appointed director of the Woodlawn Experimental Schools Project, which was a joint effort of the public schools, the University of

Upon her election to the position of superintendent of schools for the District of Columbia public school system, Barbara Sizemore became the first Black woman to head the public school system of a major city. [Moorland-Spingarn]

of School Administrators in Arlington, Virginia. The next year, her growing reputation led to her election as superintendent of schools for the District of Columbia public school system. The first Black woman to head the public schools in a major city, she was committed to involving parents in creating quality education for students. That commitment led to controversy and a difficult political situation. In 1975, her tenure in the position was terminated.

After two years as an educational consultant, Sizemore moved to Pittsburgh to become associate professor in the Department of Black Community Education and Development at the University of Pittsburgh. In 1989, she became full professor.

Since the late 1960s, Sizemore has published widely. Her first book, *The Ruptured Diamond*, appeared in 1981. It was a study of the politics of decentralization in the District of Columbia public schools. A second book, *An Abashing Anomaly*, was scheduled for publication in 1992. Sizemore is also active in local and national political movements. In the 1970s and early 1980s, she was a key figure in the Black Political Assembly and the National Black Independent political party.

Barbara Sizemore has been married twice, the second time to Jake Milliones, Jr. She has two children from her first marriage and three stepchildren.

BIBLIOGRAPHY
CBWA; NBAW; WWBA (1992).

KATHLEEN THOMPSON

Chicago, and the Woodlawn Organization, a powerful community action group. Funds for the project were provided by the federal government through Title IV of the Elementary and Secondary Education Act (1965), but the program was controlled by the Woodlawn community.

The experience of these years in public education, from the late 1940s to the early 1970s, gave Sizemore tremendous insight into the problems of education in modern urban areas. While she worked with the Woodlawn project, she also shared that insight as a teacher at the Center for Inner City Studies at Northeastern Illinois State University.

In 1972, Sizemore moved to the Washington, D.C., area and became the first woman and the first Black associate secretary of the American Association

SKLAREK, NORMA MERRICK (1928-)

It is seldom that a groundbreaker is quite so far ahead of the pack as architect Norma Merrick Sklarek. Born on April 15, 1928, in New York City, she is the daughter of Amelia Willoughby and Walter Merrick. She attended Barnard College of Columbia University, receiving a Bachelor's degree in architecture there in 1950. In 1954, she was the first Black woman to become licensed as an architect in the state of New York. She was hired in 1955 by the distinguished firm of Skidmore, Owings & Merrill and remained there for five years. At the same time, she was on the architecture faculty of City College of New York. In 1960, she moved to Los Angeles to join the firm of Gruen and Associates and to join the architecture faculty of the University of California at Los Angeles.

She was the first Black woman to be licensed as an architect in California, passing the examination in 1962; it would be twenty years before another Black woman would achieve that status.

Six years after joining Gruen, Merrick became director of architecture, managing a large staff of architects. She was the first woman to hold that position. In 1966, she became the first woman honored with a fellowship in the American Institute of Architects, but she was not yet a partner at Gruen. She married Ralf Sklarek in 1967 and had two sons. She remained with Gruen and Associates for twenty years.

From 1980 to 1985, Sklarek was vice president of Welton Becket Associates, leaving to form her own firm with two women partners. In 1984, her husband died and in 1985 she married her second husband, physician Cornelius Welch. Since 1989, she has been a principal in the Jerde Partnership.

Among Sklarek's important works are the American Embassy in Tokyo, the Pacific Design Center and Terminal One of the International Airport in Los Angeles, and Fox Plaza in San Francisco.

BIBLIOGRAPHY

Lanker, Brian. *I Dream a World* (1989); *NBAW*; *Who's Who of American Women* (1989); *WWBA* (1992).

KATHLEEN THOMPSON

SLAVE NARRATIVES

The modern reader need only read Toni Morrison's novel *Beloved* (1987) to realize the importance of the slave narrative tradition to twentieth-century Black writers. Not only is Morrison's flashback to slavery narrative dependent on her vast knowledge of the slave experience, but she also uses it to demonstrate how slavery as a curse, like Maule's or Sutpen's curses, dominates the present in a mysterious way. The slave narrative has influenced many modern works, including Ralph Ellison's *Invisible Man* (1952), Richard Wright's *Black Boy* (1945), Ernest Gaines's *The Autobiography of Miss Jane Pittman* (1971), James Weldon Johnson's *Autobiography of an Ex-Coloured Man* (1912), Alice Walker's *The Color Purple* (1982), and *The Autobiography of Malcolm X* (1964). Three of these titles contain the word "autobiography," and it is the autobiographical voice of the slave narrative that gives it its unique power and perspective.

In the nineteenth century, antebellum slave narratives gave the abolitionist movement, which financed and published many of them, an unusual voice because the best-known abolitionists were white northerners intent on bringing the peculiar institution of southern slavery to an end. Men such as William Lloyd Garrison and Wendell Phillips crusaded against slavery as a demonic other, an incarnation of Satan, and a force to be contested with both word and sword. Garrison not only wrote an introduction to Frederick Douglass's *Narrative of the Life of Frederick Douglass, an American Slave* (1845); he also edited the abolitionist newspaper the *Liberator*, and sponsored defiant attacks against any proslavery government, including the federal government, whose Compromise of 1850 allowed California to enter the union as a nonslave state while Utah and New Mexico entered without making a decision on the issue. The Fugitive Slave Law of 1850 implicated all states that ratified the new legislation as participating in the evil practice of slavery. The slave narrators spoke out against persecution by using examples from their personal experience, and because their voices were so direct and immediate, and their recollections so clearly articulated, they developed a literature that exceeded the invective and treatise writing of their sponsoring agents. Slave narratives constitute some of the most persuasive literature composed during the first half of the nineteenth century. After the Emancipation Proclamation of 1862, they practically ceased to be published, for their work was theoretically done. As Douglass prophetically observed, however, "with the Emancipation Proclamation the work of freedom is not done, it has only begun" (Gates 1985).

Douglass's "work of freedom" was effectively done by two women writers of the nineteenth century, one white and one Black. Harriet Beecher Stowe's novel *Uncle Tom's Cabin* (1852) is greatly indebted to the slave narrative and the Indian captivity narrative traditions, both of which Stowe knew extremely well. Her debts to the sentimental novel have been examined by Jane Tompkins (1985), but Stowe herself acknowledged her indebtedness to the slave narrative when she indicated that the prototype for Uncle Tom was the slave Josiah Henson, whose autobiographical narrative had been published in 1842.

The declarative autobiographical accounts of the slaves themselves, escaped or emancipated, who wrote as they emerged from slavery, provide modern readers with some vivid accounts of human brutality, but the demonic other in this tradition is the institution of slavery itself. Slavery is the antagonist in almost all of the extant antebellum slave narratives, as well as in Stowe's novel. The experience of the female slave, Harriet Jacobs, is represented by Linda Brent in *Inci-*

dents in the Life of a Slave Girl, Written by Herself (1861). The phrase "written by herself" is important because slave narrators often were charged with misrepresentation; for this reason most narratives contain a preface or introduction composed by a well-known white abolitionist who argues for the authenticity of the document. Lydia Maria Child, for example, introduced *Incidents* by saying, "The author of the following autobiography is personally known to me. ... I believe those who know her will not be disposed to doubt her veracity, though some incidents in her story are more romantic than fiction." Both Garrison and Phillips wrote similar prefaces to Douglass's 1845 *Narrative*.

The dominant theme in all slave narration is the quest for personal freedom in an oppressive and hostile context. For female slaves, however, the problems were compounded; not only were they subordinate to their male owners as slaves; they also were the sexual slaves of their masters, whose wills they were forced to obey. Harriet Jacobs's narrative indicts both men and women in white slave society for abusing the victimized Black woman. Linda's movement toward personal freedom is thwarted throughout the story by the sexual assaults of a Dr. Flint. This pattern is established very early in the story; when Linda is quite young, she assumes an identity in relation to Flint that initially terrorizes her but which creates a revulsion toward her persecutor that motivates her escape from his lustful grasp:

> For my master, whose restless, craving, vicious nature moved about day and night, seeking whom to devour, had just left me, with stinging, scorching words; words that scathed ear and brain like fire. O, how I despised him! I thought how glad I should be, if some day when he walked the earth, it would open and swallow him up, and disencumber the world of a plague. ... When he told me that I was made for his use, made to obey his command in *every* thing, that I was nothing but a slave, whose will must and should surrender to his, never before had my puny arm felt half so strong.

The imagery of the master here is biblical, alluding to Satan, the adversary who "walked to and fro upon the earth" in the Book of Job (1:7). Analogies to disease and beasts also are commonplace in the slave narratives. Using a technique of inversion, Jacobs depicts the hypocritical slaveowners as pigs, dogs, worms, and creatures below man in the hierarchy of creation, thus ironically reversing the literally subhu-

man treatment inflicted on female slaves by their white masters. Jacobs is emphatic in her insistence that the chattel slavery of America was far worse than the wage slavery suffered by serfs and peasants in Europe:

> There was no law forbidding them to learn to read and write; and if they helped each other in spelling out the Bible, they were in no danger of thirty-nine lashes, as was the case with myself and poor, pious, old uncle Fred. ... No master or overseer could come and take from him his wife, or his daughter. They must separate to earn a living; but the parents knew where their children were going, and could communicate with them by letters. The relations of husband and wife, parent and child, were too sacred for the richest noble in the land to violate with impunity.

Jacobs contrasts the misery of the wage slave with the intolerable conditions of the chattel slave by shaping her narrative around family ties, the thread that weaves throughout the story and draws the characters together in a tight bond of mutual concern, just as Toni Morrison uses family structure to bond the characters in *Beloved*. As in many slave narratives, Jacobs's account contains the dreaded slave auction scene, which dramatizes the breakup of family life just as the loving concern of slave mothers illustrates the tight bonds of family. The overpowering effect of disunion is tragically recalled:

> To the slave mother, New Year's Day comes laded with peculiar sorrows. She sits on her cold cabin floor, watching the children who may all be torn from her the next morning; and often does she wish that they might die before the day dawns. She may be an ignorant creature, degraded by the system that has brutalized her from childhood; but she has a mother's instincts, and is capable of feeling a mother's agonies.

The inhumanity of the auction scenes and the arbitrary nature of the sales, the commodification of humans as lots and labor, give the slave narratives their dramatic force. In the Jacobs narrative, as in many contemporary accounts and modern recapitulations of the slave experience, the protagonist is striving to escape from the clutches of many antagonists, slaveowners, slave breakers, slave overseers, slave catchers, and slave rapists. Each narrative relates particular instances and experiences, but it is the evil institution that victimizes everyone associated with slavery, and all the narratives long for abolition, not only to free the slaves, but also to free society from a blight that will forever tarnish the character, humanity, and democratic ideals that the United States is supposed to uphold. Thus the purpose of each narrative is twofold; there is the larger objective of abolishing the institution of slavery but also the personal objective of relating the history of a particular person. Slave narratives generally, and Harriet Jacobs's story in particular, demonstrate the dominance of the oppressor over the oppressed and the mechanisms used by empowered figures, usually male, to maintain their position in relation to the oppressed. It is emblematic of this oppression that slaves often were punished with an instrument of torture known as the bit, an iron device that surrounded the slave's head and thrust a metal plate or saucer back into the mouth against the throat so that the victim could not eat, drink, swallow comfortably, or even speak.

This unusual form of physical torture symbolizes the oppressive society's attempt to deny its victims a voice, inasmuch as slaves who were punished with the bit could not communicate with each other, their oppressors, or their family. Often slaves were forced to work while wearing the device, either in the field or in the kitchen or in the house. Toni Morrison makes reference to this punishment, as do Olaudah Equiano and Harriet Jacobs. Clearly the violation of personhood, family structure, and personal voice was central to the slave's condition. Jacobs and her successors show the value of the personal narrative as a corrective to such oppression, as a means of allowing the oppressed voice to be heard.

[See also FEDERAL WRITERS PROJECT SLAVE NARRATIVES.]

BIBLIOGRAPHY

For a complete bibliography of slave narratives published before the end of 1910, see Yellin, Jean Fagan and Cynthia D. Bond, *The Pen Is Ours* (1991).

Andrews, William. *Go Tell a Free Story: The First Century of Afro-American Autobiography, 1760-1865* (1986); Bell, Bernard W. *The Afro-American Novel and Its Tradition* (1987); Blassingame, John W. *The Slave Community: Plantation Life in the Ante-Bellum South* (1972); Davis, Charles T., and Henry Louis Gates, Jr. *The Slave's Narrative* (1985); Douglas, Ann. *The Feminization of American Culture* (1977); Jacobs, Harriet A. *Incidents in the Life of a Slave Girl, Written by Herself*, ed. Lydia Maria Child ([1861] 1987); Lowance, Mason. "Biography and Autobiography in Early America." In *The Columbia Literary History of the United States*, ed. Emory Elliott (1988); Seskora, John, and Darwin Turner. *The Art of the Slave Narrative: Original Essays in Criticism and Theory* (1982); Tompkins, Jane. *Sensational Designs: The Cultural Work of American Fiction, 1790-1863* (1985).

MASON LOWANCE

SLAVERY

The first Black females who came to the British colony of Virginia probably arrived in 1619. It was in the previous summer that the English ship *Treasurer* left Virginia on its way to acquire "officially" salt, goats, and other provisions for the colony. Shortly after it left Virginia, however, the *Treasurer* came into contact with a Dutch man-of-war, and the two ships sailed on in consort. While so doing, they "happened upon" a Spanish frigate with a cargo of African slaves en route to the Spanish West Indies. The crews of the *Treasurer* and the Dutch ship took the cargo of slaves for themselves. Separated and delayed by bad weather, the ships' provisions were diminished, and a number of the slaves died from starvation before the ships reached land. When the Dutch man-of-war arrived at Jamestown in August 1619, it carried only twenty of the one hundred slaves it had taken aboard, a few who undoubtedly were female. The *Treasurer*, which had taken the other part of the African cargo, landed only one Black person in Virginia, a female her captors called Angela.

It is not certain what became of this lone African woman, Angela, or the few others who arrived at the British colonial outpost in 1619. Slavery was not a formal, legalized institution in the colony at the time, although Europeans had been taking Africans as slaves to Europe and to the New World for more than a century. Unlike most of the other British New World colonists who embraced the institution of slavery soon after the appearance of Africans in their society, Virginians first regarded these African women as indentured servants. (The colony of Georgia outlawed the importation of Black slaves until 1750.)

By 1661, however, their status had irreversibly changed. It was in that year that a law, meant principally to quell plots of Black and white servants escaping together, legally affirmed what had been customary for at least twenty years—the perpetual enslavement of male and female Africans. The following year, the fate of the next several generations was sealed in law. In response to queries regarding the status of children born to Black women and white men, the colony decided that "all children borne in this country shall be held bond or free only according to the condition of the mother." Other colonies followed suit, reversing traditional British law and patriarchal custom that prescribed a child's status according to his or her father. Due to the shortage of European women in the early colonies (ratios were as extreme as four men to one woman in many areas), significant numbers of white men were establishing sexual relations with African women. The law of 1662 limited the size of the mulatto free class that might have resulted from these interracial intimacies if the father's status was the principal determinant of the offspring's legal identity.

Female slave property in the British mainland colonies represented numerous ethnic groups that resided in a vast expanse that stretched along the West African coast from the Senegambia region down through Angola, inland at least several hundred miles, and around the southern tip of the continent to Madagascar. While the slave ship manifests do not give distinct ethnic origins, they nonetheless provide a list of places from which slaves from the surrounding vicinity were taken—Sierra Leone, Gambia, Madagascar, Angola, Congo, Gold Coast, Benin, Guinea, Cape Verde, Senegambia, Calabar, Bonny, Windward Coast, Bonney, Bande. They were of various ethnicities, but particularly the Ibo, Ewe, Bakongo, Wolof, Serer, Fante, Bambara, Arada, Tiv, Fon, Yoruba, Dahomey, Ashanti, Fulani, Mandingo, Coromantee, and Hausa.

They came from African villages, cities, and states that had various social rules and in which they played diverse roles. Some of their indigenous ethnic groups were patriarchal, others were not. Some believed in polygamy, while others embraced monogamous marriages. Many brought with them their Islamic beliefs and rules of social behavior; others maintained the rituals and moral ideology of indigenous African religions. They were part of societies with rich and longstanding heritages in which women were traders, agriculturalists, weavers, warriors, leaders, and especially mothers. The more than 100,000 African women who arrived as slaves in the British mainland colonies were part of a much larger forced exodus that included minimally 10 million Black people, most of whom became slaves in the Caribbean and Latin America (Curtin 1975). Indeed, many of the slave women who eventually arrived in North America were first enslaved in the Caribbean, particularly during the sixteenth century, and were introduced to the institution of Black New World slavery in places like Bermuda, Barbados, Antigua, Nevis, and Jamaica.

Strangers in a foreign land, forced to comprehend a new language spoken by people who looked and behaved so differently from themselves, confronted with a hostile physical and emotional environment, along with extreme work quotas and harsh corporal punishment, these first few African females undoubtedly experienced great emotional and physical distress. Yet, their anguish and alienation did not begin on the coasts of the New World. For several weeks and sometimes months before they ever reached North America, African girls and women suffered incredibly at the hands of traders, European and African, who captured or bought them. Torn from the very fabric of their lives, these women, many of whom were already married and had children of their own, were forced to leave their families, their culture, and their ethnically prescribed identities behind. As part of a well-established international trade, African merchants bartered them for a variety of European and American items, principally iron bars, pewter, guns, gunpowder, whiskey, brandy, rum, cloth, brass pans, crystal beads, and foodstuffs. They were sold along with the other regional "treasures" for which different areas of the West African coastline were named—gold, ivory, and grain.

Much of the British trade was organized through the auspices of the Royal African Company from 1672 to 1731, but colonists also purchased slaves from other monopolistic companies and privateers. With the incredible increase in the volume of the trade during the eighteenth century, organization of the business on the African coast and in the hinterland became much less decentralized. The impact on African societies was traumatic—African rulers and traders lost more and more control of the numbers of persons taken and exported; new state rivalries and conflicts escalated; and the daily life of the millions of persons who remained in those affected societies were profoundly altered. One European living in West Africa, for example, reported in 1702 that "the English had come with two large Vessels, and had Ravaged the Country, destroyed their canoes, plundered their houses, and carried off some of their people for slaves" (quoted in Meier and Rudwick 1976). Africans, who were the target of these raids, actively resisted their enslavement and the destruction of their villages and communities. Olaudah Equiano, an Ibo man from the Benin province of Nigeria captured along with his sister and later enslaved in Virginia, noted that the phenomenon of enemies coming into the vicinity of his village in order to take prisoners as slaves was so prevalent by the mid-eighteenth century that often the men and the women took weapons to the fields in order to defend themselves. "Even our women are warriors and march boldly out to fight along with the men.

Our whole district is a kind of militia," he explained (Curtin 1967).

The immediate physical and psychological violence African women and girls experienced in the trade have been documented repeatedly by slave merchants, observers, and the Africans themselves. Exposed to the elements day and night without any type of shelter, receiving little medical attention and food, many were physically debilitated before they ever reached the holding pens or barracoons on the coast. African females taken as slaves not only were physically and emotionally impaired by the experience but also faced the threat of sexual abuse at every juncture of their forced migration. Not surprisingly, some were pregnant by the time they reached America. For many, the immediate response was to resist—to escape or perhaps get the aid of a sympathetic passerby. Some even tried to overpower their guard; others committed suicide. Relatively few succeeded in regaining their freedom.

The slave coffles of shackled men and women eventually reached the slave forts or barracoons sometimes weeks after their first capture. There they waited to be placed on ships to the Caribbean and the British mainland, most unable to even imagine that their lives could change as drastically as their New World enslavement would demand. The Middle Passage between Africa and America could only have deepened their confusion, horror, and anger as it provided even greater chance for abuse. This phase of the enslavement process undoubtedly was the most terrifying and deadly experience that Africans coming to the New World would have—mortality rates could range from 10 percent to 50 percent.

Packed tightly into boats, often forced to lie on their sides in spoon fashion for most of the trip because the holds of the ships, many constructed in the New England colonies, were too narrow and too shallow (sometimes only two to four feet in height) for women to be able to stand, the one-to-three-month journey must have been unbearable for many. During periods of good weather, slaves could come up to the deck where they could get sunlight and fresh air and wash themselves. When the weather was bad or there was some fear of a slave plot to overthrow the crew, they were forced to remain below, lying chained together in their own feces, urine, blood, and vomit. The opportunities for infection, disease, and epidemic were tremendous. "The floor of the rooms," one eighteenth-century slave ship's surgeon wrote, "was so covered with blood and mucus which had proceeded from them in consequence of dysentery, that it resembled a slaughter house. It is not in the power of human imagination to picture to itself a situation more dreadful or disgusting" (quoted in Meier and Rudwick 1967).

> Numbers of the slaves having fainted, they were carried upon deck, where several of them died. The surgeon, upon going between decks in the morning, to examine the situation of the slaves, frequently finds several dead, and among the men, sometimes a dead and living negro fastened by their irons together. When this is the case, they are brought upon the deck, and being laid on the grating, the living negro is disengaged, and the dead ones thrown overboard (Curtin 1967).

Contemporary colonists often asserted that they knew of the approach of a slave ship even before they saw it because the stench of the human cargo was so great.

Numerous attempts of onboard mutiny against such horrific conditions and enslavement occurred. Documentation exists of more than fifty-five such attempts from 1699 to 1845, some in which women figured prominently (Blassingame 1979). Suicide, self-imposed starvation, general refusals to cooperate, and violent outbursts were all resistance efforts. By the time they finally came ashore to again face physical inspection by prospective buyers, which for women included the crudest gynecological examination, and resale, they were physically debilitated, emotionally battered, and sometimes sick and dying with small pox, the "bloody flux," or other European diseases.

Female slaves were only a small portion of these first Black imports. The initial experiment with the importation of Black slaves to these colonies largely excluded females, since the emphasis was on labor, particularly agricultural labor, and colonial masters believed young men to be superior workers. Would-be slaveholders made their orders to purchasing agents clear—they wanted young, healthy male slaves, not women. Writing to his factor in June 1682, for example, tobacco planter William Fitzhugh instructed: "purchase what likely Negroes you can, either 1, 2, 3, 4, 5, or 6, what boys and men you possibly can, as few women as may be, but be sure not above two, to purchase neither men nor women above thirty years old." Despite their smaller numbers, Black women were a significant part of the growing forced exodus of Africans and Black Creoles from various West African and Caribbean locations. An appraisal of the ship merchandise on the *Margarett* of London which docked in Maryland in February 1693, for example, not only included several "Negro" males but "3

Negros Judith Moll and Maria, Girles worth 30 pounds."

The trade in women continued to increase during the pre-Revolutionary eighteenth century. It has been estimated, for example, that there were approximately 1,100 women (1,800 men) in South Carolina by 1703 (Wood 1974). Amidst the labor intensive "rice boom," their number grew even more rapidly. Thus, the colony's governor had occasion to write to the Board of Trade in 1754 that "there have been already Imported since the 1st of November upwards of 2,000 Negroes, and there are some Ships that are still expected from Africa with more, they have all been readily sold and at great Prices, the men for 250, 260, and 270 Pounds Currency and the Women for 200, the Boys and Girls for little less" (Donnan 1935).

Georgia was late to embrace the institution of slavery, legally forbidding it at the colony's founding, but, amid persistent settler criticism, repealing the act in 1750. Advertisements in the colony's *Gazette* soon read like so many others of the era: "To be Sold on Thursday next, at publick vendue, Ten Likely Gold Coast New Negroes, Just imported from the West Indies, consisting of eight stout men and two women"; or "On Tuesday the 17th inst. will be sold at Savannah, About 40 Likely New Negroes, Consisting mostly of Men and Women, Lately from Gambia and Sierreleone" (Donnan 1935).

Black women went to inhabit and work not just in southern locales but the middle and northern colonies as well. By 1690, for example, they comprised a minority of the 400 Black people in Massachusetts; 200 in Connecticut; 250 in Rhode Island; and 100 in New Hampshire (Piersen 1988). They also figured in the forty slaves in Delaware in 1670; the 2,170 in New York in 1698; the 2,581 in New Jersey by 1726; and the few thousand residing in Pennsylvania by the 1720s (U.S. Bureau of the Census 1975, 1979).

The reality of colonial American society offered additional problems to African women. Despite the trauma of enslavement and travel, their arrival and the aftermath were just as frightening. Many associations with members of their original ethnic groups made while on board the ship ceased immediately and without warning as slave women left the docks with their new masters. Language and cultural barriers that had not been complete until this time now insured a gnawing social isolation. The female slaves' familial and communal networks, which were vital to the African woman's identity and function, did not exist at those rural outposts called plantations where they went to reside. The so-called seasoning process that occurred during the first two years following enslave-ment was the time owners expected their Black female property to adjust, physically and mentally, to their new surroundings and status. It was a time when these women learned to work and communicate in order to appease owners and their supervisory staff. It was also during this period that they began to learn how to impose their aboriginal culture and "female-ness" on the New World.

Unlike voluntary immigrants, Africans did not leave or arrive in family groups. Nor did they have much of an opportunity to form families for several years after their arrival. Demographers studying the colonial era, for example, calculate that a typical slave ship cargo included twice as many men as women and very few children, most of whom also were boys. These gender and generational imbalances did not correct themselves significantly, even in the earliest settled regions of the colonies, until the mid-eighteenth century, and then only as a result of natural reproduction. Given these demographic characteristics and slaves' spatial isolation from one another, most of the first female imports suffered a lonely sociosexual existence, acute cultural isolation, starvation, and brutal physical treatment.

It is difficult to ascertain what community or family meant to these early Black slaves in the context of the rural colonial frontier. These were concepts that were important to an African woman's sense of identity and purpose. The rules of formation and activity within these social institutions were clear in their homelands. In seventeenth- and eighteenth-century America, however, peopled by a vast array of culturally and racially diverse persons, these phenomena must have seemed elusive, if not impossible, to acquire. Yet, social commitments and relations akin to marriage, family, and community slowly developed. While African women insisted on shaping their emergence, colonial officials attempted to impose their guidelines.

Seventeenth-century masters quickly established the right to define and structure the most intimate connections and activities of their slaves and servants, electing to control various aspects of their sexual behavior and family life through their power in the colonial legislature. Early lawmakers were concerned in particular with interracial bonding. Recognizing the potentially explosive social and political, to say nothing of economic, implications of such intimate alliances, they forbade intimate relations and marriages between Europeans, Africans, and Native Americans.

On September 17, 1630, for example, the Virginia colonial government decided that "Hugh Davis

[was] to be soundly whipped before an assembly of Negroes and others for abusing himself to the dishonor of God and shame of Christians by defiling his body in lying with a Negro, which fault he is to acknowledge next Sabbath day." Ten years later, the minutes of the proceedings of the Governor and Council of Virginia sentenced a white man, Robert Sweet, "to do penance in church according to the laws of England, for getting a Negro woman with child." While Mr. Sweet was left to do his penance, the unnamed Black woman was whipped for her sin.

By the end of the first half century of Black female slavery, antimiscegenation laws were being firmly set in place in that colony as elsewhere. In 1691, Virginia created legislation that "banished forever" any white, free or bond, who intermarried with a Negro, mulatto, or Indian. This same act stipulated that the mulatto children born of free or servant white women and Black men were to be "bound out" by church wardens until the age of thirty. In the next century (1765), Virginia lowered the ages of release to twenty-one years for males and eighteen for females. Legislation passed in 1753 regarding whites who intermarried with Blacks or mulattoes stipulated a six-month prison term and a fine of ten pounds. Other colonies followed suit. Yet, intimate relationships, forced or otherwise, between Africans, Europeans, and Native Americans were a reality of America's racially plural society that would never change.

The colonial households that these African women helped to form, therefore, often were not defined by blood relationships, race, or culture but rather by economic and production necessities. Documented examples of cooperation between colonial servants and slaves of various races in group escapes and other forms of resistance, as well as the creation of those early antimiscegenation laws, indicate close, kin-like relationships that these early residents attempted to form with those to whom they felt, if not cultural or blood affinity, then some political and economic kinship as well as social and emotional compatibility. Family for many of the first African and Black Creole women, therefore, existed in their memories of those whom they had to leave behind when they traveled to the British mainland colonies and perhaps as well among those relations that they formed with fellow servants and slaves with whom they lived and worked in the colony.

As long as Africans dominated the slave population, there were many problems that hindered both marriage and reproduction among themselves. Black women had a better opportunity to establish marital relations than did Black men given the severe gender imbalance of their society. Yet, African women had few children. Many began bearing children late in their twenties, in part because of their ages at the time of their arrival in the colonies. Yet, their overall poor physical health, high mortality rates, and psychological distress also discouraged fertility. Many of the first African female servants and slaves must have wondered how it would be possible for them to establish themselves as wives and mothers in a place and as part of an institution that was so profoundly hostile to them.

Native born Black slave women, in contrast, usually began bearing children at an earlier age, could provide their infants with natural immunities to local illnesses that African women could not, and generally are believed to have had superior physical and emotional health. Consequently, they experienced more live births than their African peers, and their children may have been healthier. A natural increase in the Black population first appeared in the colonies in the 1720s and 1730s and continued to improve over the next several decades. It was only then that women became part of operative slave communities based loosely on extended kin networks that often spanned two or three generations.

Despite the importance of family and marriage to slave women, their principal definition in American society was that of laborer. The relationships that female slaves had with their labor supervisors and the kind of work they performed in the colonial as well as antebellum eras, therefore, had a great impact on other aspects of their lives. Though most slave females worked very hard from childhood through old age, there were variables that affected the kinds of labor they performed, its intensity, the nature of their supervision, and their rewards and punishments. Location, generation, age, gender, level of acculturation, size of the slaveholding to which one belonged, and color all had an important impact on slave labor in the British mainland colonies and, during the antebellum era, in the American South. The nature of one's labor affected the slave woman's material status, health, fertility, family stability, and overall value in the slave market.

These are some of the most striking topics in the history of slave women's lives and labor. Yet, from the perspective of the African woman and her female descendants, life was not experienced in these scholarly terms. Living as a slave meant hard work, poor rations, sometimes brutal beatings, lost families, and illness. It also meant marriage on negotiated terms but marriage nonetheless, children who learned how to care for their elderly or ailing kin, communities of friends, and, between the hard times, some laughter, pride, romance, song, dance, and God.

In the New England and middle colonies, most female slaves worked on small farms, dairy and cattle raising estates, cultivated vegetables, tended livestock, and served as house slaves cooking, cleaning, butchering, nursing and rearing children, waiting on tables, and acting as counselors to their master's family. Silvia Du Bois, born in New Jersey in 1768, for example, served, along with her mother, as a farm worker, ferryman, and domestic in a tavern on the Pennsylvania frontier. Her personal account of bondage defies contentions that northern mainland slavery was less harsh than that of the southern colonies. It also shatters myths of slave mistress benevolence.

Silvia Dubois's biographical narrative included many examples of cruelty. It is a two-generation story, one that chronicled both her life and that of her mother, Dorcas Compton. According to Dubois, their owner forced Dorcas to start working again only three days after she gave birth. Her master then beat her with an "ox-gad because she didn't hold a hog while he yoked it." "It was in March," she went on, "the ground was wet and slippery, and the hog proved too strong for her. . . . From the exposure and the whipping, she became severely sick with puerperal fever; but after a long while she recovered." While Dorcas Compton's abuse primarily was imposed by her master, it was Silvia Dubois's mistress who often chastised her brutally. "Why, she was the very devil himself," Dubois offered. "Why, she'd level me with anything she could get hold of—club, stick of wood, tongs, fire-shovel, knife, ax, hatchet." This slaveholding woman was unrelenting in her physical abuse of Silvia when she was a child, kicking her in her stomach, whipping her with various objects, and even cracking her skull with a shovel. As she grew older, however, Dubois was determined to fight back, rescuing herself physically and emotionally from the woman's brutality (Loewenberg and Bogin 1976).

While the northern and middle colonies had a more diversified economy than those to the south, much of the diversity apparent in their shipbuilding industry, distilleries, printing shops and other such businesses did not have great impact on the labor of Black women. Throughout the British mainland, female slaves were allowed to perform little skilled labor except that of midwife, nurse or herbalist, seamstress, weaver, or cook. Few slaveowners believed women were suited for other kinds of work. Accordingly, male slaves retained almost exclusive rights to jobs and the mobility associated with them—in lumbering, iron works, distilleries, tanneries, whaling and fishing industries, and as blacksmiths, coopers, and carpenters—that women could not have.

The vast majority of "prime" slave women (about 89 percent) in the South and men (about 83 percent), worked as agriculturalists. This kind of labor was not a novel experience for African women—many had grown rice, millet, and other grains as well as cotton before they became slaves in the New World. They brought the skills attendant to cultivating these kinds of crops to the New World. African women from various ethnic groups, for example, routinely cared for vegetable gardens and livestock. They not only produced subsistence crops and reared livestock but also helped to manufacture raw materials for home consumption and marketing. Women also produced many of the utilitarian domestic objects their families used as slaves. Their contributions included textiles, baskets, containers, and buttons, and they introduced the cultivation and preparation of various West African foods such as millet, goundnuts, benne, gourds, congo peas, and yams (Hatley 1983). They too helped create the songs slaves used to regulate their labor while maintaining African-influenced religious beliefs, medicinal practices, dressing and hair styles, dancing, birthing, courtship, and marital rituals. These contributions aided both owners and slaves.

Masters, of course, centered their attention on the skills African women used to influence their profit margins. Most undoubtedly were pleased that these women had well-honed agricultural knowledge to apply to their field labor. The principal crops slave women helped to produce in the southern colonies were tobacco, wheat, corn, and other grains in Virginia, Maryland, and North Carolina; tobacco, rice, and indigo in South Carolina; and rice and indigo in Georgia.

Rising early in the morning to the sound of an overseer or driver blowing a horn and working until nightfall for five and one-half to six days a week, slave female agricultural laborers usually were responsible for almost every aspect of the planting, growing, harvesting, and preparing for market of the crops, except the initial clearing of land. Amelia Walker, for example, remembered watching her mother working in the fields. When interviewed, she noted: "Mama plowed wid three horses—ain't dat somp'n? Thought women was sposed to work 'long wid men, I did" (Perdue, Barden, and Phillips 1976).

Tobacco was a difficult plant for female slaves to grow successfully due to the delicacy of the leaf, the difficulty of insect control, the detailed technology that was necessary, and problems associated with producing a good grade. During the antebellum era, infertile land was a particularly pressing problem affecting the ability of growers to successfully produce a profitable quota of leaves. The planting of tobacco began in the late winter or early spring when the laborers prepared seedlings in special beds. Once this was done, the slaves began to ready the fields to receive the seedlings in the late spring.

Ex-slaves testified that this was particularly wrenching, backbreaking work, for they were equipped with only heavy, crude plows and hoes to break up the fields and divide them into small hills approximately three to four feet apart. Once the spring rains had made the soil damp enough, male and female slaves went to the fields to set out the young seedlings in their hills, each planting several hundred a day. Each female tobacco worker was responsible for the preparation, planting, and care of several rows of tobacco that were marked by a piece of cloth or in some other manner. In this way, supervisors could easily identify the quality and amount of work that individual slaves performed. Also, some slaves worked in specified gangs or family groups, with each unit responsible for a certain acreage.

Several weeks followed when slaves weeded and replanted seedlings washed away during rains. Experts noted that "once the plants began to mature and started to flower, slaves had to 'top' them, or remove the flower, leaving the stalk a specific height. They then had to pull off the suckers which grew from the stalk. This allowed the tobacco leaves to reach full size." Tobacco workers also intermittently had to pull hornworms from the plants' leaves. Slaves had to be particularly careful not to damage the leaf of the plant while pulling suckers, worms, or cutting the leaf, and some labor supervisors forced women to expose their bodies by pinning up their dresses in order that their skirts would not get entangled in the plants and damage the leaves. Slaves usually harvested tobacco in September (Gerald-Stevenson and Stevenson 1987).

Harvest meant that every available laborer, female and male, had to put forth an extreme effort. One ex-slave recalled that during harvest time they worked from well before sunrise until late at night and had to build bonfires to see what they were doing. Slave women too old and infirm to do fieldwork any longer brought supper to the field at night. Thus, owners compelled slaves to work most strenuously during the hot summer months.

During harvest, slaves broke off the mature tobacco leaves, strung them on sticks, and hung them in tobacco barns to dry and be cured. While slaves were working the tobacco, they also were responsible for preparing the soil and growing and harvesting other crops such as corn and wheat for home consumption. But as ex-slave Matilda Perry noted, on farms where tobacco was the primary cash crop, all emphasis was placed on producing a high yield leaf of good quality. Slaves on tobacco farms cleared fields for planting wheat in late August, harvested corn in October, and sowed wheat from October until the end of November. It was then time to begin plowing for the new tobacco crop.

Although the work was rigorous, tobacco could be produced profitably on moderate-size farms. In Virginia, for example, where the best grade of tobacco was produced during the colonial period, the average slaveholding was between nine and thirteen slaves. One of the largest slaveholders in Virginia at the end of the eighteenth century, for example, was George Washington. He owned 188 slaves in 1783, 215 in 1786, and 316 in 1799, distributed among the five farms that comprised his Mount Vernon estate. His female slaves performed much of the labor on his tobacco and grain farms. In his 1786 diary, for example, Washington listed seventeen "Labour[in]g" Women and ten men at his River Plantation; ten laboring women and eight men at his Dogue Run Plantation; ten laboring women and five men at his Ferry Plantation; and nine laboring women and five men at his Muddy Hole Plantation. Although he employed slave men as overseers and "underoverseers" on three of his farms, no women held such a supervisory role. With rare exceptions, those positions in the field, like skilled occupations, were held by males.

Wheat was less labor intensive than tobacco, allowing slaves more breaks in the intense work routine. Tobacco slaves were busy from late December until late the next fall producing their crop, whereas women working in wheat began to sow the crop in late September and had finished their harvest by July. During the intervals present in wheat production, however, owners required female slaves to complete a number of other strenuous tasks associated with the growth and harvest of corn, potatoes, and other garden crops, the care and butchering of livestock, filling the ice house, and spinning cotton. Owners also took advantage of "slack-times" by renting out idle slaves.

Ex-slave Frank Bell recalled that Black slaves on John Fallons's wheat plantation worked in family groups. The work was hard, Bell noted, particularly during harvest time, and Fallons made all of the women work in the field because he "wasn't much on no special house servants." Yet, the women on Fallons's wheat farm performed less physically demanding agricultural tasks than did the men. Male slaves were responsible for clearing the land and the actual cutting and cradling of the wheat. Women raked and bound the cut grain in stacks. Men and women both were responsible for sowing and caring for the young crops. Some overseers would not allow slaves to work in family groups, so Bell and his family were fortunate. He had four brothers and no sisters, but he felt particularly protective of his mother, "who arn't very strong" (Perdue, Barden, and Phillips 1976). He, along with his father and brothers, shared his mother's workload and provided her with ample emotional support in the field.

Rice was a much more labor intensive crop than wheat or tobacco; consequently female rice workers were part of much larger slaveholdings than those who produced other kinds of crops. Located principally along the South Carolina and Georgia coasts, slaveholdings ranged in size from thirty-five to seventy-five slaves per agricultural unit (Phillips 1918). Rice production, too, had a seasonal quality, but it employed slave women throughout the year. Preliminary breaking of the soil occurred during the fall months, and the fields were prepared for planting during the early spring. Summer brought the alternating of flooding the fields with drying them out and weeding. Harvest occurred in early September. Overseers assigned each man and woman three or four rows to cut. The following day, they bound the stalks in sheaths. Threshing began soon thereafter.

The agricultural skills that African women were able to transfer successfully to the New World were inclusive of rice technology. Many societies in precolonial West Africa produced rice quite similarly to the manner in which slaves cultivated the crop in South Carolina and Georgia. Rice cultivation was known to occur from the region south of Cape Verde to the area north of Sierra Leone from the fifteenth century through the centuries in which slaves were imported. Women were vital laborers in those rice fields. An eighteenth-century slave ship's captain commenting on rice production among the Bagas of Guinea-Conakry, for example, had occasion to note the "dexterity" of the "women and girls" who transplanted rice seedlings in the fields men prepared (Littlefield 1991).

Slave women and girls also were important rice laborers in the American South. Prices of slaves in Savannah document that planters were willing to pay equally for prime male and female rice hands. In a slave inventory dated 1852, for example, twenty-seven-year-old Callie May, a woman described as a "Prime Woman, Rice," was priced at $1,000; equally priced

was Deacon, a twenty-six-year-old "Prime Rice Hand." Both men and women in the American South hoed the rice fields, moving in unison to songs they sang to set the rhythm of their labor. Women also helped equally in harvesting. In some West African societies their harvesting tasks were distinguished by gender: women cut the stalks and men gathered them. Although women were expected to hoe and harvest with the same capacity as men, slave women were not allowed to serve as labor supervisors. Only men held this position, as on tobacco, wheat, and cotton plantations. The result undoubtedly was a hardship for women, who often found it difficult to penetrate the field labor hierarchy founded on skill, gender, and age.

Slave women traditionally cleaned and whitened the rice by using mortar and pestle, again setting the rhythm of their work by singing and timing the striking of the pestle. Both men and women constructed the winnowing baskets they used to fan the rice, although much of the basketry women produced, made from light grasses and palmetto leaves, was used for decorative purposes. African women not only brought their skills to the colonies, but owners also believed they brought a natural immunity to malaria, often transmitted by infected mosquitoes in swampy rice fields. Some undoubtedly did, but they paid for their sickle cell trait in other ways that impaired their health and fertility (Savitt 1978; Wood 1974; Vlach 1991).

As the colonial era passed, slavery disappeared in the Northeast and Midwest, freeing almost 30,000 Black women. To the south, however, the number of female slaves grew steadily, as did slave territory. The acquisition of Florida, the Louisiana Purchase, and the annexation of Texas, along with the coercive relocation of Native Americans in the Lower South, provided a tremendous boost to the expansion of the institution of slavery. The profitable cultivation and ginning of short staple cotton, along with the development of Sea Island cotton, providing raw fiber for the expanding textile industry in Britain and the northeastern United States, almost guaranteed an increase in the number of persons enslaved. Indeed, the number of female slaves grew by 262 percent, from 750,000 in 1820 to 1.97 million in 1860. (Male slaves increased by 251 percent; see Appendix.) In Mississippi alone, where cotton was the principal crop produced, the total number of slaves went from 3,489 in 1800 to 436,631 in 1860. At the same time, the national production of cotton increased from 349,000 bales in 1819 to 3.2 million bales in 1855, a 921 percent increase (Syndor 1933). Certainly there was a fundamental connection between these three indices of an expanding economy: land, increases in the slave population, and the cotton boom.

The increase in the number of slaves during the antebellum era occurred at a time when the concentration of the southern Black population also was shifting drastically, from the Upper South to the cotton states of the Deep South. There was, for example, an overall increase of the slave population of the Lower South of 34 percent just in the decade 1850-60 while the Upper South only registered a 9.7 percent increase during those ten years. During this decade before the initiation of the Civil War, cotton states documented an enormous rise in the numbers of resident slaves: Mississippi, 40.9 percent; Texas, 213.9 percent; Alabama, 27.2 percent; Arkansas, 135.9 percent; Georgia, 21.1 percent; and Louisiana, 35.5 percent. This dramatic shift in slave concentrations suggests profound changes in the lives of slave women, thousands of whom lost husbands, sons, daughters, and other kin and friends to the domestic slave trade. The rapid "peopling" of the South in general and the cotton belt specifically meant that slaveholders were placing tremendous pressure on slave women to begin to have children earlier and to have them regularly. Procreation literally became part of their job, documented by the numerous advertisements describing slave women as "breeding wenches."

Planters experimented with cotton production for years before Eli Whitney's patent of a cotton gin in 1793 provided their means to a worthwhile profit margin. Improved technology also increased the average acreage cotton hands were responsible for cultivating. In 1820, for example, slaveholders believed a "prime hand" could successfully work six acres of cotton and eight acres of corn. Some years later, they began to expect their slaves to cultivate an average of ten acres of cotton and ten acres of corn. Field slaves confined to cotton plantations began the annual routine in the winter months, when they began clearing old fields and preparing new ones. They usually planted corn in March and began cotton planting in April. Once the cotton began to grow, there were cycles of hoeing and plowing that continued until the end of July. During the mid-summer, much of the field labor was work in the corn fields. Cotton picking began in the early fall and continued until the early winter in some southern piedmont areas.

Female slaves participated in every aspect of the routine required to produce a cotton crop, although there were some differences in some of their labor and that of males, particularly on intermediate-size (sixteen to fifty slaves) and large plantations (at least

fifty-one). When masters owned at least sixteen slaves, they usually divided them into hoe gangs and plow gangs. Generally, females did not participate in plow gangs at the same rate as males; but slave women, along with boys and elderly men, dominated the hoe gangs. Of course there were many exceptions. One traveler to Mississippi noted, for example, "Seeing a wench ploughing, I asked him [the overseer] if they usually held the plough. He replied that they often did; and that this girl did not like to hoe, and, she being a faithful hand, they let her take her choice" (Syndor 1933). On farms with small holdings, however, there were few gender-specific tasks as women were compelled to participate in every aspect of cotton production.

Everyone participated in the harvest, although on intermediate-size and large farms the number of female pickers was usually greater than that of males. Overseers and drivers forced workers to pick as quickly, carefully, and thoroughly as possible, insisting on corporal reprisals for failure to do so. Slave women and girls were tremendous pickers, sometimes even surpassing males. The average daily yield of a prime picker in the latter part of the antebellum era was about 150 pounds per day. Betsy, a slave on a Yazoo River plantation, picked 712 pounds in four days; Ellin, another woman on the same plantation, picked 818 pounds during the same time period. It was difficult and demanding physical work. One Louisiana ex-slave woman remembered in particular the hard time she had picking cotton after the temperature began to drop in the late fall: "The time I hated the most was pickin' cotton when the frost was on the bolls. My hands git sore and crack open and bleed. We'd have a li'l fire in the fields, and iffen the ones with tender hands could'nt stand it no longer, we'd urn ad warm our hands a li'l bit" (Moody 1924).

Women of all ages not only helped to grow and pick cotton but also were employed in cotton gins and as spinners and weavers. Elderly slave women especially, many who were too old to continue to do fieldwork, did this kind of labor, although among those slaveholdings with sufficient numbers of females to allow full-time diversification, younger women also held these positions. Older slave women also were plantation seamstresses and knitters. "Grandma lived in de same house wid me and us chillun," Martha Colquitt recalled, "she worked in de loom house and wove cloth all the time" (Wilkes 1987). This too was difficult labor. Although "cloth houses" provided physical shelter for female workers, mistresses who insisted on closely supervised work regimentation established routines that often exceeded the physical capabilities of elderly women who may have suffered from general fatigue and other illnesses as well as rheumatism and arthritis. Elizabeth Sparks noted, for example: "[My mistress] uster make my Aunt Caroline knit all day an' she git sleepy, she'd make her stan' up and knit. She work her so hard that she'd go to sleep standin' up an' every time her haid nod an' her knees sag, the lady'd come down across her haid with a switch" (Perdue, Barden, and Phillips 1976). A substantive number of elderly females also worked as domestics and as slave nurses to white and Black children. Others proved to be skilled midwives, doctors, and herbalists.

An important minority of native-born females performed domestic service in the homes of their owners and were rented out to others. Most slavemasters refused to employ African women in these jobs because of language and cultural barriers. Slave men also worked as domestics for wealthy slaveholders with large numbers of slaves. Most owners with limited slave property stipulated that house workers only hold such positions on a part-time basis, requiring them to be available when they were needed to do fieldwork. Those with large slaveholdings could afford full-time household servants, who often lived in special quarters in their owners' homes or just behind the master's house.

Within the slave community, some females preferred the position of domestic to fieldworker for several reasons. First, they did not have to perform the same kind of hard, physically demanding labor that tobacco, rice, sugar, or cotton cultivation required. Second, most of the work that domestics performed was inside their owners' homes, away from the heat, cold, and rain that fieldworkers sometimes faced. Also, domestic slaves usually had better material support such as food, clothing, and sometimes housing than did field slaves. Others felt that their proximity to whites would quicken the process of cultural assimilation. Some hoped that as domestic servants they would be able to establish close ties with powerful whites who might eventually emancipate or by some other means reward them.

Yet domestic slavery was still slavery. Although they fared better materially, domestic slave women also had little time to tend to the needs of their own families after they completed their assigned work quotas. They worked very long hours, for some lived in their owners' home and had to be accessible to their owners' demands twenty-four hours a day. Some women, therefore, preferred fieldwork because they followed specific schedules and could go back to their individual cabins and families at the end of the day.

Moreover, the labor that domestic slaves performed was not light, or easy, or simple. Most were not responsible for one specific job but for a combination of household tasks that could include everything from the care and nurture of several children to cleaning, gardening, butchering, cooking, serving meals, ironing, and sewing. Each of these individual tasks required experience and skill, and each was physically demanding.

Female slaves who labored in the homes of whites were subject to overwhelming amounts of emotional strain because they worked so closely with and under the constant scrutiny of white authority figures. White male owners expected their wives to create pleasant, well-run households that addressed their physical and emotional needs and those of their children. Plantation mistresses tried to obtain such results through their own efforts and the supervision of slave domestic labor that was often scarce, temporary, and part time. In order to have an efficient staff, these white women believed it necessary for their domestic slaves to assimilate white cultural domestic skills and behavior patterns. Thus, many entered into an intense period of apprenticeship, with small slave girls selected to be domestic slaves in order to create well-trained, so-called civilized, house servants. This long and emotionally wrenching process sometimes resulted in the cultural alienation of house slaves in relation to fieldworkers.

The imbalance of power inherent in the slave/master relationship inevitably resulted in psychological, physical, and moral conflict. Race, class, and gender influenced these conflicts. Female agriculturalists were under the scrutiny and direction of male drivers, who were primarily white, but sometimes Black. Ex-slave testimony and the letters and wills of planters indicate that the psychological and social distance as well as the physical difference that existed between white male supervisors and Black female laborers presented a more abusive work environment for Black female agricultural laborers than domestic servants encountered under the supervision of white females. Obviously, in a society where power and control were so related to gender and race differentiation, white males considered the threats that Black women offered to their authority a more vitally important issue than did white women. Consequently, white males' response to conflict with a Black female that they viewed as potentially undermining their authority was quick and brutal, both psychologically and physically.

"Beat women! Why sure he beat women," ex-slave Elizabeth Sparks shouted excitedly. "Beat women jes' lak men. Beat women naked an' wash 'em down in brine" (Perdue, Barden, and Phillips 1976). Statements similar to Sparks's are found throughout the written histories of female slaves. As part of the seasoning process, slave women realized that they had to complete their assigned tasks in order to escape punishment. Such reprisals usually meant verbal abuse for small offenses, but owners, overseers, and drivers did not hesitate to impose severe beatings and public humiliation on females who did not or would not complete assigned tasks or who were disrespectful in their interaction with authority figures. Sale also was an option and negative incentive that owners used to dissuade female resistance.

Slaveholding women acted similarly toward their female domestic staff. Plantation mistresses struck back at slaves they considered slow, lazy, inefficient, and ungrateful, quickly resorting to verbal and physical abuse when they felt it appropriate to do so. Often they grew attached to their domestic servants and allowed them certain favors. Yet, slaveholding mistresses were quick to assert their authority if they felt it challenged in any way. Though both slave and mistress were the same gender, race and class distinctions prevented any true bonding. Mistresses, like masters, refused to recognize the humanity of their female slaves. Indeed, much of their behavior also denied a slave woman's femininity and responsibility as a woman. Loyal slave women often were dismayed by the acts of cruelty slaveholding women imposed. Cordelia Long, for example, was a devoted house servant who felt compelled to confront her mistress after she had been beaten. Long demanded to know how her owner could treat her so cruelly after so many years of service. The slave concluded that her appeal to her mistress's conscience "was to no avail" (Still 1872).

Female slaves began working as young children. The owner's decision to initiate slave children into the plantation labor force was influenced largely by the size, physical and mental development of the child, and a perceived need for a well-trained future labor force. Females developed physically at a faster pace than did male children; thus slave girls started working at about the same time as boys but probably were more productive laborers as children and adolescents than were slave boys (Fogel 1989). Most children started performing some tasks at about age six, although others did not begin until eight or older. One ex-slave who described herself as "sickly" during her childhood recalled that she did not have to work because of her health. One day, however, her owner saw her playing and decided that she was indeed well

enough to do fieldwork. The next day he assigned her to weeding corn. "Sho' foun' what fiel' work was about arter dat," she concluded. "Guess I was 'bout ten years old" (Perdue, Barden, and Phillips 1976). Another ex-slave recalled: "Children had to go to the fiel' at six on our place. Maybe dey don't do notin' but pick up stones or tote water, dey got to get used to bein' dere. Uncle Zack ... Used to set in de shade lookin' at de fiel' an' mutter, 'Slave young, slave long' " (Perdue, Barden, and Phillips 1976).

Owners wanted to create obedient, disciplined, efficient laborers who knew the work routine and the punishment for not adhering to it. Thus, they were quite interested in the early socialization of slave children as laborers. Slave girls selected to be agricultural workers not only picked up stones, pulled weeds, and carried water but also learned to care for livestock and fowl and performed other tasks such as collecting fallen fruit and nuts and picking berries for their owners' tables. Slave children on tobacco farms also were responsible for pulling horn worms from tobacco leaves. Girls on cotton farms and plantations helped their mothers pick cotton and also worked in trash gangs composed of children, older slaves, pregnant women, and others who were physically weak. An ex-slave who had lived on a wheat plantation recalled that the children, boys and girls, had to stack the bound wheat during harvest. Female children on other farms were responsible for the care of livestock and had to keep the animals out of the crops.

Slave girls may have begun to perform small domestic tasks earlier than they did agricultural labor. Owners and nurses often ordered these children as early as age four to help care for young slave children. Usually slave nurses supervised their labor, although as they grew older, slave women destined to become house servants received instruction from their owners' wives and older domestic servants, who were often their female relations. These young domestics performed duties that varied according to their maturity and skill and the size of the household staff. They helped care for small white children, cleaned, served food, ran errands for white household members, and did whatever else they were asked to do.

Once slave girls began to labor and came under the direct supervision of whites, they began to suffer psychological and physical abuse similar to that endured by their mothers. It was not unusual for supervisors of slave children to punish them if they did not complete their tasks satisfactorily and/or treat their supervisors with the appropriate respect. Many ex-slaves recalled the beatings that they received as young laborers. Delia Garlic remembered that her mistress had run a hot iron up and down her arm because her baby had hurt its hand while playing with the young domestic. Armaci Adams fainted from the severe beating her owner gave her when someone killed a turkey she was responsible for raising. Owners also threatened young slaves with sale if they did not obey commands. The notion of sale and subsequent isolation from family and friends was particularly frightening to young slaves because it was common to sell slaves at an early age. Young working females also came into contact with and fell prey to the sexual aggression of white males. Some slave masters purchased adolescent females with the conscious intention of establishing sexual relationships with them. A note that George Carter's factor wrote to the wealthy Virginia bachelor in 1805 was a telling one: "Girls are more frequently for sale than Boys—would you object to a very likely one—a *virgin*—of about 14 or 15?" (George Carter letterbook, Carter family papers, Virginia Historical Society).

Contrary to the opinions of slaveowners, evidence of female performance in the fields and homes of their masters documents that they usually strove to complete assigned work quotas. The risk of sale, floggings, or material deprivation was too great for them to behave otherwise. Yet, many women still resisted being overworked when they felt exploited and abused beyond their endurance. Female slaves understood that they contributed to the financial support of their owners and expected some reward for their efforts and reasonable work conditions and quotas. Their work ethic was part of the overall moral code of slave culture that demanded an exchange of slave labor and obedience for material support, acceptable physical and emotional treatment, and some control over their intimate relations. Slaves who felt that this silent agreement had been violated resisted the demands of owners. "Our folks will work and be reasonable as any other group about it," Virginia Shepard noted. "As slaves, Negroes did some real work, but even the Negro had his limit." Recalling a painful episode of female resistance, she noted:

This woman would work, but if you drive her too hard, she'd git stubborn like a mule and quit. . . . Julian worked in the field. She was a smart strong and stubborn woman. When they got rough on her, she got rough on them and ran away in the woods. One day she ran away and hid a long time. They found her by means of bloodhounds. . . . They took her back and chained her by her leg just as though she were a dog. The band was very tight . . . and the chain

cut a round her ankle. . . . Vermin got in the wound and ate the flesh around the bone. Her back was a mass of scars (Perdue, Barden, and Phillips 1976).

Black women were tied down, faced against a tree or wall and stripped of their few pieces of clothing, as owners and overseers symbolically stripped them of their pride and femininity, evoking longlasting memories of incredible power, sadistically enforced. The object of this kind of chastisement was not just to insure future obedience but to dehumanize. The Black driver on a tobacco plantation, Issac Williams, explained why he believed his owner had brutally beaten a young "yellow girl": "He tied her across the fence, naked and whipped her severely with a paddle bored with holes, and with a switch. Then he shaved the hair off of one side of her head, and daubed cow-filth on the shaved part, to disgrace her—keep her down" (Perdue, Barden, and Phillips 1976).

Despite the fear of physical torture, perhaps sale, separation from their children, or rape, African women and their descendants continued to resist their enslavement and its implications. Some ran away. Perhaps 10 percent of fugitive slaves in the colonies were female. The proportion increased slightly during the antebellum era probably as a result of the much larger proportion of females in this population. Of the 562 runaway slaves that owners advertised for in the Huntsville, Alabama, newspapers between 1820 and 1860, for example, 15 percent were female.

Colonial slave women who escaped were different from their male slave counterparts in other ways as well. Except for the issue of nativity, most of the traits of colonial fugitive slave women remained similar to those of the antebellum era. While a significant minority of colonial male fugitives were recently imported, most female fugitives were "seasoned" or native-born women. Moreover, most fugitive slave women traveled alone or with their young children. Men, in contrast, rarely traveled with family members. Many of the women also were running to family members, trying to see loved ones from whom they had been recently separated or perhaps hoped to take along with them. Males tended to seek more permanent avenues of escape, either removing themselves to great distances or affecting anonymity in a new environment. Many more of the women who attempted to escape were described as "mulatto" than among the male fugitives. Slave women may have realized that a disproportionate number of free women of color were light-skinned and hoped to pass themselves off as one of them. Moreover, European and

American male standards of Black feminine beauty guaranteed that these women were more likely to acquire the aid of a free man if they needed to do so.

The descriptions of the "fugitive" women placed as advertisements for their capture and return in local newspapers more than adequately document many elements of a colonial slave woman's life—the abuse, material status, family and community relations, and even some personality characteristics:

> RUN away from the subscriber, a very white Mulatto wench, named ANNAS. She is thick, well made, about 5 feet high, and had on when she went away a country cloth jacket, black and white stripes, branded on the right cheek E, and on the left R, but cannot be discerned except near to her; and observing her nicely there are several cuts on the back part of her neck, and a scar upon her left side. . . . Whoever takes her up, and brings her to me . . . shall have Forty shillings reward, besides what the law allows.

> RUN away from the Subscriber, . . . a Negro Woman named JUDITH, who carries her Child with her, a little Girl at the Breast, about twelve Months old I bought her but the Day before. . . . I am not able to give a particular Description of her, but think she is middling tall, and slender, not very black, appears to be between thirty and thirty-five Years of Age, and I have been since told she is with Child. I expect, if she is not already gone back to Middlesex, she will soon endeavor to return to her former Master and some of his Neighbours.

> RUN-AWAY from the subscriber, . . . a negro wench named SCISLEY, with a child, a girl about 4 months old. She is about 5 feet 7 or 8 inches high, about 28 years of age, and very likely; when spoke to is very huffy, and is remarkable in shewing the white of her eyes. . . . She formerly lived in King and Queen County, where she now has a child, and it is probable she may have made that way. If not, I suspect she will endeavor to get to Baltimore, where she was once apprehended when run-away (Windley 1983).

Owners pursued fugitive slave women with a fierceness that these advertisements belie. They literally hunted these women, or paid others to do so, and demonstrated little mercy when they successfully found them. The point was not just to recover one's property, it was to prevent others from trying to escape. Slaveholders believed brutal and public retaliation was the best deterrent. As noted earlier, some masters meant not only to physically hurt a slave female in response to an act of resistance, but also to strike out at objects of her "femaleness," trying to destroy her sense of female identity as well as her sense of her own humanity. Consider, for example, the fate of Aunt Cheyney, a fugitive slave woman on the Kilpatrick cotton plantation in Mississippi who, as one of her owner's concubines, bore four of his children. According to Mary Reynolds, one of Cheyney's peers:

> Aunt Cheyney was jus' out of bed with a sucklin' baby one time, and she runs away. Some say that was 'nother baby of Massa's breedin'. She don't come to the house to nurse her baby, so they misses her and old Solomon gits the nigger hounds and takes her trail. They gits near her and she grabs the limb and tried to heist herself in a tree, but them dogs grab her and pull her down. The men hollers them on to her, and the dogs tore her naked and et the breasts plumb off her body. She got well and lived to be a old woman, but 'nother woman has to suck her baby, 'cause she ain't got no sign of breasts no more (Mellon 1988).

The men employed by Kilpatrick to find Cheyney let the dogs destroy her breasts, the most visible symbols of her feminine identity. They physically and psychologically harmed her and reduced her contribution to her family and community since she was no longer able to nurse her baby. No more potent lesson to slave women hoping to escape could have been rendered. The irony, of course, is that not only was the woman "ruined" for other slave men and slave children, she also ceased to be attractive to her owner or to be able to service their mulatto "suckling baby." Mary Reynolds was not exaggerating when she spoke generally of her life as a slave and a Black woman on the Kilpatrick plantation: "Slavery was the worst days that was ever seed in the world. They was things past tellin' " (Dawson 1988).

Nonetheless, slave women ran away, refused to maintain certain work quotas, talked back to authority figures, stole food, met secretly with other slaves, plotted against masters, and brought whites physical harm. The earliest records of female slave activity document patterns of resistance and rebellion that continued throughout the antebellum era. In 1777, for example, Jenny, a slave woman to John Lewis, was condemned and executed for conspiracy; the following year, Rachel, a slave of Lockey Collier, was executed for murder. Between 1819 and 1831, seventeen female slaves in the state of Virginia were found guilty of sundry crimes such as stealing and suspected arson and were transported out of the state; six were found guilty of capital crimes such as murder, conspiracy, and arson and were executed.

While these numbers seem small, one must remember that the large majority of female slave resistance was not a matter handled by local officials but by individual slaveholders. Slave women were implicated in many crimes against their owners, including poisoning, mishandling of planter children, theft, lying, spying, feigning illness, helping to hide runaways, and writing illegal passes. Hundreds, perhaps thousands, of slave women were sold because of such acts of resistance. Many more received corporal punishment on an almost daily basis.

Slave women also resisted their enslavement and that of future generations by refusing to have children. Most owners expected female slaves to be producers of laborers; some promoted long-term slave marriages, particularly if the couple proved to be amply fertile. Others went even further to insure substantial fertility rates among slave women, forcing them to have children. If, for any reason, marriages did not endure, owners wanted slave men and women to find new spouses. Buyers interested in purchasing female adolescent and adult slaves routinely inquired about their general health and their ability to have children. "Good breeding women" were highly priced and subject to the sexual exploitation of masters through the use of "good breeding men." Sometimes slaveowners promised female slaves material rewards such as larger food allowances, better clothing, or more spacious cabins if they would have children.

Some undoubtedly accepted these incentives. Yet, unless seriously threatened with sale or severe corporal punishment, many slave women did not allow whites to control this most intimate activity. Slave women used crude contraceptive methods in order to maintain control over their procreation. Owners suspected them of using contraceptives and inducing miscarriage but rarely were able to detect such. Eliza Little, for example, spoke of her master's attempts to discover information about "a slave girl who had put her child aside" (Drew 1969). The master beat several of the slaves and inquired about the incident, but he was unable to get the details of this carefully guarded secret from the slave community.

There also are isolated incidences of slave women who went even further to make certain that their children did not grow up as slaves. Perhaps the most famous case of a slave mother murdering her child is that of Margaret Garner of Kentucky, who attempted to escape with her husband, four children, and several others across the Ohio River in 1856. When discovered by slave hunters before she and her family could complete their escape, she slit the throat of one of her young children and tried to kill the others before she was subdued.

Those who did bear and raise daughters as slaves prepared them to resist dehumanization and to survive their experience. Slave kin could not afford public challenges to white authority figures and the abuse they inflicted on their daughters. Those who did so usually failed and risked greater future abuse for themselves and the girls. Parents could, however, try to prepare their offspring for a covert defense against such abuse. Slave mothers and other kin attempted to teach their daughters that the best protection against the brutalities of the slave system was for each individual slave to develop an approach to whites that was suitable to the slave's personality and the expectations of her owners. This technique for interacting with masters allowed the slave to walk the line between the position of a chattel and that of a human being.

Thus, slave girls had to learn a manner that was pleasing to owners and other white authority figures. Slaves had to demonstrate, through hard labor and public deference, that they were willing to repay owners for their "benevolence" and material support. Concurrently, slave youth had to retain enough of their sense of self-worth and humanity to permit public submission without being emotionally crushed. Female slaves had to be able to live productive, meaningful lives with their families and within their communities.

Slave kin began their attempts to teach their girls survival methods during their early childhood. They did so through children's stories, religious lessons, and example. Many tried to instill a sense of discipline with regard to labor and obedience to persons of authority through the assignment of tasks within the quarters and an insistence on "proper" behavior. According to Della Harris, slave mothers taught their children to be seen but not heard and to respect the authority of older slaves. Parents expected children to complete assigned tasks without any opposition. Slave mothers tried to teach their daughters the difference between right and wrong and other lessons of morality essential to acceptance in the slave community as well as in the world of whites. Martha Shoveley's mother, for example, taught her to help keep peace in the quarters and on the larger plantation by not meddling in other people's business.

Most believed rigid behavioral and moral standards would not only produce good citizens of the slave community but also would help them survive as slaves. A child's failure to obey her parents' orders or those of older kin and to follow established rules of behavior was met with the same type of punishment that whites would impose, a sound beating. Marriah Hines, for example, recalled that a display of disrespect for elders or other authority figures by slave children meant corporal punishment. Such youngsters would "git de breath slapped out of 'em. Your mammies didn't have to do it either," Hines continued, for "any old person would, and send you home to git another lickin' " (Perdue, Barden, and Phillips 1976).

Mothers combined their emphasis on discipline and obedience with words of encouragement and support. Attempts by owners to teach slave girls obedience, docility, submission, and hard work through harsh words and beatings were met in the slave quarters with words and acts of kindness and care that reassured these females of their worth and humanity. Secret religious services emphasized to all members of the slave community, including children, the equality of the races before their God and the slave's inevitable freedom from bondage. Slave women taught their daughters to turn to God in times of trouble and to pray for divine protection. They also believed there were other ways to relieve the stress and depression. Amanda Harris, for example, recalled that her grandmother told her that smoking a pipe helped to ease her pain. "Tain't no fun, chile," the elder explained to the adolescent. "But it's a pow'ful lot o' easement. Smoke away trouble, darter. Blow ole trouble an' worry way in smoke" (Perdue, Barden, and Phillips 1976).

Slave mothers hoped to teach their girls how to survive as individuals in a slave society, the importance of the slave family and community, and each slave's responsibility to help other slaves. These were revolutionary lessons in a society where social relations were predicated on the inherent inequality of Blacks. Young female slaves learned not to lie or steal from other slaves; to keep the secrets of the quarters from whites; to protect and hide runaways; to help sick and disabled slaves by sharing their work loads; and to give covert aid to other slaves whenever possible. Slave parents taught their girls to protect other

This group portrait of slaves in front of their cabin was taken circa 1861. [Schomburg Center]

slaves and to give them the courtesy and respect that they deserved. Ex-slave Jane Pyatt eloquently explained the basis for relations between slaves, in contrast to those between slaves and whites, when she stated: "The respect that the slaves had for their owners might have been from fear, but the real character of a slave was brought out by the respect that they had for each other. Most of the time there was no force back of the respect the slaves had for each other, and yet, they were for the most part truthful, loving and respectful to one another" (Perdue, Barden, and Phillips 1976).

Such lessons usually did not apply to their treatment of whites. Former slave woman Cornelia Carney disclosed an important credo slave girls came to learn and live by—the necessity and ability to outsmart white folks: "Niggers was too smart for white folks to get catched. White folks was sharp too, but not sharp enough to git by ole Nat" (Perdue, Barden, and Phillips 1976). When asked about the name she responded, "Nat? I don't know who he was. Old folks used to say it all the time. De meaning I git is that the niggers could always outsmart the white folks" (Perdue, Barden, and Phillips 1976). Miss Carney did not realize that "git by ole Nat" probably was a veiled reference to Nat Turner, leader of the slave rebellion in Southampton, Virginia, in August 1831, in which slaves killed sixty whites.

Perhaps the most difficult lesson for slave mothers was how to teach their daughters to avoid the sexual advances of white men and how to live with their inability to do so. They began by teaching them to respect themselves. Minnie Folkes's mother told her not to "let nobody bother yo' principle 'cause dat wuz all you had." Consequently, Minnie, whom her mother described as "a perfect lady," even refused to have sexual relations with her husband until they received her mother's approval. Many mothers did not want their daughters to become sexually active until they were married, but few mothers openly discussed the details of sex with them, preferring instead to warn their girls against getting too close or familiar with males, Black and white.

Slave parents did not want their adolescent daughters to publicly express their sexuality. As such, adult kin, especially mothers, monitored their daughters' behavior and did not allow them to spend much time alone with men. They verbally and physically chastised daughters who they believed behaved inappropriately toward males, such as dancing too closely or not wearing sufficient clothing to cover their body while in males' presence. Most specifically warned their girls to stay physically and emotionally

distant, avoiding any type of contact when possible. In so doing, these young females would avoid male attention as well as the negative responses of jealous white females who found it easier to blame Black females than their husbands for the initiation of interracial sexual acts.

It was difficult for slave mothers to enforce their moral ideals given the pressure that owners placed on young female slaves to begin to have children as soon as possible, and given the threat of white male sexual abuse. As such, there was great empathy expressed toward young female rape victims and those forced into a life of prostitution. One ex-slave, for example, expressed the sorrow he felt for a victimized slave teen when he recounted her story. His description also documents a perverse, misogynist legacy of violence and domination that some slaveholders passed on to their sons: "[Ethel Mae] told me 'bout Marsa bringing his son Levey . . . down to the cabin," the ex-slave stated. "They both took her—the father showing the son what it was all about—and she couldn't do nothing 'bout it" (Perdue, Barden, and Phillips 1976).

Many slave female teens and young adults willingly participated in sexual activity prior to marriage. It is not possible to approximate what part of the population was sexually active prior to settling into a permanent relationship, but some slave lists and church records do provide some limited documentation that premarital sexual relations did occur. Herbert Gutman argued that this type of activity was quite prevalent among antebellum slaves and was acceptable in the quarters, particularly until after the birth of a woman's first child. Yet, the limited evidence from the slave narratives indicates that slave parents certainly did not consider premarital sex appropriate behavior for their daughters, although there is no indication that children born outside of marriage were shunned. Familial acceptance of such children, however, does not document acceptance of the conditions by which the children were conceived.

Unfounded in law, though oftentimes consummated in love, slave marriages were tenuous relationships in which couples struggled to survive given the immense and divisive pressures of slave life. Slaves regarded marriage as an important commitment and tried to impress their daughters with the seriousness of the institution and the responsibilities associated with it. Married female slaves were responsible for having acquired the domestic skills that would bring comfort and care to their future families. Most of these females learned such skills while growing up, while watching and helping their mothers, other adult female kin, and white mistresses. Unfortunately, there was no apprenticeship to give these females the emotional maturity and stability they needed to help their marriages survive. Such was built on the strong characters that slave parents tried to mold in their daughters. Slave wives expected that their husbands would be able to provide additional food for their families by hunting, fishing, and gardening. Those who had an opportunity to do so should work extra hours in order to gain some income that could be used to provide extra food and clothing.

Most slaves hoped that marriages would be permanent commitments and therefore expected couples to consider well their choices for spouses before they married. Although most slaves had to ask their owners for permission to marry, it was the custom in some slave communities for the couples to seek the blessing of an authority figure within their family or community. Caroline Johnson Harris, for example, recalled that when she wanted to marry she had to go ask "Aunt Sue" for permission. Harris recalled of the elderly slave's response: "She tell us to think 'bout it hard fo' two day, 'cause marryin' was sacred in de eyes of Jesus." After reflecting for two days, Caroline and her intended, Moses, returned to Aunt Sue's, "an' say we done thought 'bout it an' still want to git married." Aunt Sue then "called all de slaves arter tasks to pray fo' de union dat God was gonna make. Pray we stay together an' have lots of chillun an' none of 'em git sol way from de parents" (Perdue, Barden, and Phillips 1976).

Owners controlled vital aspects of slave marriage, and as such their actions often meant the success or failure of these relationships. Slave masters usually preferred that their property marry someone in their holding, but there is much evidence of large numbers of "abroad" marriages in both the colonial and antebellum eras. Most resulted from the lack of available partners at one's residence. Also, ex-slaves such as Tom Epps noted that some male slaves wanted to marry females on neighboring plantations so that they could "git a pass to go visit 'em on Saddy nights" and thus broaden their slave community network and the margins of their limited physical environment. Others may have wanted to escape the pain and humiliation of witnessing the daily abuse of their wives and so preferred some physical and emotional distance.

In any case, ex-slaves recalled that owners made the final decision as to whether or not a slave could marry, when she could do so, and to whom. If the couple had the same master, there was usually no problem in gaining permission, although sometimes the owner would question each party as to his or her feelings before giving consent for the marriage. If the couple had different owners, however, they had to receive permission from both masters and usually continued to live on separate farms after the marriage.

Slave men took the initiative and informed owners of their desire to marry a particular slave woman. The preference that male slaveholders allowed male slaves with regard to choosing wives on and off their places of residence provided the structure for the practice of polygamy. Although there is evidence of only a few occurrences of such, the polygamous marital relations did survive the antebellum era. Some of the slave women involved in these kinds of marriages obviously believed them to be less than ideal. "I'se bin' married three times; de firs' time wuz in slave'ry time an' me an dat nigger jus' jumped de broom stick; dey called him Calhoun, but he wuzn't no regular husban'; he left me an' had three or four udder wives," Polly Turner Cancer of Mississippi explained (Rawick 1977).

Slave women usually married in their late teens, although there were many exceptions. Some newly married slave women automatically moved from their parental home to live with their husbands, but others remained with their parents until they began to have children. Although some slave marriages were forced, and couples suffered from the negative implications of such arrangements, many Black female ex-slaves dearly loved their husbands and cherished memories of their courting days, weddings, and marital life. "Master married me to one of the best colored men in the world," Marriah Hines noted. "I had five chillun by him" (Perdue, Barden, and Phillips 1976).

Slave marriages, like those of any group, varied in terms of quality, length, and goals. Slave women wanted longstanding, loving, affectionate, exclusive relationships with their husbands. Most did not expect that their spouses would be able to protect them from some of the most violent and abusive aspects of slave life, but hoped that they would understand the lack of choices that their wives had. Slave husbands expected the same kind of love, support, and respect from their wives. Regardless of the commitment that slave couples made to each other, the intervention of slave-owners could be devastating. The impact of white male sexual aggression toward slave wives created a great deal of tension in the relationships between slave husbands and wives. The rape of Black women was meant to be a violent and dehumanizing experience for women, and an emasculating one for men who could ill afford to interfere with such activities. Many did, and they suffered the consequences, which often meant severe beatings, murder, or permanent separation from family through long distance sale. Many slave husbands undoubtedly felt as Charles Grandy did when he spoke of the murder of a male slave who tried to protect his wife from the advances of their overseer: "Nigger ain't got no chance" (Perdue, Barden, and Phillips 1976).

Slaveholders who insisted that Black women marry or establish continual sexual relations with a man in order to become pregnant had a severe impact on slave marriages. Mollie Dawson, an ex-slave from east Texas, explained forced breeding and its implications for slaves' social and domestic life:

Co'se, mah mother and father was slavery time married darkies. Dat didn't mean nuthin' dem days, but jest raisin' mo darkies, and every slave darkie woman had ter do dat whether she wanted to or not. Dey would let her pick out a man, or a man pick him out a woman, and dey was married, and if de woman wouldn't have de man dat picks her, dey would take her ter a big stout high husky nigger somewhere and leave her a few days, jest lak dey do stock now'days, and she bettah begin raisin' chilluns, too. If she didn't, dey would works her ter death; dey say dat she no 'count and dey soon sell her.

Mah mother and father never did love each other lak dey ought to, so dey separated as soon as dey was free (Mellon 1988).

Sometimes wives also witnessed the sexual abuse of their husbands. Owners involved in slave breeding sometimes forced married slave men to have sexual relations with women other than their wives.

Some slave husbands and wives were overwhelmed with the daily threat of such problems and other incidents that challenged their right to protect their intimate relationships and families. Consequently, some responded to their anger, frustration and guilt with behavior that was destructive to their marital and familial relationships. Alcoholism, domestic violence, jealousy, mental cruelty, and adultery were internal problems that plagued and sometimes destroyed slave families. Some husbands ran away and left behind their families and domestic problems. More than a few slave couples voluntarily separated and began new marital relationships. Other wives and husbands withdrew themselves emotionally. Most, however, stayed and tried to make their relationships successful ones within the constraints that the slave society imposed.

The most devastating problem that slave couples faced, however, was the threat of owner-imposed permanent separations. Large numbers of slave couples were pulled apart as a result of the sale of one or both persons. Slave women and especially slave men age thirteen to twenty-five comprised a large percentage of slaves sold and most without their spouse or children. It was difficult, if not impossible, for slave women to retain close ties to those husbands who had been sold. Some never heard from their husbands again, others tried to retain communication by writing or having others write for them. Many such wives remained unattached for years, hoping that by some miracle they would be reunited with their spouses. Others moved on with their lives more quickly, finding some other man to love and cherish, and hopeful that they could establish nurturing stepfamilies in which to rear their children.

Childrearing was a shared responsibility in the slave quarters. Given the precariousness of the life of the slave and her family, it is not difficult to understand that the cooperation of members of the slave nuclear, step, and extended family as well as the larger slave community was quite necessary to accomplish this important social task. Parents, grandparents, step parents, older siblings, aunts, uncles, and sometimes cousins and community associates contributed to the upbringing of slave children if circumstances of the slave family deemed it necessary to do so. "I seen chillun sold off and de mammy not sold, and sometimes de mammy sold and a little baby kept on de place and give to another woman to raise. Dem white folks didn't care nothing 'bout how de slaves grieved when dey tore up a family," Katie Rowe of Arkansas commented (Mellon 1988).

Slaveowners significantly shaped the domestic relations of slaves and the childrearing experience. Their insistence on the importance of the slave mother in the slave family, particularly in regard to childrearing, for example, helped to sustain both African and European cultural traditions that slaves could draw on when deciding how to order their social world. Owners believed that slave women, as childbearers, had a natural bond with their children and, therefore, it was their responsibility, more so than the children's fathers', to care for their offspring. Some slaveowners, for example, frowned upon separating mothers from children under twelve years old. Others did not, but rarely did any owners afford fathers the same measure of consideration.

Thus, most slave children under twelve years old lived with their mothers and many did not have constant contact with their fathers. Those men who lived on neighboring farms usually could visit their families only on Sundays and holidays. Others who lived more distantly might see their children only rarely, if at all, once they left the vicinity. Slave men who were rented out usually did not see their families except during the Christmas holidays. For all of these reasons, slave mothers assumed the most significant long-term obligation to their offspring. In the absence of the father and mother, other nuclear, step, and extended family members and sometimes "fictive" kin took on the major responsibility of childrearing. Again, these substitute childrearers were usually female. Yet, given the workloads of adult slaves, one or two persons, even parents, rarely were capable of attending to all of the components of the childrearing task and, therefore, had to share these responsibilities with others. As such, the distribution of childrearing tasks among kin also was determined by the kind, amount, and seasonal quality of the work performed by family members.

Slave mothers who worked as agriculturalists, for example, probably had much more time to attend to the needs of their children after harvest and before planting season than at other times when the farm routine required a more labor intensive schedule. Likewise, those slave women who labored on wheat farms may have had more time to devote to family life than those who worked in the more demanding tobacco industry. Some domestics were allowed to bring their small children to work with them, a practice seldom available to fieldworkers. When slave mothers did need help with childrearing tasks, they usually called on older female children and nearby grandmothers and single aunts to assist with feeding young children, attending to medical needs, caring for and repairing their clothing, cleaning them, and teaching them necessary social skills such as talking, walking, dressing, and personal hygiene. This sharing of childrearing and other domestic tasks strengthened the bonds between generations of women and prepared the younger generation to one day assume the duties of those who had come before them.

White plantation mistresses and overseers' wives also helped to rear slave females, performing a variety of tasks when owners deemed it necessary. They usually provided medical attention, some moral instruction, and especially supervised the domestic work of young slave women in the owners' homes, punishing them when these girls were inefficient or disrespectful. Certainly, some slave mistresses who became emotionally attached to the young workers took an interest in their personal lives—giving them second-hand clothing, and offering advice and supervision with regard to moral behavior, or guidance in the selection of a marital partner. White women who established such relationships with favored slave girls, however, often did so with orphans. Many such mistresses were without children or did not have geographically or emotionally close relationships with their offspring. Yet, even under the most favorable of circumstances, the maternal interest that white women took in young slaves most often was perverted by antebellum racist and ethnocentric views. Still, more than a few slaveholding women freed slaves that they had been close to since the slaves' childhood. Others left special provisions in their wills to acknowledge such ties.

Male owners rarely bothered with slave children directly, except to assign an occasional task or to prescribe a punishment for misbehavior of some kind. Some masters became attached to some of their slave wards, but few were compelled by such feelings to act differently than as described above, except to occasionally give their favorites additional food, clothing, and a kind word. Unfortunately, the attachment that slaveholders developed for slave girls was more likely to be sexual in nature. Slave girls who may have been the "pets" of their owners when quite small were often the victims of white male sexual aggression as they entered adolescence. Whispered about in the quarters as well as in the white community, the consequence of white male behavior was quite visible in the large number of mulattoes identified in the slave and free Black populations of, for instance, antebellum Virginia.

Some white owners were particularly fond of and kind to slave girls who were their natural, but illegitimate, offspring. Such actions caused tremendous problems within white planter families. Most, however, denied their connection with such children and any responsibility that accrued from such. "Us niggers knowed the doctor took a Black woman quick as he did a white, and took any on his place he wanted, and he took them often. But mostly the chillun born on the place looked like niggers, . . . but he didn't give them no mind" (Mellon 1988). Yet, this ex-slave woman went on to note, her owner bought a "yaller gal" from Baton Rouge, a seamstress whose offspring he treated somewhat differently:

This yaller gal breeds so fast she gits a mess of white younguns. She larnt them fine manners and combs out they hair. Once two them goes down the hill to the dollhouse where the Kilpatrick chillun am playin'. They wants to go in the dollhouse, and one the [master's] boys say, "That's for white chillun." They say, "We ain't no niggers, 'cause we got the same daddy you has, and he comes to see us near every day and fetches us clothes and things from town. ... He is our daddy and we call him 'Daddy' when he comes to our house to see our mama."

Despite the frankness of these children, few slaves spoke openly of white parentage, and slave mothers often hesitated to disclose to their mixed offspring their paternity, given predictable reprisals from whites and within the slave community. Many exslave mulattoes painfully recalled the shame and confusion that they felt when confronted with their paternity. Some, however, accepted their heritage and hoped that it would mean an easier lifestyle, perhaps even freedom.

Unfortunately, most of the special attention that racially mixed female slaves received from white males, who may or may not have been related through blood, was the same sexual exploitation and abuse that their mothers had experienced. Most of these women learned early in their lives that tightly drawn racial lines effectively denied parental affection, responsibility, and respect. The slave offspring of white fathers usually had to rely on Black relations and stepfathers for care, acceptance, and guidance. The evidence suggests that miscegenation created situations as explosive in the slave cabins as in planters' homes, and some marital conflict, along with ill-treatment of mulatto children by Black stepparents, undoubtedly occurred.

The rearing of slave girls was a difficult task for kin. Despite the concerns and hopes of slave kin, masters owned Black slave children. Clearly, the approach to these children differed drastically from their mothers and other slaves involved in childrearing. To maintain control of their human property, slaveholders did not hesitate to preempt the authority of slave kin by assigning slave children tasks and punishing and/ or separating them from their families without parental consultation. Some even went so far as to offer slave youth protection from their mother's disciplinary tactics, overtly challenging her position and mandating that the child clearly decide between the two. Masters also chose to share the authority that they held over slave youth with slave kin, as well as with the relatives of owners, white overseers, Black drivers, and slave nurses. Nurses were a particularly important force in the lives of young slave girls, as were drivers and overseers in the lives of adolescents. Owners furthered their attempts to undermine Black women's authority in their matrifocal families by publicly treating them like children. Young slaves obviously were confronted with a significant variety of authority figures, white and Black, each with his or her own priorities, demands, and contributions to the upbringing of children. Each had an impact on the girls' physical and psychological development.

Slave parents and white owners certainly held the most important positions of authority in the lives of slave children. Yet the balance of power was both delicate and complex and could shift quite suddenly. Slave parents were the most important authority figures in the lives of young slave children, but as these girls grew older, they increasingly realized the limited authority and power that their parents held. It was undoubtedly a confusing and difficult situation for slave children, although most managed eventually to comprehend the complexities of the situation. Parents particularly resented the intrusion of white authority in the lives of their daughters, not only because it was a reminder of the power whites held over intimate concerns of slaves, but also because slave mothers perceived that the childrearing techniques and goals of whites often were harmful to their children's development into healthy, moral, psychologically sound adults. Not surprisingly, some slave mothers argued openly with their owners regarding control over their children. One contraband slave woman, for example, recalled an argument that she had with her Virginia mistress: "I said to my Missis if folks owns folks, then folks owns their own children. 'No, they don't' [her mistress responded] ... 'white folks own niggers.'" "Well," replied the slave mother, not to be outdone, "the Government owns *you* and everything" (Perdue, Barden, and Phillips 1976).

Slaveowners balked at attempts by slave kin or any other potential authority figure to retain control of the lives of Black children in opposition to their authority as masters. They were especially incensed at the notion that their authority and power on the plantation might be challenged by one they viewed as threefold inferior—Black, female, and slave. A successful challenge to their authority by a slave mother would certainly encourage other challenges.

The manner in which slave kin and white owners perceived slave female children in relation to themselves directly influenced the ways in which they treated these youths and tried to shape their development. Slave girls were an important resource to Black kin and their white guardians/owners. Despite the oppressive and inevitably painful experiences of parents rearing children as slaves, bondwomen and men loved their offspring and, consequently, invested much of their time and energy to assure their daughters' well-being. Slaves viewed their children as extensions of themselves and a continuation of kinship lines, the importance of which is indicated in the naming patterns evident among their families. Often slave mothers named their daughters for themselves as well as other relations, especially grandmothers, aunts, and sisters. Slave children were the future of the slave families and as such, parents regarded them as providers of future security. They often spoke of their daughters as persons they could depend on for love, comfort, and service when they became older because of the greater likelihood that male children would be sold away.

Slaveowners, in contrast, regarded slave children as a financial resource, as the prices of slave children document. During the latter part of the antebellum era, when the market in slaves was particularly lucrative, children were priced as high as $250 by the time they were seven, $450 at ten years old, and $500 by age fourteen. A slave female was valuable to an owner if she survived her childhood (and only about 50 to 60 percent did) and developed into an adult who was an obedient, submissive, and efficient worker who could provide her owner with labor or capital through rental or sale.

Regardless of the emphasis that owners placed on high slave fertility rates, however, many slave women had difficulty bearing children. This is not surprising given the harsh treatment they received, heavy work loads, nutritionally deficient diets and limited access to proper medical attention. Most slave women began to have children when they were nineteen or twenty years old and then, on average, had a live birth every 2.4 years. The average numbers of children slave women bore could differ considerably according to their "generation," location, the size and labor organizational patterns of the farm on which they lived, standards of material support, general health, and longevity. While slave women of the Upper South tended to have approximately five to six children, those who lived in the Lower South had slightly bigger families (Stevenson, "compassion" 1990; Steckel 1988; Fogel 1989).

The labor that slave women performed significantly affected their ability to bear healthy children, but their general material status also had considerable impact. Slave women were concerned about the quality and quantity of their diet, clothing, housing, and medical attention, often finding ways to improve or supplement their owners' provisions. While slave children of either gender usually received the same kinds of support and accommodations, their allowances began to change as they became laborers. As adults, slave women faced the reality that their owners gave them clothes that were not as protective or functional

as those males got. Many also received smaller allowances of protein in their food rations. Slave women usually could gain, if not greater medical attention, then more time off, because of the potential profit in their childbearing ability.

Masters provided slaves with few luxuries. This reality was particularly evident in the monotonous and limited food stuffs that owners rationed out weekly to their human property. Slave mothers usually nursed their infants for the first year of their lives, routinely returning to their babies two or three times during the work day, for intervals of a half an hour, to feed them. Many slaveowners relied on contemporary instruction manuals to guide them in the appropriate material support for their human property. One such manual stipulated that each slave child over two years of age and under ten was to receive a weekly food ration of one pound of bacon, one-half peck of corn meal, and that "to the above will be added milk, buttermilk, and molasses at intervals, and at all times vegetables and fresh meat occasionally." Experts also suggested that the weekly food ration for a boy or girl who worked in the fields should be the same: two and one-half pounds of bacon and one peck of corn meal. Those older children who worked indoors were to receive two pounds of bacon and one peck of corn meal per week. Instructions for slave gardens read in part: "A vegetable or kitchen garden will be established and well cultivated, so that there may be at all seasons an abundance of wholesome and nutritious vegetables for the negroes, such as cabbages, potatoes, turnips, beets, peas, beans, pumpkins."

According to the testimonies of ex-slaves and the records of planters, owners usually followed the broadest interpretation of such instructions. The staple for young slave children consisted of some bread items, usually hoecake made from corn meal, mixed with milk to produce a mush. Many masters had wooden troughs made that served as communal bowls for small children who, equipped with crude spoons made out of shell, or with only their hands, scooped up their meal. Slaveowners designated a nurse to feed small children and supervise their activities during their parents' workday. This person usually was an elderly woman, no longer capable of strenuous agricultural labor or efficient domestic service, or an older female child, perhaps a sibling of the younger children, who owners believed was still too young to be productive at other tasks. These nurses not only fed and supervised the play of young slave children, but also punished them if they were disobedient, attended to their illnesses, and supervised some of their assigned work activities when they became old enough to begin to perform small tasks. During the evening, slave children usually ate food that their mothers or some other female kin prepared. It appears that masters rarely assigned slave personnel to prepare the evening meals of slaves who lived in family units unless fieldworkers were compelled to work very late into the night.

As children grew older, small portions of meat, primarily pork, were added to their diet. Their mothers usually received about three pounds of pork per week and one peck of corn and sometimes fish, salt and molasses. Women also supplemented their diet by gathering fruit, nuts, and vegetables, and by fishing and hunting. Others were able to enhance their diets through clandestine trade with hawkers and theft from their owners.

Slaveowners provided slave girls with clothing twice a year, during the late fall and spring. Small slave children, regardless of their gender, wore simply designed, loose fitting shifts of various lengths that usually came down to their knees. These "shirt tails," as they were called, were made of cotton for summer wear and wool or flax for the winter. Most slave children did not have shoes prior to their integration into their masters' labor forces.

When slave children reached the age of about eight, they began to wear the gender differentiated clothing ascribed to adults. Masters provided slave clothing seasonally, and women received two to four dresses per year. Owners distributed shoes and coats in the winter. Masters were particularly concerned with the winter allotment of slave clothing, for they hoped that proper clothing would stave off illness and discontent. Undergarments were scarce, but some older slave children had them made out of material from sacks and cloth bags. Slave mothers had little time or material support to care for the clothing of their children, but some ex-slaves reported that they routinely washed their clothes and those of family members in the evenings and hung them before the fire to dry.

The quality and quantity of clothing that slave children wore, like their food, were determined by the attitude and wealth of their individual owners, the occupations of their slave kin, the proximity of slave kin and children to owners, and perhaps one's gender. Preadolescent and adolescent girls, for example, concerned with feminine attractiveness, paid special attention to their clothing. Yet, the clothing slaveowners provided laborers was neither attractive nor practical. Most of it was made of homespun or inexpensive cloth purchased only for slave clothing.

Slave clothing was not made in a variety of styles or colors.

The daughters of domestics, skilled laborers, or free fathers and those who were favorites of their master's family usually had better clothing than others, often receiving cast-offs or extra clothing purchased specifically for them. Skilled weavers and seamstresses gathered scraps of thread and material to make additional clothes and remake old clothing, using natural dyes and indigo to color dresses and skirts for special occasions. Yet, few were as successful as Nancy Williams, who boasted that as an adolescent she "usta change sometimes three, four times a day" and her collection of dresses included a "Junybug silk" dress that had three ruffles, which she wore with her tasseled slippers. Williams, a favorite of her owner, earned the money to provide herself with a relatively extensive wardrobe by making quilts that she sold to local whites for as much as $10 each. Her expertise as a seamstress and her imaginative skills as a designer allowed her to alter the design and color of one of her dresses several times.

Most slave girls grew up in small one- or two-room cabins. Much slave housing, particularly during the antebellum decade, consisted of a single room with a loft where older children slept, although two-room cabins were not unusual. Colonial slave housing varied somewhat, for there is evidence that African slaves in some locations were able to transfer some aspects of their culturally traditional housing styles and building materials to the colonial landscape, including thatched roofs, circular walls, and mud flooring.

In the cabins that had lofts, small children slept downstairs in the room with adults, while infants usually slept in the same bed as their mothers. Older children occupied the loft. When both males and females shared the loft, they often constructed a makeshift partition of old clothes or blankets that allowed some privacy. Slave dwellings were characteristically crowded and provided little privacy for adults or children. Dr. Richard Eppes, for example, recorded in his diary in October 1851 that the thirty-eight Negroes (twelve men, ten women, seven boys and nine girls) at his Eppes Island plantation in Charles City lived in three houses. A week later, he recorded that the thirty-three Negroes (nine men, nine women, ten boys and five girls) at his Bermuda Hundred estate lived in four houses. Eppes noted of the latter group that they were "too confined," but made no further statement as to what he would do to relieve the situation.

Most slave housing was poorly lit and ventilated. Some did have windows and doors, but many doors were missing or poorly hung. Most small wooden structures, crude in design and comfort, characteristically had hard dirt floors and cracks in the walls and ceilings that allowed rodents and insects to enter and made the buildings cold, wet, and drafty. Some women grew up in larger and more comfortable dwellings made of stone, rather than wood. Generally, the quality of slave housing was related to when the housing was built, who built it, the natural resources available for building, the location of the slave housing in relation to the owners', and the wealth of the owners.

The slave cabins routinely were hot in the summer months and cold during winter. Furniture was scarce, crude, and uncomfortable. Perhaps a chair, or a low bench, a few beds made of straw, or pallets of rags placed on the floor at night were the most that the majority of slaves could hope to put in their cabins. Some slaves living on small farms did not live separately from their owners, but instead occupied a small portion of their masters' homes. Caroline Hunter's family, for example, lived in one room at the back of her master's house. She, her parents, and three brothers "et, slep an' done ev'ything in jus' dat one room" (Perdue, Barden, and Phillips 1976).

Most slave dwellings proved to be poor shelters for both slave children and adults. These homes, and the surrounding bushes that usually served as the communal privy, often fostered the diseases so common among slaves and other residents of the rural antebellum South. The diseases slave girls and women suffered were seasonal. They were sick with respiratory illnesses during the winter months when cold weather forced them to spend much of their time indoors in close contact with others. Tuberculosis, diphtheria, colds, influenza, pneumonia, sore throats, and scarlet fever were common. As the temperatures rose in the spring, however, young slave girls running and playing outdoors were more likely to suffer with intestinal diseases contracted from drinking infected well water and through dirt infested with worms, worm larvae, and eggs from human and animal feces. Such ailments included dysentery, typhoid fever, cholera, hepatitis, and worms (hook, tape, and round). Most diseases that slaves contracted outdoors were easily spread indoors in small spaces intimately shared by several persons.

Most of these health problems were related not only to the poor housing and sanitary conditions that slaves routinely experienced but also to the poor health of pregnant slave mothers, the poor care that slave girls received during their working mothers' absence, the lack of adequate clothing and nutrition, and the crude state of medical science, particularly as practitioners, scientists, and quacks imposed it on slaves. Slave mothers took care of most of the common health problems of their daughters, such as scrapes, bites, burns, worms, and colds, but many consulted slave herbalists and white owners when concerned about the outcome of more serious illnesses.

Slaveowners were generally solicitous of the health of their young slaves. Plantation mistresses routinely checked the quarters for sick residents and treated them with their limited medical knowledge. Owners, however, rarely brought in doctors to treat slave children, reserving this expensive option for full-time laborers. Many times common but dangerous childhood ailments such as measles, whooping cough, and smallpox that occurred in epidemic proportions throughout the South concurrently affected whites and slaves in the same locale. Slave women, therefore, sometimes benefited from the professional medical attention that children of prominent white families received, for some concerned owners relied on physician prescribed treatments or some version of them in the slave quarters as well as in their homes. Yet, most owners repeatedly applied only a very limited number of crude medications for a variety of slave child ailments.

While slaveholders and their wives provided much of the medical attention slaves received, slave women and men served as the most important doctors, nurses, and midwives among slaves. Mothers and other female kin cared for the daily medical needs of their children and each other. Serious illness called for the attention of the local slave doctor or herbalist, who often used traditional medicines and medical practices originating in African cultures. Strong evidence remains to document that slaves arrived in the New World with a tremendous amount of medical knowledge, even providing curative remedies for such serious illnesses as the yaws and small pox. One eighteenth-century account of Africans in Boston, for example, stated: "That in their [African] country *grandy-many* dye of the *Small-Pox*; But now they learn This Way: People take Juice of Small-Pox; and Cutty-Skin, and Putt in a Drop . . . . by 'nd by a little Sicky, sicky: then very few little things like *Small-Pox:* and nobody dy of it; and no body have *Small-Pox* any more" (Wood 1987). Certainly Black men and women used this kind of knowledge to help their loved ones and sometimes whites as well.

The skill and knowledge of older slave women who were midwives, "baby doctors," or just wise from experience often consoled girls as they neared childbearing age. When slave girls entered puberty, they began to suffer from a number of ailments, most of them localized in their reproductive organs. Slave masters, quite aware of the kinds of debilitating illnesses slave women could have, thoroughly investigated the health of their potential chattel, rejecting those who did not seem healthy. Robert Conrad, for example, wrote to his wife during the winter of 1843 regarding a prospective purchase of a slave woman: "It is hardly worth while to write to Doct McGuire from here about the girl's health. Get him to examine her, and if likely to be sick or complaining I would not have her for nothing. . . . Be very cautious not to have a sickly negro put upon you" (Conrad family papers, Virginia Historical Society). Adolescent and adult slave females routinely complained of amenorrhea, abnormal bleeding between cycles, and abnormal vaginal discharges associated with venereal disease, tumors, and malfunctioning or damaged uteruses.

Pregnancy brought on additional discomforts such as physical weakness and dizziness, as well as the emotional upheavals that had to be endured while maintaining heavy work schedules. Often complaints warranted, and received, reprieves from very strenuous work. John Fitzgerald, for example, stated in an affidavit submitted in late 1858 that his "servant woman" Mobrina had recently suffered with some gynecological problems. "During the month of January 57," he reported, "she was sick for a day or two, I think, as she said from too great flow of Her menses." A year later, the man who rented Mobrina from Fitzgerald informed him that she had been sick and he feared the slave was pregnant. Mobrina was then "indisposed more or less from that time [April 1858] till the 5th of May [1858]" (Fitzgerald family papers, Virginia Historical Society).

Surviving documents do not reveal Mobrina's fate, or that of her child. If she survived during the next several years, she went on to live the remainder of her life as a "free" woman. Had she been questioned at some later date about her enslavement, she might have said many things—painted a variety of elusive scenarios that captured the essence of the experience for her. She may have succeeded in uncovering for her audience what bondage really meant and felt like to Angela, the "servant" who arrived in Virginia in 1619, and to the several generations of Black slave women who followed.

The experiences of these numerous generations of slaves were colored deeply by their gender. They cost less than men and their occupations were more limited in scope than those of male slaves. Thus, they

had little opportunity to earn additional income and gain control over their labor as skilled artisans or as drivers and overseers in the fields, and they received less material support than male slaves. Slave women's ability to increase the value of their masters' slaveholdings by bearing children enhanced their "price" in one sense, but detracted from it in another. Owners were torn between their perceptions not of slave women as "chattel" on the one hand and "human" on the other, but rather of slave women as "chattel," "human," and "female."

Within their own Euro-American culture schema, slaveholders regarded women, even Black women, as mothers and they acted on this identity in ways that profoundly distinguished the female slave experience from that of male slaves. Slave masters pressured many slave women to bear children on a regular basis, but they also tried to design the slave family according to their preoccupation with their construction of "mother" and their presumption of patriarchal authority within their homes and in the homes of their slave property. They believed slave women to be the natural nurturers of their children and generally assigned them this role. Slave masters took upon themselves the role of the male head of family—leader, provider, disciplinarian, owner—thus preempting, whenever they deemed it necessary, the position of the slave husband and father. Despite the slaves' definition of family as generally including husbands and fathers, slave masters fundamentally defined the slave family as a mother and her children. To the very limited extent that slaveholders were willing to "protect" slave family life, therefore, it almost always meant keeping slave mothers with young slave children in the wake of a sale; and allowing slave women to live with and care for their children on a daily basis. The additional responsibility of motherhood placed severe strains on the slave woman's life, affording her a great amount of domestic labor and restricting her resistance efforts and general mobility.

Slave women realized their experiences as "chattel" differed from those of men, and this acknowledged difference and the conditions that prescribed it were the basis for bonding among them. They found comfort as well as challenges in each other's company. They formed an imperfect community of friends, relatives, enemies, and rivals, creating their own rules of behavior and survival while establishing indices of respect, appreciation, and honor among themselves. It was through their participation in this community that slaves who also were women were able to maintain and define their femaleness in the face of the persistent, countervailing forces of gender suppression and manipulation.

APPENDIX

Population of Male and Female Slaves in the United States, 1820-1860

Year	Female	Male
1820	750,010	788,020
1830	996,220	1,012,823
1840	1,240,938	1,246,517
1850	1,601,779	1,602,534
1860	1,971,135	1,982,625

Source: *Historical Statistics of the United States, Colonial Times to 1970* (Washington, D.C.: U.S. Bureau of the Census, 1975).

BIBLIOGRAPHY

DOCUMENTS

Ball, Charles. *Slavery in the United States: A Narrative of the Life and Adventures of Charles Ball, A Black Man* ([1859] 1970); Blassingame, John, ed. *Slave Testimony: Two Centuries of Letters, Speeches, Interviews, and Autobiographies* (1977); Bleser, Carol, ed. *Secret and Sacred: The Diaries of James Henry Hammond, A Southern Slaveholder* (1988); Brown, Mary Griffiths. *Autobiography of a Female Slave* (1857); Burton, Annie L. *Memories of Childhood's Slavery Days* (1909); Catterall, Helen Tunnicliff, ed. *Judicial Cases Concerning American Slavery and the Negro* (1929); Curtin, Philip, ed. *Africa Remembered: Narratives by West Africans from the Era of the Slave Trade* (1967); Dangerfield, Henrietta G. "Our Mammy," *Southern Workman* (1901); Donnan, Elizabeth, ed. *Documents Illustrative of the History of the Slave Trade to America* (1935); Drew, Benjamin, ed. *The Refugee: A North-Side View of Slavery* (1969); Fitzpatrick, John C., ed. *The Diaries of George Washington, 1748-1799* (1925); Greene, Jack P., ed. *The Diary of Colonel Landon Carter of Sabine Hall, 1752-1778* ([1965] 1987); Guild, June E., ed. *Black Laws of Virginia: A Summary of the Legislative Acts of Virginia Concerning Negroes from Earliest Times to the Present* ([1936] 1969); Hening, William W., ed. *Statutes at Large, Being a Collection of All the Laws of Virginia* (1819-23); Jacobs, Harriet A. *Incidents in the Life of a Slave Girl* (1861); Loewenberg, Bert James and Ruth Bogin, eds. *Black Women in Nineteenth-Century American Life* (1976); Mellon, James, ed. *Bullwhip Days: The Slaves Remember, An Oral History* (1988); Olmstead, Frederick Law. *The Cotton Kingdom: A Traveller's Observations on Cotton and Slavery in the American Slave States*, ed. Arthur M. Schlesinger (1953); Perdue, Charles L., Thomas E. Barden, and Robert K. Phillips, eds. *Weevils in the Wheat: Interviews with Virginia Ex-Slaves* (1976); Porter, Dorothy, ed. *Early Negro Writing, 1760-1837* (1971); Rawick, George P., ed. *The American Slave* (1972-1979); *Putman's Monthly Magazine*, "A Slave's Story" (June 1857); Sterling, Dorothy, ed. *We Are Your Sisters: Black Women in the Nineteenth Century* (1984); Still, William, ed. *Underground Railroad, A Record of Facts, Authentic Narratives, Letters, etc.* ([1872] 1968); Swint, Henry, ed. *Dear Ones at Home: Letters from Contraband Camps* (1966); Windley, Lathan, ed. *Runaway Advertisements: A Documentary History from the 1730s to 1790*, Vol. 1: *Virginia and North Carolina* (1983); Yetman, Norman, ed. *Voices From Slavery* (1970).

BOOKS

Blassingame, John. *The Slave Community: Plantation Life in the Antebellum South* (1979); Breen, T. H. and Stephen Innes. *"Myne Owne Ground": Race and Freedom on Virginia's Eastern Shore, 1640-1676* (1980); Brouwer, Merle Gerald. "The Negro as a Slave and as a Free Black in Colonial Pennsylvania," Ph.D. diss. (1973); Curtin, Philip D. *The Atlantic Slave Trade: A Census* (1969); Essah, Patience. "Slavery and Freedom in the First State: The History of Blacks in Delaware from the Colonial Period to 1865," Ph.D. diss. (1985); Fogel, Robert. *Without Consent or Contract: The Rise and Fall of American Slavery* (1989); Fox-Genovese, Elizabeth. *Within the Plantation Household: Black and White Women of the Old South* (1988); Genovese, Eugene. *Roll, Jordan, Roll: The World the Slaves Made* (1974); Gutman, Herbert. *The Black Family in Slavery and Freedom, 1750-1925* (1976); Jones, Jacqueline. *Labor of Love, Labor of Sorrow: Black Women, Work and the Family from Slavery to the Present* (1985); Kulikoff, Allan. *Tobacco and Slaves: The Development of Southern Cultures in the Chesapeake, 1680-1800* (1986); Lebsock, Suzanne. *"A Share of Honour": Virginia Women, 1600-1945* (1984); Levine, Lawrence. *Black Culture and Black Consciousness: Afro-American Folk Thought from Slavery to Freedom* (1977); Littlefield, Daniel C. *Rice and Slaves: Ethnicity and the Slave Trade in Colonial South Carolina* (1991); Matthei, Julie. *An Economic History of Women in America: Women's Work, the Sexual Division of Labor and the Development of Capitalism* (1982); Mbiti, John S. *African Religions and Philosophy* (1970); McColley, Robert. *Slavery and Jeffersonian Virginia* (1978); Meier, August and Elliott Rudwick. *From Plantation to Ghetto: An Interpretive History of American Negroes* (1967); Moody, V. Alton. *Slavery on Louisiana Sugar Plantations* (1924); Morgan, Edmund. *American Slavery, American Freedom: The Ordeal of Colonial Virginia* (1975); Mullin, Gerald W. *Flight and Rebellion: Slave Resistance in Eighteenth-Century Virginia* (1975); Paulme, Denise. *Women of Tropical Africa*, trans. H. M. Wright ([1960] 1974); Phillips, Ulrich Bonnell. *American Negro Slavery: A Survey of the Supply, Employment and Control of Negro Labor as Determined by the Plantation Regime* ([1918] 1966); Piersen, William D. *Black Yankees: The Development of an Afro-American Subculture in Eighteenth-Century New England* (1988); Savitt, Todd. *Medicine and Slavery in Virginia: The Diseases and Health Care of Blacks in Antebellum Virginia* (1978); Sellers, James Benson. *Slavery in Alabama* (1950); Sobel, Mechal. *The World They Made Together: Black and White Values in Eighteenth-Century Virginia* (1987); Stampp, Kenneth. *The Peculiar Institution: Slavery in the Antebellum South* (1956); Stuckey, Sterling. *Slave Culture: Nationalist Theory and the Foundations of Black America* (1987); Syndor, Charles Sackett. *Slavery in Mississippi* ([1933] 1965);

Turner, Lorenzo. *Africanisms in the Gullah Dialect* (1949); Vass, Winifred. *The Bantu Speaking Heritage of the United States* (1979); Vlach, John Michael. *By the Work of Their Hands: Studies in Afro-American Folklife* (1991); Webber, Thomas L. *Deep Like the Rivers: Education in the Slave Quarter Community, 1831-1865* (1978); White, Deborah Gray. *Ar'n't I a Woman?: Female Slaves in the Plantation South* (1985); Wood, Peter. *Black Majority: Negroes in Colonial South Carolina from 1670 through the Stono Rebellion* (1974); Woodson, Carter G. and Charles H. Wesley. *The Negro in Our History* (1972); Works Progress Administration. *The Negro in Virginia* (1940).

ARTICLES

Berlin, Ira. "The Slave Trade and the Development of Afro-American Society in English Mainland North America, 1619-1775," *Southern Studies* (Summer 1981); Dunn, Richard S. "A Tale of Two Plantations: Slave Life at Mesopotamia in Jamaica and Mount Airy in Virginia, 1799 to 1828," *William and Mary Quarterly* (January 1977); Gerald-Stevenson, Emma and James Stevenson. "Tobacco Cultivation in the Carolinas," Unpublished manuscript (June 1987); Hancock, Ian. "Gullah and Barbadian-Origins and Relationships," *American Speech* (January 1980); Hatley, Tom. "Tending Our Gardens," *Southern Changes* (October/November 1984); Kiple, Kenneth F. and Virginia H. Kiple. "Slave Child Mortality: Some Nutritional Answers to a Perennial Puzzle," *Journal of Social History* (March 1977); Klein, Herbert S. "Slaves and Shipping in Eighteenth Century Virginia," *Journal of Interdisciplinary History* (Fall 1975); Kulikoff, Allan. "The Beginnings of the Afro-American Family in Maryland." In *Law, Society, and Politics in Early Maryland,* ed. Aubrey C. Land, Lois G. Carr, and Edward C. Papenfuse (1977), and "The Origins of Afro-American Society in Tidewater Maryland and Virginia, 1700 to 1790," *William and Mary Quarterly* (April 1978); Manfra, Jo Ann, and Robert R. Dykstra. "Serial Marriage and the Origins of the Black Stepfamily: The Rowanty Evidence," *Journal of American History* (June 1985); Marks, Bayly. "Skilled Blacks in Antebellum St. Mary's County, Maryland," *Journal of Southern History* (November 1987); Saxton, Martha. "Black Women's Moral Values in the Eighteenth Century Tidewater," Berkshire Conference on Women's History, New Brunswick, New Jersey (1990); Steckel, Richard. "Slave Mortality: Analysis of Evidence from Plantation Records," *Social Science History* (October 1979); Stevenson, Brenda E. "Compassion and Powerlessness: Myths and Realities of the Plantation Mistress' Relationship with Slaves," Virginia Center for the Humanities, Charlottesville (June 5, 1990), and "Southern Black Familial Discord, 1830-1865." In *In Joy and in Sorrow: Women, Family, and Culture in the Victorian South,* ed. Carol Bleser (1990); Sutch, Richard. "The Breeding of Slaves for Sale and the Westward Expansion of Slavery, 1850-1860." In *Race and Slavery in the Western Hemisphere: Quantitative Studies,* ed. Stanley Engerman and Eugene Genovese (1975); Tadman, Michael. "Slave Trading in the Ante-Bellum South: An Estimate of the Extent of the Inter-Regional Slave Trade," *Journal of American Studies* (Spring 1979); Tanner, Nancy. "Matrifocality in Indonesia and Africa and among Black Americans." In *Woman, Culture and Society,* ed. Michelle Rosaldo and Louise Lamphere (1974); Trussel, James and Richard Steckel. "The Age of Slaves at Menarche and Their First Birth," *Journal of Interdisciplinary History* (Winter 1978); Wilkes, Leslie. "The Treatment of Elderly Women in Slavery," Unpublished manuscript (November 1987); Wood, Peter. "The Impact of Smallpox on the Native Population of the Eighteenth-Century South," *New York State Journal of Medicine* (January 1987), and " 'More Like a Negro Country': Demographic Patterns in Colonial South Carolina, 1700-1740." In *Race and Slavery in the Western Hemisphere: Quantitative Studies,* ed. Stanley L. Engerman and Eugene D. Genovese (1975).

BRENDA E. STEVENSON

SLEW, JENNY (b. c. 1719)

It is commonly assumed that women did not appear as advocates before American courts until the late nineteenth century when they were allowed to enter the legal profession. However, in 1766 John Adams, later to become the second president of the United States, wrote in his diary: "5 Wednesday. Attended Court: heard the trial of an action for trespass, brought by a mulatto woman, for damages, for restraining her of her liberty. This is called suing for liberty; the first action that ever I knew of the sort, though I have heard there have been many." The mulatto woman was forty-six-year-old Jenny Slew, who in 1765 filed suit in the Massachusetts colony, claiming she had been unlawfully kidnapped and enslaved in 1762. As Adams's diary entry points out, there are records of freedom suits as early as the seventeenth century in the states of Maryland and Virginia. However, it is difficult to find many of these cases without searching through mountains of court records. The evidence of advocacy by African-Americans, and African-American women in particular, remains undiscovered unless noted in the few newspapers of the era or in the personal diaries of prominent individuals like Adams.

Slew was able to sue on her own behalf, although enslaved, because at the time Massachusetts was one of the few states that permitted slaves, considered property, not persons, under the law, to bring civil suits. She initially lost in the lower court, but prevailed a year and a half later in a higher court.

At both trials the defendant challenged Jenny Slew's legal capacity to sue, saying that she could not sue in her own name because she had been married several times previously to slaves (presumably Black men) and thus she had no legal identity separate from her husband. However, there was a 1706 state law prohibiting interracial marriages and thus there is some question whether a marriage between a free mulatto and Black slave was valid. There also is some question about the legality of marriages between enslaved individuals. The Superior Court, without explanation, refused to dismiss Slew's claim. Perhaps the explanation lies in the court's resolution of Slew's substantive claim, namely that Jenny Slew was born free because her mother was white. Counsel for Slew argued that the legal status of an individual followed the mother, so it did not matter whether Slew's father, a Black man, was free or slave. The Superior Court judges were divided on this point and as a result Jenny Slew was awarded her freedom, four pounds, and court costs.

BIBLIOGRAPHY

Johnson, Whittington B. "The Origin and Nature of African Slavery in Seventeenth Century Maryland," *Maryland Historical Magazine* (1978); Kimmel, Ross M. "Free Blacks in Seventeenth-Century Maryland," *Maryland Historical Magazine* (1976); Moore, George H. *Notes on the History of Slavery in Massachusetts* ([1866] 1968); Quarles, Benjamin. *The Negro in the Making of America* (1964); Jenny Slew, Plaintiff versus John Whipple, Defendant. "Memorandum." Court Files of Suffolk (Essex) 808 (September 1766–March 1767); Jenny Slew, Appellant versus John Whipple, Appelle. Massachusetts Superior Court of Judicature (1766-67); Williams, George W. *History of the Negro Race in America, 1619-1800* ([1883] 1968); Wroth, L. K. and H. B. Zobel, eds. *Legal Papers of John Adams*, Vol. 2. (1965); Zilversmit, Arthur. "Quok Walker, Mumbet, and the Abolition of Slavery in Massachusetts," *William and Mary Quarterly* (1968).

TAUNYA LOVELL BANKS

SLOWE, LUCY DIGGS (1885-1936)

That deans of women at Black colleges are no longer matrons, responsible only for the morals and physical well-being of their charges, is thanks to Lucy Diggs Slowe. Slowe's work at Howard University changed forever the role of deans in Black schools.

Born on July 4, 1885, Slowe was the youngest child of Henry and Fannie Slowe. She lost both of her parents at an early age, her father when she was nine months old and her mother when she was six. After her mother's death, she went to live with her aunt,

Martha Slowe Price, in Lexington, Virginia. When she was thirteen, the family moved to Baltimore, Maryland. She graduated from the Black high school in Baltimore as salutatorian in 1904 and entered Howard University.

It was during her college years that Slowe's talents as an innovator came to the fore. She was one of the founders of the first Black college sorority. It was not to be her last first. After graduation, she began teaching English in the Baltimore and Washington, D.C., public high schools. At the same time, she completed a Master's degree in English from Columbia University.

In 1919, the first Black junior high school was established in the Washington, D.C., school system. Slowe became its principal. During her time at Shaw Junior High School, she developed an in-service training system for her teachers. She induced Columbia University to offer an extension course in education for teachers at the junior high level. The course was so successful that it was attended not only by her teachers but also by the faculty of the white junior high as well.

Three years later, Slowe was hired by Howard University as dean of women; she also taught English and education. There was a new movement in college administration at the time. Such women as Sarah Sturtevant, Harriet Hayes, Esther Lloyd-Jones, and Thyrsa Amo had begun to redefine the role of the women's dean. Slowe began working to do the same at Howard. It was Slowe's idea that the dean of women should be a specialist in women's education. She was eventually very successful, and her work inspired a similar change in Black colleges around the country.

While working as a college administrator, Slowe was also active beyond the campus. In 1935, she helped organize the National Council of Negro Women and became its first secretary. She also helped found the National Association of College Women and became its first president. She worked with a number of other national organizations, such as the Young Women's Christian Association (YWCA) and the Women's International League for Peace and Freedom. The YWCA was problematic for her because, while theoretically in favor of Black participation in policymaking, it maintained separate Black branches. However, when Eva Bowles resigned in 1932 from the staff of the national YWCA because of a reorganization that she believed was a step backwards, Slowe remained and kept up the struggle.

Slowe was also a competitive tennis player, winning seventeen cups, and she sang contralto in her church choir.

Slowe's health began to suffer from her intense schedule and, in 1936, she came down with a severe case of influenza. Weakened by that illness, she died of kidney disease. Four years after her death, the women of Howard University donated a stained glass window in her honor to the University Chapel.

[See also ASSOCIATION OF DEANS OF WOMEN AND ADVISERS TO GIRLS IN NE-GRO SCHOOLS; EDUCATION.]

BIBLIOGRAPHY
DANB; NAW; NBAW.

KATHLEEN THOMPSON

SMITH, ADA *see* BRICKTOP

SMITH, AMANDA BERRY (1837-1915)

Called "the singing pilgrim" and "God's image carved in ebony" by the newspapers of her time and by those at the various camp meetings she attended, nineteenth-century evangelist Amanda Berry Smith won international acclaim as a leader of the holiness revival that inspired widespread social and religious reform across racial lines. During a forty-five-year missionary career of arduous travel on four continents, this self-educated former slave and washerwoman became a highly visible and well-respected leader despite intense opposition to women in public ministry, a crescendo of white racist violence, and the tightening grip of segregation. Her leadership and devotion to her ministry also earned her recognition as "one of the most powerful missionaries of the nineteenth century" (Dayton 1976).

Smith led revivals throughout the United States, Europe, and India; spent eight years as an independent missionary in West Africa; wrote an autobiography that has become a classic in women's literature; and founded and operated an orphanage and industrial school while continuing to speak at camp meetings and revivals throughout the country.

Although an active member of the African Methodist Episcopal (AME) Church, she spent most of her public ministry before mainly white congregations and rose to prominence through her riveting spiritual singing and stirring testimonies at national camp meetings that attracted wealthy white worshippers to summer seaside and mountain resorts. Although some AME Church leaders accused her of neglecting her own people, her example and effectiveness helped win a more prominent role for women in the AME Church, helped lay the foundations of the sanctified church, and bridged the gap that has divided the races in the Christian church well into the twentieth century.

Born a slave January 23, 1837, in Long Green, Maryland, she was the second child of Samuel and Miriam Berry. By 1840 her father had bought his family's freedom and by 1850 he had moved them to York county in southeastern Pennsylvania. Inspired by her parents' efforts to help fugitives escape from slavery and by their many references to her duty to aid her African homeland, Smith grew up with a missionary reformer's zeal.

Denied an education because of local prejudice, she learned to read and write at home, and at thirteen, as the eldest daughter in a family of eleven children, she went to work as a domestic. At seventeen she married Calvin Devine and moved with him to Lancaster county, where she experienced a religious conversion two years later. Her first baby died, but the second one, Mary, survived. Her husband's drinking led to marital problems and they had separated by the time he joined the Union army and died fighting in the South. Amanda then moved to Philadelphia and married local AME Church deacon James Henry Smith, who was twenty years her senior.

In 1865, they moved to New York and settled in Greenwich Village. Their unhappy marriage produced three children, all of whom died in infancy, two of them from tuberculosis contracted in the dank rear apartment dwelling where Amanda Berry Smith stood long hours over a washtub and ironing board trying to eke out a living. One Sunday morning in 1868, she bypassed the Sullivan Street AME Church where she was a regular member to attend Greene Street Methodist Church and hear the Reverend John Inskip preach on the second blessing of sanctification, an experience that contemporary holiness revivalists were urging for all Christians. That morning Smith received the second blessing, which she said empowered her to launch the preaching ministry that transformed her from a washerwoman to an evangelist. In 1869, the same month her husband died of stomach cancer, she began conducting revivals at AME churches in New Jersey and New York, branched out to white Methodist churches, and began attending the popular national camp meetings convened by Inskip.

At the end of her successful career as an evangelist who appeared mainly before white audiences, Amanda Berry Smith used her entire life's savings to open an orphan home and industrial school for Black children. [Schomburg Center]

In 1872, she took part in the first AME Church general conference in the South, mounting the platform with the Fisk Jubilee Singers in Nashville, Tennessee. In 1875, she became a charter member of the Women's Christian Temperance Union (WCTU) by joining the Brooklyn branch, and in 1878, Mary Coffin Johnson, long-time WCTU national secretary, invited Smith to join her in England for a series of temperance revivals. Leaving her daughter behind with friends, Smith left for what would become a twelve-year mission to England, Scotland, India, and West Africa. She spent eight of those years in Liberia promoting Western education for women and children and preaching holiness and temperance reform.

Slowed by debilitating arthritis and frequent bouts with malaria, a weakened Smith returned to the United States in 1890 and almost immediately resumed her missionary work. She wrote her autobiography, continued conducting revivals, testified before a congressional committee on the liquor traffic, re-turned to England for treatment at a sanatorium, and in 1893 settled in Chicago where her autobiography was published. Despite advancing age, she then began raising funds to open an orphan home and industrial school for Black children in Harvey, Illinois, a new temperance settlement south of Chicago. In 1899 she opened the school in a building she purchased on Jefferson Street. She subsequently bought eighteen adjoining lots. Through a wide-ranging network of supporters, including women's club organizers Ida B. Wells and Hallie Q. Brown, Wells's attorney-husband Ferdinand Barnett, local realtors, philanthropists, and church leaders, Smith managed to operate the home without an endowment or government help. She published a newsletter and continued her desperate attempts to raise funds until 1913 when failing health forced her to retire to Sebring, Florida, where a wealthy Ohio businessman, George Sebring, had built a new town with a cottage for Smith near the lake. After a series of strokes, she died February 24, 1915. Sebring shipped her body back to Chicago for an impressive funeral at Quinn Chapel, AME Church. She was buried in Homewood, Illinois. The ill-fated industrial home, wracked by debt and decaying facilities, burned down in 1918, and the surviving orphans were placed in private homes.

BIBLIOGRAPHY

AUTOBIOGRAPHIES AND BIOGRAPHIES

Andrews, William L., ed. *Sisters of the Spirit: Three Black Women's Autobiographies of the Nineteenth Century* (1986); *BDAAM*; Bragg, George F., Jr. *Men of Maryland* (1925); Brown, Hallie Q. *Homespun Heroines and Other Women of Distinction* ([1926] 1988); Cadbury, M. H. *The Life of Amanda Smith: "The African Sybil, the Christian Saint"* (1916); Dannett, Sylvia. *Profiles of Negro Womanhood* (1964-66); Dayton, Donald. *Discovering an Evangelical Heritage* (1976); Deen, Edith. *Great Women of the Christian Faith* (1959); Harvey, E., ed. *Amanda Smith: The King's Daughter* (n.d.); Loewenberg, Bert James and Ruth Bogin, eds. *Black Women in Nineteenth-Century American Life: Their Words, Their Thoughts, Their Feelings* ([1976] 1985); Majors, Monroe A. *Noted Negro Women: Their Triumphs and Activities* ([1893] 1971); *NAW*; Smith, Amanda. *An Autobiography: The Story of the Lord's Dealing with Mrs. Amanda Smith* ([1893] 1988); Taylor, Marshall W. *The Life, Travels, and Helpers of Mrs. Amanda Smith* (1886).

MANUSCRIPT COLLECTIONS

Julius Rosenwald Papers, University of Chicago, Chicago, Illinois; Booker T. Washington Papers, Library of Congress, Washington, D.C.; Ida B. Wells-Barnett Papers, University of Chicago, Chicago, Illinois.

ADRIENNE ISRAEL

SMITH, BESSIE (1894-1937)

Bessie Smith was the undisputed "Empress" of the blues in the 1920s. More than any other woman of her time, she came to symbolize African-Americans' resurgent militancy and ràcial pride. As a cultural leader, Smith assumed a role comparable to that of Jack Johnson, the first Black heavyweight champion of the world, whose defiance of white authority was legendary, and Marcus Garvey, the charismatic prophet of Black nationalism. All three were highly visible in their advocacy of Black pride and in their resistance to the unequal treatment and the inferior social status imposed on African-Americans in the United States.

Bessie Smith was born in Chattanooga, Tennessee, on April 15, 1894. Her family was large, nine in all, and very poor. Her father, William Smith, was a Baptist preacher who operated a local mission; he died soon after Bessie Smith was born. Two other brothers as well as her mother died before Smith reached her teens. Her oldest sister, Viola, took over as the nominal head of the household, and Bessie Smith went to work on the city's street corners with her younger brother Andrew. She sang for tips, while he accompanied her on guitar. During this period, Chattanooga was a rapidly growing yet rigidly segregated southern trade and transportation center; approximately half of the 30,000 inhabitants were Black. They were crowded into the city's "Negro quarter," where unsanitary living conditions, disease, unemployment, poverty, and crime were common. Most of the jobs open to African-Americans were low-paying manual or domestic jobs, and openings were scarce. The only other opportunity for lawful employment was in the segregated entertainment business. This was to be Smith's avenue of escape from the Chattanooga slums.

Bessie Smith broke into show business in her hometown at the age of eighteen with the help of her older brother, Clarence. He had earlier joined Moses Stokes's traveling minstrel troupe as a comedian, and when he returned to Chattanooga with the show in 1912 he arranged for his sister to audition for it. She was initially hired as a dancer, and she went out on the road with the troupe that same year. One of its members was the famous Ma Rainey, at the time still married to Pa Rainey. Smith and Ma Rainey struck up a close friendship that lasted for the rest of their lives. Bessie Smith recorded two of Rainey's blues standards, "Moonshine Blues" and "Boll Weevil Blues." Smith, however, was not groomed for stardom by Ma Rainey. She had been singing publicly, if not profes-sionally, for ten years before meeting Ma Rainey (the "mother of the blues"), and she toured with her briefly on only two occasions. Bessie Smith developed her own singing style through years of hard work, mostly on her own, just as she persistently made her own way in the world of show business.

In 1913, Smith relocated to Atlanta, where she soon became a fixture at Charles Bailey's 81 Theatre. Her starting salary was a mere $10 a week, but her evocative singing style brought in a deluge of tips to supplement her income. The song she was most remembered for during her years in Atlanta is "Weary Blues," a common folk blues song first published by St. Louis ragtime pianist Artie Matthews in 1915. By 1918, Smith was already a well-known headliner throughout the South and as far north as Baltimore. Two years later she became the star of her own musical troupe.

In the early 1920s, Bessie Smith moved to Philadelphia, where she performed regularly at the Standard and Dunbar theaters, as well as at Paradise Gardens, a popular nightclub in Atlantic City, New Jersey. Her initial attempts to break into the record industry were frustrated by a voice that sounded coarse by Tin Pan Alley standards and mannerisms that many considered plebeian. She auditioned material for the Emerson Record Company in 1921, but nothing was released in her name. She auditioned for Fred Hager at Okeh Records but was turned down because her voice was "too rough." Harry Pace of Black Swan Records rejected her on similar grounds. Early in 1923, however, Smith was approached by the head of the Columbia Records segregated "race" catalogue, Frank Walker. He later claimed to have first heard her singing in a Selma, Alabama, gin mill in 1917, thereby implicitly taking credit for discovering her for the record industry. Actually, both Clarence Williams and Perry Bradford were active in attempting to negotiate a recording contract for Bessie Smith before Frank Walker showed any interest in her. Williams worked as Walker's assistant and served as the intermediary in locating her, which suggests that he may have had a hand in bringing her to Walker's attention. Williams talked Smith into taking him on as her manager and then he induced her to record material that he had copyrighted. When Smith discovered how much of her earnings from Columbia Records were earmarked for Williams's wallet, she terminated her contract with him and made new arrangements directly with Walker, who then handled her recording career from 1923 to 1931.

Smith's earliest recording sessions for Columbia were in 1923. On February 11, her first session, she recorded "Downhearted Blues" and "Gulf Coast Blues." Clarence Williams's piano accompaniment, even on the piece he had copyrighted as his own, "Gulf Coast Blues," is stiff, mechanical, and uninspired. Smith's vocals, however, are quite the opposite, in spite of the primitive acoustic recording techniques then available. Her voice is both powerful and poignant, especially in her version of "Downhearted Blues." Her next session produced no real blues numbers, but instead a string of well-known vaudeville songs, including "Aggravatin' Papa," "Beale Street Mama," "Oh Daddy," and Clarence Williams's song "Baby, Won't You Please Come Home." Her undisputed masterpiece from this second session is her rendition of Porter Grainger's saucy "Tain't Nobody's Business If I Do."

By her third Columbia session, Smith had switched piano players, dumping Williams for Fletcher Henderson, probably because of the revelation of Williams's scheme to swindle her out of half of her recording fees but also because he was a mediocre pianist at best. Henderson had a shy and accommodating personal manner better suited to Smith's fiery temperament and he was a better piano player. During this session, Smith returned to familiar blues material, recording a version of her standard, "Weary Blues," which she retitled "Mama Got the Blues." In June 1923, Bessie Smith returned to the Columbia studios in New York for a fourth session, again accompanied by Fletcher Henderson on piano. A majority of the numbers she recorded were blues; among them was the well-known "Jailhouse Blues."

The downhome folk lyrics from these songs, coupled with Smith's compelling blues vocals, struck a responsive chord among the Black record-buying public. Her first Columbia record sold approximately 780,000 copies in six months. Throughout her career as a recording artist, she drew material from African-American oral tradition. It was a practice that helped to establish her strong personal bond with Black audiences; she was the carrier of their cultural heritage.

The release of Bessie Smith's first recordings gave her stage career a dramatic boost. During the rest of 1923, and well into the next year, she toured constantly. In particular, she traveled to cities that had attracted large numbers of African-American migrants during World War I—St. Louis, Detroit, Cleveland, Pittsburgh, Cincinnati, Indianapolis, Kansas City, and especially Chicago. Black people lined up around an entire city block to hear her sing the blues, just as they waited in line to buy her latest record. She was also one of the few Black performers of her era to stage shows for white audiences and was

the first Black woman to be broadcast live in concert on local radio stations in Atlanta and Memphis.

From the beginning, Smith's stage act included some dancing and an occasional husband and wife comedy routine with a male co-worker. Perry Bradford recalled that she was "a whopping good foot dancer" when he first saw her in Atlanta; at the time, she was working with a male comedian named Buzzin Burton. Still, it was neither her dancing nor her humor that brought out the crowds; it was her vocal renditions of the blues. She sang them with a passionate conviction and stage presence. Her voice was rich and resonant; she concentrated on middle octave and center tones, although she had a much greater range. Like other great Black vocalists, Smith could bend, stretch, and slur notes to achieve a desired effect. She used her voice as a jazz instrument, like the growl of a trombone. Many musicians who worked with her commented on these vocal pyrotechnics and on her ability to hold an audience spellbound.

In 1924 and 1925, Smith was back in the recording studio for a series of sessions that would prove to

When the great Bessie Smith toured the country, Black people lined up around entire city blocks to hear her sing the blues. [Schomburg Center]

be, from a musical standpoint, the best of her career. Through her association with Fletcher Henderson, she began to use members of his New York-based dance orchestra as accompanists. These were some of the most talented jazzmen in the country, and their participation in her recording sessions vastly improved the quality of her accomplishments. They included cornetist Joe Smith, trombone player Charlie Green, clarinetist Buster Bailey, saxophonists Coleman Hawkins and Don Redman—as well as the era's premier jazz musician, Louis Armstrong. In addition, she found another pianist to her liking, Fred Longshaw. These men became key figures in Smith's best backup bands during the Columbia recording sessions from 1924 to 1930.

An especially memorable musical collaboration occurred in 1924, when Bessie Smith teamed up with Charlie Green and Joe Smith for the first in a series of recordings they would make together. On two of the 1924 recordings they made with Smith, "Weeping Willow Blues" and "The Bye Bye Blues," they are featured together, and their endeavors produced an exceptional record. They create a spontaneous interplay between the two horns that embellishes the accompaniment to the extent that even Smith's vocals sound better than usual. The Empress was duly impressed; she would continue to request Green and Smith as backup musicians in her recording sessions up until the onset of the Depression. In 1925, Louis Armstrong backed up Bessie Smith in the recording studio on three separate occasions for a total of nine songs. The best titles they recorded were W. C. Handy's classic "St. Louis Blues," Ben Harney's satirical ragtime standard "You've Been a Good Old Wagon," and "Careless Love." Unfortunately, Armstrong and Smith never worked together after the 1925 recording sessions; hence, the nine Columbia releases produced in those sessions were the only collaboration of the decade's two most important Black musicians.

The blues that Smith recorded from 1925 to 1930 give equal attention to social and sexual themes. The social material she drew from the daily plight of the African-American masses, as she saw it; topics such as poverty, bootlegging, prisons and injustice, drinking and gambling, unemployment and hard times were all commonplace in her recordings. Some of her noteworthy releases include "Rent House Blues," which tells about receiving an eviction notice from the landlord, and "Workhouse Blues," which tells the story of confinement to a prison workhouse. Other prison-related material that she recorded during this period includes "Sing Sing Prison Blues," a grim

reminder of the infamous New York State penitentiary, and "Woman's Trouble Blues," a story about the unjust incarceration of a young Black woman.

Smith's biggest-selling blues number of the decade was "Backwater Blues," a song she wrote herself after seeing a flood along the Ohio River. It detailed the flood from the point of view of a female victim, who had to be evacuated from her home before it was washed away by the raging flood waters. As if a prophecy, its release coincided with the worst flooding in the history of the Mississippi River, which may have accounted for some of its extraordinary sales. Her accompanist and collaborator on "Backwater Blues" was the stride piano virtuoso James P. Johnson. Theirs was a brief but fruitful relationship, and Smith soon thereafter recorded one of his compositions, "Black Mountain Blues," a mischievous song about life in the "Negro quarters of the South." "Money Blues," "Pickpocket Blues," and "Dying Gambler Blues" deal with residents of the urban tenderloin; "Foolish Man Blues" is about homosexuality; and "Bedbug Blues" and "Washerwoman's Blues" tell two satirical stories about city life for migrant African-Americans. Her masterpiece of social protest from this period is a song she wrote entitled "Poor Man's Blues." Smith's biographer, Chris Albertson, maintained that " 'Poor Man's Blues' could have been entitled 'Black Man's Blues' " (Albertson 1975). It was a song that much of the population could identify with, regardless of whom Smith had in mind when she wrote it.

Sex was one topic that Bessie Smith always dealt with candidly. At times, she employed risqué double entendres, as she did in her recording of "Kitchen Man" and the popular "Empty Bed Blues." When she turned to the subject of her personal relationships with men, however, she made several recordings that are critical of her male partners, like "Salt Water Blues" and "Sinful Blues"—though she did record some traditional material such as "My Man" and "Honey Man." She recorded numbers like "I Ain't Gonna Play No Second Fiddle" and "I've Been Mistreated and I Don't Like It," but she also recorded songs containing a sense of newly acquired independence and freedom of choice, as in "Young Women Blues" and "Reckless Blues."

Taken as a whole, the blues lyrics immortalized by Bessie Smith had two characteristics of great significance. First, they were drawn from the Black oral tradition's repository of rural folk blues; hence, they were very familiar to African-Americans. She avoided the more commercialized material from the vaudeville stage or Tin Pan Alley, concentrating instead on verse that evoked deeply felt responses from her audiences. The second characteristic of Smith's blues lyrics was that, although they often addressed far-reaching social issues and concerns, they expressed her own feelings and experiences as a Black woman. Their individuality and emotional honesty appealed not only to African-Americans but also to certain sectors of the white population. Smith's blues verses were poetry set to music; they were like all great art in that they expressed human emotions that were universal.

Bessie Smith's personal life was full of the excesses, conflicts, and rebelliousness that she sang about with such conviction. She was married twice, and not a stranger to heartbreak. Her first husband, Earl Love, died shortly after their marriage. When she moved to Philadelphia in 1922, she met and then married Jack Gee, a night watchman who claimed he was a policeman. They separated seven years later, after a stormy and exhausting marriage that often deteriorated into angry physical brawls. During this period of her life, Bessie also had numerous lovers, both male and female. Among her known male lovers were musicians Sidney Bechet, Porter Grainger, and Lonnie Johnson, all of whom worked with her in the 1920s. Her longest-lasting, and perhaps steadiest, relationship with a man was with Richard Morgan, a Chicago-based bootlegger and patron of Black music. Morgan became a friend in 1924, during her initial visits to Chicago; he remained close to her up until her death in 1937 and was, in fact, driving her car when the accident occurred that killed her.

Smith was open with her female lovers about her bisexuality, but does not seem to have shared much of this information with the men in her life. The sexual liaisons she had with other women tended to be short-lived and relegated to a relatively secret zone of female social activity. Most often her liaisons occurred when Smith was on the road with a show and involved other women in the troupe. They lasted for the duration of the tour or until her husband discovered her indiscretions.

Bessie Smith indulged her appetites generally. She ate and drank with gusto and was especially fond of home-cooked southern food and moonshine. She was a binge drinker who often drank to forget her troubles. Alcohol sometimes brought out a volcanic rage in her, and her drinking sprees often ended in violence. To compound the problem, Smith had a penchant for the night life of the urban underworld. She made regular nocturnal ventures into tenderloin districts all over the country and was equally at home in Chattanooga, Atlanta, Harlem, Chicago, Cincinnati, and Detroit. In Chris Albertson's biography, *Bessie Smith*, her cousin, Ruby Smith, described a

notorious "buffet flat" that Smith frequented whenever she performed at Detroit's Koppin Theatre: "It was nothing but faggots and bull dykes, a real open house. Everything went on in that house—tongue baths, you name it. They called them buffet flats because buffet means everything, everything that's in life. Bessie was well known in that place" (Albertson 1975). This pattern of excess was part of Smith's chaotic lifestyle. To escape the pressures of fame, and perhaps also the painful memories of her childhood, she turned to drunken revelry, combined with sexual and culinary gratification. Whether she was attending a party in the sporting district where "the funk was flying," as she liked to put it, or holding court in the railroad car she toured the South in, the cycle of overindulgence hampered her development as a blues artist and damaged her health.

Smith became notorious for her extreme behavior. On the one hand, she could be fun-loving and generous to a fault, lavishing gifts on her companions, picking up all their bar tabs, even sending them on paid vacations. Yet on several occasions she walked out on her road shows, leaving the cast and crew without money to pay their bills, and at times she fired her employees gratuitously. She displayed remarkable courage in the face of danger. During one altercation she pursued a male attacker even after he had buried a knife in her side; another time she single-handedly repulsed a Ku Klux Klan raiding party with a barrage of scurrilous invective. She could also be a merciless bully and beat her adversaries senseless or attack them with no provocation. Great strength of character, courage, love, and will power were contradicted by deep hurt, anger, and an unremitting rage toward the society in which she lived.

With the onset of the Depression, Smith's fortunes plummeted along with those of most Black entertainers. The advent of talking motion pictures was a death blow to vaudeville in general and Black vaudeville in particular. The record industry also suffered serious setbacks. The sales of records dwindled considerably because of the overall economic decline and the gains made by radio in the entertainment business. Swing dance music, played by white orchestras, became the popular commercial music of the era, and interest in the blues waned. Bessie Smith's recording contract with Columbia was terminated in 1931. She recorded once more in 1933 at a special session arranged and paid for by John Hammond, but other than that her career as a recording artist was over. During one of her final recording sessions for Columbia, Smith made a record that was destined to become both her personal epitaph and a Depression-era classic; it was entitled "Nobody Knows You When You're Down and Out."

If Bessie Smith's final years did not yield to her the prominence and financial rewards commensurate with her vocal artistry, they were at least less turbulent and less emotionally traumatic for her than the previous decade had been. Her control of the drinking binges improved, and her relationship with Richard Morgan deepened into a loving and supportive companionship. Smith seemed to have mellowed with age, learning from her past mistakes. With the record contract gone, she found that even singing engagements in clubs were hard to secure; at times, she had to rely on Morgan for financial help. Smith continued to perform the blues up until her death, at the age of forty-three, in 1937. Her fatal automobile accident in Mississippi came at a time when her career was on the rebound.

While Bessie Smith never received official recognition in her lifetime, her important contributions to the blues idiom were eventually acknowledged by American music historians and scholars. Within African-American culture, she will always be the greatest woman blues singer, a heroine of her race who sang the common people's music like no one else. Her influence on American culture in general is impressive. More than any other Black performer in the 1920s and 1930s, she was responsible for introducing the blues into the mainstream of popular American music. If Columbia Records reaped the financial benefits of this profitable enterprise, Smith and her public at least enjoyed the cultural fruits of these endeavors. Her music was not to be a passing commercial fad; it was an enduring and permeating contribution to the fabric of American music that would change the course of the entire culture over the next decades.

BIBLIOGRAPHY

Albertson, Chris. *Bessie Smith: Empress of the Blues* (1975); Barlow, William. *Looking Up At Down: The Emergence of Blues Culture* (1989); Bradford, Perry. *Born with the Blues: His Own Story* (1965); Harrison, Daphne Duval. *Black Pearls: Blues Queens of the 1920s* (1988); Oliver, Paul. *Bessie* (1959).

DISCOGRAPHY

For a discography, see Brooks, Edward. *The Bessie Smith Companion* (1982).

WILLIAM BARLOW

SMITH, CELESTINE LOUISE (1903-1975)

Celestine Louise Smith's lifelong quest to understand the intricacies of human relationships, together with her efforts on behalf of justice and human dignity for all, took her on many different paths during her seventy-two years. The quest for answers to her personal identity began shortly after her birth in Macon, Georgia, in 1903, the daughter of Fletcher Carrol Smith (Schmitzen), a German Jew, and Viola Jane Smith, an African-American. When she was a child, people asked Celestine's mother why she gave her daughter the name Celestine, and her mother said it came from a Spanish novel. This mixing of cultural consciousness engendered in Smith a desire to heal the divisions between races and peoples, but it also confused her. As a Jungian analyst later in life, she searched for the knowledge that would help her understand the ancestral fusion that she represented.

Celestine Smith earned a Bachelor's degree from Talladega College in Talladega, Alabama, in 1925, a certificate in social work from the University of Southern California in 1942, and a doctor of education degree in marriage and family counseling from Columbia University in 1952. Later in life she received psychological analysis training at Union Theological Seminary in New York and the Divinity School at the University of Chicago.

Her career included two years of teaching in a private high school in Florence, Alabama, and serving the Young Women's Christian Association (YWCA) from 1929 to 1968: as national student secretary in the southwest; director of counseling and casework; specialist in human relations; and, for one year, director of the Lagos, Nigeria, YWCA. As a YWCA employee she worked to desegregate public schools and institutions of higher learning. She also was an administrative director of Morningside Mental Hygiene Clinic in New York City and, in her later life, a private practitioner of Jungian psychoanalysis.

Highly intelligent, jovial, aggressive and articulate, Celestine Louise Smith died on December 19, 1975, in Mount Holly, New Jersey.

BIBLIOGRAPHY

Boyd, Nancy. *Eminaries: The Overseas Work of the American YWCA 1895-1970* (1986); *New York Times.* "Celestine L. Smith" (obituary) (December 19, 1975); Pratt, Mildred. Telephone interviews with Mary Wood, Pittsburgh, Pennsylvania (September 10, 1991), and personal interview with Elizabeth Norris, YWCA of the USA, National Board Archives, New York, New York (August 29, 1991); Smith, Celestine L. Personal file. YWCA of the

USA, National Board Archives, New York, New York; Wilson, Frank T. "Celestine L. Smith: A Tribute of Remembrance," YWCA of the USA, National Board Archives, New York, New York.

MILDRED PRATT

SMITH, IDA VAN (1917-)

I believe that anything children do very young, they will probably be able to learn better and feel more at ease with than if they wait until they were my age to begin. (Ida Van Smith, 1991)

Ida Van Smith, a pilot and air flight instructor, has spent much of her adult life teaching others about the benefits of aviation and space. The youngest of three children, she grew up in a loving, sheltered environment in Lumberton, North Carolina. Her mother was an African-American, and her father had a mixed background. The family was religious and attended church services often. Ida Van went to school in Lumberton, graduated from Redstone Academy in 1934 as valedictorian, and studied at Barber Scotia Jr. College in Concord, North Carolina, before attending Shaw University. She graduated from Shaw with a major in social studies and a minor in mathematics. She taught for two years in North Carolina; then she married Edward D. Smith and moved to New York. She taught in Queens, New York, and earned a scholarship to City College of New York. She received her M.S. from that institution in 1964.

Smith's love for airplanes began when, as a young child, she was delighted by barnstorming and wing-walking exhibitions in Lumberton. Her pursuit of her dream of piloting an airplane, however, was delayed half a century. Smith raised four children and taught for several years in the New York City public schools before she enrolled for her first flying lesson. She was fifty years old and about to sign the final official papers to begin studies in a doctoral program at New York University when she drove to LaGuardia Airport and took her first lesson in a single-engine airplane. She later decided to study aviation at a small airport in Fayetteville, North Carolina, closer to her parents' home. She became a licensed pilot, instrument rated (allowed to fly during inclement weather), and ground instructor.

Smith founded the Ida Van Smith Flight Clubs in 1967 to introduce children from three through nine-

Ida Van Smith was fifty years old and about to begin studies in a doctoral program at New York University when she decided instead to learn to fly. A few years later, she founded the Ida Van Smith Flight Clubs to introduce youngsters to careers in aviation and space. [Elizabeth Freydberg]

teen to the variety of careers in aviation and space. Adults are accepted by special request. Her students have become Air Force and Navy pilots and officers, submarine navigators, and airline and private pilots.

Smith began teaching children about aviation using a stationary airplane instrument panel in her living room. She expanded her program into the public schools and started an introductory aviation class for adults at York College in Jamaica, New York. Volunteers from diverse areas of aviation give her classes tours of airplanes and airports, take her students flying, and give lectures and demonstrations that are tailored to each age group. Children in the club and their parents fly in small airplanes, seaplanes, and helicopters and visit aerospace museums and Federal Aviation Administration (FAA) installations. All members learn the controls, the functions of the instruments, and what makes a plane fly by actually sitting in the cockpit of Smith's Cessna 172.

Smith sponsors aviation workshops once a month at York College where children meet airline pilots, flight attendants, air traffic controllers, meteorologists, aircraft mechanics, and other people whose jobs are related to the aviation industry. Initially she used only personal funds to establish her flight clubs, but she now relies on corporate and private donations and volunteer efforts as well. There are now eleven Ida Van Smith Flight Clubs in New York, Texas, North Carolina, and St. Lucia.

Smith also designed an aviation-oriented coloring book for children and produced and hosted a weekly television program about aviation. Her photographs and story lines appear in the Smithsonian National Air and Space Museum with the Tuskegee Airmen's *Black Wings*, in the Pentagon, and in the International Women's Air and Space Museum in Dayton, Ohio. In 1978-79, the FAA funded aviation career programs designed by Smith for three high schools in New York and New Jersey. These programs were later adopted by the FAA.

In 1984, Smith became the first African-American woman to be inducted into the International Forest of Friendship, in recognition of her exceptional contributions to aviation. The forest was a bicentennial gift to the United States from the International Ninety-Nines (1929), an organization of women pilots, of which Amelia Earhart was cofounder and first president. The forest contains trees from the fifty states, several territories, and forty-one countries representing the location of more than 6,000 members worldwide. On special occasions a representative flag is flown next to each tree. Since her induction, Smith has sponsored the induction of Bessie Coleman (1896-1926) and Janet Harmon Bragg (1907-).

Smith and her clubs have won numerous awards for their work with inner-city youth. She has received many honors from national and international agencies in recognition of her outstanding work in aviation and her dedication to the education of children.

Over the years, Smith has produced and published five booklets on the history of the Ida Van Smith Flight Clubs. Ida Van Smith continues to speak about aviation at schools, churches, and museums throughout New York as well as other states. She also grooms at least one junior high school student annually for preparation for summer space camp.

BIBLIOGRAPHY

American Biographical Institute. *Community Leaders and Noteworthy Americans: Outstanding, Distinguished* (1975 and 1977); Arnold, Clinton M. and Raymond Eugene Peters. *Black Americans in Aviation* (1975); Congress for Racial Equality. *Profiles in Black: Biographical Sketches of 100 Living Black Unsung Heroes* (1976); Flowers, Sandra. *Women in Aviation and Space* (n.d.); Freydberg, Elizabeth Hadley. Personal interview with Ida Van Smith (February 1991); International Historical Society. *The International Who's Who in Fraternities and Sororities* (1984); International Organization of Women Pilots. *History of the Ninety-Nines* (1979); Kay, Ernest, ed., *Dictionary of International Biography: A Biographical Record of Contemporary Achievement* (1979).

ELIZABETH HADLEY FREYDBERG

Graduates of the Ida Van Smith Flight Clubs have become Air Force and Navy pilots and officers, submarine navigators, and airline and private pilots. [Elizabeth Freydberg]

SMITH, JEAN *see* YOUNG, JEAN WHEELER SMITH

SMITH, LUCIE WILMOT (b. 1861)

Lucie Wilmot Smith was a professional journalist and articulate, outspoken defender of women's rights. Unfortunately, little is known about her life.

Lucie Wilmot Smith was born in Lexington, Kentucky, on November 16, 1861. Her mother was Margaret Smith, but her father is unknown. She prob-

Acclaimed nineteenth-century journalist Lucie Wilmot Smith was an ardent supporter of woman's suffrage and Black civil rights. [Moorland-Spingarn]

ably was born into slavery, but this is far from certain. At age sixteen, Smith was supporting both herself and her mother by working as a teacher. Smith later graduated from the normal (education) school at the state university in Louisville in 1877.

After working as a teacher, Smith went on to become private secretary to the educator William J. Simmons, a position she held until 1884, when, at his suggestion, she began to write the children's column of the *American Baptist*. She enjoyed the work and soon moved on to direct the publication of *Our Women and Children*, established in Louisville in 1888. Smith edited the "Women and Women's Work" department, a section that came to reflect her strong interest in woman's suffrage and struggle for equality. Smith also was a frequent contributor to the *Baptist Journal*, published in Saint Louis by Reverend R. H. Coles; *The Journalist*, a Black newspaper published in New York City; and the acclaimed *Indianapolis Freeman*, the country's first, and at that time only, illustrated paper for a specifically Black readership. Her articles were reprinted in many papers, including the *Boston*

Advocate and the *Freeman*. Smith also held a faculty position at the University of Louisville.

Lucie Wilmot Smith was a member of the Afro-American Press Convention, several religious societies, and other national bodies. Unfortunately, almost nothing is known about her life after 1891. From what is known about her, however, it is clear she was both a determined advocate of women's rights and suffrage as well as a highly successful journalist.

BIBLIOGRAPHY

Penn, I. Garland. *The Afro-American Press and Its Editors* (1891); Smith, Lucie Wilmot. "Women as Journalists." In *The Black Press 1827-1890*, ed. Martin E. Dann ([1889] 1971).

FENELLA MACFARLANE

SMITH, MABLE LOUISE (1924-1972)

Big Maybelle was born Mable Louise Smith on May 1, 1924, in Jackson, Tennessee. She died on January 23, 1972, following a diabetic coma.

Big Maybelle's earliest musical training was in the Sanctified Church choir in her hometown of Jackson, Tennessee. Her professional career was launched when she won first prize in the Memphis Cotton Carnival Singing Contest in 1932—she was just eight years old. Later, she worked with such noted groups as the Dave Clark Band (1930s), the International Sweethearts of Rhythm (1936-40), the Christene Chapman Orchestra (1944), the Tiny Bradshaw Orchestra (1947-50), and Jimmy Witherspoon.

Big Maybelle's career developed at an interesting time. During the 1930s there was a shift from smaller ensembles to swing bands. Along with this shift came a heavier reliance on male white singers and few if any contracts and engagements for blues singers. This was also a period when recording companies attempted to focus their markets by labeling music according to the market they hoped to attract. So, the term rhythm and blues was introduced to describe artists who considered themselves to be blues singers.

Her style was greatly influenced by the legacies of such artists as Bessie Smith and Ma Rainey, singers whose music not only validated African-American women performers as professional artists, but also transformed and adapted the rhythms of southern-based blues to an urban landscape. Yet, her delivery was not jazz in the tradition of the classic female singers, or the shout of the male Kansas City singers. It was a style that relied on raw emotional power, a power that represented a combination of these various influences and one that was characteristic of the soul tradition that developed in the 1960s.

Although her recordings span a thirty-year period, she is best remembered for those done during her heyday in the 1950s. For example, while she is often remembered for *Candy* (Savoy 1195), recorded on May 20, 1956, she also charted hits with *Grabbin Blues* (Okeh 6931), recorded on January 3, 1953, *My Way Back Home* (Okeh 6955), recorded on May 30, 1953, and *My Country Man* (Okeh 7009), recorded on November 28, 1953. Other charted national hits include *Don't Pass Me By* (Rojac 14969), recorded on November 12, 1966, and *96 Tears* (Rojac 112), recorded on January 14, 1967.

She recorded eighteen 45 rpm records for a variety of labels from 1953 to 1967.

BIBLIOGRAPHY

Bruyninckx, Walter. *60 Years of Recorded Jazz, 1917-1977* (1980); *BWW*; Hart, Mary, Brenda M. Eagles and Lisa Howorth. *The Blues: A Bibliographic Guide* (1989); Hoare, Ian, ed. *The Soul Book* (1975); Mawhinney, Paul C. *Music Master: The 45 RPM Record Directory* (1982); Oliver, Paul, ed. *The Blackwell Guide to Blues Records* (1989); Rotante, Anthony. "Big Maybelle," *Record Research* (May/June 1964); Shaw, Arnold. *The World of Soul* (1971); Whitburn, Joel. *Joel Whitburn's Top Rhythm and Blues Records, 1949-1971* (1973), and *Joel Whitburn's Top Rhythm and Blues Singles, 1942-1988* (1988).

ROBERT STEPHENS

SMITH, MAMIE (1893-1946)

In 1920, when Okeh Records released Mamie Smith's "Crazy Blues," it became one of the biggest popular hits of the early 1920s, sold close to a million copies, and set off a recording boom for Black female blues singers. Mamie Smith was born Mamie Gardener in Cincinnati, Ohio, on May 26, 1893. Not much is known about her family or childhood; however, she began her career in show business at the age of ten as a dancer with the Four Dancing Mitchells, and soon thereafter left Cincinnati. By 1910 she was touring the Midwest and the East Coast as a member of the Smart Set Company, a Black minstrel troupe. In 1912, she married singer William "Smitty" Smith, and at that time changed her stage name to Smith. A year later, the couple moved to New York, and Mamie commenced her career as a cabaret dancer, singer, and pianist. Her first major break came in 1918, when she was hired by Perry Bradford, a Black songwriter and show business entrepreneur, to appear in his musical, *Made in Harlem*. Bradford was so impressed with Smith that he chose her to be the Black female artist to break the color line in the growing record industry based in New York. After her audition for Victor Records failed to make an impression, Bradford set up a session for her at Okeh Records, a small, independent label. Initially, Okeh was interested in Bradford's songs but wanted them to be recorded by the white vaudeville star Sophie Tucker. When Tucker could not make the recording sessions due to prior commitments, Mamie Smith was given the nod. Her first release for Okeh in the spring of 1920, "That Thing Called Love" and "You Can't Keep a Good Man Down," sold well enough to warrant another session later in the year. At that historic second session, she recorded "Crazy Blues," a Bradford composition she had popularized as "Harlem Blues" in the "Made in Harlem" musical. Bradford changed the name of the song to "Crazy Blues" to avoid copyright problems. Her backup band for the session, christened the Jazz Hounds, included Willie "the Lion" Smith on piano, Jimmy Dunn on cornet, and Dope Andrews on trombone—all well-known local jazz musicians. "Crazy Blues" was a phenomenal success.

The release of "Crazy Blues" catapulted Mamie Smith into the national limelight; in a matter of months, she became one of the best known female vocalists in the country. Over the next year, she made thirty more recordings for the Okeh label. In addition, she became the star attraction in a series of Black vaudeville shows that toured the country, garnering rave reviews and packing the theaters wherever they appeared. These shows included *Follow Me* (1922), *Struttin' Along* (1923), *Dixie Review* (1924), *Syncopated Revue* (1925), and *Frolicking Around* (1926). During this period of her greatest renown, she continued to record for the Okeh label, and began to record for Ajax Records (1924) and Victor Records (1926). In addition, her backup band, the Jazz Hounds, continued to attract the decade's most accomplished jazz musicians, men like pianist Fats Waller, saxophonist Coleman Hawkins, trumpeter Bubber Miley, and clarinetist Buster Bailey. Everywhere she appeared, Mamie Smith was lauded for her poise, beauty, and stage presence.

During the Depression, Mamie Smith's career slowed. She continued to record for Okeh Records up through 1931, about the time the bottom fell out of the "race" recording industry. She continued to star in Black musical revues, including the *Sun Tan Frolics*

The release of "Crazy Blues" catapulted Mamie Smith into the national limelight. It was followed by thirty more recordings on the Okeh label. [Schomburg Center]

(1929), *Fireworks of 1930, Rhumbaland Revue* (1931), and the *Yelping Hounds Revue* (1932-34). She married her third husband, Mr. Goldberg, in 1929. Her second husband had been comedian Sam Gardner, whom she married in 1920 and divorced a few years later. The highlights of her career in the 1930s were a tour of Europe in 1936 and a leading role in the 1939 film *Paradise in Harlem*, in which she sang the famous "Harlem Blues," backed up by the Lucky Millinder orchestra. Her film career continued to flourish in the early 1940s; during this period, she appeared in *Mystery in Swing* (1940), *Sunday Sinners* (1941), *Murder on Lenox Avenue* (1941), and *Because I Love You* (1943). In 1944, Mamie Smith's health began to fail her, and she was admitted to the Harlem Hospital; after a prolonged illness, she died there in the fall of 1946.

BIBLIOGRAPHY
Barlow, William. *Looking Up At Down: The Emergence of Blues Culture* (1989); *BWW*; Harrison, Daphne Duval. *Black Pearls: Blues Queens of the 1920s* (1988).

DISCOGRAPHY
For a discography, see Allen, Daniel. *Bibliography of Discographies, Vol. 2: Jazz* (1981).

WILLIAM BARLOW

SMITH, TRIXIE (1895-1943)

Trixie Smith was a theatrical performer and blues singer. Born in Atlanta, she moved to the North and established herself as a singer in vaudeville by the time she was twenty. In the 1920s and 1930s, in addition to performing and recording as a singer, she pursued an active theatrical career, appearing in musical revues and plays and in one film, *The Black King* (1932). She appears to have performed both singing and character roles.

Her recording career began in January 1922, when she recorded for Black Swan, a Black-owned record company. In February 1922, she won a blues singing contest sponsored by the Fifteenth Regiment of the New York Infantry at the Manhattan Casino in New York City. The contest helped both her recording and performing careers. After Paramount Records bought out financially troubled Black Swan, she recorded for Paramount until 1926. Her last records were made for Decca in the late 1930s. She went into semiretirement after 1940 and died suddenly in 1943.

Trixie Smith's singing voice was light and flexible, without the hard edge or the intense tone quality of other blues singers. She was an excellent performer of jazz-tinged blues and show tunes, recording with prominent jazz musicians, among them Louis Armstrong, Fletcher Henderson, and Sidney Bechet. However, the songs she wrote for herself ("Trixie's Blues," "Railroad Blues," and "Mining Camp Blues") exhibit a more traditional orientation and the ability to appeal directly to an audience, which is characteristic of the best of the blueswomen.

BIBLIOGRAPHY
Albertson, Chris. Liner notes to Ida Cox, *Blues Ain't Nothing Else But...*, Milestone MLP 2015 (1971); *BDAAM*; *BWW*; Harrison, Daphne Duval. *Black Pearls: Blues Queens of the 1920s* (1988); Hitchcock, H. Wiley and Stanley Sadie, eds. *The New Grove Dictionary of American Music* (1986); *New York Times*, "Ida Cox Is Dead: Blues Singer, 78" (November 12, 1967); Placksin, Sally. *American Women in*

Jazz, 1900 to the Present: Their Words, Lives, and Music (1982); Reitz, Rosetta. Liner notes to Ida Cox, *Wild Women Don't Have the Blues*, Rosetta Records RR 1304 (1981); Sampson, Henry T. *Blacks in Blackface: A Sourcebook of Early Black Musical Shows* (1980); Stewart-Baxter, Derrick. *Ma Rainey and the Classic Blues Singers* (1970).

DISCOGRAPHY

Trixie Smith, Collector's Classics 29, Masters of the Blues, volume 5 (n.d.); *Trixie Smith, 1922-1939*, RST Records BD-2068, Blues Documents (1989); *Blues Ain't Nothing Else But . . .*, Milestone MLP 2015 (1971); *Wild Women Don't Have the Blues*, Rosetta Records RR 1304 (1981; previously issued as *Blues for Rampart Street*, Riverside 274 [1961]).

SUZANNE FLANDREAU

SMITH, WILLIE MAE FORD (1904-)

The African-American gospel music movement of today is irrevocably linked with three names: Thomas A. Dorsey, Sallie Martin, and Willie Mae Ford Smith. These three were the leaders of a small group that met in Chicago in 1932 to organize the National Convention of Gospel Choirs and Choruses, the parent organization that brought forth such contemporary singers as the Winans, Take Six, and Shirley Caesar. Of the three leaders, the most talented singer was Smith, who could have performed European classical music as easily as gospel, which would have been gospel's loss.

Willie Mae Ford was born, one of fourteen children, in the small village of Rolling Rock, Mississippi, in 1904. As a small child, she moved with her family to Memphis, Tennessee, and when she was twelve, the family settled in St. Louis. Her father, a devout deacon in the Baptist church, worked during the week as a railroad brakeman, and her mother was a homemaker until 1928, when she opened a restaurant in one of the poorer sections of St. Louis. Smith, an eighth-grade student at the time, left school to help her mother in the restaurant, bringing her formal education to a close. Smith was not concerned with formal education because she had already chosen music as her vocation, beginning as a soloist when she was ten. In 1922, she and her three sisters organized a group to sing Black spirituals and the emerging gospel jubilee songs that were becoming popular. This group sang at the 1922 National Baptist Convention and created a sensation.

It was not until 1926, however, that Smith heard the kind of singing for which she had been searching.

At the 1926 National Baptist Convention, Artelia Hutchins of Detroit, the co-composer with Dorsey of "God Be with You," sang "Careless Soul, Why Do You Linger?," and Smith found her voice. From her Baptist background and the singing of Hutchins, Smith developed her dark contralto into a sonorous vehicle for delivering long melodic lines, executing mild embellishments, and expanding it from a whisper into a thunderous bell. She turned to the songs that she learned as a child and added the new elements she admired. In Smith's style, the hymn "What a Friend We Have in Jesus," traditionally sung in the slow and languorous eighteenth-century Baptist lining hymn manner, became a soliloquy of conviction and pride. She was the first gospel singer to add a gospel rhythm to the hymn "Blessed Assurance" and improvise the chorus in such a way that it became a sing-along melody.

In 1929, she married James Peter Smith, who owned a small moving company. Shortly after her marriage, the stock market crashed, and in order to help with the finances of the family, she began traveling to other cities to sing. She met Thomas A. Dorsey in Chicago in 1931 and was invited back to Chicago in 1932 to help with the organization of the National Convention of Gospel Choirs and Choruses. She was such a successful soloist, both in the rendition of songs and the ability to inspire audiences, that in 1936 Dorsey asked her to head the Soloists Bureau and teach gospel singing. The following year she set the standard for solo singing with her rendition of her own composition, "If You Just Keep Still." Smith served as the director of the Soloists Bureau for over forty years. She organized a chapter of the National Convention of Gospel Choirs and Choruses in St. Louis and assisted Dorsey and Sallie Martin in traveling to cities in the Midwest to organize gospel groups.

In 1939, she joined the Pentecostal congregation of the Church of God Apostolic and took on the rhythm, bounce, and percussive attacks of the Sanctified singer. She was then able to render the Baptist hymn in the so-called Watts style, or bring a church into a holy dance through her short songs. She inspired a large number of singers, the first of whom was Mahalia Jackson. Jackson decided to leave her job as a beautician after consulting with Smith. Unlike Jackson and Roberta Martin, with whom she sang for a while, Smith made very few recordings. None of these garnered much attention, and she therefore concentrated her efforts on preaching, having become an evangelist after joining the Sanctified church. She would sing and preach for a week at one church and offer singing lessons during the day. Many of her students attained the fame that eluded her. Among them were Edna Gallmon Cooke, Martha Bass (the mother of soul singer Fontella Bass), Myrtle Scott, the Oneal twins, and, perhaps her most famous student, Brother Joe May, who was the first to call her "Mother."

Smith is credited with the introduction of the "song and sermonette" form into gospel music, whereby the singer delivers a five- or ten-minute sermon before, during, or after the performance of a song.

She has appeared at the Newport Jazz Festival and Radio City Music Hall and in 1982 was celebrated in the gospel film documentary *Say Amen, Somebody*. In 1989, she was selected as one of the African-American women to be featured in Brian Lanker's collection of photographs called *I Dream a World*.

BIBLIOGRAPHY

Heilbut, Anthony. *The Gospel Sound—Good News and Bad Times* (1985); Walker, Wyatt Tee. *Somebody's Calling My Name* (1979).

HORACE CLARENCE BOYER

SMITH-ROBINSON, RUBY DORIS (1942-1967)

Ruby Doris Smith-Robinson worked with the Student Nonviolent Coordinating Committee (SNCC) from its earliest days in 1960 until her death in October 1967. She served the organization as an activist in the field and as an administrator in the Atlanta central office. She eventually succeeded Jim Forman as SNCC's executive secretary; Ruby Smith-Robinson was the only woman ever to serve in this capacity. Her SNCC colleagues realized how important she was. SNCC freedom singer Matthew Jones recalled, "You could feel her power in SNCC on a daily basis" (Jones 1989). Smith-Robinson demanded hard work and dedication from everyone around her. Jack Minnis, a member of SNCC's research staff, insisted that people could not fool her. Minnis was convinced that she had a "100 percent effective shit detector" (Minnis 1990).

This hard-nosed administrator and legendary activist was born in Atlanta, Georgia, on April 25, 1942, and she spent her childhood in Atlanta's Black Summerhill neighborhood. She was the second oldest of seven children born to Alice and J. T. Smith. The Smith children lived a comfortable existence in their separate Black world. They had strong adult support, and they had their own churches, schools, and social activities. No matter how insulated they were, however, the reality of American racism and segregation intruded from time to time. Smith-Robinson recalled her feelings about segregation in those early years. "I was conscious of my Blackness. Every young Negro growing up in the South has thoughts about the racial situation." She also remembered her reaction to the white people she came in contact with when she was a youngster. "I didn't recognize their existence, and they didn't recognize mine. . . . My only involvement was in throwing rocks at them" (Garland 1966).

In this atmosphere, young Ruby, like many young Black Americans of her generation, became convinced that change was possible. A few years later, when Ruby Smith entered Spelman College, she quickly became involved in the Atlanta student movement. She regularly picketed and protested with her colleagues who were trying to integrate Atlanta, and she soon moved from the local scene to the national arena. As early as February 1961 she became involved in activities sponsored by the fledgling SNCC. She was a bold and daring colleague, the creator of SNCC's jail no bail policy and one of the original Freedom Riders.

Because of her attitude and her actions, Ruby Doris Smith-Robinson soon became a legend. Most early SNCC members could recount at least one Ruby Smith-Robinson story. For example, Julian Bond remembered that when a delegation of SNCC staff was preparing to board a plane for Africa in the fall of 1964, an airline representative told them the plane was overbooked and asked if they would wait and take a later flight. This angered Ruby Smith-Robinson so much that without consulting the rest of the group she went and sat down in the jetway and refused to move. They were given seats on that flight. The innovative and determined spirit displayed in her activism was also part of her administrative demeanor. By 1963, she had become a full-time member of the central office staff. Then, in 1966, she was elected to the post of executive secretary. Throughout this period Ruby Smith-Robinson devoted an enormous amount of attention to SNCC, but there was another part to her life as well. She married Clifford Robinson in 1964, and they had a son, Kenneth Toure Robinson, in 1965. In the meantime, she managed to graduate from Spelman with a Bachelor's degree in physical education.

Because of her talent and commitment, Ruby Smith-Robinson was able to juggle all of these demanding roles—for a time. By January 1967, however, her health began to decline precipitously. At that time she was admitted to a hospital. In April of that year she was diagnosed with terminal cancer. She died on October 9, 1967.

BIBLIOGRAPHY

Garland, Phyl. "Builders of a New South," *Ebony* (August 1966); Jones, Matthew. Personal interview (April 24, 1989); Minnis, Jack. Personal interview (November 4, 1990).

CYNTHIA GRIGGS FLEMING

SNOW, VALAIDA (c. 1909-1956)

Valaida Snow was born in Chattanooga, Tennessee, c. 1909. Although internationally known as Queen of the Trumpet, Snow was a versatile artist who claimed talents as a dancer, singer, conductor, arranger, and composer. She began her career in the 1920s in clubs in Pennsylvania and New Jersey. In 1922, she made her debut in New York at Barron Wilkins' Harlem cabaret and showcased her versatility by dancing, singing, and playing the violin; topping the performance off with daring trumpet solos.

Snow was born into a family of musicians. Her mother tutored her on several instruments and her sisters, Alvaida, Hattie, and Lavaida, eventually became professional entertainers as well.

She toured internationally in the 1930s, 1940s and 1950s and performed with jazz greats Count Basie, Earl Hines, Jack Carter, Teddy Weatherford, Willie Lewis, and Fletcher Henderson. Her fans in Europe called her Little Louis, because of her Louis Armstrong-influenced trumpet style. She recorded more than forty titles for record companies in Denmark, England, and Sweden.

She made her Broadway debut as Mandy in *Chocolate Dandies* (1924). She later appeared in the Broadway stage shows *Rhapsody in Black* (1924) and *Blackbirds* (1934) and the films *Take It from Me* (1937), *Irresistible You*, *L'Alibi*, and *Pièges* (1939).

In 1941, when the United States entered World War II, Snow was interned in a Nazi concentration camp. She was released about a year later, in unstable health, but shortly resumed performing in theaters and clubs.

She married twice—first to dancer Ananias Berry and later to performer and producer Earle Edwards. Her last performance was a 1956 engagement at the Palace Theater in New York. She died May 30, 1956, of a cerebral hemorrhage.

BIBLIOGRAPHY

Carr, I., D. Fairweather, and B. Priestley. *Jazz: The Essential Companion* (1988); Dahl, Linda. *Stormy Weather: The Music and Lives of a Century of Jazzwomen* (1984); Duncan, Amy. "Record Guide: Jazz/Pop." *The Christian Science Monitor* (July 13, 1982); Handy, D. Antoinette. *Black Women in American Bands and Orchestras* (1981); Placksin, Sally. *American Women in Jazz, 1900 to the Present: Their Words, Lives, and Music* (1982); Sampson, Henry T. *Blacks in Blackface: A Source Book on Early Black Musical Shows* (1980).

SELECTED DISCOGRAPHY

Hot Snow: Valaida Snow, Queen of the Trumpet, Sings and Swings, Rosetta Records RR1305; *Swing Is the Thing*, World (EMI) SH354; *Valaida: High Hat, Trumpet and Rhythm*, World (EMI) SH309.

PAULETTE WALKER

SOCIAL WELFARE MOVEMENT

Black women have had a long history of struggle over social welfare services and basic survival needs. Social welfare movements, especially efforts to improve access to health care and education, were most visible from 1890 to 1950, during the period of legalized segregation in the United States. Overall, Black Americans had to find their own solutions to the poverty, ill health, and education needs of their communities. Organized Black clubwomen, many of whom were educators, laid the foundation for the social welfare movements of the twentieth century.

Both Black and white women's civic activism has been central to the creation of social welfare programs. The task was more arduous for Black women because racism and segregation meant the creation of a separate, privately funded network of health and social services for Black people. Rural and urban Black women at the turn of the twentieth century were concerned about a wide range of social welfare issues, including health care, education, housing, child care, and family life. Much of Black women's social welfare activities developed in communities surrounding southern Black educational institutions.

Club work was midway between the work of personal charity and professional institutions, and as such, influenced the direction of social welfare work during the so-called Progressive era. Black clubwomen established day nurseries and kindergartens in response to the needs of mothers in the labor force. They also opened working girls' homes to assist young Black migrants from rural areas with housing, employment information, job training, and moral instruction in order to protect them from the sexual dangers of urban areas.

Furthermore, clubwomen organized community support for the establishment of hospitals and nursing schools throughout the country. The early history of Provident Hospital and Nurses' Training School in Chicago, one of the best-studied Black hospitals, demonstrates that it was the uncompensated labor of laywomen, along with the student nurses, that sustained such institutions.

Class differences among African-Americans influenced clubwomen's work and ultimately the development of Black social welfare movements. Indeed, the insistence on diversity within Black communities was one of the most clearly articulated messages of the rising Black middle class at the turn of the twentieth century. Black middle-class women believed they had a stake in improving the circumstances of the poor because white America did not differentiate among Black people according to class status. Members of the Black middle class hoped to gain previously denied legitimacy by constructing a position for themselves as the moral superiors and leaders of poor Black people.

A Black public health movement, called the National Negro Health Movement, grew out of Black clubwomen's health work and became a catalyst for Black community organizing from 1915 to 1950. This movement, which began with annual Negro Health Week celebrations, nationalized health activities that had existed since at least the late nineteenth century. Black women, as both health professionals and layworkers, formed the backbone of the Black health movement. Although men held most formal leadership positions, women did most of the grass-roots organizing.

Black women activists not only attempted to improve Black health conditions, but also used the health care arena as a site to advance the Black civil rights struggle. In defending their right to health services, middle-class Black women and men challenged the racially segregated health care system. Middle-class Black women's organizing efforts at the community level sustained a Black health movement that targeted health improvement as a means to racial advancement. Although not a confrontational protest movement, the cumulative effect of health activism in thousands of rural and urban communities around the country was to create a mass movement.

Building on Black women's social welfare work, Black health activists tried to turn self-help ventures into state-sanctioned programs. They were not usually successful, but they nevertheless exerted sustained pressure for government accountability to Black health needs. National Negro Health Week was a coordinated form of Black social welfare organizing through which middle-class Black activists made claims on the state in a period when most Black people were without formal political and economic power. At the national level, Black activists tried to convince the U.S. Public Health Service to take over the movement. At the local level, activists organized Negro Health Week observances and negotiated with city and county agencies for social services in Black neighborhoods.

Many middle-class Black activists hoped to shape federal health and welfare policy through Black government appointments, believing that Black officials would best represent Black interests in the development and administration of government policy. Dr. Roscoe C. Brown headed the Office of Negro Health Work at the U.S. Public Health Service from 1932 to 1950, an office created by the Black public health movement. A few Black women occupied similar positions in the federal government, although only Mary McLeod Bethune headed an office. Bethune was head of the Office of Minority Affairs of the National Youth Administration from 1936 to 1944. Vinita Lewis, a Black social worker, served as a Negro child welfare specialist at the Children's Bureau from 1936 to 1945.

It was at the local level that Black women played a vital role in advocating Black entitlement to health and welfare services. Their organizations created social welfare programs previously denied to Black citizens and lobbied local governments and private organizations to integrate Black Americans into existing programs.

Black women provided free health services to the poor in their communities, in part through lobbying local governments and voluntary agencies. For example, the Savannah Federation of Colored Women's Clubs, with over 100 separate clubs by the early 1930s, created the Cuyler Children's Free Clinic. The Federation had full control and financial responsibility for the clinic. The women convinced Black and white physicians to donate their services, and they lobbied city and county commissioners to cover the costs of the clinic and the salary of a nurse. Throughout the 1920s and 1930s the clinic provided free health services to about 400 poor children each month and a Tuesday clinic for adults, mostly the unemployed or those who worked as domestics and laborers.

The neglect and denial of health and welfare services to Black Americans during the period of legalized segregation led Black women to create social welfare movements. Black women activists not only provided social welfare services to Black communities, but they turned to the state to ensure the permanency of such programs. For the most part, when middle-class Black people called on the state they received limited benefits at best, yet through their efforts they kept alive the Black struggle for equality. Furthermore, Black women's grass-roots organizing during the early twentieth century laid part of the foundation for community mobilization that was essential to the civil rights struggles of the post-World War II era.

BIBLIOGRAPHY

Beardsley, Edward H. *A History of Neglect: Health Care for Blacks and Mill Workers in the Twentieth-Century South* (1987); Giddings, Paula. *When and Where I Enter: The Impact of Black Women on Race and Sex in America* (1984); Gordon, Linda. "Black and White Visions of Welfare: Women's Welfare Activism, 1890-1945," *Journal of American History* (September 1991); Harley, Sharon and Rosalyn Terborg-Penn. *The Afro-American Woman: Struggles and Images* (1978); Hine, Darlene Clark. *Black Women in White: Racial Conflict and Cooperation in the Nursing Profession, 1890-1950* (1989), and *When the Truth Is Told: A History of Black Women's Culture and Community in Indiana, 1875-1950* (1981); Lerner, Gerda. *The Majority Finds Its Past* (1979); Neverdon-Morton, Cynthia. *Afro-American Women of the South and the Advancement of the Race, 1895-1925* (1989); Rouse, Jacqueline Anne. *Lugenia Burns Hope: Black Southern Reformer* (1989); Salem, Dorothy. *To Better Our World: Black Women in Organized Reform, 1890-1920* (1990); Scott, Anne F. "Most Invisible of All: Black Women's Voluntary Associations," *Journal of Southern History* (February 1990); Smith, Susan Lynn. " 'Sick and Tired of Being Sick and Tired': Black Women and the National Negro Health Movement, 1915-1950," Ph.D. diss. (1991).

SUSAN SMITH

SOMERVILLE, VADA WATSON
(1885-1972)

As a civil rights activist and health care professional, Vada Watson Somerville was a leader in the African-American community in Los Angeles, California, for nearly fifty years. As a member of a new generation of professional elites—whose leadership supplanted that of the pioneering Black families—she crafted myriad organizations and strategies that shaped Black Los Angeles' response to racial discrimination.

The child of migrants from Arkansas, Somerville was born in Pomona, California, on November 1, 1885. After attending public schools, Somerville won an academic scholarship from the *Los Angeles Times* in 1903 that allowed her to enroll at the University of Southern California. After leaving the university prior to graduating, from 1906 until 1912 Somerville worked as a telephone operator and bookkeeper. In 1912, she married dentist John Somerville, who encouraged her interest in dentistry. She went back to college and in 1918, Somerville received a D.D.S. degree from the University of Southern California, practicing until 1930 when she "retired to devote her time to social welfare and civic work." In 1927, Vada and John Somerville built the Hotel Somerville, an elegant, all-Black hostelry that symbolized both the possibilities of racial advancement and the realities of racial segregation.

The Somerville home was at the center of much of the reform and political activities of Black Los Angeles. Vada Somerville was one of the founders of the Los Angeles branch of the National Association for the Advancement of Colored People in 1913, the Los Angeles chapter of the National Council of Negro Women in 1938, and the Los Angeles County Human Relations Committee in 1948. Her commitment to better health care for African-American women led Somerville to establish the Pilgrim House Community Center, to service the health needs of Black families who migrated to Los Angeles during World War II, and to support the creation of Black women's service organizations like The Links and the Alpha Kappa Alpha sorority. To foster interracial cooperation, Somerville created the Stevens House of the University of California at Los Angeles, a multiracial dormitory that she hoped would prove that a new order of race relations was possible. Vada Somerville died in Los Angeles on October 28, 1972.

BIBLIOGRAPHY

Bass, Charlotta. *Forty Years: Memoirs from the Pages of a Newspaper* (1960); Beasley, Delilah. *The Negro Trail Blazers of California* (1969); Bunch, Lonnie. *Black Angelenos: The Afro-American in Los Angeles, 1850-1950* (1988); Dummett, Clifton. "A Dental Family's Impact on the Community: The Many Contributions of John and Vada Somerville," *Bulletin of the History of Dentistry* (June 1983); Somerville, J. Alexander. *Man of Color: An Autobiography of J. Alexander Somerville* (1942); Tolbert, Emory. *The UNIA and Black Los Angeles* (1980).

LONNIE BUNCH

SOUTHEASTERN ASSOCIATION OF COLORED WOMEN'S CLUBS

The Southeastern Association of Colored Women's Clubs (SACWC) originated as the Southeastern Federation of Colored Women's Clubs through the efforts of Mary McLeod Bethune. By 1919, in the midst of the Great Migration, and shortly following their heroic efforts on the homefront during World War I, southern African-American clubwomen realized the need for a regional organization within the National Federation of Colored Women's Clubs. Representing the concerns of Black women in the politically repressive Jim Crow South, SACWC united state federation leaders and plotted common strategy on important issues.

At its first conference, held at Tuskegee Institute in January 1920, SACWC announced its intention to forge a stronger organization of southern women. Bethune of Florida was elected president, Charlotte Hawkins Brown of North Carolina was named chairperson of the executive board, and Marion B. Wilkerson of South Carolina was elected vice-president-at-large. State presidents from eight states—Alabama, Florida, Georgia, North Carolina, South Carolina, Tennessee, Mississippi, and Virginia—served as vice presidents. Rebecca Stiles Taylor of the Georgia federation assumed the position of corresponding secretary, with Floridians Emma J. Colyer and Frances R. Keyser serving as parliamentarian and auditor, respectively.

Founding a regional organization enabled southern African-American women to respond to white clubwomen's expressed interest in interracial work with a coordinated plan and united leadership; SACWC officers were among the representatives who went to Memphis in 1920 to meet with white clubwomen in order to develop an agenda for interracial cooperation. The groups worked together to issue a position paper to delineate interracial problems and to propose mutual action. Controversy over its content soon erupted, however. When the white women moved to strike the plank calling for African-American suffrage in the South, SACWC issued a pamphlet titled *Southern Negro Women and Race Co-operation*, which included their demand for voting rights. When women gained the right to vote a few months later, SACWC helped coordinate Black women's efforts to register and vote in the South.

The association also planned regional campaigns conducted by the several state federations on a variety of issues. One of the leading causes from the 1920s onward was the effort to establish homes in each state for delinquent and dependent African-American girls in order to provide an alternative to their being incarcerated with adults. The strategy, which succeeded in North Carolina and Virginia but failed repeatedly in Mississippi, involved gaining the support of the state federation of white women's clubs in order to lobby state legislatures for annual appropriations. The size of these state appropriations varied, and they were sporadic, so the primary financial burden for maintaining the homes often fell on the state federations.

Rebecca Stiles Taylor of Savannah, Georgia, followed Bethune as president, serving from 1923 until 1927, when Ora Brown Stokes assumed the post for a few months. The official history of SACWC notes that from 1927 until 1940 the organization was inactive, yet others have reported that Bethune actively promoted the work of the southeastern federations during the 1930s by encouraging citizenship departments despite political repression, by urging state delegates to attend national conventions, and by providing important connections to government agencies. Perhaps during the difficult years of the Great Depression, members were unable to pay dues to support the regional association, which forced a cutback in the official structure and led Bethune to continue its activities unofficially. Alternatively, perhaps the collapse of the southeastern regional structure during this period reflects the national association's shift away from political involvement to middle-class domesticity and Bethune's interest in her new project, the National Council of Negro Women.

In a 1940 meeting at Tuskegee Institute, birthplace of the organization, a group of women, including original founders Brown and Taylor, revived the association. Under the leadership of President Bertha L. Johnson of Mississippi, SACWC restored biennial meetings in 1946. Continuing the tradition it began in 1920 as the representative for southern African-American women who wanted to work with white women for the cause of racial justice, SACWC promoted meetings between Black and white women during the decade of integration in the 1960s. From its inception on the eve of woman's suffrage, throughout most of the twentieth century, SACWC provided a united front that encouraged southern African-American women to work to solve social problems and to participate in political activities in the face of odds that might have overwhelmed individuals working alone.

BIBLIOGRAPHY

Brown, Charlotte Hawkins. Manuscript collection, Schlesinger Library, Radcliffe College, Cambridge,

Massachusetts; Hall, Jacquelyn Dowd. *Revolt against Chivalry: Jesse Daniel Ames and the Women's Campaign Against Lynching* (1974); Lerner, Gerda, ed. *Black Women in White America: A Documentary History* (1973); Neverdon-Morton, Cynthia. *Afro-American Women of the South and the Advancement of the Race, 1895-1925* (1989); Rouse, Jacqueline Anne. *Lugenia Burns Hope: Black Southern Reformer* (1989); Salem, Dorothy. *To Better Our World: Black Women in Organized Reform, 1890-1920* (1990); Wesley, Charles Harris. *The History of the National Association of Colored Women's Clubs: A Legacy of Service* (1984).

GLENDA ELIZABETH GILMORE

SOUTHERLAND, ELLEASE (1943-)

"I got a horn / You got a horn / All God's Children got a horn" describes the talent, spirituality, and sense of communality that characterize the work of Ellease Southerland. "I Got a Horn, You Got a Horn" is the title of an autobiographical essay in which Southerland describes what she most remembers growing up the oldest daughter in a family of fifteen, a family she describes as "plagued by brilliant minds on fire." This musician, poet, novelist, teacher, and ex-social worker remembers herself at five years of age singing hymns with her family—hymns such as "O Mary Don't You Weep," "Onward, Christian Soldiers," and, especially, "I Got a Horn."

Ellease Southerland was born on June 18, 1943, in Brooklyn, New York, to Ellease Dozier and Monroe Penrose Southerland. She earned a B.A. from Queens College of the City University of New York in 1965 and an M.F.A. from Columbia University in 1974. Southerland's mother was born in North Carolina and her father in Florida, as were her two oldest brothers. Southerland says that the roots of her parents in the Black South, with its lost, but identifiable, ties to Africa, defined her family's life. Her father was a minister and a baker; her mother, a homemaker. The memories of her upbringing are the materials from which her poetry and fiction are shaped.

In "I Got a Horn," Southerland tells of the family growing to a full brass band, using horns bought by her father in a pawnshop. The gift of music evident in the family takes specific form in her poetry. She won the Gwendolyn Brooks Award from *Black World* magazine in 1972 for her poem "Warlock," which is in her first volume of poetry, *The Magic Sun Spins*, published by Paul Breman in 1975.

The Magic Sun Spins takes its title from the poem "Black is," which celebrates Blackness, ending with the words, "And the magic sun is beautiful. / Beautiful / because / Black is." Three poems, "Ellease," "Two Fishing Villages," and "Nigerian Rain," celebrate Southerland's love and affinity for the people and traditions of Nigeria. "That Love Survives" addresses the lessening of pain after four years of grieving for her dead mother with whom she had a deep spiritual and psychic bond. Southerland, in the essay "I Got a Horn," describes coming of age with her mother's intimate guidance, and understanding the depth of love of her mother for her father—in spite of their problematic relationship. Southerland says she felt like a "co-mother" rather than a daughter, an observation that foreshadows her role as mother to her brothers and sisters after her mother's death from cancer at age forty-five.

Music, religion, and family solidarity are the themes most evident in Southerland's extraordinary first novel, *Let the Lion Eat Straw* (1979), in which the protagonist, Abeba Williams, born out of wedlock in the rural South, is raised by the midwife who delivered her. Abeba is eventually claimed by her natural mother and transported to Brooklyn, New York, where she experiences traditional family life with her mother and kindly stepfather. Her exceptional musical abilities are encouraged, and she graduates from high school with honors. Against her mother's wishes, Abeba abandons a promising career as a concert pianist to marry a man who will experience recurring bouts of madness; nevertheless, she will bear fifteen children and preside over a household of exuberant, creative people. The story of Abeba is a bittersweet account of Southerland's own mother. *Let the Lion Eat Straw* was a Book-of-the-Month Club alternate selection.

After the death of her mother, Southerland became a social worker in order to help support her brothers and sisters. Her second novel in progress, a sequel to the first, tentatively titled *A Feast of Fools*, introduces Abeba's daughter, who continues the family saga. (The novel is excerpted in *Breaking Ice*, an anthology edited by Terry McMillan.) In an interview, Southerland indicates that this daughter, in love with a Nigerian, is the link between African-Americans and Africans. The story is a counterbalance to *Lion*, ending with a wedding and acknowledging human need for ceremony. The novel reflects Southerland's love of Africa and her early sense of Black heritage originating in Africa. In addition to this novel, she is working on a collection of short stories entitled *Before the Cock Crows Twice*. Ellease Southerland has published short fiction and poetry in such periodicals as *Black World*, *Massachusetts Review*,

Présence Africaine, and *Journal of Black Poetry*. Her excellent critical essay, "The Influence of Voodoo on the Fiction of Zora Neale Hurston," is published in *Sturdy Black Bridges*, an anthology of essays on the literature of Black women.

Ellease Southerland lives in Jamaica, New York, and is an adjunct professor and poet-in-residence at Pace University. She says she writes so that readers can dream their own dreams, believing that her story should not be so heavy as to overwhelm the reader's story. She has traveled five times to Nigeria and once to Egypt and is interested in Egyptology and hieroglyphics, teaching people in workshop sessions to understand the principles of this ancient form and to write their names in it. The themes in her poetry and fiction speak to family, church, and community values; her forthcoming work reflects her love for Africa. Though Southerland works slowly, publishing only when she senses her work is ready, she is a major voice in contemporary Black literature.

BIBLIOGRAPHY

BABB; CA; DLB; Mitchell, Carolyn. Personal interview with Ellease Southerland (December 12, 1991); *SBAA*; Southerland, Ellease. "A Feast of Fools." In *Breaking Ice: An Anthology of Contemporary African-American Fiction*, ed. Terry McMillan (1990), and "I Got a Horn, You Got a Horn." In *A World Unsuspected: Portraits of Southern Childhood*, ed. Alex Harris (1987), and "The Influence of Voodoo on the Fiction of Zora Neale Hurston." In *Sturdy Black Bridges: Visions of Black Women in Literature*, ed. Roseann P. Bell, Bettye J. Parker, and Beverly Guy-Sheftall (1979).

CAROLYN MITCHELL

SOUTHERN NEGRO YOUTH CONFERENCE (SNYC) *see* THE LEFT

SPEARS, CHLOE *see* FREE BLACK WOMEN IN THE ANTEBELLUM NORTH

SPELMAN COLLEGE

On April 11, 1881, Sophia B. Packard and Harriet E. Giles, white missionaries from New England to the war-torn South, started a school for Black females, later called Spelman College, in the basement of Atlanta's Friendship Baptist Church. Eleven Black girls, just out of slavery and eager to acquire basic educational skills, made up the first student body of what was then called Atlanta Baptist Female Seminary.

The Spelman story began in February 1880, when Packard went to the South as a representative of the Woman's American Baptist Home Mission Society (WABHMS) of New England so that she might gain a better understanding of the plight of freedpersons. During her travels she was disturbed by the extremely difficult conditions under which Black southerners were living, particularly Black women. Educated in female seminaries and a former teacher and administrator of several outstanding New England academies, she was particularly sensitive to the lack of educational opportunities for Black girls. When she became ill after reaching New Orleans, an urgent call went out to her longtime friend, Harriet Giles, a teacher in Boston, who joined her. They returned to Boston in late April, determined to start a school in the South for Black females. Packard and Giles solicited aid from WABHMS, but their request fell on deaf ears because of the riskiness of such a venture. Persistent in their efforts, however, the women took their plan in March 1881 to the First Baptist Church of Medford, Massachusetts, where they received a pledge of $100. Encouraged, they returned to the WABHMS and solicited support, eventually receiving it, and in March 1881 they left for Georgia. After arriving in Atlanta on April 1, 1881, they contacted Dr. Shaver, a teacher at Atlanta Baptist Seminary (later Morehouse College), who took them the next day to visit Reverend Quarles, pastor of Friendship Baptist Church and the most influential Black Baptist in Georgia. On April 4, Quarles convened a meeting of local Black ministers, introducing them to Packard and Giles and encouraging them to help the women in any way that they could. Classes began a week later. The need for such a school was immediately evident; within three months the school had grown from its original eleven pupils to eighty, and within a year enrollment was at two hundred students ranging in age from 15 to 52.

In the summer of 1882, Packard and Giles went north and at the invitation of Reverend King of Cleveland, Ohio, visited his Wilson Avenue Church. King had promised the women that if they would discuss

This photograph of Spelman Seminary students, taken in the 1890s, indicates the school's appeal to students of varying ages, including older and even pregnant women. [Spelman College Archives, Atlanta, Georgia]

their school he would invite John D. Rockefeller, a member, to hear them. When the collection plate was passed, Rockefeller emptied his pockets and later pledged $250 for the building fund. This was Rockefeller's first gift to Black education, a philanthropy that would continue for many years. In 1883, the seminary moved to its new site on property known as the barracks because it had been occupied by Union soldiers during the Civil War. In 1884, the name of the school was changed to Spelman Seminary in honor of Mr. and Mrs. Harvey Buel Spelman, the parents of Mrs. John D. Rockefeller.

Meanwhile, the future of this separate school for young women was in doubt as a result of a proposal from the American Baptist Home Mission Society that it be combined with Atlanta Baptist Seminary. Packard and Giles disagreed with the proposed coeducational scheme because it was their experience

that in coeducational schools the courses were planned primarily for men, and training for women received only secondary consideration. They also believed that the special education that women required could best be accomplished apart from the distractions caused by constant companionship with men. The solution to the problem lay in the ability of WABHMS, Packard, and Giles to raise enough money to support the separate school. They began a fund-raising campaign, raising money from Northern Baptists and Georgia Black Baptists, and in April 1884 John D. Rockefeller and his family, learning of the serious financial difficulty, donated the remaining balance, thereby ensuring the school's continued existence as a separate school for girls.

The 1883 move and expansion enabled the curriculum to expand from the initial elementary normal course to include a college preparatory department that was equivalent to high school. The industrial department taught cooking, sewing, housekeeping, laundering, and printing and assumed a high priority in the curriculum because of Packard and Giles's desire to make education practical. Spelman's founders never agonized over the need to offer their Black female students a classical education. Ever mindful of the peculiar history of Black women in this country and the realities of their everyday lives, the founders' primary aim was to provide training for teachers, missionaries, and church workers. Equally important was the imparting of those practical skills that would make Black women good homemakers and mothers.

In 1886 the Nurse Training Department opened, the first Black nurse training school in the United States. In 1891 the Missionary Training Department opened. The practical and industrial nature of the Spelman curriculum was in stark contrast to the mostly classical curriculum offered at many colleges for white women during the same era. At Spelman there was a definite emphasis on training for jobs (mainly teaching and missionary work), as well as the building of Christian character. In 1897 Spelman Seminary initiated a College Department, granting its first college degrees in 1901, but the greatest portion of the students' college work was offered on the Morehouse College campus.

In 1900, Rockefeller gave $200,000 for general improvements on the campus, which included the erection of four badly needed buildings as well as a

Clenched fists reflect the assertive mood among African-American college students of the 1960s. Sisters in Blackness, a Spelman College student organization, was formed in the late 1960s. [Spelman College Archives, Atlanta, Georgia]

Trustees walk through protesting students after the 1976 lock-in to protest the board's failure to appoint a Black woman to the presidency of Spelman College. Eleven years later, in 1987, Johnnetta Betsch Cole became the first Black woman to head the school. [Spelman College Archives, Atlanta, Georgia]

power house with a complete system of heating and lighting. One of the new buildings was MacVicar Hospital, which was needed both as a practice school for the nurses' training program and as a hospital to serve Black women patients.

In 1924, Spelman Seminary became Spelman College. When Florence Matilda Read became president in 1927, her task was to develop Spelman into a strong liberal arts college. President Read's first accomplishment was setting in motion the process for securing an endowment for Spelman. In order to conserve limited resources, the Board of Trustees voted to eliminate most of the departments that were outside the college division: the Nurses Training Department and Elementary School were closed but the high school was retained until 1930 because few public high schools existed for Black students in Georgia, and the pool of college-level Black females was

still small since opportunities for college preparation were still limited. When the high school was finally discontinued, the aim of Spelman College was to provide to a small number of students a first-rate liberal arts education that would be equal to any available elsewhere. To achieve this goal, additional college courses in the humanities, fine arts, social sciences, and natural sciences were established and the college faculty increased. In 1932, Spelman College received an "A" rating from the Southern Association of Colleges and Secondary Schools. During Florence Read's first year at Spelman, 122 students were enrolled for college work; ten years later the college enrollment totaled 312.

Before 1920, the majority of teachers were unmarried white women from New England, though there were a few Black teachers. The earliest Black female teachers were former Spelman students. These included Claudia White, 1901 college graduate, who began teaching in the high school in 1902 and, in a joint arrangement with Morehouse, taught German and Latin on the Morehouse campus from 1910 to 1914. Jane Granderson, 1901 college graduate, taught at Spelman from 1902 until her untimely death in 1905. During the 1920s and 1930s, however, Black teachers became more prominent on the faculty, both at the high school and college levels. Gradually the Spelman faculty became more evenly balanced racially and by 1937, Black teachers outnumbered white teachers by two to one, and by 1952, there were three times as many Black teachers. Women faculty outnumbered men for a longer period. In 1926, there were no men on the faculty, although there had been two in the early years, a white male from 1882 to 1887 and a Black male from 1887 to 1897; both taught music. In 1927, two men joined the Spelman faculty, one full-time and one part-time. Ten years later there were twelve men on the Spelman faculty.

Following the stewardship of four white women—Packard (1881-91); Giles (1891-1909); Lucy Tapley (1910-27); and Florence M. Read (1927-53)—Albert E. Manley, then dean of the College of Arts and Sciences of North Carolina College, elected president on July 1, 1953, bringing an end to more than half a century of New England leadership of the college. On June 15, 1976, Francis Day Rogers, chair of the board of trustees, announced that another Black man, Donald Mitchell Steward, associate dean, faculty of arts and sciences, the director of the College of General Studies, and the counselor to the provost at the University of Pennsylvania, would assume the presidency of Spelman College. Following this announcement, dramatic efforts were taken by some students and faculty members to block the appointment of a man to succeed Dr. Manley to the presidency. Many believed it was time for Spelman to have a Black woman president. During the April meeting of the board of trustees, several hundred students and a few faculty and staff members banded together and kept the board of trustees locked in the board room for more than twenty hours in a protest move to get them to reconsider Dr. Steward's appointment. The board affirmed its support of Steward, who became the sixth president of the college.

Eleven years later, on April 5, 1987, the board appointed Johnnetta Betsch Cole (Robinson), professor of anthropology and director of the Latin American and Caribbean studies program at Hunter College of the City University of New York, as Spelman's seventh president and the first Black woman to lead the institution in its 106-year history.

BIBLIOGRAPHY
    Guy-Sheftall, Beverly and Jo Moore Stewart. *Spelman: A Centennial Celebration* (1981); Read, Florence. *The Story of Spelman College* (1961).

MANUSCRIPT COLLECTIONS
    American Baptist Historical Society, Valley Forge, Pennsylvania; Rockefeller Archives Center, Tarrytown, New York; Spelman College Archives, Spelman College, Atlanta, Georgia; *Spelman Messenger*, Division of Special Collections and Archives, Woodruff Library, Clark Atlanta University, Atlanta, Georgia.

                    BEVERLY GUY-SHEFTALL

SPENCE, EULALIE (1894-1981)

Unlike many early Black women who wrote protest plays to promote social change during the 1920s and 1930s, Eulalie Spence wrote for entertainment and avoided racial themes. Spence was one of the most prolific and experienced Black female playwrights of her time. Of her thirteen known works, at least eight have been published and seven produced. With the exception of *Her* and *Undertow*, Spence wrote comedies about Harlem life. Her themes were universal, but her characters were undeniably Black.

Eulalie Spence was born June 11, 1894, on the island of Nevis, British West Indies. The daughter of a sugar planter, she was the eldest of seven girls. At the turn of the century, her father's crop was destroyed during a hurricane, and the Spence family migrated to New York City in 1902. Spence was inspired by her well-educated mother, who was a great storyteller, to become a writer.

Spence graduated from the New York Training School for Teachers, and later received a B.A. in 1937 from New York University, and an M.A. in speech from Columbia University in 1939. At Columbia, Spence studied playwriting and performed with the Drama Club.

In 1918, Spence joined the New York public school system, and in 1927, she was assigned to Eastern District High School, Brooklyn, where she taught elocution, English, and dramatics, as well as headed the drama group, until her retirement in 1958.

Spence won numerous awards during the Harlem Renaissance for her plays. *Foreign Mail* placed second in the National Association for the Advancement of Colored People's *Crisis* competition for playwriting in 1926. In 1927, Spence won the Urban League's *Opportunity* second place award for *The Hunch* and a third place award for *The Starter*. That same year, *Foreign Mail* and *Fool's Errand* were entered in the David Belasco Little Theatre Tournament, and won the Samuel French $200 prize. Both plays were then published by French. Spence's only full-length play, *The Whipping*, a three-act comedy, was sold to Paramount Pictures but was never produced.

Spence devoted most of her life to her students and work at Eastern District High School. Eulalie Spence died March 7, 1981, in Pennsylvania.

BIBLIOGRAPHY

Hatch, James V. and Ted Shine, eds. *Black Theatre U.S.A.: Forty-five Plays by Black Americans, 1847-1974* (1974); Locke, Alain, and Montgomery T. Gregory, eds. *Plays of Negro Life: A Sourcebook of Native American Drama* (1927); Perkins, Kathy Anne, ed. *Black Female Playwrights: An Anthology of Plays before 1950* (1989); Randolph, Ruth Elizabeth and Lorraine Elena Roses, eds. *Harlem Renaissance and Beyond: Literary Biographies of 100 Black Women Writers, 1900-1945* (1989).

PLAYS BY EULALIE SPENCE

Being Forty (1920); *Brothers and Sisters of the Church Council* (1920); *La Divina Pastora* (1929); *Episode* (1928); *Fool's Errand* (1927); *Foreign Mail* (1926); *Her* (1927); *Hot Stuff* (c. 1927); *The Hunch* (1926); *The Starter* (1926); *Undertow* (1929); *The Whipping* (1932); *Wife Errant* (1928).

KATHY A. PERKINS

SPENCER, ANNE (1882-1975)

Of the many women who distinguished themselves as poets during the Harlem Renaissance, Anne Spencer may be the most original and unconventional.

Annie Bethel was born in Henry County, Virginia, on February 6, 1882. Her parents, Joel Cephus and Sarah Louise, separated when she was five. Annie then moved with her mother to Bramwell, West Virginia, a mining town. While Sarah worked to support them, Annie lived with another family, the Dixies. When she was eleven, her father learned that she had never received a formal education—her mother had not wanted her to attend school in a mining town. He threatened to take Annie, and so her mother enrolled her in the Virginia Seminary in Lynchburg as Annie Bethel Scales—under Sarah's maiden name. She was the youngest student ever to attend school there.

Annie excelled in humanities courses but did not fare as well in the sciences. For these she recruited a tutor, Edward Spencer. Soon she performed well in all her courses, and in 1899 she graduated from the seminary, receiving the honor of delivering the valedictory address. After teaching school for two years in West Virginia, Annie returned to Lynchburg in 1901 to marry Edward Spencer.

Annie soon became the mother of two daughters, Bethel Calloway (Stevenson) and Alroy Sarah (Rivers), and a son, Chauncey Edward (who grew up to become a pioneer in Black aviation). Others assisted in their care; Annie spent most of her time writing and working in her garden.

When James Weldon Johnson became the guest of the Spencers, arriving in Lynchburg in 1917 to help organize a chapter of the National Association for the Advancement of Colored People, he saw some of Annie's poetry. He helped her find a publisher and suggested the pen name Anne Spencer. At thirty-eight, Anne Spencer published her first poem, "Before the Feast of Shushan," in the February 1920 *Crisis*, and Johnson published five of her poems in *The Book of American Negro Poetry* (1922). By 1927, ten of her poems were published in Countee Cullen's *Caroling Dusk* and it had become clear that she was an important new poet. From the 1920s through the 1940s, Anne Spencer was represented in every volume of Negro poetry and in *American Negro Poetry since 1900*. Her poems, receiving favorable reviews, were often characterized as private or ironic, yet conventional in structure and nonracial in theme. With recurring themes such as friendship, love, and freedom, Spencer's poems had more in common with nineteenth-century American poets than with her contemporaries in Harlem.

Her home at 1313 Pierce Street became an important resting place for Black travelers when hotels would not allow them accommodations. W.E.B. Du Bois, Paul Robeson, Langston Hughes, George Washington Carver, and Sterling Brown were often guests in her home as Anne Spencer participated in the New Negro cultural and intellectual awakening. Writers solicited her criticism of their works and exchanged ideas during their visits.

As Anne Spencer's popularity grew outside of Lynchburg, she became notorious locally. She forced the ouster of white teachers at the all-Black high school, which led to the hiring of Black teachers. She boycotted segregated public transportation and rode the trolley in defiance—refusing to move or be moved. In 1923 she walked two miles to the town's library and requested a job as librarian, thus initiating the opening of the only Black library in Lynchburg. She served as its librarian from 1923 to 1945.

Anne Spencer's local fame also was based on her gardening abilities. Her garden became well known for its varied plants and flowers. Spencer spent eight years developing a pink candy-striped Chinese peony from seed. Her devotion to her garden matched her devotion to her poetry. Indeed, she uses a garden as image or setting in many of her poems. In the last published poem of her lifetime, "For Jim, Easter Eve" (written in memory of James Weldon Johnson, who died in a car accident in 1938 shortly after visiting her home), Anne Spencer states, "if ever a garden was Gethsemane . . . this, my garden has been to me."

By 1940 Anne Spencer had become a recluse. After Edward's death in 1964, she began working on a number of historical pieces and preparing her poems for publication. When she died July 12, 1975, at the age of ninety-three, she left behind approximately fifty poems and her famous garden. Most of these poems have been compiled in J. Lee Greene's *Time's Unfading Garden: Anne Spencer's Life and Poetry* (1977) and her garden and its cottage, "Edankraal," have been placed on the National Register of Historic Places.

BIBLIOGRAPHY

Brown, Sterling. *Negro Poetry and Drama, and the Negro in American Fiction* (1969); Cullen, Countee, ed. *Caroling Dusk: An Anthology of Verse by Negro Poets* (1927); Davis, Arthur P. *From the Dark Tower: Afro-American Writers, 1900-1960* (1974); Davis, Arthur P., and Saunders Redding, eds. *Cavalcade: Negro American Writing from 1760 to the Present* (1971); *Echoes from the Garden: The Anne Spencer Story*. Documentary film, Byron Studios (1980); Glikin, Ronda. *Black American Women in Literature: A Bibliography, 1976-1987* (1989); Greene, J. Lee. "Anne Spencer." In *AAW*; and *Time's Unfading Garden: Anne Spencer's Life and Poetry* (1977); Hughes, Langston, and Arna Bontemps, eds. *The Poetry of the Negro, 1746-1970* (1970); Hull, Gloria. "Black Women Poets from Wheatley to Walker," *Negro American Literature Forum* (Fall 1975), and *Color, Sex and Poetry: Three Women Writers of the Harlem Renaissance* (1987); Johnson, James Weldon, ed. *The Book of American Negro Poetry* (1922); Kerlin, Robert T., ed. *Negro Poets and Their Poems* (1923); Locke, Alain, ed. *The New Negro: An Interpretation* (1925); Nichols, Charles H., ed. *Arna Bontemps/ Langston Hughes Letters 1925-1967* (1990); Perry, Margaret. *The Harlem Renaissance: An Annotated Bibliography and Commentary* (1982); Roses, Lorraine Elena, and Ruth Elizabeth Randolph. *Harlem Renaissance and Beyond: Literary Biographies of 100 Black Women Writers 1900-1945* (1990); Untermeyer, Louis. *American Negro Poetry since 1900* (1923).

PAULA C. BARNES

SPIKES, DELORES MARGARET RICHARD (1936-)

"Southern represents hope," said Delores Spikes, president of the Southern University System and former interim chancellor of Southern University at Baton Rouge (1988-91). "It represents a way to open the doors of America to countless young people who would otherwise be shut out."

Delores Spikes was featured in the January 1990 issue of *Ebony* as recipient of the Thurgood Marshall Educational Achievement Award. *Ebony Man* also cited her as one of the twenty "Most Influential Black Women in America" (January 1990). She is the first

Called one of the twenty most influential Black women in America by Ebony Man *magazine, Delores Spikes became the first woman in the United States to head a university system when she was chosen president of the Southern University System. [Patricia Kenschaft]*

female in the United States to head a university system, and she was the first female to lead a Louisiana public college or university.

She was born on August 24, 1936, in Baton Rouge to Mr. and Mrs. Lawrence G. Richard. She married Hermon Spikes, and they have one daughter, Rhonda Kathleen Spikes-Pete, and one granddaughter.

Delores Richard's precollege education was in the public and private schools of Baton Rouge. In 1957, she received a B.S. summa cum laude in mathematics from Southern University. In 1958, the University of Illinois at Urbana awarded her an M.S. in mathematics. After teaching four years at Mossville School in Calcasieu Parish, she joined the faculty of Southern University in 1961.

In 1971, she became the first Black graduate and the first graduate of Southern University to receive a doctorate in mathematics from Louisiana State University. Her Ph.D. was in pure mathematics with a specialty in commutative ring theory. In 1981, she became part-time assistant to the chancellor of Southern University, along with being full-time professor of mathematics.

She has received numerous awards and prestigious appointments, including being "Alumnus of the Century" at the Southern University Centennial Celebration. She was also appointed to a three-year term on the commission on women in higher education of the American Council on Education.

BIBLIOGRAPHY

Kenschaft, Patricia. "Black Women in Mathematics," *Newsletter of the Association for Women in Mathematics* (May-June 1980).

PATRICIA CLARK KENSCHAFT

SPIVEY, VICTORIA (1906-1976)

Victoria Spivey had a long and colorful career as a blues singer, recording artist, and songwriter. She was born into a musical family in Houston, Texas, on October 6, 1906, and learned to play piano as a child. By her early teens she was performing in local clubs. She admired the recordings and performances of the older women blues singers. Hoping for such a career herself, she traveled to St. Louis in 1926 and wangled an audition with Jesse Johnson, the local agent for Okeh Records. Her first record, "Black Snake Blues," was a hit. She was hired as a songwriter for the St. Louis Publishing Company, and until 1929 she recorded extensively for Okeh. In 1929, Spivey won an

ingenue role in King Vidor's all-Black film musical *Hallelujah!* though the role of the blues singer went to another actress. Throughout the Great Depression, when many musicians found work scarce, Spivey continued to record for various labels and to perform in clubs and touring shows, from *Dallas Tan Town Topics*, which toured Texas and Oklahoma in 1933, to the Minsky burlesque circuit. In 1938-39, she performed and toured in the Broadway show *Hellzapoppin'*. During these years she often appeared with her sisters, Addie and Leona, who were also blues singers, or with her husband, dancer Billy Adams.

Spivey continued to work in clubs until the 1950s, when she quit show business for church work, but in 1961 she returned, forming her own record label, Queen Vee. In 1962, it became Spivey Records, for which she produced recordings of well-known and up-and-coming blues musicians' lyrics and songs. She also recorded albums, performing her own songs for the Bluesville and Folkways labels. During the 1960s, she was a mainstay at colleges, folk clubs, and festivals, visiting Europe with the American Folk Blues Tour (1963) and performing at the Chicago (1969), Philadelphia (1971), and Ann Arbor (1973) blues festivals. She died suddenly of an internal hemorrhage in New York City on October 3, 1976. Victoria Spivey had a high, rather nasal singing voice made more evocative by a characteristic moan she called her "tiger squall." She never entirely lost the Texas country blues sound of her youth, and she was a mercurial performer, able to evoke whatever emotions each song required. Her best songs, among them "TB Blues" and "Murder in the First Degree," show an ability to portray even situations outside her personal experience vividly. The blues revival of the 1960s made it possible for her to receive the acclaim she deserved.

BIBLIOGRAPHY

BDAAM; *BWW*; Garon, Paul and Amy O'Neal. "Victoria Spivey, 1906-1976," *Living Blues* (September/October 1976); Harrison, Daphne Duval. *Black Pearls: Blues Queens of the 1920s* (1988); Hitchcock, H. Wiley and Stanley Sadie, eds. *The New Grove Dictionary of American Music* (1986); Jasen, David. Liner notes to Spivey, Victoria. *The Blues Is Life*. Folkways Records FS 3541; *New York Times*, "Victoria Spivey Is Dead at 68; A Singer of Blues in the 1920s" (October 7, 1976); Oliver, Paul. *Conversation with the Blues* (1965); Placksin, Sally. *American Women in Jazz, 1900 to the Present: Their Words, Lives, and Music* (1982); Stewart-Baxter, Derrick. *Ma Rainey and the Classic Blues Singers* (1970).

DISCOGRAPHY

The Blues Is Life. Folkways FS 3541 (1976); *Recorded Legacy of the Blues.* Spivey 2001 (n.d.); *Songs We Taught Your Mother* (Victoria Spivey, Lucille Hegamin, and Alberta Hunter). Prestige Bluesville BV 1052 (1961); *Victoria and Her Blues.* Spivey 1002 (n.d.).

SUZANNE FLANDREAU

SPORTS

To chronicle the participation of Black women in sports in the United States is to tell the story of slavery, alternative communities, Black colleges of distinction, organizations that provided safe havens for participation, and modern heroines. Above all, it is to tell a story of courage, physical skill, and centrality of purpose rarely chronicled in the sports pages and television shows of modern America.

Separation of Black from white women in sport remained long after the abolishment of slavery and the emancipation of Black women. It was not until the 1970s with the passage of Title IX of the Civil Rights Act, and the first universal offering of athletic scholarships for women, that Black women could be found training alongside white women in athletic clubs and institutions of higher education.

Most early Black American women necessarily found their physical activities conditioned by slavery. As part of "amusings" that occurred during Saturday evening respites from work or holiday observations, Black women gathered to participate in simple games, foot races, and dances. Agricultural fairs, weddings, and funerals also provided the setting for participation in contests such as corn shuckings, jumping the broom, and other competitions of skill and dexterity.

With the abolition of slavery and the procurement of land and material goods by prominent Black families, Black women began to participate in sports that required equipment and recreational facilities, heretofore considered the province of middle- and upper-class white women. As early as 1890, several Black families owned tennis courts. As a result, matches and tournaments began at Black colleges in 1895 and in suburban Washington, D.C., by 1910. Excluded by white sporting organizations, such as the U.S. National Lawn Tennis Association (USLTA), Black players formed their own governing group, the American Tennis Association, in 1916. In contrast to the traditional separation of the sexes in the dominant white culture, Black women were coparticipants in the competitions as early as 1917. Wearing ankle-length skirts, long-sleeved high-neck blouses, and leather tennis shoes, they competed in tennis tournaments with grace, style, and energy. The national tennis championship in 1917 was won by Lucy Diggs Slowe.

Throughout history, several events and movements have changed the number of opportunities for participation in sport by Black women. For example, at the end of World War I, there was a northern migration of Black Americans that brought women into contact with settlement houses, churches, industrial training schools, Young Women's Christian Associations (YWCAs), as well as public schools and parks. Such community assemblages provided the opportunity, not as readily available in southern states, for participation in sports such as basketball and track. As a result, club sports emerged and included basketball, swimming, tennis, and, eventually, elite track programs for women at Black colleges.

Track for Black women developed rapidly in the 1920s. Among the city clubs to produce champions of national stature at that time were the New York Mercury Club and the Illinois Women's Athletic Club. Along with the Tuskegee Relays in the South, which began in 1927, such clubs in the North afforded Black women an opportunity to showcase their talent. Indeed, the first Black women selected for Olympic competition (1932), Tydie Pickett and Louise Stokes, came from clubs and playgrounds in the North. Affording additional training for Black women in the cities, the YWCAs provided facilities such as basketball courts and swimming pools. Pioneering this surge of athletic talent was Anita Gant. School teacher, YWCA basketball captain, and swimming and tennis champion, Gant used her physical prowess (which had been polished to perfection at the Washington, D.C., YWCA) to attain the national American Tennis Association (ATA) mixed-doubles championships in 1929 and 1930. Similarly, Inez Patterson proved to be Philadelphia's multifaceted champion. In high school, Patterson was the only Black member of the women's field hockey team. As a member of McCoach Playground she broke swimming records and captained the girls' basketball team. Later, at Temple University, Patterson made all-collegiate teams in hockey, tennis, basketball, track, volleyball, and dancing. Black communities also provided support for women's sport. For example, the *Philadelphia Tribune* women's basketball squad dominated women's basketball from 1931 through 1940 and was founded by Ora Mae Washington. Washington, an eight-time ATA champion, was the player-coach for the basketball team, which traveled all over the country, playing the best Black and white teams. After competitions and exhibitions that often used men's rules, the team also offered clinics and coaching to members of local communities.

Because Black women in the 1930s had limited access to instruction, facilities, and equipment (as well as to the predominantly white universities), such exposure to training techniques made an important contribution to the future of competitive women's sports. In fact, Black women physical educators and sport professionals provided the necessary leadership and nurturance for the development of Black women athletes. Writing at this time, Black sport historian Edwin Henderson argued that "despite the narrowed limits prescribed for girls and women, there are girls who ought to display their skills and natural sport ability to a wider extent. These national exponents of women's sport are therefore to be commended for the prominence they have attained. The opportunities and participation ought to increase. The race of man needs the inspiration of strong virile womanhood. Honor is due the pioneers and the present competitors in the field of women's athletics" (Henderson 1949).

An increase in Black women's sport opportunities coincided with the decline of track and field and other face-to-face competition for white women. The decline resulted from policies generated by the Council on Women's Sport and similar national groups in the 1920s and 1930s. Emphasizing that face-to-face competition aligned women's sports with the male model of exploitation and elitism, white women physical educators proposed play days and other less competitive situations as appropriate activity for girls and women in sport.

In the forefront of the movement for the empowerment of Black sportswomen was the Tuskegee Institute in Alabama, which established the prototype for the training of future women Olympians. Led by Amelia C. Roberts and Cleveland Abbott, Tuskegee established a successful women's track team and included two events for women in the Tuskegee Relays as early as 1927. The only college to have varsity competition for women at that time, Tuskegee first included the 100-yard dash and the 400-meter relay in its meet. Three years later, the 50-yard dash and the discus event were added. As a result, Tuskegee dominated the Amateur Athletic Union meets from 1937 through 1948. Both Black and white northern women's athletic clubs provided Tuskegee's chief competition. The only year in which Tuskegee's winning streak was broken was 1943, when they were defeated by a Cleveland team led by 1932 Polish Olympian Stella Walsh.

Olympic success came in 1948, when four Tuskegee-trained athletes competed in the Olympic games. Alice Coachman cleared 5 feet 6 1/8 inches to win the gold medal in the high jump. Also competing from Tuskegee were Nell Jackson (200-meter dash) and Mabel Walker (100-meter dash). From the emerging power in women's track, Tennessee Agricultural and Industrial (later named Tennessee State University), Audrey Patterson (bronze medalist in the 200-meter dash), Emma Reed (running broad jump), and Therese Manuel (javelin and 80-meter hurdle) competed.

With track and field leading the way in the 1920s and 1930s, progress toward an integrated society on the national level in the 1940s came as a result of Executive Order No. 8802. Issued June 25th, 1941, it integrated federal employment practices. President Harry Truman integrated the armed forces in 1948. Integration of professional sports for men also started in the 1940s, with the signing of Jackie Robinson by the Brooklyn Dodgers.

Black sport governing bodies also pushed for integration. The ATA promoted Althea Gibson, who in 1949 participated in the USLTA eastern and national meets. When the USLTA realized that allowing Gibson into their regional and national tournaments would open the way for her to participate at Wimbledon, it decided to rethink its policies. Renowned tennis champion, Alice Marble, challenged the USLTA to cease wavering. Consequently Gibson was invited to the U.S. Open at Forest Hills in 1950. Between 1950 and 1957, Althea Gibson was coached by Dr. Robert W. Johnson and Sydney Lewellyn, both of whom had devoted considerable time and effort to the development of young Black tennis talent. As a result of their efforts and her talent, determination, and endless hours of daily practice, Gibson became not only the U.S. champion but also the Wimbledon singles champion in both 1957 and 1958. In 1957, Gibson became the first Black woman to appear on the cover of *Sports Illustrated*.

Another Black governing body to push for integration, the Unified Golf Association (UGA), also encouraged Black female talent. The UGA joined forces with the National Association for the Advancement of Colored People (NAACP) to bring concurrent legal actions against the heretofore segregated public golf courses. The purpose behind the legal actions was to force either integration of golf courses or the provision of separate but equal facilities for Black golfers. Such legal action was part of the NAACP's larger strategy, to challenge the separate but equal legal doctrine established in 1896 under *Plessy* v. *Ferguson*. By 1954, *Brown* v. *Board of Education* represented a victory for integration, but it was not until 1967 that the first Black woman, Renee Powell, joined the Ladies Professional Golf Association tour.

The Olympic games have continued to provide an arena for the integration of women's sport. The Tennessee State Tigerbelles dominated track and field between 1956 and 1972. Such premiere athletes as Wilma Rudolph, Martha Hudson, Barbara Jones, Lucinda Williams, Edith McGuire, Madeleine Manning, and Wyomia Tyus went on from the Tennessee school to win gold medals at the Olympics. Such successes also paved the way for Black women to hold leadership positions both in the sports community and in educational institutions throughout the country. For example, Dr. Dorothy Richey became the first woman athletic director for both men's and women's sports. Nell Jackson was a professor at three universities and twice a director of athletics. In addition she was a member of the board of directors of the U.S. Olympic Committee (USOC) and vice president of The Athletic Congress (TAC). Willie White, a member of five Olympic teams, also was a member of the committee.

Black women were to assume leadership positions in other sports as well. After playing on the Northeast field hockey team in the 1940s and the U.S. Women's Lacrosse Association team in the 1950s, Verneda Thomas became the first Black national field hockey official and the first Black national lacrosse official.

In the 1960s, the United States began to follow the lead of the Soviet Union and other eastern bloc countries, encouraging women's Olympic competition in order to use women athletes to help boost the medal count.

However, it was not until the 1970s that gender discrimination of all forms was addressed in the United States. With the passage of Title IX in 1972, and its implementation in 1975, American women athletes began to receive access to opportunities for training, coaching, and sports facilities in all educational institutions. As colleges came into compliance, scholarships were offered to women athletes and a wider variety of options for sports participation became available to Black women athletes. Predominantly white universities began to adopt a model of training and nurturance similar to that used at Tuskegee and Tennessee State. Basketball and track and field were the first sports to use scholarships as a means to create world-class teams by recruiting women athletes from throughout the United States. Some of the early Black women champions to benefit from the scholarship options were Marian Washington at Westchester State College, Lusia Harris-Stewart at Delta State University, Lynnette Woodard at Kansas State University, and LaTaunya Pollard at Long Beach City College. When *Sports Illustrated* honored women's basketball in 1985, Cheryl Miller of the University of Southern California was featured on the cover. Six members of the 1984 women's Olympic gold-medal basketball team were Black athletes. In 1989, Cindi Brown became one of the first professional women basketball players in Japan. Lynnette Woodard was the first woman member of the Harlem Globetrotters.

In track and field, the University of California at Los Angeles encouraged many young Black women athletes. Evelyn Ashford, Florence Griffith Joyner, and Jackie Joyner-Kersee were gold medalists in 1984 and 1988 who attended classes on the Westwood campus. Jackie Joyner-Kersee also was a gold medalist in the 1992 Olympics.

In the last two decades Black women have also received international recognition in predominantly white sports. Currently a member of the International Olympic Committee and the U.S. Olympic Committee, and president of the Amateur Athletic Foundation of Los Angeles, Anita de Frantz (Connecticut College, University of Pennsylvania) won a bronze medal in rowing in 1976. One of the most outstanding volleyball players of the twentieth century, Flora Hyman attended the University of Houston and was a member of the silver-medal team in 1984. Hyman died while playing for a Japanese club in 1986. In 1991, Antoinette White, from Long Beach City College, was named the Women's Volleyball Big West Player of the Year and the National Collegiate Athletic Association American Volleyball Coaches' Association TACHIKARA National Player of the Year.

Other Black women athletes to achieve recognition in predominantly white sports were Debi Thomas, silver medalist in the 1988 Olympic games in figure skating, Lynnette Love, gold medalist in the demonstration sport of taekwondo in 1988, and Zina Garrison, ranked fifth in the world in tennis in 1985.

In spite of the double burden of racial and gender discrimination, Black women have a rich sporting heritage. They have demonstrated that collective action can lead to social transformation in the clubs, the colleges, and sports' governing bodies. Moreover, they have shown that determination and concentration make a winning formula.

BIBLIOGRAPHY

Adkins, Vivian. *The Development of Negro Female Olympic Talent* (1982); Ashe, Arthur, Jr. *A Hard Road to Glory* (1988); Bentley, Ken. *Going for the Gold* (1983); Beverly, Robert. *The History and Present State of Virginia, in Four Parts* (1705); Brown, Alexander. *The First Republic in America* (1898); Cann, Susan Kathleen. *Coming on Strong: Gender and Sexuality in Women's Sport, 1900-1960* (1990); Grant, Anne. *Memoirs of an American Lady* (1809); Green, Tina Sloan, et al. *Black Women in Sport* (1981); Henderson, Edwin Bancroft. *The Negro in Sport* (1949); Page, James. *Black Olympian Medalists* (1991); *Report of the United States Olympic Committee, 1948 Games* (1948); *Sports Illustrated: 35 Years of Covers* (March 28, 1990); Stockard, Bessie. "The Black Female Athlete," *Crisis* (May 1983).

D. MARGARET COSTA
JANE A. ADAIR

SPRAGUE, FREDERICKA DOUGLASS (PERRY) AND ROSABELLE DOUGLASS (JONES)

"A race can rise no higher than its women" was the belief expressed by Frederick Douglass's granddaughter, Fredericka Douglass Sprague Perry, when she advocated the membership of all young girls in the Missouri Association of Colored Girls, an organization she founded in Kansas City, Missouri. Fredericka Douglass Sprague Perry and Rosabelle Douglass Sprague Jones were community activists in Kansas City, Missouri. Active in the local and state chapters of the National Association of Colored Women, Fredericka and her sister, Rosabelle, developed child welfare and other initiatives to respond to the needs of the African-American community, especially young girls, in Kansas City. The activities of both Fredericka and Rosabelle are best characterized as community caregiving activities that were an outgrowth of the voluntarism so prevalent among middle- and upper-class Black women during the first three decades of the twentieth century.

Both Fredericka and Rosabelle, like many women in the women's club movement, were married to educated, well-to-do African-American men. Fredericka was married to Dr. J. Edward Perry who founded the Perry Sanitarium (later, Wheatley Provident Hospital) in 1910. The couple had one son, Dr. E. B. Perry, who practiced medicine in Houston, Texas. Rosabelle was married to physician Thomas A. Jones.

Before moving to Kansas City, Missouri, and marrying J. E. Perry, Fredericka was an instructor in cooking at the Lincoln Institute in Jefferson City. Before and for a short time after her marriage, she worked with her husband at the Wheatley Provident Hospital. In the early days of the hospital, she provided nursing-care-related services. Later she organized the women's auxiliary and developed various fund-raising activities to support on-going and expanded services at the medical facility. She consistently supported and encouraged her spouse's medical ambitions.

The extent of Rosabelle Mary Sprague Jones's contributions in Kansas City is difficult to determine. Recorded biographical materials on Rosabelle provide more details about her sister Fredericka's contributions to the Kansas City community than about her own. Rosabelle was the younger of the two women and the youngest of the seven children in the family. Although she seemed to walk in Fredericka's shadow, she was a leader in her own right and active in civic and voluntary associations in Kansas City. For two years she served as president of the Kansas City Federation of Colored Women's Clubs. Her second annual message on May 9, 1930, described the Kansas City "race" women as a "group of women who are earnestly endeavoring to do things for humanity."

Fredericka Douglass Sprague Perry's voluntary association activities were more extensive than those of her sister. Her focus on systematic child-oriented services through the Colored Big Sister Association of Kansas City founded in 1934 is particularly noteworthy. Fredericka's leadership in the National Association for Colored Girls, the Missouri Association for Colored Girls, and the local Colored Big Sister Association led to concrete services for dependent Black girls who were not eligible for state-supported foster home services in Kansas City during the 1930s. The Colored Big Sister Home for Girls opened in April 1934, and continued as a private charity until 1943. Fredericka's concern for delinquent girls and her employment in the local court system led to broad-based community support for her pioneering efforts in child welfare reform in Kansas City. Her philosophy is reflected in the titles of the state song and the motto she composed for the girls' association—"Show Me" and "Learning as We Climb."

BIBLIOGRAPHY

Hine, Darlene Clark. "Lifting the Veil, Shattering the Silence: Black Women's History in Slavery and Freedom."

In *The State of Afro-American History*, ed. Darlene Clark Hine (1986); Kansas City Federation of Colored Women's Clubs. *Annual Message, May 30, 1930*. Frederick Douglass Papers, Moorland-Spingarn Research Center, Howard University, Washington, D.C.; *Kansas City Journal Post*, "Colored Big Sisters Home for Girls" (September 20, 1936); *Kansas City Times*, "Obituary, Mrs. John E. Perry" (October 25, 1943); *Kansas City Times*, "Biographical Sketch, Dr. John Edward Perry" (February 8, 1945); Lincoln Institute. *35th Annual Catalogue*. Jefferson City, Missouri (1906-7); National Association of Colored Women. "Biography of Mrs. Rosabelle Douglass Sprague Jones," *Lifting as They Climb* (1933); Peebles-Wilkins, W. "Black Women and American Social Welfare: The Life of Fredericka Douglass Sprague Perry," *Affilia: Journal of Women and Social Work* (1989); Perry, J. E. *Forty Cords of Wood: Memoirs of a Medical Doctor* (1947); *Report of the Kansas City Federation of Colored Women's Clubs, September 1929-June 1930*. Frederick Douglass Papers, Moorland-Spingarn Research Center, Howard University, Washington, D.C.; Schirmer, Sherry Lamb and Richard D. McKinzie. *At the River's Bend: An Illustrated History of Kansas City* (n.d.); Sterling, Dorothy, ed. *We Are Your Sisters: Black Women in the Nineteenth Century* (1984); Young, William and Nathan Young. "Dr. J. E. Perry, Physician and Builder," *Your Kansas City and Mine* (n.d.).

WILMA PEEBLES-WILKINS

SPRAGUE, ROSETTA DOUGLASS (1839-1906)

In describing the relationship of her parents, Frederick and Anna Murray Douglass, Rosetta Douglass Sprague explained: "As is the condition of most wives her identity became so merged with that of her husband's that few of their earlier friends in the North really knew and appreciated the full value of the woman who presided over the Douglass home for forty-five years" (Sprague 1923). While Sprague was concerned about the plight of African-Americans, she made her greatest historical contribution by making visible the personal life of her parents. Her famous speech, "Anna Murray Douglass—My Mother as I Recall Her," delivered at the founding meeting of the National Association of Colored Women (NACW), recaptured her mother's marital role in the life of her father, Frederick Douglass. From Rosetta's recollections, bits and pieces of her own life can be reconstructed as well.

Rosetta Douglass Sprague, the older daughter of Frederick and Anna Murray Douglass, and her offspring were social activists committed to their spouses and to the causes of the African-American community. Anna Murray Douglass was a role model for this social consciousness and activism in her anti-slavery activities in Lynn, Massachusetts. A participant in the 1896 founding of the National Association of Colored Women, Rosetta Douglass Sprague, and later her daughters Fredericka and Rosabelle, utilized civic, club-related, and educational activities as avenues for improving the legal and social circumstances of the African-American community during the late nineteenth and early twentieth centuries.

Rosetta was born in June 1839, in the two-room Douglass home overlooking Buzzards Bay on Elm Street in New Bedford, Massachusetts. Her three brothers, Lewis, Frederick, Jr., and Charles, were also born in New Bedford. When Rosetta was around six years old, her father, Frederick Douglass, moved his family to a cottage he purchased in Lynn, Massachusetts. Annie, Rosetta's younger sister, was born in Lynn. Douglass later moved his family to Rochester, New York.

Because of racial segregation and differential treatment in the schools of Rochester, New York, Rosetta Douglass was educated in business-related skills at the Oberlin College Academy. Her first secure teaching position was in Salem, Massachusetts, where she taught until she married Nathaniel Sprague in 1863. The couple moved back to Rochester to start their family. The Spragues had seven children, six daughters and one son: Annie Rosine, Harriet Bailey, Alice Louise, Estelle Irene, Fredericka Douglass, Herbert Douglass, and Rosabelle Mary.

The Spragues lived in Rochester until Nathaniel was imprisoned for removing the contents from letters on his job in the Rochester post office. Nathaniel Sprague was an uneducated ex-slave who had difficulty keeping jobs and Frederick Douglass had helped him get the job in the post office. After he was released from jail, he joined Rosetta in Washington, D.C., where she had relocated with their children to obtain work after liquidating her personal property to cover the couple's debts. She was supporting the children by working as a government clerk in the Register of Deeds Office with her father. She remained in Washington, D.C., until her death in 1906.

BIBLIOGRAPHY
Giddings, Paula. *When and Where I Enter: The Impact of Black Women on Race and Sex in America* (1984); Majors, Monroe A. "Mrs. Nathaniel Sprague." In *Noted Negro Women*, ed. M. A. Majors (1893); Clark Atlanta University Library, Special Collections, Atlanta, Georgia; Render, Sylvia Lyons. "Afro-American Women: The Outstanding

and the Obscure," *Quarterly Journal of the Library of Congress* (October 1985); Sprague, Rosetta Douglass. "Anna Murray Douglass—My Mother As I Recall Her," *Journal of Negro History* (1923); Sterling, Dorothy, ed. *We Are Your Sisters: Black Women in the Nineteenth Century* (1984); Frederick Douglass papers. Moorland-Spingarn Research Center, Howard University, Washington, D.C.

WILMA PEEBLES-WILKINS

STANLEY, SARA G. (1837-1918)

Sara Stanley, free-born in an era when millions of Black men and women were enslaved, was a pioneer integrationist in higher education, both as an antebellum college student and as a teacher.

Stanley's parents, John Stuart and Frances Griffith Stanley, ran a private school for free Black children in New Bern, North Carolina, before the Civil War. Not surprisingly, therefore, she had an excellent early education. In fact, when she went to Ohio to study at Oberlin College in the early 1850s, Stanley was so well-prepared that she did not have to take the preparatory courses that were required for many white and Black students.

The Stanleys left North Carolina in the mid-1850s, as freed people were suffering heightened persecution and were immigrating North. The family settled in Cleveland. Sara Stanley left college before receiving her degree to teach school and became involved in the abolitionist movement prior to the Civil War. A speech she gave to the Ladies Antislavery Society in Delaware, Ohio, in 1856, one of the earliest by a Black American woman, was later published as an antislavery tract.

In 1864, Stanley volunteered to teach freedpeople through the interracial, Protestant-based American Missionary Association (AMA). She taught in Norfolk, Virginia; St. Louis, Missouri; Louisville, Kentucky; and Mobile, Alabama, from 1864-70. Although she was born free, she identified with the freedpeople through "ties of consanguinity and love . . . socially and politically they are 'my people' " (Lawson 1985). However, she also considered herself the equal of her white coworkers, noting that "God is man, Christ clothed in the habiliments of flesh, the Son of God in the person of a Negro" (Lawson 1985). Therefore, she insisted, unsuccessfully at the time, on equal housing for Black teachers.

In addition to being a teacher, Stanley also was an accomplished writer. The *Weekly African-American* published her critique of John Greenleaf Whittier's

poetry in the April 19, 1862, edition, and that same year she was named to the National Young Men's Literary Association, a Black organization. In the 1860s, the AMA regularly published her reports. One report describes a visit to her classroom by a government official, who told the children that education made them different from whites. Stanley told him that the children knew better: that the difference was money stolen off the backs of Black people over the years.

In 1868, Stanley, a mulatto, married Charles Woodward, a white Civil War veteran who managed the Freedmen's Bank in Mobile, where she continued to teach. (The 1870 census lists her as white.) The couple's only child died in infancy. They moved to the North in the late 1870s, and Sara is listed as a widow in 1885. She died in 1918, place and exact date unknown.

Sara Stanley, born free, highly educated, and able to pass as white in the racist climate of the late nineteenth century, chose not to pass but, instead, to teach freedpeople in the South in a tumultuous era.

BIBLIOGRAPHY

Franklin, John Hope. *The Free Negro in North Carolina* (1943); Lawson, E. N., ed. *The Three Sarahs: Documents of Antebellum Black College Women* (1985); "Recollections of New Bern Fifty Years Ago." In Craven-Pamlico-Carteret Regional Library, New Bern, North Carolina; Stanley, Sara G. Unpublished letters c. 1864-1869, American Missionary Association Papers, Amistad Research Center, New Orleans, Louisiana; Tyron Palace Commission. *The Stanley Family and the Historic John Wright Stanley House* (1969).

ELLEN MACKENSIE LAWSON

STAPLES, MAVIS (c. 1940-) / THE STAPLE SINGERS

Music critics unanimously applaud Mavis Staples as possessing one of the most dynamic and distinctive voices in contemporary music. Along with her father and siblings, Mavis was part of the Staple Singers, who enjoyed success with both gospel and popular music fans from the 1950s through the 1970s. She is also recognized as a solo performer of pop and gospel music.

In 1934, Roebuck "Pop" Staples moved his wife, Oceola, and children, Cleotha and Pervis, from his native Mississippi to Chicago. Once there, Yvonne, Mavis, and Cynthia were born, and eventually all of

With her family, the Staple Singers, Mavis Staples told the Black world in the sixties to "Respect Yourself." The Singers consisted of, left to right, Cleotha, Roebuck ("Pop"), Yvonne, and Mavis Staples. [Steve Holsey]

the children were taught to harmonize by their father. The Staple Singers performed in a style that has been described by gospel music historian Horace C. Boyer as "characterized by folk-style simple harmonies, rendered in a country and western twang, supporting a lead by the tenor voice of Roebuck or the hard gospel alto of Mavis" (Boyer 1991). Roebuck's bluesy guitar and the group's pulsating rhythm section also were featured.

After performing in local Chicago churches, the Staple Singers recorded for a number of companies, beginning with United Records (1954) and Vee Jay Records (1955-61), with which they released several recordings, including "Uncloudy Day." Subsequent labels were Riverside (1961-64) and Epic (1964-68); for the latter, they recorded the classic "Why (Am I Treated So Bad)." Yet it was the music they made for Stax Records (1968-74) that attracted mass audiences. While there, the Staple (the final "s" got dropped

over the years) Singers were featured in the "Soul to Soul" and Wattstax concerts. Among their hits were "Respect Yourself," "If You're Ready (Come Go with Me)" and "I'll Take You There," all of which became number-one *Billboard* hits. Further success and another number one hit came with their performance on the sound track for the comedy film *Let's Do It Again* for Curtom Records. Although some fans accused the singers of selling out when they switched from gospel to "message" music, the group insisted that although the beat had gotten funkier, the message of love had never changed. The Staple Singers continue to perform with various personnel changes (Pop has also recorded as a solo performer), but the group has not been able to replicate its earlier success.

Mavis's driving performance style and husky voice, reminiscent of two of her childhood gospel idols, Dorothy Love Coates and Ruth Davis, eventually led her to a solo career. Beginning in 1970, she recorded several critically acclaimed albums on the Volt, Warner Brothers, Phono, and Curtom labels. Among the recordings making the national rhythm and blues charts were "I Have Learned to Do Without You," "Endlessly," and "A Piece of the Action" from the movie of the same name. Mavis Staples also performs gospel music and has recorded with such major artists as Aretha Franklin (1988) and BeBe and CeCe Winans (1991); with the latter, she sang on their remake of her family's hit of twenty years ago, "I'll Take You There."

BIBLIOGRAPHY

Bonds, Ray, ed. *Illustrated Encyclopedia of Black Music* (1982); Boyer, Horace Clarence. Historical notes for *Freedom Highway*, Columbia Records/Sony Music Entertainment, CK 47334 AAd/ADD (1991); Bronson, Fred. *The Billboard Book of Number One Hits* (1985); Heilbut, Anthony. *The Gospel Sound: Good News and Bad Times* ([1971] 1985); Whitburn, Joel. *Joel Whitburn's Top R & B Singles, 1942-1988* (1988).

SELECTED DISCOGRAPHY

The Staple Singers: *The Twenty-Fifth Day of December*, Riverside, monaural RLP 3513, stereo RLP 93513 (1962); *Will the Circle Be Unbroken*, Vee Jay LP 5008 (1966); *The Best of the Staple Singers*, Vee Jay 5019; *Swing Low*, Vee Jay 5014; *Let's Do It Again*, Curtom 0109 (1975). Mavis Staples: *A Piece of the Action*, Curtom 0132 (1977); *Oh What a Feeling*, Warner (1979).

DEBORAH SMITH BARNEY

STATON, DAKOTA (1932-)

Born June 3, 1932, in Pittsburgh, Pennsylvania, Dakota Staton (Rabia Aliyah) is one of the best of several little advertised jazz singers. Her artistic talents became evident at an early age, as she began singing and dancing before she entered elementary school, and by the time she graduated from high school her jazz singing talent was sufficient to launch a professional career. She began to sing at jazz clubs, jazz festivals, and theaters throughout the United States and Canada while also studying music at the Fillon School of Music in Pittsburgh.

In 1954, at the age of twenty-two, she made her first recording. Thereafter she made several additional recordings, receiving critical acclaim for her album *The Late, Late Show* (1957). Staton recorded with George Shearing in 1957 and at the Newport Jazz Festival in 1963; she also toured with Benny

Goodman around 1960. In 1965, Staton moved to England, and from 1965 to the early 1970s she both lived and performed abroad, primarily in Australia, Europe, India, Pakistan, and the Far East.

Since returning to the United States in the early 1970s, Staton's recordings have become eclectic, including both jazz and two soul-jazz albums. Staton performs standards and incorporates elements of both Dinah Washington and Sarah Vaughan into her style. She displays excellent diction, has an excellent sense of rhythm and harmony, and often uses scat techniques in her voice stylings.

BIBLIOGRAPHY

BDAAM; Dahl, Linda. *Stormy Weather: The Music and Lives of a Century of Jazz Women* (1964); Kernfeld, Barry, ed. *The New Grove Dictionary of Jazz* (1985).

SELECTED DISCOGRAPHY

The Late, Late Show, Capitol T-576 (1957); *The George Shearing Quintet with Dakota Staton: In the Night*, Capitol ST-1503 (1957).

EDDIE S. MEADOWS

STAUPERS, MABEL KEATON (1890-1989)

The history of Black nursing is characterized by a relentless struggle for equality of opportunities and a quest for recognition and acceptance into the mainstream of American nursing. Although others also played major roles in the advance of Black nursing, Mabel Keaton Staupers deserves special recognition. Staupers orchestrated the long struggle of Black nurses to win full integration into the American nursing profession during the decades of the Great Depression and World War II. Staupers is perhaps best known for her role in implementing the desegregation of the U.S. Army Nurse Corps during World War II. She published an illuminating account of this and other battles of Black nurses in *No Time for Prejudice: A Story of the Integration of Negroes in Nursing in the United States* (1961).

Born in Barbados, West Indies, on February 27, 1890, to Thomas and Pauline Doyle, in April 1903 she and her parents migrated to the United States, settling into the Harlem community in New York City. She completed primary and secondary school there and in 1914 enrolled in the Freedmen's Hospital School of Nursing (now the Howard University College of Nursing) in Washington, D.C. Three years later she graduated with honors from the nursing program and was married to Dr. James Max Keaton of Asheville, North Carolina. The marriage, however, ended in divorce. In 1931 she married Fritz C. Staupers of New York City. They remained married until his death in 1949.

When Staupers entered nursing, the vast majority of hospital nurses' training schools denied admission to Black women. These exclusionary practices reflected the dominant social system of racial segregation and discrimination in America. In response, African-American leaders embraced the ideology of racial solidarity and Black self-help, creating a parallel infrastructure of hospitals and nursing training schools and founding separate professional societies and organizations.

Like the vast majority of all graduate nurses, Staupers began her professional career by accepting private-duty cases. Opportunities for Black women to secure positions in hospital staff nursing and visiting and settlement house or public health nursing were virtually nonexistent. Staupers was an exception in that her career as a private-duty nurse was brief. In 1920, in cooperation with Black physicians Louis T. Wright and James Wilson, Staupers helped to organize the Booker T. Washington Sanitarium, the first in-patient center in Harlem for Black patients with tuberculosis and one of the few city facilities that permitted Black physicians to treat their patients.

Staupers's work with Black health care facilities and organizations enlarged her awareness of the discrimination and segregation that African-Americans encountered in their search for adequate medical treatment. After she received a 1921 working fellowship at the Henry Phipps Institute of Tuberculosis in Philadelphia, she accepted an assignment at the Jefferson Hospital Medical College. Her firsthand observations of the ill treatment and lack of respect for African-Americans by college administrators and physicians left an indelible impression on the young nurse.

In 1922, she accepted an invitation by the New York Tuberculosis and Health Association to conduct a survey of the health needs of residents in the Harlem community. Her subsequent report finding the city's efforts to meet their needs inadequate led to the establishment of the Harlem Committee of the New York Tuberculosis and Health Association. For twelve years Staupers served as the organization's executive secretary. She worked assiduously to channel aid and resources to members of minority groups afflicted with tuberculosis.

In 1934, Staupers became executive secretary of the National Association of Colored Graduate Nurses

Best known for her role in implementing the desegregation of the U.S. Army Nurse Corps during World War II, Mabel Staupers was a tireless organizer and leader who was one of the founders of the National Council of Negro Women. For her achievements in integrating Black nurses into the mainstream, she received the Spingarn Medal in 1951. [Moorland-Spingarn]

(NACGN) just as Estelle Massey Osborne (1903-1981), the superintendent of nurses at the Homer G. Phillips Hospital in St. Louis, Missouri, assumed the presidency. In 1931, Osborne had become the first Black nurse to earn a Master of Arts degree in nursing education. Together Staupers and Osborne worked to win integration and acceptance of Black nurses into the mainstream of American nursing. Both women also joined Mary McLeod Bethune in 1935 to found the National Council of Negro Women.

The NACGN's fight for nursing integration involved a series of strategies, the first of which was instituting programs that addressed the immediate needs of Black nurses. Staupers spent the first few years in her new position collecting data, organizing state and local nursing associations, advising and counseling Black nurses, and representing them in the larger community. She organized a biracial national advisory council in 1938 in order to develop greater public interest in and support for the association's programs among prominent liberal white groups.

The struggle acquired new momentum and urgency with the outbreak of World War II. Staupers adroitly seized the opportunity created by the war emergency and the increased demand for nurses to project the plight of Black nurses into the national limelight. By the time of the Japanese attack on Pearl Harbor in December 1941, Staupers had developed a sharp sense of political timing. When the army set a quota of fifty-six Black nurses and the navy refused even to consider admitting Black nurses into the Nurse Corps, Staupers swung the NACGN into action. She publicized the denial of opportunities to Black nurses who desired to serve their country and joined with other Black leaders to meet directly with army generals and high-ranking government officials to protest the imposition of quotas. Although the pressure resulted in little immediate success, shortly before the war ended, Black nurses were able to claim victory in their war against discriminatory quotas and second-class treatment in the military and the civilian nursing professions.

Exhausted by the battle to integrate Blacks into the army and navy Nurse Corps, she relinquished her position as executive secretary of the NACGN in 1946 to take a much-needed rest. It was to be of short duration, however, since Staupers had not yet accomplished her major objective, the integration of Black women into the American Nurses' Association (ANA). Since 1934, Staupers and Osborne had pressured the ANA for integration at its biennial meetings. In 1948 the ANA opened its doors to Black membership.

Staupers was elected president of the NACGN in 1949. With the removal of the overtly discriminatory barriers to membership in the ANA, Staupers and the leadership of the NACGN persuaded its members that the organization was now obsolete. The ANA agreed to take over the functions of the NACGN and to continue to award the Mary Mahoney Medal to the individual or group contributing the most to intergroup relations within a given period. During the NACGN's 1949 convention the members voted the organization out of existence.

Staupers received many accolades for her leadership. The crowning acknowledgment of her role in and contribution to the quest of Black nurses for civil rights came when the Spingarn Committee of the National Association for the Advancement of Colored People chose her to receive the Spingarn Medal for 1951. In 1967, New York mayor John V. Lindsay gave her a citation of appreciation, which read, "To an immigrant who came to the United States and by Individual Effort through Education and Personal Achievement has become an Outstanding American Leader and Distinguished Citizen of America." Three years later Howard University gave her the Alumni Award "for Distinguished Achievement in the Fields of Nursing and Community Service." Staupers lived with her sister in Washington, D.C., until her death on September 29, 1989.

[See also NURSING.]

BIBLIOGRAPHY

The Fifty Year Graduates of Freedmen's Hospital School of Nursing Tell Their Story (1986); Hine, Darlene Clark. *Black Women in White: Racial Conflict and Cooperation in the Nursing Profession, 1890-1950* (1989), and "Mabel K. Staupers and the Integration of Black Nurses into the Armed Forces." In *Black Leaders of the Twentieth Century*, ed. John Hope Franklin and August Meier (1982); *New York Times* (obituary) (October 6, 1989); Mabel Keaton Staupers's papers are housed at the Moorland-Spingarn Research Center, Howard University, Washington, D.C.

DARLENE CLARK HINE

STEELE, REBECCA WALKER (1925-)

Rebecca Walker Steele has had a highly successful career as a choral music director, voice teacher, music educator, singer, and arts administrator. Currently she is director of the Concert Chorale as well as voice teacher and director of cultural affairs at Bethune-Cookman College in Daytona Beach, Florida.

She was born Rebecca Walker on October 18, 1925, the daughter of Edward David and Julia Walker of Lakeland, Florida. At an early age she began playing the piano and singing, talents that were nurtured by her parents, who provided her with the best possible musical training.

She holds a B.S. from Alabama State University, where she studied piano with Hazel Harrison and choral music with Fredrick Hall. She also holds an

M.A. in voice, piano, and choral conducting as well as a Master's degree in music education from Columbia University and a Ph.D. in humanities and music, with a special emphasis on multicultural music education, from Florida State University.

She was in great demand as a singer while still a student in New York City and later as a teacher at Florida A & M University, performing throughout the southeast. Particularly popular were her soprano solos from Mozart's *Requiem*, numerous operatic arias, and her interpretations of spirituals.

Rebecca Steele is a dynamic, demanding teacher who accepts nothing but the best from her students. Her motto, "No half-stepping," is evident in the quality of her students, both at Florida A & M and at Bethune-Cookman College. Under her direction, the concert choir at Florida A & M was noted for its performances of major extended choral works, including Verdi's *Requiem* and Bach's *Magnificat*, and for its outstanding renditions of Negro spirituals. While teaching at Florida A & M, Steele introduced opera to many school children through her production of Verdi's *Rigoletto*, performed by college students.

At Bethune-Cookman, Steele's production of "From Bach to Gospel" features choral works, ensembles, and solos in a wide variety of styles and from many periods. A master of musical interpretation, Steele is noted for her ability to conduct different styles of music and for the beautiful tone quality and phrasing she produces in her work. Constantly in demand, her choral groups have performed throughout the United States. The Bethune-Cookman Concert Chorale, for example, has performed with the Jacksonville Symphony Orchestra and Lyric Theatre in a production of *Porgy and Bess* as well as at the Spoleto festival in Charleston, South Carolina.

In addition to her work as a choral director, Steele is an outstanding voice teacher. Her students at Florida A & M have won many contests, including the Ted Mack Amateur Hour, the Florida State Music Teachers Association Collegiate Contest, and state and regional Metropolitan Opera auditions. Her graduates include opera singers, music educators, popular and jazz singers, and music administrators.

Steele's professional affiliations include the Music Educators National Conference, the Florida State Music Teachers Association, the Association of University Professors, the Southern Arts Federation (panelist and member of the Southern Arts Exchange), and the Florida Professional Presenters Consortium. She has served as adjudicator of vocal solo and choral music festivals, clinician for numerous music festi-

vals, and evaluator for the Southern Association of Colleges and Schools.

Steele has received awards from the Music Educators National Conference (certificate of excellence), the Florida A & M University Alumni Association, and the African-American Spiritual Renaissance Festival as well as numerous service awards from Florida A & M and Bethune-Cookman College.

She lives in Florida with her husband, prominent gourmet chef and food service director, John Steele, and their son, John David Steele.

BIBLIOGRAPHY
Steele, Rebecca Walker. Personal interviews.

MARY ROBERTS

STEWARD, SUSAN McKINNEY (1847-1918)

Her patients affectionately referred to her as "Dr. Susan" because this modest but strong-willed physician acted out of a compassionate love to serve humanity. She was born of mixed European, African, and Shinnecock Indian stock in 1847, the seventh of ten children of Sylvanus and Ann S. Smith. Both Sylvanus and his wife Ann Smith were active in civic affairs and members of the Brooklyn Black elite. As a child, Susan studied the organ under the tutelage of John Zundel and Henry Eyre Brown, and this musical training made her a welcome addition as organist and chorister at Brooklyn's Siloam Presbyterian Church and the Bridge Street African Methodist Episcopal (AME) Church.

Susan McKinney Steward entered the New York Medical College for Women in 1867, graduating three years later as class valedictorian. She was the first Black female to practice medicine in New York State and the third in the nation. Her predecessors, Rebecca Lee, a graduate of the New England Female Medical College (1864), and Rebecca J. Cole, a graduate of the Woman's Medical College in Philadelphia (1867), never equaled her in social or medical prominence. There are several possible explanations for her career choice. One was that she was shocked at the untimely deaths of two brothers during the Civil War. Also, in 1866 Brooklyn had high death rates from a cholera epidemic and perhaps Steward's attention to a sick niece convinced her that she could serve as a medical practitioner. In any event, her decision to seek a medical degree in an era when "ladies" either remained at home or sought teaching positions was indicative of her pride and her unwillingness to place limitations on her possibilities.

In the mid-nineteenth century, male editors, physicians, and laymen viewed medicine as the domain of men. Indeed, women physicians were considered unsexed. Fortunately for Steward, homeopathic medical schools welcomed the presence of women.

The New York Medical College for Women, which opened on November 1, 1863, was a homeopathic medical school founded by Clarence Sophia Lozier, a wealthy abolitionist. Lozier was Steward's mentor and close friend until Lozier's death in 1888, and she took special pleasure in seeing her prized student be selected by the faculty and fellow students as valedictorian of the class of 1870. Steward achieved

Shocked by the deaths of her two brothers during the Civil War and by Brooklyn's high death rates in 1866 from a cholera epidemic, Susan McKinney Steward entered medical school and became the first Black woman to practice medicine in New York State, and only the third Black woman physician in the entire United States. [Schomburg Center]

this honor by studying while her classmates slept, for neither fatigue nor the taunts of male medical students during shared clinic hours at Bellevue Hospital could deter her from her goal. Despite her achievement, New York area newspapers chose not to print her valedictory. The *Courier* did write about the event, but the reporter only focused on her hair and her choice of clothing, going so far as to express the hope that her "modest attire" was a "good sign of the improvement of the African race."

Steward's medical practice was slow in starting but began to improve as word spread about her skill, and as her caseload grew, it also became diverse; Steward's patients were young and old as well as white and Black. The *New York Sun*, in an 1887 feature on wealthy Black New Yorkers, described her as someone who had "a handsome bank account and lives well." In 1895, the *New York Times* described her Brooklyn address at 205 DeKalb Avenue as being "in the midst of the fashionable quarter of the hill." She was active in the Kings County Homeopathic Medical Society and the Homeopathic Medical Society of the State of New York. It was before this society that she presented two important medical papers. The first, presented in 1883, described an incident when she was called in to treat a pregnant woman who had been directed by another physician to treat her mother's burns twice daily with a solution of carbolic acid. The woman shared the same bed with her mother for five days and was very sick when Steward was contacted. Steward isolated the woman and treated her, but after her symptoms disappeared, the patient removed Steward from the case. A few days later the woman went into labor and died soon after giving birth; she had been contaminated earlier when treating her mother's burns. The infant died the following day. The second paper, "Marasmus Infantum," was delivered in 1886. Childhood diseases were a specialty of Steward, and she reported that marasmus, or a wasting away of the body, was caused by chronic vomiting, diarrhea, worms, and inherited syphilis. She believed that recovery was better under homeopathic treatment.

Despite a full medical practice and surgical rounds at the Brooklyn Woman's Homeopathic Hospital and Dispensary, as well as an affiliation with the Brooklyn Home for Aged Colored People as attending physician, Steward found time to be a community activist. She was active in Bridge Street's missionary work; she was a devout supporter of female suffrage; and, as president of the Women's Christian Temperance Union Number 6 in Brooklyn, she spoke out about the dangers of alcohol. In 1884, for example, she urged readers of the New York *Freeman* to "graciously" refrain from serving alcoholic beverages during the Christmas holiday season.

Susan McKinney Steward was married twice. She married William G. McKinney, an itinerant preacher, on July 12, 1871. They had two children, William S. McKinney, who was a clergyman in the Protestant Episcopal Church in New York City, and Anna M. Carty, the former wife of M. Louis Holly and a New York City school teacher. William G. McKinney died in 1892. On November 26, 1896, she married Theophilus Gould Steward, chaplain of the Twenty-fifth U.S. Colored Infantry. Steward was a prolific writer of both sacred and secular materials, and she accompanied her husband to Montana and other western states until his retirement in 1907. Later, they both joined the faculty of Wilberforce University in Ohio. The Stewards traveled to Europe for pleasure in 1909 and again in 1911 so that Steward could deliver a paper, "Colored American Women," before the delegates at the First Universal Race Congress in London. In 1914, she presented a paper, "Women in Medicine," before the National Association of Colored Women's Clubs in Wilberforce, Ohio.

When Susan Steward died on March 7, 1918, W.E.B. Du Bois delivered the eulogy. She is buried in Brooklyn's Green-Wood Cemetery. Through the persistence of William S. McKinney, Jr., Steward's grandson, the board of education renamed Brooklyn's Junior High School 265 the Dr. Susan Smith McKinney Junior High School in 1974. Black female doctors in the New York/New Jersey/Connecticut area also honored her memory by naming their medical society after her.

BIBLIOGRAPHY

Alexander, Leslie L. "Susan Smith McKinney, M.D. 1847-1918," *National Medical Association* (1975); Homeopathic Medical Society of the State of New York. "Proceedings of the Thirty-Second Annual Meeting" (February 14, 1883), *Transactions of the Homeopathic Medical Society of the State of New York* (1884), and "Proceedings of the Thirty-Fifth Annual Meeting" (1986), *Transactions of the Homeopathic Medical Society of the State of New York* (1887); Majors, M. A. *Noted Negro Women* (1893); *New York Sun*, "Some Rich Colored Men" (June 5, 1887); *New York Times*, "Wealthy Negro Citizens" (July 14, 1895); Seraile, William. "Susan McKinney Steward: New York State's First African-American Woman Physician," *Afro-Americans in New York Life and History* (July 1985); Steward, Susan M. "Colored American Women," *Crisis* (1911), and "Women in Medicine," Paper presented to the National

Association of Colored Women's Clubs at Wilberforce University in Wilberforce, Ohio (1914).

WILLIAM SERAILE

STEWART, ELLA PHILLIPS (1893-1987)

The child of sharecroppers, Ella Phillips Stewart rose to remarkable heights of accomplishment and honor in service of both the Black women's club movement and the United States government.

Born in 1893 in Berryville, Virginia, Ella Phillips attended a local grade school, where she was an outstanding student. From there she went to Storer College, winning five major scholarship awards and marrying fellow student Charles Myers. After the death of a child, she and Myers were divorced and she moved to Pittsburgh, Pennsylvania. While working as a bookkeeper at a drug store, she became acquainted with a local physician, who persuaded her to become a pharmacist. The first Black woman to attend the pharmacy school at Pittsburgh University, she became friendly with two white classmates who, after graduation, hired her to work as a pharmacist at the drugstore they opened.

Ella Phillips owned her own drugstore when she met William Wyatt Stewart and married him. The Stewarts moved to Ohio, where they settled in Toledo, opened a pharmacy, and became important members of their community. Their store became a center of community activity and their home, above the store, offered lodgings to visiting Black celebrities such as Mary McLeod Bethune and W.E.B. Du Bois.

Ella Phillips Stewart was active in club work, becoming president in 1948 of the National Association of Colored Women. She updated Elizabeth Davis's *Lifting as They Climb* (1933), a history of the NACW, and, after traveling throughout the world for a number of groups, including the Education Exchange Service of the U.S. State Department, she was appointed by Dean Rusk to the executive board of the U.S. Commission of the United Nations Educational, Scientific, and Cultural Organization (UNESCO). A lifetime of honors was capped when the city of Toledo named a new $3 million elementary building the Ella P. Stewart Elementary School.

BIBLIOGRAPHY

CBWA; NBAW; Wesley, Charles Harris. *The History of* *the National Association of Colored Women's Clubs* (1984).

KATHLEEN THOMPSON

STEWART, ELLEN (c. 1920-)

Ellen Stewart's main criterion for deciding whether to produce any given play is at once simple and mystical: "If a play is talking to me personally, if a script *beeps* to me when I'm reading it, we do it" (Greenfield 1967). Stewart continues to combine this straightforward enthusiasm with an uncanny ability to smooth over bureaucratic, economic, and interpersonal barriers in operating La MaMa ETC, the leading experimental theater in New York since the early 1960s.

The facts about Ellen Stewart's personal life are hazy, and she likes to keep them that way. She was born around 1920, perhaps in Illinois or Louisiana. She has a son and a grandchild. She was raised in Chicago, but in 1950 left for New York, where she felt she would have better opportunities to study fashion design. She got a job at Saks Fifth Avenue and spent her Sundays exploring New York City. On an expedition to the Lower East Side, she was befriended by a clothing merchant, Abraham Diamond, who began promoting her designs. Soon she became an executive designer for Saks, but had to leave her position when she became seriously ill. While recuperating in Tangiers, a friend's remark that one must "have one's own pushcart" (Greenfield, 1967) prompted Stewart to return to New York to seek out her "pushcart": a theater of her own.

She rented a theater in the basement of 321 East Ninth Street in 1961. Cafe La MaMa began there, and relocated four times over the next four years: first to 82 Second Avenue; then to 122 Second Avenue, in a loft above a laundromat; then to 9 St. Mark's Place; and then to 74 East Fourth Street, as La MaMa ETC (Experimental Theatre Club), with the La MaMa Annex three doors away, at 66-68 East Fourth Street.

As a club La MaMa originally operated on a subscription basis, with Stewart constantly contributing money from her earnings as a fashion designer to keep the theater afloat. In part due to the experimental nature of La MaMa's productions, and in part due to Stewart's view that long runs foster a "success-failure syndrome" harmful to developing playwrights, La MaMa's finances have often teetered on the brink of disaster. In 1966 La MaMa almost closed permanently when Actors Equity decreed that its actors could not work at La MaMa unless Stewart paid them. Equity rescinded its decree in response to her appeal.

Since then, Stewart has received several grants to support the theater and pay the actors. The move to East Fourth Street was funded by grants from the Ford and Rockefeller foundations. She has received numerous grants from the National Endowment for the Arts over the years and, in 1985, a $300,000 MacArthur Fellowship. Her other honors include the Margo Jones Award for helping to develop new playwrights (1969, 1979), the Brandeis Award for distinguished contribution to the theater (1967), a New York State Council on the Arts Award (1973), a special Obie for achievement in Off Off Broadway Theatre (1980), and the Edwin Booth Award (1985), given by the Ph.D. program in Theatre of the CUNY Graduate Center for a significant contribution to New York theater.

Ellen Stewart has given new playwrights the freedom to develop, and the playwrights she fostered epitomize the New York avant-garde. A brief list of her protégés includes Sam Shepard, Jean-Claude van Itallie, Rochelle Owens, Tom Eyen, Julie Bovasso, Megan Terry, Lanford Wilson, Elizabeth Swados, Israel Horovitz, and Leonard Melfi. La MaMa also fostered important directors such as Andrei Serban and Tom O'Horgan. While rooted in the East Village theater scene, La MaMa enjoys international fame. Acting ensembles from La MaMa began touring Europe in 1965, and affiliated companies were established in London, Paris, Bogota, Tokyo, and several other cities around the world. La MaMa gave Harold Pinter his first American showing with its production of *The Room* (1962), and Stewart has brought countless other artists and companies from around the world to perform at La MaMa, the theater Elizabeth Swados has dubbed "the Marx Brothers version of the United Nations" (Swados 1986).

BIBLIOGRAPHY

BAR; *Current Biography* (1973); Greenfield, Josh. "Their Hearts Belong to La MaMa," *New York Times* (July 9, 1967); Loney, Glenn. "La MaMa: The First Twenty Years," *Performing Arts Journal* (1982); *Notable Names in the American Theatre* (1976); *NWAT*; Stewart, Ellen. "Ellen Stewart and La MaMa," *TDR* (June 1980); Swados, Elizabeth. "Stretching Boundaries: The Merlin of La MaMa," *New York Times* (October 26, 1986); *Who's Who in America* (1978-1979); *Who's Who in the Theatre* (1981).

JOEL BERKOWITZ

STEWART, MARIA W. (1803-1879)

"What if I am a woman?" intoned Maria W. Stewart during a speech in Boston on September 21, 1833. Throughout her brief oration she reminded her mixed audience of women and men that women, even in the ancient world, had been honored for their wisdom, prudence, religiosity, and achievements. Yet, her own people of color, she noted, had failed to accord her similar recognition.

Maria Stewart, born in Hartford, Connecticut, in 1803, had taken up public speaking as a means of supporting herself following husband James's death. Her marriage in 1826 at the Reverend Thomas Paul's African Baptist Church marked her as a member of Boston's small Black middle class; but she had been cheated of a comfortable inheritance by unscrupulous white Boston merchants. Before her public speaking tour (1832-33) she had published a small pamphlet, *Religion and the Pure Principles of Morality, the Sure Foundation on Which We Must Build* (1831). During her short public speaking career she also published *Meditations from the Pen of Mrs. Maria W. Stewart* (1832). William Lloyd Garrison reported all four of her speeches in the pages of his *Liberator*, the best known abolitionist newspaper of the time. Thus, it was neither a stranger nor an outside agitator that sought to address the problems faced by Black Boston and American Blacks.

Stewart's speeches were not well received due to the gender politics of nineteenth-century America. She was, after all, the first American-born woman to break the taboo against women participating in public political dialogues, a taboo shared by Black and white communities alike. Moreover, there was opposition to Stewart from within conservative Black Boston political circles.

Although married in the African Baptist Church, there is reason to believe that Stewart at the time of her public speeches was more influenced by the individuals and activities represented by Rev. Samuel Snowden's African Methodist Episcopal Church. In 1829, one of its members, David Walker, had published his controversial *Walker's Appeal*. Prior to that, in 1826, the Massachusetts General Colored Association was founded. These two events laid the groundwork for Stewart's advocacy of Black self-determination and economic independence from even well-meaning whites. All three developments were part of a burgeoning radicalism among young Black Bostonians, and perhaps an implied criticism of Rev. Thomas Paul's tendency to work consistently but not exclusively with white allies.

Although rebuffed in her attempt at public political speaking, Stewart had a distinguished career as public school teacher in New York City, Baltimore, and Washington, D.C. In 1878, when applying for a widow's pension from her second husband, Stewart was reunited with her old friend and publisher, William Lloyd Garrison. She subsequently published, at her own expense, an enlarged edition of *Meditations* (1879). Shortly after, she died, and on December 17, 1879, Maria W. Stewart was buried at Graceland Cemetery in Washington.

The emergence of Black history and women's studies has reintroduced scholars to the life and work of Maria W. Stewart, but this pioneering Black political activist still lacks a critical biographical assessment. Her life and her continuing obscurity illustrate the double pressures of racism and sexism on the lives of Black women. Rather than being recognized as a significant advocate of Black autonomy, she has been silenced for more than four decades. Stewart's speeches and writings issue a clear challenge to our contemporary world: Black women's need for self-determination cannot be addressed if it is only an adjunct to Black men's freedom.

[*See also* ABOLITION MOVEMENT.]

BIBLIOGRAPHY

Giddings, Paula. *When and Where I Enter: The Impact of Black Women on Race and Sex in America* (1984); Lerner, Gerda, ed. *Black Women in White America: A Documentary History* (1972); Loewenberg, Bert James and Ruth Bogin. *Black Women in Nineteenth-Century American Life: Their Words, Their Feelings, Their Thoughts* (1976); Porter, Dorothy. "The Organized Educational Activities of Negro Literary Societies, 1828-1846," *Journal of Negro Education* (October 1936); Quarles, Benjamin. *Black Abolitionists* (1969); Richardson, Marilyn, ed. *Maria W. Stewart, America's First Black Woman Political Writer: Essays and Speeches* (1987); Stewart, Maria W. *Religion and the Pure Principles of Morality, the Sure Foundation on Which We Must Build* (1831), and *Meditations from the Pen of Mrs. Maria W. Stewart* (1832), and *Productions of Mrs. Maria W. Stewart* (1835), and *Meditations by Mrs. Maria W. Stewart* (1879).

HARRY A. REED

STEWART, SALLIE WYATT (1881-1951)

Sallie Wyatt Stewart was a prominent figure in the flourishing Black women's club movement in Indiana during the early decades of the twentieth century. A statewide network of scores of individual clubs provided space for Black women to socialize and develop leadership skills. Such clubs were useful in galvanizing support for the establishment of an impressive array of welfare and service institutions designed to fulfill the distinct social, health care, and recreational needs of Black Indianans.

By the 1920s, Black women's clubs were found in every major city in Indiana. For example, in Terre Haute, Black women organized the Phyllis Wheatley Association, which served as a recreational center and boardinghouse for young Black girls; and Anna B. Barton, a beautician, organized the St. Pierre Ruffin Club in South Bend in 1900, where, as she asserted, Black women "could learn the finer things of life: Literature, Art and Music." Other clubwomen founded and maintained retirement homes, settlement houses, hospitals and sanitariums, and gymnasiums and raised money for scholarships for Black youths across the state of Indiana.

The woman who best epitomizes the contributions of Black women in Indiana is Sallie Wyatt Stewart. Sallie migrated with her family from Ensle, Tennessee, to Evansville in the 1880s, joining the roughly 2,600 African-Americans in the border city who shared a common inheritance of illiteracy, propertylessness, and powerlessness. Like their counterparts in cities throughout the Midwest, Black migrants to Evansville suffered low job status, poor living conditions, residential segregation, and white hostility.

When her father became disabled, Sallie shared with her mother the responsibility for raising her seven younger sisters and brothers. Through sheer will, Sallie was able to complete her education in spite of overwhelming demands at home. She graduated from the Evansville High School as valedictorian of her class and subsequently took courses at Evansville Normal School, the University of Chicago, and Indiana University. Sallie proved to be intelligent, resourceful, hard working, ambitious, and highly motivated. She completely subscribed to the ideals of self-help. After securing a teaching certificate, Sallie commenced a fifty-year career as a teacher in the Evansville school system. From 1924 to 1928, she was dean of girls at Douglass High School. She held a similar position at the all-Black Lincoln High School from 1929 to 1951, where she introduced the first courses in domestic science, stenography, and mental hygiene.

An energetic and imposing woman, she became involved in many diverse ventures. In 1912, she became the catalyst for generating much of the Black social service work in Evansville, which benefited the

Among the many organizations founded by clubwoman Sallie Wyatt Stewart was the National Association of Colored Girls, which was affiliated with the National Association of Colored Women, of which she was the fourth president. [Schomburg Center]

entire community. In 1915 she was secretary of the Evansville chapter of the National Association for the Advancement of Colored People. She was selected chairperson of the Black auxiliary of the county tuberculosis association in 1928. In the late 1920s, she founded a Black women's newspaper entitled *Hoosier Women.* This was the first, if not the only, publication devoted exclusively to Black women's concerns in Indiana. Other affiliations included president of the National Association of Colored Women (NACW) in 1930, fourth vice president of the National Council of Women, member of the Executive Committee of the National Negro Business League, member of the Executive Committee of the National Colored Merchant's Association, secretary of the Inter-Racial

Commission of Evansville, trustee of the Eastern Star and Masonic Home of Indiana, and president of the Tuberculosis Auxiliary and the Lincoln Alumni Association. She was the founder of the Evansville Federation of Colored Women, the Day Nursery Association for Colored Children, the Phyllis Wheatley Association in Evansville, and the National Association of Colored Girls, which was affiliated with the NACW. In 1942, Stewart organized a Colored Women's War Work Committee to sell war bonds and stamps.

After her marriage to Logan Stewart, the two joined forces to develop a very lucrative real estate business, which she continued to manage after his death in 1928. When she died in 1951, Stewart left an estate valued at over $100,000, all of which she stipulated in her will was to be used to help young Black girls.

BIBLIOGRAPHY

Bingham, Darrel E. *We Ask Only a Fair Trial: A History of the Black Community of Evansville, Indiana* (1987); Hine, Darlene Clark. *When the Truth Is Told: Black Women's Culture and Community in Indiana, 1875-1950* (1981).

DARLENE CLARK HINE

STEWART-LAI, CARLOTTA (1881-1952)

The Black experience in Hawaii has remained largely obscure even though a handful of Black laborers and professionals migrated to Hawaii during the nineteenth and twentieth centuries in order to improve their economic status and escape the social and political restrictions that plagued Black Americans on the mainland. Among these sojourners was Carlotta Stewart-Lai, a Black educator who, for more than four decades, taught in the Hawaiian public schools and served as a principal on the islands of Oahu and Kauai. Stewart-Lai's career illustrates that despite the presence of a small Black population and considerable discrimination directed at other racial and ethnic minorities, Hawaii was a relatively open community for Black females and that economic opportunities were available for Black women beyond domestic work and menial labor.

The third child of T. McCants Stewart and Charlotte Pearl Harris, Carlotta Stewart was born in 1881 in Brooklyn, New York, where she attended public school and spent her formative years. She was eighteen when she arrived in Hawaii in 1898,

At the age of twenty-eight, Carlotta Stewart-Lai became principal of a multiracial Hawaiian elementary school, a stunning achievement for a Black woman in 1909. She is seen here in a 1902 photograph with other members of the senior class of Oahu College. [Moorland-Spingarn]

accompanying her father and stepmother. Stewart had hoped to continue her education in Hawaii and begin planning her future. This expectation was realized in 1902, when, as one of eight members in the senior class, she graduated from Oahu College after one year. After graduation, Stewart completed the requirements for a normal (teaching) school certificate, which she received in 1902, and she promptly accepted a teaching position in the practice department of the normal school in July. Stewart remained at the normal school for several years, where she taught English, her major at Oahu College.

Stewart-Lai's teaching career illustrates many of the opportunities and challenges that Black professional women faced in Hawaii during the early twentieth century. Her annual salary of $660 in 1902 placed her comfortably in the Black middle class, both in Hawaii and on the mainland. Within four years her salary had increased to $900, which she supplemented by typing in her spare time. By 1908, her teaching salary had increased to $100 per month; this not only provided a comfortable standard of living, it also financed extensive travel throughout the islands when her classes were not in session, permitted occasional trips to the mainland by ocean steamer to visit relatives, and allowed her to provide limited financial assistance to her mother and two brothers.

Stewart was highly respected in the community as well as in the classroom. She told her brother, McCants, during the 1906 school year that in addition to teaching, she was busy with classes, vacations, camping, surfing, and frequent parties. She also attended Sunday baseball games on the islands and served as coach of the junior and senior female teams in her local community. Stewart's career advancement, her acceptance into the larger Hawaiian community, and her strong friendships were pivotal factors in her decision to remain in Hawaii following her father and stepmother's departure in 1905.

Although conditions were neither difficult nor racially oppressive for a Black professional woman in Hawaii, there was no substantial Black community before World War II, and Stewart saw few Black people in either her classrooms or outside. Most of her socializing took place in groups, thus relieving her of the pressure to find a companion with a comparable racial and social background.

Nonetheless, Stewart remained isolated from her family, and following the death of her mother in 1906 she felt particularly distraught. She had promised to help her mother financially following her divorce from T. McCants Stewart, an obligation that, by her own admission, she had neglected. Yet Stewart was not altogether to blame, for T. McCants Stewart prohibited his three children from contacting their natural mother while they were under his care following his remarriage in 1893. The news of her mother's death triggered a feeling of alienation and depression, and in 1907 Stewart considered returning to the mainland to live permanently for the first time since her arrival in Hawaii.

However, Stewart decided not to return to the mainland. Despite her intermittent loneliness, the depression following the death of her mother, and her financial problems, which stemmed in part from the Panic of 1907, she was an established professional woman in the Hawaiian schools, a status she would have been unlikely to achieve in any Pacific Coast community in the early twentieth century because of racial discrimination. She decided to remain in Hawaii.

Her decision to stay proved to be advantageous, for within two years she had been promoted to principal of an elementary school, with an increase in salary. Her rapid advancement in the space of seven years was an impressive achievement, for although many Black women had established teaching careers, and a handful were school administrators by 1909, it was unusual for a Black female at the age of twenty-eight to serve as principal of a multiracial school. This achievement was particularly striking in a society in which few Black people lived and, therefore, had no political influence to request a job of this magnitude.

Stewart's pupils reflected a true cross-section of Hawaii's school-aged population, which grew rapidly between 1900 and 1940. In 1933, for example, the composition of her pupils included Hawaiians, Japanese, Filipinos, Koreans, and Portuguese; sixteen white Americans also were listed among the student population, but no Black students were included. It is unlikely that Stewart had contact with more than a handful of Black students prior to World War II, and the majority were probably the children of U.S. military personnel and Black laborers who worked on sugar and pineapple plantations.

The number of pupils who attended Stewart's schools when she served as principal varied annually, ranging between 200 and 300 students. The *Hanamaulu School World*, for example, reported that 283 students of various races attended the Hanamaulu School where Stewart served as principal in 1933. Between 1940 and 1944, however, the school's enrollment declined to 256 students. In addition to managing the school, Stewart also supervised several classroom teachers, the school librarian, the cafeteria manager, and taught English. These responsibilities were a firm testament of the confidence that public school officials had in Stewart's administrative ability, but they also indicate how far she had come in her career.

Stewart was not a social reformer and never joined any organization designed to promote the advancement of African-Americans, Puerto Ricans, Asians, Hawaiians, or women. It is true that Hawaii did not have chapters of the most prominent Black national organizations, such as the National Association for the Advancement of Colored People (NAACP), the National Urban League, the National Association of Colored Women (NACW), or the National Council of Negro Women during those years, yet Stewart had grown up in a family of Black activists. Her brothers, McCants and Gilchrist, both attorneys, were active in civil rights activities in Portland and New York, and her father had challenged successfully several Jim Crow laws in the state of New York and won the praise of Booker T. Washington.

In 1916, as Stewart approached her thirty-fifth birthday, she married Yun Tim Lai, of Chinese ancestry, at Anahola, Kauai County. Lai, five years younger than Stewart, was sales manager of Garden Island Motors, Ltd., an automobile dealership in Lihue, Kauai, when the couple wed.

In 1944, after forty-two years of public service in the Hawaiian schools, Carlotta Stewart-Lai retired. She lived the final years of her life in Kauai on Anahola Bay, before ill health forced her to enter a Honolulu nursing home in 1951. Her health declined rapidly, and on July 6, 1952, she died.

Few Black women were employed in teaching or administrative jobs in the western states and territories when Stewart-Lai began teaching at the Normal School in 1902, and fewer still succeeded in moving up the ladder to become principals or administrators before World War II. Thus Carlotta Stewart-Lai was not only a trailblazer for Black women in Hawaii but for Black women throughout the entire West.

BIBLIOGRAPHY

Adams, Romanzo C. *Interracial Marriage in Hawaii: A Study of the Mutually Conditioned Processes of Acculturation and Amalgamation* (1937); Broussard, Albert S. Personal interviews with Mrs. Katherine Stewart Flippin (July 19, 1986; June 4, 1987); de Graaf, Lawrence B. "Race, Sex, and Region: Black Women in the American West, 1850-1920," *Pacific Historical Review* (May 1980); Du Puy, William Atherton. *Hawaii and Its Race Problem* (1923); Greer, R. A. "Blacks in Old Hawaii," *Honolulu* (November 1986); Harris, William H. *The Harder We Run: Black Workers since the Civil War* (1982); Hine, Darlene Clark. *When the Truth Is Told: A History of Black Women's Culture and Community in Indiana, 1875-1950* (1981), and "To Be Gifted, Female, and Black," *Southwest Review* (August 1982); Jones, Jacqueline. *Labor of Love, Labor of Sorrow: Black Women, Work, and the Family from Slavery to the Present* (1985); Katzman, David M. *Seven Days a Week: Women and Domestic Service in Industrializing America* (1978); Lee, Lloyd L. "A Brief Analysis of the Role and Status of the Negro in the Hawaiian Community," *American Sociological Review* (August 1948); Lerner, Gerda. "Community Work for Black Clubwomen," *Journal of Negro History* (April 1974); Neverdon-Morton, Cynthia. *Afro-American Women of the South and the Advancement of the Race, 1895-1925* (1989); Nordyke, Eleanor C. "Blacks in Hawai'i: A Demographic and Historical Perspective," *Hawaiian Journal of History* (1988); *Report of the Superintendent of Public Instruction to the Governor of the Territory of Hawaii, 1902-1904* (1904); Sterling, Dorothy, ed., *We Are Your Sisters: Black Women in the Nineteenth Century* (1984); Stewart, Theophilus Gould. *Fifty Years in the Gospel Ministry* (1921); Stewart-Flippin papers, Moorland-Spingarn Research Center, Howard University, Washington, D.C.; Takara, Kathryn, and Michi Kodama-Nishimoto. *Oral History Recorder*, Oral History Project on Black Hawaiians, Center for Oral History, the University of Hawaii at Manoa; Takara, Kay Brundage. "Who Is the Black Woman in Hawaii?" In *Montage*, ed. Nancy Foon Young and Judy R. Parrish (1977); Tate, Merze. "The Sandwich Island Missionaries Lay the Foundation for a System of Public Instruction in Hawaii," *Journal of Negro Education* (Fall 1961); Yinger, John Milton. "Integration and Pluralism Viewed from Hawaii," *Antioch Review* (Winter 1962-63).

ALBERT S. BROUSSARD

STOKES, ORA BROWN (1882-1957)

Only 7 of the 240 biographies included in the Virginia volume of A. B. Caldwell's *History of the American Negro* (1921) chronicle the lives of African-American women. Among this select group was Ora Brown Stokes, whom Caldwell described as "a rare leader whose brilliant intellect and charming personality have been put upon the altar for her people." By 1921, when Caldwell's volume appeared, Stokes had completed nearly twenty years of service to church, temperance, education, suffrage, and civic reform organizations in Virginia and had begun to acquire a national reputation as one of her state's most active and influential Black leaders.

Ora M. Brown was born on June 11, 1882, in Chesterfield County, Virginia, the second daughter of the Reverend James E. Brown, a Baptist minister, and his second wife, Olivia Quarles Brown, a schoolteacher. In 1887, Reverend Brown accepted a call to the pastorate of Shiloh (Old Site) Baptist Church in Fredericksburg, where young Ora Brown was raised and educated. Possessing a quick mind and a zest for learning that her parents encouraged, she excelled in Fredericksburg's segregated public school system, winning her class medal each year in high school and graduating at the age of thirteen. She then enrolled in the Virginia Normal and Collegiate Institute, in Petersburg, where she earned her Bachelor's degree with a major in economics. Ora Brown taught school in Milford, Virginia, for two years following graduation. On September 9, 1902, she married thirty-year-old William H. Stokes, the dynamic new pastor of Richmond's Ebenezer Baptist Church.

Ora Brown Stokes continued her education after marriage, studying at Hartshorn Memorial College, in Richmond, and at the University of Chicago's School of Civics and Social Administration. She also took an active part in the life of her husband's congregation, teaching in the Sunday school, singing in the choir, organizing a missionary society, and leading the Baptist Young People's Union. Within a few years she had also become an officer in the statewide Women's Baptist Missionary and Educational Association. The Stokeses had no natural children, but during the early years of their marriage Ora Stokes helped to care for her husband's young sister and an adopted son, Earnest Morton. From 1909 to 1911, Stokes operated a millinery shop but she soon abandoned this effort in favor of a career in civic and social work.

In 1912, Stokes founded the Richmond Neighborhood Association, a general relief and self-help organization dedicated to the needs of working women and girls. The association, with Stokes as president and superintendent, quickly grew in membership and scope to become one of Richmond's most important African-American community institutions. The association supported a day nursery and a home for young girls, sponsored satellite organizations such as the Camp Fire Girls, the Protective League for Negro Girls, and a chapter of the Council of Negro Women, held public lectures featuring Black and white community leaders, and conducted discussion groups on topics ranging from "The Home Beautiful" to "Neglected Children." Members of the association also participated in community-wide activities, providing relief to flood victims, contributing to the care of tubercular patients, and sponsoring a citywide clean-up campaign. By 1919, the association estimated that it had assisted more than 6,000 persons and had accumulated property valued at $10,000. Stokes's work on behalf of the Richmond Neighborhood Association brought her into contact with city and state welfare officials, who sought and relied upon her advice. Both the State Board of Charities and Corrections and the Richmond City Juvenile Court employed her as a probation officer, work she continued to do for the next twenty years.

Stokes's warm personality and gift for public speaking brought her many opportunities and invitations that placed great demands upon her time. She traveled extensively during the 1920s and 1930s, addressing community groups and college audiences, and she participated actively in a host of influential organizations. She served on the executive committee of the Hampton University Conference and the Negro Organization Society of Virginia and was a trustee of Hartshorn College. She was staunchly committed to the cause of woman suffrage and after 1920 served as president of the Virginia Negro Woman's League of Voters. During World War I, she served as chair of the Colored Women's Section of the Council of National Defense in Virginia, and after the war served several terms as president of the Improved Order of Shepherds and Daughters of Bethlehem and of the southeastern section of the National Association of Colored Women, as well as vice-president of the National Race Congress, the National Conference of Social Workers, and the Virginia Federation of Colored Women's Clubs. Ora Stokes curtailed her activities somewhat in the early 1930s due to her husband's failing health but resumed her hectic schedule following his death in 1936. She was serving as director of a receiving home for Black youth operated by the Virginia Department of Public Welfare when she was asked by Mary McLeod Bethune to join the staff of the National Youth Administration, in Washington, D.C.

Ora Brown Stokes continued to maintain a Richmond address until the end of World War II, when she accepted a position as a field director of the Women's Christian Temperance Union (WCTU), the only Black member of the WCTU's national staff. While working for the WCTU in Houston, Texas, Stokes met physician John Edward Perry, whom she married on March 4, 1948. The couple moved to Kansas City, Missouri, where Ora Stokes continued her work on behalf of Black women's orga-

nizations. She became ill in the spring of 1957 while in Washington, D.C., on an assignment for the National Association of Colored Women. Returning to Kansas City, she died there on December 19, 1957.

Nearly a generation younger than Maggie Lena Walker and Janie Porter Barrett, Ora Stokes's contributions to African-American life in Virginia were on a par with those of her more famous contemporaries. Well educated and deeply committed to the advancement of her gender and race, she worked tirelessly in the areas of social reform that she believed to be most pressing. Typical of college-trained southern Black women of her day, Stokes contributed to the activist tradition of Black women's organizations that later energized the men and women of the mid-twentieth-century civil rights movement.

BIBLIOGRAPHY

Caldwell, A. B., ed. *History of the American Negro (Virginia Edition)* (1921); *Calendar of the Richmond Neighborhood Association, 1919-1920* (1919); Fitzgerald, Ruth Coder. *A Black History of Fredericksburg, Stafford, and Spotsylvania, Virginia* (1979); *Fredericksburg Free Lance* (September 13, 1902); "Minutes of the Tenth Annual Session of the Women's Baptist Missionary and Educational Association of Virginia" (June 22-25, 1910). Virginia State Library and Archives, Richmond, Virginia; *Norfolk Journal and Guide* (August 10, 1946; January 4, 1958); *Program of the First Annual Session of the Negro Organization Society, November 6-7, 1913.* Virginia State Library and Archives, Richmond, Virginia; *Report of the State Board of Charities and Corrections* (1911-1920). Virginia State Library and Archives, Richmond, Virginia; *Richmond News Leader* (July 30, 1946); *Richmond Planet* (March 31, 1917; September 1928; March 23, 1929; July 27, 1929; October 11, 1930; July 25, 1936); *Souvenir Program.* National Association of Colored Women's Clubs, Twelfth Biennial Session, Richmond, Virginia (August 1922); Birth Records, Division of Vital Records and Health Statistics, Virginia Department of Health, Chesterfield County, Virginia State Library and Archives, Richmond, Virginia (1853-96).

SANDRA GIOIA TREADWAY

STOUT, JUANITA KIDD (1919-)

Juanita Kidd Stout is noteworthy for a career of firsts in the legal profession, being both the first Black woman to be elected to a judgeship and the first to serve on a state supreme court. Born in Wewoka, Oklahoma, on March 7, 1919, she was the only child of Henry and Mary Kidd. Both college educated, the Kidds raised their daughter in an environment that was conducive to learning. A very bright child, Juanita was taught to read at the age of two by her mother, who was a school teacher. Reading together was a favorite family pastime.

Juanita Kidd was educated in the segregated public schools of Wewoka, where she received an excellent education from the dedicated Black teachers. Upon graduating in 1935, she left Oklahoma because the separate Black college for African-Americans, Langston University, was unaccredited. She enrolled at the University of Iowa, where she earned a B.A. in music in 1939.

In June 1942, Juanita Kidd married Charles Otis Stout who used his educational benefits from the GI Bill so that he could go to graduate school and Juanita could go to law school. Juanita Kidd Stout earned a J.D. (1948), while Charles Otis Stout earned his Ph.D., both from Indiana University.

In 1948, the Stouts moved to Washington, D.C., where Juanita Kidd Stout became the administrative secretary for the Honorable Charles H. Houston of the law firm of Houston, Houston, and Hastie. In 1949, when William H. Hastie was appointed as a judge for the U.S. Court of Appeals for the Third Circuit in Philadelphia, Juanita Kidd Stout joined him in Philadelphia to serve as his administrative secretary. Between 1953 and 1955, she worked in private practice, specializing in civil and criminal law. In 1955, however, she accepted a post as an assistant district attorney for Philadelphia, while continuing a limited private practice. In November 1959, Juanita Kidd Stout was elected as a Philadelphia county court judge, and became the first African-American woman to be elected to a court of record. She successfully ran for retention in 1969 and in 1979. Remarkably, during these years Judge Stout's decisions were reversed fewer than ten times.

Judge Stout was appointed to the state supreme court in February 1988 and was inducted on March 3, 1988, becoming the first African-American woman to serve on a state supreme court. She was forced to retire in 1989, on her seventieth birthday, due to the mandatory retirement provision of the Pennsylvania constitution. She subsequently served as a senior judge in the Court of Common Pleas in Philadelphia.

During the course of her memorable career, Justice Stout has been awarded ten LL.D. degrees and an L.H.D., has written several articles, and has received over 250 organizational awards. An article in the *Retainer*, a publication of the Philadelphia Bar Association, proclaimed that Justice Stout "possesses all of the qualities that are necessary to be a great jurist—a keen intellect, an appreciation of the issues, compas-

sion where appropriate, an inexhaustible supply of energy and the courage to apply the law fairly and justly regardless of how controversial the issues or powerful the parties" (Rosenwald 1988).

BIBLIOGRAPHY

Ebony, "Philadelphia's Lady Judge" (March 1960); *Ebony*, "A Career of Firsts" (February 1989); *Pennsylvania Law Journal-Reporter*, "Off the Bench and Off the Cuff" (February 23, 1981); *Philadelphia Enquirer*, "A Justice of Quality" (October 30, 1988); Rosenwald, Lawrence S. "Juanita Stout: Truly a Judge for All the People," *The Retainer* (February 10, 1988); Stout, Juanita Kidd. Speech given on Heritage Day, Wewoka, Oklahoma (May 1980).

V. P. FRANKLIN

STRINGER, C. VIVIAN (1948-)

C. Vivian Stringer, coach of the University of Iowa's nationally ranked women's basketball team, is the most significant Black basketball coach in the history of the women's game. For the last two decades she has been committed to breaking gender- and race-related barriers. Stringer's leadership and the respect she commands as an exceptionally talented coach enabled her to become the first Black woman head coach of a U.S. national women's basketball team. Her squad won a bronze medal in the 1991 Pan American Games in Havana, Cuba. She successfully coached the 1989 U.S. World Championship zone qualification team. No stranger to the winner's circle in earlier years, Stringer also led a small, unknown Black Cheyney State College (Pennsylvania) basketball team to a second-place finish in the first National Collegiate Athletic Association (NCAA) Women's National Basketball Championship in 1982.

Charlene Vivian Stoner was born to Charles and Thelma Stoner in Edenborn, Pennsylvania, March 16, 1948. Participation in a variety of sports and a desire for education were the two driving forces in Vivian's early life. She played softball, basketball, and field hockey during her high school years and competed in the latter two sports at Slippery Rock State College in Slippery Rock, Pennsylvania. She received the college's Most Valuable Player Award in basketball, made the Mid-East Field Hockey Team, and played on the nationally ranked (second place) Pittsburgh Orioles softball team. She holds B.S. and M.Ed. degrees in physical education from Slippery Rock State College. In 1972, she went to Cheyney State

C. Vivian Stringer, on her way to being the first Black woman head coach of a U.S. nationally ranked women's basketball team, led a small, unknown Cheyney State College basketball team to a second-place finish in the first NCAA Women's National Basketball Championship in 1982. [Public Relations Office, University of Iowa]

College as an assistant professor of physical education and coach for women's basketball and volleyball. In 1978-79, she held the unique position of assistant coach for the University of Chihuahua, Mexico, men's basketball team. After coaching the Cheyney State College team to the second place title in the 1982 NCAA national games, she was actively recruited by many institutions. She selected the University of Iowa in 1983 and again coached the women's team to four straight Big Ten conference titles (1987-90), and a place in the NCAA national tournament every year from 1986 to 1992. Her coaching record of over 80 percent wins in eighteen years makes her one of the most successful women's basketball coaches in the country.

Vivian and her husband, William D. Stringer, live in Iowa with their three children, David, Janine, and Justin. To encourage girls in basketball, she runs her own summer basketball camp and conducts clinics throughout the country. In the summer of 1991, her basketball team toured Japan.

Stringer's contribution to the basketball world is phenomenal. She represented the NCAA on the 1992 Olympic games committee for Barcelona. She is vice-president of U.S.A. Basketball's administrative committee and serves on NCAA, U.S.A. Basketball, and Women's Basketball Coaches Association committees.

Stringer's numerous accomplishments include coaching the 1985 World University Games, the 1982 U.S. Olympic Festival East Team, the 1982 Parade All-American South Team, and the 1981 Women's Touring Team trip to China. Among Stringer's Coach of the Year awards are the Philadelphia Sports Writers Award (1979), NCAA Award (1982 and 1988) and the prestigious Converse Award (1988). Other honors include the Distinguished Faculty Award from Cheyney State, the Smithsonian Institution Black

Women in Sports Award, and a listing in *Who's Who among Black Americans.*

Sports Illustrated invited Stringer, one of ten prominent sports figures, to share her thoughts about the opportunities available to Black athletes, in the article "The Black Athlete Revisited" (August 5, 1991). She focused on three primary themes: setting priorities, combating racism, and providing direction for Black youth. Stringer reminded readers that education is more important than athletics and that the reality for Black youth is that they must overcome barriers to their educational and economic success. Black athletes and leaders must save "our own people" by providing direction and support for individual achievement. For Stringer, sports in general, and basketball in particular, offer rich opportunities for both personal and political advancement.

BIBLIOGRAPHY

Green, Tina Sloan, Carol A. Oglesby, Alpha Alexander, and Nikke Franke. *Black Women in Sport* (1981); Greenberg, Mel. "Hoops World Upheaval, NCAA." In *On the Road to the Final Four NCAA Basketball Review* (1991); Koehler, Michael D. *America's Greatest Coaches* (1990); Sports Information. "C. Vivian Stringer," *Women's Basketball* (1991).

JOAN HULT

STUDENT NONVIOLENT COORDINATING COMMITTEE

African-American women activists played a major role in the founding and development of the Student Nonviolent Coordinating Committee (SNCC). Ella Baker (1903-86), director of the Atlanta headquarters of the Southern Christian Leadership Conference (SCLC), organized the April 1960 conference in Raleigh, North Carolina, that resulted in the formation of SNCC. A strong advocate of group-centered rather than leader-centered groups, Baker encouraged student protesters attending the conference to form their own organization rather than become the student arm of SCLC or other existing civil rights groups. During its first months of existence, SNCC's operations were conducted in a corner of SCLC headquarters, and the fledgling organization made use of Baker's extensive contacts with Black activists throughout the South. Baker remained an advisor to SNCC through the mid-1960s, consistently arguing for organizing strategies that emphasized the nurturing of grass-roots leaders in areas where SNCC established projects.

Women who were active in the lunch counter sit-in movement of 1960 led in the transformation of SNCC from a coordinating office into a cadre of militant activists dedicated to expanding the civil rights movement throughout the South. In February 1961, Diane Nash (1938-) and Ruby Doris Smith (1942-67) were among four SNCC members who joined the Rock Hill, South Carolina, desegregation protests, which featured the jail-no-bail tactic—demonstrators serving their jail sentences rather than accepting bail. In May 1961, Nash led a group of student activists to Alabama in order to sustain the Freedom Rides after the initial group of protesters organized by the Congress of Racial Equality (CORE) encountered mob violence in Birmingham. During May and June, Nash, Smith, and other student freedom riders traveled on buses from Montgomery to Jackson, Mississippi, where they were swiftly arrested and imprisoned. In August, when veterans of the sit-ins and the Freedom Rides met to discuss SNCC's future, Baker helped to avoid a damaging split by suggesting separate direct-action and voter-registration wings. Nash became the leader of the direct-action wing of SNCC.

During the period from 1961 to 1964, as SNCC established a staff of full-time office workers and field secretaries, women continued to play a central role in the organization. While Nash's activity in SNCC declined after her marriage to SCLC organizer James Bevel and the birth of their first child, Smith's role in the organization increased. In 1962, Smith (later Smith-Robinson) left her position as executive secretary of the Atlanta student movement to become the full-time southern campus coordinator for SNCC. The following year, she became SNCC's administrative secretary and then its executive secretary. She remained one of SNCC's most forceful administrators until her death in 1967 from a rare form of cancer. Other African-American women served on SNCC's office staff or in its support network, including Roberta Yancy, Smith's successor as southern campus coordinator, Norma Collins, Judy Richardson, Jean Wheeler Smith, Lenora Tate, and Carol Merritt.

SNCC's community organizing projects involved many African-American women. In Georgia, Albany Movement participants Bernice Johnson Reagon (1942-), Ruth Harris, and Bertha Gober became members of SNCC's Freedom Singers. In August 1962, Prathia Hall (1940-) left Temple University to join SNCC's southwest Georgia project. Boston native Peggy Dammond also worked in southwest

Georgia. Gloria Richardson (Dandridge) sustained a protest movement in Cambridge, Maryland. Hall, Martha Norman, Annie Pearl Avery, Colia LaFayette, Ruth Howard, and Fay Bellamy (1938-) played important roles in SNCC's voting rights campaign in Alabama.

Many African-American women were active in SNCC's voting rights campaign in Mississippi. These included Victoria Jackson Gray (1937-) of Hattiesburg, who ran in the 1964 Democratic primary to represent Mississippi in the U.S. Senate and later ran for Congress on the Mississippi Freedom Democratic Party (MFDP) ticket. Muriel Tillinghast, a former Howard University student, served as SNCC's project director in Greenville and later worked under Ruby Smith-Robinson in Atlanta. Another Howard student, Cynthia Washington, also served as a project director in Mississippi. Dorrie and Joyce Ladner first became active in their hometown of Hattiesburg. Other SNCC activists and organizers in Mississippi included Brenda Travis, Mary Lane, Dona Richards, Janet Jemmott (Moses), Amanda Purdew, Eleanor Holmes (Norton), Freddye Greene, Gloria House, Doris Derby, Helen O'Neal, June Johnson, Ruth Howard (Chambers), and Emma Bell.

The best known of the local leaders who were drawn into the struggle by SNCC's organizing efforts was Fannie Lou Hamer (1917-77), a native of Ruleville, Mississippi. In 1962, after attending a SNCC meeting, Hamer attempted to register to vote and was promptly evicted from the plantation where she worked. After enduring a beating in jail, Hamer became a SNCC field secretary and, in 1964, ran for Congress as a candidate of the MFDP. Hamer received national attention in August 1964, when she testified about her beating before the credentials committee of the Democratic National Convention as part of an effort to unseat the regular Mississippi delegation to the convention. Hamer and other MFDP delegates rejected a compromise that would have given them two at-large seats.

After the convention, SNCC grew increasingly concerned with issues beyond civil rights reform. Reflecting a long-term interest among SNCC workers in Pan-Africanism, a SNCC delegation, including Hamer, Hall, Smith-Robinson, and Richards, toured Africa during fall 1964. Most African-American women in SNCC were initially reluctant to affiliate with the white-dominated women's liberation movement of the late 1960s. Nevertheless, at the November 1964 staff meeting in Waveland, Mississippi, two white SNCC workers, Casey Hayden and Mary King, wrote a controversial paper on the position of women in the group that has since been described as a pioneering statement of the modern women's liberation movement.

During SNCC's Black Power period in the late 1960s, African-American women remained active in the organization's ideological discussions. Ethel Minor edited SNCC's newspaper and worked closely with SNCC chair Stokely Carmichael. The shift in SNCC activities away from sustained community organizing toward Black Power propagandizing was accompanied by increasing male dominance. The Black Women's Liberation Committee, founded by Frances Beal, was one of SNCC's few significant initiatives of the post-1966 period. Beal later was founder of the Third World Women's Alliance. By the early 1970s, external repression and internal ideological conflicts had destroyed the organization's effectiveness.

BIBLIOGRAPHY

Carson, Clayborne. *In Struggle: SNCC and the Black Awakening of the 1960s* (1981); personal interviews by authors.

CLAYBORNE CARSON
HEIDI HESS

SUDARKASA, NIARA (1938-)

A fascination with and commitment to the African continent is one of two continuing motifs in the life of Niara Sudarkasa, born Gloria Marshall on August 14, 1938, in Fort Lauderdale, Florida. The other is a belief in the importance of education to the Black community, accompanied by a firm conviction that Black colleges provide the best opportunity for providing that education.

Sudarkasa was raised in Florida by her grandparents, who were from the Bahamas. As a result, she was thought of by those around her as a West Indian. Because her family was so large, she grew up thinking that every second person she met would be a cousin.

Her interest in Africa was sparked by a cultural connection she made while at Oberlin College. In a course on Caribbean culture, she learned that *esu*, savings associations with which she had been familiar from childhood, were a Yoruba institution. This was the first concrete link between the West Indies and Africa that she had encountered. She became very excited by this evidence of her origins and determined to go to West Africa to explore them further.

Africa was a revelation to Sudarkasa in many ways. She was fascinated by the resemblance in physical posture and mannerisms of the Yoruba people to those she had known as a child. She admired the position of women in the culture as market traders and independent workers. Moreover, the sense of being part of the majority was something she had never before experienced. Africa belonged to her in a way that the United States never had. She had always felt that the United States was her country but not her land; Africa was her land.

Her experience in Africa inspired her, among other things, to change her name. She acquired her new last name through marriage. Her new first name was an adaptation of a Swahili word, and it indicates a woman of high purpose.

Having earned an M.A. and Ph.D. in anthropology from Columbia University, Sudarkasa went to work at the University of Michigan, where she became very involved in political activities. She was soon well known as an activist-scholar. She served as the associate vice president for academic affairs at the University of Michigan at Ann Arbor and became the first Black woman there to receive tenure.

In 1987, Sudarkasa became the first woman president of Lincoln University, the nation's oldest Black college and, for much of its history, an all-male institution. With her strong feelings for the African continent, she leads a school that has a long and distinguished history of association with Africa.

BIBLIOGRAPHY

Brelin, Christa. *Who's Who among Black Americans* (1992); Lanker, Brian. *I Dream a World* (1989); *NBAW.*

KATHLEEN THOMPSON

SUFFRAGE MOVEMENT

Black women contributed significantly to passage of the Nineteenth Amendment, which in 1920 enfranchised all American women. For white women, the amendment ended battles that had begun more than seventy years before. For most African-American women, however, the struggle to maintain the ballot continued for two generations after the passage of the woman suffrage amendment, as they were robbed of their hard-won ballots by the success of white political supremacy in the South. This is the story, however, of the first seventy-two years, or the first three generations, of African-American woman suffragists and their long struggle for political equity.

Black women, in their struggle for the right to vote, fought racism and sexism simultaneously. Their battles reveal several aspects of African-American women's history. First, although Black men appeared to be in the forefront throughout the woman suffrage movement, their position of prominence occurred during the first forty years. From the last decade of the nineteenth century to the end of the struggle for the Nineteenth Amendment, a larger number of African-American women took leadership positions in local and regional woman suffrage activities.

Second, Black women's support for woman suffrage often paralleled, yet developed differently from, that of white suffragists, especially as the movement progressed. Although there were similar strategies and coalitions among Black and white supporters, the experiences of the two racial groups differed. The existence of an anti-Black woman suffrage rationale and strategy among many whites, including women, and the discrimination that Black women found at the polls, reinforced differences among African-American and white woman suffragists.

Third, Black male leaders publicly supported woman suffrage. Black women actively worked in the movement but remained invisible, a burden imposed by a sexist society. Consequently, these woman suffragists were limited politically, and as a result, the struggle for suffrage among African-American women was similar to but different from both that of white women and Black men.

The woman suffrage movement began at Seneca Falls, New York, in 1848 and ended with the passage of what was called the Susan B. Anthony amendment in 1920. In an overview of the movement, the changing status of African-American women and the changing goals of the wider woman suffrage movement can be seen as factors influenced by Black strategies.

Beginning in the antebellum years, suffrage was extended to white males but not to women or to Black men. White manhood suffrage, not universal suffrage, characterized the growth of democracy. African-Americans, both males and females, supported and argued for universal suffrage, for, along with white women, they were denied political rights. Male leaders dominated the reform movements of this era. Students of the abolitionist movement and of other early nineteenth-century reforms know that white women often worked behind the scenes in petitioning governments and in fund-raising. Similarly, this was true of the small free Black women's population. Antebellum Black female abolitionists known to have supported the movement through organizational activities included Sojourner Truth, Harriet Forten Purvis, Margaretta Forten, Sarah Remond, and Mary Ann Shadd Cary.

After the Civil War, universal suffrage continued to be the goal of woman suffrage advocates. However, during the late 1860s, a split in the movement developed over strategy. Feminists who were disillusioned by the introduction of the word "male" into the U.S. Constitution first lobbied to exclude the word from the Fourteenth Amendment, but that strategy failed. They then protested the Fifteenth Amendment, because it proposed to enfranchise Black males, leaving women disfranchised. The debate that ensued divided the universal suffrage movement into two camps, those who felt that Black men needed the vote even more than women and those who were unwilling to postpone woman suffrage.

The African-American poet Frances Ellen Watkins Harper articulated the views of the first camp. Although she regularly attended the American Equal Rights Association conventions and was committed to women's gaining the right to vote, she supported Frederick Douglass (himself a woman suffragist), who argued that the vote was a matter of life or death for Black men. Harper said she was willing to wait to gain the ballot in order not to jeopardize this right for the men of her race. She supported what was called the "Negro suffrage" side of the controversy.

Throughout the twenty years of the split, or the second generation, the suffragists used two different strategies to gain the ballot. For a brief period, the more radical members of the National Woman Suffrage Association (NWSA) held that women should focus their efforts upon challenging the Fourteenth Amendment by attempting to vote. Among the African-American women who attempted unsuccessfully to vote in the 1860s were Sojourner Truth in Michigan and Mary Ann Shadd Cary in the District of Columbia. Both women affiliated with the NWSA, as did Harriet Purvis and her daughter Hattie. For a while they focused upon state referenda, but they eventually worked toward a constitutional amendment to enfranchise women. The members of the more conservative American Woman Suffrage Association, who had supported the Fifteenth Amendment and universal suffrage, focused on state legislatures in attempts to obtain woman suffrage on state levels. A larger number of Black women affiliated with this group. During the 1870s this organization attracted Black suffragists Frances Harper of Pennsylvania, Caroline Remond Putnam of Massachusetts, and Lottie Rollin of South Carolina. All three women served as delegates representing their states at national conventions.

For this era, there has been a significant recovery of evidence about Black women in woman suffrage history. As Black women's clubs emerged, so too did goals and concerns unique to African-American women. The changing status of Black women became evident also. As free women, increasing numbers became educated and worked to uplift their communities. As a result, Black woman suffragists moved in two directions, identifying with the mainstream, white woman suffrage organizations on the one hand and developing their own agendas in Black woman suf-

The August 1915 issue of The Crisis *included a special section entitled "Votes for Women: A Symposium by Leading Thinkers of Colored America," with essays by such luminaries as Nannie Helen Burroughs and Robert H. Terrell. This photograph of suffragists opens the section. [*The Crisis*]*

frage organizations on the other. By the end of the century, thousands of African-American women joined clubs with affiliations in state federations. Most clubs included woman suffrage as one of their goals. In addition, Black women developed as leaders of this movement.

By 1890, when the two national associations merged to form the National American Woman Suffrage Association (NAWSA), only four states, all in the West, offered full suffrage to women. Although by the 1920s women gained limited suffrage in an additional ten states, most white men in the East and the South remained resolutely opposed to woman suffrage. Throughout this period, African-American women participated in growing numbers in the movement, yet the probability of their achieving suffrage was far less than that for either Black men or white women. Despite the fact that most African-American men in the South had been disfranchised during the 1890s, those who lived in all regions outside of the South could still vote, and Black politicians nationwide used a variety of strategies designed to reenfranchise Black males. As for white women, in the states where they had won full or partial voting rights, the Black female population was small. Nonetheless, Black woman suffragists and Black suffrage associations continued to grow as African-American, not white, suffragists utilized strategies in support of universal suffrage.

The growth of a nationally organized Black women's club movement in the 1890s revealed the members' belief that votes for Black women would mean regaining the votes stolen from disfranchised Black men. National leaders of the Black women's club movement presented their views to white leaders whenever possible. Ida B. Wells-Barnett, founder of the Black women's club movement in the state of Illinois, was noted by suffragist Susan B. Anthony as one of the most respected African-American woman suffragists in the nation. Wells-Barnett used this leverage to lobby Anthony to oppose the growing political expediency among white northern women, as they acceded to the anti-Black suffrage views of their southern counterparts. Josephine St. Pierre Ruffin, founder of the National Federation of Afro-American Women and editor of *Woman's Era*, told her readers how the strategy to keep Black women from obtaining the ballot would provoke Black Americans who had remained silent about the issue to defend suffrage for Black women.

At the turn of the century, at the beginning of the third generation of woman suffrage campaigns, another exclusionary strategy developed among mainstream suffragists as some form of literacy requirement was legislated in several states. Among woman suffrage advocates, this trend was known as "educated suffrage" and was obviously meant to limit Black and foreign voters. Some suffragists, therefore, adopted the strategy of trying to convince the white male electorate that the ballot should be extended to the middle-class, educated, white women of the nation. While attending the 1903 NAWSA convention in New Orleans, Susan B. Anthony visited the African-American women of the Phyllis Wheatley Club. The club president, Sylvanie Williams, used the opportunity to publicly inform Anthony that Black suffragists knew how negatively they rated among white suffragists. She made it clear, however, that African-American women would continue their struggle for the vote.

Nonetheless, most mainstream white suffrage leaders acquiesced as southern whites attempted to cancel out the Black vote by writing Black women out of state and federal suffrage proposals. These efforts of white supremacists stimulated Black men to join in the push for a Nineteenth Amendment that excluded no women. During the last eight years before ratification of this amendment, national and local coalitions of Black men and women worked to intensify support for its passage. When Mary Church Terrell of the National Association of Colored Women (NACW) discussed the suffrage controversy with Walter White of the National Association for the Advancement of Colored People, these leaders of two of the largest African-American organizations agreed that if most white woman suffragists could, they would omit Black women from the federal amendment.

While the politics of race divided the woman suffrage movement, suffrage advocates of both races identified the absence of civil and political rights as barriers to the progress of women. They also argued that female reformers could better solve the problems of their society if they were armed with the ballot. This view was especially popular during the Progressive era, when woman reformers sought to address the societal ills of intemperance, political corruption, inadequate economic and educational opportunities for women, crime, and limited consumer protection. Adella Hunt Logan is representative of the African-American women who saw the connection between social reform and electoral politics. A clubwoman in Alabama who had taught at Tuskegee Institute before marriage, Logan hoped to use the ballot to improve conditions in Black communities and address the negative treatment of her people by the courts. Similarly, Maria Baldwin, a school principal in Massachusetts,

This photograph of woman suffragists in the late 1890s includes Mary Church Terrell (center). (The identity of the two women standing is unknown.) Terrell was later an ardent supporter of the Equal Rights Amendment as well. [Moorland-Spingarn]

looked to the vote as a means of improving public education for children of all races.

Black woman suffragists argued for all social reform issues, even after middle-class white suffragists had abandoned many of them. However, white woman suffragists did not include racial discrimination and the plight of disfranchised Black women in their priorities for social reform. They either avoided the race question or openly opposed the inclusion of Black women in the suffrage goal.

Third-generation woman suffragists, for the most part, realized by the First World War years that a national strategy, rather than a state-by-state approach, was essential to the success of the movement. White southern suffragists, in the meantime, held fast to the traditional states' rights argument aimed at excluding

Black women voters. By 1918, of the forty-eight states in the union, only seventeen provided for woman suffrage. The growing interest in gaining the vote among African-American women frightened white woman suffrage leaders like Ida Husted Harper, an Indiana native. When the Northeastern Federation of Colored Women applied for membership in NAWSA, Harper wrote to the founding president of NACW, Mary Church Terrell, expressing fear that this initiative by an organization representing thousands of Black women would create racial tension among southern members and jeopardize the passage of the Nineteenth Amendment. Harper appealed to Terrell to encourage the federation to withdraw the application.

Although opposition to woman suffrage failed to check the growth of the national movement, attempts to keep Black women disfranchised continued until both houses of Congress passed the federal amendment in June 1919. Ironically, by the time the Nineteenth Amendment was ratified in August 1920, nine more states had granted woman suffrage through legislative enactment, including two southern states—Tennessee and Kentucky—where, for a period, Black women were enfranchised equally with white women.

Just as woman suffrage may not have come automatically with twentieth-century changes in the nature of electoral politics but required an effective lobby, so too African-American women may not have automatically gained inclusion in the Nineteenth Amendment. They had to struggle to remain visible in order to ensure that inclusion.

When Black women became voters, they lobbied for political candidates, several of whom were women. In addition, Black women organized voter education groups in their own communities, ran for a variety of offices, and fought attempts by southern racists to keep them from the polls. Among the African-American female candidates were Mrs. Edward Washington, who ran for the Haddonfield, New Jersey, school board in 1918. The same year, Mrs. W. L. Presto ran for the state senate from Seattle, Washington. By 1920, Grace Campbell of New York City ran for the state assembly as a Socialist party candidate.

In spite of efforts to implement their political rights, Black women in the South were disfranchised less than a decade after the Nineteenth Amendment enfranchised them in 1920, and Black women outside the South lost the political clout they had acquired. As many African-American woman suffragists suspected, white women voters ignored their plight. Having encouraged Black women earlier in the movement to join in order to bring Black male voters into the woman suffrage camp, white suffragists then abandoned disfranchised Black women. Similarly, some working-class white women believed that middle-class white suffragists had abandoned them after the passage of the Nineteenth Amendment. As a result, the coalitions established during the push for a woman suffrage amendment dissolved. Politically conscious women outside of the mainstream became disillusioned with the goals and strategies of the new middle-class feminist leadership.

In spite of the disappointing aftermath of the Nineteenth Amendment, African-American woman suffragists had participated in the enfranchisement process and learned lessons for the future. They had engaged in speech making, in petitioning federal and state governments, and in campaigning for woman suffrage referendums. African-American women founded at least thirty groups which were either woman suffrage associations or women's clubs with suffrage leaders or associations. The most significant realization of the Nineteenth Amendment was the triumph of democratic principle. The right of all women to vote was finally acknowledged in the U.S. Constitution. Attempts to implement this right, however, would have to wait for another forty-five years.

BIBLIOGRAPHY

Aptheker, Bettina. *Woman's Legacy: Essays on Race, Sex and Class in American History* (1982); Giddings, Paula. *When and Where I Enter: The Impact of Black Women on Race and Sex in America* (1984); Kraditor, Aileen. *The Ideas of the Woman Suffrage Movement, 1890-1920* (1971); Stanton, Elizabeth Cady, et al., eds. *History of Woman Suffrage, 1848-1920*, 6 vols. (1969); Sterling, Dorothy, ed. *We Are Your Sisters: Black Women in the Nineteenth Century* (1984); Terborg-Penn, Rosalyn. *Afro-Americans in the Struggle for Woman Suffrage* (1978), and "Discrimination against Afro-American Women in the Woman's Movement, 1830-1920." In *The Afro-American Woman: Struggles and Images*, ed. Sharon Harley and Rosalyn Terborg-Penn (1978).

ROSALYN TERBORG-PENN

SULLIVAN, MAXINE (1911-1987)

Born Marietta Williams on May 13, 1911, in Homestead, Pennsylvania, Maxine Sullivan grew up in a musical household; her father played mandolin, and several uncles played other instruments as well. One of her uncles, who played drums with vocalist Lois Deppe's band in 1922, formed a group of his own called the Red Hot Peppers, and young Maxine used to go along with the band and sing a few songs. Despite the fact that her voice was on the soft side and her repertoire did not contain any blues, Sullivan landed a job in the Benjamin Harrison Literary Club in downtown Pittsburgh. It was while she was working at this after-hours club that Gladys Mosier, pianist with Ina Ray Hutton's all-woman band, convinced Sullivan to go to New York, where Mosier arranged what turned out to be a successful audition with pianist/arranger Claude Thornhill. Thornhill wrote an arrangement of the old Scottish folk song "Loch Lomond" for Sullivan, and her 1937 recording became a hit. Sullivan was accompanied on the record by a small group, including bassist John Kirby. This was essentially the group that played at the Onyx Club on Fifty-second Street, where Sullivan and Kirby often worked together. Later in 1937, Kirby and Sullivan were married.

Things were looking good for the newlyweds. They recorded frequently and even became co-stars of an NBC network radio show, *Flow Gently, Sweet Rhythm*. In 1939, Sullivan took part in a stage production called *Swingin' the Dream*, a swing version of *A Midsummer Night's Dream* in which she played the part of Titania, queen of the fairies. She also appeared that year in two Hollywood films, *St. Louis Blues* and *Going Places*, in the latter co-starring with Louis Armstrong and Ronald Reagan. Things stopped going well for the couple during this time, and they were divorced in 1941. Sullivan joined the Benny Carter Orchestra for one tour and then embarked on a solo career.

In 1950, Sullivan married stride pianist Cliff Jackson, and the marriage lasted until Jackson's death in 1970. Sullivan took up the valve trombone in 1956, and later she played flugelhorn, then pocket trumpet. Also in 1956, she retired from show business, choosing to devote her time and energies to raising her daughter and working with the local school board. In 1961, she became president of the Public School 136 Parent-Teachers Association in the Bronx.

Although she was retired, Sullivan made periodic appearances at clubs and festivals, and after her well-received performances and recordings with the World's Greatest Jazz Band in the late 1960s, she officially came out of retirement. She continued to perform, touring Europe and Japan, and to record until her death in New York City on April 7, 1987.

The 1937 hit recording of "Loch Lomond" typecast Maxine Sullivan as a singer of folk songs such as "Molly Malone" and "If I Had a Ribbon Bow," which she sang in a suave, sweet, gently swinging style. In her comeback years, however, her voice ac-

quired a huskiness that gave her jazz singing an authenticity that earlier had been lacking. Maxine Sullivan will be remembered not just as "the Loch Lomond girl" but also as a truly original vocal stylist whose best work was done in the later years of her long and distinguished career.

BIBLIOGRAPHY

Friedwald, Will. *Jazz Singing* (1990); Johnson, Ron. "Maxine Sullivan," *Coda* (1974); Placksin, Sally. *American Women in Jazz, 1900 to the Present* (1982); Shaw, Arnold. *The Street That Never Slept: New York's Fabled 52nd Street* (1971).

SELECTED DISCOGRAPHY

As leader: *A Tribute to Andy Razaf*, DCC Jazz 610 (1956); *The Queen, volume 1*, Kenneth 2052 (1981); *The Queen, volume 2*, Kenneth 2053 (1982); *The Queen, volume 3*, Kenneth 2054 (1982-83); *The Queen, volume 4*, Kenneth 2055 (1984); *The Great Songs from the Cotton Club by Harold Arlen and Ted Koehler*, Stash 244 (1984); *Maxine Sullivan Sings the Music of Burton Lane*, Stash 257 (1985); *I Love to Be in Love*, Tono 101 (1985); *Spring Isn't Everything*, Audiophile 229 Z (1986); *Together: Maxine Sullivan Sings the Music of Jule Styne*, Atlantic 81783-1 (1987). As sideman, with the Scott Hamilton Quintet: *Uptown*, Concord Jazz CJ-288 (1985), and *Swingin' Sweet*, Concord Jazz CCD-4351 (1986).

VINCENT PELOTE

SUL-TE-WAN, MADAME (1873-1959)

Madame Sul-Te-Wan, born Nellie Conley on September 12, 1873, in Louisville, Kentucky, was the first African-American actress contracted to appear in one of the most pioneering and controversial films in American cinematic history: *Birth of a Nation* (1915). Her background was African-American and Hawaiian (though some thought her father was Hindu), and she was one of the "Negro Trail Blazers" of California. She did not acquiesce to false pride while experiencing seemingly insurmountable difficulties in her upward climb to be her own person. She always believed she owed it "to the future generation of Negroes to tell of this struggle that it might aid them to not lose heart" (Beasley 1919).

Madame Sul-Te-Wan helped her widowed mother, a washerwoman who worked for actresses. Described as "the little lady" from childhood through adult life, she delivered laundry to actresses at the stage door and was often allowed inside to see the shows. Every time she was permitted to watch a show, the following day she would rehearse the act at school before her classmates, avowing that she too would be an actress someday.

Her mother could not afford singing or dance lessons for Madame, but actresses Mary Anderson and Fanny Davenport inspired her. These actresses were convinced of her talent and requested the mayor of Louisville, James Whalen, who was in charge of the Buckingham Theater, to provide the young aspirant with an audition. She was one of twenty-five "buck and wing dance" contestants (all African-American), a special attraction at his theater. First prize was a dishpan and spoon made of granite. Madame Sul-Te-Wan was the undisputed winner. For Madame, the prize meant confidence in her abilities and aspirations. Her mother began allowing her daughter to perform occasionally. When she was convinced of Madame's talent, she moved with her daughter to Cincinnati, Ohio, to assist the latter's career.

Madame soon became known as "the little dancing protégé of Mary Anderson and Fanny Davenport." She performed on Vine Street at the Dime Museum and in a section of town called Over the Rhine in family theaters. She eventually joined the Three Black Coast company, using the stage name of Creole Nell. A major step in her career came when Fanny Davenport contacted her to help secure African-American performers for a play in which Davenport had been contracted to perform in Cincinnati. Of course, Creole Nell was a member of the cast. She eventually formed her own company, the Black Four Hundred, consisting of sixteen performers and twelve musicians. The next season she organized the Rair Back Minstrels. The company toured the East Coast with great success until "she was besieged to marry and did" (Beasley 1919).

Madame gave birth to three sons: Otto, Onest, and James. After her marriage she continued to work and later relocated to Arcadia, California. After two years in California, and with her youngest child three weeks old, Madame's husband had deserted her, and the money she had been sending home while performing on the road had not gone toward the rent, which was ten months in arrears.

An employment agent, J. W. Coleman, introduced Madame and her children before the Forum, an African-American organization devoted to cultural presentations and not-for-profit activities that assisted community members with food and shelter. When she attempted to address the men of the Forum "she began to cry, whereupon her oldest son, who was not yet seven years, looking up into his mother's face, said: 'Mother you are not begging. We are going to sing and earn what they give you.' He and his little brother sang and greatly impressed the Forum Club" (Beasley 1919). Madame Sul-Te-Wan

did not want to beg, but her situation was desperate. The local theatrical booking companies were white owned and offered excuses rather than jobs to African-Americans in the early 1900s. Finally the Associated Charities of Los Angeles moved Madame and her children into town, and she was engaged at the Pier Theater in Venice, a beach area near Los Angeles. The engagement was short, which meant the money barely paid for her and her children's subsistence. Neighbors tried to assist, but Madame was not comfortable accepting charity.

Madame Sul-Te-Wan heard that a man from her hometown was directing a film that was employing African-Americans. Since the booking companies claimed they did not handle independent bookings, Madame made a personal visit to the director-producer to plead her case for a job. His name was D. W. Griffith, and the film, *Birth of a Nation* (based on Thomas Dixon's novel *The Clansman*), was to become legendary. For Madame, it was successful employment at $3 a day in 1915, when the average American was fortunate to make that amount in a week. Her first day of work was so impressive that Griffith immediately raised her salary to $5 a day and had a separate sketch written in *Birth of a Nation*, making her the first contracted, featured African-American actor (or actress) in American film.

The new sketch "was to show the advancement of the Negro from antebellum days to this present period. . . . [Madame] appeared as a rich colored lady, finely gowned and owner of a Negro colony of educated colored citizens, who not only owned their own land, but she drove her own coach and four-in-hand" (Beasley 1919). She played opposite the character actress Josephine Crowell. In her first scene as a nouveau riche Black woman immediately after the Civil War, she is finely dressed and meets Crowell on the street; Crowell shuns Madame. Insults follow, and the scene climaxes with Madame spitting in Crowell's face. "After the picture was made . . . the censor cut the part out in which she appeared as a rich colored lady, and other parts, leaving only the bitter-gall portions for the insults of the Negro race throughout the nation" (Beasley 1919). The film was a historical spectacle with a running time of over three hours and broke all previous financial records. However, the censorship probably heightened the film's racial controversy; all major African-American roles (after the censoring) were played by white actors in blackface. The African-Americans who were involved were relegated to minor parts, thus encouraging the notion of racially stereotyped images.

In 1957, Madame Sul-Te-Wan, at that time the oldest active film actress in Hollywood at age eighty-six, appeared in Band of Angels, *directed by Raoul Walsh, who, forty-two years before, played John Wilkes Booth in D. W. Griffith's* Birth of a Nation. *The latter film marked Madame Sul-Te-Wan's film debut. [AP/Wide World Photos]*

Birth of a Nation was technically an innovative classic. While Griffith pushed the film in New York, it made its West Coast premiere in Los Angeles. Many in the African-American community objected to the racial images of northern Blacks after the Civil War moving to the South, "exploiting and corrupting the former slaves, unleashing the sadism and bestiality *innate* in the Negro, turning the once-congenial darkies into renegades, and using them to 'crush the white South under the heel of the Black South' "(Cripps 1977). Portraying African-Americans as eating chicken legs, drinking whiskey from bottles, and propping bare feet on their business desks as political legislators, Griffith was accused of perpetuating racial stereotypes.

Madame Sul-Te-Wan was featured in the films *The Marriage Market, Intolerance, Happy Valley's Oldest Boy,* and *Up from the Depths.* Her other films include *Narrow Street* (1925) and Josef Von Sternberg's *Thunderbolt* (1929). *Thunderbolt* was one of the earlier films to move away from the conventional images of African-Americans. Madame's eccentric dress style (flowery hats, turbans, flowing beaded necklaces, and an array of cotton/silk color combinations) won her a character role as Voodoo Sue in the 1931 Will Rogers film *Heaven on Earth,* based on a novel by Ben Lucien Burman. She was also a contract cast member in the 1934 film version of *Imitation of Life* and *Black Moon* (1934). In 1938, Madame Sul-Te-Wan appeared with George Reed in Fox Pictures' major Technicolor Christmas release, *Kentucky*—one of the many racetrack films done in the 1930s. During the same era there were attempts by filmmakers to turn the camera's eye on the social injustices of prisons. *Ladies They Talk About* (1932), for example, featured an incarcerated Barbara Stanwyck in a prison with a few Blacks, who included "a darkly ominous" Sul-Te-Wan (Cripps 1977).

Madame's other films include Zanuck's *In Old Chicago* (1938), *Uncle Tom's Cabin* (1927), and, as the character Tituba, *The Maid of Salem* (1937). When she died on February 1, 1959, at the Motion Picture Country Home in Woodland Hills, California, several papers cited her as a pioneering actress who had performed on stage and in films for over seventy of her eighty-five years. Sul-Te-Wan's last films included *Rhapsody in Blue* (1945), *Mighty Joe Young* (1949), *Carmen Jones* (1954), *Something of Value* (1957), *The Buccaneer* (1958), and Samuel Goldwyn's *Porgy and Bess* (1959).

BIBLIOGRAPHY

Beasley, Delilah L. *Negro Trail-Blazers of California* (1919); Bogle, Donald. *Brown Sugar* (1980); Cripps, Thomas. *Slow Fade to Black* (1977); Murray, Florence, ed. *The Negro Handbook* (1942); Spradling, Mary M., ed. *In Black and White* (1980); Maidie Norman collection of African-American Theater History Research (Macgowan Hall), University of California, Los Angeles.

BEVERLY J. ROBINSON

THE SUPREMES, DIANA ROSS AND

Formed in Detroit, Michigan, in 1959 as the Primettes, the group originally consisted of Florence Ballard (1943-1976), Betty McGlown (1943-), Mary Wilson (1944-), and Diana Ross (1944-). Florence Ballard was asked by Paul Williams to form a sister act that would perform with his group, the Primes (they became the Temptations in 1961). Managed by Milton Jenkins, the Primettes performed at clubs and record hops throughout Detroit, with each of the young singers taking a turn on the lead vocals. In July 1960, they won first prize in the Detroit/Windsor Freedom Festival. Although this made them local celebrities, they had no recording contract.

Coincidentally, Diana Ross (born Diane Ross) had lived in the same neighborhood as Smokey Robinson. Robinson and his group the Miracles had just been discovered by Berry Gordy, founder of Motown Records. As a favor to Ross, Robinson arranged an audition with Gordy in August 1960. Gordy liked the Primettes but did not offer them a recording contract because of their age. They were told to come back after they finished high school.

Shortly afterwards, Betty McGlown announced she was leaving the group to get married. They were now short one person in a group that used four-part harmonies. In the meantime, Robert West of LuPine Records agreed to record them on two songs, "Tears of Sorrow," on which Ross sang lead, and "Pretty Baby," which featured Mary Wilson on lead vocals. They used two other singers to fill the gap that McGlown had left. Unfortunately, West was targeted for a payola investigation and the songs were never distributed. They were eventually released, about twenty years later, in Japan and Great Britain. Today, these singles are quite valuable and in demand as collectors' items.

After their recordings with West, the young women returned to local clubwork but had difficulty in getting bookings because they still lacked a fourth member. During the 1950s and early 1960s singing groups always had a minimum of four members; for the Primettes to continue as a trio was unthinkable. They finally recruited Barbara Martin (1944-) but found bookings still scarce because they lacked a manager. Milton Jenkins had abandoned them and so had his successor, Richard Morris. Out of desperation they returned to Motown, hoping that Gordy would reconsider signing them. Gordy did not sign them but he did utilize them as handclappers for artists such as Mary Wells and Mable John.

Finally, on January 15, 1961, Gordy signed them with the stipulation that they change their name. Because she was the founder and principal lead vocalist, Ballard was given the task of selecting a suitable name. She picked "Supremes" from a list of names that included the Darleens, the Sweet P's, and the Jewelettes. None of the others liked the name Supremes but agreed to abide by Ballard's decision because their first record, "I Want a Guy," was about to be released. Contrary to popular belief, the Supremes were not overnight sensations. In fact, it was three years and eight releases before they had their first number-one hit. During this time they were known around Motown as "the no-hit Supremes." The situation was so bad that Ballard briefly toured with the Marvelettes in 1962, filling in for one of the members who was on maternity leave.

A turning point for the Supremes came in 1962. Barbara Martin left the group that spring to have a baby. They did not replace her because they didn't feel that anyone else would be as committed as they were. During the fall of that year the group went on the road to tour the chitlin circuit as an opening act in Motown's first revue. This gave them the opportunity to perfect their stage act, developing a style of dress and choreography that would later distinguish them from all other girl groups.

Still confined to the bottom of the Motown roster of stars, Berry Gordy sent them out on Dick Clark's Caravan of Stars during the summer of 1964. While on that tour Motown released "Where Did Our Love Go," a song written by the production team of Brian and Eddie Holland and Lamont Dozier. By the end of August, the "no-hit Supremes" had the number-one song in America. "Where Did Our Love Go" was the first of a string of number-one hits written for the Supremes by Holland-Dozier-Holland. The three songwriters helped define the Motown sound; the Supremes helped articulate that sound.

By the mid-1960s, the Supremes had established themselves as the most popular female recording act in America. Hardly a week passed that they were not featured on at least one television program, appearing most frequently on "The Ed Sullivan Show." They also performed at major nightclubs like the Copacabana in New York. They were featured in movies and became spokespersons for Coca-Cola. They eventually had their own "Supremes' White Bread" in 1966. They became equally popular in England, appearing on a number of British variety shows.

As the pressures of worldwide stardom began to take its toll on the group, relationships began to break down. Diana Ross increasingly separated herself from the group. This was supported by Gordy's intention to make her a solo act. After the success of "Where Did Our Love Go," Gordy decided that Ross would be the lead vocalist on all subsequent releases because her voice had the most commercial appeal. Initially, Ballard and Wilson agreed to this arrangement for the sake of the group's success. When it became clear that the Supremes had become a vehicle to launch Ross's solo career, Florence Ballard began to rebel. Known for being outspoken and steadfast in her convictions, she began to fight with Gordy and Ross, particularly over the proposed name change to Diana Ross and the Supremes. The situation worsened when Ballard began to drink heavily and became overweight. After a period of missing a number of rehearsals and performances, Gordy fired her in April 1967. Ballard signed a two-year recording contract with ABC Records but was legally prevented by Gordy from promoting herself as a former member of the Supremes. In 1968, she released two singles that went nowhere, "It Doesn't Matter How I Say It" and "Love Ain't Love." Both are considered rare and collectors' items. Disappointed with the sales of these records, ABC let her contract expire. Distraught, Ballard went into seclusion with her children. In 1971, she filed a multimillion dollar lawsuit against Motown and the Supremes, alleging that Diana Ross maliciously conspired to oust her from the group that she founded. The case was thrown out of court. In late 1974, Ballard was found living on welfare in Detroit. Despite attempts by Mary Wilson and Ballard's family to encourage a comeback, Ballard lacked the motivation to revive her career. Tragically, Florence Ballard died of cardiac arrest on February 22, 1976.

When Ballard was fired from the Supremes she was replaced by Cindy Birdsong (1939-). Birdsong previously had sung for many years with Patti LaBelle and the BlueBelles. Bearing a strong resemblance to Ballard, Birdsong merely functioned as a stage performer, filling in the gap that Ballard left behind. By late 1968, Mary Wilson and Cindy Birdsong were singing on very few recordings. Gordy would record Diana Ross on the lead vocals and use in-house singers for the background. In fact, neither one of them sang on their farewell hit, "Someday We'll Be Together."

On January 14, 1970, Diana Ross left the Supremes to embark on a solo career that would include motion pictures. She was replaced by Jean Terrell, the sister of heavyweight fighter Ernie Terrell. With Terrell as their new lead singer, the Supremes had several more major hits including "Up the Ladder to the Roof" and "Stoned Love." Cindy Birdsong left the group in 1972 and was replaced by Lynda Lawrence. The next year, when Lawrence and Terrell decided to quit the group, Birdsong returned and Scherrie Payne (1944-) took over the lead spot. When Birdsong left for a second time in 1976, Susaye Green, a backup vocalist for Stevie Wonder, joined the group. Then, in 1977, the Supremes officially disbanded.

Diana Ross became a superstar. As a soloist she had several number-one hits, including "Ain't No Mountain High Enough," "Love Hangover," and "Upside Down." In 1972, she starred in the highly acclaimed motion picture *Lady Sings the Blues*, a biographical film based on the life of Billie Holiday. For her outstanding performance, she received an Academy Award nomination for Best Actress. She also starred in *Mahogany* and *The Wiz*. Before leaving Motown in 1981 to sign with RCA Records, Ross recorded the biggest hit of her career, "My Endless Love," a duet with Lionel Richie. With the exception of a few hits such as "Mirror Mirror" and "Missing You," Ross was unable to duplicate her Motown successes. In 1988, she returned to Motown where she records sporadically and is known primarily for her lavish concerts and world tours.

In the nine years they were together, Diana Ross and the Supremes placed twelve songs in the number-one position on Billboard's Top 100. As a soloist, Ross hit number one six times, giving her eighteen number-one songs, and making Diana Ross and the Supremes the number-one female recording act in history.

[*See also* FILM.]

BIBLIOGRAPHY

Nite, Norm N. *Rock On: The Illustrated Encyclopedia of Rock 'n Roll* (1974); Turner, Tony and Barbara Aria. *All That Glittered: My Life with the Supremes* (1990); Whitburn, Joel. *Joel Whitburn's Top R & B Singles, 1942-1988* (1988); Wilson, Mary with Patricia Romanowski. *Dreamgirl: My Life as a Supreme* (1986), and *Supreme Faith: Someday We'll Be Together* (1990).

DISCOGRAPHY

For discographies, see Brown, Geoff. *Diana Ross* (1981); Taraborrelli, J. Randy. *Diana* (1985).

FRANK WILLIAM JOHNSON

SWEET HONEY IN THE ROCK

For nearly two decades this Black women's a cappella group has been singing songs of struggle. With a power rooted in the tradition of the southern Black church, Sweet Honey In The Rock delivers sermons in song that challenge us to be counted in the fight for social justice.

Since its founding in 1973 by Bernice Johnson Reagon, over twenty women have been in the group. Though the exact cluster of talents has changed over time, in the early 1990s the group included Evelyn Harris, Ysaye Barnwell, Aisha Kahlil, Nitanju Bolade Casel, and sign-language interpreter Shirley Childress Johnson.

Using the power of the unaccompanied human voice, the women of Sweet Honey weave dazzling, breathtaking harmonies with a special sound that resonates with the history of the African diaspora. The group moves effortlessly through a repertoire that includes urban blues tunes, West African chants, field hollers, Black gospel, reggae, and rap.

What distinguishes Sweet Honey In The Rock from other performers, however, is the messages contained in the group's songs. The group's repertoire of original compositions tackles such issues as apartheid, economic injustice, the AIDS crisis, homelessness, political prisoners, and the global struggle for human rights.

Sweet Honey In The Rock has built an international following through tours and performances in Africa, Asia, Europe, South America, and the Caribbean. They have performed in such historic venues as the Apollo Theatre and Carnegie Hall, recorded nine albums, and received a Grammy Award for a 1988 recording of songs by Woody Guthrie and Leadbelly.

BIBLIOGRAPHY

Personal interviews with members of the group.

DISCOGRAPHY

All for Freedom, Music for Little People (1989); *Breaths—Best of Sweet Honey In The Rock*, Cooking Vinyl (1989); *Live at Carnegie Hall*, Flying Fish, (1988); *The Other Side*, Flying Fish (1985); *Feel Something Drawing Me On*, Flying Fish (1985); *We All . . . Everyone of Us*, Flying Fish (1983); *Good News*, Flying Fish (1982); *B'lieve I'll Run On . . . See What the End's Gonna Be*, Redwood Records (1978); *Sweet Honey In The Rock*, Flying Fish (1976).

IVY YOUNG

SWEETHEARTS OF RHYTHM *see* INTERNATIONAL SWEETHEARTS OF RHYTHM

With a power rooted in the tradition of the southern Black church, Sweet Honey In The Rock delivers sermons in song that challenge us to be counted in the fight for social justice (pictured from left: Bernice Johnson Reagon, Aisha Kahlil, Shirley Childress Johnson, Evelyn Maria Harris, Nitanju Bolade-Casel, and Ysaye Maria Barnwell). [Moorland-Spingarn]

T

TALBERT, MARY MORRIS BURNETT (1866-1923)

"Clear and insistent is the call to the women of my race today—the call to self-development and to unselfish service. We cannot turn a deaf ear to the cries of the neglected little children, the untrained youth, the aged and the poor" (Mary Church Terrell Papers). These words, spoken by Mary Burnett Talbert on the eve of the twentieth century, characterize the work to which she dedicated her life as educator, lecturer, and human rights advocate.

Born in the college town of Oberlin, Ohio, on September 17, 1866, Mary Burnett was able to build upon the firm foundation that her parents, Cornelius and Caroline Nicholls Burnett, had laid for her and their other seven children. Initially members of the Episcopal church, the Burnetts later changed their affiliation to the Congregational church because of its active involvement in the abolition movement and its promotion of education for Black youth. Cornelius Burnett, who was active in the politics of both, had engaged in Reconstruction politics in his native North Carolina. Burnett continued his affiliation with the Republican party in Ohio and attended several state conventions as an elected delegate. In the heart of Oberlin's business district the Burnetts operated a restaurant, boarding house, and barber shop that catered primarily to students from Oberlin College (one of the earliest colleges to admit Black people

and women as students). From her family's affiliations and business enterprises, Burnett learned that the constraints of race and gender could be circumvented. In Oberlin's unique social environment she also learned the importance of service to both church and community.

Mary Burnett attended the public schools of Oberlin, played the organ at the Methodist church, and embraced her parents' belief in service to the community. After graduating from Oberlin High School at age sixteen, and aided by a benefactor, she attended Oberlin College, where her ideals regarding community involvement were further cemented. Mary Church (Terrell) and Anna Julia Cooper, who later became renowned for their reformist activities, also were students at the college, and Hallie Q. Brown, another important Black activist, grew up in Oberlin during this period. These women undoubtedly knew each other, and their promotion of human rights later reunited them.

Mary Burnett followed a literary track at Oberlin and received an S.P. in 1886. (Recipients of this degree later were awarded a bachelor of arts, which Talbert received in 1896.) Some biographers contend that Talbert received a Ph.D. from the University of Buffalo, but that university did not award a doctorate in arts and sciences on a regular basis until the 1930s, and so it cannot be confirmed that Talbert received this degree. Students who took continuing education

A lifetime of dedication to human rights was recognized when Mary Burnett Talbert became the first woman to receive the NAACP's coveted Spingarn Medal. [Moorland-Spingarn]

classes at the university were awarded certificates called doctorates, and it is possible that Mary B. Talbert received one of these certificates.

In 1886, she assumed a teaching position at Bethel University in the segregated school system of Little Rock, Arkansas, where she taught history, mathematics, Latin, science, and geography. In Arkansas she experienced the impact of Jim Crow laws firsthand, but at the same time, the respectability accorded Black teachers gave her high visibility, and she earned a national reputation. As a result, the superintendent of schools appointed her assistant principal of Bethel University, and she became the only woman ever to be selected for this position. It was the highest ever held by a woman in the state. Then, in 1887, she was named principal of Union High School in Little Rock.

Mary Burnett's sister, Henrietta, introduced her to her brother-in-law, William Herbert Talbert, a successful city clerk and realtor in Buffalo, New York. On September 8, 1891, they were married, at which

point Mary Burnett ended her teaching career and moved to Buffalo. The following year she gave birth to their only child, Sarah May, who later attended the New England Conservatory of Music and became an accomplished pianist and composer.

In Buffalo, Talbert spent her time managing the extended Talbert household and working in the Michigan Avenue Baptist Church, which had been founded by Talberts in the early nineteenth century and was known for its political activism. Unable to teach in the public schools of Buffalo because regulations barred married women from teaching, Talbert established classes at her church, where she trained more than 300 Sunday school teachers. She also joined forces with other Black women in Buffalo and, in 1899, became a charter member of the Phyllis Wheatley Club, the first club in the city to become an affiliate of the National Association of Colored Women (NACW). The NACW was founded in Washington, D.C., in 1896, and served as an umbrella group for many clubs throughout the United States. The Phyllis Wheatley Club established a settlement house in Buffalo and, in 1910, during Talbert's presidency, invited the National Association for the Advancement of Colored People (NAACP) to begin organizing activities in the city. Also a charter member of the Empire Federation of Women's Clubs, founded in 1911, Talbert served as its second president, from 1912 to 1916.

Mary Talbert attracted the attention of NACW members in 1901 when she challenged the all-white board of commissioners of the Buffalo Pan American Exposition to appoint an African-American and to include an exhibit on Black American life. Also in 1901, she was reunited with her Oberlin community colleagues Mary Church Terrell, Anna Julia Cooper, and Hallie Q. Brown at NACW's second biennial conference held at her home in Buffalo. Talbert subsequently held several NACW administrative positions, including parliamentarian, recording secretary, chair of the executive committee, and vice president. Delegates elected her president in 1916, and she served two terms, ending in 1920.

Mary Talbert's administration was noteworthy for several reasons. First, during this time club members embarked upon a national project to purchase and restore Anacostia, the District of Columbia home of Frederick Douglass, as a monument to a great statesman and to commemorate the contributions made by African-Americans to the United States. At the Denver conference, in 1920, President Talbert announced that the NACW owned the building outright. Second, under Talbert the organization was recognized as a full member of the International Council of Women (ICW) when she became the first official NACW delegate to be seated at ICW's fifth quinquennial conference, held in Christiana, Norway, in 1920.

Talbert was one of the Americans who addressed the ICW delegates, representing more than thirty countries. She told them that "the greatness of nations is shown by their strict regard for human rights, rigid enforcement of the law without bias, and just administration of the affairs of life." She further noted that because white women have greater opportunity, "they are duty bound to lift [their] voices against the ills that afflict [their] sisters of color, both in America and elsewhere." Talbert asked them "to appeal to your strong men to justify their claim as leaders of mankind . . . and [to] uphold law and order . . . till no individual or race shall feel the hoof of oppression upon them" (*National Notes*, October-December 1920). While in Europe, Talbert traveled to several countries, lecturing on the conditions of Black Americans, especially women and children; the press gave extensive coverage to her speeches.

During the post-World War I era, Talbert engaged in many activities to rebuild Europe and promote democracy, often under the aegis of the NACW and the NAACP. In 1919, as NACW representative, she served as YMCA secretary and Red Cross nurse in Romagne, France, where she offered classes for African-American soldiers. She led the Third Liberty Bond Drive among Black clubwomen, which raised $5 million, and Talbert was an appointee to the League of Nations committee on international relations. In 1921, as a member of an NAACP delegation of prominent Black Americans, she petitioned President Warren Harding to grant clemency to members of the African-American twenty-fourth regiment who had been falsely accused of inciting a race riot in Houston, Texas, in 1917. In 1922, Talbert joined other NACW members who founded, in Washington, D.C., the International Council of Women of the Darker Races, which was committed to uniting women of color around the globe in order to present a united attack against oppression; she was a member of the organization's committee on education. She also contributed articles to *Woman's Voice* and the *Champion*.

Talbert was an NAACP vice president and board member from 1918 until her death in 1923. By organizing NAACP chapters in Louisiana and Texas, she strengthened the organization's influence in key southern states. It has been alleged that Talbert influenced the NAACP to investigate the atrocities perpetrated by the United States against Haitian women and children in 1921. As national director of the NAACP's antilynching campaign, Talbert assiduously sought support for the bill that Leonidas Dyer introduced into Congress in 1921. Although the campaign failed to reach its financial goal, enough funds were raised to advertise the atrocities of lynching and to win greater white support for its elimination. Congress failed to ratify the Dyer bill, however, and in response, Talbert urged clubwomen to use their newly won right to vote in order to oppose those representatives who voted against it. This was to be Talbert's last major contribution to her people. In 1922, she became the first woman to be awarded the NAACP's coveted Spingarn Medal for her efforts to purchase the Douglass home as well as for her human rights activities.

After a lengthy illness, at the age of fifty-seven, Mary B. Talbert died of coronary thrombosis at her home in Buffalo, New York, on Monday, October 15, 1923. She is buried in Forest Lawn Cemetery.

[*See also* ANTILYNCHING MOVEMENT.]

BIBLIOGRAPHY

Brown, Hallie Q., comp. *Homespun Heroines and Other Women of Distinction* (1926); *Buffalo Enquirer* (October 16, 1923); *Buffalo Express* (July 15, 1923); *Crisis* (February 1923 and December 1923); *DANB*; Dannett, Sylvia. *Profiles of Negro Womanhood* (1966); Mary Church Terrell papers are located at the Library of Congress in Washington, D.C.; *National Notes* (May 1926); *NBAW*; *Oberlin Alumni Magazine* (April 1917); Robinson, Wilhelmina S. *Historical Negro Biographies* (1967); Talbert, Mary B. "Did the Negro Make in the Nineteenth Century Achievements along the Lines of Wealth, Morality, Education, etc., Commensurate with His Opportunities? If So, What Achievements Did He Make?" In *Twentieth Century Negro Literature*, ed. D. W. Culp (1969); Williams, Lillian S. "Talbert, Mary Morris Burnett." In *Encyclopedia of World Biography*, ed. David Eggenberger (1988), and "Mary Morris Burnett Talbert." In *African American Women in the United States: A Biographical Directory*, ed. Dorothy Salem (forthcoming), and *American Women Social Reformers*, ed. Gayle Hardy (forthcoming).

LILLIAN S. WILLIAMS

TANNEYHILL, ANN (ANNA) ELIZABETH (1906-)

Ann Tanneyhill has dedicated her professional life to serving others through the National Urban League. Her career with the league began in 1928 when she worked for the Springfield, Massachusetts, affiliate office as a secretary to the executive director. Between 1947 and 1961, Tanneyhill was the director of vocational services for the league's national office in New York. As director of vocational services, Tanneyhill organized vocational opportunity campaigns to provide vocational guidance and counseling to Black youth at predominantly Black high schools and at historically Black colleges and universities (HBCUs) throughout the South.

Ann Tanneyhill was born in Norwood, Massachusetts, on January 19, 1906. She is the daughter of Alfred Weems Tanneyhill and Adelaide (Grandison) Tanneyhill. In 1928, Tanneyhill earned her B.S. from Simmons College in Boston. Ten years later, she received her M.A. in vocational guidance and personnel administration from Teachers College of Columbia University in New York City. In addition, Tanneyhill was awarded a certificate from the Radio Workshop of New York University.

Tanneyhill's career within the league was particularly full. After she left the league's affiliate office

A longtime executive of the National Urban League, Ann Tanneyhill has had an extraordinary commitment to Black youth and a flair for distinctive methods of reaching those youth. She was a pioneer in the use of radio and television to inspire pride in Black heritage. [Schomburg Center]

in Springfield in 1930, she moved to New York City where she continued working for the league at its national headquarters. Between 1930 and 1940, Tanneyhill was the secretary to the director of industrial relations. The following year, she became the assistant in charge of guidance and personnel. From 1941 through 1981, the year she retired, Tanneyhill served in a number of professional posts at the league, including Secretary, Bureau of Guidance and Placement (1941-45); Executive Assistant (1946); Director of Vocational Services (1947-61); Assistant Director of Public Relations (1961-63); Associate Director of Public Relations (1964-68); Director of Conferences (1969-70); Consultant to the Executive Director of the League (1971-79); and Director of the George Edmund Haynes Fellowship Program (1979-81).

In addition to holding several key positions within the league, Tanneyhill served on the boards of many associations, including the Advisory Committee on Young Workers of the Bureau of Standards, U.S. Department of Labor; the National Vocational Guidance Association; the New York Personnel and Guidance Association; the Advisory Commission of the New York Vocational High School in New York City; and the New York Citizens Committee for Nursing Education. Tanneyhill is a charter member of the Urban League's Quarter-Century Club, which is composed of those who have been in service to the league for twenty-five years or longer.

Tanneyhill's commitment to Black youth is extraordinary. She once wrote that one of the most serious problems facing the nation was the "high rate of unemployment among black and other minority youth. . . . There is great need to place more attention on basic education, and on the guidance, counseling, and preparation of youth for jobs and careers." Tanneyhill has emphasized the need for a "massive upgrading" of inner city schools to better prepare the students for postsecondary education and employment (National Urban League 1963b). She has ardently supported voter registration efforts, declaring that "the need for a massive 'voter education' program . . . is essential" and that minority youth need to understand the "privilege of the ballot box."

The career conferences on HBCUs in the 1950s were the brainchild of Tanneyhill. Between 1950 and 1955, these conferences established the practice of inviting major companies to recruit on Black college campuses, thereby providing Black students with professional opportunities and providing employers who had records of discriminatory practices with opportunities to improve their records by hiring Black talent. Tanneyhill also established the "Tomorrow's Scientists and Technicians Project," a national effort to encourage Black youth to explore their vocational talents and interests.

Tanneyhill is the recipient of several awards and honors. In 1963, she was presented with two awards, the Merit Award of the New York Personnel and Guidance Association and the National Vocational Guidance Association Award. In 1970, the Ann Tanneyhill Award was established and named in her honor by the National Urban League. The award is presented annually to a league staff member "for excellence and extraordinary commitment to the Urban League Movement." In 1971, Tanneyhill was honored by her alma mater, Simmons College, with its Alumnae Achievement Award.

Tanneyhill authored several articles, vocational guidance aids, radio program scripts, and a number of other publications, including *From School to Job: Guidance for Minority Youth* (1953), *Program Aids for the Vocational Opportunity Campaign* (many editions), and *Whitney M. Young Jr.: "The Voice of the Voiceless"* (1977). Tanneyhill used a variety of resources to promote her work among minority youth. In the 1940s, she arranged two radio programs for CBS. In 1941, Tanneyhill supervised the radio program *The Negro and National Defense*. In 1943, Tanneyhill also promoted the *Heroines in Bronze* radio program, "which was an appeal for the inclusion of Black women in the war effort." In 1960, Tanneyhill was the primary consultant to the television documentary film *A Morning for Jimmy*, sponsored by the National Urban League.

Tanneyhill is affectionately called "Miss 'T' " by Urban League staff members who have worked with her. Her life and work testify to her dedication to the Black community and her unswerving devotion to promoting the talents of minority youth in America.

BIBLIOGRAPHY

Directory of Significant Twentieth Century American Minority Women (September 28, 1977); Donnelley, Susan. "Young Ghetto Negroes Urged to 'Reach for Stars,' " *Oregonian* (August 22, 1967); Giddings, Paula. *When and Where I Enter: The Impact of Black Women on Race and Sex in America* (1984); *Journal and Guide.* "Urban League Staffer Honored with Merit Award" (November 30, 1963); *Minority American Women: A Biographical Dictionary* (December 15, 1980); National Urban League. "Biographical Sketch of Ann Tanneyhill" (April 1963), and "Biographical Sketch of Ann Tanneyhill" (dated "after 1963," 1963b), and "Ann Tanneyhill Award" (1971), and "News from National Urban League Conference" (July 22, 1970); Parkinson, Margaret B. "How Did She Get There? Ann Tanneyhill, Vocational Counselor, Who Has Opened the Job Door for Thousands,"

Charm (May, 1957); Parris, Guichard and Lester Brooks. *Blacks in the City: A History of the National Urban League* (1971); Weiss, Nancy. *The National Urban League, 1910-1940* (1974); Ann Tanneyhill is also included in the Black Women Oral History Project, Schlesinger Library, Radcliffe College, Cambridge, Massachusetts.

LISA BETH HILL

TATE, MERZE (1905-)

In 1991, Merze Tate received the American Historical Association's prestigious Distinguished Scholar award for exceptional teaching and scholarship. Tate taught for more than fifty years on the secondary and college levels before retiring from Howard University in 1977. Her experience was primarily in segregated institutions that often gave exceptional educations to African-Americans. She was the first African-American woman to receive an advanced degree from Oxford University and provided excellent instruction to students who remembered her years later as a wonderful role model and rigorous teacher.

Born in Blanchard, Michigan, on February 6, 1905, Tate walked eight miles daily to attend Battle Creek High School. In 1927, she graduated first in her class from Western Michigan Teachers College in Kalamazoo, where she became the first African-American to earn a B.A.

Racial prejudice and Jim Crow practices kept Tate from finding a teaching position in Michigan. However, in 1928 she was hired to teach history at Crispus Attucks High School, a newly opened facility for African-American students in Indianapolis. This academic institution was one of several secondary schools built during the first third of the twentieth century for Black students in urban areas throughout the nation. Some of the country's finest African-American scholars began their teaching careers at similar institutions.

Like many African-American educators, Tate spent her summers in New York City, earning her Master's degree at Columbia University in 1930. By 1932, she had entered Oxford University, where she earned the Litt.D. in 1935. Her major field of study was international relations.

Afterward Tate began an illustrious college teaching career that spanned more than forty years in historically Black institutions. She began with the position of dean of women at Barber College in North Carolina. From there she became the chair of social science at Bennett College in Greensboro, North

A legend in the world of foreign relations, Merze Tate served on the faculty of Howard University for thirty-five years while she also acted as consultant to national and international policy makers. [Moorland-Spingarn]

Carolina. In 1941, Tate became the first African-American woman to earn a Ph.D. in government and international relations from Harvard University, writing her dissertation on U.S. disarmament policies. The following year she joined the faculty at Howard University, where she served for thirty-five years.

A significant influence among undergraduate and graduate students, Tate saw the economic and social aspects of society as central to understanding history. A mentor through the years, she has taught outstanding African-American students who themselves have made contributions to public secondary education, higher education, and the history profession. Upon retiring from Howard, she endowed the Tate Seminar in Diplomatic History, an annual lecture hosted by the university.

A prolific writer, Tate is a foreign policy expert whose advice has been sought by the United Nations. Her many books and essays include *The Disarmament Illusion: The Movement for a Limitation of Armaments to 1907* (1942), *The United States and Armaments* (1948), *The United States and the Hawaiian Kingdom: A Political History* (1965), and *Mineral Railways in Africa* (1989).

BIBLIOGRAPHY

Franklin, John Hope and Alfred Moss. *From Slavery to Freedom* (1989); Spacy, James G. "Black Women in Focus," *Philadelphia New Observer* (December 21, 1988); *WWBA* (1981).

ROSALYN TERBORG-PENN

TAYLOR, ANNA DIGGS (1932-)

Lawyer, judge, and consistent advocate for civil rights, Anna Johnston Diggs Taylor was born on December 9, 1932, in Washington, D.C. Her parents enrolled her in the Northfield School for Girls in East Northfield, Massachusetts. After graduating from Northfield in 1950, she attended Barnard College and Columbia University and received a Bachelor's degree in economics in 1954. She was attracted to Yale Law School by its standards and its offer of scholarship aid. In 1957, she graduated with a degree of LL.B. In spite of her strong scholastic record, her race and gender prevented her from being hired by a law firm. With the help of a high-ranking Black official, J. Ernest Wilkins, the assistant secretary of labor, she was hired in 1957 as an assistant solicitor in the

Solicitor's Office of the U.S. Department of Labor, where she remained until 1960. From 1960 until 1972, Anna Johnston was married to Charles C. Diggs, Jr., a mortician, politician, and a U.S. congressman serving as a democrat from Detroit since 1955. Living together in Detroit, they had two children: Douglass Johnston Diggs (1964) and Carla Cecile Diggs (1967). In 1976, she married attorney S. Martin Taylor, an executive with state government and, later, with private organizations.

Anna Diggs Taylor has held several significant positions in her professional life and has been involved in numerous civic activities. She was admitted to practice law in Washington, D.C., in 1957 and in Michigan in 1961. She served as assistant Wayne County prosecutor from 1961 to 1962, as assistant U.S. attorney for the Eastern District of Michigan from 1966 to 1967, and supervising assistant corporation counsel for the City of Detroit's Law Department from 1975 to 1979. In 1964, Taylor and Claudia Shropshire Morcom were the only women attorneys volunteering their legal services in civil rights cases handled by the National Lawyers Guild in the Mississippi "Freedom Summer." Taylor worked as an attorney with a law firm from 1970 to 1975 and also taught law courses in the 1970s. Her considerable political involvement included campaigns to reelect Charles Diggs to Congress, serving as Diggs's legislative assistant and manager of his Detroit office from 1967 to 1970 and, in 1973, aiding in the campaign to elect Coleman Young as Detroit's first Black mayor. In addition, she worked as chairperson of Lawyers for Humphrey and Lawyers for McGovern and was also prominent in the effort to elect Jimmy Carter president.

In November 1979, Taylor became a federal judge for life when President Jimmy Carter appointed her to the United States District Court, Eastern District of Michigan. Her work as a judge has attracted considerable attention, much praise, and some criticism. She is known for her fairness to all, though a few lawyers think she tends to favor the plaintiff in civil rights cases and the defendant in criminal cases. Even her critics say that she, like other judges, often produces "very good, sophisticated opinions." Vigilant in trying to sensitize others to the negative quality of their racial views, in 1984 she criticized the chief judge of her own court, John Feikens, for his published remarks to the effect that Black people had not yet learned how to run city governments and "some will not understand how to run government . . . [or to provide] leadership." Judge Taylor wrote Judge Feikens a letter that eventually became public, stating that his remarks were "an extraordinary insult to all black professionals and/or administrators, and indicates a total failure to value human individuals on their individual merit: the essence of bigotry." Taylor has received many high honors and distinctions and is frequently cited as a model for young people to emulate.

BIBLIOGRAPHY
Almanac of the Federal Judiciary (1990); Higgins, Chester. "Lady Legal Eagles Learn of 'Mississippi Way of Life,' " *Jet* (July 9, 1964); *NBAW*; "U.S. Judge Focus of Racial Dispute," *National Law Journal* (September 17, 1984); "Women in the Law—Comments from Some Women Judges," *Michigan Bar Journal* (June 1984).

DE WITT S. DYKES, JR.

TAYLOR, KOKO (1935-)

Koko Taylor is Chicago's reigning "Queen of the Blues." She was born Cora Walton on September 28, 1935, in Memphis, Tennessee. As a youth, she sang gospel music in a local church choir. She was also influenced by the recordings of Bessie Smith and "Memphis" Minnie Douglas. In 1953, Cora—or "Koko," a nickname her family gave her—moved to Chicago, where she married Robert "Pops" Taylor in 1956. She began to sing professionally in the late 1950s, and with the help of "Big" Bill Hill, a prominent Chicago blues disc jockey, made her first recordings for the U.S.A. and the Spivey labels in the early 1960s. Her big breakthrough as a blues vocalist came in 1964, when she teamed up with composer/producer Willie Dixon of Chess Records. A year later she released her first major hit, Dixon's classic "Wang Dang Doodle." Koko remained with the Chess/Checker labels for ten years, during which time she worked with many of Chicago's best blues artists, including Buddy Guy, Matt Murphy and Pinetop Perkins. In 1974, she signed with Alligator Records. By that time, Koko had formed her own band and was performing throughout the country. Since then, she has recorded six albums for the Alligator label; these recordings have won for her four W. C. Handy blues awards and five Grammy nominations. Even today, Koko Taylor continues to be acclaimed as the undisputed "Queen of the Blues" wherever she performs. Her deep, resonant voice, punctuated by sustained growls, is instantly recognizable to blues enthusiasts not only in the United States, but throughout the world.

BIBLIOGRAPHY

BWW; Feather, Leonard. *Encyclopedia of Jazz in the Seventies* (1976); *Living Blues* (Winter 1971/72); Neff, Robert and Anthony Connors. *Blues* (1975).

DISCOGRAPHY

For a discography, see *Goldmine* (May 20, 1988); Mohr, Kurt et al. "Koko Taylor," *Soul Bag* (September 1975).

WILLIAM BARLOW

TAYLOR, MILDRED (1943-)

In 1990, among the best-sellers in children's literature was one book by an African-American. That book, *Roll of Thunder, Hear My Cry*, was written fourteen years before by Mildred Taylor. Immediately hailed in 1976 as a beautifully written work of great insight, it has since established itself as a classic and its author as one of the foremost writers of children's literature in the country.

Mildred Delois Taylor was born in Jackson, Mississippi, in 1943. Three months after her birth, her family moved out of the South because of a potentially violent quarrel between her father, Wilbert Lee Taylor, and a white man. They settled in Toledo, Ohio, eventually buying a large house that served as a haven for relatives and friends escaping the racial hostilities of the South. As a child, Taylor visited the South with her parents many times. The culture, rhythms, sights, and sounds of her birthplace entered her consciousness during those visits, but she never lived in Mississippi again.

Taylor's childhood was apparently very happy, filled with the love of her family and relatively free of the pain of bigotry. She attended public schools, segregated in elementary grades and integrated in high school. She was an excellent student, a class officer, editor of the school newspaper, and a member of the honor society. After graduating from the University of Toledo, she joined the Peace Corps, a dream since high school. She characterized the two years she spent in Ethiopia teaching history and English as one of the happiest periods of her life.

On her return to the United States, Taylor taught in a Peace Corps training school and became a recruiter for the organization. After a year, she entered the University of Colorado, where, in the atmosphere of the 1960s, she became a political activist. She helped found the Black Student Alliance and lobbied for a Black Studies department. After receiving an M.A. in English, she remained at the university, working as coordinator of the study skills center.

Immediately hailed in 1976 as a beautifully written work of great insight, Roll of Thunder, Hear My Cry *has since established itself as a classic and its author, Mildred Taylor, as one of the foremost writers of children's literature in the country. [Schomburg Center]*

The urge to write, however, was strong. She quit her job and moved to Los Angeles, taking a position that did not tax her intellectual or creative energies so that she could write at night. The stories she wanted to write were about her family. In an article for *Booklist* in 1990, she explained why:

As the years passed I felt a growing need for others to know these people, too. I felt a growing need to put the stories on paper for I wanted to show the black world as I knew it, a world different from that so often portrayed. I wanted to include the teachings of my own childhood, the values and principles upon which I and so many other black children were reared. I wanted to show a family united in love and self-respect, as parents strong and sensitive who attempted to guide their children successfully, without harming their spirits, through the hazardous maze of living in a discriminatory society. I wanted to show happy, loved children, about whom other children of all colors, or all cultures, could say, "I really like them, I feel what they feel."

Taylor's father was her primary source of inspiration. Throughout their childhood, he told his children stories about strong men and women who were proud of their race and history. When Taylor tried to share these stories with her white teachers and classmates, they were often dismissed as fanciful, but Taylor believed them and wanted to tell them to others.

Starting in 1975, Taylor published a series of six novels about the Logan family in the years after World War II, just prior to the convulsive period of the modern civil rights movement. The first book, *Song of the Trees*, won a contest sponsored by the Council on Interracial Books for Children in 1973 and was published two years later. The second, *Roll of Thunder, Hear My Cry*, won the Newbery Medal in 1977. Taylor was the second African-American to receive the award. The book also was nominated for a National Book Award, and it was made into a film.

The third book in the series, *Let the Circle Be Unbroken*, won the Coretta Scott King Award in 1983 and was nominated for an American Book Award. The fourth Logan family book, *The Friendship*, also was given the Coretta Scott King Award, in 1984. The last two, *Mississippi Bridge* and *The Road to Memphis*, were both published in 1990 and named Notable 1990 Children's Books in the Field of Social Studies. In addition to this six-part series, Taylor has written *The Gold Cadillac* (1987) about the vicissitudes of a family that visits the South in a gaudy, prestigious car.

Taylor's awards assure her reputation, but children do not select a book and make it a best-seller because of its critical pedigree. They want characters who are recognizable and have traits that appeal to them. Themes must resonate without didacticism, and the action must not be contrived. Taylor's books meet these criteria, and children have taken them to their hearts. Readers share in the lives of the Logans and come away renewed, challenged, educated, entertained, and, one suspects, hopeful. Taylor's family represents, to a great extent, the best in African-American families. Thus, she makes African-

Americans visible and places their lives in the center of life in the United States.

BIBLIOGRAPHY

Fogelman, Phyllis. "Mildred D. Taylor," *The Horn Book Magazine* (August 1977); Harper, Mary T. "Merger and Metamorphosis in the Fiction of Mildred D. Taylor," *Children's Literature Association Quarterly* (Summer 1988); Senich, Gerard. "Mildred Taylor," *Children's Literature Review* (1985); Sims, Rudine. *Shadow and Substance* (1982); Taxel, Joel. "Reclaiming the Voice of Resistance: The Fiction of Mildred Taylor." In *The Politics of the Textbook*, ed. M. W. Apple and L. K. Christian Smith (1991); Taylor, M. "Newbery Award Acceptance," *The Horn Book Magazine* (August 1977), and "Growing Up with Stories," *Booklist* (December 1, 1990).

SELECTED WORKS BY MILDRED TAYLOR

Song of the Trees (1975); *Roll of Thunder, Hear My Cry* (1975); *Let the Circle Be Unbroken* (1981); *The Friendship* (1987); *The Gold Cadillac* (1987); *Mississippi Bridge* (1990); *The Road to Memphis* (1990).

VIOLET J. HARRIS

TAYLOR, SUSIE BAKER KING (1848-1912)

Susie Baker King Taylor is the only Black woman to write of her participation in the Civil War, and for these experiences—as teacher, laundress, and nurse—she is remembered.

A cursory reading of her memoir, however, reveals something as unique as Taylor's reminiscences. Through oral tradition, Taylor traces her maternal line back to a great-great-grandmother who, she believed, lived to be 120 years old. According to family tradition, five of this woman's sons served in the American Revolution, establishing the precedent for patriotism that Taylor would later follow. This female ancestor also must have been among the first African slaves brought to the colony of Georgia, which was founded in 1732. A daughter of this ancestor, Taylor's great-grandmother, was said to have given birth to twenty-five children, only one of whom was a son. One of her many daughters was Taylor's grandmother; born in 1820, she was responsible in part for Taylor's upbringing.

Taylor's mother was born in 1834, and Taylor herself, the first child, in 1848. These remarkable genealogies indicate that the matrilineal Black family was in place early, possibly from the beginning of African migration into pre-Revolutionary War Georgia. None of the men in the line, including Taylor's own father, is remembered.

Taylor's mother, known only by the last name Baker, was a domestic slave. While Taylor was still quite small, her grandmother obtained permission to remove her from plantation life to freedom in Savannah, where the older woman eked out a living primarily by bartering chickens and eggs for goods. In Savannah Taylor was fortunate enough to come into contact

The remarkable memoirs of Susie King Taylor tell of her exploits during the Civil War when she learned to handle a musket, served as a nurse with Clara Barton, and lived through a nearly fatal injury to continue working with her regiment. [Schomburg Center]

with two white children who taught her to read and write, skills forbidden to Blacks in the pre-Civil War South.

When the Civil War erupted, Taylor and her grandmother returned to the plantation, but soon thereafter Taylor departed for the Sea Islands of South Carolina with her maternal uncle and his family. Taylor was only fourteen at the time, but even in old age she vividly recalled her first sight of the Yankees who were then fighting to take over the coastal areas. Taylor was immediately pressed into service by Union forces, first as teacher to freed slave children (and some adults). Later, after marrying Sgt. Edward King of the first South Carolina Volunteers, she worked as both laundress and nurse for the Union.

Most of her wartime activities were centered in South Carolina, moving up and down the coast to Florida and Georgia. Taylor learned how to handle a musket as well as bandage and care for the dying—both Black and white. In 1863, Taylor worked with Clara Barton during the eight months Barton practiced her nursing skills in the Sea Islands. In late 1864, Taylor nearly died as a result of a boating accident, but after a few weeks of recovery she was back at work and remained with her regiment until the fall of Charleston in February 1865.

After the war, Taylor's movements exemplified those of many freed people during Reconstruction. She and her husband first settled in Savannah, where she opened a school. In 1866, upon King's death, Taylor moved to rural Georgia. Finding that country life did not agree with her, however, she returned to Savannah and opened a night school for freedmen where she taught until 1872. Then, using her husband's military pension, she traded her poorly paid career in education for service as a laundress and cook for a wealthy white family in Savannah.

When the family journeyed to New England on summer holiday, Taylor accompanied them and soon after moved to Boston. There she married Russell Taylor and became involved in civic activities as a founding member of the Corps 67 Women's Relief Corps. She was elected president of the organization in 1893.

In 1898, when her son lay dying in Louisiana, Taylor ventured to the South one last time. To her surprise, the winds of freedom had turned into the chains of segregation. She even witnessed a hanging in Mississippi. In old age she chose to overlook the devastation of the post-Reconstruction era and harkened back instead to 1861's "wonderful revolution"—the phrase she used in the closing words of her brief memoir.

BIBLIOGRAPHY

Higginson, Thomas Wentworth. *Army Life in a Black Regiment* (1870); Quarles, Benjamin. *The Negro in the Civil War* (1968); Taylor, Susie King. *A Black Woman's Civil War Memoirs: Reminiscences of My Life in Camp with the 33rd United States Colored Troops, Late 1st S.C. Volunteers*, ed. Patricia W. Romero and Willie Lee Rose (1988).

PATRICIA W. ROMERO

TEER, BARBARA ANN (1937-)

Barbara Ann Teer, award-winning actress and director, producer, writer, educator, cultural leader, businesswoman, real estate developer, and founder/executive director of the National Black Theatre Company, was born June 18, 1937, in East St. Louis, Illinois, to Fred L. and Lila (Benjamin) Teer. She received her B.S. in dance education in 1957 from the University of Illinois with honors, did further study in dance in Germany, Switzerland, and Paris, and studied acting with Sanford Meisner, Paul Mann, Phillip Burton, and Lloyd Richards. Additionally, she studied at the University of Wisconsin, University of Connecticut, Bennett College, Sarah Lawrence College, Mary Wigman Studios, and for four years at the Musical Academy of Dramatic Art.

Her Broadway credits include the controversial African musical *Kwamina*, for which she worked as the dance captain for Agnes De Mille (who won a Tony Award for choreography), and *Where's Daddy*, by William Inge, at the Billy Rose Theatre. She was the winner of the Drama Desk Vernon Rice Award in 1964-65 for outstanding achievement off-Broadway in *Home Movies*, and later appeared in twelve off-Broadway productions including *The Experiment, Who's Got His Own, Day of Absence* and *Experimental Death Unit I, The Living Premise, Does a Tiger Wear a Necktie, Young Lady of Property, Missing Rattlesnakes, Funnyhouse of a Negro, The Owl and the Pussycat*, and *The Prodigal Son*. Her television credits include three appearances on *Camera Three, Kaleidoscope*, the soap opera *As the World Turns, The Ed Sullivan Show, The David Susskind Show*, and Joseph Mankiewicz's *A Carol for Another Christmas*. Her movie credits include Sidney Lumet's *The Group* and *The Pawnbroker* and Ossie Davis's *Gone Are the Days*. Her dance tours include Brazil with the Alvin Ailey American Dance Theater, Chicago with the Duke Ellington show, Las Vegas with the Pearl Bailey show, Canada with Get Aboard the Jazz Train, and New York City with the Louis Johnson Dance Company and the Henry Street Playhouse Dance Company.

Prior to taking the boldest step in her theater career, founding the National Black Theatre Company (NBT) in Harlem in 1968, Teer had grown dissatisfied with the lack of respect for Black culture in American professional theater. In 1967, she and Robert Hooks founded the Group Theatre Workshop in Harlem to refocus their talents toward the Black community. When this endeavor evolved into the founding of the Negro Ensemble Company (NEC), she was inclined to establish her own company, which (with NEC) became one of the most prominent theater companies in the country during the Black revolutionary theater movement of the late 1960s and early 1970s. In the NBT Teer saw the opportunity to develop an art form that would address the immediate concerns of African-American people. Her endeavor to reflect the collective personality (ethos-soul) of African-Americans through theater was enhanced in 1972 by a Ford Foundation Fellowship to sponsor her visit to Africa to further her research. She spent four months in western Nigeria acquainting herself with the Yoruba culture and extended her study to South America, the Caribbean islands, and Harlem.

Out of this quest evolved Teer's ritualistic theater, developed and taught through the "Black Art Standard"—sometimes known as "Teer Technology of Soul"—as a technique for teaching "God Conscious Art" at the National Black Theatre. Teer has written, directed, and produced several productions reflecting her "Black Art Standard," including *The Ritual* on the television show *Soul* in 1970, *Change/Love Together/Organize: A Revival* (1972), *We Sing a New Song* (1972), *Sojourn into Truth* (1976), and *Softly Comes the Whirlwind, Whispering in Your Ear* (1978). She toured in Haiti, Bermuda, Trinidad, Guyana, and Nigeria. More recently, she produced the ritualistic drama *The Legacy*, by Gordon Nelson, at the 1989 National Black Theatre Festival. Additionally, she directed *Me and My Song* for the Black Heritage series on NBC television and wrote, directed, and coproduced the award-winning film *Rise: A Love Song for a Love People* (1975), based on the life of Malcolm X. Her off-Broadway directing credits include Joseph Walker and Jo Jackson's *The Believers*, Douglas Turner Ward's award-winning *Day of Absence*, and Charles Russell's *Five on the Black Hand Side*.

Teer's boldest accomplishment, developing real estate for the arts, promises to be the most ambitious building project of any traditionally Black arts organization in history. After the NBT's 137th Street home was destroyed by fire in 1983, Teer purchased property on 125th Street and Fifth Avenue for NBT, where she is completing the development of a new theater in the Harlem community: the National Black Institute of Communication through Theatre Arts (NBICTA). This ten-million-dollar theater is the first revenue-generating Black arts theater complex in the country, according to Teer, and combines commercial, retail, and office space with theater arts activities.

Teer's talent, vision, and commitment to her community and to uplifting African-American theater arts have been recognized extensively. She is the recipient of more than thirty awards, citations, and memberships including *Who's Who in America* (1991); distinguished membership in Delta Sigma Theta sorority's National Commission on the Arts (1991); Legends in Our Time, *Essence* magazine (1991); Citation, the J. Raymond Jones Democratic Club, Barbara Ann Teer Day, East St. Louis, Illinois (1991); AUDELCO (Audience Development Committee) Special Achievement Award (1989); Kwanza Expo Award (1989); Acknowledgment Award, Breakthrough Foundation New York Youth at Risk; Sojourner Truth Award, Harlem Women's Committee/New Future Foundation, Inc. (1987); and the Monarch Merit Award, National Council for Culture and Art (1984).

BIBLIOGRAPHY

Faison, Abisola. Typescript, National Black Theatre, New York (November 15, 1991); Norflett, Linda Kerr. Interview with Barbara Ann Teer (April 10, 1980); Whitten, Reena. Typescript, National Black Theatre, New York (November 20, 1991).

LINDA NORFLETT

TELEVISION

Black women have had an uneasy relationship with network television since the first season of full programming (1948-49). Arguably the most conservative of all the arenas of popular culture, television has been slow to give positive attention to Black women. The respect given to Black female musical artists such as Ella Fitzgerald, Sarah Vaughan, and Marian Anderson, who appeared in variety shows like CBS's 1948-71 *Toast of the Town* (later renamed *The Ed Sullivan Show*), was rare. Whether in situation comedies ("sitcoms") or in dramatic series, those Black actresses lucky enough to fight their way onto the small screen usually found themselves relegated to a negative stereotype.

One such stereotype depicted Black women as subservient within an otherwise white society. These roles commonly included domestics in white households such as Lillian Randolph's Louise in the long-running Danny Thomas vehicle *Make Room for Daddy* (*The Danny Thomas Show*) (1953-57 on ABC; 1957-64 on CBS). Even after the civil rights movement of the 1960s, Black women continued to be relegated to servile roles in all-white environments. Nichelle Nichols as Lieutenant Uhuru in the NBC 1966-71 cult favorite *Star Trek* did little more than punch buttons at the command of white Captain James T. Kirk (played by William Shatner). Madge Sinclair's Ernestine Shoop was a Black nurse serving predominantly white doctors and patients in the 1979-86 CBS series *Trapper John, M.D.* While nurses and lieutenants have higher professional status than domestics, the essential power structure remains the same. Rarely at the center of TV storylines, Black women have traditionally been little more than token color in an otherwise white television landscape.

The impulse to portray Black women as subordinate carried over into numerous shows that did star Black women. One such show, ABC's *Beulah* (1950-53), tried to draw audiences by recruiting three of Hollywood's best-known mammies. *Beulah*, originally a popular radio show featuring Hattie McDaniel (who won an Oscar for her role as Mammy in the 1939 blockbuster film *Gone with the Wind*), focused on the comic trials and tribulations of Beulah, a Mammyesque maid. Although Ethel Waters portrayed the TV Beulah for the show's first season, McDaniel was slated to take over in the second season. When she became too ill, Louise Beavers (costar of the 1934 tearjerker *Imitation of Life*) became the final incarnation of Beulah. Butterfly McQueen, and then Ruby Dandridge, played Beulah's brainless friend Oriole.

CBS's *Amos 'n' Andy* (1951-53), also based on a popular radio program, featured many of the cartoonish stereotypes of Black Americans familiar from earlier forms of American popular culture. Among these types were the "coon" as brought to life by the character George "Kingfish" Stevens (Tim Moore). Traditionally the coon is a flamboyant, grinning, simple-minded schemer, whose plottings are played for laughs. In the TV show, Kingfish as coon found his victims in Amos Jones (Alvin Childress) and Andy Hogg Brown (Spencer Williams). As in many other previous depictions of the coon, Kingfish finds his comeuppance in the person of his demanding wife, Sapphire (Ernestine Wade). Indeed, thanks to *Amos 'n' Andy*, "Sapphire" became the name for an-

The first Black regular on a television series, in 1963-64's East Side/West Side, *Cicely Tyson later starred in the highly successful television movie* The Autobiography of Miss Jane Pittman *(1974), for which she received two Emmy Awards. [Donald Bogle]*

other stereotype: the Black woman as a shrewish, violent, husband-emasculating wife.

From the mid-1950s through the early 1960s, Black women essentially disappeared from the television screen. Then, in the mid-1960s, presumably in response to the civil rights movement, Black women appeared in higher-status professions. In addition to Nichelle Nichols as Lieutenant Uhuru at the control panel in *Star Trek,* Judy Pace portrayed lawyer Pat Walters in ABC's short-lived series *The Young Lawyers* (1970-71).

Even when a Black woman was the show's star, she was surrounded by white characters. NBC's *Julia* (1968-71) featured the light-skinned Diahann Carroll as Julia Baker, a widowed nurse trying to raise her young son in what appeared to be an affluent all-white community. Issues of race were rarely brought up on the show. More typically the show dealt with

the mundane dilemmas familiar to sitcoms. Ironically, Carroll later starred (1984-87) as Dominique Deveraux, who, along with Troy Beyer as Deveraux's daughter Jackie, was the exception to an otherwise all-white cast on the ABC prime-time soap *Dynasty* (1981-89).

Unsurprisingly, variety shows showcasing Black women performers proved unpopular with TV audiences during the late 1960s and early 1970s. *The Leslie Uggams Show* aired in 1969 on CBS only to be canceled thirteen weeks later. *The Pearl Bailey Show* lasted for only half of ABC's 1970-71 season.

However, network programming during the 1960s did present a few notable exceptions to the Black-women-in-a-white-world scenario. ABC's series *Room 222* (1969-74) depicted a wide range of realistic issues concerning the multiracial student body of Walt Whitman High. Even more importantly, the series revolved around a Black couple, Pete Dixon (Lloyd Haynes), a history teacher, and Liz McIntyre (Denise Nicholas), the school's guidance counselor. Such an attempt to sympathetically portray complex Black characters won *Room 222* approval from the National Association for the Advancement of Colored People, although the show tended to idealize Pete Dixon and Liz McIntyre for their ability to assimilate into mainstream white values rather than to challenge them.

Two critically acclaimed series proved even more radical. *East Side/West Side*, a CBS dramatic series, featured Cicely Tyson in the recurring role of Jane Foster, a secretary in an urban welfare office. The show explored a variety of inner-city problems. One episode, entitled "Who Do You Kill?," graphically portrayed a Black couple trying to make ends meet in the ghetto. Although Diana Sands won an Emmy for her role as the wife in "Who Do You Kill?" *East Side/West Side* proved too sobering for the American television audience and was only broadcast for one season: 1963-64. Another CBS dramatic show, *The Nurses*, was slightly more successful—it ran for three seasons (1962-65). Although the series's regular cast was white, distinguished Black actors frequently guest-starred, among them Ruby Dee and Claudia McNeil, who both earned Emmy nominations for their appearances.

By the mid-1970s, such attempts at experimentation were largely abandoned. Idealistic hope for the racially harmonious world of *Room 222* seemed naive in light of continued racial tension in America. *East Side/West Side* was too hot to handle. In place of such shows, network executives introduced a group of Black sitcoms to prime time. These shows, which included NBC's *Sanford and Son* (1971-77), CBS's *Good Times* (1974-79), CBS's *The Jeffersons* (1975-85), ABC's *That's My Mama* (1974-75), and ABC's *What's Happening!!* (1976-79), all showcased a Black man in a coon role strikingly reminiscent of Kingfish Stevens. Within this formula, the coon's scheming resulted in a series of comic scrapes. His family tirelessly bailed him out of trouble. Particularly long-suffering was the family's matriarch, who was usually either the coon's wife or mother. Invariably overweight, the matriarch did little more than endlessly fret about the house. She was either a Sapphire-like volatile personality like Aunt Esther (LaWanda Page) in *Sanford and Son*, or a long-suffering comic foil like Esther Rolle's Florida Evans of *Good Times*, Mabel King's Mama Thomas of *What's Happening!!* and Isabel Sanford's Louise Jefferson from *The Jeffersons* (Sanford won an Emmy for the 1980-81

season and five other nominations for her portrayal of Louise Jefferson).

The only alternative to this return to stereotypical buffoonery was ABC's *Get Christie Love*, a 1974-75 police show starring Teresa Graves as Christie. The show presented a unique popular cultural bit of anthropology. It was a cross between the blaxploitation (Black exploitation) films of the early seventies (action/adventure movies like *Superfly* and *Shaft* that starred Black men in "stud" roles), and the "jiggle" TV shows of the late 1970s (shows featuring groups of beautiful, provocatively dressed white women, such as *Charlie's Angels*, ABC's 1976-81 series).

From the end of the 1970s until the mid-1980s, American TV once again virtually erased Black women stars from the screen. The types of Black women presented in the 1970s were no longer appropriate, yet no new ones had taken their place. There were a few isolated reworkings of the familiar theme of a Black woman surrounded by whites: Nell Carter as Nell, the mammy-like caretaker for a white policeman and his three daughters, on NBC's *Gimme a Break* (1981-86) and Kim Fields (veteran of the short-lived 1978 CBS series *Baby I'm Back*) as Tootie Ramsey, an adolescent girl attending an all-girls, apparently otherwise all-white, boarding school in NBC's *The Facts of Life* (1978-88). Once again, these women were isolated in their blackness. The people around them on the show were uniformly white.

However, the late 1970s and early 1980s did present a few stirrings of change. TV specials gave plum roles to several Black actresses. Cicely Tyson starred in the 1974 CBS movie *The Autobiography of Miss Jane Pittman*, which traced the life of a 110-year-old woman from her slave days to her involvement with the civil rights movement in the early 1960s. Tyson went on to portray Marva Collins, the innovative Chicago educator, in the 1981 CBS movie *The Marva Collins Story*. The revolutionary 1976-77 and 1978-79 ABC miniseries *Roots 1* and *Roots 2* made a major impact on Americans, generating widespread interest in Black history. Actress Olivia Cole won an Emmy for her work on *Roots* and Ruby Dee was nominated for the award. In 1979, CBS produced *I Know Why the Caged Bird Sings*, adapted from actress/writer Maya Angelou's autobiography of the same name. The show starred Constance Goods as young Angelou, costarring Esther Rolle as Angelou's grandmother.

The early 1980s also saw the flowering of Debbie Allen, who was to become a powerful force in television. Allen got her entertainment start singing, dancing, and acting on Broadway. She made two highly praised appearances on TV in the late 1970s in *Roots 2*, and in a starring role on the short-lived 1977 NBC variety show *3 Girls 3*. It was Allen's involvement with the dramatic series *Fame* (1981-85, first on NBC, then produced for syndication) that secured her high TV status. Allen's performance on the show as dance teacher Lydia Grant was strong and complex, but *Fame* also launched her career behind the scenes. She won two Emmys for her choreography for *Fame* (for the 1981-82 and 1982-83 seasons), and was nominated for two other seasons (1983-84 and 1984-85). She also began to try her hand at directing, beginning with a few *Fame* episodes, then branching out to other shows. In 1989, she won Emmy nominations for both choreographing and directing her own ABC special, *The Debbie Allen Special*.

In the mid-1980s, the women of the Huxtable family, on NBC's The Cosby Show, *were the most-watched Black women in the history of prime-time television (clockwise, from top left: Sabrina Le Beauf, Tempestt Bledsoe, Lisa Bonet, Keshia Knight Pulliam, and Phylicia Rashad).*

In 1984, NBC introduced *The Cosby Show* (1984-92), and the television image of Black women was dramatically changed forever. The show starred and was produced by TV perennial Bill Cosby, and detailed the lives of the Huxtables, a Black family nothing like previous depictions of Black families. While the Evanses and Jeffersons of the 1970s were either poor or *nouveau*-middle class, the Huxtables were comfortably upper-middle class. Cliff Huxtable (Cosby) was a doctor, and wife Clair (played by Phylicia Rashad) was a lawyer. Their five kids went to good schools, and the family lived in the wealthy neighborhood of Brooklyn Heights. The show proved to be one of the most successful of all time, and many of the women in the cast were nominated for Emmys in the mid-1980s: Rashad (twice), Lisa Bonet (who played Cosby daughter Denise), and Keshia Knight Pulliam (baby of the family Rudy).

In the derivative world of television, it is not surprising that *The Cosby Show* spawned a host of sitcoms depicting Black families, including CBS's *Charlie & Co.* (1985-86), ABC's *Family Matters* (1989-), and NBC's *The Fresh Prince of Bel Air* (1990-). While critics praised *The Cosby Show* and these popular shows for providing Black Americans with positive images, they also criticized them for two reasons. First, like *Julia* before them, the shows were termed "not Black enough," since they rarely addressed issues that shaped the lives of most Black Americans and instead relied on formulaic plots. Second, *The Cosby Show* ushered in a new age of the Black woman as fairy tale Supermom, where mothers never seemed to have a conflict between work and family. Clair Huxtable and her imitators were eerily young-looking, beautiful, successful, perpetually energetic, and relentlessly nurturing. Critics argued that these Supermoms set an example that was impossible for Black women to achieve.

In spite of these critics, the appeal of *The Cosby Show* did lead to an increase of African-American women on TV. For example, Cosby went on to produce NBC's successful *A Different World* (1987-) about an all-Black college, featuring many Black women such as the status-seeking Whitley (Jasmine Guy) and the studious, ambitious Kim (Charnele Brown). The show eventually gained a positive reputation for its opportunities for Black women behind the camera as writers, directors, and producers. The increasingly powerful Debbie Allen directed many episodes and eventually became the show's producer.

Many non-Cosby-controlled shows centered around strong Black women characters as well. For example, NBC's *227* (1985-90) starred Marla Gibbs as Mary, an urban, lower-middle-class, wisecracking wife and mother. Gibbs was also named *227*'s creative consultant, which gave her some artistic control over the show. ABC's sitcom *Head of the Class* (1986-91) focused on gifted New York City high school students in an accelerated history class, featuring three Black women: Darlene (Robin Givens), Sarah (Kimberly Russell), and T. J. (Rain Pryor). The Fox network's *21 Jump Street* (1986-91), a cop show with an ensemble cast, featured Holly Robinson as Hoffs, an intelligent and complex character. Talk show phenomenon Oprah Winfrey executive-produced and starred, along with a large cast of other talented Black actresses, in a 1989 TV-movie version of Gloria Naylor's *The Women of Brewster Place*. Winfrey's work as producer and star of *The Oprah Winfrey Show* won her three Emmys. Beginning in 1991, NBC aired the dramatic series *I'll Fly Away*, which focused partly on a single Black mother, Lilly Harper (played by Regina Taylor), living in the South during the early days of the civil rights movement.

Even daytime soap operas jumped on the bandwagon, an unprecedented move in a television genre that traditionally excluded Black characters. Daytime soaps ran from 1950 until the late 1960s before the first Black soap actresses made their appearance. Early Black women soap characters found themselves stuck with stereotypical roles and were isolated in mostly white casts. For example, accomplished singer Micki Grant played secretary Peggy Harris in NBC's *Another World* (1964-) for several seasons in the late 1960s. In 1968, Ellen Holly's character Carla Gray on ABC's *One Life to Live* (1968-) tried desperately to pass as white by calling herself Carla Benari, in order to win the heart of white Dr. James Craig (Robert Milli). On NBC's *Days of Our Lives* (1965-), a 1977 interracial romance between David Banning (Richard Guthrie) and Valerie Grant (Tina Andrews) proved too controversial for its audience, and the relationship was dissolved. Strangely enough, whenever a Black woman character during the 1960s and 1970s became too hot to handle, she was quickly married off to a Black policeman. By the late 1980s, however, virtually every soap featured Black women in a wider range of roles. In 1989, Debbi Morgan won an Emmy for her good-hearted character Angie Hubbard on ABC's *All My Children* (1970-)—a sure sign that Black women had gained respect in the world of soaps.

In 1990, Fox introduced *In Living Color*, an innovative half-hour comedy show with a multiracial cast. Fox executives and producer/director/writer/star Keenen Ivory Wayans gave *In Living Color*'s Black female performers—Kim Coles (who left after the show's first season), T'Keyah "Crystal" Keymah, and Kim Wayans—a unique opportunity. For the first time, Black women were allowed to engage in the kind of parodic social criticism and political satire that NBC's *Saturday Night Live* allowed its constantly metamorphosing cast of predominantly white men, white women, and Black men from 1975 onward (though it should be noted that remarkable comic Danitra Vance did appear on *SNL* for the 1985-86 season). In addition, *In Living Color* proved as influential as its NBC predecessor, attracting a huge following among young people, both white and Black, male and female. However, some critics charged the show with perpetuating some unfavorable Black stereotypes and also pointed to the high number of white writers on the show.

Despite these criticisms, *In Living Color* remained an example of the increasing strength of Black women in television—and not only on screen. Indeed, Keenen Ivory Wayans's direct boss in the 1991-92 season was a Black woman, Rose Catharine Pinkey, director of Current Programs at Twentieth Television, a division of Twentieth Century Fox Film Corp. Pinkey's high status at Fox, as well as Winfrey's award-winning success as a producer and Allen's meteoric rise during the 1980s, reflected another TV trend of the time—the growing numbers of successful Black women power brokers. Although according to a 1991 NAACP study, 75 percent of TV executives were still white men, by 1992 Black women had managed to penetrate some of the higher echelons of network programming. These women include Karen Burnes, vice-president of children's programming at Fox; Kim Fleary, vice-president of comedy development at ABC; Kelly Goode, senior director of comedy development at CBS; Winnifred White, director of Motion Pictures for Television at NBC; Debra Langford, director of Current Programs at Warner Bros. Television; and Charisse McGhee, director of Current Dramatic Television at NBC.

Black women were thriving at every other level of television production as well. Suzanne de Passe, president of Motown Productions, won Emmys for producing two variety specials: NBC's 1982-83 *Motown 25: Yesterday, Today, Forever*, and the 1984-85 *Motown Returns to the Apollo*. Janet Harrell and Darlene Hayes won a combined five Emmys spanning the 1980s for producing the syndicated talk show *Donahue* (1970-). Hayes was also a writer for NBC's *Amen* (1986-91). Winifred Hervey-Stalworth won a 1985-86 Emmy for producing NBC's popular sitcom *The Golden Girls* (1985-92), and wrote for

many other shows. Other successful producers included Helaine Head, who produced episodes of NBC's *L.A. Law* (1986-), CBS's *Cagney and Lacey* (1982-86), and NBC's *St. Elsewhere* (1982-88), and Neema Barnett, who produced episodes of *The Cosby Show* and a range of TV movies. Other writers include Janet Allston, Kathleen McGhee-Anderson, and Vide Spears. Make-up artist June Josef, set decorator Cheryal Kearney, and costume designer Maritza Garcia have all been nominated for Emmys.

The Public Broadcasting System (PBS) deserves special mention. Unlike the other networks, PBS is publicly funded, and generally appeals to a well-educated, liberal audience. Begun in the 1950s, PBS was always a step ahead of the commercial networks in its positive attention to Black women. Not only did its series, movies, documentaries, and specials frequently feature Black women from very early on in its history, but PBS led the way in giving Black women important opportunities. PBS's Emmy-winning reporter (for the 1983-84 and 1984-85 seasons) Charlayne Hunter-Gault from *The MacNeil/Lehrer News Hour* (1976-) was the first Black woman on a national daily news program. The acclaimed civil rights documentary series *Eyes on the Prize 1* and *Eyes on the Prize 2* (1987-88 and 1989-90) featured many Black women writers and producers, many of whom were nominated for Emmys. Finally, the only Black woman as of 1992 with the executive power to develop programs from their inception to their on-screen product was employed at PBS: Jennifer Lawson, executive vice president of national programming and promotion services.

Thus, at the beginning of the 1990s, television was changing for the better. As late as the early 1980s, it was unthinkable that so many different kinds of roles would be available on network television for Black women. Even more unthinkable was that Black women like Jennifer Lawson would be in control of the very medium that historically stereotyped them and relegated them to the shadows.

BIBLIOGRAPHY

Bogle, Donald. *Blacks in American Films and Television: An Encyclopedia* (1988); Hill, George. *Black Women in Television. An Illustrated History and Bibliography* (1990); MacDonald, J. Fred. *Blacks and White TV: Afro-Americans in Television since 1946* (1983).

SARAH P. MORRIS

TEMPERANCE WORK IN THE NINETEENTH CENTURY

If you meet in any part of the country, women lacking in breadth of soul, so that they wish to draw the color-line, when they draw the line at color, draw your line at self-respect and fight without them. You cannot fight alone if you fight with God, and all the Divine forces in the world that work for righteousness. . . . If every other woman should trail this [temperance] banner, should it not be our privilege only to grasp it with a firmer hand? (Frances E. W. Harper 1891)

With signature evangelical fervor, Frances E. W. Harper laid out the special calling Black women brought to temperance work in the nineteenth century. In doing their Christian duty, Black women needed a firmer hand to do alone the work they might have shared with white women. Thus the story of Black women's historic involvement with temperance reform moves along two fronts. First is their independent work through the Black churches, clubs, and settlements which developed a special female role in race uplift. Second is their bid for equal standing in the mostly white and often racist Women's Christian Temperance Union (WCTU).

Of course, African-Americans' involvement with temperance long preceded the WCTU's founding in 1874. Northern free Blacks embraced temperance, both as an idea and a movement, before the Civil War. Emerging somewhat later than antidrink activism among whites and growing almost solely out of the churches, temperance figured in Black self-help efforts in the 1830s, a time of rising disfranchisement and white hostility. As with the American Temperance Society and the Sons of Temperance, men led most Black organizations; clergymen combined temperance work with pastoring, abolition, and mutual aid work. Like organizations among white working-men, Black temperance societies often provided practical services like burial funds and sick benefits. The New England Colored Temperance Society was unique in its denial of membership to women; Black women more often than not formed separate groups (Philadelphians were especially active) or, occasionally, joined forces with white women. For example, in Utica, New York, in the early 1840s, Black women were a palpable if small presence in the city's so-called cold water army.

After the Civil War, the temperance impulse again came from the Black churches and fraternal organiza-tions. The African Methodist Episcopal Church frowned upon alcohol use. During Reconstruction, Black lodges affiliated with the British-based International Order of Grand Templars, and in North Carolina these Black chapters actively recruited women to full membership. Many also read about T. Thomas Fortune's flirtation with the Prohibition party during the mid-1880s. Fortune, admired as the militant and lucid editor of the widely circulated *New York Age*, made arguments that would appeal deeply to African-Americans' sense of what was wrong with the South. First, drunkenness excused white violence against Blacks. Second, a third party (even a single-issue one) spoke to the need for political independence for Black voters.

In the 1890s, temperance continued to figure in programs for Black education and advancement. Abstemiousness was one attribute in the success-through-respectability credo taught at Tuskegee Institute. As part of the success and uplift ethic, temperance injunctions took important cues from traditional gender ideology. Lay preachers in open-air meetings also exhorted southern Black Americans to temperance. In order for whites to "respect us as *men*," cried one speaker, Black people must "renounce the use of all intoxicating liquors . . . in the great struggle of life beside the white man" (Robinson 1892).

Black women also embraced temperance to meet life's demands on them. Black clubwomen's campaigns against the one-room cabin in the South often focused on domestic practices and included efforts to keep wives and mothers from dipping snuff and chewing or smoking tobacco. Black women continued these admonitions into the twentieth century: "No woman can accomplish the greatest functions of her sex, replenishing the earth and rearing her children in an atmosphere of sweet purity—with a tainted body, weakened by the ravages of alcohol—or a mind made torpid by drink. . . . Let us then be sober" (Gibbs 1907). Black women were expected to teach temperance by example and to encourage men to the same. Underscoring women's ideal role as the keeper of morals (and as dependent on men), a male writer in the *Colored American Magazine* explained in 1904: "Our young women can do much to head off the drink habit among the young men . . . and it is for their own future well-being that they exercise their decisive influence to this end."

Despite the invocation of traditional gender roles in typical temperance rhetoric, Black women's temperance work took on new meanings during and after Reconstruction, marking important shifts in their roles and expectations. In the 1870s, fiction writer Pauline Hopkins and journalist Josephine Turpin Washington inaugurated their writing careers with essays on temperance themes. Temperance offered an acceptable arena for many Black women to test a new public voice. When the *AME Church Review* published a symposium on temperance in 1891, all its contributors were women, and the keynote was struck by Frances Harper.

Frances Harper listed the "three great evils" of civilization as intemperance, the social evil (prostitution), and lawlessness (which included lynching). Christian duty dictated women's special duty to fight against alcohol: "I hold that the Women's Christian Temperance Union has in its hand one of the grandest opportunities that God ever placed in the hands of the womanhood of any country." Her formula was straightforward: "Consecrate, educate, agitate, and legislate" (Harper 1891). Prohibition was the righteous politics of any voter or any party. Temperance unions among Black women, explained Lucy Thurman, would be a grand "training school for the development of women" (Bordin 1990). Black women carried out temperance work in "colored locals" and participated in a national—even world-wide—movement for Christian liberation from vice.

Harper complained—sometimes bitterly—of white women who failed to distinguish between the goals of social equality and those of Christian commitment and drew the color line in the WCTU. Indeed, racial segregation was an organizing principle of the WCTU according to its bylaws. Harper's role as Superintendent of Colored Work was not a gesture at an idealized sisterhood, but rather affirmed Black women's equality in the work of Christian reform. The temperance battle, Harper insisted, "was not the contest of a social club, but a moral warfare for an imperiled civilization" (Harper 1888).

As citizens of the "Christian countries of the globe," Black women assumed their part in the work for "God and Home and Native Land" (the WCTU's motto) against the great curse of alcohol. This language positioned Black women ideologically within woman's era. That is, WCTU membership affirmed Black women's right to participate in a female culture of reform whose ideological pillars were Christian duty and an expanded notion of women's role in bettering society (social housekeeping). At the same time, however, Black women resisted white women's singling out of Black men for criticism (especially prevalent in the South) and downplayed the anti-male approach characteristic of white women's temperance rhetoric. Thus Black women reworked

temperance ideas to suit their particular social and political situation and negotiated a separate but equal space for themselves in the WCTU.

White priorities gave rise to official racial segregation in the WCTU, especially Frances Willard's ambition to organize the South and racist southerners' desire to take both alcohol and the vote from Black men, whom they considered enslaved equally by liquor and the Republican party. The daughter of abolitionists, Willard prided herself on a family tradition of sympathy for southern slaves. But her southern tours of the 1880s instead moved her to pity the white southerners because she felt the "problem on their hands is immeasurable." "The colored race multiplies like the locusts of Egypt," she insisted, "the grog shop is its center of power" (Willard 1890). Consistent with the national temper that ended Reconstruction in 1877, Willard deemed white southerners, not Black southerners, most in need of northern sympathy.

Willard sometimes addressed Black audiences in the southern towns she visited, often at the request of local white leaders. There is some evidence that temperance activity "broke the color line" as one enthusiastic worker reported of a Raleigh, North Carolina, meeting around 1880 (Willard 1883). In Grimes County, Texas, a winning voter bloc of 600 freedmen and 125 white people carried prohibition. Yet southern white temperance women convinced Willard that she had to choose between not organizing in the South or doing so on only a segregated basis.

Not all Black women were satisfied with the WCTU practices and policies. Northern militants like Ida B. Wells and Josephine St. Pierre Ruffin found racism in the WCTU intolerable. In the pages of the *Woman's Era*, and through direct confrontation in Wells's case, each took strong public positions against Willard's racial views, especially on lynching. Willard's most infamous statements held that "great dark-faced mobs" menaced the South such that "the safety of woman, of childhood, of the home, is menaced in a thousand localities at this moment, so that men dare not go beyond the sight of their own roof tree" (Willard 1890). Wells seems never to have joined the WCTU, but she did attend the Cleveland convention of 1894 to influence the group's position on lynching—and was unsuccessful. (Frederick Douglass and Reverdy C. Ransom also condemned Willard's position on lynching.)

Racism aside, Willard's ideas were compelling ones for Black women in this period. The "Do Everything" policy dovetailed nicely with their own broadly conceived impulse to race uplift and offered more promise than the single-issue politics then evolving in the suffrage movement. Harper and Thurman affirmed that Woman "doing everything" included Black women; Wells and Ruffin challenged whether the "everything" included racial justice. The answer to the latter, however, was generally no.

It is extremely difficult to know exactly how many Black women affiliated with the WCTU in the nineteenth century, though the organization's historian concludes that few Black women actually joined. At least three Black women, Frances Harper, Sara J. Early, and Lucy Thurman, held the national post of Superintendent of Colored Work and many others, like Frances A. Joseph of New Orleans and Georgia Swift King of Atlanta, led local unions of Black women. Many Black women admired and honored Frances Willard by naming their clubs for her and presenting flowers to her at national conventions, and they took great pride in Black women's growing leadership in the world-wide movement against drink. At the turn of the century, Black women were a small but proud presence at the World Temperance Conferences in Washington, D.C., and Edinburgh, Scotland. By about 1910, the maturing Black and white club and suffrage movements eclipsed the WCTU as standard-bearers of the first mass movement of women in America, and the National Association of Colored Women maintained its own department for temperance work.

[See also WOMEN'S CHRISTIAN TEMPERANCE UNION, SOUTH.]

BIBLIOGRAPHY

Bordin, Ruth. *Woman and Temperance: The Quest for Power and Liberty, 1873-1900* (1990); Carby, Hazel V. *Reconstructing Womanhood: The Emergence of the Afro-American Novelist* (1987); Cleagle, Rosalyn. "The Colored Temperance Movement, 1830-1860," M.A. thesis (1969); *Colored American Magazine*, "Drink Habit Among Afro-Americans" (1904); Epstein, Barbara Leslie. *The Politics of Domesticity: Women, Evangelism and Temperance in Nineteenth Century America* (1981); Gibbs, Ione E. "Woman's Part in the Uplift of the Negro Race," *Colored American Magazine* (1907); Gilmore, Glenda Elizabeth. "Lessons in the Limits of Sisterhood: Black Women, White Women, and the W.C.T.U. in North Carolina, 1880-1900." Unpublished manuscript (1991); Hamilton, Tulia K. Brown. "The National Association of Colored Women, 1896-1920," Ph.D. diss. (1978); Harper, Mrs. F.E.W. "The Women's Christian Temperance Union and the Colored Woman," *AME Church Review* (October 1888), and "Symposium—Temperance," *AME Church Review* (April 1891); Lawson, Rosetta E. "Temperance Reform a World-Wide Movement," *AME Church Review* (January 1901); "Miss Willard and the Colored People," *Woman's Era* (July 1895); "Mrs. Frances Joseph, President of the Frances Willard WCTU," *Colored American Magazine* (1903); Penn, I. Garland. *The Afro-American Press and Its Editors* (1891); Robinson, Magnus L. "A Common Sense Appeal to the Colored People in Regard to the Use of Intoxicating Liquors," *Industrial Advocate* (pamphlet, 1892); Ryan, Mary P. *Cradle of the Middle Class: The Family in Oneida County, New York, 1790-1865* (1981); Sewell, May Wright, ed. *The World's Congress of Representative Women* (1894); Sterling, Dorothy, ed. *We Are Your Sisters: Black Women in the Nineteenth Century* (1984); Terborg-Penn, Rosalyn. "Discrimination against Afro-American Women in the Woman's Movement." In *The Afro-American Woman: Struggles and Images*, ed. Sharon Harley and Rosalyn Terborg-Penn (1974); Thornbrough, Emma Lou. *T. Thomas Fortune: Militant Journalist* (1972); Willard, Frances E. "The Race Problem," *Voice* (October 23, 1890), and *Woman and Temperance or, The Work and Workers of the Woman's Christian Temperance Union* (1883); The Temperance and Prohibition Papers, 1830-1933, are on microfilm at the Ohio State Historical Society, Columbus, Ohio.

PATRICIA A. SCHECHTER

TEMPLE, RUTH JANETTA
(1892-1984)

Ruth Janetta Temple was born in Natchez, Mississippi, in 1892. Following her father's death, the family moved in 1904 to Los Angeles. Throughout high school, Ruth cared for her five siblings while her mother worked as a practical nurse to support the family. When Ruth's brother was injured in a gunpowder explosion, she became determined to enter the medical field. "At that time I thought that women were nurses. I didn't know they were doctors. When I learned that women were doctors, I said, 'Ah, that's what I want to be'" (Temple 1978).

Temple's medical training at Loma Linda University was financed by prominent Black activist T. W. Troy and his colleagues. Upon receiving her medical degree in 1918, Temple opened the first health clinic to be located in southeast Los Angeles, an area populated by 250,000 people. Unable to garner the financial support of area institutions to subsidize the Los Angeles clinic, Temple and her husband, real estate developer Otis Banks, bought a five-room bungalow in east Los Angeles and converted it into the facility that became the Temple Health Institute. Temple and Banks, displaced by the instruments and furnishings of the Health Institute, slept in a chicken coop behind the clinic. Temple later instigated the Health Study Club program, which brought together parents, teachers, and school children to educate the public on health resources available at Temple's own clinic and elsewhere, as well as on general health issues such as nutrition, sex education, immunization, and substance abuse. According to Temple, she developed the first health study club after having helplessly watched a mother in a damp tenement allow her baby to die of pneumonia out of fear of sending him to the hospital or of allowing Temple to treat him with hydrotherapy in his own home. Membership in the program grew to encompass such disparate groups as teenaged street gangs and nightclub owners and patrons. The program itself ultimately expanded beyond the borders of the state.

Temple's internship with the Los Angeles City Maternity Service (1923-28) inspired her to specialize in obstetrics and gynecology. In 1941, the city health department offered her a scholarship to pursue her Master's degree at Yale University School of Public Health. Temple held several key posts in the Los Angeles Public Health Department from 1942 to 1962 and received many awards and presidential accolades for her work in community health. She died in Los Angeles in 1984 at the age of ninety-one.

In 1978, Temple summed up her views on community health responsibility: "I think that people who can give themselves health care should do it. . . . And then I think that where persons cannot, with their best efforts, do the things they need to have done, I think it should be done for them, beautifully, graciously, and without giving them a feeling of accepting charity."

BIBLIOGRAPHY

Temple, Ruth Janetta, M.D. Interview with Tahi Mottl, *Black Women Oral History Project*, Schlesinger Library, Radcliffe College, Cambridge, Massachusetts (1978).

SUSAN SHIFRIN

TERRELL, MARY ELIZA CHURCH (1863-1954)

"A White Woman has only one handicap to overcome—a great one, true, her sex; a colored woman faces two—her sex and her race. A colored man has only one—that of race." This provocative statement was made in 1890 at the National Woman Suffrage Association convention in Washington, D.C., by Mary

Born into the Black elite of Memphis, Tennessee, Mary Church Terrell was sheltered from racism as much as possible by her parents. As her awareness of discrimination grew, so too did her resolve to prove the abilities of African-Americans in general and of African-American women in particular. [Library of Congress]

Eliza Church Terrell, one of the leading twentieth-century Black women activists. For more than sixty-six years, she was the ardent champion of racial and gender equality.

Born into the Black elite of Memphis, Tennessee, on September 23, 1863, as the Civil War was coming to a close, she was the oldest child of Robert Reed Church and Louisa Ayers. Her early years were spent in Memphis, a city convulsed by violent and bitter racism. Although she was sheltered as much as possible by her parents, who attempted to obliterate any trace of their own slave beginnings, she could not avoid encountering racism when, after her parents' divorce, her mother sent her to school in Ohio. In response to her growing awareness of discrimination, she resolved to excel academically to prove the abilities of African-Americans and especially Black women. After graduating from Oberlin College in 1884, and living with her father for one year, she took a teaching position at Wilberforce University in Ohio and, a year later, at M Street High School in Washington, D.C. It was at the high school that she met her future husband, Robert H. Terrell.

Between 1888 and 1896, Terrell was faced with two major decisions. First, as an intellectual, she had to decide whether to remain in the United States, where she would not be judged by her abilities but by her race and gender, or to seek a world free of prejudice. Second, as a woman, she had to decide whether to accept the Victorian ideal that a woman's place is in the home. She decided to go to Europe. After two years, she returned to the United States as an advocate of racial elevation.

In 1896, Terrell became the founder and first president of the National Association of Colored Women (NACW). Symbolizing unity among Black women, this self-help organization offered sisterly support for its members and created programs that addressed racial problems through the elevation of Black women. Terrell believed that the amelioration of discrimination was contingent upon "the elevation of Black womanhood, thus both struggles are the same."

Aware of the preponderance of Black married women in the work force, Terrell led the NACW in establishing socially progressive institutions such as kindergartens, day nurseries, and Mother Clubs. Mother Clubs functioned as depositories and disseminators of information on rearing children and conducting the home. Terrell's objective was to improve the moral standards of the "less favored and more ignorant sisters," because the world "will always judge the womanhood of the race through the masses of our women."

Because of the contact between Mother Clubs and the masses of women, and the rapid loss of jobs held by Black women, Terrell broadened the functions of Mother Clubs to include social as well as economic concerns. She advised directors of Mother Clubs to study the effects of the lack of employment for Black men as well as women. In addition, she launched a fund-raising campaign to establish schools of domestic science. The NACW also established homes for girls, the aged, and the infirm. It emerged as a leading women's organization, enhancing the lives of the masses and providing a vehicle for the emergence of middle-class women.

From 1896 to 1901, Terrell defined and developed her role as a "New Woman," which resulted in the development of purpose, independence, and vitality in her life. By 1901, Terrell was prepared to function as a leader outside the confines of women's organizations. She began to move from an approach of Black self-help to one of interracial understanding, advocating education as the way to this understanding. She hoped that unbiased research and intelligent dissemination of information to both white and Black peoples would spark better cooperation.

Terrell's advocacy of advancing the race through improving the lives of Black women led to opportunities to comment on broader issues facing her race. She gave numerous speeches highlighting the improved living conditions of Black people and their progress in spite of discrimination. In a stirring address delivered in 1904 at the International Congress of Women in Berlin, she vividly described the numerous contributions of the Black race. She delivered the speech in German (she spoke three languages fluently), receiving accolades for her depictions of Black life and her intellectual abilities. Through her speeches, she became a booster of Black morale, as she exhorted her people to improve themselves.

Terrell also wrote articles and short stories on lynching, chain gangs, the peonage system, defection of mulattoes, and the disfranchisement of African-Americans. In her writings, she sought to further interracial understanding by educating white people about the realities of Black life.

Terrell's actions were undertaken with the same conviction of racial equality that she demonstrated in her writings and speeches. Uncompromising and unequivocal, she never hesitated to criticize southern white liberals, northerners, or even members of her own race if she felt that their positions were not in the best interest of humanity. When Republican President Theodore Roosevelt disbanded several companies of Black soldiers, she vehemently attacked his decision, despite the fact that her husband owed his federal judgeship to the Republican party. In an article, "Disbanding of the Colored Soldiers," she asked African-Americans to "regard the terrible catastrophe which has filled the whole race with grief as an evil out of which good will eventually come" (Jones 1990).

The last two decades of her life marked a transition in her position on race relations and politics. Frustrated by the economic hardships of African-Americans during the Great Depression and the New Deal era, dismayed by the irony that African-Americans were fighting for democracy abroad during

World War II but were denied it at home, and grieved by the death of her husband, Terrell became a militant activist, working assiduously to bring a definitive end to discrimination in the United States, particularly in the nation's capital.

Terrell's later life is most noted for leading a three-year struggle to reinstate 1872 and 1873 laws in Washington, D.C., that "required all eating-place proprietors to serve any respectable well-behaved person regardless of color, or face a $1,000 fine and forfeiture of their license," which had disappeared in the 1890s when the District code was written. On February 28, 1950, Terrell, accompanied by two Black and one white collaborator, entered Thompson Res-

taurant, one of several segregated public eating establishments. Thompson refused to serve the Black members of the interracial party. Immediately Terrell and her cohorts filed affidavits. The case of *District of Columbia* v. *John Thompson* became a national symbol against segregation in the United States.

Throughout the three-year court struggle, Terrell targeted other segregated facilities. Confronted with the intransigence of proprietors of restaurants, she realized that the earlier weapons of moral suasion and interracial dialogue were incapable of abolishing segregated public facilities. She armed herself with such direct-action tactics as picketing, boycotting, and sit-ins. Finally, on June 8, 1953, the court ruled that segregated eating facilities in Washington, D.C., were unconstitutional.

This ardent fighter for civil rights lived to see the U.S. Supreme Court mandate the desegregation of public schools in *Brown* v. *Board of Education*. Two months later, on July 24, 1954, she died.

[*See also* NATIONAL COUNCIL OF NEGRO WOMEN; OBERLIN COLLEGE; SUFFRAGE MOVEMENT; WASHINGTON, BOOKER T.]

BIBLIOGRAPHY

Green, Constance. *The Secret City: A History of Race Relations in the Nation's Capital* (1969); Jones, Beverly W. *Quest for Equality: The Life and Writings of Mary Church Terrell, 1863-1954* (1990); Terrell, Mary Church. *A Colored Woman in a White World* (1940). The papers of Mary Church Terrell are located at the Library of Congress and in the Moorland-Spingarn Collection at Howard University, Washington, D.C.

SELECTED WORKS BY MARY CHURCH TERRELL

"Duty of the National Association of Colored Women to the Race," *AME Church Review* (January 1900); "Club Work of Colored Women," *Southern Workman* (August 8, 1901); "Lynching from a Negro's Point of View," *North American Review* (June 1904); "The Progress of Colored Women," *Voice of the Negro* (July 1904); "The International Congress of Women," *Voice of the Negro* (December 1904); "The National Association of Colored Women," *Voice of the Negro* (January 1906); "A Plea for the White South by a Colored Woman," *Nineteenth Century* (July 1906); "The Disbanding of the Colored Soldiers," *Voice of the Negro* (December 1906); "What It Means to Be Colored in the Capital of the United States," *Independent* (January 24, 1907); "Peonage in the United States: The Convict Lease System and the Chain Gangs," *Nineteenth Century* (August 1907); *A Colored Woman in a White World* (1940); "Needed: Women Lawyers," *Negro Digest* (September 1943).

BEVERLY JONES

By the last two decades of her life, Mary Church Terrell had become a militant activist. The most notable achievement of her later life was leading the successful three-year struggle that ended segregation in public eating places in Washington, D.C. [Afro American Newspaper Archives and Research Center]

THARPE, SISTER ROSETTA
(c. 1915-1973)

Sister Rosetta Tharpe, performer and musician, helped bring gospel music from obscure African-American storefront churches to the national music stage. Some of her more popular recordings included "Rock Me," "That's All," "I Looked down the Line," "Up above My Head," and "This Train." Influenced by the syncopated rhythms of such sanctified singers as Arizona Dranes, Tharpe created upbeat and jazzy religious songs. In the process, she ventured away from the deep and somber style that had characterized most religious music between the 1930s and 1950s. Tharpe rendered her upbeat style through abstract vocal phrasing and distinctive guitar playing. Like blues guitarists such as Big Bill Broonzy and Lonnie Johnson, Tharpe viewed her guitar as much more than a source of background rhythm to support her lyrics. In the vast majority of the songs that comprised her repertoire, Tharpe foregrounded melody

The dynamic Sister Rosetta Tharpe helped bring gospel music from obscure Black storefront churches to the national music stage. [Schomburg Center]

through guitar solos that featured single notes rather than chords. Moreover, Tharpe gave her guitar a clear and distinct presence by phrasing her guitar solos differently from her vocals.

Tharpe was born in Cotton Plant, Arkansas, on March 20, 1915 (1921?). The rhythmic power that became Tharpe's trademark was fostered in the Church of God in Christ (COGIC), where she began her career. In contrast to mainline Black churches that stressed sedate religious worship, COGIC and other Pentecostal churches stressed the importance of emotional religious expression. These churches encouraged the use of such rhythmic instruments as drums, trumpets, and tambourines in religious worship as a means of articulating devotion to God. As a singing evangelist, Tharpe's mother, Katie Bell Nubin, was very active in COGIC. Tharpe accompanied her mother on her missionary travels as a youngster. By the time she was six Tharpe was singing with her mother and touring sanctified churches. By the early thirties she had migrated from Arkansas to Chicago with her mother and was accompanying herself on guitar when she performed in churches and revivals.

Tharpe gained national attention in 1938 when she did a revival show at the Cotton Club in New York City. The exposure she received helped propel her to national celebrity status. A recording contract with Decca Records in 1938 made Tharpe the first gospel singer to record with a major label. From the late 1930s through the 1960s Tharpe performed in major entertainment venues in the United States and Europe that included concert halls, folk-jazz festivals, and radio and television programs.

Despite the national acclaim that Tharpe enjoyed, she did not let that notoriety determine the music she played. As an artist, Tharpe pushed her music to unexplored terrain. Although she was a gospel singer, Tharpe collaborated with artists of both sacred and secular music. She performed and recorded with boogie-woogie pianist Sammy Price and Lucky Millinder and his swing band, as well as such gospel groups as the Richmond Harmonizing Four and the Dixie Hummingbirds. For most of her career she was either a solo or lead singer; but in 1947 she teamed up with Marie Knight, a contralto who was also a member of the Sanctified Church. The two recorded together for several years.

While the exposure Tharpe enjoyed helped bring national recognition to gospel music, she unleashed controversy within African-American communities. As a type of religious music, gospel music primarily had predominated in Black Baptist and Pentecostal churches before the 1940s. Unlike many of her gospel contemporaries, Tharpe ventured beyond the church to carry her music to such nonreligious venues as nightclubs and theaters frequented by Black as well as white audiences. Many African-Americans believed that singing gospel music in nightclubs turned sacred music merely into entertainment. These men and women viewed Tharpe's willingness to move beyond the church as blasphemous because it made a mockery of religion.

Tharpe died on October 9, 1973, in Philadelphia. Throughout her career she resisted the censure of her critics. The controversy she sparked involved more than concerns about the proper place of performance. Through both her music and performance, she raised questions about the boundaries that separated the sacred and the secular. Tharpe dismissed the accusations directed against her by defending her behavior on evangelical grounds. She maintained that she had carried her music beyond the church in order to bring religion to, in her words, "the people who needed it" (*New York Amsterdam News*).

[*See also* GOSPEL MUSIC.]

BIBLIOGRAPHY

Boyer, Horace. "Contemporary Gospel Music," *Black Perspectives in Music* (Spring 1979); Goreau, Laurraine. *Just Mahalia Baby* (1975); Heilbut, Anthony. *The Gospel Sound: Good News and Bad Times* (1985); Levine, Lawrence. *Black Culture and Black Consciousness: Afro-American Folk Thought From Slavery to Freedom* (1977); *New York Amsterdam News* (October 13, 1973); Reitz, Rosetta. Liner notes for *Sincerely Sister Rosetta Tharpe: Sacred and Secular Gospel-Blues-Jazz* (1988); "Singer Swings Same Songs in Church and Night Club," *Life* (August 29, 1939).

DISCOGRAPHY

For a discography, see Hayes, C. J. "Sister Rosetta Tharpe: A Discography," *Matrix* (June 1968).

JERMA JACKSON

THEATER

The list of Black women who have made outstanding contributions to the American theater is long and impressive. The Hyers Sisters, Evelyn Ellis, Abbie Mitchell, Diana Sands, Lena Horne, Ethel Waters, Claudia McNeil, Ruby Dee, and Gloria Foster are just a few of the many Black performers whose work set standards of excellence. Covering a span of almost one hundred years, these actresses have fought for dignified representations of Black women on the American stage, a battle that continues to be waged.

For many of these women, the fighting extended to backstage as well.

In 1957, when Lena Horne appeared in the Broadway hit musical *Jamaica*, her performance was widely praised. Backstage, Horne had been instrumental in the fight to hire Black stagehands. Black Americans had never worked on Broadway in such a capacity, and their addition to the stage crew for *Jamaica* was a historical event in theater history.

The details of the achievements and contributions of the Black woman artist in the American theater are virtually unknown. Though many of these women have had a major impact on the development and growth of the American theater, their contributions unfortunately remain unheralded and unresearched, representing a substantial loss to the practice and history of American theater. Black women have been present in every aspect of the American theater—as producers, designers, directors, choreographers, musical directors, critics, managers, and craftspeople—but the road to the professional stage has been a long and difficult one.

Since the nineteenth century, Black women have struggled to gain an honorable place in the American theater, free from stereotypes and demeaning roles. The institution of slavery prevented Black artists from performing professionally on the American stage until after the Civil War. However, in the early 1850s a few Black singers—such as the Whitehouse Sisters, Blind Tom, and Black Swan—performed musical concerts throughout the northern states. Minstrel shows, though mainly using white performers, provided some Black performers with their first professional jobs on the American stage.

Spearheaded by white actor T. D. Rice during the late 1820s, minstrel shows became the first original American theater. Basing the material on stereotypes about Black attitudes and perspectives, minstrels became the most popular form of entertainment in America for nearly a hundred years. Applying burnt cork to "blacken-up" their faces, white males performed gross exaggerations of Black characters through dance, songs, and skits. Through these shows, stereotypes of Black Americans emerged that continue to exist. The dominant image presented was that of a singing, dancing, shiftless, oversexed, exotic, and carefree people. Black women were generally depicted as mammy figures, wenches, and hot mamas. Even with the demise of the minstrel shows, shortly after the turn of the century, these images prevailed in the Tom shows (dramatizations of Harriet Beecher Stowe's *Uncle Tom's Cabin*), coon shows (early name for Black musicals), and vaudeville/variety shows.

When Black performers were permitted in minstrel shows, only men were allowed to perform. During the 1870s, several Black artists attempted to deviate from the minstrel tradition and incorporate more accurate aspects of Black American culture into its content. Their efforts resulted in numerous original gains through skits, dance, comedy routines, and specialty acts.

Anna and Emma Hyers, billed as the Hyers Sisters, were the first Black women to gain success on the American stage. Emerging during the early 1870s, this talented operatic team toured nationally for several seasons in a series of concerts. They performed in musical plays dealing with the Black experience—such as *Out of Bondage* (1875) and *The Underground Railroad* (1879)—and toured extensively until the early 1880s. The Hyers Sisters were unique because they dared to deviate from the stereotypes imposed upon them in order to achieve success in a male-dominated business.

Most women performing on stage were relegated to musical acts and various comedy groups that carried over from the minstrel tradition. During the 1890s, the development of the Black musical comedy opened the stage to women. Aida Overton Walker, aside from being the wife of the famed comedian George Walker, was a pioneer actress, singer, and dancer, becoming one of the most popular entertainers from the late 1880s into the early part of the twentieth century. Aware of the limited roles for Black performers in the professional theater, she often spoke of the need for a "good school in which colored actors and actresses may be properly trained for good acting" (Walker 1905). Performing throughout the United States and in Europe, Walker brought dignity to the cakewalk as well as other dances originating in Black culture. In 1911, after the death of her husband, she devoted her time to producing acts with some dramatic content.

Walker would go on to become one of many female producers to emerge after the turn of the century. The early female producers began their theatrical careers as performers. Many saw producing as an alternative to the limited roles for Black women on the stage; thus by creating their own companies they could present Black life in a more realistic manner.

In 1915, Anita Bush, who along with Aida Walker had been a chorus member of the Williams and Walker team, decided to form her own dramatic theater company in New York City. To prove the capabilities of Black performers, she aspired to present them on stage in a medium different from the vaudeville and minstrel shows to which audiences had grown accustomed. She had no idea, however, that the all-Black dramatic company, which would later be called the Lafayette Players, would exist for a length of time unprecedented in the history of American theater—from 1915 to 1932—and would produce an impressive roster of great Black actors and actresses. Earlier attempts at forming all-Black dramatic companies—such as the African Grove (1820) and the Chicago Pekin Players (1906)—had been short-lived.

Anita Bush, one of many Black Americans who attempted to move beyond the roles imposed by whites, opened Broadway's doors for Black dramatic performers and served as an inspiration for many Black women.

Evelyn Ellis, who in 1927 organized the All-Star Colored Civic Repertory Company, was another actress turned producer. By 1928, Ida B. Anderson, a former Lafayette Player, also began producing dramatic presentations with her company, the Ida Anderson Players, at the Lincoln Theatre in Harlem. Bush, Anderson, and Ellis had successfully challenged the popular form of theater prescribed for Black artists during their era. In a sense, they prepared the way for Rose McClendon, hailed as one of the greatest actresses of the American stage. Trained at the American Academy of Dramatic Arts, McClendon created and performed numerous roles in Broadway and off-Broadway shows. In the 1930s, McClendon formed the Negro People's Theatre to present dramatic works, and she continued to direct various dramatic productions throughout New York. During the 1930s, when the Works Progress Administration (WPA) Federal Theatre Program (FTP) came into existence, McClendon was asked to assume the role of director for the New York City Negro Unit.

Regina Andrews, the noted librarian with the 135th Street Branch library in New York City, was one of the founders of the Harlem Experimental Theatre Company in 1927. Using the basement of the library as its theater, this organization set out to produce works by Black playwrights. This same library basement became the stage for many theater groups throughout Harlem.

During the 1940s, the dramatic actress and director Osceola Archer played a significant role in the American Negro Theatre (ANT). Archer headed the ANT school, where she trained numerous outstanding Black actors of the stage and screen, such as Sidney Poitier, Harry Belafonte, Ruby Dee, and Helen Martin.

Emma Hyers (pictured here) and her sister Anna, who were billed as the Hyers Sisters, were the first Black women to gain success on the American stage. They toured nationally in the 1870s and early 1880s, appearing in musical plays dealing with the Black experience. [Moorland-Spingarn]

In musical theater, Eva Jessye has long been considered the greatest choral director of all time. Jessye conducted countless choruses on Broadway and throughout the country. From 1938 to 1958, she conducted the choruses for every major production of *Porgy and Bess*. In 1932, America witnessed the first opera ever to be written and performed professionally by Black Americans. In Cleveland, Ohio, Shirley Graham (Du Bois) presented *Tom-Toms: An Epic of Music and the Negro* to over 25,000 people in just two performances. This opera, which had a cast of 500, traced Black history from Africa to America. Graham also wrote numerous plays, all of which received professional productions during the 1930s and 1940s.

Meta Warrick Fuller pioneered numerous developments in the area of stage design. Known primarily as a sculptor, Fuller designed costumes, scenery, lighting, and make-up as early as 1910 in the Boston area. Fuller was indeed an anomaly for her period, not only because she was one of only a few Black stage designers but also because she designed for all areas of the stage. In 1951, Louise Evans became the first Black woman to be admitted to the exclusive United Scenic Artists in the area of costume design. She designed in all areas of the theater as well as directed and performed.

Many Black women have contributed to theater at the college and university levels as well. Anne Cooke (Reid) devoted most of her life to developing theater departments at Black institutions, during a period when there were very few places where Black artists could study on any kind of professional level. Her greatest contribution was during her tenure at Howard University, where she headed the Drama Department. In 1949, Cooke brought the department and the university international acclaim when the Howard Players toured in Europe.

Black female playwrights have been neglected in the annals of theater history and so little is known about them. Black playwrights began to emerge before the Civil War, but their development as artists was extremely slow. "Both slavery and racial prejudice are certainly among the factors that hindered

Aida Overton Walker was a pioneer actress, singer, and dancer who was one of the most popular entertainers of the late 1880s and early 1890s. She brought dignity to the cakewalk and other dances originating in Black culture. [Donald Bogle]

Blacks from utilizing the stage as a medium for the expression of their political, intellectual, and social concerns" (Peterson 1990). Mr. Brown, of the African Grove Theatre in New York City, is credited with writing the first Black American play, *King Shotaway* (1823). In 1879, Pauline Hopkins wrote the first known play by a Black female, *The Underground Railroad*, first performed in Boston in 1880.

Before Lorraine Hansberry's 1959 landmark play, *A Raisin in the Sun*, Black women published over seventy discovered plays and pageants. These early works reveal the historical, social, political, economic, and racial climate of the period in which these women lived. Written primarily after 1918, these plays conveyed Black women's attitudes—concerns rarely voiced on the stage at the time. Black women frequently wrote about such topics as lynching, poverty, women's rights, motherhood, disenfranchised war heroes, miscegenation, family loyalty, education, and the church.

Washington, D.C., gave birth to the first twentieth-century full-length play written, performed, and produced by Black Americans—*Rachel*. Billed as a "race play" in three acts, Angelina Weld Grimké's *Rachel* was presented in 1916 by the Drama Committee of the National Association for the Advancement of Colored People. As stated in the playbill: "It is the first attempt to use the stage for race propaganda." *Rachel*, an angry play, explores lynching and its devastating psychological effects on a young woman. It was after seeing *Rachel* that Willis Richardson decided to become a playwright and he went on to become the first Black dramatist on Broadway.

Shortly after the appearance of *Rachel*, plays by Black women began to appear in large numbers. The major playwrights were Georgia Douglas Johnson, May Miller, Eulalie Spence, Shirley Graham Du Bois, Mary P. Burrill, Angelina Grimké, Marita Bonner, Zora Neale Hurston, and Alice Dunbar-Nelson. Both Dunbar-Nelson's 1918 drama, *Mine Eyes Have Seen*, and Burrill's 1919 work, *Aftermath*, question the Black man's loyalty in wartime to a country that deprives him of basic freedoms. In 1919, the *Birth Control Review* published Burrill's play *They That Sit in Darkness*. Possibly one of the first Black feminist plays, *They That Sit in Darkness* addresses the issues of a woman's right to knowledge concerning birth control.

Through their plays, Black women attempted to eradicate the demeaning mammy image as well as other stereotypes. They wrote realistically about Black women's experiences in America, when white dramatists—including Eugene O'Neill, Paul Green, and

DuBose and Dorothy Heyward—all achieved fame for plays about superficial aspects of Black life.

As Black women moved into the 1950s, they became more visible, but they were still pioneers. In 1955, Alice Childress—an actress turned playwright—became the first Black woman to have a play, *Trouble in Mind*, produced off Broadway. The play also won her the first Obie Award to be awarded to a Black woman. Four years later, in 1959, Lorraine Hansberry became the first Black woman and youngest playwright to have a show on Broadway with *A Raisin in the Sun*.

As the civil rights movement and the women's movement of the 1960s and 1970s progressed, Black women emerged in the theater as directors, producers, artistic directors, designers, and playwrights. Playwrights such as Adrienne Kennedy, Ntozake Shange, Kathleen Collins, Saundra Sharp, Micki Grant, and Elaine Jackson had more diverse audiences than the playwrights of the first half of the century. Works by designers such as Shirley Prendergast, Judy Dearing, and Gertha Brock began appearing on and off Broadway.

The civil rights movement also ushered in numerous companies founded by Black women. Barbara Ann Teer, Rosetta LeNoire, Vinnette Carroll, and Marla Gibbs are all actresses turned producers. Like earlier Black performers who started their own companies, these women had felt limited by stereotypical roles. In a 1968 *Negro Digest* article entitled "The Great White Way Is Not Our Way—Not Yet," the actress/producer Barbara Teer wrote: "As a Black actress, as long as this condition prevails, I can merely look forward to playing demanding roles such as prostitutes, maids, and/or every now and then, just for local color, of course, some form of exotic."

After three decades, funding for theater companies has all but disappeared. While a few Black women are appearing on the national scene, such as playwrights Cheryl West and Endesha Holland, opportunities are once again limited for Black women. In spite of limited production budgets and the lack of work spaces, they continue to write, direct, produce, and design. The struggle continues.

BIBLIOGRAPHY

DBT; Hamalian, Leo and James V. Hatch. *The Roots of African American Drama* (1991); Hill, Errol. *The Theatre of Black Americans* (1980); Perkins, Kathy A., ed. *Black Female Playwrights: An Anthology of Plays Before 1950* (1989); Peterson, Bernard L., Jr. *Early Black American Playwrights and Dramatic Writers* (1990); Sampson, Henry T. *Blacks in Blackface: A Source Book on Early Black Musical Shows* (1980); Walker, Aida Overton. "Colored Men and Women on the Stage," *Colored American* (1905); Wilkerson, Margaret. *Nine Plays by Black Women* (1986).

KATHY A. PERKINS

THOMAS, ALMA (1891-1978)

Alma Thomas, an abstract artist of world renown, was born in Columbus, Georgia, in 1891. She moved to Washington, D.C., with her family in 1907, and two years later graduated from Armstrong Technical High School, where she studied art and architectural and mechanical drawing. She then attended normal school in Washington, D.C., and after two years went to teach in Wilmington, Delaware. Returning to Washington in 1921, she enrolled at Howard University, where she became part of the newly organized art department and its first graduate in 1924. She later received an M.A. in education (1934) from Teachers College, Columbia University, New York, and was organizer and director of the School Art League Project which encouraged an appreciation of art among Black students, between 1936 and 1939. For the next twenty years Thomas continued teaching while pursuing her own art and organizing exhibitions by African-American artists in galleries in Washington, D.C., most notably the Barnett-Aden Gallery, which was one of the city's first commercial art galleries.

Thomas created her most important and exciting work after she retired from teaching in 1960 and devoted herself full time to painting. For the next eighteen years she created distinctive abstract compositions in oil paint and watercolor that featured vertical, centrifugal, and horizontal cascades of individual strokes of color. The marks left by Thomas as her strokes accumulated on the surface of canvas or paper exhibited a poetic quality of involvement by the hand. Each form sat in rows that lost their regularity as the length of the stroke varied or shifted into another direction. The pristine white of the undersurface peered through, between her battalions of gesture, evoking at once an optical delight and a landscape phenomenon.

In a work such as *Red Roses Sonata* (1972, Collection of the Metropolitan Museum of Art, New York), the curtain of red daubs covers a green background, which sets up a vibrating visual effect between the complementary colors. In addition, two vertical bands of a lighter green color are laid within the background, creating a minimalist composition that recalls the composition of Barnett Newman within the dense articulation of the surface. In a 1973 composition, *Wind and Crepe Myrtle Concerto* (Collection of the National Museum of American Art), the differentiated bands lie on the surface of the rose over-painting, contrasting with the lighter pink. Underneath is a more intricate landscape of yellows and greens, which looks like a sunny glade overhung by a curtain of rose petals. This work indicates how Thomas was able to loosen the grid-like tendency of her compositions and produce, in the words of Merry A. Foresta, "an atmospheric quality" (1981). As Foresta observes, "despite our propensity to read these compositions on multiple layers, attempting to discern what seems to be happening behind the surface, in fact Thomas intends no specific spatial illusion. Edges are merged and blended by the brushwork so that the surface constantly shifts in an evocation of fluttering and falling leaves."

Thomas's later work was informed by her earlier compositions from the 1950s and 1960s as she followed the trend toward gestural abstraction. Compositions such as *Untitled (Study for a Painting)* (1964, watercolor on paper, Collection of Michael G. Fisher, Washington, D.C.) show an intense accumulation of distinctly applied brushfuls of paint that recalls the dense painterly articulations of Hans Hofmann at the end of his career. Another, *Watusi (Hard Edge)* (1963, acrylic on canvas, Collection of Hirshhorn Museum and Sculpture Garden, Smithsonian Institution, Washington, D.C.), shows unexpected arrangements of what seem to be uncut shapes of paper whose irregular borders nonetheless suggest squares, trapezoids, and parallelograms. These shapes are arranged seemingly helter-skelter against a white background, reminiscent of Jean Arp's Dada compositions created through the seemingly random tossing of bits of paper onto a surface. What is evident is that Thomas readily absorbed the language of a variety of abstract idioms and was able to synthesize them quickly into a highly individual style.

Her work of the 1960s is characterized by a shortening and regimentation of strokes, as well as a restriction of the palette (individual colors are nonetheless brilliant and translucent), which is well suited to the more discrete surfaces and the objectification of the creative process that marked the artistic phenomena of the decade, Minimalism and Color Field Painting. Thomas was working in Washington, D.C., at the time, and it is evident that the evocative abstractions of Morris Louis and the so-called Washington Color School, which gave rise to such talents as Gene Davis and Sam Gilliam, were a prime influence on her work. Thomas never divorced the trace of her hand from her work, however. Instead, she created "curtains" of color composed of individual irregular strokes of paint that interact optically with one another. This interweaving of visual patterns is as accomplished in her watercolors as in her oils. The powerful sense of luminosity that emanates from her oil paintings, particularly those that have white in the background, is readily achieved in the watercolors, which themselves are distinctive by virtue of Thomas's use of intensely saturated hues.

Toward the end of her career, Thomas's individual tesserae of color become even more sharply defined as individual squares, rectangles, and parallelograms that occasionally curve around on one edge to conform to the more circular arrangement of her color. The forms function alternately as individual pieces of tile or ceramic and as pictograms with distinct personalities. The regularity and density of the surface also begin to break up. In *Hydrangeas Spring Song* (1976, acrylic on canvas, Collection of Harol Hart, New York), a passageway seems to have been cleared in the wake of an unexpected clearing of white color, which moves up the composition from the center of the bottom edge to the upper right-hand corner. Not only is the population of hieroglyphs much more sparse, but the forms themselves seem to be breaking up into individual forms. This adds a decidedly dynamic character to the pleasant regimentation of forms in a grand scheme that is established in each one of Thomas's compositions. If, as Foresta suggests, this was a strategy to counter accusations of decorativeness in her work, it was a development that sadly was left incomplete because of Thomas's frail health during the last year of her life.

Alma Thomas was the first African-American woman to achieve critical acclaim within an abstract medium. She had her first one-person exhibition at the Whitney Museum of American Art in New York City in 1972, the first African-American woman to have an individual show in that institution. That same year the Corcoran Gallery of Art in Washington, D.C., opened a retrospective of her work, and she also received the Two Thousand Women of Achievement award for her life's work.

Thomas died in 1978 at the age of eighty-six from complications following heart surgery.

BIBLIOGRAPHY
Foresta, Merry A. *A Life in Art: Alma Thomas, 1918-1978* (1981).

LOWERY S. SIMS

THOMAS, CORA ANN PAIR
(1875-1952)

The Lott Carey Baptist Home and Foreign Mission Convention of the United States opened its first mission in 1897 in Brewerville, Liberia, fifteen miles from Monrovia. In 1909, the convention sent Reverend William Henry Thomas, a Jamaican, and his wife, Cora Ann Pair Thomas, to work at the mission station.

Cora Ann Pair was born in Knightdale, Wake County, North Carolina on September 8, 1875. In 1895, she graduated from Shaw University (Raleigh, North Carolina) with a higher English diploma. Between 1904 and 1906, she took missionary training courses in the theological school of Fisk University (Nashville, Tennessee). Before traveling to Africa, Pair acted as principal of the orphanage for Black children in Oxford, North Carolina.

In November 1908, Cora Pair married William Henry Thomas, who had been born in Jamaica but came to the United States to complete his higher education. The couple met at Shaw University where William Thomas earned A.B. and B.Th. degrees. The following month the pair traveled to Liberia, arriving at Monrovia in January 1909. The salary and transportation expenses for Cora Thomas were paid by the Lott Carey Women's Baptist Missionary Convention of North Carolina.

At Brewerville, Cora Thomas successfully persuaded the Lott Carey mission board to establish a school, which was later named the Lott Carey Mission School. Hundreds of girls and boys and young men and women attended the school, where Cora Thomas taught.

After Reverend Thomas's death in September 1942, Cora Thomas was appointed superintendent of the mission, succeeding her husband. She served in that capacity for four years. In 1946, she left Liberia because of failing health.

Cora Thomas returned to Liberia in November 1951 with the Lott Carey Pilgrimage Group. After a severe attack of malaria, she died at Brewerville on May 10, 1952. She was buried next to her husband on the Lott Carey Mission School campus.

BIBLIOGRAPHY

Boone, Clinton C. *Liberia as I Know It* (1929); Fitts, Leroy. *Lott Carey: First Black Missionary to Africa* (1978); Freeman, Edward A. *The Epoch of Negro Baptists and the Foreign Mission Board* (1953); Jacobs, Sylvia M. " 'Say Africa When You Pray': The Activities of Early Black Baptist Women Missionaries among Liberian Women and Children," *Sage: A Scholarly Journal on Black Women* (Fall 1986); Rux, Mattie E. and Mary M. Ransome. *Fifty Years of Pioneering in Christian Missions: History of the Woman's Auxiliary to the Lott Carey Baptist Foreign Mission Convention, 1900-1956* (n.d.).

SYLVIA M. JACOBS

THOMAS, EDNA LEWIS (1886-1974)

Born in 1886 in Lawrenceville, Virginia, Thomas first came to acting prominence with the Lafayette Players, a group that existed from 1917 to 1932. Sister M. Francesca Thompson says that "this was the first major professional Black dramatic company in America." Thomas made her debut on November 8, 1920, at the Putnam Theatre, Brooklyn, in F. H. Wilson's *Confidence*, a vehicle of the Quality Amusement Corporation, the contractual name for the Lafayette Players.

Seven months later, on June 11, 1921, the *New York Age* recorded her being cast in the principal female role of Elsie Tillinger in *Turn to the Right* with the Lafayette Players in New York City.

It was during the 1920s, however, and the fervent Harlem Renaissance that Thomas received considerable recognition. A part of the wealthy A'Lelia Walker's social circle, Thomas mingled with artists, musicians, writers, actors, underworld characters, and leading citizens at one of Walker's three splendid residences. Carl Van Vechten, *bon vivant*, writer, photographer, and Negrophile, supported Thomas and served other artists of color through his wealth, media contacts, and vast photographic collection.

A "handsome" woman, according to actor-director-promoter Carlton Moss, this performer of color, fair-skinned enough to be mistaken for white, "rubbed shoulders with the dominant group" (Moss 1978). Eventually she came to the attention of young filmmaker Orson Welles and actor-director John Houseman, and finally, after a half century, went on to Hollywood and Broadway to be cast in minor roles.

Her first exposure outside the Lafayette Players came on May 15, 1923, when the Ethiopian Art Theatre cast Thomas as Adrianna's sister in a jazz version of Shakespeare's *The Comedy of Errors*, staged in a circus tent at the Frazee Theatre, New York City. Percy Hammond, critic of the *New York Herald Tribune*, referred to the then thirty-seven-year-old actor as an "ingenue," giving her "a magnificent review," according to an interview Thomas gave scholar Rich-

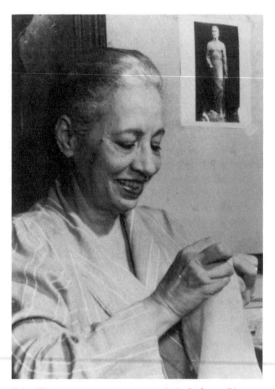

Edna Thomas came to prominence with the Lafayette Players, and went on to perform on Broadway and in films. Among her roles was that of the Mexican woman in Tennessee Williams's A Streetcar Named Desire, *which she played in the original Broadway production, several subsequent revivals, and in the film version. She is seen here in her dressing room during the 1951 revival of the Williams play. [Griffith J. Davis]*

ard France in 1972. Alexander Woollcott, also a major critic, called the troupe "an industrious darky" one.

Expansive and unflinching in a daring career against all odds for a woman of color, Thomas saw the footlights again in 1926 when producer David Belasco cast her in a small role in his famed production of the realistic drama *Lulu Belle*, by Charles G. MacArthur and Edward S. Sheldon. Lenore Ulrich and Henry Hull, both white, played the courtesan and the male lead, respectively. Larry Barretto, in *Bookman*, observed that "an enormous cast [mainly African-American] . . . must have depopulated several cotton-growing states, not to speak of emptying Harlem's black belt nightly." In a letter to Van

Vechten, Thomas wrote from Chicago on October 21, 1927:

> Carlo darling . . . *Lulu Belle* went over big—every critic (except one) praising the work of Miss U. in the most extravagant fashion. The odd man (*Tribune*) laid off until yesterday, when he used much space warning the natives against so filthy a play. The result of which will be, I hope, a forced extension of our ten weeks here. . . . Affectionately, Edna

The actor also crossed the boards in vaudeville and, according to *Variety*, was in the Theatre Guild's production of Dorothy and DuBose Heyward's *Porgy*, the 1927 play on which the 1935 Gershwin opera *Porgy and Bess* was based. However, her name does not appear in cast listings.

With the waning of the Harlem Renaissance and the onset of the Great Depression, Thomas and her husband, Lloyd Thomas, met with hard times. Finally Thomas worked again, playing Maggie in Donald Heywood's *Ol' Man Satan*, which opened at the Forest Theatre on October 3, 1932, after a year's rehearsal; this was the longest rehearsal period on record, excluding *Sing for Your Supper*, produced by the Federal Theatre. Such abuse of actors made Thomas an activist; she gave her copy of *The Revolt of the Actors* to unionizer Frederick O'Neal.

In 1933, Thomas played Sis Ella, the forgiving wife of the preacher's son at Hope Baptist Church, whose marriage is threatened by the temptress Sulamai from a pagan cult across the river, in Hall Johnson's *Run, Little Chillun*. The volatile and controversial *Stevedore*, a play by Paul Peters and George Sklar about the unionizing of Louisiana dock workers, followed; Thomas played Ruby Oxley, the romantic interest. Congress labeled the play "a Communistic lynch drama."

With such stellar performances and recognition by critics and audiences, Thomas became a leading figure in the Federal Theatre's $46 million effort under the aegis of Franklin Delano Roosevelt's Works Progress Administration (WPA) project. In 1936, Orson Welles chose Thomas to play Lady Macbeth in his voodoo adaptation of Shakespeare's tragedy; she was fifty years old. The work opened to mixed reviews, intensely hot controversy, and standing-room-only crowds that had to be quelled by riot police squads. This was her first major classical role. Roi Ottley of the *New York Amsterdam News* wrote, "In Edna Thomas's last scene as Lady Macbeth, she literally tore the heart of the audience with her sensitive and magnificent portrayal of the crazed Lady Macbeth." *Newsweek* also was favorable, but arch-conservative Percy Hammond declared, "Miss Thomas impersonated Lady Macbeth with a dainty elegance that defied all traditions except those of the WPA."

Other Federal Theatre vehicles for Thomas included the part of the slave girl, Lavinia, in a 1938 Negro version of George Bernard Shaw's *Androcles and the Lion* opposite P. Jay Sidney as the romantic interest, the captain. Six months after this play opened, Congress closed the Federal Theater, urged on by threatened Broadway producers who feared "welfare" theater and communist infiltration.

The government theater led to roles on Broadway—Sukey, a mulatto slave girl, in *Harriett*, with Helen Hayes, in 1943-44; Mamie McIntosh in Lillian Smith's novel-turned-play, *Strange Fruit*, produced by José Ferrer in 1945; and the Mexican woman in Tennessee Williams's *A Streetcar Named Desire*, both on stage in 1947, 1950, 1951, and on the screen in 1956.

Her opportunities were few, although she was well known in limited circles of Boston and New York. She spent her retirement years in New York City, where she died of a heart condition on July 22, 1974.

BIBLIOGRAPHY

Barretto, Larry. Review of *Lulu Belle, Bookman* (April 1926); de Paur, Leonard. Personal Interview (March 29 1982); Gill, Glenda E. "Edna Thomas: The Grande Dame." In her *White Grease Paint on Black Performers: A Study of the Federal Theatre, 1935-1939* (1988); Hammond, Percy. "A W.P.A. 'Macbeth,' " *New York Herald Tribune* (April 16, 1936); *New York Age*. "Mrs. Edna Lewis Thomas, Well-Known Socially, Joins Lafayette Players" (November 6, 1920); *New York Age*. "Edna Lewis Thomas Stars in 'Turn to the Right' at Lafayette" (June 11, 1921); Moss, Carlton. Telephone interview with Glenda E. Gill (November 5, 1978); *New York Times*. Obituary (July 24, 1974); Ottley, Roi. "Harlem's Lord and Lady Macbeth in Full Regalia," *New York Amsterdam News* (April 8, 1936); Thomas, Edna. Interview with Richard France (courtesy of the Research Center for the Federal Theatre Project, George Mason University, Fairfax, Virginia) (1972), and Letter to Carl Van Vechten (October 21, 1972), and Personal Interview (March 29, 1982); Thompson, Sister M. Francesca. "The Lafayette Players, 1917-1932." In *The Theater of Black Americans*, ed. Errol Hill (1980); *Variety*. Obituary (July 31, 1974); Woollcott, Alexander. "Shouts and Murmers," *New York Herald Tribune* (May 16, 1923).

GLENDA E. GILL

THOMPSON, ERA BELL (1906-1986)

The success of *Ebony* magazine owes a great deal to one of its earliest editors, Era Bell Thompson. Thompson was born in Des Moines, Iowa, on August 10, 1906, and grew up in Driscoll, North Dakota, with her parents and her three brothers. She was a track star at North Dakota State University before attending Morningside College in Iowa. There she first discovered her bent for journalism. Her autobiography states that her teacher, Mr. Lewis, responded to her first theme by saying, "Well, Miss Thompson, there isn't much of yourself; there are many misspelled words; but the general impression is so good that I can't help it. 'A.' "

Thompson hardly needed the encouragement. She began writing with a vengeance. In no time she was writing for the Chicago *Defender*. She first tackled political issues, writing a feature that attacked Marcus Garvey's "Back to Africa" movement. Readers responded with fervor, for and against. Later, Thompson contributed an ongoing column about "the wild and wooly West" under the name Dakota Dick. Still, she remained more interested in acrobatics than writing until she sold an article to *Physical Culture* magazine. The $3 she received tipped the

The success of Ebony *magazine owes a great deal to one of its earliest editors, Era Bell Thompson, who once wrote a column for the* Chicago Defender *under the name Dakota Dick.*

balance from contortionism—her great ambition at the time—to journalism. She graduated from Morningside College in 1933 and went on to study at Medill School of Journalism at Northwestern University.

However, in Depression-era Chicago, journalism jobs were not easy to find. She worked at Settlement House with Mary McDowell and got jobs through the Works Progress Administration, the Chicago Department of Public Works, the Chicago Relief Administration, the Chicago Board of Trade, and the Illinois State Employment Services office. She also worked as a waitress, domestic worker, elevator operator, and office worker. In 1945, she was awarded a Newbery fellowship that supported her while she wrote an autobiography, *American Daughter* (1946).

Two years later, John H. Johnson hired Thompson to be managing editor of his new magazine *Negro Digest*, which was later called *Black World*. In 1951, she became co-managing editor of *Ebony*, a position she held until 1964. In that year, she moved to the position of international editor and spent another twenty-two years working for the world's most popular Black magazine. She traveled all over the world and wrote stories for the magazine about her experiences.

During her time at *Ebony*, Thompson wrote *Africa, Land of My Fathers* (1954) and coedited, with Herbert Nipson White, the book *White on Black* (1963). She received numerous awards, including election to the Iowa Hall of Fame, and was chosen, in 1978, by Radcliffe College as one of fifty women to be recorded and photographed for the Black Women Oral History Project. She was a member of the board of directors of Hull House, the Chicago Council on Foreign Relations, and the Chicago Press Club. Era Bell Thompson died in Chicago in 1986.

[*See also* WESTERN TERRITORIES.]

BIBLIOGRAPHY
Anderson, Kathie Ryckman. "Era Bell Thompson: A North Dakota Daughter," *North Dakota History* (Fall 1982); *NBAW*.

KATHLEEN THOMPSON

THOMS, ADAH BELLE SAMUELS (c. 1870–1943)

Adah Belle Samuels Thoms devoted her life to nursing—working to improve nurse training, to organize and develop the National Association of Colored Graduate Nurses, and to provide equal employment opportunities in the American Red Cross and the U.S. Army Nurse Corps. Thoms also documented the struggles of Black nurses in *Pathfinders: A History of the Progress of Colored Graduate Nurses* (1929).

Adah Belle Samuels Thoms was born on January 12, circa 1870, in Richmond, Virginia, to Harry and Melvina Samuels. In 1893, she moved to New York City to study elocution and public speaking at the Cooper Union. It did not take her long to realize the need for more remunerative work. After a job at the Woman's Infirmary and School of Therapeutic Massage in New York, Thoms, the only Black student in a nursing class of thirty, graduated in 1900.

Upon receipt of her diploma, Thoms worked as a private duty nurse in New York City and as a staff nurse at St. Agnes Hospital in Raleigh, North Carolina. After only one year as head nurse of St. Agnes, Thoms returned to New York to seek additional training.

The timing of her return to New York was fortuitous. In 1903, Thoms entered the newly organized school of nursing at Lincoln Hospital and Home. Founded in 1893 by a group of white women who despaired over the impoverished plight of Black people in the city, Lincoln soon became a major provider of health care. In 1898, the women managers of Lincoln Hospital opened a nursing school for Black women. This nursing school soon became one of the most outstanding of the approximately ten Black schools of nursing formed during the 1890s. Black communities across the country joined in a nationwide movement to establish a racially separate network of parallel institutions. The entrenchment of racial segregation dictated these actions. By the 1930s, over two hundred Black hospitals, with one third of them operating nursing training schools, existed. Thoms was obviously a talented student nurse. While in her second year at Lincoln, she won appointment to the position of head nurse on a surgical ward, and upon graduation in 1905, Lincoln immediately offered her full-time employment.

In 1906, Thoms assumed the position of assistant superintendent of nurses, a position she held until her retirement eighteen years later. Only unrelenting racial discrimination explains the refusal of the white managers to promote Thoms to the superintendency of Lincoln Hospital. Still, as assistant superintendent, Thoms made noteworthy strides in improving nursing training. In 1913, she began a six-month postgraduate course for registered nurses, and in 1917, just five years after the establishment of the National

Organization for Public Health Nursing, she inaugurated a course in public health nursing.

As a long-time president of the Lincoln Nurses' Alumnae, Thoms was well situated to respond to a letter from a Black nurse, Martha Franklin. Thoms informed Franklin of the Lincoln Alumnae Association's willingness to sponsor the first meeting of what would become the National Association of Colored Graduate Nurses (NACGN). While Franklin became president of the new organization, Thoms was elected treasurer. Like many Black nurses, Thoms was eager to become more engaged in the profession. The denial of membership in the American Nurses' Association (ANA) increased her determination to raise the status of Black nurses. Through her association with Franklin, Thoms embraced the prospect of founding a Black professional nurses association.

Eventually, Thoms served as president of the NACGN from 1916 to 1923. She fought to improve the training offered in the Black hospital nursing schools and became a staunch advocate for greater employment opportunities for Black nurses. Throughout this period, Thoms set the model for Black nurse involvement in a variety of community organizations and concerns. In 1916, she began working with both the National Urban League and the National Association for the Advancement of Colored People in an attempt to improve conditions at Black hospitals and training schools. At the top of her agenda was the necessity to build NACGN's membership and to organize local and state associations of Black graduate nurses across the country. Of course, little advance was possible on this front until the NACGN found resources sufficient to employ a full-time executive director.

America's entry into World War I signaled a growing need for nurses. Thoms wanted desperately for Black nurses to become a part of the war effort. She appreciated the fact that nursing status usually increased during war. When Congress declared war on Germany in April 1917, Thoms urged Black nurses to enroll in the American Red Cross Nursing Service, the only avenue into the U.S. Army Nurse Corps. But when Black nurses applied to the American Red Cross, they met cold, silent rejection. Thoms engaged in a futile campaign to reverse the Red Cross's refusal to accept Black nurses. In the eleventh hour, Jane A. Delano, chair of the American National Red Cross Nursing Service, indicated that she was willing to accept Black nurses at home and abroad, but the surgeon general of the army remained adamant. Finally in December 1917, Thoms received word that there would be limited enrollment of Black nurses. Although the first Black nurse enrolled in July 1918, it was not until December 1918, after the war was over, that eighteen qualified Black nurses were appointed to the Army Nurse Corps with full rank and pay.

Although Thoms did not achieve the objective of having Black women participate in the war effort, she did win other kinds of recognition for herself and for Black nurses in general. In 1917, she helped establish a new order of Black war nurses, called the Blue Circle Nurses. The Circle for Negro War Relief recruited these nurses and paid them to work in local communities, instructing poor rural Black people on the importance of sanitation, proper diet, and appropriate clothing. In 1921, Thoms was appointed by the assistant surgeon general of the army to serve on the Woman's Advisory Council of Venereal Diseases of the United States Public Health Service.

Thoms retired from Lincoln in 1923 and married Henry Smith. The marriage was cut short by his death the following year. After her retirement, she continued to be active in a variety of professional organizations. In 1929, she wrote the first history of Black nurses. And in 1936, the NACGN awarded Thoms its first Mary Mahoney Award. Thoms died on February 21, 1943. In 1976, Thoms posthumously was named into nursing's Hall of Fame.

BIBLIOGRAPHY

DANB; Davis, Althea T. "Architects for Integration and Equality: Early Black American Leaders in Nursing," Ph.D. diss. (1986), and "Adah Belle Samuels Thoms 1870-1943," *American Nursing: A Biographical Dictionary*, ed. Vern L. Bullough, Olga Maranjian Church, and Alice P. Stein (1988); Hine, Darlene Clark. *Black Women in White: Racial Conflict and Cooperation in the Nursing Profession, 1890-1950* (1989); Staupers, Mabel. *No Time for Prejudice* (1961); Thoms, Adah Belle. *Pathfinders* (1929).

DARLENE CLARK HINE

TITUBA

Tituba, a slave indicted for witchcraft during the Salem witch trials in 1692, is one of the least known historical figures, despite the fact that the accusations made against her served as the catalyst for the trials. Before the hysteria about witchcraft in Salem Village came to an end, nineteen persons were hanged for witchcraft, and a man was crushed to death for refusing to testify as to his own guilt or innocence.

Tituba and her husband, John Indian, were slaves who belonged to Reverend Samuel Parris. They were not Indian but were given that last name because they came from Barbados, one of the islands of the West Indies. Parris, an impoverished, quarrelsome man, had been a trader in Barbados. After his business failed, however, he decided to return to Boston and to the ministry. He had studied theology at Harvard University, but had not completed work for his degree. Before he left Barbados with his ailing wife, his six-year-old daughter, Betsey, and his wife's nine-year-old niece, Abigail Williams, Parris purchased Tituba and John. The slaves would look after his household but, more importantly, would be hired out, thus assuring him of a small income.

In 1689, Parris finally received an offer from a church in Salem Village, a tiny community outside Salem. Once established in the parsonage, Parris hired out John to a tavern keeper and Tituba to a weaver. An expert weaver, Tituba supplied the woven goods used by the Parris family; she also managed the household, took care of Parris's invalid wife, and looked after the children.

During the long, cold winters, Tituba entertained the children with stories about Barbados, evoking the warmth and beauty of the island, telling stories of animals that could talk and of magic spells, and reading their palms. Gradually the parsonage became a meeting place for bound girls who were eager to hear Tituba's stories of a livelier, more colorful world. Meanwhile, in keeping rooms and taverns all over the Massachusetts Bay Colony, witchcraft had become a favorite—and frightening—topic of conversation.

Some of the girls listening to Tituba's stories, including Parris's daughter and niece, became hysterical, performing strange antics, crying out, and barking like dogs. Some of the girls accused Tituba; Sarah Good, a tramp; and Sarah Osborne, a sick old woman, of having bewitched them. In 1692, these three women became the first persons to be accused of practicing witchcraft in Salem Village. Tituba was beaten and abused by Parris until she confessed to being a witch. Then she was indicted for the practice of witchcraft and was jailed in Boston for thirteen months.

Prisoners were charged for food and shelter during their prison terms and by law had to reimburse the jailer before they could be released. Parris refused to pay Tituba's fees because she insisted she was not, and never had been, a witch and would state so publicly if given the opportunity. Finally she was sold to someone else. There is no further record of Tituba, a Black woman who was the unwitting catalyst of the most famous of the seventeenth-century witchcraft trials.

BIBLIOGRAPHY

Levin, David. *What Ever Happened in Salem?* (1950); Petry, Ann. *Tituba of Salem Village* (1991); Starkey, Marion L. *The Devil in Massachusetts* (1950); Upham, Charles W. *History of Witchcraft and Salem Village* (1867); Williams, Charles. *Witchcraft* (1959).

ANN PETRY

TRUTH, SOJOURNER (c. 1799-1883)

Sojourner Truth, abolitionist and woman's rights activist, is one of the two most widely known nineteenth-century Black women; the other, Harriet Tubman, was also a former slave who was not formally educated. While Tubman is known as the "Moses of her People" for having led hundreds of slaves to freedom, Truth is remembered more for her speeches than for her post-Civil War work in freedpeople's relief. She is most closely identified with the question "and a'n't I a woman?" which demands that women who are poor and Black be included within the category of *woman*. Disrupting assumptions about race, class, and gender in American society, Truth's twentieth-century persona works most effectively within the politically-minded worlds of Black civil rights and feminism. During her lifetime, however, she was deeply immersed in the Second Great Awakening's propagation of Methodist-inflected and unconstrained religiosity. Hence the making of her modern reputation entails the creative reworking of much of her life, an elaboration that she encouraged and that began during her lifetime. The emblematic character of Sojourner Truth—the slave woman who asks "and a'n't I a woman?"—is constructed upon a peculiarly nineteenth-century life experience that is nearly as obscure as the symbolic figure is well known.

The symbol of Sojourner Truth that is most popular today turns on two speeches of the 1850s: one in Akron, Ohio, in 1851, the other in Silver Lake, a small town in northern Indiana, in 1858. Like everything that happened to Truth after 1849, both events are known only through reports from other people. Truth was illiterate, and even her *Narrative of Sojourner Truth* (1878) was dictated to someone else in the late 1840s. Feminist abolitionist Frances Dana Gage recorded the popular version of Sojourner Truth's speech before a woman's rights convention held in Akron, Ohio, in May 1851. According to Gage, Truth said:

Wall, chilern, whar dar is so much racket dar must be somethin' out o' kilter. I tink dat 'twixt de niggers of the Souf and de womin at de Norf, all talkin' 'bout rights, de white men will be in a fix pretty soon. But what's all dis here talkin' 'bout? Dat man ober dar say dat womin needs to be helped into carriages, and lifted ober ditches, and to hab de best place everywhar. Nobody eber helps me into carriages, or ober mud puddles, or gibs me any best place! And a'n't I a woman? Look at me! Look at my arm! (and she bared her right arm to the shoulder, showing her tremendous muscular power). I have ploughed, and planted, and gathered into barns, and no man could head me! And a'n't I a woman? I could work as much and eat as much as a man—when I could get it—and bear de lash as well! And a'n't I a woman? I have borne thirteen chilern, and seen 'em mos' all sold off to slavery, and when I cried out with my mother's grief, none but Jesus heard me! And a'n't I a woman? (Titus 1878).

Truth's 1851 speech demands that definitions of female gender allow for women's strength as well as their suffering attendant upon poverty and enslavement. Her 1858 gesture, recorded by abolitionist William Hayward, again reclaims her female gender and defies critics who seek to silence an eloquent critic of slavery and sexism. Faced with a hostile audience that questioned a Black woman's right to speak in public and that intended to shame her out of presenting her case, Truth confronted men who claimed she was too forceful a speaker to be a woman. After they demanded that she prove her sexual identity through a performance intended to humiliate, Truth bared her breast in public, turned the imputed shame back upon her tormenters, and, transcending their small-minded test, turned their spite back upon them.

Based upon these words and gestures, the symbol of Sojourner Truth is an eloquent, inspired ex-slave who made her experience of work and victimized motherhood into an alternate model of womanhood. In a world that saw *woman* as white and *Black* as male, she is a woman who is also Black and a Black who is also woman. Although several Black women worked for the abolition of slavery and the achievement of women's rights in the middle of the nineteenth century (e.g., Sarah Mapps Douglass, Frances Ellen Watkins Harper, Sarah Remond), the ex-slave Sojourner Truth has become the emblematic nineteenth-century Black woman and the symbol of the conjunction of sex and race.

Sojourner Truth was born about 1799 in Ulster County, New York, on the west side of the Hudson River, some eighty miles north of New York City, in a region dominated culturally and economically by people of Dutch descent. She was the second youngest of ten or twelve children, and her parents, James and Elizabeth Bomefree, named her Isabella. Their first language was Dutch. As a child Isabella belonged to several owners, the most significant of whom was John Dumont, for whom she worked from 1810 until a year before she was emancipated by state law in 1827. She kept in touch with the Dumont family until they moved west in 1849.

When she was about fourteen years old, Isabella was married to another of Dumont's slaves, an older man named Thomas. Thomas and Isabella had five children: Diana, Sophia, Elizabeth, Peter, and, perhaps, Hannah. In 1826-27, the year before she became free, Isabella had several critical experiences. She left her long-time master Dumont of her own accord and went to work for the family of Isaac Van Wagenen. When her son's owner illegally sold him into perpetual slavery in Alabama, Isabella went to court in Kingston, New York, and sued successfully for his return. She also had a dramatic conversion experience and joined the recently established Methodist church in Kingston, where she met a Miss Grear, with whom she journeyed to New York City after her emancipation. Leaving her daughters in Ulster County at work or in the care of their father, Isabella took Peter, a troubled young teenager, with her.

In New York City in the early 1830s Isabella supported herself through household work. She attended the white John Street Methodist Church and the Black African Methodist Episcopal Zion Church, where she briefly encountered three of her older siblings. She also began to preach at the camp meetings held around the city and attracted the attention of white religious mavericks, some of whom became her employers. Through the dissident Methodist Latourette family, Isabella encountered the Magdalene Society, a mission to prostitutes founded by Arthur Tappan, who became a leading abolitionist in the mid-1830s. In the Magdalene Society she met Elijah Pierson, and through Pierson, the self-proclaimed prophet Matthias (Robert Matthews).

Between 1832 and 1835, Isabella was a follower of Matthias and lived in his "kingdom," a commune in Sing Sing underwritten by Pierson and another wealthy merchant family. The only Black follower among Matthias's adherents, Isabella was also one of only two of the commune's working-class members. Like that of many other independent popular prophets of the early nineteenth century, Matthias's message was eclectic and idiosyncratic. Having begun his public life as an ardent advocate of temperance and a fiery anti-Mason, Matthias advocated several of the enthusiasms that were current in the 1830s. He claimed to possess the spirit of God and taught his followers that there were good and evil spirits and that the millennium was imminent. The virtually corporeal existence of spirits was also a central tenet of the kingdom. Matthias and his followers did not believe in doctors, reasoning that illness was caused by evil spirits that must be cast out. Members of the kingdom fasted often and followed a diet that emphasized fresh fruit and vegetables and prohibited alcohol.

This famous preacher, abolitionist, and lecturer was born Isabella Bomefree, a slave. She was freed in 1827, and in 1843 she became an itinerant preacher, taking the name Sojourner Truth. A fiery orator, she spoke out on subjects ranging from abolition to temperance, prison reform, and woman suffrage. [Schomburg Center]

Although other communities with which Sojourner Truth would be connected would hold many of these same convictions, Matthias's kingdom was the only one organized around so autocratic and charismatic a prophet.

Matthias's kingdom collapsed in 1835, after an accusation of murder and a free love scandal brought the community tremendous notoriety. Matthias left for the West, and Isabella resumed household work in New York City for another eight years. Her *Narrative* contains no record of her activities between the breakup of the Matthias commune in 1835 and her assumption of a new identity in the midst of economic hard times in 1843.

The *Narrative* does indicate that in 1843 Isabella was profoundly influenced by the millenarian movement inspired by a religiously independent farmer named William Miller. Making his own calculations based on biblical prophesies, Miller had figured that the world would come to an end in 1843. Scores of itinerant preachers, who addressed hundreds of camp meetings, which were coordinated by several well-run newspapers (including the New York *Midnight Cry*), spread Miller's message. Believing herself to be part of what she called a great drama of robbery and wrong, Isabella felt that she must make a definitive break with her old way of life. On the first of June 1843, she changed her name to Sojourner Truth, which means itinerant preacher. Without informing her family or friends, she set out eastward, exhorting people to embrace Jesus, as the Spirit had commanded her. Following a network of Millerite camp meetings, she made her way from Brooklyn, across Long Island, into Connecticut, and up the Connecticut River Valley. By December 1843, the Millerites were facing the reality of the Great Disappointment, and Sojourner Truth had joined the utopian Northampton Association, located in what is now Florence, Massachusetts.

A utopian community dedicated to the cooperative manufacture of silk, the Northampton Association attracted relatively well-educated people whose reforming sentiments were broad and deep-running. Unusual at the time, the Northampton Association did not draw the color line, and there Truth encountered the retired Black abolitionist David Ruggles, who was a permanent resident, and Frederick Douglass, who visited occasionally. William Lloyd Garrison also spent months at a time at the Northampton Association, staying with his brother-in-law George Benson, who was one of the association's founders. Between residents and visitors at the association, Truth lived for the first time in an environment permeated with liberal reforms like feminism and abolitionism.

Even before the association collapsed in 1846 and its lands were subdivided and sold, Truth began to address antislavery audiences, taking her preacher's forensic skills into a new field. After 1846 she stayed on in Florence, where she bought a house on Park Street. In 1849, she joined George Thompson, an antislavery British Member of Parliament, on the antislavery and women's rights lecture circuit, selling her *Narrative* to pay off the mortgage on her house. Florence remained her base until she moved to Battle Creek, Michigan, in 1856.

As an antislavery feminist speaker, Sojourner Truth quickly gained a reputation for pungent wit and insight. Whether she said that women deserved equal rights with men, that slavery should be abolished, or that freedpeople should be allocated government lands in the West, she always prefaced her remarks and authenticated her authority by recalling her experience in slavery. In time she overstated both the duration of her enslavement and the particulars of her suffering. In the "a'n't I a woman?" speech she says she lost thirteen children to the slave trade, which more nearly approximates her mother's tragic experience than her own. After the Civil War, Truth routinely spoke of having spent her mother's forty, rather than her own thirty, years as a slave. Stressing her identification with slavery, Truth gauged her audiences well, for she, rather than her free, educated, and ladylike Black colleagues, found a fond place in American memory.

Truth continued to lecture to antislavery and women's rights audiences until she went to Washington, D.C., in 1863 to help the Black refugees who were fleeing the warfare of northern Virginia. As she nursed and taught domestic skills among destitute former slaves, she realized that the old clothes and handouts of charitable aid could not address the fundamental causes of poverty among the freedpeople: lack of paying jobs and material resources. In 1867, she initiated a job-placement effort that matched refugee workers with employers in Rochester, New York, and Battle Creek, Michigan. When that operation became too cumbersome for volunteers to manage, she drew up a petition to Congress that demanded that western land be set aside for the freedpeople's settlement. In 1870 and 1871 she traveled throughout New England and the Midwest, including Kansas, collecting signatures on her petition, on which no action was taken. In 1879, however, scores of Black southerners—who were called Exodusters—migrated to Kansas spontaneously. The Exodusters were acting independently on the same kind of millenarian fear of imminent transformation that Truth had experienced in 1843. Fearing (rightly) that ascendant Democrats would seek to reenslave them, Exodusters from Mississippi, Louisiana, Texas, and Tennessee flocked to the state that they knew as Free Kansas. By the late 1870s Sojourner Truth was in very poor health, but she applauded the Exodusters' venture. She died in Battle Creek in 1883, mourned as a stalwart of antebellum reform.

Well before her death Truth had begun to enter historical memory. Writing down Truth's autobiography, which Truth published in 1850 as *The Narrative of Sojourner Truth*, Olive Gilbert preserved the first portrait of Sojourner Truth. Harriet Beecher Stowe wrote a widely circulated profile entitled "Sojourner Truth, The Libyan Sibyl," which was published in the *Atlantic Monthly* in April 1863 and reprinted in the 1875-78 edition of *The Narrative of Sojourner Truth*. Stowe's article motivated Frances Dana Gage to write her own recollections of Truth, which were republished in the 1875-78 edition of *The Narrative of Sojourner Truth* and volume one of Elizabeth Cady Stanton et al., *History of Woman Suffrage* (1881). Subsequent Sojourner Truth biographies, long and short, have mostly repeated material from these three mid-nineteenth-century sources.

Because she was so singular and so eloquent a personage and knew how to appeal to educated American audiences without revealing her inner self, Sojourner Truth's persona has changed to reflect the needs and tastes of her audiences since she entered the public realm in the early 1830s. In camp meetings around New York City she gained renown as a preacher and singer, a reputation that she retained well after she became Sojourner Truth, the itinerant preacher, in 1843. As an antislavery lecturer, her first famous phrase, uttered in the late 1840s, as Frederick Douglass was doubting the possibility of ending slavery peaceably, was, "Frederick, is God dead?" This rhetorical question established her as a Christian of exquisite faith, in accordance with nineteenth-century evangelical sensibilities. But this phase's popularity had begun to fade by the century's end. Modern audiences are more likely to know Truth as a feminist who redefines womanhood along very contemporary lines. To reinforce the power of this Black feminist persona, it is now common practice to collapse her 1851 words and 1858 actions into one event. This combination produces an angry, defiant character that may suit modern tastes but that does not match the evangelical qualities of the historic Sojourner Truth.

[*See also* ABOLITION MOVEMENT.]

BIBLIOGRAPHY

Bernard, Jacqueline. *Journey Toward Freedom: The Story of Sojourner Truth* ([1967] 1990); Campbell, Karlyn Kohrs. "Style and Content in the Rhetoric of Early Afro-American Feminists," *Quarterly Journal of Speech* (November 1986); Collins, Kathleen. "Shadow and Substance: Sojourner Truth," *History of Photography* (July-September 1983); Fauset, Arthur Huff. *Sojourner Truth: God's Faithful Pilgrim* (1938); Lebedun, Jean. "Harriet Beecher Stowe's Interest in Sojourner Truth, Black Feminist," *American Literature* (1974); Mabee, Carleton. "Sojourner Truth, Bold Prophet: Why Did She Never Learn to Read?" *New York History* (January 1988), and "Sojourner Truth and President Lincoln," *New England Quarterly* (December 1988), and "Sojourner Truth Fights Dependence on Government: Moves Freed Slaves off Welfare in Washington to Jobs in Upstate New York," *Afro-Americans in New York Life and History* (January 1990); Ortiz, Victoria. *Sojourner Truth, A Self-Made Woman* (1974); Painter, Nell Irvin. "Sojourner Truth in Life and Memory: Writing the Biography of an American Exotic," *Gender and History* (Spring 1990), and "Introduction" to reprinted edition of Jacqueline Bernard, *Journey toward Freedom: The Story of Sojourner Truth* (1990), and "Sojourner Truth in Feminist Abolitionism: Difference, Slavery, and Memory." In *An Untrodden Path: Antislavery and Women's Political Culture*, ed. Jean Yellin and John Van Horne (1992); Pauli, Hertha. *Her Name Was Sojourner Truth* (1962); Porter, Dorothy. "Sojourner Truth Calls upon the President: An 1864 Letter," *Massachusetts Review* (1972); Smith, Grace Ferguson. "Sojourner Truth: Listener to the Voice," *Negro History Bulletin* (March 1973); Sterling, Dorothy, ed. *We Are Your Sisters: Black Women in the Nineteenth Century* (1984); Titus, Frances W., ed. *Narrative of Sojourner Truth* (1878); Yellin, Jean Fagan. *Women and Sisters: The Antislavery Feminists in American Culture* (1989).

NELL IRVIN PAINTER

TUBMAN, HARRIET ROSS
(c. 1821-1913)

Running away was one way to resist slavery. Until recently, running away has been described in general terms as a predominantly masculine form of resistance. Because of their roles as mothers, wives, and daughters, women slaves, it was argued, resorted instead to strategies consonant with their biology and with social expectations. They poisoned food, injured livestock, committed arson, aborted pregnancies, feigned illness, and some physically fought mistresses, masters, and overseers. The fact that Harriet Tubman ran away repudiates the comfortable dichotomy of race and sex in resistance strategies.

Harriet Ross Tubman has achieved mythic fame as the best known conductor on the Underground Railroad. Her heroic exploits included at least fifteen trips into the South to rescue over 200 slaves and deliver them to freedom. Since Underground Railroad operators did not keep records of their activities, the exact number of trips Tubman made is unknown. Tubman herself remembered the number as eleven.

Born around 1821 in Dorchester County on Maryland's eastern shore to Benjamin and Harriet Greene Ross, Harriet was one of eleven children. Called Araminta when young, she later chose her mother's name, Harriet. Like most slave children, Harriet performed a variety of domestic chores, including attending the owner's children and cleaning house, before becoming a field hand. Harriet preferred fieldwork since it afforded a measure of autonomy and moments of respite from the close scrutiny and relentless demands of the slaveowner. An added benefit of fieldwork was that it enabled her to develop considerable muscular strength and physical endurance.

One incident in her youth left Tubman with a lifelong affliction. An owner or overseer (accounts vary) intent on reprimanding a fleeing slave instead struck Harriet on the head. As a result of this nearly fatal head injury, Harriet suffered recurring narcoleptic seizures. In 1844, Harriet married John Tubman, a free Black man. Harriet yearned to be free, but John failed to share her mounting anxiety of being sold into the Deep South or of the possible dispersal of her family should her owner die. In 1849, upon learning that her worst fears were soon to become reality, Harriet escaped. John refused to accompany her, and when she returned for him months later, he had taken another wife. John died soon after the Civil War and in 1869, Harriet married Civil War veteran Nelson Davis.

After her escape, Tubman made her way to Philadelphia where she worked as a domestic, saving her meager earnings until she had the resources and contacts to rescue her sister, Mary Ann Bowley, and her two children. This was the first of many rescue missions Tubman would undertake as an agent of the Underground Railroad, a network of way stations situated along several routes from the South to the North to Canada, providing runaways with assistance in the form of shelter, food, clothing, disguises, money, or transportation. Most conductors on the Railroad who ventured South to seek prospective escapees and to guide them to freedom were Black station masters. In her numerous trips South, Tubman followed various routes and used different disguises. She might

Harriet Tubman has achieved fame as the best-known conductor on the Underground Railroad. Her heroic exploits included at least fifteen trips into the South to rescue personally more than 200 slaves and deliver them to freedom.

appear as a hooded, apparently mentally impaired, wretchedly dressed man loitering about or talking in tongues or as an old woman chasing hens down the street. She usually chose a Saturday night for the rescue since a day would intervene before a runaway advertisement could appear. She carried doses of paregoric to silence crying babies and a pistol to discourage any fugitive slave from thoughts of disembarking the freedom train. Within two years of her own escape she had returned to Maryland's eastern shore to lead more than a dozen slaves to freedom in northern states. Maryland planters saw her as such a threat that they offered $40,000 for her capture.

Tubman eventually developed close, mutually supportive relationships with Black abolitionist William Still of Philadelphia and white abolitionist Thomas Garrett of Wilmington, Delaware. Still was the leading Black figure in the Underground Railroad. He described Tubman as "a woman of no pretensions; indeed a more ordinary specimen of humanity could hardly be found among the most unfortunate-looking farm hands of the South. Yet in point of courage, shrewdness, and disinterested exertions to rescue her fellowman, she was without equal"

(Conrad 1943). As early as 1830, Garrett, a Quaker, had become actively involved in the Underground Railroad. By August 1854, Garrett had assisted 1,853 runaways. On numerous occasions, Tubman relied on these men and on others for assistance as she escorted fugitives North.

The Fugitive Slave Law of 1850 placed fugitive cases under federal supervision and empowered special U.S. commissioners to receive $10 for each arrest that returned a slave to his or her owner. With the passage of this legislation, the entire federal govern-

Harriet Tubman is often thought of as a figure in the distant American past, yet she lived into the twentieth century. She is shown here in a photograph taken shortly before her death in 1913. [Schomburg Center]

ment machinery and power could be called upon to assist in the capture and return of escaped slaves in any section of the country. This law cast an ominous shadow over the lives of all free African-Americans in northern communities. Tubman, having been forced to relocate many fugitives to Canada, herself moved to Saint Catharines, Ontario, just beyond Niagara Falls.

In December 1851, Harriet went South and returned with eleven slaves, including her brother and his wife. The following year she made another trip into Maryland and retrieved nine more slaves. On December 29, 1854, Thomas Garrett wrote, "We made arrangements last night, and sent away Harriet Tubman, with six men and one woman to Allen Agnew's (in Pennsylvania) to be forwarded across the country to the city. Harriet and one of the men had worn their shoes off their feet, and I gave them two dollars to help fit them out but do not yet know the expense." On June 4, 1857, Tubman achieved a long-desired goal when she rescued her parents and took them to Garrett's house in Wilmington. She made her last rescue in late 1860 when she returned to Dorchester County to free Steven Ennets, his wife, Maria, and their three children. Tubman took great pride in having never lost a passenger. These long journeys of courage and faith inspired her friends and the runaways to call her "Moses."

As is true with any social movement, a culture developed around the antislavery or abolitionist movement. Its luminaries included Frederick Douglass, William Lloyd Garrison, David Ruggles, and Gerrit Smith. Among many newspapers supporting the cause were the *Liberator*, *North Star*, *National Anti-Slavery Standard*, and the *Genius of Universal Emancipation*. Meetings, conventions, lectures, petitions, fund-raising and political activities, and dramatic rescue attempts generated newspaper headlines and kept antislavery sentiments alive. Tubman, in addition to her rescues, participated fully in this culture. Although illiterate, Tubman gave speeches and personal testimony. She conspired with John Brown on his doomed effort to provoke a massive armed slave rebellion by raiding the federal arsenal at Harpers Ferry, although illness prevented her direct participation in the raid.

When the Civil War began, free African-Americans eagerly anticipated participation in this long-awaited opportunity to help strike down slavery. Harriet Tubman, Sojourner Truth, Frederick Douglass, and other Black leaders, therefore, were shocked and angered by President Abraham Lincoln's denial that the purpose of the war was to free the slaves and his initial reluctance to accept Black volunteers into the Union army. Eventually, Lincoln gave in to pressure and issued the preliminary Emancipation Proclamation declaring that slaves in states still in rebellion on January 1, 1863, would be set free, and early in 1863, the enlistment of African-Americans into the Union army began in earnest.

Tubman, like more than 186,000 fellow African-Americans, willingly put her life on the line in the quest for emancipation. She earned distinction as the only woman in American military history to plan and execute an armed expedition against enemy forces. Serving in numerous capacities, Tubman was a spy, scout, and nurse for the Union army stationed in the Carolinas and Florida. Her most famous adventure during the war was as assistant to Colonel James Montgomery on a raid from Port Royal, South Carolina, inland up to the Combahee River in June 1863, during which many plantations that had been providing food for Confederate troops were destroyed. Tubman was also present at the Fort Wagner battle and was purported to have served the last meal to Colonel Robert Gould Shaw of the Black Massachusetts Fifty-Fourth Regiment, celebrated in the 1990 film *Glory*. She recorded a powerful description of the battle that ended in the death of approximately 1,500 Black troops: "Then we saw de lightening, and that was de guns; and then we heard de thunder, and that was de big guns; and then we heard de rain falling, and that was de drops of blood falling; and when we came to get in de crops, it was dead men that we reaped."

Following the Civil War, Tubman recounted her life story to her friend, Sarah Elizabeth Bradford, and received a small stipend from the sale of the resulting biography, *Scenes in the Life of Harriet Tubman* (1869). For thirty years, Tubman fought to receive a pension from the U.S. government for her military services and eventually won a $20 per month stipend. She purchased a home in Auburn, New York. On land she had purchased from New York governor W. H. Seward before the Civil War as a home for her parents, she established a permanent home for aged ex-slaves who could no longer perform strenuous jobs. Her postwar social reform efforts to provide relief for the recently freed slaves and the families of Black soldiers paralleled the work of many Black women, such as Harriet Jacobs and Elizabeth Keckley. These women organized relief associations, raised funds, and rendered invaluable aid. Harriet Tubman died in March 1913.

Frederick Douglass wrote to Harriet Tubman on August 28, 1868, and eloquently summed up her life.

The difference between us is very marked. Most that I have done and suffered in the service of our cause has been in public, and I have received much encouragement at every step of the way. You, on the other hand, have labored in a private way. I have wrought in the day—you the night. I have had the applause of the crowd and the satisfaction that comes of being approved by the multitude, while the most that you have done has been witnessed by a few trembling, scared, and foot-sore bondmen and women, whom you have led out of the house of bondage, and whose heartfelt "God bless you" has been your only reward. The midnight sky and the silent stars have been the witness of your devotion to freedom.

On May 30, 1974, the Department of Interior declared the Harriet Tubman Home for Aged and Indigent Colored People a National Historic Landmark. The U.S. Postal Service issued in 1978 its first stamp in the Black Heritage USA Series, appropriately enough commemorating Harriet Tubman. She was a great leader determined to gain freedom for herself and others or to die in the effort.

[See also ABOLITION MOVEMENT; CIVIL WAR AND RECONSTRUCTION.]

BIBLIOGRAPHY

Bradford, Sarah. *Harriet Tubman: The Moses of Her People* ([1886] 1961); Conrad, Earl. "I Bring You General Tubman," *Black Scholar* (January/February 1970), and *Harriet Tubman* (1943); *DANB*; *NBAW*; Quarles, Benjamin. "Harriet Tubman's Unlikely Leadership." In *Black Leaders of the Nineteenth Century*, ed Leon Litwack and August Meier (1988); Thompson, Priscilla. "Harriet Tubman, Thomas Garrett, and the Underground Railroad," *Delaware History* (Spring/Summer 1986).

DARLENE CLARK HINE

TUCKER, C. DeLORES NOTTAGE (1927-)

C. DeLores Tucker was born October 4, 1927, in Philadelphia to the Reverend Whitfield and Captilda Gardiner Nottage. She was the tenth of eleven children. She was educated in the public schools of the city and graduated from the Philadelphia High School for Girls in 1946. C. DeLores Nottage attended Temple University, where she studied finance and real estate. She also attended the North Philadelphia Realty School, and two years after her marriage to William Tucker on July 21, 1951, they established Tucker and Tucker Real Estate Company.

With the coming of the protest and demonstrations associated with the civil rights movement in the early 1960s, C. DeLores Tucker became involved in the campaigns in Philadelphia. She served as vice president of the Philadelphia branch of the National Association for the Advancement of Colored People and in 1961 she was a delegate to President John F. Kennedy's White House Conference on Civil Rights. Between 1963 and 1966 the Philadelphia NAACP, under the leadership of Cecil Moore, launched a series of protests and demonstrations to end the discriminatory practices of construction trades unions, post offices, and bus companies in the city and C. DeLores Tucker participated in and led these protests. In March 1965, she headed a Philadelphia delegation that accompanied Martin Luther King, Jr., on the famous march from Selma to Montgomery, Alabama, in support of voting rights legislation. In 1968, she became chair of the Pennsylvania Black Democratic Committee.

A Philadelphia public relations firm, C. DeLores Tucker Associates, was formed in 1967 and the following year Tucker was appointed by Mayor James H. J. Tate to the board of adjustment of the Philadelphia Zoning Commission. This was the first of many major political appointments. In 1970, she was appointed vice-chair of the Pennsylvania Democratic party, and in January 1971, Governor Milton Shapp appointed Tucker as Pennsylvania's secretary of state. She was the first African-American to serve in such a position in the United States. She was reappointed to the office in 1975 and served until 1977.

Secretary of State Tucker was instrumental in the appointment of numerous women and minorities to judgeships and political offices throughout the state. She served on numerous state boards and commissions, including the Pennsylvania Commission on Women and the State Bicentennial Commission, and she headed the governor's Affirmative Action Council. She also headed several national organizations, serving as the vice president of the National Association of Secretaries of State (1976), national president of the Federation of Democratic Women (1977), and chair of the Democratic National Committee's Black Caucus (1984).

DeLores Tucker also has served on several community boards and a number of charitable organizations. She has been a member of the board of directors of the Philadelphia branch of the Young Women's Christian Association, the New School of Music, the Urban Coalition, the United Fund, Philadelphia Tribune Charities, Inc., the Medical College of Pennsylvania (Commonwealth Board), and Messiah College, and a member of the national board of directors for People United to Save Humanity (PUSH).

Tucker has received numerous honors and awards, including the 1961 NAACP Freedom Fund Award, the National Association of Television and Radio Artists' Woman of the Year Award in 1972, the Martin Luther King Service and Achievement Award, and the Community Service Award from the Philadelphia Chapter of B'nai B'rith. She has been awarded honorary degrees from Villa Maria College in Erie, Pennsylvania, and Morris College in Sumter, South Carolina. She was listed among the 100 most influential Black Americans by *Ebony* magazine in 1973, 1974, and 1975.

In 1984, along with Shirley Chisholm, she founded the National Political Congress of Black Women to assist African-American women who are interested in running for political office, and in 1985, she founded the Bethune-Du Bois Fund to assist young Black professionals in gaining internships and employment in federal agencies in Washington, D.C. Tucker is still active in Philadelphia politics and was appointed by Mayor W. Wilson Goode to serve as Philadelphia's ambassador to Washington, D.C. In September 1991, Tucker declared her candidacy for the congressional seat from Pennsylvania's second district.

BIBLIOGRAPHY

Commonwealth of Pennsylvania. *The Pennsylvania Manual* (1971, 1975); *Philadelphia Enquirer* (September 17, October 13, 1991); Tucker, C. DeLores. Personal interview (October 21, 1991).

V. P. FRANKLIN

TURNER, TINA (1939-)

During the mid-1980s, Tina Turner epitomized the meaning of the phoenix. This fiery, thoroughbred singer made one of the biggest comebacks in recording history with *Private Dancer*, an album that sold more than 25 million copies.

Born Anna Mae Bullock in the borough of Nutbush near Memphis, Tennessee, on November 26, 1939, Turner was not yet a teen when she began her career as a singer and dancer for local trombonist Bootsie Whitelaw. After her parents separated, she moved to St. Louis, Missouri, with her mother and sister. There she was befriended by Ike Turner, an established rhythm and blues singer and guitarist. While still in her teens she joined Ike's entourage, Kings of Rhythm, when she stepped in at the last moment of a performance to sing lead on "Fool in Love."

Renamed the Ike and Tina Turner Revue, the incendiary collaboration relocated to Los Angeles and became one of the biggest recording acts in both rhythm and blues and pop. With a mixture of raw soulful delta blues, edgy rock guitars, country rockabilly, and tinges of psychedelia, the revue became a favorite in both the United States and the United Kingdom. Churning out such hits as "I Want to Take You Higher," "Proud Mary," "Tra La La La," "Poor Love," "It's Gonna Work Out Fine," and "Nutbush City Limits," the Ike and Tina Turner Revue electrified audiences with Tina's raspy pipes and pulsating go-go acrobatic dancing. During her partnership with Ike, Turner recorded a solo record with Phil Spector titled "River Deep, Mountain High" and starred as the Acid Queen in the movie version of the Who's rock opera, *Tommy*.

Despite the magical chemistry that Ike and Tina showcased onstage, behind closed doors Tina suffered physical, verbal, and emotional abuse from Ike. In 1975, she left Ike in Dallas in the middle of a tour. After her divorce, Tina tried to establish a solo career but was shunned by most promoters and booking agents in the United States. In the United Kingdom, however, her ties remained strong, and her appearances were not restricted to smaller clubs.

In 1979, Turner met Roger Davies, a young Australian manager who helped redirect her career from a lounge act back to its raw blend of rock 'n' soul. He also steered her in the direction of England's new-wave sound. The following year, Turner relocated to Europe, where, with the help of Mick Jagger, Rod Stewart, Keith Richards, and David Bowie, she began to revive her singing career.

Paired with English newcomers Martyn Ware and Ian Craig Marsh (who later became known as the new-wave group Heaven 17), Turner provided vocals on the Temptations' classic "Ball of Confusion" for the synth new-wave group British Electric Foundation. After session work with Heaven 17, Turner landed a recording contract with Capitol Records and soon asked the duo to produce her version of Al Green's hit "Let's Stay Together." Not only did it become a hit, both in the United Kingdom and the United States, but it also served as a catalyst for a string of comeback hits. The single sold more than 250,000 copies and earned a U.K. Silver Disc Award.

In 1984, the amazing Tina Turner's comeback album Private Dancer *took the world by storm. At the Grammy Awards that year, Turner won Grammys for Record of the Year, Best Pop Vocal Performance, and Best Rock Vocal Performance. That same year, she burst onto the world of film as Aunt Entity in* Mad Max beyond Thunderdome *(released in 1985).* [Schomburg Center]

Very impressed with the results, Capitol Records decided to produce a full album of material.

Turner suddenly found herself working with eight different songwriters and four producers, including Mark Knopfler of Dire Straits. In May 1984, after only two weeks of production, Turner recorded the monumental *Private Dancer*, a multiplatinum album that took the world by storm. Supported by show-stopping videos, *Private Dancer* yielded such hits as "Better Be Good to Me," "Private Dancer," and "What's Love Got to Do with It," which won a Grammy Award for song of the year. Ironically, Turner initially did not like "What's Love Got to Do with It," claiming it was too tame. Turner won three Grammys in 1984, record of the year, best pop vocal performance, and best contemporary rock vocal performance, capping one of the biggest comebacks in recording history. Turner also returned to acting in 1984, starring as Aunt Entity in the postatomic war action film *Mad Max beyond Thunderdome* (released in 1985). She also sang two songs on the soundtrack, "We Don't Need Another Hero" and "One of the Living."

In 1985, Turner was a featured artist on the single "We Are the World," a record that benefited hunger relief efforts in drought-stricken parts of Africa. She also filmed a live performance special for Home Box Office (HBO), with guests David Bowie and Bryan Adams, and published her autobiography, *I, Tina.*

In September 1986, Turner released her second solo album for Capitol Records, *Break Every Rule.* Another top seller, it went platinum with the hits "Typical Male" and "Back Where You Started," which won a Grammy for best female rock performance. Turner promoted the album on an exhausting tour that covered 145 cities in 25 countries on 5 continents. The tour was recorded on a two-disk set, *Tina Live in Europe!* (released in 1988). At Brazil's Maracana Soccer Stadium in 1988, Turner played to the largest paying crowd for a solo artist in history. Turner announced that year that she was retiring from touring in order to focus on her acting career, but after working as a consultant on the autobiographical film of her life planned by Disney she returned to the stage to support her 1989 *Foreign Affair* album. Europe's biggest tour ever, the *Foreign Affair* tour attracted more than 3 million fans to 121 sold-out performances.

In fall 1991, Capitol Records released a retrospective compact disc and home video, aptly titled *Simply the Best.* Recounting her comeback period, the release also featured three new tracks, "Love Thing," "I Want You Near Me," and "Way of the World."

The album also featured new mixes of Turner's earlier hits "Nutbush City Limits" and "River Deep, Mountain High."

Tina Turner's saga provides the measuring stick for all comebacks. From a small town farm girl to an international superstar, Tina Turner is truly a living legend.

BIBLIOGRAPHY

Current Biography (1984); *Jet.* "Tina Turner Still Sexy and Going Strong" (July 9, 1990); Norment, Lynn. "Rich, Free, and in Control—The Foreign Affairs of Tina Turner," *Ebony* (November 1989); Turner, Tina, with Kurt Loder. *I, Tina* (1986).

DISCOGRAPHY

For discographies, see Allen, Daniel. *Bibliography of Discographies, Vol. 2: Jazz* (1981); Ivory, Steven. *Tina!* (1985); Mills, Bart. *Tina* (1985); Wynn, Ron. *Tina, the Tina Turner Story* (1985).

JOHN MURPH

TURNEY, MATT (1930-)

Matt Turney was born in Americus, Georgia, in 1930. She studied at the University of Wisconsin and at the Martha Graham school in New York. Known as a "dancer's dancer," she was suited to Martha Graham's myth-oriented, highly technical choreography. She joined the Martha Graham Dance Company in 1951 and continued to perform in the company until 1972. Among the many Graham-choreographed dances in which she created roles were *Ardent Song* (1954), *Seraphic Dialogue* (1955), *Clytemnestra* (1958), *Embattled Garden* (1958), *Visionary Recital* (1961), and *Phaedra* (1969).

Turney also danced with the companies of Donald McKayle, Alvin Ailey, Paul Taylor, and Pearl Lang. In a 1960 recital by her colleagues Bertram Ross and Robert Cohan, Turney performed *Praises, The Pass,* and *Quest.*

BIBLIOGRAPHY

Clarke, Mary and David Vaughn, eds. *The Encyclopedia of Dance and Ballet* (1977); Cohen-Stratyner, Barbara Naomi. *Biographical Dictionary of Dance* (1982); *EBA*; Goodman, Saul. "Dancers You Should Know," *Dance Magazine* (1964); Long, Richard. *The Black Tradition in American Concert Dance* (1990); McDonagh, Don. *The Complete Guide to Modern Dance* (1976); Toppin, Edgar A. *A Biographical History of Blacks in America Since 1528* (1971); Willis, John, ed. *Dance World* (1967, 1976).

KARIAMU WELSH ASANTE

TYSON, CICELY (1939-)

The achievements and contributions of Cicely Tyson are a testament to the substantial gains made by African-American women in film and theater. Her parents, William and Theodosia Tyson, immigrated to the United States from Nevis, the smallest of the Leeward Islands in the West Indies. Her father was a painter and in between jobs sold fruit and vegetables from a pushcart. The family settled in East Harlem, New York, where Cicely, one of three children, was born on December 19, 1939. Her parents divorced when she was eleven and Cicely grew up with her mother, who was devoutly religious. It was at church that her talents began to develop. She sang, played the organ, and taught Sunday school in the Episcopalian and Baptist churches. Theatrical entertainment, such as movies, was strictly forbidden by her mother as sinful; the ability of the actor to capture and potentially sway an audience in an other than ordinary space could be mistaken for godliness.

After graduating from Charles Evans Hughes High School, she took a job as a secretary before she was asked by Walter Johnson, her hairdresser, to model hairstyles. He encouraged Cicely to pursue modeling, and she eventually enrolled in the Barbara Walters Modeling School, earning $65 an hour as a model. When the *Ebony* fashion editor, Freda DeKnight, discovered Cicely Tyson through an interview, it was not long before Tyson was one of the top models in the United States.

Her first starring role on stage was in *Dark of the Moon.* This 1957 production was directed by Vinnette Carroll at the Harlem Young Men's Christian Association (YMCA). It was written by Howard Richardson and William Berney and was produced by the YMCA Drama Guild in association with the Little Theatre players and the Harlem Showcase. In 1959, *Dark of the Moon* was presented at the Equity Library Theater with Cicely Tyson, James Earl Jones, Isabel Sanford, and choreography by Alvin Ailey. Her next performance was in *Moon on a Rainbow Shawl* (1962), written by Errol John and directed by George Roy Hill. This time she shared the stage with Vinnette Carroll, whom she respected as an important teacher of theater. The New York production was the winner of an Obie Award, and Tyson received the prestigious Vernon Rice Award for her role as Mavis.

When Jean Genet's *The Blacks* appeared off-Broadway (1961-62), directed by Gene Frankel, Cicely Tyson was again honored with the Vernon Rice Award, this time for her portrayal of Virtue. Frankel's epochal directing established an innovative standard for off-Broadway theater. The play had a stellar cast that included Tyson, James Earl Jones, Helen Martin, Maya Angelou, Roscoe Lee Browne, Godfrey Cambridge, and Louis Gossett, Jr. An ensemble of many of these African-American actors was later formed to develop one of the oldest continuous Black theater companies today, the Negro Ensemble Company. Though she had begun a film and television career, Tyson never forgot the stage. Films broadened her acting experience and further tested the training that she began with Lloyd Richards in 1959,

Magnificently exemplifying a new awareness of Black beauty and dignity, Cicely Tyson after The Heart Is a Lonely Hunter *(1968) refused film roles rather than appear in parts that were not positive in their image, attitude, and expression. She broke that hiatus with a stunning performance in* Sounder *(1972) as Rebecca Morgan (pictured). [Donald Bogle]*

the same year she filmed *Odds against Tomorrow* and *The Last Angry Man.*

She made her major television debut in Paule Marshall's *Brown Girl, Brownstones* (1960), and then did a series of Sunday morning dramas. She also was cast for a *Camera Three* television production, *Between Yesterday and Today*. When the prominent actor George C. Scott saw her performance in *The Blacks*, he recruited her for the 1963-64 season television show *East Side/West Side*, establishing Cicely Tyson as the first Black regular on a television series. Unfortunately, the series did not utilize her talents as an actor. Fortunately, the stage did allow her to explore and display her artistry. In 1962, she appeared in the stage production *Tiger, Tiger, Burning Bright* and in 1963 in the off-Broadway production of *The Blue Boy in Black*, directed and produced by Ashley Feinstein.

In 1963, Tyson performed in *Trumpets of the Lord* (directed by Donald McKayle). This off-Broadway production was adapted by Vinnette Carroll from folk sermons and a prayer from James Weldon Johnson's *God's Trombones* and was revived in 1968. (Tyson performed in both productions.) Other theater credits include *A Hand Is on the Gate* (1966); *Carry Me Back to Morningside Heights* (1968); the off-Broadway production of *To Be Young, Gifted, and Black* (1969); and *Desire under the Elms*, performed in Lake Forest, Illinois (1974). Between her stage, film, and television performances, she honed her craft by taking courses at New York University, Lee Strasberg's Actors' Studio, and the Paul Mann workshop.

Cicely Tyson's television appearances on *Slattery's People* (1965); *I Spy* (1965, 1966); *The Guiding Light* series (1967); and *Cowboy in Africa* (1966, 1967) were mere preludes to her stunning performances in the 1968 film *The Heart Is a Lonely Hunter* and as Rebecca Morgan in *Sounder* (1972). The several-year gap between films resulted from Tyson's refusal to accept parts that were not positive in their image, attitude, and expression of Black people. In *The Heart Is a Lonely Hunter*, based on the novel by Carson McCullers, the role of the doctor's daughter had been especially tailored for her by the screenwriter. *Sounder* was Tyson's first film after her decision not to participate in films exploiting stereotypes. As Rebecca Morgan, she played a faithful, dignified, strong, loving wife of a sharecropper. While some African-Americans were critical of the 1940s setting of *Sounder* and its southern historical base, Tyson has been adamant in her belief that the characters were drawn from lives of people "who have been through those kinds of years, [and] are the foundation upon which we are standing today" (Robinson 1974).

The 1970s saw Cicely Tyson emerge as one of America's leading dramatic performers. She brought a refreshing image of Black women to the screen by portraying perseverance, pride, and strength in a variety of settings. For her critically acclaimed performance in *Sounder*, she was named Best Actress by the National Society of Film Critics and was nominated for an Academy Award. Her ability to absorb a role as part of an organic process in the art of acting is (as she has often learned and stated) "getting into the cells, and fibre, and being of the character" (Robinson 1974). Her absorption process was truly put to the test when she was cast in the television drama *The Autobiography of Miss Jane Pittman* (1974), in which she portrayed 110-year-old Jane Pittman. Jane Pittman, born into slavery and subjected to discrimination in a racist and hostile society, finds in old age the courage at last to strike out at injustice. For her performance, Cicely Tyson received excellent reviews and numerous awards, including two Emmy Awards, as Best Lead Actress and as Actress of the Year. Her agent, Bill Haber, lauded her performance but questioned what she could possibly do after *Sounder* and *Miss Jane Pittman*. He believed she had "acted herself clean out of the business" (Robinson 1974).

Cicely Tyson returned to the stage in 1976 for the Broadway production of *The River Niger*, and that same year she received her fourth National Association for the Advancement of Colored People Woman of the Year Award. The following year she returned to television in *Wilma* (the story of Wilma Rudolph, played by Shirley Jo Finney). Subsequent television roles include the mother of Kunta Kinte in *Roots* (Emmy nomination as Best Actress); Coretta Scott King in the miniseries *King*; Harriet Tubman in *A Woman Called Moses*; and Chicago schoolteacher Marva Collins in a television movie. Most recently she appeared in a television miniseries produced by and starring Oprah Winfrey, *The Women of Brewster Place* (1989) and in the film *Fried Green Tomatoes* (1991).

Other awards and honors include an Honorary Doctor of Humane Letters from Lincoln University, an honorary Doctor of Fine Arts from Loyola-Marymount College, and honorary doctorates from Atlanta and Pepperdine universities. She has been honored by the Congress of Racial Equality (CORE), the NAACP, and the National Council of Negro Women. In 1974, she received the Best Actress award at Jamaica's First Black Film Festival (for *The Autobiography of Miss Jane Pittman*). She was inducted into the Black Filmmakers Hall of Fame (1977) and in Chicago, Operation PUSH declared a Cicely Tyson Day. In 1974 Cicely Tyson was the first actor of any

Cicely Tyson poses here with the two Emmy Awards she won for her performance in the title role of the 1974 drama The Autobiography of Miss Jane Pittman, *an account of a Black woman's life from slavery to defiance at the age of 110.*

race or sex to be honored with a day by the Harvard University Faculty Club.

She was the first vice-president of the board of directors of the Dance Theatre of Harlem, a trustee of the American Film Institute, and a Board of Governors member of Urban Gateways (an organization that exposes children to the arts). Tyson is also the former wife of the late jazz trumpeter Miles Davis.

BIBLIOGRAPHY

Andrews, Bert. *In the Shadow of the Great White Way* (1989); Mapp, Edward. *Directory of Blacks in the Performing Arts* (1978); *NA*; Ploski, Harry and James Williams. *Reference Library of Black America* (1990); Robinson, Louie. "A Very Unlikely Movie Star," *Ebony* (May 1974).

BEVERLY J. ROBINSON

U

UNIVERSAL AFRICAN BLACK CROSS NURSES

The Universal African Black Cross Nurses, organized in May 1920, was a female auxiliary of the Universal Negro Improvement Association (UNIA). The UNIA, a Black nationalist organization, was founded in Jamaica by Marcus Mosiah Garvey in 1914. Black Cross nurses, active members of the UNIA, were trained in their local divisions throughout the United States and internationally by a head nurse or registered nurse. Their aim was to provide services to their local communities and ultimately to prepare for liberation wars in Africa.

Like the Red Cross nurses, these women were primed in first aid and relief measures in case of calamities. They were encouraged to raise funds by giving public lectures and instruction in first aid. They disseminated professional knowledge on safety devices, nutrition, and geriatric care by utilizing pamphlets and a column on the woman's page in the *Negro World*, the UNIA's weekly newspaper published in New York. In addition, Black Cross nurses assisted at local hospitals and supported social service agencies.

Though there are photos of children in Black Cross nurse uniforms, only Black women between the ages of sixteen and forty-five took a solemn oath to administer medical care and educate their public on health and home care. One of many UNIA auxil-iaries, the Black Cross nurses followed protocol and each division elected a president, head nurse, secretary, and treasurer. Often featured in UNIA parades wearing long white robes with an emblem of a Black Latin cross on their caps, these women represented the epitome of activists committed to the welfare of their Black communities.

BIBLIOGRAPHY

Hill, Robert A., Emory J. Tolbert, and Deborah Forczek, eds. *The Marcus Garvey and Universal Negro Improvement Association Papers* (1983-84); Lewis, Rupert. *Marcus Garvey: Anti-Colonial Champion* (1988); "Swearing in of Black Cross Nurses of UNIA," *Blackman* (June 28, 1929); "Universal African Black Cross Nurses Child Welfare Department," *Negro World* (1923).

ULA TAYLOR

UNIVERSAL NEGRO IMPROVEMENT ASSOCIATION

Marcus Garvey's Universal Negro Improvement Association (UNIA), the grass-roots Pan-Africanist organization that began in Jamaica in 1914 and was reconstituted in the United States in 1917-18, is characteristically seen as one manifestation of the post-World War I New Negro movement—a movement in which patterns of racial accommodation were exchanged for resistance, pride, and the proclamation of Black manhood. It is less commonly recognized that the UNIA also challenged dominant definitions of Black womanhood. Women were an important part of the UNIA, making up at least half of its membership and serving in leadership positions on the local, national, and international levels. Garvey acknowledged that women made up the backbone of the grass-roots movement, but his idealized and patriarchal vision of women dominated the formal affairs of the UNIA. Nevertheless, the thousands of women who participated in the movement effectively broadened the internal debate over what women should do and be.

Garvey's view of women was consistent with his larger nationalist philosophy of racial unity, self-help, and identification with Africa. His poems, notably "The Black Woman" and "The Black Mother," idealized the African woman as a virginal goddess-queen or as the mother who is a source of unconditional support for the son. Garvey used such visions of Black womanhood to reverse white-defined standards of beauty and lift Black women above white stereotypes of immorality.

Similarly, the UNIA worshiped a Black Christ and canonized the Virgin Mary as a Black Madonna, countering white images of the holy family. While the issue of birth control was debated within the UNIA (with some seeing it as a boon to women and others as genocide), Garvey, a Catholic, denounced it as interference with divine will. At the same time, he criticized single motherhood and exalted the nuclear, patriarchal family, with women in companionate, supportive roles. He credited the UNIA with lifting Black women out of domestic service in white homes and into dignified clerical work in UNIA offices and businesses. As with his poetry and religious instruction, his views on women, work, and family addressed the historical separation of Black families and work-force exploitation of Black women. His ideal of manhood was that Black men should protect Black womanhood, and chivalry was a prevalent theme in UNIA rhetoric. While he saw the ideal woman's role as that of wife, Garvey also praised women as leaders in the UNIA and referred to successful women entrepreneurs (Maggie Lena Walker, Madam C. J. Walker, Annie Malone) as role models to emulate in building a Black economy. He admired Sojourner Truth and other Black heroines of history. Africa was often given female form in his speeches as a woman in need of rescue and redemption, and as the Motherland.

The UNIA's Declaration of Rights and Constitution defined men's and women's official roles. On the local level, each UNIA division had a general president (male) who oversaw the activities of the division as a whole. Each division also had a woman president, who had authority over the women members and female auxiliaries. Children were divided into separate courses by gender, with girls instructed by women. Female auxiliaries in the UNIA included the Black Cross Nurses, the Motor Corps, and the elite Ladies of the Royal Court of Ethiopia.

Women also played a role in UNIA enterprises, serving on the boards of the Black Star Line and the *Negro World*, and having primary roles as workers and consumers in UNIA restaurant, laundry, hat-making, and dress-making businesses. Women were delegates to the famous UNIA conventions, which also featured women's days and exhibits of women's industrial arts and crafts. Women participated in important organizational rituals, marching in UNIA parades, appearing in pageants and concerts, and singing at UNIA mass meetings. They were frequent contributors to UNIA fund-raising projects and owned Black Star Line stock. The *Negro World* newspaper featured columns, letters, articles, poetry, and short stories by women as well as men. Women participated in Garvey's African School of Philosophy, an officer-training course he developed in the 1930s, and held key positions as regional organizers.

Several women were instrumental to Garvey's success as a race leader. Amy Ashwood, who later became Garvey's first wife, helped found the UNIA in Jamaica and drew women into the movement as members and benefactors in its early years. Madam C. J. Walker gave money to help Garvey begin the *Negro World* and purchase Liberty Hall, and Ida B. Wells-Barnett was a guest speaker for the fledgling organization. Henrietta Vinton Davis also lent her fame to the movement in its beginnings, and as International Organizer, traveled on many national and international tours to found or reorganize hundreds of local divisions and to win support for the UNIA's business enterprises. Ashwood was supplanted as UNIA headquarters manager and Garvey's personal assistant by Amy Jacques, who became Garvey's second wife. Jacques emerged as a forceful speaker, writer, and administrator and carried out UNIA business according to Garvey's instructions during the years of his imprisonment. She became the movement's premier propagandist, publishing the two-volume *Philosophy and Opinions of Marcus Garvey* (1923, 1925). After Garvey's death, she devoted herself to preserving his name and reputation. M.L.T. De Mena, another great UNIA organizer, followed Davis as the leading female officer in the late 1920s. Daisy Whyte, one of a series of personal secretaries who handled Garvey's affairs, cared for the UNIA leader in his final illness in London in 1940. Ethel Collins emerged as a local leader in New York and, as UNIA Secretary General, orchestrated the reorganization of the movement after Garvey's death.

Despite women's participation in the UNIA and Garvey's praise of their abilities, their authority in policy and leadership positions remained largely token. Amy Jacques Garvey, for example, never held official office in the organization. Davis was for many years the only woman in any international office; she was also the only woman to participate in UNIA diplomatic delegations. There were no women staff members of the *Negro World* until 1924. Men far outnumbered women as business executives, diplomats, and editors and were generally granted greater status as UNIA employees, officers, and delegates. While all UNIA officials suffered from the organization's lack of financial solvency, women were more likely to be seen as fulfilling a calling or support service and thus less in need of remuneration, promotion, or personal recognition than men. Some women protested this state of affairs: women delegates rose at conventions to demand greater equality, a voice in policy, freedom from male restriction, and access to positions reserved for men. Davis, De Mena, and Jacques all made militant appeals for the recognition of and equal opportunity for women. De Mena wrote in the *Negro World* (1926), "We are sounding the call to all the women in the UNIA to line up for women's rights."

Jacques's "Our Women and What They Think" page, the women's section of the *Negro World*, details the ways in which UNIA women redefined the prevailing standard of womanhood set by Garvey. The women's page offers a full range of opinion, including antifeminism, domestic feminism, and liberal feminism as well as coverage of women in political movements around the world and in racial and party politics, accounts of outstanding Black women achievers, articles about women who succeeded in traditionally male professions and businesses, and debates about women's traditional roles as mother, wife, laborer, and homemaker.

BIBLIOGRAPHY

Bair, Barbara. "True Women, Real Men: Gender, Ideology, and Social Roles in the Garvey Movement." In *Gendered Domains: Rethinking Public and Private in Women's History*, ed. Susan Reverby and Dorothy O. Helly (1992); Ford Smith, Honor. "Women and the Garvey Movement in Jamaica." In *Garvey: His Work and Impact*, ed. Rupert Lewis and Patrick Bryan (1988); Garvey, Amy Jacques. *Garvey and Garveyism* (1978), and Amy Jacques Garvey papers. Marcus Garvey Memorial Collection, Fisk University, Nashville, Tenn.; Hill, Robert A. and Barbara Bair, eds. *Marcus Garvey: Life and Lessons* (1987); Hill, Robert A., et al., eds. *The Marcus Garvey and Universal Negro Improvement Association Papers*. 7 vols. (1983-90); Lerner, Gerda, ed. *Black Women in White America: A Documentary History* (1973); Martin, Tony. "Women in the Garvey Movement." In *Garvey: His Work and Impact*, ed. Rupert Lewis and Patrick Bryan (1988), and *Literary Garveyism: Garvey, Black Arts and the Harlem Renaissance* (1983); Matthews, Mark. "Our Women and What They Think: Amy Jacques Garvey and the *Negro World*," *Black Scholar* (May-June 1979); Seraile, William. "Henrietta Vinton Davis and the Garvey Movement," *Afro-Americans in New York Life and History* (July 1983); Smith-Irvin, Jeannette. *Footsoldiers of the Universal Negro Improvement Association* (1989); Yard, Lionel M. *Biography of Amy Ashwood Garvey* (c. 1989); Microfilm of the papers of the UNIA Central Division, New York, and the *Negro World* newspaper, along with the John E. Bruce Papers, and photographs of Garvey movement in Harlem are at the Schomburg Center for Research in Black Culture, The New York Public Library, New York; The papers of the UNIA in Cleveland are at the Western Reserve Historical Society, Cleveland, Ohio.

BARBARA BAIR

V

VASHON, SUSAN PAUL (1838-1912)

Susan Paul Vashon was a distinguished teacher, school principal, and organizer of numerous groups for women and young people, but she is perhaps best remembered for her efforts during the Civil War when she raised money and cared for wounded soldiers and Black refugees.

Susan Paul Vashon was born on September 19, 1838, in Boston, Massachusetts. Her father was Elijah W. Smith, a skilled musician and composer. Her mother, Anne Paul Smith, was a daughter of Reverend Thomas Paul, who was renowned for his abolitionist work and his efforts on behalf of Black people generally and one of the most influential Black leaders in Boston in his time. Paul was founder and pastor of the Joy Street Church, the only refuge for the American Anti-Slavery Society in Boston. The African school conducted in the basement of Paul's church educated Black children who were denied admittance to the city's segregated public schools.

Her mother died when Vashon was very young, and she then moved into the house of her maternal grandmother, Katherine Paul. Also living there was Vashon's aunt, Susan Paul, a hard-working abolitionist and advocate of woman's rights for whom Susan had been named. At sixteen, Vashon graduated from Miss O'Mears's Seminary in Somerville, Massachusetts, a private, nonsegregated school. Vashon, the only Black student in her class, graduated as valedictorian. After graduation, she went to Pittsburgh, Pennsylvania, where her father lived, and began to work as a teacher in the city's only school for Black children.

The principal of her school was George Boyer Vashon, who like Vashon, came from a family dedicated to working both for Black education and the abolition movement. They were married in 1857 and had seven children. It is probable that as newlyweds the Vashons were helpers in the Underground Railroad. Both George Vashon and his father, John Bethune Vashon, are known to have been conductors for the railroad. During the years 1864-65, Vashon helped organize a series of highly successful sanitary relief bazaars that raised thousands of dollars that were used to nurse sick and wounded soldiers as well as house Black refugees in Pittsburgh.

After the family moved to Washington, D.C., in 1872, Vashon returned to public school teaching. She later became principal of the Thaddeus Stevens School, a position she held until 1880. Vashon was widowed in 1878, and in 1882 she and her four surviving children moved to St. Louis, Missouri, where she worked with church groups and women's organizations. In 1902, she served as president of the Missouri State Federation of Colored Women's Clubs of the National Association of Colored Women's Clubs. She also played a pivotal role in the formation of the St. Louis Association of Colored Women's Clubs. She was active too in the Mother's Club for young women and the Book Lover's Club. Her children went on to hold respected positions in St. Louis, and Vashon High School was named in recognition of the family's outstanding community achievements.

Having led a busy and successful life as mother, teacher, and community organizer, Susan Paul Vashon died in 1912.

BIBLIOGRAPHY

Brown, Hallie Q. *Homespun Heroines and Other Women of Distinction* (1926); *CBWA;* Dannett, Sylvia G. *Profiles of Negro Womanhood* (1964); Manning, Erma. *Herstory Silhouettes: Profiles of Black Womanhood* (1980); *NBAW*. Biographical information on Susan Paul Vashon is located in the Missouri Historical Society, St. Louis.

FENELLA MACFARLANE

VAUDEVILLE AND MUSICAL THEATER

The world of show business mirrored American society in the early twentieth century: the races were separated in the theaters, and white and Black men dominated the ranks of owners, producers, and actors. However, as commercial success and the lure of popularity and profit increased, the willingness of theater owners to allow women, particularly Black women, to exhibit their talents as singers, dancers, and actresses increased. Show business vehicles also changed. Minstrel shows gave way to variety shows, which gave way to elaborate vaudeville and musical revues, and the lines between these genres began to blur. Like other businesses of the period, the potential for success encouraged many entrepreneurs to enter and compete in the business of entertainment. By the 1920s, consolidation and concentration had taken hold; the myriad of independent theater owners had been replaced with syndicates of producers, booking agencies, and a few theater owners monopolizing the field.

Vaudeville, the seven- or nine-act variety show, differed from musical theater while sharing many of its traits. The vaudeville show consisted of distinct acts varying widely in range and quality, from acrobats to song-and-dance numbers, to comedy, and finally, to a fully staged animal act. There was no attempt to unify all acts around a central theme. By contrast, musical theater had a plot that threaded its way throughout the musical and dance numbers, and the sets and costumes were more elaborate. However

obvious the differences, critics often commented on the similarities between the forms because both genres emphasized spectacular dance numbers, slapstick comedians, and attractive women dancers and singers. The narrative structure of much musical theater was often weak, and the show usually lapsed into a series of acts, with the headliners standing out from the rest of the production. These failings characterized both Black and white musical theater.

Many Black entertainers worked both in vaudeville and in musical theater, alternating between presenting vaudeville shows and musical comedies. Both vaudevillians and musical stars traveled the "circuit," often playing a split week: three days in one city, a day to travel, and three days in the next city. Theaters varied in quality and size and in their treatment of entertainers. Race discrimination undergirded the system, which meant, for one thing, that Black entertainers had to accommodate themselves to segregated theaters and hotels. When a singer like Edith Wilson played on a vaudeville show in which she was the only Black woman, not only could she not stay in the same hotel, she could not eat dinner with her fellow performers in the troupe.

When Black entertainers played in northern cities, the show was geared to a white audience, and the fewer Black patrons were relegated to the balcony. In the South, segregated seating also prevailed, although some theaters in both regions became predominantly Black theaters with few white patrons. Also, the content of an all-Black show had to uphold stereotypes of Black people while not being so obviously defamatory as to insult Black audiences. A delicate balance, not always achieved, became an active goal of both Black and white composers, writers, and producers of Black musical shows.

As early as 1906, Robert Mott, a Black entrepreneur, opened the Pekin Theater on Chicago's South Side. He had a resident stock company that performed both musicals and dramas. In 1909 (or 1913, depending upon the source), Sherman H. Dudley, a Black actor and producer, organized the first Black theatrical circuit. He owned several theaters in Washington, D.C., and Virginia and began to book acts into his theaters. Eventually, he owned twenty-one theaters and booked shows into Black theaters throughout the South. Black performers worked for both Dudley's circuit and, later, the Theater Owners Booking Association (TOBA), a vaudeville circuit exclusively for Black acts. Some entertainers fondly referred to TOBA as "the chitlin circuit," but others referred to it not so fondly as "Tough on Black Asses." Some Black headliners traveled on the white

Pantages Circuit or the Loews Circuit, but few appeared under the auspices of the most prestigious circuit, the Keith-Albee.

According to Henry T. Sampson, a leading authority on Black musical theater, TOBA was organized in Chattanooga in 1920 by a group of prominent theater owners in the South who wanted more control over the business. By purchasing shares of stock in the association, the members received a franchise to book acts into their theater. Of the fifteen original stockholders, four were Black men with theaters throughout the South and Southwest. Thirty-one theaters participated, and by the end of the decade more than eighty theaters were involved, with the possibility of acts being booked for a full season. Theoretically, the system benefited both the actors, who were assured continuous employment, and the owners, who could plan and profit from regularly scheduled shows throughout the year. In practice, however, the system favored the theater managers to the detriment of the workers, who often faced poor working conditions, lower-than-promised salaries if audiences were not large, and abrupt cancellations. In 1920, Indianapolis was the northernmost city in the association, and Jacksonville, Florida, was the farthest south. Texas had five TOBA members; Oklahoma had three.

Both Black and white producers, writers, and composers participated in creating the acts and shows that traveled the circuit, particularly in the early years. In the 1910-30 period, which was the height of Black musical theater and vaudeville, notable Black producers were Whitney and Tutt, Sherman Dudley, Irvin C. Miller, and Mabel Whitman, who produced a show featuring her sisters. It was a difficult business, though, and white producers and theater owners, with more resources than their Black colleagues, became dominant by the end of the 1920s.

Within this context, Black female singers and dancers became prominent participants in the growing business of entertainment. Talent played a major role in catapulting performers into the limelight, but it was a woman's physical shape and the image she projected that influenced producers and managers. In this regard, Black and white men who hired women singers and dancers and who wrote skits that included parts for women shared a general cultural view; they believed that a woman had to play the sweet young thing, the romantic interest, the sexual tease, or the butt of a joke. Black critics often lamented the fact that light-skinned mulattas succeeded far more often than dark-skinned women. Although skin color was not a significant factor for men, it was a primary

Vaudeville and the Theater Owners Booking Association provided thousands of Black entertainers with their only opportunity to perform. This group is Edwards and Delotch's "Bingham and Brevities." [Scurlock Studio]

Stump and Stello were among the Black acts that toured the vaudeville circuits. [Scurlock Studio]

consideration in choosing female dancers for the chorus line. Singers with talent, whatever their skin color or body type, had a greater chance to succeed, but Black female entertainers, like their white counterparts, were expected to embody the cultural ideal about women.

Many people have heard about—or remember—Bessie Smith and Florence Mills, two of the most popular singers in Black vaudeville and musical theater, but few have heard about the many other veterans who traveled the circuit for years, entertaining Black audiences in Macon, Georgia; Detroit,

Michigan; and Louisville, Kentucky. Ada (or Aida) Overton Walker, Edith Wilson, Adelaide Hall, and Susie Edwards (of the Butterbeans and Susie team) are examples of little-known vaudevillians who were quite famous in their day, and their careers are representative of the many Black female performers whose names appear on old posters and in frayed theatrical pamphlets.

Ada Overton Walker (1880-1914) was born in New York City. At the age of sixteen, she joined a prominent Black musical revue company called the Black Patti Troubadours. This company's headliner was Sissieretta Jones, known as Black Patti (after white opera star Adelina Patti). Touring the whole country and especially popular in California, the show followed a minstrel formula but later evolved into musical comedy. Ada Overton danced in the chorus and became a featured player. In 1898, she joined the company of Williams and Walker, a legendary team of comics who produced musical comedies to surround their humorous numbers. The following year, she married the co-star, George Walker.

Ada Walker played a leading role in the three major productions mounted by the comedy team between 1902 and 1908. To many Black historians of the era, these shows represented Black musical theater at its best. Theater critics for Black newspapers around the country singled out Walker's performances for comment. Sylvester Russell wrote in the *Freeman* (Indianapolis) that her presence in *In Dahomey* (1902) stood out and that she was "the most important female in the cast," owning the stage whenever she was on it. Walker played Rosetta Lightfoot, described as "a troublesome young thing" in this musical comedy about two Black American men who go to Dahomey, a West African country, with the intention of taking it over for their own financial advantage. The show traveled to London in 1903, and English critics echoed the Americans. Walker's singing and dancing "were a revelation," gushed a critic for London's *Sunday Dispatch*.

Ada Walker continued to receive positive reviews for her roles in *Abyssinia Company*, the 1906 Williams and Walker show, as well as in *Bandanna Land* (1908). When George Walker became ill during the Broadway run of *Bandanna Land*, Ada dressed in male attire to take his place. The great comic duo of Williams and Walker ended after *Bandanna Land*, and George Walker never performed again; he died in 1911. Meanwhile, Ada Walker continued to perform; in 1909 she organized a vaudeville act called Ada Overton Walker and the Abyssinian Girls. In a July 17, 1909 review, the *Variety* critic found her exotic dance to have "a wild, weird aspect and an immense amount of action to it." Although the critic did not like her singing voice, he noted that the audience responded favorably, especially to her popular renditions of songs such as "I'm Miss Hannah from Savannah" and "That Is Why They Call Me Shine." Ada Walker died on October 10, 1914, at the age of thirty-four.

The career of Edith Wilson (1897-1981) spanned many of the greatest years of Black vaudeville and musical theater. Wilson began singing in amateur shows in her home town of Louisville, Kentucky, in 1910 when she was only thirteen. She promised her

mother that she would return to school after a successful run, but her interest in school quickly faded, and her singing career began in earnest. She gained wide recognition at the Park Theater in Louisville in 1919 and debuted in New York City two years later at the Town Hall in the musical *Put and Take*. Her smooth, silky voice and jazzy presentation made her a popular and busy performer.

Throughout the 1920s, Wilson appeared in many of the most popular Black musicals on Broadway, including *Plantation Revue* (1922), *Dover Street to Dixie* (1926), and *Hot Chocolates* (1929). In the latter show she sang "Black and Blue," one of the songs for which she was most famous. Fats Waller's music and Andy Razaf's lyrics provided her with effective material in *Hot Chocolates*. In a June 26, 1929 review, the *Variety* critic said her rendition of "Pool Room Papa," a double entendre blues song, was "distinctively suggestive" and that Wilson delivered it with verve and style. Many of the musicals in which she appeared

Florence Mills was one of the best-known Black singers in vaudeville and musical comedy. She achieved a first for Blacks when she headlined at the famous Palace Theatre. [Moorland-Spingarn]

were not highly rated, but Wilson's performance was always singled out for praise. In *Hot Rhythm* (1930), for example, she received the evening's only "genuine encores" (Woll 1989).

Edith Wilson's voice also made her popular at Harlem cabarets such as the Cotton Club and Connie's Inn. Beginning in 1922, she recorded her blues songs for Columbia Records, eventually making twenty-six records for them. She toured with the Duke Ellington band, both in this country and in England, in the 1940s. In 1947, she went to work for the Quaker Oats Company as their Aunt Jemima spokeswoman; appearing before youth and community organizations around the country, she remained in this position until 1965. In 1966, when Derrick Stewart-Baxter asked her about the negative view of the Aunt Jemima image held by the Black community, she replied: "Jemima is a well-loved character—almost a folk figure who gives only love and kindness, so how can that be bad?" (Stewart-Baxter 1970). In a 1973 videotaped interview she appeared as vibrant and personable as she had been in her youth. Her singing voice remained strong, her pace effective, and her delivery sure. Wilson died in 1981 at the age of eighty-four.

Adelaide Hall (1901-) was a dancer and singer in Black musical revues. She began her career early, dancing in the chorus as one of the Jazz Jasmines in *Shuffle Along* (1921). This musical is usually credited with being the first of many successful Black shows, returning to Broadway after a ten-year hiatus. Hall played a major role in *Runnin' Wild* (1923), another hit, and developed a "luxuriant voice," according to one historian (Woll 1989). She and legendary dancer Bill "Bojangles" Robinson starred in the decade's longest running Black musical, *Blackbirds of 1928*. Hall sang "I Can't Give You Anything But Love," one of the most enduring songs to emerge from American musical theater.

The Depression years were hard on musical theater and indeed on all forms of entertainment. Still, *Brown Buddies* (1930), starring Hall and Robinson, ran 111 performances during the height of the 1930-31 season. In this show Hall sang "Give Me a Man Like That" and "My Blue Melody."

Hall appeared in Europe during the 1930s and 1940s and made a few Black musical shorts in Hollywood, including *All Colored Vaudeville Show* and *Dixieland Jamboree*. Although she was still a vigorous woman who wanted to work, opportunities began to dwindle in the late 1940s. Her most recent appearance was in a 1980 revival of the Black musical revue *Black Broadway*, in which she again sang "I Can't Give You Anything But Love."

Susie Hawthorne Edwards (1902-63) was part of one of vaudeville's most famous husband-and-wife teams, Butterbeans and Susie. According to one story, they married in 1917 (when Edwards was only fifteen) as part of a publicity stunt for which they were paid $50. In their routine Susie sang the blues and danced the cakewalk, while Butterbeans, dressed in tight pants, did eccentric dances and frequently played the straight man in their comic skits. Although marital conflict was often the major theme of their humor, bawdy material also was featured. Less offensive material was recorded on the Okeh label during the 1920s and helped to promote their personal appearances.

Throughout the 1920s and 1930s Butterbeans and Susie traveled on various vaudeville circuits. They worked for white producer Jimmy Cooper, who produced a Black-and-white revue for the Columbia Burlesque Circuit, and later became a popular act on the Consolidated Booking Office circuit in cities such as Louisville, Indianapolis, Kansas City, Tulsa, and Cleveland. They also produced their own revue in 1928. In 1935, they appeared in the "Cotton Club Parade" and in later years performed on the stage of Harlem's Apollo Theatre. Susie Edwards died in 1963 at the age of sixty-one.

Black women performers in vaudeville and musical theater displayed a wide range of talents. Ada Overton Walker and Adelaide Hall in particular were known as great dancers as well as dynamic singers. Susie Edwards sang and danced but is best remembered for her comic timing and effective delivery of a funny line. Edith Wilson was one of the most successful blues singers in the 1920s. Edwards and Wilson both occupied the bawdy end of the spectrum; they enjoyed doing songs and routines that were full of sexual innuendo and that allowed the audience to laugh at human foibles.

Although each of these women contributed her own unique style and talent to the entertainment world, they all acted within recognizable stereotypes available to women performers. They sang, in both serious and mocking styles, of love lost; they showed off their legs in virtuoso dance numbers; and they made fun of the sexual dalliances of their men. Like their white sisters in show business, they not only survived but also often prevailed under very difficult circumstances. Unlike their white counterparts, they endured segregation while traveling the circuits as well as race typecasting in New York City. Nonetheless, all of them—Walker, Wilson, Hall, and Edwards—brought many hours of joy and laughter to many people over a period of many years.

BIBLIOGRAPHY

Anderson, Jervis. *This Was Harlem, 1900-1950* (1982); *DBT*; Di Meglio, John E. *Vaudeville U.S.A.* (1973); Dixon, Robert M. W. and John Godrich. *Recording the Blues* (1970); Fox, Ted. *Showtime at the Apollo* (1983); Harrison, Daphne Duval. *Black Pearls: Blues Queens of the 1920s* (1988); Hughes, Langston and Milton Meltzer. *Black Magic: A Pictorial History of the Negro in American Entertainment* (1967); Lewis, Theophilus. "Theatre Column," *The Messenger* (December 1923), and "Gay Harlem," *The Messenger* (June 1927); MacDonald, J. Fred. "Interview with Edith Wilson," Northeastern Illinois University, Chicago (videotape, Fall 1973); *The Messenger*, "Whitney and Tutt" (January 1925); *The Messenger* "Sherman H. Dudley" (January 1925); Owen, Chandler. "The Black and Tan Cabaret," *The Messenger* (February 1925); Sampson, Henry T. *Blacks in Blackface: A Source Book on Early Black Musical Shows* (1930), and *The Ghost Walks: A Chronological History of Blacks in Show Business, 1865-1910* (1988); Spitzer, Marian. "The Business of Vaudeville," *Saturday Evening Post* (May 24, 1924); Stein, Charles W. *American Vaudeville as Seen by Its Contemporaries* (1984); Stewart-Baxter, Derrick. *Ma Rainey and the Classic Blues Singers* (1970); Woll, Allen. *Black Musical Theatre: From Coontown to Dreamgirls* (1989).

JUNE SOCHEN

The incomparable Sarah Vaughan had one of the biggest voices ever heard in popular music. Her control inspired awe in other musicians and fanatical devotion among audiences. The divine Sarah was one of the greatest singers of all time. [Schomburg Center]

VAUGHAN, SARAH (1924-1991)

Born in Newark, New Jersey, on March 17, 1924, Sarah Vaughan grew up in a musical family and became one of the most outstanding jazz recording artists. Her father was an amateur guitarist and singer of folk tunes. Her mother was a pianist who sang in the church choir. Vaughan's musical career began with piano lessons at the age of seven, followed by organ lessons, and at the age of twelve she became the organist at the Mount Zion Baptist Church in Newark; she also sang in the choir, often as a soloist. Sarah Vaughan's musical talents also blossomed outside the church because she played the piano in her high school orchestra and would, on selected occasions, sing popular songs at parties.

As a result of her eclectic musical talents, Vaughan was persuaded by friends to enter the famous amateur night contest at Harlem's Apollo Theatre. She entered on a Wednesday night in April 1943, when she was nineteen years old, winning the competition with her rendition of "Body and Soul." In addition to receiving congratulations from Ella Fitzgerald, a winner of a similar contest nine years earlier, Vaughan won $100 and a week's engagement at the Apollo. During her engagement, Billy Eckstine heard Vaughan sing and recommended her to his boss, Earl "Fatha"

Hines (Eckstine was a vocalist for Hines). After a successful audition, Vaughan was given a job as a vocalist, doubling as a second pianist with the Hines band.

The job with Hines afforded valuable contacts with other young, creative, and soon-to-be giants of jazz, specifically, Dizzy Gillespie and Charles Parker, two of Hines's sidemen in his 1936 band. Vaughan was infatuated with the Gillespie and Parker approaches to both harmony and rhythm. After a year with the Hines band, Billy Eckstine, Vaughan's mentor from 1944 until her death in 1991, invited her to join his newly organized big band, a band that also included Gillespie and Parker. Vaughan was quoted once as saying, "I thought Bird and Diz were the end," and that, "at that time [her tenure with Hines and Eckstine], I was singing more off key than on. I think their playing influenced my singing. Horns always influenced me more than voices. All of them—Bird, Diz, Pres, Tatum, J. J. Johnson, Benny Green, Thad Jones—listening to them and others like them, listening to good jazz, inspired me" (Gold

1957). Indeed, throughout her recording career Vaughan was accompanied by Gillespie and Parker as well as Freddie Webster, Bud Powell, Thad Jones, Clifford Brown, and Frank Foster, among others.

After her years with the Hines, Eckstine, and John Kirby bands, Vaughan pursued a solo career. Soon after a stint at the Café Society in New York, she met her first husband, George Treadwell, who abandoned his own jazz career to become his wife's manager and music director. With Treadwell's support, Vaughan took voice and stagecraft lessons, updated her wardrobe, and improved her overall physical appearance. Thereafter, although the marriage did not last, a new, polished Sarah Vaughan emerged.

Arguably, Sarah Vaughan was the first vocalist to both understand and accentuate modern harmonic and rhythmic concepts. Although Louis Armstrong, Billie Holiday, and Ella Fitzgerald had taken jazz vocals to new heights, Vaughan was best suited to *make* it to new heights. Her vocal range encompassed three octaves, her command of dynamics enabled her to make quick transitions from soft to loud within a few measures, and she exuded impeccable pitch and a keen ear for harmonic changes. She also displayed an indelible feel for rhythm, alternating between tension and relaxation, from slow ballads to jump tunes. Sarah Vaughan was more than a vocalist, she was a musician's musician.

Beyond general observations of Vaughan's vocal stylistic interpretations, one also can draw specific conclusions from analyzing specific recordings. No researcher has introduced a methodology capable of discerning and explaining all of the intangibles of vocal stylistic interpretations of jazz, but the methodology espoused by Ruth Elaine King is well suited to describe the vocal stylings of Sarah Vaughan. King adapted Cantometrics, a system developed by Alan Lomax, and a system of notating modern music advocated by David Cope. King also developed seventeen new sets, patterned after Cantometrics, to analyze elements such as harmonic suggestion in the melodic line, position of the first tone in each phrase, text painting, vibrato, timbre, melodic and rhythmic imitation and deviation, and additional elements such as falls, smears, grace notes, lower and inverted mordents, bends, scoops, and slurs. King also compared Vaughan's early vocal style with two later recordings of the same compositions. Contrasting Vaughan's 1945 and 1963 recordings of "Lover Man" and her 1946 and 1978 versions of "Body and Soul," King was able to provide some insightful comparative comments.

In the 1945 recording of "Lover Man," one of her earliest recordings, one can hear undulated phrases (mostly two-measure phrases), a nasal-like tone quality, clear enunciation, an interval range that commonly encompasses a perfect fifth to an octave, and a liberal interpretation of both the melody and rhythm. Also audible are a limited number of glissandos, falls, scoops, and inverted mordents. In short, here are the makings of an outstanding jazz vocalist, a goal that was realized soon after this recording. The 1963 recording of "Lover Man" differs in several ways from the 1945 recording. The 1963 tempo is slower, there is a key change from D to D flat, and Vaughan has developed both her vocal skill and her musicality, specifically, her explorations of vocal timbres and registers, her use of embellishments, and her use of vibrato. Also by 1963, perhaps due to Treadwell's urging, Vaughan had polished her stage presence, vocal skills, and musicianship.

The two recordings of "Body and Soul," 1946 and 1978, also offer an interesting insight into Vaughan's early and late vocal stylings. The 1946 version features the backing of a band, frequent beginning and ending of phrases on the lowest pitch of the phrase, a melodic range that extends beyond an octave, rhythmic deviation, and timbres primarily within the middle register. The 1978 version is characterized by musical contrast. Specifically, this rendition features Vaughan in a duet with Ray Brown (bass); she begins many of her phrases in both the lower and upper tonal ranges and demonstrates a wide variety of phrase contours. In addition, she uses rhythmic flexibility, timbre flexibility, a wide array of embellishments, and, on occasion, implies harmonies different from the original harmonies. In short, by 1978 Vaughan's style had matured and was characterized by freedom of interpretations including approaches to phrasing and articulation, phrase contour and length, and eclectic approaches to embellishments, reharmonization, and timbre.

The aforementioned concepts can be heard in all of her recordings after 1978, including *Sarah Vaughan: Celebration of Duke Ellington*, Pablo (1979); *Send in the Clowns*, Pablo (1981); and *Gershwin Live* (accompanied by the Los Angeles Philharmonic, conducted by Michael Tilson Thomas), CBS (1982).

BIBLIOGRAPHY

Bennett, Richard Rodney. "Technique of the Jazz Singer," *NAJE Educator* (February/March 1975); Berendt, Joachim E. *The Jazz Book: From Ragtime to Fusion and Beyond* (1982); Collier, James Lincoln. *The Making of Jazz:*

A Comprehensive History (1978); Cope, David. *New Music Notation* (1976); Dahl, Linda. *Stormy Weather* (1984); DeToledano, Ralph, ed. *Frontiers of Jazz* (1962); Feather, Leonard and Ira Gitler. *The Encyclopedia of Jazz in the Seventies* (1976); Fraser, Al. *To Be or Not to Bop: Memoirs of Dizzy Gillespie* (1979); Fredrickson, Scott. "Vocal Improvisation: A Practical Approach," *Jazz Educators Journal* (October/November 1982); Gold, Don. "Soulful Sarah," *Downbeat* (1957); Gollobin, Laurie Brooks and Harvey White. "Voice Teachers on Voice, Part 2," *Music Educators Journal* (February 1978); Hodeir, André. *Jazz: Its Evolution and Essence* (1980); King, Ruth Elaine. "The Stylistic Interpretations of Sarah Vaughan," M.A. thesis (1984); Liska, A. James. "I'm Not a Jazz Singer," *Downbeat* (May 1982); Lomax, Alan. *Folk Song Style and Culture* (1968); Long, Sharon. "Melodic Notation in Jazz Improvisation," *NAJE Educator* (October/November 1972); Lyons, Len. *The 101 Best Jazz Albums: A History of Jazz on Records* (1980); Meadows, Eddie S. *Jazz Reference and Research Materials: A Bibliography* (1981); *New Yorker*, "From the Top" (December 29, 1980); Ostransky, LeRoy. *Understanding Jazz* (1977); Placksin, Sally. *American Women in Jazz* (1982); Pleasants, Henry. "Bel Canto Singing in Jazz and Pop Singing," *Music Educators Journal* (May 1973); Quinn, Bill. "Sassy '67," *Downbeat* (July 1967); Skowronski, JoAnn. *Women in American Music: A Bibliography* (1978); Tirro, Frank. *Jazz: A History* (1977); Ulanov, Barry. *A History of Jazz in America* (1972); Williams, Martin. *Jazz Master in Transition, 1957-69* (1970), and *The Jazz Tradition* (1983).

SELECTED DISCOGRAPHY

After Hours, Sony Music Special Products A-660 (reissued 1991); *George Auld and His Orchestra with Sarah Vaughan*, vol. 2, Musicraft MVS 509 (1957); *Count Basie and Sarah Vaughan*, Roulette 42018 (1963); *Best of Sarah Vaughan*, Pablo 2310 885 (1978); *Celebration of Duke Ellington*, Pablo 2312 119 (1979); *The Complete Sarah Vaughan*, Mercury vol. 1 (1954-56); vol. 2 (1956-57); and vol. 3 (1954-56); *Consequences*, Mercury SRM 3-1700 (1956); *Copacabana—Exclusivamente Brazil*, Pablo 2312 125 (1981); *Crazy and Mixed Up*, Pablo 2312 137 (1987); *The Early Years: The Divine Sarah*, Musicraft MVS 504 (1961); *Echoes of an Era: Basie, Getz, and Vaughan Live at Birdland*, Roulette RE 126 (1962); *Echoes of an Era: Count Basie Vocal Years*, Roulette RE 107 (1963); *Echoes of an Era: Sarah Vaughan*, Roulette RE 103 (1964); *Duke Ellington Songbook*, vol. 1, Pablo 2312 111 (1983); *Duke Ellington Songbook*, vol. 2, Pablo 2312 116 (1984); *George Gershwin Songbook*, EmArcy 814 1871 (1954-57); *Gershwin Live*, CBS FM 37277 (1982); *Golden Hits*, Mercury 60645 (1958); *How Long Has This Been Going On?*, Pablo 2310821 (1978); *In the Land Hi Fi*, Columbia Encore Star Series P13084 (1955); *I Love Brazil*, Pablo 2312101 (1977); *Linger Awhile*, Columbia Special Products P14364 (1963); *Live in Japan*, Mainstream 2401 (1973); *The Man I Love*, Musicraft MVS-2002 (1946); *Misty*, Mercury 846488-2 (1990); *No Count Sarah*, Trip Jazz TPL 5562 (1958); *Recorded Live*, EmArcy 2412 (1957-58, 1963); *Sarah's Blues*, Jazz Music Yesterday JMYCD-1002 (1963); *Sassy*, Trip Jazz TPL 5562 (1956); *Sassy Swings the Tivoli*, Mercury EXPR 1035 (1988); *Send in the Clowns*, Pablo 2312 130 (1981); *The Singles Sessions*, Roulette Jazz B21Y-95331 (1960-61); *Sings George Gershwin*, vol. 1, EmArcy 846895-2 (1990); *Sings George Gershwin*, vol. 2, EmArcy 846896-2 (1990); *A Time in My Life*, Main MRL 340 (1971); *Sarah Vaughan*, EmArcy EXPR 1009 (1954); *Vaughan and Voices*, Mercury 846506-4 (1963).

EDDIE S. MEADOWS

VROMAN, MARY ELIZABETH
(c. 1924-1967)

"Writing School Marm: Alabama Teacher Finds Literary, Movie Success with First Short Story" is the title of an article about Mary Elizabeth Vroman that appeared in the July 1952 edition of *Ebony* magazine. The story, which was titled "See How They Run," had been published in *Ladies' Home Journal*; it depicted the real-life struggles of a rural school teacher trying to educate poor Black children. The story was an immediate success and received the prestigious Christopher Award. It later was adapted as the movie *Bright Road*, starring Harry Belafonte and Dorothy Dandridge. Vroman wrote the screenplay and became the first Black woman to gain membership in the Screen Writers Guild.

Born in Buffalo, New York, Vroman was a twenty-seven-year-old Alabama school teacher at the time the *Ebony* article was written. She had grown up in the West Indies and was a graduate of Alabama State Teachers College in Montgomery. A devoted educator, she later taught in Chicago and New York City.

Vroman's literary accomplishments also included two novels and one work of nonfiction. *Esther*, published in 1963, portrays the life of Esther Kennedy, the granddaughter of a midwife who overcomes seemingly insurmountable obstacles to become a nurse in a segregated hospital. Vroman's second novel, *Harlem Summer*, was published in 1967, the year of her death. Written for young adult readers, the work recounts the experiences of sixteen-year-old John who visits relatives in Harlem. Both works celebrate Black people as overcomers, attesting to their unwavering will to succeed.

Mary Elizabeth Vroman died from complications following surgery in 1967. She was survived by her husband, Oliver M. Harper.

BIBLIOGRAPHY

Bachner, Saul. "Black Literature: The Junior Novel in the Classroom—Harlem Summer," *Negro American Literature Forum* (Spring 1973), and "Writing School Marm: Alabama Teacher Finds Literary, Movie Success with First Short Story," *Ebony* (July 1952); *DLB*.

SHIRLEY JORDAN

W

WADDLES, CHARLESZETTA LINA CAMPBELL (1912-)

Charleszetta Lina Campbell Waddles, founder of the Perpetual Mission for Saving Souls of All Nations, was born October 7, 1912, in St. Louis, Missouri, the first of seven children of Henry and Ella (Brown) Campbell. Only three of the seven children lived to adulthood. Henry Campbell was a barber for many years and later did construction work until his health failed; he died in 1924 when Charleszetta was twelve. Ella Campbell was also in frail health, so Charleszetta left school when she was in eighth grade to work to support the family. Her numerous jobs included work as a maid, sorting in a rag factory, restaurant cook, day work, and dishwashing. Ella found it necessary to receive Aid to Families with Dependent Children (AFDC) as did Charleszetta, when later she was a single parent of several children. As an adult, she read to educate herself, but Charleszetta never had the opportunity to return to school.

Charleszetta has been married several times, been divorced and widowed, and is the mother of ten children. The longest of her marital relationships was with Le Roy Wash, a truck driver for a coal company, to whom she was married from 1933 until their divorce in the late 1940s, and with Payton Waddles, an employee of the Ford Motor Co., from 1957 until his death in 1980. In 1936, Charleszetta and Le Roy Wash migrated to Detroit, seeking better job opportunities. Except for a short time in the 1940s when she and her children returned to St. Louis to care for her ailing mother, she has remained in Detroit.

Her own experiences with poverty motivated Charleszetta Waddles and a small group of neighborhood women who were members of a prayer group to think creatively of how to aid others. Charleszetta had started the prayer band, continued as its leader, and began to develop the skills and practices that led to starting her mission church. She was ordained a pentecostal minister in 1956 and was reordained by Bishop M. J. Moore of the International Association of Universal Truth in 1961. In September 1957, the prayer band decided to become an organized group, and from this decision developed the Perpetual Mission for Saving Souls of All Nations, Inc. Aid is available to persons of all races and creeds. In 1980, Mother Waddles estimated that Black people constituted 75 percent of those receiving help.

The mission is best known for providing immediate relief to the needy with a minimum of red tape and qualification barriers. Those in need of food, clothing, furniture, and small amounts of money can usually get help quickly. Mother Waddles also tries to solve problems and run interference for her clients with various agencies. Receiving no governmental funds, the mission is entirely dependent for its success on voluntary donations of time, materials, and money, the amount of both varying from week to week and year to year. The mission has often moved from one location to another and increased or decreased its program due to availability of resources. At various times, the mission has offered restaurant meals free or for 35¢ for those who could pay, shelter, legal aid, assistance with housing, job placement for the unemployed, medical services, and transportation. The work of the mission has had a wide influence: governmental agencies have adopted some of Waddles's ideas and, in the 1970s, branches of the mission were established in ten African countries. Mother Waddles has written two cookbooks, a training manual for missionaries, and two autobiographies. Wide publicity has been given to her efforts and numerous awards and honors have been extended to her. Mother Waddles's work is guided by a practical application of Christian principles rather than a concern for formal theology. In her lifetime, she has aided thousands and set an example for all.

BIBLIOGRAPHY

Davis, James Kotsilibas. "Mother Waddles: The Gentle Warrior," *Life* (March 21, 1969); Edson, Lee. "Mother Waddles: Black Angel of the Poor," *Reader's Digest* (October 1972); Greenlee, Marcia. "Interview with Charleszetta Waddles," *Black Women Oral History Project*, Schlesinger Library, Radcliffe College; "Mother Waddles's Mission," *Newsweek* (May 1, 1972); *NBAW*; Smith, Vern E. "The Perpetual Mission of Mother Waddles," *Ebony* (May 1972); *WWBA*.

DE WITT S. DYKES, JR.

WALKER, AIDA OVERTON
(1880-1914)

Variety called Aida Overton Walker "easily the foremost Afro-American stage artist" of her day. The leading Black female cakewalk dancer and ragtime singer at the turn of the century, she electrified audiences with her talent, brought more authentic Black songs and dances to Broadway musical theater, and became one of the first Black international superstars.

She was born Aida Overton on February 14, 1880, in New York City, the second child of Moses and Pauline Whitfield Overton. In her teens she joined the traveling chorus of the Black Patti Troubadours. She met and married George W. Walker at the beginning of his successful stage career with Bert Williams. Aida Walker choreographed the Williams and Walker shows, played female leads, and emerged as a sensational attraction in her own right.

Williams and Walker's ragtime musicals with all-Black casts superseded minstrelsy and so helped change the nature of American vernacular entertainment. Aida Walker took major roles beginning with *The Policy Players* in 1899 and continuing in *Sons of Ham*, *In Dahomey*, *Abyssinia*, and *Bandanna Land*. In 1903, *In Dahomey* went to London for a command performance at Buckingham Palace; Aida Walker sang and danced for the royal family.

When George Walker's illness forced him to retire from the stage, Aida Walker continued in *Bandanna Land*, wearing his flashy clothes and singing his numbers. She went on to appear in various productions, including, in 1912, a spectacular vaudeville performance of *Salome* at Oscar Hammerstein's Victoria Theatre.

The leading Black woman cakewalk dancer and ragtime singer at the turn of the century, Aida Overton Walker electrified audiences with her talent, brought more authentic Black songs and dances to Broadway musical theater, and became one of the first Black international superstars. [Richard Newman]

Aida Walker died in New York City as a result of a kidney infection on October 11, 1914.

[*See also* THEATER.]

BIBLIOGRAPHY

Newman, Richard. " 'The Brightest Star': Aida Overton Walker in the Age of Ragtime and Cakewalk," *Perspectives* (forthcoming).

RICHARD NEWMAN

WALKER, A'LELIA (1885-1931)

Called "queenly," "lavish," and the "Mahogany Heiress" by some of her contemporaries, A'Lelia Walker was one of the foremost promoters of Black arts in Harlem during the 1920s. Writer/poet Langston Hughes called her "the joy goddess of Harlem's 1920s (Hughes 1981). Walker also began calling herself something other than her birth name, Lelia McWilliams. When she was about thirty-five years old, she changed her name to A'Lelia, the name by which she is most known. She had long since started using her stepfather's last name—Walker.

Walker was born to Sarah Breedlove and her husband Moses McWilliams in Vicksburg, Mississippi, on June 6, 1885. After her husband's death in 1887, Sarah and her daughter moved to St. Louis. There Sarah worked as a washerwoman until 1905, when she began to develop hair-care products and techniques for Black consumers that would make her America's first self-made woman millionaire. In July 1905, Sarah Breedlove moved to Denver, Colorado, where she married newspaperman Charles Walker and became Madam C. J. Walker. A'Lelia was probably attending Knoxville College in Knoxville, Tennessee, when her mother moved initially, but she was living in Denver, Colorado by 1907-08. Madam Walker began to sell her products door to door in Denver; then she trained agents to sell them for her and expanded her business. In 1908, she opened an office in Pittsburgh, Pennsylvania, managed by twenty-three-year-old A'Lelia (the Denver office was closed when they moved to Pittsburgh). In 1910, Madam Walker set up office in Indianapolis, Indiana, and A'Lelia continued to work for her mother in the Pittsburgh office and at Lelia College, a school Madam Walker opened to train Walker hair culturists and agents. In 1914, Madam Walker moved to a townhouse at 108-110 West 136th Street in New York City. She became one of the first Black people to own property there.

One of the foremost promoters of Black artists in Harlem during the 1920s, A'Lelia Walker was rejected by some members of the Harlem community because of her fast-paced social life and her unusual style of dress. [A'Lelia Bundles]

That same year, A'Lelia divorced her first husband and moved to New York to manage the headquarters of the Walker College of Hair Culture. She adopted a daughter named Mae Bryant in 1912.

In 1917, Madam Walker began building an Italianate country home in Irvington-on-Hudson, New York, at a cost of $250,000. One account states that the home was designed by Black architect Vertner Tandy and called "Villa Lewaro" by singer Enrico Caruso, who took the syllables from A'Lelia Walker Robinson's name.

While on a business trip to South America in spring 1919, A'Lelia wrote to her mother that she intended to marry Dr. James Arthur Kennedy, as Madam Walker wished. On May 25, 1919, Madam Walker died while A'Lelia and Mae were still in Panama. Returning to New York, A'Lelia canceled her engagement to Kennedy, buried her mother privately on June 3, and married Dr. Wiley Wilson on June 6. Soon after, however, she divorced Wilson, then reconciled with and married Kennedy.

Following Madam Walker's death, A'Lelia Walker became president of her mother's company and inherited an estate estimated to be worth about $1 million. In 1923, she gave Mae a lavish and expensive wedding at Saint Philip's Episcopal Church in Harlem.

In the mid-1920s, A'Lelia Walker, purposefully setting out to encourage the literary and artistic renaissance in Harlem, welcomed young writers and artists into her home and provided them with food and moral support. In 1927, she cemented her intentions by creating in her 136th Street home a salon where artists could exhibit their paintings, writers could discuss their work, and all could buy food and drink. Richard Bruce Nugent named the salon Dark Tower after Countee Cullen's column of the same name in *Opportunity: A Journal of Negro Life*. Manhattan designer Paul Frankel decorated the salon, placing texts of Cullen's "The Dark Tower" and Langston Hughes's "The Weary Blues" on the walls opposite each other; these were either painted directly on the wall by a local sign painter or were framed pieces.

Walker organized a planning committee and had a grand opening, but in October 1928, after only a year, Dark Tower closed. Walker went to live in her apartment on Edgecombe Avenue in Harlem's West End, but she still maintained her townhouse. In October 1929, a redecorated Dark Tower reopened as an expensive restaurant, eventually moving even further away from A'Lelia Walker's intention to become a hangout for well-to-do cafe society. The club had a hat checker and formal tea room.

During the Harlem Renaissance, A'Lelia Walker became notorious for elaborate gatherings and expensive parties, at both Dark Tower and Villa Lewaro. Her guests included European royalty, influential white Americans, and Black artists such as James Weldon Johnson, Zora Neale Hurston, Langston Hughes, Countee Cullen, Florence Mills, Rudolph Fisher, Charles Gilpin, Bruce Nugent, Aaron Douglas, and Jean Toomer. Society writer Geraldyn Dismond colorfully described the nightly excitement at Dark Tower in the *Inter-State Tattler*, a publication covering Black social life in both small and large cities.

In 1927, A'Lelia Walker created in her home on 136th Street in Harlem a salon where artists and writers could exhibit and discuss their work, and everyone could buy food and drink. The salon was known as Dark Tower, after Countee Cullen's column for Opportunity. *[A'Lelia Bundles]*

A'Lelia Walker was not accepted by everyone in the Harlem community, however. Some begrudged her the fact that she was the daughter of a washerwoman. Some also objected to her fast-paced social life and unusual style of dress, which included turbans and jewelry. Some of her contemporaries called her the "De-kink Heiress." James Weldon Johnson's wife, Grace Nail Johnson, who was known as the social dictator of Harlem, refused to attend Walker's parties.

The Great Depression had its effect on A'Lelia Walker. In 1930, she closed her restaurant and auctioned off some contents from Villa Lewaro. In 1931, she divorced Dr. Kennedy. On August 16, 1931, A'Lelia Walker died at the age of forty-six while visiting friends in New Jersey.

At her funeral, Reverend Adam Clayton Powell gave the eulogy, Mary McLeod Bethune spoke, Edward Perry read Langston Hughes's poem "To A'Lelia," and the Bon Bons, who had often entertained at her parties, performed for her one last time.

BIBLIOGRAPHY

Bundles, A'Lelia Perry. "Madam C. J. Walker to Her Daughter A'Lelia—The Last Letter," *Sage* (1984), and *Madam C. J. Walker: Entrepreneur* (1991); Hughes, Langston. *The Big Sea* (1981); Lewis, David L. *When Harlem Was in Vogue* (1981); Kellner, Bruce, ed. *The Harlem Renaissance: A Historical Dictionary for the Era* (1987); Ottley, Roi. *New World A-Coming* (1968).

TIYA MILES

WALKER, ALICE (1944-)

The title of Alice Walker's 1983 collection of essays, *In Search of Our Mothers' Gardens*, best sums up the perspective that dominates nearly everything she writes. In this collection of essays, Walker argues that Black women can survive whole only by recovering the rich heritage of their ancestors, particularly their Black sister warriors. Walker urges women to look to their mothers to find ways to heal themselves. Her message is that Black women's personal salvation hinges upon recognizing their connectedness to women who historically have built bridges for them with their indomitable and independent spirit. From these sister warriors, Black women can develop respect for possibilities.

Grange Copeland in Walker's *The Third Life of Grange Copeland* (1970) expresses Walker's vision about women and their mothers when he says that,

regardless of the cost, human beings have the capacity to enjoy spiritual health and that poor, Black, uneducated people have the potential to blossom. Walker suggests that although Black women often find themselves in the harshest of environments—ones that are physically, spiritually, economically, and mentally debilitating—they can soar by finding in their mothers' gardens the roots that can bind, nurture, guide, and sustain them.

Although Walker writes about the restrictions placed on Black women because of sexism and racism, she also writes about the transformations that are possible. In her novel, *Meridian* (1976), the civil rights workers express Walker's vision when they say that sometimes fighting is necessary to keep from becoming overwhelmed with bitterness. Walker repeatedly makes the point in her writings that Black women can ameliorate the loneliness of their lives by armoring themselves with the knowledge of the heroic lives of their foremothers. She cogently argues that when a woman goes in search of her mother's garden she will ultimately find her own.

Novelist, poet, short-story writer, essayist, educator, biographer, and editor, Alice Walker was born the last of eight children to sharecroppers Willie Lee and Minnie Tallulah (Grant) Walker on February 9, 1944, in rural Eatonton, Georgia. Growing up mostly with her five brothers, Walker learned how to defend herself. She also learned to make her way in a world of cotton fields, hogwire fences, sharecroppers' shacks, overpriced food in white-owned commissaries, and landlords who believed that Black men were invisible, Black women could be theirs for the taking, and Black children did not need an education.

Walker's early childhood in abject poverty led to feelings of loneliness and alienation, which were magnified when her brother accidentally shot her in the eye with a BB gun. Losing vision in one eye and developing what seemed to her like a monstrous white film over it, Walker became reclusive and dreamed of suicide. She discovered books and began to read texts by some of the world's master writers.

Walker has recalled that her mother, perhaps because of the sympathy she felt when she looked into the disfigured eye, allowed her time to read without interruption, even when there were chores that needed attending to. When she was growing up, Walker's mother gave her three gifts that she considered the most significant of her life. These gifts were particularly meaningful because her mother had never owned such items and had bought them for Walker on a salary of less than $20 a week earned as a maid. One gift was a sewing machine so she could make her own clothes, communicating the message to be self-sufficient and independent. The second gift was an exquisite suitcase, better than most people in Eatonton owned, giving her permission to travel the world and to come home whenever she needed to touch base with her family and community. The third gift was a typewriter, which Walker saw as a mandate to write not only her own but also her mother's stories.

Armed with her three gifts, a "rehabilitation" scholarship from the state of Georgia awarded to her as senior class valedictorian, and $75 collected from her poor community, Walker marched off to Spelman College in Atlanta, where she studied from 1961 to 1963. At the all-woman college Walker's consciousness was raised as she interacted with Black females from across the country who wanted to change the world, particularly the politics of racism. While at Spelman, Walker became an activist and also became disillusioned with the middle-class preoccupation with respectability and material possessions. During the 1960s, Spelman's aim was to produce "ladies," and Walker had learned that she did not want to sit upon a pedestal; she wanted to be a sister warrior like her foremothers.

Walker transferred to Sarah Lawrence College in Bronxville, New York, in 1963, a move that allowed her an opportunity to distance herself from the South and to begin to see the world as a global village. She traveled to Africa in her senior year, storing up experiences that would later appear in her literary works. One experience at Sarah Lawrence that spawned Walker's writing career was an unplanned pregnancy. Her recurrent childhood dreams of suicide returned as she struggled with her options. She knew that if she committed suicide her parents would be devastated but that if they learned of her pregnancy they would be disappointed and ashamed. She chose to have an abortion, which led her to write a series of poems about her ordeal, published in 1968 in *Once*.

After graduating from Sarah Lawrence with a Bachelor's degree in 1965, Walker returned to the South to work in voter registration and in promoting welfare rights in Georgia. On March 17, 1967, she married white civil rights lawyer Melvyn Rosenman Leventhal. Her work in Georgia put her in contact with the state's poorest and least educated African-Americans. She began to observe the impact of poverty on the relationships between Black men and women, namely their cruelty to family members and to each other. Funded by a National Endowment for the Arts grant, Walker completed her first novel, *The Third Life of Grange Copeland*, in 1969, three days before the birth of her daughter Rebecca Grant.

Perhaps her most passionately written work, *Grange Copeland* centers on a father and son, Grange and Brownfield, who turn to alcohol and violence as they try to survive life in a state of powerlessness. Incapable of loving, they abuse their women. Grange's wife kills herself and her child when Grange abandons her. When Brownfield's wife, Mem, tries to elevate her family out of poverty, he blows her head off. Brownfield is probably the least redeemable male character in Walker's canon, particularly because he is arrogant, cruel, unfaithful, and jealous of Mem's college training. He literally beats the newly acquired education out of Mem, which parallels the flesh that falls from her bones and the teeth and hair she loses. An emaciated, toothless nag whose newborn baby Brownfield places on the porch to freeze to death, Mem is spiritually dead long before Brownfield drunkenly sends her head flying in one direction and her body spastically hopping in another. Walker leaves only Ruth, Mem's daughter, with a possibility of surviving whole. Ironically, it is her grandfather, Grange, who makes a commitment to save Ruth from destruction by both her evil father and white people. He teaches Ruth that she must cling tightly to a place inside her where white people cannot go, essentially an inviolable place. More importantly, Grange is transformed or redeemed when he teaches Ruth independence and self-love.

Walker held several teaching jobs early in her writing career, including writer-in-residence and teacher of Black studies at Jackson State University (1968-69) and Tougaloo College (1970-71). Leaving the South in 1971 to assume a two-year Radcliffe Institute fellowship, Walker continued to reach back to her native state for characters. She worked as a lecturer in literature at Wellesley College and at the University of Massachusetts in Boston in 1972-73.

In 1973, Walker published a second volume of poetry, *Revolutionary Petunias and Other Poems*, which won the Lillian Smith Award and was nominated for a National Book Award. While the poems in this collection point to the decline of the southern revolution, there are heroines whose acts of rebellion establish Black women's role in the civil rights movement. In the same year, she published a collection of short stories, *In Love and Trouble: Stories of Black Women*, for which she won a Richard and Hinda Rosenthal Award from the National Institute of Arts and Letters. This collection focuses on the violence that dominates the lives of Black women and the mechanisms they use to fight back. One story in the collection that is frequently anthologized is "The Revenge of Hannah Kemhuff," in which a Black

For years a prolific and highly respected writer, Alice Walker became internationally known with the publication of The Color Purple *in 1982. The book won the Pulitzer Prize and the American Book Award and was made into a blockbuster movie starring Whoopi Goldberg and Oprah Winfrey. [Schomburg Center]*

woman has a conjurer cast a spell on a white woman who had denied her commodities during the Depression; the spell results in the deaths of the white woman's children. Obsessed with the curse, the white woman goes mad and begins to collect her own hair, fingernails, feces, and so on. She eventually dies from stress or, perhaps, from the curse.

An artist who believes in recovering the lives and texts of African-Americans, Walker wrote *Langston Hughes, an American Poet* (1974), a biography for children. Later she would research and recover Zora Neale Hurston's rich legacy to American literature. Walker's second novel, *Meridian*, takes up where *Grange Copeland* leaves off in terms of the civil rights movement, with the main character devoting her life to freeing her people. Meridian goes against stereotypical images of Black mothers in that she is so terrified of failing at motherhood that she gives up her son, has her tubes tied, and becomes an activist to help change a society that places restrictions on women and African-Americans. Walker elevates Meridian to the symbolic mother of the Black race.

Walker's career was well on its way by the time she was awarded the prestigious Guggenheim Fellowship in 1977-78. In 1979, she moved from New York City to a ranch outside San Francisco, where she currently resides and writes full time.

A third collection of poetry, *Good Night Willie Lee, I'll See You in the Morning* (1979), treats love relationships by restructuring them to include a healthy love of self for women. Walker's second collection of short stories, *You Can't Keep a Good Woman Down* (1981), looks closely at pornography, abortion, interracial rape, and politicization of relationships. Unlike heroines in her previous works, the women in these stories are more optimistic, spirited, and tenaciously committed to surviving whole.

Walker became internationally known with the publication in 1982 of *The Color Purple*, which was nominated for a National Book Critics Circle Award and which won the Pulitzer Prize and the American Book Award in 1983. The book was made into a movie in 1985 and had mass appeal. Using the epistolary style, Walker has Celie write to God, Nettie to Celie, and Celie to Nettie. What occurs in these letters is the story of gross abuse of Black women, subjugated by their men in both America and Africa. Focusing on incest, women's explorations of their bodies and souls, wife beating, and other violence, *The Color Purple* illustrates the dehumanization of women.

Becoming more prolific with each passing year, Walker has completed several projects since winning the Pulitzer. A collection of essays, *In Search of Our Mothers' Gardens* (1983), introduced the term *womanist*, as opposed to *feminist*, to separate Black feminists or feminists of color from white feminists, who often differ ideologically on issues of race and gender. These essays essentially bring together her ideas about art and its relationship to life, namely, that a bad person cannot write a good book because art must improve life.

Several other texts have followed, including *Horses Make the Landscape Look More Beautiful* (1984), a book of poems; *To Hell with Dying* (1987), a book for children; and *Living by the Word: Selected Writings, 1973-1987* (1988), a book of essays. Her most recent novel, a Book-of-the-Month Club featured alternate, is *The Temple of My Familiar* (1990). Steeped in mysticism, employing a dreamlike structure, and filled with ample symbols, myths, legends, and fantasy, the novel addresses issues of self-knowledge, humanity, and man's destiny.

One of America's most prolific and profound writers, Walker treats a host of subjects, including individual and collective freedom for Black people and women, the endurance or will to survive, ancestral worship, the transformation of impoverished illiterate people, and the impact of racism and sexism on Black relationships. With the releasing of the movie *The Color Purple*, Walker's vision for women and Black people became accessible to millions. Perhaps no other Black author has touched as many lives as Walker. Walker often writes about possibilities, and her very life gives testimony to the blossoms that can grow strong and tall when a woman finds her own in her mother's garden.

BIBLIOGRAPHY

CA; Christian, Barbara T. "Alice Walker." In *Afro-American Writers after 1955, DLB* (1984); Davis, Thadious. "Alice Walker." In *American Novelists since World War II* (1980); Harris, Trudier. "Violence in *The Third Life of Grange Copeland*," *College Language Association Journal* (December 1975); *NA*; Parker-Smith, Bettye. "Alice Walker's Women: In Search of Some Peace of Mind." In *Black Women Writers, 1950-1980*, ed. Mari Evans (1984); Steinem, Gloria. "Do You Know This Woman? She Knows You—A Profile of Alice Walker," *Ms.* (June 1982); Walker, Cam. Review of *The Third Life of Grange Copeland* and *Meridian, Southern Exposure* (Spring 1977); Washington, Mary Helen. "Alice Walker: Her Mother's Gifts," *Ms.* (June 1982), and "An Essay on Alice Walker." In *Sturdy Black Bridges*, ed. Roseann P. Bell, Bettye J. Parker, and Beverly Guy-Sheftall (1979).

ELIZABETH BROWN-GUILLORY

WALKER, FRANCES (1924-)

Frances Walker (Slocum) retired in 1990 from the piano faculty at Oberlin College after a forty-year career as a teacher and concert pianist. Born in Washington, D.C., on March 6, 1924, to parents of West Indian background, she was raised in a solidly middle-class environment. Her father, a prominent physician and amateur pianist, encouraged the music interests of both Frances and her brother, George, an accomplished concert pianist and composer.

Frances Walker's formal musical training began at an early age with private teachers in Washington, D.C. While still a student at Dunbar High School, she studied in the junior division of the Howard University School of Music, regarded as a spawning ground for many of the nation's talented musicians. Upon graduation, she entered the renowned Oberlin Conservatory and received a Bachelor's of Music in 1945. She continued studying privately at the Curtis Institute of Music (Philadelphia) and entered Columbia University Teachers College, earning both an M.A. in 1952 and a professional diploma in 1971.

In addition to Oberlin, where she returned to teach in 1976, Walker held faculty appointments at Barber-Scotia College (North Carolina), Tougaloo College (Mississippi), Lincoln University (Pennsylvania), and Rutgers University (New Jersey). During the early 1960s, she also taught piano at the Third Street Settlement House in New York City.

At age thirty-five, she made her debut in New York's Carnegie Hall and continued to concertize in the United States and Europe until her retirement. Besides being known for her performances of European classical composers, particularly Brahms, Schumann, Prokofiev, and Rachmaninoff, her repertoire included the work of several important African-American composers, including Samuel Coleridge-Taylor, William Grant Still, George Walker, and Margaret Bonds, whose setting of the spiritual "Wade in the Water," entitled "Troubled Water," often was featured by Walker on her concert program.

Frances Walker has recorded two albums. One, featuring compositions written for her by Wendell Logan, is titled *Five Pieces for Piano* (Orion ORS

80373); the other is a two-album set, *Samuel Cole-ridge-Taylor, Twenty-Four Negro Melodies*, and *William Grant Still, Traceries* (Orion ORAS 78305/306). Walker has been quoted as saying that the Black pianist is not accorded the luxury of being a specialist, limiting his or her repertoire to a specific composer or period. Among African-American pianists, she noted, "there is no Mozart or Beethoven specialist" (*Essence* 1974). However, she has performed on programs dedicated to Black composers, such as the February 29, 1976, piano festival in Harlem, where she was a featured pianist, and an April 1975 concert at the National Gallery of Art in Washington, D.C.

BIBLIOGRAPHY

Abdul, Raoul. *Blacks in Classical Music* (1977); *BDAAM*; *Essence*, "Blacks in Classical Music" (September 1974).

IRENE JACKSON-BROWN

Vicksburg to work as domestics. At fourteen, Breedlove married Moses McWilliams, in part to escape her sister's cruel husband. In 1887, when the McWilliamses' daughter, Lelia (later known as A'Lelia Walker), was two years old, Moses McWilliams died.

To support herself and her daughter, Sarah McWilliams moved up-river to St. Louis. During the next seventeen years she eked out a living as a laundress, educated her daughter in the public schools and at Knoxville College, and joined St. Paul African Methodist Episcopal Church. Around 1904—the same year St. Louis hosted the World's Fair and a convention of the National Association of Colored Women (NACW)—there is evidence that she worked briefly as an agent selling hair care products for Annie Turnbo Pope Malone's Poro Company.

She had used Malone's "Wonderful Hair Grower"—and some of the dozens of other commercially available hair and scalp conditioners—to remedy

WALKER, MADAM C. J. (SARAH BREEDLOVE) (1867-1919)

"I got myself a start by giving myself a start," Madam C. J. Walker often said (*New York Times Magazine*, November 4, 1917). Madam Walker was an entrepreneur, hair-care industry pioneer, philanthropist, and political activist. At the 1912 National Negro Business League convention—after League founder Booker T. Washington had refused her request to be included on the program—she stood up on the last day of the assembly and addressed the body anyway.

"I am a woman who came from the cotton fields of the South," she began. "I was promoted from there to the washtub. Then I was promoted to the cook kitchen, and from there I promoted myself into the business of manufacturing hair goods and preparations. . . . I have built my own factory on my own ground." She so astounded and impressed the mostly male audience—and Washington—that she was invited back the next year as a keynote speaker (National Negro Business League 1912).

Born Sarah Breedlove on a Delta, Louisiana, cotton plantation on December 23, 1867, she was orphaned by age 7. Her parents, Owen and Minerva Breedlove, had been slaves on Robert W. Burney's Madison Parish farm during the Civil War's siege of Vicksburg when the property served as a battle-staging area for General Ulysses S. Grant's Union troops.

In 1878, when the cotton crop failed and a yellow fever epidemic struck, ten-year-old Sarah and her older sister, Louvenia, moved across the river to

Businesswoman, philanthropist, and inventor, Madam C. J. Walker was the first self-made U.S. woman millionaire. Her Walker Company sent hundreds of agents into the field to promote her beauty care products. [A'Lelia Bundles]

*To foster cooperation among the agents who sold her beauty care products and to protect them
from competitors, Madam C. J. Walker created a national organization, the Madam C. J.
Walker Hair Culturists Union of America, which held annual conventions. This group
photograph was taken at the first convention, in 1917 in Philadelphia. [A'Lelia Bundles]*

alopecia (baldness) that was brought on by poor diet, stress, damaging hair care treatments, dandruff, psoriasis, and other scalp diseases. The ailment was common enough among Black women that Sarah Breedlove McWilliams decided she could make more money by developing her own line of products.

In July 1905, with $1.50 in savings, the thirty-seven-year-old McWilliams moved to Denver where she joined her deceased brother's wife and four daughters. In January 1906 she married a newspaper sales agent, Charles Joseph Walker, adopting his name and—following a custom practiced by many businesswomen of the era—added the title "Madam." As her husband and business partner, Charles Walker helped her design her advertisements and set up a mail-order operation.

As Madam C. J. Walker, she tried her products first on friends, then canvassed door to door for customers. Her own "hair growing" formula had come

in a dream where, she claimed, "a big black man appeared to me and told me what to mix up for my hair. Some of the remedy was grown in Africa, but I sent for it, mixed it, put it on my scalp, and in a few weeks my hair was coming in faster than it had ever fallen out" (*Literary Digest* 1917). She may also have discussed her ideas for a formula with Denver pharmacist E. L. Scholtz, for whom she worked as a cook for a short time.

While Madam Walker is often said to have invented the "hot comb" or steel straightening comb, it is more likely that she adapted metal combs and curling irons popularized by the French to suit Black women's hair. Acutely aware of the debate about whether Black women should alter the appearance of their natural hair texture, she insisted years later that her Walker System was not intended as a hair "straightener," but rather as a grooming method to heal and condition the scalp to promote hair growth, to make the hair easier to comb once it grew back, and to help Black American women find their own unique style.

"Right here let me correct the erroneous impression held by some that I claim to straighten the hair," she once told a reporter. "I want the great masses of my people to take a greater pride in their personal appearance and to give their hair proper attention" (*Indianapolis Recorder* 1919).

In September 1906 Madam Walker and her husband began a year and a half of traveling to promote her products and train sales agents while her daughter ran the mail-order operation from Denver. From 1908 to early 1910 they operated a beauty parlor and training school called Lelia College for Walker "hair culturists" in Pittsburgh. Walker hair culturists learned a philosophy of inner and outer beauty, creating an atmosphere in their salons to pamper their clients. She considered her hot combing method more natural and an improvement over previous practices using a device called "hair pullers"—popularized by her competitor, Annie Malone—that flattened the hair strands.

In 1910, they moved the company to Indianapolis—then the nation's largest inland manu-facturing center—to take advantage of the city's access to eight major railway systems. During this phase of development, Madam Walker assembled a talented and competent staff, including Freeman B. Ransom (Walker Company attorney and general manager for nearly forty years), Robert Lee Brokenburr (a graduate of Hampton College and Howard Law School and the first Black Indiana State senator), Alice Kelly (a former teacher at Eckstein Norton Institute, Madam Walker's private tutor, and Walker factory forewoman), and Marjorie Stewart Joyner (founder of Alpha Chi Pi Omega sorority and national principal of Walker Beauty Schools).

In the midst of Madam Walker's success, personal and business differences with her husband resulted in divorce, though she retained his name for the rest of her life.

Meanwhile, Walker's daughter, A'Lelia—convinced that the company needed a base in New York City—persuaded her mother to buy a townhouse in Harlem on 136th Street near Lenox Avenue. In a letter to Attorney Ransom, Madam Walker pronounced the building—with its living quarters, beauty salon, and Lelia College—"a monument. . . . There is

The significance of Madam C. J. Walker's life and career lies both in her innovative, and sometimes controversial, hair-care system and in her advocacy of Black women's independence and her creation of business opportunities for Black women. In 1919, the year Walker died, Mary McLeod Bethune called her "the greatest demonstration . . . of Negro woman's ability recorded in history." [A'Lelia Bundles]

nothing to equal it, not even on Fifth Avenue" (May 2, 1913).

After a dinner party there for board members of the National Equal Rights League, Ida B. Wells-Barnett wrote, "I was one of the skeptics that paid little heed to her predictions as to what she was going to do. To see her phenomenal rise made me take pride anew in Negro womanhood" (Duster 1970).

In 1912, A'Lelia Walker adopted thirteen-year-old Mae Bryant of Indianapolis. Initially Mae had run errands for the Walker women at company headquarters. After getting to know her, they decided Mae's long, thick hair would make her an excellent model for the Walker products, especially their "Wonderful Hair Grower." Mae's mother, Etta Bryant—persuaded that A'Lelia and Madam Walker would keep their promise to educate Mae—consented to their request to adopt her. (Mae later attended Spelman Seminary in Atlanta.)

From 1912 to 1916, Madam Walker crisscrossed the country and gave slide lectures promoting her business, as well as other Black institutions, at conventions held by Black religious, fraternal, and civic organizations. To expand her market internationally, she traveled to Jamaica, Cuba, Haiti, Costa Rica, and the Panama Canal.

Madam Walker's reputation as a philanthropist was solidified in 1911 when, in response to a massive national drive led by Jesse E. Moorland to build Young Men's Christian Associations in Black communities across the country, she contributed $1,000 to the building fund of the Indianapolis branch. This was the largest gift given to the effort by a Black woman.

In 1916, Madam Walker moved to Harlem, leaving the day-to-day management of her manufacturing operation in Indianapolis to Ransom, Kelly, and Brokenburr. Madam Walker's business philosophy stressed economic independence for women. "The girls and women of our race must not be afraid to take hold of business endeavor and . . . wring success out of a number of business opportunities that lie at their very doors. . . . I want to say to every Negro woman present, don't sit down and wait for the opportunities to come. . . . Get up and make them!" (National Negro Business League 1913).

Helping to create those opportunities, Walker hired former maids, farm laborers, housewives, and school teachers to fill jobs at all levels from factory worker to national sales agent. One satisfied agent wrote to her in 1913, "You have opened up a trade for hundreds of colored women to make an honest and profitable living where they make as much in one

week as a month's salary would bring from any other position that a colored woman can secure" (Wilson 1913). By 1916, the Walker Company claimed 20,000 agents—women and men—in the United States, Central America, and the Caribbean.

To foster cooperation among the agents and to protect them from competitors, Walker created a national organization called the Madam C. J. Walker Hair Culturists Union of America, which held annual conventions. She also organized the first federation of Black hair-care and cosmetics manufacturers.

When the United States entered World War I in the spring of 1917, Madam Walker was among those, like W.E.B. Du Bois and James Weldon Johnson, who—though with reservations and caveats—encouraged Black Americans to cooperate in the nation's war effort. Such a demonstration of loyalty, they believed, would be rewarded with long overdue equal rights. Madam Walker lent her name—by now widely known in both the Black and white communities—to the government's Black recruitment and war-bond drives.

However, after the bloody East St. Louis riot during the summer of 1917, Madam Walker joined the planning committee of the Negro Silent Protest Parade. The event drew some 30,000 Black New Yorkers, 10,000 of whom marched silently down Fifth Avenue on July 28 in a show of solidarity. Heartened by the response, Madam Walker, James Weldon Johnson, Harlem realtor John E. Nail, and *New York Age* publisher Fred Moore sought a meeting with President Woodrow Wilson to present a petition urging him to support legislation to make lynching a federal crime. When they arrived at the White House on August 1, Wilson claimed to be too busy to see them, dispatching his secretary, Joseph Tumulty, instead. Later that month, at the first annual Walker Hair Culturists' convention, Madam told the delegates, "This is the greatest country under the sun, but . . . we should protest until the American sense of justice is so aroused that such affairs as the East St. Louis riot be forever impossible" (Convention minutes 1917).

Realizing that her wealth gave her visibility and credibility, Walker became increasingly outspoken on political issues. In early 1918 she was the keynote speaker at several National Association for the Advancement of Colored People fund raisers for the antilynching effort throughout the Midwest and East. That summer she was honored at the NACW convention in Denver for having made the largest individual contribution to the effort to save the Anacostia home of abolitionist Frederick Douglass.

After the official opening of her Irvington-on-Hudson, New York, estate in August 1918, guest of honor Emmett J. Scott (former private secretary to Booker T. Washington and special assistant to the Secretary of War in Charge of Negro Affairs) wrote to her, "No such assemblage has ever gathered at the private home of any representative of our race, I am sure" (Scott 1918). During the weekend, she and her guests discussed the status of Black soldiers—especially Harlem's own Hellfighters of the 369th Regiment—and resolved to fight for the rights of returning Black veterans. Madam Walker was emphatic that they be granted full respect.

Scott's message, and the gathering of Black notables, especially delighted Madam Walker, who had intended her home not only as a showplace but also as a conference center for summits of race leaders. She thought of Villa Lewaro—designed by Black architect Vertner Woodson Tandy, named by opera singer Enrico Caruso, and located near the homes of industrialists Jay Gould and John D. Rockefeller—as a monument to inspire other African-Americans to pursue their own dreams.

During the spring of 1919, Madam Walker's long battle with hypertension exacted its toll. On Easter Sunday, while visiting friends and introducing a new line of products in St. Louis, she became so ill that she was rushed back to Irvington-on-Hudson in a private train car with her personal physician and a nurse.

Upon her return to Villa Lewaro she directed her attorney to donate $5,000 to the NAACP's antilynching campaign. News of the gift, announced a few days later by NACW president Mary B. Talbert at the group's antilynching conference at Manhattan's Carnegie Hall, brought a standing ovation from the 2,500 delegates.

During the final weeks of her life Madam Walker revamped her will, contributing thousands of dollars to Black schools, organizations, individuals, and institutions, including Mary McLeod Bethune's Daytona Normal and Industrial School, Lucy Laney's Haines Institute, Charlotte Hawkins Brown's Palmer Memorial Institute, Tuskegee Institute and numerous orphanages, retirement homes, YWCAs, and YMCAs in cities where she had lived.

When she died at age 51 on Sunday, May 25, 1919, at Villa Lewaro, she was widely considered the wealthiest Black woman in America and reputed to be the first Black American woman millionaire. In some references she is cited as the first self-made American woman millionaire.

Her daughter, A'Lelia Walker (1885-1931)—a central figure of the Harlem Renaissance—succeeded her as president of the Madam C. J. Walker Manufacturing Company.

Walker's significance lies as much in her innovative, and sometimes controversial, hair-care system as it does in her advocacy of Black women's economic independence and her creation of business opportunities at a time when most Black women were employed as servants and sharecroppers. Her entrepreneurial strategies and organizational skills revolutionized what has become a multibillion dollar Black hair-care and cosmetics industry. She was a trailblazer of Black philanthropy, using her wealth and influence to leverage social, political, and economic rights for women and Blacks.

Madam Walker's friend and colleague, Mary McLeod Bethune, called Walker's life "an unusual one." She was, Bethune said, "the clearest demonstration, I know, of Negro woman's ability recorded in history. She has gone, but her work still lives and shall live as an inspiration to not only her race but to the world" (Bethune 1919).

[See also BEAUTY CULTURE.]

BIBLIOGRAPHY

Bethune, Mary McLeod. Letter to A'Lelia Walker (June 13, 1919); Bundles, A'Lelia P. "Madam C. J. Walker—Cosmetics Tycoon," *Ms.* (July 1983), and "Madam C. J. Walker to Her Daughter A'Lelia Walker—The Last Letter," *Sage* (Fall 1984), and *Madam C. J. Walker—Entrepreneur* (1991), and "Sharing the Wealth: Madam Walker's Philanthropy," *Radcliffe Quarterly* (December 1991), and "A Letter to My Great-Great-Grandmother," *Radcliffe Quarterly* (December 1987); Duster, Alfreda, ed. *Crusade for Justice: The Autobiography of Ida B. Wells* (1970); Giddings, Paula. *When and Where I Enter* (1984); Hamilton, Charles V. and Jack Salzman, ed. *Encyclopedia of African-American Culture and History* (forthcoming); *Indianapolis Freeman*, "America's Foremost Colored Businesswoman" (December 28, 1912); *Indianapolis Recorder*, "Madam Walker Increases Line of Toilet Articles" (March 15, 1919); *Literary Digest*, "Queen of Gotham's Colored 400" (October 13, 1917); National Negro Business League. *Report of the Fourteenth Annual Convention*, Philadelphia (1913); National Negro Business League. *Report of the Thirteenth Annual Convention*, Chicago (1912); *New York Times Magazine*, "Wealthiest Negro Woman's Suburban Mansion" (November 4, 1917); Perry, Marion R. Interviews (December 1975, July 1982); Reynolds, Violet Davis. "A Remarkable Woman" (1973), and Interviews (December 1975, July 1982); Scott, Emmett. Letter to Madam Walker (September 8-9, 1918); *Textbook of the Madam C. J. Walker Schools of Beauty Culture* (1928); Walker Collection. Private collection, A'Lelia Perry Bundles; Wilson, Maggie. Letter to Madam Walker (October 1, 1913); Madam C. J. Walker papers. Indiana Historical Society, Indianapolis, Indiana.

A'LELIA PERRY BUNDLES

WALKER, MAGGIE LENA
(c. 1867-1934)

Maggie Lena Walker was always crystal clear about what she was trying to accomplish as executive head of the Independent Order of St. Luke, the organization she ran for thirty-five years and built to a membership of 100,000 in twenty-two states and the District of Columbia. She wanted to create businesses that would provide employment for Black Americans, particularly Black women, through cooperative effort and mutual support. As a vehicle for community education, the Order had, she said in 1913, "devoted itself to the teaching of the power of organization and the lesson of confidence" (*Proceedings* 1915). This spirit animated her career of public service, explains much about her personal style, and suggests why St. Luke's business enterprises, with one exception, enjoyed quiet, steady success when so many similar ones failed.

There is no official record of Maggie Lena Walker's birth. Standard sources state that she was born in Richmond, Virginia, on July 15, 1867. There is no reason to doubt the month and day, which is still celebrated in Richmond, but several lines of evidence suggest she was born two or three years before the date she used. In any case, she was a member of that remarkable generation born during or just after the Civil War. Her mother, Elizabeth Draper, worked for Elizabeth Van Lew, Richmond's famous spy for the Union. Her father, Eccles Cuthbert, was an Irish-born newspaperman who was a correspondent for the *New York Herald* for many years.

Elizabeth Draper married William Mitchell, the butler in the Van Lew house, on May 27, 1868. The little family moved to a house in College Alley just off Broad Street, close to William Mitchell's new job as a waiter in the St. Charles Hotel, at that time the city's most luxurious. Maggie's brother, John B., called Johnnie, was born in 1870. William Mitchell disappeared in February 1876, and after an intensive five-day search, his body was recovered from the James River. The coroner's report specifies suicide by drowning, but all other reports, including Maggie Walker's own, assume he was murdered.

The widowed Elizabeth Mitchell worked from her home as a laundress; of the few occupations available to Black women, this one was preferred by women with young children. The children, especially Maggie, picked up and delivered the clothes. As she later put it, "I was not born with a silver spoon in my mouth, but with a laundry basket practically on my head" (Independent Order of St. Luke 1917). Participation in her mother's work was itself an education because laundresses worked in groups rotating between houses and discussed possible solutions to community problems.

Maggie Mitchell and the Richmond public school system virtually grew up together. She attended a grammar school that had no bathrooms of any kind, but had, and had had almost from the beginning, an all-Black faculty who were outstanding community leaders. She completed her education at the Normal School, graduating in 1883, a member of a class of ten that made its mark locally, and through the Black press nationally, by demanding to use a public facility other than the Black church they were usually relegated to for their graduation ceremony. While they were unsuccessful in forcing desegregation of the Richmond Theater, where white high school graduations were held (they refused the balcony), they were considered heroic to face expulsion and their exercises were held at the school.

Right around the corner from the Mitchell home was the First African Baptist Church, the oldest and largest Black Baptist congregation in Richmond. Maggie Mitchell joined the Sunday school and was baptized during the Great Richmond Revival in the summer of 1878. The church, both in particular and in general, remained central to her life. Her speeches and diaries illustrate the depth of her religious commitment, and her wide-ranging knowledge of the Bible is a tribute to the thoroughness of her training. She was active in Baptist affairs, served on the boards of Hartshorn College, Virginia Union University, and the National Training School for Girls in Washington, D.C., and was an early member of Nannie Helen Burroughs's Women's Auxiliary of the National Baptist Convention.

After her graduation, Maggie Mitchell became a teacher, in the year the Readjuster political victory opened unprecedented, long overdue opportunities for Black professionals in the school system. Not only was there an influx of Black teachers, but there were some Black principals, all of whom were fired at the end of the year. She was assigned to Valley, her old elementary school, where she taught both primary

The daughter of a laundress who had at one time worked for Elizabeth Van Lew, Richmond, Virginia's famous Union spy, Maggie Lena Walker once said, "I was not born with a silver spoon in my mouth, but with a laundry basket practically on my head." [National Park Service]

and grammar grades for three years, starting at thirty-five dollars a month.

Her career ended, as was the rule, when she married Armstead Walker on September 14, 1886. Walker had graduated from Normal School in 1875, and he worked in his father's prosperous bricklaying and construction business, later forming a partnership with his brother. For ten years he also was a mail carrier, a coveted job. Although he was active in St. Luke affairs for some years, his participation beyond membership ceased when his wife became the Right Worthy Grand Secretary.

The Walkers had three sons: Russell Eccles Talmage in 1890, Armstead Mitchell in 1893 (who died in infancy, the same year her brother Johnnie died at age 23), and Melvin DeWitt in 1897. Another child, Margaret (Polly) Anderson, known after her marriage as Polly Payne, was adopted into the Walker household from a connection in Armstead's family in the early 1890s. She became the anchor who ran the

Taking over the meager assets of the Independent Order of St. Luke in 1899, Maggie Lena Walker transformed the society into a highly successful financial complex that greatly bolstered the Black community of Richmond, Virginia. [National Park Service]

house, cared for the Walker children as well as those of other St. Luke families while their mothers traveled, and in the end devoted herself to a severely disabled Maggie Walker. Elizabeth Mitchell, an active St. Luke member, lived with them until her death in 1922, working for many years as a midwife and "doctress."

While in Normal School, Maggie Mitchell had joined Good Idea Council No. 16 of the Independent Order of St. Luke, one of the myriad mutual aid societies in Richmond. These multipurpose organizations were so important in the life of the Black

community that people typically belonged to several for networking and insurance reasons, but usually concentrated their energies in one. Officers came and went annually, but despite periodic elections, the executive headship was typically for life. At this time the head of St. Luke was more interested in his other job as head of the Odd Fellows.

The nature of some societies was changing in the 1880s. One argument was over shifting the responsibility for caring for the sick and burying the dead from the local councils to a centrally administered system supported by special assessments from all of the society members when any member died. Ultimately, over the years, the industrial insurance principle of forwarding a small amount every week or month to a central office as a purchase of life insurance was adopted by almost all societies, and Black insurance companies formed in the 1890s. Richmond was at the forefront of these controversies and developments. Centralization, membership drives, increased income, and quickly accumulated capital to finance programs and investments transformed some societies into diversified businesses. The first organization to tread this path was Richmond's own True Reformers, who put their insurance policies in place in 1884, started their Rosebud children's division in 1885, founded what was arguably the first Black bank in 1888, and organized a regalia department, a real estate division, newspaper, hotel, and grocery store in quick succession in the 1890s.

Maggie Walker had been a delegate to several St. Luke conventions, Chief of Good Idea Council, and had held all the ritual positions. Also while she was teaching, she had worked as a collection agent and had had some business training. When she found that home and the social whirl were not enough for her talents, it was natural for her to turn to St. Luke. She started her career at the 1895 convention, when she submitted a resolution for the formation of a Juvenile Division with Circles, headed by Matrons, to be formed by each local council. With one stroke, women achieved a formal, innovative, commanding position. They created the Juvenile Department and a Council of Matrons. She was shortly elected Grand Matron, which she remained for life. A powerful vehicle of socialization into race pride, thrift, responsibility, and mutual caring, St. Luke's youth organization touched the lives of tens of thousands of children.

The next move was taken outside the formal St. Luke structure. Twenty-five Richmond councils formed a joint stock company called the St. Luke Association for the purpose of purchasing property on which to build a headquarters. Maggie Walker was secretary of the board. The association accomplished all its goals, raising money with bazaars and entertainments, and in 1903 building a three-story brick hall that it rented to the central organization, the Right Worthy Grand (RWG) Council. The building was important, not only as an office and headquarters for regalia and printing enterprises but also as meeting rooms, an auditorium, and a tremendous source of pride.

In addition to her organizational and leadership skills, Maggie Walker's dramatic talents and her love of ritual kept her in demand to run ceremonies. By the time it became obvious that St. Luke would not progress under its then executive head, who was more interested in his other job as head of the Odd Fellows, Walker was the 1899 convention's obvious choice as RWG Secretary. Taking over the meager assets, she and her associates went to work. They used charm and persuasion and an emphasis on building good will, harmony, and optimism to enforce a compulsory insurance plan, which meant added income. A big membership drive, the first of many that spread St. Luke into twenty-two states, got under way. She spoke everywhere, moving audiences to tears about disfranchisement, electrifying them with hope for co-operative enterprise, urging economic independence of the Black community from the white community and women from men, exhorting women to enter the business world and Black consumers to support Black enterprise. Her low, rich voice and storytelling style captivated people whether they agreed with her or not. Despite her emphasis on women, she always said St. Luke was a women's organization that gave equal opportunity to men, and many men were prominent activists. The development plan started with a newspaper, moved to a bank, then a store, and fantasized a factory.

Very few copies of the *St. Luke Herald* (f. 1902) survive. Always under the managing editorship of Lillian Payne, in the early years its editorials were written by the fiery lawyer James Hayes, an arch rival of John Mitchell, the editor of the *Richmond Planet*. The *Herald* was considerably more than a fraternal bulletin; it was outspoken on lynching, the position of Black women, the situation in Haiti, whatever the outrage of the day. The paper also gave rise to a profitable printing business.

Maggie Walker prepared to be a banker by spending a few hours a day for several months in the Merchants' National Bank of Richmond. When the St. Luke Penny Savings Bank opened in St. Luke Hall in 1903, she became arguably the first woman bank president in the United States, running the fourth

Black bank in Richmond. The bank grew slowly, and the constant selling job necessary to convince the St. Luke family and Richmond's Black community to trust the institution began.

About this time she bought a large house on Leigh Street that became the home for her large extended family. Her sons brought their brides there, and all the Walker grandchildren were born there. This house has been restored by the National Park Service as a national historic site, which gives the public an opportunity to experience something of her world. The library is particularly evocative. It holds over a thousand books, and the walls are covered with photographs of family, St. Luke notables, and other

When the St. Luke Penny Savings Bank opened in 1903, Maggie Lena Walker became the first woman bank president in the United States. When St. Luke's merged with two other banks to become the Consolidated Bank and Trust Company, Walker became chairman of the board of the only Black bank in Richmond. [Schomburg Center]

race leaders of all political persuasions. The last St. Luke project, the department store called the Emporium (1905-11), was the most symbolically crucial because it was to provide substantial employment for women, both in the store and on the board. Situated on Broad Street, Richmond's main thoroughfare, in a three-story building with an elevator, it struggled against overt white merchant pressure, and Black consumers' preference for the labels of Richmond's traditional stores. After a promising start, it lost more and more money each year, made up from St. Luke general revenues. Even after the insurance commissioner said the Emporium had to close, the St. Luke women were reluctant to surrender their dream.

Regulation drastically changed both the insurance and banking businesses. Too late to save True Reformers (whose empire collapsed in 1910), it forced St. Luke to restructure. Insurance policies had to be guaranteed by reserves, in each state, which meant capital had to be invested in secure bonds, not risky business enterprises. Every aspect of their activity was inspected. As Maggie Walker said, "The only secret we have left is our password." Insurance became the Order's major, very complex, business, and it did provide employment for many women clerks. In Walker's lifetime, St. Luke never missed a death payment.

To comply with the new law, the bank was separated from the Order, although the Order remained the major stock holder. Other Black banks failed in Richmond and two more were founded. When the latter weakened at the beginning of the Great Depression, St. Luke Bank and Trust was senior partner in two mergers that resulted in the Consolidated Bank and Trust Company headed by Emmett Burke, the original St. Luke cashier, with Maggie Walker as chairman of the board. As the sole Black bank in Richmond, the bank made a smooth transition after her death and flourishes today.

She entered the National Association of Colored Women (NACW) late (1912) but as a well-known achiever with the fascinating status of bank president. As chairman consecutively of the business, finance, and budget committees, she was a member of the executive committee until her death. She was part of Margaret Murray Washington's small group of prominent women who were invited to start the International Council of Women of the Darker Races. She served on the board of trustees of the Frederick Douglass Home. On the local level, she was an active member of Janie Porter Barrett's Virginia Federation of Colored Women's Clubs (f. 1907) and a staunch supporter

of their primary activity, founding and running an Industrial School for Colored Girls, with Barrett as superintendent, as an alternative to putting delinquent children in jail and thus onto chain gangs. She founded in 1912 and was lifelong president of Richmond's Council of Colored Women (CCW). The council raised $5,000 for the Industrial School and continued to support it and many other social service projects. When the school was taken over by the state, she continued on the board as the appointee of the governor.

Other activities of the CCW centered around the house they purchased at 00 Clay Street. It was a well-decorated facility where club affairs were held. It was rented to other groups, served as an office for an embattled National Association for the Advancement of Colored People (NAACP), was a canteen for Black servicemen during World War I, and was the site of a gala reception for the National Association of Colored Women women at the Richmond convention in 1922. When the Depression hit, and they could not keep up the payments, the St. Luke Bank auctioned it, bought it, and sold it to the city (at a profit) to become the first Black library in Richmond. This illustrates the levers of power Maggie Walker had accumulated. Today, 00 Clay Street houses the Black History Museum that opened in 1991.

She was one of the founders of Virginia's Negro Organization Society, which tried to bring every Black organization in the state into the fight for better health and education. As the interracial movement gained strength following World War I, she was on the board of the Community House for Colored People, which evolved into the Richmond branch of the Urban League. She was put on the State Interracial Commission. As always, her style was direct, confrontational when necessary, and impressively well informed. She and her associates formed the core of the local NAACP (f. 1917), but segregated southern branches found it difficult to be active except as fund-raisers. Her heart lay with the national organization, for which she served as a board member from 1923 to her death.

Other honors, in addition to those bestowed by St. Luke, were a Master's degree from Virginia Union University, and honorable mention in the 1927 Harmon Award for Distinguished Achievement competition in the business category. In 1921, she was chosen to run as Superintendent of Public Instruction on Virginia's Lily Black Republican ticket.

Her personal life was shattered in 1915 when her son Russell shot and killed his father while mistaking him for a burglar. He was indicted for murder and, after a traumatic trial that polarized the community, was acquitted. This tragic situation caused a serious challenge to her leadership, but she faced it down with style. Russell died in 1924, having worked in his father's construction business, at the bank, and in the Order. Melvin, who died a year after his mother, also spent his working life in St. Luke enterprises.

For reasons that are not clear, she began to lose the use of her legs in the late 1920s. In 1908, she had fractured her kneecap in a bad fall that left her with a limp, but the new condition was progressive. After several years of trips to Hot Springs, Arkansas, exercise regimens, and braces that constantly broke, one day, with characteristic decisiveness, she ordered an elevator for the house and sent her Packard to be customized to accommodate a wheel chair. During her last years of scarcely diminished activity, she was known as the Lame Lioness. She died of diabetic gangrene on December 15, 1934.

[See also THE MIDDLE CLASS; MUTUAL BENEFIT SOCIETIES.]

BIBLIOGRAPHY

Boyd [Leathers], Kim Q. "An Actress Born, a Diplomat Bred: Maggie L. Walker, Race Woman," Master's thesis (1987); Branch, Muriel and Dorothy Rice. *Miss Maggie: A Biography of Maggie Lena Walker* (1984); Brown, Elsa Barkley. "Womanist Consciousness: Maggie Lena Walker and the Independent Order of St. Luke," *Signs* (Spring 1989), and "Mothers of Mind," *Sage* (Summer 1989); Chandler, Sallie. "Maggie Lena Walker (1867-1934): An Abstract of Her Life and Activities," Master's thesis (1975); Dabney, Wendall P. *Maggie L. Walker and the I.O. of St. Luke: The Woman and Her Work* (1927); *DANB*; Daniel [St. Clair], Sadie. *Woman Builders* (1981); *Fiftieth Anniversary—Golden Jubilee: Historical Report of the R.W.G. Council, I.O. of St. Luke*. Independent Order of St. Luke (1917); Fleming, Jesse. "A History of Consolidated Bank and Trust Company (The Beginning of Black Banking in the United States)," Master's thesis (1972); Hammond, Lily Hardy. *In the Vanguard of a Race* (1922); Ovington, Mary White. *Portraits in Color* (1927); *Proceedings of the Annual Meetings, 1913-14.* Negro Organization Society (1915); *WWCA.* Manuscripts of speeches, diaries, personal papers, photographs, some oral histories, and a great deal of material about St. Luke activities (including several copies of the *St. Luke Herald*) are in the archives of the Maggie L. Walker National Historic Site, Richmond, Virginia.

GERTRUDE W. MARLOWE

WALKER, MARGARET ABIGAIL (1915-)

"I taught nearly forty years," says Margaret Walker, "and I taught my students that every person is a human being. Every human personality is sacred, potentially divine. Nobody is any more than that and nobody can be any less" (Smith 1991). This simple statement comes very close to encapsulating Walker's poetry.

Margaret Abigail Walker was born on July 7, 1915, in Birmingham, Alabama. Her father, Sigismund C. Walker, was a Methodist minister, a well-educated theologian who could speak five languages and read three more. Her mother, Marion Dozier Walker, was a music teacher who also had a college education. Because of her parents' love of learning, Walker grew up surrounded by music and books. Because of their passion for achievement, she was under constant pressure to excel. Her mother taught her to read by the time she was four years old. She finished elementary school at eleven, high school at fourteen, and college at nineteen. (She would have finished earlier, but she had to stay out a year.) Her father was determined that she complete a Ph.D. by twenty-one. "Luckily," as she later put it, "neither health nor finances would permit it" (Smith 1991).

Walker had begun writing poetry when she was eleven. Her family had moved to New Orleans, where her parents were both professors at New Orleans University. Walker attended Gilbert Academy and then enrolled at the university where her parents taught. When she was sixteen, Langston Hughes read his work at the school, and Walker approached him afterward with her own. He encouraged her to keep writing and to get out of the South.

At Northwestern University, where she did her undergraduate work, Walker again found encouragement. W.E.B. Du Bois published her poetry in *Crisis*, and E. B. Hungerford, her creative writing teacher, arranged for her to be admitted to the Northwestern chapter of the Poetry Society of America. After graduating, Walker lived in Chicago for several years. She joined the Federal Writers Project, which was funded by the Works Progress Administration (WPA). At the time, she did not realize how much less money she was receiving than the men in the project. She did realize that she was working with and enjoying the company of such writers as Gwendolyn Brooks, Arna Bontemps, and Richard Wright. Her exposure to life for Chicago's urban Black population proved to be an important ingredient in her writing.

When funding for the project stopped, Walker went to the University of Iowa to work on a Master's degree. While she was there, she completed her first book of poetry, *For My People* (1942). Its publication has been called one of the most important events in Black literary history. Not since Georgia Douglas Johnson had a Black woman published a book of poetry, and Walker was the first Black poet to be chosen for Yale University's Series of Younger Poets. *For My People* is a powerful work of poetic excellence. Written with strong rhythm and imagery, it presents a world of emotions that are both personal and mythic.

Poets, however, do not often support themselves through book sales. In the twentieth century, most of them look to academia for financial support. This was the avenue Walker chose. When she received her Master's degree, she went to teach, first at Livingstone College in Salisbury, North Carolina, and then at West Virginia State College. She also got married, to Firnist James Alexander, on June 13, 1943. In 1945, she went back to Livingstone for a year and then to Jackson State College, where she taught until 1979. She was also director of the college's Institute for the Study of the History, Life, and Culture of Black People, beginning in 1968.

Walker did not publish a book between 1942, when *For My People* appeared, and 1966, when her novel *Jubilee* and another book of poetry, *Ballad of the Free*, came out. She did, however, write poetry and essays. She received a Rosenwald Fellowship in 1944 and a Ford Fellowship in 1954. She completed work on her Ph.D. in creative writing at the University of Iowa in 1966, submitting *Jubilee* as her final creative work. She also had four children and supported her family financially because her husband was disabled.

Jubilee was well received, both critically and popularly. It was translated into six languages, was made into an opera, and is still in print. A fictionalized reconstruction of the life of Walker's great-grandmother, the book describes a woman who maintains her own positive spirituality in the face of tremendous oppression. Walker says that this aspect of the book, which has been criticized by those who see forgiveness as weakness, accurately portrays her great-grandmother, who "realized that hatred wasn't necessary and would have corroded her spiritual well-being" (Smith 1991).

Walker's third volume of poetry, *Prophets for a New Day*, was published in 1970. It is filled with reflections on the civil rights movement, tributes to its leaders, and poetic indictments of the racist world in which Black people live. In 1972, Walker published *How I Wrote Jubilee*, describing the thirty-year

process of writing that book and the obstacles that she and other women writers face. Eighteen years later, she published *Why I Wrote Jubilee*, a group of essays in which she reveals much of her anger and frustration about the lives of women, especially Black women.

Walker has written two other volumes of poetry, *October Journey* (1973) and *This Is My Century* (1989). She and poet Nikki Giovanni collaborated on the book *A Poetic Equation: Conversations between Nikki Giovanni and Margaret Walker* (1974). In *This Is My Century*, Walker's voice is that of an elder, one who teaches, heals, and admonishes. It is a rich and satisfying book in which wisdom is often cut with bitterness and frustration, but faith and humanity prevail. Walker is also the author of a biography, *Richard Wright, Daemonic Genius: A Portrait of the Man, a Critical Look at His Work* (1985).

Whether or not Margaret Walker has ever received the critical attention she deserves, there is another standard that anyone who has taught young people will recognize: the smudged and ragged pages of an often-read literary anthology. Margaret Walker belongs to an elite group of poets who qualify for this award.

BIBLIOGRAPHY

CBWA; *NA*; *NBAW*; Smith, Valerie. *African-American Writers* (1991); *WWBA* (1992).

KATHLEEN THOMPSON

WALLACE, SIPPIE (1898-1986)

Eminent blues artist Beulah ("Sippie") Wallace was born to George and Fanny Thomas on November 1, 1898, in Houston, Texas. Beulah was the fourth child of the religious couple who neither approved of nor indulged in the Saturday night house parties that spawned such blues notables as "Ragtime" Henry Thomas and Blind Lemon Jefferson. Although the Thomases did not live to see it, two of their sons, George Jr., and Hersal, and one of their daughters, Beulah, rose to stardom as a trio on the vaudeville circuit.

Beulah, nicknamed Sippie by her siblings, spent her preteen years singing and playing in the family church, Shiloh Baptist. Her musical career was encouraged by her older brother and sister, George, Jr., and Lillie. When George Jr. went to New Orleans to pursue his musical career in 1912, Sippie soon followed him there. In New Orleans she met and married

The great blues singer Sippie Wallace had a successful career in the 1920s, but the Depression stalled her progress. She made a comeback in the mid-1960s, when a new generation of blues enthusiasts discovered her mix of southwestern rolling honky-tonk and Chicago shouting moan. [Daphne Harrison]

Frank Seals; it was an unsuccessful marriage, which she later described as a mistake. Both of her parents had died when she returned home around 1918 to live with her siblings, but the stage-struck young woman could not forget her experiences in the Storyville District of New Orleans, where George's friends included King Oliver and the soon-to-be-famous Louis Armstrong.

Sippie Wallace began her road show career as maid and stage assistant to Madam Dante, a snakedancer with Philip's Reptile Show. With Madam Dante, Wallace traveled around Texas, where she soon gained a reputation as the "Texas Nightingale," singing with small bands at picnics, dances, and holiday celebrations. Later she began to sing in tent shows around the state and no longer needed to work as a maid.

Wallace's first recordings demonstrate her status as a mature, seasoned performer who had honed her craft. She owed a lot to her brother, George, who was a respected composer and music publisher when he sent for her to come to Chicago. George was on the recording staff of the music division of the W. W. Kimball Company as well as director of his own orchestra when Sippie, her niece, Hociel, and brother Hersal arrived in Chicago. Under George's influence, the three siblings formed a trio. Sippie and George developed their songwriting partnership to produce the popular songs "Shorty George" and "Underworld Blues," and the musically talented Thomases quickly became famous as recording artists. Sippie Wallace's first recordings, "Shorty George" and "Up the Country Blues" on the Okeh label, were very popular. "Shorty George" purportedly sold 100,000 copies, quite a feat for a newcomer.

Wallace's blues style was a mix of southwestern rolling honky-tonk and Chicago shouting moan, a seductive brew that fit her personality. She had a strong, smooth voice and good articulation that pushed the words straight forward. Her ability to shift moods with a song was a dimension missing in other singers. Her unorthodox sense of timing and accentuation of words gave her lyrics push and tension. Many of the ideas for her blues songs came as she mulled over her personal concerns. She repeatedly said about songwriting that she would be "thinking it over in my mind . . . and it would just come to me to make a song about what was troubling me."

Wallace's second marriage was to Houstonian Matthew ("Matt") Wallace, whose penchant for gambling created financial problems for the couple, problems Wallace wrote about in her 1926 release, "Jack o' Diamond Blues." Wallace was promoted as a recording artist in 1923 and 1924, and this enhanced her stage career as well. Soon she was a regular headliner on the Theater Owners Booking Association (TOBA) circuit, and Detroit replaced Chicago as home base for her, Matt, Hociel, and Hersal. The next few years were her peak years on the stage, but her success was at times overshadowed by great sorrow, as the three siblings who had been instrumental in her development as a singer died in close succession. In 1925, she was summoned to the bedside of her dying older sister, Lillie; then, in June 1926, her beloved Hersal died from a case of food poisoning at age sixteen; and, in 1928, George was run down by a streetcar in Chicago, bringing an end to the brilliant trio.

In 1929, Wallace was put under contract by Victor records. There she made four sides, but only two were issued, the popular "I'm a Mighty Tight Woman" and "You Gonna Need My Help." "Mighty Tight Woman," one of the few erotic blues tunes recorded by Wallace, demonstrated her superb vocal phrasing and her talent at the piano. Unfortunately,

her career greatly suffered during the Great Depression. Because she had not developed the versatility of style and the repertoire of an Edith Wilson or an Alberta Hunter, she could not find employment as a comedienne or sultry chanteuse. Wallace's stage bookings finally petered out, and by 1932 she had slipped into obscurity along with many of her singing sisters. Her husband, family, and church became the focal points of her life, as, for the next three decades, Wallace turned her song-writing and piano-playing abilities toward church music.

Sippie Wallace the blues singer might have remained in obscurity, except for an occasional club date in Detroit, had it not been for the issuance of two recordings. In 1945, Mercury Records issued her great recording "Bedroom Blues," which was excellent but did not sell well. Her next recording, on Detroit's Fine Arts Label in 1959, suffered the same fate, but it must have convinced her friend Victoria Spivey to keep urging her to come out of retirement and try the folk-blues festival circuit that was sweeping the country. As a result, Wallace went to Europe in 1966 and captivated a new, younger generation of blues enthusiasts. The Storyville recording of her Copenhagen performance demonstrated that the second coming of Sippie Wallace was long overdue. She presented new renditions of her old classics and introduced "Women Be Wise, Don't Advertise Yo' Man," the blues song that inspired a young white singer named Bonnie Raitt. One reviewer wrote, "Visiting Europe in 1966, Sippie Wallace astonished by the breadth of her singing and a delivery recalling Bessie Smith." In 1977, bathed in the spotlight of Lincoln Center's Avery Fisher Hall, Sippie Wallace, at eighty, could still evoke the deepest emotions as she sang the blues.

In numerous ways, Sippie Wallace was the archetypal woman blues singer—gutsy, yet tender; bereft, but not downtrodden; disappointed, yet hopeful; long on talent, short on funds; legendary, but not widely acclaimed; exploited, but not resentful; independent, yet vulnerable. Her life story is not resplendent with dramatic events that capture the imagination. Indeed, it might have been considered quite pedestrian had it not been for her musical talent, which did not save her from toil or drudgery or grief but did enable her to communicate her feelings about life's triumphs and disasters. Old age and crippling arthritis did not stop Wallace from singing the blues whenever and wherever she was called. In the spring of 1986, six months before her death, Wallace sang to an audience in Germany, "Women Be Wise, Don't Advertise Yo' Man."

BIBLIOGRAPHY

Chicago Defender (June 12, 1926; August 12, 1926); Harrison, Daphne DuVal. " 'Up Country . . .' and Still Singing the Blues: Sippie Wallace." In her *Black Pearls: Blues Queens of the 1920s* (1988); Kunstadt, Len. "The Comeback of Sippie Wallace," *Record Research* (January 1968); Price, Sammy. Personal interview (April 1977); *Talking Machine World* (May 15, 1925); Wallace, Sippie. Personal interview (January 24, 1975).

DISCOGRAPHY

For a discography, see O'Neal, Jim. "Sippie Wallace Discography," *Goldmine* (November 1982).

DAPHNE DUVAL HARRISON

WARD, CLARA (1924-1973), AND THE WARD SINGERS

The famous Ward Singers were the finest group during gospel's golden age, the period from 1945 to 1960, and Clara Ward was one of the supreme gospel talents: arranger, composer, pianist, and group leader. Her vocal style was closely echoed by Aretha Franklin; similarly the stylistic mannerisms of her star soloist, Marion Williams, inspired Little Richard. Traces of the Ward Singers can be detected in popular and gospel music, twenty years after Ward's death.

The group was formed by Gertrude Murphy Ward (1901-1983), a native of South Carolina who, with her husband, George, had moved to Philadelphia, where her daughters, Willia (1921-) and Clara (1924-1973), were born. In 1931, while working in a local dry-cleaning establishment, Gertrude Ward felt herself summoned to "sing the gospel and help save dying men." She became an early exponent of the gospel style pioneered by Thomas A. Dorsey and Sallie Martin, and she formed a trio with her daughters; eventually Clara became both the piano accompanist and the star attraction. By the late 1930s, the group was touring the South during summer vacation.

In 1943, the trio made a triumphant debut at the National Baptist Convention, and by that time Clara had become a remarkable soloist. However, although she became a mistress of the newest gospel sounds, she tended to favor the traditional hymns and the moans of Dr. Watts. Her inspiration was Mary Johnson Davis, the most audacious of the early gospel divas. Davis, a Pittsburgh soprano, specialized in melisma, the elaborate spinning out of syllables, also known as "slurs" or "flowers and frills," and she had

an equally strong impact on Mahalia Jackson's early career. Clara also learned from Roberta Martin, the supreme gospel pianist and founder of the premier group, the Roberta Martin Singers of Chicago. Clara toured a few times as a Martin Singer, and in 1946 Roberta presented her and Delois Barrett Campbell, the Martin Singers' soprano, in a dual concert. Five years later the Ward group returned and packed Chicago's churches for five straight weeks.

In 1946, Gertrude Ward began recruiting other members, and for the next decade she signed an unparalleled array of talent. The first was Henrietta Waddy (1901-1981), another South Carolina native who performed in traditional church fashion, albeit with great charm and showmanship. Others included stylists of Clara Ward's calibre. The most famous was Marion Williams, lead singer of the group's greatest hits, but others included Martha Bass, a St. Louis contralto with the immense, bluesy authority of her mentor, Willie Mae Ford Smith; Thelma Jackson, a powerful mezzo-soprano; Frances Steadman, a debonair contralto who recalled her twin inspirations, Roberta Martin and Billie Holiday; Kitty Parham, a flamboyant performer in the style of Dorothy Love Coates; Gloria Griffin, later a soloist with the Roberta Martin group; and Ethel Gilbert, a pianist, soloist, and evangelist who generally was considered to be the most spiritual member of the group.

Beginning in 1948, the Wards made a series of classic records, most of them led by Marion Williams, including "Surely God Is Able," "I'm Climbing Higher and Higher," and "Packin' Up." Under her own name Clara recorded an equally distinguished repertory, including new compositions such as, "How I Got Over" and "Come in the Room," and traditional hymns. Her finest solos, "The Day Is Past and Gone," "The Fountain," and "Precious Lord," were later duplicated, virtually note for note, in Aretha Franklin's first recording session. The Wards were not merely celebrated for their musicianship, however. Fierce competition required heavy doses of religious drama, and they became preeminent church-wreckers. If Marion Williams did not "shout" the people with her rockers, Clara would perform a hymn; if all else failed, Madame Gertrude Ward (as she had become known) would start up a congregational number. The Wards also specialized in flamboyant wardrobes and hairstyles, which may have diverted attention from their musical excellence. In any case, people often turned out simply to see their costumes.

Madame Ward became a leading gospel promoter, and her Cavalcades, featuring the best-selling groups and quartets, drew astonishing crowds, up to 25,000 at a time. She also was an imperious taskmaster, however, and notoriously stingy. In 1958, Marion Williams, Frances Steadman, Kitty Parham, and Henrietta Waddy quit and formed their own group, the Stars of Faith (under Steadman's leadership, the group still performs, appearing mostly in Europe). "It's a sit-down strike!" complained Madame Ward, the aggrieved gospel capitalist (*Jet* 1958). She recruited new members—the most gifted were Jessie Tucker, a wide-ranging soprano from Atlanta, and Christine Jackson, a Florida native reminiscent of Marion Williams—but the old magic was gone.

The group shifted gears; calling themselves the Clara Ward Singers, they entered the secular arena and greatly magnified their patented flamboyance. In their glittering robes and outlandish hairdos, the new group became a star attraction in Las Vegas, where their club repertoire was restricted to pop-gospel, spirituals, and inspirational ballads. During this time they moved from Philadelphia to Los Angeles. The members included Vermettya Royster (Jacksonville, Florida), Voyla Crowley (Columbus, Ohio), soprano Mildred Means (Detroit), soprano Agnes Jackson (St. Louis), Geraldine Jones (Tampa, Florida), Mavelyn Simpson (Baltimore), and Alice Houston (Oakland, California). This group continues to perform under the leadership of Madeleine Thompson, a Philadelphia native who first heard the originals when she was a schoolgirl. In 1991, they released an album comprising the Wards' biggest hits. Other albums include *The Best of the Ward Singers, Clara Ward Memorial Album, Gospel Warriors, The Gospel Sound,* and *The Great Gospel Women.*

Clara Ward adjusted to show business, but her heart remained with the Baptist hymns. "That's all I like to sing," she once told an interviewer; everything else was just a job. Clara recorded a few more hymns before her untimely death in 1973, a tragic event that prompted Gertrude Ward's last attempt at spectacle. There were two funerals, one in Los Angeles, where Marion Williams recreated "Surely God Is Able," and another in Philadelphia, which was graced by Clara's idol, Mary Johnson Davis, and her prize student, Aretha Franklin. After that Madame Ward mostly kept to herself. Occasionally she toured with Clara's group, reminding folk that "before there was a Clara Ward, I was telling the world it's a God somewhere." Whenever singers or friends would visit, she would insist on taking them to the cemetery where Clara lay buried "with all the stars." She outlived her daughter by one decade, dying in 1983.

[*See also* GOSPEL MUSIC.]

BIBLIOGRAPHY

Heilbut, Anthony. *The Gospel Sound: Good News and Bad Times* (1985); *Jet* (August 1958).

ANTHONY HEILBUT

WARING, LAURA WHEELER (1887-1948)

Laura Wheeler Waring, painter and educator, was acknowledged as a significant artist during her lifetime and continues to be appreciated today for her technical skill and imagination. Although best known for portraits, she also produced highly original landscapes and other important paintings.

Painter and educator Laura Wheeler Waring was acknowledged as a significant artist during her lifetime and continues to be appreciated today for her technical skill and imagination. [Moorland-Spingarn]

Born in 1887 in Hartford, Connecticut, Laura Wheeler grew up with the advantages available to the Black upper-class of the time. She showed promise as an artist early in her life and, after graduating from high school, chose to study at the Pennsylvania Academy of Fine Arts in Philadelphia, where she remained for six years. In 1914, she received a scholarship that allowed her to pursue her artistic interests in Europe, where she spent a large part of her time at the Louvre. These studies were interrupted by the outbreak of World War I, and Wheeler returned to the United States where, soon afterward, she was asked to direct the art and music departments at Cheyney Training School for Teachers in Philadelphia. Although her work at Cheyney was interrupted by two more trips to Europe for study and for exhibition of her work, she continued to teach there for thirty years.

After her second European trip, Wheeler's reputation as an artist grew rapidly. Her work began to be shown at major American galleries, including the Philadelphia Museum of Art, the Corcoran Gallery in Washington, D.C., and the Art Institute of Chicago. During her third European trip, Wheeler, who was now Laura Wheeler Waring, and married to Professor Walter E. Waring of Lincoln University, exhibited her work at the notable Galerie du Luxembourg.

Many of Waring's most famous paintings are portraits of celebrated figures, such as W.E.B. Du Bois, James Weldon Johnson, and Marian Anderson. Others are considered socially significant; for example, *Mother and Daughter* depicts a mixed-race woman and her child. Late in her life, Waring produced a series of paintings, including *Jacob's Ladder* and *The Coming of the Lord*, interpreting various Negro spirituals.

Waring died, after a long illness, on February 3, 1948.

BIBLIOGRAPHY
CBWA; DANB; NA; NBAW.

JAN GLEITER

WARRICK, META VAUX
see
FULLER, META VAUX WARRICK

WARWICK, DIONNE (1940-)

Born Marie Dionne Warrick on December 12, 1940, to Mancel and Lee Warrick, Warwick grew up

Twice in a lifetime, Dionne Warwick has risen to the top as a singer of popular music. Now, her Warwick Foundation raises millions to fight AIDS. [Schomburg Center]

in East Orange, New Jersey, singing in the Methodist church in which her parents were active members. Her mother was business manager for a well-known gospel group, the Drinkard Singers, and as a child, Warwick often served as a replacement singer. By the time she was fourteen, when she formed her own group with her sister, Dee Dee, and a cousin, Cissy Houston, she was an experienced entertainer. The group, called the Gospelaires, sang backup for such performers as the Drifters and Sam "the Man" Taylor on the stage of the Apollo Theatre and in New York recording studios.

Warwick left the group to attend Hartt College of Music at the University of Hartford in West Hartford, Connecticut, on a four-year scholarship to study music education. However, during summer vacation recording sessions with the Gospelaires, composer Burt Bacharach heard her. She was wearing jeans and pigtails and singing louder—and better—than anyone else. The composer and his lyricist partner, Hal David, asked Warwick to make demonstration records for them. They then promoted the demos to record companies and, in 1962, were offered a contract by Scepter Records. (Marie Dionne Warrick became Dionne Warwick because Scepter misspelled her name on the record label.) Their first single, "Don't Make Me Over," was a hit, as were thirty others by the trio that, for most of the 1960s and early 1970s, could do no wrong.

In the mid-1960s, *Time* magazine called Warwick "the best new female pop-jazz-gospel-rhythm-and-blues singer performing today." She collected many Grammy awards and gold and platinum records and was one of the strongest Black women in the entertainment business. She had a sense of who she was and how she should be treated, but when she found out, in 1972, that the partnership of Bacharach and David had split up by reading it in the papers, she was devastated. "I thought I was their friend," she told *Rolling Stone*, "but I was wrong. They didn't care about Dionne Warwick" (Holden 1979). She sued the pair for breach of contract. Then, less than three years after the Bacharach-David breakup, Warwick's eight-year marriage to Bill Elliot, father of her sons, David and Damion, ended in divorce. In 1977, her father died unexpectedly, and the next day, her mother suffered a serious stroke. To make matters worse, the woman who was accustomed to having two or three hits a year had only three hits in half a decade, between 1972 and 1979.

Then she changed record labels. Her first album with Arista, *Dionne*, produced by Barry Manilow, went platinum. One single from the album, "I'll Never Love This Way Again," went gold and hit the top five. Since then, Warwick has had a half dozen successful albums with Arista.

During the 1980s, Warwick began to become involved with political and social issues. In 1985, she was one of the performers of the song "We Are the World," recorded to benefit hunger relief in Africa. In that same year, she recorded "That's What Friends Are For" with her friends Stevie Wonder, Gladys Knight, and Elton John and donated the proceeds to the American Foundation for AIDS Research. The song was written by Burt Bacharach, with whom she had reconciled, and his wife, Carole Bayer Sager. It raised more than $1.5 million. In 1986, she won the Entertainer of the Year Award at the nineteenth annual Image Awards sponsored by the National

Association for the Advancement of Colored People (NAACP). In 1987, she announced the first of a series of concerts with friends to further benefit acquired immune deficiency syndrome (AIDS) research and education and has established the Warwick Foundation to help fight the disease.

Dionne Warwick has never been easy to label, but she is a force in contemporary music and a strong presence in the public consciousness. "Talent will prevail," she says of herself. "Nobody, bar none, can do what Dionne Warwick does" (Wiseman 1979). So far, she's right.

BIBLIOGRAPHY

BAFT; *CBWA*; Holden, Stephen. "Dionne Warwick Makes Herself Over," *Rolling Stone* (November 15, 1979); Hunt, Dennis. "Dionne Warwick Speaks Out for Strong Black Women," *Ebony* (May 1983); *Jet*, "Dionne Warwick Organizing AIDS Fund-Raiser in D.C.; Cited By Reagan and Barry" (October 12, 1987), and "Dionne Warwick Is Named NAACP Entertainer of the Year" (December 15, 1986); Lamanna, Dean. "A New High Note for Dionne Warwick," *Ladies' Home Journal* (June 1990); *NBAW*; Smith, Mary. "Dionne the Universal Warwick," *Ebony* (May 1968); *Time*, "Spreading the Faith" (July 14, 1967); Wiseman, Rich. "Dionne Warwick Knew the Way to San Jose But Not Out of a Five-Year Slump—Until Now," *People Weekly* (October 15, 1979); *WWBA* (1992).

KATHLEEN THOMPSON

WASHINGTON, BOOKER T.

Like his positions on many important issues of the day, Booker T. Washington's views on the gender roles of, and education for, Black women also were ambiguous. In his autobiography *Up from Slavery* (1901), he indicated that he did not oppose higher education for women. Two of his three wives, Olivia Davidson and Margaret Murray, and his daughter Portia, had received some college education. Yet he asserted that educated young women were knowledgeable about too many subjects that had no relevance to housekeeping. Curriculum at Tuskegee Institute focused on manual training and domestic economy and was gender-specific. Girls were expected to excel at what were termed "the household arts"—cooking, washing, sewing, and dressmaking—while boys were expected to become experts in agriculture and the trades.

Booker T. Washington was born in 1856 to a slave mother who undoubtedly influenced his ideas about women. It was, however, a white woman, Mrs.

Lewis Ruffner, who probably encouraged his lifelong devotion to the values of thrift, morality, and cleanliness for both sexes, when Washington worked for her as her houseboy. When he founded Tuskegee Normal and Industrial Institute in 1881, Washington modeled it after Hampton Institute, where he received his formal education from 1872 to 1875.

Washington had to defend his educational policy when he received scores of letters annually from wealthy white employers soliciting young Black women as cooks, maids, and washerwomen. He argued that Tuskegee girls would go into their communities as homemakers and role models for other Black women. Strict codes of discipline were enacted for all, but especially for girls, who were chaperoned by a female teacher when they left the campus. Washington permitted dancing classes for girls only, because Jane Addams found that dancing benefited the carriage and appearance of her charges at Hull House. Male students were not permitted to dance. Ruth Anna Fisher, who later became an accomplished editor and historian, came to Tuskegee in 1906 after graduating from Oberlin College but lasted only two months because of the stifling atmosphere of the school.

Atlanta University-educated Adella Hunt Logan also found life at Tuskegee confining. A teacher of domestic science, she and her husband, Warren, who served as the Institute's treasurer, lived next door to the Washingtons. In defiance of Booker T. Washington, Adella Hunt Logan worked ardently on behalf of woman suffrage. So light-skinned that she was able to join white women's suffrage groups, in 1901 Logan was the only life member of the National American Woman Suffrage Association from Alabama. She wrote on suffrage for Black periodicals; in 1912, the National Association for the Advancement of Colored People's *Crisis* carried articles by her and Mary Church Terrell, who also caused Washington trouble. Logan was so conflicted by her defiance of Washington that she had a nervous breakdown and committed suicide after his death.

Mary Church Terrell was a political pragmatist in her relations with Booker T. Washington. Willful, well educated, and a promoter of higher education for Black women, Terrell was often critical of Washington because he catered to white racism and did not stand up for the race. Her husband, Robert H. Terrell, was appointed judge in the District of Columbia in 1910, largely as a result of Washington's influence, and this tempered her criticisms. Ironically, in advertisements promoting her lectures, Mary Church Terrell was referred to as the "female Booker T. Washington," because of her oratorical skills.

Washington's views on women's roles and education greatly influenced early Black clubwomen, who promoted the teaching of domestic science in their local communities to develop values of efficiency, cleanliness, thrift, and morality. Not only in rural areas but also in urban communities, Black women in charge of social welfare centers accepted Washington's views on childcare, manual training, cooking, and dressmaking. Through her work in women's clubs, Washington's third wife, Margaret Murray Washington, promoted her husband's views about women's education and gender roles.

Margaret Murray came to Tuskegee in 1889 as Dean of Women and Head of Women's Industries and married Booker T. Washington in 1895. Apparently she had little influence on Washington's views on the larger society in general, and race relations in particular, but played a major role in Tuskegee affairs. She was a member of the school's executive council and was one of its chief divisional officers. In 1895 she founded the Tuskegee Woman's Club, and in 1896 she became president of the National Federation of Afro-American Women, one of the regional groups that formed the National Association of Colored Women (NACW) in 1897. She was president of the Alabama State Federation and was twice elected president of the NACW.

Margaret Murray Washington extended the educational and home economics role of Tuskegee Institute to Macon County to improve Black home life. As her husband had promoted the three B's—Bible, broom, and bath—at Tuskegee, she took them to rural Alabama. In 1898 she opened the Russell plantation school, close to the Institute, and adapted methods used by settlement houses in the urban north. The plantation school aimed to improve farmers' efficiency and encourage land ownership. Over fifty families with 112 children participated. Margaret Murray Washington also did missionary work at Black schools and plantation settlements in Macon County, founded Tuskegee Mothers' Clubs, and advocated rural health care clubs. Like her husband, she favored and promoted temperance. It was also during her administration that the NACW formed the Colored Women's Kindergarten Association. For many years the NACW's newsletter, *National Notes*, was printed by Tuskegee students under Margaret Murray Washington's supervision. Some clubwomen argued that this was why articles critical of Booker T. Washington and his policies never appeared there.

Through her work in Black women's clubs, Margaret Murray Washington advanced her husband's views. Like him, she did not support woman's suffrage. While Booker T. Washington publicly counseled Blacks that the vote was not important, he and most of the other men at Tuskegee voted, and privately, he contributed funds to support campaigns to reclaim Black male suffrage in the South. After her husband's death in 1915, Margaret Murray Washington continued to promote his accommodationist views through her club work and later, in 1921, founded the International Council of Women of the Darker Races.

[*See also* NATIONAL NEGRO HEALTH WEEK.]

BIBLIOGRAPHY
Harlan, Louis, et al., eds. *The Papers of Booker T. Washington* (1972-1984); Harlan, Louis. *Booker T. Washington: The Making of a Black Leader, 1856-1901* (1972), and *Booker T. Washington: The Wizard of Tuskegee 1901-1915* (1983); Rouse, Jacqueline Anne. *Lugenia Burns Hope: Black Southern Reformer* (1989); Salem, Dorothy. *To Better Our World: Black Women in Organized Reform, 1890-1920* (1990).

JACQUELINE GOGGIN

During her sixteen years with Mercury Records, Dinah Washington had forty-six hits on Billboard's *Rhythm and Blues charts, including "What a Diff'rence a Day Makes" and "Baby, You've Got What It Takes." She also helped build the careers of many other entertainers, such as Slappy White, Redd Foxx, Johnny Mathis, Lola Falana, Leslie Uggams, Patti Austin, and Quincy Jones. [Schomburg Center]*

WASHINGTON, DINAH (1924-1963)

Known as "Queen of the Blues," Dinah Washington, née Ruth Lee Jones, was one of four children born to Alice Jones in Tuscaloosa, Alabama. Like many other Black families at that time, they moved to Chicago in 1928. Although they were financially burdened, the Jones family shared a musical talent that provided them with some monetary relief. In addition to domestic work, Alice Jones played piano at St. Luke's Baptist Church for extra money. She taught Ruth to play the piano, and while still in elementary school, Ruth was singing and playing solos at the church. She was so popular that her mother formed a singing group with her to tour the country, giving recitals in Black churches.

Still known as Ruth Jones, she made little money singing gospel in churches. The family lived in poverty, a condition that left her bitter for years. She became intrigued with the secular music that was becoming popular in Chicago. She soon began to idolize Billie Holiday and sing popular songs, much to her mother's displeasure. At fifteen she won an amateur contest at Chicago's Regal Theater by singing "I Can't Face the Music." She then performed, without her mother's knowledge, at various local night clubs, using a different name so that her mother would not find out.

In 1940, Ruth Jones was discovered by Sallie Martin, one of the foremost figures in gospel music. Martin placed her in the first all-woman gospel group, the Sallie Martin Colored Ladies Quartet, with whom she performed for about three years. Still unable to earn a sufficient income, Ruth left Sallie Martin to perform in nightclubs on Chicago's South Side. During this time she met John Young, who became her agent and the first of seven men she married. The others were George Jenkins, Robert Grayson, Walter Buchanan, Eddie Chamblee, Rafael Campos, and Dick "Night Train" Lane.

Contrary to popular belief, it was not Lionel Hampton who changed her name from Ruth Jones to Dinah Washington. Washington herself stated that the change occurred in 1942 while she was singing at the Garrick Lounge in Chicago. She credits Joe Sherman, the club's manager, with changing her name for billing and promotional purposes. She did, however, tour with Hampton's orchestra as the featured vocalist from 1942 to 1945, leaving because of contractual and monetary disputes with Hampton. According to legend, she had to use a gun to persuade Hampton to release her from her contract.

As a soloist, Washington first recorded in December 1945 for Apollo Records, an independent company that had no relationship to the Apollo Theater. She recorded blues songs such as "Wise Woman Blues," "My Lovin' Papa," and "Mellow Mama Blues." In early 1946, she was approached by Ben Bart of Mercury Records, who offered her an exclusive recording contract. This was the beginning of Washington's career as a major popular vocalist, acquiring such accolades as "the poor man's Lena Horne" and "Queen of the Blues." During her sixteen-year tenure at Mercury, she placed forty-five songs on *Billboard*'s Rhythm and Blues charts including "Am I Asking Too Much," "Baby, Get Lost," "What a Diff'rence a Day Makes," and "This Bitter Earth." Her biggest hit with the label was "Baby, You've Got What It Takes," a duet she recorded with Brook Benton in 1960. Many of her hits were recorded with leading musicians like Count Basie, Dizzy Gillespie, and Mitch Miller.

Although she was infamous for having a volatile temper, Washington was also known to shower her close friends and associates with lavish gifts. She gave free concerts in the Black community; financially supported Martin Luther King, Jr.'s activities during the civil rights movement; and unselfishly helped build the careers of many now-famous entertainers like Slappy White, Redd Foxx, Johnny Mathis, Lola Falana, Leslie Uggams, Patti Austin, and Quincy Jones.

In spite of being called "Queen of the Blues," Washington's repertoire was not confined to the blues genre. In fact, she once said in an interview that she did not consider herself a blues singer but rather "a pop singer with conviction" (Maher 1957). Washington recorded many pop songs and covers of hits by white singers such as "Harbor Lights," "Pennies from Heaven," and "September in the Rain," but Mercury continued to market her solely as a rhythm and blues vocalist.

Unhappy with Mercury's promotional activities, Washington left Mercury for Roulette Records in 1961 but was unable to duplicate her previous success. It was during this time that her financial status declined and her health began to deteriorate from years of touring. Overweight for most of her career, she also taxed her health by taking diet and sleeping pills, mercury shots, and drinking heavily. In 1963, while making plans for a huge Christmas party at her Detroit home, Washington was found dead from an accidental overdose of sleeping pills.

Because of her immense popularity and unique vocal quality, many singers, including Della Reese, claim to have been directly influenced by Dinah Washington. Many of her songs have been remade by other vocalists and most of her original recordings are still available to the public.

BIBLIOGRAPHY

Haskins, Jim. *Queen of the Blues: A Biography of Dinah Washington* (1987); Hepburn, Dave. "The Stranger on This Earth," *New York Amsterdam News* (December 21, 1963); Maher, Jack. "I'm No Blues Singer Says Dinah Washington," *Metronome Music USA* (April 1957); Whitburn, Joel. *Joel Whitburn's Top R & B Singles, 1942-1988* (1988).

DISCOGRAPHY

For a discography, see Haskins, James. *Queen of the Blues* (1987).

FRANK WILLIAM JOHNSON

WASHINGTON, FREDI (1903-)

Fredi Washington (Fredericka Carolyn Washington), an actress, writer, dancer, and singer, was born in Savannah, Georgia, on December 23, 1903. Her education began in Cornwells Heights, Pennsylvania, at St. Elizabeth Convent. She then attended the Egri School of Dramatic Writing and the Christopher School of Languages, where she pursued her early interests in civil rights, casting, writing, dancing, and singing.

Her career began as a dancer in nightclub engagements. From 1922 to 1926, she toured with one of America's first musicals, *Shuffle Along*, written by Flournoy E. Miller and Aubrey Lyles, with music by Noble Sissle and Eubie Blake. Following this landmark production, she adopted the stage name Edith Warren and was cast as the lead in *Black Boy* (1926) with Paul Robeson. It was difficult to find work in New York, so she toured Europe as a dancer. The talented Florence Mills and Josephine Baker had already begun to pave the way for other African-Americans in Europe. Some of her European engagements included Gaumont Palace and Chateau Madrid (Paris); Casino (Nice); Green Park Hotel (London); Casino (Ostend), Trocadero and Floria Palast (Berlin); Barberina Cafe (Dresden); and Alkazar (Hamburg). She was cast in *Sweet Chariot* (1930) in New York, followed by *Singin' the Blues* (1931) and *Run, Little Chillun* (1933). She had also started a film career between stage performances and appeared in *Black*

Fredi Washington's performance in Imitation of Life, *as a young Black woman who passes for white, was so powerful that it caused her problems in real life. In spite of her strong commitment to the Black movement for equality, she was often thought of as a woman who denied her heritage. [Donald Bogle]*

and Tan Fantasy (1929), an all-Black musical short with Duke Ellington, *The Old Man and the Mountain*, and *The Emperor Jones* (1933). Yet the stage was her first love. When she appeared in *Mamba's Daughters*, *New York Times* critic Brooks Atkinson wrote that Fredi Washington "beautifully plays the part of Hagar's talented granddaughter . . . with intelligence as well as charm" (January 4, 1939).

One of her primary concerns was the relationships that existed between Black and white women. She brought to the screen a new conception of African-American women in general. This was best exemplified in her role as the mulatto daughter who passed for white in the movie *Imitation of Life* (1934). Thematically, the film was probably the first Hollywood attempt to portray the struggles of racially different women with similar financial woes. Claudette Colbert and Louise Beavers are both single heads of households; both have daughters; and both are determined to keep a roof over their heads. The association of these two women during America's Depression occurs through domestic employment: the mistress (Miss Bea, played by Colbert) and the maid (Delilah, played by Beavers). Washington's performance as the daughter (Peola) and that of Beavers as the mother who helps a white employer become rich by teaching her how to fry griddle cakes were two of the finest of the time. The story was wrought with melodrama, but when Washington and Beavers were paired in their one-on-one scenes, the film's power was said to "transform Hollywood trash into something unique and often powerful" (Cripps 1977). So convincing was Washington's portrayal of the tragic mulatto, many African-Americans believed Fredi Washington in real life must have been anti-Black. Friends like Bobby Short and her sister's husband, Congressman Adam Clayton Powell, Jr., said Washington never hid behind the lightness of her complexion.

Washington's commitment to equal rights was as strong as her commitment to her craft as a performer. She was one of the founders of the Negro Actors Guild and was the guild's first executive secretary in 1937-38; she was theater editor and columnist for the *People's Voice* (a New York weekly published by Adam Clayton Powell, Jr.), administrative secretary for the Joint Actors Equity-Theatre League Committee on Hotel Accommodations for Negro Actors throughout the United States, and the registrar for the Howard da Silva School of Acting.

Washington also performed on the radio and television program *The Goldbergs*, a comedy series about a Jewish immigrant family, in addition to performing in specials for National Urban League on

CBS. After her major film performance in *Imitation of Life*, she appeared in *Drums of the Jungle* (1935) and *One Mile from Heaven* (1937). She was casting consultant for the screen version of *Cry, the Beloved Country* (1952) and for the stage productions of *Carmen Jones* and *Porgy and Bess* (1943). Washington appeared in stage productions of *Lysistrata* (1946), *A Long Way from Home* (1948), and *How Long till Summer* (1949).

Fredi Washington believed in performance excellence and human rights. She believed in herself and her heritage as an African-American and never denied who or what she was. She believed in giving her best unselfishly to make room for others. She was inducted into the Black Filmmakers Hall of Fame in Oakland, California, in 1975. She is the sister of Isabel Washington, former actress, singer, and first wife of Congressman Adam Clayton Powell, Jr. In 1933, Fredi Washington married Lawrence Brown, a trombonist with the Duke Ellington band. They were married for fifteen years. In 1952, she remarried, to Anthony Bell, a Connecticut dentist.

BIBLIOGRAPHY
Bell, Fredericka Washington. Papers, Schomburg Center for Research in Black Culture, New York; Cripps, Thomas. *Slow Fade to Black* (1977); Kauser, Ernest, Otto Lindenmeyer, and Harry Ploski. "The Black Performers in Film." In *RLBA*; Kellner, Bruce, ed. *The Harlem Renaissance: A Historical Dictionary for the Era* (1984); Mapp, Edward. *Directory of Blacks in the Performing Arts* (1978); Sampson, Henry. *Blacks in Blackface* (1980).

BEVERLY J. ROBINSON

WASHINGTON, GEORGIA E. L. PATTON (1864-1900)

Georgia Patton was the first Black woman in Tennessee to be licensed to practice medicine for surgery. Born in Grundy County, Tennessee, in 1864, she graduated from Central Tennessee College in Nashville in 1890 and in 1893 was the first woman to receive a medical degree from Meharry Medical College.

On May 5, 1893, Patton sailed for Liberia as a self-supporting medical missionary. In 1894 she wrote:

> For the first few days after my arrival, the surroundings looked very discouraging for my professional work. On examining my first case, remarks made by natives were "Patients in his condition never get well; we always expect them

to die. You may as well give him up; he will die." After careful treatment and watching for two months he was able to leave his bed, and finally went to his work. The next two cases were also considered to be hopeless, yet both recovered (Hubbard 1900-1901).

Patton stated that she lost only four patients out of more than one hundred.

Due to ill health and poor finances, Patton was forced to return to Memphis, where she established a private practice. She married David W. Washington on December 29, 1897, and died only three years later, on November 8, 1900.

BIBLIOGRAPHY
Hubbard, G. W. "Dr. Georgia E. L. Patton Washington," *The Christian Educator* (1900-1901).

JANET MILLER

WASHINGTON, ISABEL (1908-)

Though 1929 was not a good year for the economy, it was a great year for Isabel Washington. She was picked from the chorus at the Alhambra to star in *Harlem*, a Broadway play written by novelist Wallace Thurman and *New York Times* feature writer William Jourdan Rapp. Brooks Atkinson wrote that she radiated "the more scarlet aspects of Harlem life with an abandon seldom seen before" (*New York Times* 1929). A few months later, the *Times* reviewer described her performance in *Bomboola* as "outstanding," "sparkling," and "lustrous," and surmised that if the show were "revised to accommodate her talent," it would "be something to mention in a breath with that permanent criterion, *Blackbirds*" (*New York Times* 1929). Then she got a part in Bessie Smith's film *St. Louis Blues*. When Isabel auditioned, she was considered too light. She agreed to be darkened, saying, "I can be dipped." The year 1929 was also the year that Isabel turned 21.

She was born in Savannah, Georgia, by her own account, on May 23, 1908. Her mother died when she was still young, and she and her older sister, Fredi, went to a Catholic boarding school in Philadelphia. Practically from the moment they moved to the North to live with their maternal grandmother, the Washington sisters set Harlem to talking about their beauty, grace, and spirit. Fredi, who had embarked on a stage career, did not want Isabel to follow in her footsteps. Fredi wanted to save her from heartbreak, but Washington was persistent. "I had a voice and I could dance" (Washington 1991).

Isabel Washington began her career as a recording artist at fifteen, recording two songs that Fletcher Henderson wrote especially for her in 1923. Isabel worked at Black Swan, W. C. Handy's record company, after school. She would sing to herself while stuffing envelopes. Henderson, the house pianist, who had one of the finest jazz bands during the 1920s, liked her voice and urged her to record for him. Paramount later reissued "I Want to Go" and "That's Why I'm Loving You," first recorded on the Black Swan label.

In the early 1930s, Isabel Washington was a soubrette at two of the leading Harlem nightspots, Connie's Inn and the Cotton Club. In 1931, she appeared with her sister in *Singin' the Blues*, which boasted songs by Jimmy McHugh and Dorothy Fields, lyricists for the Cotton Club. Eubie Blake's orchestra provided the music. Atkinson referred to Washington as "Harlem's most vivid nightingale" who gave "the blues the exultation of the spirituals" (*New York Times* 1929). She replaced Revella Hughes in the 1932 revival of *Shuffle Along*, singing in the quartet, and she later was offered the role of Julie in *Show Boat* but "Adam told me if I took it, we couldn't get married" (Washington 1991).

Isabel Washington married the Reverend Adam Clayton Powell, Jr., in 1933. Powell had to fight his father's congregation, which opposed his marriage to the Broadway star and divorced Cotton Club chorine with a son. After her marriage, Isabel Powell devoted her talent to the choir at her husband's Abyssinian Baptist Church, which at one time included a young Diahann Carroll. The marriage lasted twelve years, and Isabel Powell helped create a closer tie between church and stage.

BIBLIOGRAPHY

Albertson, Chris. *Bessie* (1973); Allen, Walter C. *Hendersonia: The Music of Fletcher Henderson and His Musicians, A Bio-Discography* (1973); Anderson, Jervis. *This Was Harlem: A Cultural Portrait, 1900-1950* (1982); Bogle, Donald. *Toms, Coons, Mulattoes, Mammies and Bucks: An Interpretive History of Blacks in American Films* (1973); Charters, Samuel and Leonard Kunstadt. *Jazz: A History of the New York Scene* (1981); Clipping file, Isabel Washington. Billy Rose Theatre Collection, The New York Public Library for the Performing Arts, New York City; Kellner, Bruce, ed. *The Harlem Renaissance: A Historical Dictionary for the Era* (1984); Mitchell, Loften. *Black Drama: The Story of the American Negro in the Theatre* (1967); *New York Times* (February 21, 1929; June 27, 1929; September 17, 1931); Scott, Freda. "Five American Playwrights on Broadway, 1923-1929," Ph.D. diss. (1990); Washington, Isabel. Personal interview (November 26, 1991).

BARBARA LEWIS

WASHINGTON, JOSEPHINE TURPIN (1861-1949)

As a writer and educator, Josephine Washington was committed to freeing America from what she described as the "monster of prejudice whose voracious appetite is appeased only when individuals are reduced to abject servitude and are content to remain hewers of wood and drawers of water." Washington was concerned with social issues from an early age, and in her teaching and many writings she was a powerful advocate of women's rights and racial justice.

Born on July 31, 1861, in Goochland County, Virginia, Washington was the daughter of Augustus and Maria Turpin. Her education began at home and continued through normal and high schools to the Richmond Institute, which later became the Richmond Theological Seminary. She entered Howard University's college department and graduated in 1886. While at the university, Washington spent her summer vacations working as a copyist for Frederick Douglass, during his tenure as Recorder of Deeds for the District of Columbia. Following her marriage to Dr. Samuel H. H. Washington, she moved to Birmingham, Alabama, in 1888. She later taught at Richmond Theological Seminary, Howard University, and Selma University, Alabama. Her commitment to education led Washington to play an important role in the development of Selma University, an educational institution for teachers and ministers alike.

Washington's literary efforts began as a teenager. Her first story, "A Talk about Church Fairs," in which she criticized the sale of wine at church fundraisers, was published in the *Virginia Star*—to a favorable reaction—when she was only sixteen years old. While her writing, and perhaps most especially her poetry, has largely been neglected, Washington addressed herself to many of the important issues of her day. Essays such as "Higher Education for Women," published in the *People's Advocate*, and her introduction to Lawson A. Scruggs's *Women of Distinction* (1893) display her concern with an array of issues affecting Black people, including job opportunities, education, motherhood, and relations between women and men. In the latter essay she powerfully defends the "progressive woman" who sought to successfully participate in both professional and domestic spheres. While chairperson of the Executive Board of the Alabama State Federation of Colored Women's Clubs, Washington also wrote their Federation Hymn, "Mother Alabama." Her work appeared in numerous publications, including the *New York Freeman*, the *New York Globe*, the *AME Review*, the *Christian Recorder*, the *Virginia Star*, the *Colored American Magazine*, and the *People's Advocate*.

Writing in 1904 for the *Colored American Magazine* on the sixth annual meeting of the State Federation of Colored Women's Clubs, held in Mobile, Alabama, Washington reported not only on the delegates' focus on Black womanhood, standards of morality, and the setting up of a youth reformatory but also on the pervasive effects of segregation and racial prejudice within the city itself. With an eye to discrimination on all levels of society, Washington noted, for instance, the playgrounds that were set aside for the exclusive use of white children, while Black children "look on longingly, but dare not touch the sacred structure" (Washington 1904).

Writer and educator Josephine Turpin Washington was committed to freeing America from what she described as the "monster of prejudice whose voracious appetite is appeased only when individuals are reduced to abject servitude and are content to remain hewers of wood and drawers of water." [Moorland-Spingarn]

While as yet little is known regarding the later years of her life, and the details of her death in 1949, Washington's numerous writings remain as testimony to her religious faith, her belief in the equality of women, and her strong commitment to ending racial discrimination.

BIBLIOGRAPHY
Brown, Hallie Q. *Homespun Heroines and Other Women of Distinction* (1926); *CBWA*; Dannett, Sylvia G. *Profiles of Negro Womanhood* (1964); Majors, Monroe A. *Noted Negro Women: Their Triumphs and Activities* ([1893] 1971); Penn, I. Garland. *Afro-American Press* ([1891] 1969); Scruggs, Lawson A. *Women of Distinction* (1893); *Twenty Nineteenth Century Black Women* (1979); Washington, Josephine. "Impressions of a Southern Federation," *Colored American Magazine* (November 1904); Wesley, Charles Harris. *The History of the National Association of Colored Women's Clubs: A Legacy of Service* (1984).

FENELLA MACFARLANE

WASHINGTON, MARGARET MURRAY (c. 1865-1925)

Few people manage to rise above the culture of their time. When someone does—Ida B. Wells-Barnett or Sojourner Truth—she lights the way for those who follow. Margaret Murray Washington was among the great majority. Her achievements were remarkable, but she remained anchored to the attitudes, prejudices, and customs of the world in which she lived.

Margaret James Murray was born in Macon, Georgia, on March 9, 1865, according to her gravestone. Evidence suggests, however, that she was actually born four years earlier. She was the daughter of Lucy Murray, who was a washerwoman, and a white father whose identity is unknown. He was apparently an Irish immigrant, and he died when Margaret was seven years old. At his death, the girl went to live with a Quaker family, a brother and sister. When she was fourteen, they suggested that she become a teacher, and she did.

Six years later, Murray decided to enter Fisk University's preparatory school. At that time many young women were teaching with scarcely more formal education than some of their students. It is at this point, perhaps, that Murray subtracted those four years from her age, thinking twenty an advanced age to begin her high school education. At any rate, that is the speculation of Louis R. Harlan, editor of the *Booker T. Washington Papers*.

Murray, working to pay her way, finished both the preparatory and college courses. She was associate editor of the student newspaper and president of one of the campus literary societies. She met her future husband, Tuskegee's Booker T. Washington, at a senior class dinner just before commencement and went to Tuskegee Institute to teach the next fall. One year later she became lady principal. A year after that, in 1891, Washington proposed. Murray was not sure, however, that she wanted marriage. For one thing, Washington had a daughter and two sons, and she did not much care for children. Paula Giddings (1984) quotes a letter from Murray to Washington in which she writes, "You do not have much sympathy with me because I feel as I do in regard to little folks. I get annoyed at myself but the feeling is there just the same." She particularly disliked Washington's daughter, Portia, and Portia felt the same about her.

Margaret Murray did marry Booker T. Washington, and she and Portia learned to live with one another. She kept her position at Tuskegee after her marriage and combined her authority on the faculty with her new authority as the president's wife to accomplish what she thought was best for the school and for the community surrounding it. She was instrumental in the establishment of an industrial department for women, housed in Dorothy Hall, and served on the committee that administered the institute when her husband was away.

Some of her most important work took place away from the campus. On March 2, 1895, she gathered together thirteen women who were connected with the institute—on the faculty or married to faculty members—to form the Tuskegee Woman's Club. One of the major activities of the club was a series of mothers' meetings that took place every Saturday in rented rooms above a Black grocery store. While students entertained the children in one room, their mothers heard a talk and enjoyed a discussion in another. The talks were on subjects such as "When Shall a Girl Be Permitted to Receive Her First Company" and "Mother's Relation to the Teacher." Eventually, these meetings attracted almost 300 women every week.

The club, under Washington's leadership, also started a school for the children of poor workers on a nearby plantation settlement. Washington persuaded the county to allocate $15 a month toward the teacher's salary, and parents contributed what they could. The Woman's Club paid the rest. Children were taught advanced farming methods and household industries, in addition to basic literacy skills. Members of the Woman's Club also worked on weekends for twelve years with the families on the plantation, teaching Sunday school, organizing boys' clubs, girls' sewing classes, and newspaper-reading clubs for men. Washington also started a small public library staffed by members of the Woman's Club.

In 1910, Washington and twelve other women who had been excluded from the annual Tuskegee Negro conference met separately. During their meeting, they conceived the Town Night School. The school taught reading, cooking, sewing, carpentry, bricklaying, painting, and tailoring to the people of the town of Tuskegee. To keep the children occupied while their mothers were in class, they were taught cooking. For a time, the school was listed in the Tuskegee catalog as an extension program, but two years after it opened, Tuskegee withdrew its support. The Woman's Club took over. They were able to keep the school open eight months of the year, supporting 103 night classes and 37 daytime classes, including cooking for the children.

Eventually, the night school began to offer some academic courses. The most successful of these was Negro history, and Washington promoted the teaching of the subject in other schools around the country. She also worked in the club movement on a national level. She was president of the National Federation of Afro-American Women, which she helped found in 1896. The organization united thirty-six women's clubs in twelve states. One year after its founding it merged with the National League of Colored Women. Together they formed the National Association of Colored Women (NACW). Washington served as president of that group from 1912 to 1918.

Some attempts were made at about this time to bring Black and white clubwomen together. Washington's home was the site of one such attempt. Nine southern white women, at the invitation of Lugenia Hope, met in Atlanta with a group of Black women. After considerable initial mistrust, the Black women began to share their daily fears, and the white women agreed to organize a conference to explore how they could help in such areas as child welfare, education, protection of Black girls, and the eradication of lynching.

The conference took place in October 1920. Many of the foremost Black women of the time spoke. Then, as Dorothy C. Salem (1990) put it, "the conference became a model for interracial meetings of the next decade. Sympathetic white women worked with articulate black women to improve the conditions for the 'educated and developed Negro,' while

Margaret Murray Washington's achievements were remarkable, but she remained anchored to the attitudes, prejudices, and customs of the world in which she lived. She worked fiercely and effectively for social improvement, never stinting herself in the service of her people, but she could not or would not take the final step into political action. [Library of Congress]

leaving the general system of segregation unchallenged."

A seven-point statement was issued by the Black women calling for, among other things, free exercise of the ballot and an end to lynching and unfair trials. However, the statement did not reach the white women as drafted. It was changed by Carrie Parks Johnson, leader of the Woman's Missionary Council. She had organized the conference and she took it upon herself to eliminate any reference to suffrage. To the point about lynching and injustice she added a qualifier deploring the actions of Black men that supposedly incited mob violence. A preamble that had articulated a feeling of pride and militance on the part of the Black women was omitted. The statement was politically gutted. Margaret Murray Washington advised Black clubwomen to respond with moderation. Lugenia Hope and others blasted the white leadership of the conference.

The process of this event is highly revealing. Washington was involved in the earliest parts of the process, as she so often was. She offered her own resources to make things happen, as she so often did. She participated actively but then came down firmly on the side of compromise and concession. It was the keynote of Washington's life that she could work fiercely and effectively for social improvement, never stinting herself in the service of her people, but that she could not or would not take the final step into political action.

Margaret Murray Washington continued to work for Tuskegee and in the Black women's club movement until her death on June 4, 1925.

[*See also* WASHINGTON, BOOKER T.]

BIBLIOGRAPHY

Brown, Hallie Q. *Homespun Heroines and Other Women of Distinction* ([1926] 1988); *CBWA*; Davis, Elizabeth Lindsay. *Lifting as They Climb* (1933); *EBA*; Giddings, Paula. *When and Where I Enter* (1984); Lerner, Gerda. "Early Community Work of Black Club Women." In *Black Women in United States History*, ed. Darlene Clark Hine (1990); *NBAW*; Neverdon-Morton, Cynthia. *Afro-American Women of the South and the Advancement of the Race, 1825-1925* (1989); Salem, Dorothy C. *To Better Our World: Black Women in Organized Reform* (1990).

KATHLEEN THOMPSON

WASHINGTON, OLIVIA DAVIDSON *see* DAVIDSON, OLIVIA AMERICA

WATERS, ETHEL (1896-1977)

In her autobiography, actress and blues singer Ethel Waters wrote, " 'Stormy Weather' was the perfect expression of my mood, and I found release in singing it each evening. When I got out there in the middle of the Cotton Club floor, I was telling things I couldn't frame in words. I was singing the story of my misery and confusion, of the misunderstanding in my life I couldn't straighten out, the story of the wrongs and outrages done to me by people I had loved and trusted."

Although the song "His Eye Is on the Sparrow" gave Ethel Waters visibility when she toured with evangelist Billy Graham after she retired from a thirty-year career in clubs, theater, and films in the late 1950s, Waters was best known for launching the Harold Arlen song "Stormy Weather" in a Cotton Club extravaganza in 1933.

Waters indeed had a hard life. Born on October 31, 1896, as a result of the rape of twelve-year-old Louise Anderson, Waters (who took her father's surname) lived in the slums of Philadelphia and Chester, Pennsylvania, raised by her grandmother, a live-in housekeeper. She would not gain the affection and admiration of her mother until much later in her life.

Her professional debut as the five-year-old Baby Star in a church production inspired her and led to performances throughout her youth. At age thirteen Waters was urged by her mother into a short-lived marriage to twenty-three-year-old Buddy Purnsley, after which she supported herself doing domestic work in hotels, singing before mirrors to an imaginary audience.

At a local Halloween party in 1917, Waters caught the attention of Braxton and Nugent, producers for a small vaudeville troupe, who offered her a job. Billed as Sweet Mama Stringbean in appearances in Philadelphia and Baltimore, she became the first woman to perform W. C. Handy's "St. Louis Blues."

Following her success as Sweet Mama Stringbean, Waters went on to perform with the Hills Sisters, touring and singing blues standards of the day. She continued to work as a blues singer on the southern vaudeville circuit, often for the TOBA (Theater Owners Booking Association or, as it became known in the trade, Tough on Black Asses). She also performed

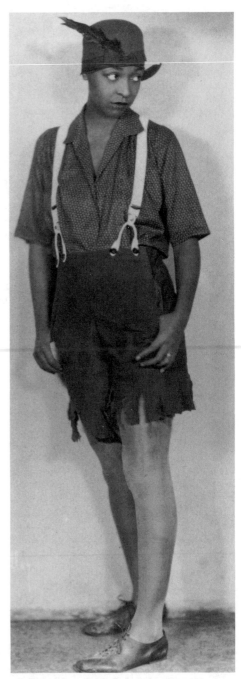

Ethel Waters was "Sweet Mama Stringbean" on the southern vaudeville circuit, star of the Cotton Club singing "Stormy Weather," the toast of Broadway in Irving Berlin's As Thousands Cheer, *and that was only the beginning. [Donald Bogle]*

during this time at Chicago's old Monogram Theater and in tent shows.

In 1919, when Harlem was the center of a national Black renaissance, Waters arrived in New York, where she became one of the leading entertainers in the clubs and on stage. Her initial New York club appearances were at the small Edmund's Cellar, a basement dive patronized by shady characters (Waters later described it as "the last step on the way down"). Her stint there, however, resulted in her first recordings for Black Swan Records in 1921. For that label owned by Harry Pace (which produced "race" recordings), Waters recorded many songs; her major hits were "Down Home Blues" and "Oh Daddy."

Waters continued to record throughout the 1920s, performing blues and fast-tempo jazz songs as well as sweet, beautiful ballads, bringing refinement and elegance to her blues style both on record and in live performances. Also during this period, Pace sent Waters on tour with the Black Swan Troubadours, a band directed by Fletcher Henderson, one of the most sought-after band leaders at the time; this was certainly a career move that benefited Waters. The singer signed a ten-year recording contract with Columbia Records.

Waters declined an invitation to tour Paris, and in 1925 Josephine Baker replaced her while Waters established her career by touring all over the United States and recording hit after hit.

Her second career, as an actress, began in 1927 in Broadway musicals: *Africana* (1927), *Blackbirds* (1930), and *Rhapsody in Black* (1931). *On with the Show* in 1929

Ethel Waters became the first Black woman to star in a Broadway drama in Mamba's Daughters *(1939), then stunned the theatrical community with her powerful performance in* The Member of the Wedding *(1950). Both she and Julie Harris repeated their Broadway roles in the 1952 film version. [Donald Bogle]*

was Waters's first film, followed in 1930 by *Check and Double Check*, a film featuring the characters of Amos and Andy.

Waters was thirty-four in 1930 when she went to Europe for a rest. By the time she returned, the Depression was at its peak and the golden era of the theater was about to begin. During this time her second marriage, to Eddie Matthews, ended.

In 1933, among other entertainment luminaries, Irving Berlin came to see the "Stormy Weather Show" at the Cotton Club. When he heard Waters, backed by the Duke Ellington Orchestra, sing the title song, he signed her for the musical *As Thousands Cheer*, a new revue produced by Sam H. Harris for which Berlin was writing the music. Waters became the first Black to perform in the all-white Broadway hit, singing Berlin originals that included "Heat Wave" and "Harlem on My Mind." Her career took off. A Radio City Music Hall version of the "Stormy Weather" act was staged. Waters subsequently appeared in the revue *At Home Abroad* (1935). She established herself with new power on the stage in 1939 as the first Black woman to star in a Broadway drama with the lead role of Hagar in *Mamba's Daughters*, receiving seventeen curtain calls on opening night.

The 1940 role of Petunia in the all-Black stage musical *Cabin in the Sky* featured Waters performing at her best, singing Vernon Blake's "Taking a Chance on Love"; she excelled again in the 1943 film version with Lena Horne. Other films Waters is known for were *Tales of Manhattan* (1949), *Pinky* (1949), and *The Sound and the Fury* (1959). For her performance in *Pinky*, she was nominated for an Academy Award as Best Supporting Actress. In 1950, she appeared on Broadway in Carson McCullers's *The Member of the Wedding*, and she repeated her performance in the 1952 film version.

Tall, big-boned, yet slender and attractive, Waters developed a tough assertiveness as a child that continued throughout her career, allowing her to eventually negotiate top salaries and to withstand the injustices and harshness of being a Black entertainer. She was always a conflicting mixture of bawdiness and piety, rawness and sweetness. Her life was a mixture of success and sadness; it was mainly through song that Waters found solace. Waters's grandmother, who had raised her, died before seeing her accomplishments on stage and screen. Waters did win the love she sought from her mother before she died. Ridden by debt and plagued by problems with the IRS whenever she hit a career slump, Waters sang and made club appearances. She died in 1977 following a long bout with cancer.

BIBLIOGRAPHY

Feather, Leonard. *The Encyclopedia of Jazz* (1960); Haskins, Jim. *The Cotton Club* (1985); Hughes, Langston and Milton Meltzer. *Black Magic* (1967); Knaack, Twile. *Ethel Waters: I Touched a Sparrow* (1978); Placksin, Sally. *American Women in Jazz* (1982); Shaw, Arnold. *Black Popular Music in America* (1986); Southern, Eileen. *The Music of Black Americans* (1983); Waters, Ethel with Charles Samuels. *His Eye Is on the Sparrow* (1951).

EVAN MORSE

WATERS, MAXINE (1938-)

"I don't have time to be polite," says Maxine Waters. "Too many Black politicians want to be in the mainstream. They don't want to talk about affirmative action, crime, or drugs. My power comes from the fact that I am ready to talk about Black people." Ready to talk. Ready to argue. Ready to fight. Congresswoman Maxine Waters seems to be ready to do anything it takes to make life better for the people she serves.

Born in the housing projects of St. Louis, Missouri, on August 15, 1938, Waters was one of thirteen children of a "sometimes single" mother. After high school, she married, had two children, and worked in factories and as a waitress in segregated restaurants. She and her husband moved to Los Angeles, where she worked in a garment factory and at the telephone company. In the late 1960s, she went to California State University to study sociology. In 1972, she was divorced and, in 1977, was remarried, to Sidney Williams.

Her political involvement grew out of her experience teaching in Head Start. Her activities increased rapidly, leading to her election, in 1976, to the California Assembly from South Central Los Angeles. In 1984, she was chair of the Democratic caucus. It took eight years, but she managed to push through legislation divesting California state pension funds from companies doing business in South Africa. In her own district, she built a vocational and education center that is an extension of the local high school and, through Project Build, brought social services from downtown Los Angeles to the Watts housing projects.

Waters served as a delegate to the Democratic National Convention in 1980 and has been a key advisor to Jesse Jackson since his presidential campaign in 1984. She was elected in 1990 to represent the Twenty-ninth District of California in the U.S. House of Representatives. She evinced no freshman

"I don't have time to be polite. . . . My power comes from the fact that I am ready to talk about Black people." Congresswoman Maxine Waters proved true to her word when she emerged as a spokesperson for the residents of South Central Los Angeles following the 1992 riots. [AP/Wide World Photos]

shyness. In 1991, she was a leader in the fight to defeat an attempt to weaken laws that require banks and savings and loans to serve minority communities and low-income areas. Shortly thereafter she attacked the chairman of the House Veterans Affairs Committee for not sufficiently representing Black soldiers and veterans of Operation Desert Storm.

In 1992, Waters rose to national prominence following the acquittal of four white Los Angeles policemen charged with the beating of Rodney King, a Black man. Amid the ensuing riots protesting both the verdict and ongoing governmental neglect of largely Black and Latino inner-city neighborhoods, Waters emerged as one of several spokespersons for the Black community of South Central Los Angeles. Her terse, angry condemnations of justice denied to Black Americans and her criticism of both the Reagan and Bush administrations demonstrated her willing-

ness to take tough stands on behalf of her constituents.

BIBLIOGRAPHY

Lanker, Brian. *I Dream a World: Portraits of Black Women Who Changed America* (1989); *WWBA* (1992).

KATHLEEN THOMPSON

WATTLETON, FAYE (1943-)

"My mother felt that I should be a missionary nurse," Faye Wattleton said in an interview for *I Dream a World*. "Her dream for me was to go abroad to Africa and other parts of the world to serve the suffering. I have been something of a disappointment to her ideal, but I think, from my own view, I have done missionary work nonetheless" (Lanker 1989). Given the dedication with which she has worked for the reproductive rights of women in today's society, there must be tens of thousands of women who would agree with her.

Alyce Faye Wattleton was born on July 8, 1943, in St. Louis, Missouri. Her father, George Wattleton, was a factory worker. Her mother, Ozie Wattleton, was a seamstress and a minister in the Church of God. The family was poor, but did not have, as Wattleton put it, "a poverty view of the world" (Lanker 1989). After graduating from high school at age sixteen, she entered Ohio State University Nursing School. She graduated in 1964, the first person in her family to earn a college degree. For two years after graduation she worked as a maternity nursing instructor at the Miami Valley Hospital School of Nursing. While there, she learned about the consequences of illegal abortion and about the consequences—and lives—of unwanted children.

In 1966, Wattleton entered Columbia University in New York. One year later, she received an M.S. in maternal and infant health care. Her time at Columbia had included an internship at Harlem Hospital, where again she confronted the problems of poor women.

From New York, she moved to Dayton, Ohio, to take a job as consultant and assistant director of Public Health Nursing Services in the Public Health Department. In Dayton, again faced with desperate women, neglected or abused children, and frightened teenage mothers, Wattleton began to volunteer her time to Planned Parenthood of Miami Valley. After serving on the board of directors for two years, she was asked to take over as executive director. She remained in that position for seven years. While she was in charge, the number of women served tripled, and the budget rose to almost $1 million a year. At the same time, right-to-life advocates began to attack the organization. In Miami Valley, the attacks were primarily verbal. In other places, such as Minnesota, Nebraska, Virginia, and Vermont, and even in other Ohio cities, clinics were being firebombed.

In 1973, Wattleton married Franklin Gordon, from whom she was divorced in 1981. In 1975, while she was pregnant with her daughter, Felicia, she was elected to chair the national executive director's council of Planned Parenthood Federation of America (PPFA). Three years later, she was chosen president of PPFA. She was the first Black person and the first woman to serve in that capacity. She was also the youngest president ever. "Even pro-life activists con-

cede," *Glamour* magazine said about Faye Wattleton in 1990, "she is everything you don't want in an opponent—articulate, strikingly telegenic, bright, and most importantly, messianic on this subject. In short, she has star quality" (Romano 1990).

The star quality contributed to her effectiveness in the battle for public opinion that has taken place in the years since Wattleton's appointment. Yet in battling the Hyde Amendment of 1977, the Reagan administration's attempt to place restrictions on abortion, Wattleton proved to be an effective, hard-working, tenacious leader as well.

In 1986, Wattleton received the Humanist of the Year Award, an award that had once been given to Margaret Sanger, founder of the family planning movement in the United States. In accepting the award she said, "We must trust the people. We must trust each other. We must recognize that private morality should be taught in the home and preached from the pulpit, but must *never* be legislated by politicians. We must protect our own basic rights by protecting those of others. Most importantly, we must never be so convinced of the rightness of our position that we blind ourselves to the possibility that the realm of truth may lie in another person's vision."

In 1992, Wattleton resigned from Planned Parenthood. She is developing her own television talk show.

BIBLIOGRAPHY

Bray, Rosemary L. "Faye Wattleton: Working for the Family," *Essence* (March 1980); Epstein, Helen. "Abortion: An Issue That Won't Go Away," *New York Times Magazine* (March 30, 1980); Huff, Ken and Nancy King. "When Teens Want Contraceptives, Should Their Parents Know? Two Impassioned Advocates Face Off," *People Weekly* (May 1982); *Jet.* "Wattleton Blasts Reagan on Harsh Abortion Stand" (August 6, 1984); Lanker, Brian. *I Dream a World* (1989); *NBAW*; Romano, Lois. "Faye: The Leader," *Glamour* (February 1990); Wattleton, Faye. "Humanist of the Year Acceptance Speech," *Humanist* (July/August 1986); *WWBA* (1992).

KATHLEEN THOMPSON

In 1978, Faye Wattleton became the first Black, the first woman, and the youngest person (at age twenty-five) ever to serve as president of Planned Parenthood. As president from 1978 to 1992, she worked tenaciously for the reproductive rights of women. [AP/Wide World Photos]

WEBSTER, KATIE (1939-)

The career of "Swamp-Boogie Queen" Katie Webster, featuring her tell-tale vocals and her barrelhouse, boogie-woogie piano, never would have started had it not been for her perseverance, especially since her deeply religious father had renounced his career as a ragtime piano player to become a minister in the sanctified Church of God in Christ. Her mother was also a gospel and classical pianist.

Born Kathryn Jewel Thorne on September 1, 1939, in Houston, Texas, she began musical training early but was forced to confine her interests to playing gospel and classical music at the insistence of her parents. So convinced were her parents that the blues was "the devil's music," the family piano was locked so Katie could be monitored by her mother when she played. On the sly, however, Webster listened to the early rock and roll of Fats Domino, Little Richard, Ray Charles, and Sam Cooke.

Webster's parents and nine siblings moved to Oakland, California, leaving the young girl with less strict relatives in Texas. It did not take the blues enthusiast long to launch her professional career. Her ability to read music landed her a debut job with a jazz band. By age thirteen, she was touring and performing in clubs from Dallas to southern Louisiana with a jazz band. About the same time, Ashton Savoy, one of southern Louisiana's most prominent rhythm and blues musicians, discovered the young pianist and took her to Louisiana to feature her piano on several of his recordings. Thorne had married pianist Earl Webster when she was fifteen, and although the marriage ended, she continued to use her married name professionally.

Two years later, she moved to Lake Charles, Louisiana, and was employed extensively as a studio musician for such Louisiana labels as Excello, Goldband, and Jin. As a result of exposure on these labels in the late 1950s and early 1960s, she garnered hundreds of recording sessions on 45s with such bluesmen as Guitar Junior (Lonnie Brooks), Clarence Garlow, Jimmy Wilson, Slim Harpo, Lazy Lester, Mad Dog Sheffield, Lightnin' Slim, and Clifton Chenier.

At the same time, Webster, leading her own band, The Uptighters, performed regular gigs in Lake Charles's major venue, The Bamboo Club. In 1964, her idol Otis Redding did a one-nighter at the club. An enthusiastic crowd called for Webster to sit in with the guest musician. So impressed was Redding with the pianist that she joined his tour the next morning and spent most of the next three years with Redding until his death in a plane crash in 1967. They became close spiritual friends since their fathers were both ministers.

Two reasons are given for Webster's failure to be on the plane with Redding. She was eight months pregnant and she either declined the offer to accompany him or she overslept and missed the plane. Whichever is true, Redding's death affected Webster to such an extent that she stopped performing for several years.

In 1982, after another hiatus from music to take care of her ailing parents in the San Francisco bay area, Webster made her debut tour of Europe, where she has since returned numerous times. Also that year, between jaunts to Europe, Webster gave her first performance since Redding's death at the San Francisco Blues Festival and performed at various clubs. In 1986, the Bay Area Women in Music group awarded Webster the Performer of the Year award, marking one of the rare times a blues artist has been so honored.

Webster has released numerous albums on the Ornament, Arhoolie, and Alligator labels. Her rousing keyboard style features her father's driving, clustered-chord bass riffs in her left hand and a unique fusion of gospel, blues, and boogie techniques in her right. Webster has been referred to as a female Muddy Waters, but she has definitely developed her own unique piano style accompanied by crisply intimate, throaty vocals tending her lyrics. In live performance, she thrives.

BIBLIOGRAPHY

BWW; liner notes, *Swamp Boogie Queen*, Alligator Records (1988); liner notes, *Two Fisted Mama*, Alligator Records (1989); Scott, Frank. *The Down Home Guide to the Blues* (1991); biographical data from Alligator Records (1992).

EVAN MORSE

WELCOME, VERDA FREEMAN (1907-1990)

"One day I am going to vote and pay back the insult to my father" (White 1979). Verda Welcome's childhood pledge propelled her into becoming one of the most outstanding legislative trailblazers of the civil rights movement in Maryland for more than twenty-five years. In 1962, Welcome was the first African-American woman elected to a state senate seat anywhere in the United States. She led the fight for legislation to open Maryland's public accommodations to all races and became a powerful and influential member of Maryland's senate finance committee.

Welcome was the third of sixteen children born to James and Docia Freeman in Uree (later Lake Lure) in North Carolina. Her mother died when Verda was young and she assumed responsibility for her family. She migrated to Baltimore, Maryland, in 1929 and soon after enrolled in Coppin State Teachers College, graduating in 1932. After marrying Dr. Henry C. Welcome in 1935, she continued teaching in the public school system as well as studying at Morgan State University, from which she graduated in 1939. In 1943, while caring for her husband and daughter Mary Sue, she received a Master's degree from New York University to improve her opportunities to teach.

Welcome's political activism began after she emerged as president of Baltimore's North West Improvement Association, which in the 1950s spearheaded the fight to lower racial barriers in public places. With the assistance of a group of fellow activists (called the Valiant Women), she ran for the Maryland House of Delegates in 1958 and defeated the powerful Jack Pollack political machine in the predominantly Black fourth legislative district in Baltimore.

Welcome was elected a Maryland state senator in 1962 and retained her seat for almost twenty years. During these years her legislative accomplishments included legislation for public accommodations, the repealing of Maryland's miscegenation law, and bills that required equal pay for equal work, gun control, and voter registration by mail. She survived an April 1964 assassination attempt. Among her numerous awards were honorary doctorates from the University of Maryland (1970), Howard University (1972), and Morgan State University (1976).

Verda Freeman Welcome died in 1990.

BIBLIOGRAPHY

Davis, Philip. "Maryland Senator and Activist Verda Welcome Is Dead," *Baltimore Sun* (April 24, 1990); *New York Times*. Obituary (April 25, 1990); Page, Sterling. "The Lady Senator," *Afro-American* (Baltimore, April 1, 1967); White, John. "Verda Welcome: The First Lady of Baltimore Politics," *Metropolitan* (Baltimore, December 1979); *WWBA* (1967).

GLENN O. PHILLIPS

WELLS-BARNETT, IDA BELL
(1862-1931)

Ida Bell Wells-Barnett was an ardent advocate of African-Americans' civil rights, women's rights, and economic rights. Throughout her life, she maintained a fearless devotion to justice, which often placed her in physical danger or social isolation. As a journalist and an activist, Ida B. Wells-Barnett made an indelible mark on the history of the United States and offered a critique of racial, sexual, and economic exploitation that still rings true.

Born on July 16, 1862, in Holly Springs, Mississippi, Ida Bell Wells was the eldest of the eight children of Jim Wells and Lizzie Warrenton. Jim Wells was born in Tippah County, Mississippi, the son of his master and a slave woman, Peggy. He was trained as a carpenter and apprenticed to a white contractor in Holly Springs. Lizzie Warrenton was one of ten children born into slavery in Virginia. Separated from her family and auctioned as a slave for several years, she began working as a cook on the plantation where Jim Wells was employed. They were married not long after and once emancipated, the couple remained in Holly Springs.

Like many Black Americans in the postbellum South, the Wellses ardently believed in education and sent their children to school as early as possible. In 1866, the Freedman's Aid Society established Shaw University in Holly Springs, later renamed Rust College, for freed Black students. As an interested father and community activist, Jim Wells became a trustee at Shaw. Lizzie Wells, having no formal education, often accompanied her children to classes so she could learn to read and write.

A yellow fever epidemic swept through Holly Springs in 1878. Jim and Lizzie Wells and their nine-month-old son, Stanley, were among the victims. Another son, Eddie, had died several years before of spinal meningitis. Sixteen-year-old Ida Wells assumed the responsibility of caring for the other five children. Her training at Shaw enabled her to pass the teacher's exam for the county schools and gain employment at a school six miles from her home at a monthly salary of $25. A year later, on the invitation of her mother's sister in Memphis, Tennessee, Wells left Holly Springs. Her paralyzed sister, Eugenia, and two brothers remained behind with relatives. She took the two younger girls with her to Memphis and secured a teaching job in the Shelby County school district at a higher salary than she had earned in Mississippi.

In May 1884, Wells boarded a train owned by Chesapeake and Ohio Railroad and sat down in the ladies' coach. The conductor informed her that he could not take her ticket where she sat and requested that she move to the segregated car. She refused to move. After scuffling with the conductor she was forcefully removed from the train. In retaliation, she hired a Black lawyer and sued the railroad. Disappointed with his lack of attention to her case, she hesitantly turned to a white lawyer. She was awarded

$500. Victory was bittersweet, however, because the state supreme court reversed the ruling of the lower court.

A prolific reader and debater, she became a member of a lyceum of public school teachers that met on Friday afternoons. After each Friday afternoon program, the lyceum closed the meeting with a reading of a weekly newspaper, the *Evening Star*. It reached hundreds and was one of the few sources of communication in the Black community. So, when the editor of the paper returned to his position in Washington, D.C., Wells took the editorship. Not long afterward, she also accepted the editorship of the weekly newspaper *Living Way*. Under the pen name "Iola," her weekly column reached mostly rural, uneducated people. She committed the column to writing "in a plain, common-sense way on the things which concerned our people" (Duster 1970). Her popularity grew, and over the years she contributed articles to local and national publications such as the Memphis *Watchman*, the *New York Age*, the *Indianapolis World*, and the Chicago *Conservator*.

In 1889, she bought one-third interest in the Memphis *Free Speech and Headlight* and later became editor. At first, she spent much of her time writing about the poor conditions of local schools for Black children. Wells argued that inadequate buildings and improperly trained teachers contributed to the mediocre education of Black children. Conservative Black leaders dismissed her argument and the white school board did not renew her contract for the following year. To financially support herself, Wells began to promote subscriptions for the *Free Speech*. She successfully canvassed and secured subscriptions throughout the Delta region in Mississippi, Arkansas, and Tennessee.

In March 1892, three Black male colleagues were lynched. Thomas Moss, Calvin McDowell, and Henry Steward were successful managers of a grocery business in a heavily populated Black section just outside Memphis. The owner of a competing white grocery store in the area charged them with conspiracy. News of the indictment spread throughout the Black community. The three men and several other Black supporters held a meeting and voiced threats against whites. They were arrested and incarcerated. Chaos erupted in the Black community. After four days of shooting, Moss, McDowell, and Steward were indicted for inciting a riot and thrown in jail. Later they were removed from the county jail, taken about a mile from the jail, shot, and hanged.

The deaths of Moss, McDowell, and Steward forced Wells to question not only the rationale of

Outrage at the lynching of three friends propelled Ida B. Wells-Barnett into a lifelong battle against racism. In her clearminded, relentless pursuit of justice and equality, she achieved true greatness. [Schomburg Center]

lynchers but also to rethink her own ideas about the reasons for lynching. She, like most Americans, Black and white, believed that lynching happened to accused rapists; that is, Black men raping white women. Yet the men brutally murdered in Memphis had not been accused of rape. Instead, they were outstanding community citizens whose only crime was economic prosperity. Wells began to investigate cases in which lynch victims were accused of rape. She concluded that lynching was a racist device for eliminating financially independent Black Americans.

Wells expressed indignation and outrage that "the city of Memphis has demonstrated that neither character nor standing avails the Negro if he dares to protect himself against the white man or become his rival." Therefore, she urged the Black citizens of Memphis to "save our money and leave a town which will neither protect our lives and property, nor give us a fair trial in the courts, when accused by white persons" (Duster 1970). In addition, she wrote a scathing editorial attacking white female purity and suggested that it was possible for white women to be attracted to Black men. The suggestion infuriated the white Memphis community.

When the editorial appeared, Wells was en route to Philadelphia to attend the African Methodist Episcopal Church's general conference. The *Free Speech* office was destroyed and threats were made that Wells's life would be in danger should she dare return to Memphis. So Wells went to New York, joined the staff of the *New York Age*, and continued her exposé on lynching. In October 1892, her thorough investigative research culminated in a feature story, "Southern Horrors: Lynch Law in All Its Phases." The publications and speaking tours on lynching and the plight of African-Americans that followed gained her a national audience.

Still, it was international pressure on the United States, she argued, that offered the best means of change for African-Americans. She toured England and Scotland using her investigations as proof of atrocities toward Black Americans. Her efforts spawned the growth of several organizations pledged to fight segregation and lynching.

Wells's second tour of England in 1894 became highly controversial when she harshly criticized and denounced the activities of prominent white leaders considered to be supporters of Black American causes. Wells argued that these leaders did not take a strong enough stance on lynching and that their silence on the issue sanctioned mob violence. In addition, she maintained that white leaders who addressed racially segregated audiences in effect condoned segregation and discrimination. These people, she concluded, were not friends of Black Americans.

The president of the Missouri Press Association, in an effort to discredit Wells, published a letter that denounced the activities of Wells and characterized Black women "as having no sense of virtue and altogether without character" (Crogman and Gibson 1902). It was in part in response to this blatant attack that Black women nationwide banded together and formed the National Association of Colored Women in 1896.

Wells was also an energetic and strong voice at the Chicago World's Fair in 1893. She solicited funds and published 20,000 copies of a protest pamphlet, *The Reason Why the Colored American Is Not in the Columbian Exposition*, to publicize the inherent racism of the fair's administration. She remained in Chicago

and helped spawn the growth of numerous Black female and reform organizations. The Ida B. Wells Club and the Negro Fellowship League were two such associations. She served as president of the Ida B. Wells Club for five years and led the club in the establishment of the first Black orchestra in Chicago and in the opening of the first kindergarten for Black children.

Wells married Ferdinand Barnett, owner of the *Chicago Conservator*, in 1895. Barnett, a widower with two children, was a strong advocate for Black equality. He contributed to her pamphlet *The Reason Why the Colored American Is Not in the Columbian Exposition*, was her strongest supporter, and encouraged her to continue her antilynching and political activities. The couple had four other children, Charles Aked, Herman Kohlsaat, Ida B. Wells, Jr., and Alfreda M. Often traveling with one or more children, she was persistent in speaking to groups about lynching and other reform activities.

In 1910, Wells opened the Negro Fellowship League to provide lodging, recreation facilities, a reading room, and employment for Black migrant males. By the end of the first year, the league boasted of finding employment for 115 Black men. Depleting funds, waning public support, and competition, however, limited the continued success of the league. Philanthropic support dwindled, the Young Men's Christian Association for Black men opened in 1913, and the Urban League opened its doors in 1916. By the end of the decade, the Negro Fellowship League disbanded altogether.

Her antilynching activities were instrumental in making her one of two Black women to sign the call for the formation of the National Association for the Advancement of Colored People in 1909. She later broke with the association because of its predominantly white board and because it was timid when confronting racial issues.

She had a strong belief that the vote for all African-Americans was the key to reform and economic, social, and political equality. In her 1910 article "How Enfranchisement Stops Lynching," she asserted that if "the constitutional safeguards to the ballot" are swept aside, then "it is the smallest of small matter ... to sweep aside ... safeguards to human life." Because she believed that economic and political empowerment for Black citizens required the cooperative effort of Black men and women, she organized the Alpha Suffrage Club. Formed in 1913, the club was the first Black female suffrage club in Illinois. The club sent Wells-Barnett as an Illinois delegate to the National American Woman Suffrage Association's suffrage parade on March 3, 1913, in Washington, D.C. White Illinois delegates pleaded with her to march with the Black delegates at the back of the procession. She refused and argued that "the southern women have tried to evade the question time and again by giving some excuse or other every time it has been brought up. If the Illinois women do not take a stand now in this great democratic parade then the colored women are lost." Moreover, she continued, "I shall not march at all unless I can march under the Illinois banner" (*Chicago Daily Tribune* 1913). Despite support from white allies, Wells-Barnett's motion to march with the state contingent fell on deaf ears.

Afterwards, Wells-Barnett disappeared from the parade site. Illinois delegates assumed she had admitted defeat and decided to march with the Black contingent; but as the delegates began marching down Pennsylvania Avenue, she quietly stepped out from the crowd of spectators and joined her state colleagues. By her bold action, she successfully integrated the suffrage movement in the United States.

In 1915, she played a pivotal role in steering the Suffrage Club to endorse the election of Oscar DePriest, an election he won, to become the first Black alderman of Chicago. The club's loyalty to the Republican machine also sustained the reign of white Republicans in Chicago politics. Throughout the twenties, Wells-Barnett maintained her interest in the political arena, and in 1930, she ran unsuccessfully for the Illinois senate as an independent candidate.

Her anti-Booker T. Washington stance and alliances with Timothy Thomas Fortune and Marcus Garvey often placed Wells-Barnett at odds with her peers and with the federal government. She believed agitation, activism, and protest were the only means of change in the United States and she saw Washington's philosophy as accommodationist. Wells-Barnett supported the editor of the *Age*, Timothy Thomas Fortune, in his efforts to resuscitate the National Afro-American League because the organization expressed some of her own grievances—disfranchisement, lynching, inequitable distribution of education funding, the convict lease system, and Jim Crow laws. She spoke at Universal Negro Improvement Association meetings and hailed Garvey as the person who had "made an impression on this country as no Negro before him had ever done. He has been able to solidify the masses of our people and endow them with racial consciousness and racial solidarity" (Duster 1970). As a result, the U.S. Secret Service branded her a dangerous radical.

Wells-Barnett continued writing and reporting despite the controversies surrounding her. She wrote exposés on several riots, including the riot in East St. Louis in July 1917, and she pointed out that similar conditions existed in Chicago. "With one Negro dead as the result of a race riot last week, another one very badly injured in the county hospital; with a half dozen attacks upon Negro children, and one on the Thirty-fifth Street car Tuesday, in which four white men beat one colored man, . . . the bombing of Negro homes and the indifference of the public to these outrages. It is just such a situation as this which led up to the East

Ida B. Wells-Barnett believed that the vote for all African-Americans was key to equality. In 1913, she formed the Alpha Suffrage Club, the first Black female suffrage club in Illinois. As a delegate to the National American Woman Suffrage Association's suffrage parade in Washington, D.C., that year, Wells-Barnett refused to march with the Black delegates, at the back of the procession, and instead joined her white colleagues in the Illinois delegation, thereby integrating the U.S. suffrage movement. [The Joseph Regenstein Library, The University of Chicago]

St. Louis riot" (*Chicago Daily Tribune*, July 7, 1919). Then, for fourteen days in July and August 1919, Black and white Chicagoans battled. In the end, thirty-eight died and 537 were injured.

After a thirty-year exile from the South, Ida Wells-Barnett returned in 1922 to investigate the case of the Arkansas Black farmers who were indicted for murder in what was known as the (Elaine) Arkansas race riot, and she published the pamphlet *The Arkansas Race Riot*.

Wells-Barnett was a reformer and one of the first Black leaders to link the oppression and exploitation of African-Americans to white economic opportunity. She believed that Black citizens had to organize themselves and take the lead in fighting for their own independence from white oppression. Through her campaigns, speeches, reports, books, and agitation, she raised crucial questions about the future of Black Americans.

Wells-Barnett died in Chicago of uremia, a kidney disease, in 1931. Her autobiography, edited by her daughter, Alfreda Duster, was published posthumously.

[*See also* ALPHA SUFFRAGE CLUB; ANTI-LYNCHING MOVEMENT; JOURNALISM; SUFFRAGE MOVEMENT; TEMPERANCE WORK IN THE NINETEENTH CENTURY.]

BIBLIOGRAPHY

Barker-Benfield, G. J. and Catherine Clinton, eds. *Portraits of American Women: From Settlement to the Present* (1991); Crogman, W. H. and John W. Gibson, eds. *Progress of a Race, or The Remarkable Advancement of the Colored American* (1902); *Chicago Daily Tribune* (March 4, 1913); Davis, Elizabeth Lindsay. *Lifting as They Climb* (1933), and *The Story of the Illinois Federation of Colored Women's Clubs* (1922); Duster, Alfreda, ed. *Crusade for Justice: The Autobiography of Ida B. Wells* (1970); *NAW*; Spear, Allan. *Black Chicago: The Making of a Negro Ghetto, 1890-1920* (1967); Ida B. Wells-Barnett Papers. University of Chicago, Chicago, Illinois.

SELECTED WORKS BY IDA B. WELLS-BARNETT

"Afro-Americans and Africa," *A.M.E. Church Review* (July 1892); *The Arkansas Race Riot* (1922); "Booker T. Washington and His Critics," *World Today* (April 1904); "How Enfranchisement Stops Lynchings," *Original Rights Magazine* (June 1910); "Lynch Law in All Its Phases," *Our Day* (May 1893); "Lynch Law in America," *Arena* (January 1900); "Lynching and the Excuse for It," *Independent* (May 16, 1901); *Mob Rule in New Orleans* (1900); "The Negro's Case in Equity," *Independent* (April 26, 1900); *On Lynchings: Southern Horrors* (1892); "Our Country's Lynching Record," *Survey* (February 1, 1913); *The Reason Why the Colored American Is Not in the World's Columbian Exposition*, with Frederick Douglass, I. Garland Penn, and Ferdinand L. Barnett (1893); *A Red Record* (1895).

WANDA HENDRICKS

WESLEY, DOROTHY BURNETT PORTER (1905-)

In the fall of 1930, when Dorothy Porter was appointed "librarian in charge of the Negro collection" at Howard University, she discovered that the bulk of the books—donated in 1914 by businessman and Young Men's Christian Association general secretary Jesse E. Moorland—were stashed away in dusty boxes. "Nothing had been done in that collection, nothing had been brought together!" recalled Wesley. With pride, passion, and love, she ripped open the boxes and over the next forty-three years helped build the specialized library into what became the Moorland-Spingarn Research Center, one of the world's largest and most comprehensive repositories of materials on the history and culture of people of African descent.

Born on May 25, 1905, in Warrenton, Virginia, the first of four children of Dr. and Mrs. Hayes J. Burnett, Dorothy Burnett received her early education in Montclair, New Jersey. After she graduated from high school, she enrolled in Minor Normal School in Washington, D.C., in 1923. In 1926, she transferred to Howard University and began work as a student assistant in the Founders Library. She graduated from Howard in 1928 with an A.B. and a resolve to continue her education to become a librarian. After working at the Howard University Library as a cataloger, Burnett enrolled in the Columbia University School of Library Science and in 1931 received a B.L.S. She received a scholarship to attend graduate school at Columbia from the Julius Rosenwald Fund and was awarded an M.L.S. in 1932, becoming the first African-American woman to do so.

Curator of the Moorland-Spingarn Research Center from 1930 to 1973, she was also a scholar. Dorothy Porter was the author of several works on nineteenth-century abolitionists. In addition, she published many bibliographical works that placed at the disposal of scholars worldwide materials that otherwise would have remained obscure. Her 1936 publication for the U.S. Government Printing Office, *A Selected List of Books by and about the Negro*, was the beginning of a facet of her career that changed forever the way people of African descent were to be studied. Her biblio-

With pride, passion, and love, Dorothy Porter Wesley turned a stockpile of books in dusty boxes into the Moorland-Spingarn Research Center, one of the world's largest and most comprehensive repositories of the history and culture of people of African descent. [Moorland-Spingarn]

graphic production included *Catalogue of the African Collection at Howard University*, published by the Howard University Press in 1958; *The Negro in American Cities: A Selected and Annotated Bibliography*, which she prepared for the National Advisory Commission on Civil Disorders in 1967; *The Negro in the United States: A Selected Bibliography*, published by the Library of Congress in 1970; and *Afro-Braziliana: A Working Bibliography*, published by G. K. Hall in 1978. The latter is thought to be one of the richest mines of information on the subject.

Wesley's awards and honors include an honorary doctorate of letters in 1971 from Susquehanna University; an appointment as a 1988-89 visiting scholar at the W.E.B. Du Bois Institute at Harvard University; an honorary doctorate of humane letters from Syracuse University in 1989; the Olaudah Equiano Award of Excellence for Pioneering Achievements in African American Culture from the University of Utah in 1989; and an honorary doctorate of humane letters

from Radcliffe College at the 1990 inauguration ceremony for Linda Smith Wilson as president.

Dorothy Burnett married James Porter, an artist, in 1929. After his death in 1970, she married Charles H. Wesley, a historian, in September 1979. He died in 1987. Retired from Howard in 1973, Wesley remains an active researcher and consultant to the Moorland-Spingarn Research Center.

BIBLIOGRAPHY

Scarupa, Harriet Jackson. "The Energy-Charged Life of Dorothy Porter Wesley," *New Directions* (January 1990); Wesley, Dorothy Burnett Porter. Manuscript collection, Moorland-Spingarn Research Center, Howard University, Washington, D.C.

SELECTED WRITINGS BY DOROTHY PORTER (WESLEY)

As compiler: *Afro-Braziliana: A Working Bibliography* (1978); *Catalogue of the African Collection at Howard University* (1958); "David M. Ruggles, An Apostle of Human Rights,"

Journal of Negro History (January 1943); "Early American Negro Writings: A Bibliographical Study," *The Papers of the Bibliographical Society of America* (1945); *The Negro in American Cities: A Selected and Annotated Bibliography* (1967); *The Negro in the United States: A Selected Bibliography* (1970); *A Working Bibliography on the Negro in the United States* (1969). As editor: *Negro Protest Pamphlets: A Compendium* (1969); *North American Negro Poets: A Bibliographical Checklist of Their Writings* ([1945] 1963); "The Organized Educational Activities of Negro Literary Societies, 1828-1846," *Journal of Negro Education* (October 1936); "Sarah Remond: Abolitionist and Physician," *Journal of Negro History* (1935); *A Selected List of Books by and about the Negro* (1936).

ARTHUR C. GUNN

WEST, DOROTHY (1907-)

As an author and journalist, Dorothy West has critically engaged the social and political issues of her day, and her early literary career was emblematic of the much celebrated Harlem Renaissance of the 1920s.

The only child of Rachel Pease Benson and Isaac Christopher West, Dorothy West was born on June 2, 1907, in Boston, Massachusetts. Her formal education began at age two under the tutelage of Bessie Trotter, sister of Monroe Nathan Trotter, then editor of the *Boston Guardian*. At age four, West entered Farragut School in Boston and proved herself already capable of doing second-grade work. Her elementary education was completed at Matin School in Boston's Mission District. At age seven, she began to write short stories. Her first story, "Promise and Fulfillment," was published in the *Boston Globe*, a paper for which West became a regular contributor and that awarded her several literary prizes. After graduating from Girl's Latin High School in 1923, West continued her education at Boston University and later at the Columbia University School of Journalism.

West's long association with Harlem began as a teenager when she and her cousin, Helen Johnson, accepted an invitation to attend *Opportunity* magazine's annual awards dinner in New York and stayed at the Harlem Young Women's Christian Association (YWCA). West later moved to New York and into an apartment that previously had been the residence of Zora Neale Hurston. West's writing career flourished in New York, and she quickly became a part of the Harlem Renaissance, surrounded by such luminaries as Hurston, Wallace Thurman, Aaron Douglas, and Langston Hughes. In 1926, West's short story "The Typewriter" won second place in a competi-

tion run by *Opportunity* magazine, an award she shared with Hurston.

In 1927, West traveled to London with the original stage production of *Porgy*, in which she had a small part. During the 1930s, West's involvement in the production of the film *Black and White* led her to the Soviet Union. The film was never completed, but West extended her visit for another year. Back in New York in 1934, she began to publish a literary magazine called *Challenge*, which was devoted to promoting the work of established Harlem Renaissance figures as well as that of lesser-known writers. In 1937, West founded *New Challenge*, with Richard Wright as associate editor. Only one issue was published, but the magazine reflected West's increasing interest in class issues as well as the struggles of Black people generally.

After her two magazines folded due to financial and editorial difficulties, West became a welfare investigator in Harlem for one and a half years. She then joined the Federal Writers Project of the Works Progress Administration (WPA) until its demise in the 1940s. West never stopped writing in this era, and

Author and journalist Dorothy West has critically engaged the social and political issues of her day. Her novel, The Living Is Easy, *published in 1948, influenced such later writers as Paule Marshall. [Moorland-Spingarn]*

several of her short stories were published, such as "Hannah Byde" (*Messenger*, July 8, 1926); "An Unimportant Man" (*Saturday Evening Quill*, June 1, 1928); "Prologue to a Life" (*Saturday Evening Quill*, April 2, 1929); and "The Black Dress" (*Opportunity*, May 12, 1934). From the 1940s to the 1960s, she was a regular contributor to the New York *Daily News*. In 1945, West moved to Martha's Vineyard in Massachusetts where she has since written weekly for the *Martha's Vineyard Gazette*.

In her novel, *The Living Is Easy*, published in 1948, West satirized affluent Black Bostonians who allowed class differences to separate them from the concerns of working-class Black communities. Although the novel received mixed reviews in the late 1940s, it became a significant influence in later decades on rising authors such as Paule Marshall. In 1982, it was reprinted by the Feminist Press, and its reemergence elicited the interest of critics and readers who are more inclined toward issues related to women, Black people, and the working class. Among the novel's original supporters was Robert Bone, who described it as a work of "primarily Renaissance consciousness" and "a diamond in the rough . . . bitingly ironic" (1965).

The talent and social awareness of Dorothy West have rightly earned her a place both as a member of the Harlem Renaissance and as a writer of enduring significance.

BIBLIOGRAPHY

Bone, Robert. *The Negro Novel in America* (1965); Daniel, Walter C. "*Challenge* Magazine: An Experiment That Failed," *College Language Association Journal* (June 1976); *DLB*; Johnson, Abby Arthur and Ronald Maberry Johnson. *Propaganda and Aesthetics: The Literary Politics of Afro-American Magazines in the Twentieth Century* (1979); *NBAW*; *Opportunity*. "Our Authors and What They Say Themselves" (July 1926); Perry, Margaret. *Silence to the Drums: A Survey of the Literature of the Harlem Renaissance* (1976); Rampersad, Arnold. *The Life of Langston Hughes, vol. 1: "I, Too, Sing America: 1902-1941"* (1986); Schraufnagel, Noel. *From Apology to Protest: The Black American Novel* (1973); Washington, Mary Helen. "I Sign My Mother's Name: Alice Walker, Dorothy West, Paule Marshall." In *Mothering the Mind: Twelve Studies of Writers and Their Silent Partners*, ed. Ruth Perry and Martine Watson Brownley (1984), and *Invented Lives: Narratives of Black Women 1860-1960* (1987); West, Dorothy. "Elephant's Dance: A Memoir of Wallace Thurman," *Black World* (November 1970), and "The Richer, the Poorer." In *The Best Short Stories by Negro Writers*, ed. Langston Hughes (1967); *WWBA* (1992); Dorothy West papers, Mugar Memorial Library, Boston University, and the James Weldon Johnson Memorial Collection, Yale University, New Haven, Connecticut.

FENELLA MACFARLANE

WESTERN TERRITORIES

Diaries, letters, census data, and anecdotal evidence indicate that Black women migrated westward in a variety of ways. Many entered western territories with fur-trading expeditions, exploring forays, and the military. For instance, when Fort Snelling was established in 1820 in what is now Minnesota, officers and their families brought slaves, both male and female, with them. In that year, an estimated two thousand to three thousand Black people, both slave and free, already lived in the upper Louisiana country. Settlers from southern states also brought slaves into western regions. In 1822, a party migrating from Virginia to Missouri included four Black slave men as well as "Mammy," the cook and household slave. Other documents of the overland trail, especially those of parties that were Texas- or Oklahoma-bound, frequently mention the presence of a slave or several slaves.

Even in those western states and territories that proclaimed themselves to be antislavery, such migrants as trappers, traders, soldiers, miners, and settlers, brought slaves with them. For instance, the 1840 Iowa census listed ten female and six male slaves even though the state prohibited slavery. Although no slaves appeared in the Iowa census after 1840, people circumvented the antislave law by indenturing Black servants.

Census data document the widespread participation of free Black people in the western experience. A handwritten county census registry of free Black people in Missouri between 1836 and 1861 listed approximately ten women and twenty men. Another Missouri county register from 1850 showed that sixteen free Black people lived in this county of over one thousand families. Of five females, two were cooks and three had no paid occupations. In that same year, in McLean County, Illinois, the register indicated the presence of several free Black female cooks and servants, as well as a twenty-year-old schoolteacher born in Kentucky.

There are several significant differences between western Black women and their counterparts in the South. Western Black women tended to bear fewer children and were of a higher median age. They also lived in urban rather than rural areas. However, like southern Black women, they experienced difficulties with racial discrimination manifested in segregation policies, denial of civil rights, exclusion from land ownership, and attempts to control Black settlers or drive them away. As a result, Black women workers in the West were usually forced to work at low-paid, exhausting domestic and agricultural tasks.

When Colorado's Black population began to increase after 1880, largely as a result of an influx of disillusioned Exodusters from Kansas, discriminatory attitudes flared. Consequently, by 1910, most of Colorado's 11,543 Black Americans lived in ghettos within white towns and cities. In these communities, Black women struggled with low wages and prejudicial attitudes. At the same time, many tried to improve the situation and their own communities, especially through an active Black women's club movement.

Evidently, many white settlers deserved Black historian William L. Katz's sharp indictment that "black laws moved westward with the pioneers' wagons." After surveying Black policies in such supposedly liberal states as Iowa, Katz concluded: "The intrepid pioneers who crossed the western plains carried the virus of racism with them" (Katz 1971).

Still, not all western settlers were anti-Black. Thousands of whites helped slaves obtain their freedom via the Underground Railroad, brought newly freed Black people home with them after the Civil War, welcomed Black settlers, and worked for the establishment of Black civil rights. In Minnesota, for example, a slave woman named Rachel, who had worked at several army posts, successfully sued for her freedom between 1831 and 1834 with the help of white supporters. Also, the two-year stint of Dred and Harriet Scott at Fort Snelling in 1836-38 resulted in the Dred Scott Case in 1857. In 1860, Eliza Winston accompanied her master on a vacation to Minnesota and, while there, received the aid of local abolitionists in seeking her freedom. Farther west, a county manumission record indicates that Mommia Travers's owner freed her at Fort Vancouver in 1851.

Numerous diary entries, letters, and memoirs of both white and Black women document the presence of female Exodusters in the American West, those Black southerners who led an "exodus" to western states. White woman Anne E. Bingham explained that in 1880 she and her husband hired a family of Exodusters, two adults and four children, to work on their Kansas farm. Bingham was especially pleased to have the woman's services as washwoman and was very disappointed when the Exoduster family "got lonesome and finally went to town" (Lockley 1916). Williana Hickman, an Exoduster, remembered an

exhausting railway journey from Kentucky to Kansas in 1878. When her husband pointed to "various smokes coming out of the ground and said, 'That is Nicodemus,' " she looked at the dugouts that served as homes and began to cry (Schwendemann 1968). Like other Black women Exodusters, however, she made the best of a difficult situation. Especially inspirational was the Black woman who also arrived in Kansas in 1878 and promptly began teaching a class of forty-five children in her tiny dugout home.

Despite discrimination, economic difficulties, and limited opportunities, Black women persevered and fought to improve their lives. In 1857, for example, Emily O. G. Grey joined a growing Black community in St. Anthony (later Minneapolis). Grey set up housekeeping in a converted barn, creating cupboards and bureaus from packing boxes covered with calico. She engaged in community reform, especially fighting problems that plagued Black Americans, including inadequate health care, poverty, and substandard education.

Black women most commonly worked outside the home as domestic servants. Often called by such names as "Nigger Ellen," Black women domestics received minimal wages sometimes supplemented by leftover scraps of food or cast-off clothing, yet some of them managed to earn local reputations as skilled workers. Before the Civil War, a woman cook known as "Black Ann" not only received the kudos of passengers on Mississippi steamboats but also earned enough money to buy her children out of slavery. In St. Paul, Minnesota, during the years following the Civil War, a family of Black women seamstresses established a thriving business.

Despite the huge odds against Black women progressing very far beyond employment as domestics, a considerable number became hotel or boardinghouse keepers and restaurant managers or owners. Perhaps the most well known of these was Mary Ellen Pleasant, also known as "Mammy" Pleasant, a California boardinghouse keeper known for her charitable acts. Yet other Black women became entrepreneurs in a variety of businesses, including millinery shops, hairdressing establishments, and food stores. The most eminent was Sarah Breedlove Walker, better known as Madam Walker, who in 1905 developed the Walker Method of straightening Black women's hair. Other Black women, including Biddy Mason of Los Angeles, Clara Brown of Denver, and Mary Elizabeth Blair of Sully County, North Dakota, were successful real estate brokers.

A number of Black women also achieved stature in the professions. In spite of state and local attempts to prohibit young Black women from attending school or to limit them to poorly funded and segregated schools, many Black women pursued whatever educational opportunities were available to them. A sizeable number of educated Black women entered the teaching profession. As teachers in segregated schools or as founders of their own schools, Black female educators usually outnumbered Black male educators in most western regions.

Other achievement-oriented women struggled to become nurses, doctors, editors, journalists, and writers. A case in point is Charlotta Spears Bass. In 1912, she became editor of the *California Eagle* (published from 1879 to 1966), the oldest Black newspaper on the West Coast. For over forty years, Bass waged a crusade against racial segregation and discrimination. In 1952, she was the first Black woman to run for vice-president of the United States.

Era Bell Thompson, who grew up in North Dakota during the early years of the twentieth century, became a noted writer. In her 1946 book, *American Daughter*, Thompson described the life of a Black family on the Plains. She recalled that during the early years, other settlers befriended her family, but as more people settled in the area prejudicial attitudes and policies increased. Thompson eventually left North Dakota for Chicago in search of an education. In later years, however, North Dakota proudly claimed Thompson as a native daughter.

Other Black women, too numerous to list here, also contributed to the growth of the American West. As Era Bell Thompson argued so eloquently in *American Daughter*, Black women were an important part of the western tradition. Indeed, they were pioneers in every sense.

BIBLIOGRAPHY

Anderson, Kathie Ryckman. "Era Bell Thompson," *North Dakota History* (Fall 1982); Armitage, Sue, Theresa Banfield, and Sarah Jacobus. "Black Women and Their Communities in Colorado," *Frontiers* (1977); Bergmann, Leola M. *The Negro in Iowa* (1969); Brady, Marilyn Dell. "Kansas Federation of Colored Women's Clubs, 1900-1930," *Kansas History* (Spring 1986); Butler, Anne A. "Still in Chains: Women in Western Prisons, 1865-1910," *Western Historical Quarterly* (February 1989); Daniels, Douglas Henry. *Pioneer Urbanites: A Social and Cultural History of Black San Francisco* (1980); de Graaf, Lawrence B. "Race, Sex, and Region: Black Women in the American West, 1850-1920," *Pacific Historical Review* (May 1980); Gill, Gerald R. " 'Win or Lose—We Win'; The 1952 Vice-Presidential Campaign of Charlotta Bass." In *The Afro-American Woman: Struggles and Images*, ed. Sharon Harley and Rosalyn Terborg-Penn (1978); Harpole, Patricia C., ed. "The Black Community in Territorial St. Anthony: A Memoir," *Minnesota History* (Summer 1984); Katz, William L. *The Black West* (1971); Lang, William L. "The Nearly Forgotten Blacks of Last Chance Gulch, 1900-1912," *Pacific Northwest Quarterly* (April 1979); Lockley, Fred. "Some Documentary Records of Slavery in Oregon," *Oregon Historical Quarterly* (June 1916); McLagan, Elizabeth. *A Peculiar Paradise: A History of Blacks in Oregon, 1788-1940* (1980); Marshall, Marguerite Mitchell, et al. *An Account of Afro-Americans in Southeast Kansas, 1884-1984* (1986); *NAW*; Riley, Glenda. "American Daughters: Black Women in the West," *Montana: The Magazine of Western History* (Spring 1988); Savage, W. Sherman. *Blacks in the West* (1976); Schwendemann, Glen. "Nicodemus: Negro Haven on the Soloman," *Kansas Historical Quarterly* (Spring 1968); Sterling, Dorothy, ed. *We Are Your Sisters: Black Women in the Nineteenth Century* (1984); Taylor, David Vassar. "The Blacks." In *They Chose Minnesota: A Survey of the State's Ethnic Groups*, ed. June Drenning Holmquist (1981); Taylor, Quintard. "Blacks in the West: An Overview," *Western Journal of Black Studies* (March 1977), and "The Emergence of Black Communities in the Pacific Northwest, 1864-1910," *Journal of Negro History* (Fall 1979); Thompson, Era Bell. *American Daughter* ([1946] 1986).

GLENDA RILEY

WHEATLEY, PHILLIS (PETERS)
(c. 1753-1784)

Phillis Wheatley was America's first Black published author. The volume was her collection *Poems on Various Subjects, Religious and Moral* (1773). She was America's second woman to publish a book of poems; Anne Bradstreet was the first.

Because she herself identifies Gambia in "Phillis's Reply" as the land of her birth and because her slender facial features (long forehead, thin lips, well-defined cheek bones, and small nose) remarkably resemble those of present-day Fulani, a people who occupied the region of the Gambia River during the eighteenth century, most scholars conclude that Phillis Wheatley was born of the Gambian Fulani. At the time of her purchase in Boston on or about July 11, 1761, she was losing her front baby teeth, suggesting that she was seven or eight at that time, and that she was born c. 1753. The name of the slaveship that transported her was the *Phillis*, and we can only speculate about the discomfort that this intelligent and sensitive child experienced because she was named after this ill-fated vessel. Her name must have served as a lifetime, moment-to-moment reminder of the horrid middle passage from Africa to America.

The only memory of her mother that Wheatley cared to recall to her white captors was that of her mother "out water before the sun at his rising" (Oddell 1834), but this self-same sun subsequently became the central image of her poetry. On the numerous occasions when the poet employs solar imagery, she infrequently articulates the commonly occurring eighteenth-century Western pun on sun-Son (Christ); rather, her sun is more often simply the life-giving sun of nature, echoing her mother's devotion. Her mother's practice of this daily ritual suggests a syncretization of hierophantic solar worship (usually practiced by the African aristocracy) and Islam, which by the mid-eighteenth century had established a presence within the Gambian region of West Africa. Wheatley's later blending in her poems of solar imagery, Judaeo-Christian thought and figures, and images from ancient classicism bespeaks complex multicultural commitments, not the least of which is to her African heritage.

Wheatley's principal biographer, Margarita Matilda Oddell, recorded that Wheatley "was frequently seen," very shortly after her purchase by John and Susanna Wheatley, "endeavoring to make letters upon the wall with a piece of chalk or charcoal" (Oddell 1834). Perhaps these letters were Arabic characters, but in any case her efforts seem to have prompted Mary Wheatley, one of the Wheatley twins (Nathaniel was the other), to teach Phillis how to read the English Bible. Her master John wrote in a letter dated November 14, 1772 (a portion of which appears in the prefatory material of her 1773 *Poems*) that "by only what she was taught in the Family, she, in sixteen Months Time from her Arrival, attained the English Language." He noted, "She has a great Inclination to learn the Latin Tongue, and has made some Progress in it" (Wheatley 1988). Indeed, she had by the next year mastered Latin so well that for *Poems* she rendered into heroic couplets the Niobe episode from Ovid's *Metamorphoses* with such dexterity that she created one of the best English translations of this episode. Significantly, Wheatley did not stop with mere translation; she added so many elements to Ovid's original (such as invocation to the muse, long speeches by Niobe and a goddess, and machinery of the gods) that she has effectively recast the Latin to create an epyllion, or short epic.

Her first memorable composition appears to have been a letter to Samson Occom, the Mohegan minister, described in the letter by her master as written in 1765. Her first published poem was printed on December 21, 1767, in the *Newport Mercury*, a colonial newspaper of Newport, Rhode Island, where her Black friend Obour Tanner resided. Some have speculated provocatively that Wheatley and Tanner came over together on the *Phillis*. In any event, Wheatley corresponded with Tanner with greater tenacity than with any other known correspondent. Recent evidence has suggested that these two visited one another frequently as well, with Wheatley traveling round-trip from Boston to Newport.

Wheatley, as a young woman, may have socialized with the other young women of Boston who joined the regular meetings of the singing schools conducted by William Billings, America's first full-time composer-choirmaster. Evidence that Wheatley and Billings knew each other has surfaced from the publication of Wheatley's elegy on Samuel Cooper's death, for appended to a six-page version of the Cooper elegy is a two-page anthem "set to Musick by Mr. Billings" to be sung at Cooper's funeral. In Billings's 1770 *The New England Psalm-Singer*, the first collection of original anthems published by an American, he included one piece entitled "Africa," which may well have been a paean to Wheatley. As early as October 2, 1769, Billings ran an ad in the *Boston Gazette* that read: "John Barrey and William Billings Begs Leave to inform the Publick, that they propose to open a Singing School This Night, near the Old South Meeting-House, where any Person inclining to learn to sing may be attended upon at said School with fidelity and Dispatch" (McKay and Crawford 1979). To be sure, the Old South Boston Meeting House was Wheatley's church and the designation "any Person," not limiting sex or race, could have appealed to her.

One possible motivation for Wheatley's patriot political position might have been her close association with Old South Church itself. This church was the site of the town meeting that followed the Boston Massacre and that resulted in the expulsion of the royal governor. Wheatley's non-extant poem "On the Affray in King Street, on the Evening of the 5th of March" was most likely about the Boston Massacre and would surely have celebrated the martyrdom of Crispus Attucks, the Black man who organized the "affray." "To Samuel Quincy, Esq; a Panegyrick," also non-extant, doubtless extolled Quincy, attorney for the Wheatley family and prosecutor of the British troops who fired on the American colonists in the massacre. This same Old South Church became the site of the massacre's anniversary orations, one of which was delivered by John Hancock, who signed Wheatley's letter of attestation as well as the Declaration of Independence. Here also was held the organizational meeting of the Boston Tea Party.

Still, Wheatley would not have required a building as a setting in which to learn the meaning of freedom. As a slave until mid-October of 1773, this poet chose the American quest for independence hardly by accident. Indeed American patriot rhetoric must have held an inexorable attraction for one who struggled so determinedly in her poetry for freedom. The fact that Wheatley was a communicant of the largely patriot Old South Church, though John and Susanna Wheatley attended the more loyalist New South Church, has gone relatively unnoticed. For example, as recently as 1982, J. Saunders Redding published in the *Dictionary of American Negro Biography* a sketch of Wheatley in which he claimed she was, along with the entire Wheatley family, a faithful loyalist.

Little could be further from the truth. Not only was Mary Wheatley married, by January 1771, to the fiery patriot John Lathrop, minister of Old North Church (largely a patriot congregation), but Wheatley herself wrote no poetry on behalf of the Tories'

predicament. It is true that John and Susanna were indeed loyalists, and it is likely that their son Nathaniel, the other twin, who remained in England when Wheatley returned to Boston in September 1773, was a staunch loyalist as well, for Benjamin Franklin, who was in England at the same time as Wheatley, remarks in a letter of July 7, 1773, that "I went to see the Black Poetess and offer'd her any Services I could do her. Before I left the House, I understood her Master was there and had sent her to me but did not come into the Room himself, and I thought was not pleased with the Visit" (Franklin 1976). The poet's political stance must have been uncomfortable to maintain in view of the divisive attitudes within the family.

Wheatley addressed patriot themes throughout her career, writing poems dedicated to George Washington, General David Wooster, and to the declaration of peace in the 1783 Treaty of Paris, for this last occasion the poem "Liberty and Peace." Such a political position, doubtless known by the citizens of

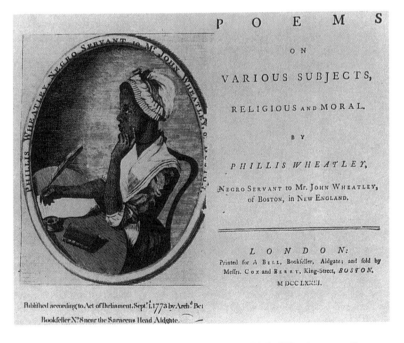

Transported by slave ship to the American colonies in 1761, Phillis Wheatley eventually became a master of eighteenth-century poetic forms, producing work that gained recognition in England and Europe as well as in America. Her book Poems on Various Subjects, Religious and Moral *was the first published by a Black person in America. [Schomburg Center]*

1253

Boston, may have discouraged publication of a volume of Wheatley's poems in Boston in 1772. Whether or not the poet's politics played a role in this, racism definitely did play a decisive role, for the Boston public would not support "anything of the kind" to be printed (Robinson 1977). Wheatley was, however, soon to find a more sympathetic backer in England. Largely because of Wheatley's publication in 1770 of her most famous elegy, "On the Death of Mr. George Whitefield," a poem widely printed in broadside on both sides of the Atlantic, the poet came to the attention of Selina Hastings, Countess of Huntingdon, a wealthy philanthropist whose personal chaplain Whitefield had been. When the Countess heard that Boston would not endorse Wheatley's volume, she agreed to back its appearance financially in London.

Wheatley's first proposal for a volume was made on February 29, 1772, and almost a year and a half elapsed before the volume finally went to press in July 1773. The collection as originally proposed was quite different from the 1773 volume; in effect it was two separate volumes. Such titles as "On America," "On the Death of Master Seider [Snider], who was killed by Ebenezer Richardson, 1770" (Snider was arguably, according to Wheatley, "the first martyr for the common good" [Wheatley 1988]), "On the Arrival of the Ships of War, and the Landing of the Troops," "On the Affray in King-Street, on the Evening of the 5th of March," and "To Samuel Quincy, Esq; a Panegyrick" had all been eliminated by July 1773 and replaced by such new titles as "To Maecenas," "Thoughts on the Works of Providence," "Hymn to the Morning," "Hymn to the Evening," "Isaiah," "On Recollection," "On Imagination," "Hymn to Humanity," "To S.M.," and "Niobe in Distress."

Though the earlier volume would have had much more appeal to an American patriot audience, Wheatley may have hoped that the 1773 *Poems* would appeal aesthetically to an audience that would find pro-American poems inflammatory. The 1772 volume's subject was American patriot politics; if published, Wheatley arguably could have been the author of the first book of Revolutionary War poems, challenging Philip Freneau's claim to this distinction. The 1773 *Poems*, however, has for its subject poetry, or rather how and why one Phillis Wheatley should write poetry.

Nonethelesss, the poems that Wheatley added to the 1773 volume are among her best; the year and a half between March 1772 and July 1773 was unusually productive, a period in which this poet matured as an artist. Finding her freedom unattainable still, Wheatley turned inward to construct a poetics of liberation. In her most powerful and best poem, "On Imagination," as a poet with absolute power over the words of *her* poems she can "with new worlds amaze th'unbounded soul" (Wheatley 1988). In the very next line of this piece, she constructs a new world not bound by winter's iron bands and instead populated by fragrant flowers and forests heavy with verdant leaves. This world into which she escapes is more redolent of her African Gambia than of a Christian paradise. As the consummate romantic poet John Keats was to learn some forty years later, Wheatley realizes that no poet can indefinitely sustain a poetic world; hence she reluctantly leaves "the pleasing views" and returns to a winter whose starkest reality is the condition of slavery.

The poet's letter of October 18, 1773, to David Wooster, enumerating her activities in London during the past summer, announces the following: "Since my return to America my Master has at the desire of my friends in England given me my freedom" (Wheatley 1988). She was freed, then, because of events that occurred in England. This same letter reveals that while Wheatley was in London she met such dignitaries as Thomas Gibbons, Granville Sharp, Brook Watson, and the Earl of Dartmouth. Dartmouth gave Wheatley five guineas with which he encouraged her to purchase Alexander Pope's *Complete Works* "as the best he could recommend to my perusal." While it is certain that Wheatley was well-acquainted with many of Pope's works before this time (for instance, her familiarity with Pope is demonstrated in "To Maecenas"), Dartmouth's recommendation to the poet that she examine Pope's complete opus suggests either that the Earl was unaware of Wheatley's knowledge of Pope or that she was not as thoroughly steeped in Pope's works as has heretofore been assumed.

Regarding Wheatley's attitude toward slavery, in a letter to Samson Occom of February 11, 1774, she presents her most eloquent and emphatic condemnation of slavery when she declares: "In every human Breast, God has implanted a Principle, which we call Love of Freedom; it is impatient of Oppression, and pants for Deliverance" (Wheatley 1988). This magnificent indictment of slavery the poet issued *after* her own manumission had been accomplished, hence putting the lie to the notion that she was unconcerned for the fate of her Black brothers and sisters still suffering under the yoke of slavery. The letter eventually saw almost a dozen reprintings in New England newspapers before 1780.

In October 1775, Wheatley wrote a poem in honor of George Washington; this piece she mailed to the commander-in-chief of the Continental Army, receiving an enthusiastic reply from the general and an invitation to visit him at his headquarters. Washington passed on Wheatley's encomium to a friend; subsequently the poem was printed several times as an instrument for the patriot cause. Wheatley accepted Washington's invitation, and met with him privately for thirty to forty-five minutes in his Cambridge headquarters. This poem and Wheatley's visit may have contributed to Washington's anguish about the slavery question in his later years.

In Wheatley's final years, nevertheless, she met with disappointment after disappointment. In 1778, the year of her marriage to John Peters, John Wheatley died, leaving her with greatly limited resources. The very next year, one senses almost a desperation in the impulse behind her decision to try to publish a new volume of poems. This attempt may have failed not because of racist reasons but because a country in revolution has little time or money for poetry. Even so, this volume projects some three hundred pages of poetry, only a small portion of which has been reclaimed. Until that manuscript is recovered (many think Peters took the manuscript south to Philadelphia after his wife's death), poems by Wheatley will probably continue to surface. During the last year of her life, Wheatley published what is perhaps her most moving funeral elegy on the death of her mentor, Samuel Cooper, as well as a poem celebrating the victory and peace of the American Revolution and another elegy. The elegy on Cooper describes its subject as "A Friend sincere, whose mild indulgent rays/Encouraged oft, and oft approv'd her lays." The paean to the Revolution boldly asserts "And newborn Rome shall give *Brittania* Law" (Wheatley 1988).

While neither of these poems suggests a weakening of her poetic powers, "An Elegy on Leaving _____" does imply that the poet's career may indeed be fast coming to an end, for she bids farewell to "friendly bow'rs" and streams, protesting that she leaves "with sorrow each sequester'd seat." She seems uncannily to know she will soon cease to visit in imagination the plains and shepherds of the pastoral land of pure poetry. Yet even in her estranged condition, "sweet Hope" may "Bring calm content to gild my gloomy seat" (Wheatley 1988).

America's first internationally respected author, Wheatley was only about thirty-one when she died. On December 5, 1784, she died in Boston, unattended, of complications arising from the birth of her third child. This child apparently died mercifully with her, the third child of hers to die.

Phillis Wheatley Peters (as she signed her name after her marriage) deserves to be remembered, not only as a first-rate author but also for the other firsts she accomplished. Wheatley is the first American woman author who tried to earn a living by means of her writing. Henry Louis Gates, Jr., identifies Wheatley as "the progenitor of the black literary tradition" and "the black woman's literary tradition" (Wheatley 1988). In the history of American letters, Wheatley's sponsors and supporters comprised the first community of women devoted to insuring the success of one of their sex. Moreover, she and her work were promoted by Susanna Wheatley, her mistress, who encouraged her literary pursuits until her death; Mary Wheatley, daughter of Susanna, who apparently taught her to read the Bible; Obour Tanner, Wheatley's Black soulmate (after William Robinson) with whom she commiserated throughout her life; and Selina Hastings, Countess of Huntingdon, who financed Wheatley's publication of her 1773 *Poems*. All of these women nourished this young artist and without their assistance her talents and achievements may never have seen the light of day.

BIBLIOGRAPHY

DANB; Franklin, Benjamin. *The Papers of Benjamin Franklin*, ed. William B. Willcox (1976); Kaplan, Sidney and Emma Nogrady Kaplan. *The Black Presence in the Era of the American Revolution* (1989); McKay, David P. and Richard Crawford. *William Billings of Boston: Eighteenth-Century Composer* (1979); Oddell, Margarita Matilda. *Memoir* (1834); Robinson, William H. *Phillis Wheatley and Her Writings* (1984), and *Black New England Letters* (1977); Shields, John C. "Phillis Wheatley and Mather Byles: A Study in Literary Relationship," *College Language Association Journal* (June 1980); Wheatley, Phillis. *The Collected Works of Phillis Wheatley*, ed. John C. Shields (1988). Wheatley's manuscripts are housed at Cambridge University (within the Countess of Huntingdon Papers), at the Massachusetts Historical Society (Phillis Wheatley Letters), at Dartmouth College, and at Harvard University's Houghton Library. The largest collection of Wheatley materials is in the Schomburg Center for Research in Black Culture, New York Public Library.

JOHN C. SHIELDS

WHIPPER, IONIA ROLLIN
(c. 1874-1953)

Ionia Rollin Whipper, M.D., was born in South Carolina. Her grandfather, William Whipper, was a conductor on the Underground Railroad. A woman's rights activist from Philadelphia, Whipper's father moved to South Carolina, became a circuit court judge, and, in 1868, founded Whipper, Elliott, and Allen, the first Black law firm in the United States. He married Frances Rollin, author of *The Life and Public Services of Martin Delaney*, which she published under the pseudonym Frank A. Rollin. In the 1880s, Ionia moved to Washington, D.C., with her mother and there studied medicine at Howard University Medical School.

Whipper graduated from Howard in 1903 with a specialty in obstetrics. She practiced in the maternity ward of the Freedmen's Hospital; served as resident physician at the Collegiate Institute in West Virginia; and during the 1920s taught obstetrics, hygiene, and pediatrics at the John A. Andrew Memorial Hospital at the Tuskegee Institute. While at Tuskegee, she also served as assistant and acting medical director and as a physician for women students.

During World War I, under the sponsorship of the War Work Council, Whipper traveled throughout the South, lecturing on health and social hygiene. From 1918 to 1920, she continued this work under the auspices of the national Young Women's Christian Association (YMCA). From 1924 through 1929, she again traveled in the southern states, this time training midwives, recording births, and conducting child health conferences for the Children's Bureau of the U.S. Department of Labor in connection with the 1921 Sheppard-Towner Act, whose purpose was to study and combat infant and maternal mortality.

When her work at the Children's Bureau ended in 1930, Whipper focused her attention on the plight of young unwed mothers in Washington, D.C. Her home became a haven for single mothers in need of shelter and medical care during and after their pregnancies. In the 1930s, she opened a permanent facility on East Capitol Street. For many years the Ionia R. Whipper Home for Unwed Mothers, now the Dr. Ionia R. Whipper Residence, remained the city's only facility providing shelter and health care for single Black mothers.

Whipper died in Washington, D.C., in 1953.

BIBLIOGRAPHY

Brown, Sarah W. "Colored Women Physicians," *Southern Workman* (1923); Fitzpatrick, Sandra and Marian R. Goodwin. *The Guide to Black Washington* (1990); Moldow, Gloria. *Women Doctors in Gilded-Age Washington* (1987); National Archives. Records of the Children's Bureau, Grace Abbott, director, letter to Mrs. Salina Shaw (December 9, 1930).

TERESA R. TAYLOR

WHITE, EARTHA MARY MAGDALENE (1876-1974)

Eartha Mary Magdalene White was born on November 8, 1876, in Jacksonville, Florida, to two ex-slaves. Her father died when she was five years old, and her mother supported the child—the only surviving one of thirteen—by working on a cruise ship. After graduation from Stanton School in Jacksonville, White attended the Madam Hall Beauty School in New York and the National Conservatory of Music. She sang for a year with the touring Oriental American Opera Company, which was an African-American company. Subsequently, she attended the Divinity School of Cookman Institute (later Bethune-Cookman College) and graduated from the Florida Baptist Academy.

White was engaged to be married to James Lloyd Jordan of South Carolina, but he died a month before their scheduled wedding day. She decided then never to marry. She taught in a rural school near Bayard, Florida, and, dissatisfied with the decayed condition of the segregated school, led a successful crusade to get the county to build a new two-room school. The rest of her life was a continuous campaign to improve the condition of all people. Most of her work was strictly voluntary, supported by her own funds and those of other private donors.

Back in Jacksonville, she began to invest in real estate. She served as acting clerk when the Afro-American Life Insurance Company was founded by her church, and she was its first woman employee. When Booker T. Washington founded the National Business League in 1900, White became a charter member and later was historian for the organization. She assisted in activating the dormant Colored Citizens' Protective League and became a speaker for that group. When a catastrophic fire struck Jacksonville, many were left homeless, and the elderly without a support system, White looked to the Afro-American Life Insurance Company for aid. White rescued the ledgers from the fire.

About this time, White revived an organization that had been dormant for sixteen years, the Union Benevolent Association (UBA). The UBA had land that had been purchased with the goal of building a home for older people. As president of the association, White raised funds for a building, and in 1902, the Old Folks Home opened.

In 1904 one of her projects resulted in the Boys' Improvement Club. Land was donated, and White used her own money to hire recreation workers. The club was in existence for twelve years before the city of Jacksonville recognized the need for it and took over its operation.

Over the years, she established, made successful, and then sold an African-American department store, a laundry, an employment agency, a taxi service, and a janitorial service. She helped organize the Jacksonville Business League. During this time, real estate was also an important part of her business ventures. She amassed an estate that was estimated at more than $1 million, when becoming a millionaire was an extremely rare achievement, and gave most of it for community services.

As a memorial to her mother, who died in 1930, White created the Clara White Mission. During the Depression she housed, fed, and sought employment for the homeless and hopeless in her community. The police brought her teenagers who would otherwise have spent the night in jail. The Works Progress Administration used the mission as an office for employment and cultural operations. The mission was a maternity home, an orphanage, and a community center. When it burned in 1944, it was rebuilt and expanded, and by 1965 it was free of debt.

Recognizing the need for child care for working mothers, White started the Milnor Street Nursery, which was supported by government funds as well as her own. She founded a tuberculosis rest home for African-Americans, who were denied access to other such institutions, and agitated for the renovation of the grossly inhumane Duval County Prison Farm. For more than fifty years she led Sunday services at the farm and served as sponsor for many prisoners who were released into her custody. She also pressured legislators to open a correctional home for girls in order to keep them out of adult prisons. During World War I and World War II, White was active in support of soldiers and their families, working closely with the American Red Cross.

White was not interested only in charity. In 1941, she joined A. Philip Randolph in organizing his March on Washington movement to protest job discrimination, which influenced President Franklin Roosevelt to issue Executive Order No. 8802 establishing fair employment in the federal government and the defense industries. White's last major project was the replacement of Mercy Hospital for the Aged, which she had founded. The result was the 122-bed Eartha M.M. White Nursing Home, which she saw dedicated when she was past 80 years of age.

Honored in her own city and in the nation, Eartha Mary Magdalene White was active in her community until her death on January 18, 1974.

BIBLIOGRAPHY

Duncan, C. Frederick. "Negro Health in Jacksonville," *Crisis* (1942); Gary, Lawrence E. "Eartha M. White." In *Biographical Dictionary of Social Welfare in America*, ed. W. I. Trattner (1986); Gibson, Harold. "My Most Unforgettable Character," *Reader's Digest* (1974); Neyland, Ledell W. "Eartha M. White: Jacksonville's 'Angel of Mercy.' " In his *Twelve Black Floridians* (1970); Obituaries, *Florida Times-Union* (Jacksonville), and *New York Times* (January 19, 1974); Taylor, Angela. "She's 94 and Still Busy," *New York Times* (December 4, 1970); Wright, Fred. "Eartha White, Florida's Rich, Black 94-Year-Old Senior Citizen of the Year, Says God Intended for All His People to Be Gray," *Floridian Magazine* (August 1, 1971).

AUDREYE JOHNSON

WHITE, WILLYE B. (1940-)

Willye B. White, five-time Olympian (1956, 1960, 1964, 1968, and 1972) and silver medalist, is a modern Olympian committed to being a Black role model and leader for female track and field athletes. She won her first silver medal in the 1956 Melbourne, Australia, games at age sixteen in the long jump, and she won another in the 1964 Tokyo Olympics. She works with youth for the city of Chicago and has for years assisted in the training of young Olympian track hopefuls and other track performers. She has competed for more years than any other female Olympian. She used her participation in her last two Olympics in particular to encourage young women to fulfill their talents, to provide good competition, and to be a goodwill ambassador in foreign countries. The longevity of her Olympic participation is a tribute to her commitment to the Olympic ideal. As a pioneering Black female athlete who had to confront both racist and sexist stereotypes, she worked to ensure that all female athletes had the opportunity and inspiration to compete successfully and to develop and prepare for leadership roles.

Willye B. White was born on New Year's Day, 1940, in Money, Mississippi. She had one sister and two brothers. Throughout her childhood, she lived in Greenwood, Mississippi, with her grandparents. She later moved to Chicago's South Side. At age eight, she started chopping cotton, using a long hoe called "the ignorant stick" and earning $2.50 for a twelve-hour day. Her training in track started early in Greenwood. In fifth grade she played on the high school varsity basketball team, where her high-scoring feats called attention to her abilities. Subsequently, the track coach at Tennessee State University, Ed Temple, invited her to attend the university's summer clinic for potential Olympians. She spent four summers at Temple's clinics and competed in the 1956 Olympics with the coaching of Temple and the colors of Tennessee State.

Returning to Chicago after the Olympics, Willye completed high school while participating in the band, choir, and basketball training every day. She won a track scholarship to Tennessee State University, but left after one year to study nursing. Perceiving that her athletic goals and her race presented barriers to a nursing degree, she became a practical nurse instead. She later returned to college, and in 1976 earned her Bachelor's degree in public health care administration and a coaching certificate at Chicago State University. By this time she held a position with the Chicago Health Department. With relatively secure employment, White was able to continue her work as a volunteer coach for Mayor Richard Daley's youth foundation and other local track clubs. She aggressively demanded more programs for young Black athletes and, despite minimal financial backing, succeeded in gaining a reputation for assisting young athletes. After over twenty years with the health department, White became director of recreation service, Chicago Park District, empowering her to better serve youth in Chicago.

White counts two events as especially important to her. The first was Willye B. White Day on March 12, 1972, when she returned to her hometown from the Olympic games. Her second was when she received the coveted Pierre de Coubertin International Fair Play Trophy in 1964 from France. During White's competitive years she was a member of thirty-nine international teams, including four Pan American teams and five Olympic teams. She held the American long-jump record for sixteen years. In addition, she has coached The Athletic Congress (TAC) international teams, U.S. Olympic Committee (USOC) Sport Festival teams, and the Special Olympics.

Among her other achievements, White has been inducted into the National Track and Field Hall of Fame, and the Black Athletes Hall of Fame. The Women Sports Foundation appointed her as a board of trustees member and an officer. She served on the President's Commission on Olympic Sports, and has been a member of and consultant to the President's Council on Physical Fitness and Sport. The Amateur Athletic Union (AAU) recognized, in the 1970s and 1980s, her contributions to track by selecting her for committee membership, and the Illinois AAU elected

her president from 1980 to 1986. White has also been a member of TAC's Athlete's Advisory Council and a representative to the USOC House of Delegates. Recently she was a candidate for membership on the powerful executive committee of the USOC.

Willye White is divorced and has one grown son. She is praised for her skill, tenacity, longevity, and her commitment to athletes and athletics. She is frequently honored, recognized with awards, and asked to speak to youth, women, and athletic organizations. She was an athlete par excellence, and she is an inspirational role model, coach, lecturer, and charismatic leader.

BIBLIOGRAPHY
CBWA; Jordan, Pat. "Sweet Home." In *Broken Patterns* (1977).

JOAN HULT

WHITE ROSE MISSION, NEW YORK CITY

A teacher at the Baylan Home for Colored Youth in Jacksonville, Florida, wrote to the superintendent of the White Rose Mission, asking her to meet one of her students who was traveling to New York to seek employment. The superintendent, Victoria Earle Matthews, arrived at the Old Dominion pier at the expected time but could not find the student. Three days later, the extremely upset young woman appeared and told of having been lured away by employment agents.

The White Rose Mission filled special needs for Black women migrating from the South. It was established by Matthews and a small group of Black women. Its principal object was "to protect self-supporting Colored girls, to direct and help them amid the dangers and temptations of New York City" (Lewis 1925). Matthews organized committees to study the living and working conditions of Black women, to contact teachers, and to locate a suitable place for the meetings.

On February 11, 1897, the White Rose Mission became a reality when it opened on East 97th Street. The White Rose Mission was nondenominational and conducted as a settlement house. It provided a social center for community women and children as well as shelter and protection to young women coming from the South in search of employment. In addition to mothers' meetings, there were vocational courses in cooking, sewing, dressmaking, woodcarving, cobbling, chaircaning, basketry, and clay modeling. There were separate boys' and girls' clubs. The children ranged in age from three to fifteen. A kindergarten class was organized and taught by Alice Ruth Moore (Dunbar-Nelson). Cultural events featured Booker T. Washington, Paul Laurence Dunbar, and other distinguished speakers and musicians.

The first travelers' aid service was formed by the White Rose Mission in 1898. Victoria Matthews and a few volunteers took turns meeting docking boats. The mission hired two agents who were Sunday school teachers, and placed Dorothy J. Boyd at the Old Dominion pier in New York City and Hattie Proctor at the same line in Norfolk, Virginia. Matthews's sister, Anna Rich, later became the New York dock agent.

In 1905 Matthews established the White Rose Travelers' Aid Society. Within approximately ten years, the Society met 50,000 women. At least 5,000 were sheltered at the White Rose Mission.

The White Rose Home and Industrial Association for Working Girls was supported through contributions and fund-raising activities. The patrons included the Rev. Adam Clayton Powell, Sr., and Booker T. Washington. Reformers such as Frances Kellor and Mary White Ovington joined the White Rose Home Association.

Victoria Matthews was superintendent of the White Rose Home until her death in 1907. Her successor, Frances Reynolds Keyser, and other Black women assumed the leadership of the Home. Its location changed several times, moving from 97th Street to 1760 Third Avenue, and later to East 95th Street. It remained at 217 East 86th Street for seventeen years. In 1918, the White Rose Home Association established permanent quarters on West 136th Street.

After 1924, financial support for the White Rose Home came from both the Empire State Federation of Women's Clubs and the Northeastern Federation of Colored Women's Clubs. As the need for separate housing facilities for Black women declined, the White Rose Home was used as a center for forums, club programs, and other community activities.

[See also ASSOCIATIONS FOR THE PROTECTION OF NEGRO WOMEN; WOMAN'S LOYAL UNION OF NEW YORK AND BROOKLYN.]

BIBLIOGRAPHY

Best, Lasalle. "History of the White Rose Mission and Industrial Association" (n.d.), Schomburg Center for Research in Black Culture, New York Public Library; Brown, Hallie Q. *Homespun Heroines and Other Women of Distinction* ([1926] 1988); Lewis, Mary L. "The White Rose Industrial Association: The Friend of the Strange Girl in New York," *Messenger* (April 1925); *New York Age* (May 25, 1905); *New York Age* (July 6, 1905); White Rose Home and Industrial Association. *Annual Report* (1911). Schomburg Center for Research in Black Culture, New York Public Library.

FLORIS BARNETT CASH

WILLIAMS, ELIZABETH BARBARA
see
FRANCISCAN HANDMAIDS OF THE MOST PURE HEART OF MARY

WILLIAMS, FANNIE BARRIER (1855-1944)

Fannie Barrier Williams recognized that racism was a central problem in the United States, but she believed that sexism played an even greater role in inequality. For "to be a colored woman," she asserted, "is to be discredited, mistrusted, and often meanly hated." She worked tirelessly, quietly, and sometimes successfully to eradicate discrimination against Black women.

Fannie Barrier grew up in the North in a sheltered and affluent environment. She was born February 12, 1855, in Brockport, New York, to Anthony J. Barrier and Harriet Prince Barrier. Anthony Barrier, a barber, coal merchant, and homeowner, was an active leader in the predominantly white community. As one of three children (two daughters and one son) of this middle-class Black family, Fannie often attended parties and socialized with others, regardless of race, and felt on equal terms with her white acquaintances. She attended the local schools and the State Normal School at Brockport, from which she graduated in 1870.

Fannie Barrier's innocence of racism and discrimination ended abruptly, however, when she joined other Black and white northern teachers who ventured South during the 1870s to teach freed Black southerners. White southerners taught her that social equality was not a right extended to Black Americans. Jim Crow laws prevailed, and white southerners expected her to strictly adhere to a racist and segregationist code. This racial etiquette, she discovered, intimated that because of her blackness, she belonged to an inferior race.

Quickly leaving the deep South, Fanny Barrier found a teaching post in Washington, D.C. While teaching in the public schools, she explored her artistic talents. She became an art student of several Washington artists and developed her skills as a portrait painter. She also spent some time extending her studies at the New England Conservatory of Music and in private studios in Boston.

While in Washington, D.C., she met a promising young law student, S. Laing Williams. He was a native of Georgia, an 1881 graduate of the University of Michigan, and a former Alabama schoolteacher.

Upon completion of his law degree in 1887, the couple married and moved to Chicago. In Chicago, S. Laing Williams worked as one of eleven assistant attorneys in Northern Illinois. With a recommendation from Booker T. Washington, he later became an assistant district attorney in Chicago.

Fannie Barrier Williams gained notoriety at the Chicago World's Fair in May 1893 when she addressed the Departmental Congress of the National Association of Loyal Women of American Liberty at the World's Congress of Representative Women. In her speech "The Intellectual Progress and Present Status of the Colored Women of the United States since the Emancipation Proclamation," she told the

Fannie Barrier Williams became famous after speaking at the 1893 Chicago World's Fair, but her greatest contributions were probably her work with Provident Hospital—a training hospital for Black staff that served both Black and white patients—and with the women's club movement. [Moorland-Spingarn]

audience that Black women "are the only women in the country for whom real ability, virtue, and special talents count for nothing when they become applicants for respectable employment" (Sewall 1894). A few months later, she told the World's Parliament of Religions that "it should be the province of religion to unite, and not to separate, men and women according to superficial differences of race line" (Barrows 1893). Within the year, Williams was deluged with speaking engagements.

In 1894, Williams was nominated for membership in the elite white Chicago Women's Club. For fourteen months, the club deliberated on admitting a Black woman. Her controversial admission caused some members to withdraw from the club and forced the General Federation of Women's Clubs to confront the issue of Black female membership.

She was an active social welfare reformer in Chicago and took a leading role in several initiatives to create new institutions. Williams was a consultant and fund-raiser for a training school for Black nurses at Provident Hospital, established in 1891. Even though Provident served Black and white patients, Williams argued that a segregated training school for Black women was imperative because "there are other training schools for white women, but none at all for colored women. Why let white women take any of the few places we'll have open."

In 1905, the Frederick Douglass Center opened as a settlement project under the auspices of white Unitarian minister Celia Parker Woolley, with the aid of several prominent Black families, including the Williamses. The center, located on the fringes of the predominantly Black Second Ward, was an interracial experiment dedicated to promoting amicable race relations.

Williams was the Chicago reporter for the *Woman's Era*, a monthly newspaper published by Josephine St. Pierre Ruffin and her daughter, Florida Ruffin Ridley. The newspaper disseminated news about and by Black women throughout the country. Williams supported the *Era*'s call for a national Black female organization in the mid-1890s. By 1896, the National Association of Colored Women was established.

In addition, Williams was chairperson of the committee on state schools for dependent children for the Illinois Woman's Alliance. She was corresponding secretary of the board of directors of the Phyllis Wheatley Home Association, and she belonged to the Prudence Crandall Study Club. The club, an exclusive twenty-five-member elite organization, was primarily a literary society. Williams headed the art and music department. From 1924 to 1926, Williams served on the Chicago Library Board. As the first Black woman to hold that position, she was a trailblazer.

Williams championed Booker T. Washington's industrial education and the need for white philanthropy. She blamed white employers for high unemployment among Black workers and was successful in persuading some white employers to hire Black women. She also abhorred housing segregation, which, she argued, led to demoralizing lifestyles steeped in poverty and crime.

In 1926, Williams returned to her home in Brockport to live with her sister. She died in 1944 at the age of eighty-nine of arteriosclerosis.

[*See also* WORLD'S COLUMBIAN EXPOSITION.]

BIBLIOGRAPHY

Barrows, John Henry, ed. *The World's Parliament of Religions* (1893); David, Jay, ed. *Black Defiance: Black Profiles in Courage* (1972); Davis, Elizabeth Lindsay. *Lifting as They Climb* (1933); *NAW*; Sewall, May Wright, ed. *The World's Congress of Representative Women* (1894); Spear, Allan. *Black Chicago: The Making of a Negro Ghetto, 1890-1920* (1967); Williams, Fannie Barrier. "A Northern Negro's Autobiography," *Independent* (July 14, 1904).

WANDA HENDRICKS

WILLIAMS, MARIE SMITH *see* SELIKA, MARIE SMITH

WILLIAMS, MARION (1927-)

Marion Williams is one of the finest vocalists gospel has produced, yet her impact extends beyond gospel. Much of the falsetto ecstasy inherent in rock 'n' roll can be traced to the style she forged while performing with the Ward Singers in the 1950s. Her greatest strength, however, is her musicianship. She is simply the finest improviser within the gospel tradition, at once the most rhythmic and the bluesiest. Her only equal is Mahalia Jackson.

Marion Williams was born on August 29, 1927, in Miami, Florida, the daughter of a West Indian barber and a South Carolinian laundress. Her father died when she was nine (she still remembers helping him campaign for Franklin Delano Roosevelt). A major influence was her great-aunt, Rebecca Edwards, a native of Cat Island who ran a preschool for the neighborhood children. Despite Edwards's plans for her, Marion was forced to leave school at fourteen to help support her mother. In an interview she said that for years she worked in the laundry, "from sun-up to sun-down," adding, "When I was coming up, we didn't know anything about what they call adolescence" (Heilbut 1985). She began singing as a child, dividing her time among local Sanctified congregations. An older brother had more secular interests, however, and he placed a jukebox ("we called it a piccolo") in the family's yard. So, as a girl, Marion was exposed to blues and jazz, although her only musical thoughts were of gospel. Jon Pareles of the *New York Times* has called her the equal of any living blues singer, and Whitney Balliett of the *New Yorker* considers her one of the greatest jazz singers. Yet she has never performed a worldly song, except for "God Bless the Child," which she transforms into a gospel moan.

Marion Williams was exposed to the pioneer gospel singers, Sanctified shouters like Sister Rosetta Tharpe, Baptist moaners like Mary Johnson Davis, and various male quartets. In 1947, she joined the Ward Singers, and for the next eleven years she was the group's undisputed star. The Ward sound, conceived by Clara Ward, was executed by Marion. Her wide vocal range and mastery of tonal colors were featured as prominently in the background as when she sang lead. Her years of studying preachers paid off; she had no trouble holding her own with the mightiest gospel men. Indeed, her stylistic versatility, encompassing lyrical poignance and a backwoods energy, inspired numerous male performers, from the gospel singer Professor Alex Bradford to Little Richard and the Isley Brothers. Her most famous recordings with the Wards were "Surely God Is Able," "I'm Climbing Higher and Higher," and "Packin' Up."

In 1958, she and several other Ward Singers formed their own group, the Stars of Faith. She stayed with them for six years, a period most notable for her appearance in *Black Nativity*, the first gospel song play. Since 1965, she has performed as a soloist, appearing at numerous festivals in America and Europe. She also was one of the first gospel singers to perform in Africa (1966).

In recent years Marion Williams has received great attention for her performances of a cappella moans. Her slurs and grunts recall old field recordings, but her stylistic authority is such that one doubts whether these traditional hymns have ever been so compellingly sung. In such performances she recalls her musical ancestors, not merely the gospel pioneers

but the nameless workers in fields and factories who expected their songs to "lift heavy burdens." Two of these performances are featured in the 1991 movie *Fried Green Tomatoes* and another is featured in the 1992 movie *Mississippi Masala*.

BIBLIOGRAPHY
Heilbut, Anthony. *The Gospel Sound: Good News and Bad Times* (1985).

SELECTED DISCOGRAPHY
I've Come So Far, Spirit Feel (1987); *Born to Sing the Gospel*, Spirit Feel (1988); *Gospel Warriors*, Spirit Feel (1988); *Surely God Is Able*, Spirit Feel (1990); *The Gospel Sound*, Spirit Feel (1991); *Strong Again*, Spirit Feel (1991); *The Great Gospel Women*, Spirit Feel (1992).

ANTHONY HEILBUT

WILLIAMS, MARY LOU (1910-1981)

Mary Lou Williams takes her rightful place as one of the most highly regarded performers, arrangers, and composers of Black American music. Her niche as projector and protector of jazz is indisputable, and her importance in the history of jazz continues to be seen in the homage paid to her by scores of her musical progeny.

Her first professional period as arranger/pianist began in 1928 when she joined Andy Kirk's band, the Twelve Clouds of Joy. The second period (1941-54) was framed by her composition *Zodiac Suite* and her hiatus in Europe. In 1954, she withdrew from performing for three years in order to explore a religious life, and her last creative period began in 1957 with her return to New York and to performance.

She was born Mary Elfreida Scruggs on May 8, 1910, in Atlanta, Georgia. Her mother, a classically trained pianist, realized when Mary was three years old that her daughter possessed a special musical gift to remember melodies. She was advised to keep Mary away from formal instruction that might restrict imaginative improvisation—and she did just that. At about the age of four, Mary and her mother moved to Pittsburgh where "the little piano girl" interacted with the great stride players, including Earl "Fatha" Hines, Count Basie, Art Tatum, and Duke Ellington. Much later, as an adult artist, Mary Lou Williams, in discussing the tension between notated music and aural sound, said, "My mother ended up not playing [the piano] at all, just reading music" (Handy 1980). During her career, however, Williams judiciously mediated the use of notation and improvisation in her arranging and composition.

As a preteen Williams joined the Buzz and Harris act managed by the Theater Owners Booking Association (TOBA). By the age of seventeen, she had married John Williams, an alto and baritone saxophone player and leader of the Holder Band (later to be Andy Kirk's Band), and moved with him to Kansas City. She worked there until 1941, when she returned to Pittsburgh and wrote for Benny Goodman ("Roll 'Em"), Louis Armstrong, Tommy Dorsey, and Duke Ellington ("Trumpet No End"). "Trumpet No End" is a piece for four trumpets that her second husband, Shorty Baker, played when they worked together in New York at the beginning of her second creative period, which began in 1941. It was during this period that she composed the *Zodiac Suite*, the first of many large compositions comprising several movements. It is a suite of dances named after the twelve signs of the zodiac with each sign dedicated to a musician or friend.

The first three dances of the suite were written for her radio show (WNEW), and a single piece was presented on the air each Sunday. "Capricorn," however, was a piece created for dancer Pearl Primus, who performed, as did Mary Lou Williams, at the Café Society. Interestingly, another Black dancer/anthropologist, Katherine Dunham, choreographed the "Scorpio" movement of the *Zodiac Suite*.

In 1946, the three items "Aquarius," "Scorpio," and "Pisces" were scored for a Carnegie Hall performance by the New York Philharmonic Orchestra. Williams often recounted that she had to copy the "Scorpio" movement overnight herself for the large orchestra (100 parts). Although Black musicians had performed on stage at Carnegie Hall on several occasions since 1919 (for example, Clef Club Orchestra, H. T. Burleigh), this symbolic performance completely eroded the whites-only barrier to Carnegie's stage, and it is especially important that a jazz composer, a Black woman, created a composition for symphony orchestra at that time.

From 1952 to 1957, Mary Lou Williams sought privacy and opted not to play publicly, explaining later that "she had stopped to pray" (Handy 1980). She did return to playing in 1957, and at the urging of her friends Dizzy and Lorraine Gillespie, "Virgo," "Libra," and "Aries" of the *Zodiac Suite* were resurrected, performed at the Newport Jazz Festival, and recorded on Verve Records.

After Williams converted to Roman Catholicism in 1956, her focus and inspiration changed, for during her third creative period she produced three large

For Black, female, and jazz musicians, history was made when three works by jazz composer Mary Lou Williams were presented at Carnegie Hall by the New York Philharmonic Orchestra in 1946. This performance completely eroded the whites-only barrier to the Carnegie Hall stage. [Lorna McDaniel]

liturgical works in jazz style. The versatility of *Mary Lou's Mass* made it suitable for professional, amateur, or children's choirs along with a jazz combo or other instruments. Williams, in preparation for a concert involving an inexperienced school choir, often refined the teacher-trained choir shortly before the concert. Performances were held at New York's Saint Patrick's Cathedral, at the First Kansas City, Missouri, Woman's Jazz Festival (1978), and in several churches throughout the United States.

During this period Williams lived in New York's Hamilton Terrace, where a concern for young people and the infirm became foremost in her mind, and she worked to ease the suffering of society. She also established the Bel Canto Foundation, a shop that collected donated articles for impoverished musicians.

Mary Lou Williams admired beautiful bass lines and composed a huge repository of bass lines for her compositional use. She often worked alone with bassists Percy Heath, Bob Cranshaw, and Buster Williams and with female bassist/singer Charlene Ray.

Her pedagogy of jazz taught that there were no positive developments immediately after bebop, the era that, in her thinking, was the pinnacle and end of the creative surge in jazz. She saw the musical detour away from bebop as a serious cultural loss that impeded not just the continuity of the music but also the functioning of the Black family. To her way of thinking, the electric sounds of the new music, rock 'n' roll, were expressive of violence and, unlike pure acoustical sound, created confusion. She promoted jazz as an art form born of suffering, and she celebrated the blues as a major healing force basic to the structure of jazz. She taught that good music must "swing" and not bounce in a meaningless and "corny" way—that the spiritual science of music, with its deepest realization in improvisation, emanates from a personal will and system of belief. She often expressed this idea to timid students by saying, "Just put your hands on the keys—and you will play."

We find in Williams's musical language the ability to shift to any style and harmonic structure in the history of jazz, from the stride of the ragtime era (with foot pumping of the loud pedal), to the boogie-woogie left-hand span of ten notes, or to the clustered and dissonant chords of avant-garde.

Musicians from all eras honored Mary Lou Williams, and they continue to pay her homage by "signifying on" and by revising her piano treatments and tunes. In 1976, the respected avant-garde pianist Cecil Taylor approached Williams with the idea of a collaboration. The astounding Carnegie Hall concert and its recording, *Embraced*, which came out of that meeting, are a testament to the continuing connection among Black pianists and to the depth of Williams's belief in the blues as the foundation of Black music. Her historic repertoire serves as the framework of the concert, overlaid with Taylor's virtuoso and layered sounds. By manipulating the stereophonic channels (restricting the sound to the left channel), one can hear the echoes of the roots of jazz engulfed within a dramatic and contemporary setting.

During her rich and productive concert, club, and recording career, Mary Lou Williams also worked for periods in the public schools of Pittsburgh, the University of Massachusetts at Amherst, and, from 1976 until her death on May 28, 1981, at Duke University in Durham, North Carolina. Williams's friend, manager, and spiritual advisor, Father Peter O'Brien, a Jesuit priest, participated with her in concert and classroom lecture/performances in which together they demonstrated the history of jazz. She received two Guggenheim Foundation grants as well as several honorary degrees. Mary Lou Williams Lane in Kansas City, the city of her first creative period, is named after her.

BIBLIOGRAPHY

Berendt, Joachim E. Liner notes from *Mary Lou Williams—Black Christ of the Andes*, Musidisc-Europe (1963); Handy, D. Antoinette. "Conversation with . . . Mary Lou Williams: First Lady of the Jazz Keyboard." In *The Black Perspective in Music*, ed. Eileen Southern (1980); Morgenstern, Dan. Liner notes from *Zodiac Suite*, Folkways Records (1945), Cecilia Music (1973); O'Brien, Peter. Liner notes from *Zoning*, Mary Records (1974); O'Brien, Peter and Hank O'Neal. Liner notes from *Mary Lou Williams—Live at the Cookery*, Chiaroscuro Records (n.d.); Williams, Mary Lou and Cecil Taylor. Liner notes from *Embraced*, Pablo Records (1978).

LORNA McDANIEL

WILLIAMS, MYRLIE BEASLEY EVERS (c. 1932-)

Myrlie Beasley was born in Vicksburg, Mississippi. She was reared by her grandmother Annie McCain Beasley and an aunt, Myrlie Beasley Polk, both teachers. After graduation from high school, Myrlie enrolled at Alcorn Agricultural and Mechanical College in Lorman, Mississippi, in 1950 as an education major and music minor.

On her first day at Alcorn, she met Medgar Evers. The fact that he was seven years older and was a veteran caused her guardians to worry, but Myrlie and Medgar were married on December 24, 1951. In 1952, after Medgar's graduation and after Myrlie's sophomore year, the couple settled in Mound Bayou, an all-Black town in the Mississippi delta. Medgar became an insurance agent for Magnolia Mutual Insurance, one of the few Black-owned businesses in Mississippi with good jobs to offer.

Myrlie became deeply involved in Medgar's civil rights work, after his 1954 appointment as the first field secretary for the Mississippi National Association for the Advancement of Colored People (NAACP). Medgar provided leadership in many important struggles: he publicized the Emmett Till murder in 1955, aided James Meredith in desegregating the University of Mississippi, fought against racist violence, and campaigned for voting rights and equal access to public accommodations. Myrlie served as his full-time secretary in the Jackson office and made valuable contributions to the civil rights movement in her own right as office director, speech researcher, hostess, chauffeur, and musician. Volumes of detailed Jackson NAACP correspondence and files for several years after 1954 bear her imprint.

The Everses had three children—Darrell Kenyatta, born in 1953 and given his middle name because of his father's respect for the African leader of the Mau Mau liberation movement in Kenya; Reena Denise, born in 1954; and James Van Dyke, born in 1960.

Medgar Evers was killed in July 1963, the victim of an assassin's bullet many believed to have been fired by Byron de la Beckwith, an avowed segregationist.

In her book *For Us the Living* (with William Peters, 1967), Myrlie Evers speaks openly and honestly about the strains and tensions Medgar's civil rights work introduced into their family life. She describes how her sheltered childhood did not prepare her for the intensity of the movement. She speaks of her resentment, her anger, and her frustration at "sharing her husband" (Evers 1967).

Her story is also one of constant growth and development, however, and she emerges as a person with a clear understanding of and commitment to the struggle. Myrlie Evers was transformed from a sheltered teenager into a coworker of Medgar as secretary in the NAACP office in Jackson. She emerged from this involvement with a powerful commentary on the movement and its significance. "I am left without my husband and my children without a father, but I am left with a strong determination to try and take up where he left off," she said, adding "you can kill a man but you can't kill an idea" (Evers 1967).

Myrlie Evers later settled in California, where she raised their three children and graduated from Pomona College in 1968. In 1987, she married Walter Williams, a retired longshoreman who was active in local civil rights activities. Myrlie worked as director of public affairs for Chevron Oil and campaigned for political office. She serves on the national board of the NAACP and on several other boards.

"You can kill a man but you can't kill an idea," said Myrlie Evers Williams, explaining her determination to continue the work begun by her husband, slain civil rights leader Medgar Evers. Here, she accepts a veterans' award on behalf of her late husband; at right is Mrs. Malcolm Peabody of Massachusetts; at center is Ralph Bunche of the United Nations. [National Archives]

In 1990, she resigned as commissioner of Public Works in Los Angeles. She had been appointed by Mayor Tom Bradley of Los Angeles and was the first Black woman to serve in that position.

Myrlie Evers Williams currently lives in Oregon and is active as a public speaker. Her efforts to keep the contributions of Medgar Evers before the public may lead to a third trial for Byron de la Beckwith for the murder of Medgar Evers.

BIBLIOGRAPHY

Bailey, Ronald. *Remembering Medgar Evers for a New Generation* (1988); Evers, Myrlie with William Peters. *For Us, the Living* (1967); Hampton, Henry and Steve Fayer. *Voices of Freedom: An Oral History of the Civil Rights Movement from the 1950s through the 1980s* (1990).

RONALD BAILEY

WILLIAMS, SHERLEY ANNE (1944-)

In one of Sherley Anne Williams's poems, "I See My Life," the speaker explains that in her male child she sees herself, her parents, her grandparents, and all her ancestors melding into a symbol of courage, strength, and wisdom. This poem is representative of Williams's philosophy that family and ancestors are crucial subjects in writing. Her writing frequently deals with both the individual and collective past of African-Americans. She feels that it is her obligation to tell the truth about Black life and to leave behind numerous models of heroes to help African-Americans understand themselves.

Literary critic, poet, and novelist Sherley Anne Williams was born in Bakersfield, California, on August 25, 1944, to Jesse Winson and Lena Silver Williams. One of four sisters, Williams grew up in the low-income housing projects where her family battled poverty. She and her sisters (Ruby, Jesmarie, and Lois) were very close and stored up ways to survive by observing their parents' indomitable spirit.

Williams attended junior high and high school in Fresno, California. After earning a Bachelor's degree in history at California State University in 1966, she moved to Washington, D.C., where she spent one year in graduate school at Howard University. After working at Federal City College in Washington, D.C., for several years, she transferred to Brown University in Providence, Rhode Island, where she taught in the Black Studies department and earned a Master's degree in 1972. She then returned to California State University as associate professor of English. In 1975,

she joined the faculty of the University of California, San Diego, where she is currently a professor of literature. As a teacher, administrator, and mother of one son, John Malcolm, she has had to carve time to write.

Williams began her writing career in 1967 with the publication of the short story "Tell Martha Not to Moan." Her first major work appeared in 1972, a literary study entitled *Give Birth to Brightness: A Thematic Study in Neo-Black Literature,* in which she analyzes works by Amiri Baraka, James Baldwin, and Ernest Gaines and concludes that true Black heroes have their origins in the Black folkloric tradition. Her own vision emerged three years later with the publication of *The Peacock Poems* (1975), which was nominated for the National Book Award in Poetry in 1976. A second collection of poems, *Someone Sweet Angel Chile* (1982), established Williams as a major African-American poet in the blues tradition. Both poetry volumes explore the struggles and triumphs of lower-income Black women, upon whose backs many professional women have stood.

The mysticism of Williams's debut novel, *Dessa Rose* (1987), links her to Toni Morrison and Alice Walker. An illuminating neo-slave narrative, the book focuses on a Black woman, Dessa, who leads an insurrection. Dessa and her companions not only escape hanging but also become successful entrepreneurs. Rufel, a white plantation mistress abandoned by a gambling husband, joins with Dessa and her friends to dupe white planters by selling them into slavery, helping them escape, and reselling them in other locations.

Williams's literary criticism, poetry, and fiction are extraordinary and place her among the most highly regarded neo-Black American writers.

BIBLIOGRAPHY

Howard, Lillie P. "Sherley Anne Williams." In *Afro-American Poets since 1955, DLB* (1985); Kubitschek, Missy Dehn. *Claiming the Heritage: African-American Women Novelists and History* (1991); Tate, Claudia, ed. *Black Women Writers at Work* (1986); Walker, Melissa. *Down from the Mountaintop: Black Women's Novels in the Wake of the Civil Rights Movement, 1966-1989* (1991).

ELIZABETH BROWN-GUILLORY

WILLIAMS, VANESSA LYNN (1963-)

Best known for her controversial ten-month stint as Miss America, Vanessa Lynn Williams has also distinguished herself as an actress and singer.

In September 1983, the twenty-year-old Syracuse University musical theater major made history as the first Black woman in the sixty-three-year history of the Miss America pageant to win the swimsuit and talent competitions and, ultimately, the crown. Her selection sparked debate within the Black community: some hailed Williams's breakthrough as on par with that of baseball great Jackie Robinson; others discounted her selection because of her fair complexion, green eyes, and straight, golden brown hair. One *Washington Post* columnist was quoted in *Ebony* as writing: "Williams's victory serves only as a bittersweet confirmation that the lighter your skin, the better your chances of being accepted" (Norment 1983). Williams's outspokenness on abortion rights, the Equal Rights Amendment, and especially race and her white boyfriend of four years only heightened the controversy.

In July 1984, Williams's reign was cut short after *Penthouse* magazine published (without her permission) a series of sexually explicit photos featuring Williams and a white woman, taken when she was eighteen. Williams later recalled "trusting a photographer whom I shouldn't have" as her "most irrational act" (Lavin 1992). Just six weeks before she was scheduled to pass on her crown, Williams again made pageant history, this time as the first woman to relinquish the title for violation of the Miss America moral code. She was succeeded by Suzette Charles, a Black woman and aspiring actress representing New Jersey. Williams's forced resignation sparked as much controversy as the pictures themselves. People of widely varying political views, from *Ms.* editors to network news commentators—even *Penthouse* publisher Bob Guccione—noted the seeming hypocrisy of pageant officials who express "shock and mortally offended morals" (Morgan 1984) yet profit off the judging of scantily clad women. Though 67 percent of women polled by *Glamour* magazine (December 1984) felt Williams should lose the title ("sexual pornography is not the same thing as acknowledging sexual attractiveness"), 44 percent believed that the Miss America pageant and *Penthouse* magazine were fundamentally the same in their exploitation of women ("Both exploit women and treat them as sexual objects"). In a significant show of support by Black women, *Essence* ran a cover story on Williams two months after the story broke, with editor Susan Taylor condemning men who "make their livings pimping off of attractive young women" and asserting that Williams "did not violate this society's ethics. This society's ethics violated you. . . . Your beauty and your gender have been exploited" (October 1984).

After abdicating, Williams abandoned her plan to continue her Syracuse studies, a decision she later regretted. In 1987, she resumed the acting career she began in college, making her film debut in *The Pick-Up Artist* (1987) and then starring in *Under the Gun* (1989). Williams's television credits include cameo appearances in a number of prime-time shows, hostessing NBC's *Showtime at the Apollo*, a starring role in Debbie Allen's made-for-television movie *Stompin' at the Savoy* (1992), and the role of Suzanne de Passe, president of Motown Productions, in *The Jacksons: An American Dream*, a miniseries about the Jackson Five (ABC, November 1992).

In January 1987, Williams married Ramon Hervey II. Hervey, the public relations specialist whom Williams's attorneys had called in when the *Penthouse* scandal broke, helped guide his wife toward a recording career. In the spring of 1988, Williams released her debut album, *The Right Stuff*, which spawned four top-ten hits on *Billboard*'s Black Singles chart: the title track, "He's Got the Look," "Dreamin'," and "Darlin' I." The album earned her three Grammy nominations and the NAACP's Best New Female Artist Award. Williams's second album, *The Comfort Zone* (1991), featured four more top-ten singles and remained on *Billboard*'s Black Album chart for over five months. She has made musical appearances on *Soul Train, Live!, Dick Clark Presents, Club MTV, Live at the Improv*, and Black Entertainment Television's *Video Soul*.

Williams, who was born March 18, 1963, in Tarrytown, New York, currently resides in Los Angeles with her husband/manager and their two daughters, Melanie and Jillian. She has one brother, Christopher, five years her junior. Her parents, Milton and Helen Williams, live in Westchester County, New York, where they are both music teachers in the public school system.

BIBLIOGRAPHY

Bennett, Lerone, Jr. "What Is Black Beauty? Selection of First Black 'Miss America' Revives Argument over Black Beauty Standards," *Ebony* (June 1984); *Billboard*. "Hot Black Singles" (1988, 1989, 1991, 1992); *Ebony*. "Letters to the Editor" (February 1984, March 1984, August 1984); *Glamour*. "This Is What You Thought" (December 1984); *Jet*. "Ex-Miss America Endures Pain, Embarrassment Sparked by Flap over Nude Pix" (August 6, 1984), and "Miss America De-throned" (July 13, 1984), and "Vanessa Williams: New Miss America Wants Character, Not Color, to Count" (October 10, 1983); Jordan, Pat. "Vanessa Redressed: Having Done the Unthinkable, Vanessa Williams Emerges Unsinkable," *Gentleman's Quarterly* (June 1990); Lavin, Cheryl. "Fast Track: Vanessa Williams:

Singer, Actress," *The Oakland* (County, Michigan) *Press* (July 3, 1992); Minnery, Tom. "The Tarnished Crown of Miss America," *Christianity Today* (September 7, 1984); Morgan, Robin. "The Vanessa Williams Controversy: What's a Feminist to Think?" *Ms.* (October 1984); Norment, Lynn. " 'Miss America' Vanessa Williams Is Black, Brainy, and Beautiful," *Ebony* (December 1983), and "Vanessa Williams Finds Success with the Right Stuff," *Ebony* (December 1988), and "Vanessa Williams: Success Is the Best Revenge," *Ebony* (April 1990); Stetler, Susan L., ed. *Biography Almanac*, 3rd ed. (1987); Taylor, Susan L. "For Vanessa," *Essence* (October 1984); Whitaker, Charles. "A New Life for Vanessa Williams: Marriage, Career Help the Former Miss America Rebound from Controversy," *Ebony* (April 1987); *WWBA* (1992).

DISCOGRAPHY

The Right Stuff, Wing Records [division of Polygram] 887-386-7 (1988); *The Comfort Zone*, Wing Records 843-522-4 (1991).

N. H GOODALL

WILLIAMSON, SARAH (1899-1986)

Sarah Williamson liked to tell how she always came back to the United States from Liberia C.O.D. (cash on delivery) until her passage could be paid by the National Baptist Convention U.S.A., Inc. During her eight years in Africa she took several furloughs in the United States where she campaigned to raise funds for mission work.

Sarah Williamson, her parents' second child, was born in Norfolk, Virginia, on December 8, 1899. She was sent to boarding school at Hampton Normal School (now Hampton University) in Hampton, Virginia, where she completed four years of high school and two years of normal school. Upon graduation from Hampton she attended the University of Rochester (New York) through her sophomore year, training in preparation for missionary work in Africa.

Williamson sailed to Liberia in November 1924, arriving six weeks later. She was stationed at Suehn Industrial Academy, becoming its third principal. It was through her efforts that Suehn became such a vital force in the National Baptist Convention's mission program, since many of the buildings on the campus were erected under her supervision.

Early in her missionary experience in Liberia, Williamson became very discouraged when she learned that her African translator was not interpreting her religious messages correctly. She decided to work with the children, believing that they could learn English more easily than their parents and that they could teach her their language. She would teach them to read and she hoped that they, in turn, would teach their parents to read the Bible.

In 1932, Williamson returned to the United States. She was married and widowed twice. In 1954, she was appointed as a missionary-at-large in West Africa, returned to Suehn Industrial Academy as dean of girls, and worked there until 1957. She died in Washington, D.C., in December 1986.

BIBLIOGRAPHY

Jacobs, Sylvia M. " 'Say Africa When You Pray': The Activities of Early Black Baptist Women Missionaries among Liberian Women and Children," *Sage: A Scholarly Journal on Black Women* (Fall 1986); *Mission Herald* (1936, 1939-40, 1954-55, 1970).

SYLVIA M. JACOBS

Through the untiring efforts of Sarah Williamson, Suehn Industrial Academy in Liberia became a vital force in the National Baptist Convention's mission program. [Sylvia Jacobs]

WILLIS, GERTRUDE POCTE GEDDES (1878-1970)

"Miss Gert," as Gertrude Willis was called by many who knew her, was a New Orleans business leader and community activist. She pioneered in a profession that was not the usual choice of women born in the nineteenth century. She succeeded as an insurance executive and funeral director and became an inspiration to later African-American women who entered the same professions.

One of three daughters born to Oscar and Louise Pocte, Gertrude was born in St. Bernard Parish in Louisiana on March 9, 1878, near the small fishing community of Happy Jack in the general area of Port Sulphur. While she was still young, her family moved to New Orleans, where she received formal schooling that did not go beyond the elementary grades. The family affiliated with St. John the Baptist Catholic Church on Dryades Street (now Oretha Castle Haley Boulevard). After the establishment of Holy Ghost Catholic Church in 1915, Willis became a parishioner and retained membership there until her death on February 20, 1970.

Twice married and twice widowed, Gertrude first married Clem Geddes, son of George Geddes, who operated a funeral home on South Rampart Street. Clem died November 12, 1913. In 1919, Gertrude married dentist and businessman Dr. William A. Willis. He died April 17, 1947. No children were born of either union.

Each·of the three sons of George Geddes chose to become funeral directors, but each established his business independently of the others. One became proprietor of Joseph Geddes Funeral Home; another formed a partnership and became coproprietor of Geddes and Richards Funeral Home. Clem established a firm in partnership with a local barber, Arnold Moss, in 1909. Gertrude was part of the venture and continued the partnership, operating as Geddes and Moss, for several years after Clem's death. Eventually she filed for reorganization and thereafter operated the business under the name Gertrude Geddes Willis Funeral Home and Life Insurance Company.

The companies formed by the other two Geddes brothers no longer survive, but family members have continued Willis's tradition of service in the funeral and insurance businesses and now operate five establishments—three in New Orleans and two in Houma, Louisiana. All trace back to the firm started by Willis and Clem in 1909 and, further, to the firm of Clem's father, George. Gertrude Geddes Willis Funeral Home and Life Insurance Company proudly boasts of "over 135 years of service." The original

A prominent New Orleans business leader and community activist, Gertrude Willis was owner and manager of a funeral parlor and life insurance company.

site on Jackson Avenue in New Orleans is still in use after periodic renovations and continual expansion.

During her long career, numerous awards came to "Miss Gert." One was a silver cup presented to her by her employees in 1915. Other honors came from organizations, both social and professional, to which she and Dr. Willis belonged. Among these groups were the Original Illinois Club; local, state, and national associations of funeral directors; and the Zulu Social Aid and Pleasure Club. Willis also held membership in the Ladies Auxiliary of the Knights of Peter Claver (Ct. no. 52), the National Association for the Advancement of Colored People, the Young Men's Christian Association, the Urban League, Crescent City Funeral Directors and Embalming Association of New Orleans, National Insurance Association, and many other organizations.

Willis is buried in the family tomb in St. Louis Cemetery Number 3, New Orleans, along with both of her husbands.

BIBLIOGRAPHY

Louisiana Weekly. Obituary (February 28, 1970); Misshore, Joseph, Jr. Personal interview (January 6, 1992); *Who's Who in Colored Louisiana*, ed. A. E. Perkins (1930).

FLORENCE BORDERS

WILSON, HARRIET E. (b. c. 1827)

On the eighteenth day of August 1859, Harriet E. Wilson registered the copyright of her novel, a fictional third-person autobiography titled *Our Nig: or, Sketches from the Life of a Free Black, in a Two-Story White House, North. Showing That Slavery's Shadows Fall Even There.* The novel's publication date was September 5. In her preface, Wilson asked her "colored brethren" to purchase her book so that she might support herself and her child. Just five months and twenty-four days later, the Amherst, New Hampshire, *Farmer's Cabinet* recorded in its obituary section the death of George Mason Wilson, seven years old, the only son of H. E. Wilson. The "color" of the child is recorded on his death certificate as "Black."

Harriet Wilson wrote a sentimental novel so that she could regain the right to care for her only son. Six months later, her son died of that standard disease, "fever." The record of his death, alone, proved sufficient to demonstrate his mother's racial identity and authorship of the book, and so Harriet Wilson entered history as probably the first African-American to publish a novel in the United States, the fifth African-American to publish fiction in English, and one of the first two Black women to publish a novel in any language.

Despite their importance to the African-American literary tradition, however, Wilson and her text seem to have been ignored or overlooked both by her "colored brethren" universally and by even the most scrupulous scholars for more than a century for reasons as curious and as puzzling as they are elusive.

Reconstructing the life and times of Harriet E. Wilson is a challenge. Even her exact birthdate and date of death are unknown. Information in the 1850 federal census of the state of New Hampshire indicates that she was born Harriet Adams in 1827 or 1828. However, the 1860 federal census of Boston, to which she had moved, indicates that she was born in Fredericksburg, Virginia, in 1807 or 1808.

It seems definite, however, that in 1850 Harriet Adams lived with a white family, the Boyles, in Milford, New Hampshire. Because the Boyles had four adult nonfamily members living with them, the home probably was a kind of boarding house, and the Boyles may very well have been remunerated by the county for sheltering aged and disabled persons.

One year after the census, in 1851, Harriet Adams married Thomas Wilson. In late May, or early June, 1852, George Mason Wilson was born, in Goffstown, New Hampshire, the first and apparently only child of the Wilsons. In Goffstown was located the Hillsborough County Farm. One of the letters ap-

pended to Wilson's novel states that, abandoned by her husband, the author of *Our Nig* was forced—after "days passed; weeks passed"—to go to the "County House," where she gave birth to a child.

It also is fairly certain that Wilson had moved to Boston by 1855 and, according to the Boston City Directory, that she remained there through 1863.

These are the bare bones of Wilson's life, drawn from public documents. They correspond dramatically to assertions about the life of the author of *Our Nig* that were made by three acquaintances who endorsed her novel in an appendix. Another source of confirmation is the plot of *Our Nig*—described as autobiographical by Wilson's supporters—which parallels those major events of her life that have been verified.

These sources help us put flesh on the biographical skeleton. According to the letter of Margareta Thorn, one of the three corroborating acquaintances, Wilson was hired out as a very young child to a family that put her to work "both in the house and in the field," allegedly ruining her health by unduly difficult work. By the time she was eighteen, her health was seriously impaired. For a time, according to the letter of an acquaintance calling herself Allida, the young woman worked as a straw sewer in Massachusetts, most probably in the area around Worcester, living in the home of a Mrs. Walker. Wilson was adept at her work, but her health prevented her from working continuously, a condition that forced Mrs. Walker to nurse her "in a room joining her own chamber."

This was the best part of Wilson's life, a time of comparative comfort with the support of kind friends. Unfortunately, she then met Thomas, whom she soon married. The two left Massachusetts and made their home in New Hampshire. Briefly. Then Thomas went to sea, abandoning his young, pregnant wife. It was at this point that she entered the county farm, which, according to George Plummer Hadley's *History of the Town of Goffstown*, consisted of a large farm house, a barn, a "small dwelling-house near the oak tree," and some smaller buildings. The "paupers" were "scattered through different buildings, which were heated by wood fires." Conditions were apparently horrid: in 1853, some of the inmates "were stricken with smallpox, and it was necessary to build a pesthouse" for their proper isolation and care.

Wilson remained at the county home until her baby was born. Then her errant husband returned just long enough to take his family out of the farm and move them to another town. For a time he supported his family well enough, but then he left again. Soon Wilson's poor health made it necessary for her to give up her child to kind, apparently white, foster parents. Oddly, at this point Wilson went into the beauty business. Having been given, by a compassionate stranger, a recipe for getting rid of grey hair, Wilson entered this trade until, again, her health broke down. It was at this point that, confined to bed, she turned to literature as a method of supporting herself and getting back her child.

Our Nig is based on this life story, but it is definitely a work of fiction; it also is definitely the work of Harriet Wilson. It is quite unlike Harriet Jacobs's *Incidents in the Life of a Slave Girl,* whose prefatory authenticator, Lydia Maria Child, admits minimal "revision," "condensation," and "arrangement." Not one of the three letters appended to *Our Nig* questions that Wilson wrote all the words in the text in their exact order. A letter of Wilson's, which Allida quotes at length, reveals the same attention to detail and event that is evident in the text of the novel; that is, it is written in the same style, giving further evidence of Wilson's authorship. Her accomplishment is all the more astonishing because the novel reads so much more fluidly, and its plot seems so much less contrived, than the novels published before *Our Nig* in the African-American tradition. Astonishment grows when we take into consideration that the authors of two of those novels, William Wells Brown and Martin R. Delany, traveled widely, published extensively, lectured regularly, and educated themselves diligently. Delany even studied medicine at Harvard.

Moreover, *Our Nig* is significant in its form. Wilson used the plot structure of her contemporary white female novelists, yet abandoned that structure when it failed to satisfy the needs of her well-crafted tale. In other words, she revised significantly what was known as the white woman's novel and thereby made the form her own. By this act of formal revision, she *created* the Black woman's novel, not merely because she was the first Black woman to write a novel in English, but because she *invented* her own plot structure through which to narrate the saga of her orphaned mulatto heroine. In this important way, Wilson inaugurated the African-American literary tradition in a fundamentally *formal* manner.

Nonetheless, this remarkable accomplishment was virtually ignored for a century after its publication. A systematic search of all extant copies of Black and reform newspapers and magazines that were in circulation contemporaneously with the publication of *Our Nig* yielded not one notice or review, nor did searches through the Boston dailies and the Amherst *Farmer's Cabinet.* Other Black fiction of the time, though not

popularly reviewed, was reviewed on occasion. That such a significant novel, the very first written by a Black woman, would remain unnoticed in Boston in 1859, a veritable center of abolitionist reform and passion, and by a growing Black press eager to celebrate all Black achievements in the arts and sciences, remains one of the troubling enigmas of African-American literary history. The list of people and publications who do *not* mention Wilson and her book is too long to insert here, but it includes Du Bois's three important bibliographies, Murray's *Preliminary List of Books and Pamphlets by Negro Authors* (prepared for the American Negro Exhibit at the Paris Exhibition of 1900), and all of the late-nineteenth- and early-twentieth-century Black biographical dictionaries.

If the historians, bibliophiles, and bibliographers overlooked Harriet Wilson, the literary historians fared only a bit better. The only references to *Our Nig* that have been discovered give the book little importance. John Herbert Nelson mentions the title only in passing in his 1926 study, *The Negro Character in American Literature.* Herbert Ross Brown, in *The Sentimental Novel in America, 1789-1860* (1940), implies that H. E. Wilson is a white male! Monroe N. Work, in his monumental compilation, *A Bibliography of the Negro in Africa and America,* does indeed list both author and title but under the category, "Novels by White Authors Relating to the Negro." In his 1972 dissertation on miscegenation in the American novel, James Joseph McKinney discusses the novel's plot. Wilson is listed in Geraldine Matthew's bibliography, *Black Writers, 1771-1949,* and in Fairbanks and Engeldinger's *Black American Fiction: A Bibliography,* but with no information beyond that found in the second column of Lyle Wright's three-volume listing of American fiction.

Curiously enough, the most complete entry for the title was made in a 1980 catalogue of the Howard S. Mott Company of Sheffield, Massachusetts, a company well regarded among antiquarians. The listing, prepared by Daniel Mott, asserted that Wilson's novel was the first by an African-American woman. Mott decided that Wilson was a Black woman because of evidence presented in the letters appended to the text.

That Wilson's novel was, to all intents and purposes, lost to the tradition for more than a century seems clear. The question of why it was so ignored is difficult to answer. Herbert Ross Brown, though mistaking the race and gender of the author, made an insightful comment in his 1940 study. "The author of *Our Nig,*" he writes, "dared to treat with sympathetic understanding the marriage of Jim, a Black, to a white woman who had been seduced and deserted." This reference to the marriage of the heroine's parents may point up one of the causes of the book's neglect—the absolute horror of interracial marriage, even among most abolitionists. It also may lead us to the more general cause.

Harriet E. Wilson's preface to *Our Nig* is an extraordinary document in the African-American literary tradition. It is, if not unique, one of the rare instances in which a Black author has openly anticipated a hostile reaction to her text from antislavery forces. She warns, in effect, that her book is not about the horrors of slavery in the South but about the horrors of racism in the North. Moreover, she states that

> I do not pretend to divulge every transaction in my own life, which the unprejudiced would declare unfavorable in comparison with treatment of legal bondmen: I have purposely omitted what would most provoke shame in our good anti-slavery friends at home.

The villains of *Our Nig* are not slaveholders and overseers. They are the women of a northern white household. Their crimes will not be destroyed by the abolition of slavery but only by a complete reexamination and amendment of the economic and social position of Black women in American society.

Literarily, Wilson's achievement was that she combined the received conventions of the sentimental novel with certain key conventions of the slave narrative to create a new form, of which *Our Nig* is the unique example. Had subsequent Black authors had this text to draw upon, perhaps the Black literary tradition would have developed more quickly and more resolutely than it did. It seems possible that, by challenging racism directly and unequivocally in a society that was not yet prepared to come to terms with the issue on that level, Harriet Wilson, through no fault of her own, condemned herself to obscurity and unwittingly slowed the emergence of a distinctive Black voice in American fiction.

BIBLIOGRAPHY

AAWW; Bell, Bernard W. "Harriet E. Wilson." In his *The Afro-American Novel and Its Tradition* (1987); *DLB*; Foster, Frances Smith. "Adding Color and Contour to Early American Self-Portraitures: Autobiographical Writings of Afro-American Women." In *Conjuring: Black Women, Fiction, and Literary Tradition*, ed. Marjorie Pryse and Hortense J. Spillers (1985); Gates, Henry Louis. "Introduction." In Harriet E. Wilson, *Our Nig: or, Sketches from the Life of a Free Black, in a Two-Story White House, North. Showing That Slavery's Shadows Fall Even There* ([1859] 1983); Gates, Henry Louis and David Ames Curtis. "Establishing the Identity of the Author of *Our Nig*." In *Wild Women in the Whirlwind: Afra-American Culture and the Contemporary Literary Renaissance*, ed. Joanna Braxton and Andree Nicola McLaughlin (1990).

HENRY LOUIS GATES, JR.

WILSON, MARGARET BUSH (1919-)

That there is no progress without struggle, a saying widely attributed to Black nationalist Marcus Garvey, must be the battle cry of Margaret Bush Wilson, whose life has been characterized by fights against unfair laws and practices, segregation, housing discrimination, and poverty. Her first victory came when, as a young lawyer, she assisted her father, James T. Bush, president of the local real estate brokers association, in what became the framework for *Shelley* v. *Kraemer*, the case that led to the 1948 U.S. Supreme Court decision declaring restrictive housing covenants unenforceable under the law.

Not all of Wilson's battles have been with the establishment, however. She stands for her beliefs, even in the face of opposition. For example, Wilson endorsed the nomination of Clarence Thomas as Associate Justice of the Supreme Court in 1991, despite his denunciation by many women's and civil rights groups, including the National Association for the Advancement of Colored People (NAACP), to which she has given her life's work.

Wilson's courage and single-mindedness typify her personality and convictions. In 1983, after years of troubled administration at the NAACP, where she had served as chairperson of the national board since 1975, Wilson tried to correct the association's continuing management problems. However, instead of a productive meeting of minds, old feuds and bitter feelings between Wilson and NAACP Executive Director Benjamin Hooks distorted the issues. Wilson suspended Hooks but was pressured to reinstate him a week later. Wilson has characterized this struggle as the "moment of truth," when she came face to face with what she calls "sexism in the most ironic place" (*Washington Post* 1983). Although ridiculed, Wilson stayed the course and fought even harder for the ideals of the organization to which she had committed herself for more than sixty years.

Born Margaret Berenice Bush on January 30, 1919, she recalls, "I was literally born and raised in the NAACP, and the issues that it faces have been a part of my earliest experiences" (Jackson 1975). Activism in the NAACP was indeed a family tradition. Both her parents were active members of the St. Louis branch. Her mother, Berenice Casey Bush, served on the executive committee. Her brother, James, Jr., and sister, Ermine, also were members. Ermine regularly modeled for the NAACP's national journal, *Crisis*.

In addition to being exposed to the inequities of life through the work of the NAACP, growing up in St. Louis during the Great Depression made Wilson sensitive to the plight of poor people. She realized very early on that the only way to help oneself and others was through education. After graduating from Sumner High School in 1935, she enrolled in Talladega College, Talladega, Alabama, where she obtained her Bachelor of Arts degree in economics cum laude. Her desire to better people's lives inspired her to pursue a career in law, and in 1943 she received her law degree from Lincoln University School of Law. At Lincoln she met Robert E. Wilson, whom she later married; they have one son, Robert Edmund Wilson III.

Wilson returned to St. Louis to practice law as U.S. Attorney at the Department of Agriculture and later as Assistant Attorney General. She also deepened her commitment to the NAACP, assuming leadership positions on the local executive board. In 1958, she was elected president of the St. Louis branch and, in 1962, president of the Missouri state branch.

In the 1960s, Wilson's commitment reached the national level. In 1963, her excellent leadership and organization of the NAACP's first statewide conference in Missouri earned her a seat on the national executive board. President Lyndon B. Johnson appointed her to the Anti-Poverty and Civil Rights Act of 1964 task force. The Johnson administration introduced the Model Cities program, a federal initiative to increase aid to severely distressed urban areas. Having worked for the Missouri Office of Urban Affairs and as founder of the Model Housing Corporation, which was designed to secure federal grants for housing, Wilson was a highly qualified candidate to fill a vacancy in the position of Deputy Director of the St. Louis Model Cities Agency in 1968.

Her other professional positions include administrator for Community Services and Continuing Education, legal specialist for the state Technical Assistance Office, professor for the Council on Legal Education Opportunity at Lincoln University School of Law, Assistant Director of the St. Louis Lawyers

for Housing, chair of the Land Reutilization Authority of St. Louis, and senior partner in the firm of Wilson, Smith, Wunderluch, and Smith.

Wilson is a member of many community, professional, and service organizations, including Alpha Kappa Alpha sorority, the Missouri Council on Criminal Justice, the St. Louis Lawyers Association, and the Mound City, Missouri, the American, and the National Bar associations. She has served on the board of the Monsanto Company and of the Police Foundation and as a trustee of Washington University and Saint Augustine's College.

Although she is the recipient of many awards, one of her most treasured is the Democracy in Action Award, given to her in 1978 by the American Jewish Conference, an organization committed to human rights.

BIBLIOGRAPHY

Black Issues in Higher Education. "Professional Appointments" (January 15, 1987); *CBWA; EBA; Ebony.* "Woman Power at the NAACP" (April 1975), and "Women at the Top: By Accepting Challenges and Sidestepping Obstacles, These Women Have Reached the Pinnacle of Their Careers" (August 1982); *Essence.* "Leading Voices: Our Styles of Protest" (October 1982); Jackson, George F. *Black Women History Makers: A Portrait* (1975); *Jet.* "Margaret Wilson Cries Foul in NAACP Board Vote" (January 23, 1984), and "NAACP Board Scraps 'Sour Grapes' Charges against Benjamin Hooks" (June 27, 1983), and "NAACP Hits Reagan's Economic Emancipation as New Black Bondage" (July 16, 1981), and "People" (January 15, 1987), and "Reagan Woos Blacks in Capitol Hill Budget Row" (July 9, 1981), and "Wilson Suspends Benjamin Hooks as NAACP Executive Director" (June 6, 1983); *New York Times.* "Ex-Chairman of NAACP Says She May Sue Board" (January 10, 1984), and "New NAACP Head: Margaret Bush Wilson" (January 14, 1975); *Newsweek.* "The NAACP: Hooks Is Back" (June 6, 1983), and "The NAACP Suspends Hooks" (May 30, 1983); *Portraits in Silhouette: The Contributions of Black Women in Missouri* (1980); *Time.* "Power Play: Mutiny at the NAACP" (May 30, 1983), and " 'Twilight Zone' for the NAACP" (July 12, 1982); *Washington Post.* "Chairwoman of NAACP on Mississippi Suit" (September 25, 1976), and "Joblessness Brings on Trouble, Two NAACP Leaders Warn" (June 30, 1975), and "New Struggles on the Long Journey: Margaret Bush Wilson Breaks Her Silence on Women's Rights and the NAACP" (November 28, 1983), and "Outgoing Chief Blasts NAACP Board" (January 10, 1975), and "A Tough Mary Poppins" (January 14, 1975).

FRANCELLO PHILLIPS-CALHOUN

WILSON, NANCY (1937-)

Born February 20, 1937, in Chillicothe, Ohio, Nancy Wilson began her musical career primarily in Columbus, Ohio. She was active as a vocalist during her teenage years, singing in nightclubs and making local television appearances, and in 1956-58 she toured the Midwest and Canada with Rusty Bryant's band. In 1959, her biggest career break came when she met Cannonball Adderley. When she sat in with the Adderley band in a 1959 gig in Columbus, Adderley was so impressed that he invited Wilson to record an album with him. She soon signed a contract with Capitol Records and in 1962 recorded an album with Adderley. Wilson's career blossomed. She received rave reviews from several prominent jazz musicians and thereafter was booked for numerous appearances in concert halls, nightclubs, and jazz clubs throughout the United States and Europe. Her recording career also blossomed, including several new albums, one with George Shearing.

Wilson's vocal style displays remarkable versatility, giving equal emphasis to both jazz and popular music. She relies upon a keen ear for both tonal and timbre nuances, an emotional intensity that draws emotion and meaning from each word of the text, and a stage presence that evokes a belief that Wilson has lived the words that she sings. It is also significant that after an experiment with popular music, primarily in the 1970s, Wilson resumed her jazz career with several leading jazz musicians in the early 1980s. She toured Japan with Hank Jones in 1981-82 and performed with the Art Farmer/Benny Golson quintet at the Playboy Jazz Festival in 1982. Since the early 1980s, Wilson has concentrated on both jazz and popular music, singing in concert halls, nightclubs, and making television appearances.

BIBLIOGRAPHY

Budds, Michael J. "Nancy Wilson." In *The New Grove Dictionary of Jazz*, ed. Barry Kernfeld (1988); Gardner, B. "The Baby Grows Up," *Downbeat* (1964).

SELECTED DISCOGRAPHY

Nancy Wilson/Cannonball Adderley, Capitol ST1657 (1962); *Yesterday's Love Songs, Today's Blues*, Capitol ST2012 (1963); *How Glad I Am*, Capitol ST2155 (1964); *Nancy Wilson with George Shearing: The Swingin's Mutual*, Capitol SM1524 (1964); *Today, Tomorrow, Forever*, Capitol T-2082 (1964); *Gentle Is My Love*, Capitol (S)T 2351 (1965); *From Broadway with Love*, Capitol (S)T 2433 (1966); *Nancy—Naturally*, Capitol (S)T 2634 (1966); *Tender Loving Care*, Capitol (S)T 2555 (1966); *A Touch of Today*, Capitol (S)T 2495 (1966); *Lush Life*, Capitol T2557 (1967); *The Very Best of Nancy Wilson*, Capitol SKA02947 (1968); *I've Never Been to Me*, Capitol ST11659 (1977); *Music on My Mind*, Capitol SMAS11786 (1978); *Nancy Wilson's Just for Now*, Capitol (S)T 2712 (1989).

EDDIE S. MEADOWS

After early encouragement from jazz great Cannonball Adderley, Nancy Wilson has been successful as both a jazz and popular singer. She has worked in nightclubs, jazz clubs, and concert halls throughout the United States, Europe, and Japan, in addition to her recording career. [Schomburg Center]

WINFREY, OPRAH (1954-)

Oprah Winfrey is a talk-show host, actress, and cultural phenomenon. Her success could almost certainly never have happened at any time in the past. That it has happened at all must be attributed to a combination of history and her own unique talents.

Winfrey was born on January 29, 1954, to Vernita Lee and Vernon Winfrey. When her parents, who were not married, separated, she went to live with her maternal grandmother on a farm. Although life was austere, the young girl thrived. She learned to read

Oprah Winfrey is a phenomenon: both an Academy Award-nominated actress and an Emmy winning talk-show host and producer, she is one of the most successful women in the history of entertainment. Here, the Reverend Jesse Jackson gives a "thumbs-up" sign at a tribute to Jackson in July 1988 in Atlanta, Georgia, as an exuberant Oprah shares the stage. [UPI/ Bettmann]

before she was three and was in the third grade by the age of six. At that point, she went to live with her mother in Milwaukee. Vernita Lee managed a subsistence-level existence with income from welfare and domestic work, and she had little time to supervise her daughter. Between the ages of nine and twelve, Winfrey was repeatedly subjected to sexual abuse by a cousin and then by other men close to her family. She began to have such serious behavioral problems that Lee gave up and sent the girl to her father in Nashville.

Life changed dramatically. Vernon Winfrey was a respected member of his community, and he put his daughter under the strictest guidance. Soon she was excelling in school again and in extracurricular activities such as speech and drama and the student council. While she was still in high school, a local radio station, WVOL, hired her to broadcast the news. She attended Tennessee State University on a scholarship she had won in an Elks Club oratorical contest.

While in her freshman year, Winfrey won the titles of Miss Black Nashville and Miss Black Tennes-

see and was a contestant in the Miss Black America pageant. This led to a job offer from the local CBS television affiliate, WTVF. In 1971, she became Nashville's first woman coanchor. She was still in the job when she graduated from college. Shortly thereafter, in 1976, she was offered a job at WJZ-TV, the ABC affiliate in Baltimore, Maryland.

The management at WTVF in Nashville had enjoyed great success with Winfrey by allowing her to be herself. The management at WJZ tried to remake the young broadcaster into a more acceptable mold, and her first year at the station was rocky as a result. The situation improved greatly when she was switched to cohosting the morning talk show, *Baltimore Is Talking*, with Richard Sher. Winfrey did the show for seven years, with ever-increasing popularity. Then, in 1984, she moved to Chicago to take over *A.M. Chicago*, a talk show that was in serious trouble in the ratings. It aired opposite Phil Donahue, a Chicago favorite, and none of its many hosts had been able to make a dent in his audience.

It took a month for Winfrey to equal Donahue's ratings. This was in a city notorious for its racial problems—not the ideal milieu for a Black woman. It took three months for Winfrey to surpass Donahue in the ratings. A year and a half after Winfrey's arrival in the windy city, *A.M. Chicago* expanded to an hour and became *The Oprah Winfrey Show*. Winfrey is smart, thinks fast on her feet, and reveals her own life and personality in a way that makes people identify with her.

In 1985, Winfrey was cast in the film version of Alice Walker's *The Color Purple*, directed by Steven Spielberg. Her performance earned her an Academy Award nomination. She has since continued her acting career in film and on television, forming a production company, Harpo Productions, to develop her own projects. In 1989, she bought her own television and movie production studio. That same year she donated $1 million to Morehouse College in Atlanta, Georgia, one of many contributions to the community.

In 1989, Winfrey produced a miniseries based on Gloria Naylor's novel *The Women of Brewster Place*; its success led to the creation of a short-lived network dramatic series, *Brewster Place* (1990). Winfrey herself appeared in both the miniseries and the drama, as the long-suffering Mattie Michael. Meanwhile, for her work on *The Oprah Winfrey Show*, Winfrey received three Emmy Awards, two (in 1987 and 1991) as outstanding host of a talk/service show and one (in 1991) as supervising producer of the outstanding talk/service show (the show itself also received Emmys in 1987 and 1988).

BIBLIOGRAPHY

Cameron, Julia. "Simply . . . Oprah," *Cosmopolitan* (February 1989); *Current Biography* (March 1987); Ebert, Alan. "Oprah Winfrey Talks Openly about Oprah," *Good Housekeeping* (September 1991); Harrison, Barbara Grizzuti. "The Importance of Being Oprah," *New York Times Magazine* (June 11, 1989); *Jet*. National Report (June 5, 1989), and "Oprah Winfrey" (December 19, 1988), and Communications (October 10, 1988); Waldron, Robert. *Oprah!* (1987); Zoglin, Richard. "Lady with a Calling," *Time* (August 8, 1988).

KATHLEEN THOMPSON

WOMANIST THEOLOGY

Womanist thought emerged within religious discourse during the 1980s. Pulitzer prize-winning novelist Alice Walker coined the term "womanist" from the Black cultural expression, "You acting womanish." Black female religious scholars adopted the term as a way of pointing to Black women's distinct experience in church and society. For instance, Cheryl Townsend Gilkes utilized the womanist concept to clarify what she identified as a "holy boldness" among sanctified church women as they created their own power base within sanctified churches. Katie Cannon identified a womanist principle in the way Black women interpreted scripture.

Womanist theology is an attempt to articulate the significance of God's movement in human history from the vantage point of Black women struggling for survival and freedom. It maintains that God speaks through the lives of these women and that Black women's experience of struggle is a starting point for discerning God's revelation. Womanist theologians understand this experience through personal observation and Black women's novels, short stories, diaries, journals, and prayers.

The starting point of womanist theology distinguishes it from its closest theological counterparts, feminist and Black theology. Though feminist theology (traditionally done by white women) claims to utilize women's experience as a primary source for what it says about God, it has historically ignored Black women's reality. Likewise, Black theology (traditionally done by Black men) claims to articulate the meaning of God for Black people in their fight for liberation. Yet, it has historically excluded the struggles of Black women. Both theologies have failed to adequately address Black women's multidimensional oppression and, hence, their theological concerns.

The concerns raised by womanist theology are sometimes like those raised by feminist and/or Black theology. This occurs because Black women share with white women a similar experience of what it means to be a female in a sexist society, and share with Black men a similar experience of what it means to be Black in a white racist society. Yet, womanist theology addresses the concerns of feminist and Black theology only as they arise from the various social and historical contexts of Black women in struggle.

Womanist theology is still in the early stages of development. Womanist theologians have just begun to identify some of the necessary characteristics for a theology that takes seriously the richness and complexity of Black women's lives. The following provides an example of what these theologians are saying about the shape of womanist theology.

First, womanist theology is a theology of survival. It gives special attention to Black women's day-to-day efforts to preserve Black life in a society that tends to devalue this life. It highlights their role as the primary caretakers and transmitters of religion and culture to their children.

Specifically, womanist theology identifies the kind of wisdom, values, spirituality, stories, and traditions that these women have "handed down" in an effort to foster the physical, psychological, emotional, and spiritual health of their sons and daughters. Womanist theology engages a religiocultural analysis. This analysis underscores those aspects of Black religion and culture that foster Black survival (i.e., self-esteem, a relationship with God) while confronting those aspects that do not.

As a theology of survival, womanist theology also draws attention to God's role as sustainer. It uses Black women's testimonies as well as the biblical witness in order to discern this role. For instance, it looks at what Black women say concerning God's presence as Holy Spirit. It also lifts up God's role in the lives of the Hebrew midwives as they worked to insure baby Moses' survival (see Exodus 2:1-10).

Second, womanist theology is a liberation theology. It confronts the complex reality of oppression that acts as a barrier to Black people's freedom. In so doing it addresses the multidimensional character of Black oppression, especially as it impacts Black women. It engages a sociopolitical analysis that challenges racism, sexism, classism, and heterosexism as they impinge upon the Black community, and as they are harbored within that community. Womanist theology seeks to make clear that the Black community cannot be free if any one Black person is discriminated against because of his/her color, gender, sexual preference, or economic condition.

As a liberation theology, womanist theology illuminates God's role as liberator. It calls attention to God's role in the lives of the Old Testament prophets as well as in the Exodus event. Womanist theology points out that after God liberated Israel from Egyptian bondage, God demanded that Israel eliminate from its community anything that kept it a divided community (i.e., persecution of the poor, stealing of land, unjust treatment of foreigners, or neglect of widows). God required that all forms of oppression be eradicated from the Israelite people. Womanist theology proclaims that the liberator God requires the same from Black people as they struggle to become free.

Third, womanist theology is global. It stresses that Black people are a part of a global community of oppressed peoples struggling for survival and freedom. It seeks to foster dialogue with other theologians of liberation, especially with women of color. (Womanist theologians are members of the Ecumeni-cal Association of Third World Theologians where much of this global dialogue takes place.) Womanist theology accents connections between oppressed people. It also confronts any of the ways in which Black people are implicated in the oppression of others around the world. It is guided by the dictum that "no human being is free if one human being is not free." As a global theology, womanist theology takes seriously the universality of God's liberating concern.

Last, it is a church theology. It affirms the involvement of women in the entire mission and ministry of the church. Moreover, it holds itself accountable to the Black women in the church pews who struggle every day to "make do and do better." It attempts to be a source of meaning and empowerment for women engaged in a fight for life and liberation.

BIBLIOGRAPHY

Brown, Kelly Delaine. "The Emergence of Black Feminist Theology in the United States." In *We Are One Voice: Black Theology in the USA and South Africa*, ed. Simon S. Maimela and Dwight N. Hopkins (1989), and "God Is as Christ Does: Toward a Womanist Theology," *Journal of Religious Thought* (Summer-Fall 1989); Cannon, Katie Geneva. "The Emergence of Black Feminist Consciousness." In *Feminist Interpretation of the Bible*, ed. Letty Russell (1985), and *Black Womanist Ethics* (1988); Eugene, Toinette M. "Moral Values and Black Womanists," *Journal of Religious Thought* (Winter-Spring 1988); Gilkes, Cheryl Townsend. "The Role of Women in the Sanctified Church," *Journal of Religious Thought* (Spring-Summer 1986); Grant, Jacquelyn. "Womanist Theology: Black Women's Experiences as a Source for Doing Theology, with Special Reference to Christology," *Journal of the Interdenominational Theological Center* (Spring 1986), and *White Women's Christ and Black Women's Jesus: Feminist Christology and Womanist Response* (1989); Weems, Renita J. *Just a Sister Away: A Womanist Vision of Women's Relationships in the Bible* (1988); Williams, Delores. "Womanist Theology: Black Women's Voices," *Christianity and Crisis* (March 2, 1987).

KELLY DELAINE BROWN

WOMAN'S IMPROVEMENT CLUB, INDIANAPOLIS

The history of the Woman's Improvement Club reflects the goals of Black clubwomen nationally at the turn of the century. The club offered its members an opportunity for further education—denied them by white society—and for self-expression and an outlet for their concerns with racial survival and uplift.

Organized in 1903 in Indianapolis by Lillian Thomas Fox as a literary club, the Woman's Improvement Club within two years of its founding broadened its stated goal of self-improvement and instruction of its members to embrace community assistance and improvement. In 1905, the club opened an outdoor tuberculosis camp—purportedly the first in the entire country—to provide care for Black tuberculous patients. To facilitate this project, club members studied medical manuals, solicited the assistance of the Black community's doctors and businessmen, and raised funds from other Black women's clubs and Black church organizations throughout the Midwest to maintain the camp's operation.

As club members became more experienced and more confident of their ability, they increased their contacts with the greater Indianapolis community. The club functioned as a member of the Indianapolis Charity Organization Society, which acted as a clearinghouse for social welfare cases. By 1911, the club established a system of referrals to the Oak Hill Tuberculosis Camp with nurses from the Metropolitan Life Insurance Company, and it regularly held public education meetings at the Young Men's Christian Association, attended by representatives from the Marion County Tuberculosis Society and the Marion County Board of Health. By 1916, the Woman's Improvement Club regularly supplied county health officials with figures for the number of cases of tuberculosis in the Black community and assisted in the opening of a publicly funded health clinic in the Black community. Thereafter the club lobbied city and state officials to provide bed space for Black patients in public hospitals, resulting in 1918 in additional bed space assigned to Black patients at Sunnyside Sanitarium and in 1935 in construction of a segregated ward at Flower Mission Hospital. Between 1922 and 1928, the Woman's Improvement Club acquired property and operated its own hospital for tuberculous patients. By 1940, Indianapolis Blacks were better able to turn to a variety of services to help people suffering from tuberculosis, and the club looked to other ways of helping the Black community, acting as a referral agency to public health organizations, providing educational scholarships for promising young students, and financially assisting poor Blacks threatened with eviction.

In June 1989, the Marion County Board of Health held a ceremony honoring the Woman's Improvement Club for its role in initiating and spearheading the drive to provide tuberculosis and health care facilities for the Indianapolis Black community.

BIBLIOGRAPHY

Ferguson, Earline Rae. "The Woman's Improvement Club of Indianapolis: Black Women Pioneers in Tuberculosis Work, 1903-1938," *Indiana Magazine of History* (September 1988); Hine, Darlene Clark, Elsa Barkley Brown, Tiffany R. L. Patterson, and Lillian S. Williams, eds. *Black Women in United States History* (1990).

EARLINE RAE FERGUSON

WOMAN'S LOYAL UNION OF NEW YORK AND BROOKLYN

The Woman's Loyal Union was founded in October 1892 by two active reformers who would later be associated with the National Association of Colored Women (NACW), Victoria Earle Matthews (1861-1907) and Maritcha Lyons (1848-1929). This Black women's club acted as an information clearinghouse for the Black communities of New York and Brooklyn (then separate cities), a center for disbursal of funds for reform work, and a locus of "race work" and community "uplift."

The Woman's Loyal Union, like many Black women's clubs in the Progressive era, supported a variety of reforms. For example, the Union encouraged and often monetarily aided Black-initiated, Black-run self-help organizations and institutions such as the Home for Aged Colored People in Brooklyn and the New Bedford Home for the Aged. The Union also nurtured ties to suffrage organizations such as the Brooklyn Equal Suffrage Club. Since many women who were members of the Loyal Union were also members of other clubs and/or active in social reform organizations such as the Urban League and the National Association for the Advancement of Colored People (NAACP), fund-raising events, efforts to lobby Congress, and public demonstrations were often performed in concert with these other groups.

Matthews, not only the cofounder of the Loyal Union but also its first president, established the White Rose Home and Industrial Association in 1897 in an attempt to address the growing problem of unscrupulous men advising or employing newly arrived Black migrants from the South. The association's White Rose Mission acted much as a settlement house for these women. It offered employment advice, a library, a kindergarten, classes in "Negro history," and courses in sewing and cooking. The Loyal Union and the White Rose Mission often shared resources. The Loyal Union, for example, contributed to Matthews's extensive collection of books and reference materials housed within the White Rose Mission's building. The Loyal Union also disseminated information (in the form of pamphlets) on the White Rose Mission both to the general public and to government agencies.

BIBLIOGRAPHY

Brown, Hallie Q. *Homespun Heroines and Other Women of Distinction* (1926); Cash, Floris. "Womanhood and Protest: The Club Movement among Black Women, 1892-1922," Ph.D. diss. (1986); Davis, Elizabeth Lindsay. *Lifting as They Climb: A History of the National Association of Colored Women* (1933); Osofsky, Gilbert. *Harlem: The Making of a Ghetto* (1963); Salem, Dorothy. *To Better Our World: Black Women in Organized Reform, 1890-1920* (1990).

THEA ARNOLD

WOMEN'S CHRISTIAN TEMPERANCE UNION, SOUTH

Southern Black women's interest in temperance predated the organization of the Women's Christian Temperance Union (WCTU) in the South in 1881. During the 1870s, African-American women formed temperance groups in their churches and joined the International Order of Grand Templars (IOGT), an interracial organization that recognized women as full members; many southern Black women became officers in the organization, which held local, state, and national conventions.

When Frances Willard, president of the WCTU, toured the South in 1881, she spoke to both Black and white audiences. Many African-American women who were long-time members of IOGT found the idea of a women's temperance organization very appealing. Originally, white and Black WCTU chapters were part of the same, but segregated, structure; Black chapters had to report to a committee of white women who oversaw work in the Black community. By the late 1880s, African-American women began to object to white women's control and lobbied for equal membership in southern statewide WCTUs. When white women refused to grant Black chapters autonomous representation in the state organization, some Black women broke rank and formed separate statewide networks, which became known in each state as the WCTU #2.

By 1898, five autonomous Black women's state unions existed in North Carolina, Tennessee, Georgia, Arkansas, and Texas. In other southern states, Black women's chapters continued to report to the Committee for Colored Work of the white women's union. Two African-American organizers from the national WCTU, Sarah Woodson Early and Lucy Thurman, visited Black chapters in the South often, and in the late 1890s several organizations of the WCTU #2 changed their name to the Lucy Thurman WCTU. Also in that decade, Black women in North Carolina founded a temperance newspaper, the *WCTU Tidings*. Southern African-American women participated in national and international interracial WCTU conventions throughout the post-Civil War period, which saw the institutionalization of segregation in the South, and the organization remained viable among southern Black women until the 1920s.

[*See also* TEMPERANCE WORK IN THE NINETEENTH CENTURY.]

BIBLIOGRAPHY

Friedman, Jean E. *The Enclosed Garden: Women and Community in the Evangelical South, 1830-1900* (1985); Gilmore, Glenda E. "Lessons in the Limits of Sisterhood: Black Women, White Women, and the WCTU in North Carolina, 1880-1900," Second Southern Conference on Women's History (June 1991); Lawson, Ellen N. "Sarah Woodson Early: Nineteenth Century Black Nationalist 'Sister,' " *UMOJA* (Summer 1981); Mossell, Mrs. N. F. *The Work of the Afro-American Woman* (1894); Neverdon-Morton, Cynthia. *Afro-American Women of the South and the Advancement of the Race, 1895-1925* (1989); Salem, Dorothy. *To Better Our World: Black Women in Organized Reform, 1890-1920* (1990); Sims, Anastatia. " 'The Sword of the Spirit': The W.C.T.U. and Moral Reform in North Carolina, 1883-1933," *North Carolina Historical Review* (1987).

GLENDA ELIZABETH GILMORE

WOMEN'S POLITICAL COUNCIL, MONTGOMERY, ALABAMA

The Women's Political Council (WPC) of Montgomery, Alabama, was a grass-roots organization of Black professional women formed to address the city's racial problems. The group led efforts in the early 1950s to secure better treatment for Black bus passengers, and in December 1955 it initiated the thirteen-month bus boycott that culminated in a U.S. Supreme Court decision ordering desegregation of the city bus system.

The WPC was founded in 1949 by Mary Fair Burks, head of the Alabama State College English Department in Montgomery, after a personal encounter with racist treatment by the police. A majority of the council's middle-class membership were teachers at the college or in local public schools; many were congregants at Dexter Avenue Baptist Church (where Martin Luther King, Jr., became pastor in 1954). The group's initial purposes were to foster women's involvement in civic affairs, to promote voter registration through citizenship education, and to aid women who were victims of rape or assault. One of its most successful programs was an annual event called Youth City, which taught Black high school students about politics and government and "what democracy could and should mean" (Burks 1990). During election campaigns the WPC worked with the white-only League of Women Voters to inform Black citizens about political candidates.

In 1949, Jo Ann Robinson, a newly hired English professor at Alabama State College, joined the council. Her firsthand experiences with segregated seating on buses prompted Robinson to succeed Burks as WPC president in 1950 and to shift the council's primary focus to challenging the seating policy. Under her leadership the council grew to over 200 members and expanded to three chapters in different areas of the city. It built a reputation as the city's most dynamic and effective Black civic organization, in part because it directly challenged racial injustice. During the early 1950s WPC leaders met regularly with Mayor W. A. Gayle and the city commission to lobby for bus reforms and other civic improvements. Although they succeeded in pressuring the city to hire its first Black police officers and to increase funding for the Black community's parks and playgrounds, they made no progress in their effort to ameliorate bus segregation. (Publicly, at least, they did not seek to end segregated seating but to make it more equitable.) Robinson expressed the group's frustration in a May 1954 letter to Mayor Gayle, four days after the Supreme Court's *Brown* v. *Board of Education* school desegregation ruling, in which she warned him of a possible bus boycott if conditions did not improve.

The WPC first considered organizing a boycott in March 1955 after Claudette Colvin, a fifteen-year-old high school junior, was arrested for refusing to give up her seat in the unreserved middle section of a city bus to a white passenger. Robinson and WPC colleagues helped arrange two meetings that Black representatives held with city and bus company officials and took the lead in demanding reform, but to no avail. Colvin's arrest and conviction angered and unified the Black community. In a spontaneous protest, large numbers refused to use the buses for several days.

When Rosa Parks was arrested on December 1, 1955, for the same offense as Colvin, WPC leaders were ready to implement the boycott that they had been discussing since the earlier incident. Parks, a longtime NAACP activist who was deeply respected in Black Montgomery, seemed the ideal community symbol around which to mobilize a mass protest. Robinson prepared a flyer calling upon Black citizens to refuse to ride the buses the following Monday, the day of Parks's trial. She spent Thursday night mimeographing the 50,000 flyers that she and two students distributed all over town the next day. The resulting one-day boycott was so successful that several thousand participants voted at a mass meeting to continue the protest until they won decent treatment.

Although Martin Luther King, Jr., and other male leaders, particularly ministers, took over the visible leadership of the boycott after it began, several WPC activists—including Robinson, Burks, Irene West, and Euretta Adair—played crucial roles in organizing and sustaining it. They served on all major committees, shared in planning and strategy, helped to manage the car pool system, and handled many of the boycott's day-to-day details. Robinson negotiated skillfully with white officials concerning the bus demands and edited the monthly newsletter. In addition, dozens of active council members assisted the boycott in various ways.

Ironically the council's indispensable role in ending city bus segregation contributed to its organizational decline. Partly because its central goal was achieved, and partly because the WPC was overshadowed by the Montgomery Improvement Association (MIA) that was created to direct the boycott, the council subsequently found itself with a diminished leadership role in the Black community. After the boycott the MIA took on some of the major issues that had animated the WPC, such as voter registration and public parks. Still, the women's organization coexisted and cooperated with the MIA for a number of years. Younger women reinvigorated the council, guided by older members serving as role models. "Members felt that young, concerned women, with their futures ahead, would benefit by the WPC," Robinson recalled, "and that we would help them to organize and select goals and directions for their future" (Robinson 1987).

Robinson and Burks left Montgomery in 1960, after several Alabama State College professors were fired for civil rights activities, to take teaching positions in California and Maryland, respectively. Information is not available on the extent to which the younger women became involved in the later civil rights movement in Montgomery and elsewhere.

BIBLIOGRAPHY

Burks, Mary Fair. "Trailblazers: Women in the Montgomery Bus Boycott." In *Women in the Civil Rights Movement: Trailblazers and Torchbearers, 1941-1965*, ed. Vicki L. Crawford, Jacqueline Anne Rouse, and Barbara Woods (1990); Garrow, David J. "The Origins of the Montgomery Bus Boycott," *Southern Changes* (October-December 1985); Millner, Steven M. "The Montgomery Bus Boycott: A Case Study in the Emergence and Career of a Social Movement." In *The Walking City: The Montgomery Bus Boycott, 1955-1956*, ed. David J. Garrow (1989); Robinson, Jo Ann Gibson. *The Montgomery Bus Boycott and the Women Who Started It* (1987).

STEWART BURNS

WOODARD, BEULAH ECTON
(1895-1955)

Beulah Ecton was born on November 11, 1895, in rural Ohio near Frankfort. The William P. Ecton family, including the youngest daughter, Beulah, migrated to California and settled near Los Angeles in what is now the city of Vernon. Through the years many unusual visitors came to the Ecton home, but none aroused Beulah's interest as much as the native African she met when she was twelve years old. This was the beginning of a lifelong interest in all things African.

While at Polytechnic High School, Beulah began showing an interest in sculpture. Possessing a natural talent that probably would have found expression even without formal training, she developed her artistic ability with courses at the Los Angeles Art School, Otis Art Institute, and the University of Southern California. She was tutored by Felix Piano, David Edstrom, Glen Lukens, and Prince Troubeskoy.

Following her marriage to Brady E. Woodard, she set to work in an improvised studio in the rear of their home. The earliest public recognition of her work came when James Rodney Smith, publisher of *California News*, exhibited her sculpture in the window of his newspaper office and advertised it in the paper's columns.

A short time later Miriam Matthews, head librarian of the Vernon Branch Library, invited Woodard to display her work at the branch and later arranged

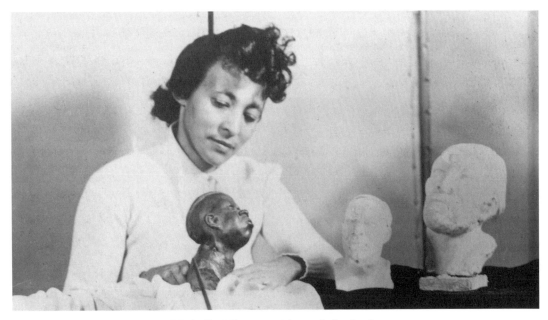

An Associated Press story about Beulah Woodard's 1935 one-person show at the Los Angeles County Museum brought her sculpture to the attention of the entire country and resulted in the earliest of many important commissions. [Miriam Matthews]

an exhibition for her at the Los Angeles Central Library downtown. This exposure led to a one-person show at the Los Angeles County Museum in fall 1935. As she was the first Black artist to be so honored, Los Angeles metropolitan newspapers headlined the event and ran photos. The Associated Press story appeared in newspapers across the nation.

Soon Woodard was in great demand throughout Southern California as a lecturer, especially in educational institutions from elementary to university graduate schools. The artist received important commissions to sculpt busts of John Anson Ford, member of the Los Angeles County Board of Supervisors; Irving Lipsteitch, noted philanthropist; Thomas Evans, first executive secretary of the University Religious Conference at the University of California at Los Angeles; and others. She won a number of awards, including first prize for sculpture at the third All-City Art Festival in 1953, and her work is in the permanent collections of various museums and in private collections on two continents.

Despite her full work schedule, Woodard always found time to support worthwhile community causes and to promote the work of other artists. She was a principal organizer of both the Los Angeles Negro Art Association in 1937 and the Eleven Associated Artists Gallery in 1950. She also stimulated public interest in the work of local and national artists, both Black and white.

Woodard died at the age of fifty-nine on July 13, 1955, just before what might have been her greatest triumph—an exhibition of her work scheduled for several German museums.

BIBLIOGRAPHY

Woodard, Beulah. Papers, Private collection, Los Angeles, California.

MIRIAM MATTHEWS

WOODARD, LYNETTE (1959-)

Reared in the game of basketball by her cousin, Hubert "Geese" Ausbie of the Harlem Globetrotters, Lynette Woodard dreamed of one day stepping into his shoes. She was born on August 12, 1959, in Wichita, Kansas, and achieved fame in 1975 and 1977 when she led her high school team in Wichita to 5A state championships for both years. A member of the Kansas Grand State Team in 1975, she was cited for All-State honors in 1975 and 1977, and made All-American her senior year. As a college freshman at the University of Kansas, Woodard led the nation in rebounds, averaging fifteen per game, and she was national leader in steals for the next three seasons. Considered at the time perhaps the most outstanding woman player in America, she single-handedly propelled the University of Kansas program into nationally recognized competition. By graduation she had amassed a total of 3,649 points, more than any other player in the history of division one women's basketball. Four-time All-American, and two-time Academic All-American, Woodard was a 1981 Wade Trophy winner. She was captain of the gold-medal-winning team representing the United States at the Pan American games in 1983 and captain of the gold-medal-winning U.S. team at the 1984 Olympics at Los Angeles.

After a brief stint as an assistant coach at the University of Kansas, Woodard won a competition against twenty-six other women athletes to become, with her cocompetitor Jackie White, the first women players to be hired by the Harlem Globetrotters. Woodard made her debut with the Globetrotters in Brisbane, Australia, in 1986. Woodard acknowledged that her cousin Ausbie, who played professionally for twenty-four years with the Globetrotters, prompted her to dream as a child of one day playing for the Harlem showteam. Named in the mid-1980s as the most outstanding one-on-one player in the world, the six-foot forward had been coached by her cousin at an early age and preferred the Globetrotters to a speculative start in the National Basketball Association. By this time she was considered the most visible professional woman player in the game.

BIBLIOGRAPHY

Ashe, Arthur. *A Hard Road to Glory, since 1946* (1988); *Boston Herald*. "In the Magic Circle" (March 26, 1987); *Buffalo News*. "We'll Play in NBA" (March 26, 1987); *Pittsburgh Courier* (February 11, 1978); Spradling, Mary M., ed. *A Guide to Magazine Articles, Newspaper Articles, and Books Concerning More Than 6,700 Black Individuals and Groups* (1985); *Women's Sports* (November 1983).

JOHN L. GODWIN

WOODBY-McKANE, ALICE (c. 1863-1946)

Dr. Alice Woodby-McKane and her husband, Dr. Cornelius McKane, established the first hospital in Monrovia, Liberia, in 1895.

Named in the mid-1980s as the most outstanding one-on-one basketball player in the world, Harlem Globetrotter Lynette Woodard was brought up in the game by her Globetrotter cousin Hubert "Geese" Ausbie. [Harlem Globetrotters]

A Pennsylvania native, Alice Woodby attended Hampton Institute from 1884 until 1886, when she entered the Institute for Colored Youth. After graduation in 1889, she entered the Woman's Medical College of Pennsylvania in 1890 and received her degree in 1892. Soon thereafter she moved to Augusta, Georgia, to establish a practice and to teach at the Haines Institute. She married Cornelius McKane, M.D., and they relocated to Savannah, Georgia, where she established the first training school for Black nurses in southeast Georgia in 1893.

In 1894, she and her husband went to Monrovia, Liberia, where they established a hospital. Woodby-McKane was also with the Monrovia Poor Home and was an assistant pension examiner for Civil War veterans. In 1896, she returned with her husband to Savannah and established the McKane Hospital for Women and Children.

About 1900, she moved to Boston with her husband and family. In addition to her practice, Woodby-McKane was a lecturer and instructor for nurses at Plymouth Hospital and was active in Massachusetts politics, serving as an elected delegate to the Republican state convention as a precinct leader. She also was director of the South End Cooperative Bank of Boston. She died of arteriosclerosis in Boston on March 6, 1946.

Of her philosophy Woodby-McKane wrote, "I work very hard that I might be able to carry out the Hampton idea of passing along what one has received" (*Southern Workman* 1911).

BIBLIOGRAPHY

Brown, Sara W. "Colored Women Physicians," *Southern Workman* (1923); *Southern Workman*. "Graduates and Ex-Students" (1911).

JANET MILLER

WORLD WAR I

The First World War transformed the consciousness of Black women in America. The war years offered Black women the opportunity for increased intergroup cooperation, the occasion to win local improvements under the guise of selfless patriotism, and the challenge to expose racial injustices in a country waging a war for international democracy. Through their wartime efforts, they proved their abilities, performed nontraditional jobs, and increased their expectations for postwar progress in pay, occupational status, and racial justice. Black women gained skills, networks, and confidence that shaped a more militant perspective—one that was a postwar amalgam of the New Negro and New Woman.

The outbreak of the European war in 1914 did not immediately concern Black women facing worsening race relations under President Woodrow Wilson, who had segregated federal restrooms and eating areas and sent the Marines to occupy Haiti. Black women had been making steady inroads into federal civil service employment until Wilson halted the progress by requiring personal interviews and application photos. Congress was considering legislation to segregate races on public carriers, to exclude Black Americans from commissions in the army and navy, and to make lynching illegal under federal law. Locally, municipal codes required residential segregation of the races, lynchings became more frequent, and *Birth of a Nation* (1915) attracted audiences to

share in the public stereotyping of Black men as beasts lusting after virtuous white women.

As individuals and groups, Black women fought against the worsening racial conditions. Black leaders from thirty-eight states protested the Wilson segregation policies. At one meeting with President Wilson, they were assured that the trend would not continue; but after a year of disappointments they returned to Wilson to complain, only to be asked to leave. A national incident resulted. Women circulated petitions, lobbied sympathetic congressmen, issued protests in the press, held public meetings with white leaders, and used the court system to stop regressive federal, state, and local legislation. To protest *Birth of a Nation*, women helped organize local boycotts to educate the public about the issues. Delilah Beasley's articles in the Oakland *Tribune* motivated her community's successful protest against the film.

As they fought against the legal and political changes, the war influenced their communities by exacerbating conditions that Black women had been attempting to improve. The war years brought nationwide inflation and a rising cost-of-living index. In the South, damaging floods, a thriving convict-lease system and the boll weevil infestation made life unbearable. The "work or fight" rules, enforced by the federal government, meant that individuals were open to arrest if neither working nor fighting for the war effort. To Black women domestics who quit their jobs, these rules led to arrest or reemployment in difficult jobs. For Black women who chose to stay home to raise their children, the rules meant mandatory employment or arrest for vagrancy.

Few organized efforts prevailed during the war years. The Women's Trade Union League called for equal treatment of Black women in the work force during a time when Black women earned 10 to 60 percent less than white women. In the North, Black women had to accept inferior positions and do the least desirable tasks. The American Federation of Labor made a superficial attempt to address the problems of Black women workers by appointing Mildred Rankin, a Black social worker, to head a national Colored Women Workers Office. Without adequate funding and power to fight the racial attitudes of the labor movement, Rankin accomplished little.

The "work or fight" rules touched even the efforts of elite Black women who tried to help their working-class sisters. Clubwomen such as Mary Church Terrell, Jeanette Carter, and Julia F. Coleman founded the Women Wage Earners Association (WWEA) in Washington, D.C., to organize and protect women workers through improved wages, working

Black women worked tirelessly throughout the war in a wide variety of projects. Here a group is shown opening a USO club for Black soldiers. [National Archives]

conditions, and adequate housing. The WWEA's organizational efforts led to strikes of waitresses, domestics, tobacco stemmers, and nurses during the war years. The strike in Norfolk, Virginia, in fall 1917 led to the arrest of strikers as "slackers" under the "work or fight" rules. As a result of the strike, the Norfolk branch of WWEA was smashed and the national organization was investigated as an attempt to interfere with the war effort. During this time period, labor organization work was construed as a threat to national security, especially when initiated by Black women.

Pushed by worsening situations and declining opportunities in the South, young Black Americans came to the cities of the North seeking employment in industries engaged in war production, in occupations previously employing European immigrants, and in jobs left open by white Americans taking bet-ter-paying factory work or serving in the armed services. As the numbers of Black migrants entered the cities, the problems of urban life—vice, housing, health and sanitation, family disintegration, social isolation, crime and education—intensified. Programs and facilities grew to serve the expanding numbers and needs. For example, the Chicago Phyllis Wheatley Home in 1915 moved to larger quarters and established an employment department to find jobs for Black women migrants. Similar conditions led to the establishment of a Black Young Men's Christian Association branch in Louisville, new quarters in Charlotte, North Carolina, and Brooklyn, New York, and new services in Detroit.

Once the United States officially entered the war in spring 1917, the wartime propaganda and intergroup cooperation provided Black women with both the rationale and the means to improve local conditions. As white women worked for the improvement of public health, Black women focused on improving the nutrition, medical care, and recreational facilities for Black children and families. Women who took Red Cross classes in home nursing and dietetics used their new knowledge in the Black community. As white women established better safeguards for women in industry, Black women improved their job opportunities by arguing that the training of Black women for new jobs freed white women and men to concentrate on the war effort. Black nurses at home meant white nurses in the European field. Black elevator operators could free white men to serve in the military. Improvement of city lighting and street conditions in Black neighborhoods and expansion of Black reformatories would lessen the potential immoral temptations for men stationed at nearby military camps. Through skillful manipulation of the wartime rhetoric, Black women helped their local communities gain municipal services and training.

Most of their efforts began, as with white women, with patriotic service. By April 21, 1917, the government had organized the Woman's Committee under the Council of National Defense. The committee incorporated all groups of women, including the National Association of Colored Women (NACW), into the domestic war effort to accomplish food conservation, production of knit goods, development of maternal and child protection activities, and creation of federal working standards for women in industry. According to Alice Dunbar-Nelson, field representative of the Woman's Committee, this was the best-organized mobilization of Black women of all the war organizations.

The racial policies of the Woman's Committee varied by state due to the reliance on state councils of defense. Most northern states incorporated Black women, yet distinctions existed. Illinois organized a Committee on Colored Women through the Urban League. Indiana's Federation of Colored Women's Clubs directed a separate division for war work. In New Jersey, the Colored Woman's Volunteer League worked through the Woman's Committee of the Council of National Defense.

Southern politics of racial segregation produced a variety of structures through which Black women served the National Council of Defense. Separate Black women's councils existed in the states of Florida, Mississippi, and Maryland. Ida Cummings, kindergarten teacher and founder of the Woman's League of Baltimore, served on the Maryland State Council of Defense. Sally Green, a graduate of Hampton Institute, chaired the state council in Mississippi.

Florida's Eartha M. White headed that state's Black women's department. In Kentucky, the Black men's organizations incorporated the women into their efforts. In Missouri, the state council saw no need to organize Black women. The West Virginia council had the state federation of Black women's clubs send a representative to the National Defense Council. Most of the southern states appointed a local Black resident to cooperate with the local county council. This approach led to well-organized local efforts that failed to influence other communities.

The American Red Cross was one of the first organizations approached by Black women seeking to serve. In many northern cities, they cooperated with white women. For example, the Black women of Freehold, New Jersey, formed an auxiliary to the Big County branch of the American Red Cross, working in the same headquarters under the same supervisor as the white women. Separate Black branches, such as the Booker T. Washington branch in Tampa, Florida, worked in Red Cross activities in the South. When nurses were called for duty overseas, Black nurses eager to serve were excluded. Their participation in Red Cross organizations coupled with protests from Black leaders and organizations led to the calling of Black women into national service in June 1918. Registered by the American Red Cross, the women served in the six Black base hospitals—Camp Funston (Kansas), Camp Grant (Rockford, Illinois), Camp Dodge (Des Moines, Iowa), Camp Taylor (Louisville, Kentucky), Camp Sherman (Chillicothe, Ohio), and Camp Dix (Wrightstown, New Jersey)—serving 38,000 Black troops. Few Black nurses had been called to overseas duty before the armistice, but Alice Dunbar-Nelson reported that over 300 Black nurses served overseas by passing for white. Denied the privilege to serve even in canteens in the South, other Black women prepared comfort kits, maintained restaurants, and did all they could within the parameters of the rigid racial etiquette of the era.

Whatever the level of training or the form of organization, Black women helped their communities during the war. When Alice Dunbar-Nelson became the field representative of the Woman's Committee, she found Black women already organized in the South. As part of the domestic war effort, they took an active part in food production and conservation, nutrition, and fund-raising through food sales to benefit both rural and urban communities. Building on the home economic demonstrations of county agents or state agricultural colleges, the women learned and then taught new canning techniques, formed clubs, and provided nutritional information to local residents. Their push for playgrounds got support from the war context because playgrounds were said to ensure strong patriotic children. Under the banner of patriotic service, health campaigns could provide information and social service.

Black women developed services similar to the Red Cross through the Circle for Negro War Relief. Started during fall 1917 in New York City, the circle expanded to sixty units by early 1918. Each circle promoted the welfare of the Black soldiers by meeting specific individual and local emergency needs. A variety of services emerged as Black women provided comfort kits, chewing gum, victrolas and records, southern dinners for homesick boys, lectures on social hygiene and race pride, and other niceties. Examples of individual units show this diversity. The ambulance unit of New York City donated a $2,000 ambulance to the 367th Regiment at Camp Upton. The Crispus Attucks circle in Philadelphia attempted to establish a base hospital for Black soldiers with a staff of Black physicians and nurses. Mary McLeod Bethune developed an emergency circle of Negro war

relief in Daytona, Florida. Boston women developed a soldiers' comfort unit. The Motor Corps of Haywood unit in New York City visited hospitals; escorted the wounded to canteens, on sightseeing tours, and on shopping trips; and wrote letters for soldiers and their families.

Black women transferred their talents as fundraisers to war work. They participated in the five Liberty loan drives, six Red Cross campaigns, the United War Work Campaign, and the thrift savings stamp program. The National Association of Colored Women, under the leadership of Elizabeth L. Davis, raised money for Liberty bonds. In the third Liberty loan campaign, they raised over $5,300,000 for the Red Cross. The National Council of Women praised the Black clubwomen for this successful fundraising, as did Emmett J. Scott, special assistant in the War Department. Black teachers encouraged student contributions as evidence of patriotism. Black schools participated in war savings stamp programs. Selma women raised money through sale of thrift stamps. Laura Brown of Pittsburgh headed the campaign to

Many local communities set up canteens for white soldiers, but Black servicemen were excluded from them. The YWCA's Colored Women's War Council organized hostess houses for them. One of the earliest (and a model for others) was the Camp Upton Hostess House, led by Lugenia Burns Hope (center). [YWCA of the USA, National Board Archives]

recruit Black women's support for these efforts, as the appointees of the National War Savings Committee under the secretary of the treasury.

In addition, the federal government indirectly stimulated Black women's involvement by mobilizing seven national organizations for the United War Work Campaign. Of these seven, only three organizations, the National War Work Councils of the Young Men's and Young Women's Christian Associations, the War Camp Community Service, and the Salvation Army, utilized the energies and skills of Black women. In June 1917, the national board of the YWCA established the War Work Council to protect the health and morals of American womanhood, especially in communities surrounding army and navy training camps. Under the leadership of Eva D. Bowles, national secretary of colored work, Black female leaders and volunteers came together to meet three needs of the Black female community. First, through the establishment of hostess houses in training camps, they provided an information bureau for female relatives and friends of Black soldiers, a pleasant atmosphere for soldiers and visitors, and a supervised environment in which to enjoy rest, refreshments, and entertainment to ease adjustment to military life and to maintain morality. Second, through an industrial department, the YWCA met the needs of Black women drawn to urban areas in search of employment. Third, the YWCA provided girls with appropriate recreation, emergency housing, and self-improvement in health, social morality, and skills.

To accomplish these goals, participation grew rapidly. Black women began in 1917 with one national secretary, sixteen local centers or branches, and nine paid workers. In 1918, the allocation of $400,000 to "colored work" supported the two-year expansion of staff to twelve national workers, three field supervisors, and sixty-three paid workers managing the work in forty-two centers, many of which later became branches of the YWCA.

Most communities set up canteens for white soldiers and their families. To meet similar needs in the Black communities, the hostess house program became the most significant achievement of the YWCA's Colored Women's War Council. The first hostess houses opened in the Northeast, where interracial cooperation and Black YWCA work was firmly established. In November 1917, Camp Upton Hostess House was opened on Long Island through the efforts of Boston Black women, including Mary Wilson, Hannah Smith, and her assistant, a Mrs. Norcomb. By early 1918, Lugenia Hope, founder of the Atlanta

Neighborhood Union, became the director of the Camp Upton House. The Upton house became a model for the succeeding fifteen facilities: Camp Custer (Michigan), Grant (Illinois), Funston (Kansas), Dodge (Iowa), Dix (New Jersey), Sherman (Ohio), Meade (Maryland), Taylor (Kentucky), Green (North Carolina), Gordon (Georgia), Alexander and Lee (Virginia), Jackson and Wadsworth (South Carolina), and Travis (Texas). Upton also served as the training center for supervisors assigned to other hostess houses. By summer 1918, training had been received by Mable Whiting for Camp Funston, Amanda Gray for Dodge, Callie Edwards and Mary Cromwell for Dix, and Ruth Hucles for Gordon.

The hostess houses served minorities shut out of other social services. When a soldier was injured or killed, the hostesses consoled and advised the women. For illiterate men from the South, the house provided a center for literacy training. During the influenza epidemic in late 1918, the houses became emergency hotels where women could stay while nursing the ill. For men drafted unjustly, the hostesses served as liaisons between the military bureaucracy and the soldier. For men away from home, the houses provided a homelike atmosphere making camp life more comfortable.

Although the YWCA provided funds, information, and direction in securing the buildings and training the hostesses, the atmosphere, furnishings, and volunteer activities originated with the Black women from surrounding communities and other centers of reform. Adapting the often paternalistic programs of the YWCA to meet the needs of the race, the Black volunteers and supervisors transformed the program into useful guidance. White journals praised the houses and the effective work done by the Black women. Leaders of the YWCA called the program a spectacular wartime achievement. Instilling both patriotism and racial pride, the hostesses encouraged the soldiers to fight to make the world safe for democracy and to improve the future of their race at home.

To meet the industrial goal of the YWCA's war work, Mary E. Jackson brought her experience in the Labor Department of Rhode Island and in the National Association of Colored Women to her task as industrial secretary of the YWCA's Committee on Colored Work in December 1917. She built on the existing employment bureaus of Phyllis Wheatley branches and developed industrial recreational centers to create training programs for improving skills and work habits, to save women from exploitation, to organize women into groups for bargaining power, and to build long-range goals from wartime opportunities.

Jackson also mobilized the women in Black communities to investigate working conditions, wages, racial problems, and occupational categories. These investigations provided the basis for Jackson's patriotic pleas to support training programs and promotional opportunities to make Black females into better war workers.

Through their separate Black branches or as agents of the industrial secretary, Black women created employment services, training bureaus, and social, educational, and recreational services to serve the communities. For example, a center in Houston provided a meeting place for the Patriotic Service League, the Rainbow Club, and the Tennis Club, as well as classes in food demonstration, wartime cookery, French, and stenography. From initially limited programs for girls working in war gardens to increase food supplies in Petersburg, Virginia, emerged a variety of multiservice centers in communities throughout the United States. Their cooperation with other wartime agencies such as the Red Cross or War Camp Community Service enabled local Black women to expand services to the community.

Although the programs and philosophy of the YWCA War Work Council did not differ considerably from those of the women's clubs or state defense councils, the characteristics of the leadership in the war work of the YWCA did differ. The clubs and women's committees of the state councils of defense had married, middle-aged women as their leaders. The YWCA national staff and war workers were younger, single women, prepared by higher education similar to the leadership in the settlement house movement. The hostess house supervisors had a higher percentage of married, middle-aged women (seven of twelve), but of 187 war workers only 51 were married. In one form or another, the war work involved Black women of all ages, marital statuses, and regions in efforts to serve the Black communities and soldiers.

Less success was evident through other national committees. The Black experience with the War Camp Community Service (WCCS) demonstrated that the armistice of November 11, 1918, had ended the fighting but not the war. The WCCS established centers to provide services and recreation for the returning soldiers. Mary Church Terrell served as an organizer for the WCCS, selecting qualified Black women to head the centers, working with local executive committees of the WCCS in program development, and

Kathryn M. Johnson (along with Addie Hunton and Helen Curtis) worked in France for the YWCA during World War I, guarding the rights of Black American soldiers in Europe. [National Archives]

ascertaining the needs of local Black communities. In some areas of the South, white leaders approved only those programs that would train domestic workers. In other areas, white organizers refused to support any recreational services for Black soldiers. Mary Terrell reported cooperation only in Memphis, the city of Terrell's family origins. In Memphis, an interracial committee established a community center that served as the headquarters for all work concerning Black people. So little was accomplished through the WCCS in the South that Terrell resigned in the spring of 1919. She sent her meticulous reports to the National Association for the Advancement of Colored People, which then called a conference at the offices of the national board of the YWCA. Eugene K. Jones of the National Urban League, Jesse Moorland of the YMCA, Eva Bowles of the YWCA, Mary Talbert of the NACW, and Mary White Ovington of the NAACP produced a letter from the five national organizations to the WCCS critical of the agency's policies and practices.

Demobilization and peace motivated Black women to ensure the safe return of their troops, to make certain that racial issues were acknowledged in the peace process, and to create a process of demobilization that protected the safety and welfare of all Black Americans. Several sought passports to go to Europe to participate in international meetings. The U.S. government, fearing embarrassing public statements about its racial injustices, denied passports to vocal Black critics such as Ida B. Wells-Barnett and Madam C. J. Walker. Other Black women won access through participation in accepted activities. Immediately following the armistice, the Paris headquarters of the YWCA sought the services of Black women to minister to the needs of the 200,000 Black troops. Kathryn Johnson, former organizer for the NAACP; Addie Hunton, organizer for the YWCA, NAACP, and NACW; and Helen Curtis, Washington clubwoman and wife of the minister to Liberia, talked with the soldiers, recorded their aspirations, and made recommendations for improving conditions. Their reports of discrimination contradicted official versions issued by the government's agents. Hunton joined Mary Talbert and Ida Gibbs Hunt in the Pan-African Congress in Paris (February 1919). Talbert and Hunt joined Mary Church Terrell at the International Congress of Women in Zurich (May 1919) to inform women of the world about the racism in the United States.

They returned to the United States, a country reverting to a peacetime economy, readjusting to civilian life, and returning to a prewar status quo. Demobilization hastened the economic and social tensions that erupted in the Red Summer of 1919. The return of Black men in uniform clashed with the revitalization of the Ku Klux Klan, persistent denial of suffrage, residential segregation, unemployment, and postwar hysteria directed against immigrants and radicals. By the end of 1919, seventy-seven Black Americans had been lynched, including eleven soldiers, and race riots had erupted in twenty-six cities. Black women had sacrificed their sons and had demonstrated their abilities during the war years only to find increased violence and intolerance. The war had transformed Black women, who could not return to the prewar patience with injustices.

Although many historians have concluded that the First World War was too brief to have a transformative effect on America, this could not be said for Black America. The war brought challenges to the women who aided Black soldiers and their families; raised money through the various Liberty loans, war savings stamps, and United War Work campaigns; helped to produce and conserve foodstuffs, clothing, and industrial goods; and spread American propaganda through the press, lectures, and schools. The war required citizens to cooperate with the government using human material resources as efficiently as possible. Often racial tensions had to be subordinated to the overall aims of the nation, thereby ignoring or lessening the elaborate systems of segregation. The women had organized to meet these challenges. Black women, proud of their achievements under adverse conditions, and possessing a power base in urban areas, emerged from their war roles resolved to bring democracy to their own people—Americans of color.

[*See also* LEAGUE OF WOMEN FOR COMMUNITY SERVICE, BOSTON; NURSING, WORLD WAR I; NATIONAL ASSOCIATION OF COLORED WOMEN.]

BIBLIOGRAPHY

Beasley, Delilah. *Negro Trailblazers of California* (1919); Blumenthal, Henry. "Woodrow Wilson and the Race Question," *Journal of Negro History* (January 1963); Breen, William. "Black Women and the Great War: Mobilization and Reform in the South," *Journal of Southern History* (August 1978); Calkins, Gladys G. "The Negro in the Young Women's Christian Association: A Study of the Development of YWCA Interracial Policies and Practices in Their Historical Setting," M.A. thesis (1960); Davis, Allen. "Welfare, Reform, and World War I," *American Quarterly* (Winter 1967); Davis, Elizabeth L. *Lifting as They Climb* (1933); Duster, Alfreda, ed. *Crusade for Justice: The Autobiography of Ida B. Wells* (1970); Hine, Darlene Clark. "The Call That Never Came: Black Women Nurses and WWI, An Historical Note," *Indiana Military History Journal* (January 1983); Hunton, Addie and Kathryn Johnson. *Two Colored Women with the American Expeditionary Forces* (n.d.); Jackson, Mary E. "Colored Girls in the Second Line of Defense," *Association Monthly* (October 1918); Lunardini, Christine A. "Standing Firm: William Monroe Trotter's Meeting with Woodrow Wilson," *Journal of Negro History* (Summer 1979); Meier, August and Elliott Rudwick. "The Rise of Segregation in the Federal Bureaucracy, 1900-1930," *Phylon* (Summer 1969); Nelson, Alice Dunbar. "Negro Women in War Work," in *Black Heritage in Social Welfare*, ed. Edyth Ross (1978); Salem, Dorothy. *To Better Our World: Black Women in Organized Reform, 1890-1920* (1990); Scheiber, Jane L. and Harry N. Scheiber. "The Wilson Administration and the Wartime Mobilization of Black Americans, 1917-1918," *Labor History* (Summer 1969); Terrell, Mary C. *A Colored Woman in a White World* (1940); Wolgemuth, Kathleen L. "Woodrow Wilson and Federal Segregation," *Journal of Negro History* (April 1959).

DOROTHY SALEM

WORLD WAR II

For African-American women, World War II was a time of fear and courage, struggle and success, opportunity and discrimination. As with all American women, they worried about sons and husbands serving in the armed forces, and they struggled to adapt to the myriad changes that were transforming everyday life in wartime America. Once the war had ended, they found that the changes they experienced during the war had been a prelude to the future.

World War II dramatically accelerated the pace of economic change for Black women. The demand for war materials and the entry of millions of men into the armed services created an unprecedented labor shortage in the United States. Millions of new jobs were created in the clerical and manufacturing fields, opening up opportunities for women and racial and ethnic minorities to secure new and better employment. Given a much wider range of choices than in the past, millions of African-American women abandoned household and rural work to take new positions in manufacturing, service, and other previously closed sectors of the economy. These jobs generally paid much higher wages and offered more benefits than did those they had left behind.

Thus, between the years of 1941 and 1945, Black women left the rural South and migrated to urban centers throughout the country. Competition for workers forced southern landowners to shift to mechanized labor in order to cultivate and harvest their crops, and this dramatically changed the face of the southern plantation economy. In the future, the South

During World War II, millions of Black women left household and farm work for other occupations. The women welders pictured here are constructing the liberty ship S.S. George Washington Carver *(ca. 1943). [National Archives]*

After the war, Black women were among the first to be fired as employers made room for returning (male) veterans. This riveter worked for Lockheed Aircraft Corporation in Burbank, California. [National Archives]

would rely on much smaller numbers of semiskilled workers, mostly men. For African-American women, the wartime shift to wage work in the cities would be a permanent one, with dramatic social consequences.

Between 1940 and 1944, the proportion of Black women workers employed in industrial work nearly tripled, from 6.8 percent to 18.0 percent. At the same time, the percentage of Black women who worked in domestic service declined from 59.9 percent to 44.6 percent. Economic opportunities were limited, however. Other fields remained virtually closed to African-American women, as the new clerical and sales jobs were given to white women, and even within the industrial sector Black women remained segregated in work that was characterized by hazardous, dirty, and poor working conditions and that paid substandard wages.

As they moved to rapidly growing cities, African-American women encountered discrimination in other areas as well. The persistence of segregation in public and private housing, coupled with the large wartime migration, resulted in extreme overcrowding and poor conditions in Black neighborhoods. Many Black workers, whose homes were located a great distance from work, found that their access to public transportation was poor. For women, the lack of adequate publicly supported child care facilities also created problems.

African-American women faced discrimination and segregation in the military as well. Segregated and limited in their assignments in the Women's Army Corps (WAC), they were totally excluded from the Women Accepted for Volunteer Emergency Service in the Navy (WAVES) until late in 1944. Under pressure from activist Black nurses led by Mabel Keaton Staupers as well as civil rights groups, the WAC eliminated racially based assignments for nurses in January 1945.

Indeed, many African-American women actively protested the discrimination they faced in formal and informal ways: They persisted in seeking jobs from employers who were reluctant to accept equal opportunity; they filed discrimination complaints with the Fair Employment Practice Committee; and they became activists in the cause of civil rights. Through their own efforts, African-American women created many of the opportunities they enjoyed during the war.

After the war was over, African-American women were among the first to be fired from defense jobs as employers openly reverted to discriminatory practices based on race and gender. Most Black women, however, did not return to the homes and jobs they had held before the war. They remained in America's cities, finding work in the growing service sector of the urban economy. The war-generated shift from farm to city proved to be permanent. Before the war, African-American women had found wage work based in their households or in the households of white employers; after 1940, however, they increasingly supported themselves and their families with paid work outside the household setting.

[See also THE MILITARY.]

BIBLIOGRAPHY

Anderson, Karen Tucker. "Last Hired, First Fired: Black Women Workers during World War II," *Journal of American History* (June 1982).

KAREN ANDERSON

WORLD'S COLUMBIAN EXPOSITION, 1893

The World's Columbian Exposition, also known as the Chicago World's Fair, in 1893 in Chicago, Illinois, celebrated the four-hundred-year anniversary of the "discovery" of America. The 27 million people who attended saw the latest innovations in technology and heard the latest developments in intellectual thought. Moreover, spectators, for the first time, witnessed the significantly active role of women at the fair.

During planning stages of the fair, Black Americans recognized that this grand celebration also symbolized and reflected the growing tide of racism and segregation underfoot nationwide. The fair, dubbed by most Americans the "White City" because the fair commission planned for all buildings to have white exteriors, was for Black Americans a "white city" because they were not adequately represented in the celebration. In the process of protesting the exclusion and organizing appropriate representation, Black women contributed to the already growing efforts to develop an effective national agenda and voice for Black women.

A 117-member Board of Lady Managers was appointed in 1890 by the commission to approve applications for space in the female exhibits. Included on the board were several prominent Chicago women—Bertha Honore Palmer, wife of tycoon Potter Palmer, Phoebe Couzins, women's rights advocate, and Matilda Carse, fund-raiser for the Women's Christian Temperance Union. No Black women were appointed to the board nor were there plans to include exhibits from Black women.

In November 1890, a group of Black women in Chicago sent a resolution admonishing the commission because "no provisions have, as yet, been made . . . for securing exhibits from the colored women of this country, or the giving of representation to them . . . and . . . under the present arrangement and classification of exhibits, it would be impossible for visitors to the Exposition to know and distinguish the exhibits and handwork of the colored women from those of the Anglo-Saxons." Thus, the group resolved that "for the purpose of demonstrating the progress of the colored women since emancipation and of showing to those who are yet doubters . . . that the colored women have and are making rapid strides in art, science, and manufacturing, and of furnishing to all information as to the educational and industrial advancement made by the race, and what the race has done, is doing, and might do . . . we, the colored women of Chicago request the World's Columbian Commission to establish an office for a colored woman whose duty it shall be to collect exhibits from the colored women of America" (Massa 1974). The commission promptly sent the letter to the Board of Lady Managers.

Still, a Black woman was not appointed to the board but the concerns of Black women became a central issue. The board appointed a southern white woman, Mary Cecil Cantrill, to represent Black women's interests. Cantrill, a friend of Palmer, was suspected by Black leaders of being just as paternalistic as other board members, and her appointment was a major disappointment to the Black community.

Because of the constant and consistent agitation by Black women, a board majority voted to provide the "same latitude and opportunity" for Black women. As a conciliatory gesture, Fannie Barrier Williams was appointed to "help supervise the installation of all exhibits in the Woman's Building." She later became secretary of the art department of the woman's branch of the Congress Auxiliaries for the fair.

Williams was also asked to address the departmental congress of the National Association of Loyal Women of American Liberty at the World's Congress of Representative Women in May 1893. A few months later, Williams was invited to speak before the World's Parliament of Religions. Although Williams was not the only Black woman who spoke at the meetings, she undoubtedly played an important role in opening the doors for several other Black women to speak before the predominantly white groups. Anna Julia Cooper, Sarah J. Early, Hallie Quinn Brown, and Frances Harper were other Black women participants.

Meanwhile, Ida B. Wells was busy soliciting funds for the publication of a protest pamphlet, *The Reason Why the Colored American Is Not in the Columbian Exposition*, to expose the problems inherent in white racism. With the aid of several Black Chicago women and $500 raised to finance the venture, 20,000 copies of the pamphlet were printed. Contributions from Frederick Douglass, Ferdinand Barnett, and I. Garland Penn, a journalist and editor, aided in the pamphlet's popularity. Douglass, former minister to Haiti, provided Wells with a desk at the Haitian building at the fairgrounds where she "spent the days putting this pamphlet in the hands of foreigners." By the end of the fair, thousands of copies had been sold.

The Black women who participated in the five-month world celebration had integrated the fair. In the process, these women put the concerns of Black Americans on the national agenda and reshaped the image of Black womanhood.

BIBLIOGRAPHY

Massa, Ann. "Black Women in the 'White City,' " *Journal of American Studies* (December 1974); Mossell, Mrs. N. F. *The Work of Afro-American Women* (1894); Rudwick, Elliott M. and August Meier. "Black Man in the 'White City': Negroes and the Columbian Exposition, 1893," *Phylon* (1965); Sewall, May Wright, ed. *The World's Congress of Representative Women* (1894); Weimann, Jeanne Madeline. *The Fair Women* (1981).

WANDA HENDRICKS

WRIGHT, ELIZABETH EVELYN (1872-1906)

Elizabeth Wright was born in a three-room cabin in Talbotton, Georgia, the seventh of twenty-one children of John Wesley Wright and Virginia Rolfe. Her father was a former slave and an illiterate carpenter. Her mother, also unschooled, was a full-blooded Cherokee. Elizabeth Wright grew up in an impoverished Black section of Talbotton known as Smith Hill. She received a haphazard primary education because the school she attended at St. Philip's Church operated only periodically. Perhaps it was her own difficulty in securing an education that made Wright so determined to provide better opportunities for others. Doggedly she persisted, despite violent opposition, financial constraints, and her own deteriorating health. Her persistence made possible Voorhees College in Denmark, South Carolina.

Without parental support and possessing a meager education, she enrolled at Tuskegee Institute in 1888. She worked days in the kitchen and attended night classes in language, reading, spelling, and mathematics as well as dressmaking, millinery, and cooking. She was physically weak and chronically sick. She could not maintain the rigorous schedule. With the help of Olivia Davidson Washington, she secured financial aid from Massachusetts Judge George W. Kelley. In poor health, she interrupted her education at Tuskegee in 1892 and taught for a year at a school in McNeill's, South Carolina, operated by a northerner, Almira S. Steele. White locals opposed the efforts of this northern white woman to educate Black people and they set fire to the school and destroyed it.

Elizabeth Wright returned to Tuskegee, finished her fifth year, and graduated in 1894. Thoroughly impressed by Booker T. Washington and fully imbued with the self-help ideology of Tuskegee, she set out to establish a similar institution in South Carolina. Repeated failure and persistent opposition did not daunt this determined woman. When Wright attempted to organize a school in McNeill's, locating it on the nine-acre site that Judge Kelley purchased from Steele, white locals burned the building materials before construction began. A second school organized in McNeill's did not survive. Her third school, opened at Hampton Court House in 1896, incited white opposition and Wright was driven out. A fourth school established at nearby Govan lasted only briefly.

Wright finally met with success in Denmark, South Carolina, when she opened Denmark Industrial School on April 14, 1897, on the second floor of a local store. With the support of a local white attorney and state senator, Stanwix G. Mayfield, she purchased twenty acres of land, moved the school, and opened it to 236 students on October 4, 1897. With the aid and persistent encouragement of Jessie Dorsey, a nurse and teacher from Coshocton, Ohio, the school grew steadily if uncertainly. Some Black people led by a local clergyman opposed the school and questioned the religious commitment of the two women, especially Dorsey, who was a Seventh-Day Adventist.

Wright served as principal of the Denmark school, supervising instruction, construction, farming, and fund-raising. Devoted to industrial and agricultural education and intensely moralistic, she was convinced that hard work, self-discipline, and the acquisition of skills combined with honesty, cleanliness, and reliability would elevate people of color. In her second annual report, she explained her mission: "We feel it is our duty to work for the ennobling of our race, and as they rise to a higher standard of citizenship and become stronger morally, physically, and intellectually, they will be a blessing to American civilization instead of a curse, and other races will be helped indirectly by them" (Coleman 1922).

She was an intrepid fund-raiser. In 1901, Ralph Voorhees, a New Jersey philanthropist, donated $4,500 to purchase 200 acres of land. The school moved to the new site and was renamed Voorhees Industrial School. Kennerly Hall and Voorhees Hall were constructed and several new programs were added, including carpentry, blacksmithing, and printing. The farm expanded with the arrival of contributions in the form of horses, mules, hogs, and poultry.

On June 2, 1906, Wright married Martin Menafee, a Tuskegee graduate and the business manager-treasurer of Voorhees. Four months later, after Wright suffered another of her repeated illnesses, Dr. James Harvey Kellogg operated on her for gastritis in Battle Creek, Michigan. She seemed to be recovering when she suffered a relapse and died on December 14.

As her legacy, Voorhees survived and prospered. It maintained its industrial mission for most of the first half of the twentieth century. In 1924, the Episcopal Church began to support Voorhees. In 1929, a junior college was added to its elementary and high school programs. In 1964, it became a four-year college.

BIBLIOGRAPHY

Coleman, J.F.B. *Tuskegee to Voorhees: The Booker T. Washington Idea Projected by Elizabeth Evelyn Wright* (1922); Morris, J. Kenneth. *Elizabeth Evelyn Wright, 1872-1906* (1983).

WILLIAM C. HINE

Y

YATES, JOSEPHINE SILONE
(1859-1912)

Josephine Silone Yates, second president of the National Association of Colored Women (NACW) from 1901 to 1906, made her most significant mark on the world as a teacher. She was also a writer—mainly for newspapers and sometimes under the pen name R. K. Potter—and lecturer.

Born in 1859 in Mattituck, New York, to a well-respected and solidly established family, Josephine Silone was taught reading, writing, and arithmetic at home before entering school. She received the favorable attention of her teachers early on for her unusual intelligence and eagerness to learn. At the age of eleven, she was sent to live with an uncle so that she could have the opportunity to study under Fanny Jackson Coppin at the Institute for Colored Youth. This, her first opportunity to interact with other Black students, seems to have been a rewarding and meaningful experience. She returned home a year later when her uncle accepted a post at Howard University but, at the age of fourteen, she accepted the invitation of an aunt to live with her in Newport, Rhode Island. This arrangement was probably made in order to provide young Josephine with the opportunity to attend the larger, and presumably better, Newport schools.

The only Black student in her high school, Yates completed the four-year course of study in three years and was the valedictorian of the class of 1877. She then attended the Rhode Island State Normal School, taking teaching courses, and graduated with honors. Again, she was the only Black student in her class. After receiving the highest score that had ever been recorded on the state teachers' examination, she became the first Black person to be certified to teach in Rhode Island.

Yates had shown an interest in and ability for science, particularly chemistry, from an early age. In 1879, she moved to Jefferson City, Missouri, to teach chemistry at the Lincoln Institute where, not long after becoming the first woman professor, she became the head of the department of natural science. Her reputation grew and she was asked by Booker T. Washington to become the "lady principal" of Tuskegee Institute, an offer she declined.

In 1889, Josephine Silone resigned her teaching position to marry W. W. Yates, the principal of the Wendell Phillips School in Kansas City. She did not, however, give up her intellectual pursuits. Although no longer teaching, she continued writing, mainly for newspaper publication, on a variety of subjects, including such wide-ranging topics as economics and Russian literature.

Yates also worked in the club movement, organizing the Kansas City Women's League in 1893 and joining, in 1896, the NACW.

After her husband's death in 1910, Yates returned to teaching for two years. She died on September 3, 1912.

BIBLIOGRAPHY

CBWA; Dannett, Sylvia. *Profiles of Negro Womanhood* (1964); Davis, Elizabeth. *Lifting as They Climb* (1933); Majors, Monroe. *Noted Negro Women* ([1893] 1986); *NBAW*; Wesley, Charles Harris. *History of the National Association of Colored Women's Clubs* (1984).

JAN GLEITER

YOUNG, JEAN WHEELER SMITH
(1942-)

The 1960s were life-changing times, particularly for those involved in the civil rights movement. For Detroit native Jean Wheeler Smith Young (who was born on April 9, 1942), a Washington, D.C., psychiatrist, writer, and former civil rights organizer in Mississippi and southwest Georgia, the movement continues to inform and enhance both her personal and professional lives. "My work with the Student Nonviolent Coordinating Committee (SNCC) was extremely fulfilling," she has said, "because it involved empowering groups of people and nurturing their ability, as a community, to act in their own behalf. Professionally, these are the same goals I have as a psychiatrist, though I now work on a more individual basis" (Richardson 1992).

The movement also enabled Young to juggle a variety of responsibilities. This proved to be a necessity when she decided, in the late 1960s, to return to college to pursue a Master's degree in food science and nutrition, having studied premed and graduated Phi Beta Kappa with a B.S. in chemistry from Howard University in 1965. While studying for her Master's degree, she raised two children, Malaika and Tarik, with the help of her former husband, D.C. City Council Chair Frank Smith. She also continued to write, receiving acclaim for her many published works, both fiction and nonfiction.

From 1970 to 1975, she was assistant professor in the Department of Interdisciplinary Sciences at the fledgling Federal City College, now the University of the District of Columbia. Never having given up her love of medicine, she decided to enter George Washington University Medical School. She graduated in 1980 and completed her residency in psychiatry, with a fellowship in child and adolescent psychology, at the university's medical center in 1985.

Always the juggler, Young currently is medical director of the women's unit of the Psychiatric Institute of Washington while also maintaining a private practice targeted to young people and serving as a consultant to several inner-city mental health programs. In this context, she serves as division chief of children's services for the Center for Family Health of the D.C. Institute of Mental Health, where the grant that she cowrote allows her to develop her specialty: the treatment of children traumatized by violence and vulnerable to the trap of drug addiction.

Young continues to bear witness to the movement that helped shape her. As she wrote in a 1966 essay in the *New Republic*, "It's too hard to find ways of giving people decent places to stay and livable incomes. It is hard because we're told that to decide to do this is also to make decisions about national fiscal policy and the social order and labor unions and the international balance of payments. And we cringe before these weighty matters. . . . I think people can get loose from the fear of deciding about things that are important by trying to consider and deal with the problems of people at the bottom."

This philosophy guides Young's practice and her life. She is supported in this by her husband, James Young, a computer program manager and retired chemist.

BIBLIOGRAPHY

Young, Jean Wheeler Smith. Personal interviews.

SELECTED WORKS OF JEAN WHEELER SMITH YOUNG

"That She Shall Dance No More," *Negro Digest*; "Something to Eat," *Negro Digest*; "O. C.'s Heart," *Black World*; "Ms. Remembered," *Essence*; "Frankie Mae." In *Black-Eyed Susans, Midnight Birds: Stories by and about Black Women*, ed. Mary Helen Washington ([1968] 1990); Richardson, Judy. Personal interview (February 1992).

JUDY RICHARDSON

YOUNG, ROGER ARLINER
(1889-1964)

Few Black women in the United States had the opportunity to engage in scientific research in the decades before World War II. Due to educational, racial, and sexual barriers, few Black women produced work that would allow them to lay full claim to the title of scientist. Roger Arliner Young, the first Black woman to earn a doctoral degree in zoology (University of Pennsylvania, 1940), also was one of the first Black women to conduct and publish research in her field. In 1924, working first with her mentor, noted Black zoologist Ernest Everett Just, she made a significant contribution to the study of structures that control salt concentration in *Paramecium*. Later she also published several notable studies on the effects of direct and indirect radiation on sea urchin eggs.

Born in Clifton Forge, Virginia, Young entered Howard University in 1916. After graduating in 1923, she was hired there as an assistant professor of zoology. She received a Master's degree in zoology in 1926 from the University of Chicago, where she was elected to Sigma Xi. From 1927 until 1936, she spent summers doing research at the leading biological research institution in the country, the Marine Biological Laboratory in Woods Hole, Massachusetts.

Although she was successful at both research and teaching, Young began to experience difficulties in both areas during the 1930s. Burdened by a heavy teaching load and few financial resources, she began to flounder. However, after losing her position at Howard University in 1935, she rallied to continue her research, publishing four papers between 1935 and 1938 and completing her doctoral work at the University of Pennsylvania under L. V. Heilbrunn in 1940. From 1940 to 1947, she taught at the North Carolina College for Negroes and at Shaw University, also in North Carolina. During the 1950s, she taught at several Black colleges in Texas, Louisiana, and Mississippi. Unfortunately, by the early 1960s she had succumbed to the effects of continuing personal and professional difficulties. Young died on November 9, 1964.

A successful scientific career is predicated on stable institutional affiliations, manageable teaching loads, financial support for research, and the continuing support of mentors, peers, and community; Young had few of these benefits throughout her career. Scientific achievement, however, is measured largely by the quality of the research produced; in this Young was successful. Further, she displayed one of the most abiding characteristics of all good scientists—a commitment to science against all odds.

BIBLIOGRAPHY

Heilbrunn, L. V. and R. A. Young. "Indirect Effects of Radiation on Sea Urchin Eggs," *Biological Bulletin* (1935); Manning, Kenneth R. "Roger Arliner Young, Scientist," *Sage: A Scholarly Journal on Black Women* (Fall 1989), and *Black Apollo of Science: The Life of Ernest Everett Just* (1983); Young, R. A. "On the Excretory Apparatus in Paramecium," *Science* (September 12, 1924).

EVELYNN M. HAMMONDS

YOUNG WOMEN'S CHRISTIAN ASSOCIATION

One Imperative: To Thrust Our Collective Power to Eliminate Racism Wherever It Exists and by Any Means Necessary. (YWCA 1970)

When the above declaration was approved by the national convention of the Young Women's Christian Association (YWCA) in 1970, it signaled a dramatic climax to the organization's century-long struggle to fulfill its social mission. At that juncture in its history, the YWCA was giving voice to its experience as the oldest and largest women's multiracial association in the world, and yet, in all of its work with, and for, women, the most overwhelming obstacle to social progress continued to be relations between the races. At the height of the civil rights and Black Power movements, and in the early stages of the modern women's movement, YWCA members asserted that by focusing on racism, women of all races could identify their positions as oppressors as well as oppressed persons and could then work more effectively to combat the ills of society.

The multiracial membership of the YWCA resulted both from incidental and deliberate actions by its membership. As early as 1870, only four years after the formation of the Boston YWCA, and only nineteen years since the first association was begun in England, Black churchwomen in Philadelphia represented a Colored Women's Christian Association at the second annual national convention of Women's Christian Associations. During the remainder of the nineteenth century, as Black women migrated in large numbers to industrial centers, similar associations were begun in an effort to meet the increasing need for social services and lodging. These early city associations were founded and operated by Black women because their race excluded them from organizations established to serve white women. However, in spite of their adoption of the name Young Women's Christian Association, and despite their unceasing efforts to affiliate with their white counterparts, these Black associations were not accepted as part of the growing national movement of women's associations that combined to form the International Board of Women's and Young Women's Christian Associations.

By contrast, as part of a separate movement of students organizing YWCAs, Black students at predominantly white colleges as well as on Black college campuses were welcomed as members. This group's national umbrella organization was known as the

American Committee of Young Women's Christian Associations. There were cordial relations between the two national bodies, but they worked as independent organizations. The American Committee associations were most often led by white students and teachers. With much emphasis on the task of evangelizing the world, this group believed that part of their Christian mission included ministering to Black and Native American students as well as working as foreign missionaries. Affiliates of the American Committee were closely aligned with the world and the international committees of the Young Men's Christian Association (YMCA), which pioneered work among minority students. Stressing prayer and Bible study in preparation for a life of service, the women's student associations grew rapidly among young Black women at the turn of the century.

When the two national organizations merged in 1906 to form one national board, fourteen Black student associations formally affiliated with the American Committee and four Black city associations were recommended for affiliation. Although these associations by no means represented all of the work being done by Black women under the name Young Women's Christian Association, Addie W. Hunton, a Black social worker who was hired by the new national board to assess the work of these groups, believed they held the most promise.

However, true to the segregationist policies of the era, white women were reluctant to accept Black affiliates, especially in city associations. Their concern centered on two main issues. First, they did not want to assume fiscal responsibility for the struggling Black associations. The second issue was equally compelling. White Southern women especially worried that "any parallel work among colored people would mean attendance by both at conferences," and they were not willing to suffer the embarrassment of being seated at regional and national meetings alongside Black women from their own cities.

The early solution was to affiliate already established Black associations directly with the national board in a separate category, independent of the white associations. This arrangement was not satisfactory in most cases, however, for a variety of reasons, not the least of which was the fact that, without financial support from the larger white associations, the small Black operations could not afford professional leadership or provide quality services. It soon became apparent that the more expedient arrangement, especially in fast-growing northern cities, was to have a central association, which usually was all white, and

so-called colored branches. Moreover, "no work was to be undertaken . . . to promote Association work among colored people in the cities in the South."

Under this arrangement, branch committees of management were mostly free to design their own programs, and a few were responsible for raising operating funds. Prior to World War I, the central association designated members of its board of directors to serve on a subcommittee for colored work. This committee, which reported back to the board, acted as liaison to maintain control over personnel and major capital decisions. Black women tolerated this structure as a trade off for fiscal support, leadership training, and credibility as part of the powerful national organization. Moreover, affiliation provided access to a national network of white Christian leaders who sometimes could influence the quality of local race relations. During this same period, according to association records, Black student association work grew to include 150 institutions. At white colleges where there were representative groups of Black students, some organized separate associations.

The benefit of affiliation was dramatically illustrated when, during World War I, the national board received $4 million from the government to supervise war-work activities for women; of this amount, $400,000 was set aside for work among Black women. During the war period, Eva Bowles, secretary for colored work for the national board, supervised the expansion of service to Black women—from sixteen affiliates to association work in forty-nine communities covering twenty-one states and the District of Columbia. In the South Atlantic region alone, at least 4,000 Black women and girls were enrolled. In a two-year period, Bowles also expanded the opportunity for hundreds of competent Black women to become employees and volunteer leaders in the association. At the end of the war, the association allocated $200,000 of its remaining funds to build the Phyllis Wheatley branch in Washington, D.C.

Association work expanded to include two principal groups of women. The first emphasis was on providing recreation and housing services for young women migrating to urban centers in search of employment. Because many of these cities were in the South, association work for this group had been almost nonexistent. YWCA workers mobilized Black leaders and with their help organized activities, some skills development, and employment and residence registries. This work, which began as a supplement to government-sponsored "hostess houses" for the families of soldiers near army camps, formed the nucleus

Prior to World War I, the YWCA was more a biracial than an interracial organization. This photograph of the Brooklyn Colored Conference, taken in 1915, includes Eva Bowles (center), secretary for colored work for the national board. [YWCA of the USA, National Board Archives]

of postwar center development. The second thrust was incorporating the large number of young women who had been organized into Girl Reserve clubs, originally formed as so-called Patriotic Leagues to support the war. These clubs contained girls between the ages of ten and eighteen in schools all over the nation.

From their beginning activities as founders, members, and participants in the YWCA, Black women petitioned in various ways to be recognized and represented in the organization's decision-making bodies. As early as 1915, Black and white women met to try and resolve racial relations between central and colored branches in southern cities where associations existed prior to the 1907 agreement and to demand Black representation on regional field committees. After World War I, having greatly increased their number as members in the association, Black women began to demand more control of the work of their own branches and to insist that their committee chairs become members of the local central committees; moreover, they pressed for representation on the national board. In 1924, Elizabeth Ross Haynes, the national board's first full-time Black staff member, was elected as the first Black member of the board. Thereafter, Black women also were represented on regional field committees. Further, in response to protests by Black members, the national board resolved to hold national conventions only in cities that would assure accommodations to all members in attendance. Although Black women were critical of the slow rate of progress, the so-called biracial policies of the organization were considered quite advanced for the time.

In 1931, the national board phased out its colored work subcommittee and assigned headquarters-based Black workers to mainstream departments. Initially this plan was greeted by the Black staff as a step toward interracial work. However, not long after it was put into place, Bowles resigned in protest, charging that in reality, "the plan would diminish the participation of Negroes in decision making." In response to her allegations, as well as to the mounting complaints of Black association leaders, the national board formed a committee on interracial policies that functioned for ten years. During this period, the board also commissioned a national study of race relations in the association.

After a careful review of local associations, the national organization adopted an interracial charter in 1946, which served as an internal sanction against all forms of segregation in instances where there were no legal restrictions. This action was preceded in 1942 by a decision by Black association leaders to disband their Negro Leadership Conference. (The conference dated back to the immediate post-war period when Black residents of the South Atlantic region had no opportunity to function as part of normal association life; from their meetings had grown a national gathering of Black YWCA representatives.) The unanimous 1946 vote was recorded as the recognition "that in the YWCA, the high value is its interrelatedness—its process of togetherness in working on the common concerns of humanity" (Bell and Wilkins 1944).

Adoption of the interracial charter was a watershed in the life of the organization. It meant that associations were expected to actively integrate Black women into programs, facilities, and governing bodies. Eventually it meant dismantling all segregated branches. In spite of strong resistance in many southern cities, including a few court battles against the national board, and more subtle resistance in other parts of the country, the YWCA desegregation effort was fairly successful. To help local associations prepare for the change, the board assigned Dorothy Height to the position of interracial education secretary. In 1963, her position was changed to director of the Office of Racial Justice, reflecting a more aggressive approach. The new office was in charge of planning strategies to overcome internal segregation and to assist in the desegregation of all facilities.

The 1970 convention that voted in favor of the association's "one imperative" to eliminate racism was preceded by a series of interracial awareness gatherings for local members and a national board-sponsored retreat for 500 Black leaders in the organization. During a period when Black members had become disillusioned with the slow rate of progress and the high emotional cost of integration, the issue had become whether to remain part of the association or separate in order to be in complete charge of services to Black women. After much agonizing, and with the thoughtful leadership of Helen Jackson Wilkins Claytor, the first Black president of the national board, the group concluded that the organization represented a historic investment for Black women as well as white women, and that they would present their "imperative" to the total convention.

Although the Young Women's Christian Association remains an organization with a predominantly white membership, its leadership has mirrored the organization's commitment to integration. Between 1973 and 1990 the organization chose two Black women as national executive director, and two Black women have served as president of the national board.

Also, the programs and projects of local associations are scrutinized to assure the inclusion of women of all races represented in the population.

[*See also* PHYLLIS WHEATLEY CLUBS AND HOMES; WORLD WAR I.]

BIBLIOGRAPHY

Bell, Juliet O. and Helen J. Wilkins. "Interracial Practices in Community Y.W.C.A.'s," pamphlet (1944); Calkins, Gladys Gilkey. "The Negro in the Young Women's Christian Association," Master's thesis (1960); Giddings, Paula. *When and Where I Enter: The Impact of Black Women on Race and Sex in America* (1984); Jones, Adrienne Lash. "Struggle among the Saints: Black Women in the YWCA, 1870-1920," typescript (1991); Lerner, Gerda. *Black Women in White America* (1972); Neverdon-Morton, Cynthia. *Afro-American Women of the South and the Advancement of the Race, 1895-1925* (1989); Rouse, Jacqueline Anne. *Lugenia Burns Hope: Black Southern Reformer* (1989); Walters, Jane Olcott, compiler. "History of Colored Work . . . 1907-1920," typescript (1920); Wilson, Elizabeth. *Fifty Years of Association Work* (1916); Young Women's Christian Association. "Report/YWCA Twenty-fifth National Convention," typescript (1970).

ADRIENNE LASH JONES

Z

ZETA PHI BETA SORORITY

The successful growth of Zeta Phi Beta Sorority is perhaps best captured in a speech by its founder, first president, and grand basileus-emeritus, Arizona Cleaver Stemons, who said, "The lamp of learning is passed from hand to hand, the seed maturing becomes the many seeds of future plantings" (Adams 1965).

Zeta Phi Beta was founded on January 16, 1920, at Howard University in Washington, D.C. The period after World War I was a paradoxical time for Black Americans. Tremendous strides had been made in creating greater opportunities for higher education and in acquiring personal property, and yet, the economic and political gains seemed minuscule because of the country's segregationist policies. There was no intermingling of the races, no engaging in interracial community and social activities. In addition, women had very limited roles to play. Women were chaperoned, they did not smoke or use profanity, and their primary pursuits were getting an education and exhibiting the finest qualities of womanhood. Thus, Zeta was founded at a time when there was a tremendous need for women to expand their roles in order to address many of the problematic issues confronting society.

Recognizing the need for an organization that would assume a leadership position in making the world a better place, Charles Robert Samuel Taylor, a member of Phi Beta Sigma fraternity (founded in January 1914), began to sow the seeds of a sister organization while escorting his friend, Arizona Cleaver Stemons, across the campus of Howard University in Washington, D.C. In 1919, Taylor and his brother, A. Langston Taylor, took Stemons's request to establish a sister organization to the Sigma conclave. After the request was approved, Stemons arranged a meeting in her dormitory room at Miner Hall with fourteen other women to determine whether there was interest in establishing a new sorority. Five of the women decided to establish a new organization, which subscribed to some of the basic tenets of the two other Black sororities on campus. Thus, the first Greek sister and brother organizations were born—Phi Beta Sigma fraternity and Zeta Phi Beta sorority.

The five founders, called the five pearls, were Myrtle Tyler Faithful and Viola Tyler Goings, both education majors from Flushing, Ohio; Pearl Neal, a music major from Charlotte, North Carolina; Fannie Pettie Watts, an education/social work major from Perry, Georgia; and Arizona Cleaver Stemons, a social work major from Pike County, Missouri. The sorority, a private nonprofit organization, was incorporated in Washington, D.C., in 1923 and in Illinois in 1939.

The Taylor brothers formally introduced the sorority to the community by holding a reception at the Whitelaw Hotel in Washington, D.C. The Zetas also were welcomed in Miner Hall by members of the other two sororities, Alpha Kappa Alpha and Delta Sigma Theta. During the organization's first year, a Zeta, Pauline Phillips, earned top academic honors at Howard by being graduated summa cum laude.

Taking blue and white as its colors, basing its constitution on that of the Sigmas, and borrowing part of its name from Phi Beta Sigma, Zeta Phi Beta sorority was chartered for the specific purpose of developing the ideals of service, educational and scholastic achievement, civic and cultural involvement, sisterhood, finer womanhood, and charity and compassion for all human beings. Cofounder Myrtle Faithful, the daughter of a former slave, emphasized that the sorority must distinguish itself by stressing its founding principles. Following the Greek alphabet, the first chapters were: Alpha at Howard; Beta at Morris Brown University in Atlanta; Gamma at Morgan State College in Baltimore; Delta at Pittsburg State College of Pittsburg (Kansas); and Epsilon in New York City.

Zeta Phi Beta's 75,000 members are primarily college-educated Black women professionals in medicine, law, dentistry, business, engineering, and education. Many prominent Americans have been Zetas, including Violette Anderson, the first Black woman admitted to practice law before the U.S. Supreme Court; Deborah Wolfe, president of the New Jersey Higher Education Commission; and Elizabeth Koontz, first Black president of the National Education Association.

There are 500 collegiate and graduate chapters in thirty-nine states, the District of Columbia, the Caribbean Islands, West Africa, and West Germany. In 1933, the sorority was decentralized, and regions, to be supervised by regional directors, were designated. Local chapters are organized and administered in these nine regions: Atlantic, Eastern, Great Lakes, Midwestern, Pacific, South Central, South Eastern, Southern, and West Africa. Since its inception, when Arizona Stemons served as grand basileus (president), nineteen grand basileis have been elected, including current international grand basileus Eunice S. Thomas. The sorority is governed by a nationally elected board of directors and administered by an executive director at its national headquarters in Washington, D.C.

Zeta Phi Beta sorority has established a phenomenal track record as the first sorority constitutionally bound to a fraternity; as a charter member of the National Pan Hellenic Council, Inc.; as the first to organize international chapters in 1948 in West Africa and West Germany; the first to organize auxiliary groups for youths (Archonettes) and adults (Amicae); and the first to establish a centralized administrative office with a paid staff. Zetas opened the Domestic Science Center in Monrovia, Liberia, in October 1965.

Prior to 1965, the sorority's program thrust was housing and juvenile delinquency projects, including the sponsorship of vocational guidance clinics, youth clubs and camps, Operation Bootstrap (a parent-child training program), and debutante cotillions. In 1965, these projects were expanded under a new program called Welfare, Education, and Health Services, with the primary emphasis being the implementation of projects designed to address the issues of poverty, education, and health care. In 1975, the sorority established a tax-exempt private corporation, the National Educational Foundation, in an effort to facilitate educational scholarship, research, and community education projects. The sorority continues to implement innovative community service projects; among them are Stork's Nest, a cooperative prenatal project with the March of Dimes; Illiteracy Eradication 2000, which includes tutorial partnerships; Project Zeta, designed to fight substance abuse; Just Say No clubs for youth; Project Z.I.P. (Zetas Investing in People); the Latch Key Children's Program; Zeta Leadership Academy; Zeta child care centers; and legislative initiatives for social and political change.

Seventy-one years after its inception, the seeds of Zeta Phi Beta Sorority, Inc., are still germinating, and the lamp of learning is still being passed from hand to hand. Perhaps the spirit of the organization is best captured in these thoughts: "Yesterday is gone. Use it as a guide, but don't dwell on it. Make the best of today by planting seeds and being agents of change. Make tomorrow better than today by cultivating and serving as living legacies" (Adams 1965).

BIBLIOGRAPHY

Adams, Ola. *Zeta Beta Sorority (1920-1965)* (1965); David, John P., ed. *The American Negro Reference Book* (1966); Emory, Frank, Doris Lucas, Tom Parramore, and Eallie Thorpe, eds. *Paths toward Freedom* (1976); Thomas, Eunice S. *Zeta Phi Beta Sorority, Inc., Membership Selection/ Intake Process Training Manual* (1990); Zeta Phi Beta Sorority, Inc. *Zeta Phi Beta Sorority, Inc.* (1989).

ALGEANIA FREEMAN

Appendices

Black Women in the United States: A Chronology

compiled by
Jamie Hart and Elsa Barkley Brown
with assistance from
N. H Goodall

1619

Twenty Africans, three of them women, are put ashore off a Dutch frigate at Jamestown, Virginia.

1624

In Jamestown, Virginia, a woman known to us only as Isabel, wife of Antoney, gives birth to William, the first black child born in English North America.

1641

Massachusetts is the first colony in North America to give statutory recognition to slavery; Connecticut follows in 1650.

1661

Virginia gives statutory recognition to slavery; Maryland in 1663; New York and New Jersey, 1664; South Carolina, 1682; Rhode Island and Pennsylvania, 1700; North Carolina, 1715; Georgia, 1750.

1662

Virginia law establishes that children born in the colony will be held bond or free according to the condition of their mother.

1692

Tituba, a West Indian slave accused of witchcraft in Salem, Massachusetts, is the catalyst for the infamous Salem witch-hunt and trials.

1708

Following a Newton, Long Island, New York, slave revolt in which seven whites were killed, a black woman is burned alive and one Indian man and two black men are hanged.

1712

Slave men and women in New York City initiate a revolt that results in the deaths of nine white men and the stiffening of restrictions on slaves. The captured conspirators are hanged or burned alive; among six who are pardoned is a pregnant woman.

1746

Lucy Terry writes "Bars of Flight," the first known poem by an African American in the United States; the poem is not published until 1895.

1765

Jenny Slew files suit in Massachusetts colony and is awarded her freedom.

1773

Phillis Wheatley publishes *Poems on Various Subjects Religious and Moral*, the first book published by a black person in North America and the second published by a woman in North America.

1777

Vermont abolishes slavery.

1780

Pennsylvania passes a gradual emancipation law; similar laws are enacted in Connecticut and Rhode Island in 1784; New York, 1799; New Jersey, 1804.

1781

Los Angeles, California, is founded by forty-four settlers, of whom at least twenty-six are black women, men, and children.

When Elizabeth Freeman, also known as Mum Bett, sues for her freedom, on the grounds that the 1780 Massachusetts state constitution declares all men born free and equal, her petition is not designed only to secure freedom for herself but also to establish slavery as inconsistent with state law and thus secure freedom for all Massachusetts slaves. Freeman is granted her freedom and 30 shillings in damages as restitution for a beating by her mistress.

1782

Deborah Sampson (Gannett), disguised as a male, begins a seventeen-month stint in the Continental Army; sources disagree as to whether Sampson was African American.

1784

The first black Catholic community in the United States is established in St. Augustine, Florida, by escaped slaves who build the fortified town of Gracia Real de Santa Teresa de Mose.

1787

The U.S. Constitution, with three clauses protecting slavery, is approved at the Philadelphia Convention.

The Northwest Ordinance prohibits slavery in the territory that would eventually become the states of Michigan, Ohio, Illinois, Indiana, and Wisconsin.

The Free African Society is established in Philadelphia, making it the first African American secret and beneficial society in the U.S.

The first African Free School is established in New York, a precursor to secular education for African Americans in New York.

1790

The black population of the United States totals 757,181: 59,557 are free and 697,624 held in slavery.

1793

The first fugitive slave law is enacted by Congress, making it a criminal offense to harbor or prevent the arrest of a fugitive slave.

The Female Benevolent Society of St. Thomas is founded by black women in Philadelphia.

A former slave, Catherine Ferguson, having purchased her freedom, opens Katy Ferguson's School for the Poor in New York, enrolling black and white children from a local almshouse.

1800

The black population of the United States totals 1,002,037: 108,435 are free and 893,602 held in slavery.

Nanny Prosser joins her husband, Gabriel, and other slaves in planning an aborted revolt near Richmond, Virginia.

1804

The Ohio legislature enacts the first of a series of Black Laws passed throughout northern states, restricting the rights and movements of free blacks in the North.

1809

The African Female Benevolent Society of Newport, Rhode Island, is founded.

1810

The black population of the United States totals 1,377,808: 186,446 are free and 1,191,362 held in slavery.

1816

The African Methodist Episcopal (AME) Church is founded.

1818

The Colored Female Religious and Moral Society of Salem, Massachusetts, is founded.

1820

The black female population of the United States totals 870,860. Total black population is 1,771,656: 233,634 are free and 1,538,022 (750,010 women) held in slavery.

Eighty-six African Americans, sailing out of New York City, emigrate to Sierra Leone, West Africa.

The African Company, the first black dramatic company, is founded, performing in the African Grove Theatre in Greenwich Village in New York City; it offers one of the first opportunities for black women to be seen on stage.

1821

The African Methodist Episcopal Zion (AMEZ) Church is founded.

Two hundred working-class women in Philadelphia band together to form the Daughters of Africa mutual benefit society.

1827

The first black newspaper, *Freedom's Journal*, is published in New York; among its main financial supporters is the Female Literary Society of New York City.

The African Methodist Episcopal Daughters of Conference organizations are officially sanctioned to provide material assistance to ministers.

The African Dorcas Association is founded by black women in New York City to supply clothing to children in the African Free Schools.

1828

The Coloured Female Roman Catholic Beneficial Society of Washington, D.C., is founded.

1829

Following a race riot, more than 1,000 black women, men, and children leave Cincinnati, Ohio, and immigrate to Canada.

The Oblate Sisters of Providence, the first Roman Catholic religious community of black women in the United States, is established in Baltimore, Maryland, with Elizabeth Lange, originally from Santo Domingo, as the Mother Superior.

St. Francis Academy of Colored Girls, a boarding school founded by the Oblate Sisters of Providence, opens in Baltimore, Maryland.

1830

Women are 1,162,366 of a total U.S. black population of 2,328,642: 319,599 are free and 2,009,043 (996,220 women) held in slavery. As a result of gradual emancipation laws, only 2,780 African Americans remain enslaved in the northern states.

1831

The first National Negro Convention meets in Philadelphia.

The Female Literary Association of Philadelphia and the Afric-American Female Intelligence Society of Boston are founded.

The History of Mary Prince, a West Indian Slave is the first slave narrative published by a black woman in the Americas.

1832

The Female Anti-Slavery Society of Salem, Massachusetts, is founded by free women of color, including Mary A. Battys, Charlotte Bell, Eleanor C. Harvey, and Dorothy C. Battys.

Maria Stewart becomes the first native-born U.S. woman to begin a public speaking career when she lectures before a "promiscuous" (male and female) audience in Boston's Franklin Hall, under the sponsorship of the African-American Society.

1833

The Philadelphia Library of Colored Persons is established to house books and sponsor concerts, lectures, and debates.

The interracial Philadelphia Female Anti-Slavery Society is founded, with nine black women among the charter members: Margaret Bowser, Grace Bustill Douglass, Charlotte Forten, Sarah Louisa Forten, Margaretta Forten, Sarah McCrummell, Harriet D. Purvis, Lydia White, and Mary Woods.

Prudence Crandall, a white Quaker schoolteacher, opens a "High school for young colored Ladies and Misses" in Canterbury, Connecticut, enrolling fifteen students. The townspeople initiate a series of efforts to close the institution, culminating in the burning of the school.

1835

Oberlin College becomes the first U.S. college to admit students without regard to race or sex.

1836

A group of black women rush a Boston courtroom and carry away to freedom two fugitive slave women before they can be returned to those claiming to be their masters; a similar rescue is executed by black women in New York.

Jarena Lee publishes *The Life and Religious Experiences of Jarena Lee, a Couloured Lady . . .*, the first autobiography by an American black woman.

1837

When the first Antislavery Convention of American Women meets in New York, at least one-tenth of the members are African American; Grace Bustill Douglass is elected a vice president and Sarah Forten's poem "We are thy sisters" is printed by the convention.

1838

The Memoirs of Elleanor Eldridge, one of the few narratives of the life of an early nineteenth-century free black woman, is published.

1840

Women total 1,440,660 in a U.S. black population of 2,873,648: 386,293 are free and 2,487,355 (1,240,938 women) held in slavery.

1841

Ann Plato writes *Essays, including Biographies and Miscellaneous Pieces in Prose and Poetry*.

1842

Henriette Delille founds the second black Roman Catholic religious congregation in the U.S., the Sisters of the Holy Family, in Louisiana.

1844

The first petition for the African Methodist Episcopal Church General Conference to license women to preach is defeated.

1846

The Colored Female Benevolent Society of Louisiana is founded in New Orleans.

Zilpha Elaw publishes *Memoirs of the Life, Religious Experience, Ministerial Travels and Labors of Mrs. Zilpha Elaw*.

1848

When Boston officials bar Sarah Roberts from a neighborhood white school and require her to pass five other white schools to attend a school designated for black children, her father, Benjamin Roberts, files the first school integration suit on her behalf. In its 1849 ruling in *Sarah C. Roberts v. City of Boston*, the Massachusetts state supreme court upholds the legality of segregation, justifying it with the first recorded use of the "separate but equal" doctrine.

Ellen Craft, along with her husband, William, escapes from slavery, with Ellen dressed as a slaveholder and William acting as her valet.

1849

The Woman's Association of Philadelphia is organized with the express purpose of raising money to support Frederick Douglass's newspaper, the *North Star*.

Harriet Tubman escapes from slavery; she will return South more than a dozen times and bring hundreds of others out of slavery.

1850

Women total 1,827,550 in a U.S. black population of 3,638,808: 434,495 are free and 3,204,313 (1,601,779 women) held in slavery.

Following the passage of the Fugitive Slave Law, which gives virtually unlimited authority to any white man claiming a black person as his runaway slave, thousands of African American women, men, and their families flee to Canada.

Lucy Sessions earns a literary degree from Oberlin College, becoming the first black woman in the U.S. to receive a college degree.

1851

In Christiana, Pennsylvania, armed black men and women resist an effort to recapture four escaped slaves; federal troops are sent to defeat the resisters, thirty-six of whom are charged with treason; all are eventually acquitted in court.

During her speech at an Akron, Ohio, women's rights convention, Sojourner Truth (Isabella Baumfree) challenges racial and gender hierarchies with her now-famous words, "And a'n't I a woman?" In 1858, while speaking before a Silver Lake, Indiana, audience, Truth is forced to bare her breasts to prove her sexual identity.

Elizabeth Taylor Greenfield ("The Black Swan"), the first black American concert singer, makes her debut in Buffalo, New York.

1852

The Institute for Colored Youth is founded in Philadelphia by the Society of Friends as the first coeducational classical high school for African Americans.

The Normal School for Colored Girls is founded in Washington, D.C., by Myrtilla Miner, a white female educator.

Mary Ann Shadd (Cary) publishes *A Plea for Emigration or Notes on Canada West, in Its Moral, Social, and Political Aspect: With Suggestions Respecting Mexico, W. Indies and Vancouvers Island for the Information of Colored Emigrants*, to educate black people on the advantages of emigrating to Canada.

1853

When Mary Ann Shadd (Cary) becomes editor and financier of the *Provincial Freeman*, published in Windsor, Canada, she is the first black woman editor of a newspaper in North America.

1854

Twenty-nine black women delegates comprise one-third of the participants at the National Emigration Convention; Mary E. Bibb is elected second vice president of the convention.

Elizabeth Jennings sues the Third Avenue Railroad Company, winning $225 in damages and a court ruling that "colored persons, if sober, well-behaved and free from disease" could ride the New York City horsecars without segregation.

Frances Ellen Watkins (Harper) publishes *Poems on Miscellaneous Subjects*.

Elizabeth Taylor Greenfield ("The Black Swan") gives a command performance at Buckingham Palace for Queen Victoria.

1855

Mary Ann Shadd (Cary) addresses the National Negro Convention in Philadelphia, where she becomes the first female corresponding member.

1856

Mary E. Bibb and Mary Ann Shadd (Cary) are elected to the Board of Publications at the National Emigration Convention.

Sarah Parker Remond becomes lecturer for the American Antislavery Society.

1857

Elizabeth Thorn Scott-Flood opens what is probably the first colored school in Alameda County, California.

1858

Mary Ellen Pleasant, the "mother of the Civil Rights Struggle in California," finances the defense of Archy Lee in California's famous fugitive slave case.

1859

In Philadelphia, Rebecca Cox Jackson founds the first black Shaker community.

Sarah Parker Remond begins a two-year lecture tour on the abolition of slavery to Scotland, Ireland, England, and France.

Harriet E. Wilson publishes *Our Nig: or Sketches from the Life of a Free Black*, the first novel published in the U.S. by an African American. Wilson is the fifth African American to publish fiction in English, and one of the first two black women to publish a novel in any language. (William Wells Brown's 1853 novel, *Clotel*, was published in London; Maria F. dos Reis publishes her novel, *Ursula*, in 1859 in Brazil.)

1860

Women total 2,225,086 in a U.S. black population of 4,441,830: 488,070 are free and 3,953,760 (1,971,135 women) held in slavery.

1861

The Civil War begins and thousands of slave women and men begin the process of self-emancipation, many fleeing to Union lines and joining their efforts to those of the Union soldiers.

Mary Peake opens a one-room day school in Hampton, Virginia, with the help of the American Missionary Association (AMA).

The Port Royal Commission is begun in the Sea Islands near South Carolina, with Charlotte Forten (Grimké) as the only black teacher in the experiment. She is joined by Susan King Taylor in 1864.

Harriet Jacobs's *Incidents in the Life of a Slave Girl* is published under the pseudonym Linda Brent.

1862

Congress abolishes slavery in Washington, D.C.

Elizabeth Keckley helps form the Contraband Relief Association to raise money to aid freed men and women.

Susan King Taylor, at fourteen, becomes the first African American army nurse in the U.S.

Mary Jane Patterson earns a B.A. degree from Oberlin College, making her the first black woman to earn a Bachelor's degree from an accredited U.S. college.

1863

Harriet Tubman leads Union troops in a raid along the Combahee River in South Carolina.

1864

Maryland abolishes slavery.

Mary Ann Shadd Cary receives a commission as a recruiting officer from Governor O. P. Morton of Indiana, becoming the only woman given official recognition as a recruiter during the Civil War.

Rebecca Lee (Crumpler) becomes the first African American woman to graduate from a U.S. college with a formal medical degree and the first and only black woman to obtain the Doctress of Medicine degree from the New England Female Medical College in Boston, Massachusetts.

1865

The Thirteenth Amendment to the U.S. Constitution, abolishing slavery, is adopted.

The Bureau of Refugees, Freedmen, and Abandoned Lands (Freedmen's Bureau) is established by Congress to coordinate aid and relief efforts, including educational opportunities, for newly emancipated slaves.

Thousands of African American women, individually and through their organizations, become depositors in the Freedman's Savings and Trust Company, chartered by the U.S. Congress, with business confined to African Americans. Most of them lose their money when the bank suspends operations in 1874.

Atlanta University (Georgia) and Shaw Institute (Raleigh, North Carolina) are founded.

Fanny Jackson (Coppin) is the second African American woman to receive an A.B. degree, when she graduates from Oberlin.

1866

Fisk University (Nashville, Tennessee), Rust College (Holly Springs, Mississippi), and Lincoln University (Jefferson City, Missouri) are founded.

In one of the bloodiest outbreaks of the Reconstruction era, three days of racial violence in Memphis, Tennessee, leave forty-six African Americans and two whites dead, five African American women raped, and hundreds of African American homes, churches, and schools destroyed by fire.

Washerwomen in Jackson, Mississippi, organize a strike and submit a formal petition to the mayor, notifying him of their intentions to demand wages commensurate with the cost of living.

Sarah Woodson Early is appointed preceptress of English and Latin and lady principal and matron at Wilberforce University, becoming the first African American woman on a college faculty.

1867

Howard University (Washington, D.C.), Talladega College (Alabama), Morgan State College (Baltimore, Maryland), Johnson C. Smith College (Charlotte, North Carolina), and St. Augustine's College (Raleigh, North Carolina) are founded.

Rebecca Cole, the second black woman to receive a medical degree in the U.S., graduates from the Women's Medical College of Pennsylvania in Philadelphia.

1868

The Fourteenth Amendment is ratified, extending citizenship rights to African Americans.

Hampton Normal and Agricultural Institute (Virginia) is founded.

The African Methodist Episcopal Church General Conference creates the position of stewardess, allowing pastors to nominate a board of stewardesses, the first official position for women in the denomination.

Elizabeth Keckley publishes her autobiography, *Behind the Scenes: or Thirty Years a Slave and Four Years in the White House.*

1869

The American Equal Rights Association, the umbrella universal suffrage organization, splits over the questions of black male suffrage and woman suffrage, prompting the creation of the National Woman Suffrage Association and the American Woman Suffrage Association.

Clark College (Atlanta, Georgia), Claflin College (Orangeburg, South Carolina), Straight College (now Dillard, New Orleans, Louisiana), and Tougaloo College (Mississippi) are founded.

Howard University Medical School opens its doors to women both black and white; by 1900, 103 women had enrolled, 48 of whom—23 black women and 25 white women—had graduated.

Mary Ann Shadd Cary chairs the Committee on Female Suffrage at the Colored National Labor Union (CNLU) convention and becomes the only woman elected to the CNLU's executive committee.

Fanny Jackson (Coppin) is named principal of the Institute for Colored Youth in Philadelphia, becoming the first black woman to head an institution for higher learning in the U.S.

1870

Women total 2,486,746 in a U.S. black population of 4,880,009.

The Fifteenth Amendment to the U.S. Constitution is ratified and interpreted as providing black male citizens with the right to vote but not the protection of that right; its enfranchisement of men sparks a debate within African American communities over woman suffrage.

The Colored Methodist Episcopal (CME) Church is founded.

Allen University (Columbia, South Carolina), Benedict College (Columbia, South Carolina), and Le Moyne-Owen College (Memphis, Tennessee) are founded.

The Philadelphia Colored Women's Christian Association is established, perhaps the first black Young Women's Christian Association.

Upon graduation from the New York Medical College for Women, Susan McKinney Steward becomes the third black female doctor in the U.S.

1871

The first tour of the Fisk Jubilee Singers, in the U.S., England, Scotland, Ireland, Holland, and Switzerland, raises $50,000 for their university.

Mary Ann Shadd Cary addresses the U.S. House of Representatives Judiciary Committee, speaking on woman suffrage.

1872

Alcorn A & M College (Lorman, Mississippi) is founded.

Following her graduation from Howard University Law School, Charlotte E. Ray, using the initials C.E. to avoid discrimination against women, is admitted to the District of Columbia bar, thus becoming the first black woman lawyer in the United States.

1873

Bennett College (Greensboro, North Carolina), Wiley College (Marshall, Texas), and Alabama State College (Montgomery) are founded.

1874

The federally sponsored Freedman's Savings and Trust Company closes, with 61,000 black depositors losing nearly $3 million.

1875

The Civil Rights Bill of 1875 provides for equal access to public accommodations without regard to race.

Alabama A & M College (Normal), Knoxville College (Tennessee), and Lane College (Jackson, Tennessee) are founded.

1876

Prairie View A & M College (Texas) is founded.

Harriet Purvis is the first African American woman to be elected vice president of the National Woman Suffrage Association.

The first permanent black musical-comedy troupe, the Hyers Sisters Comic Opera Company, is organized.

1877

On the heels of the Great Strike of 1877, which crippled the nation's railroad industry, domestic workers in Galveston, Texas, organize a strike.

The all-black town of Nicodemus, Kansas, is founded.

Jackson State College (Mississippi) is founded.

1878

Two hundred and six black emigrants set sail from Charleston, South Carolina, for Liberia, West Africa, on board the *Azor*, a ship of the Liberian Exodus Joint Stock Steamship Company.

1879

As many as 6,000 African Americans migrate to Kansas in the space of a few months; this is part of a larger westward movement of approximately 25,000 southern black people in the late 1870s-early 1880s.

Livingstone College (Salisbury, North Carolina) is founded.

Graduating from the School of Nursing, New England Hospital for Women and Children in Boston, Mary Eliza Mahoney becomes the first African American in the U.S. to receive a diploma in nursing.

Julia A. J. Foote publishes *A Brand Plucked from the Fire! An Autobiographical Sketch*.

1880

Women total 3,327,678 in a total U.S. black population of 6,580,793.

Southern University (New Orleans, later Baton Rouge, Louisiana) is founded.

Mary Ann Shadd Cary, Mrs. Nichols, Anna Montgomery, Miss Jennings, Mrs. Robinson, Mrs. Jerris, and Mrs. Monroe organize the Colored Women's Progressive Franchise Association in Washington, D.C., to gain the vote for women and to establish black women in business.

1881

Tennessee passes a state railroad segregation law. Similar laws are passed in Florida (1887); Mississippi (1888); Texas (1889); Louisiana (1890); Alabama, Arkansas, Georgia, Kentucky (1891); South Carolina (1898); North Carolina (1899); Virginia (1900); Maryland (1904); and Oklahoma (1907).

In the largest mass migration from South Carolina, 5,000 black women, men, and children leave Edgefield and relocate in Alabama; they equal approximately one-fifth of the Edgefield population.

Tuskegee Institute (Alabama) is founded.

Atlanta Baptist Female Seminary is founded in Atlanta, Georgia; the name is changed to Spelman Seminary in 1884.

Washerwomen in Atlanta form the Washing Society and organize the largest known strike by black women to date; at its peak, 3,000 strikers and supporters are mobilized.

1882

Virginia State College (Petersburg) is founded.

1882-1927

At least twenty-six black women are lynched in the United States.

1883

The U.S. Supreme Court declares the Civil Rights Act of 1875 unconstitutional.

Hartshorn Memorial College for Women is founded in Richmond, Virginia, and becomes (in 1888) the first educational institution in the U.S. chartered as a *college* for black women.

Mary Ann Shadd Cary becomes the second black woman to earn a law degree, when she graduates from Howard University.

Rebecca Lee Crumpler, M.D., publishes *A Book of Medical Discourses in Two Parts*. Based on nearly two decades of practice as a physician, it offers advice to women on how to provide medical care to themselves and their children.

1884

Anna Julia Cooper, Mary Church (Terrell), and Ida A. Gibbs (Hunt) graduate from Oberlin College.

1885

Gertrude Mossell initiates the woman's column in the *New York Age* with her article "Woman's Suffrage."

Sara E. Goode is the first black woman to receive a U.S. patent, for her "Folding Cabinet Bed."

1886

The Colored Farmers' Alliance is founded; by 1891 it has organized in twenty states with a membership of 1,125,000.

Kentucky State College (Frankfort) is founded.

Lucy Craft Laney opens a grammar school in Augusta, Georgia, which develops into the Haines Normal and Industrial Institute.

The first school for black nursing students is established at Spelman Seminary, Atlanta, Georgia.

Louise "Lulu" Fleming becomes the first black woman to be commissioned for career missionary service by the Women's Baptist Foreign Missionary Society of the West.

1887

Florida A & M College (Tallahassee) and Central State College (Wilberforce, Ohio) are founded.

Mary Ellen Morrison earns a Pharmaceutical Doctor degree from Howard University's School of Medicine.

1888

Our Women and Children begins publication. Founded by Dr. William J. Simmons, it employs a number of black women journalists, including Lucy Wilmot Smith as head of the woman's department, Mary V. Cook as editor of the educational department, Ida B. Wells (Barnett) as editor of the home department, and Ione E. Wood as editor of the temperance department.

Cornelia Bowen founds Mt. Meigs Institute, Mt. Meigs, Alabama.

Sarah Woodson Early becomes superintendent of the Colored Division of the Women's Christian Temperance Union and serves until 1892.

Sarah E. Gorham becomes the first woman missionary of the African Methodist Episcopal Church appointed to a foreign field.

Nancy Jones is the first unmarried black woman commissioned by the Congregational American Board as a missionary to Africa.

Miriam E. Benjamin is awarded a patent for a "Gong and Signal Chair," which is later adopted for use in the U.S. House of Representatives to signal pages.

1889

The federal government opens Oklahoma Territory to homestead settlement; over 7,000 African Americans migrate to the territory during the first year of settlement.

Ida B. Wells (Barnett) is elected secretary of the National Afro-American Press Association; Wells also becomes part owner and editor of the *Memphis Free Speech and Headlight*.

Maria Louise Baldwin becomes the first African American female principal in Massachusetts and the Northeast, supervising white faculty and a predominantly white student body at Agassiz Grammar School in Cambridge.

Josephine A. Silone Yates becomes professor and head of the Natural Sciences Department at Lincoln University (Jefferson City, Missouri), earning $1,000 per year.

1889-93

At least eight black women are lynched.

1890

Women total 3,753,073 in a U.S. black population of 7,488,676.

The National Afro-American League is founded.

The all-black town of Langston City, Oklahoma, is founded.

Savannah State College (Georgia) is founded.

The Locust Street Settlement House is established in Hampton, Virginia, by Janie Porter Barrett; it is one of the first African American settlement houses.

Clarence and Corinne or God's Way, by Amelia E. Johnson, is the first book by a woman to be published by the American Baptist Publication Society and the first Sunday school book published by an African American.

Receiving a degree from the University of Michigan, Ida Gray is the first African American woman to receive the Doctor of Dental Surgery degree.

1891

Delaware State College (Dover), North Carolina A & T College (Greensboro), and West Virginia State College (Institute) are founded.

Daniel Hale Williams founds Provident Hospital in Chicago, site of the second nursing school for African American students.

Lucy Parsons begins publishing her newspaper, *Freedom: A Revolutionary Anarchist-Communist Monthly*.

Julia Ringwood Coston edits and publishes *Ringwood's Afro-American Journal of Fashion*.

1892

Ida B. Wells (Barnett) launches the first phase of the antilynching movement, with her articles and editorials in the Memphis *Free Speech* and the *New York Age* and the publication of *Southern Horrors*.

The Woman's Loyal Union is founded in New York City, with Victoria Earle Matthews as its first president.

The Colored Woman's League of Washington, D.C., is founded.

Mary Moore Booze, Harriet Amanda Miller, and Dixie Erma Williams graduate with B.S. degrees from Hartshorn Memorial College, the first college degrees granted by a black woman's institution.

Anna Julia Cooper publishes *A Voice from the South by a Black Woman of the South*.

Frances Ellen Watkins Harper publishes her novel *Iola Leroy: or, Shadows Uplifted*.

The international opera star Sissieretta Jones is summoned by President Benjamin Harrison to sing at the White House.

1893

The Women's Home and Missionary Society of the African Methodist Episcopal Church is founded.

Anna Julia Cooper, Fanny Jackson Coppin, and Fannie Barrier Williams address the Women's Congress at the World's Columbian Exposition in Chicago, on the theme "The Intellectual Progress of Colored Women of the United States since Emancipation."

Meharry Medical College, founded in 1876 in Nashville, Tennessee, awards its first medical degrees to women: Georgianna Patton and Anna D. Gregg.

The Woman's Era Club is founded in Boston.

Myrtle Hart, pianist and harpist, plays at the British exhibit at the Chicago World's Fair.

1894

The *Woman's Era*, later to become the official organ of the National Association of Colored Women, begins publication.

Julia A. J. Foote becomes the first female ordained deacon in the A.M.E. Zion Church.

Gertrude (Mrs. N. F.) Mossell publishes *The Work of the Afro-American Woman*.

1894-98

At least fifteen black women are lynched.

1895

The Church of God in Christ is founded.

Black Baptist churches throughout the country organize the National Baptist Convention.

The National Medical Association is founded.

Fort Valley State College (Georgia) is founded.

Josephine St. Pierre Ruffin organizes the first National Conference of Colored Women, meeting in Boston.

The National Federation of Afro-American Women is founded, with Margaret Murray Washington as president and Josephine St. Pierre Ruffin as vice president.

Victoria Earle Matthews begins a tour of the South to report on the status of southern African American women for the National Federation of Afro-American Women.

Ida B. Wells (Barnett) publishes *Red Record: Tabulated Statistics and Alleged Causes of Lynchings in the United States, 1892-1894* after completing lecture tours in England.

Mary Church Terrell is appointed to the Washington, D.C., Board of Education, becoming the first African American woman to serve on a board of education.

1896

In the precedent-setting *Plessy* v. *Ferguson*, the U.S. Supreme Court rules "separate but equal" facilities are constitutional, thus signaling the federal government's endorsement of segregation laws.

South Carolina State College (Orangeburg) is founded.

The *Laurada* sets sail from Savannah, Georgia, with 321 African Americans from throughout the South emigrating to Liberia, West Africa.

The National League of Colored Women and the National Federation of Afro-American Women merge to form the National Association of Colored Women, with Mary Church Terrell as first NACW president.

Sissieretta Jones organizes the Black Patti Troubadours.

1897

The First Hampton Negro Conference is held; the annual meeting assesses the conditions and strategies of African Americans. At the first conference, Fanny Jackson Coppin speaks on industrial education; later conferences include sessions organized by state and national women leaders on topics such as women's education, community services, and health issues.

The American Negro Academy is founded to promote scholarly work and fellowship among leading intellectuals; Anna Julia Cooper is the only woman elected to membership.

Langston University (Oklahoma) is founded.

Elizabeth Evelyn Wright, with the help of Jessie Dorsey, founds the Denmark Industrial School in Denmark, South Carolina (later Voorhees Industrial School, now Voorhees College).

Spelman Seminary begins a College Department, with collegiate courses offered on Atlanta Baptist (Morehouse) campus.

Victoria Earle Matthews founds the White Rose Mission in New York City, to serve as a community center with special emphasis on assistance to black women migrating from the South.

1898

A Slave Girl's Story, Kate Drumgold's autobiographical narrative, is published.

1899-1903

At least four black women are lynched.

1900

Women total 4,447,447 in a U.S. black population of 8,833,994.

According to a study by W. E. B. Du Bois, 252 black women have obtained baccalaureate degrees; 65 of them are Oberlin College graduates.

The National Negro Business League is organized to promote business among African Americans.

The *Colored American* begins publication, with Pauline Hopkins as one of the founding members and editors.

At the First Pan-African Conference in London's Westminster Hall, Anna H. Jones of Missouri and Anna Julia Cooper of Washington, D.C. (an official U.S. delegate and elected member of the executive committee) are the only black women to address the international gathering.

Under the leadership of Nannie Helen Burroughs, the Women's Convention, auxiliary of the National Baptist Convention, is founded at the annual meeting in Richmond, Virginia, with S. Willie Layten as the first president.

Madam C. J. Walker (Sarah Breedlove) begins selling hair and skin treatments door-to-door and later becomes the first female African American self-made millionaire.

Pauline Hopkins publishes *Contending Forces: A Romance Illustrative of Negro Life North and South*, a forceful protest novel.

1901

Grambling College (Louisiana) is founded.

Spelman Seminary grants its first college degrees to Jane Anna Granderson and Claudia Turner White.

1902

President Theodore Roosevelt suspends postal service to Indianola, Mississippi, after white supremacists succeed in displacing Minnie Cox as postmistress, claiming her appointment represents "nigger domination."

Charlotte Hawkins Brown founds the Palmer Institute in Sedalia, North Carolina.

Susie King Taylor's *Reminiscences of My Life in Camp with the U.S. 33rd Colored Troops* is published.

1903

The Saint Luke Penny Savings Bank opens in Richmond, Virginia, with Maggie Lena Walker as president, the first African American woman to direct a bank and probably the first U.S. woman to do so other than through inheritance from her husband.

Georgia Anderson and other working-class women from Savannah submit a petition to the Georgia legislature, requesting $2,000 to emigrate to Africa.

1904

The all-black town of Boley, Oklahoma, is founded.

Mary McLeod Bethune establishes the Daytona Educational and Industrial Training School, which becomes Bethune-Cookman College.

Mary Church Terrell represents the National Association of Colored Women at the International Council of Women congress in Berlin, Germany.

The Colorado Association of Colored Women's Clubs is founded.

Virginia W. Broughton publishes *Women's Work, as Gleaned from the Women of the Bible*, an analysis of biblical precedents for gender equality.

1904-8

At least six black women are lynched.

1905

The Niagara Movement is founded.

Eva del Vakia Bowles becomes the first black woman on the Young Women's Christian Association (YWCA) staff, when she becomes secretary of the Colored Young People's Christian Association in New York City (later the 135th St. YWCA in Harlem). In 1913 Bowles becomes the first secretary of the National Board Subcommittee for Colored Work.

The Woman's Improvement Club of Indianapolis, Indiana, opens an outdoor tuberculosis camp, purportedly the first in the nation.

The Memphis Players, the first modern jazz band, makes its debut in New York, with Abbie Mitchell singing and Ida Forsyne dancing.

1906

The National League for the Protection of Colored Women is founded, uniting the work of various state and local associations in assisting migrants to the cities.

1907

C. M. Hughes and Minnie Thomas begin publishing the monthly *Colored Woman's Magazine* (1907-20), one of the longest-running periodicals under the editorial control of black women.

Meta Vaux Warrick is the first black woman artist to receive a federal commission.

1908

Josephine Leavell Allensworth, along with her husband, Allen, founds the all-black "race colony" of Allensworth, California.

Alpha Kappa Alpha Sorority, the first black Greek-letter organization for women, is founded at Howard University.

The National Association of Colored Graduate Nurses is founded, with Martha Franklin as first president.

The Empire State Federation of Colored Women's Clubs is founded.

The Atlanta Neighborhood Union is founded, under the leadership of Lugenia Burns Hope.

1909

The National Association for the Advancement of Colored People is founded.

Tennessee State A & I University (Nashville) is founded.

Nannie Helen Burroughs is founding president of the National Training School for Women and Girls in Washington, D.C.

1909-13

At least six black women are lynched.

1910

Women total 4,941,882 in a U.S. black population of 9,827,763.

North Carolina College (Durham) is founded.

Sara Winifred Brown, Mary Church Terrell, and others establish the College Alumnae Club.

1911

The National Urban League is founded.

1912

Adah B. Thoms is one of three black delegates to the International Council of Nurses in Cologne, Germany.

Charlotta Bass becomes owner and publisher of the *California Eagle*, a weekly newspaper in Los Angeles.

The Normal Vocal Institute is established in Chicago by Emma Azalia Hackley.

1913

Illinois becomes the first state east of the Mississippi River to enfranchise women.

Delta Sigma Theta Sorority, the second black Greek-letter organization for women, is founded at Howard University.

Under the leadership of Jane Edna Hunter, the Phillis Wheatley Home in Cleveland, Ohio, opens.

The Alpha Suffrage Club is founded in Illinois.

Ida B. Wells-Barnett is asked not to march with the white Illinois delegation at a National American Woman Suffrage Association parade in Washington, D.C.

Organization of the first black-theater circuit by black showman Sherman H. Dudley leads to the formation of the Theater Owners Booking Association in 1920.

1914

Institution of the Spingarn Medal award by the National Association for the Advancement of Colored People for achievement by a black individual. It is 1922 before a woman is honored.

1914-18

At least eleven black women are lynched.

1915

The National Association for the Advancement of Colored People organizes protests against D. W. Griffith's film *Birth of a Nation*.

The Association for the Study of Negro Life and History is founded by Carter G. Woodson; much of its early support comes from black clubwomen and churchwomen.

Mary Burnett Talbert becomes president of the National Association of Colored Women, serving until 1920, representing the NACW at the meeting of the International Council of Women in Norway.

In New York City, Anita Bush ("the Little Mother of Black Theater") forms the Anita Bush Players (soon to be renamed the Lafayette Players), a dramatic stock company that performs serious, nonmusical theater for black audiences.

The first woman to be awarded a certificate by the American Teachers Association, Hannah Pierce Lowe organizes the Organization of Teachers of Colored Children in New Jersey.

1916

The American Tennis Association is organized in Washington, D.C., to promote tennis among African Americans.

First colored students' conference of the Young Women's Christian Association (YWCA) is held at Spelman Seminary in Atlanta, Georgia.

Frances Elliott Davis is the first African American nurse to officially enroll in the Red Cross nursing service.

In Los Angeles, Lauretta Green Butler opens the first black professional dance studio for children.

1917

Forty African Americans are killed in the East St. Louis, Illinois, race riot.

Ten thousand African Americans march down New York City's Fifth Avenue in a National Association for the Advancement of Colored People-sponsored silent parade to protest racial discrimination and, especially, racial violence.

Black women develop the Circle for Negro War Relief, to provide medical, recreational, and other services to black soldiers.

Following state legislation initiating woman suffrage in Texas, black women throughout the state organize Negro Women Voter Leagues.

Domestic workers, waitresses, and tobacco stemmers form a union and organize a strike for higher wages in Norfolk, Virginia.

Ella Pete organizes the Domestic Servants Union in New Orleans, with more than 1,000 members.

Lucy Diggs Slowe becomes the first black woman athletic champion, winning the women's singles title at the first national American Tennis Association championships in Baltimore, Maryland.

1918

Founding of the African Blood Brotherhood, with Bertha DeBasco, Gertrude Hall, and Grace Campbell as members of this radical black nationalist organization.

Juliette Derricotte becomes secretary of the national student council of the Young Women's Christian Association (YWCA).

The Women's Political Association of Harlem is one of the first African American organizations in the country to advocate birth control.

One of the most prolific female poets, Georgia Douglas Johnson publishes her first volume of poems, *Heart of a Woman*.

Nora Douglas Holt is the first African American to earn an advanced degree in music, receiving an M.Mus. from the Chicago School of Music.

1918-27

Eleven black women are lynched; three of them were pregnant.

1919

In what is termed the "Red Summer of 1919," at least twenty-five race riots occur in cities across the country, including Longview, Texas; Chicago, Illinois; Knoxville, Tennessee; Omaha, Nebraska; and Elaine, Arkansas.

Jessie Redmon Fauset becomes literary editor of *The Crisis*, the National Association for the Advancement of Colored People's official publication.

Delilah L. Beasley publishes *The Negro Trail Blazers of California*.

The September issue of *Birth Control Review* features Mary P. Burrill's play, *They That Sit in Darkness*, possibly the first black feminist drama.

Georgia Hill Robinson becomes the first African American policewoman in the U.S., after passing the civil service exam in Los Angeles.

Under the leadership of Nora Douglas Holt, the National Association of Negro Musicians is founded.

1920

The Nineteenth Amendment to the U.S. Constitution is ratified, granting female citizens the right to vote.

The Universal Negro Improvement Association (UNIA) holds its international convention in New York City; Henrietta Vinton Davis chairs the mass meeting in Madison Square Garden.

The Universal African Black Cross Nurses, a female auxiliary of the UNIA, is organized.

Becoming the first woman to record the blues, Mamie Smith releases "Crazy Blues" and thus begins the "race record" market.

Zeta Phi Beta Sorority, the third black Greek-letter organization for women, is founded at Howard University.

The International Council of Women of the Darker Races is founded.

The Southeastern Association of Colored Women's Clubs holds its first conference at Tuskegee Institute, where Mary McLeod Bethune is elected its first president and Charlotte Hawkins Brown is elected chairperson of the executive board.

Black women in St. Louis and Cleveland launch selective buying campaigns that result in opening up some jobs in clothing and department stores heavily patronized by black women. These were the precursor to the widespread "Don't-Buy-Where-You-Can't-Work" campaigns.

The National Association for the Advancement of Colored People presents Angelina Weld Grimké's three-act play *Rachel*, the first successful stage drama by an African American.

1921

The Eubie Blake-Noble Sissle musical *Shuffle Along* opens on Broadway, running a record 504 performances and launching the careers of Josephine Baker, Caterina Jarboro, and Florence Mills.

The first black record company, Pace Phonograph Company, is founded; it releases records on the Black Swan label.

Jessie Fauset is a delegate to the Second Pan-African Congress, representing the National Association of Colored Women.

Mary Talbert's invitation to speak at a National Woman's Party (NWP) meeting is rescinded after Alice Paul, NWP president, rules that as a representative of the National Association for the Advancement of Colored People, Talbert represents an organization related to race, not sex.

The first black women to earn Ph.D. degrees in the U.S. are Georgiana R. Simpson, German, University of Chicago; Sadie Tanner Mossell (Alexander), economics, University of Pennsylvania; and Eva Dykes, English philology, Radcliffe College.

Anita Bush costars with Lawrence Chenault in the first all-black Western movie, *The Crimson Skull*.

1922

The Anti-Lynching Crusaders is organized under Mary Talbert's leadership.

Sigma Gamma Rho Sorority is the fourth black Greek-letter organization for women; it is the first established on a predominantly white campus, Butler University in Indianapolis, Indiana.

After a protest staged by women delegates at the Universal Negro Improvement Association convention, Henrietta Vinton Davis becomes fourth assistant president general of the association.

Mary B. Talbert becomes the first woman to receive the National Association for the Advancement of Colored People's Spingarn Medal.

Kathryn Johnson and Addie Hunton coauthor *Two Colored Women with the American Expeditionary Forces*, detailing their work in Europe to protect the rights of black soldiers during World War I.

Louise Evans (Briggs-Hall) is the first black woman admitted into the prestigious United Scenic Artists Association for costume, scenic, and lighting designers.

Bessie Coleman, the first licensed African American aviator, gives her first exhibition on Long Island.

1923

The U.S. Department of Labor reports that half a million African Americans migrated out of the South in the preceding year.

"Ma" Rainey (Gertrude Pridgett) and Bessie Smith record their first records. Ida Cox and Lovie Austin begin recording for Paramount Records.

Runnin' Wild is performed on Broadway, choreographed by the first-known African American choreographer, Elida Webb.

Completing the course of study at Carnegie Library School in Philadelphia, Virginia Proctor Powell (Florence) becomes the first African American woman to receive professional training in librarianship.

1924

The National League of Republican Colored Women is organized.

Spelman Seminary becomes Spelman College, now offering college courses on its own campus.

Elizabeth Ross Haynes is the first black woman elected to the National Board of the Young Women's Christian Association (YWCA), a position she holds until 1934.

Mary Montgomery Booze becomes the first black woman elected to the Republican National Committee.

Mary McLeod Bethune is elected president of the National Association of Colored Women.

Henrietta Vinton Davis is the only female member of the Universal Negro Improvement Association delegation to Liberia.

Mary Jane Watkins receives a Doctor of Dental Surgery degree and goes on to become the first woman dentist in the military services.

1925

The Hesperus Club of Harlem becomes the first ladies' auxiliary of the Brotherhood of Sleeping Car Porters.

Josephine Baker receives international acclaim for her appearance in *La Revue Nègre* in Paris.

1926

Observance of Negro History Week is inaugurated under the auspices of the Association for the Study of Negro Life and History.

The National Bar Association is founded.

Bennett College, founded as a coeducational institution in 1873, becomes a college for women.

An interracial charter is adopted by the Young Women's Christian Association (YWCA) at its national convention; it commits the YWCA to involve African American women more in its organizational life.

Selena Sloan Butler founds the National Congress of Colored Parents and Teachers.

Violette N. Anderson becomes the first black woman to argue a case before the U.S. Supreme Court.

Homespun Heroines and Other Women of Distinction is compiled and edited by Hallie Quinn Brown.

Era Bell Thompson establishes five women's track records while at the University of North Dakota.

1927

Girl Friends, Inc., a national social, civic, charitable, and cultural organization, is formed in New York City.

Minnie Buckingham-Harper, appointed to fill her husband's unexpired term in the West Virginia legislature, becomes the first black woman to serve in a U.S. legislative body.

1928

The National Association of Colored Women opens its national headquarters in Washington, D.C.

Novelist Nella Larsen publishes *Quicksand*, with *Passing* published the following year.

1929

The first major film musical with a black cast, *Hallelujah*, produced by King Vidor, debuts Nina Mae McKinney, the first black actress to gain recognition on the screen.

Lucy Diggs Slowe convenes the first annual conference of deans and advisers to girls in Negro schools, which gives birth to the Association of Deans of Women and Advisers to Girls in Negro Schools.

Anna Julia Cooper is named president of Frelinghuysen University in Washington, D.C.

Receiving a degree from Columbia University, Jane Ellen McAlister becomes the first African American woman in the U.S. to earn a Ph.D. degree in education.

Premier athlete Inez Patterson makes six all-collegiate teams at Temple University: hockey, tennis, basketball, track, volleyball, and dancing.

1930

Women total 6,035,474 in a U.S. black population of 11,891,093.

Caterina Jarboro becomes the first African American to sing with a major opera company, with her debut as Aïda at the Puccini Opera House in Milan, Italy.

Nella Larsen is the first black woman to win a creative writing award from the Guggenheim Foundation.

1931

The Share Croppers' Union is organized in Alabama.

Ella Baker becomes the first national director of the Young Negroes Cooperative League.

Under the leadership of player-coach Ora Mae Washington, the *Philadelphia Tribune*'s women's basketball team is organized, traveling the country through 1940 playing black and white teams.

Katherine Dunham founds the Negro Dance Group in Chicago.

Receiving her degree from Columbia University in New York, Estelle Massey Osborne becomes the first black nurse to earn a Master's degree in nursing from a U.S. institution of higher education.

Jane Mathilda Bolin is the first black woman to graduate from Yale University Law School.

1932

Hartshorn Memorial College, the first black woman's college, merges with Virginia Union University.

Lillian Hardin Armstrong organizes the Harlem Harlicans, an all-female swing band.

The Cleveland Opera Company produces Shirley Graham's *Tom-Toms: An Epic of Music and the Negro*, with a cast of 500.

Dorothy Porter is the first African American woman to earn an advanced degree in library science, when she receives an M.L.S. from Columbia University.

Harvard University's Peabody Museum of Archaeology and Ethnology publishes Caroline Bond Day's *A Study of Some Negro-White Families in the United States*.

Louise Stokes and Tydie Pickett are the first black women selected for Olympic competition, when they qualify in the 100-meter race for the showpiece games in Los Angeles; they are later replaced by two white athletes. Stokes goes on to qualify for the 1936 Olympics.

1933

The St. Louis, Missouri, nut-pickers' strike involves more than 1,200 black women.

Run Little Chillun by Hall Johnson is the first production on Broadway of a Negro folk opera written by a black composer.

Billie Holiday records her first album.

Elizabeth Lindsay Davis publishes *Lifting as They Climb*, the first history of the national club movement.

The Chicago Symphony Orchestra premieres composer Florence B. Price's *Symphony in E Minor* during the Chicago World's Fair.

Margaret Bonds is the first African American to be a guest soloist with the Chicago Symphony, performing with it at the Chicago World's Fair.

1934

Receiving a degree from the University of Minnesota, Ruth Winifred Howard becomes the first African American woman in the U.S. to receive a Ph.D. degree in psychology.

Zora Neale Hurston publishes her first book, *Jonah's Gourd Vine*, a novel.

Mahalia Jackson makes her first recording, "God Shall Wipe Away All Tears" (Decca Records).

Osceola Archer debuts on Broadway in the Elmer Rice play *Between Two Worlds*.

Ella Fitzgerald wins the Apollo Theatre's amateur contest.

The Domestic Workers Union, led by Dora Jones, is affiliated with the Building Service Union, local 149, in New York City.

1935

Mary McLeod Bethune is appointed by President Franklin Delano Roosevelt to the Advisory Board of the National Youth Administration (NYA) and in December begins her tenure as director of the newly created Division of Negro Affairs of the NYA.

The National Council of Negro Women is founded, with Mary McLeod Bethune serving as first president, 1935-49.

Mary McLeod Bethune begins her fifteen-year tenure as president of the Association for the Study of Negro Life and History.

Mary McLeod Bethune receives the National Association for the Advancement of Colored People's Spingarn Medal.

National Association for the Advancement of Colored People leader Lillie Mae Jackson organizes a "Buy Where You Can Work" national campaign to force merchants to employ African Americans.

Crystal Bird Fauset becomes director of Negro women's activities for the Democratic National Committee.

George Gershwin's folk opera *Porgy and Bess* (with libretto by DuBose and Dorothy Heyward) premieres at New York City's Alvin Theatre, with Eva Jessye as the choral director and Anne Wiggins Brown in the role of Bess.

Jessie Jarue Mark is the first African American woman to earn a Ph.D. degree in botany (Iowa State University).

1936

The National Negro Congress, an umbrella organization of racial advancement groups, with emphasis on black workers, is founded.

Flemmie P. Kittrell is the first African American woman to earn a Ph.D. degree in nutrition (Cornell University).

1937

The Southern Negro Youth Congress is founded.

Zora Neale Hurston publishes her novel *Their Eyes Were Watching God*.

Zelda Jackson "Jackie" Ormes initiates her first cartoon strip, "Torchy Brown in Dixie to Harlem," in the *Pittsburgh Courier*; Ormes becomes the first nationally syndicated black woman cartoonist.

Katherine Dunham receives a Guggenheim Award to pursue her investigation of dance in Haiti, Jamaica, Trinidad, and Martinique.

1938

The election of Crystal Bird Fauset to the Pennsylvania State Assembly (House of Representatives) is the first election of an African American woman to major public office in the U.S.

The National Council of Negro Women sponsors a national Conference on Governmental Cooperation in the Approach to the Problems of Negro Women and Children, held in Washington, D.C., at the Department of the Interior and the White House.

The International Ladies' Auxiliary to the Brotherhood of Sleeping Car Porters is founded.

The International Sweethearts of Rhythm, a 14-16 piece all-female swing band, is formed at Piney Woods Country Life School, Piney Woods, Mississippi, to travel throughout the U.S. raising money for the school.

When Miriam Stubbs Thomas calls together sixteen black women in Philadelphia to form a club to sponsor cultural events and opportunities for their children, Jack and Jill of America is born.

Rosetta Tharpe gains national celebrity status when she takes gospel out of the church, performing a revival show at the Cotton Club, a Harlem nightclub.

Ella Fitzgerald records "A-tisket, A-tasket."

Louise "Mamma" Harris, a tobacco worker, leads a spontaneous strike at the I. N. Vaughn Company in Richmond, Virginia; it is the first strike in the tobacco industry since 1905.

1939

Tuskegee Institute establishes a school of nurse-midwifery.

Jane Mathilda Bolin of New York City is appointed justice of the Domestic Relations Court of the City of New York by Mayor Fiorello LaGuardia, becoming the first black woman judge in the United States.

On Easter Sunday, Marian Anderson sings before a crowd of 75,000 at the Lincoln Memorial in Washington, D.C., after the Daughters of the American Revolution deny her the right to perform in Constitution Hall; later in the year the

National Association for the Advancement of Colored People awards Anderson its Spingarn Medal.

Mary T. Washington becomes the first African American female certified public accountant after graduating from Chicago's Northwestern University.

1940

Women total 6,596,480 in a U.S. black population of 12,965,038.

Sixty percent of all black women in the labor force are still employed in domestic service and 10.5 percent are in other service work; only 1.4 percent are in clerical and sales positions and 4.3 percent are in professional positions.

The American Negro Theater is formed, its players including Ruby Dee and Osceola Archer (Adams).

Hattie McDaniel wins Best Supporting Actress Academy Award for her role in the 1939 film *Gone with the Wind*.

Katherine Dunham's performances in *Tropics* and *Le Jazz Hot: From Haiti to Harlem* in New York establishes her international reputation as a dancer.

Laura Bowman appears as Dr. Helen Jackson in *Son of Ingagi*, the first all-black horror film.

Receiving a degree from the University of Chicago Graduate Library School, Eliza Atkins Gleason becomes the first African American to earn a doctorate in library science.

Roger Arliner Young is the first black woman to earn a Ph.D. degree in zoology (University of Pennsylvania).

1941

Mary Lucinda Cardwell Dawson founds the National Negro Opera Company in Pittsburgh. The first permanent black opera company, it continues through 1962.

Ruth Lloyd is the first African American woman to earn a Ph.D. degree in anatomy (Western Reserve University).

Merze Tate is the first African American woman to earn the Ph.D. degree in government and international relations from Harvard University.

Charlotte Hawkins Brown's *The Correct Thing to Do, to Say, and to Wear* is published.

Emily and Edgar ("Dooky") Chase, Sr., open Dooky Chase Restaurant in New Orleans, with Emily Chase as the chef, a position later assumed by their daughter-in-law, Leah Chase.

1942

In Chicago, the Congress of Racial Equality (CORE), an organization committed to nonviolent direct action to end racial discrimination, is founded.

Charity Adams (Earley) is the first black woman to become a commissioned officer in the Women's Army Auxiliary Corps (later renamed the Women's Army Corps, or WAC).

For My People by Margaret Walker is published. Walker is the first African American poet to be included in the Yale Series of Younger Poets.

Margurite Thomas is the first African American woman to earn a Ph.D. degree in geology (Catholic University).

The August cover of *Ladies' Home Journal* features one of designer Mildred Blount's hats.

Lena Horne appears in *Panama Hattie*, her first film role.

Jazz singer Sarah Vaughan is discovered after winning amateur night at the Apollo Theatre.

1943

A series of race riots occur in cities across the country, including Mobile, Alabama; Detroit, Michigan; Beaumont, Texas; and Harlem, New York.

The Katherine Dunham School of Arts and Research opens in New York City.

Anne Cooke receives a Ph.D. degree in theater from Yale University.

1944

Anna Arnold Hedgeman is named executive director of the National Council for the federal Fair Employment Practices Commission.

Daisy Hill Northcross founds and becomes superintendent of Mercy Hospital in Detroit, Michigan.

Jessie Abbott becomes Tennessee State University's first women's track coach.

1945

Maida Springer (Kemp) is the American Federation of Labor's delegate to the United States Division of Psychological Warfare to Observe Wartime Conditions among English Workers.

Selma Burke's bronze plaque of Franklin Delano Roosevelt, sponsored by the Fine Arts Commission of Washington, D.C., is installed at the Recorder of Deeds Building in Washington, D.C., with President Harry S Truman speaking at the installation ceremonies.

Nora Douglas Holt becomes the first black person accepted into the Music Critics Circle of New York.

Gwendolyn Brooks's first collection of poetry, *A Street in Bronzeville*, is published.

1946

Asserting that, as an interstate traveler, she is not bound by the laws of the state of Virginia, Irene Morgan refuses to sit at the back of a Greyhound bus heading from Gloucester County, Virginia, to Baltimore, Maryland. The case comes before the Supreme Court, which rules in *Irene Morgan* v. *Commonwealth of Virginia* that states cannot require segregation on interstate buses.

The Links is founded in Philadelphia by Margaret Roselle Hawkins and Sarah Strickland Scott.

Lucille Dixon, jazz bassist, forms the Lucille Dixon Orchestra.

The New York Philharmonic Symphony performs Mary Lou Williams's *Zodiac Suite* ("Aquarius," "Scorpio," and "Pisces") in Carnegie Hall.

Pearl Bailey wins the Donaldson Award for Most Promising Newcomer when she makes her Broadway theater debut as Butterfly in *St. Louis Woman*, a musical extravaganza.

While studying in Mexico in 1946-47, Elizabeth Catlett completes her graphic series on the "Negro Woman," fifteen linocuts that configure real images of black women.

Camilla Williams is the first black woman to perform with the New York City Opera.

The Street is published by novelist Ann Petry and later receives the Houghton Mifflin Literary Award.

1947

The Journey of Reconciliation project sends a biracial group of thirteen on a bus ride through the upper South to test compliance with the 1946 *Morgan* decision; it is the precursor to the 1961 Freedom Rides.

Rosa Lee Ingram, a Georgia tenant farmer and widowed mother of twelve, along with two of her sons, is convicted and sentenced to death for the murder of a neighboring white tenant farmer who she alleged had assaulted her. The case spurs a national defense campaign that includes the organization of the National Committee to Free Rosa Ingram and Her Sons, chaired by Mary Church Terrell, and the Sojourners for Truth and Justice, initiated by Charlotta Bass, Shirley Graham DuBois, Louise Thompson Patterson, Alice Childress, and Rosalie McGee. A worldwide amnesty campaign results in Ingram's 1959 pardon.

Receiving a degree from Columbia University, Marie M. Daly becomes the first African American woman to earn a Ph.D. in chemistry.

1948

In *Ada Lois Sipuel* v. *Board of Regents*, the Supreme Court orders the University of Oklahoma School of Law to admit Sipuel, arguing that a state cannot require African Americans to postpone their education until separate black graduate or professional schools are established.

While working for the Associated Negro Press (ANP), journalist Alice A. Dunnigan travels with Harry Truman, covering his presidential election campaign.

Alice Coachman becomes the first black woman Olympic champion when she wins the gold medal in the high jump and sets a new Olympic record of 5' 6 1/4".

1949

The popular music industry uses the term "rhythm and blues" for the first time, replacing the older term "race records."

Flemmie Pansy Kittrell is a U.S. delegate to the International Congress of Home Economics in Stockholm, Sweden.

Eleanora Figaro becomes the first black woman to receive the papal honor Pro Ecclesia et Pontifice.

The Women's Political Council, Montgomery, Alabama, an organization of professional black women, is founded by Mary Fair Burks to address racial discrimination in the city; the WPC is instrumental in the 1955-56 Montgomery bus boycott.

Marjorie Lee Brown (University of Michigan) and Evelyn Boyd Granville (Yale University) become the first African American women to earn Ph.D. degrees in mathematics.

Dorothea Towles, the first African American woman to earn her living entirely as a professional model, begins her career in Europe in Christian Dior's showroom.

1950

Women total 7,743,564 in a U.S. black population of 15,042,286.

Forty-two percent of all black women in the labor force are employed in domestic service and 19.1 percent are in other service work; only 5.4 percent are in clerical and sales positions and 5.7 percent are in professional positions.

Gwendolyn Brooks is the first black writer to be awarded a Pulitzer Prize, winning the poetry award for *Annie Allen* (1949).

Attorney Edith Sampson is the first African American to be appointed an alternate delegate to the United Nations General Assembly.

Norma Merrick Sklarek graduates from the School of Architecture at Columbia University and in 1954 becomes the first black woman to be licensed as an architect in the U.S.

Elma Lewis, dance and drama instructor, founds the Elma Lewis School of Fine Arts in Boston, Massachusetts.

1951

The National Negro Labor Council is formed.

The National Association of Colored Graduate Nurses merges with the American Nurses Association.

Althea Gibson becomes the first African American woman to play in the Wimbledon (England) tennis tournament.

Prima ballerina Janet Collins makes her debut in *Aïda*, becoming the first black artist to perform on the stage of the Metropolitan Opera House in New York City.

Black concert artists first appear on television shows: William Warfield and Muriel Rahn on *The Ed Sullivan Show*, followed by Marian Anderson in 1952.

High school student Barbara Johns initiates a student strike that persuades the National Association for the Advancement of Colored People to make desegregation of schools in Prince Edward County, Virginia, one of the four cases eventually decided by the Supreme Court in its 1954 *Brown* v. *Board of Education* decision, ruling segregated schools unconstitutional.

Mildred Fay Jefferson becomes the first African American woman to graduate from Harvard University's Medical School. She goes on to serve three terms as president of the National Right to Life Committee.

Arie Taylor becomes the first black person to be a Women's Air Force classroom instructor.

Life magazine features Maude Daniels Callen's work as a midwife in South Carolina.

1952

Charlotta Bass becomes the first black woman to be nominated for vice president of the U.S. by a major political party, when she runs on the Progressive Party ticket.

Daisy Bates becomes president of the Arkansas state conference of National Association for the Advancement of Colored People branches.

1953

"Big Mo" Aldredge becomes the first African American woman to make the national Amateur Athletic Union (AAU) women's basketball team.

Toni Stone, originally of St. Paul, Minnesota, signs to play professional baseball with the Indianapolis Clowns, the Negro American League champions.

Gwendolyn Brooks publishes the novel *Maud Martha*.

The first black woman to gain membership in the Screen Writers Guild, Mary Elizabeth Vroman adapts her autobiographical short story into the screenplay *Bright Road*, starring Dorothy Dandridge and Harry Belafonte.

1954

The *Brown v. Board of Education* decision makes segregated schools unconstitutional, with Constance Baker Motley playing a major role in preparing the case.

Dorothy Dandridge appears in *Carmen Jones*, one of the most publicized and successful all-black movies. For the title role, Dandridge is nominated for an Academy Award in the Best Actress category, the first black woman to be so honored.

Doris Evans McGinty earns a Ph.D. degree in musicology from Oxford University (England).

1955

Rosa Parks and the Women's Political Council are instrumental in organizing and sustaining the Montgomery, Alabama, bus boycott.

Willa Player becomes president of Bennett College.

Alice Childress's *Trouble in Mind* is the first work by a black woman playwright to be produced off-Broadway. It later wins an Obie Award, the first presented to a black woman.

Marian Anderson makes her debut with the Metropolitan Opera Company, becoming the first black soloist to sing at the Met.

A black singer first appears in a televised opera: Leontyne Price in Puccini's *Tosca* on NBC.

The Women's Amateur Athletic Union (AAU) Track and Field Championship is won by the Tigerbelles of Tennessee State University.

Jean Blackwell Hutson becomes curator of what is now the New York Public Library's Schomburg Center for Research in Black Culture and guides its development until her retirement in 1984.

1956

Alabama outlaws the National Association for the Advancement of Colored People.

Ella Baker, along with Stanley Levison and Bayard Rustin, founds the northern-based organization In Friendship, to help raise funds for the southern civil rights struggle.

Under a Supreme Court order and with the aid of Ruby Hurley, National Association for the Advancement of Colored People regional director, Autherine Lucy enrolls in the University of Alabama in Tuscaloosa, only to be expelled days later by university officials, who cite her statements regarding race relations at the school as grounds for her dismissal.

Nell Cecilia Jackson is head coach of the U.S. women's track and field team at the Olympic Games in Melbourne, Australia, the first black person to serve as head coach of an Olympic team. Jackson is head coach again at the 1972 Olympic Games in Munich, Germany.

Ann Gregory becomes the first African American to play in an integrated women's amateur golf championship.

Earlene Brown wins the South Pacific Amateur Athletic Union (AAU) shotput title.

Alice Childress publishes *Like One of the Family: Conversations from a Domestic's Life*.

1957

The first federal Civil Rights Bill since 1875 is passed.

The Southern Christian Leadership Conference (SCLC) is begun in New Orleans, with Ella Baker as organizer of the central office.

Nine students, including Minniejean Brown, Elizabeth Eckford, Thelma Mothershed, Melba Pattillo, Gloria Ray, and Carlotta Walls, integrate Central High School in Little Rock, Arkansas, despite violent assaults eventually quelled only by the presence of federal troops. Daisy Bates and the Little Rock Nine receive the National Association for the Advancement of Colored People's Spingarn Medal.

Dorothy I. Height becomes the fourth president of the National Council of Negro Women; she continues in 1992, thirty-five years later, in that position.

Althea Gibson wins both the singles and, with partner Darlene Hard, the doubles championships at Wimbledon, becoming the first black woman Wimbledon champion.

Charlemae Rollins is the first black person to be elected president of the Children's Services Division of the American Library Association.

Ebony Fashion Fair stages its first tour; in the following decades, it grows into the world's largest traveling fashion show.

1959

Opening at the Ethel Barrymore Theatre on March 11, *A Raisin in the Sun* by Lorraine Hansberry becomes the first play by an African American woman to be performed on Broadway. Awarded the New York Drama Critics Circle Award, Hansberry is the first black playwright, the youngest person, and the fifth woman to win that award.

Dorothy Dandridge wins the Golden Globe Award for best actress in a musical for her role in the film *Porgy and Bess*.

Winning the election for county court judge in Philadelphia, Juanita Kidd Stout is the first black woman *elected* to a judgeship in the U.S.

Lena Frances Edwards, M.D., subsidizes the founding of Our Lady of Guadeloupe Maternity Clinic in Hereford, Texas, to provide medical services to migrant workers.

Elizabeth Catlett heads the sculpture department of the National School of Fine Arts at the Universidad Nacional Autonoma de Mexico.

Paule Marshall publishes her first novel, *Brown Girl, Brownstones*.

1960

Women total 9,758,423 in a U.S. black population of 18,871,831.

Of all black women in the labor force 32.5 percent are employed in domestic service, 21.4 percent are in other service positions, 10.8 percent are in clerical and sales, and 6 percent are in professional positions.

The Civil Rights Act of 1960 is passed.

Black college students begin sit-ins protesting discrimination in places of public accommodation at Greensboro, North Carolina; Nashville, Tennessee; Montgomery, Alabama; Houston, Texas; and other cities throughout the South.

The Student Nonviolent Coordinating Committee (SNCC) is founded.

Wilma Rudolph becomes the first U.S. woman ever to win three Olympic gold medals and earns the title "World's Fastest Woman" when she captures the gold in the 100-meter dash, 200-meter dash, and 400-meter relay in Rome.

1961

Black and white civil rights activists initiate the Freedom Rides, traveling on buses into the South to test compliance with the Interstate Commerce Commission's desegregation order. The Freedom Riders face physical assault and legal harassment; in Rock Hill, South Carolina, the "Rock Hill Four," including Ruby Doris Smith, refuse to pay their trespassing fines and remain in jail, creating the Student Nonviolent Coordinating Committee's "jail no bail" policy.

Federal courts order Charlayne Hunter and Hamilton Holmes admitted to the University of Georgia.

Helene Hillyer Hale becomes Hawaii's county chairperson, a position equivalent to mayor.

Opera star Leontyne Price makes her debut at the Metropolitan Opera House in *Il Travatore* and receives a forty-two-minute ovation, one of the longest in Met history.

Ellen Stewart ("La Mama") founds the La Mama Experimental Theater Club, an off-off-Broadway theater in New York City.

Margaret Burroughs, with her husband, Charles, establishes the Ebony Museum of African-American History in her South Side Chicago home; the museum becomes the DuSable Museum of African American History.

1962

Four black mothers begin a sit-in at a Chicago elementary school protesting de facto segregation, unequal facilities, double shifts, and mobile classrooms.

Civil rights activist Daisy Bates publishes *The Long Shadow of Little Rock*.

1963

The March on Washington draws 250,000 people to the Lincoln Memorial to lobby Congress for passage of a civil rights bill.

Addie Mae Collins, Denise McNair, Carole Robertson, and Cynthia Wesley are murdered when the Sixteenth Street Baptist Church, Birmingham, Alabama, where they are attending Sunday school, is bombed by white racists opposing civil rights activities in the city.

Marian Anderson is awarded the Presidential Medal of Freedom by Lyndon B. Johnson.

1964

The Twenty-fourth Amendment to the U.S. Constitution eliminates the levying of a poll tax for federal elections.

The Civil Rights Act of 1964 prohibits discrimination in public accommodations and in employment.

The Mississippi Freedom Democratic Party (MFDP) is founded.

Annie Devine, Fannie Lou Hamer, Anna Mae King, Unita Blackwell, and others representing the Mississippi Freedom Democratic Party confront Democratic Party leaders at the Atlantic City national convention, where Hamer testifies before the credentials committee and a national television audience about the physical violence she and others suffered when they attempted to vote.

Constance Baker Motley becomes the first black woman elected to the New York State Senate.

Lena Frances Edwards, M.D., receives the highest civilian award, the Presidential Medal of Freedom, from President Lyndon B. Johnson, becoming the only obstetrician-gynecologist, before or since, to be so honored.

Alma Jacobs is the first African American to become a member of the executive board of the American Library Association.

Appearing on the cover of *Harper's Bazaar*, Donyale Luna becomes the first African American model to appear on the cover of a mainstream U.S. fashion magazine.

Diana Sands stars on Broadway in *The Owl and the Pussycat*; this is considered the first breakthrough, as she appears in a role not specifically written for a black actress.

Anna Arnold Hedgeman publishes her autobiography and assessment of black leadership, *The Trumpet Sounds*.

The Supremes have their first number-one hit with "Where Did Our Love Go."

1965

The Voting Rights Act is passed by Congress.

In the Watts riot, 34 are killed, 900 injured.

The Organization of African American Unity is founded.

Patricia Roberts Harris becomes the first black woman to head a U.S. embassy when she is appointed ambassador to Luxembourg.

The National Association of Media Women is organized by Rhea Callaway.

Constance Baker Motley is elected president of the borough of Manhattan in New York, the highest elected office held by a black woman in a major U.S. city.

Lucille Dixon is a founding member and manager of the Symphony of the New World.

Joan Murray becomes one of the first black newswomen at a major television station, when she joins WCBS in New York.

Leontyne Price receives the National Association for the Advancement of Colored People's Spingarn Medal.

1966

The Black Panther Party is founded in Oakland, California.

Constance Baker Motley is confirmed by the U.S. Senate as a U.S. district court judge, becoming the first black woman on the federal bench.

Barbara Charline Jordan becomes the first black woman in the Texas Senate; she is later elected to the U.S. House of Representatives and distinguishes herself during the Watergate hearings.

Twenty black women employed as nurses' aides, housekeepers, and kitchen staff at Lincoln Nursing Home in Baltimore, Maryland, create a freedom union, Maryland Freedom Local No. 1.

Ruby Doris Smith-Robinson is elected executive secretary of the Student Nonviolent Coordinating Committee (SNCC), the only woman to hold that position.

1967

In *Loving* v. *Virginia* the U.S. Supreme Court rules Virginia's antimiscegenation law unconstitutional, thus, by extension, nullifying similar laws in fifteen other states.

The founding convention of the National Welfare Rights Organization (NWRO) is held, with Johnnie Tillmon as chair, Etta Horn as first vice-chair, Beulah Saunders as second vice-chair, Edith Doering as secretary, and Marian Kidd as treasurer.

Helen Natalie Jackson Claytor becomes the first African American to serve as national president of the Young Women's Christian Association (YWCA).

Renee Powell is the first black woman to join the Ladies Professional Golf Association (LPGA) tour.

Kathleen Cleaver becomes communications secretary of the Black Panther Party.

The Urban Arts Corps, an inner-city theater program to showcase performers of color, is founded in New York City by Vinnette Carroll, who serves as its artistic director.

Aretha Franklin signs with Atlantic Records and releases *I Never Loved a Man (the Way I Loved You)*.

Nannie Mitchell Turner receives the Distinguished Editor Award from the National Newspaper Publishers Association.

1968

The National Domestic Workers Union is founded in Atlanta, under the leadership of Dorothy Lee Bolden.

Shirley Chisholm, from New York's Twelfth Congressional District, becomes the first black woman elected to the U.S. House of Representatives.

Fannie Lou Hamer, Dessie Lee Patterson, and twenty other Mississippi Freedom Democratic Party (MFDP) members unseat the regular delegation to the National Democratic Convention in Chicago.

Elizabeth Duncan Koontz becomes the first African American to serve as president of the National Education Association (NEA).

Barbara M. Watson, the first woman to be assistant secretary of state, becomes the first woman to be the administrator of the Bureau of Security and Consular Affairs of the U.S. State Department.

Attorney Marian Wright Edelman is the congressional and federal agency liaison for the Poor People's Campaign.

Clothhilde Dent Brown becomes the first African American woman to be promoted to the rank of colonel in the U.S. Army.

With the premiere of *Julia*, Diahann Carroll becomes the first black star of a television situation comedy.

Gwendolyn Brooks becomes poet laureate of Illinois.

Madeline Manning wins a gold medal in the 800-meter race in the Mexico City Olympics and later participates in the 1972 and 1976 Olympics.

The longest-running drama of the 1968-69 off-Broadway season is *To Be Young, Gifted, and Black*, adapted posthumously from the unpublished writings of Lorraine Hansberry.

Naomi Sims is the first black woman to appear on the cover of *Ladies' Home Journal*; the next year she is the first black woman on the cover of *Life*.

1969

Nell C. Jackson becomes the first African American to sit on the U.S. Olympic Committee's board of directors and is inducted into the Black Athletes Hall of Fame in 1977 for her achievements as a track star and sports administrator.

Tina Sloane-Green is the first African American woman to compete on the U.S. National Lacrosse team.

The youngest woman and the first African American to win a national fencing championship, at age eighteen Ruth White holds four national titles.

Employed with WAGA-TV in Atlanta, Xernona Clayton (Brady) becomes the first black woman to host a television show in the South.

Lucille Clifton's first book of poems, *Good Times*, is published and chosen by *The New York Times* as one of the ten best books of the year.

Maya Angelou's first autobiography, *I Know Why the Caged Bird Sings*, is published.

Fannie Lou Hamer begins a Freedom Farm Cooperative in Sunflower County, Mississippi.

Clara McBride ("Mother") Hale opens Hale House in Harlem for babies of drug-addicted mothers.

1970

Women total 11,831,973 in a U.S. black population of 22,580,289.

Of all black women in the labor force 17.5 percent are employed in domestic service, 25.7 percent are in other service positions, 23.4 percent are in sales and clerical positions, and 10.8 percent are in professional positions.

Essence magazine begins publication.

Activist and educator Angela Davis is placed on the FBI's Ten Most Wanted list, arrested after a nationwide police search, and charged with murder, kidnapping, and conspiracy. An international campaign to free Davis develops and in June 1972 a jury, after only thirteen hours of deliberation, finds her not guilty on all counts.

Norma Holloway Johnson is confirmed to a seat on the U.S. District Court in Washington, D.C., after being nominated by President Richard Nixon.

The Coalition of 100 Black Women is founded in New York.

Effie O'Neal Ellis, M.D., becomes special assistant for health services to the American Medical Association and is the first black woman physician to hold an administrative post or executive office in the AMA.

Toni Cade (Bambara), editor, publishes the pioneering collection of essays *The Black Woman: An Anthology*.

Lucille Clifton publishes her first children's book, *Some of the Days of Everett Anderson*.

Toni Morrison's first novel, *The Bluest Eye*, is published.

Poet Sonia Sanchez publishes *We a BaddDDD People*.

Alice Walker publishes her first novel, *The Third Life of Grange Copeland*.

1971

The National Women's Political Caucus is founded.

Aileen Hernandez is elected president of the National Organization for Women (NOW), the first African American woman to hold the position.

Lauranne B. Sams is a founding member of the National Black Nurses' Association and serves as its first president.

Maya Angelou's screenplay, *Georgia, Georgia*, is made into a film starring Diana Sands, making Angelou the first black woman to have an original screenplay produced.

Angela Davis publishes the pioneering essay "Reflections on the Black Woman's Role in the Community of Slaves," written from her prison cell.

Fannie Granton serves as parliamentarian of the Washington Press Club, the first African American to hold office in that organization.

1972

Three thousand delegates and 5,000 observers participate in the first National Black Political Convention in Gary, Indiana.

The first African Liberation Day march, organized by the African Liberation Support Committee, takes place in Washington, D.C.

The Coalition of Black Trade Unionists is founded.

A National Education Association study reveals that African Americans have lost 30,000 teaching positions since 1954 in seventeen southern and border states because of desegregation and discrimination.

Yvonne Braithwaite Burke cochairs the Democratic National Convention, the first black person to chair a major party's national political convention.

Shirley Chisholm makes a bid for the Democratic Party's presidential nomination.

Barbara Jordan is elected to the U.S. House of Representatives and serves three terms.

Jewel Stradford Lafontant, the first black woman to serve as assistant U.S. attorney, is appointed deputy solicitor general of the U.S. by President Richard Nixon.

Elizabeth Courtney is the first black woman nominated for an Academy Award for Costume Design, for *Lady Sings the Blues*.

The first black woman to join the Directors Guild of America, Sue Booker wins an Emmy Award for producing *As Adam Early in the Morning*.

Alma Thomas is the first African American woman to have an individual show at the Whitney Museum of American Art in New York City.

Johnnie Tillmon becomes executive director of the National Welfare Rights Organization (NWRO).

The National Association of Black Women Attorneys is founded and led by attorney Wilhelmina Jackson Rolark.

Serving as executive director of the New Jersey Medical School, College of Medicine and Dentistry, Florence Gaynor becomes the first woman to head a major teaching hospital.

Sociologist Joyce Ladner publishes *Tomorrow's Tomorrow*.

1973

In *Roe* v. *Wade*, the U.S. Supreme Court establishes a woman's constitutional right to an abortion; over the next two decades, state and federal legislators and the Supreme Court gradually impose restrictions on that right.

The National Black Feminist Organization is founded.

Lelia K. Smith Foley is elected mayor of Taft, Oklahoma, becoming the first African American female mayor in the continental U.S.

Marian Wright Edelman founds the Children's Defense Fund to lobby for health, welfare, and justice for children and their families.

Vernice Ferguson is the first African American nurse to become chief, Nursing Department, National Institutes of Health in Washington, D.C.

Sara J. Harper is the first woman appointed as a justice for the U.S. Marine Corps.

Sweet Honey In The Rock, an a cappella singing group, is founded by Bernice Johnson Reagon.

The national journal *Nursing Research* appoints Elizabeth Carnegie editor-in-chief, the first African American to hold the position.

Shirley Prendergast becomes the first black woman lighting designer on Broadway, with the production of the Negro Ensemble Company's *The River Niger*.

Cicely Tyson wins two Emmy awards for her performance in *The Autobiography of Miss Jane Pittman*.

1974

Opera Ebony is founded in Philadelphia.

Elaine Brown becomes the first and only female chairperson of the Black Panther Party.

The radical black feminist Combahee River Collective is founded in Roxbury, Massachusetts.

Virginia Hamilton publishes *M. C. Higgins, the Great*, which wins the American Library Association's Newbery Medal for the "most distinguished contribution to literature for children published in the United States," the National Book Award, the Lewis Carroll Shelf Award, and the International Board on Books for Young People Award.

1975

The Congress of African Peoples (CAP) launches Black Women United Front.

Cardiss Collins becomes the first African American and first woman to be appointed Democratic Party whip-at-large of the U.S. House of Representatives.

Margaret Bush Wilson becomes the first black woman chair of the board of the National Association for the Advancement of Colored People.

Gloria Randle Scott becomes the first black woman to serve as national president of the Girl Scouts, U.S.A.

JoAnne Little is acquitted of the charge of murdering the guard who had raped her in a Beaufort, North Carolina, jail cell; the case becomes a cause célèbre, highlighting the sexual abuse of black women and the denial of basic rights to black prisoners.

1976

The National Alliance of Black Feminists is formed.

Ntozake Shange's *For Colored Girls Who Have Considered Suicide/When the Rainbow Is Enuf* appears on Broadway.

When Barbara Jordan addresses the Democratic National Convention, she is the first African American to keynote a major party's national political convention.

Yvonne Braithwaite Burke, representative from California, becomes the first woman to chair the Congressional Black Caucus.

Elected mayor of Mayersville, Unita Blackwell becomes the first African American mayor in Mississippi.

Maxine Waters is elected to the California State Assembly.

Pauli Murray is the first African American woman priest ordained in the Episcopal Church.

Mary Frances Berry becomes chancellor of the University of Colorado at Boulder, the first African American woman to head a major research university.

Clara Stanton Jones is the first African American to be president of the American Library Association.

Linda Jefferson leads the Toledo Troopers to the National Women's Football League championship.

Josephine Riley Matthews ("Mama Jo"), credited with delivering more than 1,300 babies in South Carolina, is named that state's Woman of the Year and Outstanding Older American.

1977

In cutting off Medicaid funds for abortions, the Hyde Amendment effectively denies many women the option of abortion.

The Women's Basketball League is organized.

Lusia Harris is the first African American woman to be drafted by a National Basketball Association (NBA) team, but she declines offers from the New Orleans Jazz and the Milwaukee Bucks.

At thirteen, Donns Lynn Mosley becomes the first African American to compete in the U.S. Gymnastics Federation Junior Olympic Nationals.

Patricia Roberts Harris becomes the first black woman in the U.S. cabinet, when she is appointed secretary of housing and urban development (HUD) by President Jimmy Carter.

Appointed by President Jimmy Carter, Eleanor Holmes Norton becomes the first female chair of the Equal Employment Opportunities Commission (EEOC).

Mary Frances Berry becomes the assistant secretary for education in the Department of Health, Education and Welfare.

Jewel Prestage, the first African American woman to receive a Ph.D. degree in political science in the U.S., becomes a member of the Judicial Council of the national Democratic Party.

Ten African American delegates create the "Black Women's Action Plan" at the International Women's Year National Conference in Houston, expressing their ideas of where black women stand within the women's movement and the black liberation movement.

Jewell Jackson McCabe becomes president of the Coalition of 100 Black Women and launches a national movement in 1981.

Toni Morrison's novel *Song of Solomon* becomes a Book-of-the-Month Club selection, the first by a black author since Richard Wright's *Native Son* (1940).

1978

Faye Wattleton becomes the first black person and the first woman to serve as president of Planned Parenthood Federation of America.

Charlayne Hunter-Gault joins the Public Broadcasting System's *MacNeil/Lehrer NewsHour* as national correspondent.

The Afro-American Woman: Struggles and Images, the first anthology of black women's history, is edited by Sharon Harley and Rosalyn Terborg-Penn.

1979

When appointed brigadier general in the U.S. Army Nurse Corps, Hazel Johnson-Brown becomes the first black woman general in the history of the U.S. military; she is also appointed chief of the Army Nurse Corps, the first African American to hold that position.

Patricia Roberts Harris becomes secretary of health, education and welfare.

The National Archives for Black Women's History and the Mary McLeod Bethune Memorial Museum open in Washington, D.C.

The Association of Black Women Historians is founded.

Barbara Chase-Riboud's *Sally Hemings* wins the Janet Heidinger Kafka Prize for the best novel by a U.S. woman.

Rosa Parks is awarded the National Association for the Advancement of Colored People's Spingarn Medal.

Jenny Patrick is the first black woman in the U.S. to earn a Ph.D. degree in chemical engineering (Massachusetts Institute of Technology).

1980

Women total 14,071,000 in a U.S. black population of 26,683,000.

Of all black women in the labor force 6.5 percent are employed in domestic service, 24.3 percent are in other service work, 32.4 percent are in clerical and sales positions, and 14.8 percent are in professional positions.

With *Harris* v. *McRae*, the U.S. Supreme Court upholds the cutoff of Medicaid funds for abortion.

The National Black Independent Political Party is founded, with a charter requirement of coequal female-male representation in all leadership positions.

Mary Frances Berry is appointed to the U.S. Commission on Civil Rights by President Jimmy Carter.

Marian Wright Edelman becomes the first black person and the second woman to chair the Spelman College board of trustees.

Toni Cade Bambara receives the American Book Award for *The Salt Eaters*.

1981

The Women's Basketball League folds.

The National Black Women's Health Project is founded under the leadership of Byllye Y. Avery.

Kitchen Table: Women of Color Press begins publishing.

Zina Garrison, at age seventeen, is the first black player to win the junior singles tennis championship at Wimbledon (England).

Lena Horne: The Lady and Her Music opens on Broadway and becomes the longest-running one-woman show in Broadway history, winning a Tony Award, a Drama Desk Award, and a Drama Critics Circle citation.

Liz Byrd joins the House of Representatives of Wyoming, the first African American legislator elected since statehood in 1890.

Attorney Arnetta R. Hubbard is the first woman to be president of the National Bar Association.

1982

The first national conference on black women's health issues is sponsored by the National Black Women's Health Project under the direction of Byllye Y. Avery.

The Combahee River Collective issues "A Black Feminist Statement."

Alice Walker publishes *The Color Purple*, which wins the Pulitzer Prize and the American Book Award in 1983 and is made into a movie in 1985.

All the Women Are White, All the Blacks Are Men, But Some of Us Are Brave, a pioneering collection of essays in black women's studies, is edited by Gloria T. Hull, Patricia Bell-Scott, and Barbara Smith.

Kathleen Collins is the first African American woman to direct a feature-length film, *Losing Ground*, which she also wrote.

1983

Ronald Reagan's attempt to gut the U.S. Civil Rights Commission is thwarted when Commissioners Mary Frances Berry and Blandina Cardenas Ramirez bring suit.

Vanessa Williams becomes the first black woman to win the swimsuit and talent competitions and the Miss America crown in the sixty-three-year history of the pageant.

Barbara Smith publishes *Home Girls: A Black Feminist Anthology*.

Christine Darden is the first black woman in the U.S. to earn a Ph.D. degree in mechanical engineering (George Washington University).

1984

Leontine T. C. Kelly, the first black woman bishop of a major religious denomination in the U.S., is elected head of the United Methodist church in the San Francisco area.

Lena Horne is honored by the Kennedy Center for lifetime achievement in the performing arts.

"Libba" Cotton wins a Grammy Award for *Elizabeth Cotton Live!*, which is voted the best ethnic or traditional folk recording of the year.

Octavia E. Butler wins two of science fiction's most prestigious awards, the Hugo Award for her short story "Speech Sounds" and the Nebula Award for her novelette *Blood-child*.

Ida Van Smith becomes the first African American woman inducted into the International Forest of Friendship, in recognition of her contributions to aviation.

SAGE: A Scholarly Journal on Black Women begins publication under the editorial direction of Patricia Bell-Scott and Beverly Guy-Sheftall.

In July, Vanessa Williams is forced to abdicate her Miss America crown after *Penthouse* magazine publishes nude photos from her past.

1985

Sherian Grace Cadoria is the first black woman promoted to brigadier general in the regular U.S. Army.

1986

The U.S. Supreme Court rules unanimously that sexual harassment constitutes illegal job discrimination.

The Oprah Winfrey Show goes national, making Oprah Winfrey the first African American woman to host a nationally syndicated weekday talk show.

Charlayne Hunter-Gault receives the George Foster Peabody Award for Excellence in Broadcast Journalism for her report on South Africa, *Apartheid's People*.

Lynette Woodard becomes the first woman Harlem Globetrotter.

1987

When Mae Jemison joins NASA, she is the first black woman to be accepted as an astronaut.

Beulah Mae Donald sues United Klans of America, following her son's lynching, and wins a $7 million judgment, which destroys that unit of the Ku Klux Klan.

Carrie Saxon Perry is elected mayor of Hartford, Connecticut.

Rita Dove wins the Pulitzer Prize for Poetry for *Thomas and Beulah*.

Johnnetta Cole becomes president of Spelman College, the first black woman to head the oldest college for black women still in existence in the U.S.

Niara Sudarkasa becomes the first woman president of Lincoln University, the oldest black college in the U.S.

Gloria Dean Randle Scott becomes president of Bennett College in Greensboro, North Carolina.

Darlene Clark Hine becomes John A. Hannah Distinguished Professor of History at Michigan State University.

1988

Barbara Clementine Harris of Boston is the first woman to become a bishop in the Episcopal Church.

Lenora Fulani of the New Alliance Party is the first woman and first African American presidential candidate to get on the ballot in all fifty states.

Juanita Kidd Stout is the first black woman to serve on a state supreme court, when she is appointed to the Pennsylvania Supreme Court.

The Black Women Mayors' Caucus is founded at the National Conference of Black Mayors.

Florence Griffith-Joyner wins three gold medals and one silver medal in the Summer Olympics, becoming the first U.S. woman to win four medals in one Olympic Games.

Jackie Joyner-Kersee wins the gold medal in the heptathlon at the Summer Olympics.

Figure skater Debi Thomas wins a bronze medal, becoming the first African American woman to win a Winter Olympics medal.

Anita DeFrantz, bronze medalist for rowing in the 1976 Montreal Olympics, becomes the first black woman to serve on the ninety-member International Olympic Committee.

Toni Morrison is awarded the Pulitzer Prize for Fiction for her novel *Beloved*.

Pearl Bailey is awarded the Presidential Medal of Freedom by Ronald Reagan.

1989

When Joan Salmon Campbell is elected moderator of the Presbyterian Church, U.S.A., she is the first black woman and sixth woman to head the church.

Oprah Winfrey buys her own television and movie production studio, Harpo, becoming the first black woman and only the third woman in U.S. history to own her own production company.

Judith Jamison becomes the director of the Alvin Ailey American Dance Theater.

Illusions, a thirty-four-minute film short written, produced, and directed by Julie Dash in 1983, is named Best Film of the Decade by the Black Filmmaker Foundation.

1990

Roselyn Payne Epps, M.D., becomes the first black woman to serve as president of the American Medical Association.

Sister Cora Billings is installed as a pastor in Richmond, Virginia, becoming the first black nun to head a parish in the United States.

Sharon Pratt Dixon (Kelly) is elected mayor of Washington, D.C., becoming the first woman and the first D.C. native to be elected mayor of the nation's capital.

Marcelite J. Harris is the first African American woman to hold the rank of brigadier general in the U.S. Air Force.

Carole Gist, a twenty-two-year-old native of Detroit, Michigan, is the first African American to be crowned Miss U.S.A.

1991

Daughters of the Dust, written, produced, and directed by Julie Dash, is the first feature film by an African American woman to have a national release.

With the acquisition of her cartoon strip, "Where I'm Coming From," by Universal Press Syndicate, Barbara Brandon becomes the first black female cartoonist to be syndicated in the mainstream white U.S. press.

Anita Hill's televised testimony before the U.S. Senate Judiciary Committee during the confirmation hearings of Supreme Court Justice Clarence Thomas initiates a national discussion on sexual harassment.

1992

Mae Jemison becomes the first African American woman in space, traveling as science mission specialist in the seven-member crew aboard the space shuttle *Endeavour*.

Carol Moseley Braun of Illinois becomes the first African American woman to be elected to the U.S. Senate; she is also the first African American senator from the Democratic party.

Lusia Harris is inducted into the Basketball Hall of Fame.

Barbara J. Jacket is head coach of the U.S. women's track and field team at the Olympic Games in Barcelona, Spain; she is the second African American woman in this position (Nell Jackson was the first, in 1956).

When Vivian L. Fuller is named athletics director at Northeastern Illinois University, she becomes the first black female athletics director in the history of Division I, the National Collegiate Athletic Association's top competitive level.

Bibliography of Basic Resources

Janet Sims-Wood

MAJOR REFERENCE BOOKS

Black Literature, 1827-1940. Alexandria, Va.: Chadwyck-Healey, 1988, 200 fiche per year.

More than 150,000 items of poetry, fiction, and book reviews published in over 900 Black-owned or edited newspapers and periodicals between 1827 and 1940. Uses census records and other genealogical sources to identify thousands of African-American women and men writers. A cumulative index accompanies the collection.

Burkett, Randall K., Nancy Hall Burkett, and Henry Louis Gates, eds. *Black Biographical Dictionaries, 1790-1950.* Alexandria, Va.: Chadwyck-Healey, 1988, 1,068 microfiche.

This collection of dictionaries reproduces more than 30,000 biographical sketches of African-Americans, along with some accompanying photographs. This reference source is drawn from some 300 collective biographies located in libraries and private collections across the country. Most of the titles are obscure, and inaccessible except for major Black history collections. A valuable resource for literary, religious, historical, sociological, political, and genealogical research.

Burkett, Randall K., Nancy Hall Burkett, and Henry Louis Gates, eds. *Black Biography, 1790-1950, A Cumulative Index.* Alexandria, Va.: Chadwyck-Healey, 1991, 3 volumes.

A comprehensive index to *Black Biographical Dictionaries, 1790-1950.* The first two volumes list alphabetically the 30,000 entries, providing details on birth, gender, death, place of birth, occupations, and religious affiliation, as well as listing the location of full biographical sketches and accompanying photographs. The third volume provides names under several categories: birth place, occupation, gender, and religion. Hundreds of cross-references and added entries were added to make it a valuable name authority file.

Cederholm, Theresa Dickason. *Afro-American Artists: A Bio-Bibliographical Directory.* Boston: Trustees of the Boston Public Library, 1973, 348p.

Covers retrospective and contemporary artists from eighteenth-century slave artisans to the present. Provides data from exhibition catalogues, periodicals, books, reviews, and questionnaires. For each artist, there is a biographical statement, list of works produced, where exhibited, where collections are housed, and sources on the artist. The accompanying bibliography is divided into books, exhibit catalogs, magazines, and newspapers.

Conference on the Educational and Occupational Needs of Black Women. Washington, D.C.: The National Institutes of Health. December 16-17, 1985, Vol. 1: Overview and Recommendations, 90p., Vol. 2: Research Papers, 261p.

The Women's Research Program of the National Institutes of Health developed a program initiative to address the educational and occupational needs of African-American women. The first step was a series of conferences to establish dialogue between scholars, practitioners, grassroots people, activists, and policy makers. The goal was to establish a policy-oriented research agenda which could be used for several years to come.

Dandridge, Rita B. *Ann Allen Shockley: An Annotated Primary and Secondary Bibliography*. Westport, Conn.: Greenwood Press, 1987, 120p.

This comprehensive bibliography is intended to facilitate future research on Shockley and to allow for a total view of her writings and their critical reception by the public. Annotations are abstract and descriptive. The bibliography is arranged in four parts. Part One denotes citations and annotations of all the published and unpublished fiction by Shockley up through 1985. Each category of fiction is arranged chronologically. Part Two lists published and unpublished nonfiction writings. Part Three lists accessible reviews of Shockley's fiction and nonfiction up through 1984. This section is also arranged chronologically. Part Four chronologically organizes the relevant biography and criticism of Shockley found in books, periodicals, and newspapers.

Davis, Lenwood G. *The Black Woman in American Society: A Selected Bibliography*. Boston: G. K. Hall, 1975, 159p.

An annotated bibliography on African-American women which includes many biographical and autobiographical works. Also includes general reference books, journal articles, reports, government documents, pamphlets, and speeches. Includes information on libraries with major collections, a list of newspaper publishers, a list of elected officials, and statistics on women in rural and urban areas.

Draper, James P., ed. *Black Literature Criticism: Excerpts from Criticism of the Most Significant Works of Black Authors over the Past 200 Years*. Detroit: Gale Research, 1992, 3 volumes.

Several women are included among the 125 writers representing the United States, Nigeria, South America, Jamaica, and over a dozen other nations. The volumes present a broad selection of the best criticism of works by major African-American writers from the eighteenth century to the present. Each author entry presents a historical survey of critical response to the author's work.

Gates, Henry Louis, Jr. *The Schomburg Library of Nineteenth-Century Black Women Writers*. New York: Oxford University Press, 1988, 24 volumes.

Reprints the works of African-American women authors and unearths the nineteenth-century roots of their literary tradition. This set resurrects the salient works from 1890 to 1910, which literary historians often call "The Black Woman's Era." Makes available the works of nineteenth-century women which have remained buried in obscurity. Many works had never before been reprinted and were accessible only in research libraries; others were available only in poorly edited reprints.

Gilkin, Ronda. *Black American Women in Literature: A Bibliography, 1976 through 1987*. Jefferson, N.C.: McFarland and Co., 1989, 251p.

Cites updated bibliographical resources on African-American women writers. Includes the short fiction, essays, poetry, novels, plays by, and criticism on 300 women who have been published in periodicals and anthologies from 1976 to 1987. This multigenre bibliography includes citations for both original works and literary criticism. Science fiction and children's literature are included. Includes a section on the authors arranged by genre. Excluded are audiovisual works, dissertations, newspapers, and reprints.

Hampton University Newspaper Clipping File, 1900-1925. Alexandria, Va.: Chadwyck-Healey, 1987, 790 fiche.

A record of early twentieth-century Black politics, economics, and culture. The 55,000 clippings from nearly 100 newspapers cover the complex forces that shaped the lives of African-Americans, especially in the South. There are several individual and subject headings on women. Printed index is available.

Hill, George, et al. *Black Women in Television: An Illustrated History and Bibliography*. New York: Garland Publishing, 1990, 168p.

Lists books, periodical articles, dissertations, and theses on Black women in television. Books and articles are subdivided by topic (e.g., soap operas, drama, comedy, etc.). Includes news and sports personalities and off-camera personnel. Most of the articles are from *TV Guide*. The brief dissertations and theses section is annotated. The introduction summarizes the interaction between the television industry and African-American actresses. Included in the appendixes are awards such as the Emmy, and listings of starring and costarring roles of the women. Also indexed by author/subject, program/film, and stations by call letters.

Hill, Ruth E. *Black Women's Oral History Collection at the Schlesinger Library, Radcliffe College*. Westport, Conn.: Meckler Corporation, 1989, 10 volumes.

The Schlesinger Library began its Black Women's Oral History program in 1976. The women included have made contributions in various fields: education, civil rights, business, medicine, social work, and the arts. The interviews present an overview of the American experience up to the 1980s. Most of the interviewers were also women. The interviews detail each woman's family background, childhood, education, significant influences in her life, the place of religion and church in her life, her attitudes on the women's movement and feminism, and her most important achievements in life. Each woman also was asked about how being Black and female affected her opportunities and choices in life, about her memberships and community activities, hobbies, travel opportunities, awards and honors, and personal circumstances (marital status, children, occupation of husband and his attitude toward her career/activities, and about her friendships).

Hill, Ruth E. *Guide to the Transcripts of the Black Women's Oral History Project.* Westport, Conn.: Meckler Corporation, 1989.

Detailed guide to the ten-volume set of the Schlesinger Library's Black Women's Oral History Collection.

Hinding, Andrea, et al., eds. *Women's History Sources: A Guide to Archives and Manuscript Collections in the United States.* New York: R. R. Bowker, 1979, Vol. 1: Collections, 1,114p., Vol. 2: Index, 391p.

Volume one identifies the location of hundreds of collections containing diaries, journals, and other first-person accounts of women housed in major research collections, small county and municipal agencies, college and university archives, and professional societies. It is a compendium of women's experiences, especially minority women, documenting women of all professions. Volume two indexes volume one and was prepared by staff on the basis of questionnaires submitted by repositories or field workers who surveyed the collections. All African-American women are not listed under the general heading of "Afro-American" in the index; therefore, the user should also search under the names of individual women.

Hine, Darlene Clark, Patrick K. Bidelman, and Shirley M. Herd. *The Black Women in the Middle West Project: A Comprehensive Resource Guide: Illinois and Indiana.* Indianapolis: Indiana Historical Society, 1983, 238p.

This volume includes biographical information on approximately 300 women. The purpose was to collect and preserve photographs and other documents that record the historical experiences and accomplishments of African-American women and their organizations in Illinois and Indiana. Includes historical essays, oral histories, biographical profiles, and document collections.

Hine, Darlene Clark, Elsa Barkley Brown, Tiffany R.L. Patterson, and Lillian S. Williams, eds. *Black Women in United States History: From Colonial Times to the Present.* New York: Carlson Publishing, 1990, 16 volumes.

The essays and monographs in this series span several themes including slavery, emancipation, reconstruction, migration, urbanization, work, resistance, family, institution-building, club formation, and aesthetic expression. The editors felt that this series was "characterized by innovative methodology, imaginative use of sources and a reclamation of women long ignored and silenced in the historical record."

Index to the Schomburg Clipping File. Alexandria, Va.: Chadwyck-Healey, 1986, 176p.

The clipping file at the Schomburg Center for Research in Black Culture, which is part of the New York Public Library, is composed of periodical and newspaper clippings, along with typescripts, pamphlets, programs, broadsides, book reviews, and ephemera of all kinds. There are two indexes to the file: a general index and a subject index relating to Africa. Both indexes list, in alphabetical order, individuals or organizations plus general topics. Several subject and individual indexes on women are included.

Logan, Rayford W. and Michael R. Winston. *Dictionary of American Negro Biography.* New York: W. W. Norton, 1982, 680p.

Some 85 of the 636 biographies are of women. Many individuals included were not national figures but had a major influence in their local or regional communities. Some were important because of their participation in the development of this country. No living persons were included. The cut-off date was January 1, 1970.

Middleton, David L. *Toni Morrison: An Annotated Bibliography.* New York: Garland Publishing, 1987, 186p.

This bibliography provides comprehensive access to critical readings of Toni Morrison's works. Part One lists her novels. Part Two deals with her nonfiction works and affords a unique insight into her view of herself as Black and female. Interviews with Morrison are annotated in Part Three, and Part Four annotates criticism of her works in two categories: criticism on general topics, and criticism of particular works. There are also listings of awards/honors, anthologies, recordings, memberships, and related references. A special section includes a postscript on the novel *Beloved.*

Newman, Debra L. *Black History: A Guide to Civilian Records in the National Archives.* Washington, D.C.: National Archives Trust Fund Board, 1984, 379p.

This guide provides information about civilian records of the federal government on the history of African-Americans (textual, photographic, and audiovisual). Describes records of more than 140 nonmilitary agencies through the 1970s. The guide is arranged by record group and series. Includes more than forty photographs and a comprehensive index to the guide. Archival records on women include women workers, World War II, women's organizations, women's rights, and some records on individual women such as Mary McLeod Bethune.

Newson, Adele S. *Zora Neale Hurston: A Reference Guide.* Boston: G. K. Hall, 1987, 90p.

Arranged chronologically beginning in 1931, this bibliography includes books, articles, book reviews, chapters and passages in books, essays, dissertations, bibliographies, and manuscript locations.

Pratt, Louis H. and Darnell D. Pratt. *Alice Malsenior Walker: An Annotated Bibliography, 1968-1986*. Westport, Conn.: Meckler Corporation, 1988, 162p.

Presents descriptive rather than evaluative annotations on Alice Walker's social and literary philosophies and analyzes the growing body of critical interpretations of her work. The listing of primary sources cites collected works, recordings, and such uncollected writings as essays, letters, interviews, short fiction, book and movie reviews, and poetry. Secondary sources feature indexes and bibliographies, unpublished dissertations, biographical sketches, articles, essays, and reviews of Walker's works. The section on criticism includes critical comments on multiple primary sources or discussions of Walker in conjunction with other contemporary writers.

Richardson, Marilyn. *Black Women and Religion: A Bibliography*. Boston: G. K. Hall, 1980, 139p.

Chapter one covers books and articles on African-American women and religion. Chapters two, three, and four cover literature and the arts and contain primary and secondary materials which include criticism, commentary, and biography, all listed by author. There is also a discography of music with religious themes by African-American women.

Roberts, J.R. *Black Lesbians: An Annotated Bibliography*. Tallahassee, Fla.: Naiad Press, 1981, 93p.

Comprehensive annotated bibliography on materials by and/or about Black lesbians in the United States from the ancient legend of Black Amazons to present-day activism in the Black and Third World gay rights movement. The items cited represent a wide range of race, sex, and class perspectives, political consciousness, style, form, and content.

Robinson, William H. *Phillis Wheatley: A Bio-Bibliography*. Boston: G. K. Hall, 1981, 166p.

Lists and annotates materials on Wheatley's life and her writings that appear in anthologies, biographies, histories, introductions to books, book reviews, journals, newspapers, dictionaries, encyclopedias, and manuscripts. The index has names of important persons and locales in which Wheatley was concerned, selected titles of her writings, books on Wheatley, and selected titles with information on Wheatley.

Sims, Janet L. *Marian Anderson: An Annotated Bibliography and Discography*. Westport, Conn.: Greenwood Press, 1981, 243p.

This annotated bibliography details Anderson's personal life, her career activities, and her awards and honors. Includes a discography of some of her recordings and also lists where primary resources on Anderson can be found.

Sims, Janet L. *The Progress of Afro-American Women: A Selected Bibliography and Resource Guide*. Westport, Conn.: Greenwood Press, 1980, 378p.

Comprehensive list of materials on many subjects including citations on family life, education, medicine, and government, along with citations on suffrage, women's rights, the theater, etc. Lists names and addresses of some of the women's organizations. Other topics include mental health, religion, sexual discrimination, sports, audiovisual materials, and law enforcement. Has an extensive author/subject index.

Smith, Jessie Carney. *Notable Black American Women*. Detroit: Gale Research, 1992, 1,334p.

Entries in this biographical dictionary include pioneers in politics, journalism, business, literature, the humanities, and other fields. Includes both pioneer and contemporary women.

Southern, Eileen. *Biographical Dictionary of Afro-American and African Musicians*. Westport, Conn.: Greenwood Press, 1982, 478p.

Cites more than 1,500 musicians of African descent, including pioneer and contemporary figures. Gives concise sketches on the individuals' professional lives. In some cases, evaluative comments are included. Each entry has a bibliography, and some have discographies. Several women are included.

Sterling, Dorothy, ed. *We Are Your Sisters: Black Women in the Nineteenth Century*. New York: W. W. Norton, 1984, 535p.

Rich with pictures and primary sources (letters, newspaper accounts, excerpts from autobiographies and diaries, etc.), this book gives a view of the Black female experience. Sterling's accompanying notes add to the primary documents.

GENERAL HISTORIES

Boulware, Marcus H. *The Oratory of Negro Leaders: 1900-1968*. Westport, Conn.: Negro Universities Press, 1969, 312p.

Some well-known African-American women are included in the chapter on "Public Addresses of Negro Women," among them Mary McLeod Bethune, Mary Church Terrell, and Charlotte Hawkins Brown. Mentions the orations of lesser-known women such as Laura Crosby, Carolina Johnson, and Belle Hendon.

Brawley, Benjamin G. *Negro Builders and Heroes*. Chapel Hill: University of North Carolina Press, 1937, 315p.

Includes several chapters on African-American women, such as "Women Who Have Led in Education," "Phillis Wheatley," and "The Negro Woman in American Life."

Brawley, Benjamin G. *Women of Distinction.* Chicago: Women's American Baptist Home Mission Society, 1919, 92p.

This volume includes an introductory chapter on "The Negro Woman in American Life," a collection of short biographies and sketches on women such as Meta Warrick Fuller and Harriet Tubman, and photographs of the women.

Brown, Hallie Q. *Homespun Heroines and Women of Distinction.* Xenia, Ohio: Aldine Publishing Company, 1926, 248p.

A collection of sketches, biographies, and photographs of some fifty-five African-American women throughout history.

Brown, Sterling. *Negro Poetry and Drama and the Negro in American Fiction.* New York: Atheneum, 1969, 209p.

Includes biographical sketches and information on works by Black writers. Some of the women included are Georgia Douglas Johnson, Anne Spencer, Jessie Fauset, and Alice Dunbar-Nelson.

Carnegie, Mary Elizabeth. *The Path We Tread: Blacks in Nursing, 1854-1984.* Philadelphia: J. B. Lippincott, 1986, 254p.

A historical overview of Blacks in the nursing profession. Gives detailed information on nursing programs, the special role of the national nursing organizations, and the integration of Black nurses into the American Nursing Association. Looks at nurses in the federal government, the military, in the United States Public Health Service, and in the Veterans Administration.

Cuthbert, Marion Vera. *Education and Marginality: A Study of the Negro Woman College Graduate.* New York: Columbia University Press, 1942, 167p.

Studies the effect of the college experience on the lives of many African-American women. Gives some psychological and sociological implications for educated Black women and some of the problems in life that they encounter because of their educational background.

Daniel, Sadie Iola. *Women Builders.* Washington, D.C.: The Associated Publishers, 1931, 187p.

Biographical sketches on seven women (Maggie Lena Walker, Janie Porter Barrett, Nannie Helen Burroughs, Lucy Craft Laney, Mary McLeod Bethune, Jane Edna Hunter, and Charlotte Hawkins Brown) who contributed to the development of Black children through the educational and social institutions that they established.

Dann, Martin E. *The Black Press, 1827-1980: The Quest for National Identity.* New York: G. P. Putnam, 1971, 384p.

Portraits of ten African-American women journalists who were prominent during the 1880s: Ida B. Wells-Barnett, Victoria Earle Matthews, Mary Cook, Ione E. Wood, Kate D. Chapman, Mrs. N. F. Mossell, Lillial Kewus, Lucretia Newman Coleman, Mary E. Britton, and Amelia F. Johnson. Includes a list of sixteen other women who contributed articles to several publications.

Dannett, Sylvia. *Profiles of Negro Womanhood.* New York: Educational Heritage, 1966, Vol. 1: 1619-1900, 352p., Vol. 2: Twentieth Century, 352p.

Biographical sketches on women in the performing arts, education, medicine, law, fine arts, nursing, civil rights, government, social work, literature, etc. Comprehensive bibliography is included.

Davis, Angela Y. *Women, Race and Class.* New York: Random House, 1981, 271p.

Presents a historical analysis of the negative impact of racism and class bias on the civil rights and women's rights struggles in the United States. Depicts critical roles women have played in each movement. Compares African-American and white middle/working-class women's efforts in gaining the right to vote, in securing educational rights for African-Americans, and in influencing the women's club movement. Also presents a historical sketch of the roles of several communist women in the women's rights and civil rights struggle.

Davis, Elizabeth L. *Lifting as They Climb.* Chicago: National Association of Colored Women, 1933, 424p.

Organized in 1896, the club had as its purpose to raise to the highest plane the home life, moral standards, and civic life of the race. There were members in every state, in Canada, and in Africa. This book provides an early history of the organization.

Davis, John P., ed. *The American Negro Reference Book.* Englewood Cliffs, N.J.: Prentice-Hall, 1976, 1,026p.

Includes several chapters on the African-American woman, including "Occupational Distribution," "The College Educated Negro Woman," and "Negro Women in the Labor Force."

Davis, Michael D. *Black American Women in Olympic Track and Field: A Complete, Illustrated Reference.* Jefferson, N.C.: McFarland and Company, 1992, 272p.

Describes Olympic participation and accomplishments of such people as Tidye Pickett, Louise Stokes, Jackie Joyner-Kersee, and Florence Griffith Joyner. Through a series of first-person interviews, twenty of the most prominent women discuss their struggles on and off the track. Details the circumstances (racism, sexism, poverty, etc.) of over ninety women in Olympic track and field.

Du Bois, W.E.B. *Darkwater: Voices from within the Veil.* New York: Harcourt, Brace and Howe, 1920, 276p.

Examines the roles Black women have played throughout history. Includes a discussion of four women whom the author remembered from his childhood: his mother, and Emma, Inez, and Ida Fuller. These women represented the problems of the widow, the wife, the maiden, and the outcast.

Earley, Charity Adams. *One Woman's Army: A Black Officer Remembers the WAC.* College Station: Texas A&M University Press, 1989, 218p.

Portrays the double difficulty of being Black and female in the military during World War II. Charity Adams volunteered in 1942 and had risen to major by 1943 and to colonel by 1945. She commanded the only Black WAC unit to serve overseas: the 6888th Central Postal Directory Battalion. She notes that morale was high despite racist and sexist slurs.

Fox-Genovese, Elizabeth. *Within the Plantation Household: Black and White Women of the Old South.* Chapel Hill: University of North Carolina Press, 1988, 544p.

Examines race, class, and gender in the antebellum South. Argues that the centrality of slavery and the "domination of the master" dictated different responses from slaveholding women and slave women, precluding any proto-feminism or proto-abolitionism that transcended class and race interests. Draws upon the diaries, letters, and journals of white women and from the Works Progress Administration slave narratives.

Franklin, John Hope. *From Slavery to Freedom: A History of Negro Americans.* New York: Knopf, 1988, 579p.

Revised and expanded edition from the nineteenth century to materials dealing with popular culture. Includes information on women in African families, as plantation slaves, in the abolition movement, as free Negroes, and in military service.

Giddings, Paula. *In Search of Sisterhood: Delta Sigma Theta and the Challenge of the Black Sorority Movement.* New York: Morrow, 1988, 336p.

Delta Sigma Theta sorority was founded at a time when liberal arts education was seen as futile and impractical for African-American women. Delta Sigma Theta sorority was created to change and benefit individuals rather than society. This not only is the story of the sorority but also details the increasing involvement of African-American women in the political, social, and economic affairs of the United States.

Giddings, Paula. *When and Where I Enter: The Impact of Black Women on Race and Sex in America.* New York: Morrow, 1984, 408p.

This narrative history of African-American women from the seventeenth century to the contemporary period is thematic in approach. Giddings, whenever possible, used the words of the women themselves. The women who appear most often in the book are those who were most articulate and who had a measurable impact on the civil rights and women's struggle in this country. Giddings describes the already existing infrastructure that could mobilize African-American women to effective political action—religious-affiliated and professional women's organizations, and sororities. She suggests possible alliances with labor organizations and major national progressive coalitions, although her emphasis is clearly on the need for African-American women to band together for effective female-directed policies and political action.

Harley, Sharon and Rosalyn Terborg-Penn. *The Afro-American Woman: Struggles and Images.* Port Washington, N.Y.: Kennikat Press, 1978, 137p.

This anthology presents, from a historical and biographical perspective, African-American women as abolitionists, reformers, club organizers, educators, artists, lecturers, workers, performing artists, composers, and civil rights activists. The book details the historical experiences common to African-American women from slavery to the mid-1970s. The book also describes some individual accounts of these women from the Civil War period to the 1950s.

Harris, Middleton. *The Black Book.* New York: Random House, 1974, 198p.

Presents historical information on African-American women as well as illustrations, sketches, drawings, and photos.

Heilbut, Tony. *The Gospel Sound: Good News and Bad Times.* New York: Simon and Schuster, 1971, 350p.

Includes several women gospel singers and groups such as Sallie Martin, Bessie Griffin, Mahalia Jackson, Roberta Martin, Dorothy Love Coates, Clara Ward, Staples Singers, the Davis Sisters, Shirley Caesar, and Rosetta Tharpe. Many of the women describe the forces that inspired them to enter the gospel field. Several photographs as well as a discography of each person or group are included.

Hine, Darlene Clark. *Black Women in White: Racial Conflict and Cooperation in the Nursing Profession, 1890-1950.* Bloomington: Indiana University Press, 1989, 264p.

Integrates primary and secondary sources to analyze the impact of racism and racial conflict on the role of African-American women in the nursing profession. Traces the establishment and evolution of a national network of segregated hospitals and training schools. Examines both southern and northern schools. Includes a detailed index.

Hull, Gloria T., Patricia Bell-Scott, and Barbara Smith. *All the Women Are White, All the Blacks Are Men, But Some of Us Are Brave: Black Women's Studies*. Old Westbury, N.Y.: Feminist Press, 1982, 401p.

These essays represent the most recent research and teaching about African-American women. Includes comprehensive bibliographies and bibliographical essays, a listing of nonprint material, and selected course syllabi, all of which focus on women from various disciplinary and interdisciplinary perspectives. This anthology is permeated by an explicit Black feminist perspective characterized by a sensitivity to the peculiar conditions under which African-American women live because of the effects of racial, sexual, and class oppression. Advances the idea of establishing Black Women's Studies as a corrective to the neglect of the subject in regular Women's Studies courses.

Jones, Jacqueline. *Labor of Love, Labor of Sorrow: Black Women, Work, and the Family from Slavery to the Present*. New York: Basic Books, 1985, 432p.

Comprehensive account of the work and family life of African-American women. Starting with the slavery period and continuing through the mid-1980s, Jones details the dual responsibilities of African-American women not only as breadwinners, but also as the guardians of family and community stability.

Lanker, Brian. *I Dream a World: Portraits of Black Women Who Changed America*. New York: Stewart, Tabori, and Chang, 1989, 167p.

Portraits of seventy-five women who have changed the world. Includes interviews Lanker conducted with these high-profile women. The women have worked in the civil rights movement and the women's movement, and have achieved many firsts. They are writers, politicians, athletes, performers, college educators, doctors, bishops, etc. Also documented are women often left out of the general history books.

Lerner, Gerda. *Black Women in White America*. New York: Pantheon Books, 1972, 630p.

A thematic collection of vignettes of well- and little-known African-American women of the past two centuries. The last three chapters are a collection of accounts of grass-roots work, race pride, and womanhood. The volume presents many vivid testimonials of the perseverance and strength of African-American women in white America.

Locke, Alain. *The Negro in Art*. Chicago: Afro-Am Press, 1969 (1940), 224p.

This pictorial record of Black arts and crafts includes several women, among them Meta Warrick Fuller, Laura Wheeler Waring, Edmonia Lewis, and Lois Mailou Jones Pierre-Noel. Includes short biographical sketches as well as illustrations, many of which depict works done by the women artists.

Loewenberg, Bert James and Ruth Bogin. *Black Women in Nineteenth Century American Life: Their Words, Their Thoughts, Their Feelings*. University Park: Pennsylvania State University Press, 1976, 355p.

The women included represent a cross section of historically significant African-American women of the nineteenth century. A selection of writings by two dozen women leaders is included with a general introduction relating them to their forebears in Colonial times and to their descendants in the twentieth century. Each section has a biographical sketch and a bibliography of works by and about the woman. Grouped into four parts, the book highlights family relationships, political and reformist movements, religious activities, and education.

Majors, Monroe A. *Noted Negro Women: Their Triumphs and Activities*. Freeport, N.Y.: Books for Libraries Press, 1971 (1893), 365p.

Over 300 short biographical sketches are included. Many of the women were wives of prominent men. Includes letters, articles, poems, and photographs.

Moore, William, Jr., and Lonnie H. Wagstaff. *Black Educators in White Colleges*. San Francisco: Jossey-Bass Publishers, 1974, 226p.

Notes that African-American women's participation in higher education was primarily through teaching and administration in all-Black colleges. Concludes that much of what we know about African-American women in education has come from their autobiographies, letters, and papers.

Moutoussamy-Ashe, Jeanne. *Viewfinders: Black Women Photographers*. New York: Dodd, Mead and Company, 1986, 201p.

This work is divided into six parts, with an overview describing the triumphs and struggles of various photographers of different eras, from Black Hollywood in the 1950s and 1960s to contemporary photographers' views of life in the 1980s and 1990s.

Myrdal, Gunnar. *An American Dilemma: The Negro Problem and Modern Democracy*. New York: Harper and Row, 1944, 1,483p.

Gives some references on women in education, leadership, professions, employment, and the armed forces. Examines the parallels between the status of African-American men and women.

Neverdon-Morton, Cynthia. *Afro-American Women of the South and the Advancement of the Race, 1895-1925.* Knoxville: University of Tennessee Press, 1989, 272p.

This detailed examination of the African-American women's club movement in Maryland, Georgia, Tennessee, Virginia, and Alabama highlights the accomplishments of these women in social welfare, public and private education, public health, and civil rights. Shows the origins of female networks with national importance during and after the Progressive era and looks at the intellectual and social commitments of southern Black women in the early twentieth century.

Noble, Jeanne L. *The Negro Woman's College Education.* New York: Teachers College of Columbia University, 1956, 163p.

Details the historical development of college-educated African-American women. Discusses the roles that society permitted them to play and how their positions influenced their higher education. Discusses the important issues in the education of over 400 women who had four or more years of college.

Parker, Marjorie H. *Alpha Kappa Alpha through the Years, 1908-1988.* Chicago: Mobium Press, 1990, 333p.

Founded in 1908 on the campus of Howard University, the sorority is the oldest Greek-letter organization for Black college women. This fourth edition highlights the creativity and significance of the organization's development and recounts eight decades of contributions to American cultural heritage. The history reflects the changing patterns of human relations. The sorority has cut across racial, physical, and social barriers to help individuals develop and maintain constructive relationships.

Perkins, Kathy A., ed. *Black Female Playwrights: An Anthology of Plays before 1950.* Bloomington: Indiana University Press, 1989, 320p.

This anthology focuses on the creative life and works of seven women playwrights during the early twentieth century. Uses nineteen little-known plays of Mary P. Burrill, Eulalie Spence, May Miller, Zora Neale Hurston, Georgia Douglas Johnson, Shirley Graham, and Marita Bonner to detail the diverse styles and themes used by these pioneer women playwrights. Includes a historical essay on women dramatists and biographical essays on each of the seven playwrights.

Porter, James A. *Modern Negro Art.* New York: Dryden Press, 1943, 272p.

Gives accounts of several women and their works, including Lottie Wilson Moss, Ella D. Spencer, Lois Mailou Jones Pierre-Noel, Edmonia Lewis, Meta Warrick Fuller, Augusta Savage, Elizabeth Catlett, Elizabeth Prophet, Laura Wheeler Waring, Selma Burke, and Hilda Wilkerson. Many of the eighty-five half-tone plates illustrate works by these women.

Quarles, Benjamin. *Black Abolitionists.* New York: Oxford University Press, 1969, 310p.

Details the role Black women have played in the abolition movement.

Scruggs, Lawson A. *Women of Distinction.* Raleigh, N.C.: L. A. Scruggs, 1893, 382p.

Nearly 100 women are included in the collected biography. Some of the biographical sketches have appeared elsewhere. Photographs of many of the women are included.

Shockley, Ann Allen. *Afro American Women Writers, 1746-1933: An Anthology and Critical Guide.* Boston: G. K. Hall, 1988, 465p.

Divided into four parts, this anthology covers the Colonial Period to the Civil War, 1746-1862; Reconstruction to the end of the century, 1868-99; pre-World War I to the New Negro movement, 1900-23; and the New Negro movement, 1924-33. Introductions to each section summarize the historical, social, political, economic, and racial climate of the time, and how this affected these women writers. Gives a detailed, chronological listing of publications within each period, plus biographical sketches and bibliographies of both primary and secondary sources on each writer. Includes selections from each writer's works.

Simms, Margaret C. and Julianne Malveaux., eds. *Slipping through the Cracks: The Status of Black Women.* New Brunswick, N.J.: Transaction Books, 1986, 302p.

Proceedings of a symposium sponsored by the *Review of Black Political Economy* and the Congressional Black Caucus Foundation, this volume contains research papers and book reviews on a variety of topics, including employment and earnings in three developing countries and the United States, health issues, single-parent families, and education and training. Concludes with a research agenda by Phyllis A. Wallace and a policy agenda by the editors.

Staples, Robert. *The Black Family: Essays and Studies.* Belmont, Calif.: Wadsworth Publishing Co., 1978, 282p.

Much of this book is devoted to African-American women. Essays include "Unwed Mothers and Their Sex Partners" and "The Changing Role of the Black Woman to the Black Man."

Steady, Filomina C. *The Black Woman Cross-Culturally.* Cambridge, Mass.: Schenkman Publishing Company, 1981, 645p.

This anthology examines, in a cross-cultural perspective, literature on the Black woman. Details common themes in their experiences. Gives representations of the Black woman in the Caribbean, in Africa, in South America, and in the United States. Since Africa has a significant number of matrilineal societies and societies with varying degrees of sexual egalitarianism, this study provides many variations for the study of sex roles in cultural contexts. Studies of family and households in the Caribbean have led to insights into family organization and a redefinition of traditional concepts on the family. In the United States, variables such as race and class, as well as slavery and institutional racism, are examined to see how they have affected the lives of African-American women.

Terborg-Penn, Rosalyn, Sharon Harley, and Andrea Benton Rushing, eds. *Women in Africa and African Diaspora*. Washington, D.C.: Howard University Press, 1987, 234p.

Convened by the Association of Black Women Historians, the conference "Women in the African Diaspora: An Interdisciplinary Perspective," held June 12-14, 1983, at Howard University, examined the role and place of women in the African diaspora. The papers were grounded in three thematic divisions: (1) Theoretical Approaches and Research Methods, which examined the Black woman from broad-based anthropological, historical, psychological, and economic perspectives; (2) Women and New Roles in African Societies, which examined values that have fostered selected customs in traditional African and New World societies; and (3) Black Women in Folk Culture and Literature, which examined the various ways in which women have used the arts to advance their struggle. Three additional papers were added for the book. The concluding essay, "Research Priorities for the Study of Women in Africa and the African Diaspora," explores the relationships between development specialists, scholars, and the women they study.

Thoms, Adah B. *Pathfinders: A History of Progress of Colored Graduate Nurses*. New York: Kay Printing House, 1929, 240p.

This early book on Black nurses discusses problems that these women encountered in gaining acceptance and recognition as professionals.

Wallace, Phyllis A. *Black Women in the Labor Force*. Cambridge, Mass.: MIT Press, 1980, 163p.

Contains information derived from data compiled by the federal government and from surveys and analyses of recent economic studies. Examines characteristics such as work schedules, occupational status, age, presence of children in the home, and educational attainment. Focuses on the post-1960 occupational status of African-American women.

Weld, Theodore D. *American Slavery As It Is; Testimony of a Thousand Witnesses*. New York: American Anti-Slavery Society, 1839, 224p.

Many of the testimonies are from Black women. Much of their statements deals with their inhumane treatment by their masters. Some of the information was supplied by white abolitionists.

Wesley, Charles H. *The History of the National Association of Colored Women's Clubs: A Legacy of Service*. Washington, D.C.: National Association of Colored Women's Clubs, 1984, 562p.

A regional history of the activities of the NACW in each state. Also gives a detailed historical overview of the organization and the future challenges facing it.

White, Deborah Gray. *Ar'n't I a Woman? Female Slaves in the Plantation South*. New York: W. W. Norton, 1985, 216p.

This study of American slavery focuses exclusively on the women and evaluates their unique position. Examines the plight of the female slave in the antebellum South, drawing from the memories of former slaves.

Williams, Ora. *American Black Women in the Arts and Social Sciences: A Bibliographic Survey*. Metuchen, N.J.: Scarecrow Press, 1973, 141p.

Over 1,200 entries on African-American women including movies, recordings, and tapes based on the writings by these women. Several photographs are included.

MAJOR RESEARCH COLLECTIONS OF PRIMARY MATERIALS

Amistad Research Center
Tulane University
New Orleans, Louisiana 70118

Mary McLeod Bethune Papers, 1923-36

Carol Brice Papers, 1905

Marguerite Dorsey Cartwright Papers, 1927-

Julius Rosenwald Fund Papers, 1917-48

Fredi Washington Papers, 1925-75

Camilla Williams Papers, 1944-73

Atlanta University
Robert W. Woodruff Library
Negro Collection
Atlanta, Georgia 30314

Association of Southern Women for Prevention of Lynching Records, 1920-43

Chautauqua Circle Records, 1913-70

Cullen-Jackman Memorial Collection: Miscellany

Grace (Towns) Hamilton Papers, 1928-76

Maud Cuney Hare Papers, 1900-36

Southern Conference on Human Welfare Records, 1938-67

Nellie Towns, in George Alexander Towns Papers, 1851-1956

Bennett College
Thomas F. Holgate Library
Greensboro, North Carolina 27401

Afro-American Women Collection

Bennett College Records, 1873-

Scrapbooks, 1929-50s

Vertical File Collection

Bethune Museum and Archives
1318 Vermont Ave., N.W.
Washington, D.C. 20005

Processed Collections:

National Council of Negro Women, 1935-78

Unprocessed Collections:

Audio Visual Resources

Jeanetta Welch Brown Papers

Polly Cowan Papers

Jeanne Dogo Papers

Jennie Austin Fletcher Papers

Susie Green Papers

Mary E. C. Gregory Papers

Euphemia Lofton Haynes Papers

Dorothy Parker Koger Papers

Historical Annals of the Ladies Auxiliary, Knights of Peter Clover

National Alliance of Black Feminists

National Association of Fashion and Accessory Designers

Records of the National Committee on Household Employment

Charles C. Parlin Papers

Photographic Collection

Dovey Johnson Roundtree Papers

Ethel Emory Heywood Smith Papers

Mabel Keaton Staupers Papers

Alice Thomas Papers

Miriam H. Thomas Papers

Vertical File Collection

Chicago Historical Society
North Avenue and Clark Street
Chicago, Illinois 60614

Etta Moten Barnett Papers, 1934-66

Irene Gaines Papers, 1917-68

Detroit Public Library
Burton Historical Collection
5201 Woodward Ave.
Detroit, Michigan 48202

Housewives League of Detroit Records, 1930-73

DuSable Museum of African American History
740 E. 56th Place
Chicago, Illinois 60637

Hope I. Dunmore Papers, 1905-60

Mellissa Ann Elam Papers, 1910-25

Fisk University Library
Special Collections
Nashville, Tennessee 37208

Lizzie Crofton Anderson Papers, 1972

Dorothy Brown Papers, 1961

Carrie B. H. Collins Papers

Ophelia Settle Egypt Papers, 1925-

Grace James Papers, 1972

Cecile Barefield Jefferson Papers, 1928-70

Gerda Lerner Collection on Black Women, 1972-

Naomi Long Madgett Papers, 1941-68

Louise Meriwether Papers

Margaret Simms Papers, 1952-70

Eileen Southern Papers, 1971

Mary Spence Papers

Lillian Voorhees Papers, 1927-60

Indiana Historical Society
315 W. Ohio St.
Indianapolis, Indiana 46202

Black Women in the Middle West Project Papers

Library of Congress
Manuscript Division
Washington, D.C. 20540

National Youth Administration

Mary Church Terrell Papers, 1886-1954

Minnesota Historical Society
Archives and Manuscripts
345 West Kellogg Blvd.
St. Paul, Minnesota 55102

Hallie Q. Brown Community House Records, 1861-1960s

Ethel Ray Nance Papers, 1920-68

Oral History Tapes, 1945

Irene Persons Papers, 1937

Moorland-Spingarn Research Center
Manuscript Division
Founders Library
Howard University
Washington, D.C. 20059

Marian Anderson Papers, 1939-43

Mary Elizabeth Branch Papers, July 1909-May 3, 1944

Ralph J. Bunche Oral History Collection, 1967-73

Jeannette Carter Papers, 1927-64

Mary Ann Shadd Cary Papers, 1844-84

Anna J. Cooper Papers, 1881-1958

Donor Oral History Program, 1982-

Eva B. Dykes Papers, 1914-77

Lena Edwards Papers, 1905-85

Ophelia Settle Egypt Papers, 1930-80

Crystal Bird Fauset Papers, 1944-59

Gregoria Fraser Goins Papers, 1843-1962

Angelina Weld Grimké Papers, 1887-1958

Hazel Harrison Papers, 1900-50s

Charlotte Moton Hubbard Papers, 1934-70

Revella Hughes Papers

Pauli Murray Papers, 1943-44

Rosey Eve Pool Papers, 1959-67

Anita Thompson Dickinson Reynolds Papers, 1850-1980

Arthur and Elizabeth Schlesinger Library, Black Women's Oral History Transcripts

Lucy Diggs Slowe Papers, 1919-43

Myra L. Spaulding Papers, 1892-1922

Isabele Taliaferro Spiller Papers, 1906-54

Mabel Keaton Staupers Papers, 1937-70

Mary Church Terrell Papers, 1888-1976

Sara A. Turner Collection, 1866-1901

Washington Conservatory of Music, Harriet Gibbs Marshall Papers, 1887-1966

Schomburg Center for Research in Black Culture
New York Public Library
515 Malcolm X Blvd.
New York, New York 10037

Wilhelmina Adams Papers, 1926-62

Bessye Bearden Papers, 1923-44

Conrad and Tubman Papers, 1893-1941

Ruby Sheppard Davis Papers, 1940-75

Mary Caldwell Dawson Papers, 1937-59

Rielta Hines Herbert Papers, 1948-64

Lyons and Williams Papers, 1830-1957

Alice McInnis Papers, 1938-74

National Association of Colored Graduate Nurses Papers, 1908-51

Lucy Terry Prince Papers, 1967-72

Tuskegee University Archives
Hollis Burke Fissell Library
Tuskegee, Alabama 36088

Juanita Gilmore Brewster Papers, 1800-1970

Sadie P. Delaney Papers, 1923-58

National Committee to Abolish the Poll Tax Papers, 1943-48

Edith M. Washington Shehee Papers, 1910-64

Southern Conference Educational Fund Records, 1938-63

Margaret Murray Washington Papers, 1896-1925

University of Illinois at Chicago
Circle Library
Manuscript Collection
The Library—Box 8198
Chicago, Illinois 60607

Chicago Urban League Records, 1932-71

Gary Urban League Records, 1941-65

Greater Lawndale Conservation Commission Records, 1953-68

Phillis Wheatley Association Records, 1908-66

University of Louisville
Oral History Center
Department of History
Belknap Campus
Louisville, Kentucky 40292

Hilda H. Butler Oral History, 1977

Vivian Crowell Oral History, 1977

Ruth Harry and Vivian Crowell (2 tapes)

Abbie Clement Jackson Oral History, 1977

Susan St. Clair Minor Oral History, 1977

Estella Sales Oral History, 1976

Wayne State University
Walter P. Reuther Library
Archive of Labor and Urban Affairs
Detroit, Michigan 48202

Frances Albrier Oral History, 1968

Joseph and Rose Billups Oral History, 1967

Geraldine Bledsoe Oral History, 1970

Dorothy Jones Oral History

Layle Lane Papers

Beulah Whitby Oral History, 1969

Western Reserve Historical Society
10825 East Blvd.
Cleveland, Ohio 44106

Jane E. Hunter Papers, 1930-69

Ladies Society of Brocton, Ohio, Papers, 1866

L. Pearl Mitchell Papers, 1875-1974

Phillis Wheatley Association, 1914-60

Classified List of Biographical Entries

ABOLITIONISTS

Cary, Mary Ann Shadd
Craft, Ellen
Douglass, Sarah Mapps
Forten Sisters
Grimké, Charlotte L. Forten
Harper, Frances Ellen Watkins
Pleasant, Mary Ellen
Prince, Nancy Gardner
Remond, Sarah Parker
Stewart, Maria W.
Truth, Sojourner
Tubman, Harriet Ross

ACTRESSES

Allen, Debbie
Archer, Osceola Macarthy (Adams)
Bailey, Pearl
Beavers, Louise
Bowman, Laura
Bryant, Hazel Joan
Bush, Anita
Carroll, Diahann
Childress, Alice
Dandridge, Dorothy
Davis, Henrietta Vinton
Dee, Ruby
Douglas, Marion
Ellis, Evelyn
Goldberg, Whoopi
Hall, Juanita
LeNoire, Rosetta Olive Burton
McClendon, Rose
McDaniel, Hattie

McKinney, Nina Mae
McNeil, Claudia
McQueen, Butterfly
Menken, Adah Isaacs
Mitchell, Abbie
Moore, Melba
Preer, Evelyn
Randolph, Amanda
Reese, Della
Richards, Beah
Sands, Diana
Sul-Te-Wan, Madame
Teer, Barbara Ann
Thomas, Edna Lewis
Tyson, Cicely
Washington, Fredi
Waters, Ethel
Williams, Vanessa Lynn
Winfrey, Oprah

ANTHROPOLOGISTS

Cole, Johnnetta Betsch
Day, Caroline Stewart Bond
Diggs, Ellen Irene
Dunham, Katherine
Robeson, Eslanda Goode
Sudarkasa, Niara

ARCHITECT

Sklarek, Norma Merrick

ARMED FORCES MEMBERS

Adams-Ender, Clara Leach
Cadoria, Sherian Grace

Earley, Charity Adams
Gannett, Deborah Sampson
Harris, Marcelite Jordan
Johnson, Hazel Winifred

ARTISTS

(*see* FOLK ARTISTS, PAINTERS, QUILTMAKER, PHOTOGRAPHER, SCULPTORS)

ASTRONAUT

Jemison, Mae C.

ATHLETES

Coachman, Alice
DeFrantz, Anita
Garrison, Zina
Gibson, Althea
Glenn, Lula Mae Hymes
Harris-Stewart, Lusia
Hyman, Flora
Jacket, Barbara J.
Jackson, Nell Cecilia
Joyner, Florence Griffith
Joyner-Kersee, Jackie
Rudolph, Wilma Glodean
Stringer, C. Vivian
White, Willye B.
Woodard, Lynette

AUTHORS

(*see* WRITERS)

AVIATORS

Bragg, Janet Harmon
Brown, Willa Beatrice
Coleman, Bessie
Oglesby, Mary
Smith, Ida Van

BAND LEADERS

Ashby, Dorothy Jeanne Thompson
Austin, Lovie
Dixon, Lucille
Ennis, Ethel Llewellyn
Pierce, Billie Goodson

BANKER

Walker, Maggie Lena

BISHOPS

Harris, Barbara
Kelly, Leontine T. C.

BLUES SINGERS AND MUSICIANS

Austin, Lovie
Baker, LaVerne
Brown, Ruth
Cox, Ida
Dranes, Arizona Juanita
Hemphill, Jesse Mae
Hunter, Alberta
Rainey, Ma
Simone, Nina
Smith, Bessie
Smith, Mable Louise
Smith, Mamie
Smith, Trixie
Spivey, Victoria
Taylor, Koko
Wallace, Sippie
Washington, Dinah
Waters, Ethel

BUSINESSWOMEN

(see ENTREPRENEURS)

CARTOONISTS

Brandon, Barbara
Ormes, Zelda Jackson "Jackie"

CHILDREN'S RIGHTS ADVOCATE

Edelman, Marian Wright

CHORAL DIRECTORS

Hall, Juanita
Jessye, Eva Alberta
Lightner, Gwendolyn
Martin-Moore, Cora
Simmons, Dorothy Vernell
Steele, Rebecca Walker

CHOREOGRAPHERS

Allen, Debbie
Dunham, Katherine
Hinkson, Mary

CIVIL RIGHTS LEADERS/ COMMUNITY ACTIVISTS/ SOCIAL AND POLITICAL ACTIVISTS

Allensworth, Josephine Leavell
Avery, Byllye Y.
Baker, Ella Josephine
Bates, Daisy Lee Gatson
Bearden, Bessye
Berry, Mary Frances
Bethune, Mary McLeod
Blackwell, Unita
Bolden, Dorothy Lee
Booze, Mary Cordelia Montgomery
Boynton, Amelia
Brown, Elaine
Brown, Hallie Quinn
Brown, Linda Carol
Burks, Mary Fair
Cable, Mary Ellen
Clark, Septima Poinsette
Cleaver, Kathleen Neal
Cotton, Dorothy Forman
Davis, Angela
Davis, Henrietta Vinton
Devine, Annie Belle Robinson
Dunlap, Ethel Trew
Edmonds, Helen Gray
Foster, Autherine Juanita Lucy
Fox, Lillian Thomas
Gaines, Irene McCoy
Garrison, Memphis Tennessee
Garvey, Amy Ashwood
Grimké, Charlotte L. Forten
Hale, Clara (Mother) McBride
Hamer, Fannie Lou
Hedgeman, Anna Arnold
Height, Dorothy Irene
Higgins, Bertha G.
Hope, Lugenia Burns
Huggins, Ericka
Hunter, Jane Edna
Hurley, Ruby
Johnson, Kathryn Magnolia
Joseph-Gaudet, Frances
King, Coretta Scott
Lampkin, Daisy Elizabeth Adams
Loving, Mildred
Luper, Clara
Mason, Vivian Carter
Matthews, Victoria Earle
McCabe, Jewell Jackson
McCrorey, Mary Jackson
McMillan, Enolia Pettigen
Mitchell, Juanita Jackson
Moody, Anne E.
Moon, Mollie

Moore, Audley (Queen Mother)
Nash, Diane
Parks, Rosa
Parsons, Lucy
Patterson, Louise Thompson
Pettey, Sarah E. C. Dudley
Polite, Carlene
Powers, Georgia Montgomery Davis
Ray, Henrietta Green Regulus
Richardson, Gloria St. Clair Hayes
Roberts, Ruth Logan
Robeson, Eslanda Goode
Robinson, Jo Ann Gibson
Ruffin, Josephine St. Pierre
Shabazz, Hajj Bahiyah Betty
Simkins, Mary Modjeska Monteith
Simmons, Althea T. L.
Smith-Robinson, Ruby Doris
Somerville, Vada Watson
Talbert, Mary Morris Burnett
Taylor, Anna Diggs
Terrell, Mary Eliza Church
Thoms, Adah Belle Samuels
Wattleton, Faye
Wells-Barnett, Ida Bell
White, Eartha Mary Magdalene
Williams, Fannie Barrier
Williams, Myrlie Beasley Evers
Willis, Gertrude Pocte Geddes
Wilson, Margaret Bush
Young, Jean Wheeler Smith

CLUBWOMEN

Anderson, Violette N.
Barrett, Janie Porter
Bearden, Bessye
Bethune, Mary McLeod
Booze, Mary Cordelia Montgomery
Brown, Charlotte Hawkins
Brown, Sara Winifred
Bruce, Josephine Beall Willson
Burrell, Mary E. Cary
Cable, Mary Ellen
Cummings, Ida Rebecca
Davis, Elizabeth Lindsay
Dunbar-Nelson, Alice Ruth Moore
Ferebee, Dorothy Celeste Boulding
Fields, Mamie Elizabeth Garvin
Fox, Lillian Thomas
Gaines, Irene McCoy
Height, Dorothy Irene
Hooks, Julia Britton
Hope, Lugenia Burns
Hunton, Addie Waits
Mason, Vivian Carter
Matthews, Victoria Earle
McCoy, Mary Eleanora
McCrorey, Mary Jackson
Napier, Nettie Langston
Ridley, Florida Ruffin
Ruffin, Josephine St. Pierre
Scott, Minnie Taylor
Sprague, Fredericka Douglass (Perry)

Sprague, Rosabelle Douglass (Jones)
Sprague, Rosetta Douglass
Stewart, Ella Phillips
Stewart, Sallie Wyatt
Stokes, Ora Brown
Talbert, Mary Morris Burnett
Terrell, Mary Eliza Church
Tucker, C. DeLores Nottage
Washington, Margaret Murray
Wells-Barnett, Ida Bell
Williams, Fannie Barrier
Yates, Josephine Silone

COACHES

Jacket, Barbara J.
Jackson, Nell Cecilia
Stringer, C. Vivian
White, Willye B.

COLLEGE PRESIDENTS

Barnett, Marguerite Ross
Bethune, Mary McLeod
Cole, Johnnetta Betsch
Moten, Lucy Ella
Player, Willa B.
Scott, Gloria Dean Randle
Slowe, Lucy Diggs
Sudarkasa, Niara

COMMUNIST PARTY ACTIVISTS

Davis, Angela
Jones, Claudia
Patterson, Louise Thompson

COMMUNITY ACTIVISTS AND LEADERS

(see CIVIL RIGHTS LEADERS)

COMPOSERS

Akers, Doris
Allen, Geri
Armstrong, Lillian Hardin
Bonds, Margaret Allison Richardson
Coates, Dorothy McGriff Love
Douroux, Margaret Pleasant
Du Bois, Shirley Graham
Holt, Nora Douglas
Lee, Julia
Martin, Roberta
Martin, Sallie
Martin-Moore, Cora
Moore, Dorothy Rudd
Moore, Undine Smith
Perry, Julia Amanda
Price, Florence Smith
Rush, Gertrude E. Durden
Schuyler, Philippa Duke
Williams, Mary Lou

CONCERT MUSICIANS

Harrison, Hazel
Hinderas, Natalie Leota Henderson
Hobson, Ann
Rushen, Patrice
Schuyler, Philippa Duke
Sprague, Frederica Douglass (Perry)
Sprague, Rosabelle Douglass (Jones)

CONCERT SINGERS

Anderson, Marian
Batson, Flora
Brice, Carol
Greenfield, Elizabeth Taylor
Hackley, Emma Azalia Smith
Hall, Juanita
Maynor, Dorothy
Mitchell, Nellie B.
Selika, Marie Smith
Steele, Rebecca Walker

CONDUCTOR

McLin, Lena Johnson

DANCERS

Allen, Debbie
Baker, Josephine
Collins, Janet
DeLavallade, Carmen
Dunham, Katherine
Hinkson, Mary
Jamison, Judith
Johnson, Virginia
Mills, Florence
Primus, Pearl
Snow, Valaida
Turney, Matt

EDITORS

Bass, Charlotta Spears
Cary, Mary Ann Shadd
Coston, Julia Ringwood
Duster, Alfreda Barnett
Fauset, Jessie Redmon
Garvey, Amy Euphemia Jacques
Laney, Lucy Craft
McLin, Lena Johnson
Merritt, Emma Frances Grayson
Moten, Lucy Ella
Peake, Mary Smith Kelsey
Richards, Fannie M.
Slowe, Lucy Diggs
Terrell, Mary Eliza Church
Thompson, Era Bell
Waring, Laura Wheeler
Wells-Barnett, Ida Bell
Whipper, Ionia Rollin

EDUCATORS

Albert, Octavia Victoria Rogers
Baker, Augusta Braxston

Baldwin, Maria Louise
Barnett, Marguerite Ross
Barrett, Janie Porter
Becroft, Anne Marie
Berry, Mary Frances
Bethune, Mary McLeod
Bowen, Cornelia
Bowman, Sister Thea
Bozeman, Sylvia Trimble
Briggs, Martha B.
Brown, Charlotte Hawkins
Brown, Hallie Quinn
Brown, Letitia Woods
Brown, Sara Winifred
Browne, Marjorie Lee
Bruce, Josephine Beall Willson
Burke, Selma Hortense
Burks, Mary Fair
Burrill, Mary P.
Burroughs, Margaret Taylor Goss
Burroughs, Nannie Helen
Butcher, Margaret Just
Butler, Loretta Green
Butler, Selena Sloan
Byrd, Flossie M.
Cable, Mary Ellen
Campbell, Lucie E.
Cary, Mary Ann Shadd
Clark, Septima Poinsette
Cobb, Jewell Plummer
Cole, Johnnetta Betsch
Collins, Marva N.
Cooke, Anne (Reid)
Cooper, Anna Julia Haywood
Coppin, Fanny Jackson
Couvent, Marie Bernard
Cox, Minnie M. Geddings
Cummings, Ida Rebecca
Davidson, Olivia America
Davis, Angela
Davis, Hilda Andrea
Denning, Bernadine
Derricotte, Juliette
Douglas, Marion
Douglass, Sarah Mapps
Drumgold, Kate
Dunbar-Nelson, Alice Ruth Moore
Dunnigan, Alice Allison
Dykes, Eva Beatrice
Early, Sarah Jane Woodson
Edmonds, Helen Gray
Epps, Roselyn Payne
Fauset, Jessie Redmon
Ferebee, Dorothy Celeste Boulding
Ferguson, Catherine (Katy)
Fields, Mamie Elizabeth Garvin
Fisher, Ada Lois Sipuel
Forsythe, Ruby Middleton
Forten Sisters
Garnet, Sarah S. T.
Garrison, Memphis Tennessee
Gilmer, Gloria
Gleason, Eliza Atkins

Granson, Milla
Grimké, Charlotte L. Forten
Hackley, Emma Azalia Smith
Hamilton, Grace Towns
Harper, Frances Ellen Watkins
Holland, Annie Welthy Daughtry
Hooks, Julia Britton
Jordan, Barbara Charline
Joseph-Gaudet, Frances
Koontz, Elizabeth Duncan
Laney, Lucy Craft
Livingston, Myrtle Athleen Smith
Logan, Adella Hunt
Lyle, Ethel Hedgeman
Marshall, Harriet Gibbs
McMillan, Enolia Pettigen
Merritt, Emma Frances Grayson
Mitchell, Nellie B.
Moten, Lucy Ella
Nickerson, Camille Lucie
Patterson, Mary Jane
Peake, Mary Smith Kelsey
Player, Willa B.
Prestage, Jewel Limar
Prout, Mary Ann
Randolph, Virginia Estelle
Robinson, Bernice
Saddler, Juanita
Sanders, Maude
Shabazz, Hajj Bahiyah Betty
Simpson, Georgiana
Sizemore, Barbara
Slowe, Lucy Diggs
Smith, Celestine Louise
Spikes, Delores Margaret Richard
Stanley, Sara G.
Steele, Rebecca Walker
Stewart-Lai, Carlotta
Sudarkasa, Niara
Talbert, Mary Morris Burnett
Tate, Merze
Taylor, Susie Baker King
Vashon, Susan Paul
Walker, Frances
Waring, Laura Wheeler
Washington, Josephine Turpin
Wright, Elizabeth Evelyn
Yates, Josephine Silone

ELOCUTIONISTS

Britton, Mary E.
Brown, Hallie Quinn
Davis, Henrietta Vinton

ENTERTAINERS

Bailey, Pearl
Baker, Josephine
Bentley, Gladys
Bowman, Laura
Bricktop [Ada Smith]
Carroll, Diahann

Douglas, Marion
Hall, Adelaide
Hall, Juanita
Hawkins, Tramaine
Horne, Lena
Jones, Sissieretta Joyner
Kitt, Eartha
LaBelle, Patti
Mabley, Jackie "Moms"
Mills, Florence
Moore, Melba
Walker, Aida Overton
Washington, Isabel

ENTREPRENEURS

Bowen, Ruth
Calloway, Blanche
Cox, Minnie M. Geddings
Eldridge, Elleanor
Forth, Elizabeth Denison (Lisette)
Hinard, Eufrosina
Keckley, Elizabeth
Lafontant-Mankarious, Jewel Stradford
McCabe, Jewell Jackson
Pleasant, Mary Ellen
Randolph, Lucille Campbell Green
Teer, Barbara Ann
Walker, A'Lelia
Walker, Madam C. J. (Sarah Breedlove)
Walker, Maggie Lena
White, Eartha Mary Magdalene
Willis, Gertrude Pocte Geddes

FASHION DESIGNERS

Blount, Mildred E.
Keckley, Elizabeth

FILMMAKER

Dash, Julie

FOLK ARTISTS

Hunter, Clementine
Powers, Harriet

FOLK SINGERS AND MUSICIANS

Cotten, Elizabeth "Libba"
Molton, Flora
Odetta

FUGITIVE SLAVES

Craft, Ellen
Tubman, Harriet Ross

GOSPEL SINGERS AND MUSICIANS

Akers, Doris
Caesar, Shirley

Campbell, Lucie E.
Coates, Dorothy McGriff Love
Douroux, Margaret Pleasant
Dranes, Arizona Juanita
Griffin, Bessie
Hawkins, Tramaine
Jackson, Mahalia
James, Etta
Lightner, Gwendolyn
Martin, Roberta
Martin, Sallie
Martin-Moore, Cora
Simmons, Dorothy Vernell
Smith, Willie Mae Ford
Staple, Mavis
Tharpe, Sister Rosetta
Ward, Clara
Williams, Marion

GOVERNMENT OFFICIALS

(see also POLITICIANS AND LEGISLATORS)
Berry, Mary Frances
Cox, Minnie M. Geddings
Denning, Bernadine
Harris, Patricia Roberts
Haynes, Elizabeth Ross
Lafontant-Mankarious, Jewel Stradford
Norton, Eleanor Holmes

HARPIST

Hobson, Ann

HISTORIANS

Beasley, Delilah Leontium
Berry, Mary Frances
Brown, Letitia Woods
Edmonds, Helen Gray
Garvey, Amy Euphemia Jacques
Houston, Drusilla Dunjee

JAZZ MUSICIANS

Allen, Geri
Armstrong, Lillian Hardin
Ashby, Dorothy Jeanne Thompson
Austin, Lovie
Brown, Cleo Patra
Coltrane, Alice
Dixon, Lucille
Donegan, Dorothy
Ennis, Ethel Llewellyn
Horn, Shirley
Lee, Julia
Liston, Melba
Pierce, Billie Goodson
Scott, Hazel
Shipp, Olivia (Porter)
Snow, Valaida
Sullivan, Maxine
Taylor, Koko
Williams, Mary Lou

JAZZ SINGERS

Anderson, Ernestine
Armstrong, Lillian Hardin
Bailey, Pearl
Barrett, "Sweet Emma"
Carlisle, Una Mae
Carter, Betty
Ennis, Ethel Llewellyn
Fitzgerald, Ella
Hall, Adelaide
Holiday, Billie
Horne, Lena
Lincoln, Abbey
McRae, Carmen
Mercer, Mabel
Simone, Nina
Snow, Valaida
Staton, Dakota
Sullivan, Maxine
Vaughan, Sarah
Wilson, Nancy

JOURNALISTS

Bass, Charlotta Spears
Bates, Daisy Lee Gatson
Bearden, Bessye
Beasley, Delilah Leontium
Britton, Mary E.
Cary, Mary Ann Shadd
Coston, Julia Ringwood
Dunbar-Nelson, Alice Ruth Moore
Dunnigan, Alice Allison
Forten Sisters
Fox, Lillian Thomas
Garvey, Amy Euphemia Jacques
Holt, Nora Douglas
Houston, Drusilla Dunjee
Hunter-Gault, Charlayne
Matthews, Victoria Earle
McClain, Leanita
Mossell, Gertrude E. H. Bustill
Payne, Ethel L.
Rollin Sisters
Ruffin, Josephine St. Pierre
Smith, Lucie Wilmot
Stewart, Maria W.
Thompson, Era Bell
Washington, Margaret Murray
Wells-Barnett, Ida Bell

JUDGES

Bolin, Jane Matilda
Johnson, Norma Holloway
Motley, Constance Baker
Phillips, Velvalea Rogers
Sampson, Edith
Stout, Juanita Kidd
Taylor, Anna Diggs

LABOR ORGANIZERS/ LEADERS

Bolden, Dorothy Lee
Harris, Louise "Mamma"
Moore, Audley (Queen Mother)
Roberts, Lillian Davis

LAWYERS

Alexander, Sadie Tanner Mossell
Anderson, Violette N.
Berry, Mary Frances
Bolin, Jane Matilda
Braun, Carol Moseley
Burke, Yvonne Braithwaite
Carter, Eunice Hunton
Cleaver, Kathleen Neal
Edelman, Marian Wright
Fisher, Ada Lois Sipuel
Harris, Patricia Roberts
Johnson, Norma Holloway
Jordan, Barbara Charline
Kelly, Sharon Pratt
Kennedy, Flo
Lafontant-Mankarious, Jewel Stradford
Mitchell, Juanita Jackson
Motley, Constance Baker
Murray, Pauli
Norton, Eleanor Holmes
Phillips, Velvalea Rogers
Poe, L. Marian Fleming
Ray, Charlotte E.
Sampson, Edith
Stout, Juanita Kidd
Taylor, Anna Diggs
Wilson, Margaret Bush

LEGISLATORS

(see POLITICIANS AND LEGISLATORS)

LIBRARIANS, BIBLIOGRAPHERS, ARCHIVISTS

Andrews, Regina M. Anderson
Baker, Augusta Braxston
Brooks, Hallie Beachem
Delaney, Sara "Sadie" Marie Johnson
Fisher, Ruth Anna
Florence, Virginia Proctor Powell
Gleason, Eliza Atkins
Harsh, Vivian Gordon
Hutson, Jean Blackwell
Jones, Clara Stanton
Jones, Virginia Lacy
Latimer, Catherine Allen
Matthews, Miriam
Phinazee, Alethia Annette Lewis Hoage
Rollins, Charlemae Hill
Shockley, Ann Allen
Wesley, Dorothy Burnett Porter

MATHEMATICIANS

Bozeman, Sylvia Trimble
Browne, Marjorie Lee
Gilmer, Gloria
Granville, Evelyn Boyd
Hewitt, Gloria Conyers
Mahoney, Carolyn R.
Spikes, Delores Margaret Richard

MAYORS

Blackwell, Unita
Kelly, Sharon Pratt
Perry, Carrie Saxon

MISSIONARIES

Boone, Eva Roberta Coles
Delaney, Emma Bertha
Fearing, Maria
Fleming, Louise "Lulu" Cecilia
Gordon, Nora Antonia
Gorham, Sarah E.
Howard, Clara A.
Jones, Nancy
Smith, Amanda Berry
Thomas, Cora Ann Pair
Williamson, Sarah

MUSIC CRITIC

Holt, Nora Douglas

MUSICIANS

(see BLUES SINGERS AND MUSICIANS, CONCERT MUSICIANS, FOLK SINGERS AND MUSICIANS, GOSPEL SINGERS AND MUSICIANS, and JAZZ MUSICIANS)

NUNS

Beasley, Mathilda
Becroft, Anne Marie
Bowman, Sister Thea
Evans, Louise
Lange, Elizabeth Clovis

NURSES

Adams-Ender, Clara Leach
Banks, Anna De Costa
Bessent, Hattie
Bullock, Carrie E.
Carnegie, Mary Elizabeth Lancaster
Davis, Frances Elliott
Fleetwood, Sara Iredell
Franklin, Martha Minerva
Gafford, Alice Taylor
Hale, Mamie Odessa
Johnson, Hazel Winifred
Laurie, Eunice Rivers
Mahoney, Mary Eliza
Mason, (Bridget) Biddy

Osborne, Estelle Massey
Staupers, Mabel Keaton
Taylor, Susie Baker King
Thoms, Adah Belle Samuels
Wattleton, Faye

OPERA SINGERS

Addison, Adele
Anderson, Marian
Arroyo, Martina
Battle, Kathleen
Brown, Anne Wiggins
Bryant, Hazel Joan
Bumbry, Grace
Dawson, Mary Lucinda Cardwell
Dobbs, Mattiwilda
Evanti, Lillian Evans
Grist, Reri
Hendricks, Barbara
Jones, Sissieretta Joyner
Norman, Jessye
Price, Leontyne
Selika, Marie Smith

PAINTERS

Burroughs, Margaret Taylor Goss
Gafford, Alice Taylor
Jones, Lois Mailou
Pindell, Howardena
Ringgold, Faith
Thomas, Alma
Waring, Laura Wheeler

PAN-AFRICANISTS

Garvey, Amy Ashwood
Garvey, Amy Euphemia Jacques
Moore, Audley (Queen Mother)

PHOTOGRAPHER

Moutoussamy-Ashe, Jeanne

PHYSICIANS

Alexander, Virginia M.
Anderson, Caroline Virginia Still
  Wiley
Britton, Mary E.
Brown, Dorothy Lavinia
Brown, Lucy Hughes
Brown, Mary Louise
Brown, Sara Winifred
Chinn, May Edward
Cole, Rebecca J.
Crumpler, Rebecca Lee
Dickens, Helen Octavia
Edwards, Lena Frances
Ellis, Effie O'Neal
Epps, Roselyn Payne
Evans, Matilda Arabella
Ferebee, Dorothy Celeste Boulding
Ford, Justina Laurena Carter

Gilbert, Artishia Garcia
Grier, Eliza Anna
Hall, Julia R. (Jane)
Jemison, Mae C.
Johnson, Halle Tanner Dillon
Jones, Sarah Garland
Jones, Sophia Bethene
Jones, Verina Morton Harris
Kneeland, Frances M.
Lattimer, Agnes D.
Logan, Myra Adele
McCarroll, Ernest Mae
Moten, Lucy Ella
Nash, Helen E.
Petioni, Muriel Marjorie
Sanders, Maude
Steward, Susan McKinney
Temple, Ruth Janetta
Washington, Georgia E. L. Patton
Whipper, Ionia Rollin
Woodby-McKane, Alice
Young, Jean Wheeler Smith

PIANISTS

Hinderas, Natalie Leota Henderson
Marshall, Harriet Gibbs
Nickerson, Camille Lucie
Pittman, Portia Marshall Washington
Rushen, Patrice
Walker, Frances

PLAYWRIGHTS

Andrews, Regina M. Anderson
Bonner, Marita
Bryant, Hazel Joan
Burrill, Mary P.
Childress, Alice
DeVeaux, Alexis
Du Bois, Shirley Graham
Gaines-Shelton, Ruth
Grimké, Angelina Weld
Hansberry, Lorraine Vivian
Hare, Maud Cuney
Hopkins, Pauline Elizabeth
Johnson, Georgia Douglas
Kein, Sybil
Livingston, Myrtle Athleen Smith
Miller, May (Sullivan)
Rush, Gertrude E. Durden
Shange, Ntozake
Spence, Eulalie

POLITICAL SCIENTISTS

Barnett, Marguerite Ross
Prestage, Jewel Limar

POLITICIANS AND LEGISLATORS

Atkins, Hannah Diggs
Bass, Charlotta Spears

Braun, Carol Moseley
Burke, Yvonne Braithwaite
Chisholm, Shirley
Collins, Cardiss Robertson
Elliott, Daisy
Fauset, Crystal Bird
Hall, Katie Beatrice Green
Hamilton, Grace Towns
Harris, Patricia Roberts
Jordan, Barbara Charline
Kelly, Sharon Pratt
Kidd, Mae Street
Motley, Constance Baker
Norton, Eleanor Holmes
Perry, Carrie Saxon
Phillips, Velvalea Rogers
Powers, Georgia Montgomery Davis
Tucker, C. DeLores Nottage
Waters, Maxine
Welcome, Verda Freeman

POPULAR MUSIC SINGERS

Carroll, Diahann
Flack, Roberta
LaBelle, Patti
Moore, Melba
Reese, Della
Riperton, Minnie
Simone, Nina
Simpson, Valerie
Turner, Tina
Warwick, Dionne
Williams, Vanessa Lynn

PSYCHIATRIST

Young, Jean Wheeler Smith

QUILTMAKER

Powers, Harriet

RELIGIOUS LEADERS

Allen, Sarah
Beasley, Mathilda
Burroughs, Nannie Helen
Drumgold, Kate
Duncan, Sara J. Hatcher
Elaw, Zilpha
Foote, Julia A. J.
Harris, Barbara
Jackson, Rebecca Cox
Kelly, Leontine T. C.
Lee, Jarena
Mason, Lena Doolin
Murray, Pauli
Prince, Nancy Gardner
Prout, Mary Ann
Ransom, Emma S. Comer
Smith, Amanda Berry
Waddles, Charleszetta Lina Campbell
Whipper, Ionia Rollin

RHYTHM AND BLUES SINGERS

Franklin, Aretha
James, Etta
Webster, Katie

SCIENTISTS

Cobb, Jewell Plummer
Robeson, Eslanda Goode
Young, Roger Arliner

SCULPTORS

Burke, Selma Hortense
Burroughs, Margaret Taylor Goss
Catlett, Elizabeth
Chase-Riboud, Barbara
Fuller, Meta Vaux Warrick
Jackson, May Howard
Lewis, Mary Edmonia "Wildfire"
Prophet, Nancy Elizabeth
Ringgold, Faith
Saar, Betye
Savage, Augusta
Woodard, Beulah Ecton

SINGERS

(see BLUES SINGERS AND
MUSICIANS, CONCERT
SINGERS, FOLK SINGERS AND
MUSICIANS, GOSPEL SINGERS
AND MUSICIANS, JAZZ
SINGERS, OPERA SINGERS,
POPULAR MUSIC SINGERS, and
RHYTHM AND BLUES
SINGERS)

SLAVEHOLDERS

Coincoin
Hinard, Eufrosina

SLAVES, FUGITIVE

Craft, Ellen
Tubman, Harriet Ross

SLAVES WHO SUED FOR FREEDOM

Freeman, Elizabeth "Mum Bett"
Slew, Jenny

SPIES (CIVIL WAR, UNION)

Bowser, Mary Elizabeth
Tubman, Harriet Ross

TELEVISION JOURNALISTS, DIRECTORS, PRODUCERS, AND PERSONALITIES

Allen, Debbie
Quarles, Norma R.

Simpson, Carole
Winfrey, Oprah

TEMPERANCE ACTIVISTS

Anderson, Naomi Bowman Talbert
Brown, Hallie Quinn
Harper, Frances Ellen Watkins
Joseph-Gaudet, Frances
Wells-Barnett, Ida Bell

THEATRICAL DIRECTORS, PRODUCERS, AND DESIGNERS

Archer, Osceola Macarthy (Adams)
Bryant, Hazel Joan
Carroll, Vinnette
Cooke, Anne (Reid)
Dearing, Judy
Evans, Louise
Prendergast, Shirley
Stewart, Ellen
Teer, Barbara Ann

UNITED NATIONS DELEGATES

Bailey, Pearl
Sampson, Edith

VOODOO PRACTITIONER

Laveau, Marie

WOMAN SUFFRAGISTS

Anderson, Naomi Bowman Talbert
Burroughs, Nannie Helen
Coppin, Fanny Jackson
Higgins, Bertha G.
Logan, Adella Hunt
Pettey, Sarah E. C. Dudley
Rollin Sisters
Ruffin, Josephine St. Pierre
Terrell, Mary Eliza Church
Wells-Barnett, Ida Bell

WOMEN'S RIGHTS LEADERS/ ADVOCATES

Anderson, Naomi Bowman Talbert
Bethune, Mary McLeod
Burroughs, Nannie Helen
Cary, Mary Ann Shadd
Coppin, Fanny Jackson
Dunbar-Nelson, Alice Ruth Moore
Early, Sarah Jane Woodson
Gaines, Irene McCoy
Garvey, Amy Ashwood
Height, Dorothy Irene
Higgins, Bertha G.
Kennedy, Flo
Murray, Pauli
Norton, Eleanor Holmes

Patterson, Louise Thompson
Pettey, Sarah E. C. Dudley
Prince, Nancy Gardner
Ray, Henrietta Green Regulus
Ruffin, Josephine St. Pierre
Scott, Gloria Dean Randle
Stewart, Maria W.
Terrell, Mary Eliza Church
Truth, Sojourner
Wells-Barnett, Ida Bell
Williams, Fannie Barrier

WRITERS

Angelou, Maya
Bambara, Toni Cade
Bennett, Gwendolyn
Bonner, Marita
Brooks, Gwendolyn
Brown, Hallie Quinn
Brown, Linda Beatrice
Burroughs, Margaret Taylor Goss
Butler, Octavia E.
Chase-Riboud, Barbara
Childress, Alice
Cliff, Michelle
Clifton, Lucille
Cobb, Jewel Plummer
Cooper, Anna Julia Haywood
Danner, Margaret Essie
DeVeaux, Alexis
Dove, Rita
Du Bois, Shirley Graham
Dunlap, Ethel Trew
Fauset, Jessie Redmon
Gaines-Shelton, Ruth
Giovanni, Nikki
Greenfield, Eloise
Grimké, Angelina Weld
Grimké, Charlotte L. Forten
Guy, Rosa
Hamilton, Virginia Esther
Hansberry, Lorraine Vivian
Hare, Maud Cuney
Harper, Frances Ellen Watkins
Haynes, Elizabeth Ross
Holt, Nora Douglas
Hopkins, Pauline Elizabeth
Hunter, Kristin
Hurston, Zora Neale
Jacobs, Harriet Ann
Johnson, Georgia Douglas
Johnson, Kathryn Magnolia
Jones, Gayl
Jordan, June
Kein, Sybil
Kincaid, Jamaica
Larsen, Nella
Lorde, Audre
Madgett, Naomi Long
Marshall, Paule
McMillan, Terry
Meriwether, Louise

Miller, May (Sullivan)
Moody, Anne E.
Morrison, Toni
Murray, Pauli
Naylor, Gloria
Petry, Ann Lane
Polite, Carlene
Prince, Lucy Terry
Rollins, Charlemae Hill
Sanchez, Sonia
Schuyler, Philippa Duke
Shange, Ntozake
Shockley, Ann Allen

Southerland, Ellease
Spence, Eulalie
Spencer, Anne
Taylor, Mildred
Taylor, Susie Baker King
Terrell, Mary Eliza Church
Vroman, Mary Elizabeth
Walker, Alice
Walker, Margaret Abigail
Washington, Josephine Turpin
West, Dorothy
Wheatley, Phillis (Peters)
Williams, Sherley Anne

Wilson, Harriet E.
Young, Jean Wheeler Smith

Y.W.C.A. OFFICIALS/ WORKERS

Bowles, Eva del Vakia
Haynes, Elizabeth Ross
Hedgeman, Anna Arnold
Height, Dorothy Irene
Ransom, Emma S. Comer
Saddler, Juanita
Saunders, Cecelia Cabaniss
Smith, Celestine Louise

Notes on Editors and Contributors

THE EDITOR

Darlene Clark Hine is John A. Hannah Professor of American History at Michigan State University. She is the author of *Black Women in White: Racial Conflict and Cooperation in the Nursing Profession, 1890-1950; Black Victory: The Rise and Fall of the White Primary in Texas;* and *When the Truth Is Told: A History of Black Women's Culture and Community in Indiana, 1875-1950.* Her numerous articles have appeared in a wide variety of periodicals, and she is the editor of *The State of Afro-American History: Past Present, and Future,* as well as Carlson Publishing's sixteen-volume series *Black Women in United States History: From Colonial Times to the Present.*

ASSOCIATE EDITORS

Elsa Barkley Brown teaches in the Department of History and Center for Afro-american and African Studies, University of Michigan. Her articles have appeared in *Signs, SAGE, History Workshop,* and *Feminist Studies.* She has been the recipient of the 1989 Letitia Woods Brown Article Publication Prize and the University of Kentucky's first Martin Luther King, Jr., Prize for the best scholarly article in African-American history.

Rosalyn Terborg-Penn is professor of history at Morgan State University, where she is developing a Ph.D. program. She has published and lectured widely. Her books include *The Afro-American Woman: Struggles and Images* (edited with Sharon Harley) and *Women in Africa and the African Diaspora* (edited with Sharon Harley and Andrea Benton Rushing). Her essay "Discontented Black Feminists: Prelude and Postscript to the Passage of the 19th Amendment" has been widely reprinted. She is a founder and first National Director of the Association of Black Women Historians.

EDITORIAL ADVISORY BOARD

Kariamu Welsh Asante is an associate professor in the Department of African American Studies at Temple University. She is the editor of *The African Aesthetic: Keeper of the Traditions* and *African Dance: Artistry and History.* She has received several dance and choreography fellowships including the National Endowment for the Arts Choreography award, the New York State Council on the Arts Minority Choreographers fellowship. and the Creative Artists Public Service Award. She has been the recipient of two Fulbright Awards, both to Zimbabwe to work with its National Dance Company. She serves on the editorial board of the *Journal of Black Studies* and the Commonwealth of Pennsylvania State Council of the Arts dance panel.

Mary Frances Berry is the Geraldine R. Segal Professor of American Social Thought and professor of history at the University of Pennsylvania. A member of the U.S. Commission on Civil Rights (surviving an attempted firing by President Ronald Reagan), she was assistant secretary for education in the Department of Health, Education and Welfare during the Carter administration. Also a university administrator, she has served as provost of the University of Maryland, College Park, and chancellor at the University of Colorado at Boulder. She is the author of numerous articles and five books, including *Long Memory: The Black Experience in America* (with John W. Blassingame).

Elizabeth Brown-Guillory is a playwright and associate professor of English at the University of Houston, where she is director of the Houston Suitcase Theatre. She is the author of two royalty plays, *Bayou Relics* (1983) and *Snapshots of Broken Dolls* (1987), and one full-length play, *Mam Phyllis* (1990). She is the author of *Their Place on the Stage: Black Women Playwrights in America* (1988) and the editor of *Wines in the Wilderness: Plays by*

African-American Women from the Harlem Renaissance to the Present (1990).

Catherine Clinton has been visiting professor at Harvard University in the Department of Afro-American Studies since 1990. She has taught in the fields of the Civil War and Reconstruction, American women's history, and southern history. She is the author of *The Plantation Mistress: Woman's World in the Old South* (1982), *The Other Civil War: American Women in the Nineteenth Century* (1984), *Portraits of American Women* (1991), and *Divided House: Gender and the Civil War* (1992). She has also written numerous articles for scholarly journals, encyclopedias, and anthologies.

Paula Giddings is the author of *When and Where I Enter: The Impact of Black Women on Race and Sex in America* and *In Search of Sisterhood: Delta Sigma Theta and the Challenge of the Black Sorority Movement*. She has taught at Rutgers University, Spelman College, and Princeton University.

Sharon Harley is acting director and associate professor of Afro-American studies and history at the University of Maryland, College Park, where she teaches courses on Afro-American history, Black culture, women's history, and women and work. She received her Ph.D. in United States history from Howard University. She is coeditor of *The Afro-American Woman: Struggles and Images* (1978) and of *Women in Africa and the African Diaspora* (1987), to which she contributed scholarly articles. Her essay "For the Good of Family and Race: Gender, Work, and Domestic Roles in the Black Community, 1880-1930" was published in *Signs*, and "Mary Church Terrell: A Genteel Militant" appeared in *Nineteenth Century Black Leaders*.

Daphne Duval Harrison is a professor of African American studies at the University of Maryland, Baltimore County. She has served as the chair of the department for eleven years. She is the author of *Black Pearls: Blues Queens of the 1920s* and several articles on blues, jazz, and other genres of Black music. She is working on a book about Black women in African-American musical theater.

Evelyn Brooks Higginbotham is an associate professor of history at the University of Pennsylvania. Her research focuses on issues of race and gender in American society. Her articles have appeared in *Signs*, *Gender & History*, and *Journal of Religious Thought*. She is the author of *Righteous Discontent: The Women's Movement in the Black Baptist Church, 1880-1920* (1993).

Jacqueline Jones teaches American social history at Brandeis University. She is the author of *Soldiers of Light and Love* (1980), *Labor of Love, Labor of Sorrow* (1985), and *The Dispossessed* (1992). *Labor of Love, Labor of Sorrow*, a history of Black working women in America, won the Letitia Brown Memorial Publication Prize of the Association of Black Women Historians, as well as the Julia Spruill Prize of the Southern Association for Women Historians.

Wilma King teaches in the Department of History at Michigan State University. She received her Ph.D. in American history from Indiana University. She has taught courses on African-American history, African-American women, and the antebellum South. She has published articles on education and on slave women and book reviews in scholarly journals. She is at work on a monograph entitled *Africa's Progeny—America's Slaves: Children and Youth in Bondage in Nineteenth Century America*.

Nellie Y. McKay is professor of American and Afro-American literature at the University of Wisconsin-Madison. Her *Jean Toomer, Artist: A Study of His Literary Life and Work, 1894-1936* (1984) was the first full-length study of this profoundly influential artist. Her edited collection, *Critical Essays on Toni Morrison* (1987), was another first full-length text to appear on a well-known author. McKay's articles on Black women's writings have been published widely. Her works-in-progress include critical studies of twentieth-century Black women's autobiographies and the novels of Toni Morrison. She is coeditor, with Henry Louis Gates, Jr., of the forthcoming *Norton Anthology of Afro-American Literature*.

Cynthia Neverdon-Morton is professor of history at Coppin State College. She is the author of *Afro-American Women of the South and the Advancement of the Race, 1895-1925*.

Nell Irvin Painter is the Edwards Professor of American History at Princeton University. Her books include *Exodusters: Black Migration to Kansas after Reconstruction*, *The Narrative of Hosea Hudson: His Life as a Negro Communist in the South*, and *Standing at Armageddon: The United States 1877-1919*. She is completing a biography of Sojourner Truth and a study of sexuality in the nineteenth-century South.

Tiffany R. L. Patterson teaches in the Department of History at Spelman College. Her articles include "Sex and Class in Marable's Third Reconstruction," in *Socialist Visions*, edited by Steve Shalom; "Out of Egypt: A Talk with Nawal El Sadaawi," in *Freedomways*; and "Louise Venable Kennedy: African-American Southern Historian," in *Historians of the American South*, edited by Rameth R. Owens and William F. Steirer.

Kathy A. Perkins is an Assistant Professor of Theatre at the University of Illinois, Urbana-Champaign, where she heads the lighting design program. She has designed over two hundred productions throughout the United States and in Europe. She is a graduate of Howard University (B.F.A.) and the University of Michigan (M.F.A.). She is the editor of *Black Female Playwrights: An Anthology of Plays Before 1950*.

Linda Reed (Ph.D. Indiana University, 1986) is an associate professor of history at the University of Houston, where she also is director of the African-American Studies Program. Her book *Simple Decency and Common Sense: The Southern Conference Movement, 1938-1963* (1991) details southerners' pre-1950s struggles in civil rights campaigns. She is working on a biography of Mississippi civil rights activist Fannie Lou Hamer and was awarded a Ford Foundation fellowship (1991-92) to pursue that work.

Gwendolyn Keita Robinson is executive director of the DuSable Museum of African American History in Chicago. She received Bachelor's and Master's degrees from Roosevelt University and a Ph.D. degree in American history from the University of Illinois at Chicago. Robinson previously was curator and historian in the Department of Social and Cultural History, director of the Program in African-American Culture, and codirector of the Duke Ellington Collection at the Smithsonian Institution's National Museum of American History. Her numerous honors and awards include postdoctoral fellowships from the Ford and Rockefeller foundations and grants from the National Endowment for the Humanities.

Jacqueline A. Rouse is an associate professor of history at Georgia State University. She has served as Landmarks Professor of African American History at American University and the Smithsonian Institution, associate professor of history at Morehouse College, and assistant editor of the *Journal of Negro History*. Rouse is the author of *Lugenia Burns Hope: Black Southern Reformer*, winner of the Letitia Woods Brown Memorial Publication Prize, 1989. She is coeditor of *Women in the Civil Rights Movement: Trailblazers and Torchbearers, 1941-1965* (1990). She is at work on biographies of Margaret Murray Washington, educator, clubwoman, and activist, and Della Raney, officer, nurse, and pilot in the Army Air Force Nursing Corps during World War II.

Stephanie J. Shaw is an assistant professor in the Department of History and the Center for Women's Studies at Ohio State University. Her research and teaching focus on the experiences of Black women in the United States.

Janet Sims-Wood is assistant chief librarian for reference/reader services at the Moorland-Spingarn Research Center. Her bibliographic research in African-American women's history has resulted in six book-length bibliographies, newspaper articles, chapters in books, and journal articles, as well as several slide presentations. She is a founding associate editor of *SAGE* and the founder of Afro Resources, Inc., the publisher of the *1993 World War II Black WAC Calendar*. A doctoral candidate in women's studies at the Union Institute Graduate School, Sims-Wood received a 1993 dissertation fellowship from the National Endowment for the Humanities to complete an oral history of World War II Black WACs.

Deborah Gray White is associate professor of history and Africana studies at Rutgers University and is the author of the award-winning book *Ar'n't I a Woman? Female Slaves in the Plantation South*. Her forthcoming book is entitled *Too Heavy a Load: Race, Class and Gender in Black Women's Associational Activity, 1896-1980*.

Lillian S. Williams is assistant professor of history, Department of Women's Studies, at the University of Albany. Her publications on African-American and women's history have appeared in the *Journal of Negro Education* and *Afro-Americans in New York Life and History*, as well as in several anthologies. She is completing work on manuscripts on Buffalo, New York's African-American community and on social activist Mary Burnett Talbert. She is an associate editor of *Afro-Americans in New York Life and History* and *Black Women in United States History*. The Research Foundation of the State University of New York has awarded her grants to prepare a research guide to Black women's clubs in the state.

CONTRIBUTORS

Jane D. Adair is a research consultant for Costa Research and Management. She is a specialist in the sociocultural area of sports studies and has taught courses on women and sports, sport sociology and psychology, sport management, and sport law.

Delores P. Aldridge, Ph.D., is Grace Towns Hamilton Professor of Sociology and African American Studies at Emory University, where she founded and directs African American and African studies. She was the first two-term elected president of the National Council for Black Studies. She is the author of more than 80 scholarly publications, including *Handbook on Black Studies: Development and Significance*, coedited with Carlene Young.

Adele Logan Alexander teaches African-American and women's history at Howard University and the University of Maryland, College Park. She is a Ph.D. candidate in history at Howard University. She is the author of *Ambiguous Lives: Free Women of Color in Rural Georgia, 1789-1879* (1991) and her articles have appeared in *Ms.*, the *Washington Post*, and *Crisis*.

Lynda Allanach is a graduate of the University of Texas at San Antonio, where she wrote the prize-winning senior thesis "Women and Democracy: The Struggle for Bread and Roses." She earned an M.A. degree in urban planning at Trinity University and has worked as a planner for the U.S. Air Force.

Karen Anderson is a historian teaching in the Department of Women's Studies at the University of Arizona.

Bettina Aptheker is an associate professor of history in the Women's Studies Program at the University of California at Santa Cruz. Her publications include *Woman's Legacy: Essays on Race, Sex, and Class in American History*.

Felix Armfield is in the Ph.D. program in American history at Michigan State University. He is working on a dissertation, "Eugene Kinckle Jones and the Rise of Professional Black Social Workers."

Thea Arnold is a Ph.D. candidate at the State University of New York at Binghamton. Her research deals with gender and interracial relations within the national headquarters of the NAACP in New York City. Her dissertation is "The Politics of Race: Mary White Ovington and the NAACP, 1909-1950."

Elizabeth Fortson Arroyo is a doctoral candidate at Columbia University, concentrating on the Civil War and the history of the South. She graduated from Harvard and Radcliffe colleges, where she was both a Harvard College Scholar and the recipient of the Elizabeth Cady Stanton Certificate of Merit. She is a contributor to *Notable Black American Women*.

Kariamu Welsh Asante is on the Editorial Advisory Board of the *Encyclopedia*. See the beginning of this list for a biographical note.

Joyce Aschenbrenner is professor of anthropology at Southern Illinois University at Edwardsville. She has published articles and monographs on African-American culture, with emphasis on Black families, and on Katherine Dunham. She has also worked on a Census Bureau project dealing with causes of the census undercount in Black communities. She is at work on a biography of Katherine Dunham.

Ronald W. Bailey has been chairman and professor in the Department of African-American Studies and professor of history at Northeastern University since 1989. He has written widely in the field of African-American studies. His books include *Black Business Enterprise, Black People and the 1980 Census*, and *Introduction to Afro-American Studies: A People's College Primer*. His articles focus on Black studies, race relations, the U.S. South, higher education, and the civil rights movement. He is completing "Those Valuable People, the Africans," on the role of the slave trade in the development of Europe and the United States.

Barbara Bair is at the Virginia Center for the Humanities. She has taught American studies and women's studies at the

University of California at Santa Cruz and Brown University. She is a former Rockefeller humanist in residence with the Institute for Research on Women at Rutgers University and an associate of the African Studies Center at UCLA.

William C. Banfield is composer in residence and director of the Indiana University Soul Review of the Afro-American Arts Institute of Indiana University, where he is a professor of Afro-American studies and jazz. A graduate of the New England Conservatory, he holds a Master of Theology degree from Boston University and a Ph.D. degree in musical arts from the University of Michigan.

Taunya Lovell Banks is professor of law at the University of Maryland. She writes about gender issues and has done research on access to health care for people of color, especially women, recently focusing on the AIDS pandemic and reproductive freedom.

William Barlow is an associate professor in the School of Communications at Howard University. He is the author of *Looking Up at Down: The Emergence of Blues Culture* (1989) and coauthor of *Split Image: African Americans in the Mass Media* (1990).

Paula C. Barnes is an assistant professor of English at Hampton University. She is currently a visiting assistant professor of Afro-American studies and minority faculty fellow at Indiana University, where she is pursuing research on Nat Turner, neoslave narratives, and the recapturing of history in the African-American novel.

Deborah Smith Barney is a doctoral student in American studies at Michigan State University, completing a dissertation on Black gospel music disc jockeys. She is a graduate of Wayne State University (M.A.T.) and Michigan State University (B.A., TV and radio).

Gerri Bates is a member of the English faculty at Howard University. She completed Bachelor's and Master's studies at Morgan State University and doctoral studies at Indiana University of Pennsylvania. She has written articles for *MAWA Review* (forthcoming), *Dictionary of Literary Biography* (forthcoming), and *Notable Black American Women* (1992).

Gina Beavers holds degrees in American history from the University of Pittsburgh (B.A.) and the University of Massachusetts at Amherst (M.A.). Her academic work focuses on the development of Black feminist thought and Native and African-American women in the liberation struggle. She has been published in *Grio* magazine.

Sandra Behel, an adjunct instructor of history at Auburn University-Montgomery, specializes in contemporary United States history. She is also an archivist with the Alabama Department of Archives and History.

Pegge Bell is an assistant professor in the College of Nursing at the University of Arkansas for Medical Services, where she teaches maternal-infant courses, and a doctoral candidate in the School of Nursing at the University of Virginia. She is working on a study of the contributions of Black nurse-midwives in the South during the 1940s.

Patricia Bell-Scott, professor of child and family development and women's studies at the University of Georgia, is founding editor of *SAGE: A Scholarly Journal on Black Women* and coeditor

of *Double Stitch: Black Women Write about Mothers and Daughters* and *All the Women Are White, All the Blacks Are Men, But Some of Us Are Brave: Black Women's Studies* (1982). Bell-Scott is director and official biographer of the Hilda A. Davis Papers Project.

Tritobia Hayes Benjamin is assistant dean of the College of Fine Arts and director of the Gallery at Howard University and also teaches in the Department of Art. She holds a Ph.D. degree in art history from the University of Maryland. Her research focuses on African-American art and artists.

Barbara Bergeron is a free-lance editor in New York City. She received a B.A. in English from North Adams (Massachusetts) State College and an M.A. in English literature from the University of Illinois at Urbana-Champaign, where she was a University Fellow. She is cocompiler of the index to *Variety Obituaries 1905-1986* and its biannual supplements.

Joel Berkowitz is a doctoral candidate in theater at the Graduate Center of the City University of New York, where he is writing a dissertation on "Shakespeare on the American Yiddish Stage." He is assistant editor of the *Journal of American Drama and Theater*.

Deirdre Bibby is executive director of the Museum of African-American Art in Tampa, Florida, and is curatorial head of the Barnett-Aden Collection, which includes over 140 works by African-American artists from the 1800s to the present. Bibby pursues independent research on sculptors and art educators Augusta Savage and Sana Musasama.

Richard J. M. Blackett, professor of history at Indiana University, is the author of *Building an Anti-Slavery Wall: Black Americans in the Trans-Atlantic Abolitionist Movement* (1983), *Beating against the Barriers: Biographical Essays in Nineteenth Century Afro-American History* (1986), and *Thomas Morris Chester: Black Civil War Correspondent* (1989).

B. J. Bolden received a B.A. degree from Columbia College in Chicago and an M.A. degree in English from Chicago State University. She is a doctoral candidate at the University of Illinois at Urbana-Champaign, specializing in African-American literature. Her dissertation is on Gwendolyn Brooks, the poet laureate of Illinois.

A. Lynn Bolles is associate professor of women's studies and affiliate faculty in anthropology and Afro-American studies at the University of Maryland, College Park. She received an A.B. degree from Syracuse University and M.A. and Ph.D. degrees from Rutgers University. Bolles's research focuses on women in the African diaspora, particularly in the English-speaking Caribbean. Her works include *My Mother Who Fathered Me and Others: Gender and Kinship in the English-Speaking Caribbean* (1988); a coauthored volume, *In the Shadow of the Sun* (1990); and *Without Them We Wouldn't Have Survived: Women Trade Union Leaders in the Commonwealth Caribbean* (forthcoming). Bolles is an editor of *Feminist Studies*.

Florence Borders is a certified archivist at Southern University. She is a graduate of Southern University (B.A.) and Rosary College (M.A., library science). She is also founder of Chicory Society of Afro-Louisiana History and Culture and editor of the *Chicory Review*.

Horace Clarence Boyer holds M.A. and Ph.D. degrees from the University of Rochester's Eastman School of Music, and he teaches at the University of Massachusetts. He was music director for such Broadway productions as *Purlie*, *Blues for Mister Charlie*, and *Do Lord, Remember Me*. His gospel choirs have appeared with Mahalia Jackson, Dorothy Love Coates, Clara Ward, and James Cleveland. Boyer's articles on gospel music have appeared in *Black Perspective in Music*, *Black Music Research Journal*, and *Music Educators Journal*.

Anne Boylan is associate professor of history and women's studies at the University of Delaware. She received a Ph.D. degree from the University of Wisconsin. She is the author of *Sunday School: The Formation of an American Institution, 1790-1880* and is working on a history of women's organizations in New York and Boston, 1800-40.

Marilyn Dell Brady is an assistant professor of history at Virginia Wesleyan College, where she teaches African-American, women's, family, and social history of the United States. She received a Ph.D. degree from the University of Kansas. She has worked as a public historian and has published articles on women's organizations in Kansas.

Mary Brookhart is associate professor of English at North Carolina Central University. She has written about a number of contemporary authors, including Eudora Welty and Ellease Southerland. In press are "Spiritual Daughters of the Black American South," in *The Female Tradition in Southern Literature*, and "Margaret Walker," in *Southern Writers of the Second Renascence*.

Stephanie Brookins, currently a high school teacher, was a researcher for the Martin Luther King, Jr., Papers. She has done graduate work in history at Stanford University.

Albert S. Broussard is associate department head in the Department of History at Texas A&M University. He holds a Ph.D. degree from Duke University and has published extensively in African-American and United States history. His most recent book is *The New Racial Frontier: San Francisco's Black Community, 1900-1954* (forthcoming).

Angela D. Brown earned an A.B. degree in Afro-American studies at Harvard University, where her senior honors thesis was "Servants of the People: A History of Women in the Black Panther Party." She is in the Ph.D. program in history at Stanford University, studying twentieth-century U.S. social movements and African-American history.

Elsa Barkley Brown is an Associate Editor of the *Encyclopedia*. See the beginning of this list for a biographical note.

Kelly Delaine Brown is assistant professor of systematic theology at Howard University School of Divinity. She holds M.A. and Ph.D. degrees from Union Theological Seminary, and she is an ordained Episcopal priest. Her articles include "The Emergence of a Black Feminist Theology in the United States," in *We Are One Voice: Black Theology in the United States and South Africa*, and "Teaching Womanist Theology" (in press).

Wendy Brown is associate professor of law at Tulane Law School. She received a B.A. degree from Harvard University and a J.D. degree from New York University. She teaches constitutional, civil rights, and procedural law and is a board member of the National Conference of Black Lawyers.

Elizabeth Brown-Guillory is on the Editorial Advisory Board of the *Encyclopedia*. See the beginning of this list for a biographical note.

Flora R. Bryant is a visiting assistant professor of history at Elizabeth City State University. She has a Ph.D. degree in American history from the University of South Carolina and is a graduate of St. Augustine's College (B.A.) and the University of North Carolina at Greensboro (M.A.). Her research includes work on Arna Bontemps and the social activism of Pauli Murray.

Violet Harrington Bryant is associate professor of English at Dillard University. She received a B.A. degree, magna cum distinctione, from Mount Holyoke College and M.A. and Ph.D. degrees from Harvard University. Her articles have appeared in the *Mississippi Quarterly* and *SAGE*, and she is the author of *Dialogues of Race and Gender: The Myth of New Orleans in Literature* (forthcoming).

Karen Buhler-Wilkerson is associate professor of community health nursing at the University of Pennsylvania School of Nursing. She is also associate director of the Center for the Study of the History of Nursing at the University of Pennsylvania.

Lonnie Bunch, founding curator of the California Afro-American Museum in Los Angeles, is assistant director for curatorial affairs at the Smithsonian Institution's National Museum of American History. He is the author of *The Black Angelenos: The African American in Los Angeles 1850-1950* and coauthor of *Visions toward Tomorrow: The History of the East Bay Afro-American Community*.

A'Lelia Perry Bundles, author of *Madam C. J. Walker: Entrepreneur* (1991), is the great-great-granddaughter of Madam Walker. Bundles frequently lectures about Madam Walker and A'Lelia Walker and has written about them and other subjects in *Essence*, *SAGE*, *Ms.*, the *Radcliffe Quarterly*, *Parade*, and *The Encyclopedia of African American Culture and History*. Bundles graduated magna cum laude from Harvard and Radcliffe College and received an M.S.J. degree from Columbia University Graduate School of Journalism. An Emmy Award winner, she is a producer with ABC's *World News Tonight* in Washington, D.C.

Stewart Burns is a social historian and associate editor of the Martin Luther King, Jr., Papers at Stanford University, where he is also an associate fellow. He received a Ph.D. degree from the University of California at Santa Cruz and has taught history at Santa Cruz, Berkeley, and Stanford. He is the author of *Social Movements of the 1960s: Searching for Democracy*, coauthor of *A People's Charter: The Pursuit of Rights in America*, and editor of the King Papers volume on the Montgomery bus boycott.

Loretta M. Butler is associate professor, emeritus, of education at Roosevelt University. She received a Ph.D. degree from The Catholic University of America. She is a researcher associated with the office of Black Catholics in the Archdiocese of Washington, D.C.

Carolyn Calloway-Thomas is associate professor of speech communication and associate dean of the faculties at Indiana University. She is coeditor with John Lucaites of *Martin Luther King, Jr., and the Sermonic Power of Public Discourse* (1993) and is completing "What If I Am a Woman: The Rhetoric of Sisterhood and Struggle, 1830-1970." In 1990 she received a Fulbright Award to Nigeria, West Africa.

Jane Campbell is associate professor of English at Purdue University. She is the author of *Mythic Black Fiction: The*

Transformation of History (1986) as well as articles and reviews about Pauline Elizabeth Hopkins, Margaret Walker, Frances E. W. Harper, and other African-American women writers. She is editing a collection of short fiction and nonfiction by Pauline Hopkins.

Candie Carawan is coordinator of residential education at the Highlander Research and Education Center in New Market, Tennessee, where she has been involved in much of the cultural empowerment work of the school for close to thirty years. With her husband, Guy, Carawan has published books and documentary albums, including *Ain't You Got a Right to the Tree of Life? The People of Johns Island, South Carolina* (1989) and *Sing for Freedom: The Story of the Civil Rights Movement through Its Songs* (reissue 1990). They also serve as advisers to film projects, including the PBS series *Eyes on the Prize* and the documentary *We Shall Overcome.*

Clayborne Carson is professor of history at Stanford University and senior editor of the papers of Martin Luther King, Jr. His *In Struggle: SNCC and the Black Awakening of the 1960s* (1981) won the Frederick Jackson Turner Award of the Organization of American Historians. More recently, he published *Malcolm X: The FBI File.* Carson served as an adviser for the fourteen-part, award-winning PBS series *Eyes on the Prize* and is an editor of *Eyes on the Prize Civil Rights Reader* (1987).

Marva Griffin Carter is chair of the Music Department and associate professor of music at Morris Brown College in Atlanta. She received Bachelor's and Master's degrees in music performance from the Boston and New England conservatories and an M.A. (Boston University) and a Ph.D. (University of Illinois, Urbana-Champaign) in musicology. She is the author of *The Life and Music of Will Marion Cook.* The organist of the historic Ebenezer Baptist Church in Atlanta, she has lectured and written articles for scholarly publications.

Floris Barnett Cash is assistant professor and director of the Africana Studies Program at the State University of New York at Stony Brook. She has written articles on Black clubwomen, most recently, "Radicals or Realists: African American Women and the Settlement House Spirit in New York City," in *Afro-Americans in New York Life and History* (1991).

Joan E. Cashin is associate professor of history at Ohio State University. She is the author of *A Family Venture: Men and Women on the Southern Frontier* (1991) and *Our Common Affairs: Documents on the History of Southern Women* (1993), as well as articles on the history of the family.

Jean Cazort is a graduate of Fisk University (B.A.) and George Peabody College (M.A.L.S.). The former associate librarian at Fisk University, she is the coauthor of *Born to Play: The Life and Career of Hazel Harrison* (1983).

Bernadine S. Chapman holds an Ed.D. degree from Northern Illinois University and is the director of NIU's ACCESS program. In addition, she is an adjunct instructor in the Women's Studies Program. Her primary research area is the Jeanes Supervisor as an adult educator within the African diaspora.

M. Melinda Chateauvert recently completed her dissertation on women of the Brotherhood of Sleeping Car Porters at the University of Pennsylvania. She teaches African-American studies at the University of Maryland, College Park.

Catherine King Clark is director of the International Studies Program and associate professor of music at Norfolk State University. She holds a Ph.D. degree in philosophy from American University and has done postdoctoral work in world religions at Harvard University.

Elizabeth Clark-Lewis is director of the Public History Program and assistant professor in the Department of History at Howard University. She has received degrees from Howard University (B.A., M.A.) and the University of Maryland (Ph.D.). She is the author of *The Transition from Live-in to Day Work* (1985) and coauthor of *Northern Virginia Community College: An Oral History* (1987). Her women's history articles have appeared in *Women and Power in American History* (1991), edited by Kathryn Kish Sklar and Thomas Dublin; *Black Women in United States History* (1990), edited by Darlene Clark Hine; and *To Toil the Livelong Day: America's Women at Work* (1987), edited by Mary Beth Norton and Carol Groneman.

Eileen T. Cline is dean of the Conservatory, Peabody Institute of the Johns Hopkins University. She holds Bachelor's, Master's, and doctoral degrees in performance and in music education from Oberlin College, the University of Colorado, and Indiana University, respectively. She has won honors for her research and writing on performance competitions, most recently for her keynote presentation on the education of minority musicians for the 1991 Chicago Symphony Orchestra Centennial Symposium.

Catherine Clinton is on the Editorial Advisory Board of the *Encyclopedia.* See the beginning of this list for a biographical note.

W. Paul Coates is founder and director of Black Classic Press, which specializes in republishing significant works by and about people of African descent. He is also adjunct instructor of African-American studies at Sojourner-Douglass College and coeditor of *Black Bibliophiles and Collectors: Preservers of Black History.*

Bettye Collier-Thomas is associate professor of history and director of the Temple University Center for African American History and Culture. She was founding executive director of the Bethune Museum and Archives National Historic Site. Collier-Thomas is also project director for a Lilly Endowment-funded project for which she will write the first narrative history of Black church women. The author of more than twenty-five articles, Collier-Thomas is completing "The Howard Theatre and the National Black Theatre Movement" and a biography of Frances Ellen Watkins Harper.

Patricia Hill Collins is associate professor in the Departments of Sociology and African American Studies at the University of Cincinnati. Her research focuses on issues of gender, race, and ethnicity related to African-American women and families. She is the author of *Black Feminist Thought: Knowledge, Consciousness, and the Politics of Empowerment.*

Susan C. Cook is associate professor of music and women's studies at the University of Wisconsin-Madison. An expert on twentieth-century American music, she is writing on Billie Holiday for the Smithsonian Institution Press *Readers on American Music* series.

Paul P. Cooke, Columbia University Ph.D., is a retired president of the District of Columbia Teachers College and former professor of English at both DCTC and Miner Teachers College.

He also has been a visiting professorial lecturer at Howard University and Trinity College. In 1988 and 1989, Cooke served as editor-in-chief and contributing editor of the Association for the Study of Afro-American Life and History's "Black History" *KIT*. He has written more than 100 articles, reviews, papers, and monographs.

M. Shawn Copeland is assistant professor of theology and Black studies at Yale University Divinity School. Her articles have appeared in *Black Scholar*, the *Journal of Feminist Studies in Religion*, *Cross Currents*, and *Concilium*.

D. Margaret Costa is professor and director of interdisciplinary studies at California State University at Long Beach. She teaches courses on women in sports and sports history and is the author of *Comparative Sport* and *Womensports*. She is also the director of the Olympic Oral History Project sponsored by the Amateur Athletic Foundation of Los Angeles.

Emily Cousins is a senior at Harvard University, where she is writing a senior thesis on the theme of resistance in the theology of James Cone (principal founder of Black liberation theology) and the art of Faith Ringgold.

Vicki Crawford is assistant professor of Black women's studies at the University of Massachusetts at Amherst. She is a graduate of Spelman College (B.A.), the University of Georgia (M.A.), and Emory University (Ph.D.). A Fulbright Fellow, she is the coeditor of *Women in the Civil Rights Movement: Trailblazers and Torchbearers, 1941-1965* (1990). Her articles have appeared in *SAGE*. She is working on a book entitled "We Shall Not Be Moved: Black Women and the Civil Rights Movement."

Maureen Creamer earned a Bachelor's degree in English from the University of Texas at Austin (1983) and a Master's degree in English from Texas A&M University (1990). She is an editor, publicist, and copywriter for Texas A&M University Press.

Lorraine J. Crouchett received an M.A. degree in history from Holy Name College. She is the author of *Delilah Leontium Beasley: Oakland's Crusading Journalist* and *Filipinos in California: From the Days of the Galleons to the Present*.

Rebecca T. Cureau is professor of music and chair of the Department of Visual and Performing Arts at Southern University. She holds a B.A. degree from Bennett College, an MMus. degree from Northwestern University, and a D.A. degree from Atlanta University. She is the recipient of grants from the National Endowment for the Humanities and in 1992 received a National Black Music Caucus Achievement Award for contributions to Black music and research.

Nomalanga Dalili is a Ph.D. candidate in the Folklore and Folklife Program at the University of Pennsylvania. She is an instructor of English composition and literature and English as a second language, the author of the poetry volume *Ba Anx Heh*, and has been published in *Black Writers in San Diego*.

Rita Dandridge is professor of English at Norfolk State University. She is the author of *Ann Allen Shockley: An Annotated Primary and Secondary Bibliography*. Her articles on Black literature have appeared in *CLA Journal*, *MELUS*, *Journal of Negro History*, *Callaloo*, and *Richmond Quarterly*.

Willia E. Daughtry is professor of music at Hampton University. She has several works in progress, including "The Collected Sacred Works of Hiram Simmons," "Black Patti Revisited" (a biography of Sissieretta Jones), and "The Benefit Concert: An American Tradition."

Joanna Davenport is associate professor in the Health and Human Performance Department at Auburn University, where she served as women's athletic director from 1976 to 1985. A former member of the Education Council of the United States Olympic Committee (1977-85), she has been three times an American delegate to the International Olympic Academy in Olympia, Greece, and one time to the Olympic Academy in Taiwan. She is a former president of the National Association for Girls and Women in Sport.

Cyprian Davis, O.S.B., Benedictine monk, is professor of church history at St. Meinrad School of Theology. He is the author of *History of Black Catholics in the United States* (1990) and has written articles on monastic history, Black spirituality, and Black Catholic history.

Hilda A. Davis is cofounder and past president of the Association of Deans of Women and Advisors to Girls in Negro Schools. She has been an advocate of women since her early career at Howard University in the 1920s. A former dean of women and retired professor, Davis continues to take a leading role in local and national education and in women's civic organizations.

Thadious M. Davis is professor of English at Brown University. She is the author of *Faulkner's "Negro": Art and the Southern Context* and the forthcoming *The Fictions of Nella Larsen*. She has edited reference texts on African-American writers and Mark Twain, and she has written essays on race, gender, and region.

Arthur C. Dawkins is professor of music, director of Jazz Studies, and director of the Jazz Oral History Project at Howard University. Under the auspices of the United States Department of State, he toured six African countries as leader of the Howard University Jazz Sextet. He is clinician/performer with Clark Terry and a member of the Smithsonian Jazz Masterworks Orchestra. He earned a Ph.D. degree from Catholic University. He has published articles in the *Journal of Research in Music Education* and *The Black Perspective in Music*.

Nancy Dawson is a doctoral candidate in humanistic studies at the State University of New York at Albany. She is adjunct lecturer in the School of Arts and Humanities at the College of Saint Rose.

Alice A. Deck is associate professor of English and Afro-American studies and research at the University of Illinois at Urbana-Champaign. She has published articles on African and African-American women's literature and is completing a book on Black women's autobiography in Africa and the United States.

Dominique-René de Lerma is director of the Center for Black Music Research at Columbia College in Chicago and has served on the faculties of Morgan State University, the Peabody Conservatory of Music, the University of Miami, and Indiana University (where he was the founder-director of the Black Music Center). His more than 700 publications include work on Black music history, Mozart, and performance practice, most recently the multivolume *Bibliography of Black Music*.

Carolyn Denard is assistant professor of English at Georgia State University, where she teaches African-American and women's literature. She is the author of "The Convergence of Feminism and Ethnicity in the Fiction of Toni Morrison," in

1359

Critical Essays on Toni Morrison, and "Beyond the Bitterness of History: Teaching Toni Morrison's *Beloved*," in *Approaches to Teaching Toni Morrison* (forthcoming). She is working on a book entitled "Return to the Briar Patch: The Contemporary Black Writer's Search for a Usable Past" and a study of Morrison's use of myth and role-definition in her fiction.

Dorothy L. Denniston is assistant professor of English at Brown University. She is completing "Cultural Reclamation," a major study of Paule Marshall's fiction.

Tomika DePriest is working on her Master's degree in Africana women's studies at Clark Atlanta University. She graduated from Spelman College in 1989 and her articles have appeared in *Urban Profile, Upscale*, and the *Atlanta Tribune*.

Lynda F. Dickson is associate professor of sociology at the University of Colorado at Colorado Springs. She is the author of several works on the African-American women's club movement, including "African-American Women's Clubs in Denver: 1890-1925," in *Essays and Monographs in Colorado History*. She has also published in the areas of Black family studies, the feminization of poverty, and comparable worth.

Jacqueline Cogdell DjeDje is associate professor in the Department of Ethnomusicology and Systematic Musicology at the University of California at Los Angeles. She has done research on African music and African-American religious music and has written articles for professional journals. Her most recent work is *African Musicology: Current Trends*.

Jualynne E. Dodson received her Ph.D. in sociology from the University of California at Berkeley. She is an associate professor at the University of Colorado in the Department of Religious Studies and the Center Studies of Ethnicity and Race in America. She has published widely and is currently at work on a book on AME women and church power.

Jocelyn Hazelwood Donlon is a Ph.D. candidate in the Department of English at the University of Illinois, where she teaches twentieth-century African-American literature. Her dissertation is entitled "Orality and the South: The Personal Narrative in Black and White Southern Fiction."

Carolyn Dorsey is associate professor in the Department of Higher and Adult Education at the University of Missouri. She was formerly coordinator of Black studies on campus. Her research focuses on Blacks and women in higher education and current issues in higher education. She is completing a study of Olivia A. Davidson Washington.

Madhu Dubey is assistant professor of English at Northwestern University. She is the author of *Winged But Grounded: Black Nationalism and Black Women's Fiction in the 1970s* (forthcoming).

Troy Duster is director of the Institute for the Study of Social Change and a professor in the Department of Sociology at the University of California at Berkeley.

Dewitt S. Dykes, Jr., is assistant professor of history at Oakland University. President of the Michigan Black History Network, Dykes specializes in African-American history, family history, genealogy and biography, and Michigan Black history. The author of numerous biographical and historical articles, Dykes is at work on "Augusta Savage: African American Artist and Teacher" and "Black Family History: A Research Guide."

Carole M. Echols received her B.A. in political science magna cum laude from Clark Atlanta University in 1992. At Clark Atlanta, she held an undergraduate research assistantship, funded by the Social Science Research Council, under the supervision of Dr. Gretchen E. Maclachlan.

Lillie Johnson Edwards is associate professor of history and director of American studies at Drew University. She received a Ph.D. degree in history from the University of Chicago. She is the author of *Denmark Vesey: Slave Revolt Leader* (1991) and a contributor to *The Dictionary of Christianity in America* (1990) and *A Historical Dictionary of Civil Rights in the United States* (1992). She is completing a study of African-American missionaries in colonial Africa.

Gwendolyn Etter-Lewis is associate professor of English at Western Michigan University. She received two postdoctoral research grants from the Ford and Spencer foundations for her study of professional Black women's oral narratives, 1920-40. Her articles and reviews have appeared in *Women's Studies Quarterly, Discourse & Society*, and the *Oral History Review*. She is completing a book based on Black women's oral narratives, *My Soul Is My Own* (1993).

David Evans is professor of music at Memphis State University and director of the Graduate Program in Ethnomusicology. He has produced more than twenty albums of blues, gospel, and other types of folk music and is the author of *Tommy Johnson*, a biography of the blues musician, and *Big Road Blues: Tradition and Creativity in the Folk Blues*.

Ena L. Farley is chairperson of the Department of African and Afro-American Studies at the State University of New York at Brockport. She holds a Ph.D. degree from the University of Wisconsin. A recipient of both Rockefeller and Fulbright grants, her articles and reviews have appeared in *Journal of Negro History, Review of Black Political Economy, Integrated Education, Revista Interamericana, Civilizations*, and *American Historical Review*.

Ruth Feldstein is a doctoral candidate in American history at Brown University, where she teaches American women's history and American intellectual history. Her dissertation analyzes pathological models of both Black and white womanhood from 1939 to 1965 and explores the relationship between "sexual conservatism" and racial "liberalism."

Earline Rae Ferguson is a doctoral candidate in U.S. history at Indiana University. She is researching Black women's organizations during the Progressive years. Her articles on women's organizations have been published in *Indiana Magazine of History, Indiana Historical Society Publication*, and *Black Women in U.S. History*.

Karen E. Fields is professor of religion at the University of Rochester and founding director of the Frederick Douglass Institute for African and African-American Studies. With Mamie Garvin Fields, she is coauthor of *Lemon Swamp and Other Places: A Carolina Memoir* (1983), and she is the author of *Revival and Rebellion in Colonial Central Africa* (1985). She is working on "Time?" to be published in *Theory and Society*, and a new translation of Emile Durkheim's "Les formes élémentaires de la vie religieuse."

Paul Finkelman teaches in the Department of History at Virginia Polytechnic Institute and State University. He received a Ph.D. degree from the University of Chicago and was a fellow in law and humanities at Harvard Law School. He is the author of sixty books, articles, and collections, including *An Imperfect Union* (1981); *American Legal History* (1991), with Kermit Hall and William Wiecek; and *Race, Law, and American History* (1992). His *Slavery in the Courtroom* (1984) won the Joseph Andrews Award from the American Association of Law Libraries.

Vivian Njeri Fisher is the head of Special Collections at Morgan State University library. She is a candidate for an M.A. degree in African-American history at Morgan State.

Suzanne Flandreau is a librarian and archivist at the Center for Black Music Research at Columbia College in Chicago. She is a graduate of Wellesley College (B.A.), the University of Michigan (A.M.L.S), and the University of Mississippi (M.A.), where she also organized and headed the University of Mississippi Blues Archive.

Cynthia Griggs Fleming is associate professor and director of the African American Studies Program at the University of Tennessee. A graduate of Duke University (M.A., Ph.D.), she taught previously at Morehouse College. Her articles have appeared in the *Journal of Negro History*, *Phylon*, and the *Tennessee Historical Quaterly*.

Sheila Y. Flemming is associate professor of history at Bethune-Cookman College. She coauthored a state report, *The Status of Education of Blacks in Florida, 1974-1985*, and is writing the history of Bethune-Cookman College and compiling the speeches and writings of Mary McLeod Bethune.

Michael Flug is archivist for the Vivian G. Harsh Research Collection of Afro-American History and Literature, Chicago Public Library. He served as archivist for the Raya Dunayevskaya Collection at the Archives of Labor and Urban Affairs, Wayne State University. He is a graduate of Columbia University (B.A.) and Wayne State University (M.S.L.S.). During the 1960s, he was a field secretary for the Congress of Racial Equality.

Yvonne Fonteneau, Ph.D., is assistant professor of English at the University of Oklahoma, where she teaches modern British and African literature. Her publications have appeared in *College Literature* and *World Literature Today*. Her poetry appears in various multicultural and women's journals.

Frances Smith Foster is professor of literature at the University of California at San Diego. She is the author of *Witnessing Slavery: The Development of Antebellum Slave Narratives* (1979) and *A Brighter Coming Day: A Frances Ellen Watkins Harper Reader* (1990). She is completing a book about African-American women writers from 1746 to 1890.

Noralee Frankel is assistant director on women and minorities of the American Historical Association. She holds a B.A. degree from the State University of New York at Albany and M.A. and Ph.D. degrees from George Washington University. She is the editor of *AHA Directory on Women Historians* and coeditor, with Nancy S. Dye, of *Gender, Class, Race, and Reform in the Progressive Era* (1991).

V. P. Franklin is professor of history in the Department of History and Politics at Drexel University. He is coeditor of *New Perspectives on Black Educational History* (1978) and the author of *The Education of Black Philadelphia* (1979) and *Black Self-Determination: A Cultural History of African-American Resistance* (1992). He is at work on a book on the history of the African-

American intelligentsia and on the history of civil rights in Philadelphia.

Algeania Freeman, Ph.D., is assistant vice president for academic planning and program development at Morgan State University and the former dean of the School of Public and Allied Health at East Tennessee State University. She served on the congressionally mandated National Academy of Science Institute of Medicine Study Committee on Allied Health and as president of the National Society of Allied Health.

Elizabeth Hadley Freydberg is assistant professor of African American studies and an adjunct professor in the Department of Theater at Northeastern University. She received a Ph.D. degree in theater and drama from Indiana University. She has taught as a Fulbright Lecturer at Kenyatta University, 1989-90, and the Goethe Institute in Nairobi, Kenya. Her publications include articles on Black theater, film, and feminism, and she is working on a biobibliography on Ethel Waters and a screenplay on Bessie Coleman.

Jan Furman is assistant professor of English at the University of Michigan at Flint. She specializes in American literature, with a particular interest in nineteenth-century slave narrative and twentieth-century neoslave narrative. Her essays include "The Slave Narrative: Prototype of the Early Afro-American Novel" in Darwin Turner's *The Art of Slave Narrative*; "Gwendolyn Brooks: The 'Unconditioned' Poet," in *College Language Association Journal*; and "James Weldon Johnson," in *Dictionary of Biography and Criticism*.

Brenda Galloway-Wright is an assistant archivist in the Urban Archives, Paley Library, at Temple University. She received a B.A. degree in history from Colgate University and earned an M.A. degree in history from Temple University.

Vannessa Gamble is an assistant professor in the Department of History of Medicine, Preventive Medicine and Family Medicine and Practice at the School of Medicine of the University of Wisconsin-Madison. She is a graduate of Hampshire College (B.A.), and earned both M.D. and Ph.D. degrees at the University of Pennsylvania. She did postgraduate work at the University of Massachusetts Medical Center. She is completing a manuscript on the Black hospital movement.

Bettye J. Gardner is professor of history at Coppin State College. She is the author of articles and book reviews and has presented twenty-five lectures at professional meetings and conferences. Gardner has been the recipient of a Moton Fellowship, an NEH Fellowship for College Teachers, and a Smithsonian Fellowship.

Phyl Garland is a professor at Columbia University's Graduate School of Journalism and a contributing editor to *Stereo Review*. Previously she served as New York editor of *Ebony* magazine. She has written about Black culture and especially Black music for more than twenty-five years and is author of *Sound of Soul*. In 1992 she received the Distinguished Achievement Award of the Fine Arts Center at the University of Massachusetts at Amherst. She is at work on a biography of Nat "King" Cole with the artist's son.

David J. Garrow, Ph.D., is a fellow of the Twentieth Century Fund. He is the author of *Bearing the Cross: Martin Luther King, Jr., and the Southern Christian Leadership Conference* (1986), which won the 1987 Pulitzer Prize in biography, *The FBI and Martin*

Luther King, Jr. (1981), and *Protest at Selma* (1978). Garrow was a senior adviser to the PBS series *Eyes on the Prize*, and is completing a comprehensive history of the reproductive rights struggle entitled *Liberty and Sexuality: Privacy, Abortion and American Law* (1993).

Henry Louis Gates, Jr., is chairman of the Afro-American Studies Department, the W.E.B. Du Bois Professor of Humanities, and director of the W.E.B. Du Bois Institute at Harvard University. He received his B.A. from Yale University and his M.A. and Ph.D. from Clare College, Cambridge, England. He previously served as associate professor of English and Afro-American studies at Yale; professor of English, comparative literature, and Africana studies at Cornell; and the John Spencer Bassett Professor of English, Duke University. He is the author of *Figures in Black: Words, Signs, and the Racial Self* and *The Signifying Monkey: Towards a Theory of Afro-American Literary Criticism*; the editor of *Our Nig* by Harriet E. Wilson and *The Classic Slave Narratives*; and series editor of *The Schomburg Library of Nineteenth-Century Black Women Writers*.

Willard B. Gatewood is the Alumni Distinguished Professor of History at the University of Arkansas. A graduate of Duke University (B.A., M.A., Ph.D.), he has served on the editorial boards of the *Georgia Review*, the *Journal of Negro History*, and the *Ozark Review*. He is the author of *Aristocrats of Color: The Black Elite* (1990), *Free Man of Color* (1982), *Governors of Arkansas* (1981), and *Slave and Freeman* (1979), as well as more than seventy articles.

Judith George is a professor in the Health, Physical Education, and Recreation Department at DePauw University. She is a graduate of Miami University (B.S.) and Indiana University (M.S., Dir. in P.E.). She has written articles on sport methodology, coaching, women's sport history, and feminist writings.

Luvenia A. George is a music educator and pioneer in the development of materials and methodology for the incorporation of ethnomusicology in music education curricula. She is the author of *Teaching the Music of Six Different Cultures* (1987). She is chairperson of the Music Department of Woodrow Wilson High School in Washington, D.C., and past president of the District of Columbia Music Educators Association and the American Choral Directors Association. George is doing research on the music of Eubie Blake and Duke Ellington.

Paula Giddings is on the Editorial Advisory Board of the *Encyclopedia*. See the beginning of this list for a biographical note.

Cheryl Townsend Gilkes is John D. and Catherine T. MacArthur Associate Professor of Sociology and African American Studies at Colby College. An ordained Baptist minister, she is also an associate minister at the Union Baptist Church in Cambridge, Massachusetts. She is a graduate of Northeastern University (B.A., M.A., Ph.D.). Her articles on African-American women and social change and on the Sanctified Church have appeared in *Signs*, *Journal of Social Issues*, *Journal of Religious Thought*, and *Journal of Feminist Studies in Religion*.

Glenda E. Gill is associate professor of drama at Michigan Technological University. She is a graduate of the Alabama A&M University (B.S.), the University of Wisconsin (M.A.), and the University of Iowa (Ph.D.). She is the author of *White*

Grease Paint on Black Performers: A Study of the Federal Theatre, 1935-1939 (1988) and is completing a biography of Ethel Waters.

Glenda Elizabeth Gilmore is assistant professor of history at Queens College in Charlotte, North Carolina. She is a graduate of Wake Forest University (B.A.) and the University of North Carolina at Chapel Hill (Ph.D). She is the author of "Gender and Jim Crow: Sarah Dudley Petty's Vision of the New South," in *North Carolina Historical Review* (1991), which received the Letitia Woods Brown Memorial Article Prize of the Association of Black Women Historians.

Jan Gleiter is a professional writer. Her credits in educational publishing include authorship of programs in literature, research, reading, and the social sciences. She has also written juvenile biographies of Matthew Henson, Diego Rivera, Jane Addams, and many others. Outside the educational field, her work has appeared in such magazines as *Ellery Queen*. She is president of Sense and Nonsense, a midwestern educational development house.

John L. Godwin teaches history at the University of South Carolina. He received a B.A. degree from the University of North Carolina, an M.A. degree from the University of South Carolina, and is writing a dissertation on race relations and civil rights.

Jacqueline Goggin is the managing editor of the *Harvard Guide to African-American History* at Harvard University. She received a B.A. degree from Cleveland State University and holds M.A. and Ph.D. degrees in history from the University of Rochester. The recipient of numerous awards, fellowships, and grants, including grants to edit the J. Franklin Jameson papers at the Library of Congress, Goggin is the author of *In Pursuit of Truth: Carter G. Woodson and the Movement to Promote Black History* (1992).

Kenneth W. Goings is professor of history at Florida Atlantic University. He earned a Ph.D. degree from Princeton University and is the author of *The NAACP Comes of Age: The Defeat of Judge John J. Parker* (1990). He is working on a manuscript entitled "Aunt Jemina and Uncle Mose: Black Collectibles as American Icons of Racial and Gender Stereotypes."

David A. Goldfarb studies problems of marginalization and its literary resolutions in the Ph.D. program in comparative literature at the Graduate Center of the City University of New York. He received a B.A. degree from Cornell University, magna cum laude in philosophy, and an M.A. degree in Slavic from the University of Toronto. He has received Deep Springs, Truman, and Telluride scholarships as well as a Kosciuszko Foundation grant for research in Poland during 1989.

N. H Goodall is a part-time undergraduate student at the University of Michigan, Ann Arbor. She is a 1992 Association for the Study of Afro-American Life and History Sadie Iola Daniel Scholar.

Virginia Gould is associate director of the Institute for Women's Studies at Emory University. She holds a B.S. degree from the University of Alabama and M.A. and Ph.D. degrees from Emory. She is the author of the forthcoming "Urban Slavery—Urban Freedom: The Manumission of Jacqueline Lemelle," in *Black Women in Slavery and Freedom in the Americas*, and "The Papers and Diary of Ann and Katherine Johnson," in *Southern Women's Diaries*.

Mildred Denby Green is professor of music at LeMoyne-Owen College. She received a B.S. degree in education from Ohio State University and Master's and doctoral degrees in music education from the University of Oklahoma. She is the author of *Black Women Composers: A Genesis*. She has won several awards for excellence in teaching, including the United Negro College Fund Distinguished Faculty Scholar Award and the Sears-Roebuck Foundation Distinguished Teacher Award.

Valerie Grim is an assistant professor in the Department of African American Studies at Indiana University. She is a graduate of Tougaloo College (B.A.) and Iowa State University (M.A., Ph.D.). Her areas of expertise are agricultural history and rural studies.

Sister Mary Gschwind, FSPA, has taught at all academic levels. She also has been a high school and college administrator, as well as a diocesan superintendent of schools. She serves on the leadership team of her congregation as a vice president. She holds degrees from Viterbo College, Catholic University, and Michigan State University.

Betty K. Gubert, head of the General Research and Reference Division of the Schomburg Center for Research in Black Culture, The New York Public Library, for twenty-one years, is retired. She is editor of *Early Black Bibliographies, 1863-1918* (1982), as well as numerous articles. She is art editor for *MultiCultural Review* and is compiling an annotated bibliography on Blacks in aviation.

Arthur C. Gunn is chief librarian at Atlanta University and previously served as chief librarian at Hunter College. He is a graduate of Wilberforce University (B.S.), Atlanta University (M.S.L.S.), and the University of Pittsburgh (Ph.D.). His articles and reviews have appeared in *American Libraries*, *The Encyclopedia of Library History*, and *Black Women in United States History*.

Beverly Guy-Sheftall is Anna J. Cooper Professor of Women's Studies and director of the Women's Research & Resource Center at Spelman College. She is founding coeditor of *SAGE: A Scholarly Journal on Black Women*; coeditor of *Sturdy Black Bridges: Visions of Black Women in Literature* (1979) and *Double Stitch: Black Women Write about Mothers and Daughters* (1991); and the author of *Daughters of Sorrow: Attitudes toward Black Women, 1880-1920* (1990).

Jacquelyn Dowd Hall is Julia Cherry Spruill Professor of History and director of the Southern Oral History Program at the University of North Carolina. She also is academic director of the Duke-UNC Center for Research on Women. She received a Ph.D. degree from Columbia University. She is the author of *Revolt against Chivalry: Jessie Daniel Ames and the Women's Campaign against Lynching* (1979) and one of five authors of *Like a Family: The Making of a Southern Cotton Mill World* (1987).

Debra Newman Ham, specialist in Afro-American history and culture at the Library of Congress, is the author of *Black History: A Guide to Civilian Records in the National Archives* (1984), "Jesus and Justice: Nannie Helen Burroughs and the Struggle for Civil Rights" (1988), "The Propaganda and the Truth: Black Women and World War II" (1986), and "Black Women Workers in the Twentieth Century" (1986).

Evelynn M. Hammonds is assistant professor of the history of science in the Program in Science, Technology and Society at the Massachusetts Institute of Technology. She studied physics at Spelman College and M.I.T. and received a Ph.D. degree in the history of science from Harvard University. Her articles and reviews on Black women in science, medicine, and health care have appeared in *Science*, *Women's Review of Books*, and *Radical America*.

D. Antoinette Handy is director of the Music Program at the National Endowment for the Arts. A flutist who performs in symphony and chamber orchestras, she also organized, managed, and played with the Trio Pro Viva, a chamber group specializing in the music of Black composers. She received her training at the New England Conservatory, Northwestern University, and the Paris National Conservatory and has taught at schools around the country. She is the author of *Black Women in American Bands and Orchestras* and *The International Sweethearts of Rhythm*, and is coauthor of *On the Podium: Black Conductors* (forthcoming).

Sharon Harley is on the Editorial Advisory Board of the *Encyclopedia*. See the beginning of this list for a biographical note.

Violet J. Harris is an associate professor of education at the University of Illinois at Urbana-Champaign. She is a graduate of Oberlin College (A.B.), Atlanta University (M.Ed.), and the University of Georgia (Ph.D.). Her research interests are literacy materials created for African-American youth prior to 1950, African-American children's literature, and the historical development of literacy among African-Americans. Her articles and reviews have appeared in the *Journal of Negro Education*, *Children's Literature Association Quarterly*, and *The Lion and the Unicorn*. She is the editor of *Teaching Multicultural Literature in Grades K-8* (1992).

Alferdteen B. Harrison is professor of history at Jackson State University and director of the Margaret Walker Alexander National Research Center for the Study of the Twentieth-Century African American, which focuses on documentation through oral and archival sources. She spent a year with the National Endowment for the Humanities Outreach Office in Washington, D.C., where she furthered her research on documenting the African-American experience in the twentieth century through oral history, archival sources, material culture, and the built environment.

Daphne Duval Harrison is on the Editorial Advisory Board of the *Encyclopedia*. See the beginning of this list for a biographical note.

Jamie Hart is in the doctoral program in American history at the University of Michigan, Ann Arbor. She is an Association for the Study of Afro-American Life and History Lorenzo J. Greene Scholar.

Lynda Roscoe Hartigan is associate curator of the Painting and Sculpture Division of the National Museum of American Art in Washington, D.C. She is a graduate of Bucknell University (B.A.) and George Washington University (M.A). Her research specialties are post-1920 American sculpture, American folk art, and African-American art. In addition to writing articles, she has managed major exhibits, taught seminars on art history, and lectured around the country.

Robert C. Hayden, president of the Boston branch and a member of the National Executive Committee of the Association for the Study of Afro-American Life and History, lectures on African-American studies at Northeastern University, Boston

College, and, as an adjunct faculty member, at Curry College. He is a graduate of Boston University (B.A., M.A.), Harvard University's Graduate School of Education, and M.I.T.'s Department of Urban Studies and Planning. Hayden is the author of *Black in America: Episodes in U.S. History* (1969), *A Guide to the TV Series Eyes on the Prize: America's Civil Rights Years 1954 to 1965* (1986), *Nine Black American Inventors* (1992), and books on Boston African-American history.

Anthony Heilbut received a Ph.D. degree from Harvard University. He is the author of *The Gospel Sound: Good News and Bad Times, Exiled in Paradise: German Refugee Artists and Intellectuals in America from the 1930s to the Present*, and a forthcoming biography of Thomas Mann. His articles and reviews have appeared in the *Village Voice*, the *Nation*, and *The New York Times Book Review*. He has also produced many albums of gospel music, for which he has won a Grammy Award and a Grand Prix du Disque. His recordings have been included on the soundtracks of the movies *Fried Green Tomatoes* and *Mississippi Masala*.

Lois Rita Helmbold is coordinator of the Women's Studies Program at San Jose State University. She received a Ph.D. degree in American history from Stanford University. Her articles have appeared in *Reviews in American History, Radical America, Labor History, Feminist Studies, Frontiers, Off Our Backs, Sojourner, Women's Review of Books*, and *Women's Studies*. Hembold wrote the historical introduction to *A Lesbian Photo Album* by Cathy Cade. She is now completing "Making Choices, Making Do: Survival Strategies of Black and White Working-Class Women during the Great Depression."

Australia Tarver Henderson is professor of humanities at GMI Engineering and Management Institute in Flint, Michigan. She received a B.A. degree from Fisk University, an M.A. degree from Ohio University, and a Ph.D. degree from the University of Iowa. She has taught English and cross-cultural humanities at Florida A&M and the University of Iowa. She is working on a study of Black southern novelists.

Wanda Hendricks is assistant professor of history at the University of North Carolina at Charlotte. She is a graduate of Limestone College (B.A.), Wake Forest University (M.A.), and Purdue University (Ph.D.). She is a contributor to *A Historical Dictionary of Civil Rights in the United States* and *African American Women in the United States 1619 to the Present* (both forthcoming).

Heidi Hess is a student at Stanford University and a researcher for the Martin Luther King, Jr., Papers Project.

Evelyn Brooks Higginbotham is on the Editorial Advisory Board of the *Encyclopedia*. See the beginning of this list for a biographical note.

Lisa Beth Hill is a doctoral candidate at Emory University, writing a dissertation on "African American Womanism and Social Activism: Building Institutions of Political, Economic, and Community Reform." She is a contributor to *Notable Black American Women* and *African American Women in the United States: A Biographical Directory*.

Darlene Clark Hine is the Editor of the *Encyclopedia*. See the beginning of this list for a biographical note.

William C. Hine is professor of history at South Carolina State University. His essays have appeared in the *Journal of Southern History, Labor History, Agricultural History*, and *American Visions*.

Donna Hollie, an administrator with the Baltimore City Department of Social Services, received an M.A. degree in history from Morgan State University. She has been the recipient of the Alberta Green Memorial Scholarship, the Druscilla Dunjee Houston Memorial Scholarship, and the Morris Goldseker Fellowship.

Margaret Homans is professor of English at Yale University. She is the author of *Women Writers and Poetic Identity* (1980) and *Bearing the Word: Language and Female Experience in Nineteenth-Century Women's Writing* (1986) and essays on Gloria Naylor, Toni Morrison, Audre Lorde, and Alice Walker.

James O. Horton is professor of history at George Washington University and director of the Afro-American Communities Project at the National Museum of American History of the Smithsonian Institution. A former Fulbright senior professor and historical adviser to the ABC News series *Our World*, he is the author of *Free People of Color: Interior Issues in African American Community* (1992).

Eleanor Hinton Hoytt, a consultant, lecturer, and fund-raiser for women and minority organizations, has been with the National Council of Negro Women since 1990, first as program and management consultant and currently as national program director and management adviser to Dr. Dorothy Height. She has worked in higher education, consulted on teacher training, researched the organizational history of Black women, and lectured on educational equity and health promotion issues for minorities and women. She is the founding chair of the board of directors of the National Black Women's Health Project and has served in various board and advisory capacities in women's associations.

Michael Hucles is assistant professor of history at Old Dominion University. He earned a Ph.D. degree from Purdue University. He has contributed articles to the *Dictionary of Virginia Biography*, has coauthored (with Philip Morgan and Sarah Hughes) "*Don't Grieve After Me": The Black Experience in Virginia, 1619-1986* (1986), and is the author of "Many Voices, Similar Concerns: Traditional Methods of African-American Political Activity in Norfolk, Virginia, 1865-1875," in *Virginia Magazine of History and Biography* (1992).

Lynn Hudson is a lecturer in the Department of Afro-American Studies at Indiana University, where she is also a doctoral student in the History Department. She holds degrees from the University of California at Santa Cruz (B.A.) and the University of North Carolina (M.A.).

Gloria T. Hull is professor of women's studies at the University of California at Santa Cruz. She is a graduate of Southern University (B.A.) and Purdue University (M.A., Ph.D.). She was coeditor, with Patricia Bell-Scott and Barbara Smith, of *All the Women Are White, All the Men Are Black, But Some of Us Are Brave: Black Women's Studies* (1982) and editor of two collections of Alice Dunbar-Nelson's writings. She is the author of *Color, Sex, and Poetry: Three Women Writers of the Harlem Renaissance* (1987) and *Healing Heart: Poems 1973-1988* (1989). In addition, her essays have appeared in *Sturdy Black Bridges: Visions of Black Women in Literature* (1979) and *Home Girls: A Black Feminist Anthology* (1983).

Joan Hult is professor of physical education at the University of Maryland, College Park. She has written articles on women in sports, organized sports, and Olympic sports and is coauthor of *A Century of Women's Basketball from Frailty to Final Four* (1991).

Jean McMahon Humez is associate professor of women's studies at the University of Massachusetts at Boston. She is author of *Gifts of Power: The Writings of Rebecca Jackson, Black Visionary, Shaker Eldress* (1981), *Mother's First-Born Daughters: Early Shaker Writings on Women and Religion* (forthcoming), and articles on American women's spiritual and secular autobiographies and oral-historical life stories.

Marion Hunt is assistant director of the Program for the Humanities in Medicine at Washington University School of Medicine. She has written articles on women physicians and women hospital managers in St. Louis. She holds an undergraduate degree from Harvard and an M.S.W. degree from Washington University, where she is completing a doctoral dissertation entitled "From Childsaving to Pediatrics: A Case Study of Women's Roles at St. Louis Children's Hospital 1879-1924."

Tera Hunter is assistant professor of history at the University of North Carolina. She received a B.A. degree from Duke University and a Ph.D. degree from Yale University. She is finishing a manuscript, "Contesting the New South: The Politics and Culture of Wage Household Labor in Atlanta, 1861 to 1920."

Louise Daniel Hutchinson was director of research, Anacostia Museum, Smithsonian Institution, from 1974 to 1987. While at the Smithsonian, she curated a number of major exhibits, including "The Frederick Douglass Years," "Mary McLeod Bethune and Roosevelt's *Black Cabinet*," and "Anna J. Cooper: A Voice from the South." She is the author of *The Anacostia Story 1608-1930* (1977), *Out of Africa: From West Africa Kingdoms to Colonization* (1979), and *Anna J. Cooper: A Voice from the South* (1981).

Jean Blackwell Hutson was curator and later chief of the Schomburg Center for Research in Black Culture from 1948 to 1980. During her tenure, the Center was expanded from a reading room on the top floor of the Countee Cullen Branch Library to a major research center.

Adrienne Israel is associate professor of history and intercultural studies and coordinator of the African American Studies Concentration at Guilford College. Her publications include "The Afrocentric Perspective in African Journalism: A Case Study of the Ashanti Pioneer 1939-1957" in the *Journal of Black Studies* (March 1992), as well as writings in the *Journal of Modern African Studies* and *Essence*.

Bobi Jackson is an affiliate scholar at the Center for the Study of Women at the University of California at Los Angeles. She is the author of *Biddy Mason: Pioneer, 1818-1891* and is doing research on Black Angelenos from 1850 to 1900.

Jerma Jackson is a McKnight Fellow at Florida International University. She is working on a dissertation in the Department of History at Rutgers University in which she explores the careers and music of two African-American musicians: Sister Rosetta Tharpe and Thomas A. Dorsey.

Joyce Marie Jackson is an assistant professor in the Department of Geography and Anthropology at Louisiana State University. She earned degrees in vocal performance at LSU (B.M., M.M.)

and in folklore-ethnomusicology at Indiana University (Ph.D.). Her major research areas are African-American and West Indian music and culture. She has been a National Endowment for the Arts Fellow and a Rockefeller Foundation Post-Doctoral Fellow. In addition, she is the author/project director of a forthcoming book and LP recording on the African-American sacred a cappella quartet tradition.

Reuben Jackson is an archivist with the Smithsonian Institution's Duke Ellington Collection. He is also a music critic and contributes regularly to the *Washington Post, Washington City Paper,* and *Jazz Times Magazine.* Jackson's first book of poems, *Fingering the Keys,* won the 1992 Columbia Book Award.

Irene Jackson-Brown earned a Ph.D. degree in ethnomusicology from Wesleyan University. She has been on the faculties of Yale University and Howard University, among others. She is editor of *Afro-American Gospel Music* (1978), *More Than Drumming* (1982), and *More Than Dancing* (1982) and general editor of *Lift Every Voice and Sing* (1981). From 1990 to 1992, she was a research fellow at Yale University's Institute for Sacred Music, Worship and the Arts.

Sylvia M. Jacobs is professor of history at North Carolina Central University. She is the author of *The African Nexus: Black American Perspectives on the European Partitioning of Africa, 1880-1920* and the editor of *Black Americans and the Missionary Movement in Africa.* In addition, she is completing "Here Am I, Send Me: African American Missionaries in Africa, 1820-1980" and "Yours for Africa: Letters from African American Missionaries in Africa."

Annetta Jefferson is professor of theater at the College of Wooster. She holds a certificate from New York's Dramatic Workshop, as well as a B.A. degree from Paul Quinn College and an M.A. degree from Western Reserve University. She has been writer, producer, and host/narrator of several public television series, including *Blackpeoplehood, Brother Man,* and *The History of Black Americans.* She is completing *In Darkness with God: The Life of Joseph Gomez, Bishop of the African Methodist Episcopal Church* and *A-Inchin', A-Shufflin', and A-rriving: The History and Literature of Blacks in American Theatre,* funded by a Luce Grant for Distinguished Scholars.

Betty L. Jenkins is an associate professor at the Morris Raphael Cohen Library, Reference Division, at the City College of New York. She is a graduate of Barnard College (B.A.), Columbia University (M.S., Advanced Certificate), and New York University (M.A.). She is coauthor of "Aiming to Publish Books within the Purchasing Power of a Poor People: Black Owned Book Publishing within the United States 1817-1987" and *Black Separatism: A Bibliography* (1976).

Earnestine Jenkins is a Ph.D. candidate in African history at Michigan State University. She is a graduate of Spelman College (B.A.) and Memphis State University (M.A.). As a graduate assistant in the Art History Department, she conducted a search for collections of Ethiopian art in the United States and abroad, which will be used as the database for an exhibit on Ethiopian art at Michigan State in 1994. She was also a research assistant on *Black Women in United States History,* edited by Darlene Clark Hine.

Suzan E. Jenkins is executive director of the Rhythm and Blues Foundation. She has presided over the foundation's grants through its Pioneer Awards Program and has developed the organization's first quarterly, *Rhythm and Blues News,* and its

Oral History/Archive Project, which operates in conjunction with the Smithsonian Institution. Jenkins has a degree in psychology from Texas Southmost College and attended the Carlson School of Management at the University of Minnesota and the American Management Association.

Willard Jenkins is a jazz journalist and executive director of the National Jazz Service Organization, which supports and enhances the preservation of jazz. He helped to found the *NJSO Journal*. In addition, his jazz articles have appeared in *Cadence, Jazz Forum*, and *Jazz Times*.

Margaret Jerrido is head of the Urban Archives, Paley Library, Temple University. She received a B.A. degree in history from Temple University and an M.L.S. degree from Drexel University. She is the author of articles on nineteenth-century Black women physicians and is currently a doctoral student in history at Temple University.

Arthur J. Johnson is associate editor and film critic of *Black Film Review* and associate editor of *Association of Performing Arts Presenters*. His fiction has appeared in *Chocolate Singles, Catalyst, Lady, Alternative, Black Arts Bulletin*, and *Nommo II Anthology*. His play, *Shades of Grey*, was produced at the Takoma Theater in 1989. Johnson recently appeared in Nigerian filmmaker Olaniyi Areke's 1991 film, *Disillusions*.

Audreye Johnson is an associate professor in the School of Social Work at the University of North Carolina. She is founder of the National Association of Black Social Workers and a charter member of the National Association of Social Workers. She coedited *Removing Cultural and Ethnic Barriers to Health Care* and is the author of *The National Association of Black Social Workers, Inc.: A History for the Future* (1988).

Catherine Johnson received her M.A. in American studies from Michigan State University in 1992, and is pursuing her Ph.D. in American history at the University of Illinois at Urbana-Champaign.

Frank William Johnson is a doctoral student in urban cultural anthropology at Temple University. He holds an M.A. degree in American studies from the University of Maryland. He is a contributor to *Biographical Dictionary of African-American Women*, edited by Dorothy Salem (forthcoming).

Dianne Johnson-Feelings is assistant professor of English at the University of South Carolina. She is a graduate of Princeton University (B.A.) and Yale University (Ph.D.) and attended the University of California at Berkeley on a Chancellor's Postdoctoral Fellowship. She is the author of *Telling Tales: The Pedagogy and Promise of African American Literature for Youth* (1990).

Allison Jolly is a graduate of Oberlin College. She is currently enrolled in a graduate program at Howard University.

Adrienne Lash Jones is associate professor and acting chair of Black studies at Oberlin College. She is the author of *Jane Edna Hunter: A Case Study of Black Leadership 1910-1950*. A fellow of the National Endowment for the Humanities and the Mellon Foundation, Jones is writing a history of African-American women in the Young Women's Christian Association. A former member of the Executive Committee of the World YWCA, in 1983 she served as a member of an international team of observers in the independence election in Namibia.

Anne Hudson Jones is professor of literature and medicine in the Institute for the Medical Humanities of the University of Texas Medical Branch at Galveston. Since 1985 she has been editor-in-chief of *Literature and Medicine*. She is also the editor of *Images of Nurses: Perspectives from History, Art, and Literature* (1988). She is working on a book entitled "Medicine and the Physician in American Popular Culture."

Beverly Jones is professor of history and director of the Institute on Desegregation at North Carolina Central University. She is the author of *Quest for Equality: The Life and Writings of Mary Church Terrell* and the *History of Stanford L. Warren Library: A Phoenix in the Durham, North Carolina Community*.

Jacqueline Jones is on the Editorial Advisory Board of the *Encyclopedia*. See the beginning of this list for a biographical note.

Regina Jones is a twenty-five-year entertainment industry veteran and former owner/publisher of *Soul Newsmagazine*, a national entertainment bi-weekly tabloid. In 1983 she became vice president of publicity for Dick Griffey Productions/Solar Records, and in 1985 she opened her own publicity firm, Regina Jones & Associates.

Amy Jordan is a graduate student in the History Department at the University of Michigan and board member of the Ella Baker-Nelson Mandela Center for Anti-Racist Education at the University of Michigan.

Shirley Jordan is an assistant professor at Hampton University. Her research focuses on interactions between white and Black women in the novels of Alice Walker, Sherley Anne Williams, Fannie Hurst, and Margaret Mitchell. She is also the founder of an educational consulting firm.

Nicoletta Karam is a 1992 graduate of Swarthmore College.

Robin D. G. Kelley is an associate professor of history, African-American studies, and American culture at the University of Michigan. He is the author of *Hammer and Hoe: Alabama Communists during the Great Depression* (1990) and articles that have appeared in *Labor History*, the *Journal of American History*, the *American Historical Review, American Quarterly, Science and Society, Radical History Review*, and the *Nation*.

Shelagh Rebecca Kenney is a 1991 graduate of Harvard University.

Patricia Clark Kenschaft, Ph.D., is professor of mathematics at Montclair State College and director of the Project for Resourceful Instruction of Mathematics in the Elementary School. Her publications include "Black Women in Mathematics in the United States," in *American Mathematical Monthly* (1981), and "Black Men and Women in Mathematical Research," in *Journal of Black Studies* (1987). She edited and contributed five chapters to *Winning Women into Mathematics* (1991).

Judith N. Kerr is assistant professor of history at Towson State University.

Leslie King-Hammond is dean of graduate studies at the Maryland Institute College of Art and project director for the Philip Morris Fellowships for Artists of Color. She has curated numerous exhibitions, including "Black Printmakers and the W.P.A." (1989), "Art as a Verb" (1988) (cocurated with Lowery Sims), and "Celebrations: Myth and Ritual in African-American

Art" (1982). She is completing *We Wear the Mask: The Ethos of Spirituality in African American Art, 1750-Present* (1993).

Thomas J. Knock is associate professor of history at Southern Methodist University. He is the author of *To End All Wars: Woodrow Wilson and the Quest for a New World Order* (1992). His articles have appeared in *American Quarterly, Political Science Quarterly,* and *Reviews in American History,* as well as several anthologies.

Robert Korstad teaches history and public policy at Duke University and is involved in research on southern rural poverty and African-American life in the Jim Crow South. He received a Ph.D. degree in history from the University of North Carolina. He is coauthor of "Opportunities Found and Lost: Labor, Radicals, and the Early Civil Rights Movement," *Journal of American History* (1988), and *Like a Family: The Making of a Southern Cotton Mill World* (1987).

Linda Rochelle Lane is an instructor in the Department of History at Clark Atlanta University. She is a graduate of the University of Maryland (A.A., B.A.), Columbus College (M.A.), and Clark Atlanta University (Ph.D.).

Ellen NicKenzie Lawson was a National Endowment for the Humanities Summer Teaching Fellow at the University of Southern California, and has been a visiting assistant professor of African-American history at Cleveland State University. She has also taught at Cuyahoga Community College. She is a consulting historian and archivist. Her publications include *The Three Sarahs: Documents of Antebellum Black Coeds* (1985) and articles in historical journals and biographical dictionaries. She is at work on a manuscript on the oral histories of African-American migrants to Cleveland from 1930 to the present.

Chana Kai Lee is an assistant professor of history at Indiana University. She is a Ph.D. candidate at the University of California at Los Angeles, and is working on a biography of Fannie Lou Hamer as her dissertation.

Gerda Lerner, who recently retired as the Robinson-Edwards Professor of History at the University of Wisconsin-Madison, 1980-92, has had a long academic career that has also included directing the M.A. Program in Women's History, 1972-76, at Sarah Lawrence College, where she taught from 1968 to 1980, and serving as associate professor at Long Island University, 1965-68. One of her major fields of specialization is women's history. Her publications include *The Grimké Sisters from South Carolina: Rebels against Slavery, The Majority Finds Its Past: Placing Women in History,* and *The Creation of Patriarchy.* She edited *Black Women in White America: A Documentary History.*

Kent A. Leslie is an assistant professor at Emory University. She is the author of "A Mulatto Lady in Nineteenth Century Georgia: Amanda America Dixon 1849-1893," in *Southern Women: Histories and Identities,* and *Woman of Color, Daughter of Privilege* (both forthcoming).

Barbara Lewis, a translator, playwright, and theater critic for the *New York Amsterdam News,* teaches writing at New York University. Her work has appeared in *Ms.* and *Essence.*

Earl Lewis is an associate professor in the Department of History and the Center for Afroamerican and African Studies at the University of Michigan and is also the director of CAAS. He is the author of *In Their Own Interests: Race, Class, and Power in*

Twentieth-Century Norfolk (1991) and coauthor of *Blacks in the Industrial Age: A Documentary History* (forthcoming).

Ellistine Lewis is associate professor of music at Jackson State University. She has several ongoing research projects, including a reference work on music and musicians in Mississippi, a study of Mary Caldwell Dawson and the National Negro Opera Company from 1941 to 1961, a video entitled *The Black Composer in American Culture,* and "Studies in Twentieth-Century Afro-American Mississippi History: Essays and Articles."

Sandra Lieb is a former assistant professor of literature and popular culture at the University of Illinois at Chicago. She is the author of *Mother of the Blues: A Study of Ma Rainey* (1981). She was music and script consultant for *Wild Women Don't Have the Blues,* an NEH-sponsored documentary film (1989).

Valinda Rogers Littlefield is staff associate/editor at the Afro-American Studies and Research Program at the University of Illinois, Urbana-Champaign. She is a graduate of North Carolina Central University (B.A., M.A.) and is a Ph.D candidate in history at the University of Illinois.

Kip Lornell is the author of four books and nearly 100 articles and monographs on blues, gospel, jazz, and early country music. He is employed by the Smithsonian Institution.

Tommy Lott is professor of philosophy at San Jose State University. His articles include "A No-Theory Theory of Black Cinema," in *Black American Literature Forum* (1991), "Marooned in America: Black Urban Youth Culture and Social Pathology," in *The Underclass Question* (1992), and "DuBois on the Invention of Race," in *Philosophical Forum* (1992). He is editor of *Slavery and Social Philosophy* (1993).

Mason Lowance is professor of American literature at the University of Massachusetts at Amherst. His publications include *Increase Mather* (1974), *Massachusetts Broadsides of the American Revolution* (1976), and *The Language of Canaan* (1980), and he has coedited a volume of the *Works of Jonathon Edwards.* His current project is "*Uncle Tom's Cabin* and American Culture: The Indian Captivity Narrative, Slave Narrative, and Puritan Sermon."

William Lowe is an associate professor of African American studies and music at Northeastern University and a doctoral candidate in American studies at Yale University. He is a trombonist, tubaist, and composer with numerous recordings to his credit, including the debut albums of JUBA, James Jabbo Ware, the Me, We and Them Orchestra, and the Bill Lowe/ Andy Jaffe Repertory Big Band, a band Lowe also co-leads. Lowe has toured and performed with Dizzy Gillespie, Sam Rivers, Eartha Kitt, and the John Coltrane Memorial Ensemble. Lowe also composed an opera, *Reb's Last Funeral: Resolution of Invisible Whips.*

Christine A. Lunardini, editorial director of *Black Women in America: An Historical Encyclopedia,* has taught women's history and American history at Princeton University, Barnard College, and Pace University. She is a graduate of Mount Holyoke College (B.A.) and Princeton University (M.A., Ph.D.) and is the author of *From Equal Suffrage to Equal Rights: Alice Paul and the National Women's Party 1910-1928* (1986). Her articles have appeared in the *Political Science Quarterly* and the *Journal of Negro History.* She is doing research for a dictionary of the twentieth-century peace movement in America.

Fenella Macfarlane is a graduate student at Columbia University. She received a B.A. degree (First Class Honors) in English and history from Victoria University, Wellington, New Zealand, and an M.A. degree in English literature from Columbia University.

Gretchen E. Maclachlan teaches women's politics and history in the Political Science Department at Clark Atlanta University. Her principal research interest is southern women workers and industrialization and urbanization in the late nineteenth and early twentieth centuries. She also writes on current public policy issues in employment and labor.

Neil R. MacMillen is professor of history at the University of Southern Mississippi and the author of *The Citizens' Councils: Organized Resistance to the Second Reconstruction* (1971) and *Dark Journey: Black Mississippians in the Age of Jim Crow* (1989).

Gertrude W. Marlowe is an associate professor of anthropology at Howard University. She was director of the Maggie L. Walker Biography Project, supported by the National Park Service and Howard University. She is the author of *Ransom for Many: A Life of Maggie Lena Walker* (1993).

Gloria Richardson Marrow, an educator and public school administrator in Baltimore, Maryland, received B.A. and M.A. degrees from Morgan State University. She is currently pursuing a doctorate in urban education administration and supervision. She is the author of *A Brief Account of Afro-American Settlement in Maryland, with Emphasis on Baltimore County* and "A Narrative of the Founding and Work of the Oblate Sisters of Providence" (Master's thesis, 1976).

Frances Marsh-Ellis, singer, teacher, and civil rights activist, received a B.F.A. degree in voice and an M.F.A. degree in voice and theater from Boston University; she also holds performance diplomas from the Conservatoire de Fontainebleau and the Conservatoire de Paris. She was professor of music at Southern University from 1960 to 1989. Marsh-Ellis produced the first complete amateur production of *Porgy and Bess*, has served on the National Arts Commission for Delta Sigma Theta, and has been national director of the Arts Program for Links, Inc.

Larry L. Martin is chairperson and associate professor of history, geography, and international studies at Coppin State College in Baltimore, Maryland. He specializes in modern European and twentieth-century Russian history. He has lectured widely and recently coordinated on the campus of Coppin State College a major regional conference on Soviet politics, history, and culture. Recent publications include "Afro-Americans and the Law," in the *National Bar Association Magazine*, and "Charlotte E. Ray," in *Notable Black American Women*.

Tony Martin is professor of Africana studies at Wellesley College. He received his M.A. and Ph.D. in history from Michigan State University and the B.S. in economics from the University of Hull, England. In 1965 he qualified as a barrister-at-law at Gray's Cipriani Labour College (Trinidad) and St. Mary's College (Trinidad). He has been visiting professor at the University of Minnesota, Brandeis University, Brown University, and Colorado College. He has authored and edited ten books, including *Race First: The Ideological and Organizational Struggles of Marcus Garvey and the UNIA* and *African Fundamentalism: A Literary and Cultural Anthology of Garvey's Harlem Renaissance*.

Waldo E. Martin, Jr., is professor of history at the University of California at Berkeley. He is the author of *The Mind of*

Frederick Douglass (1984) and numerous articles on Douglass, including "Frederick Douglass: Humanist as Race Leader," in *Black Leaders of the Nineteenth Century* (1988). He has also written articles on African-American cultural and intellectual history, including "The Making of Black America," in *Making America: The Society and Culture of the United States* (1991). He is working on a study of Black cultural politics in the 1960s.

Miriam Matthews, California's first African-American librarian with professional credentials, holds degrees from the University of California at Berkeley and the University of Chicago. As regional librarian of the Los Angeles Public Library she supervised twelve branch libraries. She was appointed by Governor Edmund G. Brown to serve on the California Heritage Preservation Commission and the California State Historical Records Advisory Board.

Tracye A. Matthews is a graduate student in African-American history at the University of Michigan, Ann Arbor. She is writing her dissertation on race, class, and gender in the Black Panther party. She is also the coordinator of the Ella Baker/Nelson Mandela Center for Anti-Racist Education.

Paula D. McClain is professor of government and foreign affairs in the Woodrow Wilson Department of Government and Foreign Affairs at the University of Virginia. She received a Ph.D. degree in political science from Howard University. Her articles have appeared in the *American Political Science Review*, *National Political Science Review*, and *Urban Affairs Quarterly*. Her latest book is *Race, Place and Risk: Black Homicide in Urban America* (1990), coauthored with Harold M. Rose. She is a past president of the National Conference of Black Political Scientists and former member of the Executive Council of the American Political Science Association.

Beverly McCloud is assistant professor of religious studies at DePaul University. A graduate of Lincoln University (B.S.), Temple University School of Pharmacy (B.S.), and Temple University (M.A., Ph.D. in Islamic studies), she is the author of "African American Muslim Women," in *Muslim Communities in America* (1991).

Lorna McDaniel is associate professor of music at the University of Michigan. A graduate of the Juilliard School and the University of Maryland (Ph.D.), she has taught the history of African-American music, ethnomusicology, and the theory and literature of music. She is writing an article, "The Concept of Nation in the Big Drum of Carriacou," for *Musical Repercussions of 1492*.

Grace Jordan McFadden is associate professor of history, director of African-American studies, and director of the Oral History and Culture Project at the University of South Carolina. She received a B.A. degree in political science from California State University at Sacramento, an M.A. degree in urban education from Catholic University, and a Ph.D. degree in African-American history from Union Graduate School. She is the author of "Quest for Human Rights: The Oral Recollections of Black South Carolinians," a twenty-five-part series for the USC Instructional Services Center, and "Septima Clark and the Struggle for Human Rights," in *Women in the Civil Rights Movement: Trailblazers and Torchbearers, 1941-1965* (1990).

William S. McFeely is Richard B. Russell Professor of American History at the University of Georgia. He is the author of *Grant: A Biography* (1981), which won a Pulitzer Prize, and *Frederick Douglass* (1991).

Doris Evans McGinty is professor emerita at Howard University. A former chairperson of the Department of Music at Howard, she is the author of numerous scholarly articles and reviews. From 1975 to 1991 she was book review editor for *The Black Perspective in Music*.

Nellie Y. McKay is on the Editorial Advisory Board of the *Encyclopedia*. See the beginning of this list for a biographical note.

Edna Chappell McKenzie is a professor of history and chairperson for Black, minority, and ethnic studies at the Community College of Allegheny County. She is the author of a documentary history, *Freedom in the Midst of a Slave Society*, and writes essays on current national issues for the *Pittsburgh Post Gazette*. She holds a Ph.D. degree in history from the University of Pittsburgh and has been appointed by the governor to serve on the Higher Education Council for the State Department of Education and the executive committee of the Pennsylvania Higher Education Assistance Agency.

Catherine McKinley is an associate at Marie Brown Associates, a New York City literary agency. She attended the University of the West Indies, Jamaica, and is a graduate of Sarah Lawrence College (B.A.) and Cornell University (M.A.), where she did her thesis on captive women and infanticide.

Earnestine Green McNealey is president of Images, a communications firm in Setauket, New York. She holds a B.S. degree in English from Fort Valley State College and M.A. and Ph.D. degrees in communications from Ohio State University. She served on Alpha Kappa Alpha's board of directors for six years and served as a staff member for six years, including five as executive director.

Genna Rae McNeil is professor of history at the University of North Carolina, where she specializes in African-American history and twentieth-century United States history. She is the author of *Groundwork: Charles Hamilton Houston and the Struggle for Civil Rights*, for which she was awarded the Silver Gavel Award from the American Bar Association, and coauthor of *Historical Judgements Reconsidered*. She is working with John Hope Franklin on "African Americans and the Living Constitution."

Eddie S. Meadows holds a B.A. degree in music education from Tennessee State University, an M.S. degree in music education from the University of Illinois, and a Ph.D. degree in music from Michigan State University. He has held a number of invited visiting professorships in the U.S. and abroad. His publications include *Theses and Dissertations on Black American Music* (1980), *Jazz Reference and Research Materials* (1981), and *Afro-American Music* (1976).

Brenda Meese is assistant professor of physical education at the College of Wooster. In addition, she is the head coach for lacrosse and field hockey. She was manager of the East Team for Field Hockey at the 1985 Olympic Sports Festival and served in the Olympic Development Program from 1985 to 1990.

Marlene Deahl Merrill is a documentary editor and an affiliate scholar at Oberlin College. She collaborated with Ellen NicKenzie Lawson on the Oberlin Antebellum Co-Ed Project, coauthoring several articles and assisting with one book. She is coeditor of *Friends and Sisters: Letters between Lucy Stone and Antoinette Brown Blackwell, 1846-1893* (1987) and editor of *Growing Up in Boston's Guilded Age: The Journal of Alice Stone Blackwell, 1872-1874* (1990).

Tiya Miles is a graduate of Harvard-Radcliffe Colleges, where she majored in African-American studies and American literature. She held an internship at the Native American Women's Health Education Resource Center in 1992.

Janet Miller is director and archivist of the Archives and Special Collections on Women in Medicine at the Medical College of Pennsylvania.

Gary B. Mills is professor of history at the University of Alabama. He is currently working on a college textbook, "A History of the American Nation," and a twelve-year research project reconstituting the lives of 5,789 free Blacks in Alabama. He is the author of *The Forgotten People: Cane River's Creoles of Color* (1977), *Of Men and Rivers: The Story of the Vicksburg District, Corps of Engineers* (1978), and *Civil War Damage Claims: An Index to Cases Filed with the Southern Claims Commission* (1980).

Carolyn Mitchell is associate professor of English at Indiana University. She has written on African-American women writers and spirituality, a project that includes an essay on Ntozake Shange's *for colored girls who have considered suicide/when the rainbow is enuf* in Susan Squire's *Women Writers and the City* and an essay on Toni Morrison's *Beloved* in *Religion and Literature* (Fall 1991). She is the coauthor with Joyce E. King of *Black Mothers to Sons: Juxtaposing African American Literature with Social Practice*.

Gloria Moldow is associate dean of arts and science, director of graduate studies, and coordinator of women's studies at Iona College. In addition to publishing articles on women physicians, medical coeducation, and women's medical dispensaries in the nineteenth century, she is the author of *Women Doctors in Gilded Age Washington: Race, Gender and Professionalization* (1987), a monograph nominated for the Herbert A. Gutman Award in American Social History.

Mellasenah Morris is head of the Music Department and professor of piano at James Madison University. She earned a B.M. degree in piano performance, an M.M. degree in piano pedagogy, and a D.M.A. degree in piano performance from the Peabody Institute of Johns Hopkins University. In 1979 she made her debut at Carnegie Hall. She has taught at the Community College of Baltimore, Villa Julie College, and Peabody Conservatory and served as the dean of the School of Music and professor of piano at Alabama State University.

Robert C. Morris is director of the National Archives, Northeast Region. He received a Ph.D. degree in history from the University of Chicago and has taught at the University of Maryland, Teachers College of Columbia University, and Rutgers University. His publications include *Reading, 'Riting and Reconstruction: The Education of Freedmen in the South, 1861-1870*; *Freedmen's Schools and Textbooks*; and "Educational Reconstruction," in *The Facts of Reconstruction: Essays in Honor of John Hope Franklin*.

Sarah P. Morris is a graduate of Harvard College. She held internships with *Woman of Power* magazine, the *Atlantic*, and Blackside, Inc.

Evan Morse is four-term president of the Northeast Ohio Jazz Society. He serves on the Board of Trustees of the Cleveland Institute of Music, Hiram House, the Cleveland public radio station, and Tri-C Jazz Fest. Morse has lectured on the history of Black women in jazz. In September 1991, he was a guest panelist on the Jazz Education Forum presented at the Congressional Black Caucus in Washington, D.C.

Marie Mosley teaches in the Department of Nursing at the Hunter College-Bellevue School of Nursing, New York City. She received a Ph.D. degree from Teachers College, Columbia University, and has done research on the role of Black women in nursing and medicine.

Amal Muhammad is a processing archivist at the Manuscripts, Archives, and Rare Books Division of the Schomburg Center for Research in Black Culture. She is a Ph.D. student in the Department of History at the State University of New York at Binghamton, where she also received her Bachelor's and Master's degrees. She is doing research on Ethel Trew Dunlap.

John Murph is membership director for the National Jazz Service Organization. He graduated from Mississippi State University and served two internships with the Smithsonian Institution's National Museum of American History, working with the Duke Ellington Collection. He also was a researcher for the Rhythm and Blues Foundation.

Percy E. Murray is interim vice chancellor for development at North Carolina Central University, where he was previously professor of history and chair of the department. He is the author of *History of the North Carolina Teachers Association* (1984), a member of the North Carolina Historical Commission, and a member of the Board of Directors of Stagville Plantation.

Clifford Muse is university archivist for the Moorland-Spingarn Research Center at Howard University. He holds degrees in American history from Hartwick College (B.A.) and Howard University (M.A., Ph.D.). He has worked both on the Moorland-Spingarn Collection and at the Office of Presidential Libraries of the National Archives in Washington, D.C.

Paul Nadler is an adjunct lecturer in the Department of Theater and Film at Hunter College. He has an M.A. degree in theater and film from Hunter College and is completing his Ph.D. in theater at the City University of New York. He won the 1991 Shuster Award for his theatrical history of the Brooklyn Academy of Music, the 1990 and 1991 John Golden Awards for Playwriting, and the 1992 Association for Theatre in Higher Education Graduate Student Playwriting Award. He is a contributor to *The Bloomsbury Theater Guide*.

Mecca Nelson is a senior at Harvard University, majoring in African-American studies.

Richard Newman is managing editor of the *Encyclopedia of African American Culture and History* project, Center for American Studies, Columbia University. He is a member of the Advisory Committee to *The Harvard Guide to Afro-American History*, the Performing Arts Task Force of the Smithsonian Institution's African American Museum Project, and the Schomburg Commission for the Preservation of Black Culture.

Linda Nieman is a cultural historian who is writing a biography of artist Aaron Douglas, curating a national retrospective exhibition of his work, and coediting (with Donald Nieman) *African-Americans and the Law: An Encyclopedia of United States Court Cases*.

Linda Norflett is chairperson of the Department of Dramatic Arts at North Carolina Central University. She is founder and artistic director of the Triangle Performing Ensemble. *Of Mules and Men*, of which she was the producing manager, was one of five national winners at the American College Theater Festival in 1991. Her articles on the Black experience in American theater have appeared in *Encore Magazine* and the *Black Literary Forum*.

J. Weldon Norris is professor of music, director of the Office of Choirs and Bands, and chairman of the Department of Music at Howard University. He is a graduate of South Carolina State College, Howard University, and Indiana University.

Margaret D. Pagan is a free-lance writer. She has contributed to magazines, newspapers, and other publications.

Nell Irvin Painter is on the Editorial Advisory Board of the *Encyclopedia*. See the beginning of this list for a biographical note.

Tiffany R. L. Patterson is on the Editorial Advisory Board of the *Encyclopedia*. See the beginning of this list for a biographical note.

June O. Patton is a professor of history and public policy at Governors State University. She is currently on loan to the federal government, working as a program officer at the National Endowment for the Humanities. Patton's latest publication is "The Declining Access of Black Males to Higher Education," in Gary Oldfield's *The Closing Door of Opportunity* (1991).

Edie C. Pearson graduated summa cum laude from Clark Atlanta University in 1992 with a major in political science. She held an Undergraduate Research Assistantship, funded by the Social Science Research Council, under the supervision of Dr. Gretchen E. Maclachlan.

Wilma Peebles-Wilkins is associate dean for academic affairs at the Boston University School of Social Work. She received a B.A. degree in sociology from North Carolina State University, an M.S. degree in social administration from Case Western Reserve University, and a Ph.D. degree in educational history from the University of North Carolina. Her work is in the area of mutual aid in the Black community with a focus on the historical development of the contributions of Black women to American social welfare.

Kathy Peiss is professor of history and women's studies at the University of Massachusetts at Amherst. She is the author of *Cheap Amusements: Working Women and Leisure in Turn-of-the-Century New York* (1986) and coeditor of *Passion and Power: Sexuality in History* (1989). She is writing a history of cosmetics in American culture.

Vincent Pelote is a librarian at the Institute of Jazz Studies at Rutgers University Library, in Newark. He has written program notes for jazz recordings, and his articles and reviews have appeared in scholarly journals and professional publications. He is the editor of the semiannual *IJS Register and Indexes*.

Kathy A. Perkins is on the Editorial Advisory Board of the *Encyclopedia*. See the beginning of this list for a biographical note.

Linda M. Perkins is associate professor of educational policy studies at the University of Illinois, Urbana-Champaign, where her research areas are the history of African-American and women's higher education. She is the author of *Fanny Jackson Coppin and the Institute for Colored Youth, 1837-1902* (1987) and is completing a manuscript entitled "The Black Female Talented Tenth: A History of Black Women's Higher Education."

William Eric Perkins is an associate examiner for the Educational Testing Service and adjunct professor of communications at Hunter College. He was educated at Northwestern University, the University of Rochester, and the Graduate Center of the City University of New York. He is the author of *Droppin' Science: Essays on Rap Music and Hip-Hop Culture* (forthcoming) and coeditor of *The Black Freedom Struggle in the United States: An Encyclopedia* (forthcoming). He is working on a book and video, "Prisoners of the Image: Race and Ethnicity in American Popular Culture."

Lillian Dunn Perry is a music consultant for the Orleans Parish School System and teaches music in elementary and junior high schools. She is a graduate of Dillard University (B.A.) and Columbia University (M.A.). She is a member of the National Association of Negro Musicians and the City Council of New Orleans.

Ann Petry is a graduate of Connecticut College of Pharmacy (Ph.G.), but is best known as a writer. Her works include *The Street*, *Country Place*, *The Narrows*, and *Miss Muriel and Other Stories*. She has written books for young readers, including *Harriet Tubman*, *Tituba of Salem Village*, and *Legends of the Saints*.

Paula F. Pfeffer is associate professor of history at Loyola University of Chicago. She received a Ph.D. degree from Northwestern University. She is the author of *A. Philip Randolph: Pioneer of the Civil Rights Movement* and "The Women behind the Union: Halena Wilson, Rosina Tucker, and the Ladies' Auxiliary to the Brotherhood of Sleeping Car Porters" (1991).

Glenn O. Phillips is associate professor of history at Morgan State University. He received a Ph.D. degree in history from Harvard University. He has published four books, the most recent of which is *Seventh-Day Adventists in Barbados, 1884-1991* (1991), and was a coeditor of *The Caribbean Basin Initiative: Genuine or Deceptive?* (1987). His articles have appeared in *Journal of Negro History*, the *Americas*, *Latin American Research Review*, *Journal of Immigrants and Minorities*, *Journal of International Affairs*, and *Journal of Caribbean History*.

Francello Phillips-Calhoun is a graduate of Howard University. She conducts independent research in women's studies and public policy.

Dianne Pinderhughes is professor of political science and Afro-American studies and director of the Afro-American Studies and Research Program at the University of Illinois, Urbana-Champaign. She received degrees from Albertus Magnus College (B.A.) and the University of Chicago (M.A., Ph.D.). She is the author of *Race and Ethnicity in Chicago Politics: A Reexamination of Pluralist Theory* and of many articles and book reviews. Her current research addresses issues involving racial and ethnic interest representation, voting rights, and urban politics. The recipient of Ford and Rockefeller postdoctoral fellowships and a University Scholar at the University of Illinois in 1988-91, she has served on the councils of the American Political Science Association and the Midwest Political Science Association, and as president of the National Conference of Black Political Scientists.

Merline Pitre is dean of the College of Arts and Sciences and professor of history at Texas Southern University. She holds a Ph.D. degree in history from Temple University. Her major works are *Through Many Dangers, Toils and Snares: The Black Leadership of Texas 1868-1900* and "Black Houstonians and the Doctrine of Separate But Equal: Carter Wesely vs. Lulu White."

Sally Placksin is the author of *Mothering the New Mother* (1993) and *American Women in Jazz, 1900 to the Present* (1982), which won an ASCAP Deems Taylor Award. She wrote and produced the *American Women in Jazz* series heard on National Public Radio. She has written and produced documentaries on the International Sweethearts of Rhythm, Harlem Renaissance writer Dorothy West, and others for the National Public Radio series *Horizons* and was coproducer of the radio special *African Dawn: A Portrait of South African Musician Abdulla Ibrahim*.

Suzanne Poirier is associate professor of medical humanities at the University of Illinois College of Medicine in Chicago. Her teaching and research include work on women's health and women in the health professions. Her study of the influence of Ann Lane Petry's experience in pharmacy on her writing appeared in *Pharmacy in History*. She is an associate editor of *Literature and Medicine* and coeditor (with Timothy F. Murphy) of *Writing Aids: Gay Literature, Language, and Analysis* (forthcoming).

Shirley Poole, a graduate of Boston University, is the executive director of the National Coalition of 100 Black Women. Before joining the coalition, she was a managing editor at the National Association of Social Workers.

Mildred Pratt, Ph.D., is a founder and codirector of the Bloomington-Normal Black History and Culture Consortium at Illinois State University at Normal. She has presented more than fifty speeches at professional conferences and is the author of eight journal articles and one book.

Philip A. Presby is an associate with the law firm of Shea & Gould in New York City.

Jewel Limar Prestage is dean and honors professor of political science in the Benjamin Banneker Honors College at Prairie View A&M University. She is coauthor (with Marianne Githens) of *A Portrait of Marginality: The Political Behavior of the American Woman* (1977) and has published articles in the *Journal of Politics*, the *Social Science Quarterly*, the *Policy Studies Journal*, and the *Annals of the American Academy of Political and Social Science*. In addition, she is working on a study of African-American women in politics. Prestage was named to the National Advisory Council on Women's Educational Programs by President Jimmy Carter, the first minority woman to chair that body.

Ronald M. Radano is assistant professor of African-American studies and music at the University of Wisconsin-Madison. He is completing a study of jazz and postmodernism and is a Rockefeller Fellow at the Center for the Study of Black Literature and Culture at the University of Pennsylvania.

Benita Ramsey is writing a biography of civil rights activist Daisy Bates. She received a Bachelor's degree from Florida State University, a Master's degree in Afro-American women's history from the University of Wisconsin, and a Juris Doctorate degree from the University of Miami School of Law.

Sonya Ramsey is in the Ph.D. program in history at the University of North Carolina, Chapel Hill, where her dissertation will be a study of Josephine Clement and Durham, North

Carolina, public education. Ramsey received her Bachelor's degree in journalism from Howard University.

Barbara Ransby is a faculty member in the History Department at DePaul University. She is a member of the editorial board of the London-based journal *Race and Class* and is currently guest-editing a special issue on "Black Women: A Global View for the 21st Century." She is also completing her dissertation on the political life and thought of Ella Josephine Baker.

Lawrence N. Redd is a communication arts and sciences specialist at Michigan State University. He holds a B.A. degree from Tennessee State University and M.A. and Ph.D. degrees from Michigan State University. He has contributed to books on communication and published journal articles on music, educational technology, and telecommunications. He is the author of *Rock Is Rhythm and Blues*. Redd produces blues records for his own company and owns/manages a cable radio station.

Christopher R. Reed is associate professor of history at Roosevelt University and chairs the Center for African American Studies. He is a graduate of Los Angeles State College (B.A., M.A.) and Michigan State University (Ph.D.). He is a coeditor, with John P. Henderson, of *Studies in the African Diaspora: A Memorial to James R. Hooker (1929-1976)* (1989). His articles have appeared in *Perspectives of Black Popular Culture*, the *Zora Neale Hurston Forum*, *Studies in the Diaspora*, the *Western Journal of Black Studies*, and *Centennial Review*.

Harry A. Reed is associate professor in the Department of History at Michigan State University. He received an A.A. degree from Los Angeles City College, B.A. and M.A. degrees from Los Angeles State College, and his Ph.D. from Michigan State University. He coedited *Studies in the African Diaspora: A Memorial to James R. Hooker (1929-1976)* and has published articles and book reviews in *Studies in the Diaspora*, *Centennial Review*, the *Western Journal of Black Studies*, *Journal of Jazz Studies*, and the *American Historical Review*. He has received fellowships and other grants from the Sumner Humanities Center, the American Philosophical Society, and the Michigan State University Foundation, among others.

Linda Reed is on the Editorial Advisory Board of the *Encyclopedia*. See the beginning of this list for a biographical note.

John Reid is a graduate of the University of Nevada (B.A., M.A.) and is enrolled in the Ph.D. program in history at Michigan State University. His field of concentration is nineteenth- and twentieth-century African and American history, and he is writing his dissertation on "The Black Women Schoolteachers of the Midwest, 1860-1950."

Margaret Reid, an alumna of Morgan State College, where she teaches, received an M.A. degree in English from the University of Iowa, an M.L.A. degree in literature from Johns Hopkins University, and a Ph.D. degree in rhetoric and linguistics from Indiana University of Pennsylvania. Reid is president of the Middle-Atlantic Writers Association, is involved in several learned societies, and is on the editorial boards of numerous journals.

Susan M. Reverby is Whitehead Associate Professor in Critical Thought and chair of the Women's Studies Department at Wellesley College. She is the author of *Ordered to Care: The Dilemma of American Nursing* and the editor of the multivolume reprint series *The History of American Nursing*. She has coedited

America's Working Women: A Documentary History, *Health Care in America: Essays in Social History*, and *Gendered Domain: Beyond the Public Private in Women's History*. Her current work focuses on the multiple interpretations of Nurse Riviers.

Delia Reyes earned a B.A. degree in creative writing and an M.A. degree in English literature at the City College of New York. Her thesis was on the theater of the Harlem Renaissance. Reyes is a playwright and is writing *Requiem for the Living*, which explores how a Puerto Rican family deals with the sudden death of its matriarch.

Jane Rhodes is a visiting assistant professor in the School of Journalism at Indiana University. She has taught in the Department of Communication Studies at the State University of New York at Cortland, where she was coordinator of African American studies. She is a Ph.D. candidate in mass communication research at the University of North Carolina, and her research focuses on the history of African-American women journalists and on race and gender in the mass media.

Darrell Rice graduated from the University of Kentucky and is a journalist in his hometown, Watonga, Oklahoma.

Deborra A. Richardson graduated from Howard University's Department of Fine Arts (music history) and the University of Maryland (M.L.S.). She is an archivist for the Duke Ellington Collection at the National Museum of American History. She is working on a biobibliography of Ulysses Kay, a contemporary Black American composer. She also is a mezzo-soprano/alto voice with local choirs and plays clarinet with the local orchestra.

Judy Richardson has been associated with the PBS series *Eyes on the Prize* since 1979, most recently as series associate producer. She also is education director for Blackside, Inc., producers of *Eyes*, and for the Civil Rights Project, Inc., which supports Blackside's work. She served as director of information for the United Church of Christ Commission for Racial Justice and during the early 1960s was a staff member of the Student Nonviolent Coordinating Committee on their projects throughout the South.

Glenda Riley is Alexander M. Bracken Professor of History at Ball State University. She has written articles and books on women in the American West, her most recent being *A Place to Grow: Women in the American West* (1992). Riley is writing a biography of Annie Oakley.

Mary W. Roberts, a pianist and professor of music at Florida A&M University, received her formal music education at the University of Kansas (B.M.), Indiana University (M.M.), and Florida State University (Ph.D.). She performs frequently, both as a soloist and an accompanist, at Florida A&M, and as a guest artist at other universities. Recently she was awarded the Teacher of the Year Award from Florida A&M.

LaVonne Roberts-Jackson is a doctoral candidate in the Department of History at Howard University and a historian intern at the National Conference of State Historic Preservation. She has a B.A. degree from the University of Texas at Arlington and an M.A. degree from Atlanta University. She has presented papers on Malcolm X, civil rights, and the Harlem Renaissance, and she is writing her dissertation on "Black Women in East Texas during Reconstruction, 1865-1877."

Beverly J. Robinson is professor of theater and folklore studies at the University of California at Los Angeles. She has written articles and a book (*Aunt Phyllis*), and is internationally known for her lectures and research on films concerning African and American cultures. Robinson graduated Phi Beta Kappa from UCLA; her graduate work was undertaken at the University of California at Berkeley (M.A., folklore) and the University of Pennsylvania (Ph.D., folklore and folklife studies). She is revising her manuscript, "Jemima, Eliza, and Edith: You Have Nothing to Be Ashamed of . . . "

Jessie Rodrique holds a year-long predoctoral fellowship at the Smithsonian Institution's National Museum of American History, where she is coordinator of the Jazz Oral History Project in the Division of Musical History. She received a Ph.D. degree in American history from the University of Massachusetts at Amherst. Rodrique is the author of "The Black Community and the Birth Control Movement," in *Passion and Power: Sexuality in History* (1989), edited by Peiss and Simmons.

Patricia W. Romero is professor of history at Towson State University. She is the author of *E. Sylvia Pankhurst* (1988) and editor of *Women's Voices on Africa*.

Lorraine Elena Roses is a visiting research scholar at the Center for Research on Women at Wellesley College. She is the author of *Voices of the Storyteller: Cuba's Lina Novas Calvo* and coauthor with Ruth E. Randolph of *Harlem Renaissance and Beyond: Literary Biographies of 100 Black Women Writers, 1900-1946.*

Darlene Roth is director of programs at the Atlanta History Center, in charge of all public and school programming, exhibits, and interpretation at two historic houses and a branch history center in the heart of town. She has published articles, book reviews, and books on women's history, southern urban history, and historic preservation.

Jacqueline A. Rouse is on the Editorial Advisory Board of the *Encyclopedia*. See the beginning of this list for a biographical note.

Jacqueline Jones Royster, formerly associate professor of English at Spelman College, is associate professor of English and director of the University Writing Center at Ohio State University. She has published articles on literacy studies and Black women's studies and has been a consultant and adviser to programs across the country in these areas. She is completing work on a book entitled "Traces of a Stream: Literacy and Social Change among African American Women."

Dorothy Salem is a professor in the Division of Social and Behavioral Sciences at Cuyahoga Community College in Cleveland. She is editing *African American Women: A Biographical Dictionary* and also is contributing a chapter ("Black Women in the NAACP and National Urban League: The 'Isms' within Reform Organizations") to an anthology.

Judy Scales-Trent is a professor at the State University of New York School of Law at Buffalo. Previously, she practiced law in Washington, D.C., with the Equal Employment Opportunity Commission. She also was special assistant to the general counsel of the agency during the Carter administration. Scales-Trent has written about the intersection of race and sex in American law and the intersection of race and color in her own life.

Patricia A. Schechter received a B.A. degree from Mount Holyoke College and is completing a Ph.D. degree in history at Princeton University with a dissertation on the life and work of Ida B. Wells-Barnett.

Anne Firor Scott is W. K. Boyd Professor of History Emerita at Duke University. Her most recent book is *Natural Allies: Women's Associations in American History* (1992).

Sandra Cannon Scott is chair of the Department of Fine Arts, director of choral activities, and associate professor of music at Mississippi Valley State University. She is the author of "An Ethnographic Study of Choral Music Education in Two Selected Small Districts of Mississippi" (University of Southern Mississippi Ph.D. dissertation, 1990). She has lectured widely and served as a consultant and choral adjudicator in the Midwest and Southwest.

Megan Seaholm is a lecturer in the Department of History at the University of Texas at Austin, where she teaches American history and U.S. women's history. She holds a B.A. degree from Austin College in Sherman, Texas, an M.A.R. degree from Yale University, and a Ph.D. degree from Rice University. She worked as director of clinic services at Planned Parenthood of Austin.

Lee E. Sellers is associate professor at Hunter College (Library). He holds a B.A. degree from Wilberforce University, an M.S.W. degree from the University of Denver, and an M.S.L.S. degree from Atlanta University, and has completed course work for a Ph.D. degree in library science at the University of Pittsburgh. He has served as the director of the Wilberforce Library and director of the School of Social Work Library as well as faculty member at the University of Connecticut.

William Seraile is professor of African-American history at Lehman College. He holds a Ph.D. degree from the City University of New York; his dissertation was "New York Black Regiments during the Civil War." He is the author of numerous professional articles and the recently published *Voice of Dissent: Theophilus Gould Steward and Black America* (1991).

V. A. Shadron is associate editor of the Martin Luther King, Jr., Papers and director of the project's offices at the Martin Luther King, Jr., Center for Nonviolent Social Change at Emory University. She is a graduate of Eckerd College (B.A.) and Emory University (M.A., Ph.D.). Her areas of interest are nineteenth- and twentieth-century American social and political history, southern and African-American history, and legal history.

Stephanie J. Shaw is on the Editorial Advisory Board of the *Encyclopedia*. See the beginning of this list for a biographical note.

John C. Shields is associate professor of English at Illinois State University. He is the author of *The American Aeneas: Classical Origins of the American Self* (forthcoming) and articles published in *American Literature, Studies in Short Fiction, Literature/Film Quarterly, Studies in Philology,* and *Black American Literature Forum.* He is also the editor of *The Collected Works of Phillis Wheatley.* He was recently appointed to the advisory board of *The Oxford Companion to African-American Literature.*

Susan Shifrin is curator of textiles and costumes at the Goldie Paley Design Center at the Philadelphia College of Textiles and Science. Shifrin was the 1991 M. Louise Carpenter Gloeckner, M.D. Summer Research Fellow at the Archives and Special Collections on Women in Medicine at the Medical College of Pennsylvania.

Frank Shuffelton is professor of English at the University of Rochester. He holds degrees from Harvard (B.A.) and Stanford (M.A., Ph.D.) universities. He is the author of *Thomas Hooker 1586-1647* (1977), *Thomas Jefferson: A Comprehensive Annotated Bibliography of Writings about Him, 1826-1980* (1983), and the forthcoming *Thomas Jefferson: 1981-1990: A Comprehensive Critical Bibliography*. His articles have been published in *Early American Literature*, *Studies in Philology*, and *New England Quarterly*.

Lawrence J. Simpson is the managing consultant of the Mogus Group, a consulting firm specializing in strategic planning and organizational and management development, working principally with arts and other not-for-profit organizations. A social psychologist, he holds degrees from Kent State University (B.A.) and the University of Pittsburgh (M.A., Ph.D.). His writings and photographs have been published in *Downbeat*, *Jazz Times*, and the *National Jazz Service Organization Jazz Letter*.

Lowery S. Sims is associate curator of twentieth-century art at the Metropolitan Museum of Art. She received a B.A. degree in art history (Phi Beta Kappa) from Queens College, an M.A. degree in art history from Johns Hopkins University, and an M.Phil. degree from the Graduate Center of the City University of New York, where she is completing a Ph.D. Sims was the 1991 recipient of the Frank Jewett Mather Award for distinction in art criticism from the College Art Association.

Barbara Smith is a writer and activist whose writing has appeared in *Ms.*, the *New York Times*, the *Guardian*, the *Black Scholar*, and the *Village Voice*. She has coedited and edited three collections by Black women: *Conditions: Five. The Black Women's Issue* (1979), with Lorraine Bethel; *All the Women Are White, All the Blacks Are Men, But Some of Us Are Brave: Black Women's Studies* (1982), with Gloria T. Hull and Patricia Bell-Scott; and *Home Girls: A Black Feminist Anthology* (1983). She is the coauthor of *Yours in Struggle: Three Feminist Perspectives on Anti-Semitism and Racism* (1984), with Elly Bulkin and Minnie Bruce Pratt. She is cofounder and publisher of Kitchen Table: Women of Color Press.

Cynthia J. Smith is associate professor of African-American studies at Smith College. She is a graduate of Spelman College (B.A.) and Yale University (M.Ph., Ph.D.). Her research focuses on Phillis Wheatley, Toni Morrison, and Gayl Jones.

Deborah Smith is assistant professor in the Department of Obstetrics and Gynecology, Howard University Hospital, Howard University School of Medicine. She is a graduate of Bryn Mawr College (B.A.), the University of California at Berkeley (M.P.H.), and Howard University School of Medicine (M.D.). She was the 1991 recipient of the American College of Obstetricians and Gynecologists-Ortho Fellowship in the History of Obstetrics and Gynecology in America.

Elaine M. Smith is assistant professor of history at Alabama State University. She is a graduate of Boston University and Bethune-Cookman College. Her research on the life and times of Mary McLeod Bethune has appeared in *Afro-American History: Sources for Research* (1981), *Notable American Women: The Modern Period* (1980), and *Clio Was a Woman: Studies in the History of American Women* (1980).

Jessie Carney Smith is university librarian and professor at Fisk University. She graduated from North Carolina A&T State University (B.S.), Michigan State University (M.A.), Peabody College of Vanderbilt University (M.A.L.S.), and the University of Illinois (Ph.D). An expert in library science, she is the author of *Images of Blacks in American Culture* and *Ethnic Genealogy*. In 1991 she completed editing *Notable Black American Women*, a biographical work on 500 Black women.

Susan Smith is assistant professor of history and women's studies at the University of Alberta, Canada. She is a graduate of the University of California at Irvine (B.A.) and the University of Wisconsin (M.A., Ph.D.). She is the author of "Sick and Tired of Being Sick and Tired: Black Women and the National Negro Health Movement" (dissertation); "New Reproductive Technologies and Motherhood," in *Feminist Collections* (1988); and "Black Women's Clubs," "Harriet Tubman," "National Council of Negro Women," and "National Negro Health Movement," in *Women's History in the United States: A Handbook* (1990).

June Sochen is professor of history at Northeastern Illinois University. She is the author of *The New Feminism in Twentieth Century America* (1971), *The Unbridgeable Gap: Blacks and Their Quest for the American Dream* (1972), *Movers and Shakers: American Women Thinkers and Activists* (1973), *Enduring Values: Women in Popular Culture* (1987), *Cafeteria America: New Identities in Contemporary Life* (1988), and *She Who Laughs Lasts: Mae West, Her Life and Times* (1992).

Rawn Spearman is professor emeritus at the College of Fine Arts of the University of Massachusetts at Lowell. A former member of the Fisk Jubilee Singers, he has won the Marian Anderson Award, the Roland Hayes Award, the American Theater Award, John Hay Whitney Award, JUGG Award, and the Ville de Fontainebleau, which allowed him to study French art songs with Nadia Boulanger. He is an active performer, researcher, and teacher.

Robert Stephens is associate professor and coordinator of music education at Montclair State College. He holds degrees in music education from Savannah State College (B.S.), Teachers College of Columbia University (M.A., M.Ed.), and Indiana University (Ph.D.). The author of biographical essays, Stephens has also written articles on music education for *Western Journal for Black Studies* and *Black Perspectives in Music*.

Brenda E. Stevenson is assistant professor of history at the University of California at Los Angeles. She is the editor of *The Journals of Charlotte Forten Grimké* and is the author of numerous articles on slave women and families. She is completing a manuscript on Black and white families in the antebellum South.

Rosemary Stevenson is Afro-Americana bibliographer and assistant professor of library administration at the University of Illinois, Urbana-Champaign, Library. She has published articles and bibliographies on Black women, politics, literature, the Caribbean, and South Africa in several journals, including *Black Scholar*, *Callaloo*, *Journal of Caribbean Studies*, *SAGE*, *Race Relations Abstracts*, and *Victorian Periodicals Review*.

Rodger Streitmatter is a professor in the School of Communication at American University. He is the author of articles about Black women journalists of the nineteenth and twentieth centuries.

Patricia Sullivan teaches history at the University of Virginia and serves as assistant director of the Center for the Study of Civil Rights. She is coeditor of *New Directions in Civil Rights Studies* (1991) and author of *To Preserve Liberty and Promote Justice: The New Deal, the South and the Politics of Civil Rights* (forthcoming).

Janice Sumler-Edmond is a historian and attorney with the law firm of Mack & Bernstein in Atlanta. Before practicing law, Sumler-Edmond was an associate professor of history and law at Clark Atlanta University, where she chaired the History Department from 1987 to 1989. She completed a J.D. degree at the University of California at Los Angeles School of Law and holds a Ph.D. degree in American history from Georgetown University. Sumler-Edmond served as the national director of the Association of Black Women Historians from 1988 to 1990. One of three 1991-92 judicial fellows, Sumler-Edmond spent her fellowship year at the Supreme Court of the United States.

Jo A. Tanner is an assistant professor in the Drama, Theatre and Dance Department at Queens College. She earned B.A. and M.A. degrees from Queens College and a Ph.D. degree from the Graduate Center of the City University of New York. She contributed the essay on Vinnette Carroll for *Notable Women in the American Theatre* and is the author of *Dusky Maidens: The Odyssey of the Early Black Dramatic Actress* (1992), which includes a lengthy section on Laura Bowman. She is working on a directory of Black women on the American stage.

Gayle T. Tate is assistant professor of political science and African studies at Rutgers University. She is a graduate of City College of New York (B.A.), Columbia University (M.S.), the Sorbonne, New York University (M.A.), and City University of New York (Ph.D.). She is the author of two articles on Black Nationalism for the *Western Journal of Black Studies* (1988, 1991) and the forthcoming "The Span of Black Women's Protest and Resistance: A Comparison of Two Time Periods," in *The Black Experience Workshop: The Collective Papers*, volume III. She is a Rockefeller Humanities Fellow at the City College of New York.

Cheryl Taylor is associate professor of nursing at Louisiana State University Medical Center in New Orleans. She is a graduate (B.S.N.) of Dillard University and the University of Washington (M.N.), and she earned a Ph.D. degree in nursing from Texas Woman's University. A former American Nurses Association Fellow, Taylor is a psychiatric mental health nurse and an expert on homelessness. She has written "Homeless Women: Hidden Teardrops Surviving the Violence of Street Life" and "Homeless Families: Coping with Turmoil and Transitions" (in press).

Susan A. Taylor is researching the women's health movements of the nineteenth and twentieth centuries and is completing an M.A. degree at Morgan State University.

Teresa R. Taylor is associate archivist at the Archives and Special Collections on Women in Medicine at the Medical College of Pennsylvania.

Ula Taylor is an assistant professor in the African American Studies Department at the University of California at Berkeley. She is writing her dissertation on "The Veiled Garvey: The Life and Times of Amy Jacques Garvey." She has taught a course in African-American history to inmates at Lompoc State Penitentiary.

Rosalyn Terborg-Penn is an Associate Editor of the *Encyclopedia*. See the beginning of this list for a biographical note.

Freida High W. Tesfagiorgis is professor of African-American and contemporary African art and chair of the Department of Afro-American Studies at the University of Wisconsin-Madison.

Her essays, articles, and reviews have appeared in *SAGE, Women's Studies Encyclopedia: Literature, Arts and Learning*, and *African Arts*. Her work has been exhibited in museums and galleries around the world and is documented in *The International Review of African-American Art*. She is curating an exhibition of contemporary African art that focuses on academic artists.

Jeanne Theoharis graduated magna cum laude in Afro-American studies from Harvard University. The recipient of numerous awards and grants, Theoharis while at Harvard founded and chaired a committee on housing rights and edited Harvard's liberal monthly, *Perspective*. She works as a teacher and counselor at Jeremiah Burke High School and as a research assistant and teaching fellow at Harvard.

Dorothy Thomas has worked in various aspects of the law as editor, biographer, indexer, and researcher. She compiled and edited *Women Lawyers in the United States* (1957). From 1975 to 1985, Thomas produced and moderated a public affairs radio program covering politics, law, education, and the arts. She is completing the first volume of "Women, the Bench and the Bar" and designing and supervising the execution of a database for more than 100 oral histories of Women's City Club of New York members.

Sister Francesca Thompson, O.S.F., is assistant to the dean, associate professor of African-American studies, and associate professor in the Department of Communications at Fordham University. She lectures extensively and has directed many college plays and numerous children's theater productions. She is the author of "The Lafayette Players," in *The Theater of Black Americans*, and *Families: Black and Catholic*.

John Thompson teaches in the Department of History at Oklahoma Christian College, where he received his B.A. in history. He earned his Ph.D. in history at Purdue University. His biography of Roscoe Dunjee is forthcoming.

Kathleen Thompson is coauthor of the feminist classic *Against Rape* (1974). She is the author of a wide variety of educational programs, books, and films. Nine of her plays have been produced in Chicago. Her latest, *Politics and Old Lace*, about the Woman's Building at the Columbian Exposition of 1893, recently had its premiere performance at the University of Chicago. For four years she was president of the educational development house Sense and Nonsense, Inc.

Shirley Thompson received her Bachelor's degree in history from Harvard University in 1992.

J. Mills Thornton III is professor of history at the University of Michigan. He is the author of *Politics and Power in a Slave Society: Alabama 1800-1860*, which won the Dunning Prize of the American Historical Association. He is now completing a study of the civil rights movement in Montgomery, Birmingham, and Selma, Alabama.

Sandra Gioia Treadway is director of the Division of Publications and Cultural Affairs at the Virginia State Library and Archives. She is a graduate of Manhattanville College (B.A.) and the University of Virginia (M.A., Ph.D.). She is coeditor of *Dictionary of Virginia Biography* and editor of *Journals of the Council of the State of Virginia*, volume 5. She has also written articles, including "New Directions in Virginia Women's History," in *Virginia Magazine of History and Biography* (1992).

H. LaRue Trotter is a dramatist and board member of the East Liberty Arts Council in Pittsburgh, Pennsylvania. She is a former instructor of African-American women's literature at Chatham College and is pursuing graduate studies in theater arts at the University of Minnesota.

Joe W. Trotter, professor of history at Carnegie-Mellon University, is the author of *Coal, Class and Color: Blacks in Southern West Virginia, 1915-32* and *Black Milwaukee: The Making of an Industrial Proletariat, 1915-45.* He is working on a comparative study of Blacks in three Alabama cities in the twentieth century.

Shauna Vey has been a director and stage manager in New York City. With an M.F.A. degree in directing from Florida State University, she has directed *All's Well That Ends Well, Cry Havoc,* and *Sex and Rage in a Soho Loft.* She is pursuing a Ph.D. in theater at the City University of New York and teaching in the Department of Speech and Theatre at Lehman College.

Gloria Wade-Gayles is professor of English and women's studies at Spelman College and in 1991 was CASE Professor of the Year for the state of Georgia. She is the author of *No Crystal Stair: Race and Sex in Black Women's Novels, 1947-1976,* the first interdisciplinary study of Black women's fiction, and a volume of poetry, *Anointed to Fly.* Her essays have appeared in *Sturdy Black Bridges, Southern Women Writers,* and *The Black Woman,* and her poetry has been published in *Essence, SAGE,* and the *Black Scholar.* She is completing a book on the evolution of Alice Walker's womanist ideology, "From Brown Fields to the Universe," and conducting research on African-American women's spirituality.

Lesa Walden, M.D., trained in family medicine at Duke University. She is a television producer specializing in health and medical programming. She founded Vital Signs Productions, Inc., an independent production company utilizing television, videotape, film, and theater. Vital Signs revived National Negro Health Week in 1992 through a lecture series hosted by the Smithsonian Institution, entitled "Caretakers of the Community."

Juliette E. K. Walker is a professor in the Department of History at the University of Illinois, Urbana-Champaign. She received a Ph.D. degree from the University of Chicago and did postdoctoral research at Harvard University. Walker is the author of *Free Frank: A Black Pioneer on the Antebellum Frontier* and the forthcoming *Black Business in American History.* She is the founder of the Free Frank Historic Preservation Foundation which is dedicated to reconstructing the frontier town New Philadelphia, Illinois, founded by Free Frank McWorter in 1836.

Paulette Walker is a student in the Graduate School of Journalism at the University of Maryland. She received her B.A. from Clark Atlanta University. She has worked for the *Washington Magazine, Atlanta Journal Constitution,* and *USA Today,* as well as for the United States Army, where she was an administrative assistant to the secretary of defense while on active duty.

Peter Wallenstein is associate professor of history at Virginia Polytechnic Institute and State University. He did his undergraduate work at Columbia College and his graduate study at Johns Hopkins University. He is the author of *From Slave South to New South: Public Policy in Nineteenth Century Georgia* (1987).

Gloria V. Warren is assistant director for the Baltimore City Department of Social Services. She is a graduate of the University of Maryland School of Social Work and Community Planning (M.S.) and is a candidate for an M.A. at Morgan State University.

Judy Warwick is a graduate of the University of Maryland (B.A., English) and is a candidate for an M.A. degree in African and African-American studies at Clark Atlanta University.

Nadine Wasserman is a graduate of the University of Wisconsin (B.A. and M.A., African-American studies) and the University of Wisconsin at Milwaukee (Museum Studies Certificate). Her Master's thesis was "An Investigation of Black Women's Identity through the Art Works of Betye Saar and Howardena Pindell."

Irma Watkins-Owen is assistant professor and director of the African-American and African Studies Institute and Social Science Division at Fordham University. She received her B.A. in history from Tougaloo College, her M.A. in history from Atlanta University, and her Ph.D. in history from the University of Michigan, Ann Arbor. She is at work on a book entitled "African Americans and African Caribbeans in the Making of the Harlem Community, 1900-1940."

Walter Weare is professor of history at the University of Wisconsin at Milwaukee. He is the author of *Black Business in the New South: A Social History of the North Carolina Mutual Life Insurance Company* (1973) and "New Negroes for a New Century," in *The Adaptable South* (1991). He is working on a collective biography of five never-married sisters who migrated from Kentucky to Colorado in the late nineteenth century and became teachers, ranchers, and businesswomen.

Judith Weisenfeld is assistant professor of religion at Barnard College. She is the author of "Who Is Sufficient for These Things? Sara G. Stanley and the American Missionary Association, 1864-1868," in *Church History* (1991), and "The More Abundant Life: The Harlem Branch of the New York City Young Women's Christian Association, 1905-1945" (dissertation, Princeton University, 1992). She serves as a consultant for the *Encyclopedia of African American Culture and History.*

Paula Welch, professor of exercise and sports sciences at the University of Florida, does extensive research on the modern Olympic Games and the history of sports, with an emphasis on women. She represented the U.S. at the International Olympic Academy in Ancient Olympia, Greece, as a participant and lecturer. She was the John Betts Lecturer at the North American Society for Sports History and the Southern District Scholar of the American Alliance for Health, Physical Education, Recreation, and Dance. She is a member of the Education Committee of the U.S. Olympic Committee.

Dorothy Porter Wesley, curator emerita of the Moorland-Spingarn Research Center, was a central figure in the African-American intellectual movement at Howard University, spanning several decades. As the chief librarian and spiritual guide of the Moorland-Spingarn collection, she was a vital resource person for scholars researching African-American life and culture. She has published ten books and pamphlets and more than sixty-five articles. A recipient of numerous awards and honorary degrees, Porter was recently awarded the degree of Doctor of Humane Letters, honorus causa, from Radcliffe College.

Delores White is assistant professor of music at Cuyahoga Community College. She received a B.M. degree in piano performance from Oberlin College and an M.M. degree from Cleveland Institute of Music. She has composed for voice, piano, and choir and has arranged Negro spirituals for cello, piano, and violin. Performances of her choral and instrumental compositions have been held nationwide, and she was recently honored as one of the YWCA's Professional Women of the Year.

Katie Kinnard White is associate professor and coordinator of teacher education in biological studies at Tennessee State University. She is a graduate of Tennessee State University (B.S.), Eastern Michigan University, and Walden University (Ph.D.). She is coauthor of *Biophysical Science Laboratory Manual*, *Learning about Living Things for the Elementary School*, and *Learning about Our Physical World for the Elementary School*. She has written numerous articles for professional journals and was a recipient of the Blanche Edwards Award from the Sigma Gamma Rho sorority.

Margaret B. Wilkerson is professor and chair of the Department of African American Studies at the University of California at Berkeley. She earned a Ph.D. degree in dramatic art at Berkeley and has published articles in *Theater Journal*, the *Drama Review*, and the *Massachusetts Review*. She is the editor of *9 Plays by Black Women*, the first anthology of its kind, and is writing a literary biography of Lorraine Hansberry.

Elsie Arrington Williams is associate professor of English studies at the University of the District of Columbia, where she teaches writing and literature. She has published poetry in *Obsidian*, an essay on Richard Pryor in the *Interdisciplinary Newsletter of Satire and Humor*, an essay on Richard Wright in *Papers in the Social Sciences*, and a chapter on Moms Mabley in *Women's Comic Visions*, edited by June Sochen.

Lillian S. Williams is on the Editorial Advisory Board of the *Encyclopedia*. See the beginning of this list for a biographical note.

Ife Williams-Andoh is a postdoctoral fellow at the University of Illinois, where she has a joint position in political science and African-American studies. She matriculated at Lincoln University and Atlanta University. Her research areas are police misconduct and civil liberty violations in the drug war.

Francille Rusan Wilson is assistant professor of history in the Department of History and Philosophy at Eastern Michigan University. She is a graduate of Wellesley College (B.A.), Harvard University (M.A.T.), and the University of Pennsylvania (Ph.D.). She is the author of "Black Workers' Ambivalence towards Unions," in *International Journal of Politics, Culture, and Society* (1989), and "Re-Inventing the Past and Circumscribing the Future: *Authenticité* and the Negative Image of Women's Work in Zaire," in *Women and Work in Africa* (1982).

Martha Kendall Winnacker is coordinator for the University of California's nine-campus Pacific Rim Research Program. She also serves as an editorial consultant to the Northern California Center for History and Life in Oakland. She was project editor for "Visions toward Tomorrow," the center's major exhibit and publication on the history of the Black community in the East Bay region. She was formerly editor of *California History* and holds degrees in history from Pomona College (B.A.) and the University of California at Berkeley (M.A.).

Victoria Wolcott is a doctoral candidate in the Department of History at the University of Michigan, specializing in African-American women's history. She has delivered a number of conference papers, including "Bible, Bath, and Broom: The National Training School and the Construction of African American Female Identities," to the Sixteenth Annual Social Science History Association (1991).

Barbara Woods is head of the Department of History at Hampton University. She is a graduate of Emory University (B.A., Ph.D.) and Cornell University (M.A.). She has held a Rockefeller Fellowship at the Duke/University of North Carolina Center for Research on Women. She is coeditor of *Women in the Civil Rights Movement: Trailblazers and Torchbearers, 1941-1965* (1990). Her most recent article is "Fifty Years of Scholarly Excellence: The Career of John Hope Franklin," in the *Journal of American Ethnic History* (1992).

Lisa Woznica is a 1992 graduate of Harvard-Radcliffe Colleges, with a degree in American history.

Joyce C. Wright is acting head of the Undergraduate Library and associate professor of library administration at the University of Illinois, Urbana-Champaign. Her articles have appeared in *Journal of Library Administration*, *Reference Services Review*, the *Reference Librarian*, *Illinois Libraries*, and *Educating Black Librarians*. She has delivered addresses and spoken at conferences dealing with minority recruitment, affirmative action, and reference services in academic libraries.

Carol Yampolsky, a graduate of the Juilliard School, made her Carnegie Hall debut at the age of nine. She holds a B.S. degree in music education from the Kentucky State University, an M.A. degree from the University of Houston, and a doctorate in musical arts from the University of Maryland. Her careful blending of jazz forms of music, along with her classical background, has earned her acclaim as featured pianist. She recently completed a recording of the unpublished solo piano music of Chick Corea and David Baker, and she will soon publish her teaching pieces for young pianists.

Dorothy Cowser Yancy is a professor in the School of History, Technology and Society at Georgia Institute of Technology in Atlanta. She received her A.B. in history and social science from Johnson C. Smith University, her M.A. in history from the University of Massachusetts at Amherst, and her Ph.D. in political science from Atlanta University. Certified in labor arbitration and mediation, she is engaged in research in African-American history, labor relations, and urban politics.

Jean Fagan Yellin is Distinguished Professor of English at Pace University. She is editor of the definitive edition of *Incidents in the Life of a Slave Girl* (1987) and is working on a biography of Harriet Jacobs. She has written extensively on American literature and culture, with a focus on "uppity" nineteenth-century women, both Black and white. Her books include *The Intricate Knot: Black Figures in American Literature, 1776-1863* (1972), *Women and Sisters: The Antislavery Feminist in American Culture* (1990), and, with Cynthia D. Bond, *The Pen Is Ours: A Listing of Writings by African-American Women to 1910* (1991).

Ivy Young is a writer in Washington, D.C.

Photo Credits

Much of the photo research that made possible the splendid variety of images in these volumes was carried out by Cynthia Kennedy-Haflett. We wish to thank her for her dedication and imagination. Also, Karen Jefferson of the Moorland-Spingarn Research Center provided invaluable assistance and contributed untold hours of personal time to the project, all above and beyond the call of duty. We very much appreciate her help.

Many of the photographs in these two volumes are from two major Black archival institutions: the Moorland-Spingarn Research Center at Howard University and the Schomburg Center of the New York Public Library. Additional information about the photographs reproduced here or about the photographic collections of these two institutions can be requested by writing them directly:

Moorland-Spingarn Research Center
Howard University
Washington, DC 20059

The Schomburg Center for Research in Black Culture
515 Malcolm X Boulevard
New York, NY 10037

Portraits of some of the physicians included here were provided by the Medical College of Pennsylvania, from their Archives and Special Collections on Women in Medicine. For additional information, write:

The Photograph Curator
Archives and Special Collections on Women in Medicine
Medical College of Pennsylvania
3300 Henry Avenue
Philadelphia, PA 19129

We secured some photographs from two commercial photographic collections, The Associated Press/Wide World Photos and the Bettmann Photo Archive. Their addresses are:

The Associated Press/Wide World Photos, Inc.
50 Rockefeller Plaza
New York, NY 10020

Bettmann Photo Archive
902 Broadway
New York, NY 10011

The splendid photographs by Addison Scurlock and his son Robert are available from:

Scurlock Studio
1813 18th Street, N.W.
Washington, DC 20009

Photographs which we secured from the contributors to the *Encyclopedia* and from other institutions are so credited.

Index

entry for, 164-65
and concert music, 273
and Mary Lucinda Cardwell Dawson, 311
photograph of, 164
Brice, Ella
and Charlotte Hawkins Brown, 173
Brice, Eugene
brother of Carol Brice, 164
Brice, Jonathan
brother of Carol Brice, 164
Brice Trio
and Carol Brice, 164
Bricks without Straw
and Frances Ellen Watkins Harper, 536
BRICKTOP (ADA SMITH)
entry for, 165-66
and Mabel Mercer, 783
photograph of, 165
Bricktop's
Bricktop (Ada Smith) performs at, 166
Mabel Mercer performs at, 783
Bridge across Jordan (Boynton), 158
"Bridge over Troubled Water"
recorded by Roberta Flack, 437
Bridge Program
and Marguerite Ross Barnett, 89
Briggs, Cyril
and the Left, 709
Briggs, Fannie Bassett
mother of Martha B. Briggs, 166
Briggs, John
father of Martha B. Briggs, 166
BRIGGS, MARTHA B.
entry for, 166-67
Briggs-Hall, Austin
husband of Louise Evans, 401
Briggs v. Elliott
and Septima Poinsette Clark, 250
and Mary Modjeska Monteith Simkins, 1033
Bright, Geraldine
and the Women's Army Corps, 794
Bright Road
and Dorothy Dandridge, 299
story adapted from life of Mary Elizabeth
Vroman, 1199
Brinckerhoff, Isaac W.
and freedmen's education, 468
Briscoll, Marshall Neil
and Gwendolyn Bennett, 107
British Anti-Lynching Society, 38
British Broadcasting Company
and Adelaide Hall, 515
British Museum
and Ruth Anna Fisher, 434
British Women's Temperance Association
Hallie Quinn Brown lectures for, 177
Britton, Henry
father of Julia Britton Hooks, 572
father of Mary E. Britton, 167
Britton, Laura
mother of Mary E. Britton, 167
BRITTON, MARY E.
entry for, 167-68
photograph of, 167
Broadside Press, 200
Broadway Rhythm
and Hazel Scott, 1019
Broadway Stock Company
Louise Evans technical director for, 401
Brock, Gertha, 1165

Brodie, Fawn
on Sally Hemings, 555
Broil, Enoch
father of Bessie Griffin, 503
Broil, Victoria Walker
mother of Bessie Griffin, 503
Brokenburr, Robert Lee
and Madam C.J. Walker, 1211
Bronson, Eli
legal dispute with Lucy Terry Prince, 945-46
Bronson, Ferne Caulkner, 297
Bronx Community College
Dorothy Rudd Moore teaches at, 813
The Bronx Is Next (Sanchez), 1004
Bronx Zoo
Debbie Allen directs, 20
Bronze: A Book of Verse (Johnson), 640
Bronzeville Boys and Girls (Brooks), 168
Brook, Peter
and Diahann Carroll, 221
Brooke, Edward E., 163
Brookline Equal Suffrage Association
and Florida Ruffin Ridley, 982
Brooklyn, N.Y.
Shirley Chisholm's political activism in, 236
Verina Morton Harris Jones practices
medicine in, 656
home of Alice Wiley Seay, 392-93
Brooklyn College
Shirley Chisholm graduates from, 236
Paule Marshall graduates from, 747
Shirley Prendergast graduates from, 939
Brooklyn Colored Conference
photograph of, 1301
Brooklyn Eagle
Victoria Earle Matthews writes for, 760
Brooklyn Equal Suffrage League
and Verina Morton Harris Jones, 657
Brooklyn Institute
Maria Louise Baldwin lectures before, 80
Brooklyn Navy Yard
Selma Hortense Burke works at, 192
Brooklyn Philharmonic
Melba Liston performs with, 724
Brooks, Avery
Paul Robeson, 296
Brooks, David Anderson
father of Gwendolyn Brooks, 168
Brooks, Elaina
and fashion industry, 409
Brooks, Elizabeth C.
photograph of, 849
Brooks, Frederic Victor
and Hallie Beachem Brooks, 170
BROOKS, GWENDOLYN, 1323, 1324, 1325, 1327
entry for, 168-69
and autobiography, 59
and Black feminism, 422
and Vivian Gordon Harsh, 542
photograph of, 169
and Margaret Walker, 1219
Brooks, Hadda
influence on Ethel Llewellyn Ennis, 394
BROOKS, HALLIE BEACHEM
entry for, 169-70
Brooks, Keziah Corinne Wims
mother of Gwendolyn Brooks, 168
Brooks, L.D.
husband of Jessie Mae Hemphill, 556
Brooks, Lonnie (Guitar Junior)

and Katie Webster, 1241
Brooks, Walter H.
and Nannie Helen Burroughs, 202
and Anna Julia Haywood Cooper, 277
and Hartshorn Memorial College, 544
Brooks, William F.
and freedmen's education, 468
"Brother Freedom" (Burroughs), 200
Brotherhood of Sleeping Car Porters
International Ladies' Auxiliary of, 613-15
and Lucille Campbell Green Randolph, 960
"Brothers"
monthly column in *Essence*, 400
Brough, Louise
and Althea Gibson, 485
Broughton, Virginia W., 1318
and the Baptist Church, 86
Browder, Earl
Claudia Jones critical of, 647
Browder v. Gayle
and the Montgomery Bus Boycott, 809
Brown, Ada
and the Harlem Renaissance, 531
BROWN, ANNE WIGGINS, 1322
entry for, 170-72
and concert music, 273
photograph of, 171
Brown, Annie
and the Women's Army Corps, 794
Brown, Beuenia
president of Empire State Federation of
Women's Clubs, 392-93
BROWN, CHARLOTTE HAWKINS, 26-28, 1317,
1320, 1323
entry for, 172-74
and the antilynching movement, 40
and Annie Welthy Daughtry Holland, 569
and Lugenia Burns Hope, 574
Lois Mailou Jones studies with, 650
and the National Council of Negro Women,
854-55
and the N.C. Federation of Colored
Women's Clubs, 883
photograph of, 173
and the Southeastern Assoc. of Colored
Women's Clubs, 1089
and Madam C. J. Walker, 1213
Brown, Charnele, 1152
Brown, Cindi, 1101
Brown, Clara, 1250
BROWN, CLEO PATRA
entry for, 174
Brown, Clifford
and Blues and Jazz, 142
and Sarah Vaughan, 1198
Brown, Clothhilde Dent, 1327
Brown, David
husband of Lucy Hughes Brown, 182
Brown, David
husband of Hazel Winifred Johnson, 644
BROWN, DOROTHY LAVINIA
entry for, 174-75
Brown, E.C.
employed Lavinia Marian Fleming Poe, 934
Brown, Edith Player
mother of Linda Beatrice Brown, 179
Brown, Edmund G.
and Miriam Matthews, 758
Brown, Edmund S.
husband of Charlotte Hawkins Brown, 173

and the Mississippi State Federation of Colored Women's Clubs, 801

Coleman, Susan
mother of Bessie Coleman, 262

The Cole Porter Song Book
Pearl Bailey records, 67

Coleridge-Taylor, Samuel
Harriet Gibbs Marshall's play based on, 747
and Frances Walker, 1208

Coles, Charles Honi
and Billie Holiday, 566

Coles, Helen
and the International Sweethearts of Rhythm, 617

Coles, Kim
and *In Living Color*, 1153

Coles, R. H.
and Lucie Wilmot Smith, 1081

Collectibles
and Black memorabilia, 781-82

College Alumnae Club
and Sara Winifred Brown, 184, 1318

"College Extension for Working People" (Cooper), 281

College Temperance Society
and Hartshorn Memorial College, 545

Collier, Lockey
as slaveholder, 1058

Collier, Lucy Smith
stepdaughter of Roberta Evelyn Martin, 749

Collier-Thomas, Bettye
and the Assoc. for the Study of Afro-American Life and History, 47

Collins, Addie Mae, 1326

COLLINS, CARDISS ROBERTSON, 1329
entry for, 264-65
and Black feminism, 424
photograph of, 264

Collins, Dara
and Audley (Queen Mother) Moore, 812

Collins, Ethel
and the UNIA, 1189

Collins, George Washington
husband of Cardiss Robertson Collins, 264

COLLINS, JANET, 294-95, 1324
entry for, 265
photograph of, 265

Collins, Kathleen, 1165, 1331
Losing Ground, 301

Collins, Lee
and Lovie Austin, 55

COLLINS, MARVA N., 1150
entry for, 265-66
and the Collins Preparatory School (Cincinnati), 266
Cicely Tyson and *The Marva Collins Story*, 1150

Collins, Norma
and SNCC, 1122

Collins, Patricia Hill
and Black feminism, 424

Colonialism
and Nannie Helen Burroughs, 202
Michelle Cliff writes about, 253

Colony House (Brooklyn)
Toni Cade Bambara works at, 81

Colorado Association of Colored Women's Clubs, 1317

Colorado Medical Society
and Justina Laurena Carter Ford, 441

Colorado Teachers College
Myrtle Athleen Smith Livingston attends, 729

Color Ebony (Day), 228

Colored Agricultural and Normal University
Bessie Coleman attends, 262

Colored American, 1317
and abolition, 7
Adella Hunt Logan writes for, 731

Colored American League (Boston)
and Pauline Elizabeth Hopkins, 578

Colored American Magazine
and Pauline Elizabeth Hopkins, 577, 663
Addie Waits Hunton publishes in, 596
and Josephine Washington, 1233

Colored Co-operative Publishing Company
and Pauline Elizabeth Hopkins, 577

Colored Empty Stocking and Fresh Air Circle
and Ida Rebecca Cummings, 292

Colored Farmers' Alliance, 1315

Colored Female Benevolent Society of Louisiana, 1311

Colored Female Brass Band (East Saginaw, Mich.)
includes pioneer Black female instrumentalists, 611

Colored Female Charitable Society of Boston
and abolition, 6
and Mutual Benefit Societies, 830

Colored Female Religious and Moral Society of Salem, 1310
and abolition, 6
and Mutual Benefit Societies, 830

Colored Female Roman Catholic Beneficial Society of Washington, D.C., 1311

COLORED FEMALES' FREE PRODUCE SOCIETY
entry for, 266-67

Colored Free Produce Society
and the Colored Females' Free Produce Society, 266

The Colored Girl Beautiful (Hackley), 511

Colored High School (Washington, D.C.)
Nannie Helen Burroughs attends, 201-2

Colored Industrial and Normal School
Frances Joseph-Gaudet founds, 661

Colored Methodist Episcopal Church (CME), 1314

Colored Mission
and Assoc. for the Protection of Negro Women, 52

Colored National Convention of 1853
and freedmen's education, 463

Colored National Labor Union (CNLU), 1314

Colored Normal School (Richmond)
and the emerging Black middle class, 788

Colored Old Folks and Orphans Home Club (Memphis, Tenn.)
and Julia Britton Hooks, 573

Colored Orphan Asylum (New York City)
and Elizabeth Taylor Greenfield, 500

Colored Welfare Association of Cleveland
and Jane Edna Hunter, 593

Colored Woman's League, Washington, D.C.
and Hallie Quinn Brown, 177
and Josephine Beall Willson Bruce, 188
and Coralie Cook, 63
and Sara Iredell Fleetwood, 438
founding of, 842

Colored Women's Christian Association (CWCA), 1299

Phyllis Wheatley Club of Washington, D.C., 921

Colored Women's Civic Club (Indianapolis, Ind.)
and Mary Ellen Cable, 213

Colored Women's Congress of the United States, 844

Colored Women's Democratic League
and Bessye Bearden, 97

Colored Women's Economic Councils
and the International Ladies' Auxiliary, Brotherhood of Sleeping Car Porters, 613

Colored Women's Federation of the State of Alabama
and Cornelia Bowen, 151

Colored Women's Magazine
founded in Topeka, Kan., 663, 1318

COLORED WOMEN'S PROGRESSIVE FRANCHISE ASSOCIATION, 1315
entry for, 267
and Black nationalism, 133
and Mary Ann Shadd Cary, 225

Colored Young Women's Christian Association
and Eva del Vakia Bowles, 152

The Color Purple (Walker) 1207-08
and the slave narrative, 1043

The Color Purple (Spielberg), 432
Whoopi Goldberg appears in, 492
still from, 492
and Oprah Winfrey, 1276

Colorstruck (Hurston), 871

Coloured Female Roman Catholic Beneficial Society of Washington, D.C.
and abolition, 6

Colquitt, Martha
and slavery, 1053

Colt, Le Baron
entry for, 268
and Blues and Jazz, 143
and Bertha G. Higgins, 558
photograph of, 268

COLTRANE, ALICE
entry for, 268-69

Coltrane, John
ensemble of, 268
husband of Alice Coltrane, 268

Columbia, S.C.
Charity Adams Earley teaches in, 375
Matilda Arabella Evans founds hospital in, 402
and the Rollin sisters, 990

Columbia Clinic Association
Matilda Arabella Evans founds, 402

Columbian University (George Washington University)
Emma Frances Grayson Merritt attends, 785

Columbia Records
and LaVern Baker, 78
and Aretha Franklin, 450
and Natalie Leota Henderson Hinderas, 564
and Billie Holiday, 567
and Mahalia Jackson, 623

Columbia University
Augusta Braxston Baker teaches at, 69
Marguerite Ross Barnett teaches at, 89
Bessye Bearden attends, 97
Gwendolyn Bennett attends, 107
Hazel Joan Bryant attends, 188
Selma Hortense Burke attends, 192
Mary Fair Burks graduates from, 196

Holden, William
  and Althea Gibson, 486
Holder, Geoffrey
  husband of Carmen DeLavallade, 318
Holder, Mac
  and Shirley Chisholm, 237
HOLIDAY, BILLIE, 294, 354, 1223, 1228
  entry for, 565-69
  and Maya Angelou, 36
  and Blues and Jazz, 141
  and Ruth Brown, 183
  and Betty Carter, 222
  death of, 976
  and Lucille Dixon, 339
  and film, 432
  and Lena Horne, 580
  influence of, 394, 779-80, 975
  Lady Sings the Blues, 1134
  Abbey Lincoln compared to, 721
  Melba Liston plays with, 726
  influenced by Mabel Mercer, 783
  photographs of, 566, 567
  and Diana Ross, 1134
  influenced by Bessie Smith, 975
Holiday, Clarence
  father of Billie Holiday, 565
Holiday Inn
  Louise Beavers in, 105
Holiness Movement, 968
  Nell Cecilia Jackson active in, 626
HOLLAND, ANNIE WELTHY DAUGHTRY
  entry for, 569-70
  photograph of, 569
Holland, Brian and Eddie
  "Where Did Our Love Go" and the
    Supremes, 1133
Holland, Endesha
  emerging Black playwright, 1165
Holland, Mary
  and Catholic Church, 226
Holland, Willis Bird
  husband of Annie Welthy Daughtry Holland,
    569
Holland Limited Touring Company
  and Hazel Joan Bryant, 189
Holley, Major
  and Aretha Franklin, 450
Holley, Sallie
  and Harriet D. Forten Purvis, 444
Hollingsworth, Cecil
  helped develop Essence, 398
Hollingsworth Group
  helped develop Essence, 398
Holloway, Cecelia
  given name of Cecelia Cabaniss Saunders,
    1010
Holloway, James H.
  father of Cecelia Cabaniss Saunders, 1010
Holly, Ellen
  and One Life to Live, 1152
Holly, James T.
  and Black nationalism, 133
Holly, Theodore
  and Julia Ringwood Coston, 285
Hollywood Bowl
  Cora Martin-Moore performs at, 751
Hollywood Shuffle
  score by Patrice Rushen, 997
Hollywood Ten
  Charlotta Spears Bass supports, 93

Holm, Hanya
  Pearl Primus studies with, 943
Holman, Helen
  and Black socialism, 708
Holmes, Eva Burrell
  and Assoc. of Deans of Women and Advisers
    to Girls in Negro Schools, 50
Holmes, Hamilton
  and desegregation of University of Georgia,
    595, 824
Holsey, Kate
  daughter-in-law of Amanda America Dickson,
    336
Holsey, M. A. L.
  and Housewives' League of Detroit, 584
Holt, George W.
  husband of Nora Douglas Holt, 571
Holt, Hamilton
  editor of Independent, 657
Holt, Mary
  and gospel music, 497
HOLT, NORA DOUGLAS, 1319, 1323
  entry for, 570-72
  photograph of, 571
Holte, Patricia Louise
  given name of Patti LaBelle, 685
Holt Street Baptist Church (Montgomery, Ala.)
  and Montgomery Bus Boycott, 808
Holy Blues
  and Flora Molton, 806
Holy Comforter Church (Washington, D.C.)
  and Sharon Pratt Kelly, 676
Holy Cross-Faith Memorial Church and School
  (Pawley's Island, S.C.)
  and Ruby Middleton Forsythe, 442
Holy Redeemer School (New Orleans), 288
Holy Trinity Church (Washington, D.C.)
  and Anne Marie Becroft, 106
Holy Vessel Baptist Church (Chicago)
  Lena Johnson McLin pastor at, 773
Homecoming (Sanchez), 1004
Home Economics
  and Flossie M. Byrd, 211-12
Home for Aged and Infirm Colored People
  (Washington, D.C.)
  supported by Mary Jane Patterson, 912
Home for Aged and Infirmed Colored People
  (Philadelphia)
  and Caroline Virginia Still Wiley Anderson,
    29
  and Fanny Jackson Coppin, 282
Home for Destitute Women and Children
  (Washington, D.C.)
  Elizabeth Keckley dies in, 673
Home for Friendless Girls (Washington, D.C.),
  842
Home Girls: A Black Feminist Anthology (Smith),
  423
Home Girls and Handgrenades (Sanchez), 1004
"Home Is Where the Hatred"
  sung by Esther Phillips, 976
"Homely Philosophy"
  column by Georgia Douglas Johnson, 641
Home of Aged Colored Persons (New York
  City)
  and Elizabeth Taylor Greenfield, 500
Homer & Eddie
  Whoopi Goldberg in, 492
Homer G. Phillips Hospital (St. Louis)
  and Helen E. Nash, 836

  and Muriel Marjorie Petioni, 916
Homespun Heroines and Other Women of
  Distinction (Brown), 178
The Homesteader
  Evelyn Preer in, 938
Homophobia
  Alice Childress on, 235
  and the Combahee River Collective, 269-70
  Lorraine Vivian Hansberry on, 528
Homunculus C. F. (Perry), 271
Honey, I Love and Other Love Poems (Greenfield),
  501
Honey and Rue
  lyrics by Toni Morrison, 819
Honey Baby, Honey Baby
  and Diana Sands, 1009
"Honey Man"
  and Bessie Smith, 1076
Hood Theological Seminary, 191
Hooker, John Lee
  and Ernestine Anderson, 29
Hooker, Olivia J.
  and Coast Guard during World War II, 794-
    95
hooks, bell
  and Black feminism, 423, 424
Hooks, Benjamin L.
  and Julia Britton Hooks, 573
  on Juanita Jackson Mitchell, 805
  and Althea T.L. Simmons, 1035
  and Margaret Bush Wilson, 1272
Hooks, Charles
  husband of Julia Britton Hooks, 573
Hooks, Grace
  daughter of Sara "Sadie" Marie Johnson
    Delaney, 316
Hooks, Henry
  son of Julia Britton Hooks, 573
HOOKS, JULIA BRITTON
  entry for, 572-73
Hooks, Kevin
  photograph of, 431
Hooks, Robert
  and Barbara Ann Teer, 1147
  son of Julia Britton Hooks, 573
Hooks Brothers' Photographers Studio
  (Memphis, Tenn.), 573
Hooks Cottage School (Memphis, Tenn.)
  and Julia Britton Hooks, 573
Hooks School of Music (Memphis, Tenn.)
  and Julia Britton Hooks, 572
Hoosier Women
  and Sallie Wyatt Stewart, 1115
Hoover, Herbert
  and Mary Cordelia Montgomery Booze, 150
  and Nannie Helen Burroughs, 203
  and Selena Sloan Butler, 211
Hope, John
  and Hallie Beachem Brooks, 170
  husband of Lugenia Burns Hope, 573-74, 576
  photograph of, 575
HOPE, LUGENIA BURNS, 1318
  entry for, 573-77
  and civil rights movement, 241
  and Neighborhood Union, 612, 870, 878
  photograph of, 575, 1287
  and Margaret Murray Washington, 1234,
    1235
  and World War I, 1288
Hopkins, Arthur

I

"Negro in Aviation" (Bragg), 161
The Negro in Films
  on Butterfly McQueen, 778
The Negro in Fusion Politics in North Carolina, 1894-1901 (Edmonds), 380
"The Negro in Illinois"
  and Vivian Gordon Harsh, 542-43
The Negro in Our History (Woodson and Wesley)
  and the Assoc. for the Study of Afro-American Life and History, 46
"The Negro in the American Theater"
  and Alice Childress, 235
The Negro in the United States: A Selected Bibliography (Wesley), 1247
The Negro in Virginia
  and Federal Writers Project Slave Narratives, 417
Negro Music Journal
  edited by Agnes Carroll, 663
"The Negro People and American Art at Mid-Century" (Catlett), 232
Negro People's Theatre, 1162
  cofounded by Rose McClendon, 766
Negro Poets and Their Poems
  Naomi Long Madgett reads as a child, 741
"The Negro Problem in America" (Cooper), 278
Negro Rural School Fund
  and Jeanes Fund and Teachers, 632
The Negro Speaks of Rivers (Primus), 943, 944
Negro Theater
  program of the Works Projects Administration, 392
The Negro Trail-Blazers of California (Beasley), 98
Negro War Relief
  and Mary McLeod Bethune, 794
  supports troops during Civil War, 793
Negro Welfare League
  and Bessie Coleman, 263
"Negro Woman" (Catlett), 230
"Negro Womanhood Defended" (Hunton), 596
Negro Women Voter League, 1319
Negro Women's Auxiliary War Council
  founded in Colorado, 794
NEGRO WOMEN'S CLUB HOME, DENVER
  entry for, 876-78
Negro Women's Franchise League
  Daisy Elizabeth Adams Lampkin elected president of, 692
Negro Women's League for Service
  founded in Colorado, 794
Negro Women's Orchestral and Civic Association
  includes pioneer Black female instrumentalists, 611
  and Olivia Porter Shipp, 1029
Negro World, 134
  and the Black Cross Nurses, 1187
  and Ethel Trew Dunlap, 367
  women's features in, 1188
  and Black feminism, 422
  and Amy Ashwood Garvey, 481
  and Amy Euphemia Jacques Garvey, 483
  no women on staff of before 1924, 1189
"The Negro Writer and His Roots" (Hansberry), 526
Negro Youth Project
  and Butterfly McQueen, 778

Neighborhood Cultural Arts Center, Inc.
  and Toni Cade Bambara, 82
NEIGHBORHOOD UNION, ATLANTA, 870
  entry for, 878
  and Lugenia Burns Hope, 574, 576, 612
Nell, Creole
  early stage name of Madame Sul-Te-Wan, 1130
Nell, William C.
  helps Harriet Ann Jacobs publish her autobiography, 628
Nelson, Gordon
  The Legacy and Barbara Ann Teer, 1147
Nelson, John Herbert
  The Negro Character in American Literature and Harriet E. Wilson, 1271
Nelson, Robert J.
  husband of Alice Ruth Dunbar-Nelson, 362, 363
Nemiroff, Robert Barro
  husband of Lorraine Vivian Hansberry, 525-27, 712
Never No More
  Rose McClendon stars in, 765
Newark City (Martland) Hospital
  and Ernest Mae McCarroll, 764
Newark Department of Health
  Ernest Mae McCarroll works for, 764
New Alliance Party, 1331
New Bedford, Mass.
  early education in, 382
New Bethel Baptist Church
  and Aretha Franklin, 450
New Challenge
  and the Harlem Renaissance, 530
  and Dorothy West, 1248
The New Creole Show, 294
New Deal, 326-27
  Mary McLeod Bethune as race leader during, 121
  and Black feminism, 420-21
  discriminatory policies of, 710
  and Daisy Elizabeth Adams Lampkin, 692
  Pauli Murray during, 826
Newell, Robert Henry
  husband of Adah Isaacs Menken, 782
New England
  and music career of Nellie B. Mitchell, 805-6
  Ann Lane Petry as chronicler of, 917
New England Conservatory of Music, 270
  Mary Lucinda Cardwell Dawson graduates from
  Maud Cuney Hare attends, 529
  and Ann Hobson, 565
  Coretta Scott King enrolls in, 679
  Florence Smith Price graduates from, 940
New England Female Medical College (Boston)
  Rebecca Lee Crumpler graduates from, 291, 923
New England Freedmen's Aid Society
  and freedmen's education, 463, 464, 465, 466
  and Harriet Ann Jacobs, 628
New England Harp Trio
  Ann Hobson plays with, 565
New England Hospital for Women and Children
  Mary Eliza Mahoney graduates from, 743, 887
The New England Psalm-Singer (Billings)
  and Phillis Wheatley, 1252

New England Women's Club
  and Harriet Ann Jacobs, 629
New England Women's Press Association
  and Josephine St. Pierre Ruffin, 994
NEW ERA CLUB, 1316
  entry for, 878-80
  and origins of International Council of Women of the Darker Races, 612
  Florida Ruffin Ridley cofounds, 982
  founded by Josephine St. Pierre Ruffin, 843, 994
New Faces of 1952
  and Eartha Kitt, 680
New Federal Theatre
  Shirley Prendergast designs lighting for, 939
New Florida Club (London)
  and Adelaide Hall, 514
New Georgetown School
  Anne Marie Becroft attends, 105-6
New Haven, Conn.
  home of Sarah Boone, 618
New Haven Adult Community Council
  Constance Baker Motley secretary of, 822
New Haven Advocate
  and Alexis DeVeaux, 334
New Haven Youth Council
  Constance Baker Motley president of, 822
New Hope, Pa.
  and Selma Hortense Burke, 194
New Idea Club
  and Nettie Langston Napier, 834
New Lady
  targets Black women, 398
  unlike *Essence*, 400
New Leader
  Charlayne Hunter-Gault writes for, 596
Newman, Lydia D.
  inventor of an improved hair brush, 618
"The New Mirror" (Petry), 917
The New Negro (Locke), 230
New Negro Alliance
  and Mary McLeod Bethune, 123
New Negro Art Theater Dance Company, 296
New Negro Movement
  and the birth control movement, 129
  Georgia Douglas Johnson's contributions to, 641
  Lois Mailou Jones and Alain Locke, 651
  Nella Larsen's writing and, 696-97
  and Catherine Allen Latimer, 697
  and the UNIA, 1187-88
  See also Harlem Renaissance
"New Negro Woman"
  and beauty culture, 100
New Orleans, La.
  "Sweet Emma" Barrett and jazz style in, 91, 92
  Marie Bernard Couvent helps to establish school in, 287-88
  Eufrosina Hinard and slavery in, 562-63
  Billie Holiday appears in, 566
  in writings of Ann Battles Johnson and Katherine Johnson, 639
  Elizabeth Clovis Lange founds schools in, 695
  Marie Laveau, the Voodoo queen of, 701
  Madame Cecee McCarty in, 396
  Black-run markets in antebellum period, 395
  organizational center for the Southern Negro Youth Congress (SNYC), 710
  Phyllis Wheatley Club of, 920, 923

W

"Waco Blues"
   sung by Julia Lee, 707
WADDLES, CHARLESZETTA LINA CAMPBELL
   entry for, 1201-2
Waddles, Payton
   husband of Charleszetta Waddles, 1201
Waddy, Henrietta, 1224
   and gospel music, 496
   and the Ward Sisters, 1223
Wade, Ernestine
   as Sapphire on *Amos 'n' Andy*, 956, 1009-10,
      1148
Wadleigh High School (New York City)
   Muriel Marjorie Petioni graduates from, 916
Wagenen, Isaac Van
   and Sojourner Truth, 1173
Wagner, Robert F.
   and Anna Arnold Hedgeman, 550
   Constance Baker Motley sworn in by, 823-24
   photograph of, 823
Wagner College (London, England)
   Michelle Cliff graduates from, 253
Waites, Addie
   mother of Eunice Hunton Carter, 223
Waites, Althea
   performs work by Florence Smith Price, 940
Waiting to Exhale (McMillan), 775
Waits, Jesse
   father of Addie Waits Hunton, 596
*The Wake and Resurrection of the Bicentennial
   Negro* (Ringgold), 984
Wake Forest University (Winston-Salem, N.C.)
   Maya Angelou teaches at, 38
Wald, Lillian, 90
   and Verina Morton Harris Jones, 656
WALKER, AIDA OVERTON, 1162
   entry for, 1202-3
   photographs of, 1164, 1202
   in vaudeville and musical theater, 1194-95
Walker, Albertina
   and Shirley Caesar, 215
   and gospel music, 497
   and Bessie Griffin, 503
WALKER, A'LELIA
   entry for, 1203-5
   and the Harlem Renaissance, 531
   and Anna Arnold Hedgeman, 549
   photographs of, 1203, 1204
   and Edna Lewis Thomas, 1167
   and Madam C. J. Walker, 1209, 1211, 1213
WALKER, ALICE, 301, 531, 579, 1328, 1331
   entry for, 1205-8
   and Toni Cade Bambara, 81
   and Black feminism, 423
   The Color Purple, 1043
   works of appear in *Essence*, 400
   and film, 432
   and Whoopi Goldberg, 492
   on Nell Cecilia Jackson, 627
   photograph of, 1207
   and Ann Allen Shockley, 1030
   The Temple of My Familiar, 876
   and Sherley Anne Williams, 1266
   and womanist theology, 1276
Walker, Amelia
   and slavery, 1050
Walker, Armstead
   husband of Maggie Lena Walker, 1215

Walker, Armstead Mitchell
   son of Maggie Lena Walker, 1215
Walker, Buddy
   and Althea Gibson, 484
Walker, Charles Joseph
   stepfather of A'Lelia Walker, 1203
   husband of Madam C. J. Walker, 1210
Walker, David
   and abolition, 3
   and Black nationalism, 132
   Walker's Appeal, 1113
Walker, Edward David
   father of Rebecca Walker Steele, 1108
Walker, Edwin A.
   and Daisy Lee Gatson Bates, 96
Walker, Eliza
   and Fisk Jubilee Singers, 435
WALKER, FRANCES
   entry for, 1208-9
   and concert music, 274
Walker, Frank
   and Bessie Smith, 1074
Walker, George W., 1162
   and Laura Bowman, 153
   and Anita Bush, 206
   and Natalie Leota Henderson Hinderas, 564
   and Abbie Mitchell, 803
   husband of Aida Overton Walker, 1195, 1202
   and Frances Walker, 1208
Walker, Janice Brown
   Ph.D. in mathematics, 757
Walker, Jimmy
   and Debbie Allen, 20
Walker, Joseph
   The Believers and Barbara Ann Teer, 1147
Walker, Julia
   mother of Rebecca Walker Steele, 1108
Walker, Louise
   and Evelyn Boyd Granville, 498
Walker, Mabel, 1100
WALKER, MADAM C. J. (SARAH BREEDLOVE),
      1203, 1209, 1250, 1317
   entry for, 1209-14
   and beauty culture, 102
   and the Black middle class, 788
   and economic status, 787
   as a successful entrepreneur, 1188
   and the Harlem Renaissance, 531
   photographs of, 1209, 1211
   and World War I, 1290
WALKER, MAGGIE LENA, 1119, 1317
   entry for, 1214-19
   and the Black middle class, 788
   and Black nationalism, 133
   and the civil rights movement, 240-41
   and economic status, 787
   as a successful entrepreneur, 1188
   and Hartshorn Memorial College, 546
   develops Independent Order of St. Luke, 829-
      30, 949
   photographs of, 1215, 1216, 1217
Walker, Margaret, 200, 1027
   and Toni Cade Bambara, 81
   and Nikki Giovanni, 490
   and Vivian Gordon Harsh, 542
WALKER, MARGARET ABIGAIL, 1323
   entry for, 1219-20
Walker, Marion Dozier
   mother of Margaret Walker, 1219
Walker, Melvin DeWitt

son of Maggie Lena Walker, 1215, 1219
Walker, Minnie Tallulah Grant
   mother of Alice Walker, 1205
Walker, Russell Eccles Talmage
   son of Maggie Lena Walker, 1215, 1218
Walker, Sigismund C.
   father of Margaret Walker, 1219
Walker, Thomas
   stepfather of Mary Smith Kelsey Peake, 914
Walker, Valaida M.
   and fashion industry, 409
Walker, Willie Lee
   father of Alice Walker, 1205
Walker, Wyatt Tee
   and Maya Angelou, 37
   and Dorothy Foreman Cotton, 287
Walker's Appeal (Walker), 1113
Walk for Freedom and Freedom Now
   Carlene Polite participates in, 935
Walkin' by the River
   Una Mae Carlisle records, 218
Walking for Wellness Program
   and Byllye Y. Avery, 61
Wall, Amanda
   and freedmen's education, 465
Wall, Lillian
   and The Links, Inc., 722
Wall, O.S.B.
   and freedmen's education, 465
Wallace, Emma Benson
   mother of Ruby Dee, 313
Wallace, George, 214
   and desegregation, 824
   speaks in Cambridge, Md., 982
Wallace, Henry
   Charlotta Spears Bass supports, 93
   supported by Food, Tobacco, Agricultural,
      and Allied Workers, 712
   and Lorraine Vivian Hansberry, 524
   and Mary Modjeska Monteith Simkins, 1034
Wallace, Marshall
   father of Ruby Dee, 313
Wallace, Matthew
   husband of Sippie Wallace, 1222
Wallace, Michele
   and Black feminism, 424
   author of *Black Macho and the Myth of
      Superwoman*, 745
WALLACE, SIPPIE
   entry for, 1220-23
   and Blues and Jazz, 142
   photograph of, 1221
Wallack Theater (New York City)
   Sissieretta Joyner Jones performs at, 654
Waller, Thomas "Fats"
   and Blues and Jazz, 142
   and Cleo Patra Brown, 174
   and Una Mae Carlisle, 218
   and Mamie Smith, 1082
"The Wallflower"
   rerelease of Etta James's work, 630
Walling, William English
   and the NAACP, 838
Walls, Carlotta, 1325
   one of the Little Rock Nine, 727-29
   photograph of, 728
The Walls Came Tumbling Down
   by Mary White Ovington, 657
Walrond, Eric
   and Gwendolyn Bennett, 106

Z